Reserve
KF
2979
-C478
2015
c. 4

UNDERSTANDING INTELLECTUAL PROPERTY LAW

MSU College of Law Library

LexisNexis Law School Publishing
Advisory Board

Bridgette Carr
Clinical Professor of Law
University of Michigan Law School

Steven I. Friedland
Professor of Law and Senior Scholar
Elon University School of Law

Carole Goldberg
Jonathan D. Varat Distinguished Professor of Law
UCLA School of Law

Oliver Goodenough
Professor of Law
Vermont Law School

Paul Marcus
Haynes Professor of Law
William and Mary Law School

John Sprankling
Distinguished Professor of Law
McGeorge School of Law

UNDERSTANDING INTELLECTUAL PROPERTY LAW

Third Edition

by

Donald S. Chisum
Author, Chisum on Patents

Tyler T. Ochoa
Santa Clara University School of Law

Shubha Ghosh
University of Wisconsin Law School

Mary LaFrance
University of Nevada, Las Vegas
William S. Boyd School of Law

ISBN: 978-1-6328-0963-6 (Print)
ISBN: 978-1-6328-0964-3 (eBook)

Library of Congress Cataloging-in-Publication Data

Chisum, Donald S., 1944- author.
Understanding intellectual property law / by Donald S. Chisum, Author, Chisum on Patents; Tyler T. Ochoa, Santa Clara University School of Law; Shubha Ghosh, University of Wisconsin Law School; Mary LaFrance, University of Nevada, Las Vegas William S. Boyd School of Law. -- Third edition .
    pages cm
  Includes index.
   ISBN 978-1-63280-963-6 (softbound)
1. Intellectual property--United States. I. Ochoa, Tyler T., author. II. Ghosh, Shubha, author. III. LaFrance, Mary, 1958- author. IV. Title.
   KF2979.C478 2015
   346.7304'8--dc23

2014046847

This publication is designed to provide authoritative information in regard to the subject matter covered. It is sold with the understanding that the publisher is not engaged in rendering legal, accounting, or other professional services. If legal advice or other expert assistance is required, the services of a competent professional should be sought.

LexisNexis and the Knowledge Burst logo are registered trademarks of Reed Elsevier Properties Inc., used under license. Matthew Bender and the Matthew Bender Flame Design are registered trademarks of Matthew Bender Properties Inc.

Copyright © 2015 Matthew Bender & Company, Inc., a member of LexisNexis. All Rights Reserved.

No copyright is claimed by LexisNexis or Matthew Bender & Company, Inc., in the text of statutes, regulations, and excerpts from court opinions quoted within this work. Permission to copy material may be licensed for a fee from the Copyright Clearance Center, 222 Rosewood Drive, Danvers, Mass. 01923, telephone (978) 750-8400.

NOTE TO USERS

To ensure that you are using the latest materials available in this area, please be sure to periodically check the LexisNexis Law School web site for downloadable updates and supplements at www.lexisnexis.com/lawschool.

Editorial Offices
630 Central Ave., New Providence, NJ 07974 (908) 464-6800
201 Mission St., San Francisco, CA 94105-1831 (415) 908-3200
www.lexisnexis.com

MATTHEW◊BENDER

Table of Contents

| Chapter 1 | INTRODUCTION | . . . . | 1 |

§ 1A   LAW AND HUMAN CREATIVITY 2
§ 1B   INTELLECTUAL PROPERTY RIGHTS: AN OVERVIEW 3
   [1]   Patents 4
   [2]   Trade Secrets 4
   [3]   Copyright 5
   [4]   Trademarks 6
   [5]   Other Intellectual Property Rights 7
§ 1C   POLICY 7
§ 1D   INTELLECTUAL PROPERTY AND THE CONSTITUTION 10
   [1]   Congress' Patent and Copyright Powers 11
   [2]   Commerce Clause Regulation of Intellectual Property 14
   [3]   Preemption 15
     [a]   Copying Publicly Disclosed Subject Matter 16
     [b]   Contracts 19
     [c]   Copyright Act Preemption 23
       [i]   Subject Matter 24
       [ii]   Equivalent Rights 25
       [iii]   Examples 27
       [iv]   Moral Rights 29
   [4]   First Amendment Limits on Intellectual Property Laws 30
     [a]   Granting or Withholding Intellectual Property Rights 31
     [b]   Enforcing Intellectual Property Rights 32
       [i]   Copyright 32
       [ii]   Trademark and Rights of Publicity 33
   [5]   Eleventh Amendment and Sovereign Immunity 34
     [a]   Claims Against State Governments 34
     [b]   Claims Against the Federal Government 37

| Chapter 2 | PATENTS | . . . . | 39 |

§ 2A   INTRODUCTION 44
§ 2B   HISTORICAL DEVELOPMENT 45
   [1]   The 1790 and 1793 Acts 45
   [2]   The 1836 and 1870 Acts 46
   [3]   The First Invention Concept 48
   [4]   Shifting Supreme Court Attitudes Toward Patents 49
     [a]   Patents Under Fire: 1880–1892 49
     [b]   Patents in Favor: 1892–1930 50

Table of Contents

[c]   Patents Under Renewed Fire: 1930–1950 50

[5]   The 1952 Act 51

[6]   The 1966 *Graham* Trilogy and Beyond 52

[7]   Leahy-Smith America Invents Act of 2011 54

§ 2C   PATENTABILITY 56

[1]   Patentable Subject Matter 57

[a]   General Definitions 57

[b]   Exclusions and Exceptions 58

[c]   New Uses of Old Products 59

[d]   Products of Nature and Living Organisms 60

[e]   Business Methods and Methods of Treatment 61

[f]   Computer Software: Algorithms and Mathematical Inventions 65

[i]   Abstract Ideas — Mental Steps 65

[ii]   Supreme Court Precedent on Software Patents 67

[iii]   Examples: *Grams* and *Iwahashi* 70

[2]   Utility 71

[3]   Novelty 72

[4]   Nonobviousness 74

[a]   General Test — *Graham v. Deere* 75

[b]   Nonanalogous Art 75

[c]   Comparative Utility 76

[i]   Rationale 76

[ii]   New and Unexpected Properties 78

[iii]   Undisclosed Advantages and Properties 79

[d]   Objective Evidence 79

[i]   Long-Felt Need — Failure of Others 79

[ii]   Commercial Success 79

[iii]   Licensing and Acquiescence by Competitors 80

[iv]   Copying and Laudatory Statements by the Infringer 80

[v]   Near Simultaneous Invention 81

[e]   Other Guidelines 81

[i]   Prior Art Suggestions — Obvious to Try 81

[ii]   Combination Inventions 82

[iii]   Chemical Compounds and Intermediates 83

[iv]   Processes — Methods of Making and Using 84

[5]   Prior Art Before the AIA 85

[a]   Documentary Sources: Patents and Publications 88

[i]   Publications 88

[ii]   Patents 89

[b]   Nondocumentary Sources: Public Use and Sale 90

[i]   Known or Used by Others 90

Table of Contents

[ii]   Statutory Bars 90

[iii]   Public Use in the United States 91

[iv]   On Sale in the United States 92

[v]   Experimental Use Exception 93

[vi]   Abandonment 94

[vii]   Foreign Patenting 95

[c]   Senior-Filed Patents 95

[i]   The *Milburn* Doctrine 96

[ii]   Foreign Priority Applications 97

[iii]   Continuation Applications 98

[iv]   Issuance 98

[d]   Prior Invention and Derivation 99

[i]   Prior Invention — Section 102(g) 99

[ii]   Derivation — Section 102(f) 100

[e]   Invention Date 101

[f]   Inventive Entities 102

[6]   Prior Art Under the AIA 103

§ 2D   PATENT PROCESS 104

[1]   Patent Prosecution 104

[a]   Overview 104

[b]   Unity of Invention — Restriction 106

[c]   Confidentiality 107

[d]   Amendments 107

[e]   Duty of Candor 108

[2]   Disclosure Requirements 108

[a]   Enablement Requirement 109

[i]   Claim Scope 109

[ii]   Experimentation 109

[iii]   Other Enablement Issues 110

[iv]   Deposit of Biological Material 111

[b]   Written Description Requirement 111

[c]   Best Mode Requirement 113

[i]   In General 113

[ii]   Computer Programs 114

[iii]   Trade Secrets 115

[iv]   Time Frame 115

[d]   Inventor Identification 116

[i]   Sole Invention 117

[ii]   Joint Invention 117

[iii]   Separate Claims 118

[iv]   Inventorship Error Correction 119

Table of Contents

[3]		Claiming Requirements	120
[a]		Definiteness	120
[b]		Format	121
[c]		Jepson Claims	123
[d]		Alternative Limitations — Markush Groups	124
[e]		Functionality — Means-Plus-Function Claims	125
[f]		Negative Limitations	126
[g]		Multiple Claims — Dependent Claims	126
[4]		Related Applications	128
[a]		Double Patenting	128
	[i]	Claim Comparison	128
	[ii]	Identical Inventions	128
	[iii]	Obvious Variation	129
	[iv]	Design and Utility Patents	129
	[v]	Terminal Disclaimers	130
	[vi]	Different Inventors' Commonly Assigned Applications	130
[b]		Continuation Applications	131
	[i]	Continuity of Disclosure	132
	[ii]	Cross References	133
	[iii]	Copendency	133
	[iv]	Inventorship	134
[5]		Interferences and Derivation Procedures	134
[a]		Priority Rules — First to Invent	134
[b]		Conception	136
[c]		Reduction to Practice	136
[d]		Diligence	137
[e]		Corroboration	139
[f]		Abandonment, Suppression, and Concealment	139
[g]		Derivation Proceedings	140
[6]		Post-Issuance Procedures	141
[a]		Reexamination	141
[b]		Reissue	143
	[i]	Inoperativeness and Invalidity	144
	[ii]	Claim Scope Alteration	145
	[iii]	Error	146
	[iv]	Oath or Declaration — Examination	146
	[v]	Effect of Reissue — Intervening Rights	147
[c]		Post-Grant Review	148
[d]		Inter Partes Review	148
§ 2E		RIGHTS	149
[1]		Duration	149

Table of Contents

[2]   Exclusive Rights 151

   [a]   Basic Rights: Direct Infringement 152

   [b]   Territorial Scope: Importation and Exportation 153

     [i]   Exportation 154

     [ii]   Importation 155

     [iii]   Process Patent Protection 156

   [c]   Secondary Liability 158

     [i]   Relation to Direct Infringement 158

     [ii]   Active Inducement 159

     [iii]   Contributory Infringement 160

     [iv]   Corporations — Officers and Directors 161

[3]   First Sale — Exhaustion — Repair and Reconstruction 161

[4]   Government Use 163

§ 2F   INFRINGEMENT 163

[1]   Claim Language Interpretation 163

   [a]   Intrinsic and Extrinsic Material 164

     [i]   Other Claims — Claim Differentiation 165

     [ii]   Specification — The Patentee as "Lexicographer" 166

     [iii]   Prosecution History 168

     [iv]   Expert Testimony 168

   [b]   "Means-Plus-Function" Limitations 168

   [c]   Consistency 170

[2]   Claim Application 171

   [a]   Literal Infringement 172

     [i]   Omissions 172

     [ii]   Additions and Improvements 172

   [b]   Doctrine of Equivalents 173

     [i]   The *Graver Tank* and *Warner-Jenkinson* Decisions 174

     [ii]   The "Triple Identity" Test 175

     [iii]   Comparison Standard — The "All Elements" Rule 176

     [iv]   Range of Equivalents — Pioneer Patents 176

     [v]   Later Developed Equivalents 177

     [vi]   Reverse Doctrine of Equivalents 177

     [vii]   Limiting Effect of the Prior Art 178

   [c]   Prosecution History Estoppel 179

     [i]   Acts Giving Rise to Prosecution History Estoppel 180

     [ii]   Effect of Prosecution History Estoppel 181

[3]   Proof of Infringing Activity 182

   [a]   Burden of Proof 182

   [b]   Intent 182

   [c]   Agency — Corporate Officers and Employees 183

Table of Contents

[4]   Jurisdiction and Joinder Provisions 183
§ 2G   DEFENSES 184
[1]   Invalidity 184
[a]   Presumption of Validity 184
[b]   Standing to Challenge Validity 185
[c]   Effect of Judgment 186
[2]   Inequitable Conduct — Fraud 187
[3]   Misuse 188
[4]   Experimental or Personal Use 189
[5]   Laches and Estoppel 190
[6]   Implied License — First Sale 191
[7]   Prior Commercial Use 192
§ 2H   REMEDIES 193
[1]   Injunctions 193
[a]   Preliminary Injunctions 193
[b]   Permanent Injunctions 194
[2]   Damages 195
[a]   Compensatory Damages 195
[b]   Increased Damages — Willful Infringement 199
[c]   Notice — Patent Marking 200
[3]   Interest 201
[4]   Attorney's Fees and Expenses 203
§ 2I   OWNERSHIP AND TRANSFER 204
[1]   Employee and Contractor Inventions 204
[2]   Ability to Sue Infringers 206
[3]   Compulsory Licenses 206

Chapter 3   TRADE SECRETS LAW 209

§ 3A   INTRODUCTION 211
[1]   State Law Versus Federal Law 213
[2]   Trade Secrets Law's Relationship to Patent Law 213
§ 3B   HISTORICAL DEVELOPMENT 215
[1]   Early English Cases 215
[2]   Early United States Cases 216
[3]   The Restatement 218
[4]   The Uniform Trade Secrets Act 219
§ 3C   NATURE OF PROTECTION — RIGHTS 221
[1]   Information That Qualifies as a Trade Secret 221
[a]   Definitions 221
[b]   Eligible Subject Matter 222
[i]   Concreteness 223

Table of Contents

[ii]	Nontechnical Information		224
[iii]	Combinations		224
[iv]	Customer Lists		224
[v]	Continuous Use		226
[vi]	Negative Information		226
[c]	Secrecy		227
[i]	Definitions		228
[ii]	Application of Secrecy Requirement		228
[iii]	Ascertainability from Products and Public Sources		230
[iv]	Copyrighted Material		232
[v]	Patented Material		232
[vi]	Novelty Versus General Knowledge		232
[vii]	Disclosure to Government Agencies		233
[viii]	Laws Mandating Disclosure		234
[d]	Commercial Value and Use		234
[i]	Value		234
[ii]	Cost of Development		234
[2]	Exclusive Rights		235
[3]	Duration and Termination		235
§ 3D	TRADE SECRET MISAPPROPRIATION LITIGATION		235
[1]	Definition of Misappropriation		236
[2]	Theories of Law		237
[a]	Contract Law Theories		237
[b]	Tort Law Theories		238
[c]	Conflicts of Laws		239
[i]	Contract Law Conflicts		239
[ii]	Tort Law Conflicts		240
[iii]	Statutes of Limitations		240
[3]	Elements and Burdens of Proof		241
[4]	Trade Secret Ownership		242
[a]	Common Law		243
[i]	Information Protectability		243
[ii]	Ownership		243
[iii]	Employment as a Confidential Relationship		245
[b]	Express Agreements		245
[i]	Ownership-Assignment Agreements		245
[ii]	Timing of Creation		245
[iii]	Consideration		246
[c]	Non-Competition Agreements		246
[5]	Misappropriation		247
[a]	Confidential Relationship		247

Table of Contents

[b]   Improper and Proper Means 248

  [i]   Improper Means 248

  [ii]   Proper Means 248

  [iii]   Otherwise Lawful Conduct 249

[c]   Innocent Receipt 249

[6]   Detrimental Use or Disclosure 250

§ 3E   DEFENSES 251

[1]   Independent Development 251

[2]   Absence of Secrecy — Public Domain 251

[3]   Reverse Engineering 252

[4]   Privilege 252

[5]   Equitable Defenses 253

[a]   Unclean Hands 253

[b]   Laches 253

[c]   Estoppel 253

§ 3F   REMEDIES 253

[1]   Injunctions 254

[a]   Preliminary Injunctions 254

[b]   Scope of Injunctions 255

[c]   Duration of Injunctions 256

[2]   Damages 257

[a]   Compensatory Damages 257

  [i]   Calculation of Damages 257

  [ii]   Effect of Public Disclosure 258

[b]   Punitive Damages 258

[3]   Attorney Fees and Court Costs 259

[4]   Seizure of Embodiments 259

[5]   Criminal Penalties 259

Chapter 4   **COPYRIGHT** **261**

§ 4A   INTRODUCTION 266

§ 4B   HISTORICAL DEVELOPMENT 267

[1]   English Antecedents 267

[2]   Copyright in the United States 268

[a]   1790 to 1909 268

[b]   The 1909 Act 269

[c]   The 1976 Act to Today 270

§ 4C   COPYRIGHTABLE SUBJECT MATTER 270

[1]   Originality 271

[a]   Constitutional Standard 271

[b]   Words and Short Phrases 272

Table of Contents

[c]		Photographs	273
[d]		Aesthetic Non-Discrimination	274
[2]		Fixation	275
[a]		Background: *White-Smith v. Apollo*	276
[b]		The 1976 Act	276
[i]		Video Games	277
[ii]		Random-Access Memory	277
[c]		Live Broadcasts and Transmissions	279
[d]		Live Performances	280
[3]		Idea and Expression	280
[a]		General Principle	280
[b]		*Baker v. Selden*	281
[c]		The Merger Doctrine	282
[d]		*Scènes à Faire*	285
[4]		Works of Authorship	286
[a]		Statutory Categories	286
[i]		Literary Works	286
(a)		Characters	286
(b)		Computer Programs	288
[ii]		Musical Works	290
[iii]		Dramatic Works	291
[iv]		Pantomimes and Choreographic Works	291
[v]		Pictorial, Graphic, and Sculptural Works	292
(a)		Generally	292
(b)		Useful Articles	293
(1)		Historical Development	293
(2)		Statutory Definition	294
(3)		Separability	295
[vi]		Motion Pictures and Other Audiovisual Works	297
[vii]		Sound Recordings	299
[viii]		Architectural Works	300
(a)		Pre-1991 Law	300
(b)		Architectural Works Copyright Protection Act	301
[b]		Works Employing Preexisting Material	303
[i]		Compilations and Collective Works	303
[ii]		Derivative Works	305
[5]		Government Works	308
[6]		National Eligibility	309
§ 4D		FORMALITIES	310
[1]		Publication	311
[a]		Publication Under the 1909 Act	311

Table of Contents

[b]		Publication Under the 1976 Act	314
[2]		Notice	314
[a]		Notice Under the 1909 Act	315
[b]		Notice Under the 1976 Act	316
	[i]	Omission of Notice	317
	[ii]	Errors in Notice	318
	[iii]	Collective Works	318
[c]		Notice After the Berne Convention Implementation Act	319
[3]		Deposit and Registration	320
[a]		Deposit of Copies	320
[b]		Registration	320
§ 4E		DURATION, RENEWAL, AND RESTORATION	323
[1]		Duration	323
[2]		Renewal of Copyright in Pre-1978 Works	324
[a]		Basic Renewal Principles	324
[b]		Renewal and Derivative Works	327
[c]		Automatic Renewal	328
[3]		Restoration of Copyright in Foreign Works	329
§ 4F		OWNERSHIP, TRANSFERS, AND TERMINATIONS	331
[1]		Initial Ownership	331
[a]		Works for Hire	333
	[i]	The 1909 Act	334
	[ii]	The 1976 Act	335
[b]		Joint Works	338
	[i]	The 1909 Act	339
	[ii]	The 1976 Act	340
[c]		Collective Works	342
[2]		Transfers and Licenses	344
[3]		Termination of Transfers	349
[a]		Persons Entitled to Terminate	350
[b]		Time Periods for Termination and Notice	351
[c]		Effect of Termination	353
[d]		Agreements to the Contrary	354
§ 4G		EXCLUSIVE RIGHTS AND LIMITATIONS	355
[1]		Reproduction	356
[a]		In General	356
[b]		Electronic Reproduction	357
[c]		Exceptions and Limitations	359
[2]		Preparation of Derivative Works	360
[a]		In General	360
[b]		Exceptions and Limitations	363

Table of Contents

[3]   Public Distribution 365

  [a]   In General 365

  [b]   Electronic Distribution 366

  [c]   First-Sale Doctrine 367

  [d]   Import and Export Rights 369

[4]   Public Performance 371

  [a]   In General 371

  [b]   Secondary Transmissions 373

    [i]   The 1909 Act 373

    [ii]   The 1976 Act 374

  [c]   Exceptions and Limitations 376

  [d]   Performing Rights Organizations 378

[5]   Public Display 379

[6]   Digital Audio Transmission 381

[7]   Moral Rights 383

  [a]   In General 383

  [b]   Visual Artists Rights Act 384

[8]   Additional Rights 386

[9]   Compulsory Licenses 387

§ 4H   INFRINGEMENT 388

[1]   Ownership of a Valid Copyright 390

[2]   Derivation or Copying 391

  [a]   Access 392

  [b]   Probative Similarity 394

[3]   Substantial Similarity 396

  [a]   Protected Expression 398

    [i]   Dissection 398

    [ii]   Distinguishing Idea from Expression 400

    [iii]   Abstraction-Filtration-Comparison 402

  [b]   Ordinary Observer Test 406

  [c]   *De Minimis* Use 410

§ 4I   SECONDARY LIABILITY 411

[1]   In General 411

  [a]   Contributory Infringement 412

  [b]   Vicarious Liability 414

[2]   Providing Copying Devices or Software 416

  [a]   The *Sony* Decision 416

  [b]   Audio Home Recording Act 418

  [c]   Peer-to-Peer File Sharing 420

[3]   Secondary Liability and the Internet 423

  [a]   In General 423

Table of Contents

[b]   Limitation of Liability for Online Service Providers 426

    [i]   Safe Harbors 426

      (a)   Transitory Digital Network Communications 426

      (b)   System Caching 427

      (c)   Web Hosting 427

      (d)   Information Location Tools 430

    [ii]   Eligibility for Safe Harbors 430

    [iii]   Notice-and-Take-Down Provisions 432

[4]   Digital Millennium Copyright Act 434

   [a]   Anti-Circumvention 435

    [i]   In General 435

      (a)   Ownership of a Valid Copyright 436

      (b)   Access-Control Measures 436

      (c)   Circumvention 437

      (d)   Authorization 438

      (e)   Facilitation of Infringement 439

      (f)   Design, Use, and Marketing of Technology 439

    [ii]   Statutory Exceptions 440

    [iii]   Regulatory Exceptions 441

    [iv]   Other Defenses 442

   [b]   Copyright Management Information 443

§ 4J   FAIR USE AND OTHER DEFENSES 444

[1]   Fair Use 444

   [a]   Preamble 445

   [b]   Factors 446

    [i]   Purpose and Character of the Use 446

      (a)   Transformative Use 446

      (b)   Commercial Use 448

      (c)   Educational Use 449

      (d)   Good Faith 449

    [ii]   Nature of the Copyrighted Work 450

    [iii]   Amount and Substantiality of the Use 452

    [iv]   Effect on Potential Market 453

   [c]   Examples 456

    [i]   Comment and Criticism 456

    [ii]   Parody and Satire 458

    [iii]   News Reporting and Documentaries 460

    [iv]   Litigation Uses 461

    [v]   Reverse Engineering 461

    [vi]   Personal Uses 462

    [vii]   Internet and Database Uses 462

Table of Contents

[2]		Other Defenses	464
[a]		Inequitable Conduct	464
[b]		Misuse	464
[c]		Statute of Limitations	465
[d]		Laches and Estoppel	466
[e]		Abandonment and Forfeiture	467
§ 4K		REMEDIES	467
[1]		In General	467
[2]		Injunctions	468
[a]		Preliminary Injunctions	468
[b]		Permanent Injunctions	469
[3]		Impoundment and Disposition	469
[4]		Monetary Remedies	470
[a]		In General	470
[b]		Damages and Profits	471
[i]		Actual Damages	473
	(a)	Lost Profits	473
	(b)	Value of Use	474
	(c)	Consequential Damages	475
[ii]		Infringer's Profits	475
	(a)	In General	475
	(b)	Indirect Profits	477
	(c)	Apportionment	479
[c]		Statutory Damages	480
[i]		Number of Works Infringed	481
[ii]		Defendant's Intent	482
[iii]		Amount of Award	484
[iv]		Constitutionality	484
[5]		Costs and Attorney's Fees	485
[6]		Criminal Penalties	487

Chapter 5		**TRADEMARKS**	**489**
§ 5A		INTRODUCTION	495
§ 5B		HISTORICAL DEVELOPMENT	496
[1]		Early Common Law: Passing Off	496
[2]		Modern Common Law and State Statutes	497
[3]		Early Federal Law: *The Trademark Cases*	498
[4]		The Lanham Act	499
[a]		Overview	499
[b]		Recent Amendments	500
§ 5C		PROTECTABILITY	500

Table of Contents

[1]		Requirements for Protection	501
	[a]	In General	501
	[b]	Distinctiveness	501
	[c]	Non-Functionality	502
	[i]	Public Policy	502
	[ii]	The Evolving Definition of Functionality	503
	[iii]	Aesthetic Functionality	506
[2]		Trademark Subject Matter	510
	[a]	Distinctiveness	511
	[i]	Arbitrary or Fanciful	512
	[ii]	Suggestive	513
	[iii]	Descriptive	514
	(a)	Common Law	515
	(b)	Secondary Meaning	515
	[iv]	Generic Terms	516
	[b]	Words and Slogans	518
	[i]	In General	518
	[ii]	Personal Names	518
	[iii]	Foreign Words	520
	[iv]	Abbreviations of Generic or Descriptive Terms	521
	[v]	Titles	521
	[c]	Non-Verbal Marks	522
	[i]	Numerals and Alphanumeric Combinations	522
	[ii]	Color, Sound, Scent	522
	[iii]	Expressive Works	523
	[iv]	Celebrity Likenesses and Fictional Characters	525
	[d]	Trade Dress	525
§ 5D		ACQUISITION AND MAINTENANCE OF TRADEMARK RIGHTS	527
[1]		Use in Trade	527
	[a]	Establishing Priority of Use	528
	[i]	Actual Use	529
	[ii]	Reputation and Business Presence	529
	[iii]	Zone of Expansion	530
	[b]	Lanham Act	530
	[i]	Use in Commerce	530
	[ii]	Foreign Use	533
	[iii]	The Famous Marks Doctrine	534
	[iv]	Intent to Use Applications	536
	[v]	Constructive Use	537
[2]		Distinctiveness	537
[3]		Maintaining Trademark Rights	538

Table of Contents

[4]		Assignments and Licenses	538
	[a]	Assignments	538
	[b]	Licensing	539
§ 5E		REGISTRATION OF TRADEMARK RIGHTS	540
[1]		Marks Eligible for Federal Registration	541
	[a]	In General	541
	[b]	Service Marks	542
	[c]	Certification Marks	543
	[d]	Collective Marks	544
[2]		Marks Ineligible for Federal Registration	545
	[a]	Immoral, Deceptive, Scandalous, or Disparaging Matter	546
	[b]	National, State, or Municipal Insignia	549
	[c]	Name, Portrait, or Signature	549
	[d]	Marks Confusingly Similar to Existing Marks	549
	[i]	Priority of Use	549
	[ii]	Priority Through Analogous Use	550
	[iii]	Factors	551
	[iv]	Concurrent Use	552
	[e]	Descriptive, Misdescriptive, or Functional Marks	554
	[i]	Descriptive and Misdescriptive Marks	555
	[ii]	Primarily Geographically Descriptive Marks	556
	[iii]	Primarily Geographically Deceptively Misdescriptive Marks	556
	[iv]	Primarily Merely a Surname	558
	[v]	Functional Marks	559
	[f]	Secondary Meaning	559
	[g]	Dilutive Marks	561
[3]		Registration Process	561
	[a]	Use Applications	561
	[b]	Intent to Use Applications	562
	[c]	Who May Register a Mark	563
	[d]	Dividing Applications	564
	[e]	*Inter Partes* Proceedings	564
	[i]	Opposition	564
	[ii]	Interferences	565
	[iii]	Concurrent Use Proceedings	565
	[iv]	Cancellation	566
	(a)	Grounds for Cancellation	566
	(b)	Procedure	567
	[f]	Judicial Review	568
	[g]	Maintaining and Renewing Registration	568
	[i]	Affidavit of Use	569

Table of Contents

[ii]   Renewal 569

[4]   Incontestability 569

  [a]   Effect of Incontestable Status 569

  [b]   Establishing Incontestability 571

[5]   The Supplemental Register 572

  [a]   Eligible Marks 572

  [b]   Registration Procedure 573

  [c]   Effect of Supplemental Registration 573

  [d]   Cancellation 573

[6]   Domestic Priority Based on Foreign Registration 574

  [a]   International Agreements 574

  [b]   National Treatment 574

  [c]   Domestic Priority 575

  [d]   The Madrid Protocol 575

[7]   State Trademark Registration 576

  [a]   State Registration Statutes 576

  [b]   Federal Preemption 577

[8]   Unregistered Marks 578

§ 5F   INFRINGEMENT 578

[1]   Effect of Federal Registration 579

[2]   Ownership of a Valid Mark 581

[3]   Likelihood of Confusion 583

  [a]   Overview 583

  [b]   Factors 584

    [i]   Similarity of Marks 586

    [ii]   Competitive Proximity 589

    [iii]   Strength of Plaintiff's Mark 591

    [iv]   Consumer Sophistication 592

    [v]   Actual Confusion 593

    [vi]   Bridging the Gap 595

    [vii] Defendant's Intent 595

    [viii] Relative Quality of Defendant's Goods or Services 596

  [c]   Jurisdictional Variations on the *Polaroid* Test 597

  [d]   Reverse Confusion 598

  [e]   Confusion Before or After the Purchasing Decision 600

    [i]   Initial Interest Confusion 600

    [ii]   Post-Sale Confusion 604

[4]   Trademark Use 606

  [a]   Keyword-Triggered Advertising 608

  [b]   Metatags 611

  [c]   Domain Names 612

Table of Contents

[d]   Expressive Works 613

[5]   Use in Commerce as Jurisdictional Prerequisite 613

[6]   Territorial Limitations 615

[7]   Reverse Passing Off 619

[8]   Adjudication and Procedure 622

[a]   Subject Matter Jurisdiction 622

[b]   Standing 623

[i]   Standing to Cancel or Oppose Federal Registration 623

[ii]   Standing Under Section 32 624

[iii]   Standing Under Section 43(a) and Common Law 625

[iv]   Standing Under Section 43(c) 626

[c]   Declaratory Judgments 626

§ 5G   DILUTION 627

[1]   The Concept of Dilution 627

[2]   Dilution Under State Law 629

[3]   Federal Trademark Dilution Act 632

[a]   History 632

[b]   Elements of a Federal Dilution Claim 632

[c]   Trademark Use 633

[d]   Distinctive and Famous Mark 634

[i]   Distinctiveness 634

[ii]   Fame 634

[iii]   Trade Dress and Other Nontraditional Marks 636

[e]   Similarity 637

[f]   Actual Dilution Versus Likelihood of Dilution 637

[i]   The FTDA and the *Moseley* Decision 637

[ii]   Likelihood of Dilution Under the TDRA 638

[iii]   Judicial Interpretations 638

(a)   Likelihood of Dilution by Blurring 638

(b)   Likelihood of Dilution by Tarnishment 640

[g]   Effective Date of TDRA 641

[4]   Exceptions to FTDA 641

[a]   Fair Use 642

[b]   Noncommercial Use 643

[c]   News Reporting and Commentary 644

[d]   Federal Registration as a Defense 644

[5]   Remedies 645

§ 5H   CYBERSQUATTING 645

[1]   Anticybersquatting Consumer Protection Act 645

[a]   Elements of an ACPA Claim 646

[b]   *In Rem* Jurisdiction 649

Table of Contents

[c]	Personal Names		651
[d]	ACPA Remedies		651
[2]	Alternative Forums for Domain Name Disputes		652
§ 5I	SECONDARY LIABILITY		653
[1]	Contributory Infringement		653
[2]	Vicarious Liability		657
§ 5J	DEFENSES		658
[1]	Abandonment		658
[a]	Cessation of Use		660
[b]	Other Causes of Abandonment		661
[i]	Naked Licensing		662
[ii]	Assignment in Gross		663
[2]	First Sale Doctrine		665
[a]	Misrepresentation by Authorized Resellers		665
[b]	Materially Different Goods		666
[i]	Used, Altered, or Refurbished Goods		666
[ii]	Other Non-Genuine Goods		669
[c]	Undisclosed Repackaging		669
[d]	Parallel Imports		670
[3]	"Classic" Fair Use		673
[4]	Nominative Fair Use		675
[5]	Comparative Advertising		678
[6]	First Amendment		679
[a]	Commercial Parodies		680
[i]	Infringement and Unfair Competition		680
[ii]	Dilution		682
[b]	Noncommercial Expression		684
[i]	Infringement and Unfair Competition		684
[ii]	Dilution		687
[c]	Political Speech		689
[d]	Expressive Merchandise		690
[7]	Other Defenses		692
[a]	Laches		692
[b]	Acquiescence		695
[c]	Statute of Limitations		695
[d]	Unclean Hands		696
[8]	Federal Preemption		696
[9]	Sovereign Immunity		699
§ 5K	REMEDIES		699
[1]	Non-Monetary Remedies		699
[a]	Injunctions		699

Table of Contents

[b]   Seizure of Counterfeit Goods and Related Materials 702

[c]   Destruction of Infringing Articles 702

[d]   Cancellation of Federal Registration 702

[e]   Disclaimers 703

[2]   Monetary Remedies 703

[a]   Actual Damages, Defendant's Profits, and Costs 703

[b]   Enhanced Damages 705

[c]   Attorney's Fees 706

[d]   Statutory Damages 707

[e]   Enhanced Awards in Counterfeiting Cases 708

[f]   Marking or Actual Notice 708

[g]   Damages Under Federal Dilution Law 709

[h]   False or Fraudulent Registration 709

[3]   Limitations on Remedies Against Certain Defendants 709

[a]   Makers of Labels, Signs, Packaging, or Advertisements 709

[b]   Printers and Publishers 710

[c]   Domain Name Registration Authorities 710

[d]   Family Movie Act of 2005 711

[e]   Remedies Against Federal and State Governments 712

[4]   Criminal Penalties 712

[a]   Counterfeit Marks 712

[b]   Counterfeit Labels 713

Chapter 6   **OTHER INTELLECTUAL PROPERTY RIGHTS** **715**

§ 6A   INTRODUCTION 717

§ 6B   DESIGN PROTECTION 718

[1]   Historical Background 720

[2]   Design Patentability Requirements 721

[a]   Article of Manufacture 721

[b]   Ornamentality 722

[c]   Nonfunctionality 723

[d]   Novelty and Statutory Bars 723

[e]   Nonobviousness 724

[3]   Application and Examination 724

[4]   Exclusive Rights and Remedies — Infringement 725

[5]   Conclusion 727

§ 6C   PLANT PROTECTION 728

[1]   Plant Patent Act 728

[a]   Requirements 728

[b]   Application and Examination 730

[c]   Exclusive Rights — Infringement 731

Table of Contents

[2]		Plant Variety Protection Act	731
	[a]	Requirements	732
	[b]	Application and Examination	733
	[c]	Exclusive Rights — Infringement	733
	[d]	Essentially Derived Varieties	734
[3]		Utility Patents for Plants	735
[4]		Protection Source Choice Factors	737
[5]		Plant Breeders Rights Under TRIPS	738
§ 6D		SEMICONDUCTOR CHIP PROTECTION	738
[1]		Introduction	738
[2]		Protection Requirements	739
	[a]	Definitions	739
	[b]	Originality	740
	[c]	Owner Nationality	741
[3]		Registration	742
[4]		Exclusive Rights — Infringement	743
	[a]	Rights Granted	743
	[b]	Limitations	745
	[i]	Reverse Engineering	745
	[ii]	First Sale	746
	[iii]	Innocent Infringement	747
	[iv]	Ideas, Procedures, and Principles	748
	[c]	Infringement Actions	748
	[d]	Remedies	749
	[i]	Injunctive Relief	749
	[ii]	Damages — Attorney's Fees	750
	[iii]	International Trade Commission Remedies	751
[5]		International Protection for Semiconductor Chips	751
§ 6E		FALSE ADVERTISING	752
[1]		Historical Development	752
[2]		Current Federal Law	754
	[a]	Falsity	754
	[b]	Commercial Advertising or Promotion	756
	[c]	Other Commercial Activities	758
	[d]	Standing	759
§ 6F		MISAPPROPRIATION	759
[1]		The *INS* Decision	760
[2]		From *INS* to *Sears-Compco*	762
[3]		*Sears-Compco* and Federal Preemption	764
[4]		Contemporary Applications	765
§ 6G		RIGHTS OF PUBLICITY	769

Table of Contents

[1]   Introduction 769

[2]   Historical Development 771

[3]   Rights 773

  [a]   Names 773

  [b]   Likenesses 774

  [c]   Roles 775

  [d]   Voice and Vocal Imitations 775

[4]   Infringement and Defenses 776

  [a]   *Prima Facie* Case 776

  [b]   Newsworthiness 777

  [c]   First Amendment 779

    [i]   Works of Art 779

    [ii]   Parody and Satire 780

    [iii] Other Uses 781

  [d]   Other Defenses 782

    [i]   Copyright Preemption 782

    [ii]   First Sale Doctrine 783

    [iii] Antitrust 784

    [iv]   Statute of Limitations and Laches 784

    [v]   Other Defenses 784

[5]   Remedies 785

[6]   Ownership and Transfer 786

§ 6H   IDEA SUBMISSION 789

[1]   Novelty and Concreteness 789

  [a]   Novelty 790

  [b]   Concreteness 791

[2]   Express Contracts 792

  [a]   Novelty and Concreteness 792

  [b]   Standard Release Forms 793

[3]   Implied Contracts 794

  [a]   Unsolicited Submissions 794

    [i]   Involuntarily Received 794

    [ii]   Failure to Reject After Notice 795

  [b]   Solicited Submissions 796

  [c]   Confidential Relationship 796

[4]   Unjust Enrichment 797

[5]   Property Theory 797

[6]   Remedies 798

[7]   Federal Preemption 799

Table of Contents

INDEX **I-1**

CONTRIBUTORS TO THE SECOND AND THIRD EDITIONS

TYLER T. OCHOA: Tyler Ochoa received an A.B. (1983) and J.D. (1987) from Stanford University, and clerked for Judge Cecil Poole of the United States Court of Appeals for the Ninth Circuit. He is a Professor with the High Tech Law Institute at Santa Clara University School of Law, and Director of Santa Clara's summer program in Comparative Intellectual Property Law in Munich, Germany. He is a co-author (with Craig Joyce, Marshall Leaffer, Peter Jaszi, and Michael Carroll) of *Copyright Law* (LexisNexis 9th ed. 2013), the best-selling copyright casebook in the United States; and a co-author (with David Welkowitz) of *Celebrity Rights: Rights of Publicity and Related Rights in the United States and Abroad* (Carolina Academic Press 2010). Prior to joining the faculty at Santa Clara, he was a Professor and Co-Director of the Center for Intellectual Property Law at Whittier Law School in Costa Mesa, California.

SHUBHA GHOSH: Shubha Ghosh received a B.A. from Amherst College (1984), a Ph.D. in Economics from the University of Michigan (1988) and a J.D. from Stanford University (1994), and clerked for Judge John Noonan of the United States Court of Appeals for the Ninth Circuit. He is a Vilas Research Fellow and Professor at the University of Wisconsin Law School, and Executive Director of the Initiatives on Studies and Technology and Entrepreneurship (INSITE). He is a co-author (with Richard Gruner, Jay Kesan, and Robert Reis) of *Intellectual Property: Private Rights, the Public Interest, and the Regulation of Creative Activity* (Thomson West 2007), a co-author (with Richard Gruner and Jay Kesan) of *Intellectual Property in Business Organizations* (LexisNexis 2006), and a co-author (with Martin Adelman and Amy Landers) of a forthcoming book on *Global Issues in Patent Law* (Thomson West). Prior to joining the faculty at Wisconsin, he was a Professor at Southern Methodist University, Dedman School of Law, and the State University of New York, University of Buffalo School of Law.

MARY LA FRANCE: Mary LaFrance received an A.B. from Bryn Mawr College (1981), and an M.A. (1986) and J.D. (1986) from Duke University, where she served as Executive Editor of the Duke Law Journal. She is the IGT Professor of Intellectual Property Law at the University of Nevada, Las Vegas, William S. Boyd School of Law. She is a co-author (with David Lange and Gary Myers) of *Intellectual Property Law: Cases and Materials* (West 3rd ed. 2007) and the author of *Understanding Trademark Law* (LexisNexis 2d ed. 2009), *Copyright Law in a Nutshell* (West 2d ed. 2011), and *Global Issues in Copyright Law* (West 2009). Prior to joining the faculty at UNLV, she was an Associate Professor at Florida State University College of Law, and she clerked for Judge Harry Edwards of the United States Court of Appeals for the D.C. Circuit.

KEITH AOKI: The late Keith Aoki received a B.F.A. from Wayne State University (1978), an M.A. in Fine Arts from Hunter College (1986), a J.D. from Harvard Law School (1990) and an LL.M. from the University of Wisconsin Law School (1993). At the time of his untimely death in 2011, he was a Professor at the University of California at Davis, King Hall School of Law. Before joining the faculty at Davis, he was the Phillip H. Knight Professor at the University of Oregon Law School. He was the author of *Seed Wars: Cases and Materials on Intellectual Property and Plant Genetic Resources* (Carolina Academic Press 2008), and illustrator and co-author (with James Boyle and Jennifer Jenkins) of *Bound by Law? Tales from the Public Domain* (2006). He wished to thank his research assistant, Camille Barr, for her contributions to the project.

DANIEL H. BREAN: Daniel Brean received a B.S. in Physics from Carnegie Mellon University (2005), and a J.D. from the University of Pittsburgh School of Law (2008), where he was the Lead Articles Editor of the Pittsburgh Journal of Technology Law and Policy and the recipient of the Faculty Award for Excellence in Legal Scholarship. He was a law clerk for the Honorable Jimmie Reyna of the United States Court of Appeals for the Federal Circuit, and is currently an attorney with the Webb Law Firm in Pittsburgh. He is also a Registered Patent Attorney with the U.S. Patent and Trademark Office, and a frequent publisher and presenter on the subject of industrial design protection.

GANKA A. HADJIPETROVA: Ganka Hadjipetrova received a B.A. from the American University in Bulgaria (1996), an M.A. in International Policy Studies from Stanford University (2004), and a J.D. from Santa Clara University School of Law (2010), where she received a Certificate in Intellectual Property Law and won First Prize in the School's Nathan Burkan Memorial Competition, sponsored by the American Society of Composers, Authors and Publishers. She is a member of the California State Bar.

CONTRIBUTORS TO THE FIRST EDITION

JONATHAN BAND: Jonathan Band received an A.B. from Harvard (1982) and a J.D. from Yale (1985). He is a partner in Morrison & Foerster's Washington, D. C. office.

DONALD S. CHISUM: Donald Chisum received an A.B. (1966) and LL.B. (1968) from Stanford University, and clerked for Judge Shirley Hufstedler of the United States Court of Appeals for the Ninth Circuit. He is Of Counsel to Morrison & Foerster, specializing in intellectual property and patent law matters. Mr. Chisum is author of the multiple volume reference text, *Patents: A Treatise on the Law of Patentability, Validity & Infringement,* first published by Matthew Bender in 1978 and regularly revised thereafter. From 1969 through 1990, he was on the faculty of the University of Washington School of Law, Seattle, Washington. His professional activities include service on the Board of Directors on the American Intellectual Property Law Association and lectures at the Judicial Conference of the United States Court of Appeals for the Federal Circuit. In 1989, he received the Jefferson Medal Award from the New Jersey Patent Law Association for meritorious and outstanding contributions in support of the United States Constitutional provision for patents and copyrights.

LAURIE S. HANE: Laurie Hane received a B.A. from Knox College (1981) and a J.D. from Northwestern University (1984), and clerked for Judge Robert Peckham, of the United States District Court, Northern District of California. She is a partner in Morrison & Foerster's San Francisco office.

MICHAEL A. JACOBS: Michael Jacobs received a B. A. from Stanford University (1977) and a J.D. from Yale Law School (1983), and served in the United States Foreign Service, holding assignments in Kingston, Jamaica, and Washington D.C. He is a partner in Morrison & Foerster's San Francisco office and co-heads the firm's Intellectual Property Group. Mr. Jacobs is currently chairman of the computer program copyright protection subcommittee of the American Bar Association's Patent, Trademark and Copyright Section.

GRANT L. KIM: Grant Kim received a B.A. from Pomona College (1978) and a J.D. from Hastings College of Law (1984), clerked for the office of Staff Attorneys of the United States Court of Appeals for the Ninth Circuit, and served in the Peace Corps in the Republic of Korea. He is an associate in Morrison & Foerster's San Francisco office.

KIM J. LANDSMAN: Kim Landsman received an A.B. from Vassar College, a M.A. from Oxford University and a J.D. from Yale Law School (1979), and clerked for Judge Arlin Adams of the United States court of Appeals for the Third Circuit. He is a partner in Morrison & Foerster's New York office.

NEAL A. STENDER: Neal Stender received a B.A. from University of California Berkley (1982) and a J.D. from Stanford University (1989). He is an associate in Morrison & Foerster's San Francisco office.

PREFACE TO THE THIRD EDITION

During the past four years, there have been a number of important developments in U.S. intellectual property law. Foremost among them was the adoption, in September 2011, of the America Invents Act, the most significant change to U.S. patent law since the 1952 Patent Act. Before the AIA, if two parties applied to patent the same invention, the patent was granted to the person who first conceived the invention or reduced it to practice (first-to-invent). The first-to-invent principle still applies to all applications filed before March 16, 2013, and to all patents granted on those applications. For applications filed on or after March 16, 2013, however, the AIA grants the patent to the first person to file a patent application on the invention. This change means that patent lawyers will have to know and apply two different standards when litigating patents for the next 20 years or so. The AIA also implemented a number of other changes, including de-emphasizing the best-mode requirement and post-grant review of patents.

The Supreme Court has been unusually active in reviewing intellectual property cases in the past four years. During that period, it has reviewed and decided 15 patent cases (including three cases on patentable subject matter), four copyright cases, and four trademark or false advertising cases. In addition, the federal Courts of Appeals have decided more than 750 patent cases, 250 copyright cases, and 400 trademark and false advertising cases during that time. While not all of these decisions warrant mention in a student hornbook, all had to be considered in deciding what material needed to be updated.

Once again, this volume would not have been possible without the combined efforts of many people. Tyler Ochoa updated Chapters 1, 4, and 6; Shubha Ghosh updated Chapters 2 and 3, and Mary LaFrance updated Chapter 5. The authors would like to thank Elisabeth (Biz) Ebben, our editor at LexisNexis Publishing, for all of her work in reviewing our submissions and her careful attention to the page proofs.

We hope that find the hornbook helpful in navigating the fascinating but complex world of intellectual property law.

Tyler T. Ochoa
Shubha Ghosh
Mary LaFrance

March 15, 2015

PREFACE TO THE SECOND EDITION

Nineteen years is a long time in any field of law, but it is a lifetime in the fast-changing world of intellectual property law. So when we undertook to revise and update Don Chisum and Michael Jacob's landmark hornbook *Understanding Intellectual Property Law*, we knew we were in for a challenge. Not only did two decades worth of new developments have to be added to the text, but the length had to be shortened from over 1200 pages to a more manageable size.

Not surprisingly, the task required more than one person. While the original hornbook was largely the effort of a single individual, Donald Chisum, aided and abetted by six colleagues from Morrison & Foerster who wrote one of the chapters (on trade secret law) and six shorter sections, the Second Edition is largely the product of three authors, with some assistance from three other contributors. Tyler Ochoa revised and updated Chapter 1 (Introduction) and Chapter 4 (Copyright), and the majority of Chapter 6 (Other IP Rights), and also edited all of the other submissions for style and consistency. Shubha Ghosh was primarily responsible for updating Chapter 2 (Patent) and Chapter 3 (Trade Secret). For Chapter 5 (Trademark), we retained only some introductory language from Chisum's text; the rest was adapted by Mary LaFrance from her own hornbook, *Understanding Trademark Law* (2d ed. 2009). In Chapter 6, the section on Design Patents was revised by Daniel Brean; the section on Plant Patents was revised by Keith Aoki; and the section on Idea Submission was revised by Ganka Hadjipetrova.

The authors would like to thank all of the contributors who made the Second Edition possible, and to thank our editor at LexisNexis Publishing, Christine Frost, and her staff. We also owe a big note of thanks to Tyler's administrative assistant, Channing McCabe, who spent many tedious hours correcting formatting errors in the conversion from the previous edition. We hope you enjoy the product of our combined efforts.

Tyler T. Ochoa
Shubha Ghosh
Mary LaFrance

February 1, 2011

PREFACE TO THE FIRST EDITION

Donald Chisum began work on his basic intellectual property text in 1987. Mr. Chisum became of counsel to Morrison & Foerster in 1990, and the firm's Intellectual Property Group brought the project to fruition. Mr. Chisum wrote the major chapters on patent, copyright, and trademark law, and sections on design protection, plant protection, unfair competition and misappropriation. Michael Jacobs, San Francisco, the Group's co-chairman, wrote the trade secrets chapter with Neal Stender's substantial assistance. Mr. Jacobs also reviewed portions of the copyright chapter. Kim Landsman, New York, wrote the false advertising and trademark remedies sections. Mr. Landsman also reviewed portions of the trademark chapter. Jonathan Band, Washington, D.C., wrote the publicity rights section. Laurie Hane, San Francisco, wrote the copyright remedies and idea submission sections. Grant Kim, San Francisco, wrote the semiconductor chip protection section.

Mr. Chisum's academic background and Morrison & Foerster's spirit of inquiry, professionalism, and extensive intellectual property practice combined to make this book possible. The authors collected the relevant statues, regulations, and court decisions and describe intellectual property law's evolution up to mid-1991 as accurately and objectively as possible. The book does not present personal views or the position of Morrison & forester or its clients on any particular point of law. Nor does it predict the law's future course. United States law has always been in flux; it is a process not a structure. Like a river crossing a plain, it will meander, but when and to where no one can say with certainty; environmental changes may affect the way the river changes. In no area is this more true than with intellectual property.

Mr. Chisum acknowledges West Publishing Company's assistance in providing him access to "WESTLAW" to prepare this book. Having written a multi-volume treatise on patent law the old-fashioned way with dusty books, 3" x 5" cards, and an IBM Selectric typewriter, he appreciates the speed, thoroughness and accuracy of data searching, quotation fetching, and word processing.

Barbara Nielsen, Mr. Chisum's editorial assistant, edited the entire text and verified its citations and quotations. She encouraged us to write directly, clearly, and without excessive verbiage. To the extent our style falls short of that goal, it is not for want of effort by Ms. Nielsen.

Donald S. Chisum
Michael A. Jacobs
Morrison & Foerster

San Francisco
October 4, 1991

Chapter 1

INTRODUCTION

SYNOPSIS

§ 1A   LAW AND HUMAN CREATIVITY

§ 1B   INTELLECTUAL PROPERTY RIGHTS: AN OVERVIEW

    [1]   Patents

    [2]   Trade Secrets

    [3]   Copyright

    [4]   Trademarks

    [5]   Other Intellectual Property Rights

§ 1C   POLICY

§ 1D   INTELLECTUAL PROPERTY AND THE CONSTITUTION

    [1]   Congress' Patent and Copyright Powers

    [2]   Commerce Clause Regulation of Intellectual Property

    [3]   Preemption

       [a]   Copying Publicly Disclosed Subject Matter

       [b]   Contracts

       [c]   Copyright Act Preemption

         [i]   Subject Matter

         [ii]   Equivalent Rights

         [iii]   Examples

         [iv]   Moral Rights

    [4]   First Amendment Limits on Intellectual Property Laws

       [a]   Granting or Withholding Intellectual Property Rights

       [b]   Enforcing Intellectual Property Rights

         [i]   Copyright

         [ii]   Trademark and Rights of Publicity

    [5]   Eleventh Amendment and Sovereign Immunity

       [a]   Claims Against State Governments

       [b]   Claims Against the Federal Government

§ 1A   LAW AND HUMAN CREATIVITY

Intellectual property law is concerned with fostering human innovation and creativity without unduly restricting dissemination of its fruits. It concerns the full spectrum of human creativity: literature, the visual arts, music, drama, movies, compilations of useful information, computer programs, biotechnology, electronics, mechanics, chemistry, product design, agriculture, and symbols of human and business identity.

Intellectual property law is a growing industry in the United States and around the world. Increased interest in copyrights, patents, trademarks and related areas stems in part from a number of major legal and economic events during the past 35 years, including, in the United States, the creation in the U.S. Court of Appeals for the Federal Circuit, with exclusive appellate jurisdiction over patent matters, in 1982, which focused renewed attention on the patent system, the traditional means of stimulating research, development and investment; adoption of "intent-to-use" trademark procedures in 1988; U.S. adherence to the Berne Convention, the major international treaty concerning copyright, in 1989; the development of the World Wide Web and the subsequent commercialization and rapid spread of the Internet, leading to the Digital Millennium Copyright Act of 1998; the Federal Trademark Dilution Act of 1995 and the Trademark Dilution Revision Act of 2006; and the America Invents Act of 2011, the most significant revision of U.S. patent law in 60 years. These developments were both complemented and driven by developments in the international arena, including the formation and expansion of the European Union; negotiations on new intellectual property treaties conducted under the auspices of the World Intellectual Property Organization ("WIPO"); and adoption of the Uruguay Round of the General Agreement on Tariffs and Trade ("GATT"), including the Agreement on Trade-Related Aspects of Intellectual Property Rights ("TRIPS"), which brought intellectual property disputes into the dispute-resolution mechanism of the newly-created World Trade Organization ("WTO").

Even apart from these dramatic events, heightened interest in intellectual property is not surprising. Today more than ever before, products of the mind — aesthetic, technological, and organizational — are humankind's most valuable assets.

In the international arena, intellectual property is divided into two broad categories. The first category is copyright and related rights (or "neighboring" rights). The major international treaties in this category are the Berne Convention for the Protection of Literary and Artistic Works, first adopted in 1886, and most recently revised in Paris in 1971;[1] and the Rome Convention for the Protection of Performers, Producers of Phonograms and Broadcasting Organizations, adopted in 1961.[2] The second category is "industrial property," which includes patents,

---

[1] The U.S. became a member of the Berne Convention in 1989.

[2] The U.S. is not a member of the Rome Convention, because the U.S. lacks a general public performance right in sound recordings. However, the U.S. is a member of the 1971 Geneva Convention for the Protection of Producers of Phonograms Against Unauthorized Duplication of Their Phonograms. In addition, there are provisions on neighboring rights in both the TRIPS Agreement and the 1996 WIPO Performances and Phonograms Treaty.

trademarks, designs, and unfair competition. The major international treaty in this category is the Paris Convention for the Protection of Industrial Property, first adopted in 1883, and most recently revised in Stockholm in 1967.[3] These treaties are administered by WIPO, a United Nations agency based in Geneva.

The term "intellectual property" begs a major policy question concerning the role of law in fostering innovation and creativity: should there be property rights in creations such as ideas and the expression of ideas? To the extent there is a property interest in intellectual creations, it is an intangible interest that must be carefully distinguished from property in tangible objects that either make the creation possible or that the creation makes possible.[4] Copyright law explicitly states the distinction between intellectual property and tangible things: "Ownership of a copyright is distinct from ownership of any material object in which the work is embodied."[5] The distinction between intellectual property and tangible things is also implicit in the doctrines of exhaustion and first sale, under which the authorized sale of a tangible object embodying an intellectual property right exhausts the intellectual property owner's rights in that object, such that the buyer of the object may use or re-sell that object without further permission from the owner of the intellectual property right.

§ 1B   INTELLECTUAL PROPERTY RIGHTS: AN OVERVIEW

Intellectual property rights include utility patents,[6] trade secrets,[7] copyrights,[8] trademarks,[9] and various other rights, including design patents, plant patents, semiconductor mask work protection, false advertising remedies, misappropriation, and rights of publicity.[10]

---

[3] The U.S. became a member of the Paris Convention in 1887.

[4] *See* Moore v. University of California, 51 Cal. 3d 120, 271 Cal. Rptr. 146, 793 P.2d 479 (Cal. 1990). In *Moore*, plaintiff alleged that the defendants took cell samples from his body and, without his knowledge or consent, used them to create biotechnological inventions, including a novel cell line, for which they obtained a patent and valuable commercial rights. The court held that plaintiff's complaint stated a cause of action for breach of the physician's disclosure obligations but not for conversion of any property interest the plaintiff could claim in his cells or genetic materials or the patent. "[T]he subject matter of the . . . patent — the patented cell line and the products derived from it — cannot be Moore's property. This is because the patented cell line is both factually and legally distinct from the cells taken from Moore's body. Federal law permits the patenting of organisms that represent the product of 'human ingenuity,' but not naturally occurring organisms. . . . Human cell lines are patentable because '[l]ong-term adaptation and growth of human tissues and cells in culture is difficult — often considered an art . . .' and the probability of success is low . . . . It is this *inventive effort* that patent law rewards, not the discovery of naturally occurring raw materials." 51 Cal. 3d at 141–42, 271 Cal. Rptr. at 159–60.

[5] 17 U.S.C. § 202.

[6] *See* Chapter 2.

[7] *See* Chapter 3.

[8] *See* Chapter 4.

[9] *See* Chapter 5.

[10] *See* Chapter 6.

The basic elements of an intellectual property right are: (1) the subject matter it covers; (2) the substantive requirements for obtaining it; (3) the procedural requirements for obtaining it; (4) the substantive rights it provides; (5) the exceptions and limitations on those rights; and (6) its duration.

[1] Patents

The Patent Act defines potentially patentable subject matter as any "new and useful process, machine, manufacture, or composition of matter,"[11] which includes mechanical, chemical and electrical products and processes. It includes the two most important technologies of our era — digital computing and biotechnology. However, an invention is patentable only if it meets three requirements — utility, novelty, and non-obviousness compared to the prior art.[12]

An inventor may obtain a patent only by filing a timely application with the United States Patent and Trademark Office ("PTO"), a federal government agency.[13] The application must describe the invention and must contain at least one "claim," a legal description of the elements that define the boundaries of the invention. The PTO will issue a patent if, after a search of the prior art and an examination, it determines that the claim or claims define a patentable invention. Patent procurement (or "prosecution") is expensive and procedurally complex.

A patent confers the right to exclude others from making, using, offering for sale, or selling in the United States the product or process claimed by the patent, or for importing the patented product or products made by the patented process into the United States.[14] A patent owner may sue not only persons who directly infringe by doing one of those things without authority, but also persons who induce others to infringe or who contribute to the infringement by selling especially designed components of patented products or processes. Unlike a copyright or a trade secret, a patent protects the owner against independent development of the patented subject matter. A patent's exclusive rights last for 20 years from the date the application is filed in the PTO.

[2] Trade Secrets

Trade secret rights may extend to virtually any type of information, including formulas, data compilations, programs, devices, processes, and customer lists.[15] Information is a trade secret only if it is secret in the sense that it derives "economic value . . . from not being generally known to, and not being readily ascertainable by proper means by, other persons" and it "is the subject of efforts that are reasonable under the circumstances to maintain secrecy."[16]

---

[11] 35 U.S.C. § 101.

[12] *See* § 2C.

[13] *See* § 2D.

[14] *See* §§ 2E and 2F.

[15] *See* Chapter 3.

[16] Uniform Trade Secrets Act § 1(4).

Unlike patents, copyrights, and trademarks, there are no formalities required to obtain trade secrets rights. The owner of a trade secret may prevent its unauthorized use or disclosure by a person who acquired it by improper means or through breach of a confidential relationship. However, trade secret law does not protect the owner against independent development of the same information, or against reverse engineering. Trade secrets rights last for as long as the trade secret's owner prevents the information from becoming common knowledge.

[3]   Copyright

The Copyright Act protects original works of authorship that are fixed in a tangible medium of expression.[17] It encompasses a wide variety of modes of artistic expression, both traditional (literature, music, drama, and visual art) and contemporary (movies, sound recordings, video games, and computer programs). To qualify, a work must be original, that is, it must be the author's own creation rather than copied from another. There is no requirement that the work be novel or strikingly different from prior creations.

Under current law, copyright arises automatically at the moment that an author fixes a work in a tangible medium of expression. Before 1978, however, a work had to published with proper copyright notice in order to obtain a copyright.[18] Before March 1, 1989, all copies distributed to the public had to bear a proper copyright notice; but as a result of U.S. adherence to the Berne Convention, there is no notice requirement for copies distributed to the public on or after that date. A copyright owner may register his or her copyright by filing an application with the U.S. Copyright Office, a division of the Library of Congress. Registration is optional, but if the authors of the work were U.S. residents or the work was first published in the U.S., then the owner must register before filing suit for infringement. In addition, registration provides certain procedural and remedial advantages, including a presumption of validity and the ability to recover statutory damages and attorney's fees.

Copyright confers upon the owner the exclusive right to reproduce (or copy) the protected work, to distribute copies of the protected work to the public, and to publicly perform or publicly display the protected work.[19] Copyright also include the right to prepare derivative works based on the protected work, such as the movie version of a book. However, copyright protects only the original expression of ideas; it confers no rights over ideas themselves. Nor does copyright protect against independent creation of similar works. To establish that an accused work infringes the copyright on a protected work, the copyright owner must prove that the accused work was copied from the protected work and that the accused work is substantially similar in expression to the protected work.[20] There are a number of

---

[17] 17 U.S.C. § 102(a). *See* § 4C.

[18] *See* § 4D.

[19] *See* § 4G.

[20] *See* § 4H.

exceptions and limitations on the exclusive rights of copyright, the most important of which is the fair use doctrine.[21]

Under current law, a copyright lasts for the author's life plus 70 years after the author's death. For "works made for hire," the copyright term is 95 years from first publication or 120 years from creation, whichever ends first. For works first published or registered before 1978, the original term was 28 years plus a renewal term of 28 more years. Since then, the renewal term for such works has been increased to 67 years, for a maximum duration of 95 years from first publication. Any work first published before 1923 is currently in the public domain in the United States.[22]

[4]   Trademarks

Any word, symbol or device that a manufacturer or merchant adopts and uses to identify its goods and to distinguish them from those of others may serve as a trademark.[23] This can include "trade dress," such as the distinctive packaging of a product, or even a distinctive and non-functional configuration of a product. The Lanham Act, the federal trademark registration statute, also provides for the registration of service marks, certification marks, and collective marks, as well as trademarks.

To be protected, a mark must distinguish the origin of the goods or services to which it relates.[24] A mark is considered inherently distinctive if it is fanciful (a coined word that has no meaning other than as a mark), arbitrary (an existing word that has no relationship to the goods or services), or suggestive (a word that indirectly suggests a quality or characteristic of the goods or services). A descriptive word cannot function as a trademark unless and until it has acquired a "secondary meaning," which means that it has been used as a mark and the public has come to view it as a brand name rather than as a description. Colors and product configurations also require a "secondary meaning" in order to be protected. A generic word cannot be a valid trademark. The mark adopted need not be new or original; however, a mark must not be confusingly similar to a mark used by others on the same or similar goods or services.

A manufacturer or merchant establishes trademark rights in a mark by using the mark on goods or services in commerce.[25] After acquiring mark ownership by use in interstate commerce, the owner may file an application to register the mark under with the U.S. Patent and Trademark Office (PTO).[26] A business may also file an application to register a mark based on a good faith "intent to use" the mark in interstate commerce, but it must actually begin using the mark to complete the registration and perfect its ownership. Federal registration offers procedural and

---

[21] *See* § 4J.

[22] *See* § 4E.

[23] *See* § 5C[1].

[24] *See* § 5C[2].

[25] *See* § 5D.

[26] *See* § 5E.

remedial advantages. However, the owner of an unregistered mark can still sue for infringement under state trademark and unfair competition law, and under section 43(a) of the Lanham Act.

Ownership of a mark confers the right to exclude others from using any identical or similar mark that creates a likelihood of confusion as to the origin or sponsorship of goods or services.[27] In addition, the owner of a "famous" mark may prevent the use of a similar mark on unrelated goods or services, even in the absence of consumer confusion, if the second mark is likely to cause "dilution" of the famous mark or to harm its reputation.[28] However, a descriptive term that has become a mark may still be used in its primary meaning to describe the goods or services of another, and a mark may be used to refer to the mark owner or the goods or services of the mark owner, so long as no confusion as to sponsorship or origin results.[29] A mark remains protectable for as long as it is used and retains its distinctiveness.

[5] Other Intellectual Property Rights

Beyond the major intellectual property rights (utility patents, trade secrets, copyright, and trademarks), there are other intellectual property rights pertaining to more specific subject matter and conduct, including design patents,[30] plant patents and plant variety protection,[31] semiconductor chip protection,[32] false advertising,[33] misappropriation,[34] and rights of publicity.[35]

§ 1C POLICY

Significant human mental creations share three characteristics: (1) humans typically produce them only with great time, effort, and expense; (2) others can duplicate them without an equivalent expenditure of time, effort, and expense; and (3) others' uses of them do not physically interfere with the first creator's use.

The major intellectual property law policy issues arise from these three characteristics. Two pairs of opposing concepts encapsulate these issues: (1) incentive versus competition, and (2) property versus monopoly. Incentive and competition clash on a utilitarian and economic battleground; property and monopoly on a moral one.

Here is a flavor of the utilitarian battle. Those who favor stronger incentives ask: Will people have an incentive to create if others can copy the results without

---

[27] *See* § 5F.

[28] *See* § 5G.

[29] *See* § 5J.

[30] *See* § 6B.

[31] *See* § 6C.

[32] *See* § 6D.

[33] *See* § 6E.

[34] *See* § 6F.

[35] *See* § 6G.

permission and without paying compensation? And even if they will create, will anyone invest in the initial production and distribution of the products of that creativity if such copying is likely to arise? As applied to patents, the question becomes: will anyone invest in research and development to produce new inventions if others can copy those inventions as soon as they are made public? As applied to copyrights, the question becomes: will anyone create new literary and artistic works if others can copy those works without permission and without paying compensation? And if so, will anyone invest in the production and distribution of those works if the works can be freely copied by others? The answers to these questions are not always clear.[36]

Those who favor competition respond that a major premise of United States public policy is that consumers benefit from free competition among producers. The effect of free competition is more efficient distribution of resources and lower prices. Granting exclusive rights to an intellectual creation is wasteful and anticompetitive because the marginal cost of using such an intangible is zero. There is little doubt, for example, that copyright leads to higher book prices, and that patents lead to higher pharmaceutical prices. Indeed, that is precisely the point of patent and copyright: by providing an exclusive right, the owner of the right may charge a higher-than-competitive price and use the excess proceeds to finance the research and development effort and to compensate the creator of the invention or work, and thereby provide a financial incentive to its creation. To preserve the benefits of competition, however, an intellectual property right should be of limited duration, so that the public gets the benefit of free competition after the right owner has earned enough money to recoup the initial costs of producing the innovation.

The moral battle closely tracks the utilitarian one. People who are more persuaded by incentive arguments argue that giving exclusive rights to an author or inventor is no more a monopoly or anticompetitive than other species of real or personal property.[37] People who are more persuaded by the competition arguments argue that intellectual property rights are indeed "monopolies,"[38] though they may

---

[36] The "open-source" software movement and the prevalence of user-generated content on the Internet both argue strongly in favor of the position that only minimal incentives are needed to give people incentives to create. However, motion pictures as we know them require a huge investment of capital that needs to be financed in some manner. In the patent arena, research and development of new pharmaceuticals likewise requires a huge investment of capital. On the other hand, a great deal of innovation in software and business methods occurred before patents were available in these areas.

[37] *See, e.g.*, Panduit Corp. v. Stahlin Bros. Fibre Works, Inc., 575 F.2d 1152, 1158 n.5 (6th Cir. 1978) (Markey: "The right to exclude others from free use of an invention protected by a valid patent does not differ from the right to exclude others from free use of one's automobile, crops, or other items of personal property. Every human right, including that in an invention, is subject to challenge under appropriate circumstances. That one human property right may be challenged by trespass, another by theft, and another by infringement, does not affect the fundamental indicium of all 'property,' i.e., the right to exclude others.").

[38] *See, e.g.*, Roberts v. Sears, Roebuck & Co., 723 F.2d 1324, 1345 (7th Cir. 1983) (Posner, dissenting: "Since new knowledge is a social good, it might seem that no limits should be placed on the scope or duration of patent protection. The problem is that patent protection has a dark side, to which the term 'patent monopoly' is a clue. A patent enables its owner to monopolize the production of the things in which the patented idea is embodied. To deny that patent protection has this effect . . . is — with all due respect — to bury one's head in the sand.").

be tolerated for public policy reasons.[39]

But the moral battle also has independent content. Some people are unimpressed by arguments concerning competition and economic efficiency. There is a "natural rights" school of thought, which favors recognizing the rights of authors and inventors regardless of the economic effects. Recognizing author or inventor control is a matter of human rights and moral right.[40] This school has had more influence in Europe and other countries than in the United States, but one also encounters natural rights viewpoints in United States intellectual property jurisprudence. To counter this view, some have posited the existence of a "natural right" to copy that is implicit in both the free market and the right of freedom of speech and expression. One need only observe any child to understand that humans learn by imitation, and that imitation is a natural behavior.

A closely related argument is one of unjust enrichment or "free riding." Just as the natural rights view posits that a creator has a natural right to the economic fruits of his or her creative labor, the "free riding" argument posits that it is unjust to allow someone else to profit from the creation of another. The most well-known expression of this view in U.S. intellectual property law is found is *International News Service v. Associated Press*, a dispute involving rival news organizations, in which a majority of the Supreme Court stated:

> [T]his defendant . . . admits that it is taking material that has been acquired by complainant as the result of organization and the expenditure of labor, skill, and money, and which is salable by complainant for money, and that defendant in appropriating it and selling it as its own is endeavoring to reap where it has not sown, and . . . is appropriating to itself the harvest of those who have sown.[41]

The "free-riding" argument, however, proves too much. All copying is free riding, and without any copying the public could not reap the benefits of free competition. As Justice Brandeis stated, dissenting in *INS v. AP*:

> [T]he fact that a product of the mind has cost its producer money and labor, and has a value for which others are willing to pay, is not sufficient to ensure to it this legal attribute of property. The general rule of law is, that the noblest of human productions — knowledge, truths ascertained, conceptions, and ideas — become, after voluntary communication to others, free as the air to common use. Upon these incorporeal productions the attribute of property is continued after such communication only in certain classes of cases where public policy has seemed to demand it.[42]

---

[39] When reading court opinions, one should be alert to the terminology the judge uses. If the term "monopoly" appears frequently, it is likely that the court will give a narrow interpretation to the patent or copyright. If the term "intellectual property" is used, it is likely that the court will give a broader interpretation.

[40] *See* Universal Declaration of Human Rights, Art. 27(2) ("Everyone has the right to the protection of the moral and material interests resulting from any scientific, literary or artistic production of which he is the author.").

[41] 248 U.S. 215, 239–40 (1918).

[42] *Id.* at 250.

Nonetheless, the unjust enrichment argument is a powerful one, and it frequently influences the outcome of intellectual property disputes, even where it is not expressly stated. To counter it, one can only point to the benefits of having intellectual property eventually enter the public domain, where it is freely available for others to copy, to use, and to improve upon.[43]

To date, the utilitarian rationale has had the strongest influence in patent law. Few would argue that there is a "natural right" to a patent,[44] and patent rights are granted only after scrutiny by the government. In addition, the duration of patents today (20 years from the date of filing) is only a little longer than it was in 1790 (14 years from the date of the grant). By contrast, although historically U.S. copyright law was strongly influenced by the utilitarian view, in recent years, the natural rights view has had increased influence, as the U.S. has adopted a more "European" model of copyright in the interests of international harmonization. This influence is most easily seen in two areas: first, in the change in copyright from an "opt in" system, in which certain formalities were required to claim copyright protection, to an "opt out" system, in which all works are automatically subject to copyright protection without any formalities;[45] and second, in the extraordinary increase in the duration of copyrights from a fixed term of years in 1790 (14 years, renewable once) to a term of 70 years after the death of the author.[46]

§ 1D INTELLECTUAL PROPERTY AND THE CONSTITUTION

United States intellectual property law policy intertwines with our Constitutional system, which distributes legislative power between the federal government and state governments and restricts state and federal legislative power.

Article I of the United States Constitution gives Congress, the federal legislative body, several powers. Two are directly relevant to intellectual property: the power to regulate interstate and foreign commerce, and the power to enact patent and copyright laws. The latter, article I, section 8, clause 8, provides that Congress shall have the power:

---

[43] There can be little doubt that society has benefitted from having patented innovations such as the telephone, the automobile, and the airplane placed in the public domain, even as improvements on those inventions are patented for a limited period of time. In the copyright arena, there can be little doubt that society has benefitted from having the works of Shakespeare and Jane Austen placed in the public domain, resulting in a wide variety of adaptations instead of only authorized ones. Is it not "unjust enrichment" for those who have benefitted by drawing upon the public domain, such as Disney, to seek to prevent their own creations from ever entering the public domain?

[44] *See* Graham v. John Deere Co., 383 U.S. 1, 8–9 (1966) (noting Thomas Jefferson "rejected a natural-rights theory in intellectual property rights and clearly recognized the social and economic rationale of the patent system. The patent monopoly was not designed to secure to the inventor his natural right in his discoveries. Rather, it was a reward, an inducement, to bring forth new knowledge.").

[45] *See* § 4D.

[46] *See* § 4E.

To promote the Progress of Science and useful Arts, by securing for limited Times to Authors and Inventors the exclusive Right to their respective Writings and Discoveries.

The Patent and Copyright Clause is unusual among the Article I legislative powers because it not only confers regulatory power over a subject area (writings and discoveries), but it also specifies both the power's purpose (to promote the progress of science and useful arts) and the means for achieving it (exclusive rights for limited times).

Congress has continuously exercised its power to enact patent and copyright laws since 1790. However, serious and difficult questions arise on the Constitution's role in intellectual property policy beyond this enabling function. First, does the Constitution restrict Congress' power to define legislatively the scope and conditions of patent and copyright protection? Second, does the Patent and Copyright Clause limit Congress' power to protect intellectual property through use of the Commerce Clause? Third, to what extent does the Patent and Copyright Clause (combined with the Supremacy Clause) limit the ability of States to provide intellectual property protection? Fourth, do any other Constitutional provisions, such as the First Amendment, limit state and federal intellectual property laws?

[1]   Congress' Patent and Copyright Powers

The grammar of the Patent and Copyright Clause indicates that copyrights are granted to "Authors" for their "Writings" in order "to Promote the Progress of Science"[47] ("science" meaning "knowledge" in 18th-Century parlance), while patents are granted to "Inventors" for their "Discoveries" in order "to Promote the Progress of . . . useful Arts"[48] ("useful Arts" meaning the technological arts).[49] Moreover, in the 18th Century "progress" meant "advancement" both in the geographic sense (as in the "progress" of a fire) and in the qualitative sense (improvement).[50] In other words, the purpose of granting patents and copyrights is to encourage both the creation and widespread distribution of new knowledge and technology. Patent and copyright laws encourage creation by granting "exclusive rights" to authors and inventors;[51] and they encourage widespread dissemination

---

[47] *See* Eldred v. Ashcroft, 537 U.S. 186, 212 (2003).

[48] *See* Graham v. John Deere Co., 383 U.S. 1, 5 & n.1 (1966). Although this conventional reading of the Patent and Copyright Clause is widely shared, some scholars contend that the phrase "Science and useful Arts" should be construed as a unit, rather than disjunctively. *See* Dotan Oliar, *The (Constitutional) Convention on IP: A New Reading*, 57 UCLA L. REV. 421 (2009).

[49] *See* Bilski v. Kappos, 561 U.S. 593, 632–35 (2010) (Stevens, J., joined by Ginsburg, Breyer, and Sotomayor, JJ., dissenting) (citing early American sources distinguishing the "useful arts" from the "liberal arts" and the "fine arts."). The majority in *Bilski*, however, declined to resolve the case on Constitutional grounds, and instead held that the particular patent at issue was invalid as an "abstract idea," while remarking that "the Patent Act leaves open the possibility that there are at least some processes that can be fairly described as business methods that are within patentable subject matter under § 101." 561 U.S. at 604.

[50] *See* Malla Pollack, *What Is Congress Supposed to Promote? Defining "Progress" in Article I, Section 8, Clause 8 of the United States Constitution*, 80 NEB. L. REV. 754 (2001).

[51] *See* Goldstein v. California, 412 U.S. 546, 555 (1973) ("In other words, to encourage people to devote

first, by requiring or incentivizing publication of the work or invention;[52] second, by making the "exclusive right" assignable to a publisher or manufacturer, who will distribute the work or invention for money; and third, by granting exclusive rights only "for limited Times," thereby ensuring that the work or invention will ultimately enter the public domain, where everyone can freely copy and use it.

Congress cannot exercise its Article I, section 8, clause 8 power to protect subject matter that does not constitute a "writing" or a "discovery" in the Constitutional sense. In *The Trade-Mark Cases*, the Supreme Court held that Congress cannot use the clause to provide trademark protection, because a trademark is neither a "writing" nor a "discovery."[53] This remains the only case in which the Supreme Court has invalidated a Congressional intellectual property statute. In other cases, however, a similar limitation is implicit. Thus, in *Burrow-Giles Lithographic Co. v. Sarony*, the Court held that a photograph was a "writing" in the Constitutional sense and thus that Congress did not exceed its powers by extending copyright to photography. The Court said:

> An author . . . is 'he to whom anything owes its origin; originator; maker; one who completes a work of science or literature.' . . . By writings in that clause is meant the literary productions of those authors, and Congress very properly has declared these to include all forms of writing, printing, engraving, etching, &c., by which the ideas in the mind of the author are given visible expression.[54]

Likewise, in *Goldstein v. California*, the Court stated that "although the word 'writings' might be limited to script or printed material, it may be interpreted to include any physical rendering of the fruits of creative intellectual or aesthetic labor."[55]

Whether the Clause restricts Congress's power to define the patent and copyright requirements of novelty and originality is less clear. The Clause does not explicitly refer to those standards, but they may be implicit in the statement of purpose ("To promote the Progress of Science and useful Arts") and in the concepts of "author" and "inventor." In *Graham v. John Deere Co.*, the Supreme Court confirmed that the Clause does impose a minimum patentability standard that restricts Congress' power to authorize patents:

---

themselves to intellectual and artistic creation, Congress may guarantee to authors and inventors a reward in the form of control over the sale or commercial use of copies of their works.").

[52] Patent law requires (with certain exceptions) that all patent applications be "published" 18 months after the date of the application. 35 U.S.C. § 122(b). Disclosure "is the price paid for exclusivity secured." Eldred v. Ashcroft, 537 U.S. 186, 216 (2003). Copyright law used to require that a work be "published" in order to receive a federal statutory copyright; but today copyright attaches as soon as a work is created. 17 U.S.C. § 302(a). *See Eldred*, 537 U.S. at 216 ("For the author seeking copyright protection, . . . disclosure is the desired objective, not something exacted from the author in exchange for the copyright.").

[53] 100 U.S. 82, 94 (1880).

[54] 111 U.S. 53, 57–58 (1884).

[55] 412 U.S. 546, 561 (1973) (holding sound recordings are "writings" within the meaning of the Clause).

The Congress in the exercise of the patent power may not overreach the restraints imposed by the stated constitutional purpose. Nor may it enlarge the patent monopoly without regard to the innovation, advancement or social benefit gained thereby. Moreover, Congress may not authorize the issuance of patents whose effects are to remove existent knowledge from the public domain, or to restrict free access to materials already available. Innovation, advancement, and things which add to the sum of useful knowledge are inherent requisites in a patent system which by constitutional command must 'promote the Progress of . . . useful Arts.' This is the standard expressed in the Constitution and it may not be ignored.[56]

The Court held that the Section 103 nonobviousness requirement merely restated the standard expressed in prior judicial precedents, and that it fulfilled the constitutional minimum.[57]

Similarly, in *Feist Publications, Inc. v. Rural Telephone Service Co.*, the Court, in holding that a "white pages" telephone directory was not sufficiently original to be copyrightable, held that the Clause imposes a minimum creativity standard for copyrights:

Originality is a constitutional requirement. The source of Congress' power to enact copyright laws is Article I, § 8, cl. 8, of the Constitution, which authorizes Congress to 'secur[e] for limited Times to Authors . . . the exclusive Right to their respective Writings.' In two decisions from the late 19th Century — *The Trade-Mark Cases* and *Burrow-Giles Lithographic Co. v. Sarony* — this Court defined the crucial terms 'authors' and 'writings.' In so doing, the Court made it unmistakably clear that these terms presuppose a degree of originality.[58]

The Court's discussion arguably was *dicta*, because the current Copyright Act expressly requires copyrightable works of authorship, including compilations, to be original.[59]

The Clause also indicates that exclusive rights for "writings" and "discoveries" may only be granted "for limited Times." Thus, Congress may not grant perpetual patents or copyrights.[60] In *Eldred v. Ashcroft*, however, the Court held that the Clause does not limit Congress' power to extend existing patents and copyrights, on the ground that the Clause leaves the determination of what period of time will best "promote the Progress of Science and useful Arts" to Congress.[61] Moreover, although the Court has expressly stated (albeit in *dicta*) that "Congress may not authorize the issuance of patents whose effects are to remove existent knowledge from the public domain, or to restrict free access to materials already available,"[62]

---

[56] 383 U.S. 1, 5–6 (1966).

[57] *Id.* at 16–17.

[58] 499 U.S. 340, 346 (1991).

[59] 17 U.S.C. § 102(a).

[60] Dastar Corp. v. Twentieth Century Fox Film Corp., 539 U.S. 23, 37 (2003).

[61] 537 U.S. 186, 212–14 (2003).

[62] Graham v. John Deere Co., 383 U.S. 1, 6 (1966).

in *Golan v. Holder* the Court held that the Clause does not forbid Congress from "restoring" copyrights in works of foreign origin that had entered the public domain for reasons other than expiration of duration, such as lack of national eligibility or failure to comply with formalities like notice and renewal.[63]

[2]   Commerce Clause Regulation of Intellectual Property

An unresolved question is the extent to which Congress may use other Article I powers, especially its power to regulate interstate and foreign commerce, to provide intellectual property protection for types of subject matter or time periods beyond what the Patent and Copyright Clause authorizes, or for subject matter within the Clause (writings and discoveries) that does not meet the Clause's minimum novelty and originality standards.

That Congress may provide protection for at least some types of subject matter beyond the Patent and Copyright Clause is confirmed by *The Trade-Mark Cases*, in which the Court indicated that Congress could rely on its Commerce Clause power to provide trademark protection, so long as it restricted the protection to interstate and foreign commerce.[64] Because the 1870 Act was not so limited, the Court held it was invalid;[65] but given the Lanham Act's express limitation to interstate and foreign commerce, it is assumed to be constitutional.

It is possible, however, that some types of Congressional regulation that exceed the scope of the Patent and Copyright Clause would be unconstitutional. In *Railway Labor Executives Ass'n v. Gibbons*, the Supreme Court held that because the Bankruptcy Clause of the Constitution authorizes Congress to grant only "uniform" bankruptcy laws, Congress could not lawfully enact a "non-uniform" bankruptcy law under the Commerce Clause.[66] By analogy, therefore, legislation that attempted to evade an express restriction in the Patent and Copyright Clause might be unconstitutional.

The question has been raised with respect to civil and criminal anti-bootlegging statutes, which prohibit the unauthorized fixation or transmission of a live musical performance, and the unauthorized distribution of any such recordings. In *United States v. Moghadam*, the court rejected a constitutional challenge to the criminal statute, saying "the Copyright Clause does not envision that Congress is positively forbidden from extending copyright-like protection under other constitutional clauses, such as the Commerce Clause, to works of authorship that may not meet the fixation requirement inherent in the term 'Writings.' "[67] In dicta, however, the court stated that the "apparently perpetual" protection provided by the statute

---

[63] 132 S. Ct. 873, 884–89 (2012); *but see id.* at 885 (characterizing successive restorations as "hypothetical legislative misbehavior"). Likewise, the First Amendment does not limit the ability of Congress to restore copyrights. *See* § 1[D][4].

[64] 100 U.S. 82, 96–98 (1880).

[65] *Id.* at 94.

[66] 455 U.S. 457, 468–69 (1982).

[67] 175 F.3d 1269, 1280 (11th Cir. 1999).

might prove "fundamentally inconsistent" with the "limited Times" restriction of the Copyright Clause.[68]

Another court has reached a similar result, but via very different reasoning. In *United States v. Martignon*, the court held that the criminal statute does not "secure" an exclusive right within the meaning of the Copyright Clause, because it "does not create and bestow property rights upon authors or inventors, or allocate those rights among claimants to them," but instead is only a criminal prohibition.[69] Because the law was therefore not a "copyright" law, it was upheld under the Commerce Clause. The court's reasoning strongly suggests that it might find the civil anti-bootlegging statute to be unconstitutional.[70]

Whether Congress may undermine the clause's novelty and originality standards has no definitive answer. In the Plant Variety Protection Act[71] and the Semiconductor Chip Protection Act,[72] Congress expressly relied on both the Patent and Copyright Clause and the Commerce Clause. Both statutes protect subject matter that most likely falls within the former's concept of the "discoveries" of an "inventor," and yet both impose eligibility standards that are less strict than patent law's nonobviousness standard. It is possible, however, that a semiconductor chip might also be considered a "writing" that is subject to the less strict "originality" standard.

[3]   Preemption

Whether and to what extent federal intellectual property policy, expressed in the Patent and Copyright Clause or in the patent and copyright statutes, preempts state laws under the Supremacy Clause is the subject of a series of Supreme Court decisions. The preemption cases give insight into intellectual property law's nature and purpose. To determine preemption, courts must balance the policies underlying the federal intellectual property systems, primarily patent and copyright law, with those underlying a spectrum of state rights. This forces them to identify and articulate what those policies are.

The Supreme Court's intellectual property preemption decisions can be segregated into two groups. The first deals with federal policy's impact on state unfair competition and trade secret laws; the second deals with its impact on state contract law. In each instance, the Court began in the 1960s with a strong preemptive posture, giving state law little permissible scope, and later moved to a more balanced position that accommodates federal and state policy.

In part because of uncertainty concerning the Supreme Court's preemption jurisprudence, Congress included an express preemption provision in Section 301

---

[68] *Id.* at 1281 (reserving the question).

[69] 492 F.3d 140, 151–53 (2d Cir. 2007).

[70] *See id.* at 152 n.8 (reserving the question). *But see* KISS Catalog v. Passport Int'l Prods., 405 F. Supp. 2d 1169 (C.D. Cal. 2005) (holding that § 1101 is constitutional).

[71] *See* § 6C.

[72] *See* § 6D.

of the 1976 Copyright Act.[73] Section 301 represents Congress' partial attempt to define the parameters of federal preemption of state laws touching on intellectual property. Unfortunately, the case law concerning section 301 does not define that line with anything like the clarity that Congress hoped to achieve.

[a]   Copying Publicly Disclosed Subject Matter

In *Sears, Roebuck & Co. v. Stiffel Co.*[74] and *Compco Corp. v. Day-Brite Lighting, Inc.*,[75] the Supreme Court held that federal policy preempted any state unfair competition law that purported to prevent the copying of an article that patent or copyright law does not protect. *Sears* and *Compco* dealt with product designs that were eligible for federal design protection but that did not meet patent novelty and nonobviousness standards. Indeed, the plaintiffs had obtained design patents for the designs, but the lower courts held that the patents were invalid.

The Court's opinions are tantalizingly vague as to whether preemption stems from the Patent and Copyright Clause or rather from Congress' occupation of the field by enacting patent and copyright legislation pursuant to the Clause. *Sears* suggested a statutory occupation theory:

> Obviously a State could not, consistently with the Supremacy Clause of the Constitution, extend the life of a patent beyond its expiration date or give a patent on an article which lacked the level of invention required for federal patents. To do either would run counter to the policy of Congress of granting patents only to true inventions, and then only for a limited time. Just as a State cannot encroach upon the federal patent laws directly, it cannot, under some other law, such as that forbidding unfair competition, give protection of a kind that clashes with the objectives of the federal patent laws.[76]

Compco hinted that the preemptive policy lay in the Constitution as well as in the federal patent statutes:

> To forbid copying would interfere with the federal policy, found in Art. I, § 8, cl. 8, of the Constitution and in the implementing federal statutes, of allowing free access to copy whatever the federal patent and copyright law leave in the public domain.[77]

Nine years later, however, in *Goldstein v. California*,[78] the Court upheld the constitutionality of state laws that barred copying of pre-1972 sound recordings, which fell within the Constitutional concept of the "writings" of an "author," but which were not included in federal statutory copyright. Petitioners were convicted under a California statute making it a criminal offense to "pirate" recordings

---

[73] 17 U.S.C. § 301.

[74] 376 U.S. 225 (1964).

[75] 376 U.S. 234 (1964).

[76] 376 U.S. at 231.

[77] 376 U.S. at 237.

[78] 412 U.S. 546 (1973).

produced by others. They challenged the statute as inconsistent with the Constitution and with federal copyright policy.

The Court held that the Patent and Copyright Clause did *not*, of its own force, forbid States from enacting intellectual property laws protecting "writings." "Although the Copyright Clause . . . recognizes the potential benefits of a national system, it does not indicate that all writings are of national interest or that state legislation is, in all cases, unnecessary or precluded. . . . [Rather,] the subject matter to which the Copyright Clause is addressed may . . . be of purely local importance and not worthy of national attention or protection."[79] Allowing State intellectual property protection would not entail such inevitable and severe conflicts among the states as to compel the conclusion that "state power has been relinquished to the exclusive jurisdiction of Congress."[80] Moreover, state copyright protection of indefinite duration did not contravene the "limited Times" provision in the Patent and Copyright Clause, because "Section 8 enumerates those powers which have been granted to Congress; [w]hatever limitations have been appended to such powers can only be understood as a limit on congressional, and not state, action."[81]

The Court also considered "whether the challenged state statute is void under the Supremacy Clause," which depends on whether in the particular case the state law stands as "an obstacle to the accomplishment and execution of the full purposes and objectives of Congress."[82] The 1909 Copyright Act extended composers' rights to reproduction of their works in records but did not grant rights in the recordings themselves. The Court found no evidence that Congress intended sound recordings to be free of state control. "In regard to this category of 'Writings,' Congress has drawn no balance; rather, it has left the area unattended, and no reason exists why the State should not be free to act."[83] Two groups of Justices dissented; both found *Sears-Compco* controlling.[84]

One year later, the Court addressed preemption yet again, in *Kewanee Oil Co. v. Bicron Corp.*, holding that "Ohio's law of trade secrets is not pre-empted by the patent laws of the United States."[85] Just as states are not absolutely forbidden from

---

[79] *Id.* at 556–58.

[80] *Id.* at 558. The Court noted that "a copyright granted by a particular State has effect only within its boundaries. If one State grants such protection, the interests of States which do not are not prejudiced since their citizens remain free to copy within their borders those works which may be protected elsewhere." *Id.*

[81] *Id.* at 560.

[82] Goldstein v. California, 412 U.S. 546, 561 (1973), *quoting* Hines v. Davidowitz, 312 U.S. 52, 67 (1941).

[83] *Goldstein*, 412 U.S. at 570.

[84] Justice Douglas, joined by Justices Brennan and Blackmun, found preemption in the Constitution, saying "*Sears* and *Compco* make clear that the federal policy expressed in Art I, § 8, cl. 8, is to have 'national uniformity in patent and copyright laws.'" 412 U.S. at 573. Justice Marshall, also joined by Justices Brennan and Blackmun, found implied preemption: "In view of the importance of not imposing unnecessary restraints on competition, . . . unless the failure to provide patent or copyright protection for some class of works could clearly be shown to reflect a judgment that state regulation was permitted, the silence of Congress [should] be taken to reflect a judgment that free competition should prevail." 412 U.S. at 577–78.

[85] 416 U.S. 470, 474 (1974).

protecting constitutionally copyrightable "writings," they also are not forbidden from protecting constitutionally patentable "discoveries."[86] As in *Goldstein*, however, the Court went on to consider whether state trade secret law stood as an obstacle to the objectives of federal patent law, and held that it did not.

Patent law's objective is to promote progress of the useful arts "by offering a right of exclusion for a limited period as an incentive to inventors to risk the often enormous costs in terms of time, research, and development," in exchange for which "the patent laws impose upon the inventor a requirement of disclosure."[87] Trade secret law is consistent with these objectives, because "[t]he holder of a trade secret would not likely share his secret with a manufacturer who cannot be placed under binding legal obligation to pay a license fee or to protect the secret. The result would be to hoard rather than disseminate knowledge."[88] The Court found "no reasonable risk" that "those who can reasonably expect to be granted patents" would be deterred from filing patent applications by the existence of trade secret protection.[89] Patent protection is attractively stronger than trade secret protection, because federal patent law protects against the risk of both independent invention and reverse engineering, whereas trade secret law does not.[90] Finally, the court noted that "[t]rade secret law and patent law have co-existed in this country for over one hundred years."[91] "During this time, Congress has repeatedly demonstrated its full awareness of the existence of the trade secret system, without any indication of disapproval."[92] Thus, "[u]ntil Congress takes affirmative action to the contrary, States should be free to grant protection to trade secrets."[93]

The Court's most recent decision regarding preemption in the intellectual property field is *Bonito Boats, Inc. v. Thunder Craft Boats, Inc.*,[94] in which the Court held that federal patent policy preempted a Florida statute prohibiting the reproduction of vessel hulls by direct molding. The Court re-affirmed the holdings in *Sears* and *Compco* that "the States may not offer patent-like protection to intellectual creations which would otherwise remain unprotected as a matter of federal law."[95] It noted that "the Florida law prohibits the entire public from engaging in a form of reverse engineering of a product in the public domain. This is clearly one of the rights vested in the federal patent holder, but has never been a part of state protection under the law of unfair competition or trade secrets."[96] While "[b]oth the law of unfair competition and state trade secret law have co-existed harmoniously with federal patent protection for almost 200 years, . . .

---

[86] *Id.* at 479.

[87] *Id.* at 480.

[88] *Id.* at 486.

[89] *Id.* at 489.

[90] Kewanee Oil Co. v. Bicron Corp., 416 U.S. 470, 490 (1974).

[91] *Id.* at 493.

[92] *Id.* at 494 (Marshall, J., concurring).

[93] *Id.* at 493 (majority opinion).

[94] 489 U.S. 141 (1989).

[95] *Id.* at 156.

[96] *Id.* at 160.

[t]he same cannot be said of the Florida statute at issue here, which offers protection beyond that available under the law of unfair competition or trade secret, without any showing of consumer confusion, or breach of trust or secrecy."[97]

Nine years after the decision in *Bonito Boats*, Congress enacted the Vessel Hull Design Protection Act, which offers federal protection of limited duration for the original design of a vessel hull.[98] Protection is granted for two years from the date the design is first made public, unless the owner of the design registers it with the U.S. Copyright Office,[99] in which case it obtains protection for ten years from the earlier of that date or the date of registration.[100] An owner may not obtain duplicate protection under the VHDPA and the design patent laws.[101]

The Court's decisions in this area are consistent with each other with one exception. *Sears*, *Compco*, and *Bonito Boats* all hold that States may not protect a publicly available article that is eligible for, but is not protected by, federal patent or copyright law. *Kewanee* is consistent with these cases, because, by definition, the subject matter of a trade secret is not yet publicly known or readily ascertainable by proper means. These cases are also consistent with the fact that states offered common-law copyright protection to unpublished works prior to 1978. The one exception is *Goldstein*, which holds that states may protect sound recordings that were left unprotected by Congress, even after those sound recordings had been commercially released and sold to the public. However, given that Congress subsequently ratified the holding in *Goldstein* by expressly providing that state-law protection for sound recordings fixed before February 15, 1972 is *not* preempted until February 15, 2067,[102] it cannot be said that the Court's decision contravened the will of Congress.

[b]   Contracts

Federal intellectual property law create rights, including patents, copyrights, and trademarks, and bestows them with property status. Federal law prescribes the initial ownership of that property and the formalities required to transfer ownership.[103] Except where prescribed by federal statute, however, state property and contract laws govern ownership, transfer, and contract rights relating to federal intellectual property.[104]

Although it generally leaves control over contract and ownership matters to the states, federal intellectual property law may nonetheless preempt state-law rules and doctrines that undermine federal policies on incentives, disclosure obligations,

---

[97] *Id.* at 166–67.

[98] The Act actually offers protection for "an original design of a useful article," 17 U.S.C. § 1303(a)(1), but it defines a "useful article" as "a vessel hull or deck." 17 U.S.C. § 1303(b)(2).

[99] 17 U.S.C. § 1310(a).

[100] 17 U.S.C. §§ 1304, 1305(a).

[101] 17 U.S.C. § 1329.

[102] 17 U.S.C. § 301(c).

[103] *See* §§ 2G, 4F, 5D[4].

[104] *See, e.g.*, Foad Consulting Group, Inc. v. Musil Govan Azzalino, 270 F.3d 821, 827–28 (9th Cir. 2001); Farmland Irrigation Co. v. Dopplmaier, 308 P.2d 732, 737–39 (Cal. 1957).

and competition. The misuse doctrine is an example: a patent or copyright owner's exercise of state-based contract rights, such as imposing restrictive license conditions, can constitute misuse, causing the courts to withhold enforcement of the patent or copyright.[105] Federal policy may also preclude enforcement of state law-based contracts pertaining to actual or potential intellectual property rights.

In *Brulotte v. Thys Co.*, plaintiff sold defendants its patented machines for a flat sum and issued a license for their use in exchange for an annual royalty. Plaintiff's patents expired on or before 1957, but the license continued beyond that date. Defendants refused to make royalty payments accruing before and after the patents' expiration, and the plaintiff sued for breach of contract. The state courts granted plaintiff judgment. The Supreme Court reversed the judgment "insofar as it allows royalties to be collected which accrued after the last of the patents incorporated into the machines had expired."[106]

> A patent empowers the owner to exact royalties as high as he can negotiate with the leverage of that monopoly. But to use that leverage to project those royalty payments beyond the life of the patent is analogous to an effort to enlarge the monopoly of the patent by [tying] the sale or use of the patented article to the purchase or use of unpatented ones.[107]

The Court acknowledged that "[t]he sale or lease of unpatented machines on long-term payments based on a deferred purchase price or on use would present wholly different considerations."[108] However, the Court refused to construe the license agreement as a form of installment payment for the machines, because the licenses stated that the payments were for use of the machines, post-expiration payments were the same as pre-expiration payments, and the licenses prohibited the machines' removal from the county in which they were used. "Those restrictions are apt and pertinent to protection of the patent monopoly; and their applicability to the post-expiration period is a telltale sign that the licensor was using the licenses to project its monopoly beyond the patent period."[109]

In *Lear, Inc. v. Adkins*, the Court more explicitly articulated and applied federal patent policy to restrict state contract law. Lear hired Adkins to solve a gyroscope problem. The parties agreed that all "new ideas, discoveries, and inventions" would become Adkins' property, but that Adkins would grant Lear a license "on a mutually satisfactory royalty basis." Adkins found a solution, which he disclosed to Lear, and applied for a patent. After lengthy negotiations, the parties agreed to a license contract, which provided that "if the U.S. Patent Office refuses to issue a patent . . .

---

[105] *See* §§ 2F[4][c] and 4J[2].

[106] 379 U.S. 29, 30 (1964).

[107] *Id.* at 33.

[108] *Id.* at 32.

[109] *Id.* Although the Court initially referred to the licensees' "defense" as "misuse of the patents through extension of the license agreements beyond the expiration date of the patents," neither the facts nor the holding evoke the usual misuse doctrine, which restricts a patent's enforceability. The plaintiff was suing for breach of contract, not for patent infringement. *Brulotte* must be viewed as applying federal patent policy to preempt state contract law.

or if such a patent so issued is subsequently held invalid," then Lear could terminate the agreement.[110]

During the lengthy prosecution, Lear decided that Adkins would not obtain effective patent protection, relying on a prior art patent that it believed fully anticipated his discovery. Lear therefore stopped paying royalties on the gyroscopes it was manufacturing. In 1960, after the patent finally issued (on a much narrower claim), Adkins sued Lear for breach of contract. The California Supreme Court upheld a jury verdict in favor of Adkins, holding that Lear had improperly terminated its contract, and that as a licensee, Lear was estopped from contesting the validity of the licensed patent.[111] It said:

> [O]ne of the oldest doctrines in the field of patent law establishes that so long as a licensee is operating under a license agreement he is estopped to deny the validity of his licensor's patent in a suit for royalties under the agreement. The theory underlying this doctrine is that a licensee should not be permitted to enjoy the benefit afforded by the agreement while simultaneously urging that the patent which forms the basis of the agreement is void.[112]

On certiorari, the Supreme Court overruled the doctrine of licensee estoppel, and held that federal patent policy required that a licensee be allowed to challenge the validity of the patent. The Court explained:

> Surely the equities of the licensor do not weigh very heavily when they are balanced against the important public interest in permitting full and free competition in the use of ideas which are in reality a part of the public domain. Licensees may often be the only individuals with enough economic incentive to challenge the patentability of an inventor's discovery. If they are muzzled, the public may continually be required to pay tribute to would-be monopolists without need or justification. We think it plain that the technical requirements of contract doctrine must give way before the demands of the public interest in the typical situation involving the negotiation of a license after a patent has issued.[113]

Because Adkins and Lear had negotiated their patent license before the patent issued and was published, the Court went on to consider whether a different result should obtain in this case. The Court rejected Adkins' "extreme position" that because "Lear obtained privileged access to his ideas before 1960, . . . it should also pay royalties during the entire patent period" without regard to validity.[114] That position "would permit inventors to negotiate all important licenses during the lengthy period while their applications were still pending at the Patent Office, thereby disabling entirely all those who have the strongest incentive to show that a

---

[110] 395 U.S. 653, 657 (1969).

[111] *Id.* at 659–61.

[112] Adkins v. Lear, Inc., 435 P.2d 321, 325–26 (Cal. 1967), *rev'd*, 395 U.S. 653 (1969).

[113] Lear, Inc. v. Adkins, 395 U.S. 653, 670–71 (1969).

[114] *Id.* at 672.

patent is worthless."[115] The Court also held that "overriding federal policies would be significantly frustrated if licensees could be required to continue to pay royalties during the time they are challenging patent validity in the courts," because otherwise a licensee "will have little incentive to initiate lengthy court proceedings," and because "enforcing this contractual provision would undermine the strong federal policy favoring the full and free use of ideas in the public domain."[116] According, the licensee "must be permitted to avoid the payment of all royalties accruing after [the] patent issued if [it] can prove patent invalidity."[117]

The Court declined to decide the "much more difficult" question of the licensee's liability for royalties accruing before the patent issued, which "squarely raises the question whether, and to what extent, the States may protect the owners of unpatented inventions who are willing to disclose their ideas to manufacturers only upon payment of royalties."[118] Although this part of *Lear* was problematic, because it cast doubt on state-law contract and tort obligations pertaining to the disclosure of ideas and trade secrets in confidence, most of these concerns were dispelled by the Court's subsequent decisions in *Kewanee Oil Co. v. Bicron Corp.*,[119] which held that state trade secret law was not preempted by federal patent law, and the next decision concerning contracts, *Aronson v. Quick Point Pencil Co.*

In *Aronson*, Aronson filed a patent application on a new form of keyholder in 1955. Before the application was published, Aronson negotiated a contract with Quick Point, which provided that Quick Point would pay a 5% royalty in return for the exclusive right to make and sell keyholders "of the type shown" in her patent application; but that if her patent application was not granted within five years, Quick Point would pay a 2.5% royalty "so long as you [Quick Point] continue to sell" the keyholder. After the PTO finally rejected Aronson's application in 1961, Quick Point reduced its payments to the lower royalty figure but continued paying for 14 years. By 1975, Quick Point's sales were being eroded by competitors that copied the design. Quick Point commenced an action, seeking a declaratory judgment that its royalty obligation under state contract law was unenforceable because of federal patent policy.[120]

The Supreme Court unanimously held that the contract was not preempted, because "the parties contracted with full awareness of both the pendency of a patent application and the possibility that a patent might not issue."[121] Enforcement of the contract "is not inconsistent" with the federal patent system's purposes of fostering invention, promoting invention disclosure, and protecting the public domain, because:

> Permitting inventors to make enforceable agreements licensing the use of
> their inventions in return for royalties provides an additional incentive to

---

[115] *Id.* at 672–73.

[116] *Id.* at 673–74.

[117] *Id.* at 674.

[118] *Id.* at 674–75.

[119] 416 U.S. 470 (1974), discussed at § 1D[3][a], above.

[120] 440 U.S. 257, 259–60 (1979).

[121] *Id.* at 261.

invention. Similarly, encouraging [them] to make arrangements for the manufacture of [their inventions] furthers the federal policy of disclosure of inventions; these simple devices display the novel idea which they embody wherever they are seen. . . .

. . . Enforcement of the agreement does not withdraw any idea from the public domain. The design of the keyholder was not in the public domain before Quick Point obtained its license to manufacture it. In negotiating the agreement, Mrs. Aronson disclosed the design in confidence. Had Quick Point tried to exploit the design in breach of that confidence, it would have risked legal liability. . . . [T]he design entered the public domain as a result of the manufacture and sale of the keyholders under the contract.[122]

The Court distinguished *Lear*, saying "neither the holding nor the rationale of *Lear* controls when no patent has issued, and no ideas have been withdrawn from public use."[123] It distinguished *Brulotte* on the ground that "the reduced royalty which is challenged, far from being negotiated 'with the leverage' of a patent, rested on the contingency that no patent would issue within five years. . . . [W]hatever role the pending application played in the negotiation of the 5% royalty, it played no part in the contract to pay the 2½% royalty indefinitely."[124]

By distinguishing rather than overruling *Lear* and *Brulotte*, *Aronson* suggested that a licensing contract will be limited to a patent's validity and duration only if there is a "fixed reliance on a patent or a probable patent grant."[125]

[c] Copyright Act Preemption

Before 1978, the United States had a dual system of copyright protection. Unpublished works were protected by state law (common-law copyright), while published works were either protected by federal law or were in the public domain.[126] The primary purpose of section 301 of the 1976 Copyright Act was to eliminate the dual system of copyright protection by preempting common-law copyright, or any "equivalent" rights under state law, as soon as a work was "fixed in a tangible medium of expression."[127]

Section 301 expressly preempts all state "legal or equitable rights that are equivalent to any of the exclusive rights within the general scope of copyright . . . in works that are fixed in a tangible medium of expression and come within the subject matter of copyright."[128] Section 301 is a statutory basis for preemption; it does not supersede the Constitutional preemption standards discussed above. Thus, even if a state law survives "express preemption" under Section 301, it must still be analyzed for "conflict preemption" to determine whether it "stands as an

---

[122] *Id.* at 262–63.

[123] *Id.* at 264.

[124] *Id.* at 265.

[125] *Id.* at 266.

[126] *See* § 4D.

[127] *See* H.R. Rep. 94-1476, at 129–30 (1976).

[128] 17 U.S.C. § 301(a). The Semiconductor Chip Protection Act contains a similar preemption provision. *See* 17 U.S.C. § 912(c).

obstacle to the accomplishment of the full purposes and objectives of Congress."[129]

Section 301 imposes a two-part preemption test: First, the subject matter must "come within the subject matter of copyright" as defined in Sections 102 and 103 of the Copyright Act. Second, the rights granted under state law must be "equivalent to any of the exclusive rights within the general scope of copyright" as specified in Section 106 of the Copyright Act.[130]

[i]   Subject Matter

The "subject matter" prong is the easier of the two parts of the preemption test. Courts need only determine if the subject matter that the plaintiff contends was copied was "fixed in a tangible medium of expression," and whether it comes "within the subject matter of copyright as specified by sections 102 and 103."[131] The subject matter analysis is only whether the work is the type of literary, musical, dramatic, pictorial, graphic, sculptural, audiovisual, or architectural work or sound recording that section 102 of the Copyright Act potentially makes eligible for copyright protection (including derivative works or compilations, which are included in copyright subject matter under section 103). "As long as a work fits within one of the general subject matter categories of section 102 and 103, . . . [section 301(a)] prevents the States from protecting it even if it fails to achieve Federal statutory copyright because it is too minimal or lacking in originality to qualify, or because it has fallen into the public domain."[132]

A difficult question concerns "ideas" or "facts" that copyright law does not protect.[133] Some decisions indicate that section 301's "subject matter" test is not met if the claimant only charges misappropriation of the work's ideas — even though the misappropriated ideas are contained in a work that is a potentially copyrightable expression of ideas.[134] Most courts, however, conclude that claims concerning unauthorized use of "facts" or "ideas" meet the subject matter test, because "[o]ne function of § 301(a) is to prevent states from giving special protection to [material] that Congress has decided should be in the public domain, which it can accomplish only if 'subject matter of copyright' includes all works of a

---

[129] See, e.g., Facenda v. NFL Films, Inc., 542 F.3d 1007, 1028 (3d Cir. 2008); Foley v. Luster, 249 F.3d 1281, 1286–87 (11th Cir. 2001); Brown v. Ames, 201 F.3d 654, 659–60 (5th Cir. 2000).

[130] Forest Park Pictures v. Universal Television Network, Inc., 683 F.3d 424, 429 (2d Cir. 2012); Montz v. Pilgrim Films & Television, Inc., 649 F.3d 975, 979 (9th Cir. 2011).

[131] 17 U.S.C. § 301(a).

[132] H.R. Rep. No. 94-1476, at 131 (1976). See, e.g., Lipscher v. LRP Publications, Inc., 266 F.3d 1305, 1311 (11th Cir. 2001); Wrench LLC v. Taco Bell Corp., 256 F.3d 446, 454–55 (6th Cir. 2001); National Basketball Ass'n v. Motorola, Inc., 105 F.3d 841, 849–50 (2d Cir. 1997); Baltimore Orioles, Inc. v. Major League Baseball Players Association, 805 F.2d 663, 676 (7th Cir. 1986).

[133] 17 U.S.C. § 102(b). See § 4C[3].

[134] See, e.g., GlobeRanger Corp. v. Software AG, 691 F.3d 702, 709 (5th Cir. 2012); Dun & Bradstreet Software Services, Inc. v. Grace Consulting, Inc., 307 F.3d 197, 218 (3d Cir. 2002) ("Grace does not dispute that the customer lists are not subject to copyright and presumably escape preemption for that reason"); Dunlap v. G&L Holding Group, Inc., 381 F.3d 1285 (11th Cir. 2004) (idea for gay and lesbian bank, although expressed in a tangible medium, was not entitled to protection, and therefore a claim for its conversion was not preempted).

type covered by sections 102 and 103, even if federal law does not afford protection to them."[135]

Even if such claims survive preemption, however, they will rarely succeed under state law unless the claimant can show that the material was not publicly disclosed and was kept secret, or that there was an express or implied contract limiting its disclosure or use.[136] Further, section 301 aside, constitutional standards may operate to preempt a state remedy against copying unpatented ideas.[137]

Section 301 expressly does *not* preempt state laws concerning works that are not yet fixed in a tangible medium of expression.[138] Thus, claims of common-law copyright in unfixed works are not preempted.[139]

[ii]   Equivalent Rights

Section 106 of the Copyright Act grants to the copyright owner the exclusive rights of reproduction, preparation of derivative works, public distribution, public performance, or public display.[140] Thus, if a state law is violated merely because the defendant engaged in one or more of these activities, it typically will be held to be preempted.[141] However, determining whether a state-based right is "equivalent" to a federal copyright exclusive right has proven to be a difficult task, and case results cannot always be reconciled.[142] The label the claimant uses is not determinative of whether the asserted right is equivalent to a copyright exclusive right.[143]

---

[135] *Wrench*, 256 F.3d at 455; *see also Forest Park*, 683 F.3d at 429–30; *Montz*, 649 F.3d at 979–80; ProCD, Inc. v. Zeidenberg, 86 F.3d 1447, 1453 (7th Cir. 1996).

[136] For a discussion of trade secret law, see Chapter 3. For a discussion of misappropriation of ideas, see § 6F.

[137] *See* § 1D[3][a].

[138] H.R. Rep. No. 94-1476, at 131 (1976) ("On the other hand, section 301(b) explicitly preserves common-law copyright protection for one important class of works: works that have not been 'fixed in any tangible medium of expression.' "). The House Report lists four examples: "choreography that has never been filmed or notated, an extemporaneous speech, 'original works of authorship' communicated solely through conversations or live broadcasts, and a dramatic sketch or musical composition improvised or developed from memory and without being recorded or written down." *Id.*

[139] *See, e.g.*, Cal. Civ. Code § 980(a)(1), and cases cited in § 4C[2][d].

[140] 17 U.S.C. § 106.

[141] *See, e.g.*, Barclays Capital, Inc. v. Theflyonthewall.com, Inc., 650 F.3d 876, 893 (2d Cir. 2011); Ritchie v. Williams, 395 F.3d 283, 287–88 (6th Cir. 2005); Daboub v. Gibbons, 42 F.3d 285, 289 (5th Cir. 1995).

[142] *See Ritchie*, 395 F.3d at 287–88 n.3 ("In all but the simplest cases, the extra elements test cannot be applied with any certainty. . . . The net result is that courts seem to first decide independently whether or not they think preemption should apply, and then label the result accordingly.") (internal quotes and citations omitted).

[143] *See, e.g.*, Crow v. Wainwright, 720 F.2d 1224, 1226 (11th Cir. 1983) (section 301 preempts a state criminal law punishing dealing in "stolen property," as applied to the sale of pirated tapes of copyrighted sound recordings; "Despite the name given the offense, the elements essential to establish a violation of the Florida statute in this case correspond almost exactly to those of the tort of copyright infringement."); Patricia Kennedy & Co. v. Zam-Cul Enterprises, Inc., 830 F. Supp. 53, 56 (D. Mass. 1993) ("In applying the section 301 preemption provision, courts focus not on the label affixed to the state cause of action, but rather upon what plaintiff seeks to protect, the theories in which the matter is thought to

During Congress's consideration of the 1976 Copyright Act, section 301(b)(3) initially contained a listing of state-law claims that would not be preempted. However, controversy over inclusion of "misappropriation" led Congress to delete the entire list.[144] Because of confusion as to the deletion's purpose, most courts give this legislative history little weight.[145]

Instead, most courts apply an "extra element" test.[146] Under this test, section 301 "preempts only those state law rights that may be abridged by an act which, in and of itself, would infringe one of the exclusive rights provided by federal copyright law. But if an 'extra element' is required instead of or in addition to the acts of reproduction, performance, distribution, or display, . . . then the [state-law] right does not lie 'within the general scope of copyright' and there is no preemption."[147] However, the asserted "extra element" must be one "which changes the nature of the action so that it is *qualitatively* different from a copyright infringement claim. . . . An action will not be saved from preemption by elements such as awareness or intent, which alter the action's scope but not its nature."[148] Although results are not always consistent, elements that have been held *not* to change the nature of the action typically involve the mental state of the defendant, rather than the defendant's conduct.[149]

---

be protected and the rights sought to be enforced.") (internal quotations omitted).

[144] For a discussion of this controversy, see § 6F[4].

[145] *See, e.g.*, Baltimore Orioles, Inc. v. Major League Baseball Players Association, 805 F.2d 663, 677 n.25 (7th Cir. 1986) ("Because the House's debate concerning the effect of the amendment is ambiguous, if not contradictory, and because the Senate concurred without discussion in the House's version of § 301, almost any interpretation of the concept of equivalent rights can be inferred from the legislative history. Therefore, in determining whether a particular right is equivalent to a copyright, we place little weight on the deletion of the list of nonequivalent rights.").

[146] *See, e.g.*, Forest Park Pictures v. Universal Television Network, Inc., 683 F.3d 424, 429 (2d Cir. 2012); Tire Eng'g & Dist., LLC v. Shandong Linglong Rubber Co., 682 F.3d 292, 309 (4th Cir. 2012); Laws v. Sony Music Entertainment, Inc., 448 F.3d 1134, 1143–44 (9th Cir. 2006).

[147] Computer Associates Int'l, Inc. v. Altai, Inc., 982 F.2d 693, 716 (2d Cir. 1992) (internal quotations omitted).

[148] *Id.* at 716–17 (emphasis in original; internal quotations omitted). *See also Laws*, 448 F.3d at 1143 ("To survive preemption, the state cause of action must protect rights which are qualitatively different from the copyright rights. The state claim must have an 'extra element' which changes the nature of the action.") (*quoting* Del Madera Properties v. Rhodes & Gardner, Inc., 820 F.2d 973, 977 (9th Cir. 1987)).

[149] *See, e.g.*, Harper & Row Publishers, Inc. v. Nation Enterprises, 723 F.2d 195, 201 (2d Cir. 1983) (the "additional elements of awareness and intentional interference" are "not part of a copyright infringement claim" but merely go "to the scope of the right;" they do not "establish qualitatively different conduct on the part of the infringing party, nor a fundamental nonequivalence between the state and federal rights implicated."), *rev'd on other grounds*, 471 U.S. 539 (1985); Crow v. Wainwright, 720 F.2d 1224, 1226 (11th Cir. 1983) ("The state criminal statute differs only in that it requires the prosecution to establish scienter, which is not an element of an infringement claim. . . . The additional element of scienter traditionally necessary to establish a criminal case merely narrows the applicability of the statute. The prohibited act — wrongfully distributing a copyrighted work — remains the same"); Nash v. CBS, Inc., 704 F. Supp. 823, 833 ("the elements of 'scienter,' 'intent,' and 'commercial immorality' required for state law actions for wrongful appropriation are not sufficiently 'different in kind' to preclude preemption"), *aff'd on other grounds*, 899 F.2d 1537 (7th Cir. 1990).

Note that section 301 expressly does *not* preempt any other federal laws.[150] Thus, a plaintiff may bring a claim under the Lanham Act as well as (or in lieu of) a claim for copyright infringement. However, in *Dastar Corp. v. Twentieth Century Fox Film Corp.*, the Supreme Court held that a "reverse passing off" claim under Section 43(a) of the Lanham Act applies only to claims that the manufacturer of a physical good was misidentified, and not to claims that the creator of any intellectual property embodied in those goods was misidentified.[151] As a result, any such claims are likely to be dismissed at the pleading stage.

[iii]   Examples

Although consistent results are hard to come by in the area of section 301 statutory preemption, the following general observations can be made.

Claims for breach of express contract typically survive preemption, because they involve the "extra elements" of agreement and consideration.[152] This is true even for adhesion contracts (such as end-user license agreements) that contain standard terms and conditions that purport to bind any users.[153] Some courts, however, have found conflict preemption (rather than statutory preemption) when an end-user license contains a term that contradicts user rights found in the Copyright Act, even though freely-negotiated contracts would not be preempted.[154] And where the breach of contract concerns claims involving ownership, reproduction, public distribution, or public performance of a fixed work of authorship, such claims may be deemed preempted.[155]

Claims for breach of implied contract are more difficult, because they rely on the argument that an agreement to pay should be implied under the circumstances. Claims for breach of an agreement implied-in-fact typically survive preemption, again for the reason that the fact of agreement constitutes an "extra element."[156] Claims for "unjust enrichment," "quantum meruit," or breach of an agreement implied-in-law, however, are more problematic, because they usually rely merely on the fact of reproduction without compensation. Most courts hold that such claims are preempted;[157] but sometimes such claims survive preemption, because some

---

[150] 17 U.S.C. § 301(d) ("Nothing in this title annuls or limits any rights or remedies under any other Federal statute.").

[151] 539 U.S. 23 (2003). *See* § 5F[7].

[152] *See, e.g.*, Utopia Provider Systems, Inc. v. Pro-Med Clinical Systems, LLC, 596 F.3d 1313, 1326–27 (11th Cir. 2010).

[153] *See, e.g.*, Bowers v. Baystate Technologies, Inc., 320 F.3d 1317, 1323–26 (Fed. Cir. 2003); ProCD, Inc. v. Zeidenberg, 86 F.3d 1447, 1454–55 (7th Cir. 1996).

[154] *See, e.g., Bowers*, 320 F.3d at 1336–38 (Dyk, J., dissenting in part); Vault Corp. v. Quaid Software Ltd., 847 F.2d 255 (5th Cir. 1988) (state statute expressly validating contracts prohibiting reverse engineering was preempted).

[155] *See, e.g.*, Ritchie v. Williams, 395 F.3d 283, 287–88 (6th Cir. 2005); Wrench LLC v. Taco Bell Corp., 256 F.3d 446, 457 (6th Cir. 2001) ("If the promise amounts only to a promise to refrain from reproducing, performing, distributing or displaying the work, then the contract claim is preempted.").

[156] *See, e.g.*, Forest Park Pictures v. Universal Television Network, Inc., 683 F.3d 424, 431–33 (2d Cir. 2012); Montz v. Pilgrim Films & Television, Inc., 649 F.3d 975, 980–81 (9th Cir. 2011); *Wrench*, 256 F.3d at 456–58.

[157] *See, e.g.*, R.W. Beck, Inc. v. E3 Consulting, LLC, 577 F.3d 1133, 1148–49 (10th Cir. 2009);

courts believe it would be unfair to allow one party to copy another's work without compensation, even when federal law permits such conduct.[158]

A state-law claim for "conversion" typically will be preempted where it involves copying of intellectual property.[159] However, if the claim involves conversion of tangible property, it will not be preempted.[160]

Claims based on the common-law doctrine of "misappropriation" typically are held to be preempted, even though the plaintiff must allege an expenditure of time, effort, and money, because the state law is violated by the mere act of reproduction, public distribution, public performance, or public display.[161] The sole exception is a "hot news" misappropriation claim, of the type upheld in *International News Service v. Associated Press*. In that case, a majority of the U.S. Supreme Court held that a claim that a competitor systematically copied the facts of news stories reported by the plaintiff and used those facts to compete with the plaintiff without paying for the news gathering violated federal common law.[162] To plead a valid claim for "hot news" misappropriation, a plaintiff must allege the "extra elements" that the information is highly time-sensitive, that "defendant's use of the information constitutes free-riding on the plaintiff's costly efforts to generate or collect it," and that such free riding "would so reduce the incentive to produce the product or service that its existence or quality would be substantially threatened."[163]

A right of publicity claim presents a difficult issue. Where the basis of the claim is merely the reproduction of a copyrighted work, and the person's likeness was fixed in the work with authorization, such claims are usually held preempted.[164] However, where the basis of the claim is the use of a person's likeness or identity for advertising purposes, the claim is typically *not* preempted,[165] even though right

---

Briarpatch Ltd. v. Phoenix Pictures, Inc., 373 F.3d 296, 306–07 (2d Cir. 2004); Murray Hill Publications, Inc. v. ABC Communications, Inc., 264 F.3d 622, 638 (6th Cir. 2001); *Wrench*, 256 F.3d at 458–59.

[158] *See, e.g.*, Schuchart & Assocs. v. Solo Serve Corp., 540 F. Supp. 928, 945 (W.D. Tex. 1982). Cf. Aalmuhammed v. Lee, 202 F.3d 1227, 1236–37 (9th Cir. 2000) (vacating dismissal of implied contract, quantum meruit, and unjust enrichment claims, without discussing preemption).

[159] *See, e.g.*, Ho v. Taflove, 648 F.3d 489, 501–02 (7th Cir. 2011); Daboub v. Gibbons, 42 F.3d 285, 289–90 (5th Cir. 1995); United States ex rel. Berge v. Board of Trustees of the University of Alabama, 104 F.3d 1453, 1463 (4th Cir. 1997).

[160] *See, e.g.*, Tire Eng'g & Dist., LLC v. Shandong Linglong Rubber Co., 682 F.3d 292, 309–10 (4th Cir. 2012); Carson v. Dynegy, Inc., 344 F.3d 446, 456–57 (5th Cir. 2003).

[161] *See, e.g.*, Barclays Capital, Inc. v. Theflyonthewall.com, Inc., 650 F.3d 876, 902–06 (2d Cir. 2011); Stromback v. New Line Cinema, 384 F.3d 283, 301–02 (6th Cir. 2004); Hartman v. Hallmark Cards, Inc., 833 F.2d 117, 121 (8th Cir. 1987); Ehat v. Tanner, 780 F.2d 876, 878–79 (10th Cir. 1985).

[162] 248 U.S. 215, 239–40 (1918). *See* § 6F.

[163] National Basketball Ass'n v. Motorola, Inc., 105 F.3d 841, 852 (2d Cir. 1997); *but see Barclays*, 650 F.3d at 898–901 (criticizing *Motorola's* statements concerning extra elements as *dicta*). *See* § 6F.

[164] *See, e.g.*, Jules Jordan Video, Inc. v. 144942 Canada Inc., 617 F.3d 1146, 1153–55 (9th Cir. 2010) (reproduction of DVD); Laws v. Sony Music Entertainment, Inc., 448 F.3d 1134, 1139–45 (9th Cir. 2006) (reproduction of sound recording); Baltimore Orioles, Inc. v. Major League Baseball Players Ass'n, 805 F.2d 663, 674–79 (7th Cir. 1986) (telecasts of baseball games); Fleet v. CBS, Inc., 50 Cal. App. 4th 1911, 191921 (1996) (distribution of motion picture).

[165] *See, e.g.*, Toney v. L'Oreal USA, Inc., 406 F.3d 905, 910 (7th Cir. 2005); Downing v. Abercrombie

of publicity claims do not require any showing of competition or likelihood of confusion. Although the results are often consistent, the rationale is not. Some courts have held that right of publicity claims are not preempted because the subject matter of the claim, the "name or likeness" of a person (or, more broadly, his or her "persona") is not "fixed,"[166] even when it is embodied in a copyrighted work, such as a photo.[167] This rationale is overbroad, because it would preclude preemption of any right of publicity claim.[168] Other courts have held, more sensibly, that the rights involved are not "equivalent" when the photo is being used to advertise an unrelated product.[169]

Claims for misappropriation of trade secrets typically survive preemption, because the plaintiff must prove the "extra elements" of secrecy and improper means, such as breach of an express or implied agreement of confidentiality or industrial espionage.[170]

The label "unfair competition" encompasses a broad range of potential misconduct, from common-law trademark infringement to misappropriation of plaintiff's labor and expenditure (i.e., free riding) merely by reproduction without compensation. To the extent a claim of "unfair competition" requires a showing of "likelihood of confusion" as to source or sponsorship, as is typically required for a common-law trademark claim, it will not be preempted.[171] However, to the extent that a claim of "unfair competition" relies on a claim of "misappropriation" or mere copying, it typically will be preempted.[172]

[iv]   Moral Rights

Before 1990, several states enacted laws to provide artists with rights of attribution and integrity in their works.[173] These rights are comparable to the "moral rights" of authors recognized in Europe and under the Berne Convention.

& Fitch, 265 F.3d 994, 1003–04 (9th Cir. 2001); Brown v. Ames, 201 F.3d 654, 657–59 (5th Cir. 2000); Waits v. Frito-Lay, Inc., 978 F.2d 1093, 1100 (9th Cir. 1992) (claim based on imitation of celebrity's distinctive voice in advertisement was not preempted); Midler v. Ford Motor Co., 849 F.2d 460, 462 (9th Cir. 1988) (same).

[166] See Midler, 849 F.2d at 462.

[167] See Toney, 406 F.3d at 910; Downing, 265 F.3d at 1003–04.

[168] But see Facenda v. NFL Films, Inc., 542 F.3d 1007, 1027–32 (3d Cir. 2008) (dismissing statutory preemption for lack of fixation, but engaging in lengthy "conflict preemption" analysis).

[169] See, e.g., Toney, 406 F.3d at 910. See also Waits, 978 F.2d at 1100 (elements of distinctive voice and deliberate imitation were sufficiently "different in kind" from copyright infringement).

[170] See, e.g., Ho v. Taflove, 648 F.3d 489, 503 (7th Cir. 2011); Stromback v. New Line Cinema, 384 F.3d 283, 302–04 (6th Cir. 2004) (citing cases); Dun & Bradstreet Software Services, Inc. v. Grace Consulting, Inc., 307 F.3d 197, 218 (3d Cir. 2002); Computer Associates Int'l, Inc. v. Altai, Inc., 982 F.2d 693, 717 (2d Cir. 1992).

[171] See, e.g., Donald Frederick Evans & Assocs., Inc. v. Continental Homes, Inc., 785 F.2d 897, 914 (11th Cir. 1986); Warner Bros. Inc. v. American Broadcasting Cos., 720 F.2d 231, 247 (2d Cir. 1983).

[172] See, e.g., Kodadek v. MTV Networks, Inc., 152 F.3d 1209, 1212–13 (9th Cir. 1998); Kregos v. Associated Press, 3 F.3d 656, 666 (2d Cir. 1993); Del Madera Properties v. Rhodes & Gardner, Inc., 820 F.2d 973, 977 (9th Cir. 1987) (unfair competition based on alleged misappropriation is preempted, despite additional allegation of breach of fiduciary duty); Warner Bros., 720 F.2d at 247.

[173] See § 4G[7][a].

Two cases have held that such a statute is not preempted under section 301(a) because it involves extra elements.[174] In 1990, however, Congress enacted the Visual Artists Rights Act (VARA), which included an express preemption provision that is codified in section 301(f).[175] Because such state statutes provide rights that are "equivalent" to those provided by VARA, these statutes are now preempted under section 301(f).[176]

California also has an Artists Resale Royalties Act that allows artists to recover a percentage of the sales price when their works are resold.[177] In *Moresburg v. Balyon*, the Ninth Circuit held that this Act was not preempted under the 1909 Act, but expressly reserved the question of whether it would be preempted under section 301.[178] A subsequent district court decision also declined to reach the issue, holding instead that the Act violated the dormant Commerce Clause, because it attempted to regulate transactions occurring wholly outside of California.[179] Although a resale royalty is not "equivalent" to any of the moral rights provided in VARA, and is therefore not preempted under section 301(f), a resale royalty does conflict with the first-sale doctrine, an exception to the copyright owner's right of distribution under the 1976 Act. As a result, this Act should be preempted under either section 301(a) or general "conflict" preemption principles.

[4]   First Amendment Limits on Intellectual Property Laws

Because intellectual property laws both provide incentives for and restrict the public expression of ideas, it is not surprising that rights claimants and accused infringers have on occasion challenged particular applications of those laws as contrary to the First Amendment's proscription of laws "abridging the freedom of speech, or of the press."[180]

The First Amendment may be implicated by intellectual property laws in two ways. First, in granting intellectual property rights, Congress might grant protection to certain works while denying protection to others. In such a case, a claimant who has been denied protection may claim his or her free speech rights have been abridged. Second, in enforcing intellectual property rights, a court may

---

[174] *See* Wojnarowicz v. American Family Association, 745 F. Supp. 130, 135–36 (S.D.N.Y. 1990) (New York Artists' Authorship Rights Act not preempted); Pavia v. 1120 Ave. of the Americas Assocs., 901 F. Supp. 620, 626–27 (S.D.N.Y. 1995). *But see* Peckarsky v. American Broadcasting Co., 603 F. Supp. 688, 696 (D.D.C. 1984) ("Although section 106 does not explicitly protect the right of attribution of authorship, assertion of such a claim in an otherwise pre-empted common law action will not save the common law claim from pre-emption.").

[175] 17 U.S.C. § 301(f)(1).

[176] *See* Lubner v. City of Los Angeles, 45 Cal. App. 4th 525, 529–531 (1996); Board of Managers of Soho Int'l Arts Condominium v. City of New York, 2003 U.S. Dist. LEXIS 10221 (S.D.N.Y. June 17, 2003). For the rights provided by VARA, *see* § 4G[7][b], below.

[177] Cal. Civ. Code § 986.

[178] 621 F.2d 972, 975–78 (9th Cir. 1980).

[179] Estate of Graham v. Sotheby's, 860 F. Supp. 2d 1117 (C.D. Cal. 2012), *reh'g en banc ordered sub nom.* Sam Francis Foundation v. Christie's, Inc., 769 F.3d 1195 (9th Cir. 2014).

[180] U.S. Const., Amend. I.

enjoin or punish speech that is too similar to a protected work. In such a case, the defendant may claim that his or her free speech rights are being violated.

[a] Granting or Withholding Intellectual Property Rights

With regard to the first category of cases, copyright law does not expressly restrict the availability of copyright protection based on the content of the work. In *Mitchell Bros. Film Group v. Cinema Adult Theater*, the Fifth Circuit held that the 1909 Copyright Act "contain[s] no explicit or implicit bar to the copyrighting of obscene materials," and noted that "Congress in not enacting an obscenity exception to copyrightability avoids substantial practical difficulties and delicate First Amendment issues."[181]

Unlike the Copyright Act, the Lanham Act expressly discriminates on the basis of content, refusing registration to marks that are "immoral" or "scandalous."[182] Nonetheless, the courts have held that "the refusal to register a mark does not . . . suppress any form of expression because it does not affect the applicant's right to use the mark in question."[183] In the view of these courts, denying the benefits of registration on the basis of content does not itself violate the First Amendment.[184]

States also enjoy considerable leeway in deciding whether to grant or withhold intellectual property protection. In *Friedman v. Rogers*, the plaintiff challenged a Texas law that prohibited optometrists from doing business under a trade name. The Court noted that a trade name enjoys little First Amendment protection because it is "commercial speech that has no intrinsic meaning."[185] Use of trade names can create opportunities to deceive the public that a state may wish to prevent.[186] An *established* trade name may become a valuable property interest, but "a property interest in a means of communication does not enlarge or diminish the First Amendment protection of that communication."[187]

---

[181] 604 F.2d 852, 858 (5th Cir. 1979). The court further held that although the First Amendment and the Patent and Copyright Clause might permit an exception for obscenity, they did not require one, *id.* at 859–860; and that courts should not infer the existence of an unwritten obscenity defense to copyright infringement, *id.* at 861–63.

[182] 15 U.S.C. § 1052(a). *See* § 5E[2][a].

[183] In re Boulevard Entertainment, Inc., 334 F.3d 1336, 1343 (Fed. Cir. 2003). *See also* Ritchie v. Simpson, 170 F.3d 1092, 1099 (Fed. Cir. 1999).

[184] *But see Ritchie*, 10 F.3d at 1103–04 (Newman, J., dissenting) (contending denial of registration may raise First Amendment concerns).

[185] 440 U.S. 1, 12 (1979).

[186] "The possibilities for deception are numerous. The trade name of an optometrical practice can remain unchanged despite changes in the staff of optometrists upon whose skill and care [the] public depends when it patronizes the practice. . . . A trade name frees an optometrist from dependence on his personal reputation to attract clients, and even allows him to assume a new trade name if negligence or misconduct casts a shadow over the old one. By using different trade names at shops under his common ownership, an optometrist can give the public the false impression of competition among the shops." *Id.* at 13.

[187] *Id.* at 12 n.11. The plaintiffs did not claim that they had been deprived of their property without due process of law. *Id.*

[b]   Enforcing Intellectual Property Rights

[i]   Copyright

The Supreme Court has consistently rejected the argument the First Amendment provides an independent defense to copyright infringement, on the ground that copyright law contains limiting doctrines that prevent impingement upon First Amendment values.

In *Harper & Row Publishers, Inc. v. Nation Enterprises*, the Supreme Court held that "copyright's idea/expression dichotomy strikes a definitional balance between the First Amendment and the Copyright Act by permitting free communication of facts while still protecting an author's expression."[188] The Court rejected an argument that the First Amendment required a broader interpretation of "fair use" in a case involving unauthorized publication of former President Gerald Ford's soon-to-be-published memoirs, saying:

> In view of the First Amendment protections already embodied in the Copyright Act's distinction between copyrightable expression and uncopyrightable facts and ideas, and the latitude for scholarship and comment traditionally afforded by fair use, we see no warrant for expanding the doctrine of fair use to create what amounts to a public figure exception to copyright.[189]

In *Eldred v. Ashcroft*, the Supreme Court likewise rejected a First Amendment-based challenge to copyright term extension, holding that First Amendment considerations were adequately reflected in existing doctrinal limitations on copyright, such as the idea-expression dichotomy and the fair-use doctrine,[190] and stating that when "Congress has not altered the traditional contours of copyright protection, further First Amendment scrutiny is unnecessary."[191]

In *Golan v. Holder*,[192] plaintiffs challenged the constitutionality of the Uruguay Round Agreements Act, which restored copyrights in works of foreign origin that had entered the public domain in the United States for failure to comply with formalities.[193] Although the Tenth Circuit initially held that "[t]he principle that works in the public domain remain there is a traditional contour of copyright protection that [copyright restoration] alters,"[194] it subsequently held that copyright restoration was a "content neutral" speech restriction that was justified by Congress' "substantial interest in protecting American copyright holders' interests abroad."[195] The Supreme Court affirmed, suggesting that the "traditional contours of copyright protection" are *limited* to the idea/expression dichotomy and the

---

[188] 471 U.S. 539, 556 (1985).

[189] *Id.* at 560.

[190] 537 U.S. 186, 219–20 (2003).

[191] *Id.* at 221.

[192] 132 S. Ct. 873 (2012).

[193] *See* § 4E[3].

[194] Golan v. Gonzales, 501 F.3d 1179, 1188 (10th Cir. 2007).

[195] Golan v. Holder, 609 F.3d 1076, 1083 (10th Cir. 2010), *aff'd*, 132 S. Ct. 873 (2012).

fair-use doctrine;[196] and holding that the public acquires no "vested rights" to use works in the public domain that cannot be divested by Congress, acting to comply with its international treaty obligations.[197]

[ii]   Trademark and Rights of Publicity

In general, "[t]he Lanham Act is constitutional because it only regulates commercial speech, which is entitled to reduced protections under the First Amendment. . . . If [the defendant's] use is commercial, then, and only then, do we analyze his use for a likelihood of confusion. If [the defendant's] use is also confusing, then it is misleading commercial speech, and outside the First Amendment."[198] In addition, like copyright, trademark contains limiting doctrines that help avoid conflict with the First Amendment.[199]

First Amendment problems occasionally arise, however, when Congress or a mark owner seeks to expand trademark law beyond its traditional limits. For example, in *San Francisco Arts & Athletics, Inc. v. United States Olympic Committee*, the Supreme Court considered a challenge to a federal law that granted the USOC exclusive rights in the word "Olympic," and in certain symbols associated with the quadrennial Olympic Games, without having to show likelihood of confusion and without resort to the statutory defenses available under the Lanham Act.[200] The Supreme Court upheld the law, noting that it applied only to certain commercial and promotional uses of the word "Olympic," and therefore primarily regulated commercial speech.[201] Applying intermediate scrutiny,[202] the Court held that "Congress reasonably could conclude that most commercial uses of the Olympic words and symbols are likely to be confusing."[203] Other parts of the opinion, however, implicitly validate other rationales for trademark protection, including misappropriation or anti-free riding,[204] and trademark dilution.[205]

---

[196]   132 S. Ct. at 889–91.

[197]   *Id.* at 891–94.

[198]   Taubman Co. v. Webfeats, 319 F.3d 770, 774–75 (6th Cir. 2003). *Cf.* Friedman v. Rogers, 440 U.S. 1, 11 (1979) ("The use of trade names in connection with [a service] . . . is a form of commercial speech and nothing more.").

[199]   *See* § 5J[3] (descriptive fair use), § 5J[4] (nominative fair use).

[200]   483 U.S. 522, 531 (1987).

[201]   *Id.* at 535. The Court suggested that the statute did not prohibit "purely" expressive uses of the word "Olympic," pointing to a case in which the Olympic rings were used "on a poster expressing opposition to the planned conversion of the Olympic Village at Lake Placid, New York, into a prison." *Id.* at 536 n.14, *citing* Stop the Olympic Prison v. United States Olympic Committee, 489 F. Supp. 1112, 1118–21 (S.D.N.Y. 1980). In so holding, the Court found that the defendant's proposed use, sponsorship of a "Gay Olympic Games" sporting event, was primarily commercial and promotional in nature, rather than purely expressive. 483 U.S. at 536, 540–41.

[202]   483 U.S. at 536–37 ("The appropriate inquiry is thus whether the incidental restrictions on First Amendment freedoms are greater than necessary to further a substantial governmental interest.").

[203]   *Id.* at 539.

[204]   *Id.* at 532 ("when a word acquires value 'as the result of organization and the expenditure of labor, skill, and money' by an entity, that entity constitutionally may obtain a limited property right in the word."), *citing* International News Service v. Associated Press, 248 U.S. 215, 239 (1918); *see also* 483 U.S. at 539 ("it is clear that the SFAA sought to exploit the 'commercial magnetism' of the word given value by the USOC."). For a discussion of the doctrine of misappropriation, see § 6F.

First Amendment problems can also arise when a trademark is used in an expressive work or for an expressive purpose, rather than in an advertising context. For example, in *L.L. Bean, Inc. v. Drake Publishers, Inc.*, the First Circuit relied in part on free expression concerns to deny state anti-dilution protection against a noncommercial trademark parody.[206] Other cases have similarly had to grapple with the First Amendment in the context of commercial parodies or non-commercial expression.[207] In order to avoid First Amendment conflicts, the Federal Trademark Dilution Act contains an express exception for "any noncommercial use of a mark."[208]

The only U.S. Supreme Court case involving the right of publicity is *Zacchini v. Scripps-Howard Broadcasting Co.*, in which the Court held that the First Amendment did not require a defense for an unauthorized television news broadcast of a performer's entire 15-second "human cannonball" act without his consent.[209] The Court held that a State may grant a right of publicity both as an incentive to encourage individuals to develop entertainment talents, and to prevent "unjust enrichment" by protecting "the product of [an individual's] own talents and energy, the end result of much time, effort, and expense."[210] The Court noted, however, that the facts presented "what may be the strongest case for a 'right of publicity' involving, not the appropriation of an entertainer's reputation to enhance the attractiveness of a commercial product, but the appropriation of the very activity by which the entertainer acquired his reputation in the first place."[211] In addition, the right of publicity has very few "internal" limits that would avoid conflict with the First Amendment. As a result, the First Amendment is almost always raised as a defense in cases involving rights of publicity, and other courts have sometimes drawn a different balance in ruling on such First Amendment challenges.[212]

[5]   Eleventh Amendment and Sovereign Immunity

[a]   Claims Against State Governments

Federal law expressly provides that "any State, any instrumentality of a State, and any officer or employee of a State or instrumentality of a State acting in his or her official capacity" may be sued for infringement of a federal intellectual property right and "shall be subject to [liability] . . . in the same manner and to the same

---

[205] 483 U.S. at 539 (Congress "could also determine that unauthorized uses, even if not confusing, nevertheless may harm the USOC by lessening the distinctiveness and thus the commercial value of the marks."), *citing* Frank Schechter, *The Rational Basis of Trademark Protection*, 40 Harv. L. Rev. 813, 825 (1927), the foundational article for the doctrine of trademark dilution. *See* § 5G.

[206] 811 F.2d 26, 32–33 (1st Cir. 1987).

[207] These cases are discussed in § 5J[5].

[208] 15 U.S.C. § 1125(c)(3)(C). *See* § 5G[4].

[209] 433 U.S. 562, 575 (1977).

[210] *Id.* at 575–76.

[211] *Id.* at 576.

[212] *See* § 6G[4][c].

extent as any nongovernmental entity."[213] Furthermore, federal law expressly abrogates the sovereign immunity of states and state actors with respect to intellectual property claims brought in federal court.[214]

Despite these clear indications of congressional intent, the Supreme Court held in a pair of 1999 decisions that Congress' abrogation of sovereign immunity violated the Eleventh Amendment proviso that "[t]he Judicial power of the United States shall not be construed to extend to any suit in law or equity, commenced or prosecuted against one of the United States by Citizens of another State, or by Citizens or Subjects of any Foreign State."[215] In *College Savings Bank v. Florida Prepaid Postsecondary Education Expense Board*, the Court held that Congress could not subject the states to suit under the false advertising provisions of the Lanham Act.[216] It interpreted the Eleventh Amendment as precluding federal court jurisdiction over any suit brought against a state, subject to two exceptions: (1) where Congress validly abrogates state immunity by exercising its power under the Fourteenth Amendment, and (2) where a state waives its immunity by consenting to suit.[217] Neither exception applied in *College Savings Bank*. As to the Fourteenth Amendment, which provides that no state shall "deprive any person of . . . property without due process of law,"[218] the Court stated that there is no "property right in freedom from a competitor's false advertising about its own products."[219] As to waiver, the Court stated that the test "is a stringent one" that is met only if the state voluntarily invokes federal court jurisdiction or makes a "clear declaration" of its intent to submit to federal jurisdiction.[220]

In the companion case, *Florida Prepaid Postsecondary Education Expense Board v. College Savings Bank*,[221] the Court held that Congress' clear and express attempt to abrogate the States' sovereign immunity with respect to patent infringement was not a valid exercise of its power to enforce the Fourteenth Amendment's substantive provisions by "appropriate" legislation.[222] In reaching this conclusion, the Court stressed that the legislation was not based on a finding of a pattern of patent infringement by the States, nor on a determination that such state patent infringements as did occur rose to the level of a Due Process violation.[223]

After *College Savings Bank* and *Florida Prepaid*, lower courts have similarly invalidated Congress's attempts to abrogate Eleventh Amendment immunity for

---

[213] *See* 35 U.S.C. § 271(h) (patent); 17 U.S.C. § 501(a) (copyright); 15 U.S.C. §§ 1114(1), 1127 (definition of "person") (Lanham Act).

[214] *See* 35 U.S.C. § 296(a) (patent); 17 U.S.C. § 511(a) (copyright); 15 U.S.C. § 1122(b) (Lanham Act).

[215] U.S. Const. amend. XI.

[216] 527 U.S. 666, 670 (1999) (citation omitted).

[217] *Id.*

[218] U.S. Const. amend. XIV, § 1.

[219] *College Savings Bank*, 527 U.S. at 673.

[220] *Id.*

[221] 527 U.S. 627 (1999).

[222] U.S. Const. amend. XIV, § 5.

[223] *Florida Prepaid*, 527 U.S. at 640–43.

purposes of both copyright infringement[224] and trademark infringement.[225] No court has held to the contrary. This bar is equally applicable whether the plaintiff's claim is for monetary damages or for injunctive relief.[226] Moreover, federal courts have exclusive jurisdiction over claims under the patent and copyright laws,[227] which presumably would bar actions against states in state courts; and although state courts have concurrent jurisdiction to hear claims under the Lanham Act,[228] the Supreme Court has ruled (despite the express language of the Eleventh Amendment) that states may claim sovereign immunity against federal causes of action in state court as well.[229] However, the Eleventh Amendment does not bar a state court from adjudicating claims against states or state officials under state law; in such a case, the question of sovereign immunity would be determined by state law.

It remains unclear, however, whether and under what circumstances federal courts may consider a claim for injunctive relief under the Lanham Act that is brought against a state officer, as distinguished from the state or an agency thereof. The Supreme Court has recognized that the Eleventh Amendment does not always bar suits for injunctive relief against state officers, even where it would bar a similar suit against the state itself.[230] For example, one court has held that a state university is not an indispensable party in a suit against its employees to correct inventorship of a patent assigned to the university.[231] However, allegations that state officials may have "approved of, condoned, or acquiesced in" alleged infringement are not sufficient to state a claim for injunctive relief.[232] In addition, some courts have held that actions for damages may be maintained against state officials in their individual capacity, unless it can be shown that the judgment would inevitably be paid out of the public purse.[233] State officials are entitled to qualified

---

[224] *See* Nat'l Ass'n of Bds. of Pharmacy v. Bd. of Regents of the Univ. System of Georgia, 633 F.3d 1297 (11th Cir. 2011); Rodriguez v. Texas Comm'n on the Arts, 199 F.3d 279 (5th Cir. 2000); Chavez v. Arte Publico Press, 204 F.3d 601 (5th Cir. 2000); *see also* Romero v. Calif. Dept. of Transportation, 2009 U.S. Dist. LEXIS 23193 (C.D. Cal. Mar. 12, 2009) (sovereign immunity applies to VARA claims).

[225] Bd. of Regents of Univ. of Wisc. Sys. v. Phoenix Int'l Software, Inc., 653 F.3d 448, 458 (7th Cir. 2011).

[226] Federal Maritime Comm'n v. South Carolina State Ports Auth., 535 U.S. 743, 766 (2002); Seminole Tribe of Florida v. Florida, 517 U.S. 44, 58 (1996).

[227] 28 U.S.C. § 1338(a).

[228] *See* § 5F[8][a].

[229] *See* Alden v. Maine, 527 U.S. 706 (1999). It is possible, however, that intellectual property owners could sue states for inverse condemnation for depriving them of their "property."

[230] *Seminole Tribe*, 517 U.S. at 71 n.14; *Ex Parte* Young, 209 U.S. 123 (1908); *see, e.g.*, Nat'l Ass'n of Bds. of Pharmacy v. Bd. of Regents of the Univ. System of Georgia, 633 F.3d 1297 (11th Cir. 2011); Cambridge Univ. Press v. Becker, 863 F. Supp. 2d 1190, 1205–10 (N.D. Ga. 2012), *aff'd in relevant part, rev'd in part on other grounds sub nom.* Cambridge Univ. Press. v. Patton, 769 F.3d 1232, 1254–55 (11th Cir. 2014); Applera Corp. v. MJ Research Inc., 311 F. Supp. 2d 293 (D.D.C. 2004).

[231] Univ. of Utah v. Max-Planck-Gesellschaft zur Forderung der Wissenschaften E.V., 734 F.3d 1315 (Fed. Cir. 2013).

[232] Coyle v. University of Kentucky, 2 F. Supp. 3d 1014 (E.D. Ky. 2014).

[233] Mkt'g Info. Masters, Inc. v. Bd. of Trustees of the Calif. State Univ. Sys., 552 F. Supp. 2d 1088, 1095–96 (S.D. Cal. 2008).

immunity in such actions unless their actions violated "clearly established law."[234]

Also unclear are the circumstances under which a state may be deemed to have voluntarily waived its Eleventh Amendment immunity to suit. When a state voluntarily appears in federal court, it waives its Eleventh Amendment immunity for purposes of that lawsuit, including any counterclaims.[235] However, a state does not waive its immunity by entering into contractual and commercial arrangements with researchers or applying for patents,[236] suing others for patent infringement, or intervening in a different lawsuit involving the same patent.[237]

Sovereign immunity is also enjoyed by U.S. territories[238] and Indian tribes,[239] although unlike the immunity enjoyed by States, Congress presumably could abrogate the sovereign immunity of these entities at any time.

[b]   Claims Against the Federal Government

Congress has expressly waived the sovereign immunity of the federal government to suits for patent and copyright infringement. Such suits may only be heard in the U.S. Court of Federal Claims, which can only grant monetary relief and not an injunction.[240] However, there are several statutory exceptions to the federal government's waiver of sovereign immunity. Waiver does not apply if the patent or copyright owner was "in a position to order, influence, or induce use of the copyrighted work by the Government";[241] or where the work or invention was "prepared by a person while in the employment or service of the Untied States,"[242] or was "prepared as a part of the official functions of the employee, or in the

---

[234] *See* Ass'n for Info. Media & Equip. v. Regents of the Univ. of Calif., 2012 U.S. Dist. LEXIS 187811 (C.D. Cal. Nov. 20, 2012); Molinelli-Freytas v. University of Puerto Rico, 792 F. Supp. 2d 150, 156–158 (D.P.R. 2010).

[235] Bd. of Regents of Univ. of Wisc. Sys. v. Phoenix Int'l Software, Inc., 653 F.3d 448, 458 (7th Cir. 2011); Vas-Cath Corp. v. Curators of the Univ. of Missouri, 473 F.3d 1376, 1382–83 (Fed. Cir. 2007); Regents of the Univ. of New Mexico v. Knight, 321 F.3d 1111, 1124 (Fed. Cir. 2003). .

[236] *See* Xechem Int'l, Inc. v. Univ. of Texas M.D. Anderson Cancer Ctr., 382 F.3d 1324, 1329–31 (Fed. Cir. 2004).

[237] *See* Biomedical Patent Mgmt. Corp. v. State of Calif., Dept. of Health Servs., 505 F.3d 1328, 1339 (Fed. Cir. 2007); *see also* Tegic Communs. Corp. v. Bd. of Regents, 458 F.3d 1335, 1340–43 (Fed. Cir. 2006).

[238] DeRomero v. Institute of Puerto Rican Culture, 466 F. Supp. 2d 410 (D.P.R. 2006).

[239] Bassett v. Mashantucket Pequot Tribe, 204 F.3d 343 (2d Cir. 2000).

[240] 28 U.S.C. § 1498(a) (patent infringement); 28 U.S.C. § 1498(b) (copyright infringement). *See* Zoltek Corp. v. United States, 672 F.3d 1309 (Fed. Cir. 2012) (sovereign immunity is waived for importation or use within the U.S. of goods manufactured outside the U.S. using a process patented in the U.S.); O'Rourke v. Smithsonian Institution Press, 399 F.3d 113 (2d Cir. 2005) (Smithsonian is an agency of the "United States" within the meaning of § 1498(b)); *but see* Blueport Co. v. United States, 533 F.3d 1374 (Fed. Cir. 2008) (claims for violations of the anti-circumvention provisions of the DMCA do not fall within the waiver of sovereign immunity in § 1498(b)); Boyle v. United States, 200 F.3d 1369 (Fed. Cir. 2000) (United States retains sovereign immunity for acts of third parties unless they acted with the authorization or consent of the government).

[241] 28 U.S.C. § 1498(a),(b); *see Blueport*, 533 F.3d at 1379–82.

[242] 28 U.S.C. § 1498(a),(b); *see* Walton v. United States, 551 F.3d 1367 (Fed. Cir. 2009) (work prepared by prison inmate under federal work program was prepared in the "service of the United States").

preparation of which Government time, material, or facilities were used."[243]

The United States has expressly waived its sovereign immunity to all claims made under the Lanham Act, including trademark infringement, dilution, and false advertising.[244]

---

[243] 28 U.S.C. § 1498(a), (b).

[244] 15 U.S.C. § 1122(a), (c).

Chapter 2

PATENTS

SYNOPSIS

§ 2A INTRODUCTION

§ 2B HISTORICAL DEVELOPMENT

    [1] The 1790 and 1793 Acts

    [2] The 1836 and 1870 Acts

    [3] The First Invention Concept

    [4] Shifting Supreme Court Attitudes Toward Patents

        [a] Patents Under Fire: 1880–1892

        [b] Patents in Favor: 1892–1930

        [c] Patents Under Renewed Fire: 1930–1950

    [5] The 1952 Act

    [6] The 1966 *Graham* Trilogy and Beyond

    [7] Leahy-Smith America Invents Act of 2011

§ 2C PATENTABILITY

    [1] Patentable Subject Matter

        [a] General Definitions

        [b] Exclusions and Exceptions

        [c] New Uses of Old Products

        [d] Products of Nature and Living Organisms

        [e] Business Methods and Methods of Treatment

        [f] Computer Software: Algorithms and Mathematical Inventions

           [i] Abstract Ideas — Mental Steps

          [ii] Supreme Court Precedent on Software Patents

         [iii] Examples: *Grams* and *Iwahashi*

    [2] Utility

    [3] Novelty

    [4] Nonobviousness

        [a] General Test — *Graham v. Deere*

        [b] Nonanalogous Art

        [c] Comparative Utility

          [i] Rationale

[ii]   New and Unexpected Properties

[iii]   Undisclosed Advantages and Properties

[d]   Objective Evidence

[i]   Long-Felt Need — Failure of Others

[ii]   Commercial Success

[iii]   Licensing and Acquiescence by Competitors

[iv]   Copying and Laudatory Statements by the Infringer

[v]   Near Simultaneous Invention

[e]   Other Guidelines

[i]   Prior Art Suggestions — Obvious to Try

[ii]   Combination Inventions

[iii]   Chemical Compounds and Intermediates

[iv]   Processes — Methods of Making and Using

[5]   Prior Art Before the AIA

[a]   Documentary Sources: Patents and Publications

[i]   Publications

[ii]   Patents

[b]   Nondocumentary Sources: Public Use and Sale

[i]   Known or Used by Others

[ii]   Statutory Bars

[iii]   Public Use in the United States

[iv]   On Sale in the United States

[v]   Experimental Use Exception

[vi]   Abandonment

[vii]   Foreign Patenting

[c]   Senior-Filed Patents

[i]   The *Milburn* Doctrine

[ii]   Foreign Priority Applications

[iii]   Continuation Applications

[iv]   Issuance

[d]   Prior Invention and Derivation

[i]   Prior Invention — Section 102(g)

[ii]   Derivation — Section 102(f)

[e]   Invention Date

[f]   Inventive Entities

[6]   Prior Art Under the AIA

§ 2D   PATENT PROCESS

[1]   Patent Prosecution

[a]   Overview

  [b] Unity of Invention — Restriction
  [c] Confidentiality
  [d] Amendments
  [e] Duty of Candor
[2] Disclosure Requirements
  [a] Enablement Requirement
   [i] Claim Scope
   [ii] Experimentation
   [iii] Other Enablement Issues
   [iv] Deposit of Biological Material
  [b] Written Description Requirement
  [c] Best Mode Requirement
   [i] In General
   [ii] Computer Programs
   [iii] Trade Secrets
   [iv] Time Frame
  [d] Inventor Identification
   [i] Sole Invention
   [ii] Joint Invention
   [iii] Separate Claims
   [iv] Inventorship Error Correction
[3] Claiming Requirements
  [a] Definiteness
  [b] Format
  [c] Jepson Claims
  [d] Alternative Limitations — Markush Groups
  [e] Functionality — Means-Plus-Function Claims
  [f] Negative Limitations
  [g] Multiple Claims — Dependent Claims
[4] Related Applications
  [a] Double Patenting
   [i] Claim Comparison
   [ii] Identical Inventions
   [iii] Obvious Variation
   [iv] Design and Utility Patents
   [v] Terminal Disclaimers
   [vi] Different Inventors' Commonly Assigned Applications
  [b] Continuation Applications
   [i] Continuity of Disclosure

      [ii]   Cross References

      [iii] Copendency

      [iv] Inventorship

  [5]   Interferences and Derivation Procedures

      [a]   Priority Rules — First to Invent

      [b]   Conception

      [c]   Reduction to Practice

      [d]   Diligence

      [e]   Corroboration

      [f]   Abandonment, Suppression and Concealment

      [g]   Derivation Proceedings

  [6]   Post-Issuance Procedures

      [a]   Reexamination

      [b]   Reissue

        [i]   Inoperativeness and Invalidity

        [ii]   Claim Scope Alteration

        [iii]   Error

        [iv]   Oath or Declaration — Examination

        [v]   Effect of Reissue — Intervening Rights

      [c]   Post-Grant Review

      [d]   Inter Partes Review

§ 2E   RIGHTS

  [1]   Duration

  [2]   Exclusive Rights

      [a]   Basic Rights: Direct Infringement

      [b]   Territorial Scope: Importation and Exportation

        [i]   Exportation

        [ii]   Importation

        [iii]   Process Patent Protection

      [c] Secondary Liability

        [i]   Relation to Direct Infringement

        [ii]   Active Inducement

        [iii]   Contributory Infringement

        [iv]   Corporations — Officers and Directors

  [3]   First Sale — Exhaustion — Repair and Reconstruction

  [4]   Government Use

§ 2F   INFRINGEMENT

  [1]   Claim Language Interpretation

      [a]   Intrinsic and Extrinsic Material

      [i]   Other Claims — Claim Differentiation

      [ii] Specification — The Patentee as "Lexicographer"

      [iii] Prosecution History

      [iv] Expert Testimony

    [b] "Means-Plus-Function" Limitations

    [c] Consistency

  [2] Claim Application

    [a] Literal Infringement

    [i] Omissions

    [ii] Additions and Improvements

    [b] Doctrine of Equivalents

    [i] The *Graver Tank* and *Warner-Jenkinson* Decisions

    [ii] The "Triple Identity" Test

    [iii] Comparison Standard — The "All Elements" Rule

    [iv] Range of Equivalents — Pioneer Patents

    [v] Later Developed Equivalents

    [vi] Reverse Doctrine of Equivalents

    [vii] Limiting Effect of the Prior Art

    [c] Prosecution History Estoppel

    [i] Acts Giving Rise to Prosecution History Estoppel

    [ii] Effect of Prosecution History Estoppel

  [3] Proof of Infringing Activity

    [a] Burden of Proof

    [b] Intent

    [c] Agency — Corporate Officers and Employees

  [4] Jurisdiction and Joinder Provisions

§ 2G DEFENSES

  [1] Invalidity

    [a] Presumption of Validity

    [b] Standing to Challenge Validity

    [c] Effect of Judgment

  [2] Inequitable Conduct — Fraud

  [3] Misuse

  [4] Experimental or Personal Use

  [5] Laches and Estoppel

  [6] Implied License — First Sale

  [7] Prior Commercial Use

§ 2H REMEDIES

  [1] Injunctions

         [a]   Preliminary Injunctions

         [b]   Permanent Injunctions

    [2]   Damages

         [a]   Compensatory Damages

         [b]   Increased Damages — Willful Infringement

         [c]   Notice — Patent Marking

    [3]   Interest

    [4]   Attorney's Fees and Expenses

§ 2I   OWNERSHIP AND TRANSFER

    [1]   Employee and Contractor Inventions

    [2]   Ability to Sue Infringers

    [3]   Compulsory Licenses

§ 2A   INTRODUCTION

Patent law protects new, nonobvious, and useful inventions, such as machines, devices, chemical compositions, and manufacturing processes.

To obtain a patent grant, an inventor must file, in a timely fashion, an application with the United States Patent and Trademark Office ("PTO"). The application must include a specification describing and precisely claiming the invention. The PTO assigns each application to an examiner with technical training in the pertinent technology who conducts a search of the prior art and determines whether the applicant's invention complies with the legal requirements of patentability: novelty, utility, nonobviousness, enabling disclosure, and clear claiming. If the examiner reaches a favorable decision, he or she allows the claims. In due course, the PTO issues a patent. The patent is a printed publication and includes (1) the complete specification as filed by the inventor, with any amendments made during examination, and (2) a cover sheet giving data on the patent, such as the patent number, the issue date, the application filing date, the inventor, prior art publications and patents cited during the examination. Patents are important sources of technical information.

A patent confers the right to exclude others from making, using, offering for sale, or importing the claimed invention in the United States for a term of 20 years from the date of the application. A patent owner may file a civil suit for infringement against anyone who, without authority, makes, uses, offers for sale, or imports the patented invention.

Patents have the attributes of personal property and may be assigned or licensed.

§ 2B HISTORICAL DEVELOPMENT

[1]   The 1790 and 1793 Acts

The United States Constitution empowered Congress to establish a national patent system: it provides that Congress shall have the power "To promote the progress of science and useful arts, by securing for limited times to authors and inventors the exclusive right to their respective writings and discoveries."[1] The Clause intermixes copyright and patent concepts. The patent concepts are "useful arts," "inventors" and "discoveries."

In 1790, Congress enacted the first patent statute.[2] It authorized patents for "any useful art, manufacture, engine, machine, or device, or any improvement therein not before known or used," provided that a designated group of executive officers (the Secretary of State, the Secretary of War, and the Attorney General) determined that the invention was "sufficiently useful and important."

Three years later, Congress replaced the 1790 Act.[3] The 1793 Act omitted the importance determination and authorized patents for "any useful art, machine, manufacture, or composition of matter, or any new and useful improvement [thereon], not known or used before the application. . . ."

The 1790 and 1793 patent statutes, and court decisions interpreting them, introduced fundamental concepts that remain features of United States patent law.

One example is the 1793 Act's four-category approach to the definition of patentable subject matter; the four categories are still in force.[4]

---

[1] Article I, § 8, cl. 8. In *Graham*, the Supreme Court discussed the origins and effect of the Patent Clause:

> The clause is both a grant of power and a limitation. This qualified authority, unlike the power often exercised in the sixteenth and seventeenth centuries by the English Crown, is limited to the promotion of advances in the 'useful arts.' It was written against the backdrop of the practices — eventually curtailed by the Statute of Monopolies — of the Crown in granting monopolies to court favorites in goods or businesses which had long before been enjoyed by the public. . . . The Congress in the exercise of the patent power may not overreach the restraints imposed by the stated constitutional purpose.

Graham v. John Deere Co., 383 U.S. 1, 5–6 (1966).

During the debate on adoption of the Constitution, James Madison, later President of the United States, in Federalist Paper No. 43, commented on the Patent and Copyright Clause as follows:

> The utility of this power will scarcely be questioned. The copyright of authors has been solemnly adjudged, in Great Britain, to be a right of common law. The right to useful inventions seems with equal reason to belong to the inventors. The public good fully coincides in both cases with the claims of individuals. The States cannot separately make effectual provision for either of the cases, and most of them have anticipated the decision of this point, by laws passed at the instance of Congress.

[2] Act of Apr. 10, 1790, ch. 7, 1 Stat. 109.

[3] In *Graham*, the Court noted the involvement of Thomas Jefferson, later President of the United States, in the first two patent statutes: "Thomas Jefferson, who as Secretary of State was a member of the group, was its moving spirit. . . . He was not only an administrator of the patent system under the 1790 Act, but was also the author of the 1793 Patent Act." Graham v. John Deere Co., 383 U.S. 1, 7 (1966).

[4] The term "art" meant process or method. In 1952, Congress replaced "art" with "process" in the

Another example is invalidity defenses. The 1790 and 1793 statutes authorized a patent owner to sue for infringement but allowed the accused infringer to defend by alleging and proving the patented invention lacked novelty or was insufficiently disclosed in the inventor's specification.[5] These defenses are still important features of the United States patent system.

Yet another example is the distinction between *lack of novelty*, meaning discovery by others before the inventor's invention, and *loss of right*, meaning public use or sale by the inventor before applying for a patent. In *Pennock v. Dialogue*,[6] the inventors, Pennock and Sellers, devised a new method of making hose in 1811. They authorized Jenkins to make and sell 13,000 feet of hose using the method. In 1818, the inventors applied for and obtained a patent. The Court affirmed a jury verdict that the patent was invalid because the invention was, within the meaning of 1793 Act Section 6, "known or used before the application." The Court conceded that Section 6 could not be interpreted literally; necessarily, at least the inventor would "know" of the invention before he or she could apply for a patent thereon. For policy reasons, the Court interpreted "known or used" as including public or commercial use by the inventor.[7] This policy orientation remains to this day a feature of the law of public use and sale.[8]

[2]   The 1836 and 1870 Acts

In 1836, Congress enacted a major revision of the patent laws.[9] The 1836 Act created a Patent Office and a system of examination of patent applications for compliance with the requirement of novelty over the prior art.[10] It introduced a

---

four-category definition but emphasized that "The term 'process' means process, art, or method." 35 U.S.C. § 101.

[5] Section 6 of the 1793 Act provided the following defenses:

[T]he specification, filed by the plaintiff, does not contain the whole truth relative to his discovery, or . . . contains more than is necessary to produce the described effect, which concealment or addition shall fully appear to have been made, for the purpose of deceiving the public;

[T]he thing, thus secured by patent, was not originally discovered by the patentee, but had been in use, or had been described in some public work anterior to the supposed discovery of the patentee, or that he had surreptitiously obtained a patent for the discovery of another person.

As to the first defense, the Supreme Court held that, despite the language on "deceiving the public," a patent issuing on a defective specification was invalid without regard to the inventor's intent or purpose. Grant v. Raymond, 31 U.S. (6 Pet.) 218, 247–48 (1832) (the statute "requires, as preliminary to a patent, a correct specification and description of the thing discovered. This is necessary in order to give the public, after the privilege shall expire, the advantage for which the privilege is allowed, and is the foundation of the power to issue the patent.").

[6] 27 U.S. (2 Pet.) 1 (1829).

[7] 27 U.S. at 19.

[8] *See, e.g.*, Envirotech Corp. v. Westech Engineering Inc., 904 F.2d 1571, 1574 (Fed. Cir. 1990) ("the policies or purposes underlying the on sale bar, in effect, define it").

[9] The Act was approved on Independence Day, the 4th of July.

[10] A Report accompanying the Act cited four "evils" in the existing system of issuing patents "without any examination into the merit or novelty of the invention":

1. A considerable portion of all the patents granted are worthless and void, as conflicting with,

statutory requirement of clear claiming.[11] It codified the *Pennock* doctrine by providing that an inventor's discovery be "not, at the time of his application for a patent, *in public use or on sale*, with his consent or allowance."[12]

In 1839, Congress amended the public use and on sale provision to add a two-year grace period; henceforth, public use or on sale activity was fatal only if it dated more than two years before the inventor applied for a patent. The grace period remains a feature of United States patent law, though Congress shorted the period to one year in 1939.

In the mid-19th century, the Supreme Court, in reviewing patent infringement judgments, established fundamental patent law concepts. *Hotchkiss v. Greenwood*[13] established the obviousness standard of patentability; a literally new device was not patentable if it would have been obvious to a person of ordinary skill in the art. *Gayler v. Wilder*[14] interpreted the "known or used" novelty standard as requiring knowledge or use accessible to the public. *Winans v. Denmead*[15] established the doctrine of equivalents; a device that did not come within the literal language of the patent claim would nevertheless infringe if it obtained the same

---

and infringing upon one another, or upon, public rights not subject to patent privileges; arising either from a want of due attention to the specifications of claim, or from the ignorance of the patentees of the state of the arts and manufactures, and of the inventions made in other countries, and even in our own.

2. The country becomes flooded with patent monopolies, embarrassing to bona fide patentees, whose rights are thus invaded on all sides; and not less embarrassing to the community generally, in the use of even the most common machinery and long-known improvements in the arts and common manufactures of the country.

3. Out of this interference and collision of patents and privileges, a great number of lawsuits arise, which are daily increasing in an alarming degree, onerous to the courts, ruinous to the parties, and injurious to society.

4. It opens the door to frauds, which have already become extensive and serious. . . . [I]t is not uncommon for persons to copy patented machines in the model-room; and having made some slight immaterial alterations, they apply in the next room for patents. . . . [T]hey go forth on a retailing expedition, selling out their patent rights . . . to those who have no means at hand of detecting the imposition. . . . This speculation in patent rights has become a regular business, and several hundred thousand dollars, it is estimated, are paid annually for void patents, many of which are thus fraudulently obtained.

Report Accompanying Senate Bill No. 239, S. Doc. No. 24–338, at 3 (1836).

[11] Act of July 4, 1836, ch. 357, § 6, 5 Stat. 117. The Supreme Court had already interpreted the 1793 Act as requiring the inventor in his patent specification to "distinguish" his invention as well as provide an enabling disclosure. Evans v. Eaton, 20 U.S. (7 Wheat.) 356 (1822).

[12] Act of July 4, 1836, ch. 357, § 6, 5 Stat. 117 (emphasis added).

The requirement that public use or sale be with the inventor's "consent or allowance" was later eliminated so that any public use or on sale activity would constitute a bar. Scholars dispute whether the consent or allowance provision was eliminated by the 1839 Act or the 1870 Act. *See* D. Chisum, Patents § 6.02[1] [b][iii]. *Cf.* Andrews v. Hovey (The Driven Well Cases), 123 U.S. 267 (1887). The issue is not without contemporary significance. It remains unclear whether and to what extent Congress intended that the standards of public use and on sale activity should be the same for the inventor-patentee and others.

[13] 52 U.S. (11 How.) 248 (1850).

[14] 51 U.S. (10 How.) 477 (1850).

[15] 56 U.S. (15 How.) 330 (1853).

result in the same way as the patented invention. *O'Reilly v. Morse*[16] established the principle of undue patent claim breadth; an inventor of one means of achieving a useful result can claim only that means, not all possible means of achieving the result. *Godfrey v. Eames*[17] established the concept of a continuing application; a second patent application could obtain the benefit of the filing date of a prior application disclosing the same invention. *Seymour v. Osborne*[18] established the enablement standard for prior art publications; a publication would anticipate a later patent claim only if it provided sufficient information to enable one skilled in the art to make and use the invention. *City of Elizabeth v. American Nicholson Pavement Co.*[19] established the experimental use doctrine; use that was otherwise public was excused if it was for experimentation, to "bring the invention to perfection," rather than for profit.

In 1870, Congress replaced the 1836 Act with a new codification. For the most part, the 1870 Act retained the 1836 Act's provisions and requirements.[20] In 1897, Congress made two changes in the statutory bar provision, adding patenting and description in a printed publication to the public use and on sale bars as loss-of-right events, and specifying that public use or on sale activity must be "in this country" to be a bar.[21]

[3]   The First Invention Concept

Until the enactment of the American Invents Act in 2011, the United States patent system stood alone in the world in determining priority among competing inventors by reference to who was the "first to invent."

The 1790 and 1793 statutes did not explicitly establish a first-to-invent priority rule but did require a patentee to be "the first and true inventor." The 1836 Act established a procedure for resolving "the question of priority of right of invention." Section 15 of the 1836 Act introduced the diligence concept by providing that an inventor's patent was invalid if it was for an invention "invented or discovered by another, who was using reasonable diligence in adapting and perfecting the same."[22] The courts read section 15 to mean that one who was the first to reduce an invention to practice would lose priority to another who was the first to "invent" in the sense of conceiving the invention, provided that the latter

---

[16] 56 U.S. (15 How.) 62 (1854).

[17] 68 U.S. (1 Wall.) 317 (1864).

[18] 78 U.S. (11 Wall.) 516 (1870).

[19] 97 U.S. (7 Otto.) 126 (1877).

[20] The 1870 Act's sections were renumbered as part of the 1874 "Revised Statutes" codification. For example, Section 61 of the 1870 Act, which was based on Section 6 of the 1836 Act, became Section 4920 of the Revised Statutes. Reported court decisions construing pre-1952 Act statutes cite the appropriate Revised Statutes section number.

[21] These changes codified the Supreme Court's ruling in Gandy v. Main Belting Co., 143 U.S. 587 (1891).

[22] Act of July 4, 1836, ch. 357, § 15, 5 Stat. 117.

exercised diligence in the reduction to practice.[23]

The 1870 Act created within the Patent Office the position of "examiner in charge of interference," beginning a tradition of separating priority determinations from patentability determinations that continued until a 1984 statute merged the "Board of Appeals" and the "Board of Patent Interferences."

From about 1890 to about 1910, lower court decisions established the basic rules on priority of invention, including definitions of the key concepts: conception, reduction to practice, and diligence. Landmarks included *Mergenthaler v. Scudder*,[24] defining conception; *Mason v. Hepburn*,[25] holding that a first inventor loses priority by abandoning, suppressing or concealing the invention after reduction to practice; *Automatic Weighing Machine v. Pneumatic Scale Corp.*,[26] holding that the filing of a patent specification adequately disclosing the invention is constructive reduction to practice; and *Sydeman v. Thoma*,[27] summarizing a long series of decisions on what constitutes an actual reduction to practice. The rules thus established have enjoyed remarkable longevity. In 1952, Congress codified them in Section 102(g). The only significant new invention priority rule since 1910 is that recognized in *Paulik v. Rizkalla*,[28] which holds that one losing the benefit of an actual reduction to practice by abandonment, suppression or concealment may establish priority by reference to resumption of activity on the invention.

[4]   Shifting Supreme Court Attitudes Toward Patents

[a]   Patents Under Fire: 1880–1892

In the late 19th Century, the volume of patent cases reaching the Supreme Court increased markedly.[29] The Court's decisions began to decry abuses of the patent system. In *Atlantic Works v. Brady*, Justice Bradley complained that "It was never the object of [the patent] laws to grant a monopoly for every trifling device, every shadow of a shade of an idea, which would naturally and spontaneously occur to any skilled mechanic or operator in the ordinary progress of manufactures."[30] The Court held many patents invalid for "want of invention," a phrase that came to encapsulate the *Hotchkiss* obviousness concept.[31]

---

[23] Dietz v. Wade, 7 F. Cas. 684 (No. 3903) (C.C.D.C. 1859); Reed v. Cutter, 20 F. Cas. 435 (No. 11,645) (C.C.D. Mass. 1841).

[24] 11 App. D.C. 264 (1897).

[25] 13 App. D.C. 86 (1898).

[26] 166 F. 288 (1st Cir. 1909).

[27] 32 App. D.C. 362 (1909).

[28] 796 F.2d 456 (Fed. Cir. 1986).

[29] *See* D. CHISUM, PATENTS § 5.02.

[30] 107 U.S. (17 Otto) 192, 201 (1883).

[31] *See, e.g.*, McClain v. Ortmayer, 141 U.S. 419 (1891); Hollister v. Benedict & Burnham Mfg. Co., 113 U.S. 59 (1885).

[b] Patents in Favor: 1892–1930

Beginning in 1892, the tide turned from hostility to receptiveness.[32] The turn was attributable in part to improved economic conditions,[33] and in part to the enactment of the Evarts Act, which created regional courts of appeal and relieved the Supreme Court of the burden of reviewing appeals in all patent infringement suits.[34]

Until about 1930, the Supreme Court upheld the validity of many patents, emphasizing the importance of inference evidence, such as the commercial success of the invention after its introduction into the marketplace,[35] and warning against the use of "hindsight" in determining obviousness.[36]

The Court continued to develop doctrinal refinements. In *Mast, Foos & Co. v. Stover Mfg. Co.*,[37] it confirmed that the *Hotchkiss* mechanic of ordinary skill in the art should be conclusively presumed to have knowledge of all the prior art, such as patents and publications, even prior art that was obscure or not known to actual ordinary workmen. In *Alexander Milburn Co. v. Davis-Bournonville Co.*,[38] the Court held that the full text of patent specifications were prior art as of their Patent Office filing date, rather than their issue date, even though patent application disclosures became publicly available only upon issue and printing. The theory was the Patent Office's delay in examining and issuing a patent on a senior-filed application should not affect the patentability of an invention in a junior-filed application.

[c] Patents Under Renewed Fire: 1930–1950

Beginning in 1930, the Supreme Court reverted to pre-1892 anti-patent attitudes, reflected in several lines of decisions. First, the Court expanded the patent misuse doctrine, which rendered a patent unenforceable if the patent owner extended the scope of the patent through tying agreements and other improper practices.[39] The misuse line culminated in *Mercoid Corp. v. Mid-Continent Investment Co.*,[40] which

---

[32] In that year, the Supreme Court upheld the patent on barbed wire even though numerous other inventors had devised similar solutions: "In the law of patents it is the last step that wins." Washburn & Moen Mfg. Co. v. Beat 'Em All Barbed-Wire Co., Barbed Wire Patent, 143 U.S. 275, 283 (1892).

[33] *See* Mayers, *The United States Patent System in Historical Perspective*, 3 Pat., Trademark & Copyright J. of Research & Educ. 33 (1959).

[34] Act of March 3, 1891, ch. 517, 26 Stat. 826.

[35] *See, e.g.*, Minerals Separation, Ltd. v. Hyde, 242 U.S. 261 (1916).

[36] *See, e.g.*, Diamond Rubber Co. v. Consolidated Rubber Tire Co., 220 U.S. 428, 435–36 (1911) ("Knowledge after the event is always easy, and problems once solved present no difficulties, indeed, may be represented as never having had any, and expert witnesses may be brought forward to show that the new thing which seemed to have eluded the search of the world was always ready at hand and easy to be seen by a merely skillful attention. But the law has other tests of the invention than subtle conjectures of what might have been seen and yet was not. It regards a change as evidence of novelty, the acceptance and utility of change as further evidence, even as demonstration. . . . Nor does it detract from its merit that it is the result of experiment and not the instant and perfect product of inventive power.").

[37] 177 U.S. 485 (1900).

[38] 270 U.S. 390 (1926).

[39] *See, e.g.*, Carbice Corp. v. American Patents Development Corp., 283 U.S. 27 (1931).

[40] 320 U.S. 661 (1944).

severely curtailed remedies against contributory patent infringement by sale of specially adapted components.

Second, the Court enforced stringent requirements as to patent claim clarity and breadth.[41] *Halliburton Oil Well Cementing Co. v. Walker*[42] invalidated the common practice of defining invention elements in terms of "means" for performing a specified "function."

Third, and most important, the Court raised the "invention" patentability standard. In *Cuno Engineering Corp. v. Automatic Devices Corp.*, Justice Douglas stated, somewhat hyperbolically, that a new device, to be patentable, "must reveal the flash of creative genius."[43] In *Great Atlantic & Pacific Tea Co. v. Supermarket Equipment Co.*, the Court decreed that a combination of old mechanical elements was patentable only if it showed "unusual or surprising consequences" and cautioned that courts should "scrutinize combination patent claims with a care proportioned to the difficulty and improbability of finding invention in an assembly of old elements."[44] The Court's anti-patent bias was so pronounced that Justice Jackson would complain, in dissent, that "the only patent that is valid is one which this Court has not been able to get its hands on."[45]

The Supreme Court's anti-patent bias in the 1930s and 1940s was not total. In *Transparent-Wrap Machine Corp. v. Stokes & Smith Co.*,[46] the Court refused to hold *per se* illegal or unenforceable "grant back" clauses in patent licenses, which required the licensee to grant back to the licensor rights in the licensee's improvement inventions. In *Graver Tank & Mfg. Co. v. Linde Air Products Co.*,[47] the Court confirmed the continuing vitality of the doctrine of equivalents.

[5] The 1952 Act

In 1952, Congress passed a new Patent Act, codified in Title 35 of the United States Code, which is still in effect. To a large extent, the 1952 Act rearranged existing statutory provisions and stated in statutory form matters previously recognized only in court decisions and Patent Office practice,[48] but it did make several specific changes and additions.[49]

---

[41] *See, e.g.*, General Electric Co. v. Wabash Appliance Co., 304 U.S. 364 (1938).

[42] 329 U.S. 1 (1946).

[43] 314 U.S. 84, 91 (1941).

[44] 340 U.S. 147, 152 (1950). The patent in question was a "cashier's counter equipped with a three-sided frame, or rack, with no top or bottom, which, when pushed or pulled, will move groceries deposited within it by a customer to the checking clerk and leave them there when it is pushed back to repeat the operation." Under the Court's view, each element of the invention was old: store counters were old, and three-sided racks to push and pull goods were old. 340 U.S. at 149.

[45] Jungersen v. Ostby & Barton Co., 335 U.S. 560, 571 (1949) (Jackson, J., dissenting).

[46] 329 U.S. 637 (1947).

[47] 339 U.S. 605 (1950).

[48] An example is section 120 on continuation applications. 35 U.S.C. § 120.

[49] Some changes restricted prior patenting practices that were perceived as having been subject to abuse. For example, section 251 put a two-year limit on the filing of reissue applications to broaden the scope of patent claims. Section 253 ended the prior practice of disclaiming a portion of a patent claim.

Some 1952 Act provisions were in response to the 1930–1950 Supreme Court anti-patent decisions: (1) a paragraph in section 112 overturned *Halliburton* and confirmed use of "means-plus-function" claim limitations; (2) a sentence in section 103 disapproved of *Cuno Engineering*'s "flash of creative genius" test by providing that "Patentability shall not be negatived by the manner in which the invention was made"; and (3) a new section 271 defined infringement, inducement of infringement, and contributory infringement, subsection (d) of which overturned *Mercoid.*

Perhaps most significantly, Congress for the first time included a statutory provision on nonobviousness, section 103. Whether Congress intended to repudiate the Supreme Court's stringent "invention" decisions leading up to *Great Atlantic & Pacific Tea* or merely to codify existing standards was a matter of dispute among the lower courts and commentators.[50]

[6]   The 1966 *Graham* Trilogy and Beyond

The Supreme Court did not reach the issue of the proper interpretation of Section 103 until 1966, when the Court granted *certiorari* in three patent cases. In *Graham v. John Deere Co.*,[51] the Court pointedly confirmed that Section 103 *codified* the judicially developed nonobviousness requirement.[52] Congress did focus inquiry on objective obviousness and, in effect, directed abandonment of "invention," which the courts had previously used to encapsulate the obviousness standard. "Invention" had led to conceptual confusion. But, according to the Court, Section 103 did not, and constitutionally could not, "lower" or fundamentally alter the patentability standard. On the merits, the Court held two of three patents invalid;[53] it held a third patent valid, emphasizing that the invention, a battery that provided strong current with the addition of a water electrolyte, was met with initial skepticism by experts but later was used extensively by the United States government.[54]

Section 253 introduced the concept of terminal disclaimers, which the courts thereafter used to mold the law of double patenting.

[50] *See, e.g.,* Reiner v. I. Leon Co., 285 F.2d 501, 503 (2d Cir. 1960) (Judge Learned Hand: "There can be no doubt that the Act of 1952 meant to change the slow but steady drift of judicial decision that had been hostile to patents."); Hawley Prods. Co. v. U.S. Trunk Co., 259 F.2d 69 (1st Cir. 1958) (mere codification); Beckett, *Judicial Construction of the Patent Act of 1952 — Codification v. Substantive Change,* 37 J. Pat. Off. Soc'y 467 (1955).

[51] 383 U.S. 1 (1966).

[52] The Court noted that "while the clear language of Section 103 places emphasis on an inquiry into obviousness, the general level of innovation necessary to sustain patentability remains the same," 383 U.S. at 4, that "the section was intended merely as a codification of judicial precedents embracing the *Hotchkiss* condition, with congressional directions that inquiries into the obviousness of the subject matter sought to be patented are a prerequisite to patentability," 383 U.S. at 17, and that "[t]he standard has remained invariable in this Court," 383 U.S. at 19.

[53] 383 U.S. at 24–26; *id.* at 32–37.

[54] United States v. Adams, 383 U.S. 39 (1966).

In two decisions dealing with "combination" patents,[55] the Supreme Court held patents invalid, using language suggesting continued vitality of special "invention" tests. Neither decision had significant impact on subsequent lower court decisions. *Graham* remains the commonly-cited Supreme Court decision on the nonobviousness patentability requirement.

In the 1960s and 1970s, Supreme Court decisions introduced doctrinal refinements. In *Brenner v. Manson*,[56] the Court interpreted the utility patentability condition as requiring an inventor to discover a substantial minimal utility for an invention, including new chemical compounds. In *Gottschalk v. Benson*,[57] the Court decreed that mathematical algorithms were unpatentable, launching two decades of confusion on what types of computation inventions were proper subjects for patents.

The 1980s saw a upward surge in the role and importance of the patent system. In *Diamond v. Chakrabarty*,[58] the Supreme Court held that genetically-altered living microorganisms are patentable subject matter. The *Chakrabarty* decision spurred new interest in patents, particularly in the nascent biotechnology industry. In *Dawson Chemical Co. v. Rohm & Haas Co.*,[59] the Court applied Section 271(d) to hold that the owner of a patent claiming a process of using a certain chemical compound was not guilty of patent misuse by selling the compound and refusing to issue licenses to competing manufacturers of the compound because the compound was a "nonstaple," that is, was not suited for commercial use other than in the patented process.

In the 1980s, Congress enacted important patent legislation. In 1982, it created the Court of Appeals for the Federal Circuit with exclusive appellate jurisdiction over cases that arise in whole or in part under the patent laws.[60] Today, the Federal Circuit's patent-related decisions guide the practical administration of the patent system in the Patent and Trademark Office, in district court patent litigation, and in International Trade Commission proceedings pertaining to patents.

In the Patent Law Amendments Act of 1984, Congress adopted amendments to sections 103, 116, and 120, which changed "a complex body of case law which discourages communication among members of research teams"[61] and made exportation of the components of a patented combination an act of infringement.[62] The same year, it enacted the Drug Price Competition and Patent Term

---

[55] Sakraida v. Ag Pro, Inc., 425 U.S. 273 (1976); Anderson's-Black Rock, Inc. v. Pavement Salvage Co., 396 U.S. 57 (1969).

[56] 383 U.S. 519 (1966).

[57] 409 U.S. 63 (1972).

[58] 447 U.S. 303 (1980).

[59] 448 U.S. 176 (1980).

[60] Federal Courts Improvement Act of 1982, P.L. 97-164, 96 Stat. 25. The Act merged two existing courts, the Court of Customs and Patent Appeals, which had five judges, and the Court of Claims, which had seven judges. The Federal Circuit came into existence on October 1, 1982.

[61] P.L. 98-622, § 104, 98 Stat. 3383.

[62] 35 U.S.C. § 271(f).

Restoration Act, providing for extension of the terms of certain patents on drug and other products that are subject to regulatory review by the Food and Drug Administration.[63] In 1988, it enacted the Patent Misuse Reform Act, restricting application of the misuse doctrine to certain patent licensing and sales practices.[64] The same year, it enacted the Process Patent Amendments Act, extending to process patent owners the right to exclude unauthorized importation of unpatented products made abroad by use of the patented process.[65]

Congress continued to make statutory changes in the 1990s and 2000s. In 1999, Congress amended section 102(g)(1) to allow consideration of inventive activity outside the United States, but in a TRIPS signatory country, for the purposes of establishing priority of invention in an interference. More importantly, in the same act Congress required the publication of patent applications 18 months after filing unless the application is no longer pending, the application is subject to an order of secrecy because of a national government interest or because of national security, the application is a provisional application, or an application for a design patent. The applicant can request nonpublication upon signing an affidavit that the invention will not be the subject of a patent application in another country or under the Patent Cooperation Treaty.[66] In 2004, Congress amended section 103(c) to remove collaborative efforts among members of a joint research agreement from consideration as prior art under sections 102(e), (f), & (g).[67] This amendment was designed to promote joint ventures and collaborative research.[68]

[7]   Leahy-Smith America Invents Act of 2011

On September 16, 2011, President Obama signed into law the Leahy-Smith America Invents Act (hereinafter, "AIA"). This Act represents a substantial shift in United States patent law. Moving the U.S. patent system to a first-to-file system, the Act also introduces post-grant review proceedings for challenging a patent, prior commercial user rights, and new definitions of prior art for novelty and nonobviousness purposes. There were two broad purposes for these revisions. The first is harmonization with the patent laws of other countries, which have always had first-to-file systems and procedures for opposing patents post-grant. The second is streamlining the process of patent prosecution to ensure that applications are reviewed more efficiently and thoroughly in order to improve patent quality. This second purpose is met through post-grant opposition proceedings and a broader definition of prior art.

Specific provisions of the AIA are discussed in the appropriate sections of this volume. This section provides a general overview of the new provisions, organized around their effective dates. There are three effective dates that apply to different provisions. Some provisions apply immediately, meaning as of September 16, 2011,

---

[63] P.L. 98-417, Title II, 98 Stat. 1585.

[64] P.L. 100-73, 102 Stat. 4674. The Act added two subsections to 35 U.S.C. Section 271(d).

[65] Omnibus Trade and Competitiveness Act of 1988, P.L. 100-418, Title IX, Subtitle A, 102 Stat. 1563.

[66] P.L. 106-113, Div. B, § 1000(a)(9) [Title IV, § 4502(a)], 113 Stat. 1536 (codified at 35 U.S.C. § 122).

[67] P.L. 108-453, § 2, 118 Stat. 3596 (codified at 35 U.S.C. § 103(c)).

[68] H.R. Rep. No. 108-425, at 2–6 (2004).

the date the act was enacted into law. Other provisions are effective one year after the signing, or September 16, 2012. Finally, some provisions are effective eighteen months after signing, or March 16, 2013. The provisions of the act are described briefly according to their effective date

Provisions effective September 16, 2011:

- Inter Partes Reexamination: The AIA imposes a higher standard for bringing a reexamination, effective immediately. Under the new standard, the petitioner has to show "a reasonable likelihood that the petitioner would prevail with respect to at least one of the claims challenged." Inter partes reexamination will be replaced by inter partes review, described below.

- Tax Strategies: "Any strategy for reducing, avoiding, or deferring tax liability, whether known or unknown" at the time of invention or application is deemed to be part of the prior art. This provision does not apply to tax preparation or financial management methods.

- Best Mode: Failure to comply with the best mode requirement of Section 112 cannot be a basis for invalidating a patent or any claim in suit. The best mode requirement of Section 112 remains unchanged.

- Subject Matter Limitation: "no patent may issue on a claim directed to or encompassing a human organism."

- Virtual and False Marking: The AIA allows a patent owner to meet the marking requirements with virtual marking and limits actions for false marking to actions brought by the U.S. government and for competitive injury suffered by a private party. This provision applies to pending and future litigation.

- Venue and Jurisdiction provisions: Actions against the USPTO are to be filed in the Eastern District of Virginia, rather than the District Court for the District of Columbia. Exclusive federal jurisdiction is expanded to include any claim for relief arising under the patent statute even if the original cause of action does not arise under the patent statute.

- Joinder: A district court can join defendants or consolidate cases only if there are common issues of fact or the cases arise out of the same transaction or occurrence. Infringement of the same patent is not sufficient for joinder or consolidation.

Provisions effective September 16, 2012:

- Inventor's Oath or Declaration: An applicant can file without obtaining the oath from the inventors under some circumstances.

- Third Party Submission of Prior Art: Allows submission by a third party of a patent, a published patent application, or a printed publication that is relevant to the examination before the earlier of the date of the notice of allowance or the later of six months after the application is published or the date of the first rejection.

- Supplemental Examination: Allows a patent owner to request the USPTO to consider, reconsider, or correct information believed to be relevant to the patent. The effect of such correction or consideration is to prevent a patent from being held unenforceable on the basis of the incorrect information. This procedure limits the inequitable conduct defense.

- Inter Partes Review: Replaces inter partes reexamination. The review is available after the nine-month window for post-grant review (see below) and allows a petitioner to introduce prior art in the form of a patent or printed publication.

- Post-Grant Review: Allows a petitioner to raise any grounds for invalidity within nine months of the grant of a patent. The standard for instituting the review is "more likely than not that at least one of the claims is unpatentable."

Provisions effective March 16, 2013:

- First-Inventor to File: This is a change from the current first-inventor system for awarding patents. The change implements two critical dates, the date of the application and one year before the date of the application, for novelty and nonobviousness purposes. The date of invention will be irrelevant. The AIA also expands what constitutes prior art for the purposes of both novelty and nonobviousness purposes.

- Derivation Proceedings: Replaces interference proceedings. A derivation proceeding determines whether a first filer of an application derived the claimed the invention from a second filer. The proceeding is relevant in determining whether certain pieces of prior art fall into the one-year safe harbor under the new version of Section 102(b).

- Statutory Invention Registration: is repealed consistent with the AIA's emphasis on first inventor to file rather than first to invent as a basis for determining patentability.

§ 2C PATENTABILITY

Patent law establishes four basic conditions an invention must meet to qualify for patent protection. The invention must be (1) in a statutory subject matter category, (2) useful, (3) novel in relation to the prior art, and (4) not obvious from the prior art to a person of ordinary skill in the art at the time the invention was made. An inventor can secure a patent by promptly filing a suitably drafted patent application.[69]

The inventor defines his or her invention in claims, precise verbal expressions included at the end of the specification that is filed with the application. The claimed invention is typically broader and more abstract than the examples the inventor discloses or puts into commercial practice. Claim drafting and interpretation are critical to patentability problem resolution.

---

[69] *See* § 2D.

[1] Patentable Subject Matter

The patent statutes provide for utility,[70] design,[71] and plant[72] patents. Utility patents are the most common and cover new and useful inventions, such as measurement instruments, medical devices, chemical compounds, and processes for making fabrics. Design patents cover new and ornamental designs of useful articles, such as furniture, containers, toys, and shoes.[73] Plant patents cover new and distinct plant varieties, such as flowering plants and fruit trees.[74]

[a] General Definitions

Section 101 defines what is eligible for a utility patent: "Whoever invents or discovers any new and useful *process, machine, manufacture*, or *composition of matter*, or any new and useful improvement thereof, may obtain a patent therefor."[75] "Process" is further defined as "process, art or method" and includes "a new use of a known process, machine, manufacture, composition of matter, or material."[76]

The four utility patent categories — process, machine, manufacture, and composition of matter — first appeared in 1793.[77] The only category change was in the 1952 Act, which substituted "process" for "art."[78] The courts interpret the old categories to include developing new technologies such as electronics, computers and biotechnology.

Processes are methods and procedures (roughly speaking: how to do something). Court decisions variously define process,[79] but no one definition is accepted as the comprehensive exclusive and inclusive test of process patent eligibility.[80] The most troublesome areas are computing methods and mathematical algorithms.[81]

---

[70] 35 U.S.C. § 101.

[71] 35 U.S.C. § 171.

[72] 35 U.S.C. § 161.

[73] Design protection is discussed in § 6B.

[74] Plant protection is discussed in § 6C.

[75] 35 U.S.C. § 101 (emphasis added).

[76] 35 U.S.C. § 100(b).

[77] Act of Feb. 21, 1793, ch. 11, § 1, 1 Stat. 319.

[78] This alteration was solely for clarity. *See* Reviser's Note, 35 U.S.C. § 101, S. Rep. No. 82-1979, at 13 (1952) ("The word 'art' in the corresponding section of the existing statute has a different meaning than the same word as used in other places in the statute; it has been interpreted by the courts as being practically synonymous with process or method. 'Process' has been used as its meaning is more readily grasped than 'art' as interpreted, and the definition in section 100(b) makes it clear that 'process or method' is meant.").

[79] Cochrane v. Deener, 94 U.S. (4 Otto.) 780 (1877) ("A process is a mode of treatment of certain materials to produce a given result. It is an act, or a series of acts, performed upon the subject-matter to be transformed and reduced to a different state or thing."); *In re* Durden, 763 F.2d 1406, 1410 (Fed. Cir. 1985) ("A process . . . is a manipulation according to an algorithm . . . doing something to or with something according to a schema.").

[80] *Cf.* Gottschalk v. Benson, 409 U.S. 63, 70 (1972) ("We do not hold that no process patent could ever qualify if it did not meet the requirements of our prior precedents.").

[81] *See* § 2C[1][f].

The product categories, "machine," "manufacture," and "composition of matter," are structural (roughly speaking: things). The courts give the categories broad definitions. A "composition of matter" includes a new molecule.[82] A "manufacture" is "anything under the sun that is made by man,"[83] a residual category sweeping up all inventions not included in the other categories. A soft-contact lens with a laser-etched marking,[84] and an instant camera[85] are examples of product inventions.

A technological advance is often defined in terms of several categories. Inventors seek and obtain claims to processes and compositions, manufactures or machines in a single or related patents.[86] For example, an inventor who devises a new method of stretching polytetrafluorethylene tape to produce a product impermeable to water but not to water vapor could claim (1) the stretching method (a process); (2) an apparatus for carrying out the stretching method (a machine); and (3) products resulting from the method (a manufacture or composition of matter).[87]

A patent or application need not, and typically does not, identify the category of patentable subject matter to which the claimed invention belongs.

[b]   Exclusions and Exceptions

The only statutory exclusion from Section 101's broad patentable subject matter categories relates to inventions useful *solely* to utilize special nuclear material or atomic energy in an atomic weapon.[88]

The AIA introduces an express statutory exemption for patentable subject matter under Section 33, which excludes from patentability "a claim directed to or encompassing a human organism." On its face, the exemption precludes a claim on a human organism itself. But it is not clear what "directed to or encompassing a human organism" means. Arguably, it could include diagnostic techniques, human stem cells, human clones and cloning techniques, and other inventions in the biomedical and biotechnology fields.

The AIA implicitly removes tax strategies for reducing, avoiding, or deferring tax liability from patentable subject matter. Section 14 states that any such strategy,

---

[82] Schering Corp. v. Gilbert, 153 F.2d 428, 432 (2d Cir. 1946). *See also* Diamond v. Chakrabarty, 447 U.S. 303, 308 (1980) (" 'composition of matter' has been construed consistent with its common usage to include 'all compositions of two or more substances and . . . all composite articles, whether they be the results of chemical union, or of mechanical mixture, or whether they be gases, fluids, powders, or solids' ").

[83] S. Rep. No. 82-1979, at 5 (1952), quoted in Diamond v. Chakrabarty, 447 U.S. 303, 309 (1980).

[84] *See* claim 1 from U.S. Patent 4,194,814. The court reviewed this claim in Bausch & Lomb, Inc. v. Barnes-Hind/Hydrocurve, Inc., 796 F.2d 443, 445 (Fed. Cir. 1986).

[85] *See* claim 8 from U.S. Patent 3,753,211. The court held this claim for a self-developing camera valid and infringed in Polaroid Corp. v. Eastman Kodak Co., 789 F.2d 1556 (Fed. Cir. 1986). Successful enforcement of this and several other patents covering Polaroid's SX-70 instant camera caused Kodak to withdraw from the instant photography field.

[86] Reference to the process for making it is another way to define an article. *See* § 2D[1].

[87] The example is from W.L. Gore & Associates, Inc. v. Garlock, Inc., 721 F.2d 1540 (Fed. Cir. 1983), upholding the "Goretex" fabric patent.

[88] 42 U.S.C. § 2181(a). *See In re* Brueckner, 623 F.2d 184 (C.C.P.A. 1980).

whether known or unknown at the time of invention or application, "shall be deemed insufficient to differentiate a claimed invention from the prior art." The section expressly does not apply to inventions relating to tax preparation or financial management. The intent is to make it impossible to patent inventions related to tax strategies. Instead of expressly excluding such inventions from patentable subject matter, Congress defined the prior art in such a way to block grants of such patents. This approach indicates the general disagreement of whether questionable patents should be handled under the patentable subject matter requirement or the novelty and nonobviousness requirements. Congress' choice represents a compromise between these two contrasting views.

[c]   New Uses of Old Products

A process includes "a new use of a known process machine, manufacture, composition of matter, or material."[89] Inventors who discover a new use of a known material, for example, an existing chemical compound's previously unknown therapeutic quality, cannot claim the old product because only *new* inventions are patentable,[90] but patent law encourages the search for new uses of existing materials by authorizing method-of-use claims.[91]

A method-of-use claim cannot cover a newly discovered characteristic or advantage of an old product or process if that characteristic or advantage is inherent in the existing use of the product or process.[92]

---

[89] 35 U.S.C. § 101(b). *See generally* D. CHISUM, PATENTS § 1.02[8].

[90] Cochrane v. Badische Anilin & Soda Fabrik, 111 U.S. 293 (1884); Titanium Metals Corp. v. Banner, 778 F.2d 775 (Fed. Cir. 1985).

This novelty bar is avoided if the inventor can define the claimed product in a way that distinguishes it from the old product. *See, e.g., In re* Bergstrom, 427 F.2d 1394, 1402 (C.C.P.A. 1970) (claim to prostaglandin extract; "by definition, pure materials necessarily differ from less pure or impure materials and, if the latter are the only ones existing and available as a standard of reference . . . perforce the 'pure' materials are 'new' with respect to them"). A similar result is reached as to "products of nature." *See* § 2C [1][d].

[91] *Cf.* Dawson Chem. Co. v. Rohm & Haas Co., 448 U.S. 176, 221–22 (1980) ("[T]he characteristics of practical chemical research are such that this form of patent protection is particularly important to inventors in that field. The number of chemicals either known to scientists or disclosed by existing research is vast. It grows constantly, as those engaging in 'pure' research publish their discoveries. The number of these chemicals that have known uses of commercial or social value, in contrast, is small. Development of new uses for existing chemicals is thus a major component of practical chemical research. It is extraordinarily expensive. It may take years of unsuccessful testing before a chemical having a desired property is identified, and it may take several years of further testing before a proper and safe method for using that chemical is developed.").

[92] *See, e.g., In re* King, 801 F.2d 1324, 1326 (Fed. Cir. 1986) ("the discovery of a new use for an old structure based on unknown properties of the structure [may be] patentable to the discoverer as a process," but, "[u]nder the principles of inherency," a claim is anticipated "if a structure in the prior art necessarily functions in accordance with the limitations of a process or method claim . . ."); *In re* May, 574 F.2d 1082 (C.C.P.A. 1978) (the discovery that a known analgesic compound had the property of nonaddictiveness will not support a patent claiming the method of effecting "nonaddictive" analgesia by use of a certain generic class of compounds because the prior art showed use of a species compound within that generic class to effect analgesia).

Cf. In re Dillon, 919 F.2d 688 (Fed. Cir. 1990) (*en banc*), discussed at § 2C[4][c][iii].

[d]   Products of Nature and Living Organisms

A naturally occurring product cannot be patented even if its existence was unknown,[93] but the discoverer may claim it in a purified, isolated, or altered form.[94]

Patents claiming *processes* using living organisms have been allowed in the United States since the 1970's.[95] In 1980, the Supreme Court held that genetically-altered living organisms are patentable as "manufactures" or "compositions of matter." The utility patent statute contains no provision excluding patent protection for such living organisms, and the Court refused to infer one.

The Supreme Court's 1980 decision in *Diamond v. Chakrabarty*,[96] a landmark in biotechnology patent law history, involved using bacteria to degrade oil. Chakrabarty and an associate discovered that certain plasmids in bacteria control their ability to degrade oil components. Chakrabarty later discovered a process for transferring the plasmids in stable form from four bacteria to a single bacterium, which itself had no capacity for degrading oil. The PTO allowed claims to the process but rejected claims for the genetically-altered bacterium itself. The Supreme Court reversed, reasoning that (1) the bacterium was not a product of nature because a human made it, (2) no patent statute excluded living things, and (3) the plant patent acts were directed to other problems[97] and did not represent a Congressional determination not to allow patents on non-plant living things. Congress, not the judiciary, should weigh genetic-engineering and life form patenting policy implications.[98]

---

[93] Diamond v. Chakrabarty, 447 U.S. 303, 309 (1980) ("a new mineral discovered in the earth or a new plant found in the wild is not patentable subject matter"); General Elec. v. De Forest, 28 F.2d 641 (3d Cir. 1928); *Ex parte* Latimer, 1889 Comm'n Dec. 13 (1889); *Ex parte* Grayson, 51 U.S.P.Q. 413 (Pat. Off. Bd. App. 1941) (shrimp with head and digestive organs removed).

Cf. Funk Bros. Seed Co. v. Kalo Inoculant Co., 333 U.S. 127 (1948), discussed at § 2C[1] [f][ii](2); American Fruit Growers v. Brogdex Co., 283 U.S. 1 (1931). *Compare* Merck v. Olin Mathieson Chemical Corp., 253 F.2d 156 (4th Cir. 1958).

[94] *See, e.g.*, Scripps Clinic & Research Foundation v. Genentech, Inc., 927 F.2d 1565 (Fed. Cir. 1991) (patent relating to the human protein, pure Factor VIII:C, the blood clotting factor: Claim 24: "A human VIII:C preparation having a potency in the range of 134 to 1172 units per ml. and being substantially free of VIII:RP."); Amgen, Inc. v. Chugai Pharmaceutical Co., 927 F.2d 1200 (Fed. Cir. 1991) (two patents relating to human erythropoietin (EPO), a 165 amino acid protein that stimulates red blood cell production; U.S. Patent 4,703,008, Claim 2, to "A purified and isolated DNA sequence consisting essentially of a DNA sequence encoding human erythropoietin"; U.S. Patent 4,677,195, Claim 1, to "Homogeneous erythropoietin characterized by a molecular weight of about 34,000 daltons on SDS PAGE, movement as a single peak on reverse phase high performance liquid chromatography and a specific activity of at least 160,000 IU per absorbance unit at 280 nanometers"); *In re* Kratz, 592 F.2d 1169 (C.C.P.A. 1979); *In re* Bergy, 563 F.2d 1031, 1036 (C.C.P.A. 1977), *remanded sub nom.* Parker v. Bergy, 438 U.S. 902 (1978), *on remand*, 596 F.2d 952 (C.C.P.A. 1979) (a biologically-pure strain of a microorganism found in a soil sample is not a product of nature).

[95] *See, e.g., In re* Mancy, 499 F.2d 1289 (C.C.P.A. 1974).

[96] 447 U.S. 303 (1980).

[97] *See* § 6C.

[98] "The grant or denial of patents on micro-organisms is not likely to put an end to genetic research or to its attendant risks . . . . Whether respondent's claims are patentable may determine whether research efforts are accelerated by the hope of reward or slowed by want of incentives, but that is all. What is more important is that we are without competence to entertain these arguments . . . . The choice

The Board of Patent Appeals and Interferences has applied *Chakrabarty* to confirm the patentability of plants and animals. In *Ex parte Allen*,[99] the Board held that a genetically altered oyster was a proper subject for a utility patent. In 1988, the PTO issued the first patent claiming a multicellular animal, a genetically-altered mouse.[100] In 2001, the Supreme Court held that a bioengineered plant can be the subject of both a utility patent and a plant patent as long as the invention meets all the requirements of each system.[101]

In its 2013 decision *Ass'n for Molecular Pathology v. Myriad Genetics, Inc.*,[102] the Supreme Court unanimously held that isolated DNA sequences are not patentable subject matter because they are natural phenomena, identical in terms of the underlying genetic information to the sequences existing in an organism. However, cDNA and other synthetic forms of DNA are patentable subject matter to the extent they differ from naturally occurring counterparts.

A patent application that claims biological material has special problems in complying with the enabling disclosure requirement.[103]

[e]   **Business Methods and Methods of Treatment**

Early case law and Patent Office practice developed three vague limitations on patentable subject matter: (1) business systems, (2) printed matter, and (3) methods of treatment of humans and animals.[104] All three limitations lack firm footing in statutory language or well-reasoned, extrastatutory policy, and are, therefore, of questionable contemporary vitality.

A 1908 Second Circuit decision stated that a "system of transacting business disconnected from the means for carrying out the system" is not patentable subject matter,[105] but it offered no precise reason for the exclusion. Two decisions,

---

we are urged to make is a matter of high policy for resolution within the legislative process after the kind of investigation, examination, and study that legislative bodies can provide and courts cannot." 447 U.S. at 317.

[99] 2 U.S.P.Q.2d 1425 (BPAI 1987), *aff'd*, 846 F.2d 877 (Fed. Cir. 1988) (unpublished). In *Allen*, the applicants developed a method for producing polyploid Pacific oysters of the species *Crassostrea gigas*. Sterile oysters do not devote significant portions of their body weight to reproduction, thereby remaining edible year round. Natural oysters are considered inedible during the Summer breeding season — the non-"R" months. The examiner allowed the applicants' method claims but rejected their product-by-process claims as being directed to "living entities" and therefore beyond Section 101. The Board reversed the Section 101 rejection, relying upon *Chakrabarty*, but affirmed a Section 103 obviousness rejection.

[100] The patent, No. 4,736,866, issued on April 12, 1988 to Harvard University as assignee of Professors Phillip Leder and Timothy Stewart, claims "a transgenic non-human mammal" the cells of which are altered to contain a recombinant activated oncogene. The preferred embodiment is a rodent in the form of a mouse. The patent stresses the utility of the claimed mice for cancer research and testing.

[101] *See* J.E.M. Ag Supply, Inc. v. Pioneer Hi-Bred Int'l, Inc., 534 U.S. 124 (2001).

[102] 133 S. Ct. 2107 (2013).

[103] *See* § 2D [3][a][vi].

[104] *See generally* D. CHISUM, PATENTS §§ 1.02[4], 1.03[3], [5].

[105] Hotel Security Checking Co. v. Lorraine Co., 160 F. 467 (2d Cir. 1908) (holding unpatentable a method for maintaining restaurant records so as to prevent frauds by waiters).

apparently recognizing the excludability of business systems "as such," hold that a business or accounting system implemented on a computer is patentable subject matter.[106]

In 1998, the Federal Circuit ruled that business methods *were* patentable subject matter, distinguishing *Hotel Security Checking* as a case about nonobviousness.[107] In 1999, Congress protected prior users of a business method from an infringement claim. Prior users are those parties who had, in good faith, reduced the patented business method to practice one year before the effective filing date of the patent application.[108]

In 2010, the United States Supreme Court ruled in *Bilski v. Kappos*[109] that a process, such as a business method, could be excluded from patentability if the claim covered an abstract idea. The Court affirmed the Federal Circuit, which had upheld the rejection of the patent for a method of hedging by the PTO.[110] However, the Court avoided any one test for rejecting a claim on the grounds of lack of patentable subject matter, including a test based on whether the invention was "useful, concrete, or tangible"; and the Court's opinion criticized the Federal Circuit's "machine or transformation test" as the sole test for determining when a process is patentable subject matter. Instead, the Court stated that although the question of whether a process claim included a machine or a physical transformation was an "important clue" for determining whether the claim covered patentable subject matter, the presence of a machine or a transformation was not necessary.[111] The Court also affirmed its precedent on the patentability of software in explaining the exception for abstract ideas.[112] Although the ruling was unanimous, four justices (Stevens, Ginsburg, Breyer, and Sotomayor) would have created a categorical exception for business methods, based on their reading of the case law and the statutory history.[113]

Early court decisions held that an invention consisting of the arrangement of information on a substrate, however new and useful, is not patentable subject matter unless the invention calls for a new relationship between the information and the substrate.[114] The limitation was closely related to that on business systems

---

[106] *In re* Johnston, 502 F.2d 765 (C.C.P.A. 1974), *rev'd, on other grounds sub nom.* Dann v. Johnston, 425 U.S. 219 (1976); Paine, Webber, Jackson & Curtis, Inc. v. Merrill Lynch, Pierce, Fenner & Smith, 564 F. Supp. 1358 (D. Del. 1983).

[107] *See* State Street Bank & Trust Co. v. Signature Financial Group, Inc., 149 F.3d 1368 (Fed. Cir. 1998).

[108] 35 U.S.C. § 273(b)(1).

[109] 130 S. Ct. 3218 (2010).

[110] *In re* Bilski, 545 F.3d 943 (Fed. Cir. 2008), *aff'd sub nom.* Bilski v. Kappos, 561 U.S. 593 (2010).

[111] 130 S. Ct. at 3225–27.

[112] *Id.* at 3230. *See* § 2C[1][f], below.

[113] *Id.* at 3233–50 (Stevens, J., concurring as to result, dissenting as to reasoning). *In Alice Corp. Pty. Ltd. v. CLS Bank Int'l*, 134 S. Ct. 2347 (2014), three justices (Sotomayor, Ginsburg, and Breyer) would have struck down the business method patent at issue as unpatentable *per se*, citing Justice Stevens' concurrence in *Bilski*. However, these three justices did concur with the majority opinion in *Alice*.

[114] *See, e.g., In re* Russell, 48 F.2d 668 (C.C.P.A. 1931) (directories with surnames indexed in a certain manner are not patentable); United States Credit System Co. v. American Credit Indemnity Co., 59 F.

because most attempts to patent "printed matter" involved information arrangements designed to implement a business system.[115] The decisions give no reason for excluding printed matter independent of a desire not to subvert the business system exclusion. Recent decisions question the printed matter limitation's scope without directly repudiating it.[116]

Two instructive "printed matter" cases deal with information matter on a medium for direct machine interaction. In each instance, the claimed subject matter was found not excludable.[117]

The Patent Office has indicated that medical methods are patentable if they meet the process definition and the conditions of utility, novelty and nonobviousness.[118] The Federal Circuit has held after *Bilski* that various method claims for treating a gastrointestinal disorder are patentable subject matter.[119] In 1996, Congress limited the right of the owner of a patent on a medical procedure or technique to seek remedies for alleged infringement based on "a medical practitioner's performance of a medical activity."[120]

In 2011, the United States Supreme Court granted a certiorari petition in *Prometheus Labs v. Mayo Collaborative Services.*[121] Applying *Bilski*, the Federal Circuit upheld the patentability of process claims for correlating metabolite levels with efficacy of a drug and calibrating the proper dosage of a drug for treatment of auto-immune diseases. The Supreme Court ruled on the case in 2012, striking down

---

139 (2d Cir. 1893) (business forms with appropriate headings are not patentable).

[115] *See* Note, *Patentability of Printed Matter: Critique and Proposal*, 18 Geo. Wash. L. Rev. 475, 476 (1950) ("The origin of the printed-matter doctrine is found in the long-standing rule that abstractions, mental theories or business methods are not patentable subject matter.").

[116] *In re* Gulack, 703 F.2d 1381 (Fed. Cir. 1983); *In re* Miller, 418 F.2d 1392 (C.C.P.A. 1969).

[117] *In re* Jones, 373 F.2d 1007 (C.C.P.A. 1967); *Ex parte* Carver, 227 U.S.P.Q. 465 (BPAI 1985).

Jones concerned a certain analog-to-digital encoder in which light passes through a rotating disc with a pattern of transparent areas onto a photocell and related reading means for converting the light into digital signals. The court held Jones' claims to suitably patterned discs were patentable subject matter not subject to the printed matter exclusion. (Claims to the *method* (*i.e.* process) of encoding analog information into digital values utilizing the new disc pattern had already been allowed by the PTO.)

Carver concerned a stereophonic recording pattern. When played on a stereo player in a defined human hearing environment, the recording generated compensating signals such that the recorded left channel included signals that substantially cancelled certain sound patterns received at a left ear location from the right speaker. Correspondingly, the recording generated signals to cancel out sounds received at the right ear location from the left speaker. The PTO Board of Appeals held that the claims could not be rejected as for nonstatutory "recorded" or "printed matter" even though, again, the only difference between the claimed product and prior art recordings was in the recorded sound pattern (the software).

Some patent applicants rely on these cases to draft computer program patent claims, for example, a claim to "A computer storage disk containing a program" etc.

[118] *Ex parte* Scherer, 103 U.S.P.Q. 107 (Pat. Off. Bd. App. 1954).

[119] Prometheus Laboratories, Inc. v. Mayo Collaborative Services, 628 F.3d 1347 (Fed. Cir. 2010) (method for calibrating dosage was held to be patentable subject matter because it involved a physical transformation).

[120] 35 U.S.C. § 287(c).

[121] Mayo Collaborative Servs. v. Prometheus Labs., Inc., 131 S. Ct. 3027, 180 L. Ed. 2d 844 (2011).

the method as an unpatentable law of nature under a two part test.[122] The two part test involved first identifying whether the claimed process recited a law of nature and second determining whether the application of the law of nature entailed an inventive concept that transformed the law into patentable subject matter.

In 2014, in *Alice Corp. Pty. Ltd. v. CLS Bank Int'l*, the Supreme Court extended the two part test set forth in its *Mayo* decision to the abstract idea exception.[123] The first determination under this two part test is identifying an abstract idea in the claimed invention. The second step is to "examine the elements of the claim to determine whether it contains an 'inventive concept'" sufficient to "transform" the claimed abstract idea into a patent-eligible application."[124] Under this two part test, the Court unanimously held ineligible a patent for a method of reducing settlement risk through an automated computer intermediary. The Court concluded that the abstract idea was "intermediated settlement" and that implementation on a general computer did not entail a sufficient inventive concept.

The USPTO announced "Preliminary Instruction Guidelines" a few days after the Supreme Court's decision in *Alice*. These Guidelines present a preliminary interpretation of the Court's ruling and practical standards of how to implement it. First, the Guidelines adopt the two step test as applying to all of the excluded categories from patentable subject matter. Second, the two step test applies to both product and process claims. Finally, the Guidelines give several examples of abstract ideas and inventive concepts that are patentable subject matter. Examples of abstract ideas include: fundamental economic practices, mathematical formulas and relationships, certain methods of organizing human activities, and "an idea of itself," the last referring to a principle or a motivating cause. Examples of what would constitute an inventive concept include: improvements to a technology or field, improvements to the functioning of a computer, and meaningful limitations on the abstract idea or law. A mere statement of application of the idea or law or recitation of a generic computer would not constitute an inventive concept.[125]

Whether computing methods are patentable is the subject of much controversy, in the United States and elsewhere.[126]

Neither a mathematical formula nor an algorithm for making mathematical computations or conversions can be patented *as such*.[127] Nor can processes involving "mental steps," that is, human thought or calculation, be patented if the steps require subjective or aesthetic human judgment.[128] Systems using mathematical formulae or mental systems can be patented as processes, and a process is not precluded from eligibility for patent protection merely because one step is use

---

[122] 132 S. Ct. 1289 (2012).

[123] 134 S. Ct. 2347 (2014).

[124] 134 S. Ct. 2347 (2014).

[125] Memorandum, *Preliminary Examination Instructions in Light of the Supreme Court Decision in Alice Corp. Pty. Ltd. v. CLS Bank International, et al.*, United States Patent and Trademark Office (June 25, 2014).

[126] *See generally* D. Chisum, Patents § 1.03[6].

[127] Parker v. Flook, 437 U.S. 584 (1978); Gottschalk v. Benson, 409 U.S. 63 (1972).

[128] *In re* Musgrave, 431 F.2d 882 (C.C.P.A. 1970).

of a suitably programmed digital computer.[129] Today, it is common for patents to issue claiming computer software structures and computing methods.

Pursuant to authorization under the AIA, the USPTO implemented a Transitional Program for Covered Business Method Patents, effective September 16, 2012. The AIA defines a "covered business method patent" as "method or corresponding apparatus for performing data processing or other operations used in the practice, administration, or management of a financial product or service, except that the term does not include patents for technological inventions."[130] According to USPTO regulations, the PTO determines whether an invention is technological by examining "whether the claimed subject matter as a whole recites a technological feature that is novel and unobvious over the prior art; and solves a technical problem using a technical solution."[131] A party who is being sued for patent infringement or faces a threatened suit can initiate the proceeding to challenge the validity of the patent. The trial court may stay the pending trial while the PTO reviews the challenge.[132] The program sunsets by September 16, 2020.[133]

[f]   Computer Software: Algorithms and Mathematical Inventions

[i]   Abstract Ideas — Mental Steps

Current law on mathematical algorithm and computer software patentability can be adequately understood only by considering two lines of cases, one on principles and abstract ideas and the other on "mental steps."

As to principles and abstract ideas, Supreme Court and lower court decisions back to the mid-19th century contained language to the effect that "a principle, in the abstract, is a fundamental truth . . . [which] cannot be patented."[134] These cases did not explain clearly the distinction between a "principle," which could not be patented, and a "process," which could be patented without reference to specific hardware.[135] These cases can be explained in terms of more specific propositions, such as:

(1)   an inventor who discovers one means for achieving a useful result cannot claim all means for achieving that result;[136]

---

[129] Diamond v. Diehr, 450 U.S. 175 (1981).

[130] AIA § 18(d)(1).

[131] 37 CFR § 42.301(b).

[132] AIA §18(b)(1).

[133] AIA § 18(a)(3).

[134] See, e.g., Le Roy v. Tatham, 55 U.S. (14 How.) 156 (1852); Wyeth v. Stone, 30 F. Cas. 723 (No. 18,107) (C.C.D. Mass. 1840).

In *Wyeth*, the patentee invented a new machine for cutting ice and stated in his patent "It is claimed, as new, to cut ice of a uniform size, by means of an apparatus worked by any other power than human." Justice Story held this broad claim invalid.

[135] See Tilghman v. Proctor, 102 U.S. 707 (1880).

[136] See Dolbear v. American Bell Telephone Co., 126 U.S. 1 (1888); O'Reilly v. Morse, 56 U.S. (15 How.) 62 (1854).

(2)   an inventor who merely shows how a known product or process operates cannot obtain a patent;[137]

(3)   the discoverer of a good business "idea" cannot obtain a patent unless he or she also develops a nonobvious product or process to carry it out.[138]

The "mental steps" cases dealt with attempts to patent processes involving mathematical calculations and other "thinking steps." In 1969, the Court of Customs and Patent Appeals, in reviewing several Office actions rejecting software patent applications, addressed the mental steps doctrine.[139] The culminating decision, *In re Musgrave*,[140] involving a seismic prospecting method, noted that the mental steps doctrine was a case law creation not founded on statutory language. The court noted that nothing in the statutory definition of a process required that all of the steps of a process be physical acts. It concluded:

> We cannot agree . . . that these claims (all the steps of which can be carried out by the disclosed apparatus) are directed to non-statutory processes merely because some or all the steps therein can also be carried out in or with the aid of the human mind or because it may be necessary for one performing the processes to think. All that is necessary, in our view, to make a sequence of operational steps a statutory "process" within 35

In *O'Reilly*, the Supreme Court upheld several claims of Morse's telegraph patent but held invalid for undue breadth the following claim:

> Eighth. I do not propose to limit myself to the specific machinery or parts of machinery described in the foregoing specification and claims; the essence of my invention being the use of the motive power of the electric or galvanic current, which I call electro-magnetism, however developed, for making or printing intelligible characters, letters or signs, at any distances, being a new application of that power of which I claim to be the first inventor or discoverer.

56 U.S. (15 How.) at 84–85. Today, the PTO would not allow a claim in such loose language.

In *Dolbear* (the Telephone Case), the Court upheld the following claim in Morse's patent.

> The method of, and apparatus for, transmitting vocal or other sounds telegraphically, as herein described by causing electrical undulations, similar in form to the vibrations of the air accompanying the said vocal or other sounds, substantially as set forth.

126 U.S. at 53. The claim was broad — but not quite so broad as to cover any means for transmitting sound telegraphically. This problem is best analyzed as one of claim breadth: an inventor is entitled to claim only such means as he or she has invented and disclosed in the patent specification. The scope of the claim must be commensurate with the scope of the "enabling" disclosure. *See* § 2C[6][a].

Legal trivia buffs may be interested to know that the Telephone Case consumes the entire volume 126 of United States Reports.

[137]   *See, e.g., In re* King, 801 F.2d 1324, 1325 (Fed. Cir. 1986).

[138]   *See, e.g.,* Rubber-Tip Pencil Co. v. Howard, 87 U.S. (20 Wall.) 498 (1874).

Rubber-Tip Pencil has been cited for the proposition that "An idea of itself is not patentable." In fact, the case simply held that a patent on attaching a rubber eraser to a pencil was invalid for obviousness. The phrase — "An idea of itself is not patentable" — was meant to say that a "good idea" for a product (good from a business or marketing point of view) did not meet the nonobviousness standard if the product itself was an obvious modification of the prior art from a technical point of view.

[139]   The sequence of decisions was *In re* Prater, 415 F.2d 1378 (C.C.P.A. 1968), *on rehearing,* 415 F.2d 1393 (C.C.P.A. 1969); *In re* Bernhart, 417 F.2d 1395 (C.C.P.A. 1969); *In re* Mahony, 421 F.2d 742 (C.C.P.A. 1970); and *In re* Musgrave, 431 F.2d 882 (C.C.P.A. 1970).

[140]   431 F.2d 882 (C.C.P.A. 1970).

U.S.C. § 101 is that it be in the technological arts so as to be in consonance with the Constitutional purpose to promote the progress of "useful arts." Const. Art. 1, sec. 8.[141]

In 2007, the Federal Circuit held that a method of conducting arbitration was not patentable subject matter because the invention constituted mental steps.[142]

[ii]   Supreme Court Precedent on Software Patents

The two lines of cases — abstract ideas and mental steps — came together in the Supreme Court's *Gottschalk v. Benson* decision,[143] in which the Court held that an algorithm for converting binary-coded decimals into binary numerals could not be patented because it was an abstract idea or natural principle. Many commentators interpreted *Benson* as severely limiting computer software method patentability.

In *Benson*, the Court cited prior Supreme Court cases, which it interpreted as relating to "idea" and "phenomenon of nature" patentability. *Benson* then offered a dogmatic statement: "Phenomena of nature, though just discovered, mental processes, and abstract intellectual concepts are not patentable, as they are the basic tools of scientific and technological work."[144] This statement makes three assertions — two explicit and one implicit. The explicit assertions are that (1) natural phenomena, mental processes, and abstract intellectual concepts are to be lumped together as unpatentable subject matter, and (2) the reason for such unpatentability is that all are "basic tools" of technological work. The implicit assertion is that an algorithm is a phenomenon of nature, a mental process, or an abstract intellectual concept.

Benson also relied on the algorithm's alleged abstract nature and the sweeping scope of its potential use as grounds for finding it unpatentable.

> Here the "process" claim is so abstract and sweeping as to cover both known and unknown uses of the BCD to pure binary conversion. The end use may (1) vary from the operation of a train to verification of drivers' licenses to researching the law books for precedents and (2) be performed through any existing machinery or future-devised machinery or without any apparatus.

In support of this conclusion, the Court recited the holdings and language from two famous 19th-Century cases upholding the validity of the basic telegraph and the telephone patents.[145] These two cases stand for polar propositions on claim breadth. On the one hand, an inventor of one means of achieving a useful result cannot claim

---

[141]   431 F.2d at 893.

[142]   *In re* Comiskey, 499 F.3d 1365 (Fed. Cir. 2007).

[143]   409 U.S. 63 (1972). For an extensive critique of the *Benson* opinion, see Chisum, *The Patentability of Algorithms*, 47 U. Pitt. L. Rev. 959 (1986).

[144]   409 U.S. at 67.

[145]   Dolbear v. American Bell Telephone Co., 126 U.S. 1 (1888); O'Reilly v. Morse, 56 U.S. (15 How.) 62 (1854). *See* § 2C[1][f][i].

all possible means for achieving that result.[146] That would violate a basic tenet of the patent system — that an inventor may claim exclusive rights only over such means as he or she has invented and disclosed in the patent specification. On the other hand, an inventor should not be restricted to the particular preferred embodiment disclosed in that specification.[147] The inventor should be allowed to claim the invented "means" with an appropriate degree of generality. Apparently the Court believed that the Benson patent was more akin to the former than to the latter.

In addition, the Supreme Court in *Benson* cited prior Supreme Court decisions concerning chemical and mechanical processes. For example, *Corning v. Burden*[148] listed several examples of a process, such as tanning, dyeing, and smelting ore, which *Benson* found significant in that chemical and raw material processes "are . . . sufficiently definite to confine the patent monopoly within rather definite bounds."[149]

Cochrane v. Deener, which upheld a patent on refining flour, contains two sentences that can be interpreted as a process definition:

> A process is a mode of treatment of certain materials to produce a given result. It is an act or a series of acts, performed upon the subject-matter to be transformed and reduced to a different state or thing.[150]

Relying on *Cochrane*, *Benson* states: "Transformation and reduction of an article 'to a different state or thing' is the clue to the patentability of a process claim that does not include particular machines."[151]

What is meant by "the clue?" Is state or thing transformation a part of the definition of a patentable process — or not? The Court left the definition issue indeterminate:

> It is argued that a process patent must either be tied to a particular machine or apparatus or must operate to change articles or materials to a "different state or thing." We do not hold that no process patent could ever qualify if it did not meet the requirements of our prior precedents.[152]

Two Supreme Court decisions followed *Benson*, one expanding the algorithm unpatentability doctrine, the other contracting it. *Parker v. Flook*[153] involved a method for updating an "alarm limit" value on a variable (such as temperature) in

---

[146] *See* §§ 2C[6][a] and 2D[1][d].

[147] *See, e.g.*, Smith v. Snow, 294 U.S. 1, 11 (1935) (the patent laws require a patentee to disclose the best mode contemplated for carrying out the invention, but "he is not confined to that particular mode of use since the claims of the patent, not its specifications, measure the invention").

[148] 56 U.S. (15 How.) 252 (1853).

[149] Gottschalk v. Benson, 409 U.S. 63, 69 (1972).

[150] 94 U.S. 780, 788 (1877). The *Cochrane* court may not have intended the statement to be a comprehensive process definition. The phrase "a process is" could be interpreted to mean "a process includes at least" or "includes things such as," rather than "a process is limited to."

[151] 409 U.S. at 70.

[152] *Id.* at 71.

[153] 437 U.S. 584 (1978).

a catalytic chemical hydrocarbon conversion process. The Court treated the claimed subject matter as a method, one step of which was an "algorithm or mathematical formula" and the other steps of which were "conventional post-solution applications" of the formula. The Court reasoned that (1) the applicant's only "novel" contribution to the prior art was the algorithm or mathematical formula; (2) because that algorithm or mathematical formula was, under *Benson*, not patentable subject matter, it must be treated as though it were "prior art," *i.e.* "as if the principle or mathematical formula were well known," even if it was not well known and the applicant was the first to formulate it;[154] and (3) the claim was not for patentable subject matter because the added "post-solution" activity was conventional. The applicant argued unsuccessfully that his claim did not "preempt the mathematical formula" because it was limited to a field of use, hydrocarbon catalytic conversion. The Court responded that the same was true in *Benson* in which "there was a specific end use contemplated for the algorithm — utilization of the algorithm in computer programming."[155]

Diamond v. Diehr[156] involved a method for curing synthetic rubber in a mold. With such molding, it is necessary to avoid both undercure (cooking too short, if you will) and overcure (cooking too long). The proper cure time is calculated according to Svante Arrhenius' formula, which took into account variables such as temperature, the composition being molded, and the mold's geometry. Applicants James Diehr and Theodore Lutton claimed an improvement in rubber molding using the Arrhenius formula to calculate cure time. The method entailed, in addition to standard molding steps, (1) constantly determining temperature inside the mold, (2) repetitively calculating (i.e. updating) the cure time, (3) comparing the calculated proper cure time with the actual elapsed molding time, (4) opening the press when the two times were equal, and (5) removing the molded rubber product.

In *Diehr*, the Court held the claim was for a typical industrial process — molding rubber products — and as such was subject matter eligible for patent protection if the other patentability requirements were met. Incorporation of a computer to improve the process did not make the process unpatentable subject matter. The Court retreated from *Flook*'s direction that an unpatentable algorithm be considered as though it were prior art and stressed that whether a method falls within the Section 101 patentable subject matter categories is distinct from the question whether one or all of the elements of the method are novel or original with the inventor. The court did not overrule *Flook* and confirmed that "A mathematical formula as such is not accorded the protection of our patent laws" and that "insignificant post-solution activity will not transform an unpatentable principle into a patentable process."[157]

---

[154] In fact, the "formula" probably *was* well known in the abstract because it is a simple equation for doing a weighted average alteration of one variable when another variable changes.

[155] 437 U.S. at 590 n.11.

[156] 450 U.S. 175 (1981).

[157] 450 U.S. at 191–92.

[iii]   Examples: *Grams* and *Iwahashi*

Two 1989 Federal Circuit decisions demonstrate the difficulty of applying *Benson* and the two-inquiry step test of mathematical algorithm patentability.

In *In re Grams*,[158] the Federal Circuit held that the PTO did not err in rejecting the applicants' claims to a clinical data analysis program as being directed to nonstatutory subject matter because the claims "in essence claim . . . a mathematical algorithm." The court noted that "intuitively" the applicants' diagnostic method was a "process" even without the "physical" data-gathering step in the first limitation, but it conceded that because of *Benson*, "mathematical algorithms join the list of non-patentable subject matter not within the scope of section 101, including methods of doing business, naturally occurring phenomenon, and laws of nature." *Benson* remains the law despite the "liberal view" of Section 101 taken in *Chakrabarty*[159] and *Diehr*.[160]

In *In re Iwahashi*,[161] the Federal Circuit held that the PTO erred in rejecting the applicants' claim to a voice recognition coefficient calculation apparatus, because the PTO incorrectly found that the claim "is merely a mathematical algorithm." The claim language, which used means-plus-function terminology, was a machine or manufacture even though it embodied a mathematical formula. The court emphasized the importance of claim language:

> 'Once a mathematical algorithm has been found, the claim as a *whole* must be further analyzed. If it appears that the mathematical algorithm is implemented in a specific manner to define structural relationships between the physical elements of the claim (in apparatus claims) or to refine or limit claim steps (in process claims), the claim being otherwise statutory; the claim passes muster under § 101.'

> . . . [A]ppellants . . . characterize what they claim as apparatus with specific structural limitations. . . . [W]e . . . agree. . . . The claim as a whole certainly defines apparatus in the form of a combination of interrelated means and we cannot discern any logical reason why it should not be deemed statutory subject matter as either a machine or a manufacture as specified in § 101. The fact that the apparatus operates according to an algorithm does not make it nonstatutory.[162]

"Means" limitations are subject to Section 112's construction rule, that is, they only cover the corresponding structure, material or acts in the specification and equivalents.[163]

---

[158] 888 F.2d 835 (Fed. Cir. 1989).

[159] Diamond v. Chakrabarty, 447 U.S. 303 (1980), discussed at § 2C[1][d].

[160] Diamond v. Diehr, 450 U.S. 175 (1981).

[161] 888 F.2d 1370 (Fed Cir. 1989).

[162] *Id.* at 1374–75 (citations omitted).

[163] *See* §§ 2D[1][e] and 2F[1][b].

[2]   Utility

The utility requirement derives from the word "useful" in Section 101. The patent laws impose three related utility conditions: (1) a claimed product or process must in fact be useful;[164] (2) a person must have discovered the invention's utility to achieve a reduction to practice for the purposes of invention priority;[165] and (3) the inventor's patent specification must disclose how to use the claimed invention.[166]

Examples of inventions lacking utility include those that (1) conflict with known scientific principles, for example, a perpetual motion machine,[167] (2) require means for accomplishing an unattainable result,[168] or (3) are inevitably unreasonably dangerous.[169]

Older cases indicated that utility was lacking if the invention was "frivolous or injurious to the well-being, good policy, or sound morals of society."[170] Today, the trend is to restrict this subjective public policy approach to utility.[171]

To establish a chemical compound's utility, the inventor must show a specific practical use for the compound exists or would be obvious.[172] In *Brenner v. Manson*, Manson filed an application claiming a new process for making a known steroid compound. The Supreme Court held that utility was not satisfied by Manson's affidavit that he had used the process to synthesize the compound, because Manson did not allege that he had discovered a practical utility for the compound or that one was obvious. It was not sufficient that the compound was "the subject of serious scientific investigation."[173] *Manson* requires that practical utility for a claimed chemical compound be disclosed in a patent specification, or be obvious in view of the specification disclosures to be a constructive reduction to practice[174] and establish an effective filing date.[175]

---

[164] 35 U.S.C. § 101.

[165] Brenner v. Manson, 383 U.S. 519 (1966). *See* § 2D[4][a].

[166] 35 U.S.C. § 112. *See* § 2C[6][a].

[167] *See, e.g., In re* Ferens, 417 F.2d 1072 (C.C.P.A. 1969). *See also* Newman v. Quigg, 877 F.2d 1575 (Fed. Cir. 1989) ("Energy Generation System Having Higher Energy Output Than Input"); Fregeau v. Mossinghoff, 776 F.2d 1034 (Fed. Cir. 1985) (method for enhancing the flavor of a beverage by passing it through a magnetic field).

[168] Raytheon Co. v. Roper Corp., 724 F.2d 951 (Fed. Cir. 1983).

[169] Twentieth Century Motor Car v. Holcomb Co., 220 F. 669 (2d Cir. 1915).

[170] Lowell v. Lewis, 15 F. Cas. 1018 (No. 8,568) (C.C.D. Mass. 1817). *See, e.g.,* Richard v. DuBon, 103 F. 868 (2d Cir. 1900) (process for making cheap cigar wrapper tobacco leaf resemble leaf from choice locations).

[171] *See* Juicy Whip, Inc. v. Orange Bang, Inc., 185 F.3d 1364, 1368 (Fed. Cir. 1999) ("The requirement of 'utility' in patent law is not a directive to the [PTO] or the courts to serve as arbiters of deceptive trade practices.").

[172] Brenner v. Manson, 383 U.S. 519 (1966); *In re* Joly, 376 F.2d 906 (C.C.P.A. 1967).

[173] 383 U.S. at 532–34.

[174] For a discussion of constructive reduction to practice, see § 2D[4][c].

[175] Yasuko Kawai v. Metlesics, 480 F.2d 880 (C.C.P.A. 1973); *In re* Joly, 376 F.2d 906 (C.C.P.A. 1967).

A patent application that asserts no utility as to humans can meet the practical utility requirement by demonstrating specific effects on laboratory animals, for example, inhibiting tumors in rats, or preventing pregnancy in rabbits,[176] or by demonstrating pharmacological activity *in vitro*, the first important step in screening to identify compounds active *in vivo*, with possible human therapeutic application.[177]

A patent applicant need not establish a chemical compound's safety or effectiveness for human pharmaceutical use if the application does not assert human utility.[178] If the applicant does assert human utility, he must supply supporting evidence.[179] The evidence need only be convincing to a person of ordinary skill in the art; clinical or *in vivo* tests are not always required.[180] A pharmaceutical product or process need only be reasonably safe to meet the utility requirement.[181] The product or process need not meet regulatory commercial marketing requirements.[182]

Only one objective stated in the inventor's specification need be achieved to satisfy the utility requirement.[183] An application disclosing several distinct utilities, one adequately supported and others not adequately supported, meets the requirement, but the PTO may require deletion of nontenable utility assertions.[184]

[3]   Novelty

To qualify for a patent, an invention must meet the novelty requirement.[185]

A "single source" anticipation rule applies to lack of novelty determinations. Anticipation exists only if all the elements of the claimed invention are present in a product or process disclosed, expressly or inherently, in a single prior art reference.[186] References may be combined only to determine the separate nonobviousness patentability requirement.[187]

---

[176] Nelson v. Bowler, 626 F.2d 853 (C.C.P.A. 1980).

[177] Cross v. Iizuka, 753 F.2d 1040 (Fed. Cir. 1985) (assertion that a compound inhibited an enzyme in human or bovine platelet microsomes is sufficient).

[178] *In re* Krimmel, 292 F.2d 948 (C.C.P.A. 1961).

[179] *In re* Novak, 306 F.2d 924 (C.C.P.A. 1962).

[180] *In re* Langer, 503 F.2d 1380 (C.C.P.A. 1974); *In re* Irons, 340 F.2d 974 (C.C.P.A. 1965).

[181] *In re* Sichert, 566 F.2d 1154 (C.C.P.A. 1977).

[182] *In re* Anthony, 414 F.2d 1383 (C.C.P.A. 1969).

[183] Standard Oil Co. v. Montedison, S.p.A., 664 F.2d 356 (3d Cir. 1981).

[184] *In re* Gottlieb, 328 F.2d 1016 (C.C.P.A. 1964). *See also In re* Hozumi, 226 U.S.P.Q. 353, 354 (Comm'r Pat. & Tm. 1985) ("it is appropriate for the Office to require removal of wildly speculative statements if the integrity of a patent as a technical disclosure document is to be maintained and if the Office can avoid misleading the public. It is the policy of the Office . . . to require cancellation of such speculative statements which do not contribute to the technical content of the disclosure.").

[185] 35 U.S.C. §§ 101, 102. *See generally* D. Chisum, Patents § 3.01 *et seq.*

[186] RCA Corp. v. Applied Digital Data Sys., Inc., 730 F.2d 1440 (Fed. Cir. 1984).

[187] *See* § 2C[4][e][i].

The single source rule does not preclude use of multiple references to interpret a single reference or to show that a single reference disclosing the entire invention is "enabling."[188] For example, a reference that discloses a claimed chemical compound but no method of making it does not anticipate if one of ordinary skill in the art could not make the compound.[189] However, the single reference will anticipate if other references make obvious a suitable method of making the compound.[190]

Novelty determination compares a single prior art reference and the patent claim. The lack of novelty (anticipation) test is the same as that for literal infringement. If an item disclosed in a reference would have infringed had it occurred after the patent issued, then it will anticipate when it comes before the inventor's invention date.[191]

That a claim to a generic invention, for example, a class of chemical compounds, is anticipated by a prior art species falling within the claimed genus or class[192] follows from the infringement test of anticipation because a species later in time would infringe a claim to the genus. A claim to an element or subcombination is anticipated by the prior art disclosure of a combination that includes that element or combination.

A claim to a species is not anticipated by prior disclosure of a genus or class including that species unless disclosure actually names or clearly points to the claimed species.[193] The claimed species might exhibit unexpected properties that differentiate it from the class or genus to which it belongs and render it patentable over the generic disclosure.[194]

A product or process that appears or is inherent in a prior art reference anticipates a claim to that product or process even though the prior art product or process was used for a different purpose, in a different setting, or without recognition of valuable properties.[195]

---

[188] See, e.g., In re Donohue, 766 F.2d 531 (Fed. Cir. 1985) (when a single publication discloses, expressly or inherently, a product (such as a chemical compound) containing all of the limitations of the claim, the claim is anticipated even though additional references must be relied upon to show that one of ordinary skill in the art could have made the disclosed product).

[189] In re Brown, 329 F.2d 1006 (C.C.P.A. 1964).

[190] In re Samour, 571 F.2d 559 (C.C.P.A. 1978).

[191] Lindemann Maschinenfabrik GMBH v. American Hoist & Derrick Co., 730 F.2d 1452 (Fed. Cir. 1984); SSIH Equip. S.A. v. United States Int'l Trade Comm'n, 718 F.2d 365 (Fed. Cir. 1983).

[192] Chester v. Miller, 906 F.2d 1574 (Fed. Cir. 1990); In re Slayter, 276 F.2d 408 (C.C.P.A. 1960). See also In re Gosteli, 872 F.2d 1008, 1010 (Fed. Cir. 1989) ("Section 102(e) bars the issuance of a patent if its generic claims are anticipated by prior art disclosing individual chemical species."); Titanium Metals Corp. v. Banner, 778 F.2d 775 (Fed. Cir. 1985) (when, as by a recitation of ranges, a claim covers several compositions, the claim is anticipated if one of the compositions is in the prior art).

[193] In re Schaumann, 572 F.2d 312 (C.C.P.A. 1978).

[194] In re Ornitz, 376 F.2d 330 (C.C.P.A. 1967).

[195] See, e.g., Verdegaal Brothers, Inc. v. Union Oil Co. of California, 814 F.2d 628 (Fed. Cir. 1987) (a claim to a process is anticipated by a prior art reference that discloses all of the limitations of that claim even though the reference does not expressly disclose the "inventive concept" or desirable property discovered by the patentee; it suffices that the prior art process inherently possessed that property);

Neither the accidental, unappreciated occurrence of a product or process in the prior art,[196] nor the speculative listing of a product (such as a chemical compound) as part of a large number of possible occurrences is an anticipation.[197]

[4]   Nonobviousness

To qualify for a patent, subject matter claimed as an invention must meet the nonobviousness requirement. No valid patent may issue if the differences between the claimed subject matter and the prior art are such that the subject matter as a whole would have been obvious at the time the invention was made to a person having ordinary skill in the art to which the subject matter pertains.[198]

The nonobviousness requirement means that not all new and useful inventions qualify for patent protection. Most countries require something more than novelty to establish patentability. Europe and Japan use the concept "inventive step", but the legal test is basically the same — would the invention have been viewed, as of the relevant date, as obvious by a person of ordinary skill in the art in view of the prior art?

In the United States, courts originally developed the obviousness requirement when passing on the validity of patents in infringement suits.[199] In 1952, Congress included it in Section 103 of the patent statutes.[200] Nonobviousness is the most important patentability requirement[201] and the most difficult to apply. In practice, the most critical factors are: (1) the scope of the claims, and (2) the content of the pertinent prior art. An invention may meet the requirement if it is narrowly defined

---

W.L. Gore & Associates, Inc. v. Garlock, Inc., 721 F.2d 1540 (Fed. Cir. 1983); *In re* Bird, 344 F.2d 979 (C.C.P.A. 1965).

[196] *In re* Marshall, 578 F.2d 301 (C.C.P.A. 1978).

[197] *In re* Wiggins, 488 F.2d 538 (C.C.P.A. 1973). *Compare In re* Sivaramakrishnan, 673 F.2d 1383 (C.C.P.A. 1982) (naming of relatively small group of possible combinable ingredients is not mere speculation).

[198] *See generally* D. Chisum, Patents § 5.01 *et seq.*

[199] *See* § 2B[2].

[200] 35 U.S.C. § 103 provides as follows:

> A patent may not be obtained though the invention is not identically disclosed or described as set forth in section 102 of this title, if the differences between the subject matter sought to be patented and the prior art are such that the subject matter as a whole would have been obvious at the time the invention was made to a person having ordinary skill in the art to which said subject matter pertains.

This statutory language contains a good deal of substance. The phrase "subject matter sought to be patented" clearly refers to the inventor's claim, in a pending application or an issued patent. The "prior art" is not defined but, presumptively and subject to possible exceptions, refers to the novelty and statutory bar provisions of Section 102. The relevant time period of obviousness is "the time the invention was made." Finally, it identifies a "person of ordinary skill" as the human actor to whom the invention must be obvious. Case law confirms that a "person of ordinary skill" is neither a highly sophisticated expert nor a layman without knowledge or skill of the technology.

[201] The utility requirement may be met by demonstrating only a minimal beneficial use. *See* § 2C[2]. The novelty requirement may be met by carefully confining the claim language so that it does not read on the disclosures of any single prior art reference. *See* § 2C[3]. The nonobviousness requirement is more fundamental and is supported by the patent system's constitutional purpose of promoting the progress of the useful arts. Graham v. John Deere Co., 383 U.S. 1 (1966).

but not if broadly defined.[202] Similarly, an invention may meet the requirement if the pertinent prior art is constricted but may not if expanded.[203]

[a]   General Test — *Graham v. Deere*

Graham v. John Deere Co.,[204] the leading Supreme Court decision on nonobviousness, directed the lower courts and the Patent Office to apply the following test:

> While the ultimate question of patent validity is one of law, . . . the § 103 condition, which is but one of three conditions, each of which must be satisfied, lends itself to several basic factual inquiries. Under § 103, the scope and content of the prior art are to be determined; differences between the prior art and the claims at issue are to be ascertained; and the level of ordinary skill in the pertinent art resolved. Against this background, the obviousness or nonobviousness of the subject matter is determined. Such secondary considerations as commercial success, long felt but unsolved needs, failure of others, etc., might be utilized to give light to the circumstances surrounding the origin of the subject matter sought to be patented. As indicia of obviousness or nonobviousness, these inquiries may have relevancy.[205]

This passage is usually referred to as the "*Graham* test" or the "*Graham* factors", and, for the most part, merely restates the language of Section 103. One factor not in Section 103 is the *level* of "ordinary skill in the art." *Graham* offered no analysis of this factor: in finding two patents invalid for obviousness, the Court made scant reference to the level of skill in the art. In subsequent lower court decisions, the level of skill finding rarely plays a major role in obviousness determinations.[206]

[b]   Nonanalogous Art

Patent law's nonobviousness requirement compares a patent claim's subject matter as a whole with the "prior art."[207] Prior art includes all pertinent items, no matter how old or obscure and regardless of whether or not persons actually working in the field knew of the items.[208]

---

[202] Claim interpretation for patentability and infringement determination are discussed at § 2F.

[203] What constitutes the pertinent art is discussed at § 2C[4][b]. What items constitute sources of prior art (prior publications, matter in public use, etc.) is discussed at § 2C[5].

[204] Graham v. John Deere Co., 383 U.S. 1 (1966). *Graham* involved two patent infringement suits. The Court held both patents invalid for obviousness. In a third suit decided the same date, the Court held a patent on a battery valid. United States v. Adams, 383 U.S. 39 (1966).

[205] 383 U.S. at 17–18.

[206] *See, e.g.*, Kloster Speedsteel AB v. Crucible, Inc., 793 F.2d 1565 (Fed. Cir. 1986) (failure to make express finding as to the level of skill in the art is not alone grounds for reversal).

Factors that may be considered in determining the level of skill in the art include: type of problems encountered in the art; prior art solutions to those problems; rapidity with which innovations are made; sophistication of the technology; and educational level of active workers in the field. *See* Custom Accessories, Inc. v. Jeffrey-Allan Industries, Inc., 807 F.2d 955, 962–63 (Fed. Cir. 1986).

[207] For a discussion of prior art sources, see § 2C[5].

[208] Merit Mfg. Co. v. Hero Mfg. Co., 185 F.2d 350 (2d Cir. 1950). It has sometimes been said that the

Prior art for obviousness does not include items in nonanalogous fields.[209] Arts are analogous if one seeking to solve a problem in one art would likely look for a solution in the other art.[210] It is not proper to use the inventor's specification teachings to determine whether prior art items are analogous.[211]

In *In re Deminski*,[212] the Federal Circuit applied a two-step test for determining whether a prior art reference is nonanalogous: (1) Is the reference "within the field of the inventor's endeavor?" and (2) If not, is the reference "reasonably pertinent to the particular problem with which the inventor was involved?" The claimed invention and reference patents are within the same field of endeavor if they have essentially the same function and structure, for example, pumps and compressors, each of the double-acting piston type.

The "art" to which an invention pertains is defined in terms of the problem to be solved rather than in terms of the specific field in which the invention will be used.[213] For example, providing a proper fastener for a beehive is in the field of mechanics pertaining to fasteners, not beekeeping.[214] It matters not that beekeepers may have little knowledge of mechanics.

Courts give the PTO's classification system relatively little weight in determining whether a reference is within the same or an analogous art.[215]

[c]   Comparative Utility

[i]   Rationale

Comparative utility is pertinent to the obviousness issue. The fact that the claimed invention achieves superior results compared to the closest prior art product or process tends to show it was not obvious. Inventors commonly rely on tests results comparing the claimed invention and the closest prior art to show

---

"inventor is presumed to know all the prior art," but this presumption has been rejected as a fiction; the person for determining obviousness is not the inventor but an imaginary person who is deemed to have access to all of the references in the public domain. Kimberly-Clark Corp. v. Johnson & Johnson, 745 F.2d 1437 (Fed. Cir. 1984).

[209] *In re* Wood, 599 F.2d 1032 (C.C.P.A. 1979). *See also* King Instrument Corp. v. Otari Corp., 767 F.2d 853 (Fed. Cir. 1985) (as to a patent for loading magnetic tape into closed cassettes, a prior patent on splicing photographic textual film in the printing industry was not within the patentee's field of endeavor). *See generally* D. Chisum, Patents § 5.03[1].

[210] *In re* Shapleigh, 248 F.2d 96, 115 U.S.P.Q. 129 (C.C.P.A. 1957). For example, prior art on freezing fish carcasses to a platform for slicing was held to be analogous to an invention on holding workpieces such as gem stones to a work station. International Glass Co. v. United States, 408 F.2d 395, 404–05 (Ct. Cl. 1969). On the other hand, prior art on tire puncture sealing was held to be not analogous to an invention on identification tags for animals' ears. *Ex parte* Murphy, 217 U.S.P.Q. 479 (PTO Bd. App. 1976).

[211] *In re* Wanderham, 378 F.2d 981 (C.C.P.A. 1967).

[212] 796 F.2d 436 (Fed. Cir. 1986).

[213] *See, e.g.*, Orthopedic Equip. Co. v. United States, 702 F.2d 1005 (Fed. Cir. 1983).

[214] *In re* Grout, 377 F.2d 1019 (C.C.P.A. 1967).

[215] *In re* Mlot-Fijalkowski, 676 F.2d 666 (C.C.P.A. 1982). *Compare In re* Deminski, 796 F.2d 436, 442 n.3 (Fed. Cir. 1986) (a cross reference in the official PTO search notes is some evidence of analogy, particularly when "nearly identical classifications of the application and references . . . are the result of the close similarity in structure and function of the invention and the prior art.").

nonobviousness of their inventions. What is the "closest" prior art depends on the circumstances.[216] The closest art may not be the commercial standard in the field.[217]

Court decisions on the obviousness requirement focus on two kinds of differences between the claimed invention and the prior art. The first is the differences between the claims and the prior art purely in terms of physical structure (or, in the case of product claims, in terms of methodology or operative steps). The second is the differences between the claims and the prior art in terms of functions and advantages (comparative utility). What functions, advantages and results does the claimed product or process have that the prior art products or processes do not in fact have?[218]

The novelty patentability condition depends solely on *physical* differences between the claimed invention and prior art disclosures. An inventor cannot claim an old product or method even though he or she may discover heretofore unknown performance characteristics.[219]

Why then does the nonobviousness condition focus on both physical and performance differences? If patents issue only for physically new things and methods, should not the focus be solely on the physical differences? The relevance of evidence of comparative utility is in part direct and in part inferential. It is direct in the sense that the new function is part of the inventive concept, the "subject matter as a whole," which must be obvious under Section 103. It is inferential in the sense that the prior art's failure to reveal the claimed invention despite its advantageous qualities tends to confirm that it was unexpected and unobvious. It would be contrary to normal economic incentives for obvious, advantageous subject matter to remain dormant.

The two rationales for giving weight to performance characteristics are distinct. Inference focuses on the issue of whether a physical thing or method that is literally new but similar to prior art things or methods would in fact have been obvious to a person skilled in the art. "Subject matter as a whole" is substantive, postulating the performance characteristics as part of the invention. If those characteristics are unexpected (not obvious), then the invention is not expected. Whether patent law policy supports the second rationale is unclear.

---

[216] *In re* Merchant, 575 F.2d 865 (C.C.P.A. 1978).

[217] *In re* Wright, 569 F.2d 1124 (C.C.P.A. 1976).

[218] D. Chisum, Patents § 5.03[5][a].

[219] A good illustration is *In re* Spada, 911 F.2d 705, 708 (Fed. Cir. 1990). In *Spada*, the applicants disclosed and claimed pressure-sensitive adhesive compositions comprising a water-based latex containing a copolymer. A prior art reference, Smith, showed water-based latexes containing polymers that overlapped those of the applicants. However, Smith disclosed properties, such as hardness and abrasion resistance, that differed from those of the applicants. The court held that the PTO properly rejected the applicant's claims as *prima facie* unpatentable for lack of novelty. That the applicants discovered and disclosed properties different from or even mutually exclusive of those disclosed by the reference did not show novelty.

[ii]   New and Unexpected Properties

What is the role of properties of an invention in determining obviousness when the invention has new or unexpected properties compared to the prior art but also shares common properties with the prior art? What is the role of properties when the inventor discovers an unexpected property in a literally new product or process that is physically similar to an old product or process that, unknown to the prior art, also possesses the unexpected property? The question is most often discussed in connection with chemical inventions,[220] but it arises with all types of inventions.

For example, in *In re Dillon*,[221] the Federal Circuit, sitting en banc, held that the PTO did not err in rejecting applicant Dillon's claims to hydrocarbon fuel/*tetra*-orthoester compositions and related methods of use, which exhibited the unexpected property of reducing particulate emissions (soot) during fuel combustion, as *prima facie* obvious in view of the teachings of primary and secondary prior art references that hydrocarbon fuel/*tri*-orthoester compositions scavenge water in the fuel and that *tetra*-orthoester is equivalent to *tri*-orthoester in scavenging water in hydraulic (nonhydrocarbon) fluids.

In affirming, the Federal Circuit noted that the claimed compositions "are not structurally or physically distinguishable from the prior art compositions by virtue of the recitation of their newly-discovered use."[222] The recitation "a sufficient amount of at least one orthoester" was not "a distinguishing limitation of the claims, unless that amount is different from the prior art and critical to the use of the claimed composition. . . . That is not the case here."[223] The structural similarity between applicant's claimed compositions and methods and the prior art created a presumption of obviousness.[224] The applicant then has the burden of rebutting the presumption. "Such rebuttal or argument can consist of a comparison of test data showing that the claimed compositions possess unexpectedly improved properties or properties that the prior art does not have, that the prior art is so deficient that there is no motivation to make what might otherwise appear to be obvious changes, or any other argument or presentation of evidence that is pertinent."[225] However, "the discovery that a claimed composition possesses a property not disclosed for the prior art subject matter, does not by itself defeat a *prima facie* case."[226]

---

[220] *See* § 2C[4][e][iii].

[221] 919 F.2d 688 (Fed. Cir. 1990) (*en banc*).

[222] *Id.* at 693 n.4.

[223] *Id.* at 693–94.

[224] The court stressed that, in determining whether prior art creates *prima facie* obviousness, the art need not have provided "a suggestion . . . or expectation . . . that the claimed [invention] will have the same or a similar utility *as one newly discovered by applicant*." *Id.* at 693.

[225] *Id.* at 692–93.

[226] *Id.* at 693.

[iii]   Undisclosed Advantages and Properties

A difficult problem arises when the result or advantage later relied upon to show nonobviousness is not disclosed in the specification. The question is not free from doubt,[227] but the general rule is that an applicant or patentee may rely on an undisclosed advantage if it is inherent when the invention is used as disclosed in the specification,[228] but not if it relates to a distinct utility not disclosed in the specification.[229] The inventor may use a continuation-in-part application, or possibly reissue, to add the utility or advantage to the specification without thereby losing the benefit of the original application's filing date.[230]

[d]   Objective Evidence

Nontechnical considerations, for example, commercial success and satisfaction of long-felt need, are relevant to an obviousness determination.[231] Economic and motivational factors provide a basis for making an inference about the ultimate issue of nonobviousness and guard against use of hindsight.

At one time, courts viewed nontechnical considerations as relevant only when the technical issue was "close,"[232] but today the Federal Circuit views them as always relevant in court suits concerning validity[233] and in PTO examination.[234]

[i]   Long-Felt Need — Failure of Others

If (1) for a number of years an industry suffers a problem and efforts to solve it are unsuccessful, and (2) the invention solves that problem, then it can be inferred that the solution was not obvious to persons of ordinary skill in the art.[235] Long-felt need and failure of others will not be as persuasive if the need and failures were before the appearance of significant prior art.[236]

[ii]   Commercial Success

If a product that embodies the invention supplants prior art products and is a great commercial success, then it can be inferred that the invention was not obvious because otherwise persons lured by the prospect of success would have

---

[227] *See generally* D. Chisum, Patents § 5.03[5].

[228] *In re* Khelghatian, 364 F.2d 870 (C.C.P.A. 1966).

[229] *In re* Davies, 475 F.2d 667 (C.C.P.A. 1973).

[230] *See* § 2D[2][b][ii]. *Cf.* Carter-Wallace, Inc. v. Otte, 474 F.2d 529 (2d Cir. 1972).

[231] *See generally* D. Chisum, Patents § 5.05.

[232] *See, e.g.*, Medical Laboratory Automation, Inc. v. Labcon, Inc., 670 F.2d 671 (7th Cir. 1981).

[233] Stratoflex, Inc. v. Aeroquip Corp., 713 F.2d 1530 (Fed. Cir. 1983). Such evidence is not conclusive. *See, e.g.*, Merck & Co., Inc. v. Biocraft Laboratories, Inc., 874 F.2d 804, 809 (Fed. Cir. 1989) ("Commercial success is an indication of nonobviousness that must be considered in a patentability analysis, . . . but in the circumstances of this case, where it is the only such indication, it is insufficient to render [the patentee's] claimed invention nonobvious.").

[234] *In re* Sernaker, 702 F.2d 989 (Fed. Cir. 1983).

[235] *See, e.g.*, Under Sea Industries, Inc. v. Dacor Corp., 833 F.2d 1551 (Fed. Cir. 1987); Reeves Instrument Corp. v. Beckman Instruments, Inc., 444 F.2d 263 (9th Cir. 1971).

[236] Graham v. John Deere Co., 383 U.S. 1 (1966).

developed the invention sooner.[237] Commercial success both in the United States and in other countries is relevant under this theory.[238]

There must be a nexus between the commercial success and the claimed invention to prove nonobviousness.[239] The product success must flow from the functions and advantages disclosed or inherent in the patent specification.[240] Success attributable to other features in the product,[241] extensive advertising, or dominant market position is not persuasive.[242]

[iii]   Licensing and Acquiescence by Competitors

If major commercial competitors accept licenses under the patent, then it can be inferred that the invention was not obvious because otherwise those competitors would have challenged the patent's validity.[243] Licensing is not as persuasive if the royalty rates are low; competitors may simply have accepted the license to avoid litigation expenses.[244]

[iv]   Copying and Laudatory Statements by the Infringer

If the person challenging a patent's validity on grounds of obviousness[245] deliberately copied the patented invention, then it can be inferred that the invention was not obvious because otherwise the challenger would have either independently developed a product or copied prior art products.[246] Weight may

---

[237] See, e.g., Akzo N.V. v. U.S. Int'l Trade Comm'n, 808 F.2d 1471 (Fed. Cir. 1986); Hybritech Inc. v. Monoclonal Antibodies, Inc., 802 F.2d 1367 (Fed. Cir. 1986); Simmons Fastener Corp. v. Illinois Tool Works, Inc., 739 F.2d 1573 (Fed. Cir. 1984).

As to the discoverability of third-party sales data, see American Standard, Inc. v. Pfizer Inc., 828 F.2d 734 (Fed. Cir. 1987). In American Standard, the Federal Circuit held that the district court did not err in limiting discovery of the confidential sales data of a third party, which was sought by a patent owner to establish commercial success of the claimed invention: "Although evidence of sales of different infringing articles showing commercial success of the claimed invention cannot be cumulative . . . , one seeking discovery of confidential sales information must nevertheless establish that it is reasonably necessary for a fair opportunity to develop and prepare the case for trial." 828 F.2d at 742.

[238] Lindemann Maschinenfabrik GMBH v. American Hoist & Derrick Co., 730 F.2d 1452 (Fed. Cir. 1984).

[239] Kansas Jack, Inc. v. Kuhn, 719 F.2d 1144 (Fed. Cir. 1983).

[240] In re Vamco Machine & Tool, Inc., 752 F.2d 1564 (Fed. Cir. 1985).

[241] See, e.g., Sjolund v. Musland, 847 F.2d 1573 (Fed. Cir. 1988).

[242] Pentec, Inc. v. Graphic Controls Corp., 776 F.2d 309 (Fed. Cir. 1985); Cable Elec. Prods., Inc. v. Genmark, Inc., 770 F.2d 1015 (Fed. Cir. 1985).

[243] Eibel Process Co. v. Minnesota & Ontario Paper Co., 261 U.S. 45 (1923).

[244] EWP Corp. v. Reliance Universal, Inc., 755 F.2d 898 (Fed. Cir. 1985); Phillips Elec. & Pharmaceutical Indus. Corp. v. Thermal & Elec. Indus., Inc., 450 F.2d 1164 (3d Cir. 1971).

[245] A person charged with patent infringement may defend on the ground that the patent claims are invalid for obviousness. See § 2F[4][a].

[246] See, e.g., Fromson v. Western Litho Plate & Supply Co., 853 F.2d 1568, 1571 n.4 (Fed. Cir. 1988) ("[I]n attributing sales to various factors, the [district] court overlooked [the accused infringer's] election to sell not its [prior art product] but the infringing [product] to the newspaper market, and the efforts of numerous companies in protesting reissue, efforts unlikely in relation to an unsuccessful invention or

also be given to the infringer's praise of the invention.[247]

[v]   Near Simultaneous Invention

If others develop solutions similar to the claimed invention at about the same time, then it can be inferred that the invention was obvious to persons of ordinary skill in the art.[248] Near simultaneous inventions can have inferential force even if they are not technically prior art.[249]

[e]   Other Guidelines

No official rules set forth the nonobviousness requirement's application to particular types of inventions, but court decisions identify guidelines that are of assistance both in general and in specific situations.

[i]   Prior Art Suggestions — Obvious to Try

The primary technical focus in assessing obviousness is on whether the prior art references collectively teach, expressly or implicitly, that various disclosed features may be combined in the manner of the claimed invention.[250] An invention may be obvious in view of a combination of references even though the references' features cannot be physically substituted or combined to create the invention.[251] Furthermore, "[o]bviousness does not require absolute predictability; only a reasonable expectation that the beneficial result will be achieved is necessary to show obviousness."[252]

An "obvious to try" approach to the prior art to determine obviousness is

---

one for which noninfringing substitutes were readily available."); Vandenberg v. Dairy Equipment Co., 740 F.2d 1560 (Fed. Cir. 1984).

    Compare Cable Electric Products, Inc. v. Genmark, Inc., 770 F.2d 1015, 1028 (Fed. Cir. 1985) ("[M]ore than the mere fact of copying by an accused infringer is needed to make that action significant to a determination of the obviousness issue"; copying may be attributable to a general lack of concern for patent property or to contempt for the patentee's ability to enforce the specific patent).

[247] Deere & Co. v. International Harvester Co., 658 F.2d 1137 (7th Cir. 1981). *Compare* Medtronic, Inc. v. Cardiac Pacemakers, Inc., 721 F.2d 1563 (Fed. Cir. 1983).

[248] Concrete Appliance Co. v. Gomery, 269 U.S. 177 (1925); *In re* Merck & Co., Inc., 800 F.2d 1091 (Fed. Cir. 1986) (evidence that four other groups of inventors independently and contemporaneously discovered the antidepressant properties of a certain chemical compound based on a knowledge of investigative techniques, including a theory (bioisosterism) as to the effect of chemical structural changes on biological properties, is evidence of the level of skill in the art at the time of the claimed invention (a method of using the compound as an antidepressant)).

[249] Newell Companies, Inc. v. Kenney Manufacturing Co., 864 F.2d 757 (Fed. Cir. 1988) (though an internal memorandum may not be "technically 'prior art'. . . ," it is admissible to show that persons of ordinary skill in the art suggested solutions to the problem similar to that claimed in the patent). *Compare* Hybritech Inc. v. Monoclonal Antibodies, Inc., 802 F.2d 1367 (Fed. Cir. 1986); Environmental Designs, Ltd. v. Union Oil Co. of Calif., 713 F.2d 693 (Fed. Cir. 1983); E.I. Du Pont de Nemours & Co. v. Berkley & Co., 620 F.2d 1247 (8th Cir. 1980) (near simultaneous invention is merely one of many indicia of obviousness).

[250] *In re* Dow Chemical Co., 837 F.2d 469, 473 (Fed. Cir. 1988).

[251] Orthopedic Equipment Co., Inc. v. United States, 702 F.2d 1005 (Fed. Cir. 1983).

[252] *In re* Merck & Co., Inc., 800 F.2d 1091 (Fed. Cir. 1986).

sometimes improper.[253] Consider the following example:

> 1. Inventor A seeks a solution to a problem and decides that the solution might consist of a combination of ingredient X with a second ingredient having the general characteristics of Y.

> 2. The prior art lists 150 possible Y ingredients with defined characteristics but does not disclose any specific information as to how they may be combined with ingredient X to solve the problem confronting the inventor.

> 3. Inventor A discovers that Y(85) when combined with X achieves unexpected results in solving the problem.

The inventor's claim to the combination of X and Y(85) may not be rejected as obvious simply on the ground that it would have been obvious to try all of the 150 possibilities. There must be something in the prior art suggesting that Y(85) would achieve the desired result when combined with X.

However, the Supreme Court has held that "[w]hen there is a design need or market pressure to solve a problem and there are a finite number of identified, predictable solutions, a person of ordinary skill has good reason to pursue the known options within his or her technical grasp. If this leads to the anticipated success, it is likely the product not of innovation but of ordinary skill and common sense. In that instance the fact that a combination was obvious to try might show that it was obvious."[254]

[ii]   Combination Inventions

The patentability of combinations of mechanical elements individually well known in the art was formerly determined by special, strict tests.[255] In *KSR Int'l Co. v. Teleflex, Inc.*,[256] the Supreme Court adopted a flexible standard for determining when combination inventions could be deemed nonobvious. The Court addressed the "teaching, suggestion or motivation" test (TSM) used by the Federal Circuit to determine when a teaching, suggestion, or motivation to combine prior art elements to create a novel invention would be found obvious.[257]

In *KSR*, the district court granted summary judgment on the grounds that Teleflex's adjustable gas pedal was obvious. The Federal Circuit reversed, holding that the lower court had failed to articulate a reason for what prior art taught, suggested, or motivated the particular combination of elements in the patented adjustable brake pedal. The Supreme Court reversed the Federal Circuit, holding

---

[253] *In re Goodwin*, 576 F.2d 375 (C.C.P.A. 1978). *See generally* D. Chisum, Patents § 5.04[1].

[254] KSR Int'l Co. v. Teleflex, Inc., 550 U.S. 398, 421 (2007).

[255] *See, e.g.*, Sakraida v. Ag Pro, Inc., 425 U.S. 273 (1976) (combination of old elements must achieve "synergism"); Anderson's Black Rock, Inc. v. Pavement Salvage, 396 U.S. 57 (1969); Great Atlantic & Pacific Tea Co. v. Supermarket Equipment Corp., 340 U.S. 147 (1950). *See* § 2B[4][c].

[256] 550 U.S. 398 (2007).

[257] The TSM test originated with the CCPA in *Application of Bergel*, 292 F.2d 955, 956–7 (C.C.P.A. 1961), and was adopted by the Federal Circuit. *See In re Kotzab*, 217 F.3d 1365, 1371 (Fed. Cir. 2000); DyStar Textilfarben GmbH & Co. Deutschland KG v. C.H. Patrick Co., 464 F.3d 1356, 1367 (Fed. Cir. 2006); Alza Corp. v. Mylan Labs., Inc., 464 F.3d 1286, 1291 (Fed. Cir. 2006).

that the TSM test was being applied too rigidly.

The Court found three errors in the Federal Circuit's application of the TSM test. First, the Federal Circuit narrowly focused on the problem to be solved by the patent owner, rather than the broader problem that the invention solved. As the Supreme Court emphasized, nonobviousness is a question of what is obvious to a person having ordinary skill in the art, not what is obvious to the specific inventor.[258] Second, the Federal Circuit erred in focusing only on prior art relevant to the problem the inventor was trying to solve, rather than the complete analogous art relevant to the invention. Related to this second error was the Federal Circuit's rejection of the "obvious to try" approach to nonobviousness. According to the Supreme Court, if there are only a finite number of ways to solve a problem, a person having ordinary skill in the art may conclude that the approach chosen by the inventor was "obvious to try" given the limited number of possible paths to a solution.[259] Finally, the Supreme Court concluded that the Federal Circuit was too rigid in its application of the TSM test, and that rigidity was not a proper way to deal with the problem of hindsight bias in nonobviousness analysis (i.e., the problem that an invention may seem obvious after it is created).[260] Instead, the Supreme Court held that a flexible approach, based on common sense and a full consideration of the prior art and the invention was the more appropriate method for applying the TSM test and analyzing nonobviousness.

[iii]   Chemical Compounds and Intermediates

A novel and nonobvious chemical compound may be patented. Many new chemical compounds are structurally similar to known compounds and are considered "structurally obvious." A "structurally obvious" compound may nevertheless be patented if it has unexpected properties not possessed by the known compounds.[261]

Determining the patentability of a chemical compound is a two-step process. First, is the claimed compound structurally similar enough to prior art compounds to show *prima face* obviousness? The level of similarity is not precise.[262] A claimed compound may be part of a homologous series with the prior art compound but not necessarily *prima facie* obvious.[263] A compound disclosed in the prior art will not create *prima facie* obviousness if the prior art discloses no specific utility for the compound.[264]

---

[258] 550 U.S. at 420.

[259] *Id.* at 420–21.

[260] *Id.* at 421.

[261] *In re* Papesch, 315 F.2d 381 (C.C.P.A. 1963). *See generally* D. Chisum, Patents § 5.04[6].

[262] *See, e.g., In re* Grabiak, 769 F.2d 729, 731 (Fed. Cir. 1985) ("[G]eneralization should be avoided insofar as specific chemical structures are alleged to be *prima facie* obvious one from the other;" there can be a *prima facie* case of obviousness even in an area as unpredictable as the biological properties of chemical compounds, but such a case must be based on support in the prior art for the structural change necessary to get from the prior art compound to the claimed compound).

[263] *In re* Mills, 281 F.2d 218 (C.C.P.A. 1960).

[264] *In re* Stemniski, 444 F.2d 581 (C.C.P.A. 1971). *See also In re* Lalu, 747 F.2d 703 (Fed. Cir. 1984) (there is no *prima facie* obviousness when a prior art reference disclosed that a compound homologous

Second, does the *prima facie* obvious claimed compound exhibit new and unexpected properties when compared with the closest prior art compounds?[265] Significantly greater effectiveness is equivalent to a new property.[266] A chemical compound's ability to operate as an intermediate to produce another compound (end product) that exhibits unexpected superior properties (compared to prior art end products) may rebut *prima facie* obviousness.[267]

If the claimed compound has an unexpected property not possessed by the closest prior art compound but shares a common property with the prior art compound, *prima facie* obviousness will be rebutted only if the unexpected property is much more significant than shared property.[268]

If an inventor discovers a significant unexpected property of a compound that cannot be claimed as such because it is old or obvious, he may obtain a patent claiming a new method of using the compound.[269]

[iv]   Processes — Methods of Making and Using

If an applicant formulates claims to both products and processes, the requirements of novelty and nonobviousness must be applied independently to each such claim.[270]

In *In re Durden*,[271] the Federal Circuit held that a claim to a process of making a chemical compound from a starting material is not necessarily nonobvious even though both the starting material and the resulting compound are nonobvious and

---

to the claimed compound was useful only as an intermediate to produce other compounds with utilities differing from those of the claimed compound.).

Compare In re Dillon, 919 F.2d 688 (Fed. Cir. 1990) (en banc) (applicant did not "show that the prior art compositions and use were so lacking in significance that there was no motivation for others to make obvious variants."; "There was no attempt to argue the relative importance of the claimed compositions compared with the prior art."; *Stemniski* "rather than destroying the established practice of rejecting closely-related compounds as *prima facie* obvious, qualified it by holding that a presumption is not created when the reference compound is so lacking in any utility that there is no motivation to make close relatives.").

[265] *In re* Johnson, 747 F.2d 1456 (Fed. Cir. 1984). *See also In re* Dillon, 919 F.2d 688, 692–93 (Fed. Cir. 1990) (en banc) ("rebuttal [of a case of *prima facie* obviousness based on structural similarity] can consist of a comparison of test data showing that the claimed compositions possess unexpectedly improved properties or properties that the prior art does not have, that the prior art is so deficient that there is no motivation to make what might otherwise appear to be obvious changes, or any other argument or presentation of evidence that is pertinent.") (citations omitted).

[266] *In re* Lunsford, 357 F.2d 380 (C.C.P.A. 1966).

[267] *In re* Magerlein, 602 F.2d 366 (C.C.P.A. 1979).

[268] *In re* May, 574 F.2d 1082 (C.C.P.A. 1978). *Cf. In re* Dillon, 919 F.2d 688, 698 (Fed. Cir. 1990) (en banc) (prior cases "concerned the question whether the existence of a new property for claimed compounds in addition to a property common to both the claimed and related prior art compounds rendered the claimed compounds unobvious. We are not faced with that question today."). *See* § 2C[4][c][iii].

[269] *See, e.g., In re* Shetty, 566 F.2d 81 (C.C.P.A. 1977).

[270] Providence Rubber Co. v. Goodyear, 76 U.S. (9 Wall.) 788 (1870). *See generally* D. CHISUM, PATENTS § 5.04[8].

[271] 763 F.2d 1406 (Fed. Cir. 1985). *Compare In re* Kuehl, 475 F.2d 658 (C.C.P.A. 1973).

patentable. In *In re Pleuddemann*,[272] however, it held that *Durden* did not apply to method-of-use claims. The Federal Circuit held that the PTO erred in rejecting the claims based on method-of-making cases, such as *Durden*, and in failing to apply method-of-use cases such as *In re Kuehl*.[273] There is "a real difference between a process of making and a process of using and the cases dealing with one involve different problems from the cases dealing with the other."[274]

The *Durden* rule has implications for the territorial scope of United States patents. A patent claiming novel and nonobvious starting materials, such as genetically-altered cell cultures useful in making natural proteins, may not be effective against use of the starting materials abroad to produce an unpatented product, such as the protein, for importation into the United States.[275] Therefore, it is important to obtain *process* claims, such as to the method of *using* the cell cultures to *make* the protein.[276]

Neither *Durden* nor the *Pleuddemann* distinction between making methods and using methods make sense (or use common sense) in terms of logic or policy. How can a method of making a novel and nonobvious product be obvious if the method, as claimed, is limited to methods that begin with or result in something that is not obvious? By definition, the scope of the claim is confined to nonobvious subject matter. Saying that such a method is obvious in view of the prior art is infected by the fallacy condemned in *Pleudemann*: it assumes that the inventor's own discovery (the product) is prior art.

In *In re Dillon*,[277] discussed above, which involved soot reduction hydrocarbon fuel/tetra-orthoester compositions, the Federal Circuit declined to rule separately on the patentability of applicant's claims to methods of using the novel compositions apart from the patentability of her claims to the *compositions* themselves because applicant did not separately argue the patentability of her method claims. It noted that "We make no judgment as to the patentability of claims that Dillon might have made and properly argued to a method directed to the novel aspects of her invention, except to question the lack of logic in a claim to a method of reducing particulate emissions by combusting."

[5] Prior Art Before the AIA

This discussion of existing law applies (and will continue to apply) to any patents granted on applications filed before March 16, 2013. In addition, the AIA retains many of the terms and phrases used in existing law, so cases construing those terms and phrases will continue to be relevant for patents issued on applications filed on or after March 16, 2013. Prior art under the AIA is discussed in § 2[C][6].

---

[272] 910 F.2d 823 (Fed. Cir. 1990).

[273] 475 F.2d 658 (C.C.P.A. 1973).

[274] *Pleuddemann*, 910 F.2d at 827.

[275] *See* Amgen Inc. v. U.S. Int'l Trade Comm'n, 902 F.2d 1532, 1538 (Fed. Cir. 1990).

[276] For a discussion of the Process Patents Amendments Act, and of Tariff Act Section 337, which cover, under some circumstances, use abroad of a process patented in the United States, see § 2E[2][b][iii].

[277] 919 F.2d 688 (Fed. Cir. 1990) (en banc). *See* § 2C[4][c][iii].

"Prior art" is a term of art in patent law. The Patent Act does not expressly define prior art for obviousness. Section 103 on nonobviousness refers to the "prior art."[278] Section 112 on disclosure refers to the "art . . . to which [the invention] pertains."[279] Section 102 on novelty and loss of right does not use the term "prior art" but lists seven conditions (subsections (a) through (g)) that preclude the grant of a patent on an invention.

Four of Section 102's conditions unquestionably define what is "prior art:" (1) Section 102(a), the primary novelty-defeating provision dealing with patents and publications anywhere and matter "known or used" by others in the United States; (2) Section 102(b), the "loss of right" or "statutory bar" provision dealing with patents and publications anywhere and matter "on sale" or "in public use" in the United States by the inventor or anyone else more than the one-year "grace period" prior to the inventor's filing of a patent application;[280] (3) Section 102(e), the provision on senior-filed patents by persons other than the inventor; and (4) Section 102(g), the provision on prior inventions in the United States by other persons.

Prior art for determining obviousness includes at least the following categories:

1. A printed publication or patent anywhere:

(a) by another if dated before the inventor's invention date, or

(b) by the inventor if dated more than one year before the date the inventor applies for a patent.

2. Anything in public use or on sale in the United States by the inventor or anyone else if dated more than one year before the date the inventor applies for a patent.[281]

3. Anything in secret commercial use by the inventor if dated more than one year before the date the inventor applies for a patent.

4. Anything "known or used" in a publicly accessible form in the United States by another if dated before the inventor's invention date.

---

[278] The obviousness section, Section 103, refers to Section 102 by excluding from patentability an invention that would have been obvious in view of the "prior art" even though that invention is not "identically disclosed or described as set forth in section 102." The problem with reading this as a straightforward incorporation of Section 102 as a definition of prior art is that some of the subsections of 102 do not deal with disclosures or descriptions. For example, subsection (c) deals with abandonment of an invention.

[279] 35 U.S.C. § 112.

[280] The similarity in wording between subsections 102(a) and 102(b) is a constant source of confusion in patent law. Section 102(a) is a *novelty* provision-determining whether subject matter is new as of the inventor's invention date in view of prior art of others. Section 102(b) is a *loss of right* provision, which contemplates that the right to a patent on an invention that was patentable as of the date of invention is lost when the inventor delays too long in filing a patent application. Different policy considerations support the two subsections.

[281] Public use or on sale activity may be excused by the experimental use doctrine. *See* § 2C[5][b][v].

5. Anything described in a United States patent, regardless of when it issues, by another if the application for that patent was filed in the United States before the inventor's invention date.

6. Anything invented in the United States by another if dated before the inventor's invention date.

A useful approach to "prior art" is to view it as having limits in four dimensions: (1) *source* (printed publication, patent, device in public use or on sale, device or process in secret use, unabandoned invention), (2) *place* (in the United States or in another country), (3) *time* (before the inventor's invention date or after that date but more than one year before the inventor's patent application filing date), and (4) *person* (the inventor or one other than the inventor).[282] An item is prior art only if it falls within the limits of one of the above categories in all four dimensions. For example, the following item falls within all the limits of category 1(a) and therefore qualifies as prior art:

Source:	Printed publication
Place:	China
Time:	A day before invention date but less than one year prior to patent date.
Person:	X, a person other than the inventor.

A change in one dimension may disqualify the item as prior art. If the above reference is a device in public use but not a printed publication (change in source), it is not prior art. If it was made by the inventor (change in person), rather than X, it is not prior art. But a change in another dimension may restore the item's status as prior art. If it is a device in public use rather than a printed publication, but is in the United States (change in place), it now falls into category 2 and it is prior art. If it is a printed publication and by the inventor but is more than one year prior to the patent application filing date (change in time), it now falls into category 1(b) and it is prior art.

Why is prior art so complex? The answer lies primarily in history and inertia. The statutory language in Section 102 traces to patent statutes enacted in 1836, 1839, 1870, and 1897. These old statutes adopted distinctions, such as those between acts "in this country" and acts in "a foreign country," that made sense at the time but are now obsolete. The 1952 Patent Act adopted and supplemented these old concepts. In 1966, a Presidential Commission recommended revision of the prior art provisions,[283] but Congress took no action on those recommendations. More recently, the United States joined multinational discussions of possible "harmonization" of the patent laws of major countries, which would necessarily bring major changes in the definition of prior art.

---

[282] *See* Chisum, *Sources of Prior Art in Patent Law*, 52 WASH. L. REV. 1 (1976); Chisum, *Foreign Activity: Its Effect on Patentability Under United States Law*, 11 INT'L REV. INDUS. PROP. & CR. L. 26 (1980).

[283] President's Commission on the Patent System, "TO PROMOTE THE PROGRESS OF . . . USEFUL ARTS" IN AN AGE OF EXPLODING TECHNOLOGY (1966).

[a]   Documentary Sources: Patents and Publications

Sections 102(a) and 102(b) list patents and descriptions in printed publications as patent-defeating events. Under Section 102(a), anything "patented" or "described in a printed publication" is prior art if it occurred before the inventor's invention date and is by one other than the inventor. Under Section 102(b), anything that is "patented" or "described in a printed publication" is prior art if it occurred more than one year before the inventor filed an application to obtain a patent on the invention and is by either the inventor or by anyone else.[284]

[i]   Publications

Any document reproduced and distributed anywhere in the world in a form accessible to the public is a "printed publication.[285] A document need not be set in type and reproduced in the traditional way to be "printed."[286] For example, a patent application microfilmed and deposited at five sub-offices of the Australian Patent Office is a printed publication.[287]

Conference papers[288] and advertising circulars[289] are printed publications. Internal corporate documents[290] and documents circulated to a small group under a pledge of confidentiality[291] are not publications.

A single copy of a document deposited in a library is a printed publication if it is indexed and available to the public.[292] A poster presentation of research findings at

---

[284] To illustrate with an example, assume that inventor I invents a widget on June 1, 2006 and applies for a patent on January 1, 2007. The following publications are prior art: (1) by person J on May 31, 2006 (Section 102(a), prior to the invention date), and (2) by inventor I on December 31, 2005 (Section 102(b), by inventor but more than one year prior to application filing). The following publications are not prior art: (1) by person J on July 1, 2006 (after date of invention but within one year of the application filing), and (2) by inventor I on January 2, 2006 (before invention date but by inventor and less than one year before application filing date).

[285] *See generally* D. CHISUM, PATENTS § 3.04.

[286] Philips Elec. & Pharmaceutical Industries Corp. v. Thermal & Elec. Industries, Inc., 450 F.2d 1164 (3d Cir. 1971).

[287] *In re* Wyer, 655 F.2d 221 (C.C.P.A. 1981).

[288] Massachusetts Institute of Technology v. AB Fortia, 774 F.2d 1104 (Fed. Cir. 1985) (a paper delivered at a conference in another country constitutes a "printed publication" when (1) prior to the conference, the author gave a copy of the paper to the head of the conference, (2) from 50 to 500 persons working in the pertinent art attended the conference, and (3) copies of the paper were distributed on request, without restrictions, to as many as six persons); Deep Welding, Inc. v. Sciaky Bros. Inc., 417 F.2d 1227 (7th Cir. 1969).

[289] Jockmus v. Leviton, 28 F.2d 812 (2d Cir. 1928). *See also* Garrett Corp. v. United States, 422 F.2d 874, 877–78 (Ct. Cl. 1970).

[290] *In re* Kratz, 592 F.2d 1169 (C.C.P.A. 1979); Northern Telecom, Inc. v. Datapoint Corp., 908 F.2d 931 (Fed. Cir. 1990) (private corporate documents stored in a private corporate library not a publication).

[291] General Tire & Rubber Co. v. Firestone Tire & Rubber Co., 349 F. Supp. 345, 353 (N.D. Ohio 1972), *aff'd*, 489 F.2d 1105 (6th Cir. 1973).

[292] *In re* Bayer, 568 F.2d 1357 (C.C.P.A. 1978). *See also In re* Hall, 781 F.2d 897 (Fed. Cir. 1986). In *Hall*, the Federal Circuit held that a doctoral thesis deposited in a library in Germany prior to the critical date of one year prior to the applicant's filing date was a printed publication as of the deposit date.

an academic conference is considered a publication,[293] but an oral lecture delivered at an academic conference which made an abstract available upon request is not a publication.[294] A grant proposal is a publication if it was included in a published list of proposals and the proposal itself was available under the Freedom of Information Act.[295]

A document is effective as a publication on the date when it first reaches members of the public or becomes accessible to the public.[296]

A publication's description anticipates, that is, completely defeats the novelty of a later invention, only if it is "enabling," that is, sufficient to teach a person of ordinary skill in the art how to make and use what is described.[297] A publication that is not enabling or that discloses an inoperative product or process does not anticipate but is part of the "prior art" for determining nonobviousness.[298]

[ii]   Patents

In the United States and most other countries, utility patents are printed for distribution and are, therefore, printed publications under Section 102(a). The question of what is "patented" arises with government protection grants that are not published on grant or are effective on a date earlier than publication.[299] Utility models, for example, a German *Gebrauchsmuster*,[300] and design registrations, for example, a German *Geschmacksmuster*,[301] are "patents."

The date exclusive rights vest in the patentee and can be enforced by an infringement suit is the patent date.[302] That date is no sooner than the date the

---

[293] *In re* Klopfenstein, 380 F.3d 1345 (Fed. Cir. 2004).

[294] Norian Corp. v. Stryker Corp., 363 F.3d 1321 (Fed. Cir. 2004).

[295] E.I DuPont de Nemours & Co. v. Cetus Corp., 19 U.S.P.Q.2d (BNA) 1174 (N.D.Cal. 1990).

[296] Constant v. Advanced Micro-Devices, Inc., 848 F.2d 1560, 1568–69 (Fed. Cir. 1988).

[297] *See, e.g.*, Reading & Bates Construction Co. v. Baker Energy Resources Corp., 748 F.2d 645 (Fed. Cir. 1984). In *Reading*, the court held that a one-page promotional brochure boasting of the results of a process was insufficient to constitute an enabling disclosure.

[298] Beckman Instruments, Inc. v. LKB Produkter AB, 892 F.2d 1547 (Fed. Cir. 1989); Paperless Accounting, Inc. v. Bay Area Rapid Transit Sys., 804 F.2d 659 (Fed. Cir. 1986); EWP Corp. v. Reliance Universal, Inc., 755 F.2d 898, 907 (Fed. Cir. 1985) ("A reference must be considered for everything it *teaches* by way of technology and is not limited to the particular *invention* it is describing and attempting to protect.").

[299] Whether something has been patented is often important under the foreign patenting bar provision, 35 U.S.C. § 102(d), discussed at § 2C[5][b][vii].

[300] Bendix Corp. v. Balax, Inc., 421 F.2d 809 (7th Cir. 1970).

[301] *In re* Talbott, 443 F.2d 1397 (C.C.P.A. 1971).

[302] *In re* Monks, 588 F.2d 308 (C.C.P.A. 1978). In *Monks*, the court held, as to a patent under then existing British law, patenting occurred on the later "sealing" date, not the earlier publication date. Though a patentee could collect damages from the date of publication, an infringement suit could not be filed until the date of sealing.

See also Ex parte Fujishiro, 199 U.S.P.Q. 36 (PTO Bd. App. 1977). In *Fujishiro*, the Board held that first publication of an application for a Japanese utility model 18 months after filing does not constitute patenting because such publication only grants the right to demand compensation in the form of a royalty, which right is enforceable only after later action.

contents of the document become publicly available.[303]

[b]   Nondocumentary Sources: Public Use and Sale

[i]   Known or Used by Others

Section 102(a) bars a patent if the invention was, before the applicant's invention date, known or used by another in the United States.[304] "Known or used" means knowledge or use accessible to the public.[305] If someone uses a process or machine in a nonsecret manner to produce articles for commercial purposes, the use is accessible to the public.[306] Secret and private use are not sufficient.[307] An "abandoned experiment" is not prior art under Section 102(a).[308] Something may be "known" in the United States even though it is not reduced to practice. For example, something is known when it is described in an unpublished document available to the public.[309]

[ii]   Statutory Bars

Section 102(b) bars a patent if the invention was (1) described in a printed publication in any country; (2) patented in any country; (3) on sale in the United States; or (4) in public use in the United States, more than one year prior to the effective filing date of the patent application disclosing the invention,. These four events are referred to as "statutory bars."[310] The statutory bars also create prior art for obviousness purposes.[311]

Section 102(b) is similar to Section 102(a) but differs in two important respects. First, the events often are by the inventor or his or her assignee. For example, a publication of an inventor's own corresponding patent application in another country is a statutory bar if the publication is more than one year before the effective United States filing date. If the inventor files a continuation-in-part application in the United States with new matter that is not entitled to an earlier parent filing date, the foreign published counterpart of the parent application is a bar with respect to claims dependent on the new matter.[312]

Second, Section 102(b) relates to the date one year before the patent application's filing, commonly called the "critical date." The period from the critical date to the filing date is, in a sense, a grace period. An inventor has up to one year to file a patent application in the United States after a public disclosure or

---

[303] *In re* Ekenstam, 256 F.2d 321 (C.C.P.A. 1958).

[304] *See generally* D. Chisum, Patents § 3.05.

[305] Carella v. Starlight Archery, 804 F.2d 135 (Fed. Cir. 1986); Connecticut Valley Enterprises, Inc. v. United States, 348 F.2d 949 (Ct. Cl. 1965).

[306] W.L. Gore & Associates, Inc. v. Garlock, Inc., 721 F.2d 1540 (Fed. Cir. 1983).

[307] Gillman v. Stern, 114 F.2d 28 (2d Cir. 1940); Kimball Int'l, Inc. v. Allen Organ Co., 212 U.S.P.Q. 584 (S.D. Ind. 1981).

[308] Lyon v. Bausch & Lomb Optical Co., 224 F.2d 530 (2d Cir. 1955).

[309] *In re* Borst, 345 F.2d 851 (C.C.P.A. 1965).

[310] *See generally* D. Chisum, Patents § 6.02.

[311] *See, e.g., In re* Kaslow, 707 F.2d 1366 (Fed. Cir. 1983).

[312] *See, e.g., In re* Ruscetta, 255 F.2d 687 (C.C.P.A. 1958). *See generally* D. Chisum, Patents § 6.02[9].

commercial use of the invention. Note that most non-U.S. patent systems do not allow a one-year period before the date of filing as the United States does. Instead, most jurisdictions treat *any* public disclosure before the filing date as barring a patent regardless of how long before the filing date the act was done.

Two of the statutory bars — patents and printed publications — are documentary sources and are the same for Section 102(b) as for Section 102(a).[313] The following subsections discuss the "public use" and "on sale" bars in Section 102(b) and the judicially-created "experimental use" exception.

[iii]   Public Use in the United States

Any nonsecret, nonexperimental use of the invention in the United States prior to the critical date is a public use bar.

In *Egbert v. Lippman*,[314] the Supreme Court held that a device could be in "public use" even though in ordinary use it was hidden from view. In 1855, one Barnes made a novel corset steel and gave it to his friend, Ms. Egbert. Ms. Egbert wore the steels for a considerable period, placing them in new corsets as the old ones wore out. Thereafter, Ms. Egbert and Mr. Barnes "intermarried." In 1863, Barnes had his wife cut open a corset and display the steels to another person. Barnes obtained a patent in 1866. The Court held the patent invalid because of public use more than one year prior to Barnes' patent application: "The inventor slept on his rights for eleven years."[315]

Private noncommercial use by the inventor is not public use,[316] but nonsecret use by a person who improperly obtained the idea from the inventor is.[317]

Secret use of a machine or process to make a product sold commercially is not public use if it is by someone other than the inventor,[318] but it is public use if it is by the inventor (or the inventor's employer or assignee).[319] Policy considerations govern the inventor secret commercial use rule; it is unfair for an inventor to use the invention for commercial profit for more than a year and thereafter apply for a patent because such activity delays commencement of the limited term of patent protection.[320]

Use outside the United States is not a public use bar, but extended use by the inventor before applying for a patent may constitute an abandonment of the

---

[313] *See* § 2C[5][a].

[314] 104 U.S. (14 Otto) 333 (1881).

[315] *Id.* at 337. For an insightful discussion of the decision that draws on history, gender theory, and policy, see Kara, Swanson, *Getting a Grip on the Corset: Gender, Sexuality and Patent Law*, 23 YALE JOURNAL OF LAW & FEMINISM 57 (2011).

[316] *See* Moleculon Research Corp. v. CBS, Inc., 793 F.2d 1261 (Fed. Cir. 1986).

[317] Lorenz v. Colgate-Palmolive-Peet Co., 167 F.2d 423 (3d Cir. 1948).

[318] W.L. Gore & Associates, Inc. v. Garlock, Inc., 721 F.2d 1540 (Fed. Cir. 1983).

[319] Kinzenbaw v. Deere & Co., 741 F.2d 383 (Fed. Cir. 1984); Metallizing Engineering Co. v. Kenyon Bearing & Auto Parts Co., 153 F.2d 516 (2d Cir. 1946).

[320] *See* § 2B[2].

invention.[321]

[iv]   On Sale in the United States

An applicant loses the right to patent if the invention is "on sale" in the United States more than one year before the date of application. In *Pfaff v. Wells Electronics, Inc.*,[322] the Supreme Court held that an invention is "on sale" when two conditions are met. First, the invention must be the subject of a commercial offer for sale. Second, the invention must be ready for patenting, which occurs in one of two ways: (i) proof of reduction to practice more than one year before the date of application or (ii) proof that more than one year before the date of application, the inventor had prepared drawings or other descriptions of the inventions that were sufficiently specific to enable a person having ordinary skill in the art to practice the invention.

The *Pfaff* decision overruled Federal Circuit precedent which applied a totality of the circumstances to determine if the invention had been on sale.[323] The Supreme Court in *Pfaff* adopted a rule that was intended to provide more certainty than the Federal Circuit approach. Subsequent case law has addressed several issues raised by the Pfaff standard.

First, the Federal Circuit has held that the existence of an offer is to be determined by "the law of contracts as generally understood."[324] Inventors can avoid triggering the on-sale bar by marketing their items and quoting prices without actually selling or offering to sell the invention.[325] Offers to license the invention do not trigger the on-sale bar, but commercial offers to use can.[326] General offers that do not specify the invention do not trigger the on sale bar.[327]

Second, the ready for patenting standard has also raised several issues. The Federal Circuit has held that ready for patenting is about the enablement of the invention rather than the conception.[328] An invention can be on sale even if the parties do not know that the invention is ready for patenting as long as the subject of the sale possessed each of the elements of the claimed invention.[329] Sales by

---

[321] *See* § 2C[5][b][vi].

[322] 525 U.S. 55 (1998).

[323] UMC Electronics Co. v. United States, 816 F.2d 647 (Fed. Cir. 1987).

[324] Group One Ltd. v. Hallmark Cards., Inc., 254 F.3d 1041, 1047 (Fed. Cir. 2001). *See also* Linear Tech. Corp. v. Micrel, Inc., 275 F.3d 1040 (Fed. Cir. 2001).

[325] *See, e.g.*, Gemmy Indus. Corp. v. Chrisha Creations, Ltd., 452 F.3d 1353 (Fed. Cir. 2006); Linear Tech. Corp. v. Micrel, Inc., 275 F. 3d 1040 (Fed. Cir. 2001).

[326] *In re* Kollar, 286 F.3d 1326 (Fed. Cir. 2002) (offer to license); Scaltech, Inc. v. Retec/Tetra, LLC., 269 F.3d 1321 (Fed. Cir. 2001) (on sale bar not triggered by offer to use).

[327] *See* Tec Air, Inc. v. Denso Mfg. Mich., Inc., 192 F.3d 1353 (Fed. Cir. 1999); Sparton Corp. v. United States, 399 F.3d 1321 (Fed. Cir. 2005).

[328] *See* Space Systems/Loral, Inc. v. Lockheed Martin Corp., 271 F.3d 1076 (Fed. Cir. 2001). *Cf.* Robotic Vision Systems, Inc. v. View Engineering, Inc., 249 F.3d 1307 (Fed. Cir. 2001) (finding on sale bar even when one inventor was uncertain about the working of the invention).

[329] *See Scaltech*, 269 F.3d at 1331; Abbott Laboratories v. Geneva Pharmaceuticals, Inc., 182 F.3d 1315 (Fed. Cir. 1999).

third parties can trigger the on-sale bar if the invention on sale covers all elements of the patented invention.[330]

Finally, a sale has to be between two separate entities for the on sale bar to be triggered, but the two entities can be related.[331]

[v]   Experimental Use Exception

A public use or sale is not a statutory bar if the inventor's primary purpose is to conduct experiments on the nature and utility of the invention. This experimental use exception is not stated in the patent statutes but is recognized by the courts on policy grounds.[332]

In *City of Elizabeth v. American Nicholson Pavement Co.*,[333] the Supreme Court held that experimental use to test the invention's qualities was not a "public use" within the meaning of the statute, even though it was a use in public. The privilege of experimentation does not end when the invention is proven to be minimally workable; it continues while the inventor determines whether the invention is superior to prior art devices.[334]

The experimental use exception applies only if there is genuine experimentation directed to the features of the invention that are the subject of the patent claim.[335] It does not apply to "market testing" to determine customer preferences.[336] Testing to obtain government approval to market a product is not necessarily "experimental" in a patent law sense.[337]

In *T.P. Laboratories, Inc. v. Professional Positioners, Inc.*, the Federal Circuit listed the following factors to be considered in determining whether a given usage was experimental:

(1)   the length of the test period in relation to tests of similar devices;

---

[330] Baxter Int'l v. Cobe Laboratories, Inc., 88 F.3d 1054 (Fed. Cir. 1996).

[331] *In re* Caveney, 761 F.2d 671 (Fed. Cir. 1985); Ferag AG v. Quipp, Inc., 45 F.3d 1562 (Fed. Cir. 1995).

[332] The experimental use exception, which relates to the effect of the inventor's activity on the right to obtain a patent, should be distinguished from the experimental purpose exception, which relates to liability for patent infringement. *See* § 2F[4][d].

[333] 97 U.S. 126 (1878).

[334] Cali v. Eastern Airlines, Inc., 442 F.2d 65 (2d Cir. 1971). *Compare* RCA Corp v. Data General Corp., 887 F.2d 1056, 1061 (Fed Cir. 1989) ("under our precedent, experimental use, which means perfecting or completing an invention to the point of determining that it will work for its intended purpose, ends with an actual reduction to practice.").

[335] Western Marine Electronics, Inc. v. Furuno Electric Co., 764 F.2d 840 (Fed. Cir. 1985). *See also* RCA Corp v. Data General Corp., 887 F.2d 1056 (Fed. Cir. 1989) (the experimental use doctrine does not excuse the inventor's offer, before the critical date, of the invention, which had already been reduced to practice, merely because the offer was of a system with additional components or was an offer to do developmental work).

[336] *In re* Smith, 714 F.2d 1127 (Fed. Cir. 1983). *See also In re* Mann, 861 F.2d 1581, 1582 (Fed. Cir. 1988). In *Mann*, the Federal Circuit held that display of a design for a wrought iron table at a trade show is a public use and is not subject to the experimental use exception: "Obtaining the reactions of people to a design . . . whether or not they like it. . . is not 'experimentation.' "

[337] Pennwalt Corp. v. Akzona, Inc., 740 F.2d 1573 (Fed. Cir. 1984).

(2)   whether payment is made for the device;

(3)   whether the user agreed to secret use;

(4)   whether progress records were kept;

(5)   whether persons other than the inventor conduct the asserted experiments.[338]

The experimental use exception does not apply to the disclosures in a printed publication or patent.[339]

[vi]   Abandonment

Section 102(c) bars a patent if the inventor "has abandoned the invention." Abandonment occurs when the inventor, by word or deed, intentionally relinquishes the right to obtain a patent.[340] Abandonment is rarely invoked as a basis for rejecting or invalidating patent claims.[341]

Mere delay in applying for a patent is not abandonment,[342] but abandonment may be inferred from an extended period of unexcused delay.[343]

Section 102(c) abandonment must be carefully distinguished from two other types of abandonment: (1) abandonment of a patent application, and (2) abandonment, suppression and concealment. As to the former, an inventor may file and then abandon a patent application without necessarily thereby abandoning rights in the invention.[344] The inventor may reapply if no other event creates a bar.[345] As to the latter, an inventor's delay in applying for a patent after a reduction to practice may be "abandonment, suppression and concealment" under Section 102(g), which will preclude the inventor from relying on the reduction to practice as the invention date for purposes of determining priority over a rival inventor.[346] The same delay would not necessarily justify a finding of abandonment of the invention and the inventor could have applied for and obtained a patent had a second inventor not appeared.

---

[338] 724 F.2d 965, 971–72 (Fed. Cir. 1984). *See also* U.S. Environmental Products Inc. v. Westall, 911 F.2d 713 (Fed. Cir. 1990).

[339] Pickering v. Holman, 459 F.2d 403 (9th Cir. 1972).

[340] Westinghouse Electric & Mfg. Co. v. Saranac Lake Electric Co., 108 F. 221 (N.D.N.Y. 1901).

[341] At one time, the Patent and Trademark Office followed a policy that an applicant for a patent "dedicated" or abandoned to the public subject matter disclosed but not claimed in a patent specification if, on the date a patent issued, no continuation application had been filed claiming that subject matter. This policy was overturned in *In re* Gibbs, 437 F.2d 486 (C.C.P.A. 1971).

[342] Bates v. Coe, 98 U.S. 31 (1878); Paulik v. Rizkalla, 760 F.2d 1270 (Fed. Cir. 1985); Moore v. United States, 194 U.S.P.Q. 423 (Ct. Cl. Trial Div. 1977). However, delay in filing a patent application may preclude a patent if one of the statutory bar events of section 102(b) has occurred more than one year prior to the application date.

[343] *See, e.g.*, Levinson v. Nordskog Co., 301 F. Supp. 589 (C.D. Cal. 1969).

[344] An applicant may abandon an application either expressly or by failing to file a timely response to an office action.

[345] Foster v. Magnetic Heating Corp., 297 F. Supp. 512, 518 (S.D.N.Y. 1968), *aff'd*, 410 F.2d 12 (2d Cir. 1969).

[346] *See* § 2D[3][f].

Consistent with the first-inventor-to-file system, the AIA does not retain abandonment of an invention before filing an application as a basis for invalidating a patent. However, old section 102(c) is presented here because it is relevant for patents that issue on applications filed before March 16, 2012. There also may be some relevance to the new prior commercial use defense, discussed in section 2G[7] below. This defense does not permit commercial uses by the defendant before abandonment of the use as a basis for the defense. The case law on what constitutes an abandonment may be relevant in this new context.

[vii]   Foreign Patenting

Section 102(d) bars a patent if the inventor obtains a patent or inventor's certificate in a foreign country and does not promptly apply for a patent in the United States.[347] The bar applies only if three conditions are met: (1) the inventor (or his legal representatives or assigns) applies for a patent on the invention in another country on the invention; (2) the inventor fails to apply for a patent on the invention in the United States within twelve months; and (3) a patent in the other country issues before the application is filed in the United States.

What is a "patent" and the patenting date are discussed in connection with Section 102(a).[348] Section 102 (d) may require precise determination of when a foreign application has been "filed" and whether the patent is "on" a particular invention. A foreign patent application will not be treated as an effective filing unless it adequately discloses the invention for which a patent is later sought in the United States under United States disclosure standards.[349]

A Section 102(d) bar can be avoided if an inventor applies for a U.S. patent within one year of an effective foreign filing, which is desirable to take advantage of the Section 119 Paris Convention priority right.

[c]   Senior-Filed Patents

Section 102(e), a complicated rule that codifies *Alexander Milburn Co. v. Davis-Bournonville Co.*,[350] bars an inventor from obtaining a patent for anything (except the inventor's own work[351]) disclosed in a United States patent granted to another ("the prior applicant") based on an application filed in the United States before the subsequent applicant's invention date.[352] Stated otherwise, everything disclosed in a United States patent with an effective United States filing date before an applicant's invention date is prior art in determining novelty and nonobviousness of

---

[347] *See generally* D. Chisum, Patents § 6.04.

[348] *See* § 2C[5][a][ii].

[349] American Stainless Steel Co. v. Rustless Iron Corp., 2 F. Supp. 742 (D. Md. 1933), *aff'd*, 71 F.2d 404 (4th Cir. 1934).

[350] 270 U.S. 390 (1926). *Milburn* adopts the "whole contents" approach to prior-filed patent applications by others and applies that approach to both the novelty and "inventive step" requirements. This contrasts with the law of many other countries, which apply the "whole contents" approach to the determination of novelty but not inventive step.

[351] *See* § 2C[5][f].

[352] *See generally* D. Chisum, Patents § 3.07.

the applicant's claimed invention — unless the disclosure is the applicant's own work.

Section 102(e) does not apply to patents and applications by the same inventor because it refers to patents issued to "another." If a company or person owns different inventors' applications, Section 102(e)'s prior art effect may be avoided by careful planning.[353]

[i]   The *Milburn* Doctrine

In *Milburn*,[354] the following fact pattern came before the Supreme Court:

1. On January 31, 1911, Clifford applied for a patent. The application *disclosed* (but did not *claim*) item X.

2. On March 4, 1911, Whitford applied for a patent claiming X.

3. On February 6, 1912, a patent issued to Clifford.

4. On March 4, 1912, a patent issued to Whitford.

The issue was whether Clifford's disclosure of X was prior art as to Whitford's patent claiming X. Because pending U.S. applications were held in secrecy, as of March 4, 1911 (Whitford's filing date and presumptive invention date), Clifford's disclosure was neither a publication nor a patent and was not available to the public. Because Clifford did not *claim* X,[355] the doctrine that claimed subject matter is "constructively" reduced to practice and a prior invention did not apply.[356] Nevertheless, the Supreme Court held that Clifford's disclosure of X was prior art and rendered invalid Whitford's patent claiming X. The Court reasoned that Patent Office delays in examining and issuing patents should not impact substantive patent rights. If the Patent Office had promptly issued a patent to Clifford, the patent, as a publication, would have anticipated Whitford's claim to X.

In 1952, Congress codified the *Milburn* doctrine as Section 102(e).[357] In 1965,

---

[353] If related applications are filed on the same date, Section 102(e) will not apply upon issue of any patents.

If related applications are filed on different dates, the applications may be combined into one continuation-in-part (CIP) application. This is made possible by a 1984 amendment. *See* § 2D[4][b][v]. The application may then issue as a single patent. If the combined inventions are viewed as separate and distinct, a restriction requirement may be entered, requiring the filing of separate divisional applications. If one application issues as a patent, it cannot then be used as a "reference" against a related divisional application.

If none of the above precautions are taken as to a senior-filed, commonly-owned application by a different inventorship entity, issue of a patent on the senior application will create Section 102(e) prior art. *See, e.g., In re* Bartfeld, 925 F.2d 1450 (Fed. Cir. 1991) (a "Section 102(e)/103 rejection," which uses as prior art for obviousness purposes an earlier-filed patent's disclosures against a later-filed, different inventive entity application or patent's claims, cannot be overcome by a terminal disclaimer; the Section 103 prior art disqualifier, added by a 1984 amendment, does not apply to Section 102(e)).

[354] Alexander Milburn Co. v. Davis-Bournonville Co., 270 U.S. 390 (1926).

[355] For that reason, no interference to determine priority of invention between Clifford and Whitford could be declared.

[356] *See* § 2D[3][c].

[357] 35 U.S.C. § 102(e): "A person shall be entitled to a patent unless — . . . (e) the invention was

the Supreme Court held that Section 102(e) and the *Milburn* doctrine apply to the determination of prior art for nonobviousness as well as for novelty.[358] Consequently, everything disclosed in a United States patent is prior art as of its effective *filing* date in the United States Patent and Trademark Office.

An inventor may eliminate a United States patent as prior art by showing an invention date prior to the patent's filing date, even if the invention date is many years before the inventor's filing date.[359] "Swearing behind" a reference patent is not possible if the reference patent claims the same invention as the applicant or patentee because only an interference proceeding may resolve an invention priority issue.[360]

[ii] Foreign Priority Applications

A United States patent's filing date, for determining its prior art effect, is its actual United States filing date. A United States patent is not effective as a reference as of its foreign priority filing date.[361] In *In re Hilmer*,[362] the fact pattern was as follows:

1. On January 24, 1957, Habicht filed in Switzerland.

2. On July 31, 1957, Hilmer filed in Germany.

3. On January 23, 1958, Habicht filed in United States.

4. On July 25, 1958, Hilmer filed in United States.

5. A United States patent issued to Habicht.

The issue was whether the Habicht United States patent's disclosures were prior art as to Hilmer's claimed invention. Under the Paris Convention priority right and Section 119, Hilmer was entitled to the German filing date as the invention date, but the court held that the Habicht patent was effective as a reference only as of its actual United States filing date, after Hilmer's effective priority filing date. Section 119, which provides that a foreign priority filing shall have the "same effect" as a filing in the United States, is only a patent-protecting, not a patent-defeating provision.

International attention has focused on whether *Hilmer* is a violation of Paris Convention Article 4B, which provides that a subsequent filing within the twelve

---

described in a patent granted on an application for patent by another filed in the United States before the invention thereof by the applicant for patent, *or on an international application by another who has fulfilled the requirements of paragraphs (1), (2), and (4) of section 371(c) of this title* before the invention thereof by the applicant for patent." (The italicized language was added later to implement the Patent Cooperation Treaty.)

[358] Hazeltine Research, Inc. v. Brenner, 382 U.S. 252 (1965).

[359] *See* § 2C[5][f]. A statutory bar (such as a U.S. or other patent that *published* more than one year before the applicant/patentee's filing date) cannot be eliminated as a reference regardless of how early the date of invention of the applicant/patentee. *See* § 2C[5][c].

[360] *In re* Eickmeyer, 602 F.2d 974 (C.C.P.A. 1979). *See* § 2D[3].

[361] An international application under the Patent Cooperation Treaty designating the United States is prior art as of the date certain formalities are complied with.

[362] 359 F.2d 859 (C.C.P.A. 1966).

month priority period "shall not be invalidated by reason of any acts accomplished in the interval, in particular, another filing. . . ." This Article relates to invention priority when two parties claim a patent on the same invention. *Hilmer* recognizes the right of the applicant with the earliest priority filing date to prevail in any contest over invention priority. In *Hilmer*, the person claiming patent rights (Hilmer) was accorded his priority filing date not only for the purpose of priority of invention but also for the purpose of determining what is prior art. An argument that *Hilmer* violates Article 4B assumes that the Article not only guarantees a priority applicant the right to a patent but also guarantees the right to be free of patent protection on related developments by subsequent applicants; that is, it assumes Article 4B assures senior applicants, such as Habicht, that no subsequent filer can obtain a patent claiming anything disclosed in the senior-filed application.

Some of the unfortunate effects of *Hilmer* can be ameliorated by aspects of interference practice, such as by broadly defining the interference count, and by applying interference estoppel and the doctrine of lost counts.[363] The *Hilmer* doctrine described below will no longer be relevant to patents issued under the AIA, because the foreign filing date is the effective filing date for all patents or patent applications under the new section 102(a)(2).

[iii] Continuation Applications

A United States patent's filing date for determining its prior art effect is the filing date of a prior United States application if at least one claim in the patent is entitled to the benefit of the prior application under Section 120.[364]

Consider the following example:

1. A files a parent application disclosing X.

2. A files a continuation-in-part ("CIP") application disclosing X and Y.

3. A files a continuation application claiming X and Y.

4. A obtains a patent claiming Y.

A's Y patent, which issued on the third application is entitled to the benefit of the second application filing date (assuming the conditions of Section 120 are met) but not the first application filing date because that application does not disclose element Y. Therefore, the patent will be effective as a reference for its disclosure of X only as of the second application filing date-even though the disclosure of X was carried forward from the first application to the patent.[365]

[iv] Issuance

A United States patent application's disclosures become effective as prior art as of its filing date only if the application *issues* as a patent containing those disclosures.

---

363 *Cf. In re* Zletz, 893 F.2d 319 (Fed. Cir. 1989); *In re* Kroekel, 803 F.2d 705 (Fed. Cir. 1986). *Compare In re* McKellin, 529 F.2d 1324 (C.C.P.A. 1976).

364 *In re* Wertheim, 646 F.2d 527 (C.C.P.A. 1981); *In re* Klesper, 397 F.2d 882 (C.C.P.A. 1968).

365 *In re* Wertheim, 646 F.2d 527 (C.C.P.A. 1981).

A patent application that is abandoned is not prior art as such.[366] A citation to a prior abandoned patent application in a later issued patent does not make that abandoned application prior art as of its filing date,[367] but such citation will make the abandoned application available to the public and evidence of public knowledge under Section 102(a) as of the publication date of the later patent.[368]

A 1985 statutory procedure provides for a "statutory invention registration" ("SIR") as an alternative to a patent.[369] A patent applicant may waive the right to receive a patent and request a SIR. The PTO may issue an SIR if it finds that the application complies with Section 112 disclosure requirements.[370] The SIR does not protect the claimed invention from unauthorized use,[371] but it is a way of making the application's disclosures prior art against other persons' subsequently filed applications because the SIR's disclosures are effective as prior art as of its effective United States filing date.[372]

[d]   Prior Invention and Derivation

[i]   Prior Invention — Section 102(g)

Note that the AIA replaces interferences with the new derivation proceedings. Therefore, section 102(g) will be irrelevant once the full provisions of the AIA are in effect. However, since the first-inventor-to-file rules are not retroactive, the material below will still be relevant for applications filed before March 16, 2013.

Section 102(g) bars a patent if "before the applicant's invention thereof the invention was made in this country by another who had not abandoned, suppressed, or concealed it." Whether this subsection creates prior art has been a point of much controversy.[373]

First invention arises in priority disputes, such as an interference in the Patent and Trademark Office.[374] For example, if A and B each apply for a patent on the same invention, the person who first invented the subject matter in the United

---

[366] Brown v. Guild (The Corn-Planter Patent), 90 U.S. (23 Wall.) 181, 210–11 (1874).

As to the ways in which a patent application may become abandoned, see § 2D [1] and § 2D[2][b][iv]. An abandoned patent application is not a constructive reduction to practice of the invention by the applicant. *See* § 2D[3][c].

[367] *In re* Lund, 376 F.2d 982 (C.C.P.A. 1967).

[368] 37 CFR § 1.14(b).

[369] 35 U.S.C. § 157. *See* 37 C.F.R. § 1.297.

[370] *See* § 2C[6]. The application is not examined for compliance with the novelty or nonobviousness requirements.

[371] 35 U.S.C. § 157. Concurrently with obtaining a SIR, the applicant may file a continuation-in-part application in order to obtain patent protection. *See* § 2D[2][b]. The disclosures and claims of the SIR will not be prior art or be used to establish a double patenting rejection against a claim in such an application, provided the later claim is not for the same subject matter that is claimed in the SIR. 37 C.F.R. Sec. 1.106(e). *See* § 2D[2][a][ii].

[372] If the patent application contents are simply published, the contents are effective as prior art only as of the publication date.

[373] 35 U.S.C. § 102(g). *See generally* D. Chisum, Patents § 5.03[3][c].

[374] *See* § 2D[5].

States will prevail (unless that person derived the idea from the other party).

First invention also arises in patentability disputes. Consider the following example:

1. A reduces invention X to practice.

2. B applies for a patent on Y.

3. A applies for a patent on X.

4. A obtains a patent on X.

Section 102(e) will not apply because B has a filing date before A's filing date. Court decisions hold that A's invention of X may nevertheless be prior art against B's application on Y. In an interference, A can use evidence of reduction to practice from any country that is a member of the World Trade Organization and signatory of the Agreement on Trade Related Aspects of Intellectual Property (TRIPS). In a judicial proceeding, however, A can only use evidence of reduction to practice in the United States.[375]

A 1984 amendment to Section 103, the statutory provision on nonobviousness, provides that "subject matter developed by another person, which qualifies as prior art only under subsection . . . (g) of section 102 . . . shall not preclude patentability under this section where the subject matter and the claimed invention were, at the time the invention was made, owned by the same person or subject to an obligation of assignment to the same person." Under this amendment, in the above example, A's invention of X will not be prior art for purposes of assessing the obviousness of B's invention of Y if A and B, at the time of B's invention of Y, owe a legal obligation to assign any patent rights on inventions to a single person (such as their mutual employer).[376] The invention of A may still be used to show a complete anticipation of B's claimed invention under Section 102 because the 1984 Amendment only deals with prior art for purposes of Section 103 obviousness.

[ii]   Derivation — Section 102(f)

Note that under the AIA, derivation is important in determining when third-party prior art may serve to defeat novelty. The AIA creates a derivation proceeding to replace interference proceedings. As with section 102(g) materials, the material below will still be relevant for applications filed before March 16, 2013.

Section 102(f), which bars a patent if the applicant "did not himself invent the subject matter sought to be patented,"[377] enforces the originality requirement. A person may not obtain a patent on an invention derived from some other person or source.

The derivation issues frequently arise in invention priority disputes, such as in a

---

[375] *See* 35 U.S.C. § 102(g)(1)–(2).

[376] 37 C.F.R. 1.106(d). The same provision is made as to prior art under Section 102(f). *See* § 2C[5][e] [ii]. As to patent right ownership of inventions created in an employment relationship, see § 2G[1].

[377] *See generally* D. Chisum, Patents §§ 5.03[3][f], 10.04[4].

PTO interference.[378] For example, if A and B separately apply for a patent on the same invention, A may contend that B derived a complete conception of the invention from A.[379] If A proves his contention, he prevails in the interference.

The matter is not free from doubt, but it seems that if an inventor derives a specific item of information (but not the whole invention) from another, then the derived information is prior art.[380]

A 1984 amendment to Section 103 (the statutory provision on nonobviousness) provides that "subject matter developed by another person, which qualifies as prior art only under subsection (f) . . . of section 102 . . . shall not preclude patentability under this section where the subject matter and the claimed invention were, at the time the invention was made, owned by the same person or subject to an obligation of assignment to the same person." Under this provision, information that B derived from A will not be prior art for purposes of assessing obviousness of B's invention if A and B, at the time of B's invention, owe a legal obligation to assign any patent rights on inventions to a single person (such as their mutual employer).[381] Information from A may still be used to show a complete anticipation of B's claimed invention under Section 102 because the 1984 Amendment only deals with prior art for purposes of obviousness under Section 103.

[e]   Invention Date

Prior art must, of course, be "prior." The three novelty provisions — Sections 102(a), 102(e), and 102(g) — refer expressly to the applicant's invention date.

The applicant's invention date is presumptively the filing date of a patent application adequately disclosing the invention. Pre-filing-date references, for example, publications, patents, or items known or used in the United States, may be eliminated as prior art in three ways.

First, the applicant may establish an invention date before the reference.[382] An invention date is determined according to the same rules that apply in determining invention priority in an interference between rival inventors.[383]

---

[378] *See* § 2D[5].

[379] *See* Applegate v. Scherer, 332 F.2d 571, 573 n.1 (C.C.P.A. 1964).

[380] *See* 37 C.F.R. § 106(d).

[381] 37 C.F.R. 1.106(d). The same provision is made as to the prior art effect of prior invention under Section 102(g). As to patent right ownership of inventions created in an employment relationship, *see* § 2G[1].

[382] During the course of an examination of a patent application, an examiner may reject a claim in view of a particular reference. The applicant may eliminate that reference by filing a verified statement of facts establishing a date of invention prior to the reference. 37 C.F.R. § 1.131. Such a statement is commonly referred to as a "Rule 131 Affidavit."

A Rule 131 affidavit may be used to avoid a disclosure in a U.S. patent with a prior filing date only if that prior patent does not claim the same invention as the applicant. If the applicant and the reference patent claim substantially the same invention, then a Rule 131 affidavit is improper and the appropriate procedure is an interference to resolve the issue of priority of invention between the application and the prior patent. *See* § 2D[3]. *In re* Eickmeyer, 602 F.2d 974 (C.C.P.A. 1979).

[383] *In re* Mulder, 716 F.2d 1542 (Fed. Cir. 1983); *In re* Suska, 589 F.2d 527 (C.C.P.A. 1979). An invention date is established by showing a conception and reduction to practice in the United States. The

Second, the applicant may establish that the disclosures of the reference derive from his own work.[384]

Third, the applicant may establish that he had, before the date of the reference, invented either as much of the subject matter of the claimed invention as is disclosed in the reference[385] or enough to make the reference disclosure obvious to a person of ordinary skill in the art.[386] This showing of partial invention possession suffices only if the subject matter is part of the claimed invention (as for example a species chemical compound falling within a claim to a generic class of chemical compounds).[387]

The above rules on avoiding a reference relate only to the three novelty provisions (Section 102(a), (e), and (g)). A reference that is a Section 102(b) statutory bar cannot be eliminated as a reference by showing a prior invention date.[388]

[f]   Inventive Entities

The three novelty provisions (Sections 102(a), 102(e), and 102(g)) refer, expressly or by implication, to acts and disclosures "by another," that is, by some person other than the inventor of the patent claim's subject matter.

A separate inventive entities theory governs whether a reference is "by another." Under this theory, the sole work by one person or the joint work of a group of persons is "by another" as to later work by a different person or group of persons even though one or more persons may be members of both entities.[389] For example, a patent by A, and a publication disclosing the joint work of A, B and C are regarded as by inventive entities differing from later work by A and B jointly, B and C jointly, and B alone.[390]

---

rules on determining a date of invention are discussed at § 2D[5][a].

[384] *In re* DeBaun, 687 F.2d 459 (C.C.P.A. 1982); *In re* Katz, 687 F.2d 450 (C.C.P.A. 1982). An inventor's own prior work and disclosures are not prior art against his later attempt to obtain a patent unless such work or disclosures are Section 102(b) statutory bars. *See* § 2C[5][b][ii].

[385] *In re* Moore, 444 F.2d 572 (C.C.P.A. 1971); *In re* Stempel, 241 F.2d 755 (C.C.P.A. 1957).

[386] *In re* Rainer, 390 F.2d 771, 773 (C.C.P.A. 1968).

[387] *In re* Tanczyn, 347 F.2d 830 (C.C.P.A. 1965).

[388] 37 C.F.R. Sec. 1.131. *See In re* Foster, 343 F.2d 980 (C.C.P.A. 1965).

[389] *In re* Land, 368 F.2d 866 (C.C.P.A. 1966). *But cf.* Shields v. Halliburton Co., 667 F.2d 1232 (5th Cir. 1982).

[390] In the example, depending on the facts, the successive work by A, A+B+C, A+B and B+C may be so closely connected in nature and result as to be a single joint invention. General Motors Corp. v. Toyota Motor Co., 667 F.2d 504 (6th Cir. 1981). *See* § 2D[1][b][i].

If each inventive entity is under an obligation to assign patent rights to a single person (*e.g.*, a common employer), the separate developments are not prior art under Sections 102(f) or (g) for obviousness purposes. *See* § 2C[5][e]. Developments by separate inventive entities will still constitute prior art under Sections 102(f) and (g) for novelty purposes and are prior art under Sections 102(a) and (e) for both novelty and obviousness purposes. *See* § 2C[5][d].

[6] Prior Art Under the AIA

The AIA expands the definition of prior art and the relevant critical dates for novelty and nonobviousness purposes. For applications filed on or after March 16, 2013, there will now be only two relevant critical dates, the date of the application and one year before the date of the application.

Under the new version of Section 102(a), the following constitute prior art if they occur before the date of the application:

1. A patent or printed publication by anyone anywhere in the world.

2. Anything in public use or on sale, or otherwise available to the public, by anyone anywhere in the world.

3. Anything described in a patent issued or in a patent application published anywhere and naming another inventor.

The first two categories of prior art track the law under the 1952 Patent Act, but they expand the existing definition of prior art geographically and to include anticipations both by the applicant and by others. The phrase "otherwise available to the public" substitutes for "known or used," and the current law is presumably applicable to the new provision. The last of these six, described in the new section 102(a)(2), is what embodies the new first inventor to file system.

The AIA also substitutes a safe harbor for the existing statutory bars. While the current section 102(b) considers only prior art if dated "more than one year prior to the date of the application," the new version of section 102(b) states that certain disclosures are not prior art if made one year or less before the date of the application. These disclosures include:

1. Disclosures made by the inventor or someone who obtained the subject matter from the inventor.

2. Subject matter publicly disclosed by the inventor or someone who obtained the subject matter from the inventor.

Although there is some disagreement about what Congress meant by "disclosures" under section 102(b), the general view is that "disclosures" includes the items of prior art under section 102(a) listed above.

The AIA also excludes disclosures made in a patent or a patent application under section 102(a)(2) from the prior art if (A) the subject matter was obtained directly or indirectly from the inventor; (B) the subject matter had previously been publicly disclosed by the inventor or someone who had obtained the subject matter from the inventor; or (C) the subject matter disclosed and the claimed invention were owned by the same person or subject to an obligation of assignment to the same person not later than the effective filing date of the application. For the purposes of determining joint ownership under the third exception, a joint research agreement is relevant to determining the scope of an invention and the identities of the applicants.

A simple example will illustrate how the new rules implement a first-inventor-to-file system. Suppose Alex files a patent application on January 1, 2015. What prior art would allow rejection of the application for lack of novelty? Let us first consider what prior art would be excluded. If Alex discloses the invention in a patent or printed publication or through a public use or a sale on or after January 1, 2014, then such disclosures will not constitute prior art in the United States. Furthermore, if a third party discloses the invention on or after January 1, 2014, then this disclosure will not be prior art if the third party obtained the subject matter from Alex. If the third party did not obtain the invention from Alex, then the third party's disclosure is not prior art if made after Alex's disclosure. The grace period under new section 102(b) gives the inventor latitude in exploiting the invention for one year before filing the application and also narrows the scope of third party disclosures that become invalidating prior art.

Outside of the one year period, prior art includes the traditional categories of prior art under the old section 102(a), but the AIA expands all of them to include prior art within and outside the United States and created by the inventor and third parties. Thus, under new section 102(a)(2), if Alex files a patent application on January 1, 2015, but the patent examiner discovers a previously-filed patent or patent application that anticipates the invention and that names another inventor, this patent or application will defeat the novelty of Alex's invention. But Alex can defeat this prior art under new section 102(b)(2) by showing either that the prior art patent or application was obtained from Alex's work or that Alex or a third party who had obtained the invention from Alex had made a public disclosure before the date of patent or the application. Again, how all this works out in actual practice will not be known until after March 16, 2013, the effective date of these provisions.

Finally, the prior art described here all applies to the nonobviousness analysis. The main difference is that nonobviousness is determined as of the date of filing of the application rather than as of the date of invention under old section 103.

§ 2D   PATENT PROCESS

To obtain a patent, an inventor must file an application fully disclosing his invention in the Patent and Trademark Office (PTO). The PTO examines the application and, if the invention meets all patentability conditions, grants a patent.

[1]   Patent Prosecution

[a]   Overview

The process of obtaining a patent from the PTO is referred to as "prosecution." Patent prosecution involves the following steps:

First, a patent agent must draft the patent application. Drafting an application is an important and complex undertaking. The drafter must understand the technology surrounding an invention and describe the invention accurately and completely. The specification and drawings filed with the application must fully disclose the invention, and are printed and distributed as part of the issued patent. The patent system's primary purpose is that the information so disclosed benefit the public by promoting the progress of the useful arts.[391]

Next, the applicant files the application with the PTO. The PTO assigns an examiner, who reviews the application, searches the prior art, examines the application for compliance with the conditions of patentability, and issues an "office action" that allows or rejects each claim, and cites the statutory basis for any rejection. Within the response period,[392] the applicant must prepare and file a response,[393] which may contain amendments (including amended, canceled, or new claims); arguments why the original or amended claims are patentable in view of the cited prior art; a Rule 131 affidavit showing an invention date before the effective date of any prior art that is not a statutory bar;[394] or a Rule 132 affidavit presenting factual evidence supporting patentability (such as commercial success, long-felt need, expert opinion, or test data).[395] The examiner considers all of the material and enters another office action allowing or rejecting the claims. This process continues until the examiner either determines the remaining claims are allowable, or enters a "final action" rejecting one or more claims.

If the examiner allows the claims, the PTO sends the applicant a notice of allowance. The applicant must then pay the issue fee within three months, or the application is abandoned.[396] If the examiner finally rejects any claims, the applicant may cancel the rejected claims so that a patent can issue on the allowed claims, appeal to the Board of Patent Appeals and Interferences, or else abandon the application and, if desired, file a continuation or a continuation-in-part application.

In an appeal, the applicant may file a brief and request an oral hearing before the Board. The examiner will file an answer to the applicant's brief, and the applicant may file a reply brief to any new responses. The Board affirms or reverses the rejections and may enter new rejections. If the Board affirms the rejections or enters new ones, the applicant may either file an appeal to the Court of Appeal for the Federal Circuit, or else file a civil action in the District Court for the District of Columbia.[397] In *Kappos v. Hyatt*,[398] the Supreme Court held that the applicant can introduce evidence not previously submitted to the USPTO in a civil action filed in

---

[391] U.S. Const. Art. I, § 8, cl. 8; Kewanee Oil Co. v. Bicron Corp., 416 U.S. 470 (1974).

[392] The statutory response period is six months, but the PTO may, and habitually does, set a shorter period, typically three months. An applicant may file a response after the set period, but before the expiration of statutory period, by paying a special fee.

If the PTO receives no response within the statutory period, the application is abandoned, but applicant may revive it by showing the abandonment was unintentional, 37 C.F.R. § 1.137(b), or unavoidable. 37 C.F.R. § 1.137(a).

[393] A response to an office action may create a prosecution history estoppel. *See* § 2F[2][c].

[394] 37 C.F.R. § 1.131.

[395] 37 C.F.R. § 1.132.

[396] 35 U.S.C. § 151. An applicant may revive an application abandoned for failure to pay the issue fee by showing that the failure was unintentional or unavoidable, just as with abandonment for failure to respond to an office action. An applicant may also file a continuation or a continuation-in-part application. *See* § 2D[3][b].

[397] 35 U.S.C. §§ 141, 145. These two ways of seeking judicial review, appeal and civil action, differ substantially. An appeal to the Federal Circuit is based on the PTO record and new evidence may not be presented. The Federal Circuit reviews PTO fact findings under the Administrative Procedure Act, which allows the court to reject an agency finding only if it is "arbitrary, capricious, an abuse of

the District Court and that the District Court should review this new evidence de novo.

The AIA replaces the Board of Patent Appeals and Interferences (BPAI) with the Patent Trial and Appeals Board (PTAB). The PTAB consists of the Director and Deputy Director of the USPTO, the Commissioner for Patents, the Commissioner for Trademarks, and administrative patent judges. Through three-judge panels, the PTAB is responsible for (i) reviewing appeals of adverse rulings of patent examiners, (ii) reviewing appeals of reexaminations, and (iii) conducting derivation proceedings, inter partes reviews, and post-grant reviews. Decisions of the PTAB may be appealed directly to the United States Court of Appeals for the Federal Circuit. The provisions creating the PTAB are effective September 16, 2012, and its duties will arise as the relevant provisions creating the new derivation proceedings, inter partes reviews, and post-grant reviews become effective.

[b]   Unity of Invention — Restriction

If an inventor claims two or more independent and distinct inventions in one application, the PTO examiner may require restriction to one of the inventions.[399] The purpose of restriction is to preserve the integrity of the PTO fee and classification systems.

If the examiner requires restriction,[400] the applicant must elect one of the independent and distinct inventions,[401] and only claims reading on the elected invention will be examined. An examiner's restriction requirement cannot be appealed but is subject to review by petition to the Commissioner.[402] If the examiner does *not* require restriction and a patent issues, the patent's validity may not later be challenged for misjoinder of independent inventions.[403]

---

discretion, or . . . unsupported by substantial evidence." 5 U.S.C. § 706(2)(A),(E); Dickinson v. Zurko, 527 U.S. 150 (1999).

In a civil action, the applicant may present further evidence supporting patentability, including expert testimony, and the district court holds a trial on any disputed issue of fact, in which the entire PTO record is considered along with any testimony. *Zurko*, 527 U.S. at 164; Hyatt v. Kappos, 625 F.3d 1320 (Fed. Cir. 2010) (en banc). The applicant or the PTO may appeal the district court's decision to the Federal Circuit, which will review the district court's factual findings under the "clearly erroneous" standard. Fed. R. Civ. P. 52(a)(6).

[398] 132 S. Ct. 1690 (2012).

[399] 35 U.S.C. § 121.

[400] The restriction and election requirement may be made before examination on the merits and usually will be made by a telephone call to the applicant's attorney or agent.

[401] The applicant may request reconsideration by the examiner of the requirement but must still make a provisional election. 37 C.F.R. § 1.143. A restriction requirement is not a rejection on the merits and cannot be appealed to the Board of Patent Appeals and Interferences. 35 U.S.C. § 121; 37 C.F.R. § 1.144.

[402] *See In re* Watkinson, 900 F.2d 230, 233 (Fed. Cir. 1990) ("[N]either this court nor the board has jurisdiction in this proceeding to review the merits of a requirement for restriction under section 121, as a restriction requirement is a matter within the discretion of the examiner and is not tantamount to a rejection of claims.").

[403] 35 U.S.C. § 121.

The applicant may pursue patent protection for the non-elected inventions by filing divisional applications, which are entitled to the filing date of the application ("parent") from which they divide.[404] A patent issuing on a parent application may not be used as a "reference" against the claims in a divisional application if two conditions are met: (1) the filing of the divisional application is in response to an actual restriction requirement,[405] and (2) the claims in the divisional application are "consonant" with the restriction requirement.[406]

[c]   Confidentiality

Section 122 provides that, subject to certain exceptions, all patent applications must be published 18 months after the earliest filing date claimed by the applicant.[407] However, an application is not published if it is (1) no longer pending; (2) subject to a secrecy order; (3) a provisional application; or (4) an application for a design patent.[408] In addition, if the applicant may request that an application not be published if the applicant certifies that he or she will not file a patent application on the same invention in another country, or under a multilateral international agreement, that requires such publication.[409]

[d]   Amendments

After filing an application with the PTO, an applicant may amend the specification, claims or drawings, but only within the severe constraints of the rule barring "new matter" additions to pending patent applications.[410] The new matter prohibition severely restricts the right to add to or alter the specification[411] and forces use of continuation-in-part applications to introduce new information into a filed patent specification.[412] Claim amendments and additions are not "new matter" and are permissible if, but only if, they are supported by the original specification disclosures.[413]

---

[404] *Id.*

[405] There is no protection from such use as a reference if the applicant voluntarily files a divisional application, *In re* Ockert, 245 F.2d 467, 468–69 (C.C.P.A. 1957), or if the PTO withdraws the restriction requirement, *In re* Ziegler, 443 F.2d 1211 (C.C.P.A. 1971).

[406] Gerber Garment Technology, Inc. v. Lectra Systems, Inc., 916 F.2d 683 (Fed. Cir. 1990).

[407] 35 U.S.C. § 122(b)(1)(A).

[408] 35 U.S.C. § 122(b)(2)(A).

[409] 35 U.S.C. § 122(b)(2)(B).

[410] 35 U.S.C. § 132. *See generally* D. Chisum, Patents § 11.04.

[411] *But see In re* Lundak, 773 F.2d 1216 (Fed. Cir. 1985) (the new matter bar is not violated when an applicant (1) deposits a cell line with a recognized depository five days after filing the application, and (2) amends the specification to add depository data (including an accession number)).

[412] *See* § 2D[4][b].

[413] *In re* Rasmussen, 650 F.2d 1212 (C.C.P.A. 1981). All claims must meet the enablement requirement. *See* § 2D[2][a]. Claims added after the original filing date must also meet the description requirement. *See* § 2D[2][b].

[e] Duty of Candor

Patent applicants have a duty to disclose to the PTO information of which they are aware that is material to the examination and to refrain from misrepresenting facts.[414] Violation of this candor duty may be "inequitable conduct" that renders the patent's claims unenforceable.[415]

An applicant may submit to the PTO an "information disclosure statement" listing patents, publications, and other information relevant to patentability.[416] The statement is optional, but its submission is encouraged as a means of complying with the duty of candor. An item's inclusion is not an admission that it is a pertinent prior art reference nor a representation that a prior art search has been made.[417]

[2] Disclosure Requirements

A complete patent application has four parts: (1) a specification, including at least one claim; (2) drawings, if "necessary to the understanding of the subject matter sought to be patented";[418] (3) an inventor's oath or declaration;[419] and (4) a filing fee.[420] To obtain a filing date,[421] the applicant must file the first two items with the PTO,[422] and the last two items may be provided within a specified time period.[423]

The specification has two parts: (1) a portion describing the invention, and (2) the claims, which precisely define the scope of the exclusive rights a patent will confer.[424] The descriptive portion must comply with the disclosure requirements;[425] the claims must comply with the clarity requirements.[426]

---

[414] 37 C.F.R. § 1.56. *See generally* D. CHISUM, PATENTS §§ 11.03[4], 19.03.

[415] *See* § 2F[4][b].

[416] 37 C.F.R. § 1.97.

[417] 37 C.F.R. § 1.97(d),(h).

[418] 35 U.S.C. § 113; 37 C.F.R. § 1.81(a). If drawings are necessary, they must be submitted with the specification to establish a filing date. A drawing that illustrates the subject matter but is not necessary may be submitted after the filing date. A post-filing date drawing cannot overcome an enabling disclosure deficiency or be used to interpret the scope of any claim. 37 C.F.R. §§ 1.81(c), (d).

[419] The person or persons identified as the inventor or inventors in the application must execute an oath or declaration. 35 U.S.C. § 115. If the application is made by one other than the inventor, the oath or declaration is made by the applicant. 37 C.F.R. § 1.64.

[420] 35 U.S.C. § 111.

[421] An early filing date is important to avoid the possible statutory bars under 35 U.S.C. § 102(b) (see § 2C[5][b][ii]) and to take advantage of the right of priority based on an application previously filed in another country (see § 2H[2]). The first person to file is also the presumptive first inventor in an invention priority interference. *See* § 2D[5][a].

[422] 35 U.S.C. § 111(b); 37 C.F.R. § 1.53(c).

[423] 37 C.F.R. § 1.53(f). Another fee is due if the last two items are submitted separately.

[424] 35 U.S.C. § 112.

[425] *See* §§ 2D[2][a], [b], and [c].

[426] *See* § 2D[3].

[a]   Enablement Requirement

The specification and drawings must provide sufficient information about the invention so as "to enable any person skilled in the art to which it pertains, or with which it is most nearly connected, to make and use the same."[427]

[i]   Claim Scope

The patent claims define the "invention" for enablement purposes. The amount of supporting disclosure depends on the patent claim's breadth[428] and the degree of predictability in the pertinent art (technological area). The broader the claim and the less predictable the art, the narrower must be the claim.

In *Amgen, Inc. v. Chugai Pharmaceutical Co.*,[429] the Federal Circuit held that the district court properly held invalid for want of enablement the patentee's generic claims to all possible genetic sequences that have activity resembling that of the specific DNA sequence encoding for a protein the patentee discovered. The patent related to human erythropoietin (EPO), a 165-amino acid protein that stimulates red blood cell production. The court noted that "[T]he number of claimed DNA encoding sequences that can produce an EPO-like product is potentially enormous:" "[O]ver 3,600 different EPO analogs can be made by substituting at only a single amino acid position, and over a million different analogs can be made by substituting three amino acids."

A claim so broad that it covers products or processes in the prior art is improper because of the novelty and nonobviousness requirements, regardless of the disclosure's adequacy.[430]

[ii]   Experimentation

The specification and drawings must be enabling to a person of ordinary skill in the pertinent art, and therefore they need not disclose what is well known in the art.[431]

A specification disclosure that requires a person of ordinary skill in the art to make adjustments or experiment to make and use the claimed invention is enabling

---

[427] 35 U.S.C. § 112. *See generally* D. Chisum, Patents § 7.03.

[428] *In re* Hyatt, 708 F.2d 712, 714 (Fed. Cir. 1983). In *Hyatt*, the court stated "the enabling disclosure of the specification [must] be commensurate in scope with the claim under consideration."

An amendment that *narrows* a claim's scope by adding a specific limitation may fail to find adequate support in the specification and thus violate either the enablement requirement or the description requirement. Therefore, under some circumstances, a broader claim may be supported while a narrower claim is not. *Cf.* DeGeorge v. Bernier, 768 F.2d 1318 (Fed. Cir. 1985). In *DeGeorge*, the court construed a claim to electrical circuitry in a word processor as not including word processing features such as a printer and a data recording mechanism. Consequently, the specification was sufficiently enabling even though it made insufficient disclosure of such features.

[429] 927 F.2d 1200 (Fed. Cir. 1991).

[430] *See* §§ 2C[3] and [4].

[431] Lindemann Maschinenfabrik GMBH v. American Hoist & Derrick Co., 730 F.2d 1452, (Fed. Cir. 1984), *appeal after remand*, 895 F.2d 1403 (Fed. Cir. 1990).

if the amount and kind of experimentation required is reasonable.[432] It is not enabling if unreasonable experimentation is required.[433] How much experimentation is reasonable depends on the circumstances, including prevailing practices in the technological area. In *In re Wands*,[434] the Federal Circuit articulated the following factors to consider in determining whether experimentation is undue: (1) the quantity of experimentation necessary; (2) the amount of direction or guidance presented in the patent; (3) the presence or absence of working examples; (4) the nature of the invention; (5) the state of the prior art; (6) the relative skill of those in the art; (7) the unpredictability of the art; and (8) the breadth of the claims.

[iii] Other Enablement Issues

The specification and drawings must be enabling as of the application filing date. Prior art that becomes available after that date cannot be considered in determining sufficiency of disclosure.[435] Likewise, post-filing date developments that enable previously unknown variations cannot be relied upon to establish nonenablement.[436]

A specification may incorporate by reference other sources such as issued patents, pending patent applications, publications and other documents in lieu of reciting them in full. However, material necessary for enablement may not be incorporated by reference if the material is not publicly accessible.[437] PTO policy is that only U.S. patents or allowed U.S. patent applications may be incorporated by reference to supply information essential for enablement. Publications and foreign patents may be incorporated only as background or illustration of the state of the art.[438]

Material improperly incorporated by reference may in some circumstances be added to the specification by amendment.[439] It is best not to use incorporation by

---

[432] *See, e.g.*, Cross v. Iizuka, 753 F.2d 1040 (Fed. Cir. 1985) (the enablement requirement's how-to-use aspect was met even though the specification did not disclose dosage levels for the claimed compounds because (1) the disclosed utility was pharmacological activity in an *in vitro* environment, rather than a therapeutic use, and (2) one skilled in the art could determine the dosage level without undue experimentation).

[433] *In re* Gardner, 427 F.2d 786 (C.C.P.A. 1970). *Compare In re* Bundy, 642 F.2d 430 (C.C.P.A. 1981).

[434] 858 F.2d 731 (Fed. Cir. 1988). *Compare In re* Hata, 6 U.S.P.Q.2d 1652 (Bd. Pat. App. & Int'f 1987).

[435] *In re* Glass, 492 F.2d 1228 (C.C.P.A. 1974). In *Glass*, the court held that an applicant could not rely on four patents issuing after the filing date to show conditions necessary to produce claimed product.

[436] *In re* Hogan, 559 F.2d 595 (C.C.P.A. 1977).

[437] Quaker City Gear Works, Inc. v. Skil Corp., 747 F.2d 1446 (Fed. Cir. 1984). In *Quaker City*, the court held that a German industrial standard that was not readily accessible to persons in the United States could not be incorporated by reference.

[438] Manual of Patent Examining Procedure § 608.01(p).

[439] *In re* Hawkins, 486 F.2d 569 (C.C.P.A. 1973).

To make an amendment adding material that is secret as of the filing date, the material must be specifically identifiable. *In re* Fouche, 439 F.2d 1237 (C.C.P.A. 1971). In *Fouche*, the applicant filed one application that referred to an example in "our application No. . . . ." The applicant was allowed to amend to add the serial number and filing date of the other application since there was only one such application pending.

reference so heavily that the application is difficult to understand without continuous reference to that material.

New and unexpected properties and advantages of a claimed invention are often critical to establishing a new product's patentability if it closely resembles prior art products.[440] For policy reasons, it is desirable that the properties and advantages be disclosed in the specification,[441] but their disclosure is not necessary to comply with the enablement requirement, which relates to information on making and using the invention. Therefore, properties or advantages may be added in a continuation-in-part application, or possibly in a reissue, without losing the original filing date.[442]

An inventor need not disclose or even understand how his invention works, as long as he makes adequate disclosure of how to make and use the invention.[443]

[iv]   Deposit of Biological Material

If a product or process cannot be made without access to special materials, machinery, or methods, the applicant must assure that the public has access to the materials, machinery, or methods when the patent issues.[444]

Starting material availability is a problem when the claimed product or process requires biological material, for example, a particular strain of microorganism or genetically-altered cells, because it may be impossible to adequately describe how to isolate that particular strain without extensive effort.[445]

[b]   Written Description Requirement

The specification must contain a written description of the invention. The description requirement's purposes are to assure that the applicant was in full possession of the claimed subject matter on the application filing date and to allow other inventors to develop and obtain patent protection for later improvements and subservient inventions that build on applicant's teachings.[446]

---

[440] *See* § 2C[4][c].

[441] *In re* Davies, 475 F.2d 667 (C.C.P.A. 1973).

[442] Carter-Wallace, Inc. v. Otte, 474 F.2d 529 (2d Cir. 1972). *See* § 3D[2].

[443] *In re* Bowden 183 F.2d 115, 119 (C.C.P.A. 1950). *Compare* Newman v. Quigg, 877 F.2d 1575, 1581–82 (Fed. Cir. 1989).

[444] White Consolidated Indus., Inc. v. Vega Servo-Control, Inc., 713 F.2d 788 (Fed. Cir. 1983); *In re* Ghiron, 442 F.2d 985, 991 (C.C.P.A. 1971). In *White*, the court held that a specification did not meet the enablement requirement when it failed to set forth a necessary computer program, which could be produced only by substantial effort. In *Ghiron*, the court held that a specification did not meet the enablement requirement as to a computer method when the method required modification of computer hardware and the applicant failed to show that a person of ordinary skill in the art would have known how to make such modifications.

[445] As to when a deposit is in fact required, see *Ex parte* Rinehart, 10 U.S.P.Q.2d 1719, 1720 (Bd. Pat. App. & Int'f 1989); *Ex parte* Goeddel, 5 U.S.P.Q.2d 1449 (Bd. Pat. App. & Int'f 1987). *See also* Amgen, Inc. v. Chugai Pharmaceutical Co., Ltd., 927 F.2d 1200 (Fed. Cir. 1991) (no best mode violation by failure to deposit cell cultures transformed with the patented DNA sequence).

[446] Fields v. Conover, 443 F.2d 1386 (C.C.P.A. 1971). *See also* Ariad Pharmaceuticals, Inc. v. Eli Lilly & Co., 598 F.3d 1336, 1345 (Fed. Cir. 2010) (en banc) ("A description of the claimed invention allows the

The description requirement is distinct from the enablement requirement.[447] A specification may contain sufficient information to enable a person of ordinary skill in the art to make and use a later claimed invention but fail to describe that invention.[448] For example, a specification may discuss only a single compound (X) and contain no language indicating that a broader invention is contemplated. The disclosure of X may enable a person of ordinary skill in the art to make and use compounds Y and Z. Nevertheless, the class consisting of X, Y, and Z has not been adequately described. A claim to the class of X-Y-Z added after the filing date would not be entitled to that date.[449]

The written description requirement does not demand any particular form of disclosure, nor does it requires that the specification recite the claimed invention literally ("*in haec verba*").[450] The test for sufficiency is whether the disclosure of the application relied upon reasonably conveys to those skilled in the art that the inventor had possession of the claimed subject matter as of the filing date.[451] This does not require either examples or an actual reduction to practice; a constructive reduction to practice that in a definite way identifies the claimed invention can satisfy the written description requirement. Conversely, reduction to practice outside of the specification is not enough; rather, it is the specification itself that must demonstrate "possession."[452]

The written description requirement ensures that the inventor was in possession of the claimed invention at the time of application. Its original purpose was to allow an applicant to take advantage of an earlier filed application if the subsequent application did not add new matter.[453] The Federal Circuit has expanded the doctrine as a limitation on the scope of the patent owner's rights by limiting the claims to the scope of the written description.[454] The Federal Circuit's approach to the written description requirement has created tension with the rules of claim construction that state that specifications can be used to interpret the claims, but not limit them. This tension remains unresolved.[455]

[PTO] to examine applications effectively; courts to understand the invention, determine compliance with the statute, and to construe the claims; and the public to understand and improve upon the invention and to avoid the claimed boundaries of the patentee's exclusive rights.").

[447] *Ariad Pharmaceuticals*, 598 F.3d at 1340, 1344–45; *In re* Barker, 559 F.2d 588 (C.C.P.A. 1977).

[448] *In re* Di Leone, 436 F.2d 1404 (C.C.P.A. 1971).

[449] A continuation-in-part application may be filed adding material to the specification to support the claim to the class of X-Y-Z (see § 2D[2] [b][i]) but that application would not be entitled to the benefit of the original application's filing date as to the X-Y-Z claim.

[450] Ariad Pharmaceuticals, Inc. v. Eli Lilly & Co., 598 F.3d 1336, 1352 (Fed. Cir. 2010) (en banc).

[451] *Id.* at 1351.

[452] *Id.* at 1352.

[453] 35 U.S.C. § 120 (benefit of earlier filing date in the United States). *See* Vas-Cath Inc. v. Mahurkar, 935 F.2d 1555 (Fed. Cir. 1991); Kennecott Corp. v. Kyocera International, Inc., 835 F.2d 1419 (Fed. Cir. 1987).

[454] *See* University of Rochester v. G.D. Searle & Co., Inc., 358 F.3d 916 (Fed. Cir. 2003); The Gentry Gallery, Inc. v. The Berkline Corp., 134 F.3d 1473 (Fed. Cir. 1998); Regents of the University of Calif. v. Eli Lilly & Co., 119 F.3d 1559 (Fed. Cir. 1997).

[455] *See* Ariad Pharmaceuticals, Inc. v. Eli Lilly and Co., 598 F.3d 1336 (Fed. Cir. 2010); Lizardtech, Inc. v. Earth Resource Mapping, Inc., 424 F.3d 1336 (Fed. Cir. 2005); 424 F.3d 1336 (Fed. Cir. 2006).

[c]   Best Mode Requirement
[i]   In General

Effective September 16, 2011, failure to comply with the best mode requirement cannot be a basis for invalidating a patent or any claim under the AIA. However, the AIA does retain the requirement of disclosing the best mode under section 112. The purpose for removing best mode as a basis for invalidation was to harmonize US patent law with that of the other countries, which do not have a best mode requirement. The practical implications of retaining the best mode requirement while not including any means of policing the requirement are yet to be worked out. We retain much of the material on best mode because it may still be relevant under section 112.

The specification must set forth the "best mode contemplated by the inventor of carrying out his invention."[456] The best mode requirement's purpose is to prevent inventors from obtaining patent protection while concealing from the public preferred embodiments of their inventions.[457]

Before the 1952 Patent Act's enactment, the patent statutes stated the enablement requirement in terms similar to the first part of Section 112 (1st Paragraph). They also stated that "in case of a machine, he [the inventor] shall explain the principle thereof, and the best mode in which he has contemplated applying that principle, so as to distinguish it from other inventions." Another provision made it a defense to an infringement suit that "for the purpose of deceiving the public the description and specification filed by the patentee in the Patent Office was made to contain less than the whole truth relative to his invention."[458]

The 1952 Act broadened the "best mode" provision to cover all inventions. The legislative history is sparse; the Revisers' Notes indicate the broader provision derived not only from the "best mode" provision but also from the "whole truth" defense.

The best mode requirement differs from the enablement requirement; a patent specification may comply with the latter but not the former.[459] The "best mode" is the one the inventor considers best, not the best in fact.[460] The standard is subjective and focuses on whether the inventor failed to reveal an embodiment he knew of and preferred.[461]

---

[456] 35 U.S.C. § 112. *See generally* D. CHISUM, PATENTS § 7.05.

[457] *In re* Gay, 309 F.2d 769, 772 (C.C.P.A. 1962). *See also* Christianson v. Colt Industries Operating Corp., 870 F.2d 1292, 1302 n.8 (7th Cir. 1989) ("[T]he best mode requirement is intended to allow the public to compete fairly with the patentee following the expiration of the patents.").

[458] Rev. Stat. § 4920, *reproduced in* D. CHISUM, PATENTS, App. 19-77.

[459] Spectra-Physics, Inc. v. Coherent, Inc., 827 F.2d 1524, 1532 (Fed. Cir. 1987).

[460] *See, e.g.*, Chemcast Corp. v. Arco Industries Corp., 913 F.2d 923, 926 (Fed. Cir. 1990) ("The best mode inquiry focuses on the inventor's state of mind as of the time he filed his application — a subjective, factual question.").

[461] *In re* Bundy, 642 F.2d 430 (C.C.P.A. 1981).

The best mode requirement is not "subjective" in a culpability sense. The inventor need not have intended to conceal something from the public; indeed, the Federal Circuit need not find a best mode violation even when the inventor *did* intend to conceal something.[462]

Few decisions deal explicitly with whose intent controls. The cases recite the statutory requirement that it is the best mode contemplated by "the inventor." For many patent law purposes, the patent rights owner, such as an inventor's employer who has taken those rights by assignment, is placed in the inventor's shoes, but there is no judicial suggestion that this is the case with the best mode requirement.

Early Federal Circuit cases confirmed that best mode disclosure sufficiency depended, in part, on the prior art.[463]

Must an inventor not only set forth the best mode but also state that it is preferred? In *Randomex, Inc. v. Scopus Corp.*,[464] the Federal Circuit found that, under the particular circumstances before it, the indiscriminate disclosure of the preferred mode along with other modes did not violate the best mode requirement. The court held that the indiscriminate disclosure by tradename of the patentee's proprietary cleaning fluid along with inferior fluids satisfied the best mode requirement because (i) the patent described the brand as a "non-residue detergent solution," (ii) commercial substitutes were readily available, and (iii) the accused infringer easily "reverse engineered" the patentee's cleaning fluid.

[ii]   Computer Programs

Court decisions give a mixed message on whether a complete version, such as by source code, of a preferred computer program used in carrying out the invention must be disclosed. In *In re Sherwood*,[465] the court found no violation in the applicant's failure to disclose an existing computer program suitable for carrying out the claimed seismic prospecting method. The specification did describe the program's features. The applicant presented affidavit evidence that the specification would enable a skilled programmer to prepare a suitable program.

> In general, writing a computer program may be a task requiring the most sublime of the inventive faculty or it may be a task requiring only droning use of a clerical skill. The difference between the two extremes lies in the creation of mathematical methodology to bridge the gap between the information one starts with (the "input") and the information that is desired (the "output"). If these bridge-gapping tools are disclosed, there would

---

[462] Randomex, Inc. v. Scopus Corp., 849 F.2d 585 (Fed. Cir. 1988).

[463] W.L. Gore & Associates, Inc. v. Garlock, Inc., 721 F.2d 1540 (Fed. Cir. 1983). *Cf.* Hybritech Inc. v. Monoclonal Antibodies, Inc., 802 F.2d 1367 (Fed. Cir. 1986) (evidence that screening methods used to identify monoclonal antibodies with necessary characteristics (such as affinity, i.e., ability to bind with a particular antigen) is labor-intensive, time-consuming, and carried out by sophisticated persons does not show concealment of a best mode for screening or producing monoclonal antibodies).

[464] 849 F.2d 585 (Fed. Cir. 1988).

[465] 613 F.2d 809 (C.C.P.A. 1980).

seem to be no cogent reason to require disclosure of the menial tools known to all who practice this art.[466]

On the other hand, in *White Consolidated Industries, Inc. v. Vega Servo-Control, Inc.*,[467] the court held a patent on a computer control machine tool system invalid for noncompliance with the *enablement* requirement, because the specification indicated that a computer language named "SPLIT" was used to carry out the invention and SPLIT was a company's trade secret. The district court also invalidated the patent for best mode noncompliance, but the appeals court did not rule on that issue.

[iii]   Trade Secrets

The best mode requirement forces the inventor to disclose information he might otherwise preserve as a trade secret. Must an inventor disclose details of a contemplated best mode if they include trade secrets owned by another? In *Chemcast Corp. v. Arco Industries Corp.*,[468] the court stated that an inventor need not disclose what he or she does not know, but that otherwise trade secrecy is no excuse for failure to set forth a contemplated best mode. The patentee's claimed invention required a material of specified hardness. The inventor preferred the material of a certain supplier ("R-4467" of Reynosol Corporation), but the specification identified neither the supplier nor the trademark nor the material's characteristics. The court said: "whatever the scope of Reynosol's asserted trade secret, to the extent it includes information known by [the inventor] that he considered part of his preferred mode, section 112 requires that he divulge it."[469]

[iv]   Time Frame

Case law confirms that the best mode is that contemplated as of the *filing date;* a patentee's use of a different mode in commercial embodiments does not establish a best mode violation.[470] The date-of-filing rule entails grave risk of an inadvertent violation when a patent application discloses one mode and the inventor, still working in the laboratory, develops a better mode a day or two before the application is filed.

Whether an applicant on filing a continuation or continuation-in-part application must "update" the best mode disclosure is an issue upon which there is a dearth of authority. The statutory basis for finding a duty to update would simply be that a continuation or CIP application is still an application with a specification and Section 112 states that the specification shall set forth the best mode. On the other hand, imposing the duty to update may be a considerable burden on applicants; if a new best mode has been generated since the filing date, the applicant could not file a "continuation" because the addition of the new mode would probably be

---

[466] *Id.* at 816.

[467] 713 F.2d 788 (Fed. Cir. 1983).

[468] 913 F.2d 923 (Fed. Cir. 1990).

[469] *Id.* at 930.

[470] Texas Instruments Inc. v. U.S. Int'l Trade Comm'n, 871 F.2d 1054, 1061 (Fed. Cir. 1989) (that the patent's assignee manufactured products containing a different or better form of product than that disclosed in the patent "is not pertinent to whether the specification disclosed" the best mode).

viewed as "new matter" that would convert the application to a "continuation-in-part."[471]

When an inventor files a patent application abroad and then, within a year, files a corresponding application in the U.S., section 119 provides a right of priority.[472] Generally, a "foreign priority" application must disclose the invention in the manner required by the U.S. patent disclosure statute,[473] which includes the best mode requirement. Thus, to obtain U.S. priority benefits, the foreign inventor or company must set forth the "best mode" as of the filing date abroad, even though the laws of the country in question may not require such a disclosure. Must the best mode disclosure be updated upon filing in the United States? The district court decision in *Tyler Refrigeration Corp. v. Kysor Industrial Corp.* said "no": Section 119 "provides that the effective date of the later filed U.S. . . . application is entitled to the . . . filing date . . . in Japan. Thus, in determining the best mode under Section 112, it is the knowledge held at and before that date and not at some later date."[474]

[d]   Inventor Identification

A patent application must be "made, or authorized to be made, by the inventor"[475] except in statutorily defined exceptional circumstances.[476] The inventor or inventors must apply even if they have assigned ownership rights to another, such as an inventor's employer.[477] The inventor must read and understand the application and sign a declaration or oath stating that he believes he is the first inventor. Even in the exceptional cases in which someone other than the inventor applies, the application must identify the actual inventor or inventors. Inventor identification may be corrected upon a satisfactory proof that an error was made

---

[471] *Cf.* Johns-Manville Corp. v. Guardian Industries Corp., 586 F. Supp. 1034, 1065 (E.D. Mich. 1983) (as to refinements developed after filing and before continuation-in-part application, "[p]laintiff would have been obligated to disclose this refinement if it were essential to the successful practice of the invention, and if it related to amendments to the continuation-in-part which were not present in the parent application"), *aff'd without op.*, 770 F.2d 178 (Fed. Cir. 1985).

[472] 35 U.S.C. § 119.

[473] Kawai v. Metlesics, 480 F.2d 880 (C.C.P.A. 1973).

[474] 601 F. Supp. 590, 605 (D. Del. 1985), *aff'd*, 777 F.2d 687 (Fed. Cir. 1985).

[475] 35 U.S.C. § 111; 37 C.F.R. § 1.41(a). If an inventor's authorization is questioned, then the applicant must show authorization. 37 C.F.R. § 41(d). In an application containing multiple claims, not all the named inventors need be inventors of all the claims' subject matter. *See* § 2D[2][d][iii].

[476] 35 U.S.C. §§ 117–118. Section 117 allows a legal representative of the inventor to apply if the inventor is dead or legally incapacitated. *See* 37 C.F.R. § 1.43. Section 118 allows a person other than the inventor (including a company) to apply if that person establishes a "sufficient proprietary interest" (*i.e.* ownership of the patent rights of the inventor) and either (1) the inventor cannot be reached or found after a diligent effort, or (2) the inventor refuses to sign. *See* 37 C.F.R. §§ 1.42–.43. Similarly, in the case of a joint invention, one joint inventor may apply alone on behalf of the joint inventors if the other joint inventor cannot be found or refuses to join. 35 U.S.C. § 116; 37 C.F.R. § 1.47(a). The ownership of patent rights is discussed at § 2G.

[477] 37 C.F.R. § 1.46. After the application is filed in the name of the inventor, further prosecution of the application may be carried on by the assignee of the whole interest to the exclusion of the inventor. 37 C.F.R. § 1.32.

without deceptive intent.[478]

The AIA permits the applicant to submit a substitute statement if (i) the individual inventor is deceased, under legal incapacity, or cannot be reached or found after diligent effort; or (ii) the individual inventor is under an obligation to assign the invention but has refused to make the oath or declaration. Because the failure to include the inventor's oath or declaration may be cured under the AIA, incorrectly identifying the inventors will no longer be a basis for invalidating a patent.

An invention may be sole or joint. When more than one person works on a project, who is an inventor depends on the quality of the contributions each makes to the claimed invention.[479]

[i]   Sole Invention

A sole invention occurs when one person conceives of the essential features or elements that represent an advance over the prior art. A person remains a sole inventor even if others posed a problem to be solved (rather than devised the solution),[480] made minor contributions or suggestions,[481] or participated in reducing the invention to practice by building and testing an embodiment.[482] One who conceives of a complete invention is a sole inventor even though another discovers its novelty or distinguishing features.[483]

[ii]   Joint Invention

A joint invention occurs when two or more persons contribute to the invention conception. People may be joint inventors "even though (1) they did not physically work together or at the same time, [or] (2) each did not make the same type or amount of contribution."[484]

In *Monsanto Co. v. Kamp*, the court discussed joint invention:

> A joint invention is the product of collaboration of the inventive endeavors of two or more persons working toward the same end and producing an invention by their aggregate efforts. To constitute a joint invention, it is necessary that each of the inventors work on the same subject matter and make some contribution to the inventive thought and to the final result. Each needs to perform but a part of the task if an invention emerges from all of the steps taken together. It is not necessary that the entire inventive

---

[478] *See* § 2D[2][d][iv].

[479] Inventorship rules differ from country to country. Person A may be the sole inventor of an invention in the United States but a joint inventor with person B in another country. A United States application must comply with United States inventorship standards, even if the application relies on a priority filing in another country.

[480] Garrett Corp. v. United States, 422 F.2d 874, 881 (Ct. Cl. 1970).

[481] Shatterproof Glass Corp. v. Libbey-Owens Ford Co., 758 F.2d 613 (Fed. Cir. 1985).

[482] Minerals Separation, Ltd. v. Hyde, 242 U.S. 261 (1916).

[483] MacMillan v. Moffett, 432 F.2d 1237, 1239 (C.C.P.A. 1970); *In re* Zenitz, 333 F.2d 924 (C.C.P.A. 1964). *Compare* General Tire & Rubber Co. v. Jefferson Chem. Co., 497 F.2d 1283 (2d Cir. 1974).

[484] 35 U.S.C. § 116. The quoted phrases were added to Section 116 by a 1984 amendment.

concept should occur to each of the joint inventors, or that the two should physically work on the project together. One may take a step at one time, the other an approach at different times. One may do more of the experimental work while the other makes suggestions from time to time. The fact that each of the inventors plays a different role and that the contribution of one may not be as great as that of another, does not detract from the fact that the invention is joint, if each makes some original contribution, though partial, to the final solution of the problem.[485]

In *General Motors Corp. v. Toyota Motor Co.*,[486] the Sixth Circuit held that a joint invention may occur when one person or a group of people makes an operable but imperfect embodiment of an invention and a second person or group makes an improved embodiment, all part of a research project.

[iii]   Separate Claims

A patent application may contain more than one claim, each claim varying in coverage.[487] Early cases stated that the inventor or inventors named in the application must be the correct inventive entity as to the subject matter of all the claims. For example, it was not proper for A and B to file an application with claim 1 covering X and claim 2 covering Y if A and B were the joint inventors of X but A was the sole inventor of Y.

A 1984 amendment provides that persons may apply for a patent jointly even though "each did not make a contribution to the subject matter of every claim of the patent."[488] In the example above, A and B's application claiming X and Y is proper. In *Smithkline Diagnostics, Inc. v. Helena Laboratories Corp.*,[489] the Federal Circuit held that the amendment codifies the better rule prevailing prior to its enactment and, therefore, applies to pending cases involving pre-1984 cases.

When multiple inventors are named, it is still necessary that each has made an inventive contribution to at least one claim.[490] The PTO may require the applicants to identify the inventive entity and invention date of each claim's subject matter.[491] Identification may be necessary because one claim's subject matter may be prior art in determining the another claim's patentability.[492]

---

[485] 269 F. Supp. 818, 824 (D.D.C. 1967). The Congressional Report on the 1984 amendment to Section 116, which partially defines joint invention, cites *Monsanto*.

[486] 667 F.2d 504 (6th Cir. 1981).

[487] *See* § 2D[3][g].

[488] 35 U.S.C. § 116.

[489] 859 F.2d 878 (Fed. Cir. 1988).

[490] 37 C.F.R. § 1.45(c).

[491] 37 C.F.R. § 1.110.

[492] 37 C.F.R. § 78(c). For a discussion of prior art, see §§ 2C[5] and 2C[5][g].

In the text example, the separately claimed subject matters X and Y are not prior art to each other for obviousness purposes under Section 102(f) or 102(g) if the inventive entities A-B and A were under a duty to assign the patent rights to a single entity (such as their employer). *See* §§ 2C[5][e] and [g]. Separately invented and claimed subject matters X and Y may be prior art to each other under Sections 102(f) or 102(g) if A and B worked for different companies that separately owned the patent rights, or

Claim amendments or additions may change the inventive entities. In the example above, if the claim to X (by A and B) is cancelled, leaving only the claim to Y (by B), the application must be amended to delete A.[493] If a third claim for subject matter Z is added, and Z is a joint invention by A, B, and C, the application must be amended to add C.[494]

[iv]   Inventorship Error Correction

It is difficult to determine who is an inventor, and errors are often made in identifying inventors in patent applications. If the error was made without deceptive intention, the inventor identification may be corrected. For example, if a patent issues to A for X, and B is the correct sole inventor of X, it is possible to correct the patent and substitute B for A as the named inventor. Factual errors and judgment errors are correctable.[495]

Section 116 provides for correcting inventorship in pending patent applications.[496]

Section 256 provides two methods for correcting inventorship in issued patents.[497] First, the parties and assignees may petition the PTO. Second, a court before whom an inventorship question is raised may order correction. With the latter method, correction may be possible even if there is a dispute among the parties.[498]

In *MCV Inc. v. King-Seeley Thermos Co.*,[499] the Federal Circuit interpreted Section 256 as explicitly authorizing judicial resolution of co-inventorship contests:

---

under Section 102(a) if they have been published or patented anywhere or known or used in the United States. *See* § 2C[5][a].

Placing the subject matters of X and Y in one application rather than in separate applications eliminates the problem of one being prior art against the other under Section 102(e). *See* § 2C[5][d].

[493] 37 C.F.R. § 1.48(b). The amendment is by a petition, which must include a statement "identifying each named inventor who is being deleted and acknowledging that the inventor's invention is no longer being claimed in the application."

[494] 37 C.F.R. § 1.48(c).

[495] *In re* Schmidt, 293 F.2d 274 (C.C.P.A. 1961).

[496] 35 U.S.C. § 116; 37 C.F.R. § 1.48. The applicant must diligently seek correction after discovering the error. *See* Van Otteren v. Hafner, 278 F.2d 738 (C.C.P.A. 1960). A correcting amendment must be accompanied by (1) a verified statement of facts by the originally named inventor or inventors; (2) an oath or declaration by the actual inventors; (3) consent of any assignee of the patent application; and (4) a fee. 37 C.F.R. § 1.48. The statement of facts must be specific as to how and why the error occurred. Coleman v. Dines, 754 F.2d 353 (Fed. Cir. 1985).

Because a statement and declaration of all concerned persons is required, it is not possible to use the PTO petition correction procedure when there is a dispute among those persons as to who is the correct inventor. Competing inventors may file separate applications, resulting in an interference proceeding to determine who is the first and original inventor. In some circumstances, however, the Patent and Trademark Office may waive the requirement that all original inventors join in the statement of facts. *In re* Hardee, 223 U.S.P.Q. 1122 (Ass't Comm'r Pat. 1984).

[497] 35 U.S.C. § 256; 37 C.F.R. § 1.324.

[498] Iowa State University Research Foundation v. Sperry Rand Corp., 444 F.2d 406 (4th Cir. 1971).

[499] 870 F.2d 1568 (Fed. Cir. 1989).

Section 256 affords the opportunity to correct the patent. . . . If the patentees and their assignees agree, correction can be had on application to the Commissioner. In the event consensus is not attained, however, the second paragraph of section 256 permits redress in federal court.

The statute prescribes only one prerequisite to judicial action: all parties must be given notice and an opportunity to be heard. If that is done, there is subject matter jurisdiction in the district court over a dispute raising solely a joint inventorship issue among contending co-inventors.[500]

[3]   Claiming Requirements

The specification filed as part of the application must "conclude with one or more claims particularly pointing out and distinctly claiming the subject matter which the applicant regards as his invention."[501]

Claims serve two functions. First, they measure the invention for determining patentability.[502] The focus of the utility, novelty, nonobviousness, and disclosure requirements is on the invention defined by the claims.[503] Second, they measure the invention for determining infringement.[504] A patentee has no exclusive rights to subject matter disclosed in the specification or drawings but not covered by a claim.

The Patent Act imposes no rules on the format or terminology of claims, but the PTO imposes ordering and format requirements.[505] A claim is the object of a single sentence and contains a preamble and one or more "elements" or "limitations." "[T]he terms and phrases used in the claims must find clear support and an antecedent basis in the description so that the meaning of the terms in the claims may be ascertainable by reference to the description."[506]

[a]   Definiteness

Claims must be definite enough to provide clear warning as to what constitutes infringement and to provide a clear measure of the invention in order to facilitate the patentability determination.[507]The Supreme Court in 2014 ruled that a "patent is invalid for indefiniteness if its claims, read in light of the specification delineating

---

[500] *Id.* at 1570.

[501] 35 U.S.C. § 112 (2d paragraph).

[502] Jackson Jordan, Inc. v. Plasser American Corp., 747 F.2d 1567, 1578 (Fed. Cir. 1984) ("the *claims*, not particular embodiments, must be the focus of the obviousness inquiry.").

[503] *See generally* D. Chisum, Patents § 8.03.

[504] Sealed Air Corp. v. U.S. Int'l Trade Comm'n, 645 F.2d 976, 985 (C.C.P.A. 1981) ("it is axiomatic that the claims measure the invention, and courts may neither add to nor detract from a claim."). *See* § 2F.

[505] 37 C.F.R. § 1.75.

[506] 37 C.F.R. § 1.75(d)(1). In drafting the specification and claims, the applicant need not use generally accepted terminology and may choose his or her own terms, so long as the meaning is clear. W.L. Gore & Associates, Inc. v. Garlock, Inc., 721 F.2d 1540, 1558 (Fed. Cir. 1983) ("a patent applicant may be his own lexicographer").

[507] United Carbon Co. v. Binney & Smith Co., 317 U.S. 228, 236 (1942).

the patent, and the prosecution history, fail to inform, with reasonable certainty, those skilled in the art about the scope of the invention."[508] The Court abrogated the Federal Circuit's "insolubly ambiguous" standard for determining indefiniteness on the grounds that it set too low a bar for definiteness of claims.

A claim must reasonably apprise persons of ordinary skill in the art of the invention's scope.[509] A claim as precise as the subject matter permits complies with the definiteness requirement.[510]

In determining definiteness, a claim must not be read abstractly but rather in light of the prior art and the teachings of the specification and drawings.[511] The specification may render an apparently clear term indefinite or an apparently unclear term definite.[512]

A claim may include relation, degree, range and approximation terms if the specification provides sufficient guidance to allow a person of ordinary skill in the art to determine whether a particular product or process falls within the claim.[513]

An interesting issue is whether a claim can be fatally indefinite under Section 112 because there are two plausible interpretations, both definite in scope. Courts often assume this is a problem of proper claim interpretation, not indefiniteness.[514]

[b]   Format

Claims commonly have three parts: a preamble, a transition, and a body of elements or limitations.

Consider the following claim:

A porous material consisting essentially of highly crystalline polytetrafluo-roethylene polymer, which material has a microstructure characterized by

---

[508] Nautilus, Inc. v. Biosig Instruments, Inc., 134 S. Ct. 2120 (2014)

[509] Georgia-Pacific Corp. v. United States Plywood Corp., 258 F.2d 124, 134–38 (2d Cir. 1958).

[510] Shatterproof Glass Corp. v. Libbey-Owens Ford Co., 758 F.2d 613 (Fed. Cir. 1985).

[511] *In re* Moore, 439 F.2d 1232, 1235 (C.C.P.A. 1971). *See* § 4B[1].

Courts determine claim definiteness in view of the prior art as of the filing date and consider later issuing patents only insofar as they reflect the filing date state of the art. *In re* Voss, 557 F.2d 812, 819 n.15 (C.C.P.A. 1977). It is impermissible to rely on post-filing date developments and publications to show claim language uncertainty. W.L. Gore & Associates, Inc. v. Garlock, Inc., 721 F.2d 1540 (Fed. Cir. 1983).

[512] *In re* Cohn, 438 F.2d 989 (C.C.P.A. 1971).

[513] Seattle Box Co., Inc. v. Industrial Crating & Packing, Inc., 731 F.2d 818 (Fed. Cir. 1984); Rosemount, Inc. v. Beckman Instruments, Inc., 727 F.2d 1540 (Fed. Cir. 1984); W.L. Gore & Associates, Inc. v. Garlock, Inc., 721 F.2d 1540 (Fed. Cir. 1983); *In re* Marosi, 710 F.2d 799 (Fed. Cir. 1983). *Compare* Amgen, Inc. v. Chugai Pharmaceutical Co., Ltd., 927 F.2d 1200 (Fed. Cir. 1991).

In *Seattle Box*, the court held the phrase "substantially equal" not impermissibly indefinite. In *W.L. Gore*, the court held the phrase "stretching . . . at a rate exceeding about 10% per second" not impermissibly indefinite. In *Marosi*, the court held the phrase "essentially free of alkali metal" not impermissibly indefinite.

[514] *See, e.g.*, Hoffman-LaRoche Inc. v. Burroughs Wellcome Co., 10 U.S.P.Q.2d 1602, 1607 (D. Md. 1989).

nodes interconnected by fibrils and has a matrix tensile strength in at least one direction above about 73,000 psi.[515]

In this claim, the preamble is "a porous material," the transition is "consisting essentially of," and the remainder is the body of elements.[516]

Whether a preamble limits the claim's scope for patentability or infringement purposes is a frequently raised issue. A preamble that states an intended use or inherent property, the body of limitation being a complete definition of the product or process, is not a limitation.[517] A preamble that states the structure or steps necessary to give meaning to the claim and properly define the invention is a limitation.[518]

In *Corning Glass Works v. Sumitomo Electric U.S.A., Inc.*, the court stressed:

> No litmus test can be given with respect to when the introductory words of a claim, the preamble, constitute a statement of purpose for a device or are, in themselves, additional structural limitations of a claim. To say that a preamble is a limitation if it gives 'meaning to the claim' may merely state the problem rather than lead one to the answer. The effect preamble language should be given can be resolved only on review of the entirety of the patent to gain an understanding of what the inventors actually invented and intended to encompass by the claim.[519]

The court interpreted a claim's preamble, "an optical waveguide," as a structural limitation rather than a statement of purpose.

There are three common transitions. The first, "comprising," creates an "open" claim in which the recited elements may be only part of the product or process.[520] A claim to a product "comprising W, X, and Y" covers products with elements W, X, and Y and additional elements (such as Z). The second, "consisting of," creates a "closed" claim in which the product or process includes the recited elements and no

---

[515] This is claim 1 from U.S. Patent No. 4,187,390, held valid in W.L. Gore & Associates, Inc. v. Garlock, Inc., 721 F.2d 1540 (Fed. Cir. 1983).

[516] The three-part structure can also be used to define an element in a claim, for example, "A book comprising a plurality of pages and a cover consisting of imprinted plastic."

[517] *In re* Pearson, 494 F.2d 1399, 1402–03 (C.C.P.A. 1974); Marston v. J.C. Penney Co., 353 F.2d 976 (4th Cir. 1965); Western Broadcasting Co., Ltd. v. Capitol Records, Inc., 218 U.S.P.Q. 94 (N.D. Calif. 1981).

In *Marston*, the claim was to a "buoyant, flexible filler pad comprising a plurality of strip portions arranged in laterally disposed relation" etc. The defendant's product used the arrangement as chair webbing. The court held that the preamble reference to a buoyant pad was not a limitation and that the chair infringed the claim even though it was not buoyant.

[518] *See, e.g.*, Perkin-Elmer Corp. v. Computervision Corp., 732 F.2d 888 (Fed. Cir. 1984); Kropa v. Robie, 187 F.2d 150 (C.C.P.A. 1951).

[519] 868 F.2d 1251, 1257 (Fed. Cir. 1989).

[520] Reese v. Hurst, 661 F.2d 1222 (C.C.P.A. 1981); *Ex parte* Schaefer, 171 U.S.P.Q. 110 (Pat. Off. Bd. App. 1970). *Cf.* Moleculon Research Corp. v. CBS, Inc., 793 F.2d 1261 (Fed. Cir. 1986) (when used in a transitional phrase, "comprising" is a term of art and means that the claim does not exclude additional, unrecited elements, but when used other than in a transition, "comprising" is subject to normal interpretative rules and may mean "having" rather than "having at least.").

others.[521] A claim to a product "consisting of W, X, and Y" does not cover a product with W, X, Y, and Z. The third type uses the phrase "consisting essentially of" covers products or processes that have additional elements but only if the added elements do not materially affect the basic and novel characteristics of the product defined in the balance of the claim.[522]

The body following the transition lists one or more limitations (sometimes referred to as "elements"),[523] which define the claimed product or process. The claim covers a product or process only if it contains all claim limitations.[524] A claim to a product "comprising W, X, and Y" does not literally cover a product with only W or with W and Z.[525]

[c]   Jepson Claims

A Jepson claim is to an improvement on an existing device, process or combination,[526] and includes (1) a preamble reciting conventional elements or steps, (2) a transition phrase such as "wherein the improvement comprises," and (3) the elements or steps the applicant considers to be new.

---

[521] *In re* Certain Slide Fastener Stringers & Machines & Components Thereof for Producing Such Slide Fastener Stringers, 216 U.S.P.Q. 907 (U.S. Int'l Trade Comm'n 1981). *Cf.* Mannesmann Demag Corp. v. Engineered Metal Products Co., Inc., 793 F.2d 1279 (Fed. Cir. 1986) (when the phrase "consisting of" appears in one claim limitation, rather than in the preamble, it closes only the limitation; the phrase does not prevent the claim as a whole from reading on devices with additional elements).

[522] Atlas Powder Co. v. E.I. du Pont De Nemours & Co., 750 F.2d 1569 (Fed. Cir. 1984); *In re* Herz, 537 F.2d 549 (C.C.P.A. 1976). *See also* Water Technologies Corp. v. Calco, Ltd., 850 F.2d 660 (Fed. Cir. 1988) (the phrase "consisting essentially of" does not exclude additional ingredients that do not materially affect the invention's characteristics).

[523] The Federal Circuit prefers "limitation." *See* Perkin-Elmer Corp. v. Westinghouse Electric Corp., 822 F.2d 1528 (Fed. Cir. 1987):

> References to "elements" can be misleading. "Elements" often is used to refer to structural parts of the accused device or of a device embodying the invention. "Elements" is also used in the phrase '[a]n element of a claim' in 35 U.S.C. § 112 ¶ 6. An element of an embodiment of the invention may be set forth in the claim. . . . It is the *limitation* of a claim that counts in determining both validity and infringement, and a limitation may include descriptive terms. . . . [C]larity is advanced when sufficient wording is employed to indicate when "elements" is intended to mean a component of an accused device or of an embodiment of an invention and when it is intended to mean a feature set forth in or as a limitation in a claim.

822 F.2d at 1533 n.9.

[524] A court may extend a claim's scope of protection beyond its literal coverage by applying the doctrine of equivalents. *See* § 2F[2][b].

[525] Builders Concrete, Inc. v. Bremerton Concrete Products Co., 757 F.2d 255 (Fed. Cir. 1985).

This rule applies to both patentability and infringement determinations. In the text example, products X and W + Z will neither anticipate the claim (if they are part of the prior art) nor be direct infringements (if they are made, sold, or used during the patent term without the patentee's authority). *See* § 2C[3][a].

Sale of a component part may be contributory infringement or inducement of infringement. *See* § 2E[2][c].

[526] "Jepson" claims are named for the Patent Office decision approving this format. *Ex parte* Jepson, 1917 C.D. 62, 243 O.G. 525 (Ass't Comm'r Pat. 1917).

Jepson claims are not mandatory, but the PTO encourages their use "where the nature of the case admits."[527] Courts approve of and even favor Jepson claims because they separate old from new.[528] A Jepson claim is used when the novel elements relate to a very small part of an old product or process.

A Jepson claim preamble is a limitation, not a statement of intended use.[529] If an inventor places an element in a Jepson preamble, he or she presumptively admits that the element is prior art[530] but may rebut the presumption.[531] No presumption arises if the preamble refers to matter in the inventor's prior patent.[532]

[d]   Alternative Limitations — Markush Groups

Early Patent Office rules prohibited alternative limitations on the ground that they were inherently ambiguous.[533] For example, a claim to "a compound consisting of A and B or C or D" was improper.

The alternative limitations ban was not a serious obstacle to claiming mechanical and electrical inventions because a suitable generic term was often available to cover the alternatives.[534] The ban was more significant with chemical inventions for which there was no suitable generic term.[535] To alleviate this problem, the Patent Office allowed use of an artificial group, referred to as a "Markush" group, in chemical applications.[536] Instead of "B or C or D," the applicant could use the form "selected from a group consisting of B and C and D."

The PTO no longer prohibits alternative limitations;[537] applicants may use "or" or a Markush group.

Markush and alternative groups may cause unity of invention problems. For example, consider a claim to "A compound consisting of a first element selected

---

[527] 37 C.F.R. § 1.75(e).

[528] Williams Mfg. Co. v. United Shoe Machinery Corp., 316 U.S. 364 (1942); Blair v. Westinghouse House Elec. Corp., 291 F. Supp. 664 (D.D.C. 1968), aff'd, Blair v. Dowd's, Inc., 438 F.2d 136 (D.C. Cir. 1970).

[529] Wells Mfg. Corp. v. Littelfuse, Inc., 547 F.2d 346 (7th Cir. 1976). See § 2D[3][b].

[530] In re Fout, 675 F.2d 297 (C.C.P.A. 1982).

[531] In re Ehrreich, 590 F.2d 902 (C.C.P.A. 1979).

[532] Reading & Bates Construction Co. v. Baker Energy Resources Corp., 748 F.2d 645, 650 (Fed. Cir. 1984).

[533] Ex parte McDougall, 18 O.G. 130, 1880 C.D. 147 (Comm'r Pat. 1880).

[534] Also, inventors can use "means-plus-function" limitations to describe their inventions in suitable generic terms. See §§ 2D[3][e] and 2F[1][b].

[535] The applicant can use a separate claim for each of the elements in combination with the element A. In the text example, the applicant could include three claims: 1. A and B; 2. A and C; and 3. A and D. This significantly increases the number of claims and the fees.

[536] The group is named after the decision that approved of its use. Ex parte Markush, 1925 C.D. 126, 340 O.G. 839 (Comm'r Pat. 1924).

Prior to Markush, inventors claimed chemical structures in terms of one or more "R" groups defining optional substituents on a central nucleus. The technique was used to obtain appropriate generic claim coverage, not to avoid the Patent Office's alternative claim language prohibition.

[537] See, e.g., Ex parte Head, 214 U.S.P.Q. 551 (PTO Bd. App. 1981).

from the group consisting of O, P, Q and R, a second element selected from the group consisting of S, T, U, and V and a third element selected from the group consisting of W, X, Y and Z." This claim has 64 permutations, which may vary from each other. An examiner may not impose a restriction requirement directed to a single claim, but may reject a claim for want of unity of invention if it groups independent and distinct inventions.[538]

A Markush group is an implied representation that the group members are alternatively suitable for the invention's purpose,[539] but use of the group is not an admission on the state of the prior art.[540] For example, assume an applicant originally claims a compound selected from the group consisting of W, X, Y, and Z. If a specific compound of element Z is found in the prior art, the claim is not allowable. The applicant may amend the claim to narrow the group to W, X, and Y, and the applicant's own statement concerning the equivalency of Z and the other members of the group cannot be used to show obviousness.[541]

[e]   Functionality — Means-Plus-Function Claims

A claim may use functional language to partially define the subject matter of an invention if it meets three requirements: (1) definiteness;[542] (2) enablement (a claim for *all* means to achieve a desirable result fails to meet this requirement because the specification discloses only specified means of achieving such a result);[543] and (3) novelty-nonobviousness (if the claim covers products or processes found in the prior art, it is not allowable even if it recites a new use or intended function).[544]

Section 112's last paragraph provides that an element in a "combination" claim may be expressed as means for performing a specified function[545] and directs that "means" be construed to cover the corresponding structure, material or acts

---

[538] *In re* Harnisch, 631 F.2d 716 (C.C.P.A. 1980).

[539] *In re* Driscoll, 562 F.2d 1245 (C.C.P.A. 1977). *See* § 2D[2][b].

[540] A person's own discoveries are not prior art in patentability determinations of that person's inventions. *See* §§ 2C[5][a] and [g].

[541] *In re* Ruff, 256 F.2d 590 (C.C.P.A. 1958).

[542] *In re* Swinehart, 439 F.2d 210 (C.C.P.A. 1971). An example of a claim using functional language is that approved in *Swinehart*:

> A new composition of matter, *transparent to infra-red rays* and resistant to thermal shock, the same being a solidified melt of two components present in proportion approximately eutectic, one of said components being BaF_2 and the other being CaF_2.

What set the composition of the claim apart from prior art compositions was the desirable function of being "transparent to infra-red rays."

Another example is a claim with the limitation "an inorganic salt that is capable of holding a mixture of [a] carbohydrate and protein in colloidal suspension in water." *See In re* Fuetterer, 319 F.2d 259 (C.C.P.A. 1963).

[543] *See, e.g.*, Holland Furniture Co. v. Perkins Glue Co., 277 U.S. 245 (1928); *In re* Hyatt, 708 F.2d 712 (Fed. Cir. 1983).

[544] *See, e.g., In re* King, 801 F.2d 1324 (Fed. Cir. 1986); *In re* Pearson, 494 F.2d 1399, 1402–03 (C.C.P.A. 1974). *See* §§ 2C[3][c] and 2C[3][c][ii].

[545] 35 U.S.C. § 112 (last paragraph). This provision repudiates Halliburton Oil Well Cementing v. Walker, 329 U.S. 1 (1946), which was critical of means-plus-function phrases. *See* §§ 2B[4][c] and 2B[5]. *See also In re* Fuetterer, 319 F.2d 259 (C.C.P.A. 1963).

described in the specification and equivalents thereof.[546] A "combination" includes chemical compositions as well as mechanical combinations;[547] a "single means" claim is improper.[548]

[f] Negative Limitations

A claim may contain one or more negative limitations if the claim's meaning is clear. Older cases held that a negative limitation, such as "a metal other than copper" rendered a claim inherently indefinite or unduly broad.[549] More recent cases hold that negative limitations are proper if they define a clear alternative and the specification supports the claim breadth.[550]

[g] Multiple Claims — Dependent Claims

A patent application may include more than one claim if the claims differ substantially and are not unduly multiplied.[551] The PTO may reject patent application claims for undue multiplication if the number of claims obscures the invention.[552]

---

[546] 35 U.S.C. § 112 (last paragraph). See § 2F[1][c]. See generally D. CHISUM, PATENTS §§ 8.04[2], 18.03[5].

This inquiry into equivalents is more specific than that under the equitable doctrine of equivalents. See § 2F[2][b]. A means-plus-function clause equivalents inquiry is for the purpose of determining literal infringement. The focus is solely on whether the means in the accused device that performs the function stated in the claim is the same as or an equivalent of the corresponding structure described in the patentee's specification as performing that function. Palumbo v. Don-Joy Co., 762 F.2d 969 (Fed. Cir. 1985); D.M.I., Inc. v. Deere & Co., 755 F.2d 1570 (Fed. Cir. 1985).

See also RCA Corp. v. Applied Digital Data Sys., 730 F.2d 1440 (Fed. Cir. 1984). In RCA, the court held that, in determining novelty and anticipation, a means-plus-function format claim limitation cannot be met by a prior art reference element that performs a different function. For a comparison with doctrine of equivalents with respect to after arising technology, see Ring & Pinion Servs, Inc. v. ARM Corp, 743 F.3d 831 (Fed. Cir. 2014).

[547] In re Barr, 444 F.2d 588 (C.C.P.A. 1971). "Combination" covers processes because Section 112 refers to "steps" and "acts," which, logically, relate to process claims.

[548] O'Reilly v. Morse, 56 U.S. 62, 112 (1853); In re Hyatt, 708 F.2d 712 (Fed. Cir. 1983). Hyatt disapproved of the following claim:

A Fourier transform processor for generating Fourier transformed incremental output signals in response to incremental input signals, said Fourier transform processor comprising incremental means for incrementally generating the Fourier transformed incremental output signals in response to incremental input signals.

A single means claim necessarily violates the enablement requirement because it covers every conceivable means for achieving the stated result and the specification discloses only those means known to the inventor.

[549] In re Schechter, 205 F.2d 185 (C.C.P.A. 1953).

[550] In re Duva, 387 F.2d 402, 408 (C.C.P.A. 1967); In re Bankowski, 318 F.2d 778, 782–83 (C.C.P.A. 1963).

[551] Cf. 37 C.F.R. § 1.75(b). Separate claims often differ minimally. Cf. Wahpeton Canvas Company, Inc. v. Frontier, Inc., 870 F.2d 1546, 1553 n.10 (Fed. Cir. 1989) ("Like many, if not most, dependent claims, most of those present here present minute structural details but were allowed because they contain all the limitations of allowed claims from which they depend.").

[552] In re Wakefield, 422 F.2d 897 (C.C.P.A. 1970).

An applicant includes claims of varying scope to effectively protect the disclosed invention. Satisfactory definition of the invention in a single claim is often impossible because of uncertainty about the prior art and future embodiments. An application may put claims in dependent form by referring back to another claim.[553] A dependent claim includes all the elements of the claims on which it depends.

Consider the following four claims:

1. A composition comprising a fluid and soap.

2. The composition of claim 1 wherein the fluid is water.

3. The composition of claim 2 further including a dye.

4. The composition recited in claim 1 or 2 wherein the soap is lye soap.

Claim 1 is an *independent* claim because it is self-contained and refers to no other claim. Claim 2 is a *dependent* claim that narrows claim 1's scope by narrowing one element. The claim 1 soap element is incorporated into claim 2. Claim 3 is a dependent claim that narrows claim 2's scope by adding an element (a dye). The claim 1 soap element and the claim 2 water element are incorporated into claim 3.[554] Claim 4 is a multiple dependent claim that alternatively incorporates claim 1 and claim 2's elements and narrows claim 1 and 2's soap element.

Because a dependent claim incorporates all the elements of the claims to which it refers, nothing can fall within a dependent claim without also falling within all of the claims on which it depends.[555]

Each claim in an issued patent is presumed valid. A dependent claim is presumed valid even though it is dependent upon an invalid claim.[556]

---

[553] 35 U.S.C. § 112; 37 C.F.R. § 1.75(c).

[554] If claim 3 only referred to claim 1, it would not contain the water element of claim 2.

[555] Teledyne McCormick Selph v. United States, 558 F.2d 1000 (Ct. Cl. 1977). *See also* Wahpeton Canvas Company, Inc. v. Frontier, Inc., 870 F.2d 1546 (Fed. Cir. 1989). *Compare* Wilson Sporting Goods Co. v. David Geoffrey & Associates, 904 F.2d 677, 685 (Fed. Cir. 1990) (axiom that "dependent claims cannot be found infringed unless the claims from which they depend have been found to have been infringed" "is no doubt generally correct" but does not apply when the prior art restricts the scope of the doctrine of equivalents for the independent claim in a way that does not apply to a dependent claim).

[556] 35 U.S.C. § 282. *See* § 2F[4][a][i].

A person challenging a patent's claims validity must submit evidence supporting an invalidity conclusion as to each challenged claim. Shelcore, Inc. v. Durham Indus., Inc., 745 F.2d 621, 624 (Fed. Cir. 1984). *Compare* N.V. Akzo v. E.I. du Pont de Nemours & Co., 810 F.2d 1148 (Fed. Cir. 1987) (the district court did not err in failing to address each claim separately; because each claim contained a 5% limitation found to be insufficient to distinguish the prior art, the basis for rejecting the broadest claim applied to all claims).

[4]   Related Applications

[a]   Double Patenting

The double patenting doctrine prohibits issue of more than one patent that claims the same or substantially the same invention to the same inventorship entity or to a common assignee of several inventorship entities.[557] The doctrine's purposes are to prevent extension of the term of patent protection[558] and to protect potential accused infringers from multiple patent suits.

A terminal disclaimer in a second or subsequent patent eliminates a double patenting objection unless the two patents claim the same invention.

[i]   Claim Comparison

Double patenting analysis compares the *claims* of two patents (or a patent and an application). Subject matter *disclosed* but not claimed in the first patent is not used in determining double patenting.[559] Consider the following example:

1. A files application M, disclosing X, Y and Z and claiming X.

2. A files application N, claiming Y.

3. A patent issues to A on application M, claiming X.

Double patenting prohibits a second patent on application N claiming Y if, but only if, Y is an obvious variation of X. The first patent's disclosure of Y and Z is not prior art in making this determination.

[ii]   Identical Inventions

Double patenting absolutely prohibits issue of more than one patent claiming identical subject matter to the same inventorship entity or a common assignee of several inventorship entities. A terminal disclaimer cannot eliminate identity-type double patenting.[560]

If there is any conceivable product or process that would fall literally within one patent's claims without falling within the other patent's claims, the two patents do not claim the identical invention.[561] A claim language difference will not overcome

---

[557] *See generally* D. CHISUM, PATENTS § 9.02. For a discussion of inventive entities, see § 2C[5][g].

[558] *See* § 2E[1].

[559] *See, e.g., In re* Kaplan, 789 F.2d 1574 (Fed. Cir. 1986); Panduit Corp. v. Dennison Mfg. Co., 774 F.2d 1082 (Fed. Cir. 1985), *remanded,* 475 U.S. 809 (1986), *on remand,* 810 F.2d 1561 (Fed. Cir. 1987) (double patenting involves a comparison of the claims of the multiple patents; a prior patent is not "prior art" as to a later patent by the same inventor).

The first patent's disclosures may be used to interpret its claims. *In re* Avery, 518 F.2d 1228 (C.C.P.A. 1975). The first patent's disclosures may be prior art on some ground other than double patenting. For example, if a patent issues more than one year before the effective filing date of the second patent, it is a statutory bar. *See* §§ 2C[5] and 2C[5][c].

[560] *See* § 2D[4][a][v].

[561] *In re* Avery, 518 F.2d 1228, 1232 (C.C.P.A. 1975). For a discussion of literal infringement, see § 2E[2][a].

identity-type double patenting if there is no scope change,[562] but there is no identity-type double patenting if the respective patents' claims have independent scope.[563]

[iii] Obvious Variation

Double patenting conditionally prohibits issue of more than one patent claiming obvious modifications of the same subject matter to the same inventor or a common assignee of several inventors.[564] A terminal disclaimer eliminates obviousness-type double patenting.[565]

The test for obvious variation is the same as the nonobviousness patentability condition,[566] *i.e.*, whether the subject matter of the claim in the subsequent patent or application would have been obvious to a person of ordinary skill in the art in view of the prior art and the subject matter of the claim of the prior patent.[567] One claim may be an obvious variation of another claim even though the two claims are mutually exclusive in scope.[568]

[iv] Design and Utility Patents

Double patenting applies, in limited circumstances, to design and utility patents on related subject matter.

Design and utility patents cover conceptually distinct subject matter. A design patent claims an article's ornamental appearance;[569] a utility patent claims an article's functional aspects.[570] Separate design and utility patents may be obtained covering the same article. Design-utility double patenting exists only if (1) the claimed design is an obvious variation of the utility patent's claimed subject matter, *and* (2) the utility patent's claimed subject matter is an obvious variation of the claimed design.[571] There is no double patenting if the utility aspects do not flow

---

[562] *See, e.g., In re* Griswold, 365 F.2d 834 (C.C.P.A. 1966).

[563] *In re* Deters, 515 F.2d 1152 (C.C.P.A. 1975); *In re* Vogel, 422 F.2d 438, 441 (C.C.P.A. 1970). In *Deters*, a claim that included an element of "at least one" surface was held not identical to a claim in which the element was for "a plurality" of surfaces because the former but not the latter literally read on a one-surface structure.

[564] *See, e.g.*, Hartness Int'l, Inc. v. Simplimatic Engineering Co., 819 F.2d 1100 (Fed. Cir. 1987) (patent invalid for obviousness-type double patenting because it was "primarily a refinement" of the subject matter claimed in the inventor's prior patent).

[565] *See* § 2D[4][a][v].

[566] *In re* Vogel, 422 F.2d 438 (C.C.P.A. 1970). *See* § 2C[4].

[567] *See, e.g., In re* Kaplan, 789 F.2d 1574 (Fed. Cir. 1986) (that a claim in a second patent or patent application "dominates" subject matter claimed in a first patent does not, by itself, give rise to double patenting; to establish "obviousness-type" double patenting as to an attempt to obtain a patent on a variation of an invention claimed in a prior patent, there must be some clear evidence to establish why the variation would have been obvious. The evidence must relate to material that qualifies as prior art.).

[568] *In re* Conix, 405 F.2d 1315 (C.C.P.A. 1969).

[569] *See* § 6B.

[570] *See* § 2C[1].

[571] Shelcore, Inc. v. Durham Industries, Inc., 745 F.2d 621 (Fed. Cir. 1984); Carman Indus., Inc. v. Wahl, 724 F.2d 932 (Fed. Cir. 1983).

inevitably from the design even if the design is obvious in view of the claimed utility aspects.

[v]　　Terminal Disclaimers

An applicant or patentee may disclaim any "terminal part of the term" of a patent applied for or issued[572] to eliminate obviousness-type double patenting.[573] The applicant or patentee disclaims the time period the second patent would otherwise be in force beyond expiration of the first patent and conditions the second patent's enforceability on its being owned by the first patent's owner.[574]

Consider the following example:

1. On January 10, 2000, A files a patent claiming X that later issues.

2. A seeks a patent claiming Y, an obvious modification of X.

3. A files a disclaimer that provides (a) the term of protection of any patent claim to Y shall terminate upon expiration of the patent on X (in 2020), and (b) the patent claim to Y shall be enforceable only during such period as the patent is commonly owned with the patent claiming X.

The disclaimer eliminates any grounds for a double patenting rejection.

A terminal disclaimer eliminates the evils double patenting seeks to prevent — *i.e.*, extension of the patent term, and potential harassment of accused infringers by multiple patent owners. Allowing a second patent benefits the public by providing disclosure of additional useful information on the first patent's invention.[575]

[vi]　　Different Inventors' Commonly Assigned Applications

Double patenting applies to related applications and patents by different inventorship entities owned by the same person or company,[576] but does not apply if the related applications are not commonly owned. In the latter situation, three courses of action are possible: the PTO will (a) declare an interference proceeding to resolve invention priority; (b) reject one application's claims because of the other patents' prior art effect; or (c) allow related patents.

---

[572] 35 U.S.C. § 253 ("any patentee or applicant may disclaim or dedicate to the public the entire term, or any terminal part of the term, of the patent granted or to be granted.").

[573] *In re* Robeson, 331 F.2d 610 (C.C.P.A. 1964).

[574] 37 C.F.R. § 1.321(b); *In re* Van Ornum, 686 F.2d 937 (C.C.P.A. 1982).

[575] *In re* Eckel, 393 F.2d 848 (C.C.P.A. 1968); *In re* Jentoft, 392 F.2d 633, 641 (C.C.P.A. 1968).

Eckel and *Jentoft* note the advantages of allowing two patents on related inventions. The alternative for an inventor with a continuing research program is to file a continuation-in-part application adding improvements and abandon the parent application, thus delaying the invention's disclosure and the commencement of the parent claims' patent term. *See* § 2D[4][b].

[576] From 1967 to 1984, the PTO did not apply double patenting rejections to applications and patents by different inventors owned by the same assignee. It changed this policy because of the 1984 Patent Law Amendments Act. The prior policy was disapproved in *In re* Longi, 759 F.2d 887, 893–94 (Fed. Cir. 1984), which held that obviousness-type double patenting rejections were appropriate as to applications and patents by different inventors owned by the same assignee.

Double patenting rejections apply in common ownership situations even if one inventorship entity's disclosure is not prior art as to a second inventorship entity's claims. Consider the following example:

1. On January 3, 1991, A files an application in Japan claiming X.

2. On January 4, 1991, B files an application in Japan claiming X + Y.

3. On January 7, 1991, C files an application in Germany claiming X + Y + Z.

4. On January 2, 3, and 7, 1992, A, B, and C respectively file in the United States applications corresponding to their prior foreign filings.

5. Company J owns the A and B applications. Company G owns the C application.

6. The inventions X, X+Y, and X+Y+Z are distinct but unpatentably obvious in view of each other.

If A obtains a patent, the common assignee J must file a terminal disclaimer as to B's application. Company G need not file a disclaimer as to C's application because there is no common ownership with the A and B applications. Because of the *Hilmer* doctrine, the A and B patent disclosures will not constitute prior art as to C.[577] The PTO may seek to avoid issuing patents with closely related claims by declaring an interference between the A, B and C applications, using a generic "phantom" count and designating various claims in A, B and C's applications as corresponding to the count.[578]

[b] Continuation Applications

An application filed during the pendency of a prior application can gain the benefit of the prior application's filing date if it meets the four conditions specified in Section 120: continuity of disclosure, cross-referencing, copendency, and inventorship.[579] The benefit of an earlier application's filing date may serve to avoid prior art references or statutory bars[580] or establish invention priority in an interference.[581] There are two types of continuation applications:

A continuation application carries forward identically a prior application's disclosure. It may be used to secure further examination if some or all claims are

---

[577] *See* § 2C[5][d][ii].

[578] *See* § 2D [5][h][i].

[579] 35 U.S.C. § 120:

An application for patent for an invention disclosed . . . in an application previously filed in the United States . . . which is filed by an inventor or inventors named in the previously filed application shall have the same effect . . . as though filed on the date of the prior application, if filed before the patenting or abandonment of or termination of proceedings on the first application or on an application similarly entitled to the benefit of the filing date of the first application and if it contains or is amended to contain a specific reference to the earlier filed application.

See generally D. CHISUM, PATENTS § 13.01 *et seq.*

[580] *See* § 2C[5][b][ii].

[581] *See* § 2D[5].

under final rejection and the applicant does not wish to pursue an appeal or wishes to add or amend claims.

A continuation-in-part ("CIP") application repeats a substantial part of a prior application and adds new matter. A CIP may be used to add improvements developed after a prior application's filing date or to overcome insufficient disclosure problems.[582] A CIP application (or patent issuing thereon) may have two effective filing dates, one for originally disclosed material and one for new matter.[583] Claims dependent upon the new matter are entitled only to the later CIP filing date.[584]

When a continuation or CIP application is entitled to the benefit of a prior application, the latter is commonly referred to as a "parent" application. In a chain of applications, there may be a remote grandparent application, great grandparent, etc. In *In re Henriksen*,[585] the CCPA held that there is no limit to the number of applications that may be chained together, provided Section 120's requirements are met.

A design patent application can gain a prior utility patent application's filing date if it meets Section 120's requirements.[586]

[i]   Continuity of Disclosure

To meet Section 120's continuity condition, an application must be for an invention disclosed in the prior application as required by Section 112, first paragraph.[587] The prior application's disclosure must support claims added or amended in a continuation or CIP application, "support" meaning compliance with the enablement, description, and, possibly, best mode requirements.[588]

If a prior application does not disclose a practical use for the claimed invention, a CIP application adding such use cannot gain the prior application's filing date.[589]

---

[582] *See, e.g.*, Paperless Accounting, Inc. v. Bay Area Rapid Transit Sys., 804 F.2d 659, 663 (Fed. Cir. 1986) ("Law and policy liberally authorize the filing of [CIP] applications for a number of reasons, whether to enlarge the disclosure to include new technological information, thereby providing the public with knowledge of recent developments or improvements; or to enable more extensive prosecution or improved draftsmanship of specification or claims; or to provide a vehicle for prosecution of non-elected claims.").

[583] Litton Sys., Inc. v. Whirlpool Corp., 728 F.2d 1423 (Fed. Cir. 1984).

[584] *In re* Kyser, 588 F.2d 303 (C.C.P.A. 1978); *In re* Scheiber, 587 F.2d 59 (C.C.P.A. 1978). In *Scheiber*, the parent application disclosed a particular compound (X). The CIP application added further disclosure necessary to support a claim to a generic class of compounds that included X. The CIP was not entitled to the parent application's filing date to avoid an intervening reference disclosing X.

[585] 399 F.2d 253 (C.C.P.A. 1968).

[586] Racing Strollers Inc. v. TRI Industries Inc., 878 F.2d 1418 (Fed. Cir. 1989).

[587] 35 U.S.C. § 120. The CIP or continuation's claims need not have been asserted in a prior application if the disclosures of the prior application adequately support those claims. Kangaroos U.S.A., Inc. v. Caldor, Inc., 778 F.2d 1571 (Fed. Cir. 1985).

[588] *See* §§ 2D[2][a]–[c]. As to whether the parent application's best mode disclosure must be updated when filing a continuation or CIP, see § 2D[2][c][iv].

[589] *In re* Hafner, 410 F.2d 1403 (C.C.P.A. 1969). *See* § 2C[2]. If the parent discloses one utility, a CIP is entitled to the parent's filing date even though the CIP discloses a different utility, provided the two

If a CIP's added disclosure makes explicit what was inherent in the parent application, and if a person of ordinary skill in the art would necessarily equate the added matter with the parent's disclosure, the CIP can retain the parent's filing date.[590]

If an inventor files a CIP adding new matter after a PTO examiner rejected parent application claims for insufficient disclosure, the "acquiescence" doctrine may bar the inventor from later arguing that the claims are in fact entitled to the benefit of the parent application filing date.[591]

[ii]   Cross References

To meet Section 102's cross-reference condition, an application must contain, or be amended before issue to contain, "a specific reference to the earlier filed application."[592] The cross reference enables persons searching PTO records to determine a patent's effective filing date.[593] A reissue application may be used to add a cross-reference.[594]

The cross reference should include all immediate and remote applications on which the applicant wishes to rely.[595] Consider the following example:

1. A files application M.

2. A files application N and abandons M.

3. A files application O and abandons N.

O should refer to M and N; N should refer to M.[596]

[iii]   Copendency

To meet Section 120's copendency condition, an application must be filed prior to abandonment, patenting, or termination of proceedings on the prior application.[597] For a chain of applications M, N, and O, N must be filed during the pendency of M, and O must be filed during the pendency of N.[598]

---

utilities are not factually inconsistent. *In re* Kirchner, 305 F.2d 897 (C.C.P.A. 1962).

[590] Wagoner v. Barger, 463 F.2d 1377 (C.C.P.A. 1972).

[591] *See, e.g.*, Pennwalt Corp. v. Akzona, Inc., 740 F.2d 1573 (Fed. Cir. 1984). *Compare* State Industries, Inc. v. A.O. Smith Corp., 751 F.2d 1226 (Fed. Cir. 1985) (filing a CIP creates no presumption that the parent does not support the CIP claims when the CIP filing is not in response to a PTO rejection).

[592] 35 U.S.C. § 120. The reference should provide the following: (1) the prior application's serial number; (2) the prior application's filing date; and (3) the applications' relationship (e.g. continuation, continuation-in-part, divisional). 37 C.F.R. § 1.78(a).

[593] Sampson v. Ampex Corp., 463 F.2d 1042 (2d Cir. 1972).

[594] Sticker Industrial Supply Corp. v. Blaw-Knox Co., 321 F. Supp. 876 (N.D. Ill. 1970).

[595] Hovlid v. Asari, 305 F.2d 747 (9th Cir. 1962).

[596] Clover Club Foods Co. v. Gottschalk, 178 U.S.P.Q. 505 (C.D. Cal. 1973).

[597] 35 U.S.C. § 120. Patenting is the issue date. Abandonment may occur by express statement, failure to prosecute, or failure to pay the issue fee. Termination of proceedings may occur upon final rejection of all claims in an application and exhaustion of any appeal right.

[598] Lemelson v. TRW, Inc., 760 F.2d 1254 (Fed. Cir. 1985).

[iv]   Inventorship

To meet Section 120's inventorship condition, an application's claimed subject matter must be by an inventor named in the prior application.[599]

Before a 1984 amendment, a subsequent application's claims had to be by the same inventor or inventors as the prior application. Consider the following example:

> 1. A, B and C jointly file application M, disclosing X, Y and Z and claiming X.
>
> 2. A and B jointly file CIP application N, disclosing X, Y and Z and claiming Y.
>
> 3. A files CIP application O, disclosing X, Y, and Z and claiming Z.

Before 1984, the claims in applications N and O could not gain the benefit of M's filing date unless there was an error in the original inventorship entity designation.[600] After 1984, the N and O applications could gain the benefit of M's filing date provided that (1) the named inventors are in fact inventors of the subject matter claimed in that application and (2) there was adequate disclosure support for the claims in the prior application.

[5]   Interferences and Derivation Procedures

An interference proceeding's purpose is to resolve the question of invention priority when more than one person seeks a patent claiming substantially the same invention.[601] Interferences are complex proceedings that use unique procedures that are not covered here.[602] The following sections focus on the substantive rules for determining an invention date.[603]

[a]   Priority Rules — First to Invent

The following rules govern the determination of invention priority.

> (1)   Presumptively, the first inventor is the one who first reduces the invention to practice. Filing a patent application adequately disclosing the invention

---

[599] 35 U.S.C. § 120; 37 C.F.R. § 1.78(a).

[600] *In re* Schmidt, 293 F.2d 274 (C.C.P.A. 1961).

[601] 35 U.S.C. § 135.

[602] Interference practice was substantially revised in 1985. Under prior law, a Board of Patent Interferences had jurisdiction over issues of priority of invention. That Board could decide only invention priority issues and disputed issues "ancillary" to priority. That Board could not decide patentability issues, which were considered to be within the expertise of the regular examiners. *See, e.g.*, Case v. CPC International, Inc., 730 F.2d 745 (Fed. Cir. 1984). A 1984 statutory amendment merged the Board of Appeals and the Board of Patent Interferences into a new Board of Patent Appeals and Interferences with jurisdiction to decide both patentability and priority issues.

Current rules for interference practice and procedure are found in 37 C.F.R. §§ 41.100–41.208.

[603] The same rules govern the determination of what constitutes prior art for patentability purposes. *See* § 2C[5][f].

is a constructive reduction to practice,[604] so the invention date cannot be later than the filing date (unless the application is later completely abandoned). An actual reduction to practice occurs when a person makes and tests an embodiment of the invention.[605]

(2)   The invention date is presumed to be the filing date,[606] but evidence can establish a pre-filing invention date.[607]

(3)   The second person to reduce the invention to practice may prevail by showing (a) prior conception of the invention,[608] and (b) continuous diligent effort toward reduction to practice (actual or constructive) from a date just prior to conception of the invention by the first person.[609]

(4)   The first inventor by virtue of an actual reduction to practice loses priority if he abandons, suppresses or conceals the invention after reduction to practice.[610]

(5)   The inventor who abandons, suppresses or conceals his invention after reduction to practice but later resumes activity may rely on the date of resumption as the invention date.[611]

(6)   An inventor cannot rely upon activity outside the United States to establish a date of conception or actual reduction to practice.

(7)   If a person derived his conception of an invention from another person, the latter is entitled to priority regardless of who first reduced it to practice.[612]

---

[604] *See* § 2D[5][c].

[605] *See* § 2D[5][c].

[606] Bates v. Coe, 98 U.S. 31 (1878).

[607] *See* 37 C.F.R. § 41.207. The burden of producing evidence is met if the person introduces credible evidence to support facts showing a pre-filing invention date.

If there is a conflict in the evidence, the burden of persuasion governs its resolution. The burden of persuasion rests on the junior party (that is, the person with the later effective filing date). If the junior party filed his application before the senior party's patent issue date or publication date, the burden of persuasion is preponderance of the evidence, the normal civil suit burden. 37 C.F.R. § 41.207(a)(2). If the junior party filed his application after the senior party's patent issue date or publication date (that is, after the applicant has access to the senior party's published patent specification), the burden is clear and convincing evidence. *Id.*

If there is a "tie," that is, more than one party shows entitlement to the same invention date, priority in an interference is awarded to the first party to file an application. Oka v. Youssefyeh, 849 F.2d 581, 584 (Fed. Cir. 1988).

[608] *See* § 2D[5][b].

[609] *See, e.g.,* Brown v. Barton, 102 F.2d 193, 197 (C.C.P.A. 1939). *See* § 2D[5][d].

[610] *See* § 2D[5][f].

[611] Paulik v. Rizkalla, 760 F.2d 1270 (Fed. Cir. 1985).

[612] Applegate v. Scherer, 332 F.2d 571 (C.C.P.A. 1964). A party may prove derivation by evidence of events outside the United States. Hedgewick v. Akers, 497 F.2d 905 (C.C.P.A. 1974).

[b]   Conception

Conception is the mental formulation and the disclosure of a complete idea for a product or process.[613] Conception must be complete enough to enable one of ordinary skill in the art to reduce the invention to practice without undue experimentation or the exercise of inventive skill.[614] A conception may be disclosed in a drawing, model, or even the inventor's testimony with corroborating witnesses.[615]

An inventor must appreciate that a new structure exists.[616] For example, if a chemist experiments with reactions and produces a mixture of compounds without realizing that a new compound is present, there is no conception of the new compound.[617] The inventor need not appreciate the new or unexpected properties that make the structure patentable.

Some early decisions suggested that there can be no conception of an invention prior to testing and reduction to practice in arts (such as some areas of chemistry) that are unpredictable.[618] In such instances, there is "simultaneous conception and reduction to practice."[619] More recent decisions emphasize that there are no *per se* rules on this matter and that routine research and testing of a product to determine its operability or utility will not necessarily preclude a prior conception of the product and of its utility.[620]

[c]   Reduction to Practice

There are two types of reduction to practice: constructive and actual.

---

[613] Gunter v. Stream, 573 F.2d 77 (C.C.P.A. 1978).

A conception must be of the *means* for achieving the object of the invention. A mental formulation of a desirable result or a problem to be solved is not a conception. Morgan v. Hirsch, 728 F.2d 1449 (Fed. Cir. 1984).

[614] Coleman v. Dines, 754 F.2d 353, 359 (Fed. Cir. 1985). *See also* Oka v. Youssefyeh, 849 F.2d 581, 583 (Fed. Cir. 1988) ("Conception requires (1) the idea of the structure of the chemical compound, and (2) possession of an operative method of making it. . . . When . . . a method of making a compound with conventional techniques is a matter of routine knowledge among those skilled in the art, a compound has been deemed to have been conceived when it was described.").

Evidence of the ease or difficulty of the actual reduction of the invention to practice after the date of an alleged conception is persuasive (though not conclusive) of the completeness of that conception. Meitzner v. Corte, 410 F.2d 433, 437–38 (C.C.P.A. 1969).

[615] Hybritech Inc. v. Monoclonal Antibodies, Inc., 802 F.2d 1367 (Fed. Cir. 1986). *Hybritech* involved a patent claiming a "sandwich assay" using monoclonal antibodies with a high antigen affinity ("at least about 10^8 liters/mole").

[616] Knorr v. Pearson, 671 F.2d 1368 (C.C.P.A. 1982).

[617] Heard v. Burton, 333 F.2d 239 (C.C.P.A. 1964).

[618] Smith v. Bousquet, 111 F.2d 157 (C.C.P.A. 1940).

[619] *See, e.g.*, Amgen, Inc. v. Chugai Pharmaceutical Co., 927 F.2d 1200, 1206 (Fed. Cir. 1991). *See generally* D. Chisum, Patents § 10.04[5].

[620] Rey-Bellet v. Engelhardt, 493 F.2d 1380 (C.C.P.A. 1974).

Constructive reduction to practice occurs when an inventor files a patent application providing full invention disclosure.[621] An applicant need not have built or tested an embodiment of the invention before filing an application.[622] An application retains constructive reduction to practice status only if the applicant maintains prosecution continuity.[623] An abandoned patent application is not a constructive reduction to practice though it is evidence of a conception date.[624]

Actual reduction to practice occurs when an inventor (or someone acting on the inventor's behalf[625]) builds an embodiment of the invention and tests it to determine that it will be operable in its intended functional setting.[626] An embodiment must be tested under either actual working conditions or conditions that sufficiently simulate working conditions.[627] The testing need not establish commercial refinement or acceptability.[628]

[d]   Diligence

To establish a prior invention date, a person who is first to conceive but last to reduce to practice must show continuous diligent effort toward reduction to practice from a date just prior to conception of the invention by another person.[629] The critical diligence period is from a date just before the conception by another party to first conceiver's later reduction to practice.

Consider an example:

1. On January 1, 2002, A conceives of invention X but delays further work on X.

---

[621] Travis v. Baker, 137 F.2d 109, 111 (C.C.P.A. 1943). For a discussion of disclosure requirements, see § 2D[2].

[622] Dolbear v. American Bell Tel. Co., 126 U.S. 1, 535–36 (1888).

An application filed in another country is a constructive reduction to practice if a corresponding United States application is entitled to the benefit of that filing date.

[623] Conover v. Downs, 35 F.2d 59 (C.C.P.A. 1929). In *Conover*, A filed a patent application disclosing, but not claiming, a process X. The application issued as a patent, still with no claim to X. A then filed a second application claiming X and became involved in an interference with B over priority of invention of X. The court held that the first application filing was evidence of A's conception but was not a constructive reduction to practice because the second application was filed after issuance of the patent and was not entitled to the benefit of the first application filing date.

[624] *In re* Costello, 717 F.2d 1346, 219 U.S.P.Q. 389 (Fed. Cir. 1983).

[625] The reduction to practice need not be by the inventor personally and may be carried out by co-employees or even suppliers or customers of the inventor's employer so long as such activity is on the behalf of the inventor. Litchfield v. Eigen, 535 F.2d 72 (C.C.P.A. 1976); MacMillan v. Moffett, 432 F.2d 1237 (C.C.P.A. 1970); Hogue v. Cowling, 101 F.2d 541, 549–50 (C.C.P.A. 1939).

[626] Kimberly-Clark Corp. v. Johnson & Johnson, 745 F.2d 1437, 1445 (Fed. Cir. 1984).

[627] Paivinen v. Sands, 339 F.2d 217 (C.C.P.A. 1964).

[628] Shurie v. Richmond, 699 F.2d 1156, 1160 (Fed. Cir. 1983).

[629] There is no diligence "race." One who is first to reduce to practice need not show diligence from a prior conception, whether it was before or after the date of conception of the other party. Steinberg v. Seitz, 517 F.2d 1359, 1364 (C.C.P.A. 1975).

Lack of diligence after an alleged actual reduction to practice is relevant only insofar as it provides an inference that no reduction to practice actually occurred or that the inventor had abandoned, suppressed, or concealed the invention. *See* §§ 2D[5][c] and [f].

2. On January 1, 2004, A begins working toward a reduction to practice.

3. On February 1, 2004, B conceives and reduces X to practice.

4. On May 1, 2004, A reduces X to practice.

A is the first inventor if A shows diligent activity, or a recognized excuse for inactivity, for the entire period from just prior to February 1, 2004 until the May 1, 2004, reduction to practice.

A person must account for the entire critical period by showing either activity devoted to a reduction to practice or a recognized excuse for inactivity.[630] Any lapse in diligence during the critical period is fatal no matter how short the critical or lapse period.[631]

Activity must be directed to reducing the invention to practice, either building and testing an embodiment or preparing a patent application. Activity directed to commercial exploitation or to other inventions is not sufficient.[632]

Recognized excuses for inactivity include:

(a) the inventor's patent attorney's reasonably organized prior case work-load,[633]

(b) employment demands,[634]

(c) the need to develop a closely related invention to test the primary invention,[635] and

(d) the inventor's extreme and continuous poverty or illness.[636]

In *Griffith v. Kanamaru*,[637] a university delayed for months applying for a patent or working to reduce a professor's conceived invention to practice. As excuses, the university cited (a) its policy of requiring outside funding for projects, and (b) the professor's decision to delay work on the concept until a particular graduate student matriculated. Neither was sufficient. Courts "may consider the reasonable everyday problems and limitations encountered by an inventor," but the university's "excuses sound more in the nature of commercial development, not accepted as an excuse for delay, than the 'hardship' cases. . . . Delays in reduction to practice caused by an inventor's efforts to refine an invention to the most marketable and profitable form

---

[630] Gould v. Schawlow, 363 F.2d 908 (C.C.P.A. 1966).

[631] Wilson v. Sherts, 81 F.2d 755 (C.C.P.A. 1936). *Cf. In re* Mulder, 716 F.2d 1542 (Fed. Cir. 1983).

[632] *In re* Nelson, 420 F.2d 1079, 1080–81 (C.C.P.A. 1970); Fitzgerald v. Arbib, 268 F.2d 763, 766 (C.C.P.A. 1959).

[633] Bey v. Kollonitsch, 806 F.2d 1024 (Fed. Cir. 1986); Rines v. Morgan, 250 F.2d 365, 369 (C.C.P.A. 1957).

[634] Gould v. Schawlow, 363 F.2d 908, 919 (C.C.P.A. 1966).

[635] Watkins v. Wakefield, 443 F.2d 1207 (C.C.P.A. 1971). *Compare* Hudson v. Giuffrida, 328 F.2d 918 (C.C.P.A. 1964).

[636] Wallace v. Scott, 15 App. D.C. 157 (1899). Insufficient funds for an actual reduction to practice will not excuse a failure to seek a constructive reduction to practice by preparation and filing of a patent application. Preston v. White, 97 F.2d 160, 165 (C.C.P.A. 1938).

[637] 816 F.2d 624 (Fed. Cir. 1987).

have not been accepted as sufficient excuses for inactivity."[638]

[e]   Corroboration

The inventor's uncorroborated testimony does not establish conception, actual reduction to practice, and diligence.[639] Witnesses who are neither the inventor nor co-inventors, verified notebooks, and records can provide corroboration. A "rule of reason" applies to the corroboration requirement.[640] For example, in *Lacotte v. Thomas*,[641] the inventor's notebook kept as part of an organized and routinely practiced research program within a corporation and records of the use of related supplies by the inventor sufficiently corroborated an actual reduction to practice.

A notebook system in which researchers make regular entries on work in progress, and a person capable of understanding but not actually involved in the work regularly witnesses the entries by dated signature, is the best procedure for the verification of dates of conception and reduction to practice.

[f]   Abandonment, Suppression, and Concealment

A person who first conceives and reduces to practice an invention loses the right to rely on the reduction to practice date if he abandons, suppresses, or conceals the invention.[642]

A person is guilty of abandonment, suppression or concealment if (1) he or she makes an invention but delays filing a patent application for a long time, (2) a second person independently makes the same invention and promptly files for a patent, and (3) the first person is "spurred" back into action by knowledge of the second person's activity.[643]

Long delay in filing a patent application creates an inference of abandonment, suppression, or concealment.[644] Making the invention available to the public, for example, by a public sales demonstration, may rebut the inference if the inventor

---

[638] *Id.* at 626, 628.

[639] Coleman v. Dines, 754 F.2d 353 (Fed. Cir. 1985); Reese v. Hurst, 661 F.2d 1222 (C.C.P.A. 1981); Naber v. Cricchi, 567 F.2d 382 (C.C.P.A. 1977).

[640] Berry v. Webb, 412 F.2d 261 (C.C.P.A. 1969).

[641] 758 F.2d 611 (Fed. Cir. 1985).

[642] 35 U.S.C. § 102(g). This section codifies the abandonment, suppression, and concealment doctrine, which the leading decision, Mason v. Hepburn, 13 App. D.C. 86 (D.C. Cir. 1898), adopted for policy reasons.

[643] Engelhardt v. Judd, 369 F.2d 408 (C.C.P.A. 1966). Spurring evidence strongly supports, but is not essential to, an abandonment, suppression or concealment finding. Peeler v. Miller, 535 F.2d 647 (C.C.P.A. 1976).

[644] Lutzker v. Plet, 843 F.2d 1364, 1367 (Fed. Cir. 1988); Shindelar v. Holdeman, 628 F.2d 1337 (C.C.P.A. 1980). *Compare* Piher, S.A. v. CTS Corp., 664 F.2d 122 (7th Cir. 1981).

Evidence of the inventor's or his assignee's intention to manufacture the invention as circumstances warrant does not rebut the inference of abandonment, suppression or concealment arising from unreasonable delay. Young v. Dworkin, 489 F.2d 1277 (C.C.P.A. 1974). Evidence of commercial exploitation does not rebut the inference if the inventor intends to keep the invention secret indefinitely. Palmer v. Dudzik, 481 F.2d 1377 (C.C.P.A. 1973).

files a patent application within the one-year Section 102(b) grace period.[645] However, delay caused by working on refinements and improvements which are not reflected in the final patent application, and delay caused by activities that go to commercialization of the invention, will not be excused.[646]

A person who abandons, suppresses or conceals an invention but later resumes work before a second person's invention date may rely on the resumption date to show priority.[647] Consider the following example:

1. In November 2000, A reduces an invention to practice. A's company takes no immediate action to prepare a patent application.

2. In January 2005, A's patent agent begins diligent work to prepare a patent application.

3. In March 2005, B files an application on the invention.

4. In June 2005, A files an application.

A's long delay is abandonment, suppression or concealment that precludes A from relying on the 2000 reduction to practice, but A may rely on the January 2005 date as conception. If A shows due diligence to the June 2005 filing date, he is prior to B, assuming B's invention date is March 2005.

[g]   Derivation Proceedings

The AIA replaces interferences, designed to determine the first inventor, with derivation proceedings, which allow a second filer to show that the first filer of an application derived the invention from the second filer. A derivation proceeding can be instituted within a one-year period beginning with the first publication of the second filer's claim that is the same or substantially similar to the earlier applicant's claim. The petitioner's claim of derivation must be stated with specificity, must be made under oath, and must be supported by substantial evidence. The Director determines whether to institute a derivation proceeding based on the petition. The Director's decision to institute a derivation proceeding is final and nonappealable.

The Patent Trial and Appeal Board (PTAB) determines whether the first applicant derived the invention from the second. The AIA requires the Director to prescribe regulations setting forth standards for the conduct of derivation proceedings. The PTAB has the authority to defer the proceedings until the expiration of a three-month period after the issuance of a patent that contains the contested claim. The PTAB can also defer or stay the proceeding in there is an ongoing infringement action involving the patent of the first applicant.

The finding of the PTAB adverse to an applicant constitutes a final rejection of the claim at issue. A finding adverse to an applicant will also constitute a

---

[645] Correge v. Murphy, 705 F.2d 1326 (Fed. Cir. 1983). The one-year grace period is discussed at § 2C[5][c].

[646] Lutzker v. Plet, 843 F.2d 1364, 1367 (Fed. Cir. 1988).

[647] Paulik v. Rizkalla, 760 F.2d 1270 (Fed. Cir. 1985). *See also* Paulik v. Rizkalla, 796 F.2d 456 (Fed. Cir. 1986).

cancellation of the claim at issue. The decision of the PTAB is appealable to the Federal Circuit.

[6]   Post-Issuance Procedures

[a]   Reexamination

The AIA replaces the inter partes reexamination described in this section with the inter partes review, described in detail below. Various provisions relating to the inter partes review have different effective dates. Effective September 16, 2011, a higher standard is required to initiate an inter partes review. This higher standard applies to inter partes reexaminations initiated after September 16, 2011. Under this higher standard, the petitioner has to show "that there is reasonable likelihood that the petitioner would prevail with respect to one of the claims challenged."

A person who believes the PTO erroneously issued a patent may, if sued for patent infringement, defend by asserting invalidity.[648] A person may also file a suit for a declaratory judgment of invalidity. Neither remedy is available to a person not currently infringing the patent or making substantial preparations to do so.[649]

A person may protest patent issue,[650] but the protest right is limited in two ways. First, the PTO rule governing protests severely restricts the protestor's right to submit information or otherwise participate in examination proceedings.[651] Second, the confidentiality of pending applications prior to publication keeps interested persons unaware of the application's existence. Protests are most commonly filed on reissue applications as to which the confidentiality policy does not apply.

In 1980, Congress enacted a limited reexamination procedure.[652] Any person, including the patent owner or an accused patent infringer, may file a request for reexamination of the validity of any claim in a patent on the basis of cited prior art patents or printed publications.[653]

---

[648] *See* § 2F[4][a].

[649] *Cf.* Syntex (U.S.A.) Inc. v. U.S. Patent & Trademark Office, 882 F.2d 1570, 1576 (Fed. Cir. 1989) ("[A] potential infringer may not sue the PTO seeking retraction of a patent issued to another by reason of its improper allowance by the PTO. A remedy must await confrontation with the patent owner.").

[650] *See generally* D. CHISUM, PATENTS § 11.03[3][b].

[651] 37 C.F.R. § 1.291.

[652] 35 U.S.C. §§ 301, 302. *See generally* D. CHISUM, PATENTS § 11.07[4].

[653] *See* Syntex (U.S.A.) Inc. v. U.S. Patent & Trademark Office, 882 F.2d 1570, 1573 (Fed. Cir. 1989) ("The category of third-party requesters is . . . open-ended and includes, for example, attorneys representing a principal whose identity is not disclosed to the PTO or patentee.").

Cf. Joy Manufacturing Co. v. National Mine Service Co., 810 F.2d 1127, 1130 (Fed. Cir. 1987) (a request for reexamination by a party to a settlement agreement did not breach the provision of the agreement that the party not file any "suit" in "court" contesting the validity of the patent; reexamination and civil litigation are "distinctly different proceedings," and the relief sought by the other party — an injunction stopping the reexamination — was unavailable because the decision of the Commissioner to institute reexamination "is not subject to review"; and an injunction directed against the requesting party "would have no effect on reexamination since [the requestor] has no future role to play in that *ex parte* proceeding.").

As to a possible remedy against bad faith reexamination requests, *see* Ball Corp. v. Xidex Corp., 705

The PTO enters a reexamination order if it determines that cited art presents a new patentability question as to the claim.[654] A reexamination is conducted under the rules that apply to examination of original patent applications.[655]

Only the patent owner may actively participate in a reexamination or appeal an adverse decision.[656] A patentee may add or amend claims during a reexamination but may not enlarge the scope of any of the patent's claims.[657]

The statutory patent validity presumption does not apply during reexamination.[658] Examiners give the claims the broadest reasonable construction, as is the case with original and reissue examination.[659] The examination is limited to the patentability of the claims based on patents and printed publications.[660]

F. Supp. 1470, 1471 (D. Colo. 1988) (refusing to dismiss plaintiff's unfair competition claim alleging that the defendants, in filing a request for reexamination of plaintiff's patent, "perpetrated a fraud on the PTO by knowingly misrepresenting evidence on the commercial success and non-obviousness of [the invention described in the] patent, by withholding evidence on these issues which defendants had in their possession and by preventing [plaintiff] from submitting that evidence under the pretext of this court's protective order in prior litigation [in which plaintiff charged defendant with infringement of the patent].").

[654] 35 U.S.C. § 304. If no reexamination is ordered, a substantial portion of the reexamination request fee will be refunded. The decision not to order reexamination is nonappealable.

Cf. Patlex Corp. v. Mossinghoff, 771 F.2d 480 (Fed. Cir. 1985) (a PTO rule barring any consideration of submissions by the patent owner in the determination of whether a new question of patentability exists which warrants reexamination violates neither the reexamination statute nor the constitutional demands of due process of law. The provision for a refund of a part of the reexamination fee does not unconstitutionally bias the decision by the PTO; a policy that "doubts" are to be resolved in favor of granting reexamination is void as contrary to the intent of Congress that patentees be protected from harassment by persons requesting reexamination.).

[655] 35 U.S.C. § 305.

[656] A person other than the patent owner is limited to (1) citing patents and printed publications and (2) filing a request for reexamination, explaining the pertinency of the cited art. If a reexamination is ordered at the request of a person other than the patent owner, and the patent owner files a statement in response to the order, the requester may file a reply statement. 35 U.S.C. § 304.

See Syntex (U.S.A.) Inc. v. U.S. Patent & Trademark Office, 882 F.2d 1570 (Fed. Cir. 1989). In *Syntex*, the Federal Circuit held that a nonpatentee reexamination requester's suit alleging that the PTO failed to comply with its rules in conducting reexamination of a patent must be dismissed for want of jurisdiction and lack of standing. *Cf. In re* Opprecht, 868 F.2d 1264 (Fed. Cir. 1989) (denying a party's motion to intervene or to file a brief *amicus curiae* in a patentee's appeal from an adverse decision on reexamination of a patent; the party did not file a reexamination request or participate before the PTO in the reexamination to the limited extent authorized by statute); Boeing Co. v. Commissioner of Patents and Trademarks, 853 F.2d 878 (Fed. Cir. 1988) (a reexamination requester who was allowed to participate as an intervenor in a patentee's 35 U.S.C. Section 145 suit to review the PTO's rejection of patent claims has no standing to appeal an order dismissing the suit without prejudice and remanding the matter to the PTO).

[657] 35 U.S.C. § 305.

[658] *In re* Etter, 756 F.2d 852 (Fed. Cir. 1985).

[659] *In re* Yamamoto, 740 F.2d 1569 (Fed. Cir. 1984). During an examination or reexamination an applicant may amend the claims to clarify their scope. In an infringement suit, claims are given a more restricted interpretation in order to sustain their validity. *See* § 2F[1][e].

[660] 37 C.F.R. § 1.552. Issues such as the public use bars or inequitable conduct are not considered. Compliance with the disclosure requirements is considered only as to new or amended claims.

If a reexamined claim is found unpatentable, it will be cancelled; if it is found patentable, a certificate of confirmation will issue.[661] After confirmation, the validity presumption continues to apply.[662] The intervening rights doctrine applies to claims amended during reexamination.[663]

A patent may be involved simultaneously in a PTO reexamination and district court patent infringement litigation. In *Ethicon, Inc. v. Quigg*,[664] the court held that the PTO may not stay reexamination pending litigation over the patent's validity because the reexamination statute requires proceedings to be conducted with "special dispatch."[665] In dictum, the court commented on the effect of a court validity ruling on PTO reexamination.

> To the extent MPEP § 2286 states that the PTO is bound by a court's decision upholding a patent's validity, it is incorrect. . . . The doctrine of collateral estoppel does not prevent the PTO from completing the reexamination [in the situation where a court determines that a patent is not invalid]. Courts do not find patents 'valid' . . . only that the patent challenger did not carry the 'burden of establishing invalidity in the *particular case* before the court' under 35 U.S.C. § 282. . . . [I]f a court finds a patent invalid, and that decision is either upheld on appeal or not appealed, the PTO may discontinue its reexamination. . . . Of course, in the end it is up to the court, not the PTO, to decide if the patentee had a 'full and fair chance' to litigate the validity of the patent. But it is admissible for the PTO to act on the standing judgment unless and until a court has said it does not have res judicata effect.[666]

[b]   Reissue

A patentee may apply for a reissue patent to correct errors made without deceptive intent that cause the patent to be wholly or partly inoperative or invalid by reason of a defective specification or drawing, or by reason of the patentee claiming more or less than he has a right to claim.[667]

---

[661] 35 U.S.C. § 307.

[662] *Cf.* Greenwood v. Hattori Seiko Co., Ltd., 900 F.2d 238, 240–41 (Fed. Cir. 1990) ("In an infringement suit before a district court, the invalidity of a patent under 35 U.S.C. § 103 must be decided on the basis of prior art adduced in the proceeding before the court. The issue cannot be decided merely by accepting or rejecting the adequacy of the positions taken by the patentee in order to obtain a Certificate of Reexamination for the patent. Once issued by the PTO, a patent is presumed valid and the burden of proving otherwise rests solely on the challenger.").

[663] 35 U.S.C. § 307(b); Fortel Corp. v. Phone-Mate, Inc., 825 F.2d 1577, 1580–81 (Fed. Cir. 1987). *See* § 2D[6][b][v].

[664] 849 F.2d 1422 (Fed. Cir. 1988).

[665] 35 U.S.C. § 305.

[666] 849 F.2d at 1429 n.3.

[667] 35 U.S.C. § 251. *See generally* D. Chisum, Patents § 15.01 *et seq.*

[i] Inoperativeness and Invalidity

Reissue applicants most commonly seek to alter the original patent's claims[668] but may also correct other deficiencies.[669] Reissue applications may (1) more precisely define the subject matter;[670] (2) cure claim indefiniteness;[671] (3) correct an obviously-correctable error in the specification;[672] (4) add a specific reference or priority claim to obtain benefit of a prior application's filing date;[673] and (5) correct inventor identification.[674]

From 1977 to 1982, the PTO allowed "no defect" reissue applications to secure patent reexamination in view of newly-discovered prior art. Often, the patent was the subject of a pending patent infringement suit. The patentee's litigation opponent participated in the reissue proceeding as a protestor. In *In re Dien*,[675] the court held these "no defect" reissues to be mere advisory proceedings. An unwilling patent owner could not be ordered to file a reissue.[676] In 1982, the PTO eliminated "no defect" reissues and curtailed the rights of protestors[677] to reduce the PTO's burdens[678] and to recognize the new, more limited, statutory reexamination procedure.[679]

---

[668] *See* § 2D[6][b][ii].

[669] *Compare In re* Keil, 808 F.2d 830 (Fed. Cir. 1987); *In re* Weiler, 790 F.2d 1576 (Fed. Cir. 1986).

[670] *In re* Wadlinger, 496 F.2d 1200 (C.C.P.A. 1974). In *Wadlinger*, the court upheld the use of reissue to insert a more precise "fingerprint" description of a chemical compound. However, there must be some showing that the original claim is defective because the reissue statute does not authorize reissue to add claims of the same scope, using different language. *In re* Wittry, 489 F.2d 1299 (C.C.P.A. 1974).

[671] *In re* Altenpohl, 500 F.2d 1151 (C.C.P.A. 1974).

[672] *In re* Oda, 443 F.2d 1200 (C.C.P.A. 1971). In *Oda*, the term "nitric acid" was mistranslated from Japanese to English as "nitrous acid." The error and its correction were obvious in the context because the specification stated a specific gravity of 1.45, which cannot apply to nitrous acid.

The new matter prohibition restricts reissue. 35 U.S.C. § 251. *See* § 2D[4][b].

[673] Brenner v. State of Israel, 400 F.2d 789 (D.C. Cir. 1968). *See* §§ 2D[4][b][iii].

A reissue application cannot cure failure to comply with the fundamental requirement that a subsequent application be filed during pendency of a prior application to be entitled to the latter's filing date. *In re* Watkinson, 900 F.2d 230, 231 (Fed. Cir. 1990) ("failure to file a divisional application [claiming a nonelected invention], regardless of the propriety of the underlying restriction requirement, is not an error correctable by reissue"); *In re* Orita, 550 F.2d 1277 (C.C.P.A. 1977).

[674] *Ex parte* Scudder, 169 U.S.P.Q. 814 (Pat. Off. Bd. App. 1971).

[675] 680 F.2d 151 (C.C.P.A. 1982). *Dien* held that, if the claims were rejected as unpatentable and the applicant refused to amend the claim, the applicant could not appeal to the courts, which have jurisdiction only over actual controversies. If the claims in the reissue application were determined to be *patentable*, they would be rejected because the PTO has no statutory authority to reissue a patent that is not defective. If the claims were determined to be *unpatentable*, they would also be rejected. In the latter case, the applicant could abandon the reissue application and retain the original patent.

[676] Johnson & Johnson, Inc. v. Wallace A. Erickson & Co., 627 F.2d 57 (7th Cir. 1980).

[677] *See* § 2D[6][a].

[678] *See* PPG Industries, Inc. v. Celanese Polymer Specialties Co., Inc., 840 F.2d 1565 (Fed. Cir. 1988).

[679] *See* § 2D[6][a]. A statutory reexamination is not the same in scope as an examination pursuant to a reissue. The former is confined to documentary prior art sources (patents and publications). The latter includes nondocumentary sources (such as matter in public use and on sale). *See* § 2C[5][b].

[ii]   Claim Scope Alteration

A patent claim may be so broad as to render it invalid in view of the prior art or so narrow as to fail to cover a product embodying the invention.[680] A reissue application may add a limitation that distinguishes the prior art[681] or eliminates an unnecessary limitation that distinguishes the product.[682]

A reissue application that seeks to broaden any claim must be filed within two years of the original patent's issue.[683] A claim is broader if it is in any respect broader than the claims of the original patent (even though it may be narrower in some respects). A claim is broader if any conceivable product or process would infringe a reissue claim but not an original claim.[684]

Reissue claims must be for an invention disclosed in the original patent specification.[685]

A reissue application may not recapture subject matter intentionally surrendered during the original prosecution.[686] The recapture rule depends on direct evidence of intent and on inferences of intent drawn from comparing the originally cancelled claim and the reissue claim.[687] Consider the following example:

1.   Applicant A originally asserts a claim to X+Y.

2.   After the examiner rejects the claim, A narrows the claim by adding element Z (X+Y+Z).

The recapture rule may preclude a reissue claim to X+Y or, perhaps, to X. It will not necessarily preclude a claim to W+X+Y+Z, which is narrower because it

---

[680] *See* Hewlett-Packard Co. v. Bausch & Lomb Inc., 882 F.2d 1556, 1564–65 (Fed. Cir. 1989) ("[T]he expression 'less than he had a right to claim' generally refers to the scope of a claim. . . . [T]hat provision covers the situation where the claims in the patent are narrower than the prior art would have required the patentee to claim and the patentee seeks broader claims. Conversely, the alternative that the patentee claimed 'more . . . than he had a right to claim' comes into play where a claim is too broad in scope in view of the prior art or the specification and the patentee seeks narrower claims.").

[681] The amended claim must be supported by the original specification disclosure. Because of this, a narrowed claim may fail to comply with the description requirement. *See* § 2D[2][b].

[682] *See, e.g., In re* Peters, 723 F.2d 891 (Fed. Cir. 1983).

[683] 35 U.S.C. § 251 (last paragraph). If the application is filed within the two year period, this requirement is satisfied even if broader claims are added by an amendment filed after the period. *In re* Doll, 419 F.2d 925 (C.C.P.A. 1970).

[684] Tillotson, Ltd. v. Walbro Corp., 831 F.2d 1033 (Fed. Cir. 1987); *In re* Price, 302 F.2d 741 (C.C.P.A. 1962). Reissues that correct defects not related to claim scope do not broaden those claims and need not be filed within the two-year period. Fontijn v. Okamoto, 518 F.2d 610 (C.C.P.A. 1975) (addition of cross-reference priority claims necessary to obtain benefit of a prior application filing date did not broaden the scope of the claims).

[685] *In re* Hounsfield, 699 F.2d 1320 (Fed. Cir. 1983) (rejecting statements in prior decisions that reissue claims must be for subject matter the applicant originally "intended" to claim; "intent to claim" is not a separate test for reissue).

[686] Ball Corp. v. United States, 729 F.2d 1429 (Fed. Cir. 1984).

[687] *See, e.g.,* Whittaker Corp. v. UNR Industries, Inc., 911 F.2d 709 (Fed. Cir. 1990) (recapture rule does not invalidate a reissue claim because limitation makes it narrower in scope than a similar claim cancelled during original prosecution; the district court erred in construing the limitation added in reissue as merely making explicit what was implicit in a cancelled original claim).

requires W, or to W+Y+Z, which is narrower because it requires W, and broader because it does not require X.

[iii]   Error

A patentee may obtain reissue only if the patent's inoperativeness or invalidity resulted from an error committed without deceptive intent. A common error is the inventor's failure to adequately communicate the nature of his invention to his patent attorney or agent.[688] Error includes errors of law, judgment, or fact.[689] The error need not have been discovered by the patentee.[690]

[iv]   Oath or Declaration — Examination

The patentee must file an oath or declaration with the reissue application setting forth facts showing sufficient reissue grounds, including the existence of a defect and how the error arose.[691] If the patentee fails to establish error, the claims added by reissue are invalid.[692]

The provisions governing original patent applications apply to reissue applications,[693] but an application may be made by and sworn to by the owner of the entire interest in the patent if the application does not seek to enlarge the original patent claims' scope.[694]

Because a reissue application is examined under the same procedures as an original patent application,[695] all claims must meet the patentability conditions of

---

[688] *Cf. In re* Wilder, 736 F.2d 1516, 1519 (Fed. Cir. 1984); *In re* Richman, 424 F.2d 1388 (C.C.P.A. 1970). *Compare In re* Weiler, 790 F.2d 1576, 1579 (Fed. Cir. 1986) (although the reissue statute is remedial in nature and should be construed liberally, "not every event or circumstance that might be labeled 'error' is correctable by reissue.").

[689] Rohm & Haas Co. v. Roberts Chemicals, Inc., 245 F.2d 693 (4th Cir. 1957); Moist Cold Refrigerator Co. v. Lou Johnson Co., 217 F.2d 39 (9th Cir. 1954). In *Rohm & Haas*, the court upheld a reissue that added a method of use claim because a statutory amendment after the original patent's issue made it clear that such claims were permissible. In *Moist Cold Refrigerator*, the court upheld a reissue that added a claim to clarify impermissibly vague functional language in the original patent claims.

[690] *In re* Richman, 424 F.2d 1388 (C.C.P.A. 1970).

[691] 37 CFR § 1.175(a). *See In re* Wilder, 736 F.2d 1516 (Fed. Cir. 1984); *In re* Keller, 642 F.2d 413, 427 (C.C.P.A. 1981). *See also* Orthokinetics, Inc. v. Safety Travel Chairs, Inc., 806 F.2d 1565, 1577 (Fed. Cir. 1986) (a reissue oath stating that the inventor believed the original patent "to be wholly inoperative or invalid" because certain claims "are unpatentable over" a certain prior art reference is "not . . . a 'binding admission' of anticipation"; the trial court erred in applying the claims of the original patent as prior art in determining the patentability of the reissue claims).

[692] Hewlett-Packard Co. v. Bausch & Lomb Inc., 882 F.2d 1556 (Fed. Cir. 1989).

[693] 35 U.S.C. § 251 (third paragraph). Unlike original applications, reissue applications are not held in confidence for 18 months. Notice of a reissue filing is published in the PTO *Official Gazette*, and the public may inspect a reissue application. 37 C.F.R. § 1.11(b). This may allow the filing of a protest. *See* § 2D[6][a].

[694] 35 U.S.C. § 251 (third paragraph). If an owner files an application that seeks a claim enlargement within the two year period but erroneously makes the application without an oath or declaration by the inventor, the error may be corrected even after the two year period. *In re* Bennett, 226 U.S.P.Q. 413 (Fed. Cir. 1985).

[695] 37 C.F.R. § 1.176. The PTO acts on reissue applications before other applications but in no case sooner than two months after announcement of the filing in the *Official Gazette*, which allows members

utility, novelty, nonobviousness, and adequate support in the disclosure.[696] The PTO's original allowance of the claims is not binding during reissue examination.[697]

[v]   Effect of Reissue — Intervening Rights

The original patent is surrendered on reissue.[698] The reissue patent is effective as of its issue date and endures for the original patent's unexpired term.[699]

Damage claims for infringing acts before reissue are preserved only insofar as the claims of the original and reissue patents are identical.[700] An amended claim may be identical if the amendment clarifies but does not alter the claim's scope.[701] A patentee should retain as many claims from the original patent as possible to preserve damage claims.

A reissue patent affects the continued right of a person to use or sell a "specific thing" made prior to reissue only if the making, using, offering for sale, selling, or importing of that thing infringes a "valid claim" in both the original and reissue patents.[702]

A court may provide for equitable intervening rights to allow for continued manufacture, use or sale of a product or process after reissue if a person, prior to reissue, made, purchased or used the product or process or made substantial preparation for such making, purchase or use.[703]

The presumption of validity applies to reissued patents.[704] Statements and actions in reissue prosecution are relevant to claim interpretation, including claims carried forward from the original patent.[705]

---

of the public to submit pertinent information on the patent.

[696] Hewlett-Packard Co. v. Bausch & Lomb Inc., 882 F.2d 1556 (Fed. Cir. 1989) ("Reissue is essentially a reprosecution of all claims. For example, original claims which a patentee wants to maintain unchanged may nevertheless be rejected on any statutory ground.").

[697] *In re* Doyle, 482 F.2d 1385 (C.C.P.A. 1973).

[698] 35 U.S.C. § 252. The reissue patent is printed with brackets and italics indicating changes.

[699] 35 U.S.C. § 251.

[700] 35 U.S.C. § 252. *See* Fortel Corp. v. Phone-Mate, Inc., 825 F.2d 1577 (Fed. Cir. 1987); Seattle Box Co., Inc. v. Industrial Crating & Packing, Inc., 731 F.2d 818, 829–30 (Fed. Cir. 1984).

[701] *See, e.g.*, Tennant Co. v. Hako Minuteman, Inc., 878 F.2d 1413, 1417 (Fed. Cir. 1989) ("Claims amended during reexamination are entitled to the date of the original patent if they are without substantive change or are legally 'identical,' to the claims in the original patent. . . . If not 'identical,' the patentee has no right to recover infringement damages for periods prior to the date that the reexamination certificate issued."); Slimfold Manufacturing Co., Inc. v. Kinkead Industries, Inc., 810 F.2d 1113 (Fed. Cir. 1987).

[702] 35 U.S.C. § 252; Southern Saw Service, Inc.v. Pittsburgh-Erie Saw Corp., 239 F.2d 339 (5th Cir. 1956).

[703] *See, e.g.*, Seattle Box Co., Inc. v. Industrial Crating & Packing, Inc., 756 F.2d 1574 (Fed. Cir. 1985).

[704] *See, e.g.*, American Hoist & Derrick Co. v. Sowa & Sons, Inc., 725 F.2d 1350 (Fed. Cir. 1984).

[705] Howes v. Medical Components, Inc., 814 F.2d 638, 645 (Fed. Cir. 1987).

[c]   Post-Grant Review

The AIA creates a new post-grant review proceeding which allows a person other than the owner of the patent to institute a review of the patent within nine months of the grant of the patent or of the issuance of a reissue patent. A petitioner can seek post-grant review on any grounds for invalidating a patent. The Director may decline to institute the review, based on the petition and a response from the patent owner, if the petitioner has not demonstrated that "it is more likely than not that 1 of the claims challenged is the petition is unpatentable." The PTAB will conduct the review as an inter partes proceeding, subject to regulations created by the Director.

A petitioner cannot request a post-grant review if he has filed a declaratory judgment action challenging the validity of a claim of the patent before filing the post-grant review petition. If the petitioner or another party files a declaratory judgment after the filing of the post-grant review petition, the civil action must be automatically stayed until (i) the patent owner moves the court to lift the stay; (ii) the patent owner files a civil action or counterclaim for patent infringement; or (iii) petitioner or other party moves to dismiss the civil action. The stay provisions do not apply to counterclaims challenging the validity of a claim. In an infringement action brought within three months of the grant of patent, the court cannot stay its consideration of a motion for preliminary injunction because of the filing of a post-grant review petition.

The party bringing a post-grant review is estopped from claiming invalidity in any other administrative proceeding on grounds that could have been raised in the post-grant review petition. A final written decision of the PTAB estops the petitioner from raising invalidity defenses in an infringement action on any grounds that could have raised in the petition. Estoppel does not apply if there is a settlement of the post-grant review proceeding.

The post-grant review provisions are effective March 13, 2013.

[d]   Inter Partes Review

The AIA allows a person other than the owner of the patent to bring an inter partes review the later of either nine months after the grant of a patent or an issuance of a reissue or after the termination of an instituted post-grant review. Challenges in an inter partes review can be based only on grounds of novelty or nonobviousness and only on the basis of prior art consisting of patents or printed publications. The Director can decline to institute an inter partes review if the petition and responses from the patent owner do not show a reasonable likelihood that the petitioner would prevail with respect to at least one of the claims challenged in the petition.

The rules pertaining to declaratory judgment actions, stays, and estoppel that apply to post-grant reviews (discussed in the previous section) apply to inter partes review. The standard for bringing an inter partes review applies to inter partes reexamination actions brought on or after September 16, 2011. The remaining provisions are effective as of September 16, 2012.

§ 2E   RIGHTS

A patent grants "to the patentee, his heirs or assigns, . . . the right to exclude others from making, using, offering for sale, or selling the invention throughout the United States or importing the invention into the United States, and, if the invention is a process, . . . the right to exclude others from using, offering for sale or selling throughout the United States, or importing into the United States, products made by that process."[706]

[1]   Duration

A United States utility patent endures for twenty years from its application date.[707] Pursuant to obligations under the TRIPS Agreement, the United States term is consistent with that of major patent systems. Using the filing date rather than the issue date removes any incentive to prolong prosecution to delay patent term commencement. A United States patent owner must pay maintenance fees at three intervals to prevent patent lapse.[708]

A patent is effective only after it issues; acts of making, using, offering for sale, selling, or importing prior to issue do not automatically give rise to liability.[709] However, after the patent issues, the patent owner has the right to collect a reasonable royalty from anyone who infringed between the time the patent application was published and the time the patent issued, provided that the infringer "had actual notice of the published patent application," and that "the invention as claimed in the patent is substantially identical to the invention as claimed in the published patent application."[710] Trade secret law or an express or implied contract also may give an inventor rights against unauthorized use of an invention before a patent issues.[711] Unauthorized use of a patented device after

---

[706] 35 U.S.C. § 154(a)(1).

Section 271(a) defines infringement and incorporates the five basic exclusive rights: "whoever without authority makes, uses, offers to sell, or sells any patented invention, within the United States or imports into the United States any patented invention during the term of the patent therefor, infringes the patent." Section 271(g) makes a comparable provision for unauthorized importation, offer for sale, sale and use of products of a patented process.

[707] 35 U.S.C. § 154 (a)(2). *See generally* D. Chisum, Patents § 16.04. For design and plant patent duration, *see* §§ 6B and 6C.

[708] *See generally* D. Chisum, Patents § 11.02[1][d][iv].

[709] Foster v. American Mach. & Foundry Co., 492 F.2d 1317, 1323 (2d Cir. 1974).

"Patent pending" is commonly used to give notice to potentially infringing manufacturers but has no specific legal effect. State Industries, Inc. v. A.O. Smith Corp., 751 F.2d 1226, 1236 (Fed. Cir. 1985).

Sales before patent issue may be contributory infringement if the seller knows that issue is imminent and that customers will resell or use the patented invention after issue. Procter & Gamble Co. v. Nabisco Brands, Inc., 604 F. Supp. 1485, 1490 (D. Del. 1985).

[710] 35 U.S.C. § 154(d)(1),(2). *See* Stephens v. Tech Int'l, Inc., 393 F.3d 1269, 1275–76 (Fed. Cir. 2004); Classen Immunotherapies, Inc. v. King Pharmaceuticals, Inc., 403 F. Supp. 2d 451, 457–58 (D. Md. 2005). To obtain the reasonable royalty, the patent owner must sue within six years from the date the patent issues. 35 U.S.C. § 154(d)(3).

[711] Hoeltke v. C.M. Kemp Mfg. Co., 80 F.2d 912, 922–23 (4th Cir. 1935). Federal patent law does not preempt state trade secret and confidential idea licensing law. Aronson v. Quick Point Pencil Co., 440

issue constitutes infringement even though the device was acquired prior to issue.[712]

A patent's effectiveness ceases at the end of its term.[713] One who makes or uses another's patented device before the patent expires infringes even if the device is not sold until after expiration.[714] A patent license royalty obligation may not be based on use of the patented invention after expiration of the patent.[715]

The 20-year patent term may be extended in some circumstances. If the Patent Office delays in acting on the application or in responding to certain actions of the applicant within specific deadlines, then the patent term may be extended for the period of the delay.[716] If the Patent Office takes more than three years to issue a patent, not counting the time required for an interference or an appeal, then the patent term may be extended, unless the delay was requested by the applicant.[717] Finally, if the issuance of the patent was delayed by a secrecy order, an interference, or an appeal, then the patent term may be extended.[718] In calculating the number of days of the extension, the PTO must subtract any time during which the applicant "failed to engage in reasonable efforts to conclude prosecution of the application," including any period of time in which the applicant took more than 3 months to respond to an office action.[719] The applicant may appeal the calculation of this time period to the District Court for the District of Columbia, and ultimately, to the Federal Circuit.[720]

In addition, section 156 provides for extension of the patent term if the commercial marketing of a human or animal drug product or a medical device, food additive, or color additive covered by a patent, or the making or use of which is covered by a patent, has been delayed by a period of regulatory review.[721] On

---

U.S. 257 (1979); Kewanee Oil Co. v. Bicron Corp., 416 U.S. 470 (1974). *See* § 1D[3][a] and [b].

[712] Cohen v. United States, 487 F.2d 525 (Ct. Cl. 1973). However, if the device was acquired with the consent of the patent owner, there is an implied license to continue use after issue. *See generally* D. CHISUM, PATENTS § 16.04[3].

[713] Damages may be collected for infringing acts occurring during the term of a patent in a suit filed after patent expiration. Recovery is subject to the statutory limitation barring recovery of damages for infringing acts occurring more than six years prior to the filing of suit. *See* § 2F[4][f].

[714] Paper Converting Machine Co. v. Magna-Graphics Corp., 745 F.2d 11 (Fed. Cir. 1984). *See also* Roche Prods., Inc. v. Bolar Pharmaceutical Co., 733 F.2d 858 (Fed. Cir. 1984). Pre-expiration use solely for obtaining FDA approval to market a drug or medical device after expiration may be exempt under Section 271(e). *See* § 2F[4][d].

[715] Brulotte v. Thys Co., 379 U.S. 29 (1964). A license conveying trade secrets or know-how in addition to patent rights and providing for royalties beyond expiration of the patent is enforceable if it clearly allocates royalties between the patent and the trade secrets and know-how. Pitney-Bowes, Inc. v. Mestre, 517 F. Supp. 52 (S.D. Fla. 1981), *aff'd*, 701 F.2d 1365 (11th Cir. 1983). *Cf.* Boggild v. Kenner Prod., 776 F.2d 1315 (6th Cir. 1985).

[716] 35 U.S.C. § 154(b)(1)(A).

[717] 35 U.S.C. § 154(b)(1)(B).

[718] 35 U.S.C. § 154(b)(1)(C).

[719] 35 U.S.C. § 154(b)(2)(C).

[720] 35 U.S.C. § 154(b)(4). For the method of calculating the delay, *see* Wyeth v. Kappos, 591 F.3d 1364 (Fed. Cir. 2010).

[721] 35 U.S.C. § 156. *See generally* D. CHISUM, PATENTS § 16.04[5]. An extension application must be

occasion, Congress has also extended a particular patent's term by special legislation.[722]

[2]   Exclusive Rights

A patent's rights to exclude include making, using, offering for sale, selling, and importing the patented invention, or products made by a patented process.[723] Direct infringement is unauthorized performance of any one of these acts, in the United States, during the patent's term.[724] Indirect infringement is the active inducement of infringement, or the unauthorized sale of a specially designed component for use in a patented combination or process (contributory infringement).[725] Additional infringing acts include: (1) exporting specially adapted components of patented combinations;[726] (2) filing an application for government approval to sell a drug claimed by a patent prior to the expiration of the patent;[727] and (3) importing, offering to sell, selling, or using products made abroad with processes covered by United States patents.[728]

A patent grants only the right to *exclude* others, not an affirmative right to make, use or sell an invention.[729] The patent owner may be prevented from making, using or selling a product embodying the patented invention because another patent's claims cover the same product,[730] or because government regulations restrain its marketing.[731] A person has no privilege to infringe another's patent simply because he has a patent covering the infringing product or process. Consider the following example:

1. A invents and obtains a patent on a combination of X + Y + Z.

2. B invents and obtains a patent on an improvement in the combination in which a particular type of Z is used (Z').

B may be unable to sell its improvement (X + Y + Z') because of A's patent, and A may be unable to sell the improvement, which falls within its patent, because of B's

---

made within 60 days of receipt of the regulatory agency's permission for commercial marketing or use. Determination of the conditions for and amount of extension is extremely complex. *See, e.g.,* Wyeth Holdings Corp. v. Sebelius, 603 F.3d 1291 (Fed. Cir. 2010); Merck & Co. v. Hi-Tech Pharmacal Co., 482 F.3d 1317 (Fed. Cir. 2007); Merck & Co. v. Kessler, 80 F.3d 1543 (Fed. Cir. 1996); Glaxo Operations UK Ltd. v. Quigg, 894 F.2d 392 (Fed. Cir. 1990).

[722] For a summary of private patent laws, *see* Tyler T. Ochoa, *Patent and Copyright Term Extension and the Constitution,* 49 J. Copyr. Soc'y USA 19, 58-85 (2001).

[723] 35 U.S.C. § 154(a)(1).

[724] 35 U.S.C. § 271(a),(g).

[725] 35 U.S.C. § 271(b),(c).

[726] 35 U.S.C. § 271(f). *See* Microsoft Corp. v. AT&T Corp., 550 U.S. 437 (2007).

[727] 35 U.S.C. § 271(e)(2), (4). *See* Eli Lilly and Co. v. Medtronic, Inc., 496 U.S. 661 (1990); Merck KGaA v. Integra Lifesciences I, Ltd., 545 U.S. 193 (2005).

[728] 35 U.S.C. § 271(g).

[729] *See, e.g.,* TransCore, L.P. v. Electronic Transaction Consultants Corp., 563 F.3d 1271, 1275 (Fed. Cir. 2009); Leatherman Tool Group, Inc. v. Cooper Industries, Inc., 131 F.3d 1011, 1015 (Fed. Cir. 1997).

[730] *See, e.g.,* Atlas Powder Co. v. E.I. du Pont de Nemours, 750 F.2d 1569 (Fed. Cir. 1984).

[731] *See, e.g.,* Patterson v. Kentucky, 97 U.S. (7 Otto.) 501 (1879).

patent.

[a]   Basic Rights: Direct Infringement

Unauthorized making, using, offering for sale, and selling are distinct and independent acts of infringement.[732] Making without use or sale may infringe; for example, a person makes a machine for sale in another country or for use after expiration of the patent.[733] Using without making or sale may infringe; for example, a person purchases and uses a machine.[734] Selling without making or using may infringe; for example, a person purchases and resells a product covered by the patent.[735] Making an offer for sale infringes even if no sale or use occurs.[736]

"Making" includes manufacture of an operable assembly of a machine claimed in the patent.[737] To "use" a system means to "put the invention into service, *i.e.*, [to] control the system as a whole and obtain benefit from it."[738] Merely displaying a product at a trade show is not "use," but courts disagree whether a "demonstration" of the product at a trade show is a "use."[739] However, a demonstration accompanied by sales activity or price information could constitute "selling" or an "offer for sale."[740]

An "offer for sale" is construed in accordance with the common law of contracts, and is shown by a "manifestation of willingness to enter into a bargain, so made as to justify another person in understanding that his assent to that bargain is invited and will conclude it."[741] In order to infringe, an "offer" must include price terms.[742] A "sale" means either the transfer of a product or title to a product for a price, or

---

[732] Paper Converting Machine Co. v. Magna-Graphics Corp., 745 F.2d 11, 16 (Fed. Cir. 1984). The Patent Act does not further define these concepts. *See generally* D. Chisum, Patents § 16.02.

[733] Underwood Typewriter Co. v. Elliott-Fisher Co., 156 F. 588 (S.D.N.Y. 1907); Ketchum Harvester Co. v. Johnson Harvester Co., 8 F. 586 (N.D.N.Y. 1881).

[734] Aro Mfg. Co. v. Convertible Top Replacement Co., 377 U.S. 476 (1961); Roche Products, Inc. v. Bolar Pharmaceutical Co., Inc., 733 F.2d 858 (Fed. Cir. 1984). However, if the machine was sold with the consent of the patent owner, then the right to use that particular machine passes to the owner under the doctrine of exhaustion. *See* §§ 2E[3], 2F[4][g].

[735] American Chem. Paint Co. v. Thompson Chem. Corp., 244 F.2d 64 (9th Cir. 1957). Again, however, if the product was sold with the consent of the patent owner, then the purchaser has the right to resell that particular product under the doctrine of exhaustion. *See* §§ 2E[3], 2F[4][g].

[736] Transocean Offshore Deepwater Drilling, Inc. v. Maersk Contractors USA, Inc., 617 F.3d 1296, 1308 (Fed. Cir. 2010); 3D Systems, Inc. v. Aarotech Laboratories, Inc., 160 F.3d 1373, 1378–80 (Fed. Cir. 1998).

[737] Deepsouth Packing Co. v. Laitram Corp., 406 U.S. 518 (1972). *See* § 2E[2][b][i].

[738] Centillion Data Systems, LLC v. Qwest Communications Int'l, Inc., 631 F.3d 1279 (Fed. Cir. 2011); NTP, Inc., v. Research in Motion Ltd., 418 F.3d 1282, 1317 (Fed. Cir. 2005).

[739] Medical Solutions, Inc. v. C Change Surgical, LLC, 541 F.3d 1136, 1140–41 (citing cases holding that "the mere demonstration of an accused product, even in an obviously commercial atmosphere" is not "use," but declining to decide the issue as a general matter; even if a demonstration can qualify as a use, evidence was insufficient).

[740] *Id.* at 1140 & n.3.

[741] *See* Rotec Industries, Inc. v. Mitsubishi Corp., 215 F.3d 1246, 1254–55, 1257 (Fed. Cir. 2000).

[742] MEMC Electronic Materials, Inc. v. Mitsubishi Materials Silicon Corp., 420 F.3d 1369, 1376 (Fed. Cir. 2005); *see also* 3D Systems, Inc. v. Aarotech Laboratories, Inc., 160 F.3d 1373, 1379 (Fed. Cir. 1998) (price quotation letters are offers to sell).

the agreement by which such a transfer takes place.[743] The four elements of a sale are: "(1) parties competent to contract, (2) mutual assent, (3) a thing capable of being transferred, and (4) a price in money paid or promised."[744] Mere possession of a product without use or sale does not infringe.[745]

One who performs all of a process's operative steps directly infringes a patent claiming the process. A process patent is generally not infringed when one party performs some of the steps and another party performs the rest of the steps; however, if one party controls or directs each step of the patented process, it cannot avoid liability by having some of the steps performed by another entity.[746] In order to find liability under this theory, there must be an agency relationship between the parties who perform the steps, or one party must be contractually obligated to the other to perform the steps.[747]

Before 1988, sale or use of an unpatented product made by a patented process was not direct infringement.[748] After the 1988 Process Patents Amendments Act, however, sale or use "within the United States [of] a product made by a process patented in the United States" is direct infringement.[749] The Act restricts the remedy against retail sellers and noncommercial users.[750]

[b] Territorial Scope: Importation and Exportation

A patent's rights to exclude cover only activity occurring within the United States.[751] Activity outside the United States may be contributory infringement or inducement of infringement if it causes unauthorized making, use or sale of the invention in the United States.[752]

---

[743] NTP, Inc., v. Research in Motion Ltd., 418 F.3d 1282, 1319 (Fed. Cir. 2005) (quoting Black's Law Dictionary 1337 (7th ed. 1999)); *accord*, Transocean Offshore Deepwater Drilling, Inc. v. Maersk Contractors USA, Inc., 617 F.3d 1296, 1311 (Fed. Cir. 2010).

[744] *NTP*, 418 F.3d at 1319 (quoting Black's Law Dictionary 1337 (7th ed.1999)).

[745] Welker Bearing Co. v. PHD, Inc., 550 F.3d 1090, 1095 (Fed. Cir. 2008); Johns Hopkins Univ. v. CellPro, Inc., 152 F.3d 1342, 1366 (Fed. Cir. 1998).

[746] *See* Muniauction, Inc. v. Thomson Corp., 532 F.3d 1318 (Fed. Cir. 2008), overruling BMC Resources, Inc. v. Paymentech, L.P., 498 F.3d 1373, 1379–81 (Fed. Cir. 2007). *See generally* D. Chisum, Patents § 16.02[6].

[747] *See* Miniauction, supra note 737. The Supreme Court addressed the issue of inducement in Limelight Networks, Inc. v. Akamai Technologies, Inc., 134 S. Ct. 2111 (2014), holding that liability could not be based on a theory of inducement without a finding of direct infringement. The Court remanded for determination of liability under *Miniauction*.

[748] *Cf.* Koratron Co., Inc. v. Lion Uniform, Inc., 449 F.2d 337 (9th Cir. 1971).

[749] 35 U.S.C. § 271(g). *See* § 2E[2][b].

[750] 35 U.S.C. § 271(g) ("In an action for infringement of a process patent, no remedy may be granted for infringement on account of the noncommercial use or retail sale of a product unless there is no adequate remedy under this title for infringement on account of the importation or other use . . . or sale of that product."). *See* § 2E[2][b].

[751] 35 U.S.C. §§ 154(a)(1), 271(a). *See generally* D. Chisum, Patents § 16.05.

[752] *See, e.g.*, Honeywell, Inc. v. Metz Apparatewerke, 509 F.2d 1137, 1141 (7th Cir. 1975); Akzona, Inc. v. E.I. duPont de Nemours & Co., 662 F. Supp. 603, 613 (D. Del. 1987).

The United States includes the fifty states, territories and possessions (for example, Puerto Rico).[753] Use of a patented device aboard a vessel under a United States national's ownership and control is within the United States.[754] The rule extends to use aboard a United States controlled craft in outer space.[755]

Use of a patented system with necessary components in both the United States and other countries is within the United States.[756] However, a process or method claim cannot be infringed unless each and every step is performed within the United States.[757]

A "sale" may occur in the United States if the sale is made directly to a customer located in the United States, even if the product is delivered "f.o.b." (free on board), meaning that title passes as soon as the product is loaded for shipment in the exporting country.[758] However, mere knowledge that a product sold overseas will be imported into the United States does not constitute direct infringement (although the seller may be liable for inducing infringement).[759]

[i] Exportation

Making an entire patented product in the United States infringes even though the product is for export and use in another country.[760]

Prior to 1984, however, making and exporting the *unassembled* components of a patented combination did not infringe. In *Deepsouth Packing Co. v. Laitram Corp.*,[761] the patent was for a shrimp deveining machine. The defendant manufactured all the machine's parts and shipped them in separate boxes to customers in other countries, where the parts could be assembled in less than 1 hour. The Supreme Court found no infringement; the patent covered only the machine as a combination, and there was no "making" or sale of the combination in the United States.

A 1984 amendment overruled *Deepsouth* and established two additional acts of infringement. Under the first, a person commits infringement by, without authority, (1) supplying or causing to be supplied in or from the United States, (2) all or a substantial portion of the components of a patented invention, where such components are uncombined in whole or in part, (3) in such manner as to actively

---

[753] 35 U.S.C. § 100(c).

[754] Gardiner v. Howe, 9 F. Cas. 1157 (C.C.D. Mass. 1865).

[755] 35 U.S.C. § 105; *Ex parte* McKay, 200 U.S.P.Q. 324 (PTO Bd. App. 1975). *Cf.* Ocean Science & Eng'g, Inc. v. United States, 595 F.2d 572 (Ct. Cl. 1979).

[756] NTP, Inc. v. Research in Motion, Inc., 418 F.3d 1282, 1317 (Fed. Cir. 2005); Decca, Ltd. v. United States, 544 F.2d 1070 (Ct. Cl. 1976).

[757] *NTP*, 418 F.3d at 1317–18.

[758] Litecubes, LLC v. Northern Light Prods., Inc., 523 F.3d 1353, 1369–71 (Fed. Cir. 2008) (defining "sale" under Copyright Act, but relying on patent cases); *cf.* North American Philips Corp. v. American Vending Sales, Inc., 35 F.3d 1576, 1579 (Fed. Cir. 1994).

[759] MEMC Electronic Materials, Inc. v. Mitsubishi Materials Silicon Corp., 420 F.3d 1369, 1377 (Fed. Cir. 2005).

[760] Packard Instrument Co. v. Beckman Instruments, Inc., 346 F. Supp. 408 (N.D. Ill. 1972).

[761] 406 U.S. 518 (1972).

induce the combination of such components outside of the United States (4) in a manner that would infringe the patent if such combination occurred within the United States.[762] This provision was construed narrowly by the Supreme Court in *Microsoft Corp. v. AT & T Corp.*,[763] in which the Court held that although a fixed copy of "software" could be a "component" of a machine,[764] copies that were made outside the United States, from a master disk that was made in the United States, were not "supplied in or from the United States" within the meaning of the statute.[765]

Under the second, a person commits infringement by, without authority, (1) supplying or causing to be supplied in or from the United States, (2) any component of a patented invention that is especially made or especially adapted for use in the invention and not a staple article or commodity of commerce suitable for substantial noninfringing use, (3) knowing that such component is so made or adapted, and (4) intending that such component will be combined outside of the United States in a manner that would infringe the patent if such combination occurred within the United States.[766] This provision goes beyond overruling *Deepsouth* by making the export of less than all of the components of a patented combination an infringement. However, this subsection does not appear to include export of components for use in a patented process, or the act of purchasing a whole product in the United States and exporting it.[767]

[ii]   Importation

Before 1988, importing a patented product into the United States was not, by itself, an infringement; no direct infringement occurred unless and until a use or sale of the imported product was made in the United States. In 1988, an amendment made unauthorized importation of a product, whether patented or unpatented, an act of infringement if the product is made abroad by a patented process.[768] In 1994, another amendment made unauthorized importation of any patented invention a direct infringement.[769]

Infringement occurs only if the activity is unauthorized. Under the first-sale doctrine, one who purchases a product from the patent owner or his licensee is

---

[762] 35 U.S.C. § 271(f)(1). *See generally* D. Chisum, Patents § 16.02[7]. This provision is similar to the provision on active inducement of infringement within the United States. *See* § 2E[2][c][iii].

[763] 550 U.S. 437 (2007).

[764] *Id.* at 459–52.

[765] *Id.* at 452–54.

[766] 35 U.S.C. § 271(f)(2). This provision is similar to the provision on contributory infringement within the United States. *See* § 2E[2][c][ii]. It differs in requiring the additional element that the seller "intended" that the component be combined in a manner that would infringe.

[767] Such purchase and export have previously been held not to constitute an infringement. Dowagiac Mfg. Co. v. Minnesota Moline Plow, Co., 235 U.S. 641 (1913). In such a situation, the patent owner has a potential remedy against the manufacturer in the United States who sold to the exporter if the manufacture occurred during the patent term.

[768] 35 U.S.C. § 271(g). This section is discussed in § 2E[2][b][3].

[769] 35 U.S.C. § 271(a).

authorized to use or resell the product.[770] The Federal Circuit, however, has held that the first-sale doctrine does not apply unless the first sale was made within the United States.[771] Therefore, importation of products made and sold by the patent owner overseas is still prohibited.

Under Section 337 of the Tariff Act of 1930, a patent owner may petition the United States International Trade Commission (ITC) for an order prohibiting importation of a product.[772] The exclusion remedy is available for patent infringement only "if an industry in the United States, relating to the articles protected by the patent . . . concerned, exists or is in the process of being established."[773] Section 337 offers patent owners procedural and remedial advantages. By statute, the ITC must complete its investigation "at the earliest practicable time after the date of publication of notice of such investigation."[774] Its remedies, an exclusion order or cease and desist order,[775] are effective in preventing further importation. Because the ITC cannot award damages, a patent owner often sues for patent infringement in a district court in addition to seeking Section 337 relief.

In *Amgen, Inc. v. U.S. International Trade Commission*, the Federal Circuit held Section 337's reference to "articles . . . made . . . by means of . . . a process covered by the claims of a valid and enforceable United States patent" did not apply "to prohibit the importation of articles made abroad by a process in which a *product* claimed in a U.S. patent is used."[776]

[iii]   Process Patent Protection

Subsection 271(g) prohibits the unauthorized importation, offer to sell, sale, or use of a product which is made by a process patented in the United States.[777] Several aspects of this section are noteworthy.

First, this section refers only to the importation or sale of a "product," meaning

---

[770] *See* § 2E[3].

[771] *See* Jazz Photo Corp. v. Int'l Trade Comm'n, 264 F.3d 1094, 1105 (Fed. Cir. 2001).

[772] 19 U.S.C. § 1337(a)(1)(B).

[773] 19 U.S.C. § 1337(a)(2). Such an industry exists if there is in the United States, with respect to the patented articles, "(A) significant investment in plant and equipment; (B) significant employment of labor or capital; or (C) substantial investment in its exploitation, including engineering, research and development, or licensing." 19 U.S.C. § 1337(a)(3).

[774] 19 U.S.C. § 1337(b)(1).

[775] 19 U.S.C. § 1337(d),(f).

[776] 902 F.2d 1532, 1538 (Fed. Cir. 1990). In *Amgen*, the ITC dismissed the petition for want of subject matter jurisdiction, reasoning that the patentee's patent did not cover a process for making the imported product. The Federal Circuit agreed with the ITC's statute interpretation but directed that the matter be dismissed on the merits rather than for want of subject matter jurisdiction.

[777] 35 U.S.C. § 271(g); *see also* 35 U.S.C. § 154(a)(1).

These sections refer to a "process patent." In fact, a single United States patent commonly contains both claims to processes or methods and claims to products (that is, machines, compositions of matter or manufactures). In view of this universally-accepted practice, and the accepted rule that each claim of a patent is treated, in law, as though it were a separate patent, *see, e.g.*, 35 U.S.C. § 282, references in the legislation to a "process patent" should be interpreted as meaning "a patent claiming a process."

a physical article. If the process generates or produces information or data, that information may be sold or used in the United States without infringing the patent.[778]

Second, the product, which itself may be unpatented, must be "made by" a patented process. Congress eschewed the word "directly," used in other countries' patent laws to describe the relationship between product and process.[779] Instead, it inserted a partial negative definition: "A product which is made by a patented process will . . . not be considered to be so made after — (1) it is materially changed by subsequent processes; or (2) it becomes a trivial and nonessential component of another product."[780]

Third, Section 295 provides a presumption as to when a product is made by a patented process to ease "the great difficulty a patentee may have in proving that the patented process was used in the manufacture of the product in question where the manufacturer is not subject to the service of process in the United States."[781] However, Congress did not want the presumption to be "casually established,"[782] because "[i]mporters and subsequent purchasers may be unable to obtain the information needed to overcome such presumptions."[783] To "minimize the risk of aggressive litigation intended to discourage firms from carrying competing products,"[784] the statute requires the court to find two conditions: "(1) a substantial likelihood exists that the product was made by the patented process," and (2) "the plaintiff has made a reasonable effort to determine the process actually used in the production of the product and was unable to so determine."[785] If the court so finds, then "the burden of establishing that the product was not made by the process shall be on the party asserting that it was not so made."[786] Neither the statute's language nor its legislative history indicate when the court should determine whether the two conditions are satisfied and evoke the presumption. Resolving the matter prior to trial gives the parties a clear advanced indication of their respective trial proof burdens.

Fourth, Section 271(g) contains an "exhaustion of remedies" provision. The owner of a patented process can obtain "no remedy" against a noncommercial user or retail seller of an unpatented product made by the patented process if the owner has an adequate remedy against others, such as the manufacturer or importer. In many situations, it is uncertain whether such a remedy exists. For example, it may be unclear whether a manufacturer in another country has sufficient contacts with a State or the United States to justify personal jurisdiction in an infringement suit.

---

[778] NTP, Inc. v. Research in Motion, Inc., 418 F.3d 1282, 1317 (Fed. Cir. 2005); Bayer AG v. Housey Pharmaceuticals, Inc., 340 F.3d 1367, 1377 (Fed. Cir. 2003).

[779] See S. Rep. No. 100-83, at 49 (1987).

[780] 35 U.S.C. § 271(g).

[781] See S. Rep. No. 100-83, at 57 (1987); see also H.R. Rep. No. 100-60, at 16 (1987).

[782] H.R. Rep. No. 100-60, at 16 (1987).

[783] S. Rep. No. 100-83, at 57 (1987).

[784] Id.

[785] 35 U.S.C. § 295.

[786] Id.

Finally, Section 287(b) provides that "no remedies" shall be available "with respect to any product in the possession of, or in transit to, [a] person . . . before that person had notice of infringement with respect to that product."[787] However, this "innocent infringer" defense is not available to a person who practiced the patented process, or who owns or controls, or is owned or controlled by, the person who practiced the patented process, or who had knowledge before the infringement that a patented process was used to make the product.[788]

[c] Secondary Liability

A person may infringe a patent by (1) actively inducing others to infringe a patent, or (2) selling an unpatented component of a patented product or an unpatented material or apparatus for use in a patented process.[789]

[i] Relation to Direct Infringement

Active inducement and contributory infringement must result in direct infringement in order for the courts to impose liability.[790] In *Aro Manufacturing Co. v. Convertible Top Replacement Co.*,[791] the patent claimed an automobile convertible top mechanism with (a) mechanical parts, and (b) a cloth top. The defendant sold cloth tops to replace worn-out tops on General Motors cars, which were made and sold with a license. The Supreme Court held the owners of those cars had the right to "repair" their patented convertible tops by replacing the cloth.[792] Because the owners did not commit direct infringement, the defendant did not commit contributory infringement.[793] The defendant also sold cloth tops to replace worn-out tops on Ford cars, which were made and sold without a license. The Court held Ford car owners had no right to replace the cloth on their cars.[794] Because the Ford owners committed direct infringement, the defendant committed

---

[787] 35 U.S.C. § 287(b)(2). "Notice of infringement" may be actual notice or constructive notice. 35 U.S.C. § 287(b)(5)(A). *See generally* D. CHISUM, PATENTS § 16.02[6]. The statute provides a process by which an importer can demonstrate good faith by sending a "request for disclosure" to a competing manufacturer asking it to identify any patents use in manufacturing the product; and if any patents are identified, the importer is deemed to be on notice unless its own manufacturer or supplier presents a "well-grounded factual basis" for claiming non-infringement. 35 U.S.C. § 287(b)(4),(5).

[788] 35 U.S.C. § 287(b)(1). *See* Infosint, S.A. v. H. Lundbeck A/S, 612 F. Supp. 2d 402, 404–05 (S.D.N.Y. 2009) (suggesting in dicta that this defense is limited to "purchasers who are remote from the manufacturer and not in the position to protect themselves," and does not apply to retailers with the "resources to send agents to other countries to seek suppliers," who "should be able and willing to exercise more vigilance" in avoiding infringement).

[789] 35 U.S.C. § 271(b), (c). *See generally* D. CHISUM, PATENTS § 17.01. *See also* Hewlett-Packard Co. v. Bausch & Lomb Inc., 909 F.2d 1464 (Fed. Cir. 1990) (discussing Section 271(b) and (c)'s origins).

[790] *Cf.* Moleculon Research Corp. v. CBS, Inc., 793 F.2d 1261 (Fed. Cir. 1986) (inducement of infringement of a method claim of a patent may be established by circumstantial evidence that direct infringement occurs as a result of the accused infringer's acts).

[791] 365 U.S. 336 (1961).

[792] *See* § 2E[3].

[793] 365 U.S. at 341 ("it is settled that if there is no direct infringement of a patent there can be no contributory infringement.").

[794] Aro Mfg. Co. v. Convertible Top Replacement, 377 U.S. 476, 480 (1964) ("when the structure is unlicensed, as was true of the Ford cars, . . . even repair constitutes infringement."); *id.* at 483–85.

contributory infringement.[795]

[ii]   Active Inducement

A person commits active inducement if he actively and knowingly encourages or aids another person's infringement.[796] Inducement may include: (1) selling a component with instructions on how to make a patented combination or carry out a patented process;[797] (2) designing an infringing product for construction by others;[798] (3) providing a warranty or other services connected with a patented product;[799] (4) repairing or servicing previously sold infringing systems;[800] or (5) licensing and controlling another's manufacture of an infringing product.[801] The Supreme Court ruled in 2014 that a claim for inducement requires establishing direct infringement under either section 271(a) or some other provision of the Act.[802]

The level of knowledge that a defendant must have to be held liable for active inducement has been a point of controversy. In *Hewlett Packard Co. v. Bausch & Lomb, Inc.*, the court said that "proof of actual intent to cause the acts which constitute the infringement is a necessary prerequisite to finding active inducement."[803] While this statement did not necessarily mean that such proof was also a sufficient condition, some courts interpreted it to mean that active inducement required only general intent (intent to cause the actions that were infringing) rather than specific intent (intent to cause infringement).[804] Other courts, however, continued to require that the defendant have knowledge of the patent and intent to cause infringement in order to be held liable for active inducement.[805] In *DSU Medical Corp. v. JMS Co.*, the Federal Circuit resolved this apparent conflict by specifically holding *en banc* that "inducement requires

---

[795] *Id.* at 485–88.

[796] *See, e.g.*, DSU Medical Corp. v. JMS Co., 471 F.3d 1293, 1305–06 (Fed. Cir. 2006); Manville Sales Corp. v. Paramount Systems, Inc., 917 F.2d 544, 553 (Fed. Cir. 1990) ("It must be established that the defendant possessed specific intent to encourage another's infringement and not merely that the defendant had knowledge of the acts alleged to constitute inducement."); Water Technologies Corp. v. Calco, Ltd., 850 F.2d 660, 668 (Fed. Cir. 1988) ("While proof of intent is necessary, direct evidence is not required; rather, circumstantial evidence may suffice.").

[797] Honeywell, Inc. v. Metz Apparatewerke, 509 F.2d 1137 (7th Cir. 1975). There can be inducement under Section 271(b) even though the component has noninfringing uses and its sale does not constitute contributory infringement under Section 271(c).

[798] Baut v. Pethick Construction Co., 262 F. Supp. 350 (M.D. Pa. 1966).

[799] C. Van der Lely N.V. v. F. lli Maschio S.n.c., 222 U.S.P.Q. 399 (S.D. Ohio 1984).

[800] *See, e.g.* Preemption Devices, Inc. v. Minnesota Mining & Mfg. Co., 803 F.2d 1170 (Fed. Cir. 1986).

[801] *See, e.g.*, Water Technologies Corp. v. Calco, Ltd., 850 F.2d 660 (Fed. Cir. 1988) (the district court did not err in finding one defendant liable as an active inducer of infringement when it exerted control over the other defendant's manufacture of the infringing products, as owner of a trademark used by the latter on its product, and through license agreements).

[802] Limelight Networks, Inc. v. Akamai Technologies, Inc., 134 S. Ct. 2111 (2014).

[803] 909 F.2d 1464, 1469 (Fed. Cir. 1990).

[804] *See, e.g.*, Moba B.V. v. Diamond Automation, Inc., 325 F.3d 1306, 1318–19 (Fed. Cir. 2003).

[805] *See, e.g.*, Manville Sales Corp. v. Paramount Systems, Inc., 917 F.2d 544, 553 (Fed. Cir. 1990) ("It must be established that the defendant possessed specific intent to encourage another's infringement and not merely that the defendant had knowledge of the acts alleged to constitute inducement.").

evidence of culpable conduct, directed to encouraging another's infringement, not merely that the inducer had knowledge of the direct infringer's activities."[806]

DSU Medical did not end the controversy, however, because questions remain as to whether the defendant must have *actual* knowledge of the patent, or whether something less than actual knowledge, such as negligence ("should have known") or recklessness (deliberate indifference to a known risk) is sufficient. In *SEB S.A. v. Montgomery Ward & Co.*, the Federal Circuit held that "a claim for inducement is viable even where the patentee has not produced direct evidence that the accused infringer actually knew of the patent-in-suit."[807] The court held that defendant Pentalpha "deliberately disregarded a known risk that SEB had a protective patent,"[808] based on evidence that Pentalpha failed to inform the attorney who analyzed its product for infringement that it had intentionally copied SEB's product, and Pentalpha did not rebut the inference with affirmative evidence of its subjective innocence.[809] On *certiorari*, the Supreme Court held that inducement "requires knowledge that the induced acts constitute patent infringement," and that "deliberate indifference to a known risk" was not sufficient.[810] Nonetheless, the Court affirmed the judgment, holding that the knowledge standard could be satisfied by Pentalpha's "willful blindness,[811] which requires "(1) the defendant must subjectively believe that there is a high probability that a fact exists, and (2) the defendant must take deliberate actions to avoid learning of that fact."[812]

[iii]   Contributory Infringement

A person who sells a component may be liable for contributory infringement if (1) the component is a material part of the invention, (2) the component is especially made or adapted for infringing use, and is not a staple article suitable for noninfringing use,[813] and (3) he knows of the patent and of the purchaser's intended use.[814] For a component to be a staple or suitable for noninfringing use, it must have some "substantial" noninfringing use, as opposed to "unusual, far-fetched, illusory, impractical, occasional, aberrant, or experimental" use.[815] "One who makes and sells articles which are only adapted to be used in a patented

---

[806] 471 F.3d 1293, 1306 (Fed. Cir. 2006) (approving *Manville*).

[807] 594 F.3d 1360 (Fed. Cir. 2010), *aff'd*, Global-Tech Appliances, Inc. v. SEB, S.A., 131 S. Ct. 2060 (2011).

[808] 594 F.3d at 1377.

[809] *Id.* at 1377–78.

[810] Global-Tech Appliances, Inc. v. SEB, S.A., 131 S. Ct. 2060, at 2068 (2011).

[811] *Id.*, at 2071–72.

[812] *Id.*, at 2070–71.

[813] 35 U.S.C. § 271(c).

[814] Aro Mfg. Co. v. Convertible Top Replacement Co., 377 U.S. 476, 487–88 (1964); Fujitsu Ltd. v. Netgear, Inc., 620 F.3d 1321, 1326 (Fed. Cir. 2010). *Cf.* Trell v. Marlee Electronics Corp., 912 F.2d 1443 (Fed. Cir. 1990) (a court may not award contributory patent infringement damages for sales made prior to a contributory infringer's knowledge of the patent in question; the knowledge requirement is satisfied if the patent owner has sent a letter to the seller identifying the patent and the grounds for contributory infringement).

Knowledge is not an element of liability for direct infringement. *See* § 2F[3][b].

[815] Vita-Mix Corp. v. Basic Holding, Inc., 581 F.3d 1317, 1327 (Fed. Cir. 2009). Use of a component

combination . . . will be presumed to intend that they shall be used" to infringe.[816]

[iv] Corporations — Officers and Directors

Corporations are liable for their employees' and agents' infringing acts under agency law principles.[817]

Corporate officers and directors may be personally liable for actively inducing the corporation's infringement.[818] Under Section 271(b), "corporate officers who actively assist with their corporation's infringement may be personally liable for inducing infringement *regardless* of whether the circumstances are such that a court should disregard the corporate entity and pierce the corporate veil."[819] However, in order to find the officers liable, "[i]t must be established that the defendant possessed specific intent to encourage another's infringement and not merely that the defendant had knowledge of the acts alleged to constitute infringement."[820] Thus, in *Manville Sales Corp. v. Paramount Systems, Inc.*, the court held that two officers could not be liable for inducement when they were not aware of the patent until suit was filed, and thereafter they acted in good faith belief, based on advice of counsel, that the corporation's product did not infringe.[821]

[3] First Sale — Exhaustion — Repair and Reconstruction

The first authorized sale of a patented product exhausts the patent owner's exclusive rights.[822] The purchaser may thereafter use, repair, and resell the purchased product. Consider the following example:

1. A obtains a patent claiming product X.

2. A grants B an exclusive license to make and sell X only in California.

---

as a replacement or repair part on products originally sold with the permission of the patent owner may be a noninfringing use. *See* § 2E[3].

[816] Metro-Goldwyn-Mayer Studios, Inc. v. Grokster, Ltd., 545 U.S. 913, 932 (2005); *see also id.* ("where an article is 'good for nothing else' but infringement, there is no legitimate public interest in its unlicensed availability, and there is no injustice in presuming or imputing an intent to infringe") (citations omitted).

[817] *See, e.g.* Westinghouse Elec. & Mfg. Co. v. Independent Wireless Co., 300 F. 748 (S.D.N.Y. 1924); Poppenhusen v. New York Gutta Percha Comb. Co., 19 F. Cas. 1059 (No. 11,283) (C.C.S.D.N.Y. 1858). *See generally* D. Chisum, Patents § 16.06.

[818] *See, e.g.* Fromson v. Citiplate, Inc., 886 F.2d 1300 (Fed Cir. 1989) ("The cases are legion holding corporate officers and directors personally liable for 'participating in, inducing, and approving acts of patent infringement' by a corporation."); Orthokinetics, Inc. v. Safety Travel Chairs, Inc., 806 F.2d 1565 (Fed. Cir. 1986); Power Lift, Inc. v. Lang Tools, Inc., 774 F.2d 478 (Fed. Cir. 1985). *Compare* Manville Sales Corp. v. Paramount Systems, Inc., 917 F.2d 544 (Fed. Cir. 1990).

[819] *Manville*, 917 F.2d at 553.

[820] *Id.*

[821] *Id. See also* Wordtech Systems, Inc. v. Integrated Network Solutions, Inc., 609 F.3d 1308, 1317 (Fed. Cir. 2010) (reversing jury verdict of individual liability for contributory infringement, where there was no evidence that either individual defendant personally sold or offered to sell to the direct infringer).

[822] Keeler v. Standard Folding-Bed Co., 157 U.S. 659 (1895); Adams v. Burke, 84 U.S. (17 Wall.) 453 (1873). *See generally* D. Chisum, Patents § 16.03[2].

3. C buys an X from A in New York, takes it to California and resells it to
D for D's use.

Neither C's resale nor D's use of the product violates either A or B's rights because
the sale from A to C in New York exhausted A's exclusive patent rights.[823]

The Supreme Court has held that the first sale doctrine applies to method claims
as well as product claims.[824] Thus, in *Quanta Computer, Inc. v. LG Electronics, Inc.*,
when Quanta's licensee Intel sold semiconductor chips that "embodied essential
features of the patented invention," Intel's customers were entitled to install the
chips into a computer that practiced the patented methods when the chips were
combined with standard parts.[825] The first sale doctrine does not allow a purchaser
to make another copy of the invention.[826]

The first sale doctrine applies only to authorized sales. Sales beyond a limited
license's scope are unauthorized.[827] Thus, in the above example, if B travels to New
York and sells product X to E, B's act is unauthorized and is an infringement; and
E's use or resale of the product would also be an infringement. However, where a
license agreement allows the licensee to "make, use, and sell" products that embody
a patented method, the patentee cannot avoid exhaustion by disclaiming any license
to third parties and requiring the licensee to inform third parties that they were not
licensed.[828]

An authorized purchaser's right to use the purchased product includes the right
to repair the product, including the right to replace worn-out parts necessary to
continue use;[829] but the purchaser may not "reconstruct" a patented product from
the parts of worn-out products.[830] Numerous cases apply the repair-reconstruction

---

[823] The rule is otherwise in the international situation in which patent rights in different countries
may be owned by or subject to exclusive rights of different persons. *See* § 2E[2][b][ii].

[824] Quanta Computer, Inc. v. LG Electronics, Inc., 553 U.S. 617, 628–30 (2008).

[825] *Id.* at 630–35.

[826] *See* Bowman v. Monsanto, 133 S. Ct. 1761 (2013).

[827] General Talking Pictures Co. v. Western Elec. Co., 304 U.S. 175 (1938), *on rehearing*, 305 U.S. 124
(1938); Mallinckrodt, Inc. v. Medipart, Inc., 976 F.2d 700, 701 (Fed. Cir. 1992).

Restrictions in patent licenses are subject to scrutiny under the antitrust laws and the patent misuse
doctrine. *See* § 2F[4][c]. For example, a restriction on the price at which a purchaser may resell a product
is improper. United States v. Univis Lens Co., 316 U.S. 241 (1942). Similarly, most provisions that
attempt to fix the price at which licensees may sell products covered by a patent are improper. *See, e.g.*,
United States v. Line Material Co., 333 U.S. 287 (1948).

[828] *Quanta*, 533 U.S. at 636–37.

[829] Wilbur-Ellis Co. v. Kuther, 377 U.S. 422 (1964); Aro Mfg. Co. v. Convertible Top Replacement Co.,
365 U.S. 336 (1961); General Elec. Co. v. United States, 572 F.2d 745, 778–86 (Ct. Cl. 1978). For a
discussion of *Aro*, *see* § 2E[2][c][i].

[830] American Cotton-Tie Co. v. Simmons, 106 U.S. (16 Otto.) 89 (1882); Hydril Co. v. Crossman
Engineering, Inc., 152 U.S.P.Q. 171 (E.D. Tex. 1966). *But cf.* Dana Corp. v. American Precision Co., 827
F.2d 755 (Fed. Cir. 1987) (where plaintiff conceded that replacing individual parts of a single automobile
clutch consisting of dozens of parts was a permissible repair rather than a reconstruction, defendant
could not be held liable for disassembling used clutches, cleaning and sorting individual parts, and
reassembling those individual parts into usable clutches in a production line, because the result was no
different than repairing individual clutches one at a time).

distinction.[831] For example, in *Jazz Photo Corp. v. International Trade Commission*, the Federal Circuit held that refurbishing single-use cameras by cutting them open, replacing the film and the battery, resetting the counter, and re-sealing them was permissible repair rather than impermissible reconstruction.[832]

As part of the new defense of prior commercial use under the AIA, the sale or "other disposition of a useful end result" by a person entitled to raise the prior commercial user defense exhausts the rights of the patent owner to the extent that such sale or disposition would exhaust rights if done by the patent owner.

[4]   Government Use

With several exceptions, Congress has expressly waived the sovereign immunity of the federal government to suits for damages for patent infringement.[833] However, the Supreme Court has held that the Eleventh Amendment gives states and state entities immunity against patent infringement claims in federal court, notwithstanding Congress' express attempt to abrogate sovereign immunity.[834] For details, see § 1D[5], above.

§ 2F   INFRINGEMENT

Infringement is the unauthorized invasion of a patent owner's exclusive rights,[835] as defined by the patent's claims. Determining infringement involves interpreting the claim language, assessing the nature of the accused infringer's acts, and applying the interpreted claims to those acts. Only *acts*, such as unauthorized making of a device, constitute infringement, but it is commonplace to say that a device "infringes" when discussing the relationship of an accused device to a patent claim.

An accused infringer may assert defenses to the infringement charge, for example, invalidity, unenforceability, laches, misuse, or experimental use.

Patent infringement remedies include preliminary and permanent injunctions, damages, interest, and, in some cases, attorney fees and multiple damages.

[1]   Claim Language Interpretation

Claim interpretation is a critical and recurring problem for every patent system participant: the inventor and his or her attorney in composing claim language that both adequately distinguishes the invention from the prior art and provides

---

[831] *Compare* Jazz Photo Corp. v. ITC, 264 F.3d 1094 (Fed. Cir. 2001); Bottom Line Mgmt., Inc. v. Pan Man, Inc., 228 F.3d 1352 (Fed. Cir. 2000); Porter v. Farmers Supply Service, Inc., 790 F.2d 882 (Fed. Cir. 1986) (repair) *with* Sandvik Aktiebolag v. E.J. Co., 121 F.3d 669 (Fed. Cir. 1997) (reconstruction).

[832] *Jazz Photo*, 264 F.3d at 1101, 1105–07. Note, however, that this holding was limited to cameras originally sold in the United States, as the court held that a lawful foreign purchase did not exhaust the importation right. *See* § 2E[2][b][ii], above.

[833] 28 U.S.C. § 1498(a).

[834] Florida Prepaid Postsecondary Educ. Expense Bd. v. College Sav. Bank, 527 U.S. 627 (1999).

[835] Exclusive patent rights are discussed at § 2E.

meaningful protection against misappropriation; the PTO in determining whether the claimed invention is patentable; potential and actual licensees or competitors of the patent owner in assessing the scope and validity of the patent; and the courts in deciding whether to hold a patent claim invalid or infringed.[836]

In *Markman v. Westview Instruments, Inc.*,[837] the Supreme Court held that there was no Seventh Amendment right to a jury trial on the question of claim construction. Although the Supreme Court's decision did not mandate a procedure for construing the claims, its ruling that claim construction was purely a question of law, and therefore a matter for the judge, led lower courts to conduct pre-trial "Markman hearings." In a Markman hearing, the judge, based on evidence provided by the parties, issues an order construing the claims. This claim construction becomes the basis for determining infringement in the trial phase.[838] The Federal Circuit has held that claim construction is reviewed *de novo*, as a pure question of law, on appeal from the district court.[839] In addition, little deference is given to the PTO's claim construction on appellate review.[840] The issue of standard of review for claim construction is before the Supreme Court in its 2014–2015 Term. The specific question being considered is: "Whether a district court's factual finding in support of its construction of a patent claim term may be reviewed de novo, as the Federal Circuit requires (and as the panel explicitly did in this case), or only for clear error, as Rule 52(a) requires."[841]

In *Phillips v. AWH Corp.*,[842] the Federal Circuit addressed *en banc* the question of what methodology to follow in construing claims. The court divided evidence of construction into intrinsic and extrinsic. Intrinsic evidence includes the language of the claims, the specification, and the prosecution history. Extrinsic evidence includes expert testimony, dictionaries, and treatises. The court held that claim construction should begin with the language of the claims themselves and turn, in order, to the specification and prosecution history to address ambiguities in the claim language. Extrinsic evidence should be considered only in unusual cases. On this last point, the Federal Circuit reversed an earlier decision on the proper use of dictionaries in construing claims.[843]

[a]   Intrinsic and Extrinsic Material

To interpret a patent claim, one must consider, in addition to the claim's language, intrinsic evidence, such as other claims in the same patent, the specification, the prosecution history; and sometimes extrinsic evidence, such as expert testimony.

---

[836] *See generally* D. CHISUM, PATENTS § 18.03.

[837] 517 U.S. 370 (1996).

[838] *See, e.g.*, Endo-Surgery, Inc. v. United States Surgical Corp., 93 F.3d 1572 (Fed. Cir. 1996).

[839] *See* Cybor Corp. v. FAS Technologies, Inc., 138 F.3d 1448 (Fed. Cir. 1998).

[840] *See* SRAM Corp. v. AD-H Eng'g, Inc., 465 F.3d 1351 (Fed. Cir. 2006).

[841] *See* Teva Pharm. USA, Inc. v. Sandoz, Inc., 723 F.3d 1363 (Fed. Cir. 2013) (upholding de novo standard of review).

[842] 415 F.3d 1303 (Fed. Cir. 2005).

[843] Texas Digital Systems, Inc. v. Telegenix, Inc., 308 F.3d 1193 (Fed. Cir. 2002) (emphasizing use of dictionaries in construing claims).

[i]   Other Claims — Claim Differentiation

In construing a patent claim, one must consider the patent's other claims. The claim differentiation doctrine embodies the common-sense notion that a court should ordinarily not interpret one claim so as to make it identical to another. For example, in *Environmental Designs Ltd. v. Union Oil Co. of California*,[844] the patent claimed a process for removing sulphur from a gas stream, one step being "separating condensed water from the hydrogenated gas stream." The accused infringer argued the claimed step means separation "prior to contact with an aqueous absorption solution" because the inventor argued during the prosecution of the patent that there was a "significant utility . . . in removing water . . . prior to contact with an aqueous absorption solution." The court refused to read a "prior to" limitation into claim 1, noting that claim 11 explicitly set forth that limitation and it would be "improper for courts to read into an independent claim a limitation explicitly set forth in another claim."

Some court opinions characterize claim differentiation as an absolute, immutable rule,[845] but, in fact, it is a guide to construction and may not be determinative in a particular case.[846] In *Autogiro Co. of America v. United States*, the court stated "[c]laim differentiation is a guide, not a rigid rule. If a claim will bear only one interpretation, similarity will have to be tolerated."[847]

The extent to which claim differentiation applies to claims in separate but closely related patents is unclear. A presumption exists that, "unless otherwise compelled, the same claim term in the same patent or related patents carries the same construed meaning."[848] Consequently, some courts have used differences in closely related patents as an aid in construing claims.[849]

The Federal Circuit "takes a narrow view on when a related patent or its prosecution history is available to construe the claims of a patent at issue and draws a distinct line between patents that have a familial relationship and those

---

[844] 713 F.2d 693 (Fed. Cir. 1985). *See also* Marsh-McBirney, Inc. v. Montedoro-Whitney Corp., 882 F.2d 498 (Fed. Cir. 1989), *cert. granted, judgment vacated*, 498 U.S. 1061 (1991), *opinion reinstated in relevant part*, 939 F.2d 969, 970 (Fed. Cir. 1991).

[845] D.M.I. v. Deere & Co., 755 F.2d 1570, 1574 (Fed. Cir. 1985) ("Where, as here, the limitation sought to be 'read into' a claim already appears in another claim, the rule is far more than 'general.' It is fixed. It is long and well established. It enjoys an immutable and universally applicable status comparatively rare among rules of law. Without it, the entire statutory and regulatory structure governing the drafting, submission, examination, allowance, and enforceability of claims would crumble."). The Federal Circuit's language is hyperbolic and dictum because it was commenting on the trial court's concession that "as a general rule a limitation cannot be read into a claim to avoid infringement."

[846] *See, e.g.*, Regents of Univ. of Calif. v. Dakocytomation Calif., Inc., 517 F.3d 1364 (Fed. Cir. 2008) ("the presumption created by the doctrine of claim differentiation is 'not a hard and fast rule and will be overcome by a contrary construction dictated by the written description or prosecution history.'"), *quoting* Seachange Int'l, Inc. v. C-COR, Inc., 413 F.3d 1361, 1369 (Fed. Cir. 2005).

[847] 384 F.2d 391, 404 (Ct. Cl. 1967).

[848] Z4 Techs., Inc. v. Microsoft Corp., 507 F.3d 1340, 1348 (Fed. Cir. 2007) (internal quotes omitted). *See also* NTP, Inc. v. Research in Motion, Ltd., 418 F.3d 1282, 1293 (Fed. Cir. 2005) ("Because [the plaintiff's] patents all derive from the same parent application and share many common terms, we must interpret the claims consistently across the asserted patents.").

[849] *See, e.g.*, Kara Technology, Inc. v. Stamps.com, Inc., 582 F.3d 1341, 1347 (Fed. Cir. 2009).

that do not."[850] Thus, although an unrelated patent "sheds no light" on the claims of the patent at issue,[851] claims and statements made in prosecution of related patents can sometimes be used to construe the claims of a patent.[852]

[ii] Specification — The Patentee as "Lexicographer"

The patent specification describes the invention and methods of making and using it, but the claims, not the specification, define the patent's scope for patentability and infringement. A patent's claims are not limited to the specification's best mode, preferred embodiment, specific objects, or illustrative examples,[853] and it is error to read limitations from the specification into the claims.[854] Conversely, a patent confers no rights over subject matter disclosed but not claimed.[855]

Nonetheless, the specification is important in interpreting claim language. Claim language may, on its face, be ambiguous enough to raise questions of invalidity for indefiniteness and yet, after the specification is considered, be quite clear.[856] The converse is also possible: an apparently clear phrase may be rendered indefinite when considered in light of the specification.[857]

The line between using the specification to interpret the claims, which is mandatory, and reading limitations from the specification into the claims, which is prohibited, is thin.[858] In *E.I. du Pont de Nemours & Co. v. Phillips Petroleum*

---

[850] Goldenberg v. Cytogen, Inc., 373 F.3d 1158, 1167 (Fed. Cir. 2004).

[851] Texas Digital Systems v. Telegenix, Inc., 308 F.3d 1193, 1211 (Fed. Cir. 2002). *See also* Abbott Laboratories v. Dey, L.P., 287 F.3d 1097, 1105 (Fed. Cir. 2002).

[852] *See, e.g.*, Microsoft Corp. v. Multi-Tech Systems, Inc., 357 F.3d 1340, 1350 (Fed. Cir. 2004); Jonsson v. Stanley Works, 903 F.2d 812 (Fed. Cir. 1990).

[853] *See, e.g.*, Laitram Corp. v. Cambridge Wire Cloth Co., 863 F.2d 855, 865 (Fed. Cir. 1988) ("References to a preferred embodiment, such as those often present in a specification, are not claim limitations."; "That the inventor preferred and adopted commercially [one specific embodiment] . . . is not a basis for limiting [a claim] to [that embodiment]."); Specialty Composites v. Cabot Corp., 845 F.2d 981, 987 (Fed. Cir. 1988); Rolls-Royce Ltd. v. GTE Valeron Corp., 800 F.2d 1101, 1108 (Fed. Cir. 1987) ("Reference to an object does not constitute in itself a limitation in the claims.").

[854] *See, e.g.*, Intervet America, Inc. v. Kee-Vet Laboratories, Inc., 887 F.2d 1050 (Fed Cir. 1989).

[855] *See, e.g.*, Environmental Instruments, Inc. v. Sutron Corp., 877 F.2d 1561, 1564 (Fed. Cir. 1989) ("the disclosure of a patent is in the public domain save as the claims forbid. The claims alone delimit the right to exclude; only they may be infringed.").

[856] *See, e.g.*, In re Moore, 439 F.2d 1232, 1235–36 (C.C.P.A. 1971).

[857] *In re* Cohn, 438 F.2d 989 (C.C.P.A. 1971) (phrase "opaque finish" used in inherently inconsistent ways in the specification). *See also In re* Merat, 519 F.2d 1390 (C.C.P.A. 1975) (claim phrase "normal chickens" rendered indefinite by specification).

[858] *See, e.g.*, Corning Glass Works v. Sumitomo Electric U.S.A., 868 F.2d 1251, 1257 (Fed. Cir. 1989) ("a court may not redraft a claim for purposes of avoiding a defense of anticipation," and "'extraneous' limitations from the specification . . . [should not] be read into the claim wholly apart from any need to interpret what the patentee meant by particular *words or phrases in the claim*," but "[i]t is entirely proper to use the specification to interpret what the patentee meant by a word or phrase in the claim."); Sjolund v. Musland, 847 F.2d 1573, 1581 (Fed. Cir. 1988) ("[W]hile it is true that claims are to be interpreted *in light of* the specification and with a view to ascertaining the invention, it does not follow that limitations from the specification may be read into the claims. . . .").

Co.,[859] the Federal Circuit held that the district court erred in incorporating two properties, environmental stress crack resistance and impact strength, from the specification into the claim to distinguish the claimed subject matter (a copolymer) from a prior art disclosure:

> It is entirely proper to use the specification to interpret what the [p]atentee meant by a word or phrase in the claim. . . . But this is not to be confused with adding an extraneous limitation appearing in the specification, which is improper. By "extraneous," we mean a limitation read into a claim from the specification wholly apart from any need to interpret what the patentee meant by particular words or phrases in the claim.[860]

A venerable patent claim interpretation principle is that the inventor may act "as his own lexicographer," *i.e.*, that he may define his terms as he chooses, provided that he makes his meaning clear.[861] This typically requires that the inventor "clearly set forth a definition of the disputed claim term in either the specification or prosecution history."[862] The definition privilege has limits: the inventor must use words in the same way in the claims and the specification,[863] and he or she must not use terminology that is so confusing, inconsistent or incorrect as to render the claim language invalid for indefiniteness.[864]

An inventor's post-patenting testimony on a claim's meaning carries little weight, especially if it is inconsistent with the specification and prosecution history.[865]

See also Datascope Corp. v. SMEC, Inc., 879 F.2d 820, 824 (Fed. Cir. 1989) (a patent claim specifying "support means" should not be limited to "solid objects" merely because the embodiments in the specification use rods and wires; "The claims . . . do not limit 'support means' to solid objects and the specification states in several places that illustrations are provided for purposes of 'example and not limitation.' . . . [There was] no evidence suggesting the propriety of anything other than a plain and ordinary reading of the claims.").

[859] 849 F.2d 1430 (Fed. Cir. 1988).

[860] *Id.* at 1433.

[861] *See, e.g., In re* Castaing, 429 F.2d 461, 463 (C.C.P.A. 1970) ("Whether the terms are conventional is not necessarily controlling. An applicant is ordinarily entitled to be his own lexicographer, so long as his meaning is clear."). *See also* Helmsderfer v. Bobrick Washroom Equipment, Inc., 527 F.3d 1379, 1381 (Fed. Cir. 2008) ("A patentee may act as its own lexicographer and assign to a term a unique definition that is different from its ordinary and customary meaning; however, a patentee must clearly express that intent in the written description.").

[862] CCS Fitness, Inc. v. Brunswick Corp., 288 F.3d 1359, 1366 (Fed. Cir. 2002); *see also* Laryngeal Mask Co. v. Ambu A/S, 618 F.3d 1367, 1372 (Fed. Cir. 2010).

[863] Fonar Corp. v. Johnson & Johnson, 821 F.2d 627 (Fed. Cir. 1987), *overruled on other grounds*, Cardinal Chemical Co. v. Morton Int'l, Inc., 508 U.S. 83 (1993); Brunswick Corp. v. United States, 34 Fed. Cl. 532, 543 (1995).

[864] *See, e.g., Ex parte* Wolk, 225 U.S.P.Q. 225, 227 (PTO Bd. App. 1984) ("Appellant's specification contains inconsistent and confusing teachings. Thus the principle that a patent applicant may be his own lexicographer cannot apply here. The definition of ash as 'noncatalytic' is wrong. Therefore the statement in the claims that reaction is 'in the absence of a catalyst' is inaccurate and indefinite."). *Cf.* Codex Corp. v. Milgo Electronics Corp., 717 F.2d 622 (1st Cir. 1983).

[865] *See, e.g.,* Senmed, Inc. v. Richard-Allan Medical Industries, Inc., 888 F.2d 815, 819 n.8 (Fed. Cir. 1989). Even inventor testimony adverse to the patentee's interests is not binding. *See, e.g.,* Smithkline Diagnostics, Inc. v. Helena Laboratories Corp., 859 F.2d 878 (Fed. Cir. 1988). *Compare* Jonsson v. The Stanley Works, 903 F.2d 812, 819 (Fed. Cir. 1990) (in granting summary judgment of noninfringement,

[iii]   Prosecution History

During prosecution, the inventor, through his patent attorney or agent, may, in response to PTO examiner actions, make arguments supporting patentability or amend the claims.

Prosecution arguments and amendments affect a patent's scope in two ways. First, the arguments and amendments are pertinent to interpretation.[866] Second, the arguments and amendments may create prosecution history estoppel, which restrains the doctrine of equivalents.[867] The two effects are distinct. For example, a prosecution history event may lead to a narrow claim interpretation but not preclude resort to the doctrine of equivalents to find infringement.[868]

[iv]   Expert Testimony

Parties to infringement suits may offer expert testimony on the pertinent technology and on patent procedure and claim interpretation.[869] Expert testimony on claim interpretation and the application of claim language to accused devices or methods is not mandatory in every case,[870] but, in some cases, a trial court may err if it fails to admit expert testimony on what a term in the claim means to a person of ordinary skill in the art.[871]

[b]   "Means-Plus-Function" Limitations

Patent Act Section 112 prescribes a rule of claim interpretation for "means-plus-function" limitations:

---

the district court did not err by relying, in part, on the inventor's deposition testimony on a patent claim term's meaning).

[866] Graham v. John Deere Co., 383 U.S. 1, 33 (1966) ("an invention is construed not only in the light of the claims, but also with reference to the file wrapper or prosecution history in the Patent Office. . . . Claims as allowed must be read and interpreted with reference to rejected ones and to the state of the prior art; and claims that have been narrowed in order to obtain the issuance of a patent by distinguishing the prior art cannot be sustained to cover that which was previously by limitation eliminated from the patent"); Howes v. Medical Components, Inc., 814 F.2d 638, 645 (Fed. Cir. 1987) ("during the prosecution of a patent, claim language may take on new meanings, possibly different from that which was originally intended").

[867] *See* § 2F[2][c].

[868] *See, e.g.*, E.I. du Pont de Nemours & Co. v. Phillips Petroleum Co., 849 F.2d 1430, 1439 (Fed. Cir. 1988) ("merely because certain prosecution history is used to define the claims more narrowly, there still may be — even in light of that same prosecution history — an appropriate range of equivalents under the doctrine of equivalents.").

[869] *See, e.g.*, Snellman v. Ricoh Company, Ltd., 862 F.2d 283, 287 (Fed. Cir. 1988) ("Although claim interpretation is a question of law, expert testimony is admissible to explain the meaning of technical terms in the claims and to give an opinion on the ultimate question of infringement."). *See also* Phillips v. AWH Corp., 415 F.3d 1303, 1318 (Fed. Cir. 2005), *citing* Pitney Bowes, Inc. v. Hewlett-Packard Co., 182 F.3d 1298, 1308–09 (Fed. Cir. 1999).

[870] Moleculon Research Corp. v. CBS, Inc., 793 F.2d 1261 (Fed. Cir. 1986).

[871] Moeller v. Ionetics, Inc., 794 F.2d 653, 657 (Fed. Cir. 1986) (summary judgment was not appropriate because there was a dispute as to the meaning of the term "electrode" in the patent claim, and expert testimony by persons skilled in the art would be helpful extrinsic evidence in interpreting the claim). *Compare* Howes v. Medical Components, Inc., 814 F.2d 638 (Fed. Cir. 1987) (expert testimony on the meaning of terms was not required because they were "not technical terms or terms of art").

An element in a claim for a combination may be expressed as a means or step for performing a specified function without the recital of structure, material, or acts in support thereof, and such claim shall be construed to cover the corresponding structure, material, or acts described in the specification and equivalents thereof.[872]

Federal Circuit decisions interpret and apply means-plus-function limitations, some in the PTO examination context,[873] others in patent validity determination,[874] but most in infringement determination.[875] "Literal infringement of a means-plus-function limitation requires that the relevant structure in the accused device perform the identical function recited in the claim and be identical or equivalent to the corresponding structure in the specification."[876]

Identity of function is a straightforward claim interpretation and application exercise. Equivalency of means is more complicated. One must first examine the patent specification to determine what structure, material or acts are described that correspond to the "means" recited in the claim. One must then compare the described structure, material or act with the structure, material, or act that performs the recited function in the accused device or method (or the prior art if the issue is patentability). The claim will cover that device or method if, upon comparison, the structure, material or act is equivalent to that disclosed in the specification of the patent, and if the other elements of the claim are also found in that device or method.

The Section 112 equivalents inquiry is not the same as the doctrine of equivalents. A Section 112 inquiry determines a claim's *literal* scope,[877] and asks solely whether the means in the accused device or method that performs the stated function is equivalent to the corresponding structure described in the specification as performing that function. In contrast, the doctrine of equivalents applies only when the claim, properly interpreted, does not cover an accused device or method. Equitable considerations guide application of the doctrine of equivalents. For example, a particularly important invention — a "pioneer" — receives a wider scope of equivalents than a narrow improvement; and equivalence is more likely if the accused infringer deliberately copies the patent's technology. These considerations

---

[872] 35 U.S.C. § 112.

[873] *In re* Bond, 910 F.2d 831 (Fed. Cir. 1990) (the Section 112, last paragraph, means-plus-function limitation interpretation rule applies to claims under PTO examination). *Cf. In re* Queener, 796 F.2d 461 (Fed. Cir. 1986).

[874] Polaroid Corp. v. Eastman Kodak Co., 789 F.2d 1556, 1570 (Fed. Cir. 1986) (prior art structures performing the recited function did not render the claimed subject matter obvious because the specification and statements in the prosecution history justified giving the means-plus-function element a narrow scope of equivalence); RCA Corp. v. Applied Digital Data Sys., 730 F.2d 1440 (Fed. Cir. 1984) (a claim element stated in a means-plus-function format cannot be met by an element in a prior art reference that performs a different function).

[875] *See, e.g.,* Baran v. Medical Device Technologies, Inc., 616 F.3d 1309 (Fed. Cir. 2010); Welker Bearing Co. v. PHD, Inc., 550 F.3d 1090 (Fed. Cir. 2008); Texas Instruments, Inc. v. U.S. Int'l Trade Comm'n, 805 F.2d 1558 (Fed. Cir. 1986); Palumbo v. Don-Joy Co., 762 F.2d 969 (Fed. Cir. 1985).

[876] General Protecht Group, Inc. v. Int'l Trade Comm'n, 619 F.3d 1303, 1312 (Fed. Cir. 2010), *quoting* Applied Medical Research v. U.S. Surgical Corp., 448 F.3d 1324, 1333 (Fed. Cir. 2006).

[877] D.M.I., Inc. v. Deere & Co., 755 F.2d 1570 (Fed. Cir. 1985).

do not apply to the focused Section 112 equivalency inquiry.[878]

In *Texas Instruments, Inc. v. U.S. International Trade Commission*,[879] a Federal Circuit panel adopted a "whole subject matter" approach to a claim containing a series of means-plus-function limitations. It stated that section 112, paragraph 6 "provides, and extensive judicial analysis has reinforced, that when the claimed invention is a novel combination of steps, all possible methods of carrying out each step of the combination are not required to be described in the specification."[880] However, "where all of the claimed functions are performed in the accused devices by subsequently developed or improved means, [it is not appropriate] to view each such change as if it were the only change from the disclosed embodiments of the invention. It is the entirety of the technology embodied in the accused devices that must be compared with the patent disclosure."[881] The court concluded that "[t]aken together, [the] accumulated differences distinguish the accused calculators from that contemplated in the . . . patent and transcend a fair range of equivalents of the . . . invention."[882]

[c] Consistency

A patent claim must be interpreted consistently in determining both validity and infringement.[883] If the inventor secures a narrow interpretation to sustain validity, he cannot show infringement by giving a broader interpretation. If the inventor secures a broad interpretation to show infringement, a court can invalidate the claim if, as interpreted, it reads on the prior art.[884]

Consistent interpretation for validity and infringement is a serious problem in patent systems in which cancellation or invalidation proceedings are separate from infringement proceedings. This problem is not as serious in the United States because validity may be raised by an accused infringer as a defense. Problems do arise if validity or infringement must be re-tried because of legal error. In one case, the error directly affected only the infringement determination; however, because the infringement trial would be to a different jury panel, the court felt that it was necessary to retry validity as well.[885]

---

[878] Palumbo v. Don-Joy Co., 762 F.2d 969 (Fed. Cir. 1985).

[879] 805 F.2d 1558 (Fed. Cir. 1986), *opinion on denial of rehearing*, 846 F.2d 1369 (Fed. Cir. 1988).

[880] 805 F.2d at 1562.

[881] *Id.* at 1569–70.

[882] *Id.* at 1570. The panel denied a request for rehearing, noting that its "subject matter as a whole" approach was distinct from the reverse doctrine of equivalents. 846 F.2d at 1371; *see* § 2F[2][b][vi].

[883] *See, e.g.*, Kimberly-Clark Corp. v. Johnson & Johnson, 745 F.2d 1437, 1449 (Fed. Cir. 1984) (claims "must be construed in the identical way for both infringement and validity").

[884] Smith v. Hall, 301 U.S. 216 (1937).

A related problem is whether a narrow construction of a claim entered against a patent owner is binding in subsequent suits brought by the patent owner against other accused infringers. *See* Jackson Jordan, Inc. v. Plaser American Corp., 747 F.2d 1567 (Fed. Cir. 1984); A.B. Dick Co. v. Burroughs Corp., 713 F.2d 700 (Fed. Cir. 1983) (judicial statements on claim scope have a collateral estoppel effect in a later suit only to the extent that the scope determination was essential to a final judgment on validity or infringement).

[885] Witco Chemical Corp. v. Peachtree Doors, Inc., 787 F.2d 1545, 1549 (Fed. Cir. 1986) ("In order to

The claim interpretation consistency principle is subject to a major caveat. If a patent claim's validity is challenged, the claim will be construed narrowly, if reasonably possible, to sustain validity.[886] In contrast, during PTO examination a claim is given the "broadest reasonable construction,"[887] because at that stage, "any ambiguity or excessive breadth may be corrected by merely changing [amending] the claim."[888]

The "broadest reasonable interpretation" rule applies to patent reissue and reexamination,[889] which can cause a patent owner substantial hardship if the claim would have been held valid over the prior art under the normal interpretation standard but is considered unpatentable under the broadest interpretation standard. To save the rejected claim, the patentee must amend it. Any substantive amendment made during reissue or reexamination extinguishes the patentee's right to recover damages for infringement of that claim as to activity occurring prior to the reissue or reexamination confirmation.[890] Amendments that cure formal defects or clarify the claim do not extinguish the right,[891] but an amendment required to distinguish prior art is substantive.[892]

[2] Claim Application

Section 271(a) defines infringement as the making, using, offering for sale, selling, or importing of the "patented invention" within the United States during the patent term without the patentee's authority.[893] The "patented invention" is defined by the claims; therefore, the claims limit the exclusive rights and define what constitutes infringement.[894]

---

determine infringement, the scope of disputed claims must be construed in light of the patent's specification and prosecution history. Here the arguments against infringement are indistinguishably woven with the factual underpinnings of the validity and enforceability determinations. . . . Consequently, the entire judgment is vacated and the case remanded for a new trial."). *Compare* Perkin-Elmer Corp. v. Computervision Corp., 732 F.2d 888 (Fed. Cir. 1984) (no retrial of the validity issue is required after an appellate reversal of the noninfringement finding absent evidence that the appellate court in finding infringement interpreted the claims differently from the jury that found the patent valid).

[886] *See, e.g.,* ACS Hospital Sys., Inc. v. Montefiore Hospital, 732 F.2d 1572 (Fed. Cir. 1984).

[887] *See, e.g., In re* Heck, 699 F.2d 1331 (Fed. Cir. 1983); *In re* Prater, 415 F.2d 1393, 1404–05 (C.C.P.A. 1969).

[888] Burlington Industries, Inc. v. Quigg, 822 F.2d 1581, 1583 (Fed. Cir. 1987).

[889] *In re* Yamamoto, 740 F.2d 1569 (Fed. Cir. 1984). *See also In re* Queener, 796 F.2d 461 (Fed. Cir. 1986). For a discussion of reissue and reexamination, see §§ 2D[6][a] and [b].

[890] *See, e.g.,* Fortel Corp. v. Phone-Mate, Inc., 825 F.2d 1577 (Fed. Cir. 1987). A right to recover damages for infringement of a claim survives reissue or reexamination only if a claim in the reissued or reexamined patent is "identical" to a claim in the original patent.

[891] Slimfold Manufacturing Co., Inc. v. Kinkead Industries, Inc., 810 F.2d 1113 (Fed. Cir. 1987); Kaufman Company, Inc. v. Lantech, Inc., 807 F.2d 970 (Fed. Cir. 1986).

[892] For this reason, the PTO ruled that the broad construction rule should not apply to reexamination of expired patents. *See Ex parte* Papst-Motoren, 1 U.S.P.Q.2d 1655 (Bd. Pat. App. & Int'l 1986). The owner of an expired patent can potentially recover damages for infringing acts occurring before expiration. Amendments to the claims of an expired patent would serve no purpose other than to deprive the patent owner of a damage remedy.

[893] 35 U.S.C. § 271(a).

[894] The statute does not expressly state that "patented invention" is determined by reference to the

To determine infringement, the words of the patent claim's words must be construed or interpreted,[895] and applied to the accused product or process. If the claim covers the accused product or process in a clear, literal way, there is literal infringement.[896] If the claim does not literally cover the accused product or process but the accused product or process is substantially the same as the claimed product or process, there may be infringement under the doctrine of equivalents.[897]

[a]   Literal Infringement

Claims contain one or more limitations, sometimes referred to as "elements."[898] To establish literal infringement, "every limitation set forth in a claim must be found in an accused product [or process]."[899]

[i]   Omissions

Omission of any claim element avoids literal infringement.[900] Consider the following example:

1. The claim in the patent is for "a product comprising X, Y, and Z, said X consisting of U, V and W."

2. The accused product contains elements X, Y and Z, but the X consists of T, U, and V.

There is no literal infringement because the specified type of element X is not in the accused product.

[ii]   Additions and Improvements

Neither addition of elements not stated in the claim[901] nor improvement on a claimed element — even a patentable improvement[902] — avoids infringement. In the above example, an accused product will infringe if the claim contains the

---

claims, but that is the natural inference from the statutory requirement that the patent specification "conclude with one or more claims particularly pointing out and distinctly claiming the subject matter which the applicant regards as his invention." 35 U.S.C. § 112.

[895] *See* § 2F[1].

[896] *See* § 2F[2][a].

[897] *See* § 2F[2][b].

[898] *See* § 2D[1][b].

[899] Becton, Dickinson & Co. v. Tyco Healthcare Group, LP, 616 F.3d 1249, 1253 (Fed. Cir. 2010) (internal quotes omitted); Southwall Technologies, Inc. v. Cardinal IG Co., 54 F.3d 1570, 1575 (Fed. Cir. 1995).

[900] *See Becton, Dickinson & Co.*, 616 F.3d at 1253 ("[i]f any claim limitation is absent from the accused device, there is no literal infringement as a matter of law."), *quoting* Amgen, Inc. v. F. Hoffman-La Roche, Ltd., 580 F.3d 1370, 1374 (Fed. Cir. 2009). *See also* Lemelson v. United States, 752 F.2d 1538, 1551 (Fed. Cir. 1985) ("each element of a claim is material and essential, and . . . in order for a court to find infringement, the patent owner must show the presence of every element or its substantial equivalent in the accused device").

The "all elements" rule also applies to the doctrine of equivalents. *See* § 2F[2][b].

[901] Uniroyal, Inc. v. Rudkin-Wiley Corp., 837 F.2d 1044 (Fed. Cir. 1988) ("Adding features to an accused device will not result in noninfringement if all the limitations in the claims, or equivalents thereof, are present in the accused device.").

specified X, Y, and Z elements, even though it may add an element W or involve an improvement on the element Y.

[b]   Doctrine of Equivalents

Unauthorized manufacture, use, offer for sale, sale, or importation of an accused product or process not literally within a claim may nonetheless infringe under the doctrine of equivalents, if "the accused product or process contain[s] elements that are identical or equivalent to each claimed element of the patented invention."[903]

Courts recognize the importance of clear claiming,[904] but they are unwilling to confine patentees to the strict literal wording of their claims, and therefore they may find infringement when an accused product or process is "equivalent" to the description in the claims. Extension of the scope of a patent beyond the literal claim language is known as the "doctrine of equivalents." According to Judge Learned Hand, the doctrine is an "anomaly":

> [A]fter all aids to interpretation have been exhausted, and the scope of the claims has been enlarged as far as the words can be stretched, on proper occasions courts make them cover more than their meaning will bear. If they applied the law with inexorable rigidity, they would never do this, but would remit the patentee to his remedy of re-issue, and that is exactly what they frequently do. Not always, however, for at times they resort to the "doctrine of equivalents" to temper unsparing logical and prevent an infringer from stealing the benefit of the invention. No doubt, this is, strictly speaking, an anomaly; but it is one which courts have frankly faced and accepted almost from the beginning.[905]

The Federal Circuit has held that the doctrine of equivalents applies to design patents because the patent statute makes "any colorable imitation" an infringement.[906]

The addition of an element may avoid literal infringement if the claim is drafted in a closed form. *See* § 2C[6].

[902] Hoyt v. Horne, 145 U.S. 302 (1892); Studiengesellschaft Kohle, m.b.H. v. Dart Indus., Inc., 726 F.2d 724, 728 (Fed. Cir. 1984). *But see* Texas Instruments, Inc. v. U.S. Int'l Trade Comm'n, 805 F.2d 1558 (Fed. Cir. 1986), *opinion on denial of rehearing*, 846 F.2d 1369 (Fed. Cir. 1988), discussed at § 2F[1][c].

[903] Warner-Jenkinson Co. v. Hilton Davis Chemical Co., 520 U.S. 17, 40 (1997).

[904] *See, e.g.*, Merrill v. Yeomans, 94 U.S. (4 Otto) 568, 573–74 (1877) ("nothing can be more just and fair both to the patentee and to the public, than that the former should understand and correctly describe just what he has invented and for what he claims a patent.").

[905] Royal Typewriter Co. v. Remington Rand, Inc., 168 F.2d 691 (2d Cir. 1948).

[906] *See* Pacific Coasts Marine Windshields, Ltd. v. Malibu Boats, LLC, 739 F.3d 694 (Fed. Cir. 2014) (interpreting 35 USC § 289).

[i] The *Graver Tank* and *Warner-Jenkinson* Decisions

The Supreme Court first recognized the doctrine of equivalents in 1853.[907] Its leading decision concerning the doctrine of equivalents is *Graver Tank & Mfg. Co. v. Linde Air Products Co.*[908] In *Graver Tank*, the accused composition substituted manganese silicate for magnesium silicate, a substitution which was disclosed in the prior art. The claims, however, required an "alkaline earth metal silicate," and since manganese is not an alkaline earth metal, the claims were not literally infringed. Nonetheless, the Supreme Court affirmed the trial court's finding of infringement under the doctrine of equivalents.

The court made the following points about the doctrine of equivalents:

1. It is based on the concept that "one may not practice a fraud on a patent."[909]

2. It operates not only in favor of pioneer inventions but also in favor of secondary inventions that produce new and useful results (though the area of equivalency may vary under the circumstances).[910]

3. It may be used against, as well as in favor of, a patentee in situations in which an accused device falls within the claim's literal words but performs the same or a similar function in a substantially different way.[911]

4. Equivalency is not determined by a formula but must be determined within the context of the patent, the prior art, and the particular circumstances of the case.

5. Complete identity for every purpose and in every respect is not required.[912]

6. Things that are equal to the same thing may not be equal to each other; things for most purposes different may sometimes be equivalent to each other.

7. Consideration must be given to the purpose for which an ingredient is used in a patent, the qualities it has when combined with other ingredients, and

---

[907] Winans v. Denmead, 56 U.S. (15 How.) 330 (1853).

[908] 339 U.S. 605 (1950).

[909] *Graver Tank's* statement that the doctrine's purpose is to prevent the practicing of "a fraud on a patent" is hardly precise or accurate. Many accused infringers have been held liable for infringement under the doctrine of equivalents even though they believed in good faith that they had designed around the patented invention.

What then is the purpose of the doctrine? One can argue that it is to protect inventors from the misunderstandings and short-sightedness of their patent attorneys in drafting claims. Time and time again, patent claims contain word limitations that are unnecessary in view of the nature of the disclosed invention, the prior art, and the actions of the patent examiner. This is not a matter of negligence or incompetence on the part of claim drafters; drafting appropriate claims is extremely difficult.

[910] *See* § 2F[2][b][iv].

[911] *See* § 2F[2][b][vi].

[912] Substantial rather than exact identity is required. Perkin-Elmer Corp. v. Computervision Corp., 732 F.2d 888, 900 (Fed. Cir. 1984).

the function it is intended to perform.

8. An important factor is whether persons reasonably skilled in the art would have known of the interchangeability of an ingredient that was not included in the patent with one that was so included.[913]

9. Equivalency is a determination of fact and may be proved by expert testimony, documents, texts and treatises, and prior art disclosures.[914]

In *Warner-Jenkinson Co. v. Hilton Davis Chemical Co.*, the Supreme Court held that the *Graver Tank* decision survived Congress' revisions of the Patent Act in 1952.[915] The Court clarified that the defense of prosecution history estoppel was a limitation on the doctrine of equivalents,[916] that intent was not an element of the doctrine of equivalents,[917] and that the doctrine could apply to technologies that arose after the patented invention.[918] Finally the Court refused to endorse a particular "linguistic formulation" for the doctrine of equivalents, leaving the Federal Circuit to refine its existing formulation on a case-by-case basis.[919]

[ii]   The "Triple Identity" Test

The traditional statement of the doctrine of equivalents is the so-called tri-partite or "triple identity" test, which asks whether the accused product or device "performs substantially the same function . . . in substantially the same way to obtain substantially the same result."[920] In *Warner-Jenkinson*, however, the Supreme Court clarified that equivalency must be determined on an element-by-element basis, rather than to the invention as a whole.[921] It also declined to adopt a particular "linguistic formulation" for the doctrine of equivalents, acknowledging both the traditional triple identity test and the "insubstantial differences" test, but leaving the Federal Circuit to refine the formulation on a case-by-case basis.[922]

The triple identity test rarely provides a clear guide in determining infringement by the doctrine of equivalents. The primary reason the triple identity test is not helpful is that it does not control the level of generality that may be used in characterizing the invention's "function," "way," or "result." Patentees in litigation characterize the function, way, and result broadly to show similarity between the patented invention and the accused product; accused infringers characterize the function, way, and result narrowly to show differences. The court

---

[913] *See* § 2F[2][b][v].

[914] *See* Martin v. Barber, 755 F.2d 1564 (Fed. Cir. 1985).

[915] 520 U.S. 17, 25–28 (1997).

[916] *Id.* at 30–32. *See* § 2F[2][c].

[917] 520 U.S. at 36.

[918] *Id.* at 37.

[919] *Id.* at 39–40.

[920] Bates v. Coe, 98 U.S. (8 Otto) 31, 42 (1878). *See also* Graver Tank & Mfg. Co. v. Linde Air Products Co., 339 U.S. 605, 608 (1950) ("if two devices do the same work in substantially the same way, and accomplish substantially the same result, they are the same").

[921] Warner-Jenkinson Co. v. Hilton Davis Chemical Co., 520 U.S. 17, 29, 40 (1997).

[922] *Id.* at 39–40. *See, e.g.*, Abbott Laboratories v. Sandoz, Inc., 566 F.3d 1282, 1296–97 (Fed. Cir. 2009); Voda v. Cordis Corp., 536 F.3d 1311, 1326 (Fed. Cir. 2008).

rules for or against equivalency based on which characterization it accepts.[923]

[iii]   Comparison Standard — The "All Elements" Rule

Before *Warner-Jenkinson*, the Federal Circuit struggled with the problem of the relationship between claim limitations and an allegedly equivalent product or process. In *Pennwalt Corp. v. Durand-Wayland, Inc.*, the court, sitting *en banc*, emphasized there must be in an accused structure or process an equivalent of each claim limitation.[924] In *Corning Glass Works v. Sumitomo Electric U.S.A., Inc.*, however, a panel held that "the determination of equivalency is not subject to such a limited formula," and that *Pennwalt* only requires that "[a]n equivalent must be found for every limitation of the claim somewhere in an accused device, but not necessarily in a corresponding component."[925]

In *Warner-Jenkinson*, the Supreme Court held that "the doctrine of equivalents must be applied to individual elements of the claim, not to the invention as a whole. It is important to ensure that the application of the doctrine, even as to an individual element, is not allowed such broad play as to effectively eliminate that element in its entirety."[926] Thus, the "essential inquiry" is: "Does the accused product or process contain elements identical or equivalent to each claimed element of the patented invention?"[927] "In other words, the 'all elements' rule is applicable to infringement under the doctrine of equivalents just as it is to literal infringement."[928]

[iv]   Range of Equivalents — Pioneer Patents

The range of equivalents varies according to the importance of the claimed invention.[929] A "pioneer" invention gains a broad range of equivalents,[930] a substantial improvement enjoys a substantial range of equivalents,[931] and a narrow improvement has only a limited range of equivalents.[932] A pioneer invention covers

---

[923] *Cf.* Claude Neon Lights, Inc. v. E. Machlett & Sons, 36 F.2d 574, 575–76 (2d Cir. 1929) (L. Hand, J.) ("The usual ritual, which is so often repeated and which has so little meaning, that the same result must follow by substantially the same means, does not help much in application; it is no more than a way of stating the problem.").

[924] 833 F.2d 931, 949–53 (Fed. Cir. 1987), *disapproved on other grounds*, Cardinal Chemical Co. v. Morton Int'l, Inc., 508 U.S. 83 (1993).

[925] 868 F.2d 1251, 1259 (Fed. Cir. 1989).

[926] Warner-Jenkinson Co. v. Hilton Davis Chemical Co., 520 U.S. 17, 29 (1997).

[927] *Id.* at 40.

[928] TIP Systems, LLC v. Phillips & Brooks/Gladwin, Inc., 529 F.3d 1364, 1377 (Fed. Cir. 2008).

[929] Continental Paper Bag Co. v. Eastern Paper Bag Co., 210 U.S. 405, 414–15 (1908).

[930] Perkin-Elmer Corp. v. Westinghouse Electric Corp., 822 F.2d 1528, 1532 (Fed. Cir. 1987); Hughes Aircraft Co. v. United States, 29 Fed. Cl. 197, 209 (1993). *But see* Texas Instruments, Inc. v. U.S. Int'l Trade Comm'n, 805 F.2d 1558, 1571 (Fed. Cir. 1987) (finding no equivalence despite pioneer status of invention), *reh'g denied*, 846 F.2d 1369 (Fed. Cir. 1988).

[931] Eibel Process Co. v. Minnesota & Ontario Paper Co., 261 U.S. 45, 63 (1923); Hughes Aircraft Co. v. United States, 717 F.2d 1351 (Fed. Cir. 1983).

[932] Warner-Jenkinson Co. v. Hilton Davis Chemical Co., 520 U.S. 17, 27 n.4 (1997) ("a claim describing a limited improvement in a crowded field will have a limited range of permissible equivalents."). *See also*

"a function never before performed, a wholly novel product, or one of such novelty and importance as to mark a distinct step in the progress of the art."[933]

[v] Later Developed Equivalents

Equivalence is determined as of the time of the infringement, not at the time the patent was issued.[934] Thus, although the fact that a person of ordinary skill in the art would have known of the equivalency at the time of the invention or the filing of the patent is a positive factor that suggests equivalency,[935] equivalency may extend to elements or devices that are developed after the dates of invention and filing.[936]

In *Hughes Aircraft Co. v. United States*,[937] the patent related to synchronous communications satellite attitude control. The claim required that the satellite have a means for receiving and directly executing control signals from an earth ground control station. Later-developed satellites did not respond directly to ground control signals as required by the claims because they utilized on-board microprocessors to receive control signals and execute them after processing. The microprocessors were unknown at the time the application for the patent was filed. The court found infringement, stressing that an inventor is not required to predict all future developments that enable the practice of his invention in substantially the same way.[938]

[vi] Reverse Doctrine of Equivalents

Equivalents may operate in reverse. An accused product that apparently falls within a claim's literal language does not infringe if it is "so far changed in principle . . . that it performs the same or a similar function in a substantially different way."[939] This defense is rarely successful; indeed, the Federal Circuit has stated

---

Kinzenbaw v. Deere & Co., 741 F.2d 383, 389 (Fed. Cir. 1984).

[933] Boyden Power-Brake Co. v. Westinghouse, 170 U.S. 537, 569 (1898). *See also* Sun Studs, Inc. v. ATA Equipment Leasing, Inc., 872 F.2d 978, 987 (Fed. Cir. 1989) (the jury verdict finding infringement by equivalency is supported by substantial evidence, whether or not the patented invention "merits the encomium of 'pioneer.' ").

[934] Warner-Jenkinson Co. v. Hilton Davis Chemical Co., 520 U.S. 17, 37 (1997).

[935] Graver Tank & Mfg. Co. v. Linde Air Products Co., 339 U.S. 605, 610–12 (1950). *See also* Corning Glass Works v. Sumitomo Electric U.S.A., 868 F.2d 1251, 1261 (Fed. Cir. 1989) ("[T]he substitution of an ingredient known to be an equivalent to that required by the claim presents a classic example for a finding of infringement under the doctrine of equivalents.").

[936] *Warner-Jenkinson*, 520 U.S. at 37 (rejecting argument that "the doctrine should be limited to equivalents that were known at the time the patent was issued, and should not extend to after-arising equivalents."); Marsh-McBirney, Inc. v. Montedoro-Whitney Corp., 882 F.2d 498, 504 (Fed. Cir. 1989) ("Advances subsequent to the patent may still infringe."), *cert. granted, judgment vacated*, 498 U.S. 1061 (1991), *opinion reinstated in relevant part*, 939 F.2d 969, 970 (Fed. Cir. 1991); American Hospital Supply Corp. v. Travenol Laboratories, Inc., 745 F.2d 1, 9 (Fed. Cir. 1984).

[937] 717 F.2d 1351 (Fed. Cir. 1983).

[938] *Compare* American Hospital Supply Corp. v. Travenol Laboratories, Inc., 745 F.2d 1, 9 (Fed. Cir. 1984) (the accused product was not equivalent to the claimed product when (a) the claim contained several specific ingredient range limitations based on a certain theory, and (b) the accused product varied one such range in following later developments based on a competing theory).

[939] Westinghouse v. Boyden Power Brake Co., 170 U.S. 537, 568 (1898); Graver Tank & Mfg. Co. v. Linde Air Products Co., 339 U.S. 605, 608–09 (1950). *Cf.* Texas Instruments, Inc. v. U.S. Int'l Trade

that "[n]ot once has this court affirmed a decision finding noninfringement based on the reverse doctrine of equivalents."[940]

[vii]   Limiting Effect of the Prior Art

Numerous decisions hold that the range of equivalents cannot extend to encompass the prior art.[941]

In *Wilson Sporting Goods Co. v. David Geoffrey & Associates*,[942] Judge Rich staked out a new approach to prior art constraint of the doctrine of equivalents:

> Whether prior art restricts the range of equivalents of what is literally claimed can be a difficult question to answer. To simplify analysis and bring the issue onto familiar turf, it may be helpful to conceptualize the limitation on the scope of equivalents by visualizing a *hypothetical* patent claim, sufficient in scope to *literally* cover the accused product. The pertinent question then becomes whether that hypothetical claim could have been allowed by the PTO over the prior art. If not, then it would be improper to permit the patentee to obtain that coverage in an infringement suit under the doctrine of equivalents. If the hypothetical claim could have been allowed, then *prior art* is not a bar to infringement under the doctrine of equivalents.[943]

The patentee bears the burden of proving the patentability of the hypothetical claim literally covering the accused product or process.[944]

Comm'n, 846 F.2d 1369, 1371 (Fed. Cir. 1986) (on denial of rehearing):

> [The] so-called 'reverse doctrine of equivalents' . . . might better be called a doctrine of non-equivalence. . . . Its invocation requires both that (1) there must be apparent literal infringement of the words of the claims; and (2) the accused device must be sufficiently different from that which is patented that despite the apparent literal infringement, the claims are interpreted to negate infringement.
>
> The reverse doctrine of equivalents is invoked when claims are written more broadly than the disclosure warrants. The purpose of restricting the scope of such claims is not only to avoid a holding of infringement when a court deems it appropriate, but often is to preserve the validity of claims with respect to their original intended scope.

[940] Tate Access Floors, Inc. v. Interface Architectural Resources, Inc., 279 F.3d 1357, 1368 (Fed. Cir. 2002).

[941] *See, e.g.*, Senmed, Inc. v. Richard-Allan Medical Industries, Inc., 888 F.2d 815, 821 (Fed. Cir. 1989) ("limitations in a claim cannot be given a range of equivalents so wide as to cause the claim to encompass anything in the prior art."); Stewart-Warner Corp. v. City of Pontiac, 767 F.2d 1563 (Fed. Cir. 1985).

[942] Wilson Sporting Goods Co. v. David Geoffrey & Associates, 904 F.2d 677 (Fed. Cir. 1990), *disapproved on other grounds*, Cardinal Chemical Co. v. Morton Int'l, Inc., 508 U.S. 83 (1993).

[943] 904 F.2d at 684 (emphasis in original). *Accord*, Abbott Laboratories v. Dey L.P., 287 F.3d 1097, 1105 (Fed. Cir. 2002); Interactive Pictures Corp. v. Infinite Pictures, Inc., 274 F.3d 1371, 1380 (Fed. Cir. 2001); Marquip, Inc. v. Fosber America, Inc., 198 F.3d 1363, 1367–68 (Fed. Cir. 1999).

[944] *Wilson Sporting Goods*, 904 F.2d at 685. *Accord*, Streamfeeder, LLC v. Sure-Feed Systems, Inc., 175 F.3d 974, 982–83 (Fed. Cir. 1999).

[c]   Prosecution History Estoppel

Prosecution history estoppel (also known as "file wrapper estoppel"[945]) precludes expansion of claim scope by the doctrine of equivalents to recapture subject matter surrendered to obtain a patent. The doctrine prevents circumvention of PTO examination and appeal procedures.[946] If an applicant believes an examiner's claim rejection is erroneous, he or she should appeal the rejection rather than amend the claim or give it a narrow scope by argument and later, in an infringement suit, seek to expand the claim to its original scope by the doctrine of equivalents.

In *Warner-Jenkinson Co. v. Hilton Davis Chemical Co.*,[947] the Supreme Court held that prosecution history estoppel arises as a defense if the patent owner limited the claims through amendment during prosecution. The patent owner then bears the burden of establishing a reason for the amendment that is unrelated to patentability, or else he or she will be estopped from reclaiming the surrendered equivalents in litigation.[948] In *Festo Corp. v. Shoketsu Kinzoku Kogyo Kabushiki Co.*,[949] the Supreme Court overturned a divided *en banc* ruling of the Federal Circuit, which had held that prosecution history estoppel was an absolute bar to the doctrine of equivalents. The Supreme Court held instead that prosecution history estoppel is a flexible bar, and that the patent owner may rebut the denial of the doctrine of equivalents even when estoppel applies. The patent owner is allowed to rebut the presumption against the doctrine of equivalents in three ways: (i) by showing that the equivalent was unforeseeable at the application; (ii) that the rationale for the amendment bore only a tangential relationship to the equivalent in question; or (iii) some other reason to be determined by future courts.[950] Upon remand, the Federal Circuit held that whether the presumption of surrender has arisen and has been rebutted are questions of law for the court;[951] and that foreseeability is to be determined under an objective standard, for which the trial court may consider expert testimony and other extrinsic evidence.[952] The Federal Circuit has addressed the issue of when an amendment is tangentially related in two cases.[953]

The Federal Circuit has held that the doctrine of equivalents cannot be used to capture equivalents disclosed in the specifications, but not claimed, on the theory

---

[945] Warner-Jenkinson Co. v. Hilton Davis Chemical Co., 520 U.S. 17, 30 (1997).

[946] Musher Foundation, Inc. v. Alba Trading Co., 150 F.2d 885, 888 (2d Cir. 1945).

[947] 520 U.S. 17 (1997).

[948] *Id.* at 31–34.

[949] 535 U.S. 722 (2002).

[950] *Id.* at 740–41.

[951] Festo Corp v. Shoketsu Kinzoku Kogyo Kabushiki Co., 344 F.3d 1359, 1367–68 & n.3 (Fed. Cir. 2003).

[952] *Id.* at 1369.

[953] Primos, Inc. v. Hunter's Specialties, Inc., 451 F.3d 841, 849 (Fed. Cir. 2006) (amendment was tangentially related); Biagro Western Sales, Inc. v. Grow More, Inc., 423 F.3d 1296, 1306 (Fed. Cir. 2005) (amendment was not tangentially related).

that such disclosure is a dedication to the public.[954]

[i]   Acts Giving Rise to Prosecution History Estoppel

The most common acts giving rise to an estoppel are amendments and cancellations in response to an examiner's prior art rejection in which the applicant narrows the scope of the claimed subject matter to secure a patent.

Prosecution history estoppel may arise even though the claim was not amended — for example, when a related claim is cancelled or amended in a way that gives meaning to terms in the claim in question.[955] Estoppel may also arise without any claim amendment at all — for example, when the applicant argues for a narrow construction of the claims to distinguish the prior art.[956]

Decisions hold there is no estoppel if an amendment merely clarified the claim's meaning and was not made to distinguish prior art.[957] The reason is that the applicant did not surrender anything or circumvent PTO examination of a broad claim's substance in relation to the prior art. The clarity exception is fertile ground for dispute and litigation. Confronted with an amendment and apparent estoppel, a patent owner often retorts that the amendment was "merely for clarity."[958]

Prosecution history estoppel is not limited to changes that avoid the prior art; any amendment that is made to secure the patent and that narrows the patent's scope, including an amendment to comply with section 112 disclosure, enablement and best mode requirements, raises the presumption of estoppel.[959] Thus, "[e]stoppel may arise from amendments to overcome non-art rejections directed to the claim breadth, for example, lack of enabling support in the specification."[960]

Estoppel may also arise from amendments or arguments in proceedings other

---

[954] Johnson & Johnson Assocs. v. R.E. Service Co., 285 F.3d 1046 (Fed. Cir. 2002).

[955] Builders Concrete, Inc. v. Bremerton Concrete Products Co., 757 F.2d 255 (Fed. Cir. 1985); Keith v. Charles E. Hires Co., 116 F.2d 46 (2d Cir. 1940).

[956] Hughes Aircraft Co. v. United States, 717 F.2d 1351 (Fed. Cir. 1983); Coleco Industries, Inc. v. U.S. Int'l Trade Comm'n, 573 F.2d 1247, 1257 (C.C.P.A. 1978). Earlier decisions refused to afford the force of an estoppel to mere arguments. See, e.g., Catalin Corp. v. Catalazuli Mfg. Co., 79 F.2d 593, 594 (2d Cir. 1935).

[957] See, e.g., Hubbell v. United States, 179 U.S. 77, 80 (1900) (suggesting in dictum that little weight should be given to amendments or changes made solely for purposes of clarity: "It is quite true that, where the differences between the claim as made and as allowed consist of mere changes of expression, having substantially the same meaning, such changes, made to meet the views of the examiners, ought not to be permitted to defeat a meritorious claimant."). See also Festo Corp v. Shoketsu Kinzoku Kogyo Kabushiki Co., 535 U.S. 722, 736–37 (2002) ("If [an] amendment is truly cosmetic, then it would not narrow the patent's scope or raise an estoppel.")

[958] See, e.g., Moeller v. Ionetics, Inc., 794 F.2d 653 (Fed. Cir. 1986) (holding that an amendment changing "an electrode body" to "an electrode disposed within said body" was made for clarity and did not limit the doctrine of equivalents).

[959] Festo, 535 U.S. at 735–37.

[960] Ellipse Corp. v. Ford Motor Co., 452 F.2d 163, 168 (7th Cir. 1971). Cf. Pennwalt Corp. v. Akzona, Inc., 740 F.2d 1573 (Fed. Cir. 1984). Compare Paperless Accounting, Inc. v. Bay Area Rapid Transit Sys., 804 F.2d 659 (1986).

than the patent's original prosecution, for example, a reissue or reexamination.[961]

[ii] Effect of Prosecution History Estoppel

Prosecution history estoppel restrains the doctrine of equivalents. It is not pertinent to literal infringement,[962] but the prosecution history is an important claim language interpretation tool.[963]

Prosecution history estoppel does not completely bar application of the doctrine of equivalents.[964] Before *Festo*, Federal Circuit decisions oscillated between a hardline approach, refusing to "speculate" whether an amendment in response to a prior art rejection was necessary to distinguish the prior art, and a flexible approach, emphasizing the amendment's nature and purpose and the prior art. As noted above, in *Festo* the Supreme Court adopted the flexible approach, holding that the patent owner may rebut the denial of the doctrine of equivalents by showing that (i) the equivalent was unforeseeable at the time of the application; (ii) that the rationale for the amendment bore only a tangential relationship to the equivalent in question; or (iii) some other reason to be determined by future courts.[965]

---

[961] *See, e.g.*, Howes v. Medical Components, Inc., 814 F.2d 638, 643, 645 (Fed. Cir. 1987). *Cf.* Caterpillar Tractor Co. v. Berco, S.p.A., 714 F.2d 1110, 1116 (Fed. Cir. 1983) ("Though no authority is cited for the proposition that instructions to foreign counsel and a representation to foreign patent offices should be considered, and the varying legal and procedural requirements for obtaining patent protection in foreign countries might render consideration of certain types of representations inappropriate, there is ample such authority in decisions of other courts and when such matters comprise relevant evidence they must be considered."). *Compare* Water Technologies Corp. v. Calco, Ltd., 850 F.2d 660, 667 (Fed. Cir. 1988) (the accused infringer failed to offer a reason "why arguments made by a different attorney prosecuting *later* patent applications for a different inventor should be used to limit an earlier-issued patent.").

[962] *See, e.g.*, Fromson v. Advance Offset Plate, Inc., 720 F.2d 1565, 1571 (Fed. Cir. 1983) ("If there be literal infringement . . . the doctrine of [prosecution history ('file wrapper') estoppel] is irrelevant."). *Compare* Standard Oil Co. v. American Cyanamid Co., 774 F.2d 448 (Fed. Cir. 1985) (the prosecution history limits the interpretation of claims so as to exclude any interpretation that may have been disclaimed or disavowed during prosecution to obtain claim allowance).

See also Keith v. Charles E. Hires Co., 116 F.2d 46, 48 (2d Cir. 1940) (Learned Hand): "The 'estoppel' is itself important only as a bar to any resort to the doctrine of equivalents. Without that doctrine every claim is indeed entitled to be interpreted in the light of the specifications as a whole, and not to be read merely with a dictionary. But often even with the most sympathetic interpretation the claim cannot be made to cover an infringement which in fact steals the very heart of the invention; no matter how auspiciously construed, the language forbids. It is then that the doctrine of equivalents intervenes to disregard the theory that the claim measures the monopoly and ignores the claim in order to protect the real invention. . . . The 'estoppel' of the file-wrapper puts an end to the court's power to do this; the applicant has abandoned his privilege to resort to an equivalent of the differentia, which all infringements must therefore embody. He may still insist that his claim shall be generously interpreted, but his monopoly stops where interpretation stops."

[963] *See* § 2F[1][b][iii].

[964] Bayer Aktiengesellschaft v. Duphar International Research B.V., 738 F.2d 1237 (Fed. Cir. 1984); Tektronix, Inc. v. United States, 445 F.2d 323, 328 (Ct. Cl. 1971).

[965] 535 U.S. 722, 740–41 (2002).

[3]   Proof of Infringing Activity

[a]   Burden of Proof

The patent owner must prove infringement by a preponderance of the evidence.[966] However, the burden of proof on a specific issue may be on the accused infringer. For example, if the accused infringer claims consent, he or she bears the burden of showing that the accused product was made or sold under an express or implied license or with the patent owner's authority.[967]

In *Andrew Corp. v. Gabriel Electronics, Inc.*,[968] the trial judge ruled against the patent owner because he could not understand the technical subject matter sufficiently to resolve the conflicting testimony of the parties' experts on infringement. The Federal Circuit held that this use of the burden of proof was erroneous:

> A true equipoise of evidence may indeed defeat the party with the burden of proof, . . . but there is no authority for holding evidence to be in equipoise for the sole reason that the court could not decide between conflicting experts. . . . Given the complexity of modern technology, it may well happen that qualified experts will appear on both sides, that their testimony will conflict, and that the testimony or the technology or both of them may be difficult to understand. However, to decline to decide the issue when conflicting evidence appears to be counterbalancing solely because the subject matter is technically complex, will defeat the party with the burden of proof without a fair hearing.[969]

[b]   Intent

Patent infringement is a strict liability offense. An unauthorized act invading the patentee's exclusive rights is infringement even if committed without knowledge of the patent.[970] However, knowledge and intent are relevant to determining liability for inducement and contributory infringement,[971] and they may also affect the measure of damages.[972]

---

[966] Bene v. Jeantet, 129 U.S. 683 (1889); Wilson Sporting Goods Co. v. David Geoffrey & Associates, 904 F.2d 677, 685 (Fed. Cir. 1990) ("The patent owner has always borne the burden of proving infringement."). *See* Medtronic, Inc. v. Mirowski Family Ventures, Inc., 134 S. Ct. 843 (2014) (patent owner has burden of persuasion to show infringement even in a declaratory judgment action).

[967] Pilley v. United States, 74 Fed. Cl. 489, 494 (2006); Augustine Medical, Inc. v. Progressive Dynamics, Inc., 194 F.3d 1367, 1370 (Fed. Cir. 1999); Carborundum Co. v. Molten Metal Equip. Innovations, Inc., 72 F.3d 872, 878 (Fed. Cir. 1995); *cf.* Sherman, Clay & Co. v. Searchlight Horn Co., 225 F. 497, 500 (9th Cir. 1915) ("the burden is upon the dealer to show that he or it is dealing with an article under license from the patentee, or in articles from which the patent monopoly has been released or removed.").

[968] Andrew Corp. v. Gabriel Electronics, Inc., 847 F.2d 819 (Fed. Cir. 1988).

[969] *Id.* at 824.

[970] Thurber Corp. v. Fairchild Motor Corp., 269 F.2d 841, 845, 849 (5th Cir. 1959).

[971] *See* § 2E[2][c].

[972] *See* § 2F[5][c].

[c]   Agency — Corporate Officers and Employees

Under agency law principles, patent infringement liability extends to corporations and other organizations whose agents or employees commit acts of infringement.[973]

A corporate officer or director may be liable with his corporation for the corporation's infringing acts on either of two theories: active inducement of infringement and alter ego.[974]

[4]   Jurisdiction and Joinder Provisions

Title 28 of the U.S. Code specifies that federal subject-matter jurisdiction over all patent and copyright claims is exclusive, and that appellate jurisdiction over all patent claims is exclusive in the Federal Circuit.[975] While the appellate jurisdiction of the Federal Circuit was previously limited to claims "arising under" the patent laws, and therefore did not include actions in which the patent claim only arose as a counterclaim,[976] the AIA expands the exclusive federal jurisdiction of the Federal Circuit to include compulsory counterclaims alleging patent infringement.

Some cases involve issues of state law as well as patent law. For example, a dispute over patent licensing may implicate contract issues. Should such a case be brought in state court or does a federal district court have jurisdiction? In *Gunn v. Minton*,[977] the Supreme Court addressed the issue of whether a question of breach of professional conduct by a patent attorney could be brought in Federal Court. Minton, the patent owner initially brought the action against his attorney in Texas state court after losing an infringement case. When the Texas Supreme Court ruled against Minton, he claimed that the state court did not have proper jurisdiction over the matter and refiled the suit in federal district court. The United States Supreme Court ruled that the matter belonged in state court, not federal court, concluding that a case only arises under federal patent law when it "necessarily raise[s] a stated federal issue, actually disputed and substantial, which a federal forum may entertain without disturbing any congressionally approved balance of federal and state judicial responsibilities."

New section 299 of the Patent Act makes it more difficult to join defendants. Under this new provision, multiple defendants can be joined in one action only if the claim involves the same transaction or occurrence and there are common questions of fact to all defendants or counterclaim defendants. An allegation that each defendant has infringed the same patent or patents cannot be a basis for

---

[973] *See, e.g.*, Westinghouse Elec. & Mfg. Co. v. Independent Wireless Tel. Co., 300 F. 748 (S.D.N.Y. 1924). In *Westinghouse*, the court granted an injunction against infringement even though the defendant company had purportedly forbidden its employees to install a circuit in a fashion that would infringe the patent, where the evidence indicated that the employees were installing such circuits anyway. *Compare* Duplex Envelope Co. v. Denominational Envelope Co., 80 F.2d 179 (4th Cir. 1935).

[974] *See* Manville Sales Corp. v. Paramount Systems, Inc., 917 F.2d 544 (Fed. Cir. 1990), discussed at § 2E[2][c][iv].

[975] 28 U.S.C. § 1338(a); 28 U.S.C. § 1295(a)(1).

[976] Holmes Group, Inc. v. Vornado Air Circulation Sys., 535 U.S. 826 (2002).

[977] 133 S. Ct. 1059 (2013).

joining defendants. The provision allows an accused infringer to waive these limitations.

§ 2G   DEFENSES

An accused infringer in a patent suit may rely on a number of defenses, including invalidity of the patent, inequitable conduct, misuse, laches and estoppel.

[1]   Invalidity

A defense to a patent infringement charge is that the patent claims are invalid for failure to meet patentability standards.[978] A patent claim may be invalid because of lack of novelty,[979] occurrence of a statutory bar,[980] obviousness,[981] or lack of adequate disclosure.[982]

[a]   Presumption of Validity

A patent is presumed valid.[983] A validity challenger has the burden of proving invalidity by clear and convincing evidence.[984] The challenger also bears the initial burden of producing evidence, but may shift that burden to the patent owner by establishing a *prima facie* case of unpatentability.[985]

The presumption of validity remains in effect regardless of what evidence was before the examiner during prosecution of the application that became the patent.[986] If the challenger relies on more pertinent prior art references than those considered by the examiner, the challenger's burden of persuasion is more easily

---

[978] 35 U.S.C. § 282. *See* Constant v. Advanced Micro-Devices, Inc., 848 F.2d 1560, 1564 (Fed. 1988) (section 282 does not violate the Patent Clause of the Constitution, which states that Congress has the power to promote the useful arts by "securing" to inventors the exclusive rights to their discoveries; "securing" does not require that patents issued by the PTO be conclusively valid and unchallengeable; "Since the adoption of the first Patent Act in 1790, Congress has permitted judicial review of the validity of patents. The courts, the interpreters of the meaning of the Constitution, have consistently construed the Patent and Copyright Clause to permit judicial review of patents. . . . Public policy requires that only inventions which fully meet the statutory standards are entitled to patents. This policy is furthered when the validity of a patent, which was originally obtained in *ex parte* proceedings in the PTO, can be challenged in court. . . . Nowhere does the Constitution require that the determination of patent validity be vested solely in the PTO (or even that there be a PTO).").

[979] *See* § 2C[3].

[980] *See* § 2C[5][b][ii].

[981] *See* § 2C[4].

[982] *See* §§ 2C[6][d] and [e].

[983] 35 U.S.C. § 282.

[984] *See* Microsoft v. i4i, 131 S. Ct. 2238 (2011), affirming Radio Corp. of America v. Radio Engineering Laboratories, Inc., 293 U.S. 1 (1934). *See also* Research Corp. Technologies, Inc. v. Microsoft Corp., 627 F.3d 859, 870 (Fed. Cir. 2010); Laryngeal Mask Co. v. Ambu, 618 F.3d 1367, 1374 (Fed. Cir. 2010).

[985] *Research Corp.*, 627 F.3d at 870. For example, if a challenger makes a *prima facie* case of public use, the burden of production on experimental use shifts to the patent owner. Lisle Corp. v. A.J. Mfg. Co., 398 F.3d 1306, 1316 (Fed. Cir. 2005). *See* § 2C[5][b][ii].

[986] Uniloc USA, Inc. v. Microsoft Corp., 632 F.3d 1292, 1321 (Fed. Cir. 2011); i4i Ltd. Partnership v. Microsoft Corp., 598 F.3d 831, 848 (Fed. Cir. 2010), *aff'd*, 131 S. Ct. 2238 (2011). In *i4i*, the Supreme

carried.[987] If the challenger relies on the same references as the examiner, the burden is less easily carried.[988]

The presumption of validity applies independently to each claim of a patent.[989]

[b]   Standing to Challenge Validity

A person may challenge patent validity even though he is a licensee. In *Lear, Inc. v. Adkins*,[990] a California state court held that a licensee could not, in a suit for enforcement of a patent license contract, contest the patent's validity. The United States Supreme Court reversed, overruling the licensee estoppel doctrine on policy grounds. Federal policy favoring the removal of invalid patents overrides contract law policy:

> Licensees may often be the only individuals with enough economic incentive
> to challenge the patentability of an inventor's discovery. If they are muzzled
> the public may continually be required to pay tribute to would-be monopo-
> lists without need or justification.[991]

If a licensee successfully challenges validity, he may escape liability for unpaid royalties that have accrued since he first raised the challenge.[992]

Lear reflects judicial skepticism of PTO examination and the presumption of validity. Subsequent lower court decisions decline to extend *Lear* beyond licensee estoppel. For example, in *Cordis Corp. v. Medtronic, Inc. I*,[993] the Federal Circuit held that *Lear* does not authorize a court to permit a licensee to deposit royalties due under a license into an escrow account during a lawsuit challenging a patent's validity. It also held that *Lear* does not authorize a preliminary injunction barring the licensor from cancelling a license for nonpayment of royalties in breach of the

---

Court rejected the argument that the burden should be lower when the prior art involved was not cited to the Patent Office.

[987] Aktiebolaget Karlstads Mekaniska Werkstad v. U.S. Int'l Trade Comm'n, 705 F.2d 1565 (Fed. Cir. 1983).

[988] Hughes Aircraft Co. v. United States, 717 F.2d 1351 (Fed. Cir. 1983).

[989] 35 U.S.C. § 282; Preemption Devices, Inc. v. Minnesota Mining & Mfg. Co., 732 F.2d 903 (Fed. Cir. 1984).

[990] 395 U.S. 653 (1969), discussed at § 1D[3][b][ii].

[991] 395 U.S. at 670.

[992] *See, e.g.*, Rite-Nail Packaging Corp. v. Berryfast, Inc., 706 F.2d 933 (9th Cir. 1983). A licensee must pay unpaid royalties that have accrued prior to the date the licensee challenges the validity of the patent. Royalties already paid may not be recovered unless the licensee was defrauded into entering into the license. Transitron Electronic Corp. v. Hughes Aircraft Co., 649 F.2d 871 (1st Cir. 1981).

Compare Hemstreet v. Spiegel, Inc., 851 F.2d 348 (Fed. Cir. 1988). In *Hemstreet*, the court held that a settlement order signed by the parties and the court, which provided for the payment of license royalties "notwithstanding that [the patent] may be held invalid and/or unenforceable in any other proceeding at a later date," is binding even though the patent in question was later found unenforceable because of inequitable conduct in its procurement. "The enforcement of settlement of litigation involves another public policy totally absent in *Lear*: the encouragement of settlement of litigation and the need to enforce such settlements in order to encourage the parties to enter into them." *Id.* at 350.

[993] 780 F.2d 991 (Fed. Cir. 1985).

license. In *Cordis Corp. v. Medtronic, Inc. II*,[994] it held that the district court did not err in preliminarily enjoining the patentee from terminating a license agreement covering pacemaker endocardial leads. The licensee paid royalties on one form of lead ("tined") but not on another form ("finned"). After the patentee threatened to terminate the license unless the licensee paid royalties on the finned lead devices, the licensee filed a declaratory judgment suit. The district court found (1) the harm to the licensee if relief were not granted outweighed the injury to the patentee if it were, and (2) the licensee showed sufficient likelihood of success on the issues that finned lead devices do not infringe and that the patentee was guilty of laches or estoppel.

In *Diamond Scientific Co. v. Ambico, Inc.*,[995] the Federal Circuit applied assignor estoppel to bar an inventor and his new company from challenging the validity of a patent on his own invention, which he had assigned to the plaintiff, his previous employer.

In *Medimmune, Inc. v. Genentech, Inc.*,[996] the Supreme Court held that a licensee had standing under the Constitution and the Declaratory Judgment Act to challenge the validity of a patent even if the licensee had not terminated the license or stopped paying royalties. The Court overturned the "reasonable apprehension of suit" test used by the Federal Circuit to determine standing to bring a declaratory judgment and held that the implicit coercion to continue under the license even if a patent were invalid was sufficient to give the licensee standing to bring a declaratory judgment action against the patentee-licensor.

[c]   Effect of Judgment

A judgment of invalidity judgment binds the patent owner in suits against other accused infringers unless "he did not have 'a fair opportunity procedurally, substantively, and evidentially to pursue his claim the first time.' "[997] A final judgment of invalidity is usually the equivalent of cancellation of the claim. However, an invalidity judgment extends only to the claims that were contested by an infringement charge or a declaratory judgment counterclaim.[998]

---

[994] 835 F.2d 859 (Fed. Cir. 1987).

[995] 848 F.2d 1220 (Fed. Cir. 1988). *See also* Pandrol USA, LP v. Airboss Railway Prods., Inc., 424 F.3d 1161, 1166–67 (Fed. Cir. 2005); Shamrock Technologies, Inc. v. Medical Sterilization, Inc., 903 F.2d 789 (Fed. Cir. 1990) (assignor estoppel precludes the accused infringers' invalidity and inequitable conduct defenses).

[996] 549 U.S. 118 (2006).

[997] Blonder-Tongue Laboratories, Inc. v. University of Illinois Foundation, 402 U.S. 313, 332 (1971). *See also* Dana Corp. v. NOK, Inc., 882 F.2d 505, 508 (Fed. Cir. 1989) (an appellate holding that a patent is invalid in a suit against one infringer collaterally estops the patent owner from asserting that the patent is valid in litigation against another infringer, even when the invalidity holding in the former suit occurs after the patent has been held valid and an appeal taken in the latter suit).

An invalidity decision by the International Trade Commission does not have the same preclusive effect in later court suits. *See* Tandon Corp. v. U.S. Int'l Trade Comm'n, 831 F.2d 1017, 1019 (Fed. Cir. 1987) ("any disposition of a Commission action by a Federal Court should not have a res judicata or collateral estoppel effect in cases before such courts.") (quoting S.Rep. No. 93-1298 at 196 (1974)). *See* § 2E[2][b][ii].

[998] Jervis B. Webb Co. v. Southern Sys., Inc., 742 F.2d 1388 (Fed. Cir. 1984); Stearns v. Beckman

A final judgment of *validity* does not bind accused infringers who are not in privity with the first accused infringer,[999] although the results of the first suit may carry some weight.[1000]

[2] Inequitable Conduct — Fraud

Inequitable conduct or fraud during a patent's prosecution may render the patent unenforceable.

Under USPTO Rule 56, an applicant has a duty to disclose information material to patentability.[1001] Failure to disclose material information can give rise to a defense of inequitable conduct and a remedy of the unenforceability of the entire patent.[1002] The failure to disclose by the patent owner can also give rise to an antitrust claim under the Sherman Antitrust Act against the owner if the failure constitutes fraud and the patent owner has market power.[1003]An antitrust action also arises when the patent owner enters into a reverse settlement agreement with an alleged infringer, particularly in the context of patented pharmaceuticals and generic drugs.[1004] Information is material to patentability if it is not cumulative of information already on record and the information refutes or is inconsistent with an argument the applicant makes as to patentability.[1005]

The issue of what level of culpability is required for a showing of inequitable conduct has long been a controversial one. In *Therasense, Inc. v. Becton, Dickinson, & Co.*,[1006] the Federal Circuit held *en banc* that

> To prevail on a claim of inequitable conduct, the accused infringer must prove that the patentee acted with the specific intent to deceive the PTO. A finding that the misrepresentation or omission amounts to gross negligence or negligence under a "should have known" standard does not satisfy this

---

Instruments, Inc., 737 F.2d 1565 (Fed. Cir. 1984). A finding of inequitable conduct renders all the patent's claims unenforceable. *See* § 2F[4][b].

[999] *See, e.g.*, Allen Archery, Inc. v. Browning Manufacturing Co., 819 F.2d 1087, 1091 (Fed. Cir. 1987) ("The *Blonder-Tongue* rule . . . 'is of necessity a one-way street,' . . . and does not bar someone charged with infringement from challenging the validity of patent claims that were upheld in a prior infringement suit to which it was not a party.").

[1000] *See, e.g.*, Gillette Co. v. S.C. Johnson & Son, Inc., 919 F.2d 720, 723 (Fed. Cir. 1990) ("The fact that the validity of [the patent] claims [in suit] has previously been upheld in an earlier litigation is . . . to be given weight, though not *stare decisis* effect."); Mendenhall v. Cedarapids, Inc., 5 F.3d 1557, 1569–72 (Fed. Cir. 1993) (*Gillette* requires only that prior decision be given "weight" in terms of precedent, and does not require prior opinion be placed in evidence for jury to consider; and rejecting argument that *stare decisis* requires jury to consider whether the evidence proffered in second suit is different from the first; *but see Allen Archery*, 819 F.2d at 1091 ("The statutory presumption of patent validity . . . is not augmented by an earlier adjudication of patent validity.").

[1001] 37 C.F.R. 1.56(a), (b).

[1002] *See* J.P. Stevens & Co. v. Lex Tex Ltd., 747 F.2d 1553 (Fed. Cir. 1984).

[1003] *See* Walker Process Equip. Inc. v. Food Mach. & Chem. Corp., 382 U.S. 172 (1965).

[1004] FTC v. Actavis, Inc., 133 S. Ct. 2223 (2013).

[1005] 37 C.F.R. 1.56(b)(2)(ii)(1996). *See* Critikon, Inc. v. Becton Dickinson Vascular Access, Inc., 120 F.3d 1253 (Fed. Cir. 1997).

[1006] 649 F.3d 1276 (Fed. Cir. 2011) (en banc).

intent requirement. In a case involving nondisclosure of information, clear and convincing evidence must show that the applicant *made a deliberate decision* to withhold a *known* material reference. In other words, the accused infringer must prove by clear and convincing evidence that the applicant knew of the reference, knew that it was material, and made a deliberate decision to withhold it.[1007]

The court further held that "[i]ntent and materiality are separate requirements. A district court should not use a 'sliding scale,' where a weak showing of intent may be found sufficient based on a strong showing of materiality, and vice versa. Moreover, a district court may not infer intent solely from materiality. Instead, a court must weigh the evidence of intent to deceive independent of its analysis of materiality."[1008] "[I]n assessing the materiality of a withheld reference, the court must determine whether the PTO would have allowed the claim if it had been aware of the undisclosed reference."[1009]

Changes under the AIA potentially diminish the impact of inequitable conduct. Effective September 11, 2012, the AIA introduces a supplemental examination proceeding under a new section 257. The patent owner can initiate this proceeding in order to have the USPTO consider, reconsider, or correct information pertaining to patentability of a granted patent. The Director, pursuant to its regulations, reviews the patent owner's petition to see if it raises a substantial new question of patentability. If the petition meets this standard, the Director orders a reexamination. The effect of the supplemental examination proceeding is to preclude holding a patent unenforceable on the basis of the information that had not been considered or had been inadequately considered by the PTO.

[3]   Misuse

If a patent owner commits misuse by improperly exploiting his patent,[1010] the courts withhold any remedy for infringement or for breach of a license agreement.[1011] If the patent owner abandons the improper practice and purges its harmful consequences, the courts restore his rights.[1012] An accused infringer may assert the misuse defense even though he is not harmed by the improper practice.[1013] The misuse defense "is an extension of the equitable doctrine 'of unclean hands' to the patent field,"[1014] and deters improper "extension" of a patent's exclusivity. Examples of misuse include price fixing[1015] and patent license

---

[1007] *Id.* at 1290 (internal quotations and citations omitted; emphasis in original).

[1008] *Id.* at 1290 (internal citation omitted).

[1009] *Id.* at 1291–92. There is an exception to the "but-for" standard "in cases of affirmative egregious misconduct, . . . such as the filing of an unmistakably false affidavit." *Id.* at 1292.

[1010] *See generally* D. CHISUM, PATENTS § 19.04.

[1011] B.B. Chem. Co. v. Ellis, 314 U.S. 495 (1942); Morton Salt Co. v. G.S. Suppiger Co., 314 U.S. 488 (1942).

[1012] *See, e.g.,* Preformed Line Prod. Co. v. Fanner Mfg. Co., 328 F.2d 265, 278 (6th Cir. 1964).

[1013] Morton Salt Co. v. G.S. Suppiger Co., 314 U.S. 488 (1942).

[1014] United States Gypsum v. National Gypsum, 352 U.S. 457, 465 (1957).

[1015] *See, e.g.,* United States Gypsum v. National Gypsum, 352 U.S. 457 (1957).

provisions tying the right to use a patented invention to purchase of unpatented supplies.[1016]

Some critics have questioned the misuse doctrine's soundness insofar as it prescribes practices that do not violate the antitrust laws.[1017] Section 271(d), added by the 1952 Patent Act, limits the doctrine of misuse with respect to contributory infringement.[1018] A 1988 amendment to Section 271(d) further limited misuse.[1019] Relying on the language of Section 271(d)(5), which requires that the defendant show market power in order to establish tying as misuse, the Supreme Court has held that ownership of a patent by itself does not create a presumption of market power in antitrust cases.[1020]

In *Dawson Chemical Co. v. Rohm & Haas Co.*, the Supreme Court applied section 271(d) in holding that a patent owner on a method of applying an unpatented herbicide was not guilty of misuse when it sued defendants for contributory infringement for selling the chemical with instructions on how to use it, where it was conceded that the chemical had no substantial non-infringing use.[1021]

[4]   Experimental or Personal Use

Unauthorized making and using a patented process or product is not infringement if done solely for research or experimentation.[1022] However, the experimental use defense has been read narrowly to include only uses for philosophical investigation. Commercial uses are not protected as experimental uses.[1023] The research exception does not apply if the infringer conducts experiments to adapt the patented invention to his business.[1024]

[1016] *See, e.g.*, Senza-Gel Corp. v. Seiffhart, 803 F.2d 661 (Fed. Cir. 1986). In *Senza-Gel*, the court found misuse when (1) the patent owner indicated that it never licensed a process patent without also leasing a machine for carrying out the patented process, (2) a witness testified that his request to license the process without the machine was refused, and (3) the machine as leased was suitable for substantial non-infringing use and therefore a staple article of commerce.

[1017] *See, e.g.*, USM Corp. v. SPS Technologies, Inc., 694 F.2d 505 (7th Cir. 1982).

[1018] *See* 35 U.S.C. § 271(d). *See also* § 2E[2][c][ii].

[1019] The 1988 amendment provides that a patent owner is not guilty of misuse by reason of having: "(4) refused to license or use any rights to the patent; or "(5) conditioned the license of any rights to the patent or the sale of the patented product on the acquisition of a license to rights in another patent or purchase of a separate product, unless, in view of the circumstances, the patent owner has market power in the relevant market for the patent or patented product on which the license or sale is conditioned." 35 U.S.C. § 271(d).

[1020] Illinois Tool Works Inc. v Independent Ink, Inc., 547 U.S. 28 (2006).

[1021] 448 U.S. 176 (1980). *See* § 2E[2][c][ii] (discussing contributory infringement).

[1022] Chesterfield v. United States, 159 F. Supp. 371 (Ct. Cl. 1958). *See generally* D. CHISUM, PATENTS § 16.03[1].

[1023] Madey v. Duke University, 307 F.3d 1351 (Fed. Cir. 2002).

[1024] Roche Products, Inc. v. Bolar Pharmaceutical Co., 733 F.2d 858 (Fed. Cir. 1984); Pitcairn v. United States, 547 F.2d 1106 (Ct. Cl. 1976).

In *Roche Products, Inc. v. Bolar Pharmaceutical Co.*,[1025] the patent covered a pharmaceutical drug. Near the end of the patent's term, the accused infringer obtained the drug outside the United States and used it in a limited testing program to obtain regulatory approval to market a generic version of the patented drug after the patent expired. The court held that the testing was an infringement not excused by the experimental use exception.[1026]

A 1984 amendment partially abrogates *Roche* by providing that it is not infringement to make, use or sell a patented invention solely for uses reasonably related to the development and submission of information under a Federal law that regulates the manufacture, use or sale of drugs.[1027] In *Eli Lilly & Co. v. Medtronic, Inc.*,[1028] the Supreme Court held this exemption applies to medical devices as well as drugs. In *Merck KGaA v. Integra Lifesciences I, Ltd.*,[1029] the Supreme Court held that Section 271(e)(1) also protected general scientific investigation in developing a new drug "as long as there is a reasonable basis for believing that the experiments will produce" information relevant to drug approval.[1030] This decision is generally understood to have expanded the scope of experimental use under section 271(e)(1).

[5]   Laches and Estoppel

There is no statute of limitations on patent infringement suits, but a patent owner may not recover damages for infringing acts committed more than six years before filing suit.[1031] However, the equitable doctrines of laches and estoppel may limit or bar relief against patent infringement.[1032]

Laches applies if a patent owner unreasonably delays filing suit after he knows or should reasonably know of the infringement and the delay prejudices the infringer.[1033] If the delay is more than six years, courts presume unreasonableness and prejudice.[1034] The patent owner may show an excuse for the delay, for

---

[1025] 733 F.2d 858 (Fed. Cir. 1984).

[1026] The court also refused to imply a limitation from federal drug regulation policies.

[1027] 35 U.S.C. § 271(e)(1). This amendment was part of the Drug Price Competition and Patent Term Restoration Act of 1984 (commonly known as the Hatch-Waxman Act).

[1028] 496 U.S. 661 (1990).

[1029] 545 U.S. 193 (2005).

[1030] *Id.* at 208.

[1031] 35 U.S.C. § 286. *See* A.C. Aukerman Co. v. R.L. Chaides Constr. Co., 960 F.2d 1020, 1030 (Fed. Cir. 1992) (en banc); Standard Oil Co. v. Nippon Shokubai Kagaku Kogyo Co., Ltd., 754 F.2d 345 (Fed. Cir. 1985) (Section 286's six-year damage limitation for an alleged contributory infringement by sale of a catalyst useful in carrying out a patented process begins on the date the catalyst was sold, not the later date when the purchaser used the catalyst to practice the process.).

[1032] *A.C. Aukerman Co.*, 960 F.2d at 1029–32; *see generally* D. CHISUM, PATENTS § 19.05.

[1033] *See, e.g.*, *A.C. Aukerman Co.*, 960 F.2d at 1032; Jamesbury Corp. v. Litton Industrial Products, Inc., 839 F.2d 1544 (Fed. Cir. 1988). *Compare* Sun Studs, Inc. v. ATA Equipment Leasing, Inc., 872 F.2d 978 (Fed. Cir. 1989) (a jury verdict of laches cannot stand where there is no substantial evidence of prejudice to the infringer from the patentee's delay in filing suit).

[1034] *A.C. Aukerman Co.*, 960 F.2d at 1034–36; Leinoff v. Louis Milona & Sons, Inc., 726 F.2d 734 (Fed. Cir. 1984).

example, pursuit of other litigation on the patent after giving the infringer notice of intent to sue.[1035] Laches bars damages for infringing acts before filing suit but not an injunction or damages for post-filing acts.[1036] Laches does not apply if the infringer was guilty of "egregious conduct," for example, willful, secret infringement or misrepresentations.[1037]

Estoppel applies if a patent owner represents to an infringer, expressly or implicitly, that he will not enforce his patent against the infringer's business, and the infringer relied on that representation and would be prejudiced by the patentee's change in position.[1038] A patent owner's silence does not create an estoppel,[1039] but an estoppel may arise if (1) the patent owner threatens suit and then unreasonably delays filing suit, and (2) the infringer, relying on the owner's silence and inaction, continues and expands his business.[1040]

[6]　　　Implied License — First Sale

A license is a defense to a patent infringement charge,[1041] because the definition of infringement includes absence of the patent owner's authority.[1042]

A license may be implied as well as express.[1043] For example, if a process patent owner sells a machine that has no practical use except in carrying out the process, the purchaser gains an implied license to use the process.[1044] If the machine has other uses, the purchaser gains no implied license.[1045] In *Met-Coil Systems Corp. v. Komers Unlimited, Inc.*, the court identified "two requirements for the grant of an implied license by virtue of a sale of nonpatented equipment used to practice a patented invention: First, the equipment involved must have no noninfringing uses. . . . Second, the circumstances of the sale must 'plainly indicate that the

---

[1035] *See, e.g.*, Meyers v. Brooks Shoe Inc., 912 F.2d 1459 (Fed. Cir. 1990); Jamesbury Corp. v. Litton Industrial Products, Inc., 839 F.2d 1544 (Fed. Cir. 1988); Hottel Corp. v. Seaman Corp., 833 F.2d 1570 (Fed. Cir. 1987) (because the patent owner failed to provide adequate notice of the patents and the nature of the other proceeding involving them, the "other litigation" exception did not apply).

[1036] *See, e.g.*, *A.C. Aukerman Co.*, 960 F.2d at 1039–41; Olympia Werke Aktiengesellschaft v. General Elec. Co., 712 F.2d 74 (4th Cir. 1983).

[1037] *See, e.g.*, Bott v. Four Star Corp., 807 F.2d 1567 (Fed. Cir. 1986). *Cf.* Fromson v. Western Litho Plate & Supply Co., 853 F.2d 1568 (Fed. Cir. 1988).

[1038] A.C. Aukerman Co. v. R.L. Chaides Constr. Co., 960 F.2d 1020, 1042–43 (Fed. Cir. 1992) (en banc); Jensen v. Western Irrigation & Mfg., Inc., 650 F.2d 165 (9th Cir. 1980).

[1039] *See, e.g.*, Hottel Corp. v. Seaman Corp., 833 F.2d 1570 (Fed. Cir. 1987).

[1040] *Cf.* MCV, Inc. v. King-Seeley Thermos Co., 870 F.2d 1568 (Fed. Cir. 1989).

[1041] *See, e.g.*, Lisle Corp. v. Edwards, 777 F.2d 693 (Fed. Cir. 1985).

[1042] 35 U.S.C. § 271(a) ("whoever *without authority* makes, uses, offers to sell, or sells any patented invention within the United States or imports into the United States any patented invention during the term of the patent therefore, infringes the patent.") (emphasis added).

[1043] An implied license is closely related to the first sale doctrine. *See* § 2E[3].

[1044] *See, e.g.*, Devices for Medicine, Inc. v. Boehl, 822 F.2d 1062, 1068 (Fed. Cir. 1987) (the law "implies a license to practice [the patentee's] claimed method [to the use of a product] to anyone who purchases one of [the patentee's] claimed [products].").

[1045] *See, e.g.*, Bandag, Inc. v. Al Bolser's Tire Stores, Inc., 750 F.2d 903 (Fed. Cir. 1984).

grant of a license should be inferred.' "[1046] The patentee sold roll-forming machines its customers used to shape flanges on metal heating ducts. The patentee also sold specially shaped corner pieces to fit on the shaped flanges. The patentee sued the defendant, who sold corner pieces to plaintiff's customers, for contributory infringement, arguing that the corner pieces had no use other than carrying out its patented duct connection process. The court held that sale of the machines conferred on the buyer an implied license to the patented process because they had no other use. The patentee's written notices to customers warning against purchase of corner pieces from unlicensed sources were to no avail because they were *after* the sale of the machine: "The subsequent notices are not a part of the circumstances at the time of the sale, when the implied license would have arisen." Because the defendant sold corner pieces only to those with an implied license, it could not be a contributory infringer.[1047]

As part of the new defense of prior commercial use under the AIA, the sale or "other disposition of a useful end result" by a person entitled to raise the prior commercial user defense exhausts the rights of the patent owner to the extent that such sale or disposition would exhaust rights if done by the patent owner.

[7]   Prior Commercial Use

In new section 273, the AIA introduces the defense of prior commercial use, expanding the current defense of prior user rights available only for business method patents. This expanded defense applies to all patents issued on or after September 16, 2011.

This defense applies to subject matter consisting of any process or a machine, manufacture, or composition of matter used in a manufacturing or other commercial process. The defense can be raised if the alleged infringer used the subject matter in good faith within the United States either in connection with an internal commercial use or an arm's length sale or transfer of a useful end result of the process. The prior commercial use must occur at least one year before the earlier or the effective filing date of the claimed invention or the date on which claimed invention was disclosed to the public in a way that qualifies as an exception from prior art under the new section 102(b). The statute states that (i) a premarketing regulatory review for safety and efficacy and (ii) nonprofit laboratory use are commercial uses for the purposes of this defense.

The defense cannot be raised if the patent owner is an institution of higher education or a technology transfer office unless the invention was not made with federal funds. The defense can be used only by a party that actually made the commercial use. If the use has been abandoned for some time but subsequently restarted, uses before the time of abandonment cannot support the defense.

[1046] 803 F.2d 684, 685 (Fed. Cir. 1986) (citation omitted).

[1047] 803 F.2d at 686–87. *See also* King Instrument Corp. v. Otari Corp., 814 F.2d 1560 (Fed. Cir. 1987) (an infringer's payment of a judgment for damages for sales of infringing devices provides full compensation to the patent owner; after such payment, the infringer receives an implied license as to those sales for the useful life of the devices and may provide to its customers spare parts needed for repairs of those devices).

Furthermore, if the defendant derived the subject matter from the patent owner or those in privity with the patent owner, then the subject matter cannot be a basis for a defense. The new provision states expressly that the defense is not a general license and cannot be used as a basis for invalidity on novelty or nonobviousness grounds. Finally, if the defense is not successful and there was no reasonable basis for raising the defense, the unreasonableness can be a basis for making the case an exceptional one for the award of attorney's fees.

§ 2H   REMEDIES

A court may grant the following remedies for patent infringement: injunctions, monetary damages, interest, and attorney fees.[1048]

[1]   Injunctions

A court may grant an injunction to prevent patent infringement "in accordance with the principles of equity . . . on such terms as the court deems reasonable."[1049] One who violates an injunction may be found in contempt and face severe sanctions.[1050]

[a]   Preliminary Injunctions

A preliminary injunction restrains an accused infringer while a lawsuit is pending to prevent irreparable injury to the patent owner. The four traditional factors governing preliminary injunctions are likelihood of success on the merits, irreparable harm, balance of hardships, and the public interest.[1051]

Courts formerly granted preliminary injunctions in patent cases only when the patent owner established validity and infringement "beyond question."[1052] The Federal Circuit rejected the "beyond question" rule and equated patent infringe-

---

[1048] For imported products that infringe or are produced by a process covered by a United States patent, the patent owner may have an additional remedy in the United States International Trade Commission. *See* § 2E[2][b][ii].

[1049] 35 U.S.C. § 283.

[1050] *See* Spindelfabrik Suessen-Schurr v. Schubert & Salzer Maschinenfabrik Aktiengesellschaft, 903 F.2d 1568 (Fed. Cir. 1990); Graves v. Kemsco Group, Inc., 864 F.2d 754 (Fed. Cir. 1988); Eli Lilly and Co. v. Premo Pharmaceutical Laboratories, Inc., 843 F.2d 1378 (Fed. Cir. 1988); Amstar Corp. v. Envirotech Corp., 823 F.2d 1538 (Fed. Cir. 1987); Joy Manufacturing Co. v. National Mine Service Co., 810 F.2d 1127 n.2 (Fed. Cir. 1987); Preemption Devices, Inc. v. Minnesota Mining & Mfg. Co., 803 F.2d 1170 (Fed. Cir. 1986); KSM Fastening Sys., Inc. v. H.A. Jones Co., Inc., 776 F.2d 1522 (Fed. Cir. 1985); MAC Corporation of America v. Williams Patent Crusher & Pulveriser Co., 767 F.2d 882 (Fed. Cir. 1985); Paper Converting Machine Co. v. Magna-Graphics Corp., 745 F.2d 11 (Fed. Cir. 1984).

[1051] *See, e.g.*, Titan Tire Corp. v. Case New Holland, Inc., 566 F.3d 1372, 1375–76 (Fed. Cir. 2009), *citing* Winter v. NRDC, Inc., 555 U.S. 7 (2008); Chrysler Motors Corp. v. Auto Body Panels of Ohio Inc., 908 F.2d 951, 953 (Fed. Cir. 1990) ("no one factor, taken individually, is necessarily dispositive. If a preliminary injunction is granted by the trial court, the weakness of the showing regarding one factor may be overborne by the strength of others."); Hybritech Inc. v. Abbott Laboratories, 849 F.2d 1446, 1451 (Fed. Cir. 1988) (the four factors guiding the issuance of preliminary injunctions "taken individually, are not dispositive; rather the district court must weigh and measure each factor against the other factors and against the form and magnitude of the relief requested.").

[1052] *See, e.g.*, Rosenberg v. Groov-Pin Corp., 81 F.2d 46 (2d Cir. 1936).

ment preliminary injunction standards with those in other areas, such as copyright law, which require only a "reasonable" likelihood of success on the merits.[1053] The Supreme Court's formulation of the standard, however, omits any such qualifiers.[1054]

Until recently, if the patent owner clearly shows validity and infringement, the court would presume irreparable injury.[1055] However, in light of the *eBay* case, discussed below, most courts have concluded that such a presumption is now improper.[1056]

The balance of hardship factor requires the court to weigh "[t]he magnitude of the threatened injury to the patent owner . . . in the light of the strength of the showing of likelihood of success on the merits, against the injury to the accused infringer if the preliminary decision is in error."[1057]

"[I]n a patent infringement case, although there exists a public interest in protecting rights secured by valid patents, the focus of the district court's public interest analysis should be whether there exists some critical public interest that would be injured by the grant of preliminary relief."[1058]

[b]   Permanent Injunctions

In *eBay, Inc. v. MercExchange, LLC*,[1059] the Supreme Court held that a grant of a permanent injunction after a finding of infringement was discretionary and not mandatory. The court's discretion is based on the traditional four-factor balancing test:

> According to well-established principles of equity, a plaintiff seeking a permanent injunction . . . must demonstrate: (1) that it has suffered an irreparable injury; (2) that remedies available at law, such as monetary damages, are inadequate to compensate for that injury; (3) that, considering the balance of hardships between the plaintiff and defendant, a remedy in equity is warranted; and (4) that the public interest would not be disserved by a permanent injunction.[1060]

[1053] H.H. Robertson, Co. v. United Steel Deck, Inc., 820 F.2d 384, 387 (Fed. Cir. 1987) ("The standards applied to the grant of a preliminary injunction are no more nor less stringent in patent cases than in other areas of the law."); Atlas Powder Co. v. Ireco Co., 773 F.2d 1230 (Fed. Cir. 1985) (a patent owner seeking a preliminary injunction must make a "clear showing" of the validity and infringement of the patent but need not make a showing "beyond question.").

[1054] *See Titan Tire Corp.*, 566 F.3d at 1377 ("It is not clear whether the addition of 'reasonable' adds anything substantive to the test, but in any event, . . . the Supreme Court's current statement of the test is the definitive one.").

[1055] *See, e.g.*, Smith Int'l, Inc. v. Hughes Tool Co., 718 F.2d 1573 (Fed. Cir. 1983).

[1056] *See, e.g.*, FieldTurf USA, Inc. v. Astroturf, LLC, 725 F. Supp. 2d 609, 617 (E.D. Mich. 2010) (citing cases).

[1057] H.H. Robertson, Co. v. United Steel Deck, Inc., 820 F.2d 384 (Fed. Cir. 1987).

[1058] Hybritech Inc. v. Abbott Laboratories, 849 F.2d 1446, 1458 (Fed. Cir. 1988).

[1059] 547 U.S. 388 (2006).

[1060] *Id.* at 391. This test is similar to the four-factor test for a preliminary injunction, except that the "likelihood of success on the merits" factor is no longer applicable, and it has therefore been replaced by the "inadequate remedies at law" factor. Given that the definition of "irreparable injury" is an injury

On remand, the district court held that a presumption of irreparable harm would no longer follow from the finding of infringement. Instead, the court examined all four factors, including the balance of hardships, in ruling against the grant of a permanent injunction.[1061] No injunction may issue or continue after a patent expires.[1062]

A court may stay an injunction pending appeal. In *Standard Havens Products, Inc. v. Gencor Industries, Inc.*,[1063] the Federal Circuit granted a stay because, *inter alia*, "without a stay [the appellant] is likely to suffer irreparable harm in the form of employee layoffs, immediate insolvency, and, possibly, extinction." The stay applicant showed a "substantial case" that it would prevail on invalidity and proposed that it be subject to financial restrictions and obligations pending the appeal. The court cautioned against mechanical application of the oft-heard admonition that "One who elects to build a business on a product found to infringe cannot be heard to complain if an injunction against continuing infringement destroys the business so elected."[1064] Instead, the court applied the traditional four factors applicable to preliminary injunctions, and also expressly considered the possibility of harm to third parties.[1065]

The AIA adds section 298, entitled "Advice of Counsel." This new provision states that failure of an infringer to obtain advice of counsel with respect to the allegedly infringed patent or the failure to present advice of counsel to the court or jury "may not be used to prove that the accused infringer willfully infringed the patent or that the infringer intended to induce infringement of the patent." This provision is intended to end some of the confusion in the case law on willful infringement and inducement.

[2]   Damages

[a]   Compensatory Damages

Compensatory damages may include the patentee's lost profits, an established royalty, and a reasonable royalty.[1066] The patentee may not recover the infringer's illicit profits,[1067] except in design patent infringement cases.[1068]

"that cannot be adequately measured or compensated by money," BLACK'S LAW DICTIONARY 801 (8th ed. 2004), this additional factor would not seem to add anything substantive to the test.

[1061] MercExchange, LLC v. eBay, MercExchange, L.L.C. v. eBay, Inc., 500 F. Supp. 2d 556 (E.D. Va. 2007), *appeal dismissed*, 273 Fed. Appx. 857 (Fed. Cir. 2008). *Accord*, z4 Techs., Inc. v. Microsoft Corp., 434 F. Supp. 2d 437 (E.D. Tex. 2006), *aff'd on other grounds*, 507 F.3d 1340 (Fed. Cir. 2007).

[1062] *See* Clark v. Wooster, 119 U.S. 322 (1886). *See* § 2E[1].

[1063] 897 F.2d 511 (Fed. Cir. 1990).

[1064] Windsurfing International, Inc. v. AMF, Inc., 782 F.2d 995, 1003 n.12 (Fed. Cir. 1986).

[1065] 897 F.2d at 512–13.

[1066] 35 U.S.C. § 284 ("Upon finding for the claimant the court shall award the claimant damages adequate to compensate for the infringement, but in no event less than a reasonable royalty for the use made of the invention").

[1067] *See* Water Technologies Corp. v. Calco, Ltd., 850 F.2d 660, 672 (Fed. Cir. 1988) ("[U]nlike copyright and trademark infringements, patent infringement carries no remedy of an accounting for an infringer's profits."). A 1946 statute eliminated the equitable remedy of accounting for a patent

A court may award lost profits when the patent owner, or an exclusive licensee, manufactures, uses or sells the patented invention.[1069] The patent owner must establish, to a reasonable probability, that, but for the infringement, he would have made greater sales, charged higher prices, or incurred lower costs.[1070] The court may infer "but for" causation if (1) the patented product was in demand, (2) no acceptable non-infringing alternative was available, and (3) the patentee or his licensees had the capacity to produce the demanded quantity.[1071] A lost profits award is most appropriate when the patent owner and the infringer were the only two significant competitors in the market.[1072] Courts use the incremental income method to measure lost profits,[1073] and they may consider the infringer's actual profits in estimating the patent owner's lost profits.[1074] A court may award lost profits for unpatented auxiliary components if the evidence shows that the patentee, or a hypothetical licensee, would anticipate selling the components along with the patented device.[1075]

---

infringer's profits. *See* D. CHISUM, PATENTS § 20.02 [4].

[1068] 35 U.S.C. § 289. *See* § 6B[4].

[1069] An exclusive licensee, including a person who has an exclusive right to distribute in the United States without any right to manufacture, may recover lost profits. Weinar v. Rollform, Inc., 744 F.2d 797 (Fed. Cir. 1984). *See also* Kalman v. Berlyn Corp., 914 F.2d 1473 (Fed. Cir. 1990) (the district court erred in denying a patentee's motion to add as co-plaintiff a sole manufacturing licensee, of which the patentee was a 50% owner, and in limiting the patentee's damages to 50% of the licensee's lost profits).

[1070] Dowagiac Mfg. Co. v. Minnesota Moline Plow Co., 235 U.S. 641 (1915); Railroad Dynamics, Inc. v. A. Stucki Co., 727 F.2d 1506 (Fed. Cir. 1984); Lam, Inc. v. Johns-Manville Corp., 718 F.2d 1056 (Fed. Cir. 1983). In *Lam*, the court affirmed an award for profits lost due to retarded sales growth caused by the infringement.

[1071] Gyromat Corp. v. Champion Spark Plug Co., 735 F.2d 549 (Fed. Cir. 1984); Panduit Corp. v. Stahlin Bros. Fibre Works, Inc., 575 F.2d 1152 (6th Cir. 1978). *See also* Datascope Corp. v. SMEC, Inc., 879 F.2d 820 (Fed. Cir. 1989) (the district court committed clear error in finding that a certain device sold by a third party (Kontron) was an acceptable noninfringing alternative; it also erred in considering alleged customer preference for the infringer's product as relevant to the third element of the *Panduit* test — "the manufacturing/marketing *capability* of the patentee to meet the demand" for the patented product). *Compare* Water Technologies Corp. v. Calco, Ltd., 850 F.2d 660 (Fed. Cir. 1988).

[1072] Marsh-McBirney, Inc. v. Montedoro-Whitney Corp., 882 F.2d 498 (Fed. Cir. 1989) (the district court did not err in awarding the patentee lost profits for infringement in view of the court's finding that the patentee and the infringer "operate in a unique sector of the domestic market," a "separate niche"), *cert. granted, judgment vacated*, 498 U.S. 1061 (1991), *opinion reinstated in relevant part*, 939 F.2d 969, 970 (Fed. Cir. 1991); Lam, Inc. v. Johns-Manville Corp., 718 F.2d 1056 (Fed. Cir. 1983).

[1073] Paper Converting Machine Co. v. Magna-Graphics Corp., 745 F.2d 11 (Fed. Cir. 1984). Under this approach, gross profit is reduced by the incremental costs of making that sale. Fixed costs are disregarded because the patent owner or exclusive licensee would have incurred those costs whether or not the additional sale was made.

[1074] *See* Water Technologies Corp. v. Calco, Ltd., 850 F.2d 660, 673 (Fed. Cir. 1988) (the infringer's profits "are not, as such, a measure of the patent owner's damages," but may be "used for comparison purposes with the profit margin figure of the patent owner to determine the reasonableness of the latter figure."); Kori Corp. v. Wilco Marsh Buggies & Draglines, Inc., 761 F.2d 649 (Fed. Cir. 1985).

[1075] *See, e.g.*, Beatrice Foods Co. v. New England Printing & Lithographing Co., 899 F.2d 1171, 1175 (Fed. Cir. 1990) ("The law does not bar the inclusion of convoyed sales" in an award of lost profits damages.); Del Mar Avionics, Inc. v. Quinton Instrument Co., 836 F.2d 1320, 1327 (Fed. Cir. 1987) ("in appropriate circumstances the patentee may prove the extent of its lost profits by the 'entire market value rule' . . . based on a showing that the patentee could reasonably anticipate the sale of the unpatented components together with the patented components."); Kori Corp. v. Wilco Marsh Buggies

An established royalty is a royalty rate agreed to and paid by enough persons to indicate general acquiescence.[1076] A court will adopt a market-established royalty as the best measure.[1077] A single license or offer is usually not sufficient to establish a royalty.[1078]

A court must award "in no event less than a reasonable royalty."[1079] A reasonable royalty is the amount that a willing licensor and a willing licensee would have agreed to had they negotiated a license the day infringement began.[1080] The court

---

& Draglines, Inc., 761 F.2d 649 (Fed. Cir. 1985) (recovery of profits lost on unpatented components is appropriate if the patentee (or his licensee can normally anticipate selling such components together with the patented device); Paper Converting Machine Co. v. Magna-Graphics Corp., 745 F.2d 11 (Fed. Cir. 1984) (lost profits may be awarded for auxiliary units that are not integral parts of the patented machine if, in all reasonable probability, the patent owner would have made the sales of those units which the infringer made). *Compare* King Instrument Corp. v. Otari Corp., 767 F.2d 853 (Fed. Cir. 1985) (there was no evidence to support the award of profits on "spare parts" that were allegedly sold as part of a package with the original machine; the touchstone for including non-patented spare parts in a damage award is whether the patentee would normally anticipate the sale of the non-patented component together with the sale of the patented components).

A court may award damages for loss of sales of an unpatented product made by a patented process. Central Soya Co., Inc. v. Geo. A. Hormel & Co., 723 F.2d 1573 (Fed. Cir. 1983).

[1076] Rude v. Westcott, 130 U.S. 152, 165 (1889); Hanson v. Alpine Valley Ski Area, Inc., 718 F.2d 1075, 1078 (Fed. Cir. 1983); Deere & Co. v. International Harvester Co., 710 F.2d 1551 (Fed. Cir. 1983). The established royalty must be for rights under the patent that are commensurate with what the infringer has appropriated. A royalty that includes other rights or services will not suffice to set an established royalty. Bandag, Inc. v. Gerrard Tire Co., 704 F.2d 1578 (Fed. Cir. 1983).

[1077] Seymour v. McCormick, 57 U.S. (16 How.) 480 (1853); Nickson Industries, Inc. v. Rol Manufacturing Co., Ltd., 847 F.2d 795, 798 (Fed. Cir. 1988) ("Where an established royalty rate exists, it will usually be the best measure of what is a 'reasonable' royalty. . . . [A] higher figure may be awarded when the evidence clearly shows that widespread infringement made the established royalty artificially low.").

Compare Beatrice Foods Co. v. New England Printing & Lithographing Co., 899 F.2d 1171 (Fed. Cir. 1990) (the district court did not err in awarding the patentee's lost profits on the infringer's sales even though, at the time the patentee first gave notice of infringement, it offered the infringer a license at a modest royalty rate and has since offered and granted royalty-bearing licenses to others).

[1078] Trell v. Marlee Electronics Corp., 912 F.2d 1443 (Fed. Cir. 1990); Railroad Dynamics, Inc. v. A. Stucki Co., 727 F.2d 1506 (Fed. Cir. 1984).

[1079] 35 U.S.C. § 284. *Compare* Lindemann Maschinenfabrik GmbH v. American Hoist & Derrick Co., 895 F.2d 1403, 1407 (Fed. Cir. 1990) ("the statute obviates the need to show the fact of damage when infringement is admitted or proven, but that does not mean that a patentee who puts on little or no satisfactory evidence of a reasonable royalty can successfully appeal on the ground that the amount awarded by the court is not 'reasonable' and therefore contravenes section 284.").

[1080] Trans-World Mfg. Corp. v. Al Nyman & Sons, Inc., 750 F.2d 1552 (Fed. Cir. 1984); Panduit Corp. v. Stahlin Bros. Fibre Works, 575 F.2d 1152 (6th Cir. 1978).

In setting the reasonable royalty, the court may consider the fact that the party using the invention is an infringer rather than an actual willing licensee. Stickle v. Heublein, Inc., 716 F.2d 1550, 1563 (Fed. Cir. 1983). *See also* Sun Studs, Inc. v. ATA Equipment Leasing, Inc., 872 F.2d 978 (Fed. Cir. 1989) ("compensation for infringement can take cognizance of the actual commercial consequences of the infringement, and that the hypothetical negotiators need not act as if there had been no infringement, no litigation, and no erosion of market position or patent value."). For a table of adjudicated reasonable royalty rates, *see* D. CHISUM, PATENTS, § 20.03[3][d].

The measuring date is the commencement of infringement, but post-commencement evidence may be relevant. *See, e.g.*, Studiengesellschaft Kohle, m.b.H. v. Dart Industries, Inc., 862 F.2d 1564, 1571 (Fed.

considers numerous factors,[1081] including:

    (a)   the infringer's anticipated profits,[1082]

    (b)   estimated cost savings,[1083]

    (c)   comparable licenses,[1084]

    (d)   typical industry licensing practices,[1085]

    (e)   noninfringing alternatives,[1086] and

Cir. 1988) (no rigid rule that "all post-infringement evidence is irrelevant to a reasonable royalty calculation.").

[1081] Georgia-Pacific Corp. v. U.S. Plywood Corp., 318 F. Supp. 1116, 1120 (S.D.N.Y. 1970), *modified*, 446 F.2d 295 (2d Cir. 1971).

[1082] TWM Manufacturing Co., Inc. v. Dura Corp., 789 F.2d 895 (Fed. Cir. 1986); Trans-World Mfg. Corp. v. Al Nyman & Sons, Inc., 750 F.2d 1552 (Fed. Cir. 1984). Evidence of the infringer's *actual* profits from the infringement is admissible as probative of the profits that would have been anticipated. *But see* Datascope Corp. v. SMEC, Inc., 879 F.2d 820 (Fed. Cir. 1989) (the district court did not err in selecting a 5% royalty even though the patentee and the infringer enjoyed large gross profit margins (71% for the infringer)).

It is error to set the reasonable rate at a level that would have left the licensee with no anticipated profits or a profit less than the licensee would ordinarily make on its sales. Lindemann Maschinenfabrik GmbH v. American Hoist & Derrick Co., 895 F.2d 1403 (Fed. Cir. 1990); Hughes Tool Co. v. Dresser Industries, Inc., 816 F.2d 1549, 1558 (Fed. Cir. 1987) ("[A] reasonable royalty must be fixed so as to leave the infringer a reasonable profit."); Tektronix, Inc. v. United States, 552 F.2d 343 (Ct. Cl. 1977); Georgia-Pacific Corp. v. United States Plywood Corp., 446 F.2d 295 (2d Cir. 1971). *Compare* Radio Steel & Mfg. Co. v. MTD Products, Inc., 788 F.2d 1554, 1557 (Fed. Cir. 1986) (10% royalty not unreasonable even though it may have exceeded the infringer's actual profits because "the determination of a reasonable royalty . . . is based not on the infringer's profit, but on the royalty to which a willing licensor and a willing licensee would have agreed at the time the infringement began."; also, the infringer's products may have been utilized as loss-leaders).

[1083] Hanson v. Alpine Valley Ski Area, Inc., 718 F.2d 1075 (Fed. Cir. 1983).

[1084] Rates in licenses the patent owner granted are probative of a reasonable royalty even when such rates do not qualify as an established royalty. Trio Process Corp. v. L. Goldstein's Sons, Inc., 533 F.2d 126 (3d Cir. 1976). Rates in a license that confers rights other than to the patent are not probative of a reasonable royalty. *See, e.g.*, Trell v. Marlee Electronics Corp., 912 F.2d 1443 (Fed. Cir. 1990).

Actual rates are less probative when the patent owner is forced to lower the rates in the face of industry-wide infringement of the patent. *See, e.g.*, Fromson v. Western Litho Plate & Supply Co., 853 F.2d 1568, 1577 n.15 (Fed. Cir. 1988). *Compare* Studiengesellschaft Kohle, m.b.H. v. Dart Industries, Inc., 862 F.2d 1564 (Fed. Cir. 1988) (proper to consider settlement agreement with another infringer entered after patent held valid and infringed).

License offers are admissible as evidence of a reasonable royalty unless the offers are to settle existing or threatened litigation. Deere & Co. v. International Harvester Co., 710 F.2d 1551 (Fed. Cir. 1983); Pitcairn v. United States, 547 F.2d 1106 (Ct. Cl. 1976).

[1085] *See, e.g.*, Stickle v. Heublein, Inc., 716 F.2d 1550 (Fed. Cir. 1983). In *Stickle*, the court held that it was error to base a reasonable royalty on a percentage of the sale price of products produced by the infringing machine when there was no evidence that the particular industry accepted those types of licenses. Typical industry practice was to pay a sum per machine for a paid-up license.

[1086] *See, e.g.*, State Industries, Inc. v. Mor-Flo Industries, Inc., 883 F.2d 1573, 1581 (Fed Cir. 1989). *Compare* TWM Manufacturing Co., Inc. v. Dura Corp., 789 F.2d 895 (Fed. Cir. 1986) (argument that a lower rate was proper because of the existence of an alternative was undercut by evidence of (1) the infringer's failure to design independently its own device; (2) the infringer's election to infringe "despite having expended only minimal sums when notified of infringement"; (3) willful infringement; (4) failure

(f)   benefits from sales of parts or related components.[1087]

The court has discretion in selecting a damage computation method.[1088] It may apply different damages measures to distinct infringing activities, for example, lost profits for some infringing sales and a reasonable royalty for others.[1089]

The court may order an accounting to determine infringing sales volume.[1090]

[b]   Increased Damages — Willful Infringement

Section 284 provides that the court "may increase the damages up to three times the amount found or assessed."[1091]

The most common basis for increased damage awards is willful infringement.[1092] The court will not increase damages if the infringer acted in good faith, for example, without knowledge of the patent,[1093] or with a reasonable belief he did not infringe or the patent was invalid.[1094]

In *In re Seagate Technology, Inc.*, the Federal Circuit held that "proof of willful infringement permitting enhanced damages requires at least a showing of objective recklessness."[1095] The Federal Circuit considers nine factors to determine a finding of willfulness: (1) whether the infringer deliberately copied the ideas or design of

---

of the infringer successfully to market alternative designs; (5) violation of an injunction against infringement; and (6) withdrawal from the business after enforcement of the injunction).

Alternatives availability is determined as of the date infringement begins. Panduit Corp. v. Stahlin Bros. Fibre Works, 575 F.2d 1152 (6th Cir. 1978).

[1087] TWM Manufacturing Co., Inc. v. Dura Corp., 789 F.2d 895 (Fed. Cir. 1986); Deere & Co. v. International Harvester Co., 710 F.2d 1551, 1559 (Fed. Cir. 1983).

[1088] State Industries, Inc. v. Mor-Flo Industries, Inc., 883 F.2d 1573, 1576 (Fed. Cir. 1989) ("Deciding how much to award as damages is not an exact science, and the methodology of assessing and computing damages is committed to the sound discretion of the district court.").

[1089] *See, e.g.,* Bio-Rad Laboratories, Inc. v. Nicolet Instrument Corp., 739 F.2d 604 (Fed. Cir. 1984).

[1090] *See* Beatrice Foods Co. v. New England Printing & Lithographing Co., 899 F.2d 1171 (Fed. Cir. 1990); Nickson Industries, Inc. v. Rol Manufacturing Co., Ltd., 847 F.2d 795, 799 (Fed. Cir. 1988); Amstar Corp. v. Envirotech Corp., 823 F.2d 1538, 1545 (Fed. Cir. 1987) ("During an accounting, as during the liability trial, a patentee must prove infringement by a preponderance of the evidence.").

[1091] 35 U.S.C. § 284. The "up to" language means that a court may award less than full trebling. *See, e.g.,* Del Mar Avionics, Inc. v. Quinton Instrument Co., 836 F.2d 1320 (Fed. Cir. 1987) (doubling).

[1092] *See, e.g.,* In re Seagate Technology, Inc., 497 F.3d 1360, 1368 (Fed. Cir. 2007) (en banc); Beatrice Foods Co. v. New England Printing && Lithographing Co., 923 F.2d 1576, 1578 (Fed. Cir. 1991); Avia Group International, Inc. v. L.A. Gear California, Inc., 853 F.2d 1557 (Fed. Cir. 1988); Rosemount, Inc. v. Beckman Instruments, Inc., 727 F.2d 1540 (Fed. Cir. 1984).

Compare Modine Manufacturing Co. v. Allen Group, Inc., 917 F.2d 538, 543 (Fed. Cir. 1990) (the district court did not abuse its discretion by refusing to award increased damages even though the jury found willful infringement by clear and convincing evidence; "a finding of willful infringement merely *authorizes*, but does not *mandate*, an award of increased damages.") *Accord,* Odetics, Inc. v. Storage Tech. Corp., 185 F.3d 1259, 1274 (Fed. Cir. 1999).

[1093] State Industries, Inc. v. A.O. Smith Corp., 751 F.2d 1226, 1235–36 (Fed. Cir. 1985).

[1094] Paper Converting Machine Co. v. Magna-Graphics Corp., 745 F.2d 11, 20 (Fed. Cir. 1984).

[1095] 497 F.3d 1360, 1371 (Fed. Cir. 2007) (en banc); *see also id.* ("to establish willful infringement, a patentee must show by clear and convincing evidence that the infringer acted despite an objectively high likelihood that its actions constituted infringement of a valid patent.").

another; (2) whether the infringer, upon learning of the patent, investigated the scope of the patent and formed a good faith belief that it was invalid or that it was not infringed; (3) the infringer's behavior as a party to the litigation; (4) defendant's size and financial condition; (5) closeness of the case; (6) duration of the defendant's misconduct; (7) remedial action by the defendant; (8) defendant's motivation for harm; (9) whether the defendant attempted to conceal its misconduct.[1096]

In *Knorr-Bremse Systeme Fuer Nutzfahrzeuge GmbH v. Dana Corp.*,[1097] the Federal Circuit addressed the issue of whether failure to obtain an opinion letter from counsel could be considered in determining willfulness or was protected by the attorney-client privilege. The court held that no adverse inference for willfulness could be found from (1) invocation of attorney-client privilege and (2) failure to obtain an opinion letter.[1098] In *Seagate*, the Federal Circuit clarified that invocation of an advice-of-counsel defense waives the attorney-client and work product privileges only with respect to counsel that provided the opinion, and not with respect to trial counsel.[1099]

[c]   Notice — Patent Marking

A patent owner may place a mark consisting of the word "patented" or "pat." and the patent's number on patented products he or a licensee sells.[1100] If the patent owner or his licensee fails to mark products, the patent owner may not recover damages for infringements that occur before giving the infringer notice.[1101] This damage limitation is the only consequence of failure to mark.

If the patent is for a machine or a process, there is no duty to mark products made by the machine or process.[1102]

Failure to mark does not limit the reasonable compensation that a patent owner may recover for United States government use.[1103]

False and counterfeit patent markings are prohibited, with a maximum fine of $500 "for every such offense."[1104] In *Forest Group, Inc. v. Bon Tool, Inc.*, the Federal Circuit held that the penalty must be imposed for each article that is falsely

---

[1096] Read Corp. v. Portec, Inc., 970 F.2d 816, 827 (Fed. Cir. 1992).

[1097] 383 F.3d 1337 (Fed. Cir. 2004) (en banc).

[1098] *Id.* at 1344–46. The court also declined to create a *per se* rule that the existence of a substantial defense would defeat a finding of willfulness. *Id.* at 1347.

[1099] 497 F.3d at 1372–76.

[1100] 35 U.S.C. § 287(a). If a patent owner licenses others to make and sell the product, he must take reasonable steps to assure that the licensees mark the products. Butterfield v. Oculus Contact Lens Co., 332 F. Supp. 750 (N.D. Ill. 1971).

[1101] 35 U.S.C. § 287(a). The patent owner must give the infringer actual notice. It is not sufficient that the infringer has knowledge of the patent from other sources. Lemelson v. Fisher Price Corp., 545 F. Supp. 973 (S.D.N.Y. 1982). "Filing of an action for infringement shall constitute such notice." 35 U.S.C. § 287(a).

[1102] Wine Railway Appliance Co. v. Enterprise Railway Equip. Co., 297 U.S. 387 (1936); Bandag, Inc. v. Gerrard Tire Co., 704 F.2d 1578, 1581 (Fed. Cir. 1983).

[1103] Motorola, Inc. v. United States, 729 F.2d 765 (Fed. Cir. 1984).

[1104] 35 U.S.C. § 292(a).

marked, and not just for an entire product.[1105] The decision set off a wave of "false marking" lawsuits, because under the *qui tam* provisions of the statute, "[a]ny person may sue for the penalty," with half of the proceeds going to the person suing and half to the United States.[1106] In *Pequignot v. Solo Cup Co.*, the Federal Circuit affirmed that articles covered by an expired patent are "unpatented" within the meaning of the statute,[1107] and that an intent to deceive may be inferred from a false marking with knowledge of its falsity;[1108] but it also held that the inference is rebuttable, and that defendant had successfully rebutted it by showing that it consulted counsel and replaced molds with the patent number when they became worn, rather than replacing them when the patent expired.[1109]

The AIA responded to these developments in Federal Circuit jurisprudence on patent marking by statutorily changing the cause of action for false marking. Under the new provision, only the United States government can sue for the $500 statutory penalty. A private action can be brought only to recover actual damages that arise from "competitive injury." In addition, the AIA allows a patent owner to comply with the marking requirements through virtual marking, that is, by placing the information on a website to which someone can be directed through information on the product. In addition, marking a product with expired patents is no longer a violation of the marking requirements. These new provisions are effective as of September 16, 2011, and apply to pending cases.

[3] Interest

Section 284 provides for a damage award "together with interest . . . as fixed by the court."[1110] In *General Motors Corp. v. Devex Corp.*, the Supreme Court held "prejudgment interest should ordinarily be awarded where necessary to afford the plaintiff full compensation for the infringement."[1111]

> In the typical case an award of prejudgment interest is necessary to ensure that the patent owner is placed in as good a position as he would have been in had the infringer entered into a reasonable royalty agreement. An award of interest from the time that the royalty payments would have been received merely serves to make the patent owner whole, since his damages consist not only of the value of the royalty payments but also of the foregone use of the money between the time of infringement and the date of the judgment.[1112]

[1105] 590 F.3d 1295, 1300–04 (Fed. Cir. 2009).

[1106] 35 U.S.C. § 292(b). *See* Stauffer v. Brooks Brothers, Inc., 619 F.3d 1321 (Fed. Cir. 2010) (any person seeking *qui tam* penalty for false patent marking has standing to sue).

[1107] 608 F.3d 1356, 1361–62 (Fed. Cir. 2010).

[1108] *Id.* at 1362–63.

[1109] *Id.* at 1363–65.

[1110] 35 U.S.C. § 284.

[1111] 461 U.S. 648, 654 (1983).

[1112] *Id.* at 655–56.

In *Devex*, the Court recognized that a court may limit or deny prejudgment interest under special circumstances, such as when the patent owner causes undue delay in filing and prosecuting the infringement suit.[1113] Federal Circuit decisions emphasize that prejudgment interest is the rule, not the exception,[1114] and narrowly restrict the circumstances justifying denial of interest.[1115]

The district court has discretion to set the interest rate and whether it should be simple or compound.[1116] Most decisions award compound interest at a market rate.[1117]

The court may not grant prejudgment interest on the increased portion of a damage award,[1118] but it may award interest on an attorney fee award.[1119]

[1113] *Id.* at 657 & n.11.

[1114] *See, e.g.*, Nickson Industries, Inc. v. Rol Manufacturing Co., Ltd., 847 F.2d 795, 800 (Fed. Cir. 1988) ("Generally, prejudgment interest should be awarded from the date of infringement to the date of judgment. District courts have discretion to limit prejudgment interest where, for example, the patent owner has caused undue delay in the lawsuit, but there must be justification bearing a relationship to the award.").

[1115] Kalman v. Berlyn Corp., 914 F.2d 1473 (Fed. Cir. 1990) (not error to award interest even though the patentee delayed six years to file suit after it learned of the defendant's infringement; during the delay period, the patentee engaged in litigation against one of defendant's customers, and defendant controlled and financed the customer's defense of that litigation); Allen Archery, Inc. v. Browning Manufacturing Co., 898 F.2d 787 (Fed. Cir. 1990) (error to exclude from the interest period the time during which the present case for infringement was stayed pending the decision in another case involving the validity of the same patent); Richardson v. Suzuki Motor Co., Ltd., 868 F.2d 1226 (Fed. Cir. 1989) (error to deny interest on the damage awards for patent infringement and violation of trade secret rights); Hughes Tool Co. v. Dresser Industries, Inc., 816 F.2d 1549, 1558 (Fed. Cir. 1987) (district court's withholding of prejudgment interest for the period of time after the patent had been held invalid by another district court in a suit against another accused infringer and the reversal of that holding on appeal "was based on [a] misunderstanding that prejudgment interest can never be awarded in such a circumstance."); Radio Steel & Mfg. Co. v. MTD Products, Inc., 788 F.2d 1554, 1558 (Fed. Cir. 1986) (the patentee's failure to remove a patent notice from its products for one-and-one-half years after the patent expired is not a justification for the denial of prejudgment interest; a justification "must have some relationship to the award of prejudgment interest.").

[1116] *See, e.g.*, Studiengesellschaft Kohle, m.b.H. v. Dart Industries, Inc., 862 F.2d 1564 (Fed. Cir. 1988) (district court did not abuse its discretion in adopting the special master's award of quarterly-compounded, prime rate prejudgment interest); Nickson Industries, Inc. v. Rol Manufacturing Co., Ltd., 847 F.2d 795 (Fed. Cir. 1988) (the patentee failed to show that the district court abused its discretion by awarding simple interest).

Compare Bio-Rad Laboratories, Inc. v. Nicolet Instrument Corp., 807 F.2d 964, 969 (Fed. Cir. 1986) (the district court erred in limiting prejudgment interest to the State judgment interest rate of 7% uncompounded; "The rate of prejudgment interest and whether it should be compounded or uncompounded are matters left largely to the discretion of the district court"; however, the district court must be guided by the purpose of prejudgment interest, which is to provide full compensation to the patent owner; the only evidence in the record suggested use of either the prime rate or the rate the patentee paid on its corporate borrowings during the period of infringement).

[1117] *See, e.g.*, Datascope Corp. v. SMEC, Inc., 879 F.2d 820, 829 (Fed. Cir. 1989) (district court did not err in providing for annual rather than quarterly or monthly compounding, where infringer's president testified that it "would have been unable to comply with any requirement to report royalties more frequently than annually."); Studiengesellschaft Kohle, m.b.H. v. Dart Industries, Inc., 862 F.2d 1564 (Fed. Cir. 1988) (prime rate compounded quarterly); Lam, Inc. v. Johns-Manville Corp., 718 F.2d 1056 (Fed. Cir. 1983) (average year-by-year prime rate).

[1118] Lam, Inc. v. Johns-Manville Corp., 718 F.2d 1056 (Fed. Cir. 1983).

[4] Attorney's Fees and Expenses

Section 285 provides that "[t]he court in exceptional cases may award reasonable attorney fees to the prevailing party."[1120] This is an exception to the general American law rule that prevailing litigants bear their own attorney fees.

If the patent owner prevails, the court may find the case exceptional because the infringement was willful[1121] or the litigation was pursued in bad faith.[1122]

If the accused infringer prevails, the court may find the case exceptional because of inequitable conduct in patent procurement[1123] or bad faith litigation.[1124]

The trial court has discretion whether to award fees,[1125] but it cannot make an award without finding a sufficient basis for declaring the case exceptional.[1126]

[1119] Mathis v. Spears, 857 F.2d 749 (Fed. Cir. 1988).

[1120] 35 U.S.C. § 285.

[1121] *See, e.g.*, Ryco, Inc. v. Ag-Bag Corp., 857 F.2d 1418 (Fed. Cir. 1988); Avia Group Int'l, Inc. v. L.A. Gear California, Inc., 853 F.2d 1557, 1567 (Fed. Cir. 1988) ("Although an award of attorney fees, because discretionary, does not automatically follow from the willfulness of an infringement, the willfulness of the infringement by the accused infringer may be a sufficient basis in a particular case for finding the case 'exceptional' for purposes of awarding attorney fees to the prevailing patent owner.").

[1122] *See* Beckman Instruments, Inc. v. LKB Produkter AB, 892 F.2d 1547, 1551–53 (Fed. Cir. 1989) (the district court did not commit clear error in finding the case "exceptional" because of the infringer's "*strategy* of vexatious activity" but abused its discretion by awarding the patentee its entire attorney fees in view of the finding that the infringer was not guilty of willful infringement and the infringer's success in showing invalidity and noninfringement of some of the claims in suit).

[1123] *See, e.g.*, A.B. Chance Co. v. RTE Corp., 854 F.2d 1307, 1312 (Fed. Cir. 1988) ("Inequitable conduct is a separate defense to patent infringement and, either alone or in conjunction with trial conduct, may constitute the basis for an award of attorney fees under 35 U.S.C. § 285.").

Compare J. P. Stevens Company, Inc. v. Lex Tex. Ltd., Inc., 822 F.2d 1047, 1052 (Fed. Cir. 1987) (the district court did not err in failing to award attorney fees to the accused infringer even though it had found the patent unenforceable because of inequitable conduct); Gardco Manufacturing, Inc. v. Herst Lighting Co., 820 F.2d 1209 (Fed. Cir. 1987) ("[I]t has not been held that every case of proven inequitable conduct must result in an automatic attorney fee award, or that every instance of inequitable conduct mandates an evaluation of the case as 'exceptional.' After the district court determines that a case is exceptional, there remains in every case its freedom to exercise its discretion 'informed by the court's familiarity with the matter in litigation and the interest of justice.' ").

[1124] *See, e.g.*, Eltech Systems Corp. v. PPG Industries, Inc., 903 F.2d 805, 811 (Fed. Cir. 1990) (the district court neither committed clear error in finding the case exceptional nor abused its discretion by awarding attorney fees against the patentee for filing and pursuing a groundless infringement suit; "Where . . . the patentee is manifestly unreasonable in assessing infringement, while continuing to assert infringement in court, an inference is proper of bad faith, whether grounded in or denominated wrongful intent, recklessness, or gross negligence."); Mathis v. Spears, 857 F.2d 749, 754 (Fed. Cir. 1988) ("The only deterrent to the . . . improper bringing of clearly unwarranted suits on obviously invalid or unenforceable patents is Section 285.").

[1125] *See, e.g.*, Modine Manufacturing Co. v. Allen Group, Inc., 917 F.2d 538, 543 (Fed. Cir. 1990) ("An express finding of willful infringement is a sufficient basis for classifying a case as 'exceptional,' and indeed, when a trial court denies attorney fees in spite of a finding of willful infringement, the court must explain why the case is *not* 'exceptional' " within the meaning of section 285; "Nevertheless, the decision whether or not to award fees is still committed to the discretion of the trial judge, and '[e]ven an exceptional case does not require in all circumstances the award of attorney fees.'").

[1126] *See, e.g.*, Advance Transformer Co. v. Levinson, 837 F.2d 1081 (Fed. Cir. 1988) (a finding of exceptional circumstances requires proof of actual wrongful intent or gross negligence).

If a suit combines patent and nonpatent claims, Section 285 authorizes an award only for attorney services pertaining to the patent claims.[1127] If, in a suit with multiple patents or claims, each party prevails to some extent, "the amount of fees awarded to the 'prevailing party' should bear some relation to the extent to which that party actually prevailed."[1128]

In *Octane Fitness, LLC. v. Icon Health & Fitness, Inc.*,[1129] the Supreme Court abrogated the rigid approach adopted by the Federal Circuit in *Brooks Furniture Mfg., Inc. v. Dutailier Int'l, Inc.*[1130] Under the Federal Circuit's approach, the party seeking attorney's fees would have to establish that the case was objectively baseless and not brought in good faith. In place of this standard, the Supreme Court held that the district courts should adopt a more flexible standard, under which an exceptional case is one that stands out in comparison to other cases with respect to the strength of the case or one that was litigated in an unreasonable manner. The Court also held that a moving party had to show that a case was exception under a preponderance of the evidence standard. In a companion case, announced on the same day, the Court ruled that the district court's ruling on an award of attorney's fees was subject to the abuse of discretion standard upon appellate review, overruling the Federal Circuit's application of a de novo standard.[1131]

§ 2I OWNERSHIP AND TRANSFER

Ownership rights in a patent vest initially in the inventor or inventors.[1132] A patent has "the attributes of personal property,"[1133] and a person may transfer ownership in a patent or patent application to another by written instrument.[1134] A patent owner may grant exclusive or nonexclusive licenses.

[1]   Employee and Contractor Inventions

An employee owns the patent rights to his or her inventions conceived or reduced to practice during the course of employment,[1135] with two important exceptions. First, an employee must assign patent rights to his employer if he was

---

[1127] *See, e.g.*, Water Technologies Corp. v. Calco, Ltd., 850 F.2d 660 (Fed. Cir. 1988) (award of the full amount of the patentee's fees cannot stand because some of the fees were for a nonpatent claim of unfair competition).

[1128] Beckman Instruments, Inc. v. LKB Produkter AB, 892 F.2d 1547, 1554 (Fed. Cir. 1989).

[1129] Octane Fitness, LLC v. Icon Health & Fitness, Inc., 134 S. Ct. 1749 (2014).

[1130] 393 F.3d 1378 (Fed. Cir. 2005).

[1131] *See* Highmark Inc. v. Allcare Health Mgmt. Sys., Inc., 134 S. Ct. 1744 (2014).

[1132] Joint inventors acquire equal, undivided interests in a patent. Absent an agreement to the contrary, each joint owner may use or authorize others to use the subject matter claimed in the patent without accounting to the other owner or owners. 35 U.S.C. § 262.

[1133] 35 U.S.C. § 261.

[1134] 35 U.S.C. § 261. State contract, tort, and fiduciary laws govern most patent ownership, transfer and licensing questions. Farmland Irrigation Co., Inc. v. Dopplmaier, 308 P.2d 732 (Cal. 1957). *See* D. CHISUM, PATENTS § 22.03[4].

[1135] United States v. Dubilier Condenser Corp., 289 U.S. 178 (1933). *See generally* D. CHISUM, PATENTS

initially hired or later directed to solve a specific problem or to exercise inventive skill.[1136] Second, an employee must assign patent rights if he signed an assignment contract.[1137] Companies commonly use such assignment contracts. An Executive Order controls the ownership by federal government employees of patent rights in their inventions.[1138] A court may order a contractually obligated employee to assign and cooperate in the patent application process.[1139] An employer or other person with a proprietary interest in the invention may file a patent application if the inventor refuses to do so.[1140]

If an employee uses his employer's resources to conceive of or reduce to practice an invention, the employer acquires a "shop right," a nonexclusive, royalty-free, non-transferable license to make and use the invention.[1141] A shop right is not an ownership interest because the employee as patentee retains all other rights, including licensing and filing infringement suits. A shop right continues even if the inventor leaves the employment.[1142] Shop rights usually arise in employment but may also arise in other relationships, for example, supplier and customer.[1143]

---

§ 22.03. See discussion in Board of Trustees of Leland Stanford Junior University v. Roche Molecular Systems, Inc., 131 S. Ct. 2188 (2011) (holding that Bayh-Dole Act did not change rules of employee assignment for inventions created under federal contract).

[1136] Standard Parts Co. v. Peck, 264 U.S. 52 (1924); National Development Co. v. Gray, 55 N.E.2d 783 (Mass. 1944).

[1137] See, e.g., United Aircraft Products, Inc. v. Warrick, 72 N.E.2d 669 (Ohio Ct. App. 1945). Cf. Shamrock Technologies, Inc. v. Medical Sterilization, Inc., 903 F.2d 789, 794 (Fed. Cir. 1990) ("Employment, salary and bonuses are valid consideration for [an employee's] assignment [of patent rights in his or her work-related inventions]"). Such contract provisions vary in wording as they are privately prepared and negotiated documents. Several state statutes restrict employee invention assignment agreements. See, e.g., Cal. Labor Code, § 2870–72; Wash. Rev. Code 49.44.140–.150; Minn. Stat. § 181.78; N.C. Gen. Stat. § 66.57.1–.2, which invalidate agreements requiring assignment of inventions made by the employee on his or her own time and do not relate to the employer's business or its actual or demonstrably anticipated research and development.

[1138] See, e.g., Heinemann v. United States, 796 F.2d 451 (Fed. Cir. 1986) (administrative determination of the ownership of patent rights in inventions by federal employees under Executive Order 10096 is subject to judicial review under the Administrative Procedure Act; such review is governed by the "arbitrary or capricious" standard; Order 10096 supersedes the common law standard of property rights that previously controlled, is not contrary to statute, and does not constitute a taking of property in violation of the Constitution's due process clause).

[1139] See, e.g., Grove v. Grove Valve & Regulator Co., 4 Cal. App. 3d 299 (1970).

[1140] 35 U.S.C. § 118. See also D. CHISUM, PATENTS § 11.02[2].

[1141] Wommack v. Durham Pecan Co., Inc., 715 F.2d 962 (5th Cir. 1983). The scope of the shop right depends on the circumstances; it is not limited to the particular machines on which the invention had been used during the time of the inventor's employment. Tin Decorating Co. of Baltimore v. Metal Package Corp., 29 F.2d 1006 (S.D.N.Y. 1928), aff'd on other grounds, 37 F.2d 5 (2d Cir. 1930).

[1142] Wiegand v. Dover Mfg. Co., 292 F. 255 (N.D. Ohio 1923).

[1143] Francklyn v. Guilford Packing Co., 695 F.2d 1158, 1160–61 (9th Cir. 1983); Kurt H. Volk, Inc. v. Foundation for Christian Living, 534 F. Supp. 1059, 1083–84 (S.D.N.Y. 1982).

[2]   Ability to Sue Infringers

A patent owner or exclusive licensee may file a suit against an accused infringer.[1144] A nonexclusive licensee may not sue for infringement.[1145] A license is exclusive if the licensee receives exclusivity over a geographic area, a field of use, or a time period.[1146] A license may be exclusive even if the patent owner has previously granted nonexclusive licenses or reserved the right to make, use or sell the invention himself.[1147]

If an exclusive licensee files a patent infringement suit, the patent owner/licensor is a necessary party and, if unwilling to join voluntarily, will be joined as an "involuntary plaintiff."[1148]

[3]   Compulsory Licenses

A patent owner has discretion to grant or refuse licenses.[1149] Statutes provide for compulsory licensing of patents relating to inventions in certain areas.[1150] In an antitrust case, a court may order compulsory patent licensing at reasonable royalty rates if patents are intimately associated with and contributed to anticompetitive

---

[1144] D. CHISUM, PATENTS § 21.03[2]. If there are joint owners of a patent (*e.g.*, A owns 50% and B owns 50%), normally both should join in bringing any suit against an alleged infringer. See Willingham v. Lawton, 555 F.2d 1340 (6th Cir. 1977); Catanzaro v. International Tel. & Tel. Corp., 378 F. Supp. 203 (D. Del. 1974).

[1145] Waterman v. Mackenzie, 138 U.S. 252 (1891); Life Time Doors, Inc. v. Walled Lake Door Co., 505 F.2d 1165 (6th Cir. 1974). *Cf.* Kalman v. Berlyn Corp., 914 F.2d 1473, 1481 (Fed. Cir. 1990) ("It is well settled that a non-exclusive licensee of a patent has no standing to sue for infringement.").

In *Kalman*, 914 F.2d at 1481–82, the Federal Circuit held that the district court erred in denying a patentee's motion to add as co-plaintiff a sole manufacturing licensee, of which the patentee was a 50% owner, and in limiting the patentee's damages to 50% of the licensee's lost profits:

> [W]e do not give any licensee who joins the patentee standing to sue an infringer. When the sole licensee, however, has been shown to be directly damaged by an infringer in a two supplier market, and when the nexus between the sole licensee and the patentee is so clearly defined as here, the sole licensee must be recognized as the real party in interest. . . . [I]n determining that [the licensee] has standing to join as a co-plaintiff, we not only give effect to principles of equity, but also the Congressional mandate that, in patent actions, '[u]pon finding for the claimant the court shall award the claimant damages adequate to compensate for the infringement . . .' 35 U.S.C. § 284.

A nonexclusive licensee may extract a contractual commitment requiring the patent licensor to sue infringers. The licensor's failure to sue infringers is a breach of contract but is not grounds for allowing the licensee to sue. Philadelphia Brief Case Co. v. Specialty Leather Prod. Co., Inc., 145 F. Supp. 425, 430 (D.N.J. 1956), *aff'd*, 242 F.2d 511 (3d Cir. 1957).

[1146] Independent Wireless Telegraph Co. v. Radio Corp. of America, 269 U.S. 459 (1926); Weinar v. Rollform, Inc., 744 F.2d 797 (Fed. Cir. 1984); Pratt & Whitney v. United States, 153 F. Supp. 409, 411, (Ct. Cl. 1957).

[1147] *See, e.g.*, Western Elec. Co. v. Pacent Reproducer Corp., 42 F.2d 116, 119 (2d Cir. 1930). *Cf.* Weinar v. Rollform, Inc., 744 F.2d 797 (Fed. Cir. 1984) (one who is an exclusive distributor in the United States, but lacks authority to manufacture, may properly be awarded damages in an infringement suit).

[1148] Independent Wireless Telegraph Co. v. Radio Corp. of America, 269 U.S. 459 (1926). *See* Fed. R. Civ. P. 19.

[1149] *See, e.g.*, United States v. Studiengesellschaft Kohle, 670 F.2d 1122 (D.C. Cir. 1981); SCM Corp. v. Xerox Corp., 645 F.2d 1195 (2d Cir. 1981).

[1150] *See, e.g.*, Clean Air Act, 42 U.S.C. 7608; Atomic Energy Act, 42 U.S.C. § 2183.

conduct and licensing is necessary to restore competition in the relevant market.[1151]

[1151] *See* United States v. Glaxo Group, Ltd., 410 U.S. 52 (1973).

Chapter 3

TRADE SECRETS LAW

SYNOPSIS

§ 3A   INTRODUCTION
   [1]   State Law Versus Federal Law
   [2]   Trade Secrets Law's Relationship to Patent Law

§ 3B   HISTORICAL DEVELOPMENT
   [1]   Early English Cases
   [2]   Early United States Cases
   [3]   The Restatement
   [4]   The Uniform Trade Secrets Act

§ 3C   NATURE OF PROTECTION — RIGHTS
   [1]   Information That Qualifies as a Trade Secret
      [a]   Definitions
      [b]   Eligible Subject Matter
       [i]   Concreteness
       [ii]   Nontechnical Information
       [iii]   Combinations
       [iv]   Customer Lists
       [v]   Continuous Use
       [vi]   Negative Information
      [c]   Secrecy
       [i]   Definitions
       [ii]   Application of Secrecy Requirement
       [iii]   Ascertainability from Products and Public Sources
       [iv]   Copyrighted Material
       [v]   Patented Material
       [vi]   Novelty Versus General Knowledge
       [vii]   Disclosure to Government Agencies
       [viii]   Laws Mandating Disclosure
      [d]   Commercial Value and Use
       [i]   Value
       [ii]   Cost of Development

    [2]   Exclusive Rights

    [3]   Duration and Termination

§ 3D   TRADE SECRET MISAPPROPRIATION LITIGATION

    [1]   Definition of Misappropriation

    [2]   Theories of Law

        [a]   Contract Law Theories

        [b]   Tort Law Theories

        [c]   Conflicts of Laws

          [i]   Contract Law Conflicts

          [ii]   Tort Law Conflicts

          [iii]   Statutes of Limitations

    [3]   Elements and Burdens of Proof

    [4]   Trade Secret Ownership

        [a]   Common Law

          [i]   Information Protectability

          [ii]   Ownership

          [iii]   Employment as a Confidential Relationship

        [b]   Express Agreements

          [i]   Ownership-Assignment Agreements

          [ii]   Timing of Creation

          [iii]   Consideration

        [c]   Non-Competition Agreements

    [5]   Misappropriation

        [a]   Confidential Relationship

        [b]   Improper and Proper Means

          [i]   Improper Means

          [ii]   Proper Means

          [iii]   Otherwise Lawful Conduct

        [c]   Innocent Receipt

    [6]   Detrimental Use or Disclosure

§ 3E   DEFENSES

    [1]   Independent Development

    [2]   Absence of Secrecy — Public Domain

    [3]   Reverse Engineering

    [4]   Privilege

    [5]   Equitable Defenses

        [a]   Unclean Hands

        [b]   Laches

        [c]   Estoppel

§ 3F REMEDIES

[1] Injunctions

    [a] Preliminary Injunctions

    [b] Scope of Injunctions

    [c] Duration of Injunctions

[2] Damages

    [a] Compensatory Damages

      [i] Calculation of Damages

      [ii] Effect of Public Disclosure

    [b] Punitive Damages

[3] Attorney Fees and Court Costs

[4] Seizure of Embodiments

[5] Criminal Penalties

§ 3A INTRODUCTION

Trade secret law reflects economic policy judgments about how to encourage innovation, competition, and consumer welfare and ethical notions about proper business behavior, the general norms of morality and good faith that are also reflected in the torts of unfair competition and breach of confidence.

Originating in the early 19th Century, trade secret law has evolved to accommodate the changing nature of business secrets, competition, technology, and employment patterns. Accelerating technological change, increased spending on research and development, greater employee mobility and entrepreneurial activity, the internationalization of business competition, and the growing complexity of integrating different technologies have heightened trade secrets law's significance.

Defining "secret" and reconciling confidentiality obligations with policies favoring free competition and employee mobility are complexities that have led to well-developed trade secrets doctrine, but the underlying moral principles retain force and may lead to judicial intervention when fact patterns do not conform to trade secrets doctrine.

Courts base trade secrets doctrine on two distinct principles: (1) a property interest in secret business information; and (2) a duty to respect the confidentiality of information. In applying the property principle, courts examine whether particular information is sufficiently secret and valuable to be considered private property. In applying the duty principle, courts put primary emphasis on the circumstances under which an alleged misappropriator obtained the information and may impose a duty to avoid its use or disclosure if it was obtained through a confidential relationship or improper means — even if its secrecy has not been definitely established.

Some courts and commentators reject the concept of a property interest in a trade secret, usually citing *E.I. du Pont de Nemours Powder Co. v. Masland*, a 1917 Supreme Court case, which stated:

The word "property" as applied to . . . trade secrets is an unanalyzed expression of certain secondary consequences of the primary fact that the law makes some rudimentary requirements of good faith. Whether the plaintiffs have any valuable secret or not[,] the defendant knows the facts, whatever they are, through a special confidence that he accepted. The property may be denied, but the confidence cannot be.[1]

This language is frequently misconstrued; as a recent Supreme Court decision put it, the opinion "did not deny the existence of a property interest," it only "deemed determination of the existence of that interest irrelevant to resolution of the case."[2] The concept of a property interest in trade secrets is in fact indispensable to the logic of trade secrets law. In *Ruckelshaus v. Monsanto Co.*, the Supreme Court held trade secrets to be a property right protectable under the Due Process Clause of the Constitution.[3]

In some situations, a case outcome may depend on which principle the court emphasizes. For example, if information's secrecy is not clearly established but a defendant acquired information through improper means, a court emphasizing the property principle would find no protectable trade secret; a court emphasizing the duty principle would penalize the defendant. Trade secrets law's equitable nature and ethical roots invite emphasis on the duty principle when a defendant's conduct offends the court's notions of fairness and morality.

Courts emphasizing the property principle have developed an extensive body of precedents defining protectable trade secrets.[4] As for courts emphasizing the duty principle, some apply broad definitions of trade secrets; others accept narrower definitions but find duties of non-use and non-disclosure even if information does not qualify as a trade secret. The divergent emphases lead to occasional lack of clarity and predictability in trade secrets law.

In addition to confusion about underlying principles, two other factors enhance the potential for inconsistent decisions in trade secrets cases. First, trade secrets law defines the secrecy underlying the property principle in relative terms.[5] Second, the duty principle relies on the blurry distinction between proper and improper behavior.[6]

Notwithstanding these ambiguities, it is clear in many fact-patterns which principle courts will emphasize and what results they will reach. In a case of theft or industrial espionage, the obvious misconduct may call for sanctions whether or not the information technically qualifies as protectable property. In contrast, where information is voluntarily disclosed to a party with merely an implied duty to maintain it in confidence, the absence of misconduct usually leads courts to require

---

[1] 244 U.S. 100, 102 (1917).

[2] Ruckelshaus v. Monsanto Co., 467 U.S. 986, 1004 n.9 (1983).

[3] *Id.* at 1000–05. *See also* Thomas v. Union Carbide Agricultural Prods. Co., 473 U.S. 568, 584 (1985).

[4] *See* § 3C[1].

[5] Today, secrecy must only be "relative," or the subject of efforts that are "reasonable under the circumstances." *See* § 3C[1][c].

[6] For a discussion of proper and improper means, see § 3D[4][b].

that the secrecy and value of the information be established as a prerequisite to restricting the recipient's use of it.

Trade secrets cases became less predictable in the late 20th Century, perhaps because the increased pace of technological change made it harder for reasonable people to agree about when asserted secrets differ from information widely known in an industry,[7] or perhaps because increased mobility and entrepreneurial activity by erstwhile employees have changed assumptions about employment relationships and the extent of one's duty to an employer. Whether these or other explanations are preferred, it is difficult to predict how courts will apply traditional trade secrets principles to situations in new high-tech industries.

Because not all the fine lines can be clearly drawn, prudent businesspersons are usually advised to err on the side of caution in designing programs to protect trade secrets and avoid inadvertent or apparent misappropriation of others' trade secrets.

[1]   State Law Versus Federal Law

Unlike patent, trademark and copyright laws, in which federal statutes played an early and increasingly dominant role, trade secrets remain a matter of state law. Each state is free to develop its own rules, as long as they do not conflict with federal intellectual property law policy. In practice, however, states' laws are substantially similar because modern trade secrets law has been dominated by two major sources, the 1939 Restatement of Torts and the 1979 Uniform Trade Secrets Act.

In 1996, Congress enacted the Economic Espionage Act as the first comprehensive statute to combat corporate espionage. It is also the first federal statute that protects trade secrets, historically the domain of state courts and legislatures. Unlike state statutes and common law rules that govern trade secrets, the Economic Espionage Act of 1996 is a criminal statute that does not recognize a private right of action.

[2]   Trade Secrets Law's Relationship to Patent Law

Accused trade secret misappropriators sometimes argue that trade secret protection under state law conflicts with, and should be preempted by, federal patent law because it diminishes the incentive for inventors to publicly disclose their inventions to obtain limited patent rights. In *Kewanee Oil Co. v. Bicron Corp.*, the Supreme Court rejected this argument, noting that, although Congress has the power to preempt state laws conflicting with federal patent and copyright laws, "Congress, by its silence over these many years, has seen the wisdom of allowing the States to enforce trade secret protection."[8] As a policy matter, federal patent law does not preempt state trade secret laws because the latter (1) do not protect any matter once it has been publicly disclosed, (2) are weaker than patent law because they do not bar reverse engineering or independent development, and (3) protect non-economic interests such as privacy.

---

[7] *See* § 3C[1][c][vi].

[8] 416 U.S. 470, 493 (1974).

In holding that patent law does not preempt trade secret law, the Supreme Court relied on both the ethical and economic bases of trade secret doctrine:

> Trade secret law and patent law have co-existed in this country for over one hundred years. Each has its particular role to play, and the operation of one does not take away from the need for the other. Trade secret law encourages the development and exploitation of those items of lesser or different invention than might be accorded protection under the patent laws, but which items still have an important part to play in the techno-logical and scientific advancement of the Nation. Trade secret law promotes the sharing of knowledge, and the efficient operation of industry; it permits the individual inventor to reap the rewards of his labor by contracting with a company large enough to develop and exploit it.[9]

The Court painted a bleak picture of life without trade secrets law:

> The holder of a trade secret would not likely share his secret with a manufacturer who cannot be placed under binding legal obligation to pay a license fee or to protect the secret. The result would be to hoard rather than disseminate knowledge. Instead . . . of licensing others to use his invention and making the most efficient use of existing manufacturing and marketing structures within the industry, the trade secret holder would tend either to limit his utilization of the invention, thereby depriving the public of the maximum benefit of its use, or engage in the time-consuming and economically wasteful enterprise of constructing duplicative manufac-turing and marketing mechanisms for the exploitation of the inven-tion. . . .
>
> In addition to the increased costs for protection from burglary, wire-tapping, bribery, and the other means used to misappropriate trade secrets, there is the inevitable cost to the basic decency of society when one firm steals from another. A most fundamental human right, that of privacy, is threatened when industrial espionage is condoned or is made profitable.[10]

In short, the coexistence of patent and trade secret law is well-established, and the two are in harmony because they serve different economic and ethical functions. Nonetheless, courts must sometimes police the boundary between the two. In *Brulotte v. Thys Co.*, the Supreme Court refused to enforce trade secret royalties after the expiration of licensed patents because the royalties for each were not clearly distinguished. The court inferred that the provision for post-expiration royalties had been subject to the "leverage" (bargaining power) of the patent monopoly and held that those provisions were an unenforceable attempt to "project the [patent] monopoly beyond the patent period."[11]

In contrast, in *Aronson v. Quick Point Pencil Co.*, the Supreme Court refused to invalidate a license for perpetual royalty payments for the disclosure of a trade secret, even though a patent application for the idea was later rejected, because the

---

[9] *Id.*

[10] *Id.* at 486–87. *See also* Painton & Co. v. Bourns, Inc., 442 F.2d 216, 223 (2d Cir. 1971).

[11] 379 U.S. 29, 32 (1964), discussed at § 1D[3][b][i].

pending patent application had "played no part in the contract to pay the . . . royalty indefinitely."[12] The key facts supporting this conclusion were that the parties knew the patent might be rejected and had negotiated for a lower royalty in the event of such rejection. Thus, the Court concluded that the licensee-manufacturer had clearly agreed to pay for "the opportunity to be the first in the market."[13]

§ 3B HISTORICAL DEVELOPMENT

Originating in early 19th-Century England, trade secret law was adopted and developed in the United States by common law court decisions, "restated" in 1939, and codified in many states beginning in 1979. Its basic principles have changed remarkably little.

[1]   Early English Cases

The first United States trade secret cases cited English equity court decisions. Equity was a body of legal principles administered without juries by the English Court of Chancery. Instead of monetary damage awards available from law courts, equity courts issued decrees enjoining or compelling specified conduct. Equity courts acted when monetary damages were an inadequate remedy for the plaintiff. Judicial reform measures have merged courts of equity and law, but equitable principles and remedies live on in United States jurisprudence.

As early as 1817, English courts acknowledged that an agreement to preserve a non-patented secret was binding. In *Newberry v. James*,[14] the court considered a request to order specific performance of a manufacturer-supplier's agreement to refrain from disclosing medicinal recipes and manufacturing techniques learned in confidence from an inventor-distributor. The court advised the plaintiff to seek damages in a law court, because it considered issuance and enforcement of a specific performance injunction to be impossible without destroying the secret by requiring its disclosure to the court. In *Williams v. Williams*,[15] the court upheld an injunction ordering a defendant-son-employee to return to the plaintiff-father-employer recipes and medicine that had been misused, together with profits from medicine that had been sold. Finding the alleged recipes' secrecy to be unproven (and difficult for a court to ascertain), the court declined to order non-disclosure, but it stated that if an agreement of confidentiality were proven, the plaintiff's entitlement to a court order of specific performance would be "a question which would require great consideration."

Within a few years, English equity courts overcame their ambivalence toward protecting trade secrets and abandoned their assumption that confidentiality could not be ordered and enforced without disclosing and destroying the secrets. In

---

[12] 440 U.S. 257, 265 (1979), discussed at § 1D[3][b][iii].

[13] *Id.* at 266.

[14] 2 Mer. 446, 35 Eng. Rep. 1011 (1817).

[15] 3 Mer. 157 (1817).

Yovatt v. Winyard,[16] a veterinary trainee surreptitiously copied medicine recipes and usage directions in violation of an understanding that his job training would be confined to more general knowledge. The court enjoined the trainee-defendant from using or disclosing the information, but, as was traditional in equity courts, accommodated non-parties' welfare by refusing to interrupt veterinary treatment already in progress.[17]

In *Bryson v. Whitehead*,[18] the first reported case concerning secrets other than medicinal recipes, the court ordered the seller of a dyeing business to perform his contractual obligations of non-disclosure, non-use, and non-competition. The court accommodated non-party interests and the public policy against excessively broad non-competitive agreements by interpreting the non-competition covenant to be limited in duration and territory. This case was a forerunner of the later tendency for trade secret claims to become entangled with questions of whether to enforce anti-competitive contractual provisions.[19]

[2] Early United States Cases

United States courts faced with confidential information misappropriation controversies looked to the early English cases for authority and sought to "do equity" in light of progressively more diverse factual situations and more complex industrial relationships, and to elaborate the principles that underlay their decisions. They developed a body of judicial precedent constituting each state's common (i.e., non-statutory) trade secrets law.[20]

Vickery v. Welch,[21] the first reported United States trade secrets case, involved a dispute about the sale of a chocolate-making business that included secret manufacturing methods. The seller had initially promised to convey exclusive title to his secrets, and the buyer had used the seller's written promises to secure investor participation. The seller then refused to do more than communicate the secrets to the buyers with an express reservation of the right to communicate the same secrets to others. Citing *Bryson*, the Massachusetts court rejected the seller's argument that the obligation of non-disclosure was void as a trade restraint:

The public are not prejudiced by the transfer of [the defendant's secret art] to the plaintiff . . . [because] it is of no consequence to the public whether the secret art be used by the plaintiff or by the defendant.[22]

---

[16] 1 Jac. & W. 394, 37 Eng. Rep. 425 (1820).

[17] 1 Jac. & W. at 395.

[18] 1 Sim. & St. 74, 57 Eng. Rep. 29 (1822).

[19] For a discussion of covenants not to compete, see § 3D[3][c].

[20] After 1979, many states codified their trade secrets law in statutes modeled after the Uniform Trade Secrets Act, which is discussed in § 3B[4], but the law's common-law flavor remains intact.

[21] 1837 Mass. LEXIS 124 (Oct. 1837).

[22] *Id.* at *9 (Oct. 1837).

In *Taylor v. Blanchard*,[23] the parties manufactured and sold shoe-cutting equipment and accessories as business partners. Defendant, who "was wholly ignorant of the business," promised plaintiff, who was experienced and established in the business, not to disclose any business secrets. The court acknowledged the principle that "the public has no right to" a businessman's trade secrets and that a contract for their exclusive use is not a restraint of trade, but it did not regard the information as a secret because "[a]lthough it was not generally known to the public, it was carried on in three different towns in the Commonwealth, by three different parties."[24]

In *Peabody v. Norfolk*,[25] the court enforced a defendant-employee's agreement not to disclose secret inventions and adaptations of gunny cloth manufacturing machinery, despite his argument that the information had lost its secrecy through disclosure to other workers. Emphasizing the time and money that the plaintiff-employer had expended to develop the information, and noting that the defendant had greater access to the information than had other employees, the court held that "A secret of trade or manufacture does not lose its character by being confidentially disclosed to agents or servants, without whose assistance it could not be made of any value."[26]

In *Salomon v. Hertz*,[27] the court granted a preliminary injunction restraining two former employees from using the employer's secret methods in violation of an alleged oral non-disclosure agreement, but it permitted the former employees to disclose prices and suppliers and customers because that information was of a character that, in the absence of a proven contractual restriction, employees should be free to use after an employment relationship.[28]

In *Tabor v. Hoffman*,[29] the court upheld an injunction restraining a trade secrets owner's competitor from using pump design drawings surreptitiously copied by a repairman. It implicitly held that a duty of confidentiality extends to parties who have no direct relationship with a trade secret owner, ignoring the dissent's observation that "[t]he cases cited to sustain the judgment arose out of the relation of master and servant, or between partners."[30] The misappropriation was not excused by the fact that defendants could have learned the secrets by combining study of plaintiff's product with additional experimentation. The information could "only be ascertained by a series of experiments, involving the expenditure of both time and money"; even though "discovery may be possible by fair means, it would not justify a discovery by unfair means."[31]

---

[23] 1866 Mass. LEXIS 257 (Nov. 1866).

[24] *Id.* at *8.

[25] 1868 Mass. LEXIS 319 (Jan. 1868).

[26] *Id.* at *16.

[27] A. 379 (Oct. 1885).

[28] 2 A. at 381.

[29] 23 N.E. 12 (N.Y. 1889).

[30] 23 N.E. at 13 (Follett, C.J., dissenting).

[31] 23 N.E. at 13.

Three other cases of historical significance warrant mention. In *O. & W. Thum Co. v. Tloczynski*,[32] a sticky fly-paper manufacturer persuaded the court to enjoin a former employee from disclosing manufacturing processes or machinery designs despite the absence of a written non-disclosure (or employment) agreement.

In *Stone v Goss*,[33] a chemical manufacturer's former employee disclosed to his new employer secret methods of mixing and treating non-secret hair-removing compound ingredients. The court enjoined the employee from making further disclosures and enjoined the new employer from using the disclosed methods, having found that the new employer had known of the employee's duty of confidentiality.

In *Pressed Steel Car Co. v. Standard Steel Car Co.*,[34] a railroad car manufacturer gave car-design blueprints to prospective and actual customers to enable them to (1) verify that the design met their requirements, (2) verify that cars did not vary from the required specifications, and (3) order spare parts and make repairs. The blueprints were not labeled confidential but were circulated only to customer-railroad companies, and receipts were required from every recipient. The court held that a competitor's acquisition of blueprint copies from customers violated an implied customer agreement that the blueprints and the design information in them would be used only for limited purposes. It enjoined the defendant-competitor from using the copies and ordered them returned to the plaintiff.

The decisions discussed above were widely cited by courts in later cases; they were the most significant contributors to the body of precedent that was the primary authority for United States trade secrets law until the late 1930s.

[3]   The Restatement

As part of the early 20th-Century United States movement to make state laws more uniform, prominent lawyers, judges and professors collected and synthesized opinions and underlying principles of particular areas of law into a series of "Restatements." The 1939 *Restatement of Torts* included two sections on trade secrets.[35]

The Restatement proved persuasive in the area of trade secret law because it adopted a core concept of "commercial morality" that was sufficiently elastic and circumstance-specific to permit the Restatement and the courts to rationalize doctrinally contradictory decisions. The Restatement's trade secret provisions used previous case law mainly as examples for broad generalizations. Most courts adopted the Restatement, but in the few areas where the Restatement sought to simplify trade secrets law's rationale, it was not widely followed. For example, the Restatement rejected the premise that trade secrets law encourages invention,

---

[32] 72 N.W. 140 (Mich. 1897).

[33] 55 A. 736 (N.J. 1903).

[34] 60 A. 4 (Pa. 1904).

[35] RESTATEMENT OF TORTS §§ 757, 758 (1939). A third section, 759, discussed protection for non-confidential information.

commenting that its protection "is not based on a policy of rewarding or otherwise encouraging the development of secret processes or devices. The protection is merely against breach of faith and reprehensible means of learning another's secret."[36] This comment failed to persuade the courts, which eventually came to consider commercial morality to be merely a means to the greater end of encouraging inventions and their most efficient exploitation.[37]

The Restatement's authors also sought to purge the property principle from trade secrets law, stating:

> The suggestion that one has a right to exclude others from the use of his trade secret because he has a right of property in the idea has been frequently advanced and rejected . . . . The theory that has prevailed is that the protection is afforded only by a general duty of good faith.[38]

To the contrary, the theory that has prevailed in the post-Restatement era is that a property right in a trade secret, although terminable by public disclosure, will be upheld against misappropriators and protected in a variety of contexts.[39]

On the whole, the Restatement led to a greater consistency of authority, language and, to a lesser extent, substantive doctrine among different states' trade secrets decisions. Substantial inconsistencies remained, however, in part because the Restatement emphasized general and subjective concepts such as "relative" secrecy[40] and "generally accepted standards of commercial morality and reasonable conduct,"[41] giving courts substantial room to differ on the application of its principles to various factual situations. The Restatement also suggested avenues outside trade secrets law for protecting non-secret information.

The *Restatement (Second) of Torts*, published in 1978, omitted trade secrets because trade secrets law had become "no more dependent on Tort law than it is on many other general fields of the law and upon broad statutory developments."[42] Trade secrets are now included in the *Restatement (Third) of Unfair Competition*,[43] reflecting the view that trade secret law is best understood as preventing unfair means of competition.

[4]   The Uniform Trade Secrets Act

Further standardization of trade secret law was taken up by another legal reform movement, which sought to codify various areas of law by means of uniform acts designed to be adopted by individual states. The National Conference of Commissioners on Uniform State Laws published the Uniform Trade Secrets Act

---

[36] RESTATEMENT OF TORTS § 757 cmt. b.

[37] *See, e.g.*, Kewanee Oil Co. v. Bicron Corp., 416 U.S. 470 (1974).

[38] RESTATEMENT OF TORTS § 757 cmt. a.

[39] For a discussion of the property principle, see § 3A.

[40] For a discussion of relative secrecy, see § 3C[1][c].

[41] For a discussion of improper means, see § 3D[4][b].

[42] Introductory Note to Division 9, in 4 RESTATEMENT (SECOND) OF TORTS 1 (1979) 1.

[43] RESTATEMENT (SECOND) OF TORTS §§ 39–44 (1995).

("UTSA") in 1979, with the stated goals of unifying definitions of trade secrets and misappropriation and standardizing statutes of limitations.[44] By the end of 2009, the UTSA, with state-to-state modifications, had been adopted in 45 states and two territories.[45]

Generally, the UTSA codified state-court common-law decisions, many of which followed the 1939 Restatement, but it also used post-Restatement experience to develop clearer guidelines on remedies.[46] By stating a goal of increased uniformity, it caused UTSA state courts to give greater attention to decisions of courts in other UTSA jurisdictions.

The UTSA and the Restatement are largely consistent, but the Act differs on a few points where the Restatement was not widely followed. The Act dropped the Restatement requirement that a trade secret be "continuously used in one's business,"[47] and rejected the Restatement's conferral of absolute immunity on innocent purchasers for value.[48] The Act also defined misappropriation to include mere acquisition by improper means, dropping the traditional requirement of actual or threatened use or disclosure.[49] Four UTSA amendments published in 1985 clarified (1) injunctive relief requirements, (2) alternative measures of damages,[50] (3) the Act's lack of preemptive effect on contract-law remedies, and (4) the Act's inapplicability to misappropriation that began before its effective date.

Consistent with the goal of uniformity, a number of jurisdictions have held that the UTSA preempts common-law tort claims, such as misappropriation and conversion.[51] However, individual state statutes may differ from the UTSA definitions and comments quoted below, where state legislatures adopted modified

---

[44] Uniform Trade Secrets Act ("UTSA"), prefatory note.

[45] In alphabetical order: Alabama, Alaska, Arizona, Arkansas, California, Colorado, Connecticut, Delaware, District of Columbia, Florida, Georgia, Hawaii, Idaho, Illinois, Indiana, Iowa, Kansas, Kentucky, Louisiana, Maine, Maryland, Michigan, Minnesota, Mississippi, Missouri, Montana, Nebraska, Nevada, New Hampshire, New Jersey, New Mexico, North Dakota, Ohio, Oklahoma, Oregon, Pennsylvania, Rhode Island, South Carolina, South Dakota, Tennessee, Texas, Utah, Vermont, Virgin Islands, Virginia, Washington, West Virginia, Wisconsin, and Wyoming.

As of this writing, three states have not adopted the UTSA: Massachusetts, New York, and North Carolina.

[46] *See* § 3F.

[47] For a discussion of continuous use, see § 3C[1][b][v].

[48] For a discussion of innocent receipt, see § 3D[4][c].

[49] For a discussion of use or disclosure as an element of misappropriation, see § 3D[5].

[50] For a discussion of the amended provision, see § 3F[2][a][i].

[51] *See* Spectrum Scan, LLC v. AGM California, 519 F. Supp. 2d 655, 656–657 (W.D. Ky. 2007) (finding conversion claim preempted); Patriot Homes, Inc. v. Forest River Housing, Inc., 489 F. Supp. 2d 865, 871–873 (N.D. Ind. 2007) (no preemption of unfair competition and taking of tangible property, but partially preempting claims for tortious interference); DSMC, Inc. v. Convera Corp., 479 F. Supp. 2d 68, 83–84 (D.D.C. 2007) (common law and statutory conspiracy claims preempted); RK Enterprise, LLC v. Pro-Comp Management, Inc., 158 S.W.3d 685, 689–90 (Ark. 2004) (finding broad preemption of alternative tort claim); Savor, Inc. v. FMR Corp., 812 A.2d 894, 898 (Del. 2002) (affirming UTSA preemption at the pleading stage); Frantz v. Johnson, 999 P.2d 351, 357–58 (Nev. 2000) (finding broad preemption of various tort claims); Mortgage Specialists, Inc. v. Davey, 904 A.2d 652, 665 (N.H. 2006) (affirming broad preemption of alternative claims); Weins v. Sporleder, 605 N.W.2d 488, 492 (S.D. 2000) (finding broad preemption). *But see* Burbank Grease Services, LLC v. Sokolowski, 717 N.W.2d 781, 793–

versions or adopted and retained pre-1985 language of the Act that has been subsequently amended by the Uniform Laws.[52]

§ 3C NATURE OF PROTECTION — RIGHTS

[1]   Information That Qualifies as a Trade Secret

To qualify as a trade secret, information must be eligible for protection, be secret, and have commercial value.

[a]   Definitions

Trade secret law traditionally emphasized application of equitable principles to specific facts rather than providing precise definitions. The Restatement stated that "[a]n exact definition of a trade secret is not possible,"[53] and contented itself with non-exclusive description and a list of factors to be considered. UTSA-based statutes created statutory definitions, but the definitions contain only "general concepts."[54] As one court stated, "[i]n the law of trade secrets, . . . examples may be more helpful than definition or attempted redefinition."[55]

The Restatement defined a trade secret as:

> [A]ny formula, pattern, device or compilation of information which is used in one's business, and gives him an opportunity to obtain an advantage over competitors who do not know or use it . . . [if] it is not simply information as to a single or ephemeral events . . . [but rather] is a process or device for continuous use in the operation of the business. . . .
>
> . . . Matters of public knowledge or of general knowledge in an industry cannot be appropriated by one as his secret. . . . [A] substantial element of secrecy must exist, so that, except by the use of improper means, there would be difficulty in acquiring the information.[56]

The Restatement listed the following six factors to "be considered in determining whether given information is one's trade secret."

(1) the extent to which the information is known outside of his business;

(2) the extent to which it is known by employees and others involved in his business;

---

94 (Wis. 2006) (ruling against preemption of alternative claims and narrowly construing Wisconsin UTSA).

[52] All quotes are from the amended 1985 version. The few pre-amendment differences are described in the accompanying footnotes. For an annotated version of the UTSA, with listings of state variations and clear indications of the pre- and post-amendment text, see 14 UNIFORM LAWS ANNOTATED (West 1990).

[53] RESTATEMENT OF TORTS § 757, cmt. b.

[54] UTSA, prefatory note.

[55] K & G Oil Tool & Serv. Co., Inc. v. G & G Fishing Tool Serv., 314 S.W.2d 782, 790 (Tex. 1958).

[56] RESTATEMENT OF TORTS § 757, cmt. b.

(3) the extent of measures taken by him to guard the secrecy of the information;

(4) the value of the information to him and to his competitors;

(5) the amount of effort or money expended by him in developing the information;

(6) the ease or difficulty with which the information could be properly acquired or duplicated by others."[57]

The UTSA defines a trade secret as:

information, including a formula, pattern, compilation, program, device, method, technique, or process, that:

(i) derives independent economic value, actual or potential, from not being generally known to, and not being readily ascertainable by proper means by, other persons who can obtain economic value from its disclosure or use, and

(ii) is the subject of efforts that are reasonable under the circumstances to maintain secrecy.[58]

The Third Restatement defines a trade secret simply as "any information that can be used in the operation of a business or other enterprise and that it is sufficiently valuable and secret to afford an actual or potential economic advantage over others."[59] The comments confirm that "[i]nformation that is generally known or readily ascertainable through proper means . . . is not protectable as a trade secret,"[60] and that "[p]recautions taken to maintain the secrecy of information are relevant in determining whether the information qualifies for protection as a trade secret."[61]

[b] Eligible Subject Matter

Virtually any "concrete" information can be a trade secret. Non-technical information has long been eligible, as have combinations of otherwise unprotectable information. A few jurisdictions, however, condition protection of customer lists on express contractual covenants. The Restatement "continuous use" requirement was never widely accepted and has been largely abandoned. The UTSA endorses the majority position protecting "negative information" as a trade secret.

One instance of dismissal due to ineligible subject matter occurred in *Lehman v. Dow Jones & Co.*, in which a trade secret claim was made for alleged misappropriation of information on a company's availability and attractiveness as a "takeover candidate." The court held that "the availability information could never

---

[57] *Id.*

[58] UTSA § 1(4).

[59] RESTATEMENT (THIRD) OF UNFAIR COMPETITION § 39.

[60] *Id.* § 39 cmt. f.

[61] *Id.* § 39 cmt. g.

have been a trade secret [because the plaintiff] had no control over its disclosure," and that the plaintiff's opinion about a takeover candidate's attractiveness to a defendant "is simply not the kind of information that qualifies as a trade secret."[62]

[i]   Concreteness

The Restatement phrase "a process or device"[63] reflects a traditional requirement that a trade secret be more concrete than an idea, theory, possibility or emotion, and relatively specific in its intended implementation. The UTSA does not mention concreteness, thereby leaving courts free to apply or reject this traditional requirement as they see fit.

In *Jones v. Ulrich*,[64] the inventor of a fertilizer spreader orally disclosed his idea to a manufacturer who later disputed whether the information was concrete enough to be protectable. The court noted that trade secret law does not require information to be in tangible or material form, found that the idea was for a specific device, as shown by the manufacturer's ability to construct the device within 24 hours of learning the details, and held that it was not a mere theory and was concrete enough for protection.[65]

In *Epstein v. Dennison Manufacturing Co.*,[66] the court denied a claim based on confidential oral disclosure of an idea for a clothes-tag design, because the idea, which the plaintiff acknowledged was just a "possibility," did not meet the requirement that "[t]he disclosure must be in sufficient detail and have such definiteness that there is no doubt as to what is disclosed."[67]

In *Vekamaf Holland B.V. v. Pipe Benders, Inc.*,[68] a group of companies engaged in designing, manufacturing and marketing industrial equipment alleged misappropriation of eleven distinct trade secrets by a prospective customer to whom disclosures had been made in confidence. One asserted trade secret was an assurance, based on experience and experimentation, of the quality of the plaintiff's techniques for bending pipes. Finding no authority for protecting "an emotion" as a trade secret, the court stated that a trade secret must be something "of form and substance":[69]

> It is difficult to see how an expression of confidence can in any way constitute a trade secret. It is nothing more than a representation of the superiority of a product comparable to those expounded by every manu-

---

[62] 783 F.2d 285, 299 (2d Cir. 1986). The court also rejected a common-law "idea submission" claim on the same grounds. *See generally* § 6H.

[63] RESTATEMENT OF TORTS § 757, cmt. b.

[64] 95 N.E.2d 113 (Ill. App. Ct. 1950).

[65] 95 N.E.2d at 120.

[66] 314 F. Supp. 116 (S.D.N.Y. 1969).

[67] *Id.* at 126.

[68] 211 U.S.P.Q. 955 (D. Minn. 1981), *aff'd*, 696 F.2d 608 (8th Cir. 1982).

[69] 211 U.S.P.Q. at 978.

facturer of a product offered for public sale. Certainly, plaintiffs did not intend to keep this confidence secret.[70]

In *Sun Media Systems, Inc. v. KDSM, LLC*, the plaintiff claimed trade secret protection for its methods of conducting a successful direct-mail advertising campaign.[71] The court suggested that this was "not the sort of definite information to which we have previously afforded trade-secret protection, such as for chemical formulae, price lists, and customer lists,"[72] and held that "such concepts are simply too ephemeral to qualify as trade secrets."[73]

[ii]   Nontechnical Information

Trade secrets can protect nontechnical information including sales data,[74] market research and marketing plans,[75] and bid price information,[76] as well as pricing and cost information[77] and financial statements.[78]

[iii]   Combinations

Although not explicitly stated in the First Restatement or the UTSA, case law holds that trade secrets may include a combination of characteristics or components, each individually in the public domain, where the unified combination affords a competitive advantage and is not publicly known.[79] For example, in the computer software industry, the "manner in which . . . generic utility programs interact" may be protectable even if the component utility programs are not.[80]

[iv]   Customer Lists

Customer lists are the subject of much litigation, yielding differing results. Courts often focus on the ease with which a particular list could be duplicated. Facts relevant to this determination include the nature of the industry, the effort invested in compiling the list, the inclusion of information in addition to names and

---

[70] *Id.* at 980.

[71] 564 F. Supp. 2d 946, 973 (S.D. Iowa 2008) ("Sun Media asserts that its trade secrets . . . are the methods, *i.e.*, the 'how' and the 'why' used to determine those prices, markets, layouts, and language to create an effective campaign.").

[72] *Id.* at 972 (citation and internal quotes omitted).

[73] *Id.* at 973.

[74] *See, e.g.*, American Standard Inc. v. Pfizer Inc., 828 F.2d 734 (Fed. Cir. 1987).

[75] *See, e.g.*, Whyte v. Schlage Lock Co., 101 Cal. App. 4th 1443, 1456 (2002); Clark v. Bunker, 453 F.2d 1006 (9th Cir. 1972).

[76] *See, e.g.*, Ovation Plumbing, Inc. v. Furton, 33 P.3d 1221, 1223–25 (Colo. Ct. App. 2001). *But cf.* Area Landscaping, LLC v. Glaxo-Wellcome, Inc., 586 S.E.2d 507, 512 (N.C. Ct. App. 2003) (bid information was not a trade secret where plaintiff did not take reasonable measures to protect its secrecy).

[77] *Whyte*, 101 Cal. App. 4th at 1455–56 (distinguishing specific cost and pricing data from "commonly used industry formulas for setting prices").

[78] *See, e.g.*, Alpha School Bus Co. v. Wagner, 910 N.E.2d 1134, 1154 (Ill. App. Ct. 2009).

[79] *See, e.g.*, Imperial Chem. Indus. Ltd. v. National Distillers and Chem. Corp., 342 F.2d 737 (2d Cir. 1965). *See also* RESTATEMENT (THIRD) OF UNFAIR COMPETITION § 39 cmt f ("The fact that some or all of the components of the trade secret are well-known does not preclude protection for a secret combination, compilation, or integration of the individual elements.").

[80] *See* Integrated Cash Mgmt. Services, Inc. v. Digital Transactions, Inc., 920 F.2d 171 (2d Cir. 1990).

addresses, and the extent to which listed customers seek to make themselves known to plaintiff's competitors.

In *American Paper & Packaging Prods., Inc. v. Kirgan*, the court noted:

> [L]ists of customers who operate manufacturing concerns and who need shipping supplies to ship their products . . . may not be generally known to the public [but] they certainly would be known or readily ascertainable to other persons in the shipping business. The compilation process in this case is neither sophisticated nor difficult nor particularly time consuming.[81]

In *Morlife, Inc. v. Perry*, however, the court distinguished *American Paper's* facts because of the work effort that went into a list:

> [W]here the employer has expended time and effort identifying customers with particular needs or characteristics, courts will prohibit former employees from using this information to capture a share of the market. . . . As a general principle, the more difficult information is to obtain, and the more time and resources expended by an employer in gathering it, the more likely a court will find such information constitutes a trade secret.[82]

In *SI Handling Systems, Inc. v. Heisley*, the identity of key decisionmakers within General Motors was held not to be a trade secret. The court distinguished such information from a typical customer list because it "involves only one customer that is well-known in the industry and that . . . actively seeks to disseminate the information."[83]

A customer list is particularly likely to be protected if it contains not only names and addresses but also the "identity of the person to be contacted at each customer location, a detailed sales history revealing products purchased, quantities purchased, container sizes, prices paid, and frequency of purchases."[84]

Before Wisconsin adopted the UTSA, its courts were notable for refusing trade secret protection to customer lists on public policy grounds.[85] After the UTSA was adopted, however, the state Supreme Court acknowledged that "[s]ome customer lists are afforded protection under the UTSA."[86] Moreover, Wisconsin courts will enforce contractual covenants against customer list use.[87]

---

[81] American Paper & Packaging Products, Inc. v. Kirgan, 183 Cal. App. 3d 1318, 1325–26 (1986).

[82] 56 Cal. App. 4th 1514, 1521–22 (1997). *See also* Courtesy Temporary Serv., Inc. v. Camacho, 222 Cal. App. 3d 1278, 1287–88 (1990).

[83] 753 F.2d 1244, 1258 (3d Cir. 1985). This distinction, and the true degree of G.M.'s active dissemination, is questionable in light of the lower court's finding that "[i]t was only after peeling through layer and layer of personnel and following many false leads that SI was finally able to reach the real decisionmakers as to its product." *Id.*

[84] NCH Corp. v. Broyles, 749 F.2d 247, 252 (5th Cir. 1985).

[85] *See, e.g.*, Corroon & Black-Rutters & Roberts, Inc. v. Hosch, 325 N.W.2d 883, 887–88 (Wis. 1982), superseded by Wisc. Stat. § 134.90 (UTSA).

[86] *See* Minuteman, Inc. v. Alexander, 434 N.W.2d 773, 779 (Wis. 1989).

[87] *See, e.g.*, Star Direct, Inc. v. Dal Pra, 767 N.W. 2d 898 (Wis. 2009) (upholding contract prohibiting employee from contacting customers for 24 months after employment).

[v] Continuous Use

The Restatement required that information be put to "continuous use" in business operations.[88] For example, in *Lehman v. Dow Jones & Co.*, the court refused to characterize information on the availability and attractiveness of a company as a takeover candidate as a trade secret, citing the Restatement continuous use requirement, and distinguishing such information from information "used in running [a] business."[89]

Many courts ignored or rejected the Restatement's "continuous use" requirement when faced with information that had demonstrable business value, even if plaintiff was not using it when the alleged breach occurred.[90] Both the Third Restatement and the UTSA endorse the business value view with a definition of trade secret that does not require continuous use.[91]

[vi] Negative Information

Under the Restatement, the issue of whether "negative information" was protected was a matter of some debate. Most decisions, recognizing the "competitive edge the competitor gains by avoiding the developer's blind alleys"[92] and the helpfulness of information demonstrating "what pitfall to avoid,"[93] upheld the protectability of information, gained by experience, showing which research avenues are not worth pursuing.[94] Some decisions, however, distinguished negative know-how from affirmative manufacturing know-how,[95] questioned the protectability of negative know-how,[96] and excluded it from trade secret protection.[97] This position was based on the Restatement's requirement that the information be "used in one's business."[98]

---

[88] Restatement of Torts § 757, cmt. b: "It is not simply information as a single or ephemeral events in the conduct of the business, as, for example, the amount or other terms of a secret bid for a contract or the salary of certain employees, or the security investments made or contemplated, or the date fixed for the announcement of a new policy or for bringing out a new model or the like. A trade secret is a process or device for continuous use in the operation of the business."

[89] 783 F.2d 285, 298 (2d Cir. 1986).

[90] *See, e.g.*, Ferroline Corp. v. General Aniline & Film Corp., 207 F.2d 912 (7th Cir. 1953); Sikes v. McGraw-Edison Co., 665 F.2d 731 (5th Cir. 1982); and Sinclair v. Aquarius Electronics, Inc., 42 Cal. App. 3d 216 (1974).

[91] Restatement (Third) of Unfair Competition § 39 cmt. d; UTSA Comment to § 1.

[92] Johns-Manville Corp. v. Guardian Indus. Corp., 586 F. Supp. 1034, 1073 (E.D. Mich. 1983), *modified*, 223 U.S.P.Q. 974 (E.D. Mich. 1984), *citing* Allis-Chalmers Mfg. Co. v. Continental Aviation & Eng. Corp., 255 F. Supp. 645 (E.D. Mich. 1966).

[93] Syntex Opthalmics, Inc. v. Novicky, 214 U.S.P.Q. 272, 278 (N.D. Ill. 1982), *aff'd*, 701 F.2d 677 (7th Cir. 1983).

[94] Gillette Company v. Williams, 360 F. Supp. 1171, 1173 (D. Conn. 1973).

[95] Megapulse, Inc. v. Lewis, 672 F.2d 959, 970 (D.C. Cir. 1982).

[96] Hurst v. Hughes Tool Co., 634 F.2d 895, 899 (5th Cir. 1981). *See also* Detachable Bit v. Timkin Roller Bearing Co., 133 F.2d 632, 635 (6th Cir. 1943).

[97] *See, e.g.*, Materials Development Corp. v. Atlantic Advanced Metals, Inc., 172 U.S.P.Q. 595, 606 (Mass. Super. Ct. 1971).

[98] Restatement of Torts § 757, cmt. b.

The distinction between positive and negative information is often "unintelligible."[99] As one court said, "every human process" results "from realizations of what not to do":

> [T]he selection of one action at a given moment involves the rejection of every other conceivable one that might have been chosen. . . . Knowing what not to do often leads automatically to knowing what to do.[100]

The UTSA resolves the debate in favor of protection. The UTSA definition of trade secret includes:

> information that has commercial value from a negative viewpoint, for example, the results of lengthy and expensive research which proves that a certain process will not work could be of great value to a competitor."[101]

This principle has been applied to customer lists. For example, in *Courtesy Temporary Service, Inc. v. Camacho*, the court stated that "[i]f a customer list is acquired by lengthy and expensive efforts which, from a negative viewpoint, indicate those entities that have not subscribed to plaintiff's services, it deserves protection as a 'trade secret'."[102]

[c]   Secrecy

Under trade secrets law's property principle, secrecy is "the threshold issue in every case,"[103] but the secrecy's sufficiency is judged in light of the circumstances, including the industry's level of general knowledge, the information's ascertainability, the offensiveness of a misappropriator's conduct, and anything else that affects a court's perception of a situation's equities. As discussed in the following sections, secrecy can be destroyed by insufficient precautions, by the marketing of a product that discloses the secret, by compliance with patent laws, or by disclosure in judicial proceedings or to government agencies. Any substantial efforts will usually be enough to avoid dismissal based solely on insufficient precautions, but lackadaisical efforts may affect a court's overall balancing of equities both in the initial liability determination and in any subsequent remedies determination.

In general, relative secrecy survives confidential disclosure on a "need to know" basis to employees, joint venturers, customers and suppliers.[104]

Secrecy questions involve three related issues: (1) the owner's precautions, (2) the level of general knowledge in an industry, and (3) the ascertainability of

---

[99] Metallurgical Industries Inc. v. Fourtek, Inc., 790 F.2d 1195, 1203 (5th Cir. 1986).

[100] *Id.* at 1203.

[101] UTSA Comment to § 1.

[102] 222 Cal. App. 3d 1278, 1287–88 (1990), *citing* Hollingsworth Solderless Terminal Co. v. Turley, 622 F.2d 1324 (9th Cir. 1980).

[103] Microbiological Research Corp. v. Muna, 625 P.2d 690, 698 (Utah 1981); *see also* Selection Research Inc. v. Murman, 433 N.W.2d 526 (Neb. 1989).

[104] RESTATEMENT OF TORTS § 757, cmt. b ("It is not requisite that only the proprietor of the business know [the secret]. He may, without losing his protection, communicate it to employees involved in its use. He may likewise communicate it to others pledged to secrecy.").

information by proper means. These often intermingle, because ineffective precautions may permit information to become generally known in an industry, and the level of general knowledge is a crucial determinant of whether otherwise secret information is readily ascertainable.

[i]　　　Definitions

The Restatement states that:

> Matters of public knowledge or of general knowledge in an industry cannot be appropriated by one as his secret. . . . It is not requisite that only the proprietor of the business know it. . . . Nevertheless, a substantial element of secrecy must exist, so that, except by the use of improper means, there would be difficulty in acquiring the information.[105]

The UTSA "does not require that information be generally known to the public for trade secret rights to be lost. If the principal persons who can obtain economic benefit from information are aware of it, there is no trade secret."[106]

Drawing upon the Restatement-influenced common law, the UTSA requires that efforts to maintain secrecy be "reasonable under the circumstances." A UTSA comment approvingly summarizes the common law requirements as follows:

> [R]easonable efforts to maintain secrecy have been held to include advising employees of the existence of a trade secret, limiting access to a trade secret on "need to know basis," and controlling plant access. On the other hand, public disclosure of information through display, trade journal publications, advertising, or other carelessness can preclude protection.[107]

Courts do not require that extreme and unduly expensive procedures be taken to protect trade secrets against flagrant industrial espionage.[108]

A 1948 case illustrates the secrecy requirement by stating that trade secrets law is concerned with secrecy "in the legal and equitable sense. Was it secret in the sense that a disclosure by an employee would lessen its value? Was it a secret in the sense that third parties would be willing to pay for a breach of trust in order to ascertain its nature?"[109]

[ii]　　　Application of Secrecy Requirement

Precautions to preserve secrecy can be categorized as procedures for (1) *security*, to prevent intrusion by outsiders, and (2) *confidentiality*, to identify secret information to, and secure obligations of confidentiality from, insiders and business contacts.

Electro-Craft Corp. v. Controlled Motion, Inc.,[110] a UTSA case, illustrates the

---

[105] RESTATEMENT OF TORTS § 757, cmt. b.

[106] UTSA Comment to § 1.

[107] UTSA Comment to § 1.

[108] UTSA Comment to § 1.

[109] L.M. Rabinowitz & Co. v. Dasher, 1948 N.Y. Misc. LEXIS 3129, at *7–*8.

[110] 332 N.W.2d 890 (Minn. 1983).

importance of circumstances in evaluating both procedures. The court forgave lax *security* where most plant entrances were unguarded and had no signs warning of limited access, a badge system was abandoned, documents were not in locked storage, and discarded drawings and plans were not destroyed, because there was little industrial espionage in the industry; but it declined to forgive plaintiff's lax *confidentiality* procedures where plaintiff "treated its information as if it were not secret."

> None of its technical documents were marked "Confidential," and drawings, dimensions and parts were sent to customers and vendors without special marking. Employee access to documents was not restricted. [The plaintiff] never issued a policy statement outlining what it considered to be secret. Many informal tours were given to vendors and customers without warnings as to confidential information. Further, two plants each had an "open house" at which the public was invited to observe manufacturing processes.[111]

The court stated that the plaintiff's "efforts were especially inadequate because of the nonintuitive nature of [plaintiff's] claimed secrets here. The dimensions, etc., of [plaintiff's] motors are not trade secrets in as obvious a way as a 'secret formula' might be."[112]

In *Dickerman Associates, Inc. v. Tiverton Bottled Gas Co.*,[113] the court reached a contrary result with respect to the sufficiency of confidentiality measures, holding that preliminary demonstrations of accounting and management software to potential customers who were not asked to sign confidentiality agreements did not destroy secrecy. The demonstrations did not reveal the program's entire menu, all its submenus or any user's guide or manual, and therefore did not permit the customers to understand the program's design and architecture.

Syntex-Opthalmics, Inc. v. Novicky[114] illustrates the link between circumstances and courts' holdings on secrecy sufficiency, stating "where the security lapses were not the cause of the misappropriation, those lapses should not be the basis for denying protection."[115] In *Defiance Button Machine Co. v. C&C Metal Products. Corp.*,[116] however, the court reached a contrary result, strictly applying the property principle to information inadvertently made accessible to a competitor. The plaintiff sold the defendant a computer without erasing secret information from the computer's memory. The filename or password needed to access the information was contained in a book that was not subject to secrecy precautions. The defendant obtained the password from the plaintiff's former employee rather than from the unprotected book. The plaintiff was held to have forfeited protection of the information by failing to erase it.

---

[111] *Id.* at 903.

[112] *Id.* at 902.

[113] 594 F. Supp. 30, 33–34 (D. Mass. 1984).

[114] 214 U.S.P.Q. 272 (N.D. Ill. 1982), *aff'd sub nom.* Syntex Ophthalmics, Inc. v. Tsuetaki, 701 F.2d 677 (7th Cir. 1983).

[115] 214 U.S.P.Q. at 277.

[116] Defiance Button Mach. Co. v. C & C Metal Products, 759 F.2d 1053, 1063–64 (2d Cir. 1985).

Because of the fact-specific nature of the inquiry, courts sometimes reach inconsistent results. In *In re Innovative Construction Systems, Inc.*,[117] the court found a manufacturer's relatively loose secrecy procedures to be sufficient. The fact that suppliers, job applicants and employees' friends had free access to the manufacturing area was not relevant to the secrecy of a formula, which was kept out of view in a notebook in the plant manager's office. Plaintiff's reliance on oral non-disclosure agreements from prospective buyers of the plaintiff's company was reasonable because this was standard industry practice. In *Wheelabrator Corp. v. Fogle*,[118] however, the court found insufficient secrecy. Plaintiff's fence and guard-posts protected the entire plant, including non-secret facilities, but provided no special security for facilities where allegedly secret processes were used. Plaintiff routinely admitted technically sophisticated customers and contractors to the plant without any express confidentiality notice or agreement and published a photo-graph of allegedly secret equipment.

One case found sufficient secrecy even though (1) a cut-away model of a ski disclosed its interior construction at a public conference (because the alleged misappropriator did not attend the conference), and (2) plaintiff gave tours of its factory (because no competitors were permitted to see the manufacturing proce-dure during the tours).[119] Another case found sufficient secrecy even though a computer manufacturer distributed thousands of circuitry drawings to customers, third party users, vendors and trainees. The drawings bore a restricted use legend prohibiting unauthorized reproduction and use.[120]

Three other cases that found insufficient secrecy emphasized specific facts: (1) drawings were distributed without restrictive use legends,[121] (2) employees were not instructed as to the secrecy of technical information,[122] and (3) an allegedly secret design was embodied in a sample displayed for two months in one relatively small store.[123]

[iii]   Ascertainability from Products and Public Sources

An alleged trade secret is readily ascertainable if, in light of the general knowledge in an industry, information available through proper means (e.g., examination of publicly available products, publicly circulated materials and public records) effectively reveals the purported trade secrets to any interested competitor without substantial research time or expense.[124]

The First Restatement required that "except by the use of improper means, there would be difficulty in acquiring the information," and specified that

---

[117] 793 F.2d 875 (7th Cir. 1986).

[118] 317 F. Supp. 633 (W.D. La. 1970), *aff'd*, 438 F.2d 1226 (5th Cir. 1971).

[119] K-2 Ski Co. v. Head Ski Co., Inc., 506 F.2d 471 (9th Cir. 1974).

[120] Data General Corp. v. Digital Computer Controls, Inc., 357 A.2d 105 (Del. Cir. Ch. 1975).

[121] Midland-Ross Corp. v. Yokana, 293 F.2d 411, 413 (3d Cir. 1961).

[122] National Rejectors, Inc. v. Trieman, 152 U.S.P.Q. 120, 135 (Mo. 1966).

[123] Skoog v. McCray Refrigerator Co., 211 F.2d 254 (7th Cir. 1954).

[124] *See* RESTATEMENT (THIRD) OF UNFAIR COMPETITION § 39 cmt. f.

"[m]atters which are completely disclosed by the goods which one markets cannot be his secret."[125]

The UTSA comment states that "Information is readily ascertainable if it is available in trade journals, reference books, or published materials. Often, the nature of a product lends itself to being readily copied as soon as it is available on the market."[126]

The product disclosure paradigm is a "simple device, widely circulated, the construction of which [is] ascertainable at a glance."[127]

There is no clear test for distinguishing readily ascertainable information from information ascertainable only with difficulty. One court stated that the time needed for reverse engineering is a factor in determining whether information is readily ascertainable;[128] another disagreed, citing the UTSA for the proposition that "the possibility of reverse engineering a trade secret . . . is not a factor in determining whether an item is a trade secret, but rather is a factor in deciding how long the injunctive relief should last."[129]

One court held:

> [A plaintiff] cannot recover for appropriation of information which had been so completely disclosed to the public as to dispel the existence of a trade secret and thus to negate the confidential relationship which had been established . . . . [However] where the extent of disclosure is arguable, and where the information had not been clearly placed in the public domain . . . [the defendant should not be allowed] to avoid the consequences of the breach of confidence by piecing together in retrospect bits of information which had been disclosed in a variety of places and which as a combination were not clearly a matter of public knowledge.[130]

Information is often ascertainable from a product only if substantial time is invested examining the product. If many competitors ascertain the information in this way, courts reach a variety of holdings; but if a particular defendant obtained the information by improper means, courts tend to focus on the value gained by the misappropriator's "head start" and may extend protection for the period of time needed to obtain the information by proper means.[131] If competitors have not ascertained the information, however, "[a]ny finding of discoverability must be reconciled with the fact of non-discovery."[132]

---

[125] RESTATEMENT OF TORTS § 757, cmt. b.

[126] UTSA Comment to § 1.

[127] Smith v. Dravo Corp., 203 F.2d 369, 375 (7th Cir. 1953). *See also* Carver v. Harr, 132 N.J. Eq. 207, 27 A.2d 895 (1942).

[128] Electro-Craft Corp. v. Controlled Motion, 332 N.W.2d 890, 899 (Minn. 1983).

[129] Minuteman, Inc. v. Alexander, 434 N.W.2d 773, 778–79 (Wis. 1989).

[130] Servo Corp. of America v. General Elec. Co., 393 F.2d 551, 555 (4th Cir. 1968).

[131] *See* §§ 3F[1][c] and 3F[2][a][ii].

[132] Zotos Intern., Inc. v. Young, 830 F.2d 350, 353 (D.C. Cir. 1987).

[iv]   Copyrighted Material

Public distribution of copyrighted materials[133] causes any trade secrets disclosed therein to enter the public domain. One decision holds that a "limited publication" for copyright purposes,[134] if subject also to appropriate trade secret restrictions, is not inconsistent with retaining a work's secret character.[135]

[v]   Patented Material

Issuance of a United States patent causes all information (whether claimed or merely disclosed) in the patent application to become a public record and enter the public domain even if the patent is subsequently declared invalid by a court. A technology rights owner can be left with neither patent nor trade secret protection if a patent is declared invalid.[136] In the United States, patent applications are published eighteen months after filing unless the application is not filed in another country that requires publication.[137] The Patent Act allows the patent owner to sue for misappropriation of the information in the published application if the patent is granted.[138]

Patent law requires that a patent specification claiming an invention disclose not only sufficient information to enable persons skilled in the art to make and use that invention but also the "best mode" the inventor contemplates, as of the patent application filing date, for carrying out the invention.[139] The "best mode" requirement restricts an owner's ability to seek a patent on some facets of an invention while retaining trade secrets rights over preferred embodiments or techniques.[140]

[vi]   Novelty Versus General Knowledge

Courts sometimes characterize the distinction between a trade secret and information generally known within an industry as a "novelty" requirement.[141] Protectable information must differ from widely known information, and the difference must have commercial value: "Mere variations in general processes known in the field which embody no superior advances are not protected."[142] The

---

[133] *See* § 4D[1].

[134] Because the Copyright Act no longer forfeits copyright for publication without proper notice, the distinction between "limited" and "general" publications is of limited utility today. *See* § 4D[1]. The Copyright Office allows registration of computer program and "secure test" works in a form that will not necessarily cause disclosure of the trade secrets expressed in the works. *See* § 4D[3].

[135] Technicon Medical Info. Systems Corp. v. Green Bay Packaging, Inc., 687 F.2d 1032, 1039 (7th Cir. 1982).

[136] The UTSA Prefatory Note cites this as a key reason for businesses to rely on trade secrets protection.

[137] 35 U.S.C. § 122.

[138] 35 U.S.C. § 154(d). *See* § 2E[1].

[139] *See* § 2D[3][c][viii].

[140] *See, e.g.*, Chemcast Corp. v. Arco Indus. Corp., 913 F.2d 923 (Fed. Cir. 1990).

[141] *See, e.g.*, Anaconda Co. v. Metric Tool & Die Co., 485 F. Supp. 410 (E.D. Pa. 1980).

[142] Jostens, Inc. v. National Computer Systems, 318 N.W.2d 691, 698 (Minn. 1982) (surveying and summing up a variety of judicial comments on novelty requirements).

Supreme Court, in summarizing trade secret law requirements, stated: "some novelty will be required if merely because that which does not possess novelty is usually known; secrecy, in the context of trade secrets, thus implies at least minimal novelty."[143]

[vii] Disclosure to Government Agencies

Government agencies collect information with potential trade secret status in connection with regulatory, purchasing and research activities. The agencies' practices differ, and most have regulations protecting trade secrets, but companies that must submit trade secrets to the government continue to run a substantial risk of having them disclosed to third parties.

Disclosure to a government agency that does not have a duty to maintain the information's confidentiality causes forfeiture of trade secret status.[144] Disclosure to an agency in confidence does not terminate trade secret protectability,[145] but an agency promise to keep the information confidential can be overridden. An agency subpoena may be denied enforcement if a court finds the agency unwilling or unable to prevent detrimental disclosure of subpoenaed trade secrets.[146]

The Freedom of Information Act ("FOIA")[147] provides that each federal government executive branch agency shall promptly make available to any person upon request all records unless one or more exemptions apply. The statute has an exemption for trade secrets;[148] however, an agency promise to a submitter that information will be kept confidential does not by itself protect the information from mandated FOIA disclosure.[149] If an FOIA exemption applies to the information, the agency is permitted, but not required,[150] to withhold it from a requestor.[151]

The Fifth Amendment protects trade secrets that are products of individuals' labor and invention as property; government agency disclosure of a person's trade secrets is a "taking" of that property if the person had a reasonable expectation

---

[143] Kewanee Oil Co. v. Bicron Corp., 416 U.S. 470, 476 (1974). *See also* RESTATEMENT (THIRD) OF UNFAIR COMPETITION § 39 cmt. f ("Although trade secret cases sometimes announce a 'novelty' requirement, the requirement is synonymous with the concepts of secrecy and value . . . and the correlative exclusion of self-evident variants of the known art.").

[144] *See* Thomas v. Union Carbide Agricultural Products Co., 473 U.S. 568, 584 (1985). *See also* Ruckelshaus v. Monsanto Co., 467 U.S. 986, 1005–08 (1983).

[145] *See, e.g.,* Boeing Co. v. Sierracin Corp., 738 P.2d 665 (Wash. 1987).

[146] Wearly v. FTC, 462 F. Supp. 589 (D.N.J. 1978), *vacated on other grounds*, 616 F.2d 662 (3d Cir. 1980). *See also* St. Michael's Convalescent v. State of Cal., 643 F.2d 1369 (9th Cir. 1981); South Fla. Growers Ass'n v. U.S. Dept. of Agr., 554 F. Supp. 633 (S.D. Fla. 1982).

[147] 5 U.S.C. § 552. FOIA was enacted by Congress in 1966 to revise § 3 of the Administrative Procedures Act, and has been amended many times since.

[148] 5 U.S.C. § 522(b)(4).

[149] *See, e.g.,* AT &T Information Sys., Inc. v. Gen. Servs. Admin., 627 F. Supp. 1396 (D.D.C. 1986), *rev'd on other grounds*, 810 F.2d 1233 (D.C. Cir. 1987).

[150] The statutory language is not clear on this point, but the U.S. Supreme Court held that the exemptions are permissive. Chrysler Corp. v. Brown, 441 U.S. 281 (1979).

[151] Withholding of trade secrets may be required by the Federal Trade Secrets Act, 18 U.S.C. § 1905. For an extensive discussion of the relation between the Trade Secrets Act and the FOIA, *see* CNA Financial Corp. v. Donovan, 830 F.2d 1132 (D.C. Cir. 1987).

that the trade secret submitted to the agency was to be kept confidential.[152]

[viii]   Laws Mandating Disclosure

Laws or regulations sometimes mandate disclosure of someone else's trade secrets. For example, federal securities law has "disclose or abstain" rules that prohibit a party from trading a corporation's stock while possessing material inside information about the corporation.[153] If the inside information is a trade secret, a party caught between the securities law disclosure requirements and trade secret law's non-disclosure requirements can be forced to delay, or even abort, plans to buy stock.[154] Court decisions on this question have come to a variety of conclusions but have generally scrutinized the degree of competitive harm that would result from public disclosure of alleged trade secret information.[155] As in most trade secret cases, the decisions usually consider the particular situation's equities.[156]

[d]   Commercial Value and Use

[i]   Value

A "value" requirement is implicit in the Restatement's formulation of "advantage over competitors,"[157] but it is intermingled with the secrecy, novelty, concreteness, and continuous use requirements. Plaintiff's efforts to protect secrecy may show value.[158] The UTSA makes the value requirement explicit by requiring that the information "derives independent economic value" from its secrecy.[159] It has been held that the UTSA requirement of "economic value" excludes the purely "spiritual value" of scriptural materials for which no commercial value was asserted.[160]

[ii]   Cost of Development

Expenditures of money and time to develop information are not required for trade secret protection (i.e., fortuitous discoveries are protectable), but courts sometimes refer to such expenditures as evidence of commercial value[161] and as an

---

[152] Ruckelshaus v. Monsanto Co., 467 U.S. 986, 1000–04 (1983).

[153] See, e.g., Rule 10(b), 15 U.S.C. § 78(b), and Rule 14e-3, 17 C.F.R. 240, of the Securities and Exchange Act of 1934.

[154] See, e.g., General Portland, Inc. v. LaFarge Coppee S.A., Fed. Sec. L. Rep. (CCH) ¶ 99, 148 (N.D. Tex. 1981).

[155] See, e.g., A. Copeland Enterprises, Inc. v. Guste, Fed. Sec. L. Rep. (CCH) ¶ 95,001 (E.D. La. 1988).

[156] See Cendali & Juceam, Enjoining a Tender Offer for Misuse of Confidential Information: Is it a Show-Stopper or Can the Bidder Cure? The Journal of Proprietary Rights, Vol. 1, No. 12, Dec. 1989, and Vol. 2, No. 1, Jan. 1990.

[157] Restatement of Torts § 757, cmt. b.

[158] See Rockwell Graphic Systems, Inc. v. DEV Indus., Inc., 925 F.2d 174, 178–9 (7th Cir. 1991).

[159] UTSA § 1(4). See also Restatement (Third) of Unfair Competition § 39 cmt. e.

[160] Religious Technology Center v. Wollersheim, 796 F.2d 1076, 1091 (9th Cir. 1986). In a later appeal, the Ninth Circuit explained and limited its holding. Technology Center, Church of Scientology v. Scott, 869 F.2d 1306, 1309–10 (9th Cir. 1989).

[161] See, e.g., Metallurgical Indus. Inc. v. Fourtek, Inc., 790 F.2d 1195, 1201 (5th Cir. 1986); Cybertek Computer Prods., Inc. v. Whitfield, 203 U.S.P.Q. 1020, 1023 (Dep't. Super. Ct. 1977).

indicator of damages.[162] If an alleged trade secret is but marginally protectable, courts may be more lenient to defendants if a plaintiff spent little time, effort or expense to develop it.[163]

[2]   Exclusive Rights

A trade secret's owner has the right to prevent its unauthorized use or disclosure by a person who acquired it through improper means. The owner has no rights against any person who acquires the purported secret through other means, "as, for example, by inspection or analysis of the commercial product embodying the secret, or by independent invention, or by [unrestricted] gift or purchase from the owner."[164]

[3]   Duration and Termination

Trade secrets may be protected as long as the owner successfully prevents them from becoming widely known.[165] In contrast, patents last only 20 years from the date of filing but offer broader protection.[166] If information becomes common knowledge, it ceases to be a trade secret.[167]

§ 3D   TRADE SECRET MISAPPROPRIATION LITIGATION

A threshold practical issue in litigation is the danger of disclosure of the trade secret through the public records of judicial proceedings or in open court. The Restatement states:

> In order to protect trade secrets against disclosure in the course of litigation, testimony involving such disclosure is generally taken by the court privately rather than in public and the record of such testimony is appropriately safeguarded against public disclosure.[168]

The UTSA provides that courts shall preserve secrecy by:

> granting protective orders in connection with discovery proceedings, holding in-camera hearings, sealing the records of the action, and ordering any person involved in the litigation not to disclose an alleged trade secret without prior court approval.[169]

---

[162] *See, e.g., Fourtek*, 790 F.2d at 1208.

[163] *See, e.g.*, Arnold's Ice Cream Co. v. Carlson, 171 U.S.P.Q. 333 (E.D.N.Y. 1971).

[164] RESTATEMENT OF TORTS § 757, cmt. a. *See also* RESTATEMENT (THIRD) OF UNFAIR COMPETITION § 43 & cmt. b.

[165] *See id.* ("protection . . . not limited to a fixed number of years.").

[166] Patents cover unauthorized manufacture, use or sale of the claimed invention even if independently developed. *See* § 2F[3][b].

[167] Protection may continue for a "head start" or "lead time" period against a person who is found to have misappropriated it before it became common knowledge. *See* §§ 3F[1][c] and 3F[2][a][ii].

[168] RESTATEMENT OF TORTS § 757, cmt. f.

[169] UTSA § 5. *See, e.g.*, Fed. R. Civ. P. 26(c)(1)(G); Cal. Civ. Code § 3426.5.

The accompanying Comment states that "a court must ensure that a respondent is provided sufficient information to present a defense and a trier of fact sufficient information to resolve the merits,"[170] and approvingly mentions that courts sometimes preserve secrecy by:

> restricting disclosures to a party's counsel and his or her assistants and by appointing a disinterested expert as a special master to hear secret information and report conclusions to the court.[171]

Federal and many state civil procedure rules explicitly balance a trade secret owner's interest in non-disclosure against the court's need for the information.[172] Discovery rules require an inquiry into:

> [W]hether the material sought is likely to be sufficiently useful to justify the burden imposed by the discovery request, [and] whether the information could be obtained through some less burdensome or less intrusive device, etc.[173]

Some states give judges discretion to exclude a party from *in camera* hearings that take evidence on whether, and what, trade secrets exist.[174]

[1] Definition of Misappropriation

The Restatement definition of conduct triggering liability and the UTSA definition of misappropriation are substantially identical, with one exception. The Restatement included disclosure or use as an essential element. The UTSA provides that mere wrongful acquisition — without use or disclosure — can be a misappropriation.

The Restatement stated:

> One who discloses or uses another's trade secret, without a privilege to do so, is liable to the other if
>
> (a) he discovered the secret by improper means, *or*
>
> (b) his disclosure or use constitutes a breach of confidence reposed in him by the other in disclosing the secret to him, *or*
>
> (c) he learned the secret from a third person with notice of the facts that it was a secret and that the third person discovered it by improper means or that the third person's disclosure of it was otherwise a breach of his duty to the other, *or*

---

[170] UTSA Comment to § 5.

[171] *Id.*

[172] *See, e.g.* Fed. R. Civ. P. 26(b)(2)(C).

[173] Advanced-Semiconductor v. Tau Laboratories, 229 U.S.P.Q. 222, 224 (N.D. Cal. 1986).

[174] *See, e.g.*, Cal. Civ. Code § 3426.5; Air Products and Chemicals Inc. v. Johnson, 442 A.2d 1114, 1128–29 (Pa. 1982) (discussing Pennsylvania Rule of Civil Procedure 223).

(d) he learned the secret with notice of the facts that it was a secret and that its disclosure was made to him by mistake.[175]

The UTSA defines misappropriation as

(i) acquisition of a trade secret of another by a person who knows or has reason to know that the trade secret was acquired by improper means; *or*

(ii) disclosure or use of a trade secret of another without express or implied consent by a person who

(A) used improper means to acquire knowledge of the trade secret; *or*

(B) at the time of the disclosure or use, knew or had reason to know that his knowledge of the trade secret was

(I) derived from or through a person who had utilized improper means to acquire it;

(II) acquired under circumstances giving rise to a duty to maintain its secrecy or limit its use; *or*

(III) derived from or through a person who owed a duty to the person seeking relief to maintain its secrecy or limit its use; *or*

(C) before a material change of his or her position, knew or had reason to know that it was a trade secret and that knowledge of it had been acquired by accident or mistake.[176]

The Third Restatement likewise defines "appropriation" to include acquisition by improper means, as well as use or disclosure in the circumstances prohibited by the UTSA.[177]

[2]   Theories of Law

The common law of trade secrets originated in tort, but alternative causes of action include breach of express or implied contract. The Restatement includes "breach of contract" in the "general duty of good faith" affording protection to trade secrets,[178] and the UTSA expressly leaves intact any contract claims.[179] Thus, in both UTSA and non-UTSA states, plaintiffs typically plead various tort and contract causes of action.

[a]   Contract Law Theories

The UTSA provides that it "displaces conflicting tort, restitutionary, and other law of [the enacting] State providing civil remedies for misappropriation of a trade secret"[180] but it expressly does not affect any contractual remedies or criminal

---

[175] RESTATEMENT OF TORTS § 757 (emphasis added).

[176] UTSA § 1(2) (emphasis added).

[177] RESTATEMENT (THIRD) OF UNFAIR COMPETITION § 40.

[178] RESTATEMENT OF TORTS § 757, cmt. a.

[179] UTSA § 7(b)(1).

[180] UTSA § 7(a). The text of § 7 was modified as part of the 1985 Amendments discussed in § 3B[4].

remedies, whether or not based upon misappropriation of a trade secret, or "other civil remedies that are not based upon misappropriation of a trade secret."[181] The UTSA Comment further explains that the Act:

> applies to a duty to protect competitively significant secret information that is imposed by law. It does not apply to a duty voluntarily assumed through an express or implied-in-fact contract . . . [or to] a duty imposed by law that is not dependent upon the existence of competitively significant secret information.[182]

A trade secret owner may allege breach of contractual obligation against use or disclosure of the trade secret in a variety of situations. A duty of confidentiality may arise from express contractual provisions, implied-in-fact contract terms based on a court's interpretation of the parties' understanding, or implied-in-law contract terms based on public policy.

Implied-in-law contractual obligations frequently arise from employment or other confidential relationships.[183] Implied-in-fact contractual obligations arise when parties' conduct indicates that they intended confidentiality as a condition of disclosure.

Because contract law theories are based on confidentiality obligations that defendants actually or implicitly undertake voluntarily, the theories support broader definitions of protectable information[184] and tighter restrictions on defendants' activities.[185] Also, contract law can provide a basis for suits against the United States government.[186] On the other hand, an attempt to disclaim a confidential relationship is more likely to be upheld for purposes of contract law than for tort law.[187] Contract and tort theories also involve different rules for conflicts of law, statutes of limitations, and damages.

[b]   Tort Law Theories

The tort of breach of confidence, the original basis for trade secrets law,[188] has always been the most broadly used theory in trade secret actions. A tort law claim exists whether or not the same confidence creates implied or express contractual obligations.

---

[181] UTSA § 7(b).

[182] UTSA Comment to § 7.

[183] See discussion of employer-employee in § 3D[3][a][i](2) and other confidential relationships in § 3D[4][a].

[184] See discussion of protectable information in § 3C[1] and discussion of customer lists in Wisconsin etc. in § 3C[1][b][iv].

[185] See discussion of agreements not to compete in § 3D[3][c].

[186] The United States has waived its sovereign immunity for most contract claims, see 28 U.S.C. § 1491, but only for a restricted list of tort claims, *see* 28 U.S.C. 1346(b).

[187] *See* Burten v. Milton Bradley Co., 763 F.2d 461 (1st Cir. 1985).

[188] For a discussion of early English cases, see § 3B[1].

[c]   Conflicts of Laws

Because different states' laws may conflict, courts must decide which states' laws apply to a claim. States' conflicts of laws rules vary, and, in some states, may depend on whether an action is based on contract or tort.

Absent a contractual choice of law agreement, a court addressing potentially conflicting laws first applies the conflict of laws rules of the state in which it sits (the "forum state").[189] This entails (1) examining whether the rules are different for actions based, respectively, on contract and tort; (2) applying these rules to select the procedural and substantive laws applicable to each cause of action; (3) applying to each action the statute of limitations of the state whose procedural laws have been selected; and, if the statute has not run; (4) applying to each action the law of the state whose substantive laws have been selected.[190]

For substantive issues, the forum state's conflicts rules may require use of its own law or the law of the state where the wrong is alleged to have occurred. If the applicable state law on substantive questions is vague, federal courts hearing trade secret cases must either attempt to predict how the state courts would rule,[191] perhaps guided by the "general law" of other states,[192] or else they may certify the question to the state's highest court where certification is available.[193]

[i]   Contract Law Conflicts

If a breach of contract claim is alleged, most states apply the law of the forum where a contract was entered into, but some look to the forum having the greatest number of contacts with the transaction, and some to the forum where performance occurs.[194] California applies the law of the state whose interest would be "more impaired if its policy were subordinated to the policy of the other state."[195] Some courts will disregard a contractual governing law clause if substantive issues involve a public policy of a state that has materially greater interests in the transaction than those of the contractually stipulated state.[196]

---

[189] In federal court, this result is dictated by the *Erie* doctrine. *See* Klaxon Co. v. Stentor Elec. Mfg. Co., 313 U.S. 487 (1941).

[190] *See, e.g.*, Rohm and Haas Co. v. Adco Chemical Co., 689 F.2d 424 (3d Cir. 1982); Goldberg v. Medtronic, Inc., 686 F.2d 1219 (7th Cir. 1982); FMC Corp. v. Varco Int'l, Inc., 677 F.2d 500 (5th Cir. 1982); Smith v. Dravo Corp., 203 F.2d 369 (7th Cir. 1953); Lehman v. Dow Jones & Co., Inc., 606 F. Supp. 1152 (S.D.N.Y. 1985), *aff'd*, 783 F.2d 285 (2d Cir. 1986).

[191] Wheelabrator Corporation v. Fogle, 317 F. Supp. 633, 636 (W.D. La. 1970), *aff'd*, 438 F.2d 1226 (5th Cir. 1971). *See* Erie R.R. Co. v. Tompkins, 304 U.S. 64 (1938).

[192] Telex Corp. v. International Business Mach. Corp., 510 F.2d 894, 930 (10th Cir. 1975).

[193] *See, e.g.*, BlueEarth Biofuels, LLC v. Hawaiian Elec. Co., 235 P.3d 310 (Haw. 2010) (answering certified questions).

[194] *See, e.g.*, Crater Corp. v. Lucent Technologies, Inc., 625 F. Supp. 2d 790, 800–01 (E.D. Mo. 2007).

[195] Lehman v. Dow Jones & Co., Inc. 606 F. Supp. 1152, 1157 (S.D.N.Y. 1985), *aff'd*, 783 F.2d 285 (2d Cir. 1986).

[196] *See, e.g.*, Barnes Group, Inc. v. C & C Products, Inc., 716 F.2d 1023, 1029 (4th Cir. 1983). *See also* RESTATEMENT (SECOND) OF CONFLICT OF LAWS § 186 (1971).

[ii]   Tort Law Conflicts

If a tort claim is alleged, most states apply the law of the state where the injury occurred, but some apply the contracts-style contacts or relationship test that the *Restatement (Second) of Conflict of Laws* endorses.[197] Under this test, factors to be considered include the place of the injury, the place where the conduct causing the injury occurred, the parties' domicile, and the place where the parties' relationship, if any, is centered.[198] In some states, a contractual choice-of-law provision may apply to tort claims as well, if "the tort claim is sufficiently intertwined with the contract claim or the interpretation of the contract."[199]

[iii]   Statutes of Limitations

At common law, it is unsettled whether trade secrets misappropriation is a continuing wrong for statute of limitations purposes. This issue is significant because it dictates whether the period within which an action must be brought starts when the misappropriation begins, or whether the statute is tolled as long as the misappropriation continues.

In *Underwater Storage, Inc. v. U.S. Rubber Co.*, a federal court applying District of Columbia law noted that the Restatement protects against not only disclosure but also use of a trade secret and held that continuing wrongful use of a trade secret is a continuing tort.[200]

In *Monolith Portland Midwest Co. v. Kaiser Aluminum & Chem. Corp.*,[201] a federal court applying California law attributed the *Underwater* holding to a property theory of trade secrets law, concluded that California law used a duty theory, and held that, under a duty theory, misappropriation is not a continuing wrong. Rather than protecting a property right which is damaged with each adverse use, *Monolith* held that California law protects only a confidential relationship, the fabric of which "once rent is not torn anew with each added use or disclosure."[202]

The UTSA rejects the *Underwater* theory of a continuing wrong, adopts most of the *Monolith* court approach, but provides for a three-year limitation period that does not begin until the trade secrets owner knows or should know of the misappropriation.[203] Because wrongful acquisition constitutes misappropriation

---

[197] RESTATEMENT (SECOND) OF CONFLICT OF LAWS § 145.

[198] *Id. See, e.g., Crater Corp.*, 625 F. Supp. 2d at 801.

[199] Peter Kiewit Sons', Inc. v. ATSER, L.P., 684 F. Supp. 2d 1126 (D. Neb. 2010). *See also* Facility Wizard Software, Inc. v. Southeastern Tech. Servs., LLC, 647 F. Supp. 2d 938, 943–45 (N.D. Ill. 2009).

[200] 371 F.2d 950, 955 (D.C. Cir. 1966). *See also* Anaconda Co. v. Metric Tool & Die Co., 485 F. Supp. 410 (E.D. Pa. 1980).

[201] 407 F.2d 288 (9th Cir. 1969).

[202] *Id.* at 293. *Monolith* also stated that the limitation period's start should not be delayed until the plaintiff's discovery of the misappropriation because discovery was not an element of the cause of action. *Id.* This holding, however, pre-dated a number of California cases which effectively made the discovery rule the default rule. *See* Stephen v. O'Neal, Comment, *Accrual of Statutes of Limitations: California's Discovery Exceptions Swallow the Rule*, 68 CAL. L. REV. 106 (1980).

[203] UTSA § 6.

under the UTSA,[204] the limitation period begins when the owner knows or should know of any wrongful acquisition.[205]

[3] Elements and Burdens of Proof

The trade secret owner has the burden of proving, by a preponderance of the evidence, the existence, ownership and misappropriation of a protectable trade secret.[206]

In most UTSA states, a trade secret claim's formal elements are: (1) the information qualifies as a statutory "trade secret";[207] and (2) the defendant's conduct constitutes statutory "misappropriation" of the trade secret.[208] The "ownership" element is implicit in the definition of "misappropriation," which requires acquisition, use, or disclosure "of the trade secret *of another.*"[209] The plaintiff must have owned the secret at the time of the misappropriation; there is no "current ownership" rule requiring that the plaintiff own the trade secret at the time of trial.[210]

In both UTSA and non-UTSA states, the underlying factual elements are best understood and organized as follows:

(1)   Specified information qualifies as a trade secret because it meets the applicable state trade secret law's secrecy and subject matter protection requirements.[211]

(2)   Plaintiff owns the trade secret because plaintiff (a) either developed the information or acquired it through proper means *and* (b) subsequently made reasonable efforts to maintain its secrecy.

(3)   Defendant either (a) acquired the secret by improper means, or (b) disclosed or used the trade secret, if the requisite knowledge was present.

(4)   Defendant has a duty to the plaintiff of non-use and/or non-disclosure, either because (a) defendant acquired the trade secret through an express

---

[204] See definitions of misappropriation in § 3D[1].

[205] Ashton-Tate Corp. v. Ross, 916 F.2d 516 (9th Cir. 1990). *See also* Cadence Design Systems, Inc. v. Avant! Corp., 57 P.3d 647, 653–654 (Cal. 2002) ("We conclude that a plaintiff's claim for misappropriation of a trade secret against a defendant arises only once, when the trade secret is initially misappropriated.").

[206] *See, e.g.,* Rusty's Weigh Scales & Service, Inc. v. North Texas Scales, Inc., 314 S.W.3d 105, 109 (Tex. App. 2010); Softchoice Corp. v. MacKenzie, 636 F. Supp. 2d 927, 936–37 (D. Neb. 2009); Vekamaf Holland B.V. v. Pipe Benders, Inc., 211 U.S.P.Q. 955, 978 (D. Minn. 1981), *aff'd,* 696 F.2d 608 (8th Cir. 1982); Greenberg v. Croydon Plastics Co., Inc., 378 F. Supp. 806, 811 (E.D. Pa. 1974); GTI Corporation v. Calhoon, 309 F. Supp. 762, 767 (S.D. Ohio 1969).

[207] For the UTSA definition of "trade secret," see § 3C[1][a].

[208] For the UTSA definition of "misappropriation," see § 3D[1].

[209] UTSA § 1(2)(i),(ii) (emphasis added).

[210] Jasmine Networks, Inc. v. Superior Court, 180 Cal. App. 4th 980, 997–1010 (2009).

[211] A plaintiff must plead sufficient facts to demonstrate a trade secret exists without disclosing the secret in order that the court and the defendant has reasonable notice of the trade secret claims. *See* Brian Lichtenberg LLC v. Alex & Chloe, Inc., 2014 U.S. Dist. LEXIS 18607 (C.D. Cal. Feb. 13, 2014).

or implied confidential relationship with the plaintiff, or through improper means, *or* (b) defendant knew or should have known that its knowledge was derived from one who acquired the secret through a confidential relationship or improper means.

Courts articulate these elements in a variety of ways, generally "without greatly affecting the concept."[212]

Most courts consider whether a trade secret existed and whether a breach of confidence occurred to be questions of fact, to which a clearly erroneous appellate review standard applies. A minority view treats trade secret existence as a question of law,[213] or as a "mixed question of law and fact,"[214] giving appellate courts a free hand to reconsider a lower court's determination that a trade secret did or did not exist.[215]

With regard to misappropriation, although the trade secret owner has the burden of proof, some courts permit the owner to satisfy its burden by introducing circumstantial evidence of access and similarity.[216] This shifts the burden of producing evidence to the defendant to show that the secret was acquired by proper means. The ultimate burden of persuasion, however, remains with the plaintiff.[217]

[4] Trade Secret Ownership

To establish ownership, plaintiff must show he or she learned the information through means that were proper and gave rise to no use restrictions. This most typically occurs through independent development, but a person may have ownership and standing to sue based on acquisition of the information by gift, sale, license (if the license confers sufficient rights), reverse engineering, or other lawful means. Most disputes are over a protectable trade secret's existence, but ownership is sometimes disputed, most frequently between an employer and employee or between joint venturers.

Issues particular to the employer/employee context include the original source of the information (employer or employee), the nature of an employee's job and responsibilities, the scope of the employment relationship, and the time when information is developed.

As between an employee and an employer, if there is no enforceable express agreement, common-law rules apply to (1) information protectability, (2) ownership, and (3) the existence of a confidentiality obligation. Protectability

---

[212] Vekamaf Holland B.V. v. Pipe Benders, Inc., 211 U.S.P.Q. 955, 978 (D. Minn. 1981), *aff'd*, 696 F.2d 608 (8th Cir. 1982).

[213] *See, e.g.*, Agriculture Labor Rel. Bd. v. Richard A. Glass Co., 175 Cal. App. 3d 703, 711–713 (1985); Uribe v. Howie, 19 Cal. App. 3d 194, 205–207 (1971).

[214] Corroon & Black-Rutters & Roberts v. Hosch, 325 N.W.2d 883, 885 (Wis. 1982).

[215] *Corroon*, 325 N.W.2d at 885.

[216] *See, e.g.*, USA Power, LLC v. PacifiCorp., 235 P.3d 749, 761 (Utah 2010) (collecting cases); Aries Information Sys., Inc. v. Pacific Mgmt. Sys. Corp., 366 N.W.2d 366, 369 (Minn. Ct. App. 1985).

[217] Moore v. Kulicke & Soffa Indus., Inc., 318 F.3d 561, 566–74 (3d Cir. 2003).

depends on whether information differs from the general knowledge, skill and experience which a typical employee gains from employment. Ownership depends on the original source of the information and the scope of the employment. An employee's duty of confidentiality depends on his or her position and responsibilities.

Express agreements can establish protectability, ownership and duties where they would not otherwise exist, but various public policies may limit the enforceability of such agreements against employees.

[a]   Common Law

[i]   Information Protectability

Every employee has the right to use and disclose all information that falls within the scope of the general knowledge, skill and experience that a typical employee gains from an employer during employment.[218] This test corresponds closely to the "novelty" requirement, and depends in large part on the state of "general knowledge" within an industry.[219]

In *Rohm & Haas Co. v. Adco Chemical Co.*,[220] a paint manufacturer sued a competitor for misappropriation of information disclosed in confidence to a former employee subsequently hired by the competitor. The employee's admission that he relied on memory rather than ability was held to be persuasive evidence that the information was not general knowledge, experience or skill.[221] Other courts, however, consider an employee's residual memory (as opposed to deliberate memorization[222]) to be more akin to general knowledge, skill, and experience.[223]

[ii]   Ownership

Employers own any trade secrets they impart to employees and may claim ownership of an employee-developed trade secret. The key issue is the scope of the employment contract.[224]

Whether trade secret ownership resides in an employer or an employee depends upon (1) the nature of the work the employee was hired to perform; (2) the invention's relation to the employer's business; and (3) the extent to which the

---

[218] *See, e.g.*, Jet Spray Cooler, Inc. v. Crampton, 282 N.E.2d 921, 924 (Mass. 1972).

[219] For a discussion of novelty and general knowledge, see § 3C[1][c][vi].

[220] Rohm and Haas Co. v. Adco Chem. Co., 689 F.2d 424 (3d Cir. 1982).

[221] *Id.* at 433.

[222] Stampede Tool Warehouse, Inc. v. May, 651 N.E.2d 209, 216–17 (Ill. App. Ct. 1995) ("Using memorization to rebuild a trade secret does not transform that trade secret from confidential information into non-confidential information.").

[223] Avnet, Inc. v. Wyle Laboratories, Inc., S.E.2d 302, 304–05 (Ga. 1993); Moss, Adams & Co. v. Shilling, 179 Cal. App. 3d 124, 129 (1986) (former employee "cannot be expected to wipe his or her memory clean."). *But see* Morlife, Inc. v. Perry, 56 Cal. App. 4th 1514, 1525–27 (1997) (disagreeing with *Moss* on this point).

[224] Rules on employer-employee trade secret ownership resemble the rules on ownership of patent rights on employee inventions. *See* § 2G[1]. For a discussion of copyright ownership in the employment context, see § 4F[1].

employee used the employer's resources in the invention's conception and development.[225] Ownership is heavily fact-dependent, and must be considered on a case-by-case basis. Other factors may be important in special situations. For instance, an employee-inventor who is a corporate officer or director may be required to assign rights to the company because of a fiduciary duty not to compete with the company.

If an employee is hired to invent or develop particular information or is assigned the duty of accomplishing a specific task, the employer is generally deemed to have an implied contractual and equitable right to require the employee to assign his or her rights to any resulting protectable information. At the other extreme, if an employee is not hired to use any inventive or creative skills, there is no implied agreement and the employer is not entitled to an assignment.

The middle ground, and harder question, involves an employee who is hired to pursue his or her inventive skills generally, but not to create anything in particular. In this case an employer may own rights to particular information if it was developed during working hours, it is in the scope of business of the employer and the employee-inventor was assigned tasks related to the creations.

In *Wexler v. Greenberg*,[226] plaintiff, a sanitation and maintenance chemical manufacturer, sought to enjoin a former employee and a competing company of which the employee had become an officer from using or disclosing formulas and processes the employee developed during his employment with plaintiff. The employee was a skilled chemist whose work for the plaintiff had been limited to modifying competitors' formulas and had included no research, experimentation or invention. The court noted that the plaintiff provided no appreciable assistance or supervision beyond usual employee job expenses, found nothing that should have put the employee on notice that proprietary formula development was the employment relationship's purpose, and held that the formulas were part of the employee's technical knowledge and skill.[227]

In *Q-Co Industries, Inc. v. Hoffman*,[228] the plaintiff, a computer software manufacturer, sued former employee programmers, who had no express confidentiality agreements, for misappropriation of software the former employees had developed for plaintiff. The court applied the following language to find that the plaintiff-employer had established a likelihood of successfully proving misappropriation:

> When an individual is expressly employed to devote his time to the development of process and machinery and was to receive therefore [sic] a stated compensation, the resulting development is the property of him who engage [sic] the services and paid for them.[229]

If an employer does not own an employee's invention or idea, it may have a more

---

[225] *See* Wexler v. Greenberg, 160 A.2d 430, 435–37 (Pa. 1960).

[226] 399 Pa. 569, 160 A.2d 430 (1960).

[227] 399 Pa. at 581, 160 A.2d at 436–37.

[228] 625 F. Supp. 608 (S.D.N.Y. 1985).

[229] 625 F. Supp. at 617 (citations and internal quotes omitted).

limited "shop right" to use the invention if the employee used a sufficient amount of the employer's time, facilities, or materials.[230] A "shop right" is a non-exclusive, non-transferable, royalty-free license for the employer to use an employee's intellectual property.[231] It is an equitable right given to the employer because of the employee's use of the employer's time, facilities, or materials. If an employer is entitled to a shop right, the employer may manufacture, use and sell devices that embody the employee's creation before and after termination of the employment relationship. The employee also may use, manufacture and market the invention, or license the employer's competitors to do so.

[iii]   Employment as a Confidential Relationship

An individual employee's position and responsibilities define the degree to which confidentiality obligations will be implied in the employment contract. At common law, a confidential relationship, and a corresponding duty not to use or disclose the employer's inventions or trade secrets, will generally be implied where employees were in a position to gain an intimate knowledge of the employer's business.[232]

[b]   Express Agreements

Express agreements can establish employer trade secret ownership and employee confidentiality duties, even in circumstances where they would not be created by implication, but information protectability is determined according to trade secret law principles, and information characterized as a trade secret by agreement still may be held unprotectable by courts.

[i]   Ownership-Assignment Agreements

Express agreements by which employees obligate themselves to assign intellectual property rights to their employer are generally enforceable, subject to traditional contract doctrines such as fraud, duress, mutual mistake, and lack of consideration. A few states have passed statutes making such agreements unenforceable unless equipment, supplies, facilities or trade secret information of the employer are used or the idea relates directly to the business of the employer or its actual or anticipated research and development, or resulted from work performed for the employer.[233]

[ii]   Timing of Creation

Employers have no implied (non-contractual) rights to valuable ideas conceived by an employee before or after the employment period. "Hold-over" clauses requiring assignment of post-employment ideas are strictly construed[234] and are only enforceable if limited to reasonable times and to ideas based on the employer's proprietary information or other subject matter which the employee worked on or

---

[230] *See* U.S. v. Dubilier Condenser Corp., 289 U.S. 178 (1932).

[231] *See* § 2G[1].

[232] Zoecon Indus. v. American Stockman Tag Co., 713 F.2d 1174, 1178 (5th Cir. 1983).

[233] *See* § 2G[1].

[234] *See, e.g.*, Armorlite Lens Co. v. Campbell, 340 F. Supp. 273, 275 (S.D. Cal. 1972).

had knowledge of during his former employment.[235]

A hold-over clause is reasonable if it is (1) no greater than needed to protect the employer's legitimate interests; (2) not unduly harsh and oppressive to the employee; and (3) not injurious to the public.[236]

If a former employee reduces an idea to practice or commercialization quickly after employment termination, courts may infer that the idea was conceived during the employment.[237]

[iii]   Consideration

Employee non-disclosure agreements must be supported by consideration. Courts often require that they be executed at the time of hiring or promotion, but one court held an agreement enforceable where the subsequently executed written non-disclosure agreement memorialized a prior oral agreement.[238]

Another court surveyed the authorities on consideration for employee non-disclosure agreements: "Where no raises or promotions resulted, where other employees with similar access [to the employer's information] were not asked to sign, the mere continuation of employment for [plaintiffs] is not enough."[239]

[c]   Non-Competition Agreements

Agreements not to compete, also known as restrictive covenants, technically lie outside the scope of trade secrets law, but their enforcement is often sought in actions that also allege trade secret misappropriation, and trade secret protection is often put forth as the reason why such an agreement should be enforced.

Agreements not to compete are strictly construed and are unenforceable under most states' public policy unless they are reasonable under the circumstances. Common law tests for reasonableness include: (1) whether the restriction is ancillary to a legitimate business purpose or agreement; (2) whether there is a legitimate business interest to protect; (3) whether the restrictions are reasonable with respect to subject matter, time, and territory; and (4) whether there is adequate consideration.[240] Legitimate business purposes may include the sale or transfer of a business, creation of an employment contract,[241] or the protection of trade secrets.[242]

State laws differ on reasonableness standards and on what constitutes adequate consideration. Many states will enforce those terms of a restrictive covenant that

---

[235] Dorr-Oliver, Inc. v. United States, 432 F.2d 447, 452 (Ct. Cl. 1970).

[236] See, e.g., GTI Corp. v. Calhoon, 309 F. Supp. 762, 773 (S.D. Ohio 1969) (five-year holdover clause void).

[237] See, e.g., Syntex Opthalmics, Inc. v. Tsuetaki, 701 F.2d 677 (7th Cir. 1983).

[238] Cybertek Computer Prod., Inc. v. Whitfield, 203 U.S.P.Q. 1020, 1022 (Dep't. Super. Ct. 1977).

[239] Jostens, Inc. v. National Computer Sys., 318 N.W.2d 691, 703 (Minn. 1982).

[240] See, e.g., Jostens, Inc., v. National Computer Sys., Inc., 318 N.W.2d 691 (Minn. 1982).

[241] See Modern Controls, Inc. v. Andreadakis, 578 F.2d 1264, 1267–68 (8th Cir. 1978).

[242] See, e.g., Mixing Equip. Co. v. Philadelphia Gear, Inc., 436 F.2d 1308 (3d Cir. 1971); Gillette Co. v. Williams, 360 F. Supp. 1171 (D. Conn. 1973).

are reasonable by reforming or deleting unenforceable terms. Other states have a strong public policy against non-competition agreements and will refuse to restrictive covenants.[243] Courts sitting in a state that has such a policy against restrictive covenants may decline to apply the law of another state that would violate the policy.[244]

Reasonableness of geographical area depends on the facts, and many states will uphold broad geographical restrictions if justified by a business' multistate or international scope,[245] but the type and scope of activity restricted must not be overbroad.

Business interests need not qualify as a trade secret to be protectable by restrictive covenants in most states, and might include customer relationships, specialized training of an employee, or even goodwill. The covenant may be given greater scope if it is protecting a trade secret.

[5]   Misappropriation

A trade secret claimant must prove that the accused misappropriator acquired the information from the claimant through a confidential relationship or improper means. If the claimant proves the accused had *access* to the information in either way, then many courts shift to the defendant the burden of producing evidence that the secret was acquired by proper means. The ultimate burden of persuasion, however, remains with the plaintiff.[246]

[a]   Confidential Relationship

A confidential relationship may arise expressly by contract or implicitly from the parties' conduct or relationship.[247] Persons subject to implied confidential obligations may include employees,[248] student-trainees,[249] independent contractors,[250] negotiators,[251] licensees, customers,[252] suppliers,[253] and joint venturers.[254]

---

[243] *See, e.g.*, Cal. Bus. & Prof. Code § 16600; Edwards v. Arthur Andersen LLP, 189 P.3d 285, 290–93 (Cal. 2008) (disapproving "narrow restraint" exception); Dowell v. Biosense Webster, Inc., 179 Cal. App. 4th 564, 574–77 (2009); Hill Medical Corp. v. Wycoff, 86 Cal. App. 4th 895, 900–01 (2001).

[244] *See, e.g.*, NCH Corp. v. Broyles, 749 F.2d 247, 250–51 (5th Cir. 1985).

[245] *See, e.g.*, Mixing Equip. Co. v. Philadelphia Gear, Inc., 436 F.2d 1308 (3d Cir. 1971).

[246] Moore v. Kulicke & Soffa Indus., Inc., 318 F.3d 561, 566–74 (3d Cir. 2003).

[247] Restatement (Third) of Unfair Competition § 41.

[248] *See* discussion in § 3D[3][a][i].

[249] *See, e.g.*, By-Buk Co. v. Printed Cellophane Tape Co., 163 Cal. App. 2d 157 (1958).

[250] *See, e.g.*, Jones v. Ulrich, 95 N.E.2d 113 (Ill. App. Ct. 1950).

[251] *See, e.g.*, Schreyer v. Casco Products Corp., 190 F.2d 921 (2d Cir. 1951).

[252] *See, e.g.*, Pressed Steel Car Co. v. Standard Steel Car Co., 60 A. 4 (Pa. 1904).

[253] *See, e.g.*, Williams v. Williams, 3 Mer. 157 (1817).

[254] *See, e.g.*, Morison v. Moat, 9 Hare 241 (1851).

[b]   Improper and Proper Means

Trade secrets law concerns the means by which access is gained to information. If the information is in fact a trade secret, as opposed to general knowledge, skill, and experience, the fact that the defendant memorized the information, as opposed to taking physical copies, will not be excused.[255] Nonetheless, surreptitious physical copying may still be significant in various ways, for example, by undermining an employee's argument that information was general knowledge, skill, and experience, or adding to the impression that the defendant acted willfully and maliciously, thus affecting the balance of equities and expanding the remedies available.

[i]   Improper Means

The Restatement stated that improper means are those "which fall below the generally accepted standards of commercial morality and reasonable conduct,"[256] including

> theft, trespass, bribing or otherwise inducing employees or others to reveal the information in breach of duty, fraudulent misrepresentations, threats of harm by unlawful conduct, wiretapping, procuring one's own employees or agents to become employees of the other for purposes of espionage, and so forth.[257]

The UTSA defines improper means to include "theft, bribery, misrepresentation, breach or inducement of a breach of a duty to maintain secrecy, or espionage through electronic or other means."[258]

The Third Restatement defines improper means to include "theft, fraud, unauthorized interception of communications, inducement of or knowing participation in a breach of confidence, and other means either wrongful in themselves or wrongful in the circumstances of the case."[259]

[ii]   Proper Means

The UTSA states that proper means include:

1.   Discovery by independent invention;

2.   Discovery by "reverse engineering";

3.   Discovery under a license from the owner of the trade secret;

---

[255] *See, e.g.*, Stampede Tool Warehouse, Inc. v. May, 651 N.E.2d 209, 216–17 (Ill. App. Ct. 1995) ("Using memorization to rebuild a trade secret does not transform that trade secret from confidential information into non-confidential information."); Ed Nowogroski Ins., Inc. v. Rucker, 971 P.2d 936 (Wash. 1999). Some courts, however, classify residual memory (as opposed to deliberate memorization) as general knowledge, skill, and experience. *See, e.g.*, Avnet, Inc. v. Wyle Laboratories, Inc., 437 S.E.2d 302, 304–05 (Ga. 1993).

[256] RESTATEMENT OF TORTS § 757, cmt. f.

[257] RESTATEMENT OF TORTS § 757, cmt. c.

[258] UTSA § 1(1).

[259] RESTATEMENT (THIRD) OF UNFAIR COMPETITION § 43.

4. Observation of the item in public use or on public display; and

5. Obtaining the trade secret from published literature.[260]

[iii]   Otherwise Lawful Conduct

The Third Restatement states that "[t]he acquisition of a trade secret can be improper even if the means of acquisition are not independently wrongful."[261] The UTSA states that "[i]mproper means could include otherwise lawful conduct which is improper under the circumstances."[262]

Both the Third Restatement and the UTSA endorse the leading case on this point, *E.I. duPont de Nemours & Co. v. Christopher*,[263] which found improper means when an airplane was used to ascertain secret aspects of the layout of a competitor's plant under construction. The court held that "we need not require the discoverer of a trade secret to guard against the unanticipated, the undetectable, or the unpreventable methods of espionage now available."[264] The Supreme Court has cited *duPont* with approval,[265] and it continues to be good law and reliable authority.[266] Nonetheless, monitoring of competitors is commonplace, and the circumstances in which otherwise lawful conduct will be held to be improper generally will be limited to situations in which taking additional precautions would be impractical.[267]

[c]   Innocent Receipt

A person who obtains another's secret through neither improper means nor a confidential relationship has no duty prior to receiving notice of the owner's rights in the secret. Innocent receipt may occur through mistake or through a third party's misappropriation. Even after receiving notice, remedies may be limited (UTSA) or liability nonexistent (Restatement) if the defendant has in good faith paid value for the secret or has otherwise detrimentally relied on the right to use or disclose the secret.

The Restatement's general rule on indirect receipt of information was:

> One who learns another's trade secret from a third person without notice that it is a secret and that the third person's disclosure is a breach of his duty to the other, or who learns the secret through a mistake without notice of the secrecy and the mistake,

---

[260] UTSA Comment to § 1. *See also* RESTATEMENT (THIRD) OF UNFAIR COMPETITION § 43.

[261] RESTATEMENT (THIRD) OF UNFAIR COMPETITION § 43 cmt. c. *See also* RESTATEMENT OF TORTS § 757, cmt. f.

[262] UTSA Comment to § 1.

[263] 431 F.2d 1012 (5th Cir. 1970).

[264] *Id.* at 1016.

[265] Kewanee Oil Co. v. Bicron Corp., 416 U.S. 470, 476 (1974).

[266] *See also* Drill Parts & Service Co. v. Joy Mfg. Co., 439 So.2d 43 (Ala. 1983) (defendant held liable for removing drawings from trash bin outside office of one of plaintiff's subcontractors).

[267] *See, e.g.*, RESTATEMENT (THIRD) OF UNFAIR COMPETITION § 43, cmt. b (taking photographs of a construction site "clearly visible from a major highway" is proper means); *id.* cmt. c (factors include foreseeability of the conduct and availability and cost of effective precautions).

(a) is not liable to the other for a disclosure or use of the secret prior to receipt of such notice, and

(b) is liable to the other for a disclosure or use of the secret after the receipt of such notice, *unless prior thereto he has in good faith paid value for the secret or has so changed his position that to subject him to liability would be inequitable.*[268]

In contrast to this Restatement language, which provides for no liability in good faith payment or reliance cases, the UTSA provides that "an injunction may condition future use upon payment of a reasonable royalty" to the trade secrets owner.[269]

The key factor is defendant's notice of the information's confidentiality. The UTSA does not define notice, but the Restatement discusses it at some length, stating that no particular form of notice is required:

The question is simply whether in the circumstances B knows or should know that the information is A's trade secret and that its disclosure is made in confidence.[270]

The UTSA includes, within its definition of misappropriation, use or disclosure by a person who:

(B) at the time of disclosure or use, knew or had reason to know that his knowledge of the trade secret was

(I) derived from or through a person who had utilized improper means to acquire it;

(II) acquired under circumstances giving rise to a duty to maintain its secrecy or limit its use;

(III) derived from or through a person who owed a duty to the person seeking relief to maintain its secrecy or limit its use.[271]

Therefore, "a trade secret owner's notification to a good faith third party that the third party has knowledge of a trade secret as a result of misappropriation by another . . . suffices to make the third party a misappropriator thereafter."[272]

[6]   Detrimental Use or Disclosure

Under the Restatement, it was not enough that a defendant be shown to possess the secret information. Damages normally required proof that the defendant used or disclosed the trade secrets to plaintiff's detriment;[273] injunctive relief was

---

[268] RESTATEMENT OF TORTS § 758 (emphasis added).

[269] UTSA § 2(b). *See* § 3F[1][d].

[270] RESTATEMENT OF TORTS § 757, cmt. j.

[271] UTSA § 1(b). The Third Restatement tracks the UTSA on this point. *See* RESTATEMENT (THIRD) OF UNFAIR COMPETITION § 40(b).

[272] UTSA Comment to § 2.

[273] For a discussion of damages, see § 3F[2].

available upon proof that detrimental use or disclosure was imminent or inevitable.[274] Detrimental use included the acceleration of product or process development.[275] The UTSA definition of misappropriation, however, includes mere acquisition by improper means, without a further use or disclosure requirement.[276]

The Restatement states that:

[A recipient] may be liable even if he uses [the secret] with modifications or improvements upon it effected by his own efforts . . . . The liability is avoided only when the contribution by the other's secret is so slight that the actor's process can be said to be derived from other sources.[277]

The UTSA makes no special provision for a misappropriator's modifications aside from considering it as a factor in balancing harms in the determination of remedies. However, variation between the plaintiff's trade secrets and the information the defendant uses may be evidence that a defendant received or developed the information from a source other than plaintiff's trade secrets.[278]

§ 3E DEFENSES

Most defenses in trade secret cases are a mirror image of misappropriation claim elements, including independent development, public domain/absence of secrecy, and reverse engineering. If all of the elements of the claim are established, a defendant may still prevent recovery through the equitable defenses of unclean hands and laches.

[1]   Independent Development

A person who independently discovers or develops information identical to another's trade secrets without relying on confidentially received information or improper means incurs no liability under trade secrets law.[279] Independent development is a complete defense to a claim of trade secret misappropriation.

[2]   Absence of Secrecy — Public Domain

If a purported trade secret fails the Restatement test of "substantial secrecy," so that others have no "difficulty acquiring the information," or fails the UTSA test of "reasonable efforts" in relation to "other persons who can obtain economic value" from the information, or fails to meet other requirements for protection,[280] then it

---

[274] For a discussion of injunctive relief, see § 3F[1].

[275] Engelhard Indus., Inc. v. Research Instrumental Corp., 324 F.2d 347, 353 (9th Cir. 1963).

[276] For a discussion of definitions of misappropriation, see § 3D[1].

[277] RESTATEMENT OF TORTS § 757, cmt. c. In such a case the actor is still subject to liability for harm caused by his disclosure of the secret.

[278] See RTE Corp. v. Coatings, Inc., 267 N.W.2d 226, 233–34 (Wis. 1978).

[279] See §§ 3C[2] and 3D[4].

[280] See discussion of requirements in § 3C[1].

is in the public domain and is completely unprotectable under trade secrets law's property principle.[281]

[3]   Reverse Engineering

Reverse engineering trade secrets from products obtained by proper means is a complete defense to a claim of trade secret misappropriation.[282] The Restatement lists "inspection or analysis of the commercial product embodying the secret" as an example of proper discovery means.[283] The UTSA Comment describes reverse engineering as:

> Starting with the known product and working backward to find the method by which it was developed. The acquisition of the known product must, of course, also be by a fair and honest means, such as purchase of the item on the open market for reverse engineering to be lawful.[284]

Defendants often assert that information "could have been" reverse engineered from a publicly available product and that no protectable trade secret exists.[285] This defense is rarely successful where nobody else has legitimately reverse-engineered the trade secret.[286] Even where others have successfully reverse-engineered the product, the courts often give primacy to trade secrets law's duty principle and enjoin the defendant from reaping the fruits of improper conduct.

[4]   Privilege

The Restatement provides that liability only exists where use or disclosure is not privileged[287] by the general need to promote a public interest or by an individual's need to defend against an infringement charge.[288] The paradigm of privilege is where a witness is compelled by law to disclose trade secrets in testimony.[289] This testimonial privilege does not protect a defendant from liability for breach of contract based on a voluntary disclosure, as an expert witness, in violation of a non-disclosure contract.[290]

---

[281] Any liability must be based either on the trade secrets law's duty principle or by reaching outside trade secrets law for broader equity principles. For a discussion of the duty and property principles, see § 3A.

[282] This is critical to the Supreme Court's *Kewanee* holding that federal patent law does not preempt trade secrets law. *See* Bonito Boats, Inc. v. Thunder Craft Boats, Inc., 489 U.S. 141, 156 (1989), discussed at § 1D[3][a][iv].

[283] RESTATEMENT OF TORTS § 757, cmt. a.

[284] UTSA Comment to § 1.

[285] *See, e.g.*, Electro-Craft Corp. v. Controlled Motion, 332 N.W.2d 890 (Minn. 1983): Minuteman, Inc. v. Alexander, 434 N.W.2d 773 (Wis. 1989); Sheridan v. Mallinckrodt, Inc., 568 F. Supp. 1347 (N.D.N.Y. 1983).

[286] For a discussion of ascertainability, see § 3C[1][c][iii].

[287] RESTATEMENT OF TORTS § 757.

[288] RESTATEMENT OF TORTS § 757, cmt. d.

[289] *Id.*

[290] ITT Telecom Products Corp. v. Dooley, 214 Cal. App. 3d 307 (1989).

[5]   Equitable Defenses

[a]   Unclean Hands

Under equity's morality-based principles, courts may deny relief to a claimant who has "unclean hands." Unclean hands includes willful and intentional deceit related to a trade secret claim or bad faith prosecution of a claim. In *A.H. Emery Co. v. Marcan Products Corp.*,[291] however, the negligent signing of an untrue oath on a patent application could have constituted unclean hands in connection with a patent infringement claim, but it was not sufficiently egregious or related to the trade secret claim to prevent relief.[292]

[b]   Laches

In *Anaconda Co. v. Metric Tool & Die Co.*, the court described the equitable laches defense in the usual way, as "inexcusable delay in instituting suit and prejudice resulting to the defendant from such delay," but it held that if the defendant was a conscious wrongdoer, "he can prevail only if the plaintiff's delay is so prolonged and inexcusable that it amounts to a virtual abandonment of the right by the plaintiff for a long period of time."[293] "Prejudice" to the defendant "must be more than the mere continued use of a misappropriated trade secret," but "the expansion of one's business and the expenditure of capital to undertake an activity" is sufficient.[294] After balancing the defendant's "conscious wrongdoing" against the plaintiff's "apparent acquiescence," the court denied a damage claim but granted a lead time injunction.[295]

[c]   Estoppel

Estoppel may also bar equitable relief. If a defendant changes its position to its detriment in reasonable reliance on the plaintiff's representation that no misappropriation claim will be made, then the plaintiff may be estopped from pursuing a claim.

§ 3F   REMEDIES

The Restatement states merely that a trade secret owner

> may recover damages for past harm, or be granted an injunction against future harm by disclosure or adverse use, or be granted an accounting of the wrongdoer's profits, or have the physical things embodying the secret

[291] A.H. Emery Co. v. Marcan Products Corp., 389 F.2d 11 (2d Cir. 1968).

[292] 389 F.2d 11, 17–18 (2d Cir. 1968). *See also* Ferroline Corp. v. General Aniline & Film Corp., 207 F.2d 912, 916 (7th Cir. 1953).

[293] 485 F. Supp. 410, 427 (E.D. Pa. 1980), *disapproved on other grounds*, Santana Products, Inc. v. Bobrick Washroom Equipment, Inc., 401 F.3d 123, 139–40 (3d Cir. 2005). For a discussion of the laches defense in patent cases, see § 2F[4][f].

[294] *Id.* at 429.

[295] *Id.* at 429–31.

. . . surrendered by the wrongdoer for destruction [and] may have two or more of these remedies in the same action.[296]

The UTSA and the Third Restatement have a much more detailed discussion of remedies than the Restatement, primarily because trade secrets remedies were an area of confusion and inconsistency under the Restatement.

[1] Injunctions

United States courts grant injunctive relief only when monetary damages are inadequate, but they traditionally issue injunctions in trade secret cases because trade secret rights can be destroyed by disclosure and the competitive advantage at stake may be immeasurable.

[a] Preliminary Injunctions

Injunctions to maintain the status quo between the parties during discovery and trial are common in trade secret cases.[297] The four traditional factors governing preliminary injunctions are likelihood of success on the merits, irreparable harm, balance of hardships, and the public interest.[298] Because public disclosure of a trade secret terminates its protectability, an imminent threat of disclosure constitutes irreparable injury.[299] However, "[w]here a misappropriator seeks only to use [the] secrets — without further dissemination or irreparable impairment of value — in pursuit of profit, . . . an award of damages will often provide a complete remedy."[300]

A preliminary injunction against disclosure or use need not set forth the trade secrets themselves, but must describe the restricted acts in "reasonable detail":[301]

Risk of harm . . . is not sufficient to satisfy the standard for granting a preliminary injunction. There must be an imminent threat of the allegedly harmful disclosure. . . . [I]njunctions will not be issued merely to allay the fears and apprehensions or to soothe the anxieties of the parties. Nor will

---

[296] RESTATEMENT OF TORTS § 757, cmt. e.

[297] *See* Salomon v. Hertz, 2 A. 379 (N.J. Eq. 1886) (preliminary injunction granted for technical business information). *See also* Dekar Industries, Inc. v. Bissett-Berman Corp., 434 F.2d 1304 (9th Cir. 1970); National Chemsearch Corp. of Missouri v. Schultz, 173 U.S.P.Q. 218 (D. Ind. 1972); Gillette Co. v. Williams, 360 F. Supp. 1171 (D. Conn. 1973).

[298] *See, e.g.*, Titan Tire Corp. v. Case New Holland, Inc., 566 F.3d 1372, 1375–76 (Fed. Cir. 2009), *citing* Winter v. Natural Resources Defense Council, Inc., 555 U.S. 7, 374 (2008); American Can Co. v. Mansukhani, 742 F.2d 314, 325 (7th Cir. 1984).

[299] *See, e.g.*, Bimbo Bakeries USA, Inc. v. Botticella, 613 F.3d 102, 118 (3d Cir. 2010); Faiveley Transport Malmo AB v. Wabtec Corp., 559 F.3d 110, 118 (2d Cir. 2009); FMC Corp. v. Varco International, Inc., 677 F.2d 500, 503 (5th Cir. 1982). *See also* UTSA § 2(a) ("Actual or threatened misappropriation may be enjoined."); RESTATEMENT (THIRD) OF UNFAIR COMPETITION § 44 cmt. c.

[300] *Faiveley*, 559 F.3d at 118–19.

[301] Dekar Industries, Inc. v. Bissett-Berman Corp., 434 F.2d 1304, 1306 (9th Cir. 1970).

an injunction be issued "to restrain one from doing what he is not attempting and does not intend to do."[302]

[b] Scope of Injunctions

Injunctions must generally be narrow, reaching only activities and information whose restriction is necessary to protect the threatened trade secrets.[303] An injunction's scope must balance the need to cover derivations from the original trade secrets[304] with the need to permit the defendant to use any information that is not a trade secret.

In *American Can Co. v. Mansukhani,*[305] an ink manufacturer sought to enjoin an ex-employee chemist from using secret formulas for printer ink. After reviewing the decisional law on injunction scope, the court of appeal held that "functional or practical similarity between its protected inks and the defendants new inks" could not be enjoined, even if the inks were similar in composition, because the ingredients themselves were widely known and were in the public domain, and the plaintiff's secret only covered the precise proportions of those ingredients.[306] The court noted that

> The owner of a trade secret is not entitled to prevent others from using public information to replicate his product, nor may the owner prevent others from making similar products which are not derived from the trade secret. Particularly in the case of a former employee, whose livelihood may well depend on the scope of the former employer's trade secret protection, it is important to permit the employee to use his or her skill, training and experience.[307]

Some courts will grant an injunction based on the "inevitability" of disclosure which would result from an employment relationship.[308] In the leading case, *Pepsico, Inc. v. Redmond,*[309] a competitor hired away an executive with intimate knowledge of plaintiff's strategic marketing plans. The plaintiff successfully argued that any decisions the executive would make in his new position would inevitably be influenced by his knowledge of the plaintiff's plans. As a result, the court of appeals affirmed an injunction preventing the executive from assuming his new position for six months. Other courts, however, have rejected the "inevitable disclosure"

---

[302] Continental Group, Inc. v. Amoco Chem. Corp., 614 F.2d 351, 358–59 (3d Cir. 1980) (citations omitted).

[303] Faiveley Transport Malmo AB v. Wabtec Corp., 559 F.3d 110, 119 (2d Cir. 2009) ("In all cases, the relief should be narrowly tailored to fit specific legal violations and to avoid unnecessary burdens on lawful commercial activity.") (internal quotes and citation omitted).

[304] For a discussion of modifications, see § 3D[5].

[305] 742 F.2d 314 (7th Cir. 1984).

[306] *Id.* at 326–27.

[307] *Id.* at 329.

[308] Bimbo Bakeries USA, Inc. v. Botticella, 613 F.3d 102, 110–12 (3d Cir. 2010). Air Products and Chemicals, Inc. v. Johnson, 442 A.2d 1114 (Pa. Super. Ct. 1982); FMC Corp. v. Varco International, Inc., 677 F.2d 500 (5th Cir. 1982). (*But see* Continental Group, Inc. v. Amoco Chem. Corp., 614 F.2d 351 (3d Cir. 1980)).

[309] 54 F.3d 1262 (7th Cir. 1995).

doctrine on the grounds that it gives the former employer the equivalent of a covenant not to compete without the necessity of having bargained for such an agreement.[310]

The UTSA provides that "[i]n appropriate circumstances, affirmative acts to protect a trade secret may be compelled by court order."[311] An "affirmative act" order may include "[m]andatory injunctions requiring that a misappropriator return the fruits of misappropriation to an aggrieved person," for example, "the return of stolen blueprints or the surrender of surreptitious photographs or recordings."[312]

[c]   Duration of Injunctions

Like trade secrets themselves, injunctions can theoretically last indefinitely, but questions about their duration and termination often arise because of the tendency for trade secrets, especially those that have been misappropriated, to lose their secrecy and protectability.

Post-Restatement common law cases split over whether injunctive relief should be available against a misappropriator if the secret became public after the misappropriation. The "*Shellmar* Rule"[313] called for injunctions whenever information was obtained by improper means, whereas the "*Conmar* Rule"[314] prohibited injunctions when the misappropriated information was public. Decisions to follow one or the other rule often depended on the question of who (owner, misappropriator or third person) had caused the trade secret to become public. Some decisions narrowed the split by granting limited "lead time" injunctions, intended to eliminate any competitive advantage that might otherwise result from the misappropriation.[315] Because the length of "lead time" gained may be indefinite, courts sometimes would issue a perpetual injunction and permit the defendant to apply to the court to have the injunction lifted if and when the information ceased to be secret.[316]

The UTSA adopts the "lead time" approach, stating that:

> An injunction shall be terminated when the trade secret has ceased to exist, but the injunction may be continued for an additional reasonable period of time in order to eliminate commercial advantage that otherwise would be derived from the misappropriation.[317]

The comment to this section explains:

---

[310] *See* Whyte v. Schlage Lock Co., 101 Cal. App. 4th 1443, 1461–63 (2002). *Accord*, LeJeune v. Coin Acceptors, Inc., 849 A.2d 451, 470–71 (Md. 2004); Kelly Services, Inc. v. Marzullo, 591 F. Supp. 2d 924, 941–43 (E.D. Mich. 2008).

[311] UTSA § 2(c).

[312] UTSA Comment to § 2.

[313] *See* Shellmar Products Co. v. Allen-Qualley Co., 87 F.2d 104 (7th Cir. 1937).

[314] *See* Conmar Products Corp. v. Universal Slide Fastener Co., 172 F.2d 150 (2d Cir. 1949).

[315] *See, e.g.*, Schreyer v. Casco Products Corp., 190 F.2d 921 (2d Cir. 1951).

[316] *See, e.g.*, Boeing Co. v. Sierracin Corp., 738 P.2d 665, 682 (Wash. 1987).

[317] UTSA § 2(a).

If a misappropriator either has not taken advantage of lead time or good faith competitors already have caught up with a misappropriator at the time that a case is decided, future disclosure and use of a former trade secret by a misappropriator will not damage a trade secret owner and no injunctive restraint of future disclosure and use is appropriate.[318]

In the case of a defendant's innocent reliance on the trade secrets, or other "exceptional circumstances," the UTSA provides that "an injunction may condition future use upon payment of a reasonable royalty for no longer than the period of time for which use could have been prohibited."[319]

[2] Damages

[a] Compensatory Damages

Prerequisite to any damage recovery, misappropriated trade secrets must be not merely known but "used," which can mean not only embodiment in a product, but also acceleration of a product's development,[320] solicitation of sales and service contracts,[321] or any activity which unjustly enriches another party or causes economic detriment to the trade secrets owner.[322]

[i] Calculation of Damages

Calculation of damages under the common law of trade secrets has gone through various permutations. Prominent decisions have allowed recovery of plaintiff's lost profits (including certain fixed costs),[323] recovery of defendant's profits,[324] and recovery of both plaintiff's lost profits and defendant's profits,[325] taking care to prevent double recovery.[326] Some states allow recovery of the greater of the two measures, illicit profits and damages.

The UTSA uses both measures but attempts to avoid double recovery, stating that "[d]amages can include both the actual loss caused by misappropriation and the unjust enrichment caused by misappropriation that is not taken into account in computing actual loss."[327] If the plaintiff meets the burden of proving the fact of damages, the burden shifts to the defendant to show that no part of its profits is attributable to the trade secret.[328] If the amount of damages is uncertain, a jury's

---

[318] UTSA Comment to § 2.

[319] UTSA § 2(b).

[320] Engelhard Indus., Inc. v. Research Instrumental Corp., 324 F.2d 347, 353 (9th Cir. 1963).

[321] University Computing Co. v. Lykes-Youngstown Corp., 504 F.2d 518, 540–42 (5th Cir. 1974).

[322] Von Brimer v. Whirlpool Corp., 367 F. Supp. 740, 743 (N.D. Cal. 1973), *modified*, 536 F.2d 838 (8th Cir. 1976).

[323] Sperry-Rand Corp. v. A-T-O, Inc., 447 F.2d 1387, 1392–94 (4th Cir. 1971).

[324] International Industries v. Warren Petroleum Corp., 248 F.2d 696, 699, *reh'g denied*, 248 F.2d 696 (3d Cir. 1957).

[325] Clark v. Bunker, 453 F.2d 1006, 1011 (9th Cir. 1972).

[326] Telex Corp. v. International Business Mach. Corp., 510 F.2d 894, 930–33 (10th Cir. 1975).

[327] UTSA § 3.

[328] Jet Spray Cooler, Inc. v. Crampton, 385 N.E.2d 1349, 1358 n.14 (Mass. 1979).

estimate will receive great deference.[329] Evidence of the amount of damages can be evaluated at a special hearing,[330] by a special master,[331] or at a separate trial.[332]

The UTSA provides, as an alternative measure of damages, a reasonable royalty to be paid for the defendant's use or disclosure of the trade secret.[333]

[ii] Effect of Public Disclosure

Under trade secret law, damages are generally not recoverable for activities occurring after the misappropriated trade secret enters the public domain, but damages may be recoverable for any unjust enrichment caused by the misappropriator's wrongfully acquired "head start" in understanding and using the (former) trade secret.[334]

A Restatement provision that one may be liable for procuring by improper means any business information, whether or not a trade secret,[335] has been applied to award post-publication damages for formerly secret information,[336] and for information that had not qualified as a trade secret at the time it was improperly acquired.[337]

The UTSA allows monetary recovery only for the period during which information is protectable, plus the value of any lead-time advantage.[338]

[b] Punitive Damages

Punitive damages are available for willful and wanton tortious acts. Courts have found malicious breach of trade secret contracts to be tortious breaches of a confidential relationship,[339] and have awarded punitive damages for "willful and malicious misappropriation."[340] The UTSA limits punitive damages to an amount

---

[329] *In re* Innovative Const. Systems, Inc., 793 F.2d 875, 887–88 (7th Cir. 1985).

[330] *See, e.g.*, K-2 Ski Co. v. Head Ski Co., Inc., 506 F.2d 471 (9th Cir. 1974).

[331] International Industries v. Warren Petroleum Corp., 248 F.2d 696, *reh'g denied*, 248 F.2d 696 (3d Cir. 1957).

[332] Rohm & Haas Co. v. AZS Corp., 229 U.S.P.Q. 399 (N.D. Ga. 1986) (bifurcated for trial but not discovery).

[333] UTSA § 3(a). This alternative was added as part of the 1985 Amendments. For a discussion of the 1985 Amendments, see § 3B[4]. *See* Storagecraft Technology Corp. v. Kirby, 744 F.3d 1183 (10th Cir. 2014) (identifying three possible measures of damages under the UTSA: (1) defendant's unjust enrichment; (2) plaintiff's actual loss; and (3) reasonable royalties).

[334] Schreyer v. Casco Products Corp., 190 F.2d 921 (2d Cir. 1951); Engelhard Industries, Inc. v. Research Instrumental Corp., 324 F.2d 347, 353 (9th Cir. 1963); Molinaro v. Burnbaum, 201 U.S.P.Q. 83 (D. Mass. 1977), *damage accounting settled*, 201 U.S.P.Q. 150 (D. Mass. 1978).

[335] RESTATEMENT OF TORTS § 759, cmt. b.

[336] Crocan Corp. v. Sheller-Globe Corp., 385 F. Supp. 251, 255 (N.D. Ill. 1974).

[337] Nucor Corp. v. Tennessee Forging Steel Service, Inc., 476 F.2d 386 (8th Cir. 1973).

[338] UTSA § 2(b).

[339] *See* Cherne Indus., Inc. v. Grounds & Associates, Inc., 278 N.W.2d 81 (Minn. 1979); Crutcher-Rolfs-Cummings, Inc. v. Ballard, 540 S.W.2d 380, 388 (Tex. App. 1976).

[340] *See, e.g.*, Boeing Co. v. Sierracin Corp, 738 P.2d 665 (Wash. 1987); Aries Information Systems, Inc. v. Pacific Management Systems Corp., 366 N.W.2d 366 (Minn. Ct. App. 1985).

not exceeding twice the compensatory damage award.[341]

[3] Attorney Fees and Court Costs

Most states follow the "American Rule" that parties should generally pay their own attorneys' fees, but awards in trade secret cases are sometimes made, for example, in cases of blatantly "oppressive and bad faith conduct."[342]

The UTSA provides that:

> If (i) a claim of misappropriation is made in bad faith, (ii) a motion to terminate an injunction is made or resisted in bad faith, (iii) willful and malicious misappropriation exists, the court may award reasonable attorney's fees to the prevailing party.[343]

The accompanying Comment states that this remedy is available for its deterrent value and allows the judge to determine whether attorney's fees should be awarded even if the trial is to a jury.[344]

[4] Seizure of Embodiments

Where trade secret theft involves tangible embodiments of the secrets, state replevin statutes can be used to remove the embodiments from the control of the misappropriator and put them under the control of the owner or of a neutral third party. A trade secret violation may form the basis of a United States International Trade Commission exclusion or cease and desist order.[345]

[5] Criminal Penalties

Neither the UTSA nor the Restatement addresses criminal penalties for trade secret misappropriation. Criminal penalties for trade secret misappropriation may be available through (1) statutes specifically designed to cover trade secrets[346] or (2) statutes generally covering property misappropriation. The former were enacted to overcome the actual and potential deficiencies of the latter, but the more general statutes may reach more broadly if it is established that trade secrets are "property" within the meaning of the relevant statute.[347]

---

[341] UTSA § 3(b).

[342] Sperry-Rand v. Electronic Concepts, Inc., 325 F. Supp. 1209, 1219 (E.D. Va. 1970), *vacated on other grounds, sub nom.* Sperry Rand v. A-T-O, Inc., 447 F.2d 1387 (4th Cir. 1971).

[343] UTSA § 4.

[344] UTSA Comment to § 4.

[345] *See, e.g.,* Viscofan, S.A. v. U.S. Int'l Trade Comm'n, 787 F.2d 544 (Fed. Cir. 1986). For a discussion of International Trade Commission proceedings involving patents, see § 2E[2][b][ii].

[346] *See, e.g.,* 18 U.S.C. § 1905 (prohibiting unauthorized disclosure of confidential information, including trade secrets, by a government employee). As of 1996, at least 24 states had criminal statutes directed at the theft of trade secrets. James H.A. Pooley, *et al., Understanding the Economic Espionage Act of 1996,* 5 Tex. Intell. Prop. L.J. 177, 186 (1997).

[347] *But see* Dowling v. United States, 473 U.S. 207 (1985) (holding that National Stolen Property Act is limited to theft of tangible property, and does not include intellectual property); United States v. Brown, 925 F.2d 1301 (10th Cir. 1995) (same).

The Economic Espionage Act of 1996 ("EEA") is a criminal statute under which the United States Attorney General is authorized to bring criminal and civil actions.[348] The EEA has eight substantive provisions and one definition section. The first two provisions lay out the elements of culpable offenses and the remaining six are remedial and procedural. Section 1831 deals with economic espionage, while Section 1832 covers the theft of a trade secret. The elements of economic espionage include the purposeful or knowing misappropriation of a trade secret, for the benefit of a foreign government, instrumentality, or agent.[349] The elements of theft of a trade secret include the purposeful or knowing misappropriation of a trade secret for the benefit of someone other than the trade secret owner, that harms the economic interest of the owner.[350] Both provisions also impose liability for attempt and conspiracy.[351]

The EEA also includes remedial and jurisdictional provisions. Available remedies include criminal sentencing, forfeiture of property or profits earned by the defendant,[352] and injunctions against conduct illegal under the Act.[353] Federal district courts have exclusive original jurisdiction, and this jurisdiction applies extraterritorially to acts committed overseas by citizens or permanent residents of the United States, or if an act in furtherance of the offense was committed in the United States.[354] The Act also requires the court to ensure the confidentiality of trade secrets that are the subject of controversy in a case.[355] Finally, given the high-profile nature of the cases, Congress required the Department of Justice to pursue these actions only upon review and authorization by the Attorney General. In 2002, Attorney General Ashcroft approved the continued enforcement of the Act, but required his authorization only for claims brought under Section 1831, not under Section 1832. This difference represents the potential effects of Section 1831 claims on foreign sovereigns and is an explanation for why there are so few indictments under Section 1831.[356]

---

[348] 18 U.S.C. §§ 1831–1839 (2009).

[349] 18 U.S.C. § 1831.

[350] 18 U.S.C. § 1832. *See* United States v. Hsu, 155 F. 3d 189, 195–96 (3d Cir. 1998).

[351] 18 U.S.C. § 1831(a)(4),(5); 18 U.S.C. § 1832(a)(4),(5). *See Hsu*, 155 F.3d at 203 (government may prove attempt "by proving beyond a reasonable doubt that the defendant sought to acquire information which he or she believed to be a trade secret, regardless of whether the information actually qualified as such.").

[352] 18 U.S.C. § 1834.

[353] 18 U.S.C. § 1836.

[354] 18 U.S.C. § 1837.

[355] 18 U.S.C. § 1835.

[356] The only reported Court of Appeal decision concerning section 1831 is United States v. Ye, 436 F.3d 1117 (9th Cir. 2006). Leading cases concerning section 1832 are United States v. Yang, 281 F.3d 534 (6th Cir. 2002); United States v. Krumrei, 258 F.3d 535 (6th Cir. 2001); United States v. Martin, 228 F.3d 1 (1st Cir. 2000); and United States v. Hsu, 155 F.3d 189 (3d Cir. 1998).

Chapter 4

COPYRIGHT

SYNOPSIS

§ 4A   INTRODUCTION

§ 4B   HISTORICAL DEVELOPMENT

    [1]   English Antecedents

    [2]   Copyright in the United States

        [a]   1790 to 1909

        [b]   The 1909 Act

        [c]   The 1976 Act to Today

§ 4C   COPYRIGHTABLE SUBJECT MATTER

    [1]   Originality

        [a]   Constitutional Standard

        [b]   Words and Short Phrases

        [c]   Photographs

        [d]   Aesthetic Non-Discrimination

    [2]   Fixation

        [a]   Background: *White-Smith v. Apollo*

        [b]   The 1976 Act

         [i]   Video Games

         [ii]   Random-Access Memory

        [c]   Live Broadcasts and Transmissions

        [d]   Live Performances

    [3]   Idea and Expression

        [a]   General Principle

        [b]   *Baker v. Selden*

        [c]   The Merger Doctrine

        [d]   *Scènes à Faire*

    [4]   Works of Authorship

        [a]   Statutory Categories

         [i]   Literary Works

          (a)   Characters

         (b)   Computer Programs

[ii]　Musical Works

[iii]　Dramatic Works

[iv]　Pantomimes and Choreographic Works

[v]　Pictorial, Graphic, and Sculptural Works

　(a)　Generally

　(b)　Useful Articles

　(1)　Historical Development

　(2)　Statutory Definition

　(3)　Separability

[vi]　Motion Pictures and Other Audiovisual Works

[vii]　Sound Recordings

[viii]　Architectural Works

　(a)　Pre-1991 Law

　(b)　Architectural Works Copyright Protection Act

[b]　Works Employing Preexisting Material

[i]　Compilations and Collective Works

[ii]　Derivative Works

[5]　Government Works

[6]　National Eligibility

§ 4D　FORMALITIES

[1]　Publication

[a]　Publication Under the 1909 Act

[b]　Publication Under the 1976 Act

[2]　Notice

[a]　Notice Under the 1909 Act

[b]　Notice Under the 1976 Act

[i]　Omission of Notice

[ii]　Errors in Notice

[iii]　Collective Works

[c]　Notice After the Berne Convention Implementation Act

[3]　Deposit and Registration

[a]　Deposit of Copies

[b]　Registration

§ 4E　DURATION, RENEWAL, AND RESTORATION

[1]　Duration

[2]　Renewal of Copyright in Pre-1978 Works

[a]　Basic Renewal Principles

[b]　Renewal and Derivative Works

[c]　Automatic Renewal

    [3]   Restoration of Copyright in Foreign Works

§ 4F   OWNERSHIP, TRANSFERS, AND TERMINATIONS

    [1]   Initial Ownership

        [a]   Works for Hire

          [i]   The 1909 Act

          [ii] The 1976 Act

        [b]   Joint Works

          [i]   The 1909 Act

          [ii] The 1976 Act

        [c]   Collective Works

    [2]   Transfers and Licenses

    [3]   Termination of Transfers

        [a]   Persons Entitled to Terminate

        [b]   Time Periods for Termination and Notice

        [c]   Effect of Termination

        [d]   Agreements to the Contrary

§ 4G   EXCLUSIVE RIGHTS AND LIMITATIONS

    [1]   Reproduction

        [a]   In General

        [b]   Electronic Reproduction

        [c]   Exceptions and Limitations

    [2]   Preparation of Derivative Works

        [a]   In General

        [b]   Exceptions and Limitations

    [3]   Public Distribution

        [a]   In General

        [b]   Electronic Distribution

        [c]   First-Sale Doctrine

        [d]   Import and Export Rights

    [4]   Public Performance

        [a]   In General

        [b]   Secondary Transmissions

          [i]   The 1909 Act

          [ii] The 1976 Act

        [c]   Exceptions and Limitations

        [d]   Performing Rights Organizations

    [5]   Public Display

    [6]   Digital Audio Transmission

    [7]   Moral Rights

    [a] In General

    [b] Visual Artists Rights Act

  [8] Additional Rights

  [9] Compulsory Licenses

§ 4H INFRINGEMENT

  [1] Ownership of a Valid Copyright

  [2] Derivation or Copying

    [a] Access

    [b] Probative Similarity

  [3] Substantial Similarity

    [a] Protected Expression

      [i] Dissection

      [ii] Distinguishing Idea from Expression

      [iii] Abstraction-Filtration-Comparison

    [b] Ordinary Observer Test

    [c] *De Minimis* Use

§ 4I SECONDARY LIABILITY

  [1] In General

    [a] Contributory Infringement

    [b] Vicarious Liability

  [2] Providing Copying Devices or Software

    [a] The *Sony* Decision

    [b] Audio Home Recording Act

    [c] Peer-to-Peer File Sharing

  [3] Secondary Liability and the Internet

    [a] In General

    [b] Limitation of Liability for Online Service Providers

      [i] Safe Harbors

        (a) Transitory Digital Network Communications

        (b) System Caching

        (c) Web Hosting

        (d) Information Location Tools

      [ii] Eligibility for Safe Harbors

      [iii] Notice-and-Take-Down Provisions

  [4] Digital Millennium Copyright Act

    [a] Anti-Circumvention

      [i] In General

        (a) Ownership of a Valid Copyright

        (b) Access-Control Measures

　　　　(c)　Circumvention

　　　　(d)　Authorization

　　　　(e)　Facilitation of Infringement

　　　　(f)　Design, Use and Marketing of Technology

　　　[ii]　Statutory Exceptions

　　　[iii]　Regulatory Exceptions

　　　[iv]　Other Defenses

　　[b]　Copyright Management Information

§ 4J　FAIR USE AND OTHER DEFENSES

　[1]　Fair Use

　　[a]　Preamble

　　[b]　Factors

　　　[i]　Purpose and Character of the Use

　　　　(a)　Transformative Use

　　　　(b)　Commercial Use

　　　　(c)　Educational Use

　　　　(d)　Good Faith

　　　[ii]　Nature of the Copyrighted Work

　　　[iii]　Amount and Substantiality of the Use

　　　[iv]　Effect on Potential Market

　　[c]　Examples

　　　[i]　Comment and Criticism

　　　[ii]　Parody and Satire

　　　[iii]　News Reporting and Documentaries

　　　[iv]　Litigation Uses

　　　[v]　Reverse Engineering

　　　[vi]　Personal Uses

　　　[vii]　Internet and Database Uses

　[2]　Other Defenses

　　[a]　Inequitable Conduct

　　[b]　Misuse

　　[c]　Statute of Limitations

　　[d]　Laches and Estoppel

　　[e]　Abandonment and Forfeiture

§ 4K　REMEDIES

　[1]　In General

　[2]　Injunctions

　　[a]　Preliminary Injunctions

　　[b]　Permanent Injunctions

[3]   **Impoundment and Disposition**

[4]   **Monetary Remedies**

   [a]   **In General**

   [b]   **Damages and Profits**

    [i]   **Actual Damages**

     (a)   **Lost Profits**

     (b)   **Value of Use**

     (c)   **Consequential Damages**

    [ii]   **Infringer's Profits**

     (a)   **In General**

     (b)   **Indirect Profits**

     (c)   **Apportionment**

   [c]   **Statutory Damages**

    [i]   **Number of Works Infringed**

    [ii]   **Defendant's Intent**

    [iii]   **Amount of Award**

    [iv]   **Constitutionality**

[5]   **Costs and Attorney's Fees**

[6]   **Criminal Penalties**

§ 4A   INTRODUCTION

Copyright law protects original works of authorship that are fixed in a tangible medium of expression. Copyrightable subject matter includes literature, music, drama, choreography, the visual arts, movies, sound recordings, architecture, and computer programs. Copyright arises automatically when an author creates a work and generally lasts for the author's life plus 70 years after the author's death.

Copyright law confers exclusive rights to reproduce the work, to prepare derivative works based on the work, to distribute copies or phonorecords of the work, and to publicly perform or publicly display the work. Copyright protects only the original expression of ideas contained in a work, and not the ideas themselves, and it confers no rights over the independent creation and dissemination of similar works. A non-literal paraphrase or modified version of a work may infringe a copyright, but only if it is substantially similar in expression to the copyrighted work. The doctrine of "fair use" permits the use of some copyrightable expression when doing so would encourage the creation of new works of authorship without significantly harming the market for the original work or licensed derivatives.

The United States Constitution authorizes Congress "[t]o Promote the Progress of Science and useful Arts, by securing for limited Times to Authors and Inventors the exclusive Right to their respective Writings and Discoveries."[1] The grammar of

---

[1] U.S. Const., Art. I, § 8, cl. 8.

the clause indicates that copyrights are granted to "Authors" for their "Writings" in order "to Promote the Progress of Science."[2] In the 18th Century, "science" meant "knowledge" in general, while "progress" meant both "advancement" in the qualitative sense and "spread" in the geographic sense.[3] In other words, copyright law serves to encourage "the creation and spread of knowledge and learning," in the form of new works of authorship.[4] This utilitarian view of copyright is confirmed in Supreme Court case law:

> The monopoly privileges that Congress may authorize are neither unlimited nor primarily designed to provide a special private benefit. Rather, the limited grant is a means by which an important public purpose may be achieved. It is intended to motivate the creative activity of authors and inventors by the provision of a special reward, and to allow the public access to the products of their genius after the limited period of exclusive control has expired.[5]

The Supreme Court has held that copyright is exclusively statutory, and that there is no common-law right to prevent copying of a work after it has been published.[6] In continental European countries, however, copyright is seen as a natural right of the author. Indeed, most European countries use the term "author's rights" rather than "copyright."[7] In recent years, the "natural right" model of copyright has gained influence as the United States has moved closer to a European model of copyright in the interests of international harmonization.

§ 4B   HISTORICAL DEVELOPMENT

[1]   English Antecedents

Copyright law evolved in England out of efforts by the Crown to control the use of the printing press by granting a monopoly on publishing to the Stationers' Company, a group of London printers and booksellers who were required to submit their publications for approval by official censors. To prevent competition among themselves, the Stationers devised a system of registration, under which no member would reproduce a book that had been registered to another. Once secured by registration, the right to print a book continued forever and could be bequeathed or sold, but only to other members of the guild.[8]

Under a series of licensing acts, no book could be printed in England unless it had first been registered with the Stationers. In 1695, the last licensing act expired,

---

[2] *See* Eldred v. Ashcroft, 537 U.S. 186, 212 (2003).

[3] *See* Malla Pollack, *What is Congress Supposed to Promote? Defining "Progress" in Article I, Section 8, Clause 8 of the Constitution*, 80 NEB. L. REV. 754 (2001).

[4] Golan v. Holder, 132 S. Ct. 873, 888 (2012).

[5] Sony Corp. of America v. Universal City Studios, Inc., 464 U.S. 417, 429 (1984). *See also* Twentieth Century Music Corp. v. Aiken, 422 U.S. 151, 156 (1975).

[6] *See* Wheaton v. Peters, 33 U.S. 591, 657–62 (1834).

[7] In France, *droit d'auteur*; in Germany, *Urheberrecht*; and in Spain, *derecho de autor*.

[8] *See* L. RAY PATTERSON, COPYRIGHT IN HISTORICAL PERSPECTIVE 20–56 (1968).

throwing the book trade into disarray. The Stationers petitioned Parliament for relief, seeking a statute under which authors would have the exclusive right to print their works — an exclusive right that could be transferred to a publisher and owned in perpetuity. Parliament responded by enacting the first modern copyright statute, the Statute of Anne, in 1710.[9] It granted to authors the exclusive right to publish their works for an initial term of 14 years, renewable for an additional 14 years.[10] After that, the work entered the public domain, meaning that anyone was free to copy or publish it.

At first, the Stationers simply ignored the term-limit provision and continued to buy and sell copyrights as if they were still perpetual. But as the terms of copyright began to expire, Scottish booksellers began publishing competing reprints, igniting a great debate in England concerning the nature of literary property. The Stationers argued that an author had a natural right of property in his works that passed to the publisher when the manuscript was purchased. Under this view, the Statute of Anne merely provided supplemental remedies to an underlying common-law right that was perpetual.[11] In 1774, however, in the landmark decision of *Donaldson v. Beckett*, the House of Lords rejected the claim of perpetual common-law copyright and established that copyright was limited in term under the Statute of Anne.[12]

[2]   Copyright in the United States

In the United States, copyright law evolved through three major eras: (1) from adoption of the Constitution to enactment of the 1909 Act; (2) the 1909 Act; and (3) the current Copyright Act of 1976.

[a]   1790 to 1909

In 1790, the first Congress enacted a statute granting copyright protection to "maps, charts, and books," for a period of 14 years, which could be renewed once for another 14 years if the author was still alive at the end of the first term. The 1790 Act also required that a work be registered before it was published in order to secure copyright protection. Except for the addition of maps and charts, the 1790 Act was copied almost verbatim from the Statute of Anne.

In 1831, at the instigation of Noah Webster,[13] Congress enacted a new Copyright Act, which extended copyright to musical compositions for the first time, along with prints and engravings, in addition to maps, charts, and books. The initial term was extended to 28 years, while the 14-year renewal term was made available to an author's heirs.

---

[9] *See* Tyler T. Ochoa & Mark Rose, *The Anti-Monopoly Origins of the Patent and Copyright Clause*, 49 J. COPYR. SOC'Y USA 675, 680–82 (2001).

[10] 8 Anne c. 19 § 1 (1710).

[11] *See* MARK ROSE, AUTHORS AND OWNERS: THE INVENTION OF COPYRIGHT 69–78 (1993); Patterson, at 158–68.

[12] 4 Burr. 2408, 98 Eng. Rep. 257 (H.L. 1774). *See also* Ochoa & Rose, at 682–84.

[13] *See* Tyler T. Ochoa & Mark Rose, *The Anti-Monopoly Origins of the Patent and Copyright Clause*, 49 J. COPYR. SOC'Y USA 675, 697–99 (2001).

Three years later, the Supreme Court ruled in *Wheaton v. Peters* that an author did *not* have a common-law right to control reproduction after the first publication of the work, and that strict compliance with statutory formalities was required to recover under the federal statute.[14] Thus, *Wheaton* recognized a dual system of copyright protection: before a work was published, it was protected by common-law copyright, which provided a right of first publication of potentially unlimited duration. When a work was published, however, one of two things happened: if the statutory formalities (such as registration and notice) were satisfied, the work received a federal statutory copyright of limited duration; but if the formalities were not observed, the work entered the public domain.

In 1870, Congress revised and codified the patent and copyright laws. Among other provisions, the 1870 Act extended copyright to paintings, drawings, statues, and other works of the fine arts; and it centralized registration of copyright in the Library of Congress. In 1891, Congress extended copyright to citizens of other countries, provided those countries had reciprocal copyright relations with the United States. However, the copyright owner still had to register the copyright before the work was published.

[b]   The 1909 Act

In 1909, Congress enacted a comprehensive new copyright law. Section 4 provided that "the works for which copyright may be secured under this Act shall include all the writings of an author." Although this language was identical to that used in the Constitution, courts held that the statutory definition of "writings" was narrower than the constitutional definition, and that there were types of works that could constitutionally be included but were not.[15] Section 5 of the 1909 Act listed 11 categories of works for purposes of registration, including books, periodicals, dramatic compositions, musical compositions, maps, works of art, photographs, and pictorial illustrations. Motion pictures were added in 1912; and sound recordings were added in 1972.

Instead of requiring registration before publication, the 1909 Act granted federal statutory copyright when a work was published with proper copyright notice. However, registration was still required before a copyright owner could file an infringement action, and registration of the initial 28-year term was required in order to register and obtain the 28-year renewal term. The 1909 Act retained a dual system of protection, under which unpublished works were protected by common-law copyright under state law; but the Act also allowed certain unpublished works to be registered, in order to obtain federal protection. If a work was published without proper notice, it entered the public domain.

The 1909 Act continues to govern copyrights that were obtained by publication or registration prior to 1978, subject to some important changes (such as duration and renewal) made in the 1976 Act and later. Because some copyrights obtained

---

[14] 33 U.S. 591, 657–58, 661–62 (1834). *See also* Ochoa & Rose, at 699–701.

[15] *Cf.* Mazer v. Stein, 347 U.S. 201, 210 (1954) ("Some writers interpret this section as being co-extensive with the constitutional grant, but the House Report, while inconclusive, indicates that it was 'declaratory of existing law' only.").

under the 1909 Act will endure until December 31, 2072, knowledge of the 1909 Act remains important today.

[c]   The 1976 Act to Today

In 1976, Congress replaced the 1909 Act with a new Copyright Act, which went into effect on January 1, 1978. The 1976 Act made a number of fundamental changes in copyright law. First, it extended federal statutory copyright protection to unpublished as well as published works, restricting state common-law copyright protection to works not yet fixed in a tangible medium of expression. Second, it altered the basic copyright term to provide protection for the life of the author plus 50 years after the author's death.[16] Congress also codified a number of important case-law doctrines, including the idea-expression dichotomy and the fair-use doctrine.

Effective March 1, 1989, the United States joined the Berne Convention, the major international treaty concerning copyright protection. To do so, Congress eliminated the requirement of notice on all published copies of the work, and it eliminated the requirement of registration before filing suit for works of foreign origin. However, for all works, registration is still required in order to obtain statutory damages or attorney's fees. Adherence to the Berne Convention also prompted additional changes: the Architectural Works Protection Copyright Act of 1990; the Visual Artists Rights Act of 1990 (effective June 1, 1991), enacting a limited form of moral rights protection; and the 1994 "restoration" of copyrights in certain works of foreign origin that had entered the public domain for failure to comply with U.S. formalities.

In 1998, Congress enacted two major pieces of legislation: the Digital Millennium Copyright Act of 1998, which added measures prohibiting the circumvention of technological protection measures and the removal of copyright management information (codified in Chapter 12), and limited the liability of Internet service providers; and the Sonny Bono Copyright Term Extension Act of 1998, which added 20 years to the terms of all existing and future copyrights.

§ 4C   COPYRIGHTABLE SUBJECT MATTER

Section 102(a) defines copyrightable subject matter: "Copyright protection subsists . . . in original works of authorship fixed in any tangible medium of expression . . . ." This section sets forth two basic conditions of copyrightability: a work must be (1) original, and (2) fixed in a tangible medium of expression. The scope of copyright protection, however, is limited by section 102(b), which codifies the principle that copyright protects only the original *expression* of ideas, not the ideas themselves. In addition, a work must fall within the constitutional and statutory definitions of a work of authorship.

---

[16] The two-term structure was retained for existing copyrights, however, with the renewal term extended to 47 years, for a maximum duration of 75 years from first publication.

[1] Originality

[a] Constitutional Standard

"To qualify for copyright protection, a work must be original to the author."[17] In codifying copyright law in the 1976 Act, Congress purposely left the standard of "originality" undefined.[18] In its landmark decision in *Feist Publications, Inc. v. Rural Telephone Service Co.*, however, the U.S. Supreme Court emphasized that "[o]riginality is a constitutional requirement," and it held that

> Original, as the term is used in copyright, means only that the work was independently created by the author (as opposed to copied from other works), and that it possesses at least some minimal degree of creativity.[19]

Prior to *Feist*, a number of courts had held that directories were copyrightable *per se*, under a theory of "industrious collection" or "sweat of the brow," under which "copyright was a reward for the hard work that went into compiling facts."[20] The Supreme Court rejected the "sweat of the brow" doctrine in *Feist*, holding that "copyright rewards originality, not effort."[21]

Feist emphasized that "originality does not signify novelty; a work may be original even though it closely resembles other works so long as the similarity is fortuitous, not the result of copying."[22] The court cited Judge Learned Hand's famous dictum: "if by some magic a man who had never known it were to compose anew Keats's *Ode on a Grecian Urn*, he would be an 'author,' and, if he copyrighted it, others might not copy that poem, though they might of course copy Keats's."[23] Of course, independent creation of a complex, fanciful work, such as Keats's *Ode*, is so highly improbable that courts can, and do, consider evidence of prior similar works in deciding whether the plaintiff's work is original.[24] Nevertheless, evidence of prior

---

[17] Feist Publications, Inc. v. Rural Telephone Service Co., 499 U.S. 340, 346 (1991).

[18] *See* H.R. Rep. No. 94-1476, at 51 (1976) ("the phrase 'original works of authorship,' which is purposely left undefined, is intended to incorporate without change the standard of originality established by the courts under the present copyright statute. This standard does not include requirements of novelty, ingenuity, or aesthetic merit, and there is no intention to enlarge the standards of copyright protection to require them.").

[19] 499 U.S. 340, 345 (1991).

[20] 499 U.S. at 352, citing Leon v. Pacific Telephone & Telegraph Co., 91 F.2d 484 (9th Cir. 1937); Jeweler's Circular Publishing Co. v. Keystone Publishing Co., 281 F. 83 (2d Cir. 1922).

[21] 499 U.S. at 364; *see also id.* at 352–54.

[22] *Id.* at 346. *See also* Alfred Bell & Co., Ltd. v. Catalda Fine Arts, Inc., 191 F.2d 99, 102 (2d Cir. 1951) (noting the ambiguity of the word "original"; "It may mean startling, novel or unusual, a marked departure from the past. . . . [However,] 'Original' in reference to a copyrighted work means that the particular work 'owes its origin' to the 'author.' No large measure of novelty is necessary."); Baltimore Orioles, Inc. v. Major League Baseball Players Ass'n, 805 F.2d 663, 668 n.6 (7th Cir. 1986) ("It is important to distinguish among three separate concepts — originality, creativity, and novelty. A work is original if it is the independent creation of its author. A work is creative if it embodies some modest amount of intellectual labor. A work is novel if it differs from existing works in some relevant respect. For a work to be copyrightable, it must be original and creative, but need not be novel.").

[23] Sheldon v. Metro-Goldwyn Pictures Co., 81 F.2d 49, 54 (2d Cir. 1936), *aff'd*, 309 U.S. 390 (1940).

[24] *See, e.g.*, Peters v. West, 692 F.3d 629, 635–36 (7th Cir. 2012) (prior use of saying "what does not kill me, makes me stronger"); Acuff-Rose Music, Inc. v. Jostens, Inc., 155 F.3d 140, 144 (2d Cir. 1998)

similar works will not always negate a finding of originality.[25]

Feist also states that "the requisite level of creativity is extremely low; even a slight amount will suffice. The vast majority of works make the grade quite easily, as they possess some creative spark, 'no matter how crude, humble or obvious' it might be."[26] For example, the fact that a plaintiff's work was "filled with generalizations, platitudes, and observations of the obvious," contained "not-so-stunning revelation[s]," and at its "creative zenith" taught "common-sense communication skills," did not render the work unoriginal.[27] However, although "[t]he standard of originality is low, . . . it does exist."[28] Thus, in *Feist* itself, the court held that the telephone white pages, listing names, addresses, and telephone numbers in alphabetical order by last name, was "devoid of even the slightest trace of creativity."[29]

[b]   Words and Short Phrases

Words and short phrases do not contain enough creative expression to be copyrightable works of authorship.[30] Similarly, very short musical phrases and simple geometric shapes are not protected,[31] although original combinations of these elements can be protected.[32] These exclusions encourage the creation of new

---

("prior usage of the saying was sufficiently widespread as to make it exceedingly unlikely" that plaintiff originated the phrase "You've got to stand for something or you'll fall for anything"); Meade v. United States, 27 Fed. Cl. 367, 372 (1992) (relying on evidence that similar works "have existed for centuries").

[25] *See, e.g.*, Fred Fisher, Inc. v. Dillingham, 298 F. 145 (S.D.N.Y. 1924). In *Dillingham*, Judge Hand held that a musical phrase, an "ostinato" or constantly repeated figure accompanying the melody in the copyrighted work, plaintiff's "Dardanella," was original and infringed by the accompaniment in the accused work, defendant's "Kalua," even though the exact same phrase appeared in several prior published musical works. Judge Hand found that the plaintiff was unaware of the prior musical compositions, and that the defendant, at least unconsciously, copied the plaintiff's work, with which he was familiar.

[26] Feist Publications, Inc. v. Rural Telephone Service Co., 499 U.S. 340, 345 (1991).

[27] Situation Mgmt. Systems, Inc. v. ASP Consulting LLC, 560 F.3d 53, 60 (1st Cir. 2009).

[28] *Feist*, 499 U.S. at 362.

[29] For more on *Feist*, see § 4C[4][b][i].

[30] 37 C.F.R. § 202.1(a) ("The following are examples of works not subject to copyright . . . : (a) Words and short phrases such as names, titles, and slogans"); Acuff-Rose Music, Inc. Jostens, Inc., 155 F.3d 140 (2d Cir. 1998) (song title "You've Got to Stand for Something"); Alberto-Culver Co. v. Andrea Dumon, Inc., 466 F.2d 705 (7th Cir. 1972) (slogan "most personal sort of deodorant"); *but see* Heim v. Universal Pictures Corp., 154 F.2d 480 (2d Cir. 1946) (suggesting in dicta that copyright would protect single lines such as "Euclid alone has looked on Beauty bare" or " 'Twas Brillig and the slithely toves."). Note, however, that names, titles and slogans may be protected under trademark law if they are sufficiently distinctive to serve as a source identifier. *See* § 5C[2][b].

[31] Newton v. Diamond, 204 F. Supp. 2d 1244 (C.D. Cal. 2002) (three-note sequence), *aff'd on other grounds*, 349 F.3d 591 (9th Cir. 2003); Baby Buddies, Inc. v. Toys R Us, Inc., 611 F.3d 1308, 1311 (11th Cir. 2010) (X-shaped ribbon bow with two loops and two arms); John Muller & Co. v. New York Arrows Soccer Team, Inc., 802 F.2d 989 (8th Cir. 1986) (logo of soccer team consisting of three pairs of angled lines).

[32] Bright Tunes Music Corp. v. Harrisongs Music, Ltd., 420 F. Supp. 177 (S.D.N.Y. 1977) (although neither three-note motif A nor five-note motif B was novel, combination of "four repetitions of A, followed by four repetitions of B, is a highly unique pattern."), *aff'd sub nom.* ABKCO Music, Inc. v. Harrisongs Music, Ltd., 722 F.2d 988 (2d Cir. 1983); Atari Games Corp. v. Oman, 888 F.2d 878 (D.C. Cir. 1989) (video game "Breakout," in which a "ball" operated by a "paddle" chips away at rows of colored "bricks"); Kelley

works by ensuring that the fundamental building blocks of expression remain in the public domain so that they can be used by subsequent creators.

For the same reason, individual numbers and lists of numbers (such as part numbers for replacement parts) typically are not protected by copyright.[33] Copyright protection also has been denied to part numbers which were assigned in a systematic way, rather than in a creative manner.[34] However, some numerical classification schemes have been held to display enough creativity in selection and arrangement to qualify for copyright protection.[35]

[c]   Photographs

In *Burrow-Giles Lithographic Co. v. Sarony*, the U.S. Supreme Court upheld Sarony's copyright in a photograph of Oscar Wilde. The Court noted the trial court's finding that

> [P]laintiff made the same . . . entirely from his own original mental conception, to which he gave visible form by posing the said Oscar Wilde in front of the camera, selecting and arranging the costume, draperies, and other various accessories in said photograph, arranging the subject so as to present graceful outlines, arranging and disposing the light and shade, [and] suggesting and evoking the desired expression.[36]

In *Mannion v. Coors Brewing Co.*,[37] involving a dispute as to whether a billboard for Coors Light beer infringed the plaintiff's copyright in a photograph of basketball star Kevin Garnett, the court opined that photos were capable of originality in three respects: rendition, timing, and creation of the subject.

Rendition comprises various aspects of the subject's depiction, including "angle of shot, light and shade, exposure, [and] effects achieved by means of filters [or] developing techniques."[38] According to the *Mannion* court, "[u]nless a photograph replicates another work with total or near-total fidelity, it will be at least somewhat original in the rendition."[39]

---

v. Chicago Park Dist., 635 F.3d 290 (7th Cir. 2011) (although common geometric shapes, such as ellipses, cannot be copyrighted, an original creative arrangement of shapes may be).

[33] Toro Co. v. R & R Products Co., 787 F.2d 1208, 1213 (8th Cir. 1986) ("The random and arbitrary use of numbers in the public domain does not evince enough originality to distinguish authorship."); Mitel, Inc. v. Iqtel, Inc., 124 F.3d 1366, 1374 (10th Cir. 1997) (same).

[34] Southco, Inc. v. Kanebridge Corp., 390 F.3d 276, 283 (3d Cir. 2004) (en banc); ATC Distrib. Group, Inc. v. Whatever It Takes Transmissions & Parts, Inc., 402 F.3d 700, 708–09 (6th Cir. 2005).

[35] American Dental Ass'n v. Delta Dental Plans Ass'n, 126 F.3d 977 (7th Cir. 1997) (taxonomy classifying dental procedures and assigning numbers to each was an original work of authorship).

[36] 111 U.S. 53, 60 (1884).

[37] 377 F. Supp. 2d 444 (S.D.N.Y. 2006).

[38] *Id.* at 452. *See also* Leigh v. Warner Bros. Inc., 212 F.3d 1210 (11th Cir. 2000) (photo of Bird Girl sculpture in Savannah cemetery used on cover of book "Midnight in the Garden of Good and Evil"); Ets-Hokin v. Skyy Spirits, Inc., 225 F.3d 1068 (9th Cir. 2000) (photo of vodka bottle for magazine ad).

[39] 377 F. Supp. 2d at 352. *See also* Jeweler's Circular Publishing Co. v. Keystone Publishing Co., 274 F. 932, 934 (S.D.N.Y. 1921) (L. Hand, J.) ("no photograph, however simple, can be unaffected by the personal influence of the author, and no two will be absolutely alike."), *aff'd on other grounds*, 281 F. 83 (2d Cir. 1922).

Timing involves the photographer's decision to seize a moment in time and reduce it to an image ("being at the right place at the right time").[40] Examples include "Alfred Eisenstaedt's photograph of a sailor kissing a young woman on VJ Day in Times Square,"[41] or the Zapruder film of the assassination of John F. Kennedy.[42]

Creation of the subject consists of contriving or "creat[ing] the scene or subject to be photographed."[43] For example, the photographer may pose the subject in a particular setting, such as a couple on a park bench with eight puppies on their laps,[44] or the photo of Oscar Wilde in *Burrow-Giles*. Photos that are original in this respect have a broader scope of protection against infringement than those that are original in rendition or timing only.[45]

This analysis suggests that most photographs are copyrightable in at least one of these aspects. However, a work that is merely a "slavish imitation" of another work, one that strives (and succeeds) in reproducing the underlying work with as much fidelity as possible, is not copyrightable, no matter how much time, effort, or skill went into the reproduction. For example, in *Bridgeman Art Library, Ltd. v. Corel Corp.*, color photographs of public domain paintings were held not to be original, despite the skill and effort which went into the photographs;[46] and in *Meshwerks, Inc. v. Toyota Motor Sales U.S.A., Inc.*, unadorned digital wire-frame models of Toyota cars, lacking any color, texture, lighting, or animation, were held not to be original, despite the 80 to 100 man-hours that were required to produce the digital models.[47]

[d]　　Aesthetic Non-Discrimination

Courts eschew substantive standards of artistic or literary merit in determining originality. In *Bleistein v. Donaldson Lithographing Co.*,[48] the works were advertisements, circus posters with portraits and figures of performers. The lower court held that the works' copyrights were invalid because the posters had "no intrinsic value other than [their] function as an advertisement,"[49] and therefore granting copyright would not "promote the progress of science and useful arts."[50] The Supreme Court reversed. In a famous passage, Justice Holmes wrote:

---

[40] 377 F. Supp. 2d at 452.

[41] *Id.* at 453.

[42] *See* Time, Inc. v. Bernard Geis Assocs., 293 F. Supp. 130 (S.D.N.Y. 1968).

[43] 377 F. Supp. at 453.

[44] *Id.* at 454, *citing* Rogers v. Koons, 960 F.2d 301 (2d Cir. 1996).

[45] *See, e.g.,* Harney v. Sony Pictures Television, Inc., 704 F.3d 173 (1st Cir. 2013) (plaintiff's photo of father and daughter was not infringed by defendant's photo, in which actors portrayed the father and daughter, because defendant copied only the subject and not plaintiff's expressive elements).

[46] 25 F. Supp. 2d 421 (S.D.N.Y. 1998) (U.K. law), *on reconsideration,* 36 F. Supp. 2d 191 (S.D.N.Y. 1999) (U.S. law).

[47] 528 F.3d 1258 (10th Cir. 2008).

[48] 188 U.S. 239 (1903).

[49] Courier Lithographing Co. v. Donaldson Lithographing Co., 104 F. 993, 996 (6th Cir. 1900), *rev'd sub nom.* Bleistein v. Donaldson Lithographing Co., 188 U.S. 239 (1903).

[50] *See* U.S. Const., Art. I, § 8, cl. 8.

It would be a dangerous undertaking for persons trained only to the law to constitute themselves final judges of the worth of pictorial illustrations, outside of the narrowest and most obvious limits. At the one extreme some works of genius would be sure to miss appreciation. Their very novelty would make them repulsive until the public had learned the new language in which their author spoke. . . . At the other end, copyright would be denied to pictures which appealed to a public less educated than the judge. Yet if they command the interest of any public, they have a commercial value, — it would be bold to say that they have not an aesthetic and educational value, — and the taste of any public is not to be treated with contempt.[51]

Applying this standard, which has become known as the "aesthetic non-discrimination principle," courts have generally declined to impose any content-based limitations on the types of works eligible for copyright protection. For example, in *Mitchell Bros. Film Group v. Cinema Adult Theater*, the court held that a work's allegedly obscene character did not render the work ineligible for copyright protection.[52] Similarly, in *Dream Games of Arizona, Inc. v. PC Onsite*, the court held that the fact that the work, an electronic video bingo game, was being operated illegally in two states did not affect the amount of damages the plaintiff could recover.[53]

[2]   Fixation

To be copyrightable subject matter, a work of authorship must be fixed in a tangible medium of expression "from which [it] can be perceived, reproduced, or otherwise communicated, either directly or with the aid of a machine or device."[54] The work must be fixed "by or under the authority of the author,"[55] and it must be "sufficiently permanent or stable to permit it to be perceived, reproduced, or otherwise communicated for a period of more than transitory duration."[56] The material object in which a work is fixed is either a "copy" or a "phonorecord." Phonorecords are defined as material objects in which only sounds are fixed, and copies are defined as material objects in which all other types of works are fixed.[57]

---

[51] 188 U.S. at 251–52.

[52] 604 F.2d 852, 854–58 (5th Cir. 1979). *Accord*, Jartech, Inc. v. Clancy, 666 F.2d 403, 405–06 (9th Cir. 1982); *but see* Devils Films, Inc. v. Nectar Video, 29 F. Supp. 2d 174 (S.D.N.Y. 1998) (declining to order seizure of allegedly infringing films on grounds of obscenity).

[53] 561 F.3d 983, 990–92 (9th Cir. 2009).

[54] 17 U.S.C. § 102(a).

[55] 17 U.S.C. § 101 (definition of "fixed"). Although the same definition also applies to infringement of the reproduction right, see § 4F[1], it cannot be applied literally in the infringement situation. Because consent is a defense to infringement, obviously the accused infringer must have fixed the work *without* the authority of the author or copyright owner.

[56] 17 U.S.C. § 101 (definition of "fixed"). *See* Kelley v. Chicago Park Dist., 635 F.3d 290, 305 (7th Cir. 2011) (a living garden is "naturally in a state of perpetual change"; "[a]lthough the planting material is tangible and can be perceived for more than a transitory duration, it is not stable or permanent enough to be called 'fixed.' ").

[57] 17 U.S.C. § 101 (definitions of "copies" and "phonorecords"). Both terms include the material object

[a]   Background: *White-Smith v. Apollo*

Although the 1909 Act did not expressly require fixation, because that Act typically protected only published works, such a requirement was implicit.[58] Arguably, a fixation requirement is also implicit in the Copyright Clause of the U.S. Constitution.[59]

In *White-Smith Music Publishing Co. v. Apollo Co.*,[60] the Supreme Court indicated that fixation must be in a form that allows a human to perceive the work directly, without the aid of a machine. Defendants encoded performances of musical compositions on player-piano rolls, perforated rolls of paper that caused the piano to play the tune. The Court held that the rolls were not "copies" of the work because humans could not readily read the musical work. It defined a "copy" of a musical composition narrowly, as "a written or printed record of it in intelligible notation."[61]

White-Smith dealt with copyright infringement, not the form in which a work must be fixed to qualify for copyright protection; but because the copyright statute in effect at that time required an author to deposit two "copies" of his work to secure protection, it followed that a copyrightable work must be fixed in a "copy" as defined by *White-Smith*.

In the 1909 Act, Congress did not alter the *White-Smith* definition of a "copy," but it did give composers the exclusive right to make "mechanical reproductions" of their compositions.[62]

[b]   The 1976 Act

In the 1976 Act, Congress expressly stated the requirement that a work be permanently fixed by or under the authority of the author, and it altered the *White-Smith* definition. The Act's definitions of "copies" and "phonorecords" both include objects from which the work can be perceived "*either* directly *or* with the aid of a machine or device."[63] The House Report states that "[t]his broad language is intended to avoid the artificial and largely unjustifiable distinctions, derived from cases such as *White-Smith Publishing Co. v. Apollo Co.*, 209 U.S. 1 (1908), under which statutory copyrightability . . . has been made to depend upon the form or medium in which the work is fixed."[64] Nonetheless, the legacy of *White-Smith*

---

in which the work is first fixed. *Id.* For example, an original manuscript or painting is nonetheless a "copy" of the literary or pictorial work embodied in it.

[58] 1909 Act, § 9 (codified at 17 U.S.C. § 10 in 1947, repealed 1978). Similarly, although unpublished works could be protected by registration, registration required deposit of a copy of the work. 1909 Act, § 11 (codified at 17 U.S.C. § 12 in 1947, repealed 1978).

[59] Cf. Goldstein v. California, 412 U.S. 546, 561 (1973) ("the word 'writings' . . . may be interpreted to include any *physical* rendering of the fruits of creative intellectual or aesthetic labor.") (emphasis added).

[60] 209 U.S. 1 (1908). For the impact of *White-Smith* on the protectability of sound recordings, see § 4C[4][a][vii].

[61] 209 U.S. at 17.

[62] 1909 Act, § 1(e) (repealed 1978). *See also* § 4C[4[a][7].

[63] 17 U.S.C. § 101 (definitions of "copies" and "phonorecords") (emphasis added).

[64] H.R. Rep. No. 94-1476, at 52 (1976).

persists in the 1976 Act's otherwise inexplicable distinction between "copies" and "phonorecords."[65]

The House Report states that "the definition of 'fixation' would exclude . . . purely evanescent or transient reproductions such as those projected briefly on a screen, shown electronically on a television or other cathode ray tube, or captured momentarily in the 'memory' of a computer."[66] As a result, case law has addressed two issues involving electronic versions of copyrighted works. The first is whether a video game meets the fixation requirement, insofar as it is treated as an audio-visual work, as distinct from the computer program that generates the game.[67] The second is whether data stored only in random-access memory (or "RAM") meets the fixation requirement.

[i]   Video Games

The sights and sounds of a video game change as players operate it in the "play" mode. Most arcade video games have, in addition to the "play" mode, an "attract" mode (that is, one that runs repetitively to attract the attention of potential customer-players). Courts uniformly have found sufficient permanency in the game's visual and aural characteristics, including its "attract" mode, to satisfy the fixation requirement.[68]

[ii]   Random-Access Memory

Generally speaking, computers use two types of "memory." Electronic reproductions of copyrighted works may be stored in some permanent form, such as a hard disk or flash memory. These reproductions persist, even when the power to the computer is turned off. It is clear that these permanent reproductions are fixed "copies" within the meaning of the Act. But computers cannot directly manipulate the digital data stored in such media. Instead, digital data must be downloaded from permanent storage (or inputted directly) into the "random-access memory" (or "RAM") of the computer for processing. Unlike other electronic media, RAM requires electricity to function. While the power is on, data held in RAM can be "perceived, reproduced, or otherwise communicated" (e.g., by transmitting the data to a monitor, a permanent storage medium, or the RAM of a networked computer); but when the power is turned off, any data remaining in RAM disappears.

When a user composes a work on a computer, it is typically stored only in RAM

---

[65] Under the 1976 Act, a piano roll would be a "phonorecord" rather than a "copy." Most (but not all) Copyright Act rights apply to both copies and phonorecords. See, e.g., 17 U.S.C. § 106(1) (conferring the exclusive right to "reproduce the copyrighted work in copies or phonorecords.").

[66] H.R. Rep. No. 94-1476, at 53 (1976).

[67] See § 4C[4][a][i](c). The computer program itself is clearly fixed — usually in several tangible media of expression (paper print-outs of source code, ROM chips, CD-ROMs, hard disks, and/or flash drives).

[68] See Stern Electronics, Inc. v. Kaufman, 669 F.2d 852, 855–57 (2d Cir. 1982); Williams Electronics, Inc. v. Artic Int'l, Inc., 685 F.2d 870, 874 (3d Cir. 1982); Midway Mfg. Co. v. Artic Int'l, Inc., 547 F. Supp. 999, 1007–08 (N.D. Ill. 1982), aff'd, 704 F.2d 1009 (7th Cir. 1983); M. Kramer Mfg. Co. v. Andrews, 783 F.2d 421, 440–42 (4th Cir. 1986).

until the user instructs the computer to "save" the work.[69] The question arises whether such RAM versions are "fixed" within the meaning of the Act. Although courts have not directly addressed the issue, they have addressed the related issue of whether data reproduced in RAM is "fixed" for purposes of the reproduction right.[70]

As noted above, the House Report states that "the definition of 'fixation' would exclude . . . purely evanescent or transient reproductions such as those . . . captured momentarily in the 'memory' of a computer."[71] Nonetheless, in *MAI Systems Corp. v. Peak Computer, Inc.*,[72] the court held that a company that provided service for computer hardware systems infringed when it "booted up" computers running the plaintiff's copyrighted operating system software. The court approved the theory that in turning on the machine, the defendant had downloaded a "copy" of the program into RAM.[73] Many subsequent courts have accepted *MAI*'s holding that transferring data into RAM creates a "fixed" copy within the meaning of the Copyright Act.[74]

In *Cartoon Network v. CSC Holdings, Inc.*,[75] however, the court limited the holding in *MAI v. Peak*. *Cartoon Network* involved a particular type of RAM known as a "buffer." A buffer is working memory that temporarily holds a stream of data while it is being processed; but the data in the buffer is automatically overwritten by new data entering the buffer in real time. Thus, although an entire data stream representing a copyrighted work passes through the buffer, only a small amount of the data (in the case, up to 1.2 seconds of the work) is contained in the buffer at any one time. Parsing the definition of "fixed," the court stated:

> We believe that this language plainly imposes two distinct but related requirements: the work must be embodied in a medium . . . (the "embodiment requirement"), and it must remain thus embodied "for a period of more than transitory duration" (the "duration requirement"). . . . Unless both requirements are met, the work is not "fixed" in the buffer, and, as a result, the buffer data is not a "copy" of the original work whose data is buffered.[76]

---

[69] Many computer programs, however, now routinely save "back-up" copies of works being composed, so that the data can be recovered in the event the power is interrupted. In such cases, the question of whether RAM is "fixed" is moot.

[70] Section 106(1) grants the exclusive right "to reproduce the copyrighted work in copies or phonorecords." Because "copies" and "phonorecords" are defined as material objects in which a work is fixed, the same definition of "fixed" applies to the reproduction right as to the initial creation of the work. *See* 4F[1] below.

[71] H.R. Rep. No. 94-1476, at 53 (1976).

[72] 991 F.2d 511 (9th Cir. 1993).

[73] *Id.* at 518. Congress later overruled the specific result, but not the rationale, of *MAI*. *See* 17 U.S.C. § 117(c), discussed in § 4G[1][c].

[74] *See, e.g.*, Stenograph LLC v. Boussard Assocs., Inc., 144 F.3d 96, 101–02 (D.C. Cir. 1998); Advanced Computer Services of Michigan, Inc. v. MAI Systems Corp., 845 F. Supp. 356, 362–64 (E.D. Va. 1994).

[75] 536 F.3d 121 (2d Cir. 2008).

[76] *Id.* at 127. *See also* CoStar Group, Inc. v. LoopNet, Inc., 373 F.3d 544, 551 (4th Cir. 2004) ("While temporary copies may be made in this transmission process, they would appear not to be 'fixed' in the

The court distinguished *MAI* and its progeny, saying "it seems fair to assume that in these cases the program was embodied in the RAM for at least several minutes."[77]

[c]   Live Broadcasts and Transmissions

Section 101's definition of "fixed" addresses the problem of live works, that is, those created simultaneously with their performance or broadcast. The definition requires that the fixation be permanent or stable, which excludes an unrecorded broadcast; but it provides that "A work consisting of sounds, images, or both, that are being transmitted, is 'fixed' for purposes of this title if a fixation of the work is being made simultaneously with its transmission."[78] This provision covers virtually all live radio and television broadcasts, which are routinely recorded.[79]

A broadcast may entail several layers of fixed and therefore copyrighted works. A live, simultaneously-recorded broadcast of a sporting or news event, such as a football game or press conference, involves copyrightable authorship only in the broadcast itself (in the selection of camera angles, etc.).[80] The event itself is not a work of authorship, and no copyright in the broadcast would be infringed if another made a similar but independent broadcast or description of the uncopyrightable event.[81] On the other hand, the live, simultaneously-recorded broadcast of an event that is itself a copyrightable work, such as an original dance, play, or comic routine, may give rise to both a copyrighted broadcast and a copyrighted choreographic, dramatic, or literary work (the recording of the performance being the fixation if one has not previously occurred).[82]

---

sense that they are 'of more than transitory duration.' ").

[77] 536 F.3d at 128.

[78] 17 U.S.C. § 101 (definition of "fixed").

[79] *See* H.R. Rep. No. 94-1476, at 52–53 (1976).

[80] A live broadcast of sporting event is a copyrightable work of authorship. *See* Baltimore Orioles, Inc. v. Major League Baseball Players Ass'n, 805 F.2d 663 (7th Cir. 1986) ("The many decisions that must be made during the broadcast of a baseball game concerning camera angles, types of shots, the use of instant replay and split screens, and shot selection . . . supply the creativity required for the copyrightability of the telecasts."); H.R. Rep. No. 94-1476, at 52 (1976) ("When a football game is being covered by four television cameras, with a director guiding the activities of the four cameramen and choosing which of their electronic images are sent out to the public and in what order, there is little doubt that what the cameramen and the director are doing constitutes 'authorship.' ").

[81] *Cf.* Production Contractors, Inc. v. WGN Continental Broadcasting Co., 622 F. Supp. 1500 (N.D. Ill. 1985). In *Production Contractors*, the plaintiff organized a Christmas parade to take place on public streets in Chicago. Plaintiff sold "exclusive" television rights to a network and its affiliated Chicago station. The defendant, another station, proposed to telecast the parade, using its own personnel and equipment. The court dismissed the plaintiff's suit for copyright infringement because a parade is not an original work of authorship and because defendant would not infringe any copyright in the broadcast.

Unauthorized photographing or broadcast of an event may violate rights other than those arising from the copyright laws. *See, e.g.*, Zacchini v. Scripps-Howard Broadcasting Co., 433 U.S. 562 (1977) (broadcast of plaintiff's "human cannonball" act violated state right of publicity and was not immunized by the First Amendment).

[82] *Cf.* Martha Graham School and Dance Foundation, Inc. v. Martha Graham Center of Contemporary Dance, 380 F.3d 624, 632 (2d Cir. 2004) (choreography is eligible for statutory copyright when filmed or videotaped).

[d]   Live Performances

Article 14(1) of the TRIPS Agreement provides that "performers shall have the possibility of preventing . . . the fixation of their unfixed performance and the reproduction of such fixation," and "the broadcasting by wireless means and the communication to the public of their live performance." In partial fulfillment of this obligation, in 1994 the U.S. added section 1101, which gives performers a civil cause of action for the unauthorized fixation, transmission or communication to the public of their live musical performances, and for trafficking in such unauthorized reproductions.[83] Criminal penalties supplement the civil cause of action.[84]

Two courts of appeals have upheld the criminal anti-bootlegging statute against a challenge that Congress could not enact a statute under the Commerce Clause that violated the "writings" requirement of the Patent and Copyright Clause.[85] The reasoning of those cases, however, suggests that the courts might find the civil statute, section 1101, is unconstitutional.[86]

Unfixed works, such as lectures and live performances, may also qualify for state common-law copyright protection.[87]

[3]   Idea and Expression

[a]   General Principle

Section 102(b) codifies the established principle that copyright protects only original expression, not ideas. It provides: "In no case does copyright protection for an original work of authorship extend to any idea, procedure, process, system, method of operation, concept, principle, or discovery, regardless of the form in which it is described, explained, illustrated, or embodied in such work."[88] This

---

[83] 17 U.S.C. § 1101.

[84] 18 U.S.C. § 2319A.

[85] *See* United States v. Moghadam, 175 F.3d 1269 (11th Cir. 1999); United States v. Martignon, 492 F.3d 140 (2d Cir. 2007).

[86] *See Martignon*, 492 F.3d at 152 n.8 (reserving the question); *Moghadam*, 175 F.3d at 1281 (section 1101 might violate the "limited Times" provision). *But see* KISS Catalog v. Passport Int'l Prods., 405 F. Supp. 2d 1169 (C.D. Cal. 2005) (holding that § 1101 is constitutional). For details, see § 1D[2].

[87] Section 301 of the Copyright Act preempts state law only as to works of authorship that are "fixed in a tangible medium of expression." 17 U.S.C. § 301(a). Similarly, section 1101(d) states that "Nothing in this section may be construed to annul or limit any rights or remedies under the common law or statutes of any State."

For cases on state-law protection of unfixed conversations, see Estate of Hemingway v. Random House, Inc., 244 N.E.2d 250 (N.Y. 1969); Falwell v. Penthouse International, Ltd., 521 F. Supp. 1204 (W.D. Va. 1981).

California provides protection by statute to "any original work of authorship that is not fixed in any tangible medium of expression . . . as against all persons except one who originally and independently creates the same or similar work." Cal. Civ. Code § 980(a)(1). *Cf.* Williams v. Weisser, 273 Cal. App. 2d 726 (1969) (recognizing a common-law copyright in a university professor's lectures).

[88] 17 U.S.C. § 102(b). For recent cases applying the statute, see Brooks-Ngwenya v. Indianapolis Public Schools, 564 F.3d 804 (7th Cir. 2009) (ideas for better educating students are not protectible); Hutchins v. Zoll Medical Corp., 492 F.3d 1377 (Fed. Cir. 2007) (method of treating victims using CPR or

principle is known as the idea/expression dichotomy.

The idea/expression dichotomy serves two purposes. First, it serves to keep copyright from being applied to protect certain types of subject matter, such as procedures, processes, systems, and methods of operation, that are potentially patentable, and should instead be evaluated under the more demanding standards of patent law.[89] Second, it serves "to promote the progress of science" or knowledge, by ensuring that ideas remain in the public domain, so that future authors and creators can repeat, discuss, criticize, debate, modify, and improve upon the ideas of those that have gone before.[90]

[b]   *Baker v. Selden*

In *Baker v. Selden*,[91] Selden published a series of books that explained a new book-keeping system. The books each consisted of an explanatory essay and blank forms with ruled lines and headings for carrying out the system. Baker made and sold account books with blank forms that used a "similar plan" as Selden's, but that made "a different arrangement of the columns, and use[d] different headings."[92] The widow of the copyright owner sued Baker for infringement and prevailed in the trial court. The Supreme Court reversed.

Baker set forth three distinct propositions, each of which has influenced subsequent copyright law development. The first proposition was that Baker copied only Selden's system, that is, his "idea," not his expression of it, because Baker's and Selden's explanations and forms were different. Ideas receive protection, if at all, under the patent system.[93] Selden's copyright on a book explaining a system does not prevent another from explaining or using the same system.[94]

The second proposition is that a person may copy even the expression of the author "for the purpose of practical application" rather than for the purpose of "explanation."[95] This proposition later became critical to the scope of copyright

---

[89] See discussion of *Baker v. Selden*, 101 U.S. 99 (1879), below.

[90] *Cf. Baker*, 101 U.S. at 103 ("The very object of publishing a book on science or the useful arts is to communicate to the world the useful knowledge which it contains. But this object would be frustrated if the knowledge could not be used without incurring the guilt of piracy of the book.").

[91] 101 U.S. 99 (1879).

[92] The forms can be viewed in Pam Samuelson, *The Story of* Baker v. Selden: *Sharpening the Distinction Between Authorship and Invention*, in INTELLECTUAL PROPERTY STORIES 158 (Jane C. Ginsburg & Rochelle C. Dreyfuss eds. 2005).

[93] The Court stated: "To give to the author of the book an exclusive property in the art described therein, when no examination of its novelty has ever been officially made, would be a surprise and a fraud upon the public. That is the province of letters-patent, not of copyright." 101 U.S. at 102. Later, the Court added: "Whether the art might or might not have been patented, is a question which is not before us. It was not patented, and is open and free to the use of the public." *Id.* at 104. For a discussion of printed matter and business system patentability, *see* § 2C[1][e].

[94] "The description of the art in a book, though entitled to the benefit of copyright, lays no foundation for an exclusive claim to the art itself. . . . The former may be secured by copyright. The latter can only be secured, if it can be secured at all, by letters patent." 101 U.S. at 105.

[95] The Court stated: "[W]here the art it teaches cannot be used without employing the methods and diagrams used to illustrate the book, or such as are similar to them, such methods and diagrams are to

protection in useful articles and computer programs.[96]

The third proposition is that "blank account-books are not the subject of copyright."[97] This proposition persists in the rule that "[b]lank forms, such as time cards, graph paper, account books, diaries, bank checks, scorecards, address books, report forms, order forms and the like, which are designed for recording information and do not in themselves convey information" are not copyrightable.[98] The vast majority of cases involving blank forms have denied copyright protection.[99] Occasionally, however, courts have upheld copyright in blank forms, either because the forms were integrated with expressive text,[100] or because the selection and arrangement of headings on the forms displayed more than a minimal amount of creativity.[101]

[c]   The Merger Doctrine

In dealing with functional and fact-based works, courts postulate that, in some instances, there may be so limited a number of ways of expressing an idea that the expression "merges" with the idea. These courts deny copyright protection to the merged expression in order to avoid protecting the underlying idea.

In *Morrissey v. Procter & Gamble Co.*,[102] the seminal merger case, plaintiff secured copyright in rules for a simple sales promotion contest that used participants' social security numbers. Defendants launched a promotion using virtually identical rules.[103] The First Circuit found there was some, though not much, creativity in plaintiff's expression of the rules, and that the defendant's rules were

---

be considered as necessary incidents to the art, and given therewith to the public; not given for the purpose of publication in other works explanatory of the art, but for the purpose of practical application." 101 U.S. at 103.

[96] *See* §§ 4C[4][a][i](c) (computer programs) and 4C[4][a][v](b) (useful articles).

[97] 101 U.S. at 107.

[98] 37 C.F.R. § 202.1(c).

[99] *See, e.g.*, Utopia Provider Systems, Inc. v. Pro-Med Clinical Systems, LLC, 596 F.3d 1313 (11th Cir. 2010) (denying protection to medical charts containing spaces for patient information, history of illness, results of physical exam, clinical impressions, consultation, disposition, and instructions); Bibbero Systems, Inc. v. Colwell Systems, Inc., 893 F.2d 1104 (9th Cir. 1990) (denying protection to plaintiff's "superbills," each of which contained simple instructions for filing insurance claims, boxes for patient information, and checklists for doctors to indicate the diagnosis and any services performed); Advanz Behavioral Mgmt. Resources, Inc. v. Miraflor, 21 F. Supp. 2d 1179, 1184 (C.D. Cal. 1991) (analyzing four possible rationales for the blank forms doctrine).

[100] *See, e.g.*, Edwin K. Williams & Co. v. Edwin K. Williams & Co.-East, 542 F.2d 1053 (9th Cir. 1976) (account books containing "several pages of instructions" and blank forms were "an integrated work entitled to copyright protection"; defendant copied both the instructions and the forms).

[101] *See, e.g.*, Kregos v. Associated Press, 937 F.2d 700, 708–09 (2d Cir. 1991) (pitching form displaying nine categories of information concerning the past performances of the opposing pitchers was potentially copyrightable as a compilation). On remand, the trial court held that the plaintiff's form was not infringed by a different selection and arrangement, and the ruling was upheld on appeal. 3 F.3d 656 (2d Cir. 1993).

[102] 379 F.2d 675 (1st Cir. 1967).

[103] For example, plaintiff's rule 1 began: "Entrants should print name, address and social security number on a boxtop, or a plain paper." Defendant's rule 1 began "Entrants should print name, address and Social Security number on a *Tide* boxtop, or *on* [a] plain paper." (additions in italics; omissions in brackets). 379 F.2d at 678.

almost identical. Nonetheless, it ruled for the defendant:

> When the uncopyrightable subject matter is very narrow, so that the 'topic necessarily requires,' . . . if not only one form of expression, at best only a limited number, to permit copyrighting would mean that a party or parties, by copyrighting a mere handful of forms, could exhaust all possibilities of future use of the substance. . . . [I]n these circumstances, we hold that copyright does not extend to the subject matter at all, and plaintiff cannot complain even if his particular expression was deliberately adopted.[104]

Similarly, in *Herbert Rosenthal Jewelry Corp. v. Kalpakian*,[105] the Ninth Circuit applied the merger doctrine to deny copyright protection to a jeweled bee pin:[106]

> What is basically at stake is the extent of the copyright owner's monopoly — from how large an area of activity did Congress intend to allow the copyright owner to exclude others? We think the production of jeweled bee pins is a larger private preserve than Congress intended to be set aside in the public market without a patent. A jeweled bee pin is therefore an 'idea' that defendants were free to copy. . . . [But] on this record the 'idea' and its 'expression' appear to be indistinguishable. There is no greater similarity between the pins of plaintiff and defendants than is inevitable from the use of jewel-encrusted bee forms in both.

> When the 'idea' and its 'expression' are thus inseparable, copying the 'expression' will not be barred, since protecting the 'expression' in such circumstances would confer a monopoly of the 'idea' upon the copyright owner free of the conditions and limitations imposed by the patent law.[107]

Some courts prefer a narrower form of the merger doctrine, holding that even when there are only a few ways to express an idea, the merger doctrine merely limits the scope of the plaintiff's copyright, so that it protects only against "virtually identical" copying.[108] For example, in *Herbert Rosenthal Jewelry Corp. v. Grossbardt*,[109] the court found infringement of a jeweled bee pin (the same pin as in *Kalpakian*) where the defendant used a rubber mold to duplicate the pin. Thus,

---

[104] 379 F.2d at 678–79. *See also* Toro Co. v. R&R Prods. Co., 787 F.2d 1208, 1212 (8th Cir. 1986) ("the doctrine is designed to prevent an author from monopolizing an idea merely by copyrighting a few expressions of it."); R.W. Beck, Inc. v. E3 Consulting LLC, 577 F.3d 1133, 1145 (10th Cir. 2009); Schoolhouse, Inc. v. Anderson, 275 F.3d 726, 730 (8th Cir. 2002).

[105] 446 F.2d 738 (9th Cir. 1971).

[106] The plaintiff's pin had 19 small white jewels on its back. Plaintiff claimed infringement by "defendants' entire line of a score or more jeweled bees in three sizes decorated with from nine to thirty jewels of various sizes, kinds, and colors." *Id.* at 740.

[107] *Id.* at 742. *See also* Ho v. Taflove, 648 F.3d 489 (7th Cir. 2011) (plaintiffs failed to demonstrate that mathematical model for behavior of electrons in nature could be expressed using different equations, diagrams, or text).

[108] *Compare* Apple Computer, Inc. v. Microsoft Corp., 35 F.3d 1435, 1444 (9th Cir. 1994) ("when an idea and its expression are indistinguishable, or 'merged,' the expression will only be protected against nearly identical copying"), *with* Superior Form Builders, Inc. v. Dan Chase Taxidermy Supply Co., 74 F.3d 488, 493 (4th Cir. 1996) ("where idea and expression are indistinguishable, copying the expression would not be barred").

[109] 436 F.2d 315 (2d Cir. 1970).

although the merger doctrine is occasionally used in deciding whether a work is copyrightable at all,[110] more often it is used at the infringement stage of the analysis, in determining whether protected expression has been copied.[111]

Applying the merger doctrine, courts have denied or limited copyright protection to such works as games,[112] recipes,[113] maps,[114] designs of useful articles,[115] computer software,[116] and depictions of humans[117] and animals.[118] However, courts have sometimes "withheld" application of the merger doctrine to ideas "that are infused with the author's taste or opinions," as opposed to "those ideas that undertake to advance the understanding of phenomena and the solution of problems."[119] Thus, in two highly questionable decisions, two courts have upheld copyright protection for the estimated values of *individual* used cars and collectible coins, respectively.[120]

---

[110] *See, e.g.*, Lexmark Int'l, Inc. v. Static Control Components, Inc., 387 F.3d 522, 537–39 (6th Cir. 2004).

[111] *See, e.g.*, Oracle Am. Inc. v. Google, Inc., 750 F.3d 1339, 1358 (Fed. Cir. 2014) (merger doctrine relates to infringement, not copyrightability); Ets-Hokin v. Skyy Spirits, Inc., 225 F.3d 1068, 1082 (9th Cir. 2000) (same), *on appeal after remand*, 323 F.3d 763 (9th Cir. 2003) (same); Kregos v. Associated Press, 937 F.2d 700, 705 (2d. Cir. 1991) (merger is considered "in determining whether actionable infringement has occurred, rather than whether a copyright is valid").

[112] *See* Allen v. Academic Games League of America, Inc., 89 F.3d 614 (9th Cir. 1996) (merger doctrine "is particularly applicable with respect to games, since they consist of abstract rules and play ideas.").

[113] *Compare* 37 C.F.R. § 202.1(a) (a "mere listing of ingredients or contents" is not copyrightable) *and* Publications Int'l, Ltd. v. Meredith Corp., 88 F.3d 473 (7th Cir. 1996) (individual recipes not protected) *with* Barbour v. Head, 178 F. Supp. 2d 758 (S.D. Tex. 2001) (creatively-worded recipes may be protected against virtually identical copying, even though the recipes themselves are unprotected).

[114] *See* § 4C[4][a][v](a).

[115] *See* § 4C[4][a][v](b).

[116] *See* § 4C[4][a][i](c).

[117] *See* Blehm v. Jacobs, 702 F.3d 1193, 1204 (10th Cir. 2012) ("Blehm has no copyright over the idea of a cartoon figure holding a birthday cake, catching a Frisbee, skateboarding, or engaging in various other everyday activities," nor in "common anatomical features such as arms, legs, faces, and fingers.").

[118] *Compare* Satava v. Lowry, 323 F.3d 805 (9th Cir. 2003) (allegedly protected elements of glass-in-glass jellyfish sculpture — "a vertically oriented, colorful, fanciful jellyfish with tendril-like tentacles and a rounded bell encased in an outer layer of rounded clear glass" — were protected only against virtually identical copying) *with* Coquico, Inc. v. Rodriquez-Miranda, 562 F.3d 62 (1st Cir. 2009) (although merger doctrine foreclosed copyright protection for a realistic depiction of a coquí, a Puerto Rican tree frog, plush toy featured combination of protected elements, including distinctive stitching, color combination, pose, placement of flag on underbelly, and dimensions).

[119] CCC Information Services, Inc. v. Maclean Hunter Market Reports, Inc., 44 F.3d 61, 71 (2d Cir. 1994).

[120] *See id.* (individual used car prices were "approximative statements of opinion" to which the merger doctrine should not apply); *CDN Inc. v. Kapes*, 197 F.3d 1256 (9th Cir. 1999) (individual used coin prices were "compilations" rather than "ideas"). *But see* New York Mercantile Exchange, Inc. v. IntercontinentalExchange, Inc., 497 F.3d 109 (2d Cir. 2007) (distinguishing *CCC* and holding NYMEX's futures contracts settlement prices were subject to the merger doctrine, in part because the incentive rationale for copyright did not apply to prices which NYMEX was required to make and report).

[d] *Scènes à Faire*

Closely related to the merger doctrine are *scènes à faire*, usually defined as "incidents, characters or settings which are as a practical matter indispensable, or at least standard, in the treatment of a given topic."[121] The courts equate *scènes à faire* with ideas and accordingly refuse to extend copyright protection to them.[122]

For example, in *Hoehling v. Universal Studios, Inc.*, involving two works about the destruction of the German dirigible *Hindenburg* in 1937, "a scene in a German beer hall, in which the airship's crew engages in revelry prior to the voyage," as well as the greeting "Heil Hitler" and the German national anthem, were considered unprotectible *scènes à faire*.[123] Likewise, "parties, alcohol, co-eds, and wild behavior are natural elements in a story about a college fraternity,"[124] "[e]lements such as drunks, prostitutes, vermin and derelict cars would appear in any realistic work about . . . policemen in the South Bronx,"[125] and "[a]ttempted escapes, flights through the woods pursued by baying dogs, the sorrowful or happy singing of slaves," "scenes portraying sex between male slaveowners and female slaves and the resentment of the female slave owners; the sale of a slave child away from her family and the attendant agonies; [and] the horror of punitive mutilation" are common in works about slavery.[126]

As with the merger doctrine, the doctrine of *scènes à faire* typically is applied at the infringement stage to limit the scope of copyright protection.[127] Although the *scènes à faire* doctrine has most often been applied to narrative works, such as novels and motion pictures, courts have also applied the doctrine to limit copyright protection in such works as video games[128] and architectural works.[129]

---

[121] Alexander v. Haley, 460 F. Supp. 40, 45 (S.D.N.Y. 1978); *accord,* Incredible Technologies, Inc. v. Virtual Technologies, Inc., 400 F.3d 1007, 1012 (7th Cir. 2005); Stromback v. New Line Cinema, 384 F.3d 283, 296 (6th Cir. 2004); Sturdza v. United Arab Emirates, 281 F.3d 1287, 1295 (D.C. Cir. 2002); Hoehling v. Universal Studios, Inc., 618 F.2d 972, 979 (2d Cir. 1980). The French phrase *scènes à faire* is usually translated as "scenes which must be done." Schwarz v. Universal Pictures Co., 85 F. Supp. 270, 275 (S.D. Cal. 1945).

[122] *Hoehling,* 618 F.2d at 979 ("Because it is virtually impossible to write about a particular historical era or fictional theme without employing certain 'stock' or standard literary devices, we have held that *scènes à faire* are not copyrightable as a matter of law.").

[123] *Id.*

[124] *Stromback,* 384 F.3d at 283 (dicta).

[125] Walker v. Time-Life Films, 784 F.2d 44, 50 (2d Cir. 1986) (also denying protection to "[f]oot chases, and the morale problems of policemen, not to mention the familiar figure of the Irish cop.").

[126] *Alexander,* 460 F. Supp. at 45 & n.7.

[127] *See, e.g.,* Satava v. Lowry, 323 F.3d 805, 810 n.3 (9th Cir. 2003).

[128] *See, e.g.,* Incredible Technologies, Inc. v. Virtual Technologies, Inc., 400 F.3d 1007, 1014–15 (7th Cir. 2005) (menu screens, club selection feature, wind meter, and distance-to-hole prompt in a "PGA Golf Tour" video game); Data East USA, Inc. v. Epyx, Inc., 862 F.2d 204, 209 (9th Cir. 1988) (common karate moves, time element, referee, computer graphics and bonus points); Atari, Inc. v. North American Philips Consumer Elecs. Corp., 672 F.2d 607, 617 (7th Cir. 1982) (mazes, tunnels, and scoring tables in plaintiff's "Pac-Man" video game).

[129] *See, e.g.,* Zalewski v. Cicero Builder Dev., Inc., 794 F.3d 95, 105–06 (2d Cir. 2014) (elements dictated by Colonial style or consumer expectations); *Sturdza,* 281 F.3d at 1297 (domes, wind towers, parapets, and arches are unprotected ideas, and certain "Islamic patterns" are *scènes à faire*); Trek

[4]   Works of Authorship

[a]   Statutory Categories

Section 102(a) lists eight categories of "works of authorship." The list is "illustrative and not limitative"; the eight categories "do not necessarily exhaust the scope of 'original works of authorship.' "[130] A work may fall into more than one category.[131]

[i]   Literary Works

The definition of "literary works" is broad, encompassing works "expressed in words, numbers, or other verbal or numerical symbols or indicia, regardless of the nature of the material objects, such as books, periodicals, manuscripts, phonorecords, film, tapes, disks, or cards, in which they are embodied."[132] It includes not only fiction and non-fiction works but also such works as directories, databases, and computer programs.[133]

(a)   Characters

Whether copyright protects characters, graphical and literary, apart from the works in which they appear, is a thorny issue.

Graphical characters, such as cartoon figures, are conceptually simpler than literary characters because "while many literary characters may embody little more than an unprotected idea, a comic book character, which has physical as well as conceptual qualities, is more likely to contain some unique elements of expression."[134] In a series of cases dating back to 1914, courts have held that comic strip and cartoon characters are protected by copyright in the works in which they appear.[135] For example, in *Walt Disney Prods. v. Air Pirates*, the court found infringement in defendant's use of characters closely resembling Mickey and Minnie Mouse, Donald Duck, and Goofy.[136] Nonetheless, sometimes one

---

Leasing, Inc. v. United States, 66 Fed. Cl. 8, 14–16 (2005) (elements dictated by BIA Pueblo Revival building style).

[130] H.R. Rep. No. 94-1476, at 53 (1976). Congress adopted the phrase "original works of authorship" rather than the phrase "all of the writings of an author," which Section 4 of the 1909 Act used, "to avoid exhausting the constitutional power of Congress to legislate in this field." *Id.* at 51. Congress did "not intend either to freeze the scope of copyrightable subject matter at the present stage of communications technology or to allow unlimited expansion into areas completely outside the present congressional intent." *Id.* at 51.

[131] "[A] work falling within one class may encompass works coming within some or all of the other categories." *Id.* at 53.

[132] 17 U.S.C. § 101.

[133] H.R. No. 94-1476, at 54 (1976). For directories and databases, see § 4C[4][b][i].

[134] Walt Disney Productions v. Air Pirates, 581 F.2d 751, 755 (9th Cir. 1979).

[135] *See, e.g.,* Detective Comics, Inc. v. Bruns Publications Inc., 111 F.2d 432 (2d Cir. 1940) ("the pictorial representations and verbal descriptions of 'Superman' "); Fleischer Studios v. Freundlich, 73 F.2d 276 (2d Cir. 1934) ("Betty Boop"); King Features Syndicate v. Fleischer, 299 F. 533 (2d Cir. 1924) (horse "Spark Plug" from comic strip "Barney Google"); Hill v. Whalen & Martell, Inc., 220 F. 359 (S.D.N.Y. 1914) ("Mutt and Jeff").

[136] 581 F.2d at 754–55. *See also* Warner Bros. Inc. v. American Broadcasting Cos., 720 F.2d 231 (2d

encounters an audiovisual character that "embod[ies] little more than an unprotected idea."[137]

As to literary characters, in *Nichols v. Universal Pictures Corp.*, Judge Learned Hand suggested in dicta that a character could be so distinctly described and developed as to be separately protectable:

> If Twelfth Night were copyrighted, it is quite possible that a second comer might so closely imitate Sir Toby Belch or Malvolio as to infringe, but it would not be enough that for one of his characters he cast a riotous knight who kept wassail to the discomfort of the household, or a vain and foppish steward who became amorous of his mistress. These would be no more than Shakespeare's 'ideas' in the play. . . . It follows that the less developed the characters, the less they can be copyrighted; that is the penalty an author must bear for marking them too indistinctly.[138]

By contrast, in *Warner Bros. Pictures, Inc. v. Columbia Broadcasting System, Inc.*, Dashiell Hammett and his publisher assigned to Warner the motion picture rights to his classic detective novel "The Maltese Falcon," featuring detective Sam Spade. Hammett used the Sam Spade character in subsequent books (sequels) and assigned those motion picture rights to others. Warner sued for copyright infringement. The Ninth Circuit denied relief, relying primarily on its interpretation of the contract. In a cryptic remark, however, it added: "It is conceivable that the character really constitutes the story being told, but if the character is only the chessman in the game of telling the story he is not within the area of the protection afforded by the copyright."[139]

Warner's result and dubious reasoning were colored by the case's equities. Judge Posner says flatly: "[t]hat decision is wrong, though perhaps understandable on the 'legal realist' ground that Hammett was not claiming copyright in Sam Spade — on the contrary, he wanted to reuse his own character but to be able to do so he had to overcome Warner Brothers' claim to own the copyright."[140]

A problem with copyright protection for characters is that the characters may appear in a series of works, some copyrighted and some not, or may be changed in

---

Cir. 1983) ("Superman" is a protected character, but was not infringed by Ralph Hinkley in TV series "Greatest American Hero").

[137] *See, e.g.*, Rice v. Fox Broadcasting Co., 330 F.3d 1170 (9th Cir. 2003) (title character of "The Mystery Magician" video not protected by copyright); *but see* Halicki Films, LLC v. Sanderson Sales & Marketing, 547 F.3d 1213 (9th Cir. 2008) (remanding for determination whether customized Ford Mustang "Eleanor" from movie "Gone in 60 Seconds" was a distinctive character that "displays consistent, widely-identifiable traits").

[138] 45 F.2d 119, 121 (2d Cir. 1930). *See also* Olson v. Nat'l Broadcasting Co., 855 F.2d 1446 (9th Cir. 1988) ("lightly sketched" characters described in three- or four-line summaries in unpublished screenplay 'Cargo' were not protected, and were therefore not infringed by characters in TV series "The A-Team").

[139] 216 F.2d 945, 950 (9th Cir. 1945).

[140] Gaiman v. McFarlane, 360 F.3d 644, 660 (7th Cir. 2004) (holding characters from comic book "Spawn" were sufficiently distinctive; but copyright would not protect stereotyped characters such as "a drunken old bum, . . . a gesticulating Frenchman, a fire-breathing dragon, a talking cat, [or] a Prussian officer who wears a monocle and clicks his heels").

later works.[141] In *Klinger v. Conan Doyle Estate Ltd.*, for example, Klinger proposed to publish an anthology of stories featuring the characters of Sherlock Holmes and Dr. Watson.[142] He sued for a declaratory judgment that he was free to use the characters, because they were described in 46 stories and four novels that were in the public domain in the U.S. The Estate demanded a license fee, because it owned the copyrights in 10 short stories that were still under copyright.[143] The court held that the characters were in the public domain, and that only the "incremental additions" in the 10 later stories were protectable.[144]

(b)   Computer Programs

The 1976 Copyright Act did not expressly mention computer programs, but it defined "literary works" broadly enough to include them.[145] The House Report affirmed that "the term 'literary works' includes . . . computer programs to the extent that they incorporate authorship in the programmer's expression of original ideas, as distinguished from the ideas themselves."[146]

In 1974, Congress created the Commission on New Technological Uses of Copyrighted Works ("CONTU") to study and report to Congress on several topics, including computer uses of copyrighted works. In 1979, CONTU recommended that the copyright law be amended "to make it explicit that computer programs, to the extent that they embody an author's original creation, are proper subject matter of copyright."[147] It recommended two specific statutory changes: a definition of computer programs, and a limitation on exclusive rights "to ensure that rightful possessors of copies of computer programs may use and adapt these copies to their use."

In 1980, Congress followed CONTU's recommendation,[148] adding a definition —

---

[141] *See, e.g.*, Toho Co. v. William Morrow & Co., 33 F. Supp. 2d 1206 (S.D.N.Y. 1998) ("While Godzilla may have shifted from evil to good, . . . Godzilla is a well-defined character with highly delineated consistent traits"); Metro-Goldwyn-Mayer, Inc. v. American Honda Motor Co., 900 F. Supp. 1287 (C.D. Cal. 1995) (James Bond character is protected by copyright, even though the character has changed "from year to year and film to film").

[142] 755 F.3d 496 (7th Cir. 2014).

[143] *Id.* at 497.

[144] *Id.* at 501. *See also* Silverman v. CBS, Inc., 870 F.2d 40 (2d Cir. 1989) (characters of "Amos 'n Andy" from public-domain radio shows first broadcast before 1948 could be used, but "increments of expression" from radio and TV shows first broadcast after 1948 were still under copyright); *but cf.* Burroughs v. Metro-Goldwyn-Mayer, Inc., 683 F.2d 610 (2d Cir. 1982) (even after license to use first "Tarzan" book and eight others was terminated, license to use the remaining five works included license to use characters from previous works, including title character, that appeared in subsequent works).

[145] The Copyright Office began accepting computer programs for registration in 1964.

[146] H.R. Rep. No. 94-1476, at 54 (1976).

[147] National Commission on New Technological Uses of Copyrighted Works, Final Report 1 (1979). The members of the Commission differed in their views on the copyrightability of computer programs. *See id.* at 28–30 (dissent of Commissioner Hersey). For a scholarly critique of CONTU's work on computer program copyrightability, see Pamela Samuelson, *CONTU Revisited: The Case Against Copyright Protection for Computer Programs in Machine-Readable Form*, 1984 Duke L. J. 663.

[148] Act of Dec. 12, 1980, Pub. L. No. 96-517, § 10, 94 Stat. 3028. *See* H.R. Rep. No. 96-1307, at 23 (1980). In assessing computer program copyrightability, courts consider the CONTU Report. *See, e.g.*,

"A 'computer program' is a set of statements or instructions to be used directly or indirectly in a computer in order to bring about a certain result"[149] — and amending section 117 to set forth adaptation and archival copying limitations.[150]

At one level, the copyrightability of computer programs is relatively uncontroversial. For example, to the extent that a videogame displays audiovisual expression comparable to that found in a motion picture, few would contest the proposition that the audiovisual aspects of the videogame are copyrightable.[151] In addition, few would contest the proposition that a computer program in its source code form meets the statutory definition of a "literary work," that is, a work "expressed in words, numbers, or other verbal or numerical symbols or indicia." The major difficulty is presented by object code, the binary 1s and 0s into which source code must be translated in order to function in a computer. Such a translation (which occurs when a program is "compiled") strips the source code of its most expressive features and leaves something which, although it also meets the statutory definition, is arguably purely functional or utilitarian.

In *Apple Computer, Inc. v. Franklin Computer Corp.*,[152] the Third Circuit confirmed that computer programs are copyrightable in both source code and object code form,[153] regardless of storage medium (hard disks, floppy disks, or ROM chips) or the nature of the program (both operating systems and application programs).[154] In so holding, the court rejected Franklin's argument, based on *Baker* and section 102(b), that an operating system program is an uncopyrightable "process," "system," or "method of operation."[155]

The holding in *Apple v. Franklin* has been extended to "microcode," which is "a series of instructions that tell a microprocessor which of its thousands of transistors to actuate in order to perform the tasks directed by the macroinstruction set."[156] The court rejected the argument that many of the routines in Intel's microcode were uncopyrightable because they were very short, consisting of a few obvious steps dictated by functional considerations (the architecture of the microprocessor), saying "[T]he issue of the limited number of

---

Vault Corp. v. Quaid Software Ltd., 847 F.2d 255, 261 (5th Cir. 1988) ("The absence of an extensive legislative history and the fact that Congress enacted proposed section 117 with only one change have prompted courts to rely on the CONTU Report as an expression of legislative intent.").

[149] 17 U.S.C. § 101.

[150] *See* § 4F[1][c].

[151] The only serious question presented by videogames is whether player participation in altering the audiovisual display interactively prevents the work from being considered "fixed in a tangible medium of expression." As noted above, courts have uniformly held that the "fixation" requirement is satisfied by the repetitive portions of such screen displays. *See* § 4C[a][2][i].

[152] 714 F.2d 1240 (3d Cir. 1983).

[153] *Id.* at 1248–49. *See also* Apple Computer, Inc. v. Formula Int'l, Inc., 725 F.2d 521, 525 (9th Cir. 1984) (expression in a computer program does not need to be communicated to the computer user in order to be protected).

[154] 714 F.2d at 1249.

[155] *Id.* at 1252 (quoting Mazer v. Stein, 347 U.S. 201, 218 (1954)). *Mazer* held that a traditional piece of sculpture could be copyrighted, even though it was intended to be reproduced as part of a useful article. *See* § 4C[4][a][v](b).

[156] NEC Corp. v. Intel Corp., 10 U.S.P.Q.2d 1177, 1178 (N.D. Cal. 1989).

ways to express an idea is relevant to infringement, but should not be the basis for denying the initial copyright."[157]

Most early computer software copyright cases involved either mechanical or near-literal copying of code. Later cases dealt with allegations of infringement through nonliteral copying of a program's "structure, sequence, and organization," or of its "look and feel," including its user interface. These cases probe the limits of copyright protection for computer programs. Copying of the functional aspects or any "idea, procedure, process, system, [or] method of operation" in a computer program is not copyright infringement, and protection for functional features and ideas is available only under the patent system.[158] As a result, most courts have held that the scope of protection in computer programs is very narrow, precluding only virtually identical copying.[159]

[ii]   Musical Works

Musical works include both the musical notes themselves and any accompanying words. Fixation may be accomplished in various media, including in "copies" (e.g., printed sheet music or written notation on paper) or "phonorecords" (e.g., vinyl disc, audiotape, CD, hard drive, or flash drive). The originality requirement may be satisfied through melody, harmony or rhythm, individually or in combination.[160] A new arrangement of a musical work is a derivative work of that musical work, and it is eligible for a separate copyright if it is made lawfully.[161]

It is important to distinguish the musical work — the notes and lyrics, in whatever form they occur — from a sound recording, which is a fixation of sounds — typically, a particular recorded performance of a musical work.[162] A sound recording of a musical work is a derivative work of that musical work, and it is eligible for a separate copyright if it is made lawfully.[163] The copyright in a musical work is initially owned by the composer and the lyricist, and is typically assigned to a musical publisher. The copyright in a sound recording is in theory owned by the performers and the sound engineers, but in practice it is typically owned by a recording company under a "work made for hire" agreement.[164]

The owner of the copyright in a musical work has the exclusive right to make

---

[157] *Id.* at 1179. Nonetheless, the court found that Intel's microcode was not infringed, because none of the routines in NEC's microcode were identical, and because the merger doctrine precluded protection for routines that were "capable of only a limited range of expression" due to hardware constraints, and which therefore "may be protected only against virtually identical copying." *Id.* at 1188.

[158] For patent protection of computer programs, see § 2C[1][f].

[159] For cases involving the scope of infringement in computer software, see § 4G[3].

[160] *See, e.g.,* Newton v. Diamond, 204 F. Supp. 2d 1244, 1249 (C.D. Cal. 2002), *aff'd,* 388 F.3d 1189 (9th Cir. 2004); Tempo Music, Inc. v. Famous Music Corp., 838 F. Supp. 162 (S.D.N.Y. 1993) (dispute involving Duke Ellington, Billy Strayhorn and Johnny Mercer over rights in melody, harmony and lyrics of jazz classic "Satin Doll").

[161] *See, e.g.,* Baron v. Leo Feist, Inc., 173 F.2d 288 (2d Cir. 1949); *but see* Woods v. Bourne Co., 60 F.3d 978 (2d Cir. 1998) (piano-vocal arrangement of existing lead sheet was not sufficiently original).

[162] *See* § 4C[4][a][vii].

[163] See § 4C[4][b][ii] for information on derivative works.

[164] *See* § 4C[4][a][vii]. For ownership of copyright generally, including works made for hire, see § 4F.

and distribute what used to be called "mechanical reproductions," and what are now called "phonorecords," or material objects in which a sound recording of that musical work is fixed.[165] However, that right is limited by section 115, which creates a compulsory license for musical works. Once authorized phonorecords of a nondramatic musical work have been made and distributed to the public in the United States, any other person who follows the statutory procedures and pays the required royalty can obtain a compulsory license to make and distribute phonorecords of the musical work, without the express permission of the copyright owner — so long as the new version does not "change the basic melody or fundamental character of the work."[166] Note that the compulsory license grants the right to make a *new* sound recording of the musical work (i.e., a "cover"), and that an *existing* sound recording may be duplicated only with the express permission of the copyright owner in the sound recording, in addition to the compulsory license for the use of the musical work.[167]

[iii]   Dramatic Works

A "dramatic work" is simply a work that dramatizes a story. The category of "dramatic works" demonstrates how the statutory categories may overlap with one another. Literary works (plays), musical works (operas and musicals), choreographic works, and motion pictures and other audiovisual works all may be dramatic or non-dramatic in nature. The characterization of a work as "dramatic" has little consequence, except that some statutory provisions (such as the § 115 compulsory license) and some standard industry contracts (such as the ASCAP and BMI public performance licenses) are limited only to "nondramatic" works.

[iv]   Pantomimes and Choreographic Works

"Pantomime is the art of imitating, presenting, or acting out situations, characters, or events through the use of physical gestures and bodily movements," and is typically performed without music or dialog.[168] Choreography, by contrast, is "a related series of dance movements and patterns organized into a coherent whole," and "is usually accompanied by a specific musical composition."[169] Under the 1909 Act, choreography could only be registered as a "dramatic composition." Therefore, choreography "was protectible only if it told a story, developed or characterized an emotion, or otherwise conveyed a dramatic concept or idea."[170] The 1976 Act expressly includes choreography, "to insure protection for 'abstract'

---

[165] 17 U.S.C. § 106(1) (reproduction right), § 106(3) (distribution right). *See* § 4G[1].

[166] 17 U.S.C. § 115(a)(1). In practice, "[m]ost music publishers . . . employ the Harry Fox Agency, Inc. ('HFA') as their agent to receive notice of the intention to obtain a compulsory license, and to collect and distribute royalties . . . [HFA] substitutes a quarterly accounting and payment schedule for the monthly schedule prescribed by Section 115." Rodgers & Hammerstein Org. v. UMG Recordings, Inc., 60 U.S.P.Q.2d 1354, 1355 (S.D.N.Y. 2001).

[167] 17 U.S.C. § 115(a)(1)(ii).

[168] Compendium of Copyright Office Practices §§ 806.1, 806.2(C) (3d ed. 2014) (Compendium III). *See* Teller v. Dogge, 8 F. Supp. 3d 1228 (D. Nev. 2014) (copyright in pantomime is valid even if it includes a magic trick as its central feature).

[169] Compendium III, at §§ 805.1, 805.2(C).

[170] Horgan v. Macmillan, Inc., 789 F.2d 157, 160 (2d Cir. 1986).

as well as traditional dramatic ballet."[171] To be protected, the work must be fixed either on film or videotape, or by written notation such as the Laban or Benesh systems.[172] The work must also be original.[173] The House Report, however, indicates that "social dance steps and simple routines" are not protectible.[174]

[v] Pictorial, Graphic, and Sculptural Works

(a) Generally

"Pictorial, graphic, and sculptural works" include "two-dimensional and three-dimensional works of fine, graphic, and applied art, photographs, prints and art reproductions, maps, globes, charts, diagrams, models, and technical drawings, including architectural plans."[175]

The first copyright act in 1790 included "maps" and "charts" in addition to "books"; and in 1802, Congress added "prints." In *Burrow-Giles Lithographic Co. v. Sarony*, the U.S. Supreme Court relied in part on these enactments in holding that the Framers interpreted the word "Writings" in the Copyright Clause broadly, to include "all forms of writing, printing, engravings, etchings, etc. by which the ideas in the mind of the author are given visible expression."[176] Accordingly, the court held that Congress did not violate the Constitution in making "photographs" eligible for copyright in 1865.

Some courts have erroneously suggested that "originality" with respect to maps depends on independent observation of the terrain.[177] Such cases are inconsistent with the Supreme Court's opinion in *Feist*, which rejected the "sweat of the brow" doctrine and held that originality requires only independent creation and a minimal amount of creativity.[178] Thus, "originality" in maps lies in the selection and arrangement of which facts to depict, as well as the selection and arrangement of colors, typefaces, symbols, labels, and other graphic elements used to depict them.[179] Accordingly, most maps display the "minimal amount of creativity"

---

[171] *Id.*

[172] *Id.* at 160 n.3; *see also* Martha Graham School and Dance Foundation, Inc. v. Martha Graham Center of Contemporary Dance, 380 F.3d 624, 632 (2d Cir. 2004).

[173] *Cf.* Open Source Yogan Unity v. Choudhury, 2005 U.S. Dist. LEXIS 10440 (N.D. Cal. Apr. 1, 2005) (finding triable issue as to whether yoga sequence consisting of 26 asanas was original). *But see* COMPENDIUM III, at § 805.5(B)(3) (excluding "functional physical movements" that "purportedly improve one's health or physical or mental condition").

[174] H.R. Rep. No. 94-1476, at 53–54 (1976); *see also* COMPENDIUM III, at § 805.5(A) (excluding "individual dance steps and short dance routines" as "the building blocks of choreographic expression"); *Id.* at § 805.5(B)(2) (excluding "social dances" which "are intended to be performed by members of the general public for their own enjoyment.").

[175] 17 U.S.C. § 101. For photographs, see § 4C[1][c]; for architectural plans, see § 4C[4][a][viii]. *But see* Kelley v. Chicago Park Dist., 635 F.3d 290 (7th Cir. 2011) (although a living garden is original, it is neither "authored" nor fixed; "a garden owes most of its form and appearance to natural forces.").

[176] 111 U.S. 53, 58 (1884).

[177] *See, e.g.*, Amsterdam v. Triangle Publications, Inc., 93 F. Supp. 79, 82 (E.D. Pa. 1950), *aff'd*, 189 F.2d 104 (3d Cir. 1951).

[178] Feist Publications, Inc. v. Rural Telephone Service Co., 499 U.S. 340, 345 (1991). *See* § 4C[1][a].

[179] *See, e.g.*, Streetwise Maps, Inc. v. Vandam, Inc., 159 F.3d 739, 748 (2d Cir. 1998) (selection,

required for copyright protection, although the scope of protection may be limited by the merger doctrine.[180] In extreme cases, a map may not display sufficient originality to qualify for copyright protection.[181]

(b)   Useful Articles

(1)   Historical Development

In *Mazer v. Stein*,[182] the seminal Supreme Court decision concerning useful articles, plaintiffs created statuettes of male and female dancing figures, copies of which they used as lamp bases. Defendant copied the statuettes and sold them as lamp bases without plaintiffs' authorization. The plaintiffs sued for copyright infringement. The Court held that the statuettes did not lose their eligibility for copyright simply because the creator intended to reproduce the creation in a useful article.[183] The Court declined to decide whether obtaining a design patent would preclude the plaintiff from also obtaining a copyright (or vice versa), but it rejected the argument that "because a thing is patentable it may not be copyrighted."[184]

After *Mazer*, the Copyright Office amended its regulations to allow protection for "features, such as artistic sculpture, carving, or pictorial representation, which can be identified separately and are capable of existing independently as a work of art."[185] Congress codified this regulation in the 1976 Act, in the definition of "pictorial, graphic, and sculptural works":

> Such works shall include works of artistic craftsmanship insofar as their form but not their mechanical or utilitarian aspects are concerned; the design of a useful article, as defined in this section, shall be considered a pictorial, graphic, or sculptural work only if, and only to the extent that, such design incorporates pictorial, graphic, or sculptural *features* that can

---

coordination, and arrangement of "expressive elements in its map, including color"); Mason v. Montgomery Data, Inc., 967 F.2d 135, 141–42 (5th Cir. 1992) ("selection, coordination, and arrangement" of factual information, and depiction in pictorial or graphic manner); U.S. v. Hamilton, 583 F.2d 448, 452 (9th Cir. 1978) ("selection, design, and synthesis" of public domain information).

[180] *See, e.g., Streetwise Maps*, 159 F.3d at 747 (no protection for "street locations, landmass, bodies of water and landmarks"), *id.* at 748 (map not infringed by another fold-out laminated map that identified different places of interest and used different symbols and colors, despite common use of color purple for water and white for streets). For background on the merger doctrine, see § 4C[3][c].

[181] *See, e.g.*, Darden v. Peters, 488 F.3d 277 (4th Cir. 2007) (maps of basic outlines of states and counties; slight variations in color, shading, and labeling made to U.S. Census maps were not sufficiently original); Kern River Gas Transmission Co. v. Coastal Corp., 899 F.2d 1458 (5th Cir. 1990) (map of location for proposed pipeline, plotted as lines added to public domain maps, merged with idea of where to locate the proposed pipeline and was therefore unprotectible).

[182] 347 U.S. 201 (1954).

[183] *Id.* at 218.

[184] *Id.* at 217. Since *Mazer*, both the lower courts and the Copyright Office have taken the position that a work may receive both copyright and design patent protection, regardless of which was obtained first. *See* Application of Yardley, 493 F.2d 1389 (C.C.P.A. 1974); 37 C.F.R. § 201.10(a). For design patent protection, see § 6B.

[185] 37 C.F.R. § 202.10(c) (1959), quoted in Esquire, Inc. v. Ringer, 591 F.2d 796, (D.C. Cir. 1978). *Esquire* thoroughly reviews the administrative and legislative developments from *Mazer* to enactment of the 1976 Act.

be *identified separately from, and are capable of existing independently of, the utilitarian aspects* of the article.[186]

This statutory limitation has two parts: first, it applies only to "useful articles"; and second, it requires courts to determine whether the article possesses aesthetic features that are separable from the rest of the article.

(2)   Statutory Definition

The separability test only applies to a "useful article," which is defined as "an article having an intrinsic utilitarian function that is not merely to portray the appearance of the article or to convey information."[187]

The apparent purpose of the first exclusion is to avoid classifying an object as a "useful article" merely because it is aesthetically pleasing. For example, in *Masquerade Novelty, Inc. v. Unique Industries, Inc.*,[188] the court held that the plaintiff's "nose masks" (representing the characteristic noses of pigs, elephants, parrots, and other animals) were *not* useful articles, because "[t]he utilitarian nature of an animal nose mask . . . inheres solely in its appearance, regardless of the fact that the nose mask's appearance is intended to evoke mirth."[189]

The reasoning in *Masquerade* seemed to conflict with a previous case involving Halloween costumes, in which another Court of Appeal stated that "the Copyright Office considers costumes to be wearing apparel and consistently rejects applications to register them."[190] The conflict led the Copyright Office to clarify its position. It agreed that masks were not useful articles, but it maintains that costumes "serve a dual purpose of clothing the body and portraying their appearance." Since the former is "an intrinsic utilitarian function," the Copyright Office continues to treat "fanciful" costumes as "useful articles" subject to separability analysis.[191] Moreover, "the general policy of nonregistrability of garment designs [is] applied not only to ordinary wearing apparel, but also to period and historical dress, and uniforms."[192]

The second limitation is that an article is not "useful" if its only utility is "to convey information." Thus, "the mere fact that an intellectual work is useful or functional — be it a dictionary, directory, map, book of meaningless code words, or computer program — does not mean that none of the elements of the work can be

---

[186] 17 U.S.C. § 101 (emphasis added).

[187] 17 U.S.C. § 101.

[188] 912 F.2d 663 (3d Cir. 1990).

[189] *Id.* at 671. *See also* Gay Toys, Inc. v. Buddy L Corp., 703 F.2d 970, 974 (6th Cir. 1983) (a toy airplane is not a "useful article" because "toys do not have an intrinsic function other than the portrayal of the real item.").

[190] Whimsicality, Inc. v. Rubie's Costume Co., 891 F.2d 452, 454 (2d Cir. 1989).

[191] *See Registrability of Costume Designs*, 56 Fed. Reg. 56530 (Nov. 5, 1991); *see also* Chosun Int'l, Inc. v. Chrisha Creations, Ltd., 413 F.3d 324, 329 & n.3 (2d Cir. 2005) (reversing District Court's holding that "Halloween costumes may not be copyrighted" and remanding for determination of separability).

[192] 56 Fed. Reg. at 56532; *see* Galiano v. Harrah's Operating Co., 416 F.3d 411, 416 (5th Cir. 2005) (finding "little doubt" that casino uniforms were "useful articles").

copyrightable."[193] For example, in *Lotus Development Corp. v. Paperback Software Int'l*, the district court held that plaintiff's user interface for its spreadsheet computer program was not a "useful article" within the meaning of the statute.[194] Nonetheless, a result similar to the "separability" test may sometimes be reached through a straightforward application of the idea-expression dichotomy, which excludes copyright protection for "*any* idea, procedure, process, system, method of operation, concept, principle, or discovery."[195] Thus, in *Lotus Development Corp. v. Borland Int'l, Inc.*, the First Circuit held that the menu command structure of the same spreadsheet user interface was an uncopyrightable "method of operation."[196]

(3)   Separability

According to the House Report, the "separability" standard was intended "to draw as clear a line as possible between copyrightable works of applied art and uncopyrightable works of industrial design."[197] However, "[c]ourts have twisted themselves into knots trying to create a test to effectively ascertain whether the artistic aspects of a useful article can be identified separately from and exist independently of the article's utilitarian function."[198] At least six different tests have been proposed for determining whether artistic features are "separable" from the utilitarian aspects of the article.[199]

1. In *Kieselstein-Cord v. Accessories By Pearl, Inc.*, the Second Circuit held that two decorative belt buckles were copyrightable, because "the primarily ornamental aspect of the [two] buckles is conceptually separate from their subsidiary utilitarian function."[200] It provided little guidance as to how to determine whether an article was "primarily" ornamental or useful; but the court relied in part on evidence that the Metropolitan Museum of Art accepted a donation of the two buckles for its collection, and that a few purchasers wore the buckles as pendants rather than as belts.[201]

2. Three Courts of Appeals have endorsed a test proposed in the Nimmer treatise, which inquires whether "there is any substantial likelihood that even if the article had no utilitarian use it would still be marketable to some significant segment of the community simply because of its aesthetic qualities."[202]

---

[193] Lotus Development Corp. v. Paperback Software Int'l, 740 F. Supp. 37, 58 (D. Mass. 1990). It should be noted that many of the listed examples, including computer programs, are "literary works," and that the separability test applies only to "pictorial, graphic, and sculptural works."

[194] *Id.* at 56–58.

[195] 17 U.S.C. § 102(b) (emphasis added).

[196] 49 F.3d 807, 815–19 (1st Cir. 1995), *aff'd by an equally divided Court*, 516 U.S. 233 (1996). *But see* Oracle Am., Inc. v. Google, Inc., 750 F.3d 1359, 1365–67 (Fed. Cir. 2014) (rejecting *Lotus* and holding that a method of operation "may nevertheless be copyrightable"). For a discussion, see § 4H[3].

[197] H.R. Rep. No. 94-1476, at 55 (1976).

[198] Masquerade Novelty Inc. v. Unique Industries, Inc., 912 F.2d 663, 670 (3d Cir. 1990).

[199] *See* Pivot Point Int'l, Inc. v. Charlene Prods., Inc., 372 F.3d 913 (7th Cir. 2004). A seventh test was dismissed in a footnote, and is discussed below.

[200] 632 F.2d 989, 993 (2d Cir. 1980).

[201] *Id.* at 991.

[202] 1 NIMMER ON COPYRIGHT § 2.08[B][3] (2010). *See* Galiano v. Harrah's Operating Co., 416 F.3d 411,

3. In *Carol Barnhart, Inc. v. Economy Cover Corp.*, the Second Circuit applied the *Kieselstein-Cord* standard in holding that four life-size human torso forms made of styrene, which were designed and used to display clothes, were not copyrightable.[203] Dissenting, Judge Newman proposed a test that asks whether "the design creates in the mind of the ordinary observer two different concepts that are not inevitably entertained simultaneously."[204] In other words, this test asks whether an ordinary observer could view the object as a work of art, without simultaneously thinking of it as a useful article.[205] No court has yet adopted Judge Newman's test.

4. In *Brandir Int'l, Inc. v. Cascade Pacific Lumber Co.*, the Second Circuit considered the "Ribbon Rack," a bike rack constructed of metal tubing bent into a serpentine form. The court adopted a test proposed in an article by Prof. Robert Denicola:

> [I]f design elements reflect a merger of aesthetic and functional consider-ations, the artistic aspects of a work cannot be said to be conceptually separable from the utilitarian aspects. Conversely, where the design elements can be identified as reflecting the designer's artistic judgment exercised independently of functional influences, conceptual separability exists.[206]

Because the artist had modified his original sculpture in order to produce a more useful bike rack, the court concluded that the bike rack was not copyrightable. This test was also adopted by the Seventh Circuit in *Pivot Point Int'l, Inc. v. Charlene Prods., Inc.*, in holding that a female head mannequin, allegedly used in beauty schools to practice makeup application, was eligible for copyright;[207] and by the Fourth Circuit in *Universal Furniture Int'l, Inc. v. Collezione Europa U.S.A., Inc.*, in holding that the decorative ornamentation on a line of furniture, such as "a carved scroll of leaves on a nightstand post," is protectable.[208]

5. Both the district court opinion and the dissent in *Pivot Point* endorse a test proposed by Professor Goldstein in his treatise. Goldstein's test asks whether there is a pictorial, graphic or sculptural feature that "can stand on its own as a work of art traditionally conceived," and whether "the useful article in which it is embodied would be equally useful without it."[209] The Seventh Circuit's reversal in *Pivot Point*

---

422 (5th Cir. 2005) (casino uniforms not copyrightable); Magnussen Furniture, Inc. v. Collezione Europa, USA, Inc., 43 U.S.P.Q.2d 1218, 1220 (4th Cir. 1997) (unpublished) (design features of iron tables not copyrightable); Poe v. Missing Persons, 745 F.2d 1238, 1243 (9th Cir. 1984) (finding triable issue of fact whether plaintiff's plastic-and-crushed-rock swimsuit was a "useful article," because it was unclear whether one could actually walk or swim in it).

[203] 773 F.2d 411, 419 (2d Cir. 1985).

[204] *Id.* at 422 (Newman, J., dissenting).

[205] *Id.* at 422–23.

[206] 834 F.2d 1142, 1145 (2d Cir. 1987), *citing* Denicola, *Applied Art and Industrial Design: A Suggested Approach to Copyright in Useful Articles*, 67 MINN. L. REV. 707 (1983).

[207] 372 F.3d 913, 930–31 (7th Cir. 2004).

[208] 618 F.3d 417, 432–34 (4th Cir. 2010).

[209] *Pivot Point*, 372 F.3d at 933 (Kanne, J., dissenting); *see also* 170 F. Supp. 2d 828, 833 (N.D. Ill.

leaves only a single district court decision using the Goldstein test.[210]

6. In *Esquire, Inc. v. Ringer*, the D.C. Circuit affirmed the Copyright Office's refusal to register the design of an outdoor lighting fixture.[211] The court rejected an argument that "conceptual separability" was sufficient, holding that the House Report, when read "in its entirety," indicated "unequivocally that the overall design or configuration of a utilitarian object, even if it is determined by aesthetic as well as functional considerations, is not eligible for copyright."[212] Courts have interpreted this decision as requiring physical separability.[213] Although the physical separability test is the one that is most consistent with the statutory language, other courts have relied on the fact that the House Report refers to "conceptual" separability in the alternative.[214]

As should be evident, the state of the law concerning "separability" is in a confused mess, because of the inability of the courts to agree on a determinative test. The first four tests can be criticized for sometimes permitting the "overall" design of a useful article to be eligible for copyright, despite the clear indication in the statute and the House Report that only separable pictorial, graphic, and sculptural "features" may be copyrighted.[215] In addition, the House Report appears to expressly reject a test closely resembling the *Brandir*-Denicola test adopted in *Pivot Point*.[216] For this reason, the sixth test is most compatible with the statutory language and the legislative history. Case law, however, seems to favor the *Brandir*-Denicola test.

[vi]   Motion Pictures and Other Audiovisual Works

In 1894, the Copyright Office registered its first claim to copyright in a motion picture under the nearest plausible category: "photographs." The 1909 Act did not expressly protect motion pictures until 1912, when they were added by the

---

2001) (Easterbrook, J., sitting by designation). The majority in *Pivot Point* also identified a sixth test: "the artistic features are not utilitarian." 372 F.3d at 923, *citing* William F. Patry, 1 Copyright Law & Practice 284 (1994). The court did not comment further on this test, and no court has adopted it. The sixth test discussed below was not listed separately in the *Pivot Point* opinion, but was dismissed in a footnote.

[210] *See* Collezione Europa USA, Inc. v. Hillsdale House, Ltd., 243 F. Supp. 2d 444, 455 (M.D.N.C. 2003).

[211] 591 F.2d 796 (D.C. Cir. 1978). Although *Esquire* arose under the 1909 Copyright Act, the court referred to the 1976 Act and its legislative history for guidance in interpreting the Copyright Office regulation on which the language of the 1976 Act was based. *Id.* at 802–03.

[212] *Id.* at 803–04. *See also* Inhale, Inc. v. Starbuzz Tobacco, Inc., 755 F.3d 1038 (9th Cir. 2014) ("The shape of a container is not independent of the container's utilitarian function — to hold the contents within its shape.").

[213] *See Pivot Point*, 170 F. Supp. 2d at 833 (*Esquire* "opted for physical separability"), *rev'd*, 372 F.3d at 922 n.8 (agreeing with the district court's interpretation of *Esquire*, but holding that "conceptual" separability is sufficient).

[214] *See Pivot Point*, 372 F.3d at 922 n.8 (listing cases).

[215] H.R. Rep. No. 94-1476, at 55 (1976).

[216] *Id.* ("*even if* the appearance of an article is determined by [a]esthetic (as opposed to functional) considerations, only elements, if any, which can be identified separately from the useful article as such are copyrightable.") (emphasis added).

Townsend Amendment.[217]

The 1976 Act defines "audiovisual works" as "works that consist of a series of related images which are intrinsically intended to be shown by the use of machines or devices such as projectors, viewers, or electronic equipment, together with accompanying sounds, if any."[218] The most common types of audiovisual works are "motion pictures," which are defined as "a series of related images which, when shown in succession, impart an impression of motion, together with accompanying sounds, if any."[219]

The definition raises a few interesting issues. First, although the definition uses the word "series," it is not necessary that the images be presented serially, in a fixed, invariable order.[220] Copyright has been sustained in videogames, in which the sequence of images is affected by player intervention.[221] Second, the word "related" has been interpreted flexibly to include textual material broadcast simultaneously with and as part of the same signal as a news broadcast, but intended to be viewed separately using a decoder, "provided [it] is intended to be seen by the same viewers as are watching the nine o'clock news, during the same interval of time in which that news is broadcast, and is an integral part of the news program."[222] Third, one recent case raises the issue of whether an actor's performance may be protected separately from the motion picture in which it appears.[223]

In many European countries, the "author" of a motion picture is statutorily defined and typically includes the principal director, the principal screenwriter, and the composer.[224] In the United States, questions as to "authorship" are typically avoided through routine application of the "work made for hire" doctrine.[225]

---

[217] Act of Aug. 24, 1912, Pub. L. No. 62-303, 37 Stat. 488.

[218] 17 U.S.C. § 101.

[219] *Id.*

[220] WGN Continental Broadcasting Co. v. United Video, Inc., 693 F.2d 622, 629 (7th Cir. 1982) ("we do not think the statutory term 'series' must be interpreted to mean a rigid, predetermined sequence.").

[221] *See* § 4C[2][b][i].

[222] *WGN*, 693 F.2d at 629.

[223] Garcia v. Google, Inc., 766 F.3d 929 (9th Cir. 2014). In *Garcia*, an actress alleged that her performance was incorporated into an anti-Muslim propaganda film without her consent. On motion for a preliminary injunction, the panel majority held that it was likely that her performance was independently copyrightable. The Copyright Office, however, refused to register her performance separately. *Id.* at 935. The Ninth Circuit subsequently granted a petition for rehearing en banc, vacating the panel opinion. 771 F.3d 647 (9th Cir. 2014).

[224] *See* Council Directive 93/98/EEC of 29 Oct. 1993, Harmonizing the Term of Protection of Copyright and Certain Related Rights, Art. 2.

[225] For ownership of copyright, including works made for hire, see § 4F.

[vii]   Sound Recordings

"Sound recordings" are defined as "works that result from the fixation of a series of musical, spoken, or other sounds."[226] A sound recording may be a derivative work of a preexisting literary or musical work, or it may simply be a recording of ambient sounds. If it is a derivative work, the sound recording is eligible for a separate copyright only if it is made lawfully.[227]

The Copyright Act severely limits the exclusive rights in a sound recording: the reproduction right extends only to the duplication of the actual sounds fixed in the recording, and the right to prepare derivative works extends only to the rearranging, remixing or other alteration of those actual sounds.[228] As a result, a sound recording copyright includes no rights against others who independently fix sounds that imitate or simulate those in the copyrighted work.[229] In addition, the copyright in a sound recording does not include a general public performance right; instead, the public performance right in a sound recording is limited to digital audio transmissions only.[230] Thus, when a sound recording of a musical work is broadcast on traditional AM or FM radio, only the musical work copyright owner is entitled to royalties; but when the same sound recording is broadcast in digital form (such as over the Internet), both the musical work copyright owner and the sound recording copyright owner are entitled to royalties.

The history of the legal protection against unauthorized reproduction of sound recordings is long and complex. One year before the 1909 Act was enacted, when the recording industry was in its infancy, the Supreme Court held in *White-Smith Music Publishing Co.* that player piano rolls — perforated rolls that caused player pianos to perform the musical compositions — were parts of machines and were not "copies" of the musical compositions, because humans could not "read" the perforations on the rolls.[231] It defined a "copy" of a musical composition narrowly, as "a written or printed record of it in intelligible notation."[232]

In the 1909 Act, Congress guardedly responded to *White-Smith*. To protect composers' economic interests, it extended the copyright in a musical work to "any form of record" from which the musical composition could be reproduced, but it imposed a compulsory license on such "mechanical reproductions" of the musical work.[233] Significantly, however, Congress did not address whether the recording itself was a copyrightable work, and it did not alter the *White-Smith*'s definition of

---

[226] 17 U.S.C. § 101. The statutory definition excludes "the sounds accompanying a motion picture or other audiovisual work," which are covered by the copyright in the audiovisual work. *Id.*

[227] 17 U.S.C. § 103(a). See § 4C[4][b][ii] for information on derivative works.

[228] 17 U.S.C. § 114(b).

[229] *Id.*

[230] 17 U.S.C. §§ 106(4), 106(6), 114(a). In addition, the digital audio transmission right is further limited by a complicated compulsory licensing scheme. *See* 17 U.S.C. § 114(d)–(j); *see also* § 4G[6].

[231] White-Smith Music Publishing Co. v. Apollo Co., 209 U.S. 1, 17 (1908). *White-Smith's* impact on the fixation requirement is discussed at § 4C[2][a].

[232] 209 U.S. at 17.

[233] *See* 1909 Act, Pub. L. No. 60-349, § 1(e), 35 Stat. 1075 (later codified at 17 U.S.C. § 1(e), repealed 1978). The compulsory license for musical works was carried forward in the 1976 Act. *See* 17 U.S.C. § 115.

a "copy," which excluded recordings. Because copyright could only be secured in works as to which "copies" could be deposited with the Copyright Office, the 1909 Act implicitly excluded copyright protection for sound recordings.[234]

Attempts to prevent unauthorized commercial copying of records and tapes therefore focused on state-law remedies: first, common-law remedies such as misappropriation and unfair competition,[235] and, later, criminal and civil statutes enacted by state legislatures.[236] In time, the Supreme Court held that federal law did not preempt such state-law remedies.[237]

Faced with the need for a uniform national solution, Congress in 1971 extended copyright protection to sound recordings.[238] The 1976 Act made the extension permanent, but only for sound recordings fixed on or after February 15, 1972.[239] State-law remedies continue to govern sound recordings fixed before that date, and such state-law protection will not be preempted by federal law until February 15, 2067.[240]

The House Report on the 1976 Act suggests that usually both "the performers whose performance is captured" and "the record producer responsible for . . . capturing and electronically processing the sounds, and compiling and editing them to make the final sound recording" are joint "authors" of the sound recording.[241] In practice, such difficult questions have usually been avoided under the "work made for hire" doctrine. However, because "sound recordings" are not expressly included in the list of works by independent contractors that are eligible for "work made for hire" treatment, the issue of "authorship" may become relevant in the event of attempted terminations.[242]

[viii]   Architectural Works

The United States' adherence to the Berne Convention and the 1990 Architectural Works Copyright Protection Act significantly altered copyright protection for an architect's work product.

(a)   Pre-1991 Law

Under the 1909 Act, architectural plans were protected as "drawings . . . of a scientific or technical character."[243] In the 1976 Act, the category of "pictorial,

---

[234] *See* Capitol Records v. Mercury Records Corp., 221 F.2d 657, 659–62 (2d Cir. 1955).

[235] *See, e.g., id.* at 663.

[236] *See, e.g.,* 1968 Cal. Stat. 1256, c. 585, § 1 (codified as amended at Cal. Pen. Code § 653h).

[237] *See* Goldstein v. California, 412 U.S. 546 (1973). *See* § 1D[3][a][ii].

[238] *See* Sound Recordings Amendments Act, Pub. L. No, 92-140, § 1, 85 Stat. 391.

[239] *See* H.R. Rep. No. 94-1476, at 133 (1976).

[240] *See* 17 U.S.C. § 301(c).

[241] H.R. Rep. No. 94-1476, at 56 (1976).

[242] For ownership of copyright, including works made for hire and terminations of transfers, see § 4F.

[243] 1909 Act, § 5(i) (repealed 1978); Imperial Homes Corp. v. Lamont, 458 F.2d 895, 898 (5th Cir. 1972); *see also id.* at 897 ("the architect who originates a set of blueprints for a dwelling is as much an author for copyright purposes as the writer who creates an original novel").

graphic, and sculptural works" includes "diagrams, models, and technical drawings, including architectural plans."[244] The copyright owner could therefore prevent others from making copies of such plans, even for the purpose of constructing a building.[245] However, buildings themselves were not copyrightable, no matter how novel and ornamental, because buildings are useful articles and their ornamental features cannot be identified separately from, and are not capable of existing independently of, their utilitarian aspects.[246] Thus, a copyright in architectural drawings did not give the owner the right to exclude others from constructing the depicted structure.[247] Nonetheless, the right to prevent copying of plans provided substantial protection against unauthorized construction of the building depicted, because, as a practical matter, it is difficult, if not impossible, to construct a building without making multiple copies of plans for the use of contractors, building inspectors, etc.[248]

In adhering to the Berne Convention, effective March 1, 1989, the United States assumed the obligation of providing adequate copyright protection for the subject matter covered by the Berne Convention, including architectural works. Congress amended the definition of "pictorial, graphic and sculptural works" by adding the reference to "architectural plans" but it expressed its intent to codify existing law on the scope of protection for architectural plans and works.[249]

(b)   Architectural Works Copyright Protection Act

The 1990 Architectural Works Copyright Protection Act makes a building design itself a copyrightable work. The Act is prospective, protecting only works created on or after the date of enactment (December 1, 1990) and works "unconstructed and embodied in unpublished plans or drawings" on that date.[250]

---

[244] 17 U.S.C. § 101. The House Report expressly stated that "[a]n architect's plans and drawings would, of course, be protected by copyright," subject to the "conceptual separability" doctrine for useful articles. H.R. Rep. No. 94-1476, at 55 (1976).

[245] Imperial Homes Corp. v. Lamont, 458 F.2d 895, 899 (5th Cir. 1972) ("nothing in *Baker v. Selden* prevents . . . a copyright [in architectural plans] from vesting the law's grant of an exclusive right to make copies of the copyrighted plans so as to instruct a would-be builder on how to proceed to construct the dwelling pictured."); Demetriades v. Kaufman, 680 F. Supp. 658, 665 (S.D.N.Y. 1988) ("the unauthorized reproduction of copyrighted architectural plans constitutes infringement").

[246] H.R. Rep. No. 94-1476, at 55 (1976). *See* § 4C[4][a][v](b).

[247] *Imperial Homes*, 458 F.2d at 898 ("no architect who copyrights his blueprints could thereby acquire a monopoly on the right to build a house with 2 x 4s or with a pitched roof or with a slab foundation or any other particular feature, no matter how unique"); *Demetriades*, 680 F. Supp. at 666 ("Construction of a building imitating that depicted in copyrighted architectural plans does not . . . constitute infringement of those plans.").

[248] *Cf. Demetriades*, 680 F. Supp. at 666 n.13 (noting that "the effect of our ruling may be to shut down construction for a certain period of time, at least until new plans can be drawn up and submitted to the Scarsdale Architectural Review Board for consideration.").

[249] S. Rep. No. 100-352, at 7–9 (1988).

[250] Pub. L. No. 101-650, Title VII, § 706, 104 Stat. 5133; *see* Richard J. Zitz, Inc. v. Dos Santos Pereira, 232 F.3d 290, 292–93 (2d Cir. 2000) (Act does not protect works that were "substantially constructed" on effective date). The Act also provided that protection for unconstructed works embodied in unpublished plans or drawings would terminate unless the building was constructed by December 31, 2002. *Id.*

The Act added "architectural works" to section 102(a)'s list of copyrightable work categories and defined architectural works as "the design of a building as embodied in any tangible medium of expression, including a building, architectural plans, or drawings. The work includes the overall form as well as the arrangement and composition of spaces and elements in the design, but does not include individual standard features."[251]

The definition contains several facets. First, it is limited to *building* designs and does not extend to other three-dimensional structures, such as "interstate highway bridges, cloverleafs, canals, dams, and pedestrian walkways," that are not characterizable as buildings.[252] Second, the building design may be "fixed" in any tangible medium of expression, and not solely in an actual building.[253] Third, it includes "overall form" and "the arrangement and composition of spaces and elements," but it excludes "individual standard features," such as "common windows, doors, and other staple building components."[254] This is consistent with the general treatment of "building block" elements, such as words and short phrases.[255]

The Act disentangles architectural works from the separability test applicable to designs of other useful articles, but the legislative history indicates that the Copyright Office and courts should not "ignore functionality." Instead, if there are original design elements present, the court should "examine whether the design elements are functionally required." If they are, copyright is excluded;[256] but "[i]f the design elements are not functionally required, the work is protectible without

---

[251] 17 U.S.C. § 101.

[252] H.R. Rep. No. 101-735, at 18 (1990). During consideration of the 1990 Act, Congress deleted the phrase "or three dimensional structure" in order to exclude such items. *Id.* Congress added that the term "building" includes both "habitable structures such as houses and office buildings" and "structures that are used, but not inhabited by human beings, such as churches, pergolas, gazebos, and garden pavilions." *Id.*

[253] *See* Hunt v. Pasternack, 192 F.3d 877, 879 (9th Cir. 1999) (an architectural work may be embodied only in plans and drawings); Shine v. Childs, 382 F. Supp. 2d 602, 608 (S.D.N.Y. 2005) (an architectural work may be embodied only in a model, and need not be embodied in plans from which a building could be constructed). Despite this provision, Congress intended to keep separate copyright in the architectural work and in plans and drawings:

> An individual creating an architectural work by depicting that work in plans or drawing will have two separate copyrights, one in the architectural work (section 102(a)(8)), the other in the plans or drawings (section 102(a)(5)). Either or both of these copyrights may be infringed and eligible separately for damages.

H.R. Rep. No. 101-735, at 17 (1990). *See* Scholz Design, Inc. v. Sard Custom Homes, LLC, 691 F.3d 182 (2d Cir. 2012) (architectural plans are protected as pictorial works, even if no building has been or could be constructed from them).

[254] H.R. Rep. No. 101-735, at 16 (1990). "The phrase 'arrangement and composition of spaces and elements' recognizes that . . . creativity in architecture frequently takes the form of a selection, coordination, or arrangement of unprotectable elements into an original, protectable whole." *Id.*; *see also* Oravec v. Sunny Isles Luxury Ventures, LLC, 527 F.3d 1218, 1225 (11th Cir. 2008) ("while individual standard features . . . are not themselves copyrightable, an architect's original combination of such features may be.").

[255] *See* § 4C[1][b].

[256] *See, e.g.* Zalewski v. Cicero Builder Dev., Inc., 754 F.3d 95, 105 (2d Cir. 2014) (elements dictated by efficiency, building codes, or engineering necessity are not protected by copyright).

regard to the physical or conceptual separability."[257]

Finally, "[t]the copyright in an architectural work . . . does not include the right to prevent the making, distributing, or public display of pictures, paintings, photographs, or other pictorial representations of the work, if the building in which the work is embodied is located in or ordinarily visible from a public place."[258] Thus, the copyright in a building only prevents the reproduction and distribution of three-dimensional replicas of the building, not two-dimensional ones.[259] In addition, the owner of the building has the right to "make or authorize the making of alterations to such building, and destroy or authorize the destruction of such building," without the consent of the copyright owner.[260]

[b]   Works Employing Preexisting Material

In addition to the eight categories of "works of authorship" listed in section 102, section 103 lists two additional categories of works that contain preexisting material: compilations and derivative works. Under section 103, "a compilation or derivative work is copyrightable if it represents an 'original work of authorship' and falls within one or more of the categories listed in section 102."[261] Copyright protection for such works, however, is subject to two important limitations. First, "protection for a work employing preexisting material in which copyright subsists does not extend to any part of the work in which such material has been used unlawfully."[262] Second, "[t]he copyright in a compilation or derivative work extends only to the material contributed by the author of such work, as distinguished from the preexisting material employed in the work, and does not imply an exclusive right in the preexisting material."[263]

[i]   Compilations and Collective Works

A compilation is "a work formed by the collection and assembling of preexisting materials or of data that are selected, coordinated, or arranged in such a way that the resulting work as a whole constitutes an original work of authorship."[264] This

---

[257] H.R. Rep. No. 101-735, at 18 (1990).

[258] 17 U.S.C. § 120(a). *See* Leicester v. Warner Bros., 232 F.3d 1212 (9th Cir. 2000) (holding that "streetwall" portion of outdoor sculpture adjoining building was part of the building itself and was therefore subject to § 120(a)).

[259] Be aware of the possibility of trademark protection for distinctive buildings; although such protection will not protect against ordinary commercial exploitation of photographs of the building. *See* Rock & Roll Hall of Fame & Museum, Inc. v. Gentile Prods., 134 F.3d 749 (6th Cir. 1998).

[260] 17 U.S.C. § 120(b).

[261] H.R. 94-1476, at 57 (1976); *see* 17 U.S.C. § 103(a) ("The subject matter of copyright as specified by section 102 includes compilations and derivative works.").

[262] 17 U.S.C. § 103(a). This section "prevents an infringer from benefiting, through copyright protection, from committing an unlawful act, but preserves protection for those parts of the work that do not employ the preexisting work. Thus, an unauthorized translation of a novel could not be copyrighted at all, but the owner of copyright in an anthology of poetry could sue someone who infringed the whole anthology, even though the infringer proves that publication of one of the poems was unauthorized." H.R. Rep. No. 94-1476, at 57–58 (1976).

[263] 17 U.S.C. § 103(b).

[264] 17 U.S.C. § 101.

definition "identifies three distinct elements and requires each to be met for a work to qualify as a copyrightable compilation: (1) the collection and assembly of pre-existing material, facts, or data; (2) the selection, coordination, or arrangement of those materials; and (3) the creation, by virtue of the particular selection, coordination, or arrangement, of an 'original' work of authorship."[265] "Not every selection, coordination, or arrangement will pass muster. . . . [T]he statute envisions that there will be some fact-based works in which the selection, coordination, and arrangement are not sufficiently original to trigger copyright protection."[266]

In *Feist Publications, Inc. v. Rural Telephone Service Co.*,[267] the Supreme Court held that a "white pages" telephone directory was not copyrightable for lack of originality. The Court emphasized that facts and data are not copyrightable, "because facts do not owe their origin to an act of authorship. . . . [T]he first person to find and report a particular fact has not created the fact; he or she has merely discovered its existence."[268] However, "[a] factual compilation is eligible for copyright if it features an original selection or arrangement of facts, but the copyright is limited to the particular selection or arrangement. In no event may copyright extend to the facts themselves."[269] Thus, a competitor may copy the facts from another's compilation, "so long as the competing work does not feature the same selection and arrangement."[270]

In *Feist*, both the selection of information — name, town, and telephone number of all subscribers — and the arrangement of that information — alphabetical order by last name — were held to lack the required originality.[271] However, a selection or arrangement that depends on subjective opinion or judgment will suffice. Thus, a selection of 5,000 baseball cards (out of 18,000) that were deemed to be "premium" cards was sufficiently original to qualify for copyright.[272] However, "the

---

[265] Feist Publications, Inc. v. Rural Telephone Service Co., 499 U.S. 340, 357 (1991).

[266] *Id.* at 358.

[267] 499 U.S. 340 (1991).

[268] *Id.* at 347.

[269] *Id.* at 350–51.

[270] *Id.* at 349. The Court remarked: "It may seem unfair that much of the fruit of the compiler's labor may be used by others without compensation. . . . [H]owever, this is not 'some unforeseen byproduct of a statutory scheme.' It is, rather, 'the essence of copyright,' and a constitutional requirement. The primary objective of copyright is not to reward the labor of authors, but '[t]o promote the Progress of Science and useful Arts.' To this end, copyright assures authors the right to their original expression, but encourages others to build freely upon the ideas and information conveyed by a work. . . . [Thus,] assuming the absence of original written expression, only the compiler's selection and arrangement may be protected; the raw facts may be copied at will. This result is neither unfair nor unfortunate. It is the means by which copyright advances the progress of science and art." *Id.* at 349–50 (internal citations omitted).

[271] *Id.* at 362–64. *See also* Silverstein v. Penguin Putnam, Inc., 522 F. Supp. 2d 579 (S.D.N.Y. 2007) (finding plaintiff's selection of all uncollected poems by Dorothy Parker that he could find was not sufficiently original).

[272] Eckes v. Card Prices Update, 736 F.2d 859, 863 (2d Cir. 1984). *See also* Key Publications, Inc. v. Chinatown Today Publishing Enterprises, Inc., 945 F.2d 509, 513–14 (2d Cir. 1991) (Yellow Pages are copyrightable); *but see* Bellsouth Advertising & Publishing Corp. v. Donnelly Info. Publishing, Inc., 999 F.2d 1436, 1441–44 (11th Cir. 1993) (en banc) (yellow pages are not copyrightable); Warren Publishing,

copyright in a factual compilation is thin."[273] Thus, even minor changes in selection and arrangement may result in a finding of non-infringement. For example, although a selection of 576 legal forms was original, it was not infringed by defendant's selection of 406 forms, even though 350 forms, or 61%, were common to both.[274]

The category of "compilations" also includes "collective works." A "collective work" is defined as "a work, such as a periodical issue, anthology, or encyclopedia, in which a number of contributions, constituting separate and independent works in themselves, are assembled into a collective whole."[275] For example, in an anthology of 24 poems, there are separate copyrights in each of the poems, and there is an additional compilation copyright in the original selection and arrangement of those poems to form a single collective work. The copyrights in the individual contributions are owned by the authors of those contributions, while the copyright in the collective work is owned by the editor or compiler.[276]

[ii] Derivative Works

"A 'derivative work' is a work based upon one or more preexisting works, such as a translation, musical arrangement, dramatization, fictionalization, motion picture version, sound recording, art reproduction, abridgement, condensation, or any other form in which a work may be recast, transformed, or adapted."[277] In addition, a "work consisting of editorial revisions, annotations, elaborations, or other modifications which, as a whole, represent an original work of authorship, is a 'derivative work.' "[278]

A derivative work based on a previous work is copyrightable if, but only if, the second work meets the originality requirement. Some courts have suggested that any "distinguishable variation" from a previous work is copyrightable, even if the differences were inadvertent.[279] However, in *L. Batlin & Son v. Snyder*, the Second Circuit held that "to support a copyright there must be at least some substantial

---

Inc. v. Microdos Data Corp., 115 F.3d 1509, 1517–19 (11th Cir. 1997) (cable television industry factbook is not copyrightable).

[273] *Feist*, 499 U.S. at 349.

[274] Ross, Brovins & Oehmke v. LexisNexis Group, 463 F.3d 478, 482–83 (6th Cir. 2006); *see also Key Publications*, 945 F.2d at 515–16 (finding no infringement where defendants directory had only 28 categories and 2000 entries, compared with 260 categories and 9000 entries in plaintiff's directory, despite deliberate copying of 1500 entries).

[275] 17 U.S.C. § 101.

[276] 17 U.S.C. § 201(c). For ownership of copyright generally, including compilations, see § 4F.

[277] 17 U.S.C. § 101. Similarly, section 7 of the 1909 Act provided that "Compilations or abridgments, adaptations, arrangements, dramatizations, translations, or other versions of works in the public domain or of copyrighted works when produced with the consent of the proprietor of the copyright in such works, or works republished with new matter, shall be regarded as new works subject to copyright."

[278] 17 U.S.C. § 101.

[279] Alfred Bell & Co. v. Catalda Fine Arts, 191 F.2d 99, 104–05 (2d Cir. 1951) (mezzotint engravings based on public domain paintings were copyrightable). However, *photographic* reproductions of paintings in the public domain were held *not* to be sufficiently original in Bridgeman Art Library, Ltd. v. Corel Corp., 25 F. Supp. 2d 421 (S.D.N.Y. 1998) (U.K. law), *on reconsideration*, 36 F. Supp. 2d 191 (S.D.N.Y. 1999) (U.S. law). See § 4C[1][c].

variation, not merely a trivial variation such as might occur in the translation to a different medium."[280] Thus, the court held that a plastic replica of a traditional cast-iron "Uncle Sam" coin bank that was in the public domain was not copyrightable. "To extend copyrightability to minuscule variations would simply put a weapon for harassment in the hands of mischievous copiers intent on appropriating and monopolizing public domain work."[281]

In *Gracen v. Bradford Exchange*, the Seventh Circuit held that "a derivative work must be substantially different from the underlying work to be copyrightable."[282] Thus, the court held that plaintiff's painting, based on the MGM movie *The Wizard of Oz*, was not copyrightable.[283] According to Judge Posner, "the purpose of the term ['original'] in copyright law is not to guide aesthetic judgments but to assure a sufficiently gross difference between the underlying and the derivative work to avoid entangling subsequent artists depicting the underlying work in copyright problems."[284]

In *Shrock v. Learning Curve Int'l, Inc.*,[285] the plaintiff was hired to photograph the defendant's licensed toys based on characters from "Thomas the Tank Engine." Retreating from the "substantially different" standard, the Seventh Circuit attempted to synthesize the previous cases into a single standard:

> (1) the originality requirement for derivative works is not more demanding than the originality requirement for other works; and (2) the key inquiry is whether there is sufficient nontrivial expressive variation in the derivative work to make it distinguishable from the underlying work in some meaningful way. This focus on the presence of nontrivial "distinguishable variation" adequately captures the concerns articulated in *Gracen* without unduly narrowing the copyrightability of derivative works.[286]

Applying this standard, the court concluded that "Schrock's photos of the 'Thomas & Friends' toys are highly accurate product photos but contain minimally sufficient variation in angle, perspective, lighting, and dimension to be distinguishable from the underlying works."[287]

---

[280] 536 F.2d 486, 491 (2d Cir. 1976) (en banc).

[281] *Id.*

[282] 698 F.2d 300, 305 (7th Cir. 1983).

[283] *Id.* The 1939 movie, of course, was itself a derivative work of the book by L. Frank Baum, first published in 1900. The book entered the public domain in 1956, but the visual elements of the movie, on which Gracen's design was based, were covered by MGM's derivative work copyright in the movie.

[284] *Id.* For example, "Suppose Artist A produces a reproduction of the Mona Lisa, a painting in the public domain, which differs slightly from the original. B also makes a reproduction of the Mona Lisa. A, who has copyrighted his derivative work, sues B for infringement. B's defense is that he was copying the original, not A's reproduction. But if the difference between the original and A's reproduction is slight, the difference between A's and B's reproductions will also be slight, so that if B had access to A's reproductions the trier of fact will be hard-pressed to decide whether B was copying A or copying the Mona Lisa itself." *Id.* at 304.

[285] 586 F.3d 513 (7th Cir. 2009).

[286] *Id.* at 521.

[287] *Id.* at 522.

As mentioned above, copyright protection for derivative works is subject to two important limitations. First, because the owner of copyright in the underlying work has the exclusive right to prepare derivative works based upon that work,[288] copyright protection for a derivative work based on a copyrighted work "does not extend to any part of the work in which such material has been used unlawfully."[289] This provision sometimes denies copyright to a work that would otherwise meet the standard of sufficient originality.[290] Thus, in *Anderson v. Stallone*, the court held that an author who created a derivative work based on characters from the movie "Rocky" without permission could not claim copyright protection in the derivative work.[291]

Despite this limitation, however, the "copyright in a derivative work, like copyright in any other work, arises by operation of law once the author's original expression is fixed in a tangible medium."[292] Thus, a person who creates a derivative work with permission of the owner of copyright in the underlying work does not need further permission to claim a copyright in the derivative work.[293] The Seventh Circuit, however, has held that the parties to an agreement may change this "default rule" by agreement: "[I]f the pertinent agreement between the parties affirmatively bars the licensee from obtaining copyright protection even in a licensed derivative work, that contractual provision would appear to govern."[294]

The second limitation is that the copyright in a derivative work extends only to the "new matter" added by the creator of the derivative work. The derivative work copyright implies no exclusive right in the "preexisting material employed in the work," and it "does not affect or enlarge the scope, duration, ownership, or subsistence of, any copyright protection in the preexisting material."[295]

---

[288] 17 U.S.C. § 106(2). *See* § 4G[2].

[289] 17 U.S.C. § 103(a). The same was true under section 7 of the 1909 Act, which provided that a derivative work shall be regarded as a copyrightable "new work" only "when produced with the consent of the proprietor of the copyright" in the original work, unless the original work was in the public domain.

[290] *See, e.g.*, Palladium Music, Inc. v. EatSleepMusic, Inc., 398 F.3d 1193 (10th Cir. 2005) (holding karaoke sound recording copyrights invalid and unenforceable for failure to obtain compulsory or consensual licenses from the copyright owners of the underlying musical works).

[291] 11 U.S.P.Q. 2d 1161 (C.D. Cal. 1989).

[292] Schrock v. Learning Curve Int'l, Inc., 586 F.3d 513, 523 (7th Cir. 2009).

[293] In Gracen v. Bradford Exchange, 698 F.2d 300 (7th Cir. 1983), Judge Posner's opinion for the court suggested in dicta that separate permission was needed to claim a copyright in the derivative work. *Id.* at 303 ("the question is not whether Miss Gracen was licensed to make a derivative work but whether she was also licensed to exhibit the painting and to copyright it."). However, in *Schrock*, the Seventh Circuit disavowed this statement, holding that "the dicta was mistaken; there is nothing in the Copyright Act requiring the author of a derivative work to obtain permission to copyright his work from the owner of copyright in the underlying work." 586 F.3d at 523.

[294] *Schrock*, 586 F.3d at 524, *quoting* 1 NIMMER ON COPYRIGHT § 3.06 (2009). *Accord*, Liu v. Price Waterhouse, LLP, 302 F.3d 749, 755 (7th Cir. 2001). *But see* Gaylord v. U.S., 595 F.3d 1364, 1380 (Fed. Cir. 2010) (holding that sculptor Gaylord was not bound by agreement between the United States and the prime contractor for the Korean War Veterans Memorial, which provided that the copyrights in the Memorial would be owned by the U.S. government); *id.* at 1382 (Newman, J., dissenting) (quoting the pertinent agreements).

[295] 17 U.S.C. § 103(b). *Cf.* Stewart v. Abend, 495 U.S. 207, 223 (1990) ("The aspects of a derivative work added by the derivative author are that author's property, but the element drawn from the

[5]   Government Works

Section 105 excludes copyright in "any work of the United States Government."[296] A "work of the United States Government" is defined as "a work prepared by an officer or employee of the United States Government as part of that person's official duties."[297] Thus, the prohibition does not extend to works created by independent contractors,[298] nor does it extend to works that are not within the employee's official duties.[299] In addition, "the United States Government is not precluded from receiving and holding copyrights transferred to it by assignment, bequest, or otherwise."[300]

Because section 105 by its terms applies only to the Federal government, nothing in the statute precludes state and local governments from claiming copyright in works produced by public officials as part of their official duties.[301] Provisions of state law, however, may dictate that otherwise protectible works be made publicly available.[302] In addition, case law holds that statutes, regulations and judicial opinions are part of the public domain and cannot be subject to copyright ownership by any government, whether state or federal.[303]

Somewhat more contentious is the situation in which the statute or ordinance is drafted by a private party. For example, in *Veeck v. Southern Building Code*

---

pre-existing work remains on grant from the owner of the pre-existing work.").

[296] 17 U.S.C. § 105. Likewise, section 8 of the 1909 Act provided that "No copyright shall subsist . . . in any publication of the United States Government." The word "publication" in the 1909 Act was construed narrowly to refer only to "printed works." *See* Scherr v. Universal Match Co., 297 F. Supp. 107, 110–11 (S.D.N.Y. 1967) (statue created by two enlisted men on active duty was not a "publication of the United States Government"). No such ambiguity would arise under the 1976 Act, which uses the broader term "work."

[297] 17 U.S.C. § 101.

[298] *See, e.g.*, Schnapper v. Foley, 667 F.2d 102, 109 (D.C. Cir. 1981) (government-commissioned television documentary produced by public broadcasting entities).

[299] *See, e.g.*, Public Affairs Assocs. v. Rickover, 268 F. Supp. 444, 448–50 (admiral entitled to copyright in speeches prepared and delivered on his own time, even though the subject of the speech related to his duties).

[300] 17 U.S.C. § 105. *See, e.g.*, U.S. v. Washington Mint, LLC, 115 F. Supp. 2d 1089, 1096–97 (design of Sacagawea dollar coin by private individual).

[301] *See, e.g.*, County of Suffolk v. First American Real Estate Solutions, 261 F.3d 179 (2d Cir. 2001) (county could assert copyright in "tax maps" showing ownership, size and location of each parcel of real property; copyright was not abrogated by state freedom of information law).

[302] *See, e.g.*, County of Santa Clara v. Superior Court, 170 Cal. App. 4th 1301 (2009) (county is required to provide copies of its Geographic Information Systems (GIS) maps, and may not claim copyright or require an end-user license agreement); Seago v. Horry County, 663 S.E.2d 38 (S.C. 2008) (county must provide copies of GIS maps on request, but may pass ordinance or require license agreement to restrict commercial dissemination); Microdecisions, Inc. v. Skinner, 889 So.2d 871 (Fla. Dist. Ct. App. 2004) (tax maps produced by county employee within scope of his employment are public records not subject to copyright).

[303] *See, e.g.*, Wheaton v. Peters, 33 U.S. (8 Pet.) 591 (1834) (opinions of U.S. Supreme Court); Banks v. Manchester, 128 U.S. 244 (1888) (opinions of Ohio Supreme Court); State of Georgia v. Harrison Co., 548 F. Supp. 110, 113–14 (N.D. Ga. 1982) (state statutes), *vacated upon settlement*, 559 F. Supp. 37 (N.D. Ga. 1983).

Congress Int'l,[304] a model building code drafted by SBCCI was adopted by two towns in North Texas. Veeck posted a copy of the model code on his website. A majority of the Fifth Circuit, sitting *en banc*, held that the model code was not copyrightable for public policy reasons.[305] Alternatively, the *Veeck* majority held that once the model code was enacted, it became a "fact" that could not be protected under the merger doctrine.[306] However, in *Practice Management Info. Corp. v. American Medical Ass'n*,[307] the Ninth Circuit upheld the trial court's ruling that the AMA's medical procedure coding system did *not* enter the public domain when it was adopted by a federal health care agency as the sole permissible system for use by applicants for Medicaid reimbursement.

[6] National Eligibility

Until 1891, no work by a foreign author was entitled to copyright protection in the United States unless the author resided here. After the 1891 Act,[308] the United States entered into a number of bilateral treaties with countries that provided reciprocal protection to U.S. authors. Alternatively, works of nationals of other countries became eligible for protection as the result of Presidential proclamations based on findings that those countries provided equivalent protection to the works of U.S. citizens under their national laws. In 1954, the United States signed its first multilateral copyright treaty, the Universal Copyright Convention.

Section 104 of the 1976 Act codified these various bases for the protection of works of foreign origin. Protection for foreign works was amended and expanded in 1988 by the Berne Convention Implementation Act,[309] and again in 1998 by the Digital Millennium Copyright Act, which recognized U.S. adherence to the TRIPS Agreement, the WIPO Copyright Treaty, and the WIPO Performances and Phonograms Treaty.[310]

As to *unpublished* works, section 104(a) provides, without reservation, that works within the statutory definition of copyrightable subject matter, "while unpublished, are subject to protection under this title without regard to the nationality or domicile of the author."[311]

---

[304] 293 F.3d 791 (5th Cir. 2002) (en banc).

[305] *Id.* at 795–800. *See also* Building Officials & Code Admins. Int'l v. Code Technology, Inc., 628 F.2d 730 (1st Cir. 1980) (vacating preliminary injunction; suggesting strongly that nonprofit organization's building code entered the public domain when enacted by Massachusetts).

[306] 293 F.3d at 800–02. For a discussion of the merger doctrine, see § 4C[3][c].

[307] 121 F.3d 516 (9th Cir. 1997).

[308] Act of Mar. 3, 1891, 26 Stat. 1106.

[309] Under 17 U.S.C. § 104(c), the Berne Convention is not "self-executing"; it is effective only to the extent it is implemented in domestic law.

[310] Under 17 U.S.C. § 104(d), "no works other than sound recordings shall be eligible for protection . . . solely by virtue of the adherence of the United States to the Geneva Phonograms Convention or the WIPO Performances and Phonograms Treaty."

[311] 17 U.S.C. § 104(a). Before the 1976 Act, common-law copyright protected unpublished works without regard to national origin. *See, e.g.*, Palmer v. DeWitt, 47 N.Y. 532 (1872). When Congress extended federal statutory copyright protection to unpublished works in the 1976 Act, it preserved this rule of neutrality with regard to national origin.

As to *published* works, section 104(b) provides that works receive protection if they fall into one of six categories: (1) any author is a national or domiciliary of the United States or of any "treaty party";[312] (2) works that are "first published in the United States or in a foreign nation that, on the date of first publication, is a treaty party";[313] (3) sound recordings that are first fixed in a "treaty party";[314] (4) pictorial, graphic, sculptural, or architectural works embodied in a building located in the U.S. or in a treaty party;[315] (5) works "first published by the United Nations or any of its specialized agencies, or by the Organization of American States";[316] or works that come "within the scope of a Presidential proclamation,"[317] if the President finds that the foreign nation extends copyright to United States authors, or to works first published in the United States, "on substantially the same basis as" it does to works of its own authors, or works first published in its territory.[318]

§ 4D FORMALITIES

Under the 1976 Act, copyright protection arises automatically upon creation of a work,[319] which occurs when the work "is fixed in a copy or phonorecord for the first time."[320] Currently, no formalities are required to obtain a copyright, to license a copyright, or to enforce a copyright by non-judicial means.[321] However, registration remains a pre-condition to filing suit for infringement of United States works,[322] and it remains a pre-condition to obtaining statutory damages and attorneys fees for all works.[323]

Historically, United States copyright law imposed formalities as a condition of obtaining copyright protection. Before the 1909 Act, a work had to be registered before it was published to obtain copyright protection; and notice of the copyright was required on published copies of the work. Under the 1909 Act, a work had to be

---

[312] 17 U.S.C. § 104(b)(1). A "treaty party" is defined as any country "that is a party to an international agreement" concerning copyright. 17 U.S.C. § 101. For a list of countries with whom the United States maintains copyright relations, see U.S. Copyright Office, Circular 38a, *International Copyright Relations of the United States.*

[313] 17 U.S.C. § 104(b)(2). This category includes works that are published in the U.S. or a treaty party within 30 days after first publication in a foreign country that is not a treaty party. 17 U.S.C. § 104(b).

[314] 17 U.S.C. § 104(b)(3).

[315] 17 U.S.C. § 104(b)(4).

[316] 17 U.S.C. § 104(b)(5).

[317] 17 U.S.C. § 104(b)(6).

[318] *Id.*

[319] 17 U.S.C. § 302(a).

[320] 17 U.S.C. § 101 (definition of "created"). Section 101 further provides that "where a work is prepared over a period of time, the portion of it that has been fixed at any particular time constitutes the work as of that time, and where the work has been prepared in different versions, each version constitutes a separate work." *Id.* For a discussion of what constitutes "fixation," see § 4C[2].

[321] The repeal of formalities that were previously required occurred as a result of U.S. adherence to the Berne Convention, which states that "[t]he enjoyment and exercise of these rights shall not be subject to any formality." Berne Convention, 1971 Paris Text, Art. 5(2).

[322] 17 U.S.C. § 411(a). *See* § 4D[3][b].

[323] 17 U.S.C. § 412. *See* § 4D[3][b].

published with proper notice to obtain copyright protection, and it had to be registered in order to have its copyright term renewed, or to file an infringement suit. The 1976 Act retained the notice requirement but moderated the consequences of notice errors and omissions. The 1988 Berne Convention Implementation Act eliminated the mandatory notice requirement for all copies publicly distributed after the Act, and it eliminated registration as a condition of suit for foreign works. However, registration remains important even today, and knowledge of the formalities required under previous law is important in assessing the validity of copyright for works published before March 1, 1989.

[1] Publication

[a] Publication Under the 1909 Act

Before January 1, 1978, the effective date of the 1976 Act, unpublished works were protected by state law (so-called "common-law copyright"). Once a work was "published," state-law protection ended, and one of two things happened. If the work was published with proper copyright notice, it obtained a federal statutory copyright under the 1909 Act. If the work was published without proper copyright notice, it immediately entered the public domain. Publication, therefore, was the principal dividing line between state and federal protection, and the initial term of 28 years was measured from the date of first publication.[324]

Because so much depended on the concept of publication, over time courts developed a body of case law that distinguished two kinds of publication. A "general" publication divested perpetual common-law (state-law) copyright in an unpublished work, and it had the potential to *invest* "statutory" (federal) copyright, running for a limited time from the date of publication. By contrast, a "limited" publication was a publication only in lay terms — an event that left the legal *status quo* unaffected, even if the author, in publishing, failed to observe the statutory formalities of copyright.

Under the case law, a "publication" was deemed to occur "when by consent of the copyright owner, the original or tangible copies of a work are sold, leased, loaned, given away, or otherwise made available to the general public, or when an authorized offer is made to dispose of the work in any such manner even if a sale or other such disposition does not in fact occur."[325] Such a publication was a "general" publication when copies of the work were "made available to members of the [general] public regardless of who they are or what they will do with it."[326] By contrast, a publication was deemed to be "limited" when copies of the work were distributed "both (1) to a "definitely selected group," and (2) for a limited purpose,

---

[324] Authors could also secure federal statutory copyrights in certain kinds of unpublished works by registering them under § 12 of the 1909 Act. In such cases, state-law protection was terminated, and the initial 28-year federal term began, on the date of registration.

[325] American Vitagraph, Inc. v. Levy, 659 F.2d 1023, 1027 (9th Cir. 1981), quoting 1 NIMMER ON COPYRIGHT § 4.04 (1981); *accord*, Academy of Motion Picture Arts & Sciences v. Creative House Promotions, Inc., 944 F.2d 1446, 1450 n.1 (9th Cir. 1991).

[326] *Academy of Motion Picture Arts & Sciences*, 944 F.2d at 1452.

without the right of further reproduction, distribution or sale."[327]

Courts expressly applied the concept of "limited" publication so as to avoid forfeiture of the copyright when possible. For example, in *Academy of Motion Pictures Arts & Sciences v. Creative House Promotions, Inc.*, the court held that the distribution of 158 "Oscar" statuettes without proper copyright notice between 1929 and 1941 was a "limited" publication, because the Oscars were distributed to a "definitely selected group" (members and performers in the film industry selected for outstanding achievement), and because the Oscars had a limited purpose of honoring achievement in the film industry.[328] More questionably, the court found that there was an "implied" restriction on further distribution or sale of the Oscar statuette, because no living recipient had ever sold or given away his or her Oscar.[329] In another case, however, the distribution to theaters of publicity materials (movie posters and lobby cards) was held to be a "general" publication, notwithstanding a contractual agreement to return the materials, because the clause was not enforced and redistribution and sale of the materials was encouraged.[330]

The concept of "publication" was based on a book model of publishing, in which tangible copies of the work are fixed, and those fixed copies are then distributed to the public. As a result, courts encountered difficulties in applying the concept of "publication" to other types of works. In 1912, the Supreme Court held that public performances of a play were *not* a publication of the play.[331] Applying this precedent, two courts have held that Martin Luther King's famous "I Have a Dream" speech was not published when he delivered the speech in front of thousands of people at the Lincoln Memorial, and millions more listening on the radio.[332] However, a motion picture was "published" when it was commercially released in theaters — not because of the public performances themselves, but because "copies of [the] film are placed in the regional exchanges for distribution to theatre operators."[333] Similarly, the public display of a painting in a gallery is not

---

[327] *Id.*

[328] *Id.* at 1452–53.

[329] *Id.* at 1453–54. *See also* Soc'y of Holy Transfiguration Monastery, Inc. v. Gregory, 689 F.3d 29, 45–46 (1st Cir. 2012) (authorized distribution of translations to religious congregations to solicit editorial feedback was a "limited" publication).

[330] Warner Bros. Ent'mt, Inc. v. X One X Prods., 644 F.3d 584 (8th Cir. 2011).

[331] Ferris v. Frohman, 223 U.S. 424 (1912).

[332] *See* King v. Mister Maestro, Inc., 224 F. Supp. 101 (S.D.N.Y. 1963); Estate of Martin Luther King Jr., Inc. v. CBS, Inc., 194 F.3d 1211 (11th Cir. 1999). King also distributed tangible copies of the speech to the press, but the *Mister Maestro* court held that this was a "limited" publication, even though King likely intended the speech to be reproduced, while the *CBS* court held that there was a triable issue of fact as to whether the distribution of copies was in fact "limited" to the press.

[333] American Vitagraph, Inc. v. Levy, 659 F.2d 1023, 1038 (9th Cir. 1981) (nonetheless holding that one week of "preview" performances to paying customers, for the limited purpose of gauging audience reaction to the film, was a "limited" publication). *See also* Burke v. National Broadcasting Co., Inc., 598 F.2d 688 (1st Cir. 1979) (finding a "limited" publication where an individual gave a copy of his film footage to a professor to use in his lectures and in a noncommercial television program); Martha Graham School & Dance Foundation, Inc. v. Martha Graham Center of Contemporary Dance, Inc., 380 F.3d 624, 644–45 (2d Cir. 2004) (affirming finding of publication for choreographic works which were listed in business

a "publication";[334] however, an "unrestricted" sale of an original painting was a "general" publication of the painting, meaning that copyright protection was forfeited upon such a sale if the canvas lacked proper copyright notice.[335]

A special problem concerned "publication" of musical works. A musical work was "published" if copies of the sheet music were distributed to the general public. But many musical works were distributed to the public only in the form of phonograph records. Because the Supreme Court in 1908 had defined a "copy" of a musical work as "a written or printed record of it in intelligible notation,"[336] most courts held that a phonograph record was *not* a "copy" of a musical work, and therefore that distribution of a phonograph record to the public was not a "publication" of the musical work.[337] In 1995, however, the Ninth Circuit disagreed, holding that distribution of a phonograph record to the public *was* a publication of the musical work.[338] Congress responded by enacting section 303(b) of the Copyright Act, which provides that "[t]he distribution before January 1, 1978, of a phonorecord shall not for any purpose constitute a publication of the musical work embodied therein."[339] Courts have upheld the retroactive application of this statute to conduct occurring before its enactment.[340]

Finally, it should be noted that under the 1909 Act, "publication" of a derivative work generally was *not* deemed to be publication of the underlying work on which it was based.[341] Thus, if the derivative work entered the public domain because it was published without notice, it still could not be reproduced without infringing the copyright in the underlying work.[342] There was one established exception to this

---

records as "filmed and sold" or "commercially produced films and videotapes," and for works listed in the catalog of the New York Public Library).

[334] American Tobacco Co. v. Werckmeister, 207 U.S. 284 (1907).

[335] *See* Grandma Moses Properties, Inc. v. This Week Magazine, 117 F. Supp. 348 (S.D.N.Y. 1953).

[336] White-Smith Music Publishing Co. v. Apollo Co., 209 U.S. 1, 17 (1908). For a discussion of *White-Smith*, see § 4C[2][a].

[337] The leading case for this view was Rosette v. Rainbo Record Mfg. Corp., 354 F. Supp. 1183, *aff'd per curiam*, 546 F.2d 461 (2d Cir. 1976).

[338] La Cienega Music Co. v. ZZ Top, 53 F.3d 950 (9th Cir. 1995).

[339] 17 U.S.C. § 303(b). *See also* Capitol Records, Inc. v. Naxos of America, Inc., 830 N.E.2d 250 (N.Y. 2005) (holding that public distribution of a phonorecord also did not constitute a "publication" of the *sound recording* embodied in that phonorecord).

[340] *See* Mayhew v. Allsup, 166 F.3d 821 (6th Cir. 1999) (concluding that § 303(b) applies to cases pending at the time of enactment); ABKCO Music, Inc. v. LaVere, 217 F.3d 684 (9th Cir. 2000) (holding that retroactivity is appropriate because the act provided a clarification rather than a change in the law).

[341] Former 17 U.S.C. § 7 (enacted 1909, renumbered and codified in 1947, repealed 1978) ("the publication of any such new works shall not affect the force or validity of any subsisting copyright upon the matter employed or any part thereof."). *See, e.g.*, Rushton v. Vitale, 218 F.2d 434 (2d Cir. 1955) (publication of a photograph of a three-dimensional doll did not place the doll itself in the public domain).

[342] *Cf.* Grove Press, Inc. v. Greenleaf Publishing Co., 247 F. Supp. 518 (E.D.N.Y. 1965) (even though English translation of a French novel had entered the public domain, defendant could not reprint the English translation without infringing the valid copyright in the underlying novel). *But see* Warner Bros. Ent'mt v. X One X Prods., 644 F.3d 584 (8th Cir. 2011) (where publicity materials were published without notice before motion picture was released, defendants could copy those materials in whole or in part, but they could not combine images from those materials in a way that infringed the "incremental expression" added in the later copyrighted movies).

general rule: publication of a motion picture was held to be a "publication" of the unpublished screenplay on which it was based, which was sufficient to divest the common-law copyright in the previously unpublished screenplay.[343]

[b]   Publication Under the 1976 Act

The 1976 Act defines "publication" as "the distribution of copies or phonorecords of a work to the public by sale or other transfer of ownership, or by rental, lease, or lending."[344] It adds that "offering to distribute copies or phonorecords to a group of persons for purposes of further distribution, public performance, or public display, constitutes publication."[345] Thus, only certain offers to distribute constitute "publication" under the 1976 Act. Finally, the 1976 Act specifies that "[a] public performance or display of a work does not of itself constitute publication."[346] This retains the old rule that a public performance is not a publication, but it rejects the interpretation of some courts that public display of a work of art without restrictions against its reproduction is a publication.

Although publication is no longer the dividing line between state common-law and federal statutory protection, it is still an important event for a number of reasons, including (1) eligibility of foreign works;[347] duration of works made for hire;[348] termination of transfers;[349] deposit and registration requirements;[350] and the availability of statutory damages.[351]

Most importantly, when a work was published between January 1, 1978 and March 1, 1989, it had to bear proper copyright notice, including the year of first publication. If the work was published without proper notice, it entered the public domain, although the omission could be "cured" in some instances if registration was made within five years of first publication.[352]

[2]   Notice

From 1790 to 1989, U.S. law required that some form of public notice of a claim of copyright be given. The 1790 Act required publication of notice in a newspaper for four consecutive weeks. The requirement of notice on all published copies was introduced in 1802. The prescribed form of notice ran to 100 words, more or less, depending on the particulars of the work in question. The 1870 Act reduced the

---

[343] *See* Batjac Prods., Inc. v. GoodTimes Home Video Corp., 160 F.3d 1223 (9th Cir. 1998); Shoptalk, Ltd. v. Concorde-New Horizons Corp., 168 F.3d 586 (2d Cir. 1999). These courts construed the language of former § 7 to refer only to federal statutory copyright protection, not to common-law protection.

[344] 17 U.S.C. § 101.

[345] *Id.*

[346] *Id.*

[347] 17 U.S.C. § 104. *See* § 4C[6].

[348] 17 U.S.C. § 302(c). *See* § 4E.

[349] 17 U.S.C. § 203(a)(3), 304(c). *See* § 4E.

[350] 17 U.S.C. § 407, 17 U.S.C. § 410(c). *See* § 4D[3][a], [b].

[351] 17 U.S.C. § 412. *See* § 4D[3][b].

[352] *See* § 4D[2][b].

required notice to a single sentence of 25 words. The short form of notice familiar today was first introduced in 1874.

The 1909 Copyright Act required that a work be published with proper copyright notice to obtain copyright protection. The 1976 Act extended the notice requirement to all copies published anywhere in the world, although it also codified some limited circumstances under which the omission of notice could be "cured." Finally, the 1988 Berne Convention Implementation Act made notice optional for copies publicly distributed after March 1, 1989, the effective date of the Act. However, knowledge of the notice requirement remains important in determining the copyright status of works first published before that date.

[a]   Notice Under the 1909 Act

Section 9 of the 1909 Act (later renumbered section 10) provided that "[a]ny person . . . may secure copyright for his work by publication thereof with the notice of copyright required by this title; and such notice shall be affixed to each copy thereof published or offered for sale in the United States by authority of the copyright proprietor."[353] Proper notice consisted of the word "Copyright" or the symbol ©, the name of the copyright owner, and the year of first publication.[354] If a work was published without proper notice, it immediately and irrevocably entered the public domain.[355]

The 1909 Act codified an earlier Supreme Court decision that held that publication without notice in a foreign country would not invalidate a properly obtained U.S. copyright.[356] However, the language of the 1909 Act, which required publication "with the notice of copyright required by this title" in order to obtain a U.S. copyright, left it ambiguous whether notice had to be used if the work was first published abroad, before being published in the United States. Although early cases were in conflict on this question, both the Second and Ninth Circuits have now expressed the view that first publication in a foreign country without notice did *not* place the work in the public domain in the United States.[357] However, the two courts

---

[353] 1909 Act, § 9, 35 Stat. 1077 (codified at 17 U.S.C. § 10 in 1947, repealed 1978).

[354] 1909 Act, § 18, 35 Stat. 1077 (codified at 17 U.S.C. § 19 in 1947, repealed 1978). Section 19 (later codified at 17 U.S.C. § 20) specified that the notice be placed "in such manner and location as to give reasonable notice of the claim of copyright." For books, notice had to be placed "upon its title page or the page immediately following."

[355] *See, e.g.*, American Code Co. v. Bensinger, 282 F. 829, 833 (2d Cir. 1922). There were some exceptions. Section 20 (later codified at 17 U.S.C. § 21) provided that "the omission by accident or mistake of the prescribed notice from a particular copy or copies shall not invalidate the copyright or prevent recovery against" a deliberate infringer, "but [it] shall prevent the recovery of damages against an innocent infringer who has been misled by the omission of the notice." This section did not apply, however, to the omission of notice from an entire edition. Data Cash Systems, Inc. v. JS&A Group, Inc., 628 F.2d 1038, 1043 (7th Cir. 1980) ("section 21 does not prevent forfeiture where, as here, notice was omitted from all copies"); National Comics Publications v. Fawcett Publications, 191 F.2d 594, 601 (2d Cir. 1951).

[356] United Dictionary Co. v. G. & C. Merriam Co., 208 U.S. 260 (1908).

[357] *See* Heim v. Universal Pictures Co., 154 F.2d 480 (2d Cir. 1946); Twin Books Corp. v. Walt Disney Co., 83 F.3d 1162 (9th Cir. 1996).

still disagree as to whether such a publication secures a United States copyright,[358] or whether the work, in effect, remains an "unpublished" work for purposes of U.S. law.[359]

[b]   Notice Under the 1976 Act

The 1976 Act retained the requirement that copies of a work publicly distributed with the copyright owner's authority must bear a copyright notice.[360] The mandatory notice requirement applied to works published "in the United States *or elsewhere*," meaning that a work's U.S. copyright could be forfeited if the work was published without notice anywhere in the world, between January 1, 1978 and March 1, 1989.[361] However, the 1976 Act also included provisions that mitigated the consequences of errors in or omissions of the required notice.[362]

Under the 1976 Act, a proper notice consists of (1) the symbol ©, the word "Copyright," or the abbreviation "Copr.";[363] (2) the year of first publication;[364] and (3) the name of the copyright owner.[365] As to "position of notice," the notice "shall be affixed in such manner and location as to give reasonable notice of the claim of copyright."[366] Pursuant to the statute, the Register of Copyrights has adopted

---

[358] *Heim*, 154 F.2d at 486–87; *but see id.* at 488 (Clark, J., concurring, but disagreeing on this point).

[359] *Twin Books*, 83 F.3d at 1167. *See also* Société Civile Succession Richard Guino v. Renoir, 549 F.3d 1182 (9th Cir. 2008) (holding that sculptures published in France in 1917 with no notice were neither "in the public domain [n]or copyrighted" in 1978, and were therefore entitled to the life-plus-70-years term of § 303). For a criticism of these cases, see Tyler T. Ochoa, *Protection for Works of Foreign Origin Under the 1909 Copyright Act*, 26 Santa Clara Comp. & High Tech. L.J. 285 (2010).

[360] Former 17 U.S.C. § 401 (1976). Section 401 applied to the distribution of "copies," while section 402 applied to the distribution of "phonorecords." Former 17 U.S.C. § 402. For phonorecords, the required symbol is a "P" in a circle, instead of a "C" in a circle or the word "Copyright." *Id.* The "P" stands for "phonogram," an internationally used synonym for sound recording, and not for the word "phonorecord," which refers to the material object in which the sound recording, or phonogram, is fixed. *See* § 4C[2].

[361] 17 U.S.C. § 401(a). *See also* H.R. Rep. No. 94-1476, at 144; Hasbro Bradley, Inc. v. Sparkle Toys, Inc., 780 F.2d 189 (2d Cir. 1985).

[362] 17 U.S.C. §§ 405–06.

[363] 17 U.S.C. § 401(b)(1). *See* Forry Inc. v. Neundorfer Inc., 837 F.2d 259, 266 (6th Cir. 1988) (suggesting that "(c)," *i.e.*, a "c" in parentheses, may suffice to fulfill the notice requirement's "purpose of preventing innocent person from infringing the copyright"); Videotronics, Inc. v. Bend Electronics, 586 F. Supp. 478 (D. Nev. 1984) (a "C" in a hexagon is sufficient).

[364] Section 401(b) states that "in the case of compilations or derivative works incorporating previously published material, the year date of first publication of the compilation or derivative work is sufficient." It also states that the year date may be omitted "where a pictorial, graphic, or sculptural work, with accompanying text matter, if any, is reproduced in or on greeting cards, postcards, stationery, jewelry, dolls, toys, or any useful articles."

[365] 17 U.S.C. § 401(b)(3). The notice may provide, in lieu of the name of the copyright owner, "an abbreviation by which the name can be recognized, or a generally known alternative designation of the owner."

[366] 17 U.S.C. § 401(c). *See* Forry Inc. v. Neundorfer Inc., 837 F.2d 259, 266 (6th Cir. 1988) (copyright notice for a computer program embodied in a microprocessor may be placed on the underside of the chip; the location was adequate because "the only way to copy the program is to physically remove the chip from the board"); Videotronics, Inc. v. Bend Electronics, 586 F. Supp. 478, 482 (D. Nev. 1984) (copyright

regulations on affixation and positions of notice.[367]

Section 403 imposed a special condition with regard to works "consisting predominantly of one or more works of the United States Government." The notice on such copies had to include "a statement identifying, either affirmatively or negatively, those portions" of the work in which copyright could be claimed.[368]

Despite the liberalizing approach of the 1976 Act, forfeiture of copyright for failure to comply with the notice requirement could still occur if the copyright owner did not meet the conditions of the provisions mitigating the consequences of omission of notice.

[i]   Omission of Notice

Section 405(a) provided that omission of notice "from copies or phonorecords publicly distributed by authority of the copyright owner [did] not invalidate copyright in a work" if any one of three conditions was met.

The first condition was that "the notice has been omitted from no more than a relatively small number of copies or phonorecords distributed to the public."[369] Literally, this condition would apply when either (1) a large number of copies were distributed to the public and notice was omitted from a "relatively small number" of those copies or (2) only a "relatively small number" of copies were distributed to the public and notice was omitted from all such copies.[370]

The second condition was that "registration for the work has been made before or is made within five years after the publication without notice, and a reasonable effort is made to add notice to all copies or phonorecords that are distributed to the public in the United States after the omission has been discovered."[371] Several cases address the issues of whether and how an omission is "discovered,"[372] and

---

notice for videogame was not adequate when notice appeared on screen "on a random and infrequent basis," and on pushing of reset button).

[367] *See* 17 U.S.C. § 401(c); 37 C.F.R. § 201.20.

[368] 17 U.S.C. § 403.

[369] 17 U.S.C. § 405(a)(1).

[370] *Compare* Original Appalachian Artworks, Inc. v. Toy Loft, Inc., 684 F.2d 821, 827 (11th Cir. 1982) ("only approximately 1% of . . . total sales [of 40,000] at the time of trial lacked the sewn-in copyright notice. . . . [T]his percentage meets the 'relatively few' test") *with* Donald Frederick Evans & Associates v. Continental Homes, Inc., 785 F.2d 897, 910 (11th Cir. 1986) ("2500 copies . . . which totaled approximately 2.4 percent of the total number of copies, constitutes more than a relatively small number. . . . Furthermore, 2,500 copies is a significant number in the absolute sense."). *See also* Cooling Systems and Flexibles, Inc. v. Stuart Radiator, Inc., 777 F.2d 485, 489 (9th Cir. 1985) (20,000 out of 25,000 is more than a relatively small number).

[371] 17 U.S.C. § 405(a)(2). Note that the obligation is only to add notice to copies distributed *in the United States. See* H.R. Rep. No. 94-1476, at 147 (1976) ("it would be burdensome and impractical to require an American copyright owner to police the activities of foreign licensees in this situation.").

[372] *Compare* Charles Garnier, Paris v. Andin Int'l, Inc., 36 F.3d 1214 (1st Cir. 1994) (deliberate omission is "discovered" when party is apprised of the legal significance of failure to provide notice) and Hasbro Bradley, Inc. v. Sparkle Toys, Inc., 780 F.2d 189 (2d Cir. 1985) (subsequent licensee may discover foreign copyright owner's omission) *with* O'Neill Developments, Inc. v. Galen Kilburn, Inc., 524 F. Supp. 710 (N.D. Ga. 1981) (discovery occurs when a copyright holder finds out that someone else is copying the work).

whether an effort to add notice is "reasonable."

The third condition is that "the notice has been omitted in violation of an express requirement in writing that, as a condition of the copyright owner's authorization of the public distribution of copies or phonorecords, they bear the prescribed notice."[373]

Section 405(b) protected the rights of "innocent infringers" who relied on a copy of the work from which copyright notice was omitted.[374] Section 405(c) provides that protection is not affected if the notice is removed or destroyed without the authorization of the copyright owner.[375]

[ii] Errors in Notice

Section 406 specified the effect of errors in name or date in the notice when the work was published with the copyright owner's authority. An error in the name of the copyright claimant did not affect the validity or ownership of the copyright. Instead, section 406(a) provided "a complete defense" to a person who began an undertaking in good faith under a purported transfer from the person named.[376] With regard to the date, if the year in the notice was *earlier* than the year of actual first publication, the only consequence was that if duration was computed from the year of first publication, it was computed from the year in the notice. If the year in the notice was "more than one year later than the year in which publication first occurred, the work was considered to have been published without notice and is governed by the provisions of section 405."[377]

[iii] Collective Works

Section 404 deals with notice on contributions to collective works, such as magazine and journal articles. Typically, the publisher of a collective work provides only a single copyright notice for the collective work as a whole, and does not provide individual notices for each contribution. When both the contribution and the collective work share the same ownership and the same year of first publication, omission of notice for the contribution scarcely matters in a practical sense. But what if the copyrights in the two works are owned by different persons, or the works were first published in different years, or both?

---

[373] 17 U.S.C. § 405(a)(3). *See* Fantastic Fakes, Inc. v. Pickwick International, Inc., 661 F.2d 479, 484 n.3 (5th Cir. Unit B 1981) ("The logical inference from this requirement is that an implied condition, or even an express condition if not in writing, will not preserve a copyright against the effects of publication without notice or publication with inadequate notice.").

[374] 17 U.S.C. § 405(b).

[375] 17 U.S.C. § 405(c).

[376] 17 U.S.C. § 406(a). This section does not apply to cases in which the defendant obtained rights from a total interloper. That is, it applies only when X authorizes Y to make copies of X's copyrighted work but X or Y puts Y's name in the notice. *See, e.g.*, Bagdadi v. Nazar, 84 F.3d 1194 (9th Cir. 1996). It does not apply when Y publicly distributes copies without X's permission.

[377] 17 U.S.C. § 406(b). This subsection is consistent with the rule developed under prior case law. *See* Callaghan v. Myers, 128 U.S. 617, 657–58 (1888); American Code Co. v. Bensinger, 282 F. 829, 836 (2d Cir. 1922); Baker v. Taylor, 2 Fed. Cas. 478, 478–79 (S.D.N.Y. 1848) (No. 782).

Cases decided under the 1909 Act reached conflicting results.[378] The 1976 Act resolved the problem by providing that a separate contribution may bear its own notice, but that a single notice applicable to the collective work as a whole is sufficient "regardless of the ownership of the copyright in the contributions and whether or not they have been previously published."[379] Section 404(b) provides that if a person named in the single notice is not the owner of the copyright in a separate contribution, the case is treated as one of an error in name under Section 406(a).[380]

[c]   Notice After the Berne Convention Implementation Act

The 1988 Berne Convention Implementation Act made notice optional for copies publicly distributed by authority of the copyright owner after March 1, 1989, the effective date of the Act.[381] The Act retained a mild incentive for using notice by inserting section 401(d), which provides that "no weight shall be given to . . . a defense based on innocent infringement in mitigation of actual or statutory damages," so long as proper copyright notice "appears on the published copy or copies to which a defendant in a copyright infringement suit had access."[382] Courts have interpreted this provision broadly, so that innocent infringement may not be claimed if the copyright owner used proper notice on published copies or phonorecords, even if the actual copy which the defendant accessed was an unlawful copy made available online without notice.[383] Nonetheless, the best incentive to use notice remains a practical one: the absence of a notice may encourage copying, because of a persistent but mistaken belief that notice is still legally required. Thus, the use of notice may deter copying by law-abiding citizens.

---

[378] *See* New York Times Co. v. Tasini, 533 U.S. 483, 494 (2001) (describing the problem); Goodis v. United Artists Television, Inc., 425 F.2d 397 (2d Cir. 1970).

[379] 17 U.S.C. § 404(a). The statute excepts "advertisements inserted on behalf of persons other than the owner of copyright in the collective work." *Id. See also* Canfield v. Ponchatoula Times, 759 F.2d 493, 496 (5th Cir. 1985) ("[T]his exception was regarded as necessary because . . . when an advertiser gives a publisher an advertisement which has been published previously in another publication and has no copyright notice affixed, it would be logical for the publisher to presume both that no copyright was claimed by the prior publisher and that reprinting of the advertisement verbatim would not infringe any right of the prior publisher."); TransWestern Publishing Co. v. MultiMedia Marketing Associates, Inc., 133 F.3d 773 (10th Cir. 1998).

[380] 17 U.S.C. § 404(b).

[381] Pub. L. No. 100-568, 102 Stat. 2853 (1988). The BCIA accomplished this change in sections 401 and 402, the basic notice provisions, by replacing the words "shall be placed on all" with "may be placed on"; and in sections 405 and 406, the provisions on omissions of and errors in notice, by adding the introductory phrase "With respect to copies and phonorecords publicly distributed by authority of the copyright owner before the effective date of the Berne Convention Implementation Act of 1988."

[382] 17 U.S.C. § 401(d). Section 402(d) contains an identical provision regarding notice on phonorecords. The House Report notes: "While innocent intent does not constitute a defense to copyright liability, the courts have taken account of the relative innocence or guilt of the defendant in assessing both actual and statutory damages. . . . The intent of new sections 401(d) and 402(d) is to direct the courts not to consider the defendant's claim of innocence if the copyright owner has marked the copies properly with notice of copyright and the defendant has access to the marked copies." H.R. Rep. No. 100-609, at 45 (1988).

[383] *See* BMG Music v. Gonzalez, 430 F.3d 888 (7th Cir. 2005).

[3]   Deposit and Registration

The Copyright Act imposes two related but distinct administrative requirements — deposit of copies, which is mandatory, and registration, which is optional.

[a]   Deposit of Copies

The owner of copyright or of the exclusive right of publication of a work published in the United States, must, within three months of publication, deposit two complete copies of the best edition with the Copyright Office for the use or disposition of the Library of Congress.[384] Deposit is mandatory,[385] but noncompliance will not invalidate the copyright.[386] The 1988 Berne Convention Implementation Act left the deposit requirement unchanged.[387]

A deposit of copies must also be made if and when a copyright owner seeks to register. An applicant may avoid double deposit by promptly applying for registration and having the mandatory deposit serve to satisfy the deposit-for-registration requirement.[388] The Register of Copyrights may exempt categories of material from deposit or require deposit of only a single copy.[389]

[b]   Registration

The owner of a copyright or any exclusive right in a work may register his claim by filing an application, paying the required fee, and depositing copies with the Copyright Office.[390] Registration is a relatively simple process; most works may now be registered by filling out an electronic form on the Copyright Office's website.[391] The Register of Copyrights issues a certificate of registration if it determines that the deposit material is copyrightable subject matter.[392]

The 1976 Act continued the prior law making registration a prerequisite to filing an infringement suit.[393] However, in order to comply with the Berne Convention,

---

[384] 17 U.S.C. § 407. In Ladd v. Law & Technology Press, 762 F.2d 809 (9th Cir. 1985), the court rejected Fifth Amendment taking and First Amendment free press challenges to the mandatory deposit law's constitutionality.

[385] The Register of Copyrights may demand deposit any time after publication in the United States. If no deposit is made within three months of demand, the defaulting persons are liable to fines of not more than $250 per work ($2,500 in the case of willful or repeated failures to comply) plus the cost of obtaining a copy. 17 U.S.C. § 407(d).

[386] 17 U.S.C. § 407(a) ("Neither the deposit requirements of this subsection nor the acquisition provisions of subsection (e) are conditions of copyright protection.").

[387] See H.R. Rep. No. 100-609, at 44 (1988) ("Since noncompliance with the mandatory deposit requirement does not result in forfeiture of any copyright protection, mandatory deposit is compatible with Berne.").

[388] 17 U.S.C. § 408(b).

[389] 17 U.S.C. § 407(c). See 37 C.F.R. § 202.19.

[390] 17 U.S.C. § 408(a).

[391] See www.copyright.gov. Paper forms must still be used for vessel-hull designs, semiconductor chip designs (mask works), restored copyrights, renewal registrations for pre-1978 copyrights, and group registrations. See U.S. Copyright Office, Circular 1: Copyright Basics, at 8 (2012).

[392] 17 U.S.C. § 410(a).

[393] Former 17 U.S.C. § 411(a) (as enacted in 1976).

which prohibits conditioning the "enjoyment and exercise" of copyrights on any formalities,[394] the 1988 Berne Convention Implementation Act exempted works of foreign origin from the registration requirement.[395] Today, registration is only required as a prerequisite to filing a civil action for infringement of "any United States work."[396] In addition, the 1976 Act provides two important additional incentives to prompt registration. First, if registration is made before or within five years after first publication, then the certificate "shall constitute *prima facie* evidence of the validity of the copyright and of all the facts stated in the certificate."[397] As a practical matter, this means that the copyright owner need only introduce the certificate as proof of ownership, and that the defendant bears the burden of introducing evidence contesting ownership or validity.[398] Second, in order to recover statutory damages or attorneys fees, registration must be made before the infringement commenced, or, for infringement of a published work, within three months after first publication.[399] Both of these incentives apply to foreign works as well as to United States works.

For United States works, section 411(a) provides that "no civil action for infringement . . . shall be instituted until . . . registration of the copyright claim has been made in accordance with this title."[400] Because the effective date of a registration is the day on which all of the required materials have been received in the Copyright Office,[401] some courts treat the submission of an application, accompanied by payment of the required fee and deposit of the requisite copies, as sufficient compliance.[402] Other courts hold that the prerequisite is not satisfied until the Copyright Office has acted on the application.[403] The Supreme Court has held that section 411(a) is not "jurisdictional," so that failure to register does not deprive

---

[394] *See* Berne Convention, 1971 Paris Text, Art. 5(2).

[395] Pub. L. 100-568, § 9(b), 102 Stat. 2853 (1988). The Act amended 17 U.S.C. § 411 by including the introductory phrase "Except for actions for infringement of copyright in Berne Convention works whose country of origin is not the United States."

[396] 17 U.S.C. § 411(a). A "United States work" is a work that is first published in the United States, or published simultaneously in the United States and a foreign country; or, for an unpublished work, a work for which all of the authors are nationals or domiciliaries of the United States. 17 U.S.C. § 101. *See* Moberg v. 33T LLC, 666 F. Supp. 2d 415 (D. Del. 2009) (assuming Swedish author's photos were "published" when they were posted on a German website, they were not simultaneously "published" in the United States, and were therefore not "United States works," for purposes of § 411(a)); Kernal Records Oy v. Mosely, 694 F.3d 1294 (11th Cir. 2012) (plaintiff failed to meet burden of proving that his work was first published in Australia, and therefore he was not exempt from the registration requirement for "United States work[s].").

[397] 17 U.S.C. § 410(c).

[398] *See* § 4H[1].

[399] 17 U.S.C. § 412.

[400] 17 U.S.C. § 411(a).

[401] 17 U.S.C. § 410(d).

[402] *See, e.g.*, Cosmetic Ideas, Inc. v. IAC/Interactive Corp., 606 F.3d 612 (9th Cir. 2010); Apple Barrel Productions, Inc. v. Beard, 730 F.2d 384 (5th Cir. 1984).

[403] *See, e.g.*, LaResolana Architects v. Clay Realtors Angel Fire, 416 F.3d 1195 (10th Cir. 2005) (collecting cases); M.G.B. Homes, Inc. v. Ameron Homes, Inc., 903 F.2d 1486 (11th Cir. 1990). Many of these courts, however, allow the plaintiff to file an amended complaint once the registration in fact issues. *See, e.g.*, *M.G.B. Homes*, 903 F.2d at 1489. The dispute could make a difference if, for example, the statute

the trial court of subject-matter jurisdiction.[404] However, the Court did not resolve the circuit split noted above.[405]

If the application for registration is denied, the applicant may seek judicial review under the Administrative Procedure Act.[406] Alternatively, section 411(a) allows the rejected applicant to file an action for infringement, so long as the Register of Copyrights is given notice and an opportunity to intervene.[407] While a court has power to adjudicate the validity of a copyright, it lacks the power to order the Register to register a copyright,[408] or to cancel a registration.[409]

With respect to collective works, if the owner of the individual contribution and the owner of the collective work are the same, then registration for the collective work will cover the individual contribution as well.[410] If the copyright claimants are not the same, however, then registration for the collective work does not apply to the individual contributions.[411] With respect to derivative works, if the same person owns both the copyright in the underlying work and the copyright in the derivative work, then registration of the underlying work will cover those elements in the derivative work which appear in both works,[412] but will not cover those elements that only appear in the derivative work.[413] Conversely, although the copyright in a derivative work "extends only to the material contributed by the author of such work, as distinguished from the preexisting material employed in the work,"[414] some courts have held that where the same person owns both copyrights, registration of the derivative work will support an action for infringement of the underlying work.[415]

---

of limitations expires before the amended complaint is filed. *See* Morgan v. Hanna Holdings, Inc., 635 F. Supp. 2d 404 (W.D. Pa. 2009).

[404] Reed Elsevier, Inc. v. Muchnick, 559 U.S. 154 (2010).

[405] *Id.* at 171.

[406] 17 U.S.C. § 701(e). *See, e.g.*, Darden v. Peters, 488 F.3d 277 (4th Cir. 2007) (reviewing denial for abuse of discretion).

[407] *See, e.g.*, Paul Morelli Design, Inc. v. Tiffany and Co., 200 F. Supp. 2d 482 (E.D. Pa. 2002) (giving "some deference" to Register's decision, rather than abuse of discretion or *de novo* review); *but see* Brooks-Ngwenya v. Indianapolis Public Schools, 564 F.3d 804 (7th Cir. 2009) (although notice rule is mandatory, failure to notify does not deprive court of jurisdiction).

[408] *See* Proline Concrete Tools, Inc. v. Dennis, 2013 U.S. Dist. LEXIS 188384 (S.D. Cal. Mar. 28, 2013).

[409] *See* Brownstein v. Lindsay, 742 F.3d 55 (3d Cir. 2014).

[410] *See* Alaska Stock, LLC v. Houghton Mifflin Harcourt Pub. Co,, 747 F.3d 673 (9th Cir. 2014); Metro. Regional Info. Sys., Inc. v. Am. Home Realty Network, Inc., 722 F.3d 591 (4th Cir. 2013).

[411] *See* Morris v. Business Concepts, Inc., 283 F.3d 502 (2d Cir. 2002); Xoom, Inc. v. Imageline, Inc., 323 F.3d 279 (4th Cir. 2003); Educational Testing Services v. Katzman, 793 F.2d 533 (3d Cir. 1986).

[412] *See* Montgomery v. Noga, 168 F.3d 1282 (11th Cir. 1999).

[413] *See* Well-Made Toy Mfg. Corp. v. Goffa Int'l Corp., 354 F.3d 112 (2d Cir. 2003); Murray Hill Publications, Inc. v. ABC Communications, Inc., 264 F.3d 622 (6th Cir. 2001).

[414] 17 U.S.C. § 103(b).

[415] *Murray Hill*, 264 F.3d at 631–32; Streetwise Maps, Inc. v. VanDam, Inc., 159 F.3d 739 (2d Cir. 1998).

§ 4E   DURATION, RENEWAL, AND RESTORATION

[1]   Duration

The Patent and Copyright Clause of the Constitution empowers Congress to grant patents and copyrights "for limited Times" only.[416] The 1790 Act followed the Statute of Anne in prescribing an initial term of 14 years, with a second term of 14 years if the author survived to the commencement of that term (and complied with certain statutory formalities). The 1831 Act increased the initial term to 28 years, retaining a 14-year renewal term, which could be claimed by an author's heirs.

Under the 1909 Act, copyright lasted for an initial term of 28 years from the date of first publication of the work. The author or, if the author was not living, specified heirs, could obtain a 28-year renewal term by filing an application during a period of one year before expiration of the initial term.

The 1976 Act changed the duration of copyrights for new works to a single term of life of the author plus 50 years. Works for hire were given an alternative term of 75 years from the date of first publication, or 100 years from the date of creation. The renewal term for subsisting copyrights granted under the 1909 Act was extended to 47 years, which, when added to the initial 28-year term, resulted in a duration of 75 years from first publication. Works created but not published or registered before 1978 were given the same term as new works, subject to a statutory minimum.

The Sonny Bono Copyright Term Extension Act of 1998 added 20 years to the terms of all subsisting copyrights, resulting in the duration provisions that we have today:

1. For works created on or after January 1, 1978, copyright subsists from creation and endures for a term consisting of the life of the author plus seventy years after the author's death.[417] For joint works, the term lasts until 70 years after the death of the last surviving author.[418] For works made for hire and anonymous and pseudonymous works, copyright lasts for 95 years from the date of first publication or 120 years from creation, whichever is shorter.[419]

2. For works first published or registered before January 1, 1978, and therefore subject to copyright under the 1909 Act, the current Act preserves the two-term renewal structure. Such works received a 28-year initial term, and they could obtain a 67-year renewal term if they were properly renewed,[420] for a total duration of 95 years from first publication.[421]

---

[416] U.S. Const., Art. I, § 8, cl. 8.

[417] 17 U.S.C. § 302(a).

[418] 17 U.S.C. § 302(b).

[419] 17 U.S.C. § 302(c).

[420] 17 U.S.C. § 304(a). For the details regarding renewal, see § 4E[2].

[421] 17 U.S.C. § 304(b) (applicable to works already in their renewal term on October 27, 1998, when the Copyright Term Extension Act was enacted).

3. Works created but not published or registered before January 1, 1978, were previously protected by state law (common-law copyright).[422] These works were brought under federal statutory copyright on January 1, 1978, and were given the same term as new works (life plus 70 years, or the alternative term for works made for hire), subject to a statutory minimum: All such works were under copyright at least through December 31, 2002; and if the work was published on or before that date, its copyright will endure at least through December 31, 2047.[423]

4. "All terms of copyright provided [above] run to the end of the calendar year in which they would otherwise expire."[424]

The 1998 Copyright Term Extension Act did not revive any copyrights on works that were already in the public domain prior to its effective date.[425] Therefore, all works published or registered in the United States before 1923 are in the public domain in the United States. In addition, all still-unpublished works by authors who died more than seventy years before the current year are now in the public domain in the United States.[426]

In *Eldred v. Ashcroft*, the Supreme Court upheld the 1998 Copyright Term Extension Act against a constitutional challenge under the "limited Times" provision of the Copyright Clause and the First Amendment.[427] With regard to the latter, the court noted that "copyright law contains built-in First Amendment accommodations," namely the idea-expression dichotomy and the fair use doctrine;[428] and it concluded that "when, as in this case, Congress has not altered the traditional contours of copyright protection, further First Amendment scrutiny is unnecessary."[429]

[2]   Renewal of Copyright in Pre-1978 Works

[a]   Basic Renewal Principles

The 1909 Act granted to authors a 28-year initial copyright term, and it granted to authors and specified heirs the right to renew the copyright for an additional 28-year term.[430] The renewal term's purpose was, in part, to protect authors and their heirs against unremunerative copyright transfers and licenses made before a work's value was recognized.[431] The renewal owner took a new property right that

---

[422] *See* § 4D.

[423] 17 U.S.C. § 303(a).

[424] 17 U.S.C. § 305.

[425] 17 U.S.C. § 304(b).

[426] Indeed, by virtue of section 303(a), works created by such authors are in the public domain so long as they remained unpublished as of December 31, 2002.

[427] 537 U.S. 186 (2003).

[428] *Id.* at 219–20.

[429] *Id.* at 221.

[430] 1909 Act, § 23, 35 Stat. 1080 (codified at 17 U.S.C. § 24 in 1947, repealed 1978). The renewal term was extended to 47 years in the 1976 Act, and to 67 years in the 1998 Copyright Term Extension Act. *See* § 4E[1].

[431] *See* Fred Fisher Music Co. v. M. Witmark & Sons, 318 U.S. 643, 653 (1943) ("By providing for two

was independent of any encumbrances and transfers of the initial term.[432]

Under the 1909 Act, the renewal right generally vested in "the author . . . , if still living, or the widow, widower, or children of the author, if the author be not living, or if such author, widow, widower, or children be not living, then the author's executors, or in the absence of a will, his next of kin."[433] In *DeSylva v. Ballentine*, the Supreme Court held that (1) when the author dies prior to renewal, the widow or widower and any children take as a class, rather than successively, and (2) whether an illegitimate offspring constitutes one of the author's "children" depends on the law of the state in which the author was domiciled at the time of his death.[434] The 1976 Act clarified the situation by defining "children" to mean "a person's immediate offspring, whether legitimate or not, and any children legally adopted by that person."[435] Although earlier cases assumed without discussion that the widow or widower and children took the renewal copyrights on a *per capita* basis, two Courts of Appeals have now held that ownership is divided *per stirpes*, so that the widow or widower owns a half-share of the renewal copyrights, and the children divide a half-share.[436]

In four cases, however, the 1909 Act provided that the renewal term would not vest in the author's heirs, but in the proprietor of the initial term at the time of renewal.[437] Those categories were posthumous works,[438] periodic, cyclopedic, or

---

copyright terms, each of relatively short duration, Congress enabled the author to sell his 'copyright' without losing his renewal interest. If the author's copyright extended over a single, longer term, his sale of the 'copyright' would terminate his entire interest. . . . [T]his is the basic consideration of policy underlying the renewal provision of the Copyright Act of 1909.").

[432] *See* G. Ricordi & Co. v. Paramount Pictures, Inc., 189 F.2d 469, 471 (2d Cir. 1951) (the renewal right "creates a new estate . . . clear of all rights, interests or licenses granted under the original copyright").

[433] 1909 Act, § 23, 35 Stat. 1080 (codified at 17 U.S.C. § 24 in 1947, repealed 1978). The same language was carried forward in § 304(a) of the 1976 Act. *See also* Film Corp. v. Knowles, 261 U.S. 326, 329 (1923) ("if there is no widow or child the executor may exercise the power [of renewal] that the testator might have exercised if he had been alive.").

[434] 351 U.S. 570 (1956).

[435] 17 U.S.C. § 101. *See also* Stone v. Williams, 970 F.2d 1043 (2d Cir. 1992) (applying *DeSylva* to copyrights renewed prior to 1978, and applying 1976 Act definition to copyrights renewed after January 1, 1978).

The 1976 Act also defines "widow" or "widower" as "the author's surviving spouse under the law of the author's domicile at the time of his or her death, whether or not the spouse has later remarried." 17 U.S.C. § 101. This definition is consistent with pre-1978 case law. *See* Edward B. Marks Music Corp. v. Borst Music Publishing Co., 110 F. Supp. 913, 918 (D.N.J. 1953) (rejecting argument that remarriage bars widow's renewal rights); Hill & Range Songs, Inc. v. Fred Rose Music, Inc., 403 F. Supp. 420, 428–29 (M.D. Tenn. 1975) (same), *aff'd on other grounds*, 570 F.2d 554 (6th Cir. 1978).

[436] *See* Broadcast Music, Inc. v. Roger Miller Music, Inc., 396 F.3d 762 (6th Cir. 2005); Venegas-Hernandez v. Asociacion de Compositores y Editores de Musica Latinoamericana, 424 F.3d 50 (1st Cir. 2005).

[437] 1909 Act, § 23, 35 Stat. 1080 (codified at 17 U.S.C. § 24 in 1947, repealed 1978). The same language was carried forward in § 304(a) of the 1976 Act.

[438] In Bartok v. Boosey & Hawkes, Inc., 523 F.2d 941, 944 (2d Cir. 1975), the court construed a "posthumous work" to be one for which "a contract for copyright was never executed by the author during his life," meaning that the proprietor of the copyright in such a situation would be the author's heirs. The House Report to the 1976 Act specifically approved this definition. *See* H.R. Rep. No. 94-1476,

other composite works,[439] any work copyrighted by a corporate body (other than as an assignee or licensee),[440] and any work copyrighted by an employer for whom the work was made for hire.[441]

Under the 1909 Act, the claimant was required to register the renewal application "within one year prior to the expiration of the original term of copyright" (in other words, during the 28th year).[442] For example, the proper period for the renewal of a copyright first published on July 1, 1930 was the period between July 1, 1957 and June 30, 1958.[443] After January 1, 1978, however, all terms of copyright were extended "to the end of the calendar year in which they would otherwise expire."[444] This change simplified the renewal calculation, so that renewal registration had to be filed within the calendar year prior to expiration. For example, a work copyrighted on July 1, 1960 was eligible for renewal only between December 31, 1987 and December 31, 1988, and applications filed earlier or later would be ineffective.

The renewal provisions spawned many problems and much litigation. In particular, the Congressional purpose of protecting authors against unremunerative transfers was largely thwarted by *Fred Fisher Music Co. v. M. Witmark & Sons*, in which the Supreme Court held that the author could by written assignment convey his renewal rights in advance of their vesting.[445] After *Fred Fisher Music*, it became standard practice to require an assignment of the author's renewal rights at the time of the initial assignment. Courts did insist, however, that such an assignment had to expressly refer to the renewal term in order to be valid.[446] Moreover, in

---

at 139 (1976) ("one as to which no copyright assignment or other contract for exploitation of the work has occurred during an author's lifetime.").

[439] This phrase refers to what the 1976 Act calls "collective works." *See* § 4C[4][b][i]. Thus, the renewal copyright covers primarily the editor's selection and arrangement; the right to renew copyright in the individual contributions remains with the authors, see Abend v. MCA, Inc., 863 F.2d 1465, 1470–72 (9th Cir. 1988), *aff'd on other grounds sub nom* Stewart v. Abend, 495 U.S. 207 (1990), except for any individual contributions that were assigned to the proprietor of the collective work prior to publication. *See* Self-Realization Fellowship Church v. Ananda Church of Self-Realization, 206 F.3d 1322, 1329 (9th Cir. 2000).

[440] According to one court, the parameters of this exception are so unclear that "apparently no reported case has ever found it applicable." Schmid Brothers, Inc. v. W. Goebel Porzellanfabrik KG, 589 F. Supp. 497, 504 (E.D.N.Y. 1984).

[441] *See, e.g.*, Twentieth Century Fox Film Corp. v. Entertainment Distributing, 429 F.3d 869 (9th Cir. 2005) (holding that Doubleday was entitled to the renewal term in General Eisenhower's memoirs); Estate of Hogarth v. Edgar Rice Burroughs, Inc., 342 F.3d 149 (2d Cir. 2003) (holding that ERB, Inc., and not the illustrator, was entitled to the renewal term in two graphic novels based on *Tarzan of the Apes*). As to when a work was made "for hire" under the 1909 Act, see § 4F.

[442] 1909 Act, § 23, 35 Stat. 1080 (codified at 17 U.S.C. § 24 in 1947, repealed 1978). The same language was carried forward in § 304(a) of the 1976 Act.

[443] *See, e.g.*, Mayhew v. Gusto Records, Inc., 960 F. Supp. 1302, 1308–10 (M.D. Tenn. 1997) (attempted renewal of musical works copyrights invalid because applications filed three days before commencement of one-year period prior to expiration of original term).

[444] 17 U.S.C. § 305.

[445] 318 U.S. 643, 656–57 (1943).

[446] *See, e.g.*, Edward B. Marks Music Corp. v. Charles K. Harris Music Publishing Co., 255 F.2d 518, 521 (2d Cir. 1958) (assignment of "all right, title and interest" in the work conveyed only the initial term);

Miller Music Corp. v. Charles N. Daniels, Inc., the Supreme Court held that such an advance assignment was contingent on the assignor living until the renewal term vested, so that the assignment would not bind the statutory heirs if the author died prior to renewal.[447]

In enacting the 1976 Act, Congress partially mitigated the consequences of *Fred Fisher Music* by enacting a procedure by which authors who had assigned their renewal terms (and their heirs) were given a five-year period in which to terminate those assignments and recapture their copyrights.[448]

[b]   Renewal and Derivative Works

In *Stewart v. Abend*,[449] the Supreme Court resolved a conflict in the lower courts about continued utilization of a derivative work after renewal of the original work's copyright. The case involved the rights to reproduce and distribute the motion picture "Rear Window," directed by Alfred Hitchcock and starring James Stewart and Grace Kelly. The movie was based on the short story "It Had to Be Murder" by Cornell Woolrich, first published in 1942. Woolrich assigned the motion picture rights to the story in 1945; the movie was produced and released in 1954. Woolrich died in 1968, before the renewal term in the short story began. His executor renewed the copyright in the short story and assigned it to Sheldon Abend, a literary agent. When MCA-Universal re-released the movie in theaters and on video in 1983, Abend sued for infringement. The question presented was whether the owner of rights in a derivative work could continue to exploit the derivative work during the renewal term without the permission of the owner of the renewal copyright in the underlying work.

The Supreme Court held that when "[t]he author of a pre-existing work . . . assigns to another the right to use it in a derivative work" and "agreed to assign the rights in his renewal copyright term to the owner of [the] derivative work, but died before the commencement of the renewal period,"[450] then under *Miller Music*, the contingent assignment of the renewal term was ineffective, and "the assignee may continue to use the original work only if the author's successor transfers the renewal rights [in the original work] to the assignee."[451] Therefore, "the owner of the derivative work infringed the rights of the successor owner of the pre-existing work by continued distribution and publication of the derivative work during the renewal term of the pre-existing work."[452]

Subsequent developments have limited the holding in *Stewart v. Abend* in two ways. First, in adopting automatic renewal in 1992, Congress limited the decision in

---

Roger Miller Music, Inc. v. Sony/ATV Publishing, LLC, 477 F.3d 383 (6th Cir. 2007) ("express use of the term 'renew'. . . evinces an intent to convey the renewal interest"); *but see P.C. Films Corp. v. MGM/UA Home Video Inc.*, 138 F.3d 453 (2d Cir. 1998) (grant of the "perpetual and exclusive right to distribute" was sufficient to convey renewal term).

[447] 362 U.S. 373, 376–78 (1960).

[448] For details regarding the termination of transfers provisions, see § 4E[3].

[449] 495 U.S. 207 (1990).

[450] 495 U.S. at 211.

[451] *Id.* at 221.

[452] *Id.* at 211.

Stewart to those cases in which the person entitled to renew the underlying work timely registers the renewal term with the Copyright Office. If the renewal is not timely registered, "then a derivative work prepared under authority of a grant . . . may continue to be used under the terms of the grant during the renewed and extended term of copyright without infringing the copyright."[453] Second, both the Second and Ninth Circuits have held that the rationale of *Stewart* applies only where the underlying work is covered by a federal statutory copyright. Thus, when a motion picture has entered the public domain for failure to renew, the motion picture cannot be distributed without the permission of the owner of the renewal copyright in the underlying published work on which it was based;[454] but the owner of a common-law copyright in the underlying unpublished screenplay on which the movie was based cannot prevent the movie from being distributed.[455]

[c]   Automatic Renewal

In 1992, Congress amended the renewal provisions of the 1976 Act. To avoid due process problems, the 1992 amendments were made applicable only to works which were first published or registered between January 1, 1964, and December 31, 1977.[456]

Beginning in 1992, renewal was made permissive, so that it was no longer necessary to register a renewal copyright in order to obtain the renewal term.[457] If no renewal was registered, then the renewal term vested automatically in the person or persons entitled to the renewal term on the last day of the original term.[458] However, if a renewal was registered, then the renewal term vested in the person or persons who were entitled to the renewal term at the time that the application for renewal was made.[459] These provisions on vesting resolved a conflict in the pre-1992 case law concerning when the persons entitled to renewal were to be identified.[460]

In addition, the 1992 amendments provided three additional incentives to encourage claimants to register their renewal terms. First, if a renewal was timely registered, then the owner of the renewal term was entitled to the benefit of the Supreme Court's ruling in *Stewart v. Abend*, meaning that the owner of copyright

---

[453] 17 U.S.C. § 304(a)(4)(A) (as amended in 1992).

[454] *See, e.g.*, Russell v. Price, 612 F.2d 1123 (9th Cir. 1979) (film version of George Bernard Shaw's play *Pygmalion*); Filmvideo Releasing Corp. v. Hastings, 668 F.2d 91 (2d Cir. 1981).

[455] *See* Shoptalk, Ltd. v. Concorde-New Horizons Corp., 168 F.3d 586 (2d Cir. 1999); Batjac Prods., Inc. v. GoodTimes Home Video Corp., 160 F.3d 1223 (9th Cir. 1998). These courts reasoned that the underlying screenplay was "published" to the extent it was included in the motion picture, thereby losing its common-law copyright. *See* § 4D[1][a].

[456] Copyright Renewal Act of 1992, Pub. L. 102-307, title I, § 2, 106 Stat. 266.

[457] 17 U.S.C. § 304(a)(3)(B) ("Such an application is not a condition of the renewal and extension of the copyright in a work for a further term of 67 years.").

[458] 17 U.S.C. § 304(a)(2)(A)(ii), § 304(a)(2)(B)(ii).

[459] 17 U.S.C. § 304(a)(2)(A)(i), § 304(a)(2)(B)(i). *See, e.g.*, Roger Miller Music, Inc. v. Sony/ATV Pub'g, LLC, 672 F.3d 434 (6th Cir. 2012).

[460] *Compare* Frederick Music Co. v. Sickler, 708 F. Supp. 587 (S.D.N.Y. 1989) (renewal vests in those persons entitled to it on the date of the renewal application) *with* Marascalco v. Fantasy, Inc., 953 F.2d 469 (9th Cir. 1991) (renewal vests in those persons entitled to it at the beginning of the renewal term).

in any derivative work could not continue to exploit that derivative work during the renewal term without the express permission of the owner of the renewal copyright in the underlying work.[461] If the renewal was not timely registered, however, "then a derivative work prepared under authority of a grant . . . may continue to be used under the terms of the grant during the renewed and extended term of copyright without infringing the copyright."[462] Second, if a renewal was timely registered, then the registration certificate "shall constitute *prima facie* evidence of the validity of the copyright during its renewed and extended term and of the facts stated in the certificate."[463] Third, the definition of "registration" was amended to include renewal registrations, thereby conferring on renewal registrations many of the other benefits of registration, including the ability to sue for infringement in United States works and statutory damages and attorneys fees.[464]

[3]   Restoration of Copyright in Foreign Works

Article 18 of the Berne Convention states that the Convention "shall apply to all works, which, at the moment of its coming into force, have not yet fallen into the public domain in the country of origin through the expiry of the term of protection."[465] Therefore, when the United States joined the Berne Convention, effective March 1, 1989, it obligated itself to protect works from other Berne nations that were not yet in the public domain in their source countries, even if they were in the public domain in the United States for some reason other than expiration, such as failure to comply with formalities.[466] However, the United States did not undertake to implement this article until after the 1994 TRIPS Agreement, which made the substantive provisions of the Berne Convention enforceable between nations under the dispute resolution mechanism of the World Trade Organization.[467]

In response, Congress enacted section 104A, which restored copyright in any work of foreign origin[468] that was "not in the public domain in its source country through expiration of term of protection," but that was "in the public domain in the

---

[461] 495 U.S. 207 (1990). See the discussion of *Stewart v. Abend* in § 4E[2][b].

[462] 17 U.S.C. § 304(a)(4)(A).

[463] 17 U.S.C. § 304(a)(4)(B). This was a change from previous law, under which only the certificate for the original registration constituted *prima facie* evidence of the validity of the copyright. Epoch Producing Corp. v. Killiam Shows, Inc., 522 F.2d 737, 745–46 (2d Cir. 1976).

[464] 17 U.S.C. § 101 (defining "registration" as "a registration of a claim in the original or the renewed and extended term of copyright."). For the benefits of registration, see § 4D[3][b].

[465] Berne Convention, 1971 Paris Text, Art. 18(1).

[466] The Convention provides some flexibility, however, by also providing that "the respective countries shall determine, each in so far as it is concerned, the conditions of application of this principle." *Id.*, Art. 18(3).

[467] *See* Golan v. Holder, 132 S. Ct. 873, 879–81 (2012).

[468] A work was eligible for restoration only if it "has at least one author or rightholder who was, at the time the work was created, a national or domiciliary of eligible country, and if published, was first published in an eligible country and not published in the United States during the 30-day period following publication in such eligible country." 17 U.S.C. § 104A(h)(6)(D). An "eligible country" is one with whom the U.S. has copyright treaty relations. 17 U.S.C. § 104A(h)(3).

United States" for one of three reasons.[469] Copyrights in all such works were restored effective January 1, 1996,[470] and are owned by "the author or initial rightholder of the work as determined by the law of the source country of the work."[471] Such works are protected "for the remainder of the term of copyright that the work would have otherwise been granted in the United States if the work never entered the public domain in the United States."[472]

The statute makes special provisions for "reliance parties," defined as any person who, before the date of enactment,[473] acquired one or more copies of a work, or engaged in acts that would have been infringing if the work had been subject to copyright protection and continues to engage in such acts after the copyright is restored.[474] Such a reliance party must be placed on actual or constructive notice of the restoration,[475] after which the reliance party is given a 12-month period to sell off any existing copies or to cease public performance or public display.[476] Moreover, if the reliance party created a derivative work based on the restored work before the date of enactment, then the "reliance party may continue to exploit that derivative work for the duration of the restored copyright" upon payment of "reasonable compensation" to the copyright owner.[477]

---

[469] 17 U.S.C. § 104A(h)(6)(B), (C). The three reasons are: (i) "noncompliance with formalities imposed at any time by United States copyright law, including failure of renewal [or] lack of proper notice"; (ii) "lack of subject matter protection in the case of sound recordings fixed before February 15, 1972," or (iii) "lack of national eligibility." 17 U.S.C. § 104A(h)(6)(C).

[470] 17 U.S.C. § 104A(a)(1)(A) ("Copyright subsists . . . in restored works, and vests automatically on the date of restoration."); 17 U.S.C. § 104A(h)(2)(A) (defining "date of restoration" as January 1, 1996, "if the source country of the restored work is a nation adhering to the Berne Convention or a WTO member country on such date."). Otherwise, the date of restoration is the date the source country adheres to one of those agreements, or is the subject of a Presidential proclamation to that effect. 17 U.S.C. § 104A(h)(2)(B).

[471] 17 U.S.C. § 104A(b). *See* Alameda Films S.A. de C.V. v. Authors Rights Restoration Corp., 331 F.3d 472 (5th Cir. 2003) (under Mexican law, film production companies were "authors" of movies entitled to restored U.S. copyrights); La Parade v. Ivanova, 387 F.3d 1099 (9th Cir. 2004) (same).

[472] 17 U.S.C. § 104A(a)(1)(B).

[473] The statutory phrase is "before the source country of that work becomes an eligible country." 17 U.S.C. § 104A(h)(4)(A). Any country that was a member of the WTO or the Berne Convention became an "eligible country" on the date of enactment. 17 U.S.C. § 104A(h)(3); Cordon Holding, B.V. v. Northwest Publ. Corp., 63 U.S.P.Q.2d 1013 (S.D.N.Y. 2002). Other countries become "eligible countries" on the date they adhere to one of the specified copyright treaties. 17 U.S.C. § 104A(h)(3).

[474] 17 U.S.C. § 104A(h)(4) (definition of "reliance party"). *See* Troll Co. v. Uneeda Doll Co., 483 F.3d 150 (2d Cir. 2007) (defendant was not a reliance party where it had ceased production before restoration and reentered the market after restoration).

[475] There are two methods for giving notice. Constructive notice is given to all reliance parties if the owner of the restored copyright "file[d] with the Copyright Office, during the 24-month period beginning on the date of restoration, a notice of intent to enforce the restored copyright." 17 U.S.C. § 104A(d)(2)(A)(i). In such a case, notice is deemed to have been given on the date the notice was published in the Federal Register. 17 U.S.C. § 104A(d)(2)(A)(ii). Alternatively, actual notice is given when the owner of the restored copyright "serves upon a reliance party a notice of intent to enforce a restored copyright." 17 U.S.C. § 104A(d)(2)(B)(i). In such a case, notice is deemed to have been given on the date the notice was received. 17 U.S.C. § 104A(d)(2)(B)(ii).

[476] 17 U.S.C. § 104A(d)(2)(A)(ii), 17 U.S.C. § 104A(d)(2)(B)(ii).

[477] 17 U.S.C. § 104A(d)(3). *See, e.g.*, Dam Things from Denmark v. Russ Berrie & Co., 290 F.3d 548, 565 (3d Cir. 2002) (to be eligible, a derivative work need only have minimal creativity: "The fact that the

In *Golan v. Holder*, the Supreme Court upheld copyright restoration against a constitutional challenge based on the Copyright Clause and the First Amendment.[478] With regard to the Copyright Clause, the Court held that the "limited Times" restriction was not violated because restored foreign works were given the same fixed term as domestic works, and that dissemination of existing works was a permissible objective under the Copyright Clause.[479] With regard to the First Amendment, the Court held that the "traditional contours" of copyright protection referred to in *Eldred* were limited to the idea-expression dichotomy and the fair use doctrine, and did not include protection of the public domain; and that the public did not have any "vested rights" in works that had entered the public domain.[480]

§ 4F   OWNERSHIP, TRANSFERS, AND TERMINATIONS

[1]   Initial Ownership

Copyright "vests initially in the author or authors of the work."[481] A work's "author" is the individual human or humans who actually created it, with one important exception: the "author" of a work made for hire is the human creator's employer, or in limited circumstances, the person who commissioned the work.[482]

If more than one person (A and B) participate in a work's creation, it may be (1) a work made for hire, (2) a joint work, (3) a derivative work, or (4) a collective work. The work's category affects copyright ownership, duration, and termination transfer rights.

A "work made for hire" results if A and B are employer and employee and B creates the work in the course of her employment.[483] Alternatively, a "work made for hire" may result if A commissions B to create a work and other conditions are met.[484] A, the employer or the commissioning party, is deemed to be the work's sole "author" by operation of law,[485] whether or not A participated in the actual creation of the work.[486] Copyright ownership therefore vests initially in A,[487] and B

---

two companies' dolls have the 'same aesthetic appeal' or 'are very similar in appearance' does not rule out the applicability of the safe harbor for derivative works.").

[478] 132 S. Ct. 873 (2012).

[479] *Id.* at 884–85, 888–89.

[480] *Id.* at 889–92.

[481] 17 U.S.C. § 201(a).

[482] 17 U.S.C. § 201(c). *See* § 4F[1][a].

[483] 17 U.S.C. § 101(1) (definition of "work made for hire").

[484] 17 U.S.C. § 101(2) (definition of "work made for hire").

[485] 17 U.S.C. § 201(b). A corporation or other legal entity may therefore be the "author" of a work made for hire.

[486] If the work is a work made for hire, A is the author and that ends further inquiry. If the work is not a work made for hire, it may be necessary to determine whether A is a joint author with rights of co-ownership with B. *See* Community for Creative Non-Violence v. Reid, 490 U.S. 730 (1989), discussed at § 4F[1][a].

[487] 17 U.S.C. § 201(b).

has no termination rights.[488] The work's copyright term is 95 years from first publication or 120 years from creation, whichever expires first.[489]

A "joint work" results if A and B each contribute original expression to a work "with the intention that their contributions be merged into inseparable or interdependent parts of a unitary whole."[490] A and B are joint authors and are co-owners of the copyright in the work, so each may authorize others to make copies, public performances, or derivative works.[491] The work's copyright term is "the life of the last surviving author and 70 years after such last surviving author's death."[492] If two or more authors execute a transfer, a majority of the joint authors may terminate that transfer.[493]

Two works, an "original work" and a "derivative work," result if A creates a work and then B, with A's consent, modifies A's work.[494] A and B are sole authors and owners of their respective copyrights — A of the original work and B of the derivative work. B's copyright covers only the new material added to the original work, so B's copyright gives B no right to reproduce or use A's original work without A's permission.[495] Conversely, A's copyright gives A no right to reproduce or use B's derivative work without B's permission.[496]

A and B may create separate works that are assembled into a collective work.[497] For example, A and B may write poems, which C compiles, with A's and B's permission, into an anthology. A and B remain sole authors of their separate works, with individual rights to terminate any transfers of copyright interests in those works. No joint work of A and B results because there was no intention that the contributions be merged into a unitary whole. Neither poem is a derivative work of the other because neither is based on the other. C's collective work may itself be a copyrightable selection and arrangement;[498] but, absent a written transfer or a

---

[488] 17 U.S.C. §§ 203(a), 304(c). *See* § 4F[3].

[489] 17 U.S.C. § 302(c).

[490] 17 U.S.C. § 101 (definition of a "joint work"). *See* § 4F[1][b].

[491] 17 U.S.C. § 201(a). *See* § 4F[1][b].

[492] 17 U.S.C. § 302(b).

[493] 17 U.S.C. § 203(a) (termination of grants executed in 1978 or later). By contrast, termination of pre-1978 grants may be exercised separately. 17 U.S.C. § 304(c)(1). *See* § 4F[3].

[494] *See* § 4C[4][b][ii]. If B does not obtain consent, copyright protection may be withheld because of the statutory direction that "protection for a work employing preexisting material in which copyright subsists does not extend to any part of the work in which such material has been used unlawfully." 17 U.S.C. § 103(a).

[495] 17 U.S.C. § 103(b). Thus, even if the derivative work enters the public domain, a third party may not reproduce or use the derivative work without the further permission of A, the owner of copyright in the underlying work. *See* § 4D[1][a], § 4E[2][b].

[496] *See, e.g.*, G. Ricordi & Co. v. Paramount Pictures, Inc., 189 F.2d 469 (2d Cir. 1951), discussed in § 4C[4][b][ii]. This result obtains even when the original work is jointly authored by A and B. *See* Weissmann v. Freeman, 868 F.2d 1313, 1318 (2d Cir. 1989) ("Even though one co-author has the right to revise a joint work in order to create an individual derivative work, the other co-author acquires no property rights in the newly created work prepared without his involvement.").

[497] *See* § 4F[1][c].

[498] *See* § 4C[4][b][ii].

valid work-for-hire agreement, A and B retain ownership of the copyrights in their contributions, while C, the creator of the collective work, acquires only the privilege of reproducing and distributing the contribution as part of that particular collective work, or a revision of that collective work.[499]

## [a]	Works for Hire

Under copyright law's "work made for hire" provisions, the employer is the author of works prepared by employees within the scope of their employment unless there is a written agreement to the contrary. The same is true of certain types of specially commissioned works.

A work for hire determination differs from a copyright transfer. With a transfer, the transferee acquires copyright ownership but does not become the author. With a work for hire, the employer or commissioning party is deemed to be the "author" for all Copyright Act purposes,[500] and the human creator has no transfer termination rights.[501] Also, copyright duration for a work for hire is set at 95 years from first publication or 120 years from creation, whichever comes first, rather than being based on the life of the human creator.[502] As the Supreme Court noted in *Community for Creative Non-Violence v. Reid*, "[t]he contours of the work for hire doctrine . . . carry profound significance for freelance creators — including artists, writers, photographers, designers, composers, and computer programmers — and for the publishing, advertising, music, and other industries which commission their works."[503]

The 1976 Act's work for hire provision differs from the prior copyright statute, the 1909 Act. Because the 1976 Act does not operate retroactively to alter ownership of works created prior to its effective date, January 1, 1978,[504] the interpretation of the 1909 Act is still important.

---

[499] 17 U.S.C. § 201(c).

[500] 17 U.S.C. § 201(b). *See* Community for Creative Non-Violence v. Reid, 490 U.S. 730, 737 (1989):

> As a general rule, the author is the party who actually creates the work, that is, the person who translates an idea into a fixed, tangible expression entitled to copyright protection. § 102. The Act carves out an important exception, however, for 'works made for hire.'. . . If the work is for hire, 'the employer or other person for whom the work was prepared is considered the author' and owns the copyright, unless there is a written agreement to the contrary. § 201(b).

[501] "Works made for hire" are not subject to the Copyright Act's termination provisions. 17 U.S.C. §§ 203(a), 304(c).

[502] 17 U.S.C. § 302(c).

[503] 490 U.S. 730, 737 (1989).

[504] Real Estate Data, Inc. v. Sidwell Co., 809 F.2d 366 (7th Cir. 1987); Roth v. Pritikin, 710 F.2d 934 (2d Cir. 1983). The *Roth* court noted that retroactive application of the 1976 Act to work for hire questions would "raise a serious issue concerning the Act's constitutionality," because "[a]n interest in a copyright is a property right protected by the due process and just compensation clauses of the Constitution." 710 F.2d at 939.

[i]   The 1909 Act

The 1909 Act provided that "the word 'author' shall include an employer in the case of works made for hire,"[505] but did not define "employer" or "works made for hire." The courts initially "concluded that the work for hire doctrine . . . referred only to works made by employees in the regular course of their employment. As for commissioned works, the courts generally presumed that the commissioned party had impliedly agreed to convey the copyright, along with the work itself, to the hiring party."[506] Beginning in 1966, however, courts merged these two lines of cases, expanding the concept of "work made for hire" to include works made by independent contractors.[507] These courts concluded that the employer is the author "whenever an employee's work is produced at the instance and expense of his employer,"[508] or "in other words, when the motivating factor in producing the work was the employer who induced its creation."[509] Although in theory the presumption that such a work was a work made for hire was rebuttable,[510] "at [the] time of the adoption of the 1976 Act, the simple rule . . . had developed into an almost irrebuttable presumption that any person who paid another to create a copyrightable work was the statutory 'author' under the 'work for hire' doctrine."[511] Because the 1976 Act does not operate retroactively to alter ownership of works created prior to its effective date,[512] courts have continued to apply the "instance and expense" test to determine authorship and ownership of commissioned works created before January 1, 1978.[513]

---

[505] 1909 Act, § 62, 35 Stat. 1075 (codified at 17 U.S.C. § 26 in 1947, repealed 1978).

[506] Community for Creative Non-Violence v. Reid, 490 U.S. 730, 744 (1989), citing, *inter alia*, Yardley v. Houghton Mifflin Co., 108 F.2d 28, 31 (2d Cir. 1939).

[507] *See, e.g.*, Brattleboro Publishing Co. v. Winmill Publishing Corp., 369 F.2d 565, 568 (2d Cir. 1966) ("We see no sound reason why these same principles are not applicable when the parties bear the relationship of employer and independent contractor.").

[508] *Id.* at 567. *See also* Picture Music, Inc. v. Bourne, Inc., 457 F.2d 1213, 1216 (2d Cir. 1972); Siegel v. National Periodical Publications, Inc., 508 F.2d 909, 914 (2d Cir. 1974).

[509] *Siegel*, 508 F.2d at 914 (quoting *Picture Music*, 457 F.2d at 1216). *See also* Murray v. Gelderman, 566 F.2d 1307, 1310 (5th Cir. 1978).

[510] *See* May v. Morganelli-Heumann & Associates, 618 F.2d 1363, 1368 (9th Cir. 1980) ("the doctrine is based on the presumed mutual intent of the parties, and does not operate as a matter of law"); Sargent v. American Greetings Corp., 588 F. Supp. 912, 921 (N.D. Ohio 1984) ("the presumption . . . operates only in the event it is not possible to ascertain the express or implied contractual intent of the parties").

[511] Easter Seal Society for Crippled Children and Adults of Louisiana, Inc. v. Playboy Enterprises, 815 F.2d 323, 327 (5th Cir. 1987). Judge Gee noted that "this most delightful of casenames [is] seriously rivaled, in our judgment, only by *United States v. 11 1/4 Dozen Packages of Article Labeled in Part Mrs. Moffat's Shoo Fly Powders for Drunkenness*, 40 F. Supp. 208 (W.D.N.Y. 1941) . . . and *United States ex rel. Mayo v. Satan and his Staff*, 54 F.R.D. 282 (W.D. Pa. 1971)." 815 F.2d at 324 n.1.

[512] Real Estate Data, Inc. v. Sidwell Co., 809 F.2d 366 (7th Cir. 1987); Roth v. Pritikin, 710 F.2d 934 (2d Cir. 1983).

[513] *See, e.g.*, Estate of Hogarth v. Edgar Rice Burroughs, Inc., 342 F.3d 149 (2d Cir. 2003) (illustrator who created graphic novel adaptations of Tarzan novels worked at the "instance and expense" of the publisher); Twentieth Century Fox Film Corp. v. Entertainment Distributing, 429 F.3d 869 (9th Cir. 2005) (General Eisenhower's memoirs were created at the "instance and expense" of the publisher, despite tax treatment as sale of a capital asset rather than payment of salary).

[ii]   The 1976 Act

The 1976 Act provides that, in the case of a work made for hire, "the employer or other person for whom the work was prepared is considered the author . . . and, unless the parties have expressly agreed otherwise in a written instrument signed by them, owns all of the rights comprised in the copyright."[514]

Section 101 of the 1976 Act provides that a work is a "work made for hire" under two sets of circumstances:

(1) a work prepared by an employee within the scope of his or her employment; or

(2) a work specially ordered or commissioned for use as a contribution to a collective work, as a part of a motion picture or other audiovisual work, as a translation, as a supplementary work, as a compilation, as an instructional text, as a test, as answer material for a test, or as an atlas, if the parties expressly agree in a written instrument signed by them that the work shall be considered a work made for hire.[515]

In *Community for Creative Non-Violence v. Reid ("CCNV")*, the Supreme Court held that the word "employee" in the 1976 Act's definition refers to "a hired party in a conventional employment relationship" as determined by general agency law: "To determine whether a work is for hire under the Act, a court first should ascertain, using principles of general common law of agency, whether the work was prepared by an employee or an independent contractor. After making this determination, the court can apply the appropriate subsection of § 101."[516]

CCNV was an organization devoted to ending homelessness in America. It commissioned Reid to sculpt three life-size human figures for a modern Nativity scene depicting a homeless family huddled on a steam grate. Relying on the *Restatement (Second) of Agency*, the Court set forth a multi-factor balancing test under agency law.[517] Applying this test, the Court concluded that Reid was not an employee of CCNV but an independent contractor. Reid was a professional sculptor who supplied his own tools and worked in his own studio; he was hired for a specific project and was paid a single lump sum, rather than a salary; and "CCNV did not pay payroll or social security taxes, provide any employee benefits, or contribute to unemployment insurance or workers' compensation funds."[518] Since Reid was an independent contractor, but there was no signed written agreement and the work

---

[514] 17 U.S.C. § 201(b). *See* Baltimore Orioles, Inc. v. Major League Baseball Players Ass'n, 805 F.2d 663, 671–72 (7th Cir. 1986) (Section 201(b) "represents a substantial change in the 'work made for hire' doctrine. Under prior law, 'such an agreement could be either *oral* or *implied.*' . . . However, § 201(b) requires that an agreement altering the statutory presumption be both *written* and *express*. In essence, this provision is a statute of frauds.").

[515] 17 U.S.C. § 101 (definition of "work made for hire").

[516] 490 U.S. 730, 750 (1989). The court specifically held that the determination should be made as a matter of federal common law, rather than state agency law, to ensure a uniform nationwide application of the Act. *Id.* at 740.

[517] 490 U.S. at 751.

[518] *Id.* at 752.

did not fall within one of the nine categories specified in clause (2), the sculpture could not be a work made for hire.[519]

Although no single factor is determinative of employee status, in practice courts have treated the financial relationship between the parties, including payroll formalities and tax treatment, as highly probative.[520] Note that failing to identify the work as "made for hire" on the registration certificate is not dispositive.[521]

Following *CCNV*, courts have also looked to the general common law of agency (as set forth in the Restatement) to determine whether a work was prepared "within the scope of [the employee's] employment." The Restatement employs a three-part test: (1) whether the work was of the type the employee was hired to perform; (2) whether the creation of the work in question occurred "substantially within the authorized time and space limits" of the employee's job; and (3) whether the employee was "actuated, at least in part, by a purpose to serve" the employer's purpose.[522]

Although the "plain language" of the 1976 Act would seem to preclude any implied exceptions for works written by employees, two opinions (written by former law professors) have concluded that there is a "teacher exception" under which professors own the copyrights to their works.[523] Even if such an exception exists, however, it is likely limited to academic books and articles, as opposed to software with commercial applications,[524] or materials prepared specifically for classroom use.[525]

With regard to commissioned works, the 1976 Act provides much greater protection for independent contractors than did the case law under the 1909 Act.

---

[519] *Id.* at 738. The Court nonetheless agreed with the D.C. Circuit that the case should be remanded to determine whether the sculpture was a "joint work" because of CCNV's contributions to the finished product. *Id.* at 753.

[520] *See* Garcia v. Google, Inc., 766 F.3d 929, 936 (9th Cir. 2014); Kirk v. Harter, 188 F.3d 1005 (8th Cir. 1999); Carter v. Helmsley-Spear, Inc., 71 F.3d 77 (2d Cir. 1995); Aymes v. Bonelli, 980 F.2d 857 (2d Cir. 1992) (noting that "every case since *Reid* . . . has found the hired party to be an independent contractor where the hiring party failed to extend benefits or pay social security taxes"). *But see* JustMed, Inc. v. Byce, 600 F.3d 1118 (9th Cir. 2010) (finding programmer was an employee, despite the fact that he worked at home, was not paid benefits, and did not have taxes withheld).

[521] *See* Pritchett v. Pound, 473 F.3d 217 (5th Cir. 2006).

[522] RESTATEMENT (SECOND) OF AGENCY § 228 (1958). *See, e.g.*, Gilpin v. Siebert, 419 F. Supp. 2d 1288 (D. Or. 2006) (finding genuine issues of material fact as to whether instruction manual written by college counselor was a work made for hire); Genzmer v. Public Health Trust of Miami-Dade County, 219 F. Supp. 2d 1275 (S.D. Fla. 2002) (computer program written by graduate research fellow at hospital was within scope of employment); McKenna v. Lee, 318 F. Supp. 2d 296 (E.D.N.C. 2002) (license plate designed by prison inmate was within inmate's scope of employment), *aff'd*, 53 Fed. Appx. 268 (4th Cir. 2002).

[523] *See* Hays v. Sony Corp. of America, 847 F.2d 412, 415 (7th Cir. 1988) (Posner, J.) (a contrary conclusion would wreak "havoc . . . in the settled practices of academic institutions"); Weinstein v. University of Illinois, 811 F.2d 1091, 1094 (7th Cir. 1987) (Easterbrook, J.) (teacher exception "has been the academic tradition since copyright law began").

[524] *See* Rouse v. Walter & Assocs., LLC, 513 F. Supp. 2d 1041 (S.D. Iowa 2007).

[525] *See* Shaul v. Cherry Valley-Springfield Central School Dist., 363 F.3d 177 (2d Cir. 2004), and Vanderhurst v. Colorado Mountain College District, 16 F. Supp. 2d 1297 (D. Colo. 1998).

Such works must fall within one of the nine categories specified in Clause (2) of the definition,[526] *and* there must a signed written agreement that the work is a work made for hire. Courts disagree as to whether the writing must exist before the work is created.[527] To avoid the uncertainties of the work-made-for-hire doctrine, many hiring parties routinely draft agreements specifying both that a work is made for hire *and* that the copyright is assigned to the hiring party. Some courts will even construe an invalid work-for-hire agreement as effecting an assignment.[528] The major drawback to an assignment, when compared with a work made for hire, is that an assignment of copyright can be terminated 35 years after the date of the grant, if the author or his or her heirs decide to do so.[529]

Two major categories of collaborative works — computer programs and sound recordings — do not fit comfortably within the nine categories specified in section 101.[530] In 1999, a "technical amendment" temporarily added sound recordings as a tenth category of works that could qualify as "works made for hire" under the second clause. After a storm of protest, however, the amendment was repealed, with Congress specifying that neither the amendment nor the repeal "shall be considered or otherwise given any legal significance" in any future proceedings.[531] Because sound recordings are routinely made under written "work made for hire" agreements, legal experts predict that there will be a flood of litigation concerning whether those agreements are valid, which would render such agreements ineligible for termination; or whether they are invalid, which could allow some performing artists to recapture their copyrights in post-1978 sound recordings through termination of those assignments.[532]

---

[526] The nine statutory categories are: "a work specially ordered or commissioned for use as a contribution to a collective work, as a part of a motion picture or other audiovisual work, as a translation, as a supplementary work, as a compilation, as an instructional text, as a test, as answer material for a test, or as an atlas." 17 U.S.C. § 101(2). The Act further defines two of those categories. An "instructional text" is "a literary, pictorial, or graphic work prepared for publication . . . [for] use in systematic instructional activities"; and a "supplementary work" is "a work prepared for publication as a secondary adjunct to a work by another author . . . such as forewords, afterwords, pictorial illustrations, maps, charts, tables, editorial notes, . . . bibliographies, appendixes, and indexes." *Id.*

[527] *Compare* Playboy Enterprises v. Dumas, 53 F.3d 549 (2d Cir. 1995) (parties must agree before the work is created, but agreement may be either oral or implied, as long as it is later confirmed in a signed writing; printed legend on the back of a check, just below the signature where the check is endorsed, will suffice) *with* Schiller & Schmidt v. Nordisco Corp., 969 F.2d 410 (7th Cir. 1992) ("the writing requirement must precede the creation of the property in order to serve its purpose of identifying the (non-creator) owner unequivocally.").

[528] *See, e.g.*, Compaq Computer Corp. v. Ergonome, Inc., 210 F. Supp. 2d 839 (S.D. Tex. 2001).

[529] 17 U.S.C. § 203(a). *See* § 4F[3].

[530] Note, however, that if a computer program or sound recording is made "as part of a motion picture or other audiovisual work," including a videogame, then it falls within the second category. Alternatively, certain programs or sound recordings might be considered to be "a contribution to a collective work" or "a compilation" in certain circumstances.

[531] 17 U.S.C. § 101. Congress further specified that "Paragraph (2) shall be interpreted as if both" the enactment and the repeal "were never enacted, and without regard to any inaction or awareness by the Congress at any time of any judicial determinations." *Id.*

[532] For a review of the legal issues, see Nimmer & Menell, *Sound Recordings, Works for Hire, and the Termination of Transfers Time Bomb*, 49 J. Copyright Soc'y 387 (2001); and Jaffee, *Defusing the*

[b] Joint Works

A "joint work" (or, more precisely, a work of joint authorship) results when two or more authors make contributions of original authorship "with the intention that their contributions be merged into inseparable or interdependent parts of a unitary whole."[533] For example, a joint work results when a composer and a lyricist write a song, an author and illustrator create a children's book, or several scholars produce a law-school textbook. The contributions of multiple authors "may be either 'inseparable' (as in the case of a novel or painting) or 'interdependent' (as in the case of a motion picture, opera, or the words and music of a song)."[534]

"The authors of a joint work are co-owners of copyright in the work."[535] "[C]o-owners of a copyright . . . [are] treated generally as tenants in common, with each co-owner having an independent right to use or license the use of a work, subject to a duty of accounting to the other co-owners for any profits."[536] Thus, "[a] co-owner of a copyright cannot be liable to another co-owner for infringement of the copyright."[537] Each joint author may also use the joint work to create derivative works, such as revisions.[538] However, "the other co-author acquires no property rights in the newly created work prepared without his involvement."[539]

Time Bomb Once Again — Determining Authorship in a Sound Recording, 53 J. COPYRIGHT SOC'Y 139 (2006).

[533] 17 U.S.C. § 101 (definition of "joint work").

[534] H.R. Rep. No. 94-1476, at 120 (1976).

[535] 17 U.S.C. § 201(a). *See, e.g.*, Picture Music, Inc. v. Bourne, Inc., 314 F. Supp. 640, 645 (S.D.N.Y. 1970) ("When two or more authors pursuing a common design together create a single work, they become joint owners of the work in undivided shares which are owned by each author."), *aff'd on other grounds*, 457 F.2d 1213 (2d Cir. 1972). The intent of the 1976 Act was to confirm existing law on the rights of co-ownership. *See* H.R. Rep. No. 94-1476, at 121 (1976) ("There is also no need for a specific statutory provision concerning the rights and duties of the co-owners of a work; court-made law on this point is left undisturbed.").

[536] H.R. Rep. No. 94-1476, at 121 (1976). *See, e.g.*, Oddo v. Ries, 743 F.2d 630, 633 (9th Cir. 1984) ("each co-owner has an independent right to use or license the use of the copyright" but "[a] co-owner of a copyright must account to other co-owners for any profits he earns from licensing or use of the copyright."); Picture Music, Inc. v. Bourne, Inc., 314 F. Supp. 640, 646–47 (S.D.N.Y. 1970) ("compensation obtained from the unilateral exploitation of the joint work by one of the co-owners without the permission of the others is held in a 'constructive trust' for the mutual benefit of all co-owners and there is a duty to account therefore."), *aff'd on other grounds*, 457 F.2d 1213 (2d Cir. 1972).

[537] Oddo v. Ries, 743 F.2d 630, 632–33 (9th Cir. 1984), citing Picture Music, Inc. v. Bourne, Inc., 314 F. Supp. 640, 646 (S.D.N.Y. 1970) ("a joint author cannot be held liable for copyright infringement to another joint owner."), *aff'd on other grounds*, 457 F.2d 1213 (2d Cir. 1972). *See also* Weissmann v. Freeman, 868 F.2d 1313, 1318 (2d Cir. 1989) ("an action for infringement between joint owners will not lie because an individual cannot infringe his own copyright. The only duty joint owners have with respect to their joint work is to account for profits from its use."); Warren Freedenfeld Assocs., Inc. v. McTigue, 531 F.3d 38, 47–48 (1st Cir. 2008).

[538] *See* Weissmann v. Freeman, 868 F.2d 1313, 1318 (2d Cir. 1989) ("one co-author has the right to revise a joint work in order to create an individual derivative work").

[539] *Id.*; *see also* Ashton-Tate Corp. v. Ross, 916 F.2d 516, 522 (9th Cir. 1990) ("Joint authorship in a prior work is insufficient to make one a joint author of a derivative work.").

[i]   The 1909 Act

The 1909 Act did not expressly refer to multiple or joint authorship, but the courts acknowledged that more than one human author may contribute jointly to a single work and that the result was joint authorship with each author being a co-owner of the copyright in the work.[540]

When two or more persons collaborate to create a single work, the work is clearly joint. More difficult to classify is a work that results from a merger of parts created by two or more persons at different times and without collaboration. In a series of cases, the Second Circuit extended joint authorship status to musical compositions in which composer and lyricist worked separately and in which the contribution of one was completed before the other contributor was even selected.

In *Edward B. Marks Music Corp. v. Jerry Vogel Music Co.*, the court found joint authorship when a lyricist wrote words to be set to music by some unknown composer and sold the words to another who then engaged a composer who wrote the music.[541]

The *Melancholy Baby* case involved a song consisting of music written by a husband and lyrics by his wife. Later, with the husband's consent, a music publisher engaged a second lyricist to write new words. The court held that the resulting song was a "joint work," even though the composer had originally intended his music to be joined with his wife's lyrics.[542]

The *12th Street Rag* case extended *Melancholy Baby* to a situation where the first author, the composer of an instrumental piano solo, had no intention at the time of creation that lyrics be added. The composer later assigned his copyright to a music publisher, who then commissioned a lyricist to write lyrics for it. After the copyrights in the piano solo and the song were renewed, the assignee of the composer sued the assignee of the lyricist for infringement by publication of the song. The court rejected the view that the composer must have intended at the time he wrote the music that lyrics be added later before joint authorship could arise. It held that the intent of the assignee, rather than that of the author, should govern.[543]

If accepted and applied widely, the *12th Street Rag* rule would substantially alter common understandings as to what constitutes a joint work and the rights of

---

[540] *See* Picture Music, Inc. v. Bourne, Inc., 314 F. Supp. 640, 645 (S.D.N.Y 1970) ("The doctrine of joint authorship is nowhere referred to in the basic federal copyright enactment, Title 17 U.S.C., which derives from the Copyright Act of March 4, 1909, 35 Stat. 1075. Rather, it is one of judicial creation which was imported wholesale from English Law by Judge Learned Hand. *See* Maurel v. Smith, 220 F. 195 (S.D.N.Y. 1915), *aff'd*, 271 F. 211 (2d Cir. 1921), citing Levy v. Rutley, L.R. 6 C.P. 523 (1871)."), *aff'd on other grounds*, 457 F.2d 1213 (2d Cir. 1972).

[541] 140 F.2d 266, 267 (2d Cir. 1944).

[542] Shapiro, Bernstein & Co. v. Jerry Vogel Music Co., 161 F.2d 406, 409 (2d Cir. 1946) ("Melancholy Baby"). The names "Melancholy Baby" and "12th Street Rag," after the titles of the songs at issue, are commonly used to distinguish two cases, which, though dealing with independent controversies, bear the same case caption.

[543] Shapiro, Bernstein & Co. v. Jerry Vogel Music Co., 221 F.2d 569, 570 (2d Cir. 1953), *modified on rehearing*, 223 F.2d 252 (2d Cir. 1955) ("12th Street Rag").

contributors to related works.[544] Not surprisingly, subsequent court decisions and legislation restrict or reject the *12th Street Rag* rule that a joint work can arise if, after creation of a work of authorship, an author or his or her assignee forms an intent to merge the work with a contribution by another.[545]

[ii]   The 1976 Act

The 1976 Act defines a joint work as "a work prepared by two or more authors with the intention that their contributions be merged into inseparable or interdependent parts of a unitary whole."[546] The House Report says: "The touchstone here is the intention, *at the time the writing is done*, that the parts be absorbed or combined into an integrated unit."[547] Thus, the intent to merge must exist at the time of preparation, not later.[548] This language has been interpreted as overruling the *12th Street Rag* case.[549]

Because joint authorship results in equal co-ownership of the resulting work, courts have been reluctant to find joint authorship where one person makes a relatively small contribution to a work predominantly created by another.[550] Accordingly, courts have added two requirements to the statutory criterion that the parties intend to merge their contributions into a unitary whole. The first is that each author must have contributed copyrightable expression to the final work.[551] Thus, an author who merely contributes ideas, parameters or

---

[544] For a critique of *12th Street Rag*, see George B. Cary, Copyright Law Revision Study No. 12, "Joint Ownership of Copyrights," at 92 (1958).

[545] *See, e.g.*, Picture Music, Inc. v. Bourne, Inc., 314 F. Supp. 640 (S.D.N.Y. 1970) (holding that the contribution of a subsequent person to the alteration of an existing copyrighted work must be "substantial" or "significant" before that person becomes a joint author of the altered work), *aff'd on other grounds*, 457 F.2d 1213 (2d Cir. 1972); Gilliam v. American Broadcasting Cos., 538 F.2d 14, 22 (2d Cir. 1976) ("The joint work theory as extended in *Shapiro* has been criticized as inequitable unless 'at the time of creation by the first author, the second author's contribution [is envisaged] as an integrated part of a single work' and the first author intends that the final product be a joint work."). In *Gilliam*, the court relied on provisions in the contract between the writers of "Monty Python" and the BBC in holding that the scripts to the series and the television programs based on the scripts were separate works, rather than joint works.

[546] 17 U.S.C. § 101.

[547] H.R. Rep. No. 94-1476, at 120 (1976) (emphasis added).

[548] *See* Eckert v. Hurley Chicago Company, Inc., 638 F. Supp. 699, 702 (N.D. Ill. 1986) ("The narrower and better view is that each author when making his or her contribution must intend it to constitute a part of a total work to which another shall make (or has already made) a contribution.").

[549] *See* Batiste v. Island Records, Inc., 179 F.3d 217, 222 n.7 (5th Cir. 1999) ("Congress overruled [*12th Street Rag*] in 1976 by adopting the current definition for 'joint work,' which requires that each author intend the merger at the time the author prepares his or her contribution.").

[550] *See, e.g.*, Eckert v. Hurley Chicago Company, Inc., 638 F. Supp. 699, 704 (N.D. Ill. 1986) ("While a co-author's contribution need not equal the other author's, at least when the authors are not immediately and obviously collaborating, the co-author's contribution must be 'significant' both in quality and quantity in order to permit an inference that the parties intended a joint work.").

[551] *See* Aalmuhammed v. Lee, 202 F.3d 1227, 1231 (9th Cir. 2000) ("A 'joint work' . . . 'requires each author to make an independently copyrightable contribution' to the disputed work.' ") (citation omitted); Erickson v. Trinity Theatre, Inc., 13 F.3d 1061, 1071 (7th Cir. 1994) ("Trinity must show that its contributions to the works were independently copyrightable."); Childress v. Taylor, 945 F.2d 500, 507 (2d Cir. 1991) ("It seems more consistent with the spirit of copyright law to oblige all joint authors to make

specifications for a work to be created by another is not a joint author.[552] Note, however, that both Nimmer and at least one court have disagreed with this added requirement, suggesting that only the combined result of the two parties' joint efforts must be copyrightable.[553]

Second, in addition to intending that their contributions be merged, courts have required that the parties intend themselves to be joint authors.[554] For example, in *Childress v. Taylor*, actress Clarice Taylor asked playwright Alice Childress to write a play about legendary comedienne Jackie "Moms" Mabley. Taylor supplied Childress with research material, and she made numerous suggestions while the play was being written and produced. Before the dispute arose, Childress registered the copyright in her own name. Later, Taylor produced another play about "Moms" Mabley, written by playwright Ben Caldwell, and Childress sued, alleging that the second play was an unauthorized derivative work. The court held that Taylor was not a joint author of the first play:

> The wording of the statutory definition appears to make relevant only the state of mind regarding the unitary nature of the finished work. . . . However, an inquiry so limited would extend joint author status to many persons who are not likely to have been within the contemplation of Congress. . . . What distinguishes the writer-editor relationship and the writer-researcher relationship from the true joint author relationship is the lack of intent of both participants in the venture to regard themselves as joint authors.[555]

Although not conclusive in all cases, the court suggested that "in many instances, a useful test will be whether . . . each participant intended that all would be identified

---

copyrightable contributions, leaving those with non-copyrightable contributions to protect their rights through contract.").

[552] *See, e.g.*, Gaylord v. United States, 595 F.3d 1364, 1377 (Fed. Cir. 2010) ("To be an author, one must supply more than mere direction or ideas: one must 'translate an idea into a fixed, tangible expression entitled to copyright protection.' "); *id.* at 1379 ("A person who merely describes to an author what the commissioned work should do or look like is not a joint author for purposes of the Copyright Act."), *quoting* S.O.S., Inc. v. Payday, Inc., 886 F.2d 1081, 1087 (9th Cir. 1989); M.G.B. Homes, Inc. v. Ameron Homes, Inc., 903 F.2d 1486, 1493 (11th Cir. 1990) ("involvement by a client in the preparation of architectural plans . . . does not, however, ordinarily render the client an 'author' of the architectural plans.") (citation omitted).

[553] *See* 1 NIMMER ON COPYRIGHT § 6.07 (2010) ("Thus if authors A and B work in collaboration, but A's contribution is limited to plot ideas which standing alone would not be copyrightable, and B weaves the ideas into a completed literary expression, it would seem that A and B are joint authors of the resulting work."); Gaiman v. McFarlane, 360 F.3d 644, 658–59 (7th Cir. 2004) (approving Nimmer's suggestion as an "exception" to the general rule that "[each] contribution must be independently copyrightable").

[554] *See Childress*, 945 F.2d at 508–09 ("Joint authorship entitles the co-authors to equal undivided interests in the work. That equal sharing of rights should be reserved for relationships in which all participants fully intend to be joint authors."); *Erickson*, 13 F.3d at 1070 ("the parties must have intended to be joint authors at the time that the work was created.").

[555] *Childress*, 945 F.2d at 507. *Accord*, Thomson v. Larson, 147 F.3d 195, 202–04 (2d Cir. 1998) (dramaturg who contributed to the musical "Rent" was not a joint author); Seshadri v. Kasraian, 130 F.3d 798, 803 (7th Cir. 1997) ("the assistance that a research assistant or secretary or draftsman or helpfully commenting colleague provides in the preparation of a scholarly paper does not entitle the helper to claim the status of a joint author.").

as co-authors."[556]

Similarly, in *Aalmuhammed v. Lee*, the Ninth Circuit held that "authorship is not the same thing as making a valuable and copyrightable contribution."[557] In determining joint authorship for the motion picture *Malcom X*, it set forth a three-factor test, looking at "who has decision making authority" or exercises creative control, "objective manifestations of a shared intent to be coauthors," and whether "the audience appeal of the work turns on both contributions."[558] Applying this test, the court held that even though the plaintiff, an Islamic technical consultant, made a valuable creative contribution to the movie, he was not a co-author, because his contributions were merely "recommendations" that the director, Spike Lee, was free to accept or reject.[559]

[c]   Collective Works

A "collective work" is "a work, such as a periodical issue, anthology, or encyclopedia, in which a number of contributions, constituting separate and independent works in themselves, are assembled into a collective whole."[560]

Section 201(c) provides that "[c]opyright in each separate contribution to a collective work is distinct from copyright in the collective work as a whole and vests initially in the author of the contribution."[561] Thus, in a periodical such as the *New York Times*, each article, photograph, and advertisement has a separate copyright, and there is an additional copyright in the collective work as a whole, *i.e.*, in the selection and arrangement of the contributions.[562] The *Times* owns the copyright in the collective work as the publisher and compiler. The *Times* also owns the copyrights in the individual contributions created by its employees, as works made for hire.[563] Freelance authors, however, are independent contractors. Because a "contribution to a collective work" is one of the nine categories of works eligible for

---

[556] *Childress*, 945 F.2d at 508. *See also Thomson*, 147 F.3d at 204 (relying on "evidence that Larson retained decisionmaking authority over the final work, that he was billed as the sole author, and that he entered into written agreements with third parties as sole author."); Janky v. Lake County Convention & Visitors Bureau, 576 F.3d 356 (7th Cir. 2009) (relying on pre-dispute copyright registration in which plaintiff listed another as having provided "additional lyrics" to a "joint work").

[557] 202 F.3d 1227, 1232 (9th Cir. 2000).

[558] *Id.* at 1232, 1234. *See also* Richlin v. Metro-Goldwyn-Mayer Pictures, Inc., 531 F.3d 962 (9th Cir. 2008) (co-author of unpublished treatment on which movie *Pink Panther* was based was not co-author of the motion picture; although "audience appeal" factor favored Richlin, he lacked creative control and was credited only as author of original story, and screenplay based on treatment was written as a work made for hire).

[559] *Aalmuhammed*, 202 F.3d at 1235. *See also* Gaylord v. United States, 595 F.3d 1364 (Fed. Cir. 2010) (sculptor who translated "ideas, comments, and suggestions of multiple committee members" into sculpture for Korean War Veterans Memorial was sole author); Garcia v. Google, Inc., 766 F.3d 929, 942–44 (9th Cir. 2014) (dissenting opinion) (actress was not a joint author of motion picture; *but cf. id.* at 933–34 (majority opinion) (agreeing that actress was not a joint author, but concluding that her performance was an independently copyrightable contribution).

[560] 17 U.S.C. § 101.

[561] 17 U.S.C. § 201(c).

[562] *See* § 4C[4][b][i].

[563] 17 U.S.C. § 101(1) (definition of "work made for hire"). *See* § 4F[1][a].

work-made-for-hire treatment, "specially ordered or commissioned" contributions by freelance authors may also be owned by the *Times*, but only if there is a signed written agreement that they are works made for hire.[564]

Frequently, however, a freelancer submits an article for publication and gets paid without signing a written agreement. If so, the copyright in the article is owned initially by the individual author. Clearly, the publisher has acquired some sort of license; but the potential for future litigation over the scope of such an implied license is evident. Accordingly, section 201(c) sets forth a default rule: "In the absence of an express transfer of the copyright or of any rights under it, the owner of copyright in the collective work is presumed to have acquired only the privilege of reproducing and distributing the contribution as part of that particular collective work, any revision of that collective work, and any later collective work in the same series."[565]

In 1993, six freelance authors brought a test case concerning 21 articles that they had contributed to the *New York Times* and two other periodicals. The question presented was whether the default privilege in section 201(c) gave publishers the authority to reproduce and distribute all of the contents of their publications, including articles written by freelance authors, in various electronic databases, including LexisNexis. In *New York Times Co. v. Tasini*,[566] the Supreme Court held that the databases did not constitute a "revision" of the collective works in which the articles were first published. The Court viewed the electronic databases as a "new anthology" or compendium, rather than as a "revision" of the individual periodical issues.

The *Tasini* opinion also rejected a proffered analogy between the databases and microform publications, noting that microfilm and microfiche faithfully reproduce, page by page, all of the contents of the periodicals they record, whereas electronic databases reproduce individual articles without any of the surrounding context present in the original periodicals. Before *Tasini* was decided, however, another court had held that *The Complete National Geographic*, a page-by-page reproduction of the entire contents of the magazine on CD-ROM, violated the section 201(c) privilege.[567] Revisiting the question after *Tasini*, two courts of appeals have now concluded that such an "electronic replica" was more analogous to microfilm than to the electronic databases in *Tasini*, and was therefore permissible under section 201(c).[568]

Meanwhile, in 2005, the parties to four consolidated class actions filed in the wake of *Tasini* agreed to settle the cases by creating an $18 million fund to compensate freelancers for previous infringing electronic uses. That settlement was threatened when the Second Circuit ruled that the district court could not assert subject-

---

[564] 17 U.S.C. § 101(2) (definition of "work made for hire"). *See* § 4F[1][a].

[565] 17 U.S.C. § 201(c).

[566] 533 U.S. 483 (2001).

[567] *See* Greenberg v. National Geographic Society, 244 F.3d 1267 (11th Cir. 2001).

[568] *See* Faulkner v. National Geographic Enterprises, Inc., 409 F.3d 26 (2d Cir. 2005); Greenberg v. National Geographic Society, 533 F.3d 1244 (11th Cir. 2008) (en banc).

matter jurisdiction over unregistered copyrights, even for settlement purposes.[569] In 2010, however, the Supreme Court held that the lack of registration did not deprive the District Court of subject-matter jurisdiction.[570] On remand, the Second Circuit vacated and remanded the settlement, holding that the class representatives did not adequately represent all members of the class.[571]

[2]   Transfers and Licenses

When a work is "created" by fixing it in a tangible medium of expression,[572] the author typically owns both the copyright in the work and the material object in which the work is first fixed, such as a manuscript, canvas, or hard drive.[573] That material object is the first "copy" of the work.[574] Section 202 provides that "[o]wnership of a copyright . . . is distinct from ownership of any material object in which the work is embodied."[575] Thus,

> Transfer of ownership of any material object, include the copy or phonorecord in which the work is first fixed, does not of itself convey any rights in the copyrighted work embodied in the object; nor, in the absence of an agreement, does transfer of ownership of a copyright . . . convey property rights in any material object.[576]

In other words, even if the author sells the original embodiment of the work, such as "the original manuscript, the photographic negative, the unique painting or statue, [or] the master tape recording," the author retains ownership of the copyright, absent further agreement.[577] The purchaser of the material object acquires only the right to publicly display that object and the right to sell or

---

[569] *See In re* Literary Works in Electronic Databases Copyright Litigation, 509 F.3d 116 (2d Cir. 2007), *rev'd sub nom.* Reed Elsevier, Inc. v. Muchnick, 559 U.S. 154 (2010).

[570] *See* Reed Elsevier, Inc. v. Muchnick, 559 U.S. 154 (2010).

[571] *In re* Literary Works on Electronic Databases Copyright Litigation, 654 F.3d 242 (2d Cir. 2011).

[572] *See* 17 U.S.C. § 101 ("A work is 'created' when it is fixed in a copy or phonorecord for the first time.").

[573] There are exceptional circumstances, however, in which someone else might own the material object in which the work is fixed. For example, if a building owner hires an artist to paint a mural on a wall of his building, or if a graffiti artist paints a mural on a wall without permission, then the artist owns the copyright, but the building owner still owns the material object (the wall) in which the work is fixed.

[574] *See* 17 U.S.C. § 101 ("The term "copies" includes the material object, other than a phonorecord, in which the work is first fixed."). If the work is a sound recording, then the material object in which the work is first fixed is a "phonorecord." *Id.* (definition of "phonorecord").

[575] 17 U.S.C. § 202.

[576] *Id.* The same was true under the 1909 Act. 1909 Act, § 41, 35 Stat. 1075 (codified at 17 U.S.C. § 27 in 1947, repealed 1978). However, the 1909 Act applied only to federal statutory copyrights in works that were published or registered. For unpublished works, some courts held that "authors or artists [were] generally presumed to transfer *common law* literary property rights when they sell their manuscript or work of art, unless those rights [were] specifically reserved." H.R. Rep. No. 94-1476, at 124 (1976) (emphasis added), *citing* Pushman v. New York Graphic Society, Inc., 39 N.E.2d 249 (N.Y. 1942). By bringing unpublished works under federal statutory copyright, the 1976 Act effectively overruled the *Pushman* doctrine. *Id.*

[577] H.R. Rep. No. 94-1476, at 124 (1976).

otherwise dispose of the possession of that copy of the work.[578]

The copyright is a property interest that can be subdivided in any way,[579] and "may be transferred, in whole or in part, by any means of conveyance or by operation of law."[580] Transfers "other than by operation of law" are valid only if made in a signed writing.[581] As one court explained: "Common sense tells us that agreements should routinely be put in writing. This simple practice prevents misunderstanding by spelling out the terms of a deal in black and white, forces parties to clarify their thinking and consider problems that could potentially arise. . . . Copyright law dovetails nicely with common sense by requiring that a transfer of copyright ownership be in writing."[582]

In applying the writing requirement, however, most courts have insisted that "the terms of any writing purporting to transfer copyright interests, even a one-line statement, must be clear."[583] Thus, an exchange of faxes that referred to a "deal," but did include any further information about the terms of the deal, was held to be insufficient.[584] However, courts have held that "an oral assignment may be confirmed later in writing,"[585] so long as the writing is "substantially contempora-

---

[578] 17 U.S.C. § 109(a), (c). *See* § 4G[[3][b].

[579] 17 U.S.C. § 201(d)(2). By contrast, under the 1909 Act, the courts applied a doctrine of "indivisibility."

[580] 17 U.S.C. § 201(d)(1).

[581] 17 U.S.C. § 204(a). *See* Effects Associates Inc. v. Cohen, 908 F.2d 555, 556 (9th Cir. 1990) ("section 204 of the Copyright Act invalidates a purported transfer of ownership unless it is in writing."). *But see* Latin Am. Music Co. v. ASCAP, 593 F.3d 95 (1st Cir. 2010) (although a transfer of ownership must be in writing, termination of such a transfer may be accomplished orally). The federal E-SIGN Act, 15 U.S.C. §7001, validates a transfer with an electronic signature or click-through agreement. *See* Metro. Regional Info. Sys., Inc. v. Am. Home Realty Network, Inc., 722 F.3d 591 (4th Cir. 2013).

The 1909 Act also required a signed writing to transfer a copyright. 1909 Act, § 42, 35 Stat. 1075 (codified at 17 U.S.C. § 28 in 1947, repealed 1978). However, the 1909 Act applied only to federal statutory copyrights in works that were published or registered. For unpublished works, common-law copyrights could be transferred orally or by conduct. *See, e.g.*, Martha Graham School and Dance Foundation, Inc. v. Martha Graham Center of Contemporary Dance, Inc., 380 F.3d 624, 643–44 (2d Cir. 2004) (holding that unpublished dances created by Martha Graham prior to 1956 were assigned to the Center she founded), *on appeal after remand*, 466 F.3d 97 (2d Cir. 2006) (affirming finding that unpublished dances created between 1956 and 1965 were likewise assigned to the Center); Pushman v. New York Graphic Society, Inc., 39 N.E.2d 249 (N.Y. 1942) (transfer of original painting also transferred common-law right to reproduce the painting).

[582] *Effects Associates*, 908 F.2d at 556–57.

[583] Papa's-June Music, Inc. v. McLean, 921 F. Supp. 1154, 1159 (S.D.N.Y. 1996). *See also* Bieg v. Hovnanian Enterprises, Inc., 157 F. Supp. 2d 475 (E.D. Pa. 2001) ("any ambiguity concerning the alleged transfer must be interpreted in favor of the original copyright holder" in order to avoid inadvertent transfers).

[584] *See* Radio Television Espanola S.A. v. New World Entertainment, Ltd., 183 F.3d 922 (9th Cir. 1999). *But see* SCO Group, Inc. v. Novell, Inc., 578 F.3d 1201 (10th Cir. 2009) (signed writing that referred to "copyrights" but was ambiguous as to *which* copyrights were being transferred, was sufficient to satisfy section 204; parol evidence may be admitted to interpret agreement).

[585] Billy-Bob Teeth, Inc. v. Novelty, Inc., 329 F.3d 586, 591 (7th Cir. 2003). *See also* Imperial Residential Design, Inc. v. Palms Development Group, Inc., 70 F.3d 96 (11th Cir. 1995) ("a copyright owner's later execution of a writing which confirms an earlier oral agreement validates the transfer *ab initio*").

neous" with the oral agreement and is "a product of the parties' negotiations."[586] Courts are more lenient in interpreting the writing requirement when the assignment is being challenged by a third party rather than by the purported licensor.[587]

Transfers "by operation of law," include transfers occurring in bankruptcy,[588] by mortgage foreclosure, or by intestate succession. Although courts disagree about the interaction of federal copyright law with state community property law,[589] the prevailing view is that in the event of divorce, the author-spouse retains exclusive control and management of the copyrights, but the non-author spouse is entitled to "an undivided one-half interest in the net economic benefits generated by or resulting from copyrighted works created by [the author-spouse] during the existence of the community and from any derivatives thereof."[590]

A copyright owner may also grant a license, or permission to use a work, to another person. A license may be either exclusive, including the right to prevent others from a similar use, or non-exclusive. A "transfer of copyright ownership" is defined as "an assignment, mortgage, exclusive license, or any other conveyance, alienation, or hypothecation of a copyright or of any of the exclusive rights comprised in a copyright . . . but not including a nonexclusive license."[591] Thus, an exclusive license is subject to the writing requirement; but a non-exclusive license may be granted orally or implied by conduct.[592] Although a gratuitous implied license remains valid until it is revoked,[593] an implied license supported by consideration may be irrevocable.[594] Under limited circumstances, however, the

---

[586] Konigsberg Int'l, Inc. v. Rice, 16 F.3d 355, 357 (9th Cir. 1994) (holding signed writing executed 18 years after purported oral transfer was insufficient).

[587] See, e.g., Eden Toys, Inc. v. Florelee Undergarment Co., 697 F.2d 27 (2d Cir. 1982) ("informal license" was later confirmed in a signed writing; because "the copyright owner appears to have no dispute with its licensee on this matter, it would be anomalous to permit a third-party infringer to invoke [§ 204] against the licensee."); Dean v. Burrows, 732 F. Supp. 816 (E.D. Tenn. 1989) (check legend stating payment was for "molds and mold designs" was sufficient against a third-party infringer).

[588] See, e.g., Thompkins v. Lil' Joe Records, Inc., 476 F.3d 1294 (11th Cir. 2007) (rejection in bankruptcy of contract to pay royalties did not result in reversion of copyright to author); ITOFCA, Inc. v. Mega Trans Logistics, Inc., 322 F.3d 928 (7th Cir. 2003).

[589] See, e.g., In re Marriage of Worth, 195 Cal. App. 3d 768 (1987) (state community property law effects a transfer by operation of law of a one-half interest to the non-author spouse).

[590] Rodrigue v. Rodrigue, 218 F.3d 432, 443 (5th Cir. 2000).

[591] 17 U.S.C. § 101.

[592] Effects Associates, Inc. v. Cohen, 908 F.2d 555, 557 (9th Cir. 1990) See, e.g., Baisden v. I'm Ready Prods., 693 F.3d 491 (5th Cir. 2012); Estate of Hevia v. Portrio Corp., 602 F.3d 34 (1st Cir. 2010); Latimer v. Roaring Toyz, Inc., 601 F.3d 1224 (11th Cir. 2010); but see Garcia v. Google, Inc., 766 F.3d 929, 937–38 (9th Cir. 2014) (finding no implied license because actress was defrauded by inclusion of her performance in an anti-Muslim propaganda film).

Courts disagree whether such an implied license is governed by state law or by federal common law. Compare Foad Consulting Group, Inc. v. Musil Govan Azzalino, 270 F.3d 821 (9th Cir. 2001) (state law determines whether implied license exists) with Cincom Systems, Inc. v. Novelis Corp., 581 F.3d 431, 436–37 (6th Cir. 2009) (applying federal common law without discussion).

[593] See, e.g., Wilchombe v. Tee Vee Toons, Inc., 555 F.3d 949 (11th Cir. 2009).

[594] See, e.g., Asset Marketing Systems, Inc. v. Gagnon, 542 F.3d 748 (9th Cir. 2008).

author or the author's heirs may terminate a license or transfer previously granted to another person.[595]

As noted above, a co-owner of a copyright may grant a license to use the work with or without the permission of the other co-owners, subject only to a duty to account for any profits earned.[596] Some courts have held, however, that a co-owner cannot grant or transfer an *exclusive* license without the consent of the other co-owners.[597] One court has also held that a transfer or license operates prospectively only, so that an alleged infringer cannot settle an infringement claim brought by one co-owner by obtaining an assignment or license from another co-owner.[598]

In general, "a license is presumed to be non-assignable and nontransferable in the absence of express provisions to the contrary," because a contrary rule would "transform every licensee into a potential competitor of the patent or copyright holder."[599] By definition, however, an *exclusive* licensee does not compete with the transferor. Moreover, the 1976 Act abrogated the doctrine of indivisibility, allowing exclusive rights to be subdivided and owned separately;[600] and section 101 defines a "copyright owner" as the owner of any exclusive right.[601] Arguably, therefore, an exclusive licensee should be able to assign or sublicense its rights freely without permission from the transferor. In *Gardner v. Nike, Inc.*, however, the Ninth Circuit held that an exclusive licensee does *not* have the right to sublicense its rights without the express consent of the licensor.[602] Other courts and commentators have criticized the *Gardner* decision.[603]

Because "conditions precedent are disfavored and will not be read into a contract unless required by plain, unambiguous language,"[604] most courts have held that a promise to pay royalties in exchange for a license constitutes a covenant rather than a condition precedent, so that non-payment of royalties gives rise to a cause of action for breach of contract, rather than to a claim for copyright infringement.[605] However, in *Jacobson v. Katzer*, the court held that the terms of an open-source license were conditions that could be enforced by an infringement action, rather

---

[595]   17 U.S.C. §§ 203, 304(c). *See* § 4F[3].

[596]   *See* § 4F[1][b].

[597]   *See, e.g.*, Davis v. Blige, 505 F.3d 90, 101 (2d Cir. 2007).

[598]   *See* Davis v. Blige, 505 F.3d 90 (2d Cir. 2007). For criticism of the decision, see 1 NIMMER ON COPYRIGHT § 6.10[A][3] (2010); 1 PATRY ON COPYRIGHT § 5:103 (2010). For an analysis, see Rothstein, *Unilateral Settlements and Retroactive Transfers: A Problem of Copyright Co-Ownership*, 157 U. PA. L. REV. 881 (2009).

[599]   Cincom Systems, Inc. v. Novelis Corp., 581 F.3d 431 (6th Cir. 2009) (discussing a non-exclusive license).

[600]   17 U.S.C. § 201(d)(2).

[601]   17 U.S.C. § 101.

[602]   279 F.3d 774 (9th Cir. 2002).

[603]   *See* Traicoff v. Digital Media, Inc., 439 F. Supp. 2d 872 (S.D. Ind. 2006); *In re* Golden Books Family Entertainment, Inc., 269 B.R. 311 (Bankr. D. Del. 2001); 2 NIMMER ON COPYRIGHT § 10.02[B][4] (2010); 1 PATRY ON COPYRIGHT § 5:103 (2010).

[604]   Effects Associates, Inc. v. Cohen, 908 F.2d 555, 559 n.7 (9th Cir. 1990).

[605]   *See, e.g.*, Sun Microsystems, Inc. v. Microsoft Corp., 188 F.3d 1115, 1121 (9th Cir. 1999); Graham v. James, 144 F.3d 229, 236–38 (2d Cir. 1998).

than independent covenants that could only be enforced by an action for breach of contract.[606]

A recurring problem in interpreting licenses concerns whether a license grants the right to use the work in subsequently invented new media.[607] The courts of appeals are split as to the proper approach to resolving such issues. The Ninth Circuit holds that a license of rights in a given medium generally "includes only such uses as fall within the unambiguous core meaning of the term . . . and exclude[s] any uses which lie within the ambiguous penumbra."[608] The Second Circuit, however, holds that the licensee "may properly pursue any uses which may reasonably be said to fall within the medium as described in the license."[609] Most recent cases concern the question of whether a previously granted license includes the right to distribute the work in electronic form.[610] As noted above, the 1976 Act provided a statutory default license for the owners of collective works,[611] under which the Supreme Court held that, absent a signed written agreement, a publisher does not have a privilege to license an individual contribution to a collective work to electronic databases without the consent of the individual freelance author.[612]

The Copyright Act includes a provision for recording transfers or "other document[s] pertaining to a copyright," including non-exclusive licenses, in the U.S. Copyright Office.[613] Recording a document provides constructive notice of its contents, but only if it specifically identifies the work to which it pertains, and the work has been registered.[614] "As between two conflicting transfers, the one executed first prevails if it is recorded" in such a manner within one month of its execution.[615] Otherwise, the later transfer prevails if it is recorded first, and it was

---

[606] 535 F.3d 1373 (Fed. Cir. 2008). *See also* Wallace v. Int'l Business Machines Corp., 467 F.3d 1104 (7th Cir. 2006) (providing software under GPL open-source license does not violate antitrust laws).

[607] *See, e.g.*, Manners v. Morosco, 252 U.S. 317 (1920) (1912 license to "produce, perform, and represent" stage play did not include right to make a silent film based on the play); L.C. Page & Co. v. Fox Film Corp., 83 F.2d 196 (2d Cir. 1936) (1923 grant of "exclusive motion picture rights" included right to produce a motion picture with sound); Bourne v. Walt Disney Co., 68 F.3d 621 (2d Cir. 1995) (1939 grant of right to use musical works in motion picture includes right to reproduce works on videocassette); Welles v. Turner Entertainment Co., 503 F.3d 728 (9th Cir. 2007) (finding triable issue of fact whether "motion picture and television rights" in *Citizen Kane* screenplay included home video distribution).

[608] NIMMER ON COPYRIGHT § 10.10[b]; *see, e.g.*, Cohen v. Paramount Pictures Corp., 845 F.2d 851 (9th Cir. 1988).

[609] Bartsch v. Metro-Goldwyn-Mayer, Inc., 391 F.2d 150, 155 (2d Cir. 1968). *Accord*, Boosey & Hawkes Music Publishers, Ltd. v. Walt Disney Co., 145 F.3d 481, 486 (2d Cir. 1998).

[610] *See* Random House, Inc. v. Rosetta Books LLC, 283 F.3d 490 (2d Cir. 2002) (right to "print, publish and sell the work in book form" does not include electronic books); Chambers v. Time Warner, Inc., 282 F.3d 147 (2d Cir. 2002) (whether recording contracts include right to distribute digital versions of musical works and sound recordings could not be resolved on motion to dismiss); Reinhardt v. Wal-Mart Stores, Inc., 547 F. Supp. 2d 346 (S.D.N.Y. 2008) (contract defining "records" to include "all forms of reproduction . . . now or hereafter known" unambiguously includes digital downloads).

[611] 17 U.S.C. § 201(c).

[612] *See* New York Times Co. v. Tasini, 533 U.S. 483 (2001), discussed in § 4F[1][c].

[613] 17 U.S.C. § 205(a),(b).

[614] 17 U.S.C. § 205(c).

[615] 17 U.S.C. § 205(d). The time period is two months for a transfer executed outside the United States. *Id.*

"taken in good faith, for valuable consideration . . . , and without notice of the earlier transfer."[616] "A nonexclusive license, whether recorded or not, prevails over a conflicting transfer" if it is in a signed writing, and if it was taken before the conflicting transfer was executed, or it was taken in good faith before the transfer was recorded and without notice of it.[617]

Although Article 9 of the Uniform Commercial Code governs perfection of security interests in unregistered copyrights,[618] one court has held that the federal system for recording transfers preempts state law with respect to registered copyrights.[619]

[3] Termination of Transfers

The 1976 Act allows authors or their heirs an opportunity to recapture their copyrights by providing a five-year period within which to terminate transfers and licenses, whether exclusive or nonexclusive.[620] There are three termination provisions which are similar, but not identical. All three termination provisions, however, do not apply to transfers of copyright in works made for hire, or transfers made by will.[621]

Section 203 establishes a right to terminate transfers or licenses executed by the author on or after January 1, 1978.[622] Section 203 does not apply to transfers or licenses executed by the author's heirs or beneficiaries.[623]

Section 304(c) establishes a right to terminate transfers and licenses of the renewal term in a work published or registered before 1978, executed by either the author or one of the author's designated beneficiaries before January 1, 1978.[624] The primary purpose of section 304(c) is to provide authors and their heirs the opportunity to benefit from the 19-year extension of the renewal term added in 1976, and the 20-year extension of the renewal term added in 1998.[625]

---

[616] *Id. See, e.g.*, Latin American Music Co. v. Archdiocese of San Juan, 499 F.3d 32, 40–41, 43 (1st Cir. 2007) (first transferee registered before second transfer, providing constructive notice).

[617] 17 U.S.C. § 205(e).

[618] *See In re* World Auxiliary Power Co., 303 F.3d 1120 (9th Cir. 2002).

[619] *See In re* Peregrine Entertainment, Ltd., 16 U.S.P.Q.2d 1017 (C.D. Cal. 1990) (Kozinski, J.).

[620] 17 U.S.C. §§ 203(a), 304(c), 304(d).

[621] *Id. See, e.g.*, Marvel Characters, Inc. v. Kirby, 726 F.3d 119 (2d Cir. 2013) (comics drawn by Kirby for Marvel were works made for hire not subject to termination); Siegel v. Warner Bros. Ent'mt, Inc., 542 F. Supp. 2d 1098, 1127 (C.D. Cal. 2008) (although bulk of Superman comics were created by Siegel as works made for hire, initial comic, including the character of Superman, was "completely developed long before the employment relationship was instituted."), *later opinion at* 658 F. Supp. 2d 1036 (C.D. Cal. 2009) (finding additional comics also existed before Siegel's employment, and were therefore also subject to termination), *rev'd on other grounds, sub nom.* Larson v. Warner Bros. Ent'mt, Inc., 504 Fed. Appx. 586 (9th Cir. 2013).

[622] 17 U.S.C. § 203(a).

[623] For a critique of this distinction, see NIMMER ON COPYRIGHT § 11.02[A][4][a] (2010).

[624] 17 U.S.C. § 304(c).

[625] *See* § 4E[1].

Section 304(d) establishes a right to terminate transfers and licenses of the renewal term, executed by either the author or one of the author's designated beneficiaries before January 1, 1978, but only if they had not previously exercised their right to terminate the grant under section 304(c), and the opportunity to terminate under section 304(c) had expired on or before October 27, 1998, the effective date of the Sonny Bono Copyright Term Extension Act.[626] This condition means that the work must have been published or registered on or before October 26, 1939.[627] The primary purpose of section 304(d) is to provide authors and their heirs the opportunity to benefit from the 20-year extension of the renewal term added in 1998.[628]

The three termination provisions set forth in detail the conditions and effect of terminations. The three provisions are similar, but there are important differences between section 203, on the one hand, and sections 304(c) and 304(d), on the other.[629]

[a]   Persons Entitled to Terminate

Both section 203 and Section 304(c) vest the right of terminate in (1) the author, if living; (2) if the author is dead, the widow or widower of the author, any surviving children of the author, and the surviving children of any dead child of the author; or (3) if none of the above survive, the author's executor or administrator.[630] Both sections adopt the principle of *per stirpes* representation, so that if both the widow or widower and any children or grandchildren are alive, the widow or widower owns one-half of the termination interest, and the children share the other half, with any children of a deceased child sharing that child's share.[631] To avoid a holdout, both the termination and any agreement to make a further grant may be effected by those holding a majority of the termination interest, with the caveat that the share of any deceased child can only be exercised by a majority of that child's children.[632]

---

[626] 17 U.S.C. § 304(d).

[627] 37 C.F.R. § 201.10. For works published or registered on October 26, 1939, the five-year window for termination opened on October 26, 1995 ("fifty-six years from the date copyright was originally secured"), and closed on October 26, 2000. However, in order to exercise the termination right, notice must have been served between two and ten years in advance of a date within that window. Therefore, the last day to serve notice was October 26, 1998, meaning the termination right under section 304(c) had expired before October 27, 1998. *Id.*

[628] *See* § 4E[1].

[629] The only differences between section 304(c) terminations and 304(d) terminations are (1) the condition that the opportunity to terminate under section 304(c) must have expired before enactment of the Bono Act, and (2) the calculation of the five-year period within which termination may be effected. Otherwise, "the conditions specified in [§ 304(c)] apply to terminations" under section 304(d). 17 U.S.C. § 304(d)(1). For the sake of convenience, all reference to section 304(c) that follow also apply to section 304(d), unless otherwise specified.

[630] 17 U.S.C. § 203(a)(2), § 304(c)(2).

[631] *Id.* The House Report gives the following example: "Take, for example, a case where a dead author left a widow, two living children and three grandchildren by a third child who is dead. The widow will own half of the reverted interests, the two children will each own 16 2/3 percent, and the three grandchildren will each own a share of roughly 5 1/2 percent." H.R. Rep. No. 94-1476, at 125–26 (1976).

[632] 17 U.S.C. §§ 203(a)(2) & (b)(3); 17 U.S.C. §§ 304(c)(2) & (c)(6)(C). Thus, in the example in the note above, the termination interest may be exercised either by the widow and one of the two surviving

Upon termination, however, the rights in the terminated grant are owned by all of the persons owning termination interests, "including those owners who did not join in signing the notice of termination."[633]

In general, section 304(c) vests the termination interest in the same class of beneficiaries as section 203 and adopts both the *per stirpes* principle and the principle of majority rule. However, because of differences between transfers and licenses made after the effective date of the 1976 Act, and transfers and licenses made before that date, section 304(c) makes different provisions as to joint works,[634] grants not executed by the author,[635] and further grants.[636]

[b]   Time Periods for Termination and Notice

Under all three sections, a termination "may be effected at any time during a period of five years" beginning on a specified date. For section 203 terminations, the specified date is 35 years from the date of execution of the grant, unless "the grant covers the right of publication of the work," in which case the date is 35 years from the date of publication or 40 years from the date of execution of the grant, whichever term ends earlier.[637] For section 304(c) terminations, the specified date is 56 years from the date copyright was originally secured.[638] For section 304(d) terminations, the specified date is 75 years from the date copyright was originally secured.[639]

The appropriate owners effect termination by "serving an advance notice in writing."[640] The notice must (1) state the effective date of the termination, which

---

children, or by the widow and two of the grandchildren. H.R. Rep. No. 94-1476, at 126 (1976).

[633] 17 U.S.C. § 203(b), § 304(c)(6).

[634] *Compare* 17 U.S.C. § 203(a)(1) ("In the case of a grant executed by two or more authors of a joint work," a majority of the authors are required to terminate; a dead author's share is exercised as a unit by his beneficiaries) *with* 17 U.S.C. § 304(c)(1) (each joint author's share may be terminated independently of the other joint authors).

[635] *Compare* 17 U.S.C. § 203(a) (termination applies only to grants "executed by the author") *with* 17 U.S.C. § 304(c)(1) ("a grant executed by a person or persons other than the author" may be terminated "by the surviving person or persons who executed it.") & 17 U.S.C. § 304(c)(4) (same); *see* H.R. Rep. No. 94-1476, at 141 (1976) ("where the grant was executed by a person or persons other than the author, termination can be effected only by the *unanimous* action of the survivors of those who executed it.") (emphasis added).

[636] *Compare* 17 U.S.C. §§ 203(b)(3) (majority rule for further grants) *with* 17 U.S.C. §§ 304(c)(6) (majority rule applies only to each author's share for joint works); *see* H.R. Rep. No. 94-1476, at 141 (1976) ("Where the extended term reverts to joint authors or to a class of renewal beneficiaries who have joined in executing a grant, their rights would be governed by the general rules of tenancy in common; each co-owner would have an independent right to sell his share, or to use or license the work subject to an accounting.").

[637] 17 U.S.C. § 203(a)(3). The alternative computation method for publications is "intended to cover cases where years elapse between the signing of a publication contract and the eventual publication of the work." H.R. Rep. No. 94-1476, 94th Cong., 2d Sess. 126 (1976).

[638] 17 U.S.C. § 304(c)(3). For works that Congress extended in anticipation of the enactment of the 1976 Act, which were therefore already in their extended term on the effective date of the 1976 Act, licenses and transfers became immediately subject to termination on the effective date, January 1, 1978. *Id.*

[639] 17 U.S.C. § 304(d).

[640] 17 U.S.C. §§ 203(a)(4), 304(c)(4).

must fall within the five-year period, and (2) comply, in form, content, and manner of service, with requirements prescribed by the Register of Copyrights.[641] The notice "shall be served not less than two or more than ten years" before the effective date.[642] The notice must be served "upon the grantee or the grantee's successor in title,"[643] and must "be recorded in the Copyright Office before the effective date, as a condition to its taking effect."[644]

The timing of the termination provisions means that choosing an effective date and serving a notice must be done with great care. For example, although the first issue of *Action Comics*, featuring the first appearance of Superman, bore a cover date of "June 1938," it was actually published on April 18, 1938, meaning the termination window opened 56 years later, on April 18, 1994, and closed on April 18, 1999. Thus, a notice of termination served on April 3, 1997, listing an effective date of April 16, 1999, was effective to terminate an assignment of the co-author's rights in *Action Comics No. 1*, but it was not effective to recapture his rights in two "promotional announcements" that were published on April 5 and April 10, 1938, more than 61 years before the effective date of the termination notice.[645]

---

[641] *Id. See* 37 C.F.R. § 201.10. Notable among the requirements of the Copyright Office regulation is that the notice contain a "brief statement reasonably identifying the grant to which the notice of termination applies." 37 C.F.R. § 201.10(b)(1)(iv). *See* Burroughs v. Metro-Goldwyn-Mayer, Inc., 683 F.2d 610, 621 (2d Cir. 1982) (notice of termination listing 33 of the author's works, including "Tarzan of the Apes," but omitting five of the Tarzan books, was not effective to terminate the grantee's interest in those five books). However, the regulation also states that "Harmless errors in a notice that do not materially affect the adequacy of the information . . . shall not render the notice invalid." 37 C.F.R. § 201.10(e)(1); *see* Siegel v. Warner Bros. Ent'mt, Inc., 542 F. Supp. 2d 1098, 1131–32 (C.D. Cal. 2008) (where termination notice identified three grants of copyrighted work, including stipulation settling 1948 litigation, but failed to identify consent judgment entered two days later confirming stipulation, error was "harmless error"), *later opinion at* 690 F. Supp. 2d 1048 (C.D. Cal. 2009) (reiterating and confirming harmless error analysis), *rev'd on other grounds sub nom.* Larson v. Warner Bros. Ent'mt, Inc., 504 Fed. Appx. 586 (9th Cir. 2013).

[642] 17 U.S.C. §§ 203(a)(4)(A), 304(c)(4)(A). For example, if the grant was made on September 1, 1987, the earliest the date could be terminated under section 203 would be 35 years from that date, or September 1, 2022. To get the earliest effective date, the notice would have to be served between September 1, 2012, and September 1, 2020. H.R. Rep. No. 94-1476, at 126 (1976). The last possible effective date would be September 1, 2027, for which the last date to serve advance notice would be September 1, 2025.

[643] 17 U.S.C. §§ 203(a)(4), 304(c)(4). The disjunctive phrase leaves unclear whether service of the notice on the grantee is sufficient when the original grantee has made further grants or issued nonexclusive licenses to others. *See* Burroughs v. Metro-Goldwyn-Mayer, Inc., 683 F.2d 610, 633–34 (2d Cir. 1982) (Newman, concurring).

In *Burroughs*, the author of the "Tarzan" books conveyed his literary property rights to a family-held corporation that, in turn, conveyed certain motion picture rights to MGM. Later, the author's statutory successors served a notice of termination listing 33 of the author's works on the family-held corporation. The majority held that because the notice failed to list five other Tarzan works, MGM retained certain rights to use the Tarzan character. Judge Newman disagreed, but he concurred in the judgment on the ground that the heirs had failed to serve the real party in interest, MGM. Judge Newman agreed with the district court that in serving the family-held corporation, the heirs were "essentially serving themselves." *Id.* at 635.

[644] 17 U.S.C. §§ 203(a)(4)(A), 304(c)(4)(A).

[645] *See* Siegel, 542 F. Supp. 2d at 1118–20. The court concluded, however, that the promotional announcements only depicted "a person with extraordinary strength who wears a black and white leotard and cape." Superman's blue, yellow, and red costume, "and his superhuman ability to leap tall

[c]   Effect of Termination

Under section 203(b), "termination means that ownership of the rights covered by the terminated grant reverts to everyone who owns termination interests on the date the notice of termination was served, whether they joined in signing the notice or not."[646] Because the future rights vest on the date the notice of termination is served,[647] the heirs of a beneficiary who dies before the effective date will inherit his or her share.[648]

After a Section 203 termination, further grants or agreements as to the terminated rights may be made by the appropriate proportion of owners.[649] The further grant or agreement is effective as to all the owners, including those who did not join in signing it.[650] Generally, the further grant "is valid only if it is made after the effective date of the termination."[651] "As an exception, however, an agreement for such a further grant may be made between [the owners] and the original grantee or such grantee's successor in title."[652]

As noted above, in general the same rules apply to terminations under section 304(c).[653] However, section 304(c) contains different provisions for joint works, grants not executed by the author, and further grants.[654]

Under both sections, "[t]ermination of a grant . . . affects only those rights covered by grants that arise under this title, and in way affects rights arising under any other Federal, State, or foreign laws."[655] Thus, if an author assigns his entire copyright interest to a publisher, then on termination he recovers only the U.S. copyright, and is not entitled to any money from continued exploitation of the work in foreign countries.[656] Likewise, the author is not entitled to any profits attributable to any trademarks obtained by the grantee.[657]

---

buildings, repel bullets, and run faster than a locomotive" were not apparent in the black-and-white promotional announcements, and were therefore subject to termination. *Id.* at 1126.

[646] H.R. Rep. No. 94-1476, at 127 (1976).

[647] 17 U.S.C. § 203(b)(2).

[648] *See* Bourne Co. v. MPL Communications Inc., 675 F. Supp. 859, 862 (S.D.N.Y. 1987) ("Because [the author's statutory successor] died after the notice of termination was served, her rights under the terminated grant had vested and thus passed to her estate.").

[649] 17 U.S.C. § 203(b)(3).

[650] *Id.*

[651] 17 U.S.C. § 203(b)(4).

[652] 17 U.S.C. § 203(b)(4). *See* Bourne Co. v. MPL Communications Inc., 675 F. Supp. 859, 865 (S.D.N.Y. 1987) ("The statute neither compels the terminating party to negotiate with the terminated grantee, nor forbids him from negotiating with anyone else. All it requires is that prior to the effective date of termination, the terminated grantee is the only person with whom the author or his successor can make an enforceable and effective agreement to transfer those rights.").

[653] *See* § 4F[3][a].

[654] *Id.*

[655] 17 U.S.C. §§ 203(b)(5), 304(c)(6)(E).

[656] *See* Siegel v. Warner Bros. Ent'mt, Inc., 542 F. Supp. 2d 1098, 1140–42 (C.D. Cal. 2008), *rev'd on other grounds sub nom.* Larson v. Warner Bros. Ent'mt, Inc., 504 Fed. Appx. 586 (9th Cir. 2013).

[657] *Id.* at 1142.

Both sections also contain an exception to termination allowing continued utilization of a derivative work after termination of a grant. It provides:

> A derivative work prepared under authority of the grant before its termination may continue to be utilized under the terms of the grant after its termination, but this privilege does not extend to the preparation after the termination of other derivative works based upon the copyright work by the terminated grant.[658]

The House Report illustrates the distinction: "[A] film made from a play could continue to be licensed for performance after the motion picture contract had been terminated but any remake rights covered by the contract would be cut off."[659]

[d]   Agreements to the Contrary

Both section 203 and section 304(c) provide that termination "may be effected notwithstanding any agreement to the contrary, including an agreement to make a will or to make any future grant."[660] The purpose of this provision was to avoid replicating the result of *Fred Fisher Music*, which largely defeated the purpose of the 1909 Act's renewal provision.[661]

For example, in *Marvel Characters, Inc. v. Simon*,[662] the court held that a settlement agreement that stipulated that a previously created work was a "work made for hire" constituted an "agreement to the contrary" which could not defeat the purported sole author's right of termination. Otherwise, "publishers would be able to utilize their superior bargaining power to compel authors to agree that a work was created for hire in order to get their works published." Thus, "[i]t is the relationship that in fact exists between the parties, and not their description of that relationship, that is determinative."[663]

In the House Report, Congress stated that "[s]ection 203 would not prevent the parties to a transfer or license from voluntarily agreeing at any time to terminate an existing grant and negotiating a new one, thereby causing another 35-year period to start running."[664] However, Congress failed to anticipate that voluntary termination and renegotiation after 1978 of a grant made before 1978 could eliminate the future termination rights of an author's heirs altogether. Section 304

---

[658] 17 U.S.C. §§ 203(b)(1), 304(c)(6)(A).

[659] H.R. Rep. No. 94-1476, at 127 (1976). *See, e.g.*, Mills Music Co. v. Snyder, 469 U.S. 153 (1985) (where exclusive licensee of musical work sub-licensed over 400 sound recordings of the work, licensee was entitled to receive royalties from such sub-licenses after termination, although licensee could not license any more recordings); Fred Ahlert Music Corp. v. Warner/Chappell Music, Inc., 155 F.3d 17 (2d Cir. 1998) ("terms of the grant" were limited to sale and distribution of records, and did not include use of the song in motion picture soundtrack).

[660] 17 U.S.C. §§ 203(a)(5), 304(c)(5). The House Report states that "A provision of this sort is needed because of the unequal bargaining position of authors, resulting in part from the impossibility of determining a work's value until it has been exploited." H.R. Rep. No. 94-1476, at 124 (1976).

[661] *See* Fred Fisher Music Co. v. M. Witmark & Sons, 318 U.S. 643, 656–57 (1943), discussed in § 4E[2][a].

[662] 310 F.3d 280 (2d Cir. 2002).

[663] *Id.* at 290–91.

[664] H.R. Rep. No. 94-1476, at 127 (1976).

would not apply, because the new grant was made after 1978; and section 203 would not apply, because the new grant was not made by the "author," but by the author's heirs.

In both *Milne v. Stephen Slesinger, Inc.*,[665] which involved rights in *Winnie-the-Pooh*, and *Penguin Group (USA) Inc. v. Steinbeck*,[666] the courts held that a post-1978 renegotiation of a pre-1978 agreement was a new agreement to which neither section 304 nor section 203 applied. The courts reasoned that the purposes of termination had been served, because the author's son (in *Milne*) or widow (in *Steinbeck*) had used the threat of termination to negotiate a more favorable deal. Accordingly, they held that a renegotiated agreement was not an "agreement to the contrary," even though it had the effect of eliminating the later-enacted § 304(d) rights of the author's heirs (Milne's granddaughter and Steinbeck's two sons), who were not parties to the renegotiated agreements. By contrast, in *Classic Media, Inc. v. Mewborn*,[667] the court held that the daughter of author Eric Knight could terminate a 1976 agreement granting rights in her father's story *Lassie Come Home*, notwithstanding a 1978 agreement confirming and modifying the 1976 agreement. The court distinguished *Milne*, noting that although Milne used the threat of termination to negotiate a more favorable deal, Mewborn did not "intend to relinquish a known termination right" and did not receive any additional consideration.

§ 4G   EXCLUSIVE RIGHTS AND LIMITATIONS

Section 106 of the 1976 Act gives the author a bundle of five exclusive rights in a work: (1) reproduction, (2) preparation of derivative works, (3) public distribution, (4) public performance, and (5) public display.[668] (A sixth exclusive right, added in 1995, provides a limited public performance right in sound recordings only.[669]) The first three of these rights "extend to every type of copyrighted work,"[670] while the last three extend only to selected categories of works. The exclusive rights are subject to the exceptions and limitations contained in sections 107 through 122.[671] In addition, in 1990 Congress provided a set of limited "moral rights" to authors of certain works of visual art, which are subject only to section 107 (fair use).[672]

The exclusive rights are independent of one another. For example, a printer violates the reproduction right by reproducing a work without authority, even if he does not sell the copies; and a retailer violates the distribution right by selling

---

[665] 430 F.3d 1036 (9th Cir. 2005).

[666] 537 F.3d 193 (2d Cir. 2008).

[667] 532 F.3d 978 (9th Cir. 2008).

[668] 17 U.S.C. § 106.

[669] 17 U.S.C. § 106(6).

[670] H.R. Rep. No. 94-1476, at 61 (1976).

[671] 17 U.S.C. § 106. *See* H.R. Rep. No. 94-1476, at 61 (1976) ("The approach . . . is to set forth the copyright owner's exclusive rights in broad terms in section 106, and then to provide various limitations, qualifications, or exemptions in the . . . sections that follow.").

[672] 17 U.S.C. § 106A.

unauthorized copies of a work, even if he did not make the copies or know that they were made without permission.[673]

Copyright infringement is the unauthorized exercise of one or more of the copyright owner's exclusive rights.[674] Once a prima facie case has been established, a court must then consider whether any of the exceptions or limitations in sections 107 through 122 applies. In an infringement action, these exceptions and limitations are treated as affirmative defenses.

[1]   Reproduction

[a]   In General

The first right is the exclusive right "to reproduce the copyrighted work in copies or phonorecords."[675] Copies and phonorecords are defined as material objects in which a work is fixed.[676] Therefore, the reproduction right is the exclusive right to make new fixations of the copyrighted work.[677] According to the House Report,

> As under the [1909 Act,] a copyrighted work [is] infringed by reproducing it in whole or in any substantial part, or by duplicating it exactly or by imitation or simulation. Wide departures or variations from the copyrighted work would still be an infringement as long as the author's "expression" rather than merely the author's "ideas" are taken.[678]

Thus, the reproduction right overlaps the derivative work right to some extent.[679]

The reproduction right is defined broadly. It is infringed if a single unauthorized copy is made, "even if it is used solely for the private purposes of the reproducer."[680] It is irrelevant whether the reproducer has "finished" his or her work; "the Act prohibits the creation of copies, even if the creator considers those copies mere interim steps toward some final goal."[681] Finally, it does not matter whether the reproducer realizes any kind of financial benefit from the reproduction.[682] While all of these facts may be considered in deciding whether the reproduction was a "fair

---

[673] H.R. Rep. No. 94-1476, at 61 (1976). *See* Walt Disney Prods. v. Filmation Assocs., 628 F. Supp. 871, 876 (C.D. Cal. 1986) ("the fact that the articles may never be published or, indeed, may be prepared only for the use of Filmation's animators, does not obviate the possibility of infringement.").

[674] 17 U.S.C. § 501.

[675] 17 U.S.C. § 106(1).

[676] 17 U.S.C. § 101. For the distinction between "copies" and "phonorecords," see § 4C[2].

[677] H.R. Rep. No. 94-1476, at 61 (1976) (the reproduction right is "the right to produce a material object in which the work is duplicated, transcribed, limited, or simulated in a fixed form").

[678] H.R. Rep. No. 94-1476, at 61 (1976).

[679] H.R. Rep. No. 94-1476, at 62 (1976).

[680] *See* Walt Disney Prods. v. Filmation Assocs., 628 F. Supp. 871, 876 (C.D. Cal. 1986) (citation omitted). *See also* H.R. Rep. No. 94-1476, at 61 (1976) ("The references to 'copies' or 'phonorecords,' although in the plural, are intended here and throughout . . . to include the singular.").

[681] *Filmation*, 628 F. Supp. at 876. *See also* 17 U.S.C. § 101 (definition of "created": "where a work is prepared over a period of time, the portion of it that has been fixed at any particular time constitutes the work as of that time.").

[682] H.R. Rep. No. 94-1476, at 61 (1976).

use," in each case a *prima facie* violation of the reproduction right exists, so long as "any substantial part" of the original expression from the copyrighted work has been fixed in some tangible form.[683]

[b] Electronic Reproduction

As noted above,[684] computers generally make two types of electronic reproductions of copyrighted works. Electronic reproductions may be made in some permanent form, such as a hard disk or "flash" memory. These permanent reproductions are fixed "copies" that are subject to the reproduction right. In addition, digital information must be downloaded from permanent storage into the "random-access memory" (or "RAM") of the computer for processing. Unlike other electronic media, RAM requires electricity to function; if the power is turned off, any data remaining in RAM disappears. The issue is whether such "RAM" data is a fixed "copy" of the work that is subject to the reproduction right.

The House Report states that "the definition of 'fixation' would exclude from the concept purely evanescent or transient reproductions such as those . . . captured momentarily in the 'memory' of a computer."[685] Despite this language, several cases have held that data residing only in RAM is a fixed "copy" subject to the reproduction right. For example, in *MAI Systems Corp. v. Peak Computer, Inc.*,[686] the court held that a company that provided service for computer hardware systems infringed when it "booted up" computers running the plaintiff's copyrighted operating system software. The court approved the theory that in turning on the machine, the defendant had downloaded a "copy" of the program into RAM.[687] Although Congress later overturned the specific result of *MAI* by enacting a new exception,[688] in so doing it appeared to implicitly accept *MAI*'s rationale that incidental reproductions, however fleeting, are "copies" subject to the reproduction right.

Treating all technologically necessary temporary reproductions as "copies," however, leads to several undesirable results. For example, an e-mail message may pass through dozens of "servers" on its way from origin to destination. On each server, a relatively short-lived "copy" of the message is created — only to be deleted or overwritten when its role in facilitating the transmission is complete. Similarly, a user can read the contents of a website only because a digital version of the website resides temporarily in the user's RAM. Applying *MAI v. Peak* would render such a user liable for copyright infringement.[689] The use of automated programs to copy information from various websites, for purposes such as facilitating search

---

[683] H.R. Rep. No. 94-1476, at 61 (1976). As for whether a reproduction or other use is a "fair use," see § 4I[1].

[684] *See* § 4C[2][b][ii].

[685] H.R. Rep. No. 94-1476, at 53 (1976).

[686] 991 F.2d 511 (9th Cir. 1993).

[687] *Id.* at 518. *See also* Stenograph LLC v. Boussard Assocs., Inc., 144 F.3d 96, 101–02 (D.C. Cir. 1998).

[688] *See* 17 U.S.C. § 117(c), discussed in § 4G[1][c].

[689] *See* Intellectual Reserve, Inc. v. Utah Lighthouse Ministry, Inc., 75 F. Supp. 2d 1290, 1294 (D. Utah 1999) (holding that browsing of infringing websites is a violation of the reproduction right).

engines, could likewise violate the reproduction right. While some or all these activities might escape liability on other grounds, such as an implied license or "fair use,"[690] the scope of potential infringement (and potential litigation) would be staggering.

Accordingly, courts and legislators have used various techniques to limit the liability of defendants accused of making temporary but technologically necessary copies. In one influential case, *Religious Technology Center v. Netcom On-Line Communication Services, Inc.*, a district court held that an Internet service provider was not directly liable for copyright infringement for automatically transmitting documents posted by a user, stating that "[a]lthough copyright is a strict liability statute, there should still be some element of volition or causation which is lacking where a defendant's system is merely used to create a copy by a third party."[691] This enabled the court to decide the case instead on grounds of contributory infringement, which requires that the defendant have knowledge of the infringing activity to be held liable.[692]

Following *Netcom*, Congress enacted section 512, which limits the liability of Internet service providers for automated technical copying if they comply with a host of specific conditions. This section is considered in detail below.[693]

Courts have also looked to the definition of "fixation" to limit liability for making technologically necessary temporary copies. *Cartoon Network v. CSC Holdings, Inc.* involved a particular type of RAM known as a "buffer." A buffer is working memory that temporarily holds a stream of data while it is being processed; but the data in the buffer is automatically overwritten by new data entering the buffer in real time. Thus, although an entire data stream representing a copyrighted work passes through the buffer, only a small amount of the data (in this case, up to 1.2 seconds of the work) is contained in the buffer at any one time. The court held that the data stream was not a "copy" of the work, because it was not fixed in the buffer "for a period of more than transitory duration."[694] Similarly, in *CoStar Group, Inc. v. LoopNet, Inc.*, in which customers posted infringing photos on the defendant's website, the court held that "[w]hile temporary electronic copies may be made in this transmission process, they would appear not to be 'fixed' in the sense that they are 'of more than transitory duration.' "[695]

---

[690] *See, e.g.*, Field v. Google, Inc., 412 F. Supp. 2d 1106 (D. Nev. 2006) (plaintiff who posted works, knowing that Google would automatically copy and index them unless certain HTML codes were included, had granted an implied license to copy those works and was estopped from claiming infringement; or alternatively, Google's use was a fair use).

[691] 907 F. Supp. 1361, 1370 (N.D. Cal. 1995). *Accord*, Cartoon Network v. CSC Holdings, Inc., 536 F.3d 121, 130 (2d Cir. 2008); CoStar Group, Inc. v. LoopNet, Inc., 373 F.3d 544, 550 (4th Cir. 2004); *see also* Fox Broadcasting Co. v. DISH Network, LLC, 747 F.3d 1060, 1067–68 (9th Cir. 2013) (concluding the user of the DVR provided by the defendant makes the copies, without quoting the "volition or causation" language).

[692] *See* § 4J.

[693] *See* § 4J.

[694] 536 F.3d 121, 127 (2d Cir. 2008).

[695] 373 F.3d 544, 551 (4th Cir. 2004).

[c] Exceptions and Limitations

In addition to "fair use," the reproduction and distribution rights are subject to a number of exceptions and limitations, including temporary "ephemeral" reproductions of a work made to facilitate licensed broadcasts,[696] and certain reproductions in specialized formats, such as Braille, for use by the blind or other disabled people,[697] and the following:

Section 108 permits libraries and archives to make and distribute single copies of a work at the request of a user or for interlibrary loan,[698] or to make up to three copies of a work for purposes of preservation and security, or replacement of a copy that is damaged, deteriorating, lost, stolen, or stored in an obsolete format,[699] under specified limited conditions.[700]

Section 113 concerns reproductions of pictorial, graphic, and sculptural works in useful articles. It leaves intact pre-1978 case law holding that copyright in a work depicting a useful article does not include the right to prevent others from making the useful article itself.[701] It also provides that if a work is lawfully reproduced in a useful article, others may make, distribute, or display pictures or photographs of the article in connection with advertising, commentaries, or news reports.[702]

Section 114 severely limits the exclusive rights in a sound recording: the reproduction right extends only to the duplication of the actual sounds fixed in the recording, and the right to prepare derivative works extends only to the rearranging, remixing or other alteration of those actual sounds.[703] As a result, a sound recording copyright includes no rights against others who independently fix sounds that imitate or simulate those in the copyrighted work.[704] Section 114 also contains a complicated compulsory licensing scheme for sound recordings that further limits the digital audio transmission right.[705]

Section 115 creates a compulsory license for the reproduction and distribution of musical works. Once authorized phonorecords of a nondramatic musical work have been distributed to the public in the United States, any other person who follows the statutory procedures and pays the required royalty can obtain a compulsory license to make and distribute new phonorecords of the musical work, without the

---

[696] 17 U.S.C. § 112.

[697] 17 U.S.C. § 121.

[698] 17 U.S.C. § 108(d), (e).

[699] 17 U.S.C. § 108(b), (c).

[700] Section 108 was initially enacted largely as a response to Williams & Wilkins Co. v. United States, 487 F.2d 1345 (Ct. Cl. 1973), aff'd by an equally divided Court, 420 U.S. 376 (1975), in which a divided Court of Claims held that photocopying of journal articles by the National Library of Medicine and the National Institutes of Health at the request of users was a fair use.

[701] 17 U.S.C. § 113(b). See, e.g., Niemi v. American Axle Mfg. & Holding, Inc., 2006 U.S. Dist. LEXIS 50153 (E.D. Mich. July 24, 2006).

[702] 17 U.S.C. § 113(c). Section 113(d) limits the "moral rights" of an author. See § 4G[7].

[703] 17 U.S.C. § 114(b).

[704] Id.

[705] See 17 U.S.C. § 114(d)–(j). For more details on the digital audio transmission right, see § 4G[6].

permission of the copyright owner, so long as the new version does not "change the basic melody or fundamental character of the work."[706] The compulsory license for musical works also applies to distribution by means of "digital phonorecord delivery," *i.e.*, iTunes and similar authorized download services.[707] In practice, the compulsory license is usually replaced by a form license, at the same royalty rate, issued by a private organization, the Harry Fox Agency.[708]

Section 117 permits the "owner" of a copy of a computer program to make or authorize the making of another copy or adaptation of that program, but only if, "such a new copy or adaptation is created as an essential step in the utilization of the computer program,"[709] or for archival purposes.[710] Because many software providers purport only to "license" their software to users, rather than "selling" it, the requirement that one be an "owner" of a copy of the program has limited the usefulness of section 117.[711]

Section 120 provides that the copyright owner in an architectural work cannot prevent others from making, distributing, or displaying pictures, paintings, or photographs of a building located in or ordinarily visible from a public place.[712]

[2] Preparation of Derivative Works

[a] In General

Early case law indicated that translations and dramatizations were not "copies" of a work.[713] In 1870, Congress conferred on authors the exclusive rights "to dramatize or translate their own works."[714] The 1909 Act expanded the list of

---

[706] 17 U.S.C. § 115(a)(1), (a)(2).

[707] 17 U.S.C. § 115(c)(3)(A), § 115(d).

[708] *See* www.harryfox.com. *See, e.g.*, EMI Entertainment World, Inc. v. Karen Records, Inc., 603 F. Supp. 2d 759 (S.D.N.Y. 2009) (defendant properly acquired mechanical licenses by faxing forms with non-material errors to the Harry Fox Agency).

[709] 17 U.S.C. § 117(a)(1). *See* Vault Corp. v. Quaid Software Ltd., 847 F.2d 255, 261 (5th Cir. 1988) ("Congress recognized that a computer program cannot be used unless it is first copied into a computer's memory, and thus provided the § 117[(a)](1) exception to permit copying for this essential purpose.").

[710] 17 U.S.C. § 117(a)(2). While some courts have construed this section narrowly to permit archival copies only "to guard against destruction or damage by mechanical or electrical failure," *see, e.g.*, Atari, Inc. v. JS & A Group, Inc., 597 F. Supp. 5, 9 (N.D. Ill. 1983), other courts have rejected such a limitation. *See, e.g.*, Vault Corp. v. Quaid Software Ltd., 847 F.2d 255, 266–67 (5th Cir. 1988).

[711] *See, e.g.*, WallData, Inc. v. Los Angeles County Sheriff's Dept., 447 F.3d 769, 784–86 (9th Cir. 2006) (Department was not an "owner" of software subject to click-through licenses, and copies of software were not "essential" but were made for convenience). *But see* Krause v. Titleserv, Inc., 402 F.3d 119, 124 (2d Cir. 2005) ("absence of formal title may be outweighed by evidence that the possessor of the copy enjoys sufficiently broad rights over it to be sensibly considered its owner").

[712] 17 U.S.C. § 120(a). *See* Leicester v. Warner Bros., 232 F.3d 1212 (9th Cir. 2000) (holding that "streetwall" portion of outdoor sculpture adjoining building was part of the building itself and was therefore subject to § 120(a)).

[713] *See, e.g.*, Stowe v. Thomas, 23 F. Cas. 201 (E.D. Pa. 1893) (unauthorized publication of a German translation of Stowe's "Uncle Tom's Cabin" was not a "printing" of "such book" within the meaning of the 1831 Copyright Act).

[714] 1870 Act, § 86, 16 Stat. 212.

derivative uses reserved to the author, and it granted the author the right "to make any other version" of a literary work.[715]

The 1976 Act grants the author the exclusive right "to prepare derivative works based on the copyrighted work."[716] A derivative work is "a work based upon one or more preexisting works," and it includes "any other form in which a work may be recast, transformed, or adapted."[717] Examples include "a translation, musical arrangement, dramatization, fictionalization, motion picture version, sound recording, art reproduction, abridgement, [or] condensation."[718] The statute also specifies that "[a] work consisting of editorial revisions, annotations, elaborations, or other modifications which, as a whole, represent an original work of authorship, is a 'derivative work.' "[719]

As the statutory examples indicate, infringing derivative works may be prepared in media different from the original work. For example, a three-dimensional work may be infringed by a two-dimensional photograph,[720] and a two-dimensional photograph may be infringed by a three-dimensional sculpture.[721] In an extreme example, one court held that a choreographic work could be infringed by a book of photographs if the photos captured the movement and flow of some of the steps, even though the entire ballet could not be re-created from the photos.[722]

The question of how similar a second work must be to a first work to be a derivative work is a difficult one, because the derivative work right, if carried too far, would give the copyright owner control over all uses of a work's ideas, contrary to fundamental copyright law policy.[723] "To narrow the statute to a manageable level, [courts] have developed certain criteria a work must satisfy in order to qualify as a derivative work."[724]

First, as with the reproduction right, to constitute a derivative work, the allegedly infringing work must have been copied from ("based upon") the original work, *and* it must be "substantially similar" to protected expression in the original work.[725] This requirement is discussed in detail in the next section.[726]

---

[715] 1909 Act, § 1(b), 35 Stat. 1075.

[716] 17 U.S.C. § 106(2).

[717] 17 U.S.C. § 101.

[718] *Id.*

[719] *Id.*

[720] *See* Ty, Inc. v. Publications Int'l, Ltd., 292 F.3d 512, 519 (7th Cir. 2002) (photographs of Beanie Babies stuffed animals are derivative works).

[721] *See* Rogers v. Koons, 960 F.2d 301 (2d Cir. 1992) (photograph of a couple on a bench holding eight puppies was infringed by a sculptural re-creation of the photo).

[722] *See* Horgan v. Macmillan, Inc., 789 F.2d 157 (2d Cir. 1986).

[723] *See* Micro Star, Inc. v. Formgen, Inc., 154 F.3d 1107, 1110 (9th Cir. 1998) ("The statutory language is hopelessly overbroad, however, for '[e]very book in literature, science and art, borrows and must necessarily borrow, and use much which was well known and use before.' "), *quoting* Emerson v. Davies, 8 F. Cas. 615, 619 (D. Mass. 1845).

[724] *Micro Star*, 154 F.3d at 1110.

[725] *See* Litchfield v. Spielberg, 736 F.2d 1352, 1357 (9th Cir. 1984) ("The little available authority suggests that a work is not derivative unless it has been substantially copied from the prior work. . . .

Second, the House Report states that "to constitute a violation . . . , the infringing work must incorporate a portion of the copyrighted work in some form."[727] Thus, for example, "a detailed commentary on a work or a programmatic musical composition inspired by a novel would not normally constitute infringements" of the derivative work right.[728] In many cases, this requirement is easily satisfied.[729] On the other hand, some courts have found infringement of the derivative work right where the underlying work did not appear at all in the derivative work.[730]

Another consideration is the role of "fixation." Unlike the reproduction right, the derivative work right does not refer to "copies" or "phonorecords" or any other term that requires fixation; and the House Report states that "the preparation of a derivative work . . . may be an infringement even though nothing is ever fixed in tangible form."[731] In *Lewis Galoob Toys, Inc. v. Nintendo of America, Inc.*, the court agreed, stating that "a derivative work must be fixed to be protected under the Act, but not to infringe."[732] In a seemingly contradictory statement, however, *Galoob* also held that "a derivative work must incorporate a protected work in some *concrete or permanent* form."[733] The requirement of some "concrete or permanent" form is simply "fixation" by another name.[734] Thus, in *Galoob*, the court held that the Game Genie, a plug-in device designed to work with the Nintendo Entertainment System, did not create "derivative works" of Nintendo videogames, because it only temporarily altered the play of the games and did not create any permanent copies of the altered versions.[735] Similarly, "pop-up" advertisements do not permanently alter, and therefore do not infringe, the websites that they obscure.[736] By contrast, in *Micro Star, Inc. v. Formgen, Inc.*, the court held that a company that reproduced and sold a CD containing 300 new "levels" for a copyrighted videogame infringed that game, because "the audiovisual displays assume a concrete or

---

To prove infringement, one must show substantial similarity.").

[726] *See* § 4H.

[727] H.R. Rep. No. 94-1476, at 62 (1976).

[728] *Id. See, e.g.*, Ty, Inc. v. Publications Int'l, Ltd., 292 F.3d 512, 520–21 (7th Cir. 2002) (a collectors' guide to plaintiff's line of Beanie Babies stuffed animals was not a derivative work, because "guides don't recast, transform, or adapt the things to which they are guides.").

[729] *See, e.g.*, Grove Press, Inc. v. Greenleaf Publishing Co., 247 F. Supp. 518 (E.D.N.Y. 1965) (translation of a novel); Metro-Goldwyn-Mayer, Inc. v. Showcase Atlanta Cooperative Productions, Inc., 479 F. Supp. 351 (N.D. Ga. 1979) (musical stage production based on *Gone With the Wind*).

[730] *See, e.g.*, Addison-Wesley Publishing Co. v. Brown, 223 F. Supp. 219 (E.D.N.Y. 1963) (physics textbook was infringed by a manual providing the answers to questions posed in the textbook).

[731] H.R. Rep. No. 94-1476, at 62 (1976).

[732] 964 F.2d 965, 968 (9th Cir. 1992).

[733] *Id.* at 967 (emphasis added).

[734] *See* 17 U.S.C. § 101 (2000) ("A work is 'fixed' in a tangible medium of expression when its embodiment in a copy or phonorecord . . . is sufficiently *permanent* or stable . . . .") (emphasis added).

[735] 964 F.2d at 968.

[736] *See* 1-800 Contacts, Inc. v. WhenU.com, Inc., 309 F. Supp. 2d 467 (S.D.N.Y. 2003), *rev'd on other grounds*, 414 F.3d 400 (2d Cir. 2005); Wells Fargo & Co. v. WhenU.com, Inc., 293 F. Supp. 2d 734 (E.D. Mich. 2003); U-Haul Int'l, Inc. v. WhenU.com, Inc., 279 F. Supp. 2d 723 (E.D. Va. 2003).

permanent form in the MAP files" that described the levels.[737]

While it is clear that a "concrete or permanent form" (or fixation) is required in some cases, it is also clear that it is not required in others. The House Report gives three examples of unfixed derivative works: "a ballet, pantomime, or improvised performance."[738] It is reasonable to assume that all three examples involve public performances; there is nothing to suggest that Congress intended to prohibit the *private* performance of a derivative work. The best way to reconcile the statutory language and the case law is to hold that a derivative work must *either* be fixed, violating the reproduction right and creating a "copy" which can be publicly distributed or displayed, *or* it must be publicly performed. Purely private performances of modified works, such as those involved in *Galoob*, do not infringe the derivative work right.[739]

Another controversy concerns the interaction of the derivative work right with the first-sale doctrine. In *Mirage Editions, Inc. v. Albuquerque A.R.T. Co.*, the Ninth Circuit held that the derivative work right was infringed when the defendant bought lawful copies of an artist's work, mounted the prints on ceramic tiles, and resold them.[740] In *Lee v. A.R.T. Co.*, the Seventh Circuit held that the same practice did not infringe the derivative work right, because the copyrighted pictorial work was not "recast, transformed, or adapted": "The art . . . was not changed in the process; it still depicts exactly what it depicted when it left Lee's studio."[741] The court reasoned that mounting art on a ceramic tile was "no different in form or function from displaying a painting in a frame or placing a medallion in a velvet case."[742] The court rejected the argument that "a change in a work's appearance may infringe the [derivative work] right . . . even if the alteration is too trivial to support an independent copyright," because it would not accept "a definition of derivative work that makes criminals out of art collectors and tourists."[743]

[b]   Exceptions and Limitations

In addition to "fair use," the derivative work right is specifically subject to the following exceptions and limitations:

Section 110(11) exempts software that makes "limited portions of [the] audio or video content of a motion picture . . . imperceptible" at the direction of a home viewer, "if no fixed copy of the altered version of the motion picture is created."[744]

---

[737] 154 F.3d 1107, 1112 (9th Cir. 1998).

[738] H.R. Rep. No. 94-1476, at 62 (1976). For an extensive analysis, see Tyler T. Ochoa, *Copyright, Derivative Works and Fixation: Is* Galoob *a* Mirage, *or Does the* Form(Gen) *of the Alleged Derivative Work Matter?*, 20 Santa Clara Computer & High Tech. L.J. 991 (2004).

[739] Alternatively, one could conclude that purely private performances do infringe, and rely on *Galoob*'s alternative holding that the use of the Game Genie to alter game play was a fair use.

[740] 856 F.2d 1341 (9th Cir. 1988); *see also* Munoz v. Albuquerque A.R.T. Co., 829 F. Supp. 309 (D. Alaska 1993), *aff'd mem.*, 38 F.3d 1218 (9th Cir. 1994).

[741] 125 F.3d 580, 582 (7th Cir. 1997).

[742] *Id.* at 581.

[743] *Id.* at 582.

[744] 17 U.S.C. § 110(11).

This exemption was enacted while litigation was pending concerning such software, rendering the case moot.[745]

Although most copyrighted works can be infringed by imitation or simulation, section 114 provides that a sound recording is infringed only by use of the actual fixed sounds.[746] In particular, the derivative work right in a sound recording "is limited to the right to prepare a derivative work in which the actual sounds fixed in the sound recording are rearranged, remixed, or otherwise altered in sequence or quality."[747] This section is implicated by digital sampling, a frequently used technique in which a recording artist copies or "samples" a short segment of an existing sound recording, electronically manipulates the sample, and incorporates it into a new sound recording.[748] In *Bridgeport Music, Inc. v. Dimension Films*, the Sixth Circuit held that *any* sampling of an existing sound recording is an infringement of copyright *per se*, without regard to whether the amount sampled was *de minimis* or whether the allegedly infringing work was "substantially similar" to the original.[749]

Section 117 permits the "owner" of a copy of a computer program to make or authorize the making of another copy or adaptation of that program if, but only if, "such a new copy or adaptation is created as an essential step in the utilization of the computer program."[750] In *Krause v. Titleserv, Inc.*, the court rejected the narrow view that "essential" meant only those steps without which the program would not function, and instead took the broader, more practical view that "essential" included "the addition of features so that a program better serves the needs of the customer for which it was created."[751]

Because a two-dimensional photograph of a three-dimensional work is a derivative work, the exemption in section 120(a) that permits making, distributing and displaying pictorial representations of an architectural work embodied in a building that is visible from a public place is implicitly a limitation on the right to prepare derivative works.[752] Section 120(b) also contains an express limitation on the derivative work right, permitting the owners of a building to modify the building without the consent of the architectural work copyright owner.[753]

---

[745] *See* Huntsman v. Soderbergh, No. 02-M-1662 (D. Colo. 2005). The case also involved retailers who were renting fixed copies of movies that had been edited. The district court ruled that preparing and renting edited versions was not a fair use. Clean Flicks of Colorado, LLC v. Soderbergh, 433 F. Supp. 2d 1236 (D. Colo. 2006).

[746] *See* § 4G[1][c].

[747] 17 U.S.C. § 114(b).

[748] *See, e.g.*, Grand Upright Music Ltd. v. Warner Bros. Records, Inc. 780 F. Supp. 182 (S.D.N.Y. 1991); Jarvis v. A&M Records, 827 F. Supp. 282 (D.N.J. 1993).

[749] 410 F.3d 792, 800–02 (6th Cir. 2005). *But cf.* Newton v. Diamond, 349 F.3d 591 (9th Cir. 2003) (use of three-note "sample" from a musical work was *de minimis* as a matter of law, in part because defendant had licensed the use of the sound recording).

[750] 17 U.S.C. § 117(a)(1).

[751] 402 F.3d 119, 128 (2d Cir. 2005). *See also* Vault Corp. v. Quaid Software Ltd., 847 F.2d 255, 261 (5th Cir. 1988).

[752] *See* 17 U.S.C. § 120(a), discussed in § 4C[4][a][viii](b).

[753] 17 U.S.C. § 120(b).

[3]   Public Distribution

[a]   In General

The third right is the exclusive right "to distribute copies or phonorecords of the copyrighted work to the public by sale or other transfer of ownership, or by rental, lease, or lending."[754] The same language is used in the statute to define the term "publication."[755] Thus, a few courts have held that Congress intended the terms "distribution" and "publication" to be synonymous,[756] and have concluded that merely making an unauthorized copy available to others, i.e., offering to distribute a copy or phonorecord, is a "distribution."[757] A majority of courts, however, have pointed to the second sentence of the definition of "publication," which includes certain offers to distribute,[758] and have concluded that the term "publication" is broader than "distribution," and that the public distribution right is limited to actual distribution.[759] The dispute has arisen primarily in cases involving peer-to-peer file sharing, in which the technology makes it relatively easy to prove that an electronic file was "made available" to the public, but more difficult to prove that an electronic file was actually "downloaded" by an unauthorized recipient.[760]

Courts also disagree how to define "to the public." One might borrow the similar term "publicly," which expressly applies to the public performance and public display rights, and conclude that unauthorized copies must be offered to "a

---

[754] 17 U.S.C. § 106(3).

[755] 17 U.S.C. § 101 (" 'Publication' is the distribution of copies or phonorecords of a work to the public by sale or other transfer of ownership, or by rental, lease, or lending.").

[756] *See, e.g.,* Elektra Entertainment Group, Inc. v. Barker, 551 F. Supp. 2d 234, 241–42 (S.D.N.Y. 2008). *See also* H.R. Rep. No. 94-1476, at 62 (1976) ("Clause (3) of section 106 establishes the exclusive right of publication: the right to 'distribute copies or phonorecords of the copyrighted work to the public . . .' ").

[757] *See* Hotaling v. Church of Jesus Christ of Latter-Day Saints, 118 F.3d 199, 203 (4th Cir. 1997) ("When a public library adds a work to its collections, lists the work in its index or catalog system, and makes the work available to the borrowing or browsing public, it has completed all the steps necessary for distribution to the public."); Arista Records LLC v. Greubel, 453 F. Supp. 2d 961, 969–70 (N.D. Tex. 2006).

[758] 17 U.S.C. § 101 ("The offering to distribute copies or phonorecords to a group of persons for purposes of further distribution, public performance, or public display, constitutes publication.").

[759] *See, e.g.,* National Car Rental Systems, Inc. v. Computer Assocs. Int'l, Inc., 991 F.2d 426, 434 (8th Cir. 1993) (section 106(3) "requires an actual distribution of either copies or phonorecords"); Capitol Records, Inc. v. Thomas, 579 F. Supp. 2d 1210, 1223 (D. Minn. 2008); Atlantic Recording Corp. v. Howell, 554 F. Supp. 2d 976, 981 (D. Ariz. 2008); London-Sire Records, Inc. v. Doe 1, 542 F. Supp. 2d 153, 166–69 (D. Mass. 2008). *See also In re* Napster, Inc. Copyright Litigation, 377 F. Supp. 2d 796, 802–05 (N.D. Cal. 2005) (criticizing *Hotaling*).

[760] Some courts have concluded that the copy or phonorecord downloaded by an investigator is direct evidence of "actual distribution." *See, e.g., Thomas,* 579 F. Supp. 2d at 1215–16; *Howell,* 554 F. Supp. 2d at 985. *See also* Olan Mills, Inc. v. Linn Photo Co., 23 F.3d 1345, 1348 (8th Cir. 1994) (involving distribution of unauthorized copies of studio photographs). Other courts have expressed doubt about this theory, pointing out that the investigator was "acting as an agent of the copyright holder, and copyright holders cannot infringe their own rights." *London-Sire Records,* 542 F. Supp. 2d at 166. Alternatively, courts have suggested that circumstantial evidence will suffice, and that a jury could infer that an "actual distribution" took place from the fact that a copy or phonorecord was "made available" to the public. *London-Sire Records,* 542 F. Supp. 2d at 169; *Thomas,* 579 F. Supp. 2d at 1225.

substantial number of persons outside of a normal circle of a family and its social acquaintances."[761] Alternatively, one might borrow the meaning given to the term "publication" at common law, meaning that a distribution "to the public" could be accomplished through distribution to "only one member of the public."[762]

[b]   Electronic Distribution

The public distribution right contemplates a "book model" of distribution, in which a work is first fixed in tangible "copies" or "phonorecords" (defined as "material objects" in which a work is fixed), and those copies or phonorecords are then distributed to the public. On the Internet, however, distribution occurs in the opposite order: a work is first transmitted to the public in the form of intangible digital information, and it is then fixed (if at all) on the receiving end. The "material object" in such a case is "the appropriate segment of the hard disk" or other electronic medium on which the digital data is fixed;[763] but no material object has changed hands. In other words, read literally, an electronic transfer may be a distribution of the "work" (an intangible), but it is not a distribution of a "copy" or "phonorecord" (a "material object") of the work. Instead, the transaction may be more properly characterized as a "reproduction" (by the downloader) instead of a "distribution" (by the uploader), although the uploader might be liable for contributory infringement if he or she intended to encourage unlawful downloading.

It is entirely possible that, in 1976, Congress intended such a result. At the time, people commonly used "material objects" such as tapes or removable "floppy" disks to transfer information from one computer to another. However, Congress later amended the section 115 compulsory license to include the right "to distribute . . . a phonorecord of a nondramatic musical work by means of a digital transmission which constitutes a digital phonorecord delivery." Moreover, the economic effect of electronic delivery is the same as a traditional distribution, *i.e.*, copies or phonorecords of the work end up in the hands of the public. Accordingly, most courts have glossed over the semantic difficulties and have concluded that an electronic transfer of a copyrighted work is a "distribution" within the meaning of the statute.[764]

---

[761] 17 U.S.C. § 101(1) (definition of 'publicly'). The 1995 "White Paper" states that "transmission of a copyrighted work from one person to another in a private e-mail message would not constitute a distribution to the public." Final Report, INTELLECTUAL PROPERTY AND THE NATIONAL INFORMATION INFRASTRUCTURE 215 (1995).

[762] *See* Ford Motor Co. v. Summit Motor Prods, Inc., 930 F.2d 277, 299–300 (3d Cir. 1991). Courts and commentators have criticized *Ford* on this point. *See, e.g.*, Cartoon Network L.P. v. CSC Holdings, Inc., 536 F.3d 121, 139 (2d Cir. 2008), citing 2 NIMMER ON COPYRIGHT § 8.11[A] (2008).

[763] London-Sire Records, Inc. v. Doe 1, 542 F. Supp. 2d 153, 171 (D. Mass. 2008).

[764] *See, e.g.*, New York Times Co. v. Tasini, 533 U.S. 483, 498 (2001) (stating without analysis that "LEXIS/NEXIS, by selling copies of the Articles through the NEXIS database, 'distribute[s] copies' of the Articles 'to the public by sale.' "); London-Sire Records, 542 F. Supp. 2d at 173 ("there is no reason to limit 'distribution' to processes in which a material object exists throughout the entire transaction — as opposed to a transaction in which a material object is created elsewhere at its finish."), *id.* at 174 ("the court concludes that an electronic file transfer can constitute a 'transfer of ownership' as that term is used in § 106(3).").

[c]   First-Sale Doctrine

Copyright law, like patent law[765] and trademark law,[766] has a first-sale doctrine, the theory of which is that a copyright owner's authorized sale of an item "exhausts" the exclusive public distribution right with respect to that item. The purchaser may use or resell the item free of any charge of infringement.

Early copyright acts contained no express first-sale provision. In *Bobbs Merrill Co. v. Straus,*[767] a publisher sold a book to wholesalers with the following notice printed on each copy: "The price of this book at retail is $1 net. No dealer is licensed to sell it at a less price, and a sale at a less price will be treated as an infringement of the copyright." Defendants bought copies from wholesalers and resold them for less than $1. The publisher sued for copyright infringement, relying solely on copyright and asserting no contract claim. The Supreme Court held that there was no violation of the copyright owner's exclusive right to vend copies of the work.[768]

The 1909 Act codified the first-sale doctrine,[769] as does the 1976 Act, which states: "the owner of a particular copy or phonorecord, lawfully made under this title, . . . is entitled, without the authority of the copyright owner, to sell or otherwise dispose of the possession of that copy or phonorecord."[770] The House Report explains: "This does not mean that conditions on future disposition of copies or phonorecords, imposed by a contract between their buyer and seller, would be unenforceable between the parties as a breach of contract, but it does mean that they could not be enforced by an action for infringement of copyright."[771]

The copyright owner can avoid application of the first-sale doctrine by retaining *title* to the copy or phonorecord, even if possession is transferred by rental, lease or loan. By contrast, any transfer of ownership, even a gratuitous transfer, brings the doctrine into play.[772] Even involuntary transfers, such as a judicial sale for the benefit of creditors, may qualify.[773] Courts have reached different conclusions on whether the permanent transfer of a copy of a computer program for a fixed price

---

[765] *See* § 2[E][3].

[766] *See* § 5[J][2].

[767] 210 U.S. 339 (1908).

[768] *Id.* at 350–51.

[769] 1909 Act, § 41, 35 Stat. 1084 (codified in 1947 at 17 U.S.C. § 27, repealed in 1978) ("nothing in this Act shall be deemed to forbid, prevent, or restrict the transfer of any copy of a copyrighted work the possession of which has been lawfully obtained.").

[770] 17 U.S.C. § 109(a).

[771] H.R. Rep. No. 94-1476, at 79 (1976).

[772] *See* UMG Recordings, Inc. v. Augusto, 628 F.3d 1175 (9th Cir. 2011) (resale of free promotional CDs on eBay was permitted under first-sale doctrine; label on CDs with alleged resale restriction did not create a license).

[773] *See* Platt & Munk Co. v. Republic Graphics, Inc., 315 F.2d 847, 854 (2d Cir. 1963); Bryant v. Gordon, 483 F. Supp. 2d 605 (N.D. Ill. 2007) (first-sale doctrine applies to copies sold in bankruptcy, where copyright owner had notice and did not object). *But see* Denbicare U.S.A., Inc. v. Toys R Us, Inc., 84 F.3d 1143, 1150 (9th Cir. 1996) (stating in dicta that a bankruptcy trustee's sale of copies without authorization of the copyright owner would be an infringement).

is a "sale" or a "license" under the statute.[774]

The first-sale doctrine is a limitation only on the copyright owner's public distribution and public display rights.[775] The first-sale doctrine does not limit the distinct exclusive rights of reproduction and public performance. For example, an electronic copy or phonorecord cannot be transferred to another without transferring the entire device on which it is fixed, because under current technology, an electronic transfer can occur only by first making a reproduction of the work and then deleting the original copy.[776] Similarly, if a person buys a lawful copy of a DVD or a song, he or she does not acquire the right to publicly perform the DVD or the song; a separate performance license from the copyright owner is necessary.[777] The first-sale doctrine also does not expressly apply to the derivative work right; however, courts have reached differing conclusions on whether a derivative work is created when an authorized copy of the work is altered.[778]

Congress has enacted two exceptions to the first-sale doctrine. In the Record Rental Amendment Act of 1984, Congress provided an exception to the first-sale doctrine for rental of phonorecords.[779] In the Computer Software Rental Amendments Act of 1990, Congress extended the record-rental exception to prohibit the rental of computer software for direct or indirect commercial advantage.[780] This exception does not apply to software embedded in products, such as "[a]utomobiles, calculators, and other electronic consumer products [that] contain computer programs,"[781] so long as the program "cannot be copied during the ordinary operation or use of the machine or product."[782]

European countries recognize a "*droit de suite*," or resale royalty right, as an exception to the first-sale doctrine.[783] Under the *droit de suite*, the author of a work of fine art is entitled to receive a royalty when the original of that work is re-sold at a profit. One state, California, has enacted a statute that likewise requires

---

[774] *Compare* Vernor v. Autodesk, Inc., 621 F.3d 1102 (9th Cir. 2010) (license); Adobe Systems, Inc. v. Stargate Software, Inc., 216 F. Supp. 2d 1051 (N.D. Cal. 2002) (same); Adobe Systems, Inc. v. One Stop Micro, Inc., 84 F. Supp. 2d 1086 (N.D. Cal 2000) (same) *with* Softman Products Co., LLC v. Adobe Systems, Inc., 171 F. Supp. 2d 1075 (C.D. Cal 2001) (sale). *Cf.* Krause v. Titleserv, Inc., 402 F.3d 119, 124 (2d Cir. 2005) ("absence of formal title may be outweighed by evidence that the possessor of the copy enjoys sufficiently broad rights over it to be sensibly considered its owner.").

[775] 17 U.S.C. § 109(a) (public distribution), 17 U.S.C. § 109(c) (public display).

[776] Capitol Records, LLC v. ReDigi, Inc., 934 F. Supp. 2d 640, 655–56 (S.D.N.Y. 2013).

[777] *See, e.g.*, Columbia Pictures Industries, Inc. v. Aveco, Inc., 800 F.2d 59, 63–64 (3d Cir. 1986) (lawful possession of video cassettes does not confer a right to use the cassettes for unauthorized public performances).

[778] *See* § 4G[2].

[779] 17 U.S.C. § 109(b)(1)(A) ("the owner of a particular phonorecord" may not, "for purposes of direct or indirect commercial advantage, dispose of, or authorize the disposal of, the possession of that phonorecord . . . by rental, lease, or lending"). The exception applies only to sound recordings of musical works, and not to sound recordings of literary works, see Brilliance Audio, Inc. v. Haights Cross Communications, Inc., 474 F.3d 365 (6th Cir. 2007), nor to motion pictures or other audiovisual works.

[780] 17 U.S.C. § 109(b)(1)(A). *See* Action Tapes, Inc. v. Mattson, 462 F.3d 1010 (8th Cir. 2006).

[781] H.R. Rep. No. 101-735, at 8 (1990).

[782] 17 U.S.C. § 101(b)(1)(B)(i).

[783] *See* Directive 2001/84/EC of the European Parliament and of the Council of 27 September 2001.

payment to the artist upon resale of "a work of fine art," defined as "an original painting, sculpture, or drawing or an original work of art in glass." Either the seller must be a resident of California at the time of resale, or the resale must take place in California.[784] One court has held that the California statute is unconstitutional under the Commerce Clause, because it attempts to regulate transactions occurring wholly outside California.[785]

[d]   Import and Export Rights

Subject to three exceptions,[786] section 602 provides that that unauthorized "[i]mportation into the United States . . . of copies or phonorecords of the work that have been acquired outside the United States is an infringement of the exclusive right to distribute copies or phonorecords under section 106."[787] If the copies would have been infringing "if this title had been applicable," their importation is prohibited; and if the copies were unlawfully made, they can be seized at the border by U.S. Customs.[788] Where the copies or phonorecords were lawfully made, however, the Customs Service is not authorized to seize the goods.[789]

In 2008, section 602(a)(2) was added, providing that unauthorized "[i]mportation into the United States *or exportation from* the United States . . . of copies or phonorecords, the making of which either constituted an infringement of copyright, or which would have constituted an infringement of copyright if this title had been applicable, is an infringement of the exclusive right to distribute copies or phonorecords under section 106."[790] The provisions on importation in section 602(a)(2) are redundant, because former section 602(a) (now section 602(a)(1)) already makes importation an infringement. What was new is infringement by exportation, and an express reference to criminal penalties for unauthorized importation and exportation.

The statutory language left it unclear whether section 602 rendered unlawful importation of copies that were made or sold abroad by the copyright owner or his licensee.[791] Section 501(a) provides that "Anyone who violates any of the exclusive rights of the copyright owner as provided by sections 106 through 122 . . . , or who imports copies or phonorecords into the United States in violation of section 602, is

---

[784] *See* California Resale Royalties Act, Cal. Civ. Code § 986.

[785] *See* Estate of Graham v. Sotheby's, Inc., 860 F. Supp. 2d 1117 (C.D. Cal. 2013), *reh'g en banc ordered sub nom.* Sam Francis Foundation v. Christie's, Inc., 769 F.3d 1195 (9th Cir. 2014). *But cf.* Morseburg v. Balyon, 621 F.2d 972 (9th Cir. 1980) (holding California statute was not preempted by the 1909 Copyright Act).

[786] 17 U.S.C. § 602(a)(3).

[787] 17 U.S.C. § 602(a)(1).

[788] 17 U.S.C. § 602(b).

[789] *Id.*

[790] 17 U.S.C. § 602(a)(2) (emphasis added).

[791] The House Report indicates a Congressional intent to bar importation of copies lawfully made abroad by licensees but imported into the United States in violation of license restrictions. H.R. Rep. No. 94-1476, at 169 (1976) ("Section 602 . . . deals with two separate situations: importation of 'piratical' articles (that is, copies or phonorecords made without any authorization of the copyright owner), and unauthorized importation of copies or phonorecords that were lawfully made.").

an infringer of the copyright."[792] This suggests that the importation right is independent of the exceptions and limitations to the public distribution right, including the first-sale doctrine. However, section 602 itself states that violation of the importation right "is an infringement of the exclusive right to distribute copies or phonorecords under section 106,"[793] and section 106, in turn, is limited by sections 107 through 122,[794] including section 109(a), the first-sale doctrine.[795]

In *Quality King Distributors, Inc. v. L'Anza Research Int'l, Inc.*,[796] the Supreme Court held that the importation right was subject to the first-sale doctrine. Plaintiff L'Anza manufactured hair care products (with copyrighted labels) in the United States. L'Anza's distributor in the United Kingdom sold the products to a distributor in Malta. Some of those products were "acquired outside the United States" by Quality King and were resold to domestic retailers at a discount, without L'Anza's permission. L'Anza sued Quality King for copyright infringement, asserting that the importation and resale of its products infringed its exclusive rights to import and distribute its copyrighted labels.

The Supreme Court held that the importation right was subject to all of the exceptions and limitations in sections 107 through 122, including the first-sale doctrine.[797] In response to the argument that this interpretation would render the importation right a nullity, the Court noted that section 109(a) is limited to copies and phonorecords "lawfully made under this title." "This title" refers to Title 17 of the United States Code; and because the Copyright Act generally does not apply extraterritorially, the phrase "lawfully made under this title" must mean copies lawfully manufactured in the United States (like the labels in *Quality King*).[798]

In *Kirtsaeng v. John Wiley & Sons, Inc.*, however, a majority of the Supreme Court rejected this passage from *Quality King* as *dictum*,[799] holding instead that the phrase "lawfully made under this title" means copies that are lawfully made under the legal standards of Title 17, regardless of where in the world they were manufactured. Accordingly, the first-sale doctrine allows anyone who has bought an authorized copy of a work overseas to import and resell that copy domestically without the authorization of the copyright owner, even if those copies were made in another country.[800] Thus, section 602 only prohibits importation of pirated copies

---

[792] 17 U.S.C. § 501(a).

[793] 17 U.S.C. § 602(a)(1).

[794] 17 U.S.C. § 106 ("Subject to sections 107 through 122, the owner of copyright under this title has the exclusive right to do and to authorize any of the following").

[795] *See* § 4G[3][c].

[796] 523 U.S. 135 (1998).

[797] *Id.* at 150.

[798] 523 U.S. at 146–47, 148–49; *see also id.* at 154 (Ginsburg, J., concurring) ("This case involves a 'round trip' journey, travel of the copies in question from the United States to places abroad, then back again. I join the Court's opinion recognizing that we do not today resolve cases in which the allegedly infringing imports were manufactured abroad.").

[799] 133 S. Ct. 1351, 1368 (2013); *but see id.* at 1375–76 (dissenting opinion).

[800] *Id.* at 1355 (majority opinion). In *Kirtsaeng*, a foreign student studying in the United States purchased copies of textbooks printed overseas and resold them in the United States at a profit.

and importation of lawful copies by one who possesses those copies without acquiring ownership of them.[801]

[4]   Public Performance

[a]   In General

The fourth right is the exclusive right "to perform the copyrighted work publicly."[802] This right applies only to "literary, musical, dramatic, and choreographic works, pantomimes, and motion pictures and other audiovisual works."[803] This omits (1) pictorial, graphic, and sculptural works and architectural works, which by their nature cannot be performed; and (2) sound recordings.[804] Congress later added a limited right to publicly perform sound recordings by means of digital audio transmission only.[805]

"To 'perform' a work means to recite, render, play, dance, or act it, either directly or by means of any device or process or, in the case of a motion picture or other audiovisual work, to show its images in any sequence or to make the sounds accompanying it audible."[806] In order for a digital download to constitute a "performance," it must be "transmitted in a manner designed for contemporaneous perception."[807] Thus, "streaming" a musical work or motion picture over the Internet is a performance,[808] but merely downloading or transmitting a file over the Internet, without simultaneously making it audible or visible, is not.[809]

To perform or display a work "publicly" means:

---

[801] *Id.* at 1361, 1368.

[802] 17 U.S.C. § 106(4).

[803] *Id.*

[804] *Cf.* 17 U.S.C. § 114(a) ("The exclusive rights of the owner of copyright in a sound recording are limited to the rights specified . . . and do not include any right of performance under section 106(4).").

Because federal law only covers sound recordings fixed on or after February 15, 1972, it is possible that a state could recognize a right of public performance in a sound recordings fixed before that date. *Compare* RCA Mfg. Co. v. Whiteman, 114 F.2d 86 (2d Cir. 1940) (no common-law right of public performance in published sound recordings) *with* Waring v. WDAS Broadcasting Station, 194 A. 631 (Pa. 1939) (finding common-law right of public performance in published sound recordings) *and* Flo & Eddie, Inc. v. Sirius XM Radio, Inc., 2014 U.S. Dist. LEXIS 139053 (C.D. Cal. Sept. 22, 2014) (finding statutory right of public performance in pre-1972 sound recordings under California law).

[805] 17 U.S.C. § 106(6). *See* § 4G[6].

[806] 17 U.S.C. § 101.

[807] United States v. ASCAP, 627 F.3d 64, 72–75 (2d Cir. 2010). *Accord,* American Broadcasting Cos. v. Aereo, Inc., 134 S. Ct. 2498, 2508 (2014) ("to transmit a performance of . . . an audiovisual work means to communicate contemporaneously visible images and contemporaneously audible sounds of the work.").

[808] *Aereo,* 134 S. Ct. at 2509 ("when Aereo streams the same television program to multiple subscribers, it "transmit[s] . . . a performance" to all of them."). *But cf.* Flava Works, Inc. v. Gunter, 689 F.3d 754 (7th Cir. 2012) (questioning whether a public performance occurs when an infringing video is uploaded to a website or when it is streamed to individual users; the former "is better at giving meaning to 'public' in public performance but worse at giving meaning to 'performance.' ").

[809] *ASCAP,* 627 F.3d at 73. Instead, downloading or transmitting a file over the Internet is a "digital phonorecord delivery," subject to the reproduction and distribution rights. *Id.* at 446–47; *see* §§ 4G[1][b] and [3][b].

(1) to perform or display it at a place open to the public or at any place where a substantial number of persons outside of a normal circle of a family and its social acquaintances is gathered; or

(2) to transmit or otherwise communicate a performance or display of the work to a place specified by clause (1) or to the public, by means of any device or process, whether the members of the public capable of receiving the performance or display receive it in the same place or in separate places and at the same time or at different times.[810]

In *Columbia Pictures Industries, Inc. v. Redd Horne, Inc.*,[811] and *Columbia Pictures Industries, Inc. v. Aveco, Inc.*,[812] the defendants provided private rooms or booths in which customers could view videocassettes of motion pictures rented from defendants. In *Redd Horne*, the videocassette players were in a central location; in *Aveco*, they were in the rooms under control of the customer. In both cases, the court held that the performances were "public," because the rooms were "open to the public," even though they were occupied only by one party at a time.[813] In *Columbia Pictures Industries, Inc. v. Professional Real Estate Investors, Inc.*, however, the court held that "a hotel did not violate the Copyright Act by renting videodiscs for viewing on hotel-provided video equipment in guests' rooms," reasoning that "[w]hile the hotel may indeed be 'open to the public,' a guest's hotel room, once rented, is not. . . . The movies are viewed exclusively in guest rooms, places where individuals enjoy a substantial degree of privacy, not unlike their own homes."[814]

The second paragraph of the definition of "publicly" encompasses transmissions to a place listed in the first paragraph, and transmissions directly to the public,[815] even if they receive the transmission in a private place.[816] This paragraph is phrased broadly enough to encompass both traditional broadcast radio and television and

---

[810] 17 U.S.C. § 101. The purpose of the second clause of subparagraph (1) is "to make clear that, contrary to the decision in Metro-Goldwyn-Mayer Distribution Corp. v. Wyatt, 21 C.O. Bull, 203 (D. Md. 1932), performances in 'semipublic' places such as clubs, lodges, factories, summer camps and schools are 'public performances' subject to copyright control." H.R. Rep. No. 94-1476, at 64 (1976). *See also* Fermata Int'l Melodies Inc. v. Champions Golf Inc., 712 F. Supp. 1257, 1260 (S.D. Tex. 1989) (performance before 21 members plus guests in the dining room of a private golf club was a "public" performance), *aff'd mem.*, 915 F.2d 1567 (5th Cir. 1990).

[811] 749 F.2d 154 (3d Cir. 1984).

[812] 800 F.2d 59 (3d Cir. 1986).

[813] *Aveco*, 800 F.2d at 63.

[814] 866 F.2d 278, 281 (9th Cir. 1989).

[815] *See* 17 U.S.C. § 101(2) (definition of "publicly"). "To 'transmit' a performance or display is to communicate it by any device or process whereby images or sounds are received beyond the place from which they are sent." *Id.* (definition of "transmit").

[816] This result is consistent with case law under the 1909 Act, which was drafted before wireless sound and image transmission were invented. *See* Jerome H. Remick & Co. v. American Automobile Accessories Co., 5 F.2d 411, 412 (6th Cir. 1925) ("Nor can a performance . . . be deemed private because each listener may enjoy it alone in the privacy of his home."). *See also* Twentieth Century Music Corp. v. Aiken, 422 U.S. 151, 158 (1975) ("Although Congress did not revise the statutory language, . . . it was soon established in the federal courts that the broadcast of a copyrighted musical composition by a commercial radio station was a public performance of that composition for profit — and thus an infringement of the copyright if not licensed.").

"asynchronous" transmissions, such as online streaming and "video on demand" (VOD) services.[817]

In *Cartoon Network LP v. CSC Holdings, Inc.*,[818] the court considered a "remote storage" DVR system, which allowed customers to make copies of TV programs and store them on hard drives at Cablevision's premises for later viewing. Among other claims, the plaintiffs contended that transmission of the stored programs to customers violated the public performance right. The Second Circuit rejected this argument, holding that each transmission "made to a single subscriber using a single unique copy produced by that subscriber" should be treated as a separate "performance" that was private rather than public,[819] because the "members of the public capable of receiving the performance" were limited to the household of that subscriber.

In *American Broadcasting Cos. v. Aereo, Inc.*, however, a majority of the Supreme Court rejected the "single subscriber/single unique copy" argument and held that a similar system that allowed subscribers to view broadcast television over the Internet for a fee was "publicly performing" television programs without authorization.[820] The Court relied on legislative history indicating that cable television systems publicly perform copyrighted works when they retransmit television signals to their subscribers.[821] The majority rejected the dissent's contention that Aereo could not be directly liable because it merely set up a system that was controlled by its subscribers;[822] and in *dicta*, it suggested that cloud-based storage services could be distinguished if the consumers using such services only transmit content that they have already lawfully acquired.[823]

[b] Secondary Transmissions

In order to understand the 1976 Act's treatment of secondary transmissions, it is necessary to review the history of how retransmissions were treated under the 1909 Act.

[i] The 1909 Act

In *Buck v. Jewell-LaSalle Realty Co.*, a hotel installed a radio receiving set and piped sound into speakers in its public and private rooms. The receiver retransmitted a radio station's unlicensed broadcast of a copyrighted musical composition. The Supreme Court held that the hotel publicly performed the work,

---

[817] *See, e.g.*, American Broadcasting Cos. v. Aereo, Inc., 134 S. Ct. 2498 (2014) (retransmitting broadcast television to subscribers over the Internet is a public performance); On Command Video Corp. v. Columbia Pictures Industries, 777 F. Supp. 787 (N.D. Cal. 1991) (transmission of signals from video cassette players located in lobby to guest rooms was a "public" performance).

[818] 536 F.3d 121 (2d Cir. 2008).

[819] *Id.* at 139. The Supreme Court denied a petition for *certiorari*, based on the Solicitor General's view that the case should be interpreted narrowly. Brief for the United States as *Amicus Curiae*, in Cable News Network, Inc. v. CSC Holdings, Inc., No. 08-448, at 20–21 (2009).

[820] 134 S. Ct. 2498 (2014).

[821] *Id.* at 2504–06. *See* § 4G[4][b][ii], below.

[822] *Id.* at 2507. *See* § 4I[3][a], below.

[823] *Id.* at 2510–11.

giving birth to the "multiple performances" doctrine — a single transmission results in several performances by different persons.[824]

Despite this precedent, *Buck* was rejected when the Supreme Court considered cable television systems, in which a central antenna received authorized TV broadcasts and retransmitted them via cable to its subscribers. The problem went to the Supreme Court twice; in each case, it held that cable retransmission was not a "public performance" under the 1909 Copyright Act.[825] Stating that "[b]roadcasters perform. Viewers do not perform," the Court held that cable "falls on the viewer's side of the line," because it merely "enhances the viewer's capacity to receive the broadcaster's signals."[826] Moreover, to allow copyright owners to extract one royalty from the original broadcaster and another from the cable television retransmitter would be unfair multiple tribute because copyright owners based broadcast royalties on estimated audience size.[827] The Court confined *Buck* to its facts and urged Congress to resolve the difficult policy problems that cable television created.

Before Congress could act, however, the Court decided another case that buried whatever was left of the "multiple performances" doctrine. In *Twentieth Century Music Corp. v. Aiken*, the owner of a small fast-food chicken restaurant had a radio with four speakers that he turned on for the enjoyment of his customers. Relying on the two cable television cases, the Court held that Aiken did not "perform" copyrighted works broadcast by licensed radio stations and received through his radio-speaker system, because "to hold all in Aiken's position 'performed' these musical compositions would be to authorize the sale of an untold number of licenses for what is basically a single public rendition of a copyrighted work."[828]

[ii]   The 1976 Act

In the 1976 Act, Congress reinstated the "multiple performances" doctrine by including "secondary transmissions" within the public performance right. The House Report states that public performance and public display "cover not only the initial rendition or showing, but also any further act by which that rendition or showing is transmitted or communicated to the public."

> Thus, for example, a singer is performing when he or she sings a song; a broadcasting network is performing when it transmits his or her performance (whether simultaneously or from records); a local broadcaster is performing when it transmits the network broadcast; a cable television system is performing when it retransmits the broadcast to its subscribers;

---

[824] 283 U.S. 191 (1931). A lower court extended *Buck* to a hotel that retransmitted a licensed broadcast into private rooms only. Society of European Stage Authors & Composers, Inc. v. New York Hotel Statler Co., 19 F. Supp. 1 (S.D.N.Y. 1937).

[825] Fortnightly Corp. v. United Artists Television, Inc., 392 U.S. 390 (1968); Teleprompter Corp. v. Columbia Broadcasting Systems, 415 U.S. 394 (1974).

[826] *Fortnightly*, 392 U.S. at 398–99.

[827] *Teleprompter*, 415 U.S. at 412–13.

[828] 422 U.S. 151, 162–63 (1975).

and any individual is performing whenever he or she plays a phonorecord [of] the performance or communicates the performance by turning on a receiving set.[829]

Congress tempered the multiple performances doctrine in a number of ways. First, the exclusive rights extend only to performances and displays that are done "publicly." For example, "[n]o license is required by the Copyright Act . . . to sing a copyrighted lyric in the shower," or to play a song on an MP3 player, because the Act confers no exclusive right to *private* performances.[830] In *American Broadcasting Cos. v. Aereo, Inc.*, however, the Supreme Court held that a system that allowed subscribers to view broadcast television over the Internet for a fee was liable for "publicly" performing television programs by retransmission.[831]

Second, Congress codified *Aiken* by enacting an exemption for "the public reception of the transmission on a single receiving apparatus of a kind commonly used in private homes."[832] Third, in section 111, Congress enacted an exemption for "the relaying, by the management of a hotel, apartment house, or similar establishment, of signals transmitted by a [FCC-licensed] broadcast station . . . to the private lodgings of guests or residents of such establishment, [if] no direct charge is made to see or hear the secondary transmission."[833] Fourth, also in section 111, Congress enacted a complicated compulsory licensing scheme for secondary transmissions by cable television systems.[834] Because Internet retransmission services are not licensed by the FCC, courts have held that such services do not qualify as "cable systems" under section 111.[835]

In 1988, after satellite television became a reality, Congress enacted a similar compulsory license for certain satellite retransmissions of copyrighted works, codified at section 119, with a sunset date of December 31, 1994. This license has been re-enacted, with amendments, for successive five-year periods ever since. The current version of the satellite compulsory license is due to expire on December 31, 2019.[836] In addition, in 1999, Congress added a permanent, royalty-free compulsory license for retransmission of a local television broadcast into its local market in section 122.[837]

In 2008, the Copyright Office issued a report concluding that sections 111 and 119 were "arcane, antiquated, complicated, and dysfunctional," and that they should be significantly modified and phased out by the end of 2014.[838] Congress adopted some

---

[829] H.R. Rep. No. 94-1476, at 63 (1976).

[830] Twentieth Century Music Corp. v. Aiken, 422 U.S. 151, 155 (1975).

[831] 134 S. Ct. 2498 (2014). *See* § 4G[4][a], above.

[832] 17 U.S.C. § 110(5)(A). This exception is discussed in more detail in § 4G[4][c].

[833] 17 U.S.C. § 111(a)(1).

[834] 17 U.S.C. § 111(c)–(f).

[835] *See* WPIX, Inc. v. ivi, Inc., 691 F.3d 275 (2d Cir. 2012).

[836] 17 U.S.C. § 119(h); *see* Pub. L. No. 113–200, §§ 201.202(a), 128 Stat. 2066.

[837] 17 U.S.C. § 122.

[838] U.S. Copyright Office, Satellite Home Viewer Extension and Reauthorization Act Section 109 Report 219 (2008).

of the recommendations, but not others, in the Satellite Television Extension and Localization Act (STELA) of 2010.[839]

[c]　　Exceptions and Limitations

The 1909 Act granted owners of *dramatic* works exclusive rights over all public performances, but it granted owners of *musical* works exclusive rights only over public performances "for profit."[840] The courts, however, applied the "for profit" label broadly. In *Herbert v. Shanley Co.*,[841] for example, the Supreme Court held that performance of copyrighted musical compositions in a hotel dining room violated the copyright owner's exclusive right to authorize public performances for profit, even though the hotel did not charge admission.[842]

The 1976 Act abolished the general exclusion of nonprofit music performances and substituted a series of more specific limitations. In addition to the cable and satellite television compulsory licenses in Sections 111, 119 and 122, public performances and public displays are subject to the following exceptions and limitations:

Section 110 includes eleven exceptions to the public performance right, several of which also apply to public displays. These include specific, limited exceptions for certain face-to-face teaching activities,[843] distance education activities,[844] religious services,[845] live educational, religious, or charitable non-profit performances,[846] agricultural and horticultural fairs,[847] promotional performances at retail stores,[848] transmissions to blind or other handicapped persons,[849] and charitable performances at nonprofits veterans or fraternal organizations.[850] Two subsections warrant further comment.

---

[839] Pub. L. No. 111-175, 124 Stat. 1218.

[840] 1909 Act, § 1(d) (dramatic works), § 1(d) (musical works), 35 Stat. 1075. The apparent reason for the distinction was that even a single performance diminishes the public's appetite for a play but that non-profit performances do not similarly diminish the appetite for music.

[841] 242 U.S. 591 (1917).

[842] Justice Holmes wrote: "The defendants' performances are not eleemosynary. They are part of a total for which the public pays. . . . It is true that the music is not the sole object, but neither is the food, which probably could be got cheaper elsewhere. The object is a repast in surroundings that . . . give a luxurious pleasure not to be had from eating a silent meal. If music did not pay, it would be given up. If it pays, it pays out of the public's pocket. Whether it pays or not, the purpose of employing it is profit, and that is enough." *Id.* at 594.

[843] 17 U.S.C. § 110(1).

[844] 17 U.S.C. § 110(2).

[845] 17 U.S.C. § 110(3). This section does *not* apply to services that are broadcast on the radio. *See* Simpleville Music v. Mizell, 451 F. Supp. 2d 1293 (M.D. Ala. 2006).

[846] 17 U.S.C. § 110(4).

[847] 17 U.S.C. § 110(6).

[848] 17 U.S.C. § 110(7).

[849] 17 U.S.C. §§ 110(8), 110(9).

[850] 17 U.S.C. § 110(10). However, "the social functions of any college or university fraternity or sorority" are not included "unless the social function is held solely to raise funds for a specific charitable purpose." *Id.*

As originally enacted, section 110(5) codified *Aiken* by providing an exemption for "the public reception of [a] transmission on a single receiving apparatus of a kind commonly used in private homes," unless "a direct charge is made to see or hear the transmission" or "the transmission thus received is further retransmitted to the public."[851] This open-ended definition led to a significant amount of litigation, with inconsistent results.[852] In 1998, Congress enacted the Fairness in Music Licensing Act, which retained the existing exemption in subsection (A), but also added a new subsection (B), providing a "safe harbor" for establishments of a specified size using specified equipment.[853] In 2001, a panel of the World Trade Organization found that subsection (B) exempts about 70 percent of all restaurants and bars and nearly half of the retail stores in the United States, and concluded that it violates Article 13 of the TRIPS Agreement.[854] Congress has not yet amended the statute to bring U.S. law into compliance with the treaty.

Section 110(11) exempts software that makes "limited portions of [the] audio or video content of a motion picture . . . imperceptible" at the direction of a home viewer, "during a performance in or transmitted to that household for private home viewing," "if no fixed copy of the altered version of the motion picture is created."[855] Although this section addresses *private* performances, which are not within the exclusive right, without this section a transmission to more than one household might have been deemed to be a public performance, and the software might have been deemed to assist in the preparation of a derivative work.[856]

As originally enacted, section 116 gave owners of "coin-operated phonorecord players" (*i.e.*, jukeboxes) a compulsory license to perform musical works embodied in phonorecords. As later amended, the compulsory license takes effect only in the absence of a negotiated license reached through voluntary collective negotiations between copyright owners and jukebox operators.[857] Section 118 provides a compulsory license for the use of published nondramatic musical works and published pictorial, graphic and sculptural works by noncommercial public broadcasting entities, which may be superseded by voluntary negotiations.[858]

---

[851] 17 U.S.C. § 110(5)(A).

[852] *Compare* Sailor Music v. Gap Stores, Inc., 668 F.2d 84 (2d Cir. 1981) (chain store with four speakers in 2,769 square feet did not qualify) *and* Broadcast Music, Inc. v. United States Shoe Corp., 678 F.2d 816 (9th Cir. 1982) (commercial sound system was not "commonly used in private homes," and establishment was of sufficient size to warrant a commercial music service) *with* Broadcast Music, Inc. v. Claire's Boutiques, Inc., 949 F.2d 1482 (7th Cir. 1991) (size of stores and financial ability to pay are irrelevant; chain with 669 stores qualified where each store used one homestyle receiver) *and* Springsteen v. Plaza Roller Dome, Inc., 602 F. Supp. 1113 (M.D.N.C. 1985) (radio wired to six speakers over 7,500 square-foot miniature golf course qualified for exemption).

[853] 17 U.S.C. § 110(5)(B).

[854] *See* World Trade Organization, Report of the Panel on Section 110(5) of the U.S. Copyright Act, available at www.wto.org/english/tratop_e/dispu_e/cases_e/ds160_e.htm (last visited March 1, 2015).

[855] 17 U.S.C. § 110(11).

[856] *See also* § 4G[2][b].

[857] 17 U.S.C. § 116.

[858] 17 U.S.C. § 118. *See* H.R. Rep. No. 94-1476, at 119 (1976).

[d]   Performing Rights Organizations

Making public performances subject to copyright creates practical problems for both owners and users of copyrighted works, especially music. How can a composer monitor performances by thousands of concert halls, taverns, restaurants, broadcast stations and other establishments? How can an establishment owner, who wants to respect copyright and obtain performance licenses, contact composers of the numerous works that he may wish to use?

To solve these problems, musical-work copyright owners formed performing rights organizations that (1) issue licenses and collect fees from users; (2) monitor public performances of their members' works and initiate copyright infringement suits against unlicensed public performances; and (3) distribute collected royalties to their members under an agreed formula.[859]

The two major United States performing rights organizations are the American Society of Composers, Authors and Publishers ("ASCAP") and Broadcast Music, Inc. ("BMI"). ASCAP and BMI hold nonexclusive rights to grant licenses for public performances of nondramatic musical works. Each offers a "blanket license" that gives broadcasters and networks unlimited use of all works in their respective repertories for a fixed fee, typically a percentage of gross revenue. In addition, by virtue of antitrust consent decrees negotiated with the U.S. Department of Justice, ASCAP and BMI must offer per-program and per-time period licenses for a set fee. If the parties cannot agree on a fee, the licensee may apply to the U.S. District Court for the Southern District of New York to set a reasonable fee.[860] In addition, the 1998 Fairness in Music Licensing Act provides that an individual proprietor may apply to have a reasonable license fee determined by either the Southern District of New York, or "a district court that is the seat of the Federal circuit . . . in which the proprietor's establishment is located."[861]

In *Broadcast Music, Inc. v. Columbia Broadcasting System*,[862] the Supreme Court held that the standard ASCAP and BMI "blanket licenses" were not *per se* unlawful under the antitrust laws, but had to be judged under the "rule of reason." On remand, the Second Circuit upheld the blanket licensing system.[863]

Note that ASCAP and BMI license only public performances of nondramatic musical works, or of individual songs from dramatic musical works when performed outside of a dramatic context. Copyright owners of musical works typically retain, and license separately, so-called "grand" performing rights, *i.e.*, rights to perform

---

[859] In other countries, performing rights societies are often governmental or quasi-governmental in nature. In the United States, private organizations have been regulated through antitrust suits and consent decrees to control the potentially anticompetitive and monopolistic aspects of their practices.

[860] *See, e.g.*, United States v. Broadcast Music, Inc., 426 F.3d 91 (2d Cir. 2005); ASCAP v. Showtime/The Movie Channel, Inc., 912 F.2d 563 (2d Cir. 1990).

[861] 17 U.S.C. § 513(2).

[862] 441 U.S. 1 (1979).

[863] CBS, Inc. v. ASCAP, 620 F.2d 930 (2d Cir. 1980). *See also* Buffalo Broadcasting Co. v. ASCAP, 744 F.2d 917 (2d Cir. 1984) (same result for blanket license for local television stations).

dramatic musical works as a whole, and to perform individual songs in a dramatic setting.[864]

[5]   Public Display

The fifth right is the exclusive right "to display the copyrighted work publicly."[865] This right applies only to "literary, musical, dramatic, and choreographic works, pantomimes, and pictorial, graphic, and sculptural works, including the individual images of a motion picture or other audiovisual work."[866] This omits (1) sound recordings, the public display of which is pointless; and (2) architectural works, which must be publicly displayed when constructed.[867]

A "display" is infringing only if it is done "publicly," and that word is defined the same way for both public performances and public displays.[868] "To 'display' a work means to show a copy of it, either directly or by means of a film, slide, television image, or any other device or process or, in the case of a motion picture or other audiovisual work, to show individual images nonsequentially."[869] Under the first-sale doctrine, however, the owner of a lawful copy of a work, such as a painting or a book, may display that copy to the public, without the permission of the copyright owner, "either directly or by the projection of no more than one image at a time, to viewers present at the place where the copy is located."[870] Thus, the public display right is primarily of value only for broadcasting or other transmissions of images of the work.[871]

In *Perfect 10, Inc. v. Amazon.com, Inc.*,[872] the Internet search engine Google used software that automatically copied images found on the Web, stored "thumbnail" versions of the images, displayed the thumbnail images to users, and provided a hyperlink to the full-size image when a user clicked on a thumbnail. When Google indexed infringing images that were posted by unknown third parties, Perfect 10 sued Google for infringement. Because the definition of "display" is "to show a 'copy' of" the work, the court held that Google was directly liable for publicly displaying the image only if it possessed a fixed "copy" of the

---

[864] *See, e.g.*, Robert Stigwood Group Ltd. v. Sperber, 457 F.2d 50, 56 (2d Cir. 1972) (concert promoter who obtained ASCAP license could not stage concert performances of *Jesus Christ Superstar* "in which the story line of the original play is preserved" without infringing the reserved right of dramatic performance).

[865] 17 U.S.C. § 106(5).

[866] *Id.*

[867] In addition, section 120 expressly permits the public display of pictures of a building that is "located in or ordinarily visible from a public place." 17 U.S.C. § 120(a).

[868] *See* discussion in § 4G[4][a]. *See also* Thomas v. Pansy Ellen Prods., Inc., 672 F. Supp. 237 (W.D.N.C. 1987) (display at a members-only trade show was a "public" display).

[869] 17 U.S.C. § 101.

[870] 17 U.S.C. § 109(c).

[871] *See* H.R. Rep. No. 94-1476, at 80 (1976) ("the display of a visual image of a copyrighted work would be an infringement if the image were transmitted by any method . . . from one place to members of the public located elsewhere. . . . [Moreover,] even where the copy and the viewers are located at the same place, the simultaneous projection of multiple images of the work would not be exempted.").

[872] 508 F.3d 1146 (9th Cir. 2007).

image on its servers. Thus, Google could not be held directly liable for providing a hyperlink to the full-size image (although it might be liable for contributory infringement).[873] And although Google conceded that it was publicly displaying thumbnails, which are fixed "copies" of the works at issue, the court held that making and displaying thumbnails as part of an automated indexing system was a fair use.[874] Accordingly, Google was liable for infringing copies posted by others only if it had notice of the infringement and did not act promptly to remove the images from its index.[875]

The public display right is implicated when a work is incorporated in or appears in the background of a motion picture or other audiovisual work.[876] For example, in *Ringgold v. Black Entertainment Television, Inc.*, the defendants displayed a lawfully made poster of plaintiff's artwork in the background of an episode of the television series "Roc." The poster was visible (at least in part) in nine shots of a few seconds each, for a total of about 27 seconds. The court held that the use was not *de minimis*, and it remanded for an analysis of whether it was fair use.[877] In several other cases, however, courts have relied on the fact that the work appeared only for a few seconds or was out of focus in concluding that such a background use was *de minimis*.[878]

Most of the exceptions and limitations that apply to public performances also apply to public displays.[879] Moreover, in addition to fair use and the first-sale doctrine, the Copyright Act also permits the public display of pictures of useful articles in advertisements, commentaries, and news reports;[880] and the public display of pictures of buildings "located in or ordinarily visible from a public place."[881]

---

[873] *Id.* at 1160–61 (direct infringement of display right); *id.* at 1170–73 (contributory infringement).

[874] *Id.* at 1163–68.

[875] *Id.* at 1172.

[876] *See, e.g.*, Woods v. Universal City Studios, Inc., 920 F. Supp. 62 (S.D.N.Y. 1996) (use of plaintiff's drawing as scenic design in movie "12 Monkeys").

[877] 126 F.3d 70, 76–77, 81 (2d Cir. 1997).

[878] *See, e.g.*, Gordon v. Nextel Communications, 345 F.3d 922 (9th Cir. 2003) (display of dental illustrations in background of a TV commercial); Sandoval v. New Line Cinema Corp., 147 F.3d 215, 217 (2d Cir. 1998) (photos on light box in background of movie "Seven" were "not displayed with sufficient detail for the average lay observer to identify" them); Gottlieb Development LLC v. Paramount Pictures Corp., 590 F. Supp. 2d 625 (S.D.N.Y. 2008) (copyrighted pinball machine in background of movie "What Women Want"); Straus v. DVC Worldwide, Inc., 484 F. Supp. 2d 620 (S.D. Tex. 2007) (display of photo on product box at end of TV commercial was *de minimis*).

[879] *See, e.g.*, 17 U.S.C. § 110(1) (face-to-face teaching); § 110(2) (distance education); § 110(3) (religious services); § 110(5) (public reception on home-style equipment); § 111 (cable television retransmissions), § 112 (ephemeral recordings); § 118 (public television compulsory license); § 119 (satellite retransmissions); and § 122 (local-to-local retransmissions).

The following exemptions do *not* apply to public displays: § 110(4) (not-for-profit performances); § 110(6) (agricultural and horticultural fairs); § 110(7) (promotional use in record stores); § 110(8) (transmissions of nondramatic literary works to the blind and handicapped); § 110(9) (transmissions of dramatic literary works to the blind and handicapped); and § 110(10) (veterans' and fraternal organizations).

[880] 17 U.S.C. § 113(c).

[881] 17 U.S.C. § 120(a).

[6]   Digital Audio Transmission

As noted above, the general public performance right does not apply to sound recordings.[882] Hence, when a song is played on traditional analog radio, only the owner of copyright in the musical work gets paid royalties; neither the record company nor the performers receive any royalties from such performances. This limitation dates back to 1971, when Congress first added sound recordings to the Copyright Act.[883] At that time, the primary concern of record companies was stronger protection against record piracy.[884] In order to overcome the objections of broadcasters to the creation of a sound recording copyright, the record companies grudgingly accepted the limits imposed on that copyright in sections 114(a) through (c). Ever since, however, record companies have been lobbying Congress to enact a full-fledged public performance right for sound recordings.

In 1995, in response to the advent of digital broadcasting, Congress added a sixth exclusive right: "in the case of sound recordings, to perform the copyrighted work publicly by means of a digital audio transmission."[885] The legislative history explains that this amendment was "a narrowly crafted response to one of the concerns expressed by representatives of the recording community, namely that certain types of subscription and interact[ive] audio services might adversely affect sales of sound recordings."[886] Accordingly, the amendment preserved the royalty-free status of traditional over-the-air broadcasts, but it added provisions addressing subscription and interactive digital audio services. These provisions were further amended in 1998 by the Digital Millennium Copyright Act.

The digital audio transmission right is subject to section 114, which divides the digital audio world into three types of services. The first category is non-subscription, non-interactive broadcast transmissions, which are exempt.[887] This category includes digital over-the-air broadcasts by FCC-licensed radio and television stations; but it does *not* include Internet simulcasts of such broadcasts.[888]

The second category is non-interactive subscription services, i.e., services for which the listener pays a monthly fee; and eligible non-subscription services, such as webcasting.[889] These services may avail themselves of a compulsory license to

---

[882] 17 U.S.C. § 106(4); 17 U.S.C. § 114(a).

[883] Because federal law only applies to sound recordings fixed on or after February 15, 1972, it is possible that a state could recognize a public performance right in sound recordings fixed before that date. *See* § 4G[4][a], above.

[884] *See* H.R. Rep. No. 92-487, at 1–2 (1971).

[885] 17 U.S.C. § 106(6).

[886] H.R. Rep. No. 104-274, at 16 (1995).

[887] 17 U.S.C. § 114(d)(1)(A). Also exempt are retransmissions of broadcast transmissions, § 114(d)(1)(B), and transmissions to and within a business establishment, § 114(d)(1)(C). The latter exemption permits existing music background services, such as Muzak, to continue operation without an additional royalty.

[888] *See* Bonneville Int'l Corp. v. Peters, 347 F.3d 485 (3d Cir. 2003) (upholding Copyright Office's rulemaking concerning Internet simulcasts of broadcast transmissions).

[889] 17 U.S.C. § 114(d)(2).

publicly perform sound recordings, which is subject to a host of specific conditions.[890] Congress specified that the net royalties from the compulsory license shall be divided as follows: 50 percent is paid to the sound recording copyright owner; 5 percent is paid to non-featured musicians and vocalists; and 45 percent is paid to featured artists.[891] In addition, such services must obtain a license to perform the musical works embodied in those recordings,[892] which is typically a blanket license from a performing rights organization such as ASCAP and BMI.[893]

The rate-setting process for the compulsory license for category two services has been the source of considerable controversy. Although the D.C. Circuit has upheld almost all of the royalty rates established in administrative proceedings,[894] twice small webcasters succeeded in lobbying Congress for a statute that allowed them to negotiate alternative agreements with SoundExchange, the royalty collecting agency for the recording industry, on a one-time basis.[895] Those agreements typically provided for royalties calculated as a percentage of expenses or gross revenue, subject to an annual minimum, rather than the per-performance royalties that were sought in administrative proceedings.

The third category of digital audio transmissions is interactive services, defined as "one that enables a member of the public to receive a transmission of a program specially created for the recipient, or on request, a transmission of a particular sound recording . . . which is selected by or on behalf of the recipient."[896] An interactive service must negotiate a license with the sound recording copyright owner,[897] in addition to obtaining a license to perform the musical works embodied

---

[890] *Id.* For example, the compulsory license limits the number of times a particular sound recording may be performed (the so-called "sound recording performance complement"), and prohibits a service from publishing or announcing in advance when a particular sound recording will be performed. 17 U.S.C. § 114(d)(2)(C)(i)–(ii), § 114(j)(13). To make things still more complicated, the DMCA added additional conditions, resulting in one set of rules for "grandfathered" services that were licensed or in operation before July 31, 1998, and another set of rules for newer services. *Compare* 17 U.S.C. § 114(d)(2)(B) *with* § 114(d)(2)(C).

[891] 17 U.S.C. § 114(g).

[892] 17 U.S.C. § 114(d)(4)(B)(i), § 114(i) ("It is the intent of Congress that royalties payable to copyright owners of musical works for the public performance of their works shall not be diminished in any respect as a result of the rights granted by section 106(6).").

[893] *See* § 4G[4][d].

[894] *See, e.g.*, Beethoven.com LLC v. Librarian of Congress, 394 F.3d 939 (D.C. Cir. 2005) (upholding CARP determination for 1998–2002); Intercollegiate Broadcast System, Inc. v. Copyright Royalty Board, 574 F.3d 748 (D.C. Cir. 2009) (upholding CRJs determination for 2006–2010, except for $500 minimum annual fee, which was determined to be arbitrary and capricious).

[895] *See* Small Webcaster Settlement Act of 2002, Pub. L. No. 107-321, 116 Stat. 2780; Webcaster Settlement Act of 2008, Pub. L. No. 110-435, 122 Stat. 4974. The deadline for the latter was extended by the Webcaster Settlement Act of 2009, Pub. L. No. 111-36, 123 Stat. 1926.

[896] 17 U.S.C. § 114(j)(7). *See* Arista Records LLC v. Launch Media, Inc., 578 F.3d 148, 162 (2d Cir. 2009) (service that allowed users to rate songs and created a customized "playlist" for each user, while still including some random selections, was not "interactive," because the user could not choose particular songs, and the playlist was not "so predictable that users will choose to listen to the webcast in lieu of purchasing music.").

[897] 17 U.S.C. § 114(d)(3). The statute places a number of conditions on the grant of exclusive licenses, in order to encourage sound recording copyright owners to grant nonexclusive licenses or to grant

in those recordings.[898]

[7] Moral Rights

[a] In General

Continental European countries traditionally protect authors' "moral rights." Moral rights are inalienable natural rights that an author retains by virtue of his or her authorship, even after he or she has transferred the copyright in the work to another. Article 6*bis* of the Berne Convention recognizes two moral rights, the right of attribution and the right of integrity:

> Independently of the author's economic rights, and even after the transfer of the said rights, the author shall have the right to claim authorship of the work, and to object to any distortion, mutilation or other modification of, or any other derogatory action in relation to, the said work, which would be prejudicial to his honor or reputation.[899]

United States copyright law traditionally did not protect moral rights. Authors have exclusive copyright rights and may assign or license them under contractual conditions that guarantee integrity and attribution; but if an author transfers copyright without such conditions, he or she loses this power.

Aside from copyright, authors have attempted various state and federal legal theories to protect moral rights. Two in particular deserve special attention. First, before the 1976 Act, many authors attempted to claim attribution rights on the basis of section 43(a) of the Lanham Act, which prohibited any "false designation of origin."[900] Section 43(a) was even used to simulate the right of integrity. In *Gilliam v. American Broadcasting Cos.*, defendant ABC obtained a license to broadcast several television shows created by the British comedy group Monty Python. When the shows were broadcast, however, ABC cut 24 minutes from each 90-minute program. The court held that this truncation violated the terms of the license and infringed the plaintiff's right to prepare derivative works.[901] The court also held that the defendant violated section 43(a) of the Lanham Act by falsely presenting the mutilated shows as the work of Monty Python.[902]

When the United States joined the Berne Convention in 1989, Congress relied on the *Gilliam* case in asserting that no amendment was needed to expressly provide moral rights protection. In 2003, however, the Supreme Court substantially undercut the legal basis for the *Gilliam* ruling. In *Dastar Corp. v. Twentieth Century Fox Film Corp.*, Dastar edited a TV series for which the copyright had

---

licenses to non-affiliated entities. For example, an exclusive license ordinarily may not be granted for more than 12 months, and may not be re-granted to the same licensee for a period of 13 months after that. 17 U.S.C. § 114(d)(3)(A).

[898] 17 U.S.C. § 114(d)(3)(C).

[899] Berne Convention, 1971 Paris Text, Art. 6*bis*.

[900] *See, e.g.*, Smith v. Montoro, 648 F.2d 602 (9th Cir. 1981). Section 43(a) is discussed in more detail in § 5F[7].

[901] 538 F.2d 14, 20–21 (2d Cir. 1976).

[902] *Id.* at 24–25.

expired, and presented the edited version as its own. Fox, the former copyright owner, sued for a violation of section 43(a) of the Lanham Act. The Supreme Court held that the phrase "origin of goods" in section 43(a) "refers to the producer of tangible goods that are offered for sale, and not to the author of any idea, concept, or communication embodied in those goods."[903] To hold otherwise, said the Court, "would create a species of mutant copyright law that limits the public's federal right to copy and use expired copyrights."[904] Although *Dastar* was decided in the context of an expired copyright, its reasoning is much broader, and subsequent cases have rejected almost every attempt to use section 43(a) to vindicate moral rights.[905]

The second avenue by which authors attempted to protect moral rights was through the enactment of artists' rights statutes. Prior to 1990, eleven states had enacted some type of artists rights statute.[906] New York's, for example, provides that "no person . . . shall knowingly display [publicly] . . . or publish a work of fine art . . . or a reproduction thereof in an altered, defaced, mutilated or modified form if the work is displayed, published or reproduced as being the work of the artist . . . and damage to the artist's reputation is reasonably likely to result therefrom."[907]

Despite these occasional and fragmentary attempts at protecting author's moral rights, and the enactment of the Visual Artists Rights Act of 1990, it is apparent that the United States is not in compliance with Article 6*bis* of the Berne Convention. Accordingly, when the TRIPS Agreement brought the substantive provisions of Berne under the dispute resolution mechanism of the World Trade Organization, it specifically excluded Article 6*bis* from that protection.[908]

[b]   Visual Artists Rights Act

In 1990, Congress enacted the Visual Artists Rights Act (VARA), providing limited attribution and integrity rights to the authors of "works of visual art." However, the phrase "work of visual art" is defined narrowly to include only "a painting, drawing, print, or sculpture," or "a still photographic image produced for exhibition purposes only," that exists "in a single copy [or] in a limited edition of 200 copies or fewer that are signed and consecutively numbered by the author."[909] The definition excludes works made for hire,[910] advertising and promotional material,[911]

---

[903] 539 U.S. 23, 37 (2003).

[904] *Id.* at 34.

[905] *See* § 5F[7].

[906] *See* H.R. Rep. No. 101-514, at 10 & n.18 (1990). These statutes are now partially preempted by federal law. *See* 17 U.S.C. § 301(f).

[907] N.Y. Cultural Affairs Law, § 14.03. *See, e.g.*, Wojnarowicz v. American Family Ass'n, 745 F. Supp. 130 (S.D.N.Y. 1990). Note that Congress subsequently enacted 17 U.S.C. § 301(f), which largely preempts state artists' rights laws.

[908] *See* TRIPS Agreement, Art. 9(1).

[909] 17 U.S.C. § 101. *See* Kelley v. Chicago Park Dist., 635 F.3d 290 (7th Cir. 2011) (questioning in *dicta* whether a living garden is a "painting, drawing, print, or sculpture," but declining to resolve the issue).

[910] *See* 17 U.S.C. § 101(B) (excluding "any work made for hire"); Carter v. Helmsley-Spear, Inc., 71 F.3d 77 (2d Cir. 1995) (concluding that "walk-through sculpture" in lobby of defendant's building was a work made for hire that was not protected by VARA).

[911] *See* 17 U.S.C. § 101(a)(ii) (excluding "any merchandising item or advertising, promotional,

literary works, motion pictures, and applied art.[912] As a result of this definition, the limited rights provided by VARA apply only to material objects, and not to reproductions or other images of the work.[913] Hence, VARA is really an art preservation statute couched in the language of moral rights, rather than a true moral rights statute.

VARA provides the author of a work of visual art with limited rights of attribution and integrity which are subject to fair use, but independent of the exclusive rights in section 106.[914] An author's attribution right consists of the right to claim authorship of the work, to prevent use of his or her name on any works of visual art that he or she did not create, and to prevent use of his or her name on a work that has been distorted, mutilated, or modified in a way "which would be prejudicial to his or her honor or reputation."[915] The author's integrity right consists of the right "to prevent any intentional distortion, mutilation, or other modification of that work which would be prejudicial to his or her honor or reputation," and "the right to prevent any [intentional or grossly negligent] destruction of a work of recognized stature."[916]

In addition to the narrow definition of a "work of visual art," VARA contains several exceptions. "The modification of a work of visual art which is a result of the passage of time or the inherent nature of the materials" is not actionable.[917] "The modification of a work of visual art which is the result of conservation, or of the public presentation, including lighting and placement, of the work" is not actionable unless it "is caused by gross negligence."[918] For works of visual art that have been incorporated into a building, such that removal of the work would cause its "destruction, distortion, mutilation, or other modification," VARA does not apply if the author consented to installation of the work before the effective date of VARA, or if the author and the building owner acknowledge in a signed writing that removal may destroy the work.[919] If the work can be removed from the building without destroying it, then the owner must merely make a "diligent, good faith

---

descriptive, covering, or packaging material or container"); Pollara v. Seymour, 344 F.3d 265 (2d Cir. 2003) (10-foot by 30-foot mural removed from Albany's Empire State Plaza was intended to promote a political message, and was therefore "advertising [or] promotional material" that was not protected by VARA).

[912] 17 U.S.C. § 101(A)(i) (excluding "any poster, map, globe, chart, technical drawing, diagram, model, applied art, motion picture or other audiovisual work, book, magazine, newspaper, periodical, data base, electronic information service, electronic publication, or similar publication").

[913] See 17 U.S.C. § 106A(c)(3) ("The rights described [above] . . . shall not apply to any reproduction, depiction, portrayal, or other use of the work in, upon, or in any connection with any item described in subparagraph (A) or (B) of the definition of 'work of visual art' ").

[914] 17 U.S.C. § 106A(a).

[915] 17 U.S.C. § 106A(a)(1)(A),(B) and (a)(2).

[916] 17 U.S.C. § 106A(a)(3)(A),(B). See Martin v. City of Indianapolis, 192 F.3d 608 (7th Cir. 1999) (concluding that a large metal sculpture that was dismantled without notice was a "work of recognized stature," on the basis of newspaper and magazine articles and letters from art experts about the work).

[917] 17 U.S.C. § 106A(c)(1).

[918] 17 U.S.C. § 106A(c)(2).

[919] 17 U.S.C. § 113(d)(1). Cf. Cohen v. G&M Realty, LP, 988 F. Supp. 2d 212 (E.D.N.Y. 2013) (denying preliminary injunction to prevent destruction of graffiti art on "5Pointz" building slated for demolition).

attempt" to notify the author before removal, and if notice succeeds, the owner must give the author 90 days "to remove the work or to pay for its removal."[920]

Case law disagrees on protection for "site-specific art," or art for which "the location of the work is an integral element of the work."[921] Because site-specific art cannot be moved from its location without destroying it, and because requiring that site-specific art be preserved in its location "would entail radical consequences for owners of land,"[922] one court has concluded that "VARA does not apply to site-specific art at all."[923] In *dicta*, another court disagree, suggesting that some site-specific art may be entitled to some protection.[924]

The rights created by VARA apply to works of visual art created on or after its effective date (June 1, 1991), and endure for the life of the author.[925] They also apply to works created before the effective date if title to the works has not been transferred as of that date, in which case the rights last for the full term of copyright, or life of the author plus 70 years.[926] The rights are nontransferable, but the author may expressly waive the rights in a signed writing.[927]

[8]   Additional Rights

Since 1976, Congress has added five chapters to Title 17, but outside of the Copyright Act itself.[928] These additional rights have been or will be discussed elsewhere. They are:

Chapter 9 is the Semiconductor Chip Protection Act of 1984.[929]

Chapter 10 is the Audio Home Recording Act of 1992.[930]

Chapter 11 contains the anti-bootlegging provisions enacted as part of the Uruguay Round Agreements Act of 1994.[931]

---

[920] 17 U.S.C. § 113(d)(2).

[921] Phillips v. Pembroke Real Estate, Inc., 459 F.3d 128, 134 (1st Cir. 2006).

[922] *Id.* at 142, *quoting* Phillips v. Pembroke Real Estate, Inc., 819 N.E.2d 579 (Mass. 2004) (holding on certification that Massachusetts Art Protection Art did not apply site-specific art).

[923] *Phillips*, 459 F.3d at 143. *Cf.* Serra v. General Services Administration, 847 F.2d 1045 (2d Cir. 1988) (pre-VARA case holding that removal of site-specific government-owned work of art from federal property did not violate free speech or due process rights of the artist).

[924] *See* Kelley v. Chicago Park District, 635 F.3d 290, 306–07 (7th Cir. 2011).

[925] 17 U.S.C. § 106A(d)(1).

[926] 17 U.S.C. § 106A(d)(2). This is clearly a drafting error, as no public policy basis exists or has been suggested for giving greater rights to authors whose works were created before the effective date. The probable explanation is that the statute was drafted so that the rights of both groups would expire with the copyright, but that only the former section was amended when Congress decided to reduce the term to life of the author.

[927] 17 U.S.C. § 106A(e)(1).

[928] The Copyright Act of 1976, as amended, is codified in Chapters 1 through 8 of Title 17.

[929] Pub. L. No. 98-620, Title III, 98 Stat. 3347. *See* § 6E.

[930] Pub. L. No. 102-563, 106 Stat. 4237. *See* § 4J[3].

[931] Pub. L. No. 103-465, Title V, Subtitle A, § 512(a), 108 Stat. 4974. *See* § 4C[2][d].

Chapter 12 contains the anti-circumvention and copyright management information provisions of the Digital Millennium Copyright Act of 1998.[932]

Chapter 13 contains the Vessel Hull Design Protection Act, which was also enacted in the Digital Millennium Copyright Act of 1998.[933]

[9]   Compulsory Licenses

A compulsory license is "[a] permission to use intellectual property, compelled by the government in order to accomplish some political or social objective."[934]

> Compulsory licensing forces an intellectual property owner to allow others to use that property at a fee set by the government. The owner is not allowed to refuse to license or to negotiate voluntary license fees in a free market, but is compelled to license at a rate thought to be 'reasonable' by the government.[935]

United States intellectual property law rarely provides for compulsory licenses, but the 1976 Copyright Act, as amended, contains eight: (1) cable television retransmissions,[936] (2) ephemeral recordings to facilitate digital transmissions,[937] (3) digital audio transmissions of sound recordings,[938] (4) phonorecords of musical works, including digital phonorecord delivery,[939] (5) jukeboxes,[940] (6) noncommercial broadcasting,[941] (7) satellite retransmissions,[942] and (8) local-to-local satellite retransmissions.[943] In addition, the Audio Home Recording Act of 1992 requires manufacturers and importers of digital audio recording equipment to pay statutory "royalties" into a fund for the benefit of copyright owners.[944]

The 1976 Act established an independent agency, the Copyright Royalty Tribunal ("CRT"), with compulsory license rate-setting and fee collection and distribution responsibilities. From the beginning, however, the CRT was embroiled in a near-constant stream of litigation and criticism.[945] As a result, the Copyright Royalty Tribunal Reform Act of 1993 eliminated the CRT and transferred its

---

[932] Pub. L. No. 105-304, Title I, § 103(a), 112 Stat. 2863. *See* § 4J[4].

[933] Pub. L. No. 105-304, Title V, § 502, 112 Stat. 2905. *See* § 1[D][3][a].

[934] J. Thomas McCarthy, Desk Encyclopedia of Intellectual Property 51–52 (1991).

[935] *Id.* at 52.

[936] 17 U.S.C. § 111. *See* § 4G[4][b].

[937] 17 U.S.C. § 112(e). *See* § 4G[1][c].

[938] 17 U.S.C. § 114(d). *See* § 4G[6].

[939] 17 U.S.C. § 115. *See* § 4G[1][c].

[940] 17 U.S.C. §§ 116. *See* § 4G[4][c].

[941] 17 U.S.C. §§ 118. *See* § 4G[4][c].

[942] 17 U.S.C. § 119. *See* § 4G[4][b].

[943] 17 U.S.C. § 122. Uniquely, the local-to-local satellite license is royalty-free. *See* § 4G[4][b].

[944] *See* § 4J[3].

[945] *See, e.g.*, Recording Industry Ass'n of America v. Copyright Royalty Tribunal, 659 F.2d 252 (D.C. Cir. 1981); Recording Industry Ass'n of America v. Copyright Royalty Tribunal, 662 F.2d 1 (D.C. Cir. 1982); Amusement and Music Operators Ass'n v. Copyright Royalty Tribunal, 676 F.2d 1144 (7th Cir. 1982).

functions to *ad hoc* "Copyright Arbitration Royalty Panels," or CARPs. CARPs were convened from time to time by the Librarian of Congress, on the advice of the Register of Copyrights, to consider particular rates or resolve particular disputes over royalty distribution that could not be settled through private negotiation.

In 2003, however, the CARPs themselves came under fire after a controversial ratesetting proceeding that was partially rejected by the Librarian of Congress and later superseded by Congress itself. The criticism resulted in the Copyright Royalty and Distribution Reform Act of 2004, which replaced the CARPs with three full-time Copyright Royalty Judges ("CRJs").[946] The role of the CRJs is limited to fact-finding and rate determinations; they are required to request a decision from the Register of Copyrights on any "novel material question of substantive law."[947] The Register also may review and comment on the CRJs' resolution of any "material question of substantive law" (without regard to novelty), and the Register's interpretations of substantive law are binding on the CRJs in any subsequent proceedings.[948] Decisions of the CRJs are subject to judicial review in the U.S. Court of Appeals for the D.C. Circuit.[949]

§ 4H INFRINGEMENT

The Copyright Act provides little assistance in determining infringement. Section 501 defines infringement as the violation of "any of the exclusive rights of the copyright owner."[950] The House Report discusses infringement standards only briefly:

> *As under the present law*, a copyrighted work would be infringed by reproducing it in whole or in any substantial part, and by duplicating it exactly *or by imitation or simulation. Wide departures or variations* from the copyrighted work would still be an infringement as long as the author's "expression" rather than merely the author's "ideas" are taken.[951]

Accordingly, it has been left to the courts to define copyright infringement with more specificity.

To prove a claim of copyright infringement, the plaintiff must prove three elements: (1) that he or she is the owner of a valid copyright; (2) that the defendant's work was derived from (or "copied") the copyrighted work; and (3) that the

---

[946] 17 U.S.C. § 801 *et seq.* To comply with the Appointments Clause of the Constitution, the D.C. Circuit held that the CRJs must be removable without cause by the Librarian of Congress, thus rendering them "inferior officers" that need not be appointed by the President and confirmed by the Senate. *See* Intercollegiate Broadcasting System, Inc. v. Copyright Royalty Board, 684 F.3d 1332 (D.C. Cir. 2012).

[947] 17 U.S.C. § 802(f)(1)(B).

[948] 17 U.S.C. § 802(f)(1)(D).

[949] 17 U.S.C. § 803(d)(1).

[950] 17 U.S.C. § 501(a).

[951] H.R. Rep. No. 94-1476, at 61 (1976) (emphasis added). The idea/expression dichotomy is discussed at § 4C[3].

defendant's work is substantially similar to protected expression in the copyrighted work.[952]

Where it is clear that the plaintiff's work contains protected expression and that the defendant has copied the plaintiff's entire work verbatim, no extensive analysis of similarity is necessary, and the court will focus on which of the six exclusive rights are implicated, if any.[953] However, when the question is whether the defendant has prepared a derivative work based upon the plaintiff's work, then the above analysis is appropriate. Moreover, because the derivative work right overlaps with the other exclusive rights, the above analysis is also appropriate whenever the plaintiff alleges that the defendant has reproduced, distributed, publicly performed, or publicly displayed any work that is alleged to have been copied from or based upon the plaintiff's work, or to imitate or simulate it in any way.

The derivation requirement does not mean that copyright infringement must be knowing or willful.[954] Copyright is a strict liability offense, meaning that infringement may be entirely innocent. For example, a publisher or broadcaster infringes when it reproduces or transmits an infringing work, even it does so in good faith without knowledge of the infringement.[955] The Internet, however, is causing some courts to re-think this basic axiom of copyright law. Thus, some courts have held that when copying occurs by an automated technical process, such as an Internet retransmission, there must be "some element of volition or causation" to hold the Internet service provider directly liable for the reproduction.[956]

---

[952] *See* Armour v. Knowles, 512 F.3d 147, 152 (5th Cir. 2007). *Accord*, Zalewski v. Cicero Builder Dev., Inc., 794 F.3d 95, 100–01 (2d Cir. 2014). These elements are all found in the case law, although sometimes the elements are grouped or combined in different ways. *See* Feist Publications, Inc. v. Rural Telephone Service Co., 499 U.S. 340, 361 (1991) ("To establish infringement, two elements must be proven: (1) ownership of a valid copyright, and (2) copying of constituent elements of the work that are original."); Arnstein v. Porter, 154 F.2d 464, 468 (2d Cir. 1946) ("it is important to avoid confusing two separate elements essential to a plaintiff's case in such a suit: (a) that defendant copied from plaintiff's copyrighted work and (b) that the copying (assuming it to be proved) went so far as to constitute improper appropriation."); Laureyssens v. Idea Group, Inc., 964 F.2d 131, 139 (2d Cir. 1992) ("In order to establish a claim for copyright infringement, a plaintiff must show ownership of a valid copyright and the defendant's infringement by unauthorized copying."); *id.* at 140 ("A plaintiff must first show that his or her work was actually copied. . . . If actual copying is established, a plaintiff must then show that the copying amounts to an improper appropriation by demonstrating that substantial similarity to protected material exists between the two works."); Selle v. Gibb, 741 F.2d 896, 900 (7th Cir. 1984) ("In establishing a claim of copyright infringement . . . , the plaintiff must prove (1) ownership of the copyright in the complaining work; (2) originality of the work; (3) copying of the work by the defendant, and (4) a substantial degree of similarity between the two works.").

[953] *See* § 4G.

[954] Willfulness may affect the monetary remedy available to the copyright owner, see § 4K below, but it is not an element of an infringement case. *See* Buck v. Jewell-LaSalle Realty Co., 283 U.S. 191, 198 (1931) ("Intention to infringe is not essential under the act.").

[955] *See, e.g.,* DeAcosta v. Brown, 146 F.2d 408 (2d Cir. 1944).

[956] Religious Technology Center v. Netcom On-Line Communication Services, Inc., 907 F. Supp. 1361, 1370 (N.D. Cal. 1995). *See* § 4G[1][b].

[1]   Ownership of a Valid Copyright

To prevail in a copyright infringement action, the plaintiff must first show that he or she is the owner of a valid copyright.[957] This element, in turn, consists of five sub-elements. First, the work must be an original work of authorship that is fixed in a tangible medium of expression.[958] Second, the identity of the author must be shown, because the author is the initial owner of the copyright.[959] Third, if the work is published, either the author must be a citizen or permanent resident of the United States or a country with whom the U.S. has copyright treaty relations, or the work must have been first published in such a country.[960] Fourth, any statutory formalities that are required must have been complied with,[961] including registration if the work is a United States work.[962] Fifth, if the plaintiff is not the author, then the plaintiff must show that he or she obtained ownership of an exclusive right from the author.[963]

The plaintiff's task with respect to these five sub-elements is greatly simplified by section 410(c), which provides that a timely certificate of registration "shall constitute *prima facie* evidence of the validity of the copyright and of the facts stated in the certificate."[964] Thus, if the plaintiff has registered the work in a timely fashion, the plaintiff need only introduce the registration certificate into evidence to satisfy his or her burden of production on this element. If the work is registered but the plaintiff is not the registered owner, then the plaintiff "needs only to show the registration and evidence of his or her chain of title from the original copyright registrant to establish *prima facie* ownership."[965] The presumption of validity, however, is rebuttable; and if the defendant introduces evidence to rebut the presumption, then the burden of production shifts back to the plaintiff, who retains the ultimate burden of persuasion.[966]

---

[957] *See* Feist Publications, Inc. v. Rural Telephone Service Co., 499 U.S. 340, 361 (1991). *See also* 17 U.S.C. § 501(a) ("Anyone who violates any of the exclusive rights *of the copyright owner . . .*") (emphasis added); 17 U.S.C. § 501(b) ("The legal or beneficial owner of an exclusive right under a copyright is entitled . . . to institute an action for any infringement of that particular committed while he or she is the owner of it.").

[958] 17 U.S.C. § 102(a). *See* § 4C[1] (originality) and 4C[2] (fixation).

[959] 17 U.S.C. § 201. *See* § 4F[1].

[960] 17 U.S.C. § 104. *See* § 4C[6].

[961] *See* § 4D.

[962] 17 U.S.C. § 411(a).

[963] *See* § 4F[2].

[964] 17 U.S.C. § 410(c). A timely certificate of registration is one obtained "before or within five years after first publication of the work." *Id.* If the work is registered more than five years after first publication, then "[t]he evidentiary weight to be accorded the certificate . . . shall be within the discretion of the court." *Id.*

[965] Peer Int'l Corp. v. Latin American Music Corp., 161 F. Supp. 2d 38, 45 (D.P.R. 2001).

[966] *See* H.R. Rep. No. 94-1476, at 157 (1976); Ets-Hokin v. Skyy Spirits Inc., 225 F.3d 1068, 1076 (9th Cir. 2000) ("To rebut the presumption, an infringement defendant must simply offer some evidence or proof to dispute or deny the plaintiff's *prima facie* case"); Entertainment Research Group, Inc. v. Genesis Creative Group, Inc., 122 F.3d 1211, 1218 (9th Cir. 1998).

[2]   Derivation or Copying

To infringe, an accused work must have been derived or copied from the copyrighted work. An independently created work does not infringe, no matter how similar to the copyrighted work.[967] Likewise, if both works are similar because they copied from a common source, then the defendant's work does not infringe the plaintiff's.[968]

The copyright owner bears the initial burden of producing evidence on the issue of copying. The copyright owner may satisfy this burden by offering direct evidence of copying, such as testimony or an admission, or by offering circumstantial evidence of copying.[969] Copying may be inferred from evidence that the defendant had access to the copyrighted work, and that the two works are sufficiently similar that it is likely that one was copied from the other ("probative similarity").[970] Alternatively, sometimes the two works are so strikingly similar that copying may be inferred without any independent evidence of access ("striking similarity").[971]

Once the copyright owner satisfies his burden of producing evidence, the burden of production shifts to the defendant to offer some evidence rebutting the inference of copying, such as evidence of independent creation or common source.[972] If the defendant does so, then the trier of fact must decide whether or not the defendant copied the plaintiff's work. The burden of persuasion on the issue of copying remains with the plaintiff, who must prove copying by a preponderance of the

---

[967] *See* Zalewski v. Cicero Builder Dev., Inc., 794 F.3d 95, 101 (2d Cir. 2014) ("Independent creation is a defense to copyright infringement."); Ty, Inc. v. GMA Accessories, Inc., 132 F.3d 1167, 1169 (7th Cir. 1997) ("The Copyright Act forbids only copying; if independent creation results in an identical work, the creator of that work is free to sell it.").

[968] *Id.* at 1170 ("two works may be strikingly similar — may in fact be identical — not because one is copied from the other but because both are copies of the same thing in the public domain."); La Resolana Architects, P.A. v. Reno, Inc., 555 F.3d 1171, 1178 (10th Cir. 2009) ("One work does not violate the copyright in another simply because there is a similarity between the two if the similarity results from the fact that both works deal with the same subject or have the same common source.").

[969] *See* Johnson v. Gordon, 409 F.3d 12, 18 (1st Cir. 2005); Laureyssens v. Idea Group, Inc., 964 F.2d 131, 140 (2d Cir. 1992). Note that an admission of copying is not equivalent to admitting copyright infringement, because the copier may still contend that he copied only ideas and not copyrightable expression, or that the two works are not substantially similar. *See, e.g.*, Nihon Keizai Shimbun, Inc. v. Comline Business Data, Inc., 166 F.3d 65, 70 (2d Cir. 1999).

[970] *See* La Resolana Architects, P.A. v. Reno, Inc., 555 F.3d 1171, 1178 (10th Cir. 2009); Armour v. Knowles, 512 F.3d 147, 152 (5th Cir. 2007); Johnson v. Gordon, 409 F.3d 12, 18 (1st Cir. 2005); Laureyssens v. Idea Group, Inc., 964 F.2d 131, 140 (2d Cir. 1992).

[971] *See* Ferguson v. National Broadcasting Co., 584 F.2d 111, 113 (5th Cir. 1978); Lipton v. Nature Co., 71 F.3d 464, 471 (2d Cir. 1995). *See also* Bucklew v. Hawkins, Ash, Baptie & Co., 329 F.3d 923, 926 (7th Cir. 2003) ("[Some] cases say that access can be inferred from a sufficiently striking similarity between the two works, and that is true; but . . . it is more straightforward to say that in some cases proof of access isn't required.").

[972] *See* Armour v. Knowles, 512 F.3d 147, 152 (5th Cir. 2007); *see also* Original Appalachian Artworks, Inc. v. Toy Loft, Inc., 684 F.2d 821, 829 (11th Cir. 1982) ("Proof of access and substantial similarity raises only a presumption of copying which may be rebutted by the defendant with evidence of independent creation."); *accord*, Calhoun v. Lillenas Publishing, 298 F.3d 1228, 1232 (11th Cir. 2002); Keeler Brass Co. v. Continental Brass Co., 862 F.2d 1063, 1065 (4th Cir. 1988).

evidence.[973] In other words, the trier of fact must decide whether it is more likely than not that the defendant copied the plaintiff's work.

Copying may be subconscious rather than deliberate.[974] For example, in *Bright Tunes Music Co. v. Harrisongs Music, Ltd.*,[975] former Beatle George Harrison's 1970 song "My Sweet Lord" was held to have infringed plaintiff's song "He's So Fine," copyrighted in 1962. After a bench trial, the court found:

> I conclude that the composer, in seeking musical materials to clothe his thoughts, was working with various possibilities. As he tried this possibility and that, there came to the surface of his mind a particular combination that pleased him as being one he felt would be appealing to a prospective listener; in other words, that this combination of sounds would work. Why? Because his subconscious knew it already had worked in a song his conscious mind did not remember. . . . Did Harrison deliberately use the music of "He's So Fine"? I do not believe he did so deliberately. Nevertheless, it is clear that "My Sweet Lord" is the very same song as "He's So Fine" with different words, and Harrison had access to "He's So Fine." This is, under the law, infringement of copyright, and is no less so even though subconsciously accomplished.[976]

Similarly, in *Three Boys Music Corp. v. Bolton*, the Ninth Circuit affirmed a jury's finding that pop singer Michael Bolton's 1991 song "Love is a Wonderful Thing" infringed a 1964 song of the same name, saying "It is entirely plausible that two Connecticut teenagers obsessed with rhythm and blues music could remember an Isley Brothers' song that was played on the radio and television for a few weeks, and subconsciously copy it twenty years later."[977]

[a]   Access

Although a few courts have required evidence that the defendant "actually viewed" the plaintiff's work, most courts only require evidence that the defendant had a "reasonable opportunity" to view or hear the plaintiff's work.[978] In order for copying to have occurred, access must have existed before the defendant's work was created; if the evidence demonstrates that the defendant's work was created before the defendant had access to the plaintiff's work, then the defendant will be entitled

---

[973] *See* Keeler Brass Co. v. Continental Brass Co., 862 F.2d 1063, 1066 (4th Cir. 1988).

[974] *See* Sheldon v. Metro-Goldwyn Pictures Corp., 81 F.2d 49, 54 (2d Cir. 1936) ("unconscious plagiarism is actionable quite as much as deliberate."); Fred Fisher, Inc. v. Dillingham, 298 F. 145, 148 (S.D.N.Y. 1924) ("Once it appears that another has in fact used the copyright as the source of his production, he has invaded the author's rights. It is no excuse that in so doing his memory has played him a trick."). Both of these landmark opinions were written by Judge Learned Hand.

[975] 420 F. Supp. 177 (S.D.N.Y. 1976), *aff'd sub nom.*, ABKCO Music, Inc. v. Harrisongs Music, Ltd., 722 F.2d 988 (2d Cir. 1983).

[976] 420 F. Supp. at 180. On appeal, the Second Circuit rejected the argument that "it is unsound policy to permit a finding of copyright infringement on the basis of subconscious copying." 722 F.2d at 998.

[977] 212 F.3d 477, 484 (9th Cir. 2000).

[978] Three Boys Music Corp. v. Bolton, 212 F.3d 477, 482 (9th Cir. 2000). *See also* Bouchat v. Baltimore Ravens, Inc., 241 F.3d 350, 354–44 (4th Cir. 2001) ("mere opportunity to see the work").

to summary judgment.[979]

Access to a work may be inferred from a work's widespread dissemination in the market.[980] For example, in *Bright Tunes*, access was shown by evidence that the song "He's So Fine" was "No. 1 on the billboard charts for five weeks" in the United States, and that it was "one of the top hits in England" for seven weeks in 1963, when one of the Beatles' songs was No. 1.[981] However, in another case, annual sales of 2,000 t-shirts and evidence that the design was posted on a website, where it could not be seen without scrolling down, was held not to be sufficient to show "widespread dissemination."[982]

Alternatively, "[a] court may infer that the alleged infringer had a reasonable possibility of access if the author sent the copyrighted work to a third party intermediary who has a close relationship with the infringer."[983] For example, in *Bouchat v. Baltimore Ravens, Inc.*, the plaintiff introduced evidence that John Moag, chairman of the Maryland Stadium Authority, offered to deliver Bouchat's drawings to the Ravens; that Bouchat faxed a drawing of the proposed logo to the MSA; that such faxes were routinely delivered to Moag's law offices; that David Modell, the owner of the Ravens, had an office "within earshot" of Moag's; and that Modell communicated with the design team that developed the team's new logo. The majority held that this evidence was sufficient to permit the jury to find that the Ravens had access to Bouchat's drawings.[984] However, "there must be evidence of a reasonable possibility of access. Access must be more than a bare possibility and may not be inferred through speculation or conjecture."[985] Accordingly, many attempts at establishing access in this manner fall short.[986] Indeed, it has been held that "evidence of corporate receipt of unsolicited work is insufficient to raise a triable issue of access where there is no evidence of any connection between the individual recipients of the protected work and the [individual] alleged infring-

---

[979] *See, e.g.,* Fogerty v. MGM Group Holdings Corp., 379 F.3d 348, 352–53 (6th Cir. 2004) (evidence that defendants received plaintiff's song on February 4, 1999, after defendant completed its song on January 6, and that defendant's song did not change after that date); Grubb v. KMS Patriots, L.P., 88 F.3d 1, 4 (1st Cir. 1996) (uncontroverted evidence that designer created the defendant's logo 12 days before the plaintiff's logo was submitted).

[980] *ABKCO Music,* 722 F.2d at 998; Art Attacks Ink, LLC v. MGA Entertainment, Inc., 581 F.3d 1138, 1144 (9th Cir. 2009).

[981] 420 F. Supp. at 179. *See also* Cholvin v. B. & F. Music Co., 253 F.2d 102, 103–04 (7th Cir. 1958) (200,000 records of plaintiff's song were sold, and song was broadcast frequently on radio).

[982] *See Art Attacks Ink,* 581 F.3d at 1144–45. *See also* Rice v. Fox Broadcasting Co., 330 F.3d 1170, 1178 (9th Cir. 2003) (evidence that 17,000 copies of video were sold over a 13-year period was insufficient).

[983] Towler v. Sayles, 76 F.3d 579, 583 (4th Cir. 1996).

[984] 241 F.3d 350, 353–55 (4th Cir. 2001). The dissenting judge criticized the jury's verdict as "the result of an illogical and impermissible series of inferences." *Id.* at 362 (King, J., dissenting).

[985] Gaste v. Kaiserman, 863 F.2d 1061, 1066 (2d Cir. 1988). *Accord,* Three Boys Music Corp. v. Bolton, 212 F.3d 477, 482 (9th Cir. 2000).

[986] *See, e.g., Towler v. Sayles,* 76 F.3d at 582–83 (evidence that an employee agreed to forward screenplay to defendant, and that her supervisor worked at a company that distributed two of defendant's films, was insufficient to show access, where there was no evidence either had any contact with defendant during the relevant period).

ers."[987]

[b]   Probative Similarity

"Obviously, access does not entail copying. An eyewitness might have seen the defendant buy the copyrighted work; this would be proof of access, but not of copying."[988] Thus, evidence of access must be coupled with evidence of "similarities that are probative of copying,"[989] meaning that the two works are sufficiently similar that the trier of fact could reasonably infer that one was copied from the other.[990]

> When evaluating probative similarity, a court should compare the works in their entirety, including both protectable and unprotectable elements. This is appropriate because although the plaintiff must ultimately establish infringement by showing that the defendant copied a substantial amount of protectable elements, (*i.e.*, meet the "substantial similarity" standard), the fact that non-protectable elements were copied, although not a basis for liability, can be probative of whether protected elements were copied (*i.e.*, help establish probative similarity).[991]

Thus, for example, although a title cannot be protected by copyright, the fact that two works share the same title may be evidence of copying.[992] Similarly, the fact that the defendant's work contains a digital watermark or even the plaintiff's name may be compelling evidence of copying, but neither element by itself would constitute protectable expression.

Copying may also be demonstrated by the presence of similar "errors" in both works.[993] For example, mapmakers and publishers of directories often insert

---

[987] Jorgensen v. Epic/Sony Records, 351 F.3d 46, 48 (2d Cir. 2003). *See also* Jones v. Blige, 558 F.3d 485 (6th Cir. 2009) (demo CD was received by Universal Music, where Blige had a recording contract, but no evidence of any connection between employee who received it and Blige); Armour v. Knowles, 512 F.3d 147 (5th Cir. 2007) (only evidence of access was that demo tape was sent to a "mysterious and unidentified" associate of defendant).

[988] Ty, Inc. v. GMA Accessories, Inc., 132 F.3d 1167, 1170 (7th Cir. 1997).

[989] *See* La Resolana Architects, P.A. v. Reno, Inc., 555 F.3d 1171, 1178 (10th Cir. 2009); Armour v. Knowles, 512 F.3d 147, 152 (5th Cir. 2007); Johnson v. Gordon, 409 F.3d 12, 18 (1st Cir. 2005); Laureyssens v. Idea Group, Inc., 964 F.2d 131, 140 (2d Cir. 1992).

[990] *See, e.g.*, Johnson v. Gordon, 409 F.3d 12, 18 (1st Cir. 2005) ("a sufficient degree of similarity exists between the copyrighted work and the allegedly infringing work to give rise to an inference of actual copying."); Positive Black Talk, Inc. v. Cash Money Records, Inc., 394 F.3d 357, 369 (5th Cir. 2004) ("whether the similarities between the two works suggest that the later-created work was factually copied."). *See also* Alan Latman, *"Probative Similarity" as Proof of Copying: Toward Dispelling Some Myths in Copyright Infringement*, 90 Colum. L. Rev. 1187, 1214 (1990) ("such similarities between the works which, under all the circumstances, make independent creation unlikely.").

[991] Positive Black Talk, Inc. v. Cash Money Records, Inc., 394 F.3d 357, 370 n.9 (5th Cir. 2004) (citation omitted).

[992] Shaw v. Lindheim, 919 F.2d 1353, 1362 (9th Cir. 1990).

[993] *See* Bucklew v. Hawkins, Ash, Baptie & Co., 329 F.3d 923, 926–27 (7th Cir. 2003) (identifying residual errors in plaintiff's spreadsheet form that were duplicated without change in defendant's form); Eckes v. Card Prices Update, 736 F.2d 859, 863–64 (2d Cir. 1984).

fictitious listings in order to detect copying.[994] In one case, copying was shown by the fact that the defendant's sculpted female head had the same double hairline as the plaintiff's.[995] However, "while common errors may often be strong evidence of copying as a factual matter, they do not assist in determining what material is protectable under copyright law."[996]

"There is an inverse relationship between access and probative similarity such that the stronger the proof of similarity, the less the proof of access is required."[997] In an extreme case, the two works may be so strikingly similar that copying may be inferred without any independent evidence of access.[998] For "striking similarity" to suffice, "the similarities should appear in a sufficiently unique or complex context as to make it unlikely that both pieces were copied from a prior common source, or that the defendant was able to compose the accused work as a matter of independent creation."[999] Thus, in *Selle v. Gibb*, the court affirmed a judgment notwithstanding the verdict for the defendant on the issue of "striking similarity," despite the testimony of a music professor that the two songs could not have been written independently of one another, because there was no evidence addressing "the possibility of common source in earlier compositions" or "the relative complexity or uniqueness of the two compositions."[1000]

Conversely, the Ninth Circuit has held that "a lesser showing of similarity" is permissible "if there is a strong showing of access."[1001] While this may be true up to a point, "[t]he logical outcome of the claimed principle is" the nonsensical proposition "that proof of actual access will render a showing of similarities entirely

---

[994] *See, e.g.*, Feist Publications, Inc. v. Rural Telephone Service Co., 499 U.S. 340, 344 (1991) (noting the presence of four "fictitious listings that Rural had inserted into its directory to detect copying"). *See also* Rockford Map Publishers, Inc. v. Directory Service Co. of Colo., 768 F.2d 145, 147 (7th Cir. 1985) (map company inserted bogus middle initials in names of parcel owners that spelled out "Rockford Map Inc.").

[995] *See* Pivot Point Int'l, Inc. v. Charlene Prods., Inc., 372 F.3d 913, 915–16 (7th Cir. 2004).

[996] Gates Rubber Co. v. Bando Chemical Industries Ltd., 9 F.3d 823, 845 (10th Cir. 1993).

[997] Positive Black Talk, Inc. v. Cash Money Records, Inc., 394 F.3d 357, 371 (5th Cir. 2004); Jorgensen v. Epic/Sony Records, 351 F.3d 46, 56 (2d Cir. 2003); *see also* Ellis v. Diffie, 177 F.3d 503, 506 (6th Cir. 1999) ("the stronger the similarity between the two works in question, the less compelling the proof of access needs to be.").

[998] *See* Ferguson v. National Broadcasting Co., 584 F.2d 111, 113 (5th Cir. 1978) ("If the two works are so strikingly similar as to preclude the possibility of independent creation, 'copying' may be proved without a showing of access"); Lipton v. Nature Co., 71 F.3d 464, 471 (2d Cir. 1995) (same). *See also* Bucklew v. Hawkins, Ash, Baptie & Co., 329 F.3d 923, 926 (7th Cir. 2003) ("[Some] cases say that access can be inferred from a sufficiently striking similarity between the two works, and that is true; but . . . it is more straightforward to say that in some cases proof of access isn't required.").

[999] Selle v. Gibb, 741 F.2d 896, 904 (7th Cir. 1984); *see also* La Resolana Architects, P.A. v. Reno, Inc., 555 F.3d 1171, 1178 (10th Cir. 2009); Arnstein v. Porter, 154 F.2d 464, 468 (2d Cir. 1946) ("If evidence of access is absent, the similarities must be so striking as to preclude the possibility that plaintiff and defendant independently arrived at the same result.").

[1000] 741 F.2d at 905. *See also* Benson v. Coca-Cola Co., 795 F.2d 973, 975 n.2 (11th Cir. 1986) ("An opinion establishing striking similarity should address the uniqueness or complexity of the protected work as it bears on the likelihood of copying.").

[1001] *See* Three Boys Music Corp. v. Bolton, 212 F.3d 477, 486 (9th Cir. 2000).

unnecessary."[1002] Thus, it bears repeating that "[n]o amount of proof of access will suffice to show copying if there are no similarities."[1003]

It should be noted that many courts regularly confuse or conflate the second and third elements of infringement, asking only whether the plaintiff has demonstrated "copying" by showing "access and substantial similarity of protected expression." It is true that similarities as to protected expression may be used as evidence of copying as well. However, copying may also be demonstrated by direct evidence, or by non-actionable similarities involving unprotected expression. For that reason, distinguishing between "probative similarity" as evidence of copying and "substantial similarity of protected expression" as the standard for infringement is preferable,[1004] and this terminology has increasingly been adopted by the courts.[1005]

[3]   Substantial Similarity

"Assuming that adequate proof is made of copying, that is not enough; for there can be 'permissible copying,' copying which is not illicit."[1006] Thus, in addition to factual copying, the plaintiff must also prove that the copying was impermissible both as to type and to amount.[1007]

First, the plaintiff must demonstrate that what the defendant copied from the plaintiff's work was protected expression. Because copyright does not protect facts or ideas, anyone can copy facts or ideas from a copyrighted work.[1008] Similarly, because copyright protects only original expression,[1009] anyone can copy public domain material that has been incorporated into the plaintiff's work,[1010] or any

---

[1002] Arc Music Corp. v. Lee, 296 F.2d 186, 187 (2d Cir. 1961).

[1003] Wickham v. Knoxville Int'l Energy Exposition, Inc., 739 F.2d 1094, 1097 (6th Cir. 1984). *See also* Arnstein v. Porter, 154 F.2d 464, 468 (2d Cir. 1946) ("Of course, if there are no similarities, no amount of evidence of access will suffice to prove copying.").

[1004] *See* Alan Latman, *"Probative Similarity" as Proof of Copying: Toward Dispelling Some Myths in Copyright Infringement*, 90 COLUM. L. REV. 1187 (1990); Laureyssens v. Idea Group, Inc., 964 F.2d 131, 139–40 (2d Cir. 1992).

[1005] *See, e.g.*, Zalewski v. Cicero Builder Dev., Inc., 794 F.3d 95, 101 (2d Cir. 2014); La Resolana Architects, P.A. v. Reno, Inc., 555 F.3d 1171, 1178 (10th Cir. 2009); Armour v. Knowles, 512 F.3d 147, 152 (5th Cir. 2007); Johnson v. Gordon, 409 F.3d 12, 18 (1st Cir. 2005).

[1006] Arnstein v. Porter, 154 F.2d 464, 472 (2d Cir. 1946). *See also* Feist Publications, Inc. v. Rural Telephone Service Co., 499 U.S. 340, 361 (1991) ("Not all copying, however, is copyright infringement.").

[1007] *See* Ringgold v. Black Entertainment Television, Inc., 126 F.3d 70, 75 (2d Cir. 1997) ("substantial similarity requires that the copying is quantitatively and qualitatively sufficient to support the legal conclusion that infringement (actionable copying) has occurred. The qualitative component concerns the copying of expression, rather than ideas. . . . The quantitative component generally concerns the amount of the copyrighted work that is copied, a consideration that is especially pertinent to exact copying.").

[1008] *See* § 4C[1][c].

[1009] *See* § 4C[[1][a].

[1010] Works can enter the public domain after expiration of the copyright, *see* § 4E[1], or for failure to renew pre-1978 copyrights, *see* § 4E[2], or for failure to comply with other formalities, such as publication with proper copyright notice before March 1, 1989, *see* § 4D. Works may also be categorically ineligible for copyright, such as U.S. Government works, *see* § 4C[5], or works published in countries

other ideas or expression that did not originate with the author.[1011]

Second, the plaintiff must demonstrate that the intended audience for the two works will deem the protected expression in the two works to be "substantially similar." "The fundamental question is whether, having seen, heard, read, or otherwise experienced the defendant's work, the relevant audience for the plaintiff's work would be less interested in experiencing the plaintiff's work. *De minimis* takings do not interfere with the plaintiff's market and do not infringe his or her copyright."[1012]

A defendant may produce a substantially similar work in two ways. First, the defendant may copy verbatim an impermissibly large portion of the plaintiff's work.[1013] This is what Nimmer calls "fragmented literal similarity," or what Leaffer calls "verbatim similarity."[1014] However, copyright "cannot be limited literally to the text, else a plagiarist would escape by immaterial variation."[1015] Thus, non-literal copying is actionable if the defendant copies the overall pattern of a work, including the plaintiff's "selection and arrangement" of otherwise unprotected facts, plot elements, or other contents.[1016] This is what Nimmer calls "comprehensive nonliteral similarity," or what Leaffer calls "pattern similarity."[1017] As this nomenclature suggests, substantial similarity does *not* include "fragmented nonliteral similarity," in which there are "random similarities scattered throughout the works," but the overall structure, pattern or arrangement of elements is not similar.[1018]

---

with whom the U.S. does not have copyright relations, see § 4C[6]. Be aware, however, that certain works of foreign origin that were previously in the public domain have had their copyrights restored by Congress. *See* § 4E[3].

[1011] *Cf.* Feist Publications, Inc. v. Rural Telephone Service Co., 499 U.S. 340, 361 (1991) (characterizing infringement as "copying of constituent elements of the work that are original.").

[1012] CRAIG JOYCE, MARSHALL LEAFFER, PETER JASZI, TYLER OCHOA & MICHAEL CARROLL, COPYRIGHT LAW 652 (9th ed. 2013). *See* Arnstein v. Porter, 154 F.2d 464, 473 (2d Cir. 1946) ("The question . . . is whether defendant took from plaintiff's works so much of what is pleasing to . . . the audience for whom such [works are] composed").

[1013] *See* Nichols v. Universal Pictures Corp., 45 F.2d 119, 121 (2d Cir. 1930) ("When plays are concerned, the plagiarist may excise a separate scene or he may appropriate part of the dialogue. Then the question is whether the part so taken is 'substantial,' and therefore not a 'fair use' of the copyrighted work.").

[1014] NIMMER ON COPYRIGHT, § 13.03[A][2] (2010); MARSHALL LEAFFER, UNDERSTANDING COPYRIGHT LAW 425 (5th ed. 2010).

[1015] Nichols v. Universal Pictures Corp., 45 F.2d 119, 121 (2d Cir. 1930).

[1016] *See* Feist Publications, Inc. v. Rural Telephone Service Co., 499 U.S. 340, 358, 362 (1991) (original "selection, coordination, or arrangement" of unprotected facts is protected); Metcalf v. Bochco, 294 F.3d 1069, 1074 (9th Cir. 2002) ("The particular sequence in which an author strings a significant number of unprotectable elements can itself be a protectable element."); *Nichols*, 45 F.2d at 121 (defendant may infringe by taking "an abstract of the whole," including "the characters and sequence of incident").

[1017] NIMMER ON COPYRIGHT, § 13.03[A][1] (2010); MARSHALL LEAFFER, UNDERSTANDING COPYRIGHT LAW 425–27 (5th ed. 2010). Nimmer's terminology has been adopted by some courts. *See, e.g.*, Palmer v. Braun, 287 F.3d 1325, 1330 (11th Cir. 2002); Warner Bros. v. American Broadcasting Cos., 720 F.2d 231, 240 (2d Cir. 1983).

[1018] *See* Litchfield v. Spielberg, 736 F.2d 1352, 1356 (9th Cir. 1984) (also cautioning that "lists of similarities" are "inherently subjective and unreliable"); Herzog v. Castle Rock Entertainment, 193 F.3d 1241, 1257 (11th Cir. 1999).

[a]   Protected Expression

[i]   Dissection

Because copyright protects only original expression and does not protect ideas, there are many elements of a copyrighted work that may freely be copied. One court listed five categories of unprotected expression: "matters of historical or contemporary fact"; "material traceable to common sources, the public domain, or folk custom"; "*scènes à faire*"; "clichéd language, metaphors and the very words of which the language is constructed"; and "theme or setting."[1019] Accordingly, some courts have found it useful to analyze the plaintiff's work to determine which elements, if any, are protected by copyright, and to consider only those elements in comparing the two works for substantial similarity. In other words, these courts subtract or exclude any unprotected elements in comparing the two works.[1020] This is known as the "subtractive" approach, or "analytic dissection" of the plaintiff's work.

However, "in distinguishing between themes, facts, and *scènes à faire* on the one hand, and copyrightable expression on the other, courts may lose sight of the forest for the trees."[1021] Although individual elements of a copyrighted work may be unprotectable, the selection and arrangement of those elements may be protected.[1022] Thus, some courts have expressed the opinion that "analytic dissection" of the plaintiff's work is inappropriate, and that the two works should instead be compared as a whole to determine if they have the same "total concept and feel."[1023] Thus turn of phrase is particularly unhelpful, because a "concept" is not protected by copyright,[1024] and the "feel" or mood of a work is unacceptably vague,[1025] and it is also unprotectable to the extent it results from a similar

---

[1019] Alexander v. Haley, 460 F. Supp. 40, 44–46 (S.D.N.Y. 1978). Facts, common sources, the public domain, folk custom, words and metaphors are excluded for lack of originality. *See* § 4C[1]. Theme, setting, and *scènes à faire* are excluded by the idea/expression dichotomy. *See* § 4C[3].

[1020] *See, e.g.*, Zalewski v. Cicero Builder Dev. Co., 754 F.3d 95, 102–03, 105–06 (2d Cir. 2014); Harney v. Sony Pictures Television, Inc., 704 F.3d 173, 179–80 (1st Cir. 2013); Blehm v. Jacobs, 702 F.3d 1193, 1200 (10th Cir. 2012); Funky Films, Inc. v. Time Warner Ent'mt Co., 462 F.3d 1072, 1077 (9th Cir. 2006).

[1021] Hoehling v. Universal City Studios, Inc., 618 F.2d 972, 979 (2d Cir. 1980).

[1022] *See, e.g.*, Metcalf v. Bochco, 294 F.3d 1069, 1074 (9th Cir. 2002) ("The particular sequence in which an author strings a significant number of unprotectable elements can itself be a protectable element."); Warner Bros., Inc. v. American Broadcasting Cos., 720 F.2d 231, 243 (2d Cir. 1983) (individual elements, although perhaps not protectible in isolation, contribute to "the expressive aspect of the combination").

[1023] *See, e.g.* Benay v. Warner Bros. Entertainment, Inc., 607 F.3d 620, 624 (9th Cir. 2010); Taylor Corp. v. Four Seasons Greetings, LLC, 315 F.3d 1039, 1043 (8th Cir. 2003); Cavalier v. Random House, Inc., 297 F.3d 815 (9th Cir. 2002); Sid & Marty Krofft Television Prods., Inc. v. McDonald's Corp., 562 F.2d 1157, 1164 (9th Cir. 1977) (disapproving dissection), *id.* at 1167 (concluding the two works share a "total concept and feel").

[1024] *See* 17 U.S.C. § 102(b) ("In no case does copyright protection for an original work of authorship extend to any idea, . . . *concept*, principle, or discovery.") (emphasis added); Tufenkian Import/Export Ventures, Inc. v. Einstein Moomjy, Inc., 338 F.3d 127, 134 (2d Cir. 2003) ("one may wonder whether a copyright doctrine whose aspiration is to protect a work's 'concept' could end up erroneously protecting 'ideas.' ").

[1025] *See Tufenkian*, 338 F.3d at 134 ("Some commentators have worried that the 'total concept and

style.[1026] Nonetheless, many courts continue to employ the formula. However, although the "totality" test was initially used to hold that two works were substantially similar because of a similar selection and arrangement,[1027] it is used equally often in holding that two works are so *dissimilar* in "total concept and feel" that summary judgment may be granted for the defendant.[1028]

Many courts have stated that, while dissection and expert testimony are appropriate in determining probative similarity or copying, both are inappropriate in determining substantial similarity, which is a question of ultimate fact for the jury.[1029] However, courts agree that expert testimony may be admitted in assessing substantial similarity when "specialized expertise" is needed, as with computer programs.[1030] In addition, even courts that generally disapprove of dissection at the latter stage agree that dissection is sometimes appropriate in deciding whether only unprotected expression was copied.[1031] Thus, the disagreement concerning dissection may boil down to whether the dissection should occur *before* comparison for similarities, as the subtractive approach would suggest, or *after* such comparison, as the totality approach would suggest.

---

feel' standard may 'invite[ ] an abdication of analysis' because 'feel' can seem a 'wholly amorphous referent.' ").

[1026] *See, e.g.*, Mattel, Inc. v. MGA Entertainment, Inc., 616 F.3d 904, 916 (9th Cir. 2010) (disapproving district court's holding that two lines of dolls were substantially similar because they shared an "aggressive, contemporary, youthful style"); Trek Leasing, Inc. v. U.S., 66 Fed. Cl. 8, 13 (2005) ("The hallmarks of a popular architectural style, as such, are not protectable"); Jewelry 10, Inc. v. Elegance Trading Co., 1991 U.S. Dist. LEXIS 9988, at 11 (S.D.N.Y. July 22, 1991) ("a painter who develops a style or technique, such as the rendition of perspective, impressionism, pointillism, fauve coloring, cubism, abstraction, psychedelic colors, minimalism, etc., cannot prevent others from adopting those ideas in their work.").

[1027] *See* Roth Greeting Cards v. United Card Co., 429 F.2d 1106, 1110 (9th Cir. 1970) (although the textual material in plaintiff's greeting cards was in the public domain and was not copyrightable, and the artwork was not infringed, "the combination of art work conveying a particular mood with a particular message, and the arrangement of the words on the [defendant's] greeting card[s] are substantially the same as in Roth's cards.").

[1028] *See, e.g.*, Williams v. Crichton, 84 F.3d 581 (2d Cir. 1996) (novel and movie "Jurassic Park" were not substantially similar to plaintiff's "Dinosaur World" children's books).

[1029] *See, e.g.*, Arnstein v. Porter, 154 F.2d 464, 468 (2d Cir. 1946) ("the trier of the facts must determine whether the similarities are sufficient to prove *copying*. On this issue, analysis (dissection) is relevant, and the testimony of experts may be received. . . . If copying is established, then only does there arise the second issue, that of *illicit copying* (unlawful appropriation). . . . [O]n that issue, 'dissection' and expert testimony are irrelevant."); Sid & Marty Krofft Television Prods., Inc. v. McDonald's Corp., 562 F.2d 1157, 1164 (9th Cir. 1977).

[1030] *See, e.g.*, Computer Associates Int'l, Inc. v. Altai, Inc., 982 F.2d 693, 719 (2d Cir. 1992); Whelan Assocs. v. Jaslow Dental Laboratory, Inc., 797 F.2d 1222, 1232–33 (3d Cir. 1986). *See also* Kohus v. Mariol, 328 F.3d 848, 857–58 (6th Cir. 2003) (technical drawings); Dawson v. Hinshaw Music, Inc., 905 F.2d 731, 736 (4th Cir. 1990) (choral arrangements of public domain melody). Of course, the reports of such experts must meet the usual standards for admissibility. *See, e.g.*, R.C. Olmstead, Inc. v. CU Interface, LLC, 606 F.3d 262, 270–72 (6th Cir. 2010) (affirming exclusion of expert's report in a computer software case).

[1031] *See, e.g.*, Apple Computer, Inc. v. Microsoft, Inc., 35 F.3d 1435, 1443 (9th Cir. 1994); Gates Rubber Co. v. Bando Chemical Industries, Ltd., 9 F.3d 823, 832 & n.7, 835 (10th Cir. 1993); Shaw v. Lindheim, 919 F.2d 1353, 1356–57 (9th Cir. 1990) (redefining admissibility of expert testimony to include "objective analysis" of expression). *See also* Corwin v. Walt Disney Co., 475 F.3d 1239, 1250–51 (11th Cir. 2007) (expert reports may be excluded when they rely only on similarity of concepts and ideas rather than protected expression).

While both tests are objectionable if applied mechanically, both are suitable if they are applied with sensitivity toward their limitations. Thus, when dissection is used, a court should be careful to consider protected selection and arrangement in addition to individual elements.[1032] Likewise, when totality is used, the court must "take into account that the copyright laws preclude appropriation of only those elements of the work that are protected by the copyright."[1033]

[ii]   Distinguishing Idea from Expression

"The distinction between an idea and its expression is an elusive one."[1034] As Learned Hand observed, "[o]bviously, no principle can be stated as to when an imitator has gone beyond copying the 'idea,' and has borrowed its 'expression.' Decisions must therefore inevitably be ad hoc."[1035] Nonetheless, in *Nichols v. Universal Pictures Corp.*, Judge Hand supplied the most well-known approach to thinking about the problem:

> Upon any work, and especially upon a play, a great number of patterns of increasing generality will fit equally well, as more and more of the incident is left out. The last may perhaps be no more than the most general statement of what the play is about, and at times might consist only of its title; but there is a point in this series of abstractions where they are no longer protected, since otherwise the playwright could prevent the use of his "ideas," to which, apart from their expression, his property is never extended.[1036]

Although some courts and commentators treat Hand's statement as a "test" for drawing the line between substantial similarity of expression and mere similarity of ideas, Judge Hand himself recognized that the so-called "test" simply stated the problem to be analyzed without resolving it.[1037] As Judge Posner has elaborated:

> [A]ll depends on the level of abstraction at which the court conceives the interest protected by the copyright. If the court chooses a low level (say, only the words the first author employed), then a copier may take the plot, exposition, and all other original material, even though these may be the most important ingredients of the first author's contribution. As a practical matter this would mean that anyone could produce the work in a new medium without compensating the original author, despite the statute's grant to the author of the privilege to make "derivative works." If on the

---

[1032] *See, e.g.,* Coquico, Inc. v. Rodriguez-Miranda, 562 F.3d 62, 68 (1st Cir. 2009); Tufenkian Import/Export Ventures, Inc. v. Einstein Moomjy, Inc., 338 F.3d 127, 134–35 (2d Cir. 2003).

[1033] Atari, Inc. v. North American Philips Consumer Electronics Corp., 672 F.2d 607, 614 (7th Cir. 1983).

[1034] Williams v. Crichton, 84 F.3d 581, 587–88 (2d Cir. 1996).

[1035] Peter Pan Fabrics, Inc. v. Martin Weiner Corp., 274 F.2d 487, 489 (2d Cir. 1960).

[1036] 45 F.2d 119, 121 (2d Cir. 1930).

[1037] *Id.* at 121 ("Nobody has ever been able to fix that boundary, and nobody ever can."); *id.* at 122 ("while we are as aware as any one that the line, wherever it is drawn, will seem arbitrary, that is no excuse for not drawing it."). *See also* Nash v. CBS, Inc., 899 F.2d 1537, 1540 (7th Cir. 1990) ("Sometimes called the 'abstractions test,' Hand's insight is not a 'test' at all. It is a clever way to pose the difficulties that require courts to avoid either extreme of the continuum of generality.").

other hand the court should select a high level of abstraction, the first author may claim protection for whole genres of work ("the romantic novel" or, more modestly, any story involving doomed young lovers from warring clans, so that a copyright on *Romeo and Juliet* would cover *West Side Story* too). Even a less sweeping degree of abstraction creates a risk of giving copyright protection to "the idea" although the statute protects only "expression."[1038]

Thus, "[w]hat is basically at stake is the extent of the copyright owner's monopoly — from how large an area of activity did Congress intend to allow the copyright owner to exclude others?"[1039]

In *Nichols*, the plaintiff alleged that her play, "Abie's Irish Rose," was infringed by defendant's movie "The Cohens and the Kellys." After describing the two works in great detail, Hand found that "[t]he only matter common to the two is a quarrel between a Jewish and an Irish father, the marriage of their children, the birth of grandchildren and a reconciliation," and concluded:

> If the defendant took so much from the plaintiff, it may well have been because her amazing success seemed to prove that this was a subject of enduring popularity. Even so, granting that the plaintiff's play was wholly original, . . . there is no monopoly in such a background. Though the plaintiff discovered the vein, she could not keep it to herself; so defined, the theme was too generalized an abstraction from what she wrote. It was only a part of her "ideas."[1040]

By contrast, in *Sheldon v. Metro-Goldwyn Pictures Corp.*, Judge Hand concluded that the movie "Letty Lynton" infringed the copyrighted play "Dishonored Lady," even though both works were based in part on the same historical incident.[1041] Thus, if two works are similar only when described at a "high" level of abstraction, there is no substantial similarity of expression;[1042] but if they are similar when described with much greater specificity, then a court may conclude that protected expression was copied.[1043]

[1038] *Nash*, 899 F.2d at 1540. In *Nash*, the court concluded that a TV show that copied the plaintiff's theory that John Dillinger survived when the FBI killed a "look-alike" in Chicago in 1934 did not infringe, because it "use[d] Nash's analysis of history but none of his expression." *Id.* at 1543.

[1039] Herbert Rosenthal Jewelry Corp. v. Kalpakian, 446 F.2d 738, 742 (9th Cir. 1971). *See also* Blehm v. Jacobs, 702 F.3d 1193, 1208 (10th Cir. 2012) ("we must be careful not to grant Mr. Blehm a monopoly over all [stick] figures . . . representing the human form.").

[1040] 45 F.2d at 122. *See also id.* ("A comedy based upon conflicts between Irish and Jews, into which the marriage of their children enters, is no more susceptible of copyright than the outline of *Romeo and Juliet*.").

[1041] 81 F.2d 49, 55–56 (2d Cir. 1936), *on appeal after remand*, 106 F.2d 45 (2d Cir. 1939), *aff'd*, 309 U.S. 390 (1940).

[1042] *See, e.g.*, Oravec v. Sunny Isles Luxury Ventures, L.C., 527 F.3d 1218, 1227 (11th Cir. 2008) (while two building designs "have a number of features in common, those elements are similar only at the broadest level of generality."); Funky Films, Inc. v. Time Warner Entertainment Co., 462 F.3d 1072, 1078 (9th Cir. 2006) ("The 'prodigal son' characters of the two works, while similar at the abstract level, are markedly different in the two scripts.").

[1043] *See* Cavalier v. Random House, Inc., 297 F.3d 815, 824–27 (9th Cir. 2002) (finding triable issue of

Although "originality" is usually held to be a question of fact for the jury,[1044] courts have recognized that the task of separating ideas from expression is "far more heavily loaded with public policy implications than most other standards more commonly used in law," and is therefore a question of law for the court.[1045]

[iii]   Abstraction-Filtration-Comparison

Most early computer software copyright cases involved either verbatim or near-literal copying of code.[1046] Later cases dealt with allegations of infringement through nonliteral copying of a program's "structure, sequence, and organization," or of its "look and feel," including its user interface. These cases probe the limits of copyright protection for computer programs. Copying of the functional aspects or any "idea, procedure, process, system, [or] method of operation" in a computer program is not copyright infringement,[1047] and protection for functional features and processes is available, if at all, only under the patent system.[1048]

Initially, however, some courts departed from these principles and accorded broad protection to computer programs. Because computer programs meet the definition of a "literary work,"[1049] these courts reasoned that since literary works in general enjoy broad protection against non-literal copying, computer programs should likewise enjoy broad protection.[1050] For example, in *Whelan Associates, Inc. v. Jaslow Dental Laboratory, Inc.*, the plaintiff was commissioned by the defendant to write a computer program to handle the bookkeeping and administrative tasks for a dental laboratory. Later, the defendant developed a program to perform essentially the same operations on a personal computer. The court held that, under *Baker v. Selden*, "the purpose or function of a utilitarian work [is] the work's idea, and everything that is not necessary to that purpose or function [is] part of the expression of the idea."[1051] Applying this standard, it found that "the idea [of the plaintiff's program" is the efficient organization of a dental laboratory," and that "[b]ecause there are a variety of program structures through which that idea can be expressed, the structure is not a necessary incident to that

---

fact as to similarity of two pairs of illustrations in children's books, but not as to the books in their entirety). *See also* Warner Bros. Inc. v. American Broadcasting Cos., 654 F.2d 204, 208 (2d Cir. 1981) ("in determining whether two such works are so substantially similar as to reveal an infringement of one by the other, courts must decide whether the similarities shared by the works are something more than mere generalized ideas or themes.").

[1044] *See, e.g.*, CMM Cable Rep., Inc. v. Ocean Coast Properties, Inc., 97 F.3d 1504, 1517 (1st Cir. 2006).

[1045] Lotus Development Corp. v. Borland Int'l, Inc., 788 F. Supp. 78, 95–96 (D. Mass. 1992). *See also* Intervest Construction, Inc. v. Canterbury Estate Homes, Inc., 554 F.3d 914, 920 (11th Cir. 2008).

[1046] *See* § 4C[4][a][i](b).

[1047] 17 U.S.C. § 102(b). *See* § 4C[2].

[1048] For patent protection for computer programs, see § 2C[1][f].

[1049] 17 U.S.C. § 101 (" 'Literary works' are works . . . expressed in words, numbers, or other verbal or numerical symbols or indicia").

[1050] *See, e.g.*, Whelan Assocs., Inc. v. Jaslow Dental Laboratory, Inc., 797 F.2d 1222, 1234 (3d Cir. 1986) ("By analogy to other literary works, it would . . . appear that the copyrights of computer programs can be infringed even absent copying of the literal elements of the program.").

[1051] *Id.* at 1236.

idea."[1052] Accordingly, it granted broad protection to the program's "structure, sequence, and organization,"[1053] finding infringement based on expert testimony concerning the two programs' file structures,[1054] screen outputs, and subroutines.[1055]

Whelan's approach to determining substantial similarity of computer programs has been rejected in other circuits. In the leading case, *Computer Associates Int'l, Inc. v. Altai, Inc.*, the court said:

> [*Whelan's*] standard for distinguishing idea from expression has been widely criticized for being conceptually overbroad. . . . "[T]he crucial flaw in [*Whelan's*] reasoning is that it assumes that only one 'idea,' in copyright law terms, underlies any computer program, and that once a separable idea can be identified, everything else must be expression." 3 Nimmer § 13.03(F). . . . [A] computer program's ultimate function or purpose is the composite result of interacting subroutines. Since each subroutine is itself a program, and thus, may be said to have its own "idea," *Whelan's* general formulation that a program's overall purpose equates with the program's idea is descriptively inadequate.[1056]

Instead, the court in *Computer Associates* set forth its own three-step test for assessing substantial similarity in computer programs. First, "a court should dissect the allegedly copied program's structure and isolate each level of abstraction contained within it."[1057] The court explained:

> At the lowest level of abstraction, a computer program may be thought of in its entirety as a set of individual instructions organized into a hierarchy of modules. At a higher level of abstraction, the instructions in the lowest-level modules may be replaced conceptually by the functions of those modules. At progressively higher levels of abstraction, the functions of higher-level modules conceptually replace the implementations of those modules in terms of lower-level modules and instructions, until finally, one is left with nothing but the ultimate function of the program.[1058]

[1052] *Id.* at 1240.

[1053] *Id.* at 1248. The court stated that "We use the terms 'structure,' 'sequence,' and 'organization' interchangeably when referring to computer programs, and we intend them to be synonymous in this opinion." *Id.* at 1225 n.1.

[1054] Jaslow argued that file structures are irrelevant to copyright infringement because they are analogous to blank forms, which are not copyrightable, see § 4C[2][b], but the court disagreed, citing cases upholding copyright in forms that "are sufficiently innovative that their arrangement of information is itself informative." 797 F.2d at 1242.

[1055] Despite characterizing the case as one of "comprehensive non-literal similarity," 797 F.2d at 1234 n.26, the court rejected the defendant's argument that substantial similarity of the programs' *structures* cannot be established by a comparison of only a small fraction of the two works (five subroutines), saying "the court must make a qualitative, not quantitative, judgment about the character of the work as a whole and the importance of the substantially similar portions of the work." 797 F.2d at 1245.

[1056] 982 F.2d 693, 705 (2d Cir. 1992).

[1057] *Id.* at 707.

[1058] *Id., quoting* Steven R. Englund, *Idea, Process, or Protected Expression?: Determining the Scope of Copyright Protection of the Structure of Computer Programs*, 88 MICH. L. REV. 866, 897–98 (1990).

Next, the court should "examin[e] the structural components at each level of abstraction to determine whether their particular inclusion at that level was 'idea' or was dictated by considerations of efficiency, so as to be necessarily incidental to that idea; required by factors external to the program itself; or taken from the public domain and hence is nonprotectable expression."[1059] More specifically, under the merger doctrine and the doctrine of *scènes à faire*, the court should filter out design choices that were "circumscribed by extrinsic considerations such as (1) the mechanical specifications of the computer on which a particular program is intended to run; (2) compatibility requirements of other programs with which a program is designed to operate in conjunction; (3) computer manufacturers' design standards; (4) demands of the industry being serviced; and (5) widely accepted programming practices within the computer industry."[1060]

Finally, "[o]nce a court has sifted out all elements of the allegedly infringed program which are 'ideas' or are dictated by efficiency or external factors, or taken from the public domain, there may remain a core of protectable expression. . . . At this point, the court's substantial similarity inquiry focuses on whether the defendant copied any aspect of this protected expression, as well as an assessment of the copied portion's relative importance with respect to the plaintiff's overall program."[1061]

Altai's three-step "abstraction-filtration-comparison" analysis apparently satisfied a previously unmet need. Since *Altai* was decided, each circuit newly confronting the choice between the *Whelan* and *Altai* approaches has adopted the latter.[1062] Only the Third Circuit stubbornly clings to *Whelan*, rejecting an argument based on *Altai* that interoperability justifies a certain amount of copying.[1063] Moreover, although *Altai* itself was a case involving nonliteral copying, its test has been extended by some courts to encompass the copying of literal code as well.[1064] In addition, one panel of the Tenth Circuit has stated that "we see no reason to limit the abstraction-filtration-comparison approach to cases involving computer programs."[1065]

[1059] 982 F.2d at 707.

[1060] *Id.* at 709–10.

[1061] *Id.* at 710.

[1062] *See, e.g.*, Gates Rubber Co. v. Bando Chemical Industries, Ltd., 9 F.3d 823 (10th Cir. 1993); Apple Computer, Inc. v. Microsoft Corp., 35 F.3d 1435 (9th Cir. 1994) (similar standard "differently articulated"); Engineering Dynamics, Inc., v. Structural Software, Inc., 26 F.3d 1335 (5th Cir. 1994); MiTek Holdings, Inc. v. Arce Engineering Co., 89 F.3d 1548 (11th Cir. 1996); Mitel, Inc. v. Iqtel, Inc., 124 F.3d 1366 (10th Cir. 1997); Computer Management Assistance Co. v. Robert F. DeCastro, Inc., 220 F.3d 396 (5th Cir. 2000); R.C. Olmstead, Inc. v. CU Interface, LLC, 606 F.3d 262 (6th Cir. 2010); Oracle Am., Inc. v. Google, Inc., 750 F.3d 1339, 1357–58 (Fed. Cir. 2014).

[1063] *See* Dun & Bradstreet Software Services, Inc. v. Grace Consulting, Inc., 307 F.3d 197 (3d Cir. 2002). In addition, the Federal Circuit has held that interoperability does not limit the scope of copyright in a computer program, but that it is relevant, if at all, only to fair use. *See Oracle*, 750 F.3d at 1368–72, discussed below.

[1064] *See, e.g.*, General Universal Systems, Inc. v. Lee, 379 F.3d 131 (5th Cir. 2004); Bateman v. Mnemonics, Inc., 79 F.3d 1532 (11th Cir. 1996). *But see* Stenograph LLC v. Bossard Associates, Inc., 144 F.3d 96 (D.C. Cir. 1998).

[1065] Country Kids 'N City Slicks, Inc. v. Sheen, 77 F.3d 1280, 1285 n.5 (10th Cir. 1996) (dolls); *see also*

Altai's abstraction-filtration-comparison test also has been used in analyzing the similarity of graphical user interfaces (GUIs), which use visual images such as icons, pointers, windows and menus to make a program easier to use. In *Apple Computer, Inc. v. Microsoft Corp.*, the court held that "analytic dissection" similar to *Altai* was an appropriate method of analyzing the GUIs of two competing operating systems. Because Apple had licensed certain elements of its GUI to Microsoft in settling an earlier claim of infringement, and other elements were "filtered out" because of merger or *scènes à faire*, the court held that "any claim of infringement . . . must rest on the copying of Apple's unique selection and arrangement of all of those features."[1066] "Having correctly found that almost all the similarities sprang either from the license or from basic ideas and their obvious expression, [the district court] correctly concluded that illicit copying could occur only if the works as a whole are virtually identical."[1067]

The First Circuit took a somewhat different approach in *Lotus Development Corp. v. Borland International, Inc.*,[1068] which considered whether plaintiff's "Lotus 1-2-3" spreadsheet program was infringed by Borland's competing program "Quattro Pro." In addition to its own original GUI, Quattro Pro also included a "Lotus emulation interface" that allowed users already familiar with Lotus to use the same menus and commands that Lotus did. Because it found that "[a] very satisfactory spreadsheet menu tree can be constructed using different commands and a different command structure from those of Lotus 1-2-3," the district court concluded that the entirety of Lotus' menu command structure was protected expression.[1069] Analogizing the menu commands to the buttons on a video cassette recorder, the First Circuit reversed, holding that the entire menu command structure was an uncopyrightable "method of operation" within the meaning of section 102(b).[1070] Concurring, Judge Boudin acknowledged that "[a] new menu may be a creative work, but over time its importance may come to reside more in the investment that has been made by users in learning the menu."[1071] He drew an analogy to the familiar QWERTY keyboard, which "dominates the market because that is what everyone has learned to use."[1072] Rather than eliminate all protection for such menus by categorizing them as "methods of operation," Judge Boudin instead proposed a "privileged use" doctrine, under which a competitor would be

---

Kohus v. Mariol, 328 F.3d 848, 855 n.1 (6th Cir. 2003) (endorsing the test to "filter out the unoriginal, unprotectible elements" of a drawing of a useful article). *But see* Jacobsen v. Deseret Book Co., 287 F.3d 936, 943 n.5 (10th Cir. 2002) ("While abstraction-filtration-comparison analysis is useful in a variety of copyright cases, not every case requires extensive analysis."); Transwestern Publishing Co. v. Multimedia Marketing Assocs., Inc., 133 F.3d 773, 777 (10th Cir. 1998).

[1066] 35 F.3d 1435, 1446 (9th Cir. 1994).

[1067] *Id.* at 1447. *See also* MiTek Holdings, Inc. v. Arce Engineering Co., 89 F.3d 1548 (11th Cir. 1996) (analyzing user interface as a compilation and adopting the "virtually identical" standard); Dream Games of Arizona, Inc. v. PC Onsite, 561 F.3d 983 (9th Cir. 2009) (although individual elements of electronic bingo videogame screen displays are unprotected, jury may properly consider whether a combination of unprotected elements warrants protection).

[1068] 49 F.3d 807 (1st Cir. 2005), *aff'd by an equally divided Court*, 516 U.S. 233 (1996).

[1069] *Id.* at 810.

[1070] *Id.* at 815–17.

[1071] 49 F.3d at 819 (Boudin, J., concurring).

[1072] *Id.* at 820.

allowed to copy such menus, but only if it had contributed something important of its own to the resulting product, as Borland had done.[1073] On *certiorari*, the Supreme Court divided 4-4, affirming the result without a written opinion.[1074]

Although over time *Lotus v. Borland* came to be regarded as settled law, the Federal Circuit reopened the debate in *Oracle America, Inc. v. Google, Inc.*[1075] In creating its Android operating system, Google copied the "structure, sequence and organization" of 37 Java software "packages," comprising more than 600 "classes" and 6,000 "methods."[1076] Google wrote its own code to implement each method, but it copied the "header" or "declaration" for each method, reasoning that doing so was necessary so that programmers familiar with Java could write programs with the same functionality in Android. The district court held that because each header had to be written in a certain way in the Java language, the structure, sequence and organization was an uncopyrightable "method of operation."[1077] The Federal Circuit reversed, holding that the district court erred in focusing on the choices available to Google at the time of copying, rather than the choices available to Sun (Oracle's predecessor in interest) at the time Java was created.[1078] It also rejected *Lotus v. Borland* and held that Google's desire for interoperability was relevant, if at all, only to fair use, and that it did not affect the scope of copyright protection in the Java packages.[1079] For now, this circuit split remains unresolved.

[b]   Ordinary Observer Test

Regardless of whether a court filters out unprotected expression before or after comparing the two works, there is general agreement that the comparison should be made from the viewpoint of an "ordinary observer." In *Peter Pan Fabrics, Inc. v. Martin Weiner Corp.*, Judge Learned Hand acknowledged that two fabric designs were not identical, but the court nonetheless found infringement on the ground that "the ordinary observer, unless he set out to detect the disparities, would be inclined to overlook them, and to regard their aesthetic appeal as the same."[1080] This statement of the infringement standard remains the most common,[1081] although some courts have phrased the concept in different ways, referring instead to the

---

[1073] *Id.* at 821.

[1074] 516 U.S. 233 (1996).

[1075] 750 F.3d 1339 (Fed. Cir. 2014).

[1076] *Id.* at 1350–51. The software "packages" are also referred to as Application Programming Interfaces, or APIs.

[1077] 872 F. Supp. 2d 974, 999–1001 (N.D. Cal. 2012), *rev'd*, 750 F.3d 1339 (Fed. Cir. 2014).

[1078] 750 F.3d at 1361–62.

[1079] *Id.* at 1365–72. This holding is somewhat similar to Judge Boudin's proposed "privileged use," except that a jury will decide the issue of fair use, rather than a court deciding the issue of "privileged use."

[1080] 274 F.2d 487, 489 (2d Cir. 1960). *See also* Nichols v. Universal Pictures Corp., 45 F.2d 119, 123 (2d Cir. 1930) (approach to assessing similarity should be "more like that of a spectator, who would rely upon the complex of his impressions of each character").

[1081] *See, e.g.*, Zalewski v. Cicero Builder Dev. Co., 754 F.3d 95, 102 (2d Cir. 2014); Harney v. Sony Pictures Television, 704 F.3d 173, 179 (1st Cir. 2013); Blehm v. Jacobs, 702 F.3d 1193, 1202 (10th Cir. 2012); Sturdza v. United Arab Emirates, 218 F.3d 1287, 1296 (D.C. Cir. 2002).

"ordinary reasonable observer,"[1082] the "ordinary reasonable person,"[1083] the "ordinary lay person,"[1084] or the "average lay observer."[1085] There are, however, two variations of the ordinary observer test that seem to be substantively different.

First, some courts have stated that "where a [work] contains both protectible and unprotectible elements, . . . the observer's inspection must be more 'discerning,' ignoring those aspects of [the] work that are unprotectible in making the comparison."[1086] This "more discerning ordinary observer" test is a variation of the "subtractive" approach discussed above. Obviously, a judge is better equipped to be "more discerning" than a jury. Thus, if a jury is to decide the issue of "substantial similarity," it should be instructed as to which elements are protected expression and which elements are unprotected ideas.[1087]

Second, some courts have held that the ordinary observer test is simply the most common application of a more general rule, the "intended audience" test. Thus, in *Dawson v. Hinshaw Music, Inc.*, the court said:

> If, as will most often be the case, the lay public fairly represents the intended audience, the court should apply the lay observer formulation of the ordinary observer test. However, if the intended audience is more narrow in that it possesses specialized expertise, relevant to the purchasing decision, that lay people would lack, the court's inquiry should focus on whether a member of the intended audience would find the two works to be substantially similar.[1088]

Dawson, involved two arrangements of the public domain spiritual "Ezekiel Saw De Wheel." The court remanded the case, instructing the trial court to consider whether the "intended audience" for the plaintiff's musical arrangement was the "general, undifferentiated lay public" or "choral directors who possess specialized expertise relevant to their selection of one arrangement rather than another."[1089] Other courts applying the "intended audience" test have held that "the similarity of child-oriented works must be viewed from the perspective of the child audience for

---

[1082] *See, e.g.*, Jada Toys, Inc. v. Mattel, Inc., 518 F.3d 628, 637 (9th Cir. 2008).

[1083] *See, e.g.*, *Blehm*, 702 F.3d at 1202; JCW Investments, Inc. v. Novelty, Inc., 482 F.3d 910, 916 (7th Cir. 2007).

[1084] *See, e.g.*, Kay Berry, Inc. v. Taylor Gifts, Inc., 421 F.3d 199, 208 (8th Cir. 2005). *See also* Arnstein v. Porter, 154 F.2d 464, 468 (2d Cir. 1946) ("ordinary lay hearer" for music).

[1085] *See, e.g.*, Baby Buddies, Inc. v. Toys R Us, Inc., 611 F.3d 1308, 1315 (11th Cir. 2010).

[1086] Laureyssens v. Idea Group, Inc., 964 F.2d 131, 141 (2d Cir. 1992). *See also Zalewski*, 754 F.3d at 102; Trek Leasing, Inc. v. United States, 66 Fed. Cl. 8, 19 (2005); Boisson v. Banian, Ltd., 273 F.3d 262, 272, 274 (2d Cir. 2001).

[1087] *See* Baby Buddies, Inc. v. Toys R Us, Inc., 611 F.3d 1308, 1314 (11th Cir. 2010) ("once the court separates out the protectable elements of a work, it can become clear that no reasonable jury could find the defendant's work infringing."); *id.* at 1316–17 ("we approach the analysis in this case as would a properly instructed jury: focusing on only the elements protected by the copyright laws (that is, setting aside the unoriginal and nonexpressive elements of the [plaintiff's work]), is the [defendant's work] substantially similar to the [plaintiff's work]?").

[1088] 905 F.2d 731, 736–37 (4th Cir. 1990).

[1089] *Id.* at 737.

which the products were intended."[1090] The "intended audience" test has also been held appropriate in cases involving technical drawings[1091] and computer programs.[1092]

What is it that the ordinary observer or the intended audience is supposed to decide? In *Arnstein v. Porter*, the court stated that "the plaintiff's legally protected interest is . . . his interest in the potential financial returns from his compositions which derive from the lay public's approbation of his efforts. The question, therefore, is whether defendant took from plaintiff's works so much of what is pleasing to the ears of lay listeners, who comprise the audience for whom such popular music is composed, that defendant wrongfully appropriated something which belongs to the plaintiff."[1093] Although this statement of the standard is somewhat circular, it is consistent with Learned Hand's later statement in *Peter Pan Fabrics*, asking whether "the ordinary observer, unless he set out to detect the disparities, would be inclined to overlook them, and to regard their aesthetic appeal as the same."[1094] Some courts have asked instead "whether an average lay observer would recognize the alleged copy as having been appropriated from the copyrighted work."[1095] But this formulation seems to confuse the issue of copying with the issue of substantial similarity. An ordinary observer might recognize that a work was copied or derived from (or inspired by) another work (at least in part), without believing that the two works are substantially similar in protected expression.[1096]

Learned Hand also famously stated that "[n]o plagiarist can excuse the wrong by showing how much of his work he did not pirate."[1097] This has led some courts to state that the ordinary observer should focus on the similarities in the two works rather than the differences. However, other courts have observed that "numerous differences tend to undercut substantial similarity,"[1098] especially where "pattern"

[1090] Lyons Partnership, L.P. v. Morris Costumes, Inc., 243 F.3d 789, 802 (4th Cir. 2001). *See also* Data East, Inc. v. Epyx, Inc., 862 F.2d 204, 20910 n.6 (9th Cir. 1988) (viewing two videogames from the perspective of the average purchaser, "a discerning 17.5 year-old boy"); Aliotti v. R. Dakin & Co., 831 F.2d 898, 902 (9th Cir. 1987) ("Because children are the intended market for the dolls, we must filter the intrinsic inquiry through the perception of children.").

[1091] *See* Kohus v. Mariol, 328 F.3d 848, 858 (6th Cir. 2003).

[1092] *See* Computer Assocs. Int'l, Inc. v. Altai, Inc., 982 F.2d 693, 713 (2d Cir. 1992).

[1093] 154 F.2d 464, 473 (2d Cir. 1946).

[1094] Peter Pan Fabrics, Inc. v. Martin Weiner Corp., 274 F.2d 487, 489 (2d Cir. 1960). *See also* CRAIG JOYCE, MARSHALL LEAFFER, PETER JASZI, TYLER OCHOA & MICHAEL CARROLL, COPYRIGHT LAW 652 (9th ed. 2013) ("The fundamental question is whether, having seen, heard, read, or otherwise experienced the defendant's work, the relevant audience for the plaintiff's work would be less interested in experiencing the plaintiff's work.").

[1095] Idea Toy Corp. v. Fab-Lu Limited, Inc., 360 F.2d 1021, 1022 (2d Cir. 1966). To date, this standard has largely been confined to the Second and Eleventh Circuits. *See, e.g.*, Baby Buddies, Inc. v. Toys R Us, Inc., 611 F.3d 1308, 1315 (11th Cir. 2010); Rogers v. Koons, 71 F.2d 301, 307 (2d Cir. 1992).

[1096] *See, e.g.*, Warner Bros. Inc. v. American Broadcasting Cos., 654 F.2d 204, 211 (2d Cir. 1981) (character of Ralph Hinkley in TV series "The Greatest American Hero" was not substantially similar to "Superman"), *on appeal after remand*, 720 F.2d 231, 243 (2d Cir. 1983) (same); Reyher v. Children's Television Workshop, 533 F.2d 87, 91–93 (2d Cir. 1976) (no substantial similarity between two works based on the theme of a child viewing her mother as "The Most Beautiful Woman in the World").

[1097] Sheldon v. Metro-Goldwyn Pictures Corp., 81 F.2d 49, 56 (2d Cir. 1936).

[1098] Durham Industries, Inc. v. Tomy Corp., 630 F.2d 905, 913 (2d Cir. 1980). *See also* Blehm v.

similarity is involved,[1099] or where the two works are graphic or three-dimensional works that are "created to be perceived as an entirety."[1100] "As a matter of logic as well as law, the more numerous the differences between two works the less likely it is that they will create the same aesthetic impact."[1101] Similarly, it has been said that "a defendant may legitimately avoid infringement by intentionally making sufficient changes in a work that would otherwise be regarded as substantially similar to the plaintiff's."[1102] In trying to reconcile these statements, the following (generalized) observation may be helpful:

> Ultimately, care must be taken to draw the elusive distinction between a substantially similar [work] that infringes a copyrighted [work] despite slight differences in [specific details], and a somewhat similar though non-infringing [work] whose [specific details], and especially their combination, significantly differ from those of a copyrighted [work], even though the second [work] is reminiscent of the first one. Stirring one's memory of a copyrighted [work] is not the same as appearing to be substantially similar to that [work], and only the latter is infringement.[1103]

Finally, one should note that the Ninth Circuit's approach to "substantial similarity" differs greatly from the other circuits. The Ninth Circuit divides the "substantial similarity" inquiry into an "extrinsic" test and an "intrinsic" test. As originally set forth in *Sid & Marty Krofft Television Prods., Inc. v. McDonald's Corp.*, the "extrinsic test" referred to "substantial similarity in ideas," while the "intrinsic" test referred to "substantial similarity in the expressions of the ideas."[1104] As reformulated in *Shaw v. Lindheim*, the "extrinsic" test is an "objective" test that considers similarities in expression as well as ideas, while the "intrinsic" test is a "subjective judgment as to whether two . . . works are or are not similar."[1105] In applying the "extrinsic" test, a court may "dissect" the work and analyze specific similarities or differences in "theme, plot, sequence of events, mood, setting, pace, characters, and dialogue."[1106] If the "extrinsic" analysis demonstrates there are substantial similarities in the "objective" criteria, then a court may not grant summary judgment unless all of the similarities concern unprotected expression, because the "intrinsic" test is for the trier of fact.[1107] While *Shaw's*

Jacobs, 702 F.3d 1193, 1208 (10th Cir. 2012) (rejecting argument that "we should focus on the images' similarities, not their differences" in comparing two sets of stick figures).

[1099] Warner Bros. Inc. v. American Broadcasting Cos., 654 F.2d 204, 210–11 (2d Cir. 1981).

[1100] Warner Bros. Inc. v. American Broadcasting Cos., 720 F.2d 231, 241 (2d Cir. 1983).

[1101] Durham Industries, Inc. v. Tomy Corp., 630 F.2d 905, 913 (2d Cir. 1980).

[1102] 4 NIMMER ON COPYRIGHT § 13.03[B][1][b] (2010); *accord Warner Bros.*, 720 F.2d at 241; Eden Toys, Inc. v. Marshall Field & Co., 675 F.2d 498, 501 (2d Cir. 1982).

[1103] Warner Bros. Inc. v. American Broadcasting Cos., 720 F.2d 231, 242 (2d Cir. 1983).

[1104] 562 F.2d 1157, 1164 (9th Cir. 1977). It is likely that this "bifurcated" approach arose out of a fundamental misunderstanding of *Arnstein v. Porter*, 154 F.2d 464 (2d Cir. 1946), which the court cited with approval.

[1105] 919 F.2d 1353, 1356–57 (9th Cir. 1990).

[1106] *Id.* at 1356–57 (listing elements in a different order); *id.* at 1362–63 (analyzing elements in the order listed in the text).

[1107] *Id.* at 1359–61.

reformulation is an improvement compared to *Krofft*, the Ninth Circuit's approach is still unnecessarily baroque and unhelpful. It is difficult to see what is gained by attempting to separate "extrinsic" or "objective" factors from "intrinsic" or "subjective" ones.

[c]   *De Minimis* Use

In determining whether any similarity of protected expression was "substantial," courts sometimes ask whether the amount of protected expression that was copied was "more than *de minimis*."[1108] In *Ringgold v. Black Entertainment Television, Inc.*, however, the court explained that the phrase *de minimis* can been used in three different ways in copyright infringement cases:

> The legal maxim "*de minimis non curat lex*" (sometimes rendered, "the law does not concern itself with trifles") insulates from liability those who cause insignificant violations of the rights of others. In the context of copyright law, the concept of *de minimis* has significance in three respects. . . .

> First, *de minimis* in the copyright context can mean what it means in most legal contexts: a technical violation of a right so trivial that the law will not impose legal consequences. . . .

> Second, *de minimis* can mean that copying has occurred to such a trivial extent as to fall below the quantitative threshold of substantial similarity, which is always a required element of actionable copying. . . .

> Third, *de minimis* might be considered relevant to the defense of fair use. . . . [However, if] the allegedly infringing work makes such a quantitatively insubstantial use of the copyrighted work as to fall below the threshold required for actionable copying, it makes more sense to reject the claim on that basis and find no infringement, rather than undertake an elaborate fair use analysis in order to uphold a defense.[1109]

In *On Davis v. The Gap, Inc.*, the court elaborated on the first meaning:

> Trivial copying is a significant part of modern life. Most honest citizens in the modern world frequently engage, without hesitation, in trivial copying that, but for the *de minimis* doctrine, would technically constitute a violation of law. We do not hesitate to make a photocopy of a letter from a friend to show to another friend, or of a favorite cartoon to post on the refrigerator. Parents in Central Park photograph their children perched on [a copyrighted] sculpture. . . . Waiters at a restaurant sing "Happy Birthday" at a patron's table. When we do such things, it is not that we are breaking the law but unlikely to be sued given the high cost of litigation. Because of the *de minimis* doctrine, in trivial instances of copying, we are in fact not breaking the law.[1110]

[1108] Tufenkian Import/Export Ventures, Inc. v. Einstein Moomjy, Inc., 338 F.3d 127, 131 (2d Cir. 2003).

[1109] 126 F.3d 70, 75–76 (2d Cir. 1997).

[1110] 246 F.3d 152, 173 (2d Cir. 2001).

Other courts, however, have expressed a more skeptical view of the *de minimis* doctrine, stating that "the overwhelming thrust of authority upholds liability even under circumstances in which the use of the copyrighted work is of minimal consequence."[1111]

The argument that any copying was merely *de minimis* is frequently made but is only rarely successful. In *Ringgold*, for example, the court held that the use of plaintiff's artwork in the background of a television show in nine shots totaling less than 27 seconds was *not* a *de minimis* use (although it remanded for the court to consider the fair use doctrine). Other courts, however, have relied on the fact that the work appeared only for a few seconds or was out of focus in concluding that such a background use was *de minimis*.[1112] In another case, *de minimis* use was found when the defendant copied three notes from a musical work, when the defendant had licensed the sound recording of that musical work.[1113] The Sixth Circuit, however, has held, based on a dubious interpretation of section 114(b), that *any* unauthorized sampling of a sound recording is an infringement *per se*, without regard to *de minimis* use or substantial similarity.[1114]

§ 4I SECONDARY LIABILITY

Where infringing activity is widely dispersed, it may be a practical impossibility for the copyright holder to sue all of the individual infringers. This fact, together with the usual search for "deep-pocket" defendants, has led copyright owners to try to impose liability on various intermediaries — manufacturers of copying equipment, Internet service providers, software designers, and others — instead of, or in addition to, the individuals who are actually infringing. This section discusses the legal theories under which such intermediaries may be held liable for the infringing conduct of others, together with legislation that expands or limits such liability in particular circumstances.

[1]   In General

"The Copyright Act does not expressly render anyone liable for infringement committed by another. . . . [However,] [t]he absence of such express language in the copyright statute does not preclude the imposition of liability for copyright infringements on certain parties who have not themselves engaged in the infringing activity. For vicarious liability is imposed in virtually all areas of the law, and the concept of contributory infringement is merely a species of the broader

---

[1111] Situation Management Systems, Inc. v. ASP Consulting LLC, 560 F.3d 53, 59 (1st Cir. 2009).

[1112] *See, e.g.*, Gordon v. Nextel Communications, 345 F.3d 922 (9th Cir. 2003) (display of dental illustrations in background of a TV commercial); Sandoval v. New Line Cinema Corp., 147 F.3d 215, 217 (2d Cir. 1998) (photos on light box in background of movie "Seven" were "not displayed with sufficient detail for the average lay observer to identify" them); Gottlieb Development LLC v. Paramount Pictures Corp., 590 F. Supp. 2d 625 (S.D.N.Y. 2008) (copyrighted pinball machine in background of movie "What Women Want"); Straus v. DVC Worldwide, Inc., 484 F. Supp. 2d 620 (S.D. Tex. 2007) (display of photo on product box at end of TV commercial was *de minimis*).

[1113] Newton v. Diamond, 349 F.3d 591 (9th Cir. 203).

[1114] Bridgeport Music, Inc. v. Dimension Films, 410 F.3d 792 (6th Cir. 2005).

problem of identifying the circumstances in which it is just to hold one individual accountable for the actions of another."[1115]

Although the Copyright Act lacks express language concerning secondary liability, such as the language that exists in the Patent Act,[1116] the Copyright Act does contain an indirect reference to such liability. Section 106 states that the copyright owner has the exclusive right "to do *and to authorize* any of the following."[1117] The House Report states that "[u]se of the phrase 'to authorize' is intended to avoid any questions as to the liability of contributory infringers. For example, a person who lawfully acquires an authorized copy of a motion picture would be an infringer if he or she engages in the business of renting it to others for purposes of unauthorized public performance."[1118] Thus, courts have held that this language "was intended to invoke the preexisting doctrine of contributory infringement."[1119]

For there to be secondary liability, there must be a direct infringement.[1120] Thus, the plaintiff must plead and prove an act of direct infringement in addition to the elements that warrant the imposition of secondary liability.

[a]   Contributory Infringement

"Contributory infringement originates in tort law and stems from the notion that one who directly contributes to another's infringement should be held accountable."[1121] "[O]ne who, with knowledge of the infringing activity, induces, causes or materially contributes to the infringing conduct of another, may be held liable as a 'contributory' infringer.' "[1122] Thus, to allege a claim of contributory infringement, "a plaintiff must allege: (1) direct copyright infringement of a third-party; (2) knowledge by the defendant that the third-party was directly infringing; and (3)

[1115] Sony Corp. of America v. Universal City Studios, Inc., 464 U.S. 417, 434–35 (1984). Note that here the Supreme Court uses "vicarious liability" as an umbrella term for all types of secondary liability, including contributory infringement. In other cases, however, "vicarious liability" is a specific doctrine that is distinguished from "contributory infringement," and both are considered types of "secondary liability."

[1116] *See* § 2E[2][c].

[1117] 17 U.S.C. § 106 (emphasis added).

[1118] H.R. Rep. No. 94-1476, at 61 (1976).

[1119] Subafilms, Ltd. v. MGM-Pathe Communications Co., 24 F.3d 1088, 1092 (9th Cir. 1994). *See also id.* at 1093 (" 'to authorize' [wa]s simply a convenient peg on which Congress chose to hang the antecedent jurisprudence of third party liability."), *quoting* 3 NIMMER ON COPYRIGHT § 12.04[A][3][a] (1993).

[1120] *Subafilms*, 24 F.3d at 1092 ("there [can] be no liability for contributory infringement unless the authorized or otherwise encouraged activity itself could amount to infringement."); Bridgeport Music, Inc. v. Diamond Time, Ltd., 371 F.3d 883, 889 (6th Cir. 2004) ("There can be no contributory infringement without a direct infringement"); Matthew Bender & Co. v. West Publishing Co., 158 F.3d 693, 706 (2d Cir. 1998) ("For a defendant to be held contributorily or vicariously liable, a direct infringement must have occurred.").

[1121] Fonovisa, Inc. v. Cherry Auction, Inc., 76 F.3d 259, 264 (9th Cir. 1996).

[1122] *Id., quoting* Gershwin Publishing Corp. v. Columbia Artists Mgmt., Inc., 443 F.2d 1159, 1162 (2d Cir. 1971).

material contribution to the infringement."[1123]

With respect to the knowledge element, contributory infringement requires that the defendant must "know or have reason to know" of the direct infringement.[1124] It is not sufficient that the defendant has constructive knowledge that some of its customers or users will infringe; instead, the defendant must know of specific infringing acts or material.[1125] The defendant must not only know of the direct infringer's conduct, but he must also know or have reason to know that the direct infringer's conduct is illegal.[1126] Finally, the defendant must possess such knowledge either before it materially contributes to the infringing conduct or while its contribution is still ongoing, so that it can act in time to avoid aiding the infringement.[1127] For example, in *Perfect 10, Inc. v. Amazon.com, Inc.*, the court held that although Google could not be held liable for automatically generating links to images posted by third parties that turned out to be infringing, it could be held liable for maintaining those links after it learned that the images were infringing.[1128]

With respect to the material contribution, the defendant's participation in or contribution to the infringing activity must be "substantial."[1129] For example, in *Fonovisa, Inc. v. Cherry Auction, Inc.*, the plaintiffs alleged that that defendant was "aware that vendors in its swap meet were selling counterfeit recordings."[1130] The court held that "providing the site and facilities for known infringing activity is sufficient to establish contributory liability."[1131] It remarked that "it would be difficult for the infringing activity to take place in the massive quantities alleged without the support services provided by the swap meet," including "the provision of space, utilities, parking, advertising, plumbing, and customers."[1132] Similarly, in *A&M Records, Inc. v. Napster, Inc.*, the court held that providing an indexing service for MP3 files was a material contribution, because "[w]ithout the support services defendant provides, Napster users could not find and download the music

---

[1123] NCR Corp. v. Korala Assocs., Ltd., 512 F.3d 807, 816 (6th Cir. 2008), *quoting* Parker v. Google, Inc., 2007 U.S. App. LEXIS 16370 (3d Cir. July 10, 2007).

[1124] *NCR Corp.*, 512 F.3d at 816. *Accord*, Arista Records, LLC v. Doe 3, 604 F.3d 110, 118 (2d Cir. 2010); A&M Records, Inc. v. Napster, Inc., 239 F.3d 1004, 1020 (9th Cir. 2001).

[1125] Luvdarts, LLC v. AT&T Mobility, LLC, 710 F.3d 1068, 1072 (9th Cir. 2013); *Napster*, 239 F.3d at 1020–21.

[1126] *See, e.g.*, Faulkner v. National Geographic Society, 211 F. Supp. 2d 450, 474–75 (S.D.N.Y. 2002) ("actual knowledge of adverse claims" is not sufficient, because "plaintiffs' allegations of infringement are anything but readily verifiable"), *aff'd on other grounds*, 409 F.3d 26, 40 (2d Cir. 2005); Religious Tech. Ctr. v. Netcom On-Line Communication Services, Inc., 907 F. Supp. 1361, 1374 (N.D. Cal. 1995) ("Where a [defendant] cannot reasonably verify a claim of infringement[,] . . . the [defendant]'s lack of knowledge will be found reasonable and there will be no liability for contributory infringement").

[1127] *See Faulkner*, 211 F. Supp. 2d at 474 ("this prong is satisfied if the defendant 'knew or should have known' of the infringing activity *at the time of* its material contribution.") (emphasis added).

[1128] 508 F.3d 1146, 1172 (9th Cir. 2007). *See also Napster*, 239 F.3d at 1021.

[1129] *Faulkner*, 211 F. Supp. 2d at 473; Demetriades v. Kaufman, 690 F. Supp. 689, 694 (S.D.N.Y. 1988).

[1130] 76 F.3d at 259, 261 (9th Cir. 1996).

[1131] *Id.* at 264.

[1132] *Id.*

they want with the ease of which defendant boasts."[1133] It also has been held that providing advertising, financial, accounting, and administrative services for a direct infringer is sufficient to constitute a material contribution.[1134]

However, the material contribution must have a "direct connection to the infringement."[1135] For example, in *Demetriades v. Kaufman*, where the named defendants built an infringing house on property they had purchased, the realtor who brokered the real estate transaction was not contributorily liable.[1136] And in *Faulkner v. National Geographic Society*, the court held that although advertising an infringing work is a material contribution, advertising a non-infringing work in a magazine that contains infringing photographs is not.[1137]

Contributory infringement also has been used to hold an officer or director of a corporation personally liable where he or she "knowingly participates in the infringement."[1138] However, the mere fact that an individual is an officer or shareholder of an infringer is not sufficient to hold the individual personally liable.[1139]

[b]   Vicarious Liability

Vicarious liability was initially developed "as an outgrowth of the agency principles of *respondeat superior*."[1140] However, "even in the absence of an employer-employee relationship one may be vicariously liable if he has the right and ability to supervise the infringing activity and also has a direct financial interest in such activities."[1141]

The "right and ability to control" prong has been held satisfied whenever the defendant reserves a contractual right to terminate its contract with the direct infringer. Thus, in *A&M Records, Inc. v. Napster, Inc.*, this prong was satisfied by a notice on the defendant's website that expressly reserved the "right to refuse service and terminate accounts in [its] discretion, including, but not limited to, if Napster believes that user conduct violates applicable law . . . or for any reason in Napster's sole discretion, with or without cause."[1142] Similarly, in *Fonovisa, Inc. v.*

[1133] 239 F.3d 1004, 1022 (9th Cir. 2001).

[1134] Columbia Pictures Industries, Inc. v. Redd Horne, Inc., 749 F.2d 154, 161 (3d Cir. 1984).

[1135] Perfect 10, Inc. v. Visa Int'l Service Assn., 494 F.3d 788, 796 (9th Cir. 2007). *See also* Faulkner v. National Geographic Society, 211 F. Supp. 2d 450, 473 (S.D.N.Y. 2002) ("The authorization or assistance must bear a direct relationship to the infringing acts, and the contributory infringer must have acted in concert with the direct infringer."), *aff'd on other grounds*, 409 F.3d 26, 40 (2d Cir. 2005).

[1136] 690 F. Supp. 289, 294 (S.D.N.Y. 1988) ("The mere fact that the Doernberg defendants brokered a real estate transaction that ultimately was connected to a copyright infringement is not enough.").

[1137] 211 F. Supp. 2d 450, 473–74 (S.D.N.Y. 2002), *aff'd on other grounds*, 409 F.3d 26, 40 (2d Cir. 2005).

[1138] Columbia Pictures Industries, Inc. v. Redd Horne, Inc., 749 F.2d 154, 160 (3d Cir. 1984).

[1139] *See* Softel, Inc. v. Dragon Medical & Scientific Communications, Inc., 118 F.3d 955, 971 (2d Cir. 1997). *See also* UMG Recordings, Inc. v. Shelter Capital Partners, LLC, 718 F.3d 1006, 1032–33 (9th Cir. 2013) (investors who obtained seats of the Board of Directors did not make a material contribution, unless they acted in concert to direct the infringing activity).

[1140] Fonovisa, Inc. v. Cherry Auction, Inc., 76 F.3d at 259, 261–62 (9th Cir. 1996).

[1141] Gershwin Publishing Corp. v. Columbia Artists Mgmt. Inc., 443 F.2d 1159, 1162 (2d Cir. 1971).

[1142] 239 F.3d 1004, 1023 (9th Cir. 2001).

Cherry Auction, Inc., the court held that a swap meet "had the right to terminate vendors for any reason whatsoever and through that right had the ability to control the activities of vendors on the premises."[1143] However, in *Perfect 10, Inc. v. Amazon.com, Inc.*, the court held that Google did *not* have the right or ability to control the infringing activity of third parties who posted infringing images on the Internet.[1144] And in *Luvdarts, LLC v. AT&T Mobility, LLC*, the court held that a wireless network carrier did not have the right or ability to control the allegedly infringing activity of its users.[1145]

The financial interest must be "direct," meaning that the defendant financially benefits from the infringing activity itself. This prong was satisfied when a department store received 10% of the gross receipts of a concessionaire who was selling counterfeit recordings.[1146] This element, however, has been stretched to include situations in which the financial benefit was arguably "indirect" rather than direct. For example, in *Fonovisa, Inc. v. Cherry Auction, Inc.*, the court held that a swap meet had a "direct" financial interest in the infringing activities of vendors who sold counterfeit recordings on its premises, even though it charged vendors a fixed fee, because "the defendants reap substantial financial benefits from admission fees, concession stand sales and parking fees, all of which flow directly from customers who want to buy the counterfeit recordings at bargain basement prices."[1147] This holding means that the swap meet could be held vicariously liable for the sales of its vendors, even if it had no reason to suspect that its vendors were selling counterfeit recordings.

Vicarious liability may be illustrated by the distinction between the so-called "landlord" cases and the so-called "dance hall" cases. "If [a] landlord lets his premises without knowledge of the impending infringement by his tenant, exercises no supervision over him, charges a fixed rental and receives no other benefit from the infringement, and contributes in no way to it, . . . [then] the landlord is not liable for his tenant's wrongdoing."[1148] However, if the proprietor of an establishment hires "a band or orchestra whose activities provide the proprietor with a source of customers and enhanced income . . . [, then] [h]e is liable whether the bandleader is considered . . . an employee or an independent contractor, and whether or not the proprietor has knowledge of the compositions to be played or any control over their selection."[1149]

[1143] 76 F.3d at 259, 262 (9th Cir. 1996).

[1144] 508 F.3d 1146, 1173–75 (9th Cir. 2007).

[1145] 710 F.3d 1068, 1071–72 (9th Cir. 2013). *See also* Flava Works, Inc. v. Gunter, 689 F.3d 754 (7th Cir. 2012) (vacating preliminary injunction against website that allowed users to "bookmark" videos found on other sites for others to view; website did not encourage or assist the people who uploaded the videos, and there was no evidence that users accessed the videos through the defendant's website).

[1146] *See* Shapiro, Bernstein & Co. v. H.L. Green Co., 316 F.2d 304, 307 (2d Cir. 1963).

[1147] 76 F.3d at 259, 263 (9th Cir. 1996).

[1148] *Shapiro*, 316 F.2d at 307, *citing* Deutsch v. Arnold, 98 F.2d 686 (2d Cir. 1938).

[1149] *Shapiro*, 316 F.2d at 307, *citing*, *inter alia*, Dreamland Ball Room, Inc. v. Shapiro, Bernstein & Co., 36 F.2d 354 (7th Cir. 1929). *See also* Broadcast Music, Inc. v. Meadowlake, Ltd., 754 F.3d 353 (6th Cir. 2014) (95% owner of restaurant was vicariously liable for copyright infringement committed by bands hired by 5% owner, even if he lacked knowledge).

Unfortunately, the two-element formula described above has extended vicarious liability well beyond its agency law roots to situations in which the direct infringers could not plausibly be considered agents of the defendant. For example, in *A&M Records, Inc. v. Napster, Inc.*, the court held that the defendant, which provided software that helped facilitate peer-to-peer file sharing by indexing MP3 files, was vicariously liable for the infringing activities of its users. In addition to the contractual right to terminate users, the court held that a "[f]inancial benefit exists where the availability of infringing material acts as a 'draw' for customers."[1150] Even though Napster was providing its service for free, the court found that "[a]mple evidence supports the district court's finding that Napster's future revenue is directly dependent upon 'increases in userbase.' More users register with the Napster system as the 'quality and quantity of available music increases.' "[1151] The opinion can be criticized on its own terms, since it allows hypothetical *future* revenue to constitute a "direct" financial benefit. But the more fundamental problem is that the opinion focuses solely on the two elements as phrased rather than considering whether an agency relationship existed between Napster and its users. While the allegations plausibly stated a claim for contributory infringement, holding Napster vicariously liable for its users essentially approved the absurd notion that the users were Napster's employees or agents.

Like contributory infringement, vicarious liability also has been used to hold an officer or director of a corporation personally liable for infringement. For example, both the president of a company who personally approved the sale of infringing copies (and had a financial interest as the sole shareholder of the company), and the agent who negotiated the sale and received a commission from it, have been held to be vicariously liable.[1152]

[2]   Providing Copying Devices or Software

[a]   The *Sony* Decision

In *Sony Corp. of America v. Universal City Studios, Inc.*, two movie studios, Universal and Disney, sued Sony for manufacturing and selling to the public the Betamax, the first video tape recorder (VTR) designed for home use. Their theory was that home users would use the Betamax to infringe by making unauthorized reproductions of copyrighted works, and that Sony was liable for contributory infringement by making and selling the copying equipment to home users.[1153] By a 5-4 vote, the Supreme Court held that home videotaping for time-shifting purposes was fair use, and that Sony was not liable for any infringing activity committed by its users.

On the question of contributory infringement, the Court borrowed the "staple article of commerce" doctrine from patent law, which expressly provides by statute that the sale of a "staple article or commodity of commerce suitable for substantial

---

[1150] 239 F.3d 1004, 1023 (9th Cir. 2001).

[1151] *Id.*

[1152] Pinkham v. Sara Lee Corp., 983 F.2d 824, 834 (8th Cir. 1992).

[1153] 464 U.S. 417, 419–20 (1984).

noninfringing use" is not contributory infringement.[1154] Thus, it held that "the sale of copying equipment . . . does not constitute contributory infringement if the product is widely used for legitimate, unobjectionable purposes. Indeed, it need merely be capable of substantial noninfringing uses."[1155] Having announced this standard, the Court then considered "whether the Betamax is capable of commercially significant noninfringing uses."[1156] It held that "private, non-commercial time-shifting in the home" was non-infringing and commercially significant, because some copyright owners were willing to allow home users to record their shows (authorized time-shifting), and because even unauthorized time-shifting was a fair use.[1157]

Although the motion picture industry forecasted dire consequences if it lost the *Sony* case, the result turned out to be a win-win proposition for everyone. The widespread availability of VTRs led to an entirely new market for exploiting motion pictures: namely, the home video market. Beginning two decades after *Sony*, movie studios made more money from rentals and sales of videotapes than they did from theatrical releases.

Today, however, the picture is a little less clear. Movie studios were happy to make the transition from videotape to DVDs, and now Blu-Ray, because DVD and Blu-Ray players do not also record works, which allows the studios to exploit the home video market with less risk of copying. The legacy of *Sony* has instead manifested itself in digital video recorders (DVRs), such as TiVo, which allow users to record television shows at home for time-shifting purposes, but also enable users to easily skip the advertising that supports broadcast television.[1158]

Movie studios are reluctant to challenge *Sony* directly, but they have fought attempts to expand its reach. In 2001, studios sued ReplayTV, seeking to enjoin a DVR that allowed users to automatically delete commercials and to send recorded programs to other users over the Internet. The lawsuit settled when ReplayTV agreed to remove the offending features.[1159] In 2006, several copyright owners sued Cablevision, seeking to enjoin a "remote storage" DVR, which allowed users to record shows on servers operated by the cable system at a central location, rather than on stand-alone DVRs at home. The copyright owners carefully avoided pleading contributory infringement, however. Instead, they relied solely on a theory of direct infringement for reproducing and publicly performing the works, which

---

[1154] 35 U.S.C. § 271(c). *See* § 2E[2][c].

[1155] 464 U.S. at 442.

[1156] Sony Corp. of America v. Universal City Studios, Inc., 464 U.S. 417, 442 (1984). The Court did not explain whether "commercially significant" noninfringing uses was equivalent to "substantial" noninfringing uses.

[1157] *Id.* at 442–56. This aspect of the decision is discussed in § 4J[1][c].

[1158] Before remote controls were common, the majority in *Sony* rejected the argument that commercial skipping would harm the market for advertiser-supported broadcast television. 464 U.S. at 452 n.36. Today, estimates of commercial-skipping on playback for DVR owners range between a low of 6.5% and a high of 75%.

[1159] *See* Paramount Pictures Corp. v. ReplayTV, 298 F. Supp. 2d 921 (C.D. Cal. 2004).

the Second Circuit rejected.[1160] And in 2013, the Ninth Circuit affirmed the denial of a preliminary injunction against DISH Network, which provided a DVR that allowed users to automatically record all prime-time network TV shows ("Prime-Time Anytime") and to automatically skip commercials on playback ("AutoHop"), reasoning that although commercial-skipping caused economic harm, it did not itself infringe.[1161]

[b]   Audio Home Recording Act

In the 1980s, the recording industry began to move away from conventional analog recording formats (like vinyl discs and magnetic tapes) and toward the new digital formats of compact discs ("CDs") and digital audio tape (or "DAT"). While the risk to sales posed by analog home taping was limited by the fact that sound quality degrades noticeably with each "generation" of copies, with digital media there is little appreciable difference between the sound quality of a CD and a DAT recording copied from it.

When DAT technology was first introduced in the U.S. market, the industry's response was to sue manufacturers and importers of DAT recording and playback devices, based on their alleged contributory liability for private acts of copyright infringement. While it is doubtful such an action would have succeeded in the face of *Sony*, the possibility of *Sony*-like litigation was enough to delay the introduction of DAT technology until a legislative solution could be devised.

The result was the Audio Home Recording Act of 1992, which added a new Chapter 10 to Title 17. The AHRA prohibits the manufacture, importation, or distribution of any "digital audio recording device" unless it contains technology designed to prevent "serial copying," and it prohibits the manufacture, importation, or distribution of equipment or services designed to circumvent such technology.[1162] The AHRA also imposes a royalty on all digital audio recording devices and media, based on a percentage of the "transfer price" of such devices and media, subject to a statutory minimum and maximum royalty.[1163] The royalties are deposited in the Copyright Office,[1164] which is charged with distributing the royalties as follows: 1/3 of the royalties are allocated to musical work copyrights, and are split 50-50 between publishers and authors;[1165] while 2/3 of the royalties are allocated to sound recording copyrights, of which 4% is set aside for "nonfeatured musicians," with 40 percent of the remainder going to "featured recording artists," and the remaining 60 percent going to sound recording copyright owners.[1166]

[1160] *See* Cartoon Network, L.P. v. CSC Holdings, Inc., 536 F.3d 121 (2d Cir. 2008), discussed at §§ 4[G][1][b], 4G[4][a], above.

[1161] *See* Fox Broadcasting Co. v. DISH Network, LLC, 747 F.3d 1060 (9th Cir. 2013).

[1162] 17 U.S.C. § 1002(a),(c).

[1163] 17 U.S.C. §§ 1003(a), 1004. There are special provisions for digital audio recording devices that are integrated with other components. 17 U.S.C. § 1004(a)(2). Although the percentage royalty is fixed by statute, the Copyright Royalty Judges may adjust the maximum royalty. 17 U.S.C. § 1004(a)(3).

[1164] 17 U.S.C. § 1005.

[1165] 17 U.S.C. § 1006 (b)(2).

[1166] 17 U.S.C. § 1006(b)(1). The Copyright Royalty Judges are charged with resolving any disputes between interested parties in the distribution of the royalties. 17 U.S.C. §§ 1006(c), 1007.

In exchange for the imposition of royalties on digital audio recording devices and media, the AHRA provides an exemption from copyright infringement for the use of such devices and media:

> No action may be brought under this title alleging infringement of copyright based on the manufacture, importation, or distribution of a digital audio recording device, a digital audio recording medium, an analog recording device, or an analog recording medium, or based on the noncommercial use by a consumer of such a device or medium for making digital musical recordings or analog musical recordings.[1167]

If the AHRA applied to computers, it would authorize peer-to-peer file sharing of sound recordings of musical works. However, computer manufacturers were unwilling to pay the royalty imposed on digital audio recording devices and media. Therefore, in a series of nested definitions, Congress made it clear that the AHRA applies only to special-purpose digital audio recording devices, and not to general-purpose computers (or computer playback devices).[1168]

A "digital audio recording device" is defined as "any machine or device of a type commonly distributed to individuals for use by individuals, . . . which is designed or marketed for the primary purpose of . . . making a digital audio copied recording for private use."[1169] A "digital audio copied recording" is defined as "a reproduction in a digital recording format of a digital musical recording, whether that reproduction is made directly from another digital musical recording or indirectly from a transmission."[1170] A "digital musical recording" is defined as "a material object . . . in which are fixed, in a digital recording format, only sounds, and material, statements, or instructions incidental to those fixed sounds, if any."[1171] The definition excludes material objects "in which the fixed sounds consist entirely of spoken word recordings" (such as audio books), or those "in which one or more computer programs are fixed," other than "statements or instructions constituting the fixed sounds and incidental material."[1172]

Working backward through the definitions, a computer hard drive is not a "digital musical recording," even if it contains MP3 files, because "almost all hard drives contain numerous programs (e.g., for word processing, . . . etc.) and databases that are not incidental to any sound files that may be stored on the hard drive."[1173] Because a "digital audio copied recording" is "a reproduction . . . of a

---

[1167] 17 U.S.C. § 1008.

[1168] *See* Recording Industry Assn. of America v. Diamond Multimedia Systems, Inc., 180 F.3d 1072, 1078 n.6 (9th Cir. 1999) (citing evidence "that the exclusion of computers from the Act's scope was part of a carefully negotiated compromise between the various industries with interests at stake, and without which, the computer industry would have vigorously opposed passage of the Act.").

[1169] 17 U.S.C. § 1001(3). The definition also excludes "professional model products," and recording equipment designed and marketed primarily to record "non-musical sounds," such as dictation and answering machines. *Id.*

[1170] 17 U.S.C. § 1001(1).

[1171] 17 U.S.C. § 1001(5)(A).

[1172] 17 U.S.C. § 1001(5)(B).

[1173] Recording Industry Assn. of America v. Diamond Multimedia Systems, Inc., 180 F.3d 1072, 1076

digital musical recording," but a computer hard drive is not a "digital musical recording," any reproduction of an MP3 file that is made from a computer hard drive is not a "digital audio copied recording." And because a typical MP3 player (such as an Apple iPod) can only download songs from a computer hard drive, such an MP3 player is not a "digital audio recording device," because its "primary purpose" is not to make "digital audio copied recordings."[1174] This reasoning is confirmed by the legislative history, which expressly states Congress' intent to exclude computers from the scope of the AHRA.[1175]

Accordingly, when the recording industry challenged the legality of the Diamond Rio, an early MP3 player, the Ninth Circuit held that the Rio was *not* a "digital audio recording device," and that it did not have to pay royalties. Although the music industry lost that battle, in doing so it inadvertently won a much larger battle, because when it sued Napster, a website that facilitated peer-to-peer file-sharing by helping users locate infringing MP3 files on other users' computers, the Ninth Circuit dismissed Napster's defense that file sharing was authorized by the AHRA, stating that "the Audio Home Recording Act does not cover the downloading of MP3 files to computer hard drives."[1176] Had the recording industry succeeded in the Diamond Rio case, the AHRA would have exempted peer-to-peer file sharing from liability for copyright infringement.

[c] Peer-to-Peer File Sharing

The first case involving peer-to-peer file sharing was *A&M Records, Inc. v. Napster, Inc.*[1177] Napster operated a website and provided software that facilitated peer-to-peer file sharing by uploading the names of all of a user's MP3 files in a designated directory to a central server operated by Napster, which maintained a real-time index of all file names of all users who were currently logged onto the Napster website. Users could search the index for file names and select a file name to download.[1178] The Ninth Circuit held that the reproduction of MP3 files of copyrighted sound recordings or musical works was an infringement and was not a

---

(9th Cir. 1999). *See also id.* ("a hard drive is a material object in which one or more programs are fixed; thus, a hard drive is excluded from the definition of digital music recordings.").

[1174] *Id.* ("the Rio [MP3 player] does not record 'directly' from 'digital music recordings,' and therefore [it] could not be a digital audio recording device unless it makes copies 'from transmissions.'"); *see also id.* at 1078 ("Under the plain meaning of the Act's definition of digital audio recording devices, computers (and their hard drives) are not digital audio recording devices because their 'primary purpose' is not to make digital audio copied recordings."); *id.* at 1081 ("Because the Rio cannot make copies from transmissions, but instead, can only make copies from a computer hard drive, it is not a digital audio recording device.").

[1175] *See* S. Rep. No. 102-294, at 49 (1992) (definition "cover[s] those objects commonly understood to embody sound recordings and their underlying works, such as recorded compact discs (CD's), digital audio tapes (DAT's), audio cassettes and long-playing albums (LP's), and in the near future, digital compact cassettes (DCC's) and mini-discs (MD's)"); *id.* at 51 ("If the 'primary purpose' of the recording function is to make objects other than digital audio copied recordings, then the machine or device is not a 'digital audio recording device,' *even if the machine or device is technically capable of making such recordings.*") (emphasis added); *id.* ("the typical personal computer would not fall within the definition of 'digital audio recording device'").

[1176] A&M Records, Inc. v. Napster, Inc., 239 F.3d 1004, 1024 (9th Cir. 2001).

[1177] 114 F. Supp. 2d 896 (N.D. Cal. 2000), *aff'd in part, rev'd in part*, 239 F.3d 1004 (9th Cir. 2001).

[1178] 239 F.3d at 1012.

fair use.[1179] It then held that Napster was liable for its users' actions under both contributory infringement[1180] and vicarious liability theories.[1181] Ultimately, Napster was ordered to install a new filtering mechanism which searched user files for specific "audio fingerprints."[1182] Following the second appeal, Napster filed for bankruptcy protection, its assets were sold, and Napster was re-launched as an authorized, fee-based service.[1183]

Following the original Napster's demise, attention shifted to other peer-to-peer file sharing services. In particular, several services developed file-sharing software that did not maintain an index of file names on a central server. Grokster used "FastTrack" technology in which the index was distributed to various "supernodes," or computers on the network with free hard disk space; while Streamcast's Morpheus software used the open-source "Gnutella" technology, in which each computer maintains its own index, and a search request is simply passed from computer to computer until a match is located.[1184] Because neither service maintained its index on a central server, an injunction against further distribution of the software would not halt any infringement, because existing users could continue sharing files without the active assistance of the website.[1185] In addition, both defendants submitted evidence that their software was capable of and was actually used to share non-infringing files, including public domain works.[1186] In part for these reasons, the district court granted summary judgment to Grokster and Streamcast,[1187] and the Ninth Circuit affirmed.[1188]

[1179] *Id.* at 1013–17. The court also rejected Napster's argument that "sampling" a recording to decide whether to purchase it and "space-shifting" a recording that one already owned on CD were fair uses. *Id.* at 1018–19.

[1180] *Id.* at 1022.

[1181] *Id.* at 1024. For criticism of this holding, see § 4I[1][b].

[1182] A&M Records, Inc. v. Napster, Inc., 284 F.3d 1091, 1097–98 (9th Cir. 2002). The panel that heard the second appeal did not appear to understand that the MP3 files were not themselves located on the Napster index.

[1183] After a long-running dispute over whether companies which invested in Napster bore any responsibility for its conduct, see UMG Recordings, Inc. v. Bertelsmann AG, 222 F.R.D. 408 (N.D. Cal. 2004) (denying motion to dismiss), settlements were reached between the investors and copyright owners.

[1184] Metro-Goldwyn-Mayer Studios, Inc. v. Grokster, Ltd., 545 U.S. 913, 921–22 (2005).

[1185] Metro-Goldwyn-Mayer Studios, Inc. v. Grokster, Ltd., 259 F. Supp. 2d 1029, 1041 (C.D. Cal. 2003) ("If either Defendant closed their doors and deactivated all computers within their control, users of their products could continue sharing files with little or no interruption."), *aff'd*, 380 F.3d 1154 (9th Cir. 2004), *rev'd*, 545 U.S. 913 (2005).

[1186] 259 F. Supp. 2d at 1035 ("it is undisputed that there are substantial noninfringing uses for Defendants' software").

[1187] *Id.* at 1037 ("Defendants correctly point out that in order to be liable under a theory of contributory infringement, they must have actual knowledge of infringement at a time when they can use that knowledge to stop the particular infringement."); *id.* at 1045 ("While the parties dispute what Defendants feasibly could do to alter their software, here, unlike in *Napster*, there is no admissible evidence before the Court indicating that Defendants have the ability to supervise and control the infringing conduct (all of which occurs *after* the product has passed to end-users).") (emphasis in original).

[1188] 380 F.3d 1154 (9th Cir. 2004), *rev'd*, 545 U.S. 913 (2005).

The Supreme Court granted certiorari and reversed. Although the concurring opinions in *Grokster* reveal that the Justices were deeply divided about the merits of the *Sony* case,[1189] the unanimous opinion by Justice Souter side-stepped the contentious issue of *Sony* almost entirely. First, the Court re-interpreted *Sony* as a case involving the *knowledge* element of contributory infringement, saying: "*Sony* barred secondary liability based on *presuming or imputing intent* to cause infringement *solely* from the design or distribution of a product capable of substantial lawful use, which the distributor knows is in fact used for infringement."[1190] The Court then held that the Ninth Circuit erred in holding that the distributor of a device capable of substantial non-infringing use could never be held liable, "even when an actual purpose to cause infringing use is shown by evidence independent of design and distribution of the product."[1191]

Next, again borrowing from patent law,[1192] the Court held that "active inducement" of infringement could render a defendant liable for the direct infringement of another. It stated that "one who distributes a device with the object of promoting its use to infringe copyright, as shown by clear expression or other affirmative steps taken to foster infringement, is liable for the resulting acts of infringement by third parties."[1193] Departing from previous patent case law, however, the Court held that the plaintiff need not show that the defendants actually "communicated an inducing message to their software users."[1194] Instead, it was sufficient to show that the defendants "acted with a purpose to cause copyright violations by use of software suitable for illegal use."[1195]

The Court held that this standard was satisfied by three types of evidence. "First, each company showed itself to be aiming to satisfy a known source of demand for copyright infringement, the market comprising former Napster users."[1196] Second, "neither company attempted to develop filtering tools or other mechanisms to diminish the infringing activity using their software."[1197] Third,

---

[1189] Three justices, in an opinion by Justice Ginsburg, thought that even though there was evidence that the software was *capable* of substantial non-infringing use, the defendants should be held liable because "Grokster's and StreamCast's products were . . . overwhelmingly used to infringe." 545 U.S. at 948 (Ginsburg, J., concurring). Three justices, in an opinion by Justice Breyer, praised the *Sony* standard as "clear," "strongly technology protecting," "forward looking," and "mindful of the limitations facing judges where matters of technology are concerned," and thought that the evidence in the lower court easily met the *Sony* standard. 545 U.S. at 952, 957–58 (Breyer, J., concurring).

[1190] Metro-Goldwyn-Mayer Studios, Inc. v. Grokster, Ltd., 545 U.S. 913, 933 (2005).

[1191] *Id.* at 934.

[1192] *See* 35 U.S.C. § 271(b) ("Whoever actively induces infringement of a patent shall be liable as an infringer."). *See* § 2E[2][c].

[1193] 545 U.S. at 919. The Court repeated the language of the second sentence later in the opinion. *Id.* at 936–37.

[1194] *Id.* at 937.

[1195] *Id.* at 938. *See also* Columbia Pictures Indus., Inc. v. Fung, 710 F.3d 1020, 1033 (9th Cir. 2013) (*Grokster's* inducement rule applies to the provision of services as well as devices or software).

[1196] Metro-Goldwyn-Mayer Studios, Inc. v. Grokster, Ltd., 545 U.S. 913, 939 (2005).

[1197] *Id.* Reliance on this evidence of "a failure to take affirmative steps to prevent infringement," *id.* at 939 n.12, contradicts the Court's earlier statement that the defendant's intent or purpose must be shown by evidence of "other *affirmative* steps taken to foster infringement."

because both companies distributed their software for free and made money by selling advertising directed to users, the Court found that "the commercial sense of their enterprise turns on high-volume use, which the record shows is infringing."[1198] From this evidence, the Court concluded that "[t]he [defendants'] unlawful objective is unmistakable."[1199]

Although some have expressed the view that the Supreme Court's "inducement" standard is a new, third type of secondary liability, the better view is that it is simply a specific application of the existing standard for contributory infringement. The most common statement of the standard for contributory infringement is "one who, with knowledge of the infringing activity, *induces*, causes or materially contributes to the infringing conduct of another."[1200] In addition, the Supreme Court stated in *Grokster* that "[o]ne infringes contributorily by intentionally inducing or encouraging direct infringement,"[1201] and it added that "[b]ecause we resolve the case based on an inducement theory, there is no need to analyze separately MGM's vicarious liability theory."[1202]

[3]   Secondary Liability and the Internet

[a]   In General

The leading case regarding secondary liability on the Internet is *Religious Technology Center v. Netcom On-Line Communication Services, Inc.*,[1203] in which the Church of Scientology alleged that Netcom provided Internet access for a computer bulletin board operated by Klemesrud, over which former Church member Dennis Erlich made proprietary Church documents available. The bulk of the court's opinion concerned Netcom's potential liability for direct infringement, contributory infringement, and vicarious liability.

Although Netcom's computers had actually reproduced and re-transmitted the infringing copies, the district court refused to hold Netcom directly liable for the infringement. The court noted that "Netcom did not take any affirmative action that directly resulted in copying plaintiffs' works other than by installing and maintaining a system whereby software automatically forwards messages received from

---

[1198] *Id.* at 939–40. *See also Fung*, 710 F.3d at 1035–36 (defendant who actively encouraged uploading of infringing BitTorrent files, failed to develop filtering tools, and relied primarily on advertising revenue was liable for inducement).

[1199] *Grokster*, 545 U.S. at 940. After the Supreme Court's decision, Grokster settled, leaving StreamCast as the only remaining defendant. The District Court then granted summary judgment against StreamCast on the inducement theory. *See* Metro-Goldwyn-Mayer Studios, Inc. v. Grokster, Ltd., 454 F. Supp. 2d 966 (C.D. Cal. 2006), *permanent injunction granted* at 518 F. Supp. 2d 1197 (C.D. Cal. 2007).

[1200] Gershwin Publishing Corp. v. Columbia Artists Mgmt., Inc., 443 F.2d 1159, 1162 (2d Cir. 1971) (emphasis added). *See also* Perfect 10, Inc. v. Amazon.com, Inc., 508 F.3d 1146, 1171 (9th Cir. 2007) ("Our tests for contributory liability are consistent with the rule set forth in *Grokster*.") (citing *Gershwin*).

[1201] Metro-Goldwyn-Mayer Studios, Inc. v. Grokster, Ltd., 545 U.S. 913, 930 (2005) (citing *Gershwin*).

[1202] *Id.* at 930 n.9.

[1203] 907 F. Supp. 1361 (N.D. Cal. 1995).

subscribers,"[1204] and it held that "[a]lthough copyright is a strict liability statute, there should still be some element of volition or causation which is lacking where a defendant's system is merely used to create a copy by a third party."[1205]

With regard to contributory infringement, the court found that there was a genuine issue of material fact concerning whether Netcom "knew or should have known that Erlich has infringed plaintiffs' copyrights":

> Where a [provider] cannot reasonably verify a claim of infringement, either because of a possible fair use defense, the lack of copyright notices on the copies, or the copyright holder's failure to provide the necessary documentation to show that there is a likely infringement, the operator's lack of knowledge will be found reasonable and there will be no liability for contributory infringement for allowing the continued distribution of the works on its system.[1206]

The court also concluded that "[p]roviding a service that allows for the automatic distribution of all Usenet postings, infringing and noninfringing," constituted "substantial participation" in the infringing activity.[1207] It therefore declined to grant summary judgment to Netcom on the issue of contributory infringement.

With regard to vicarious liability, the court found that there was a genuine issue of fact as to whether Netcom had the right and ability to supervise the conduct of its subscribers.[1208] However, the court found that the plaintiff did not "provide any evidence of a direct financial benefit received by Netcom from Erlich's infringing postings," because "Netcom receives a fixed fee," and "[t]here is no evidence that infringement by Erlich, or any other user of Netcom's services, in any way enhances the value of Netcom's services to subscribers or attracts new subscribers."[1209] Accordingly, the court held that Netcom was not vicariously liable for any infringement committed by Erlich.

The *Netcom* court's analysis, refusing to hold providers of computer services directly liable for infringing activity committed by others using their computers, and instead analyzing their conduct under the principles of secondary liability, has subsequently been endorsed by a number of other courts.[1210] And although the

---

[1204] *Id.* at 1368.

[1205] *Id.* at 1370. This limitation on direct liability has been widely accepted in the lower courts. *See* American Broadcasting Cos. v. Aereo, Inc., 134 S. Ct. 2498, 2512 (2014) (dissenting opinion) ("Every Court of Appeals to have considered an automated-service provider's direct liability for copyright infringement has adopted [the volitional conduct] rule."). Although the majority in *Aereo* rejected the application of the volitional conduct rule in the factual situation before it, it acknowledged that "[i]n other cases involving different kinds of service or technology providers, a user's involvement in the operation of the provider's equipment and selection of the content transmitted may well bear on whether" the equipment provider is directly liable. *Id.* at 2507 (majority opinion).

[1206] 907 F. Supp. 1361, 1374 (N.D. Cal. 1995).

[1207] *Id.* at 1375.

[1208] *Id.* at 1375–76.

[1209] *Id.* at 1377.

[1210] *See* CoStar Group, Inc. v. LoopNet, Inc., 373 F.3d 544, 548–51 (4th Cir. 2004); Cartoon Network, L.P. v. CSC Holdings, Inc., 536 F.3d 121, 130–31 (2d Cir. 2008); Field v. Google, Inc., 412 F. Supp. 2d 1106,

Netcom principles were partially codified in the Digital Millennium Copyright Act, courts have held that prior case law was specifically preserved and was *not* preempted by the DMCA.[1211]

After the Supreme Court's ruling in the *Grokster* case, the Ninth Circuit decided a trio of cases involving secondary liability brought by Perfect 10, a purveyor of soft-core pornography. First, in *Perfect 10, Inc. v. CCBill LLC*, the court addressed a number of issues concerning the DMCA's statutory immunity for internet service providers.[1212] Second, in *Perfect 10, Inc. v. Amazon.com, Inc.*, the court held that Google could not be held directly liable for automatically generating links to images posted by third parties that turned out to be infringing,[1213] but that it could be held liable for maintaining those links after it learned that the images were infringing. "Google could be held contributorily liable if it had knowledge that infringing Perfect 10 images were available using its search engine, could take simple measures to prevent further damage to Perfect 10's copyrighted works, and failed to take such steps."[1214] The court further held that Google was *not* vicariously liable, because it did not have the right or ability to control the infringing activity of third parties who posted the infringing images on the Internet.[1215]

Third, in *Perfect 10, Inc. v. VISA Int'l Service Ass'n*, the court considered whether financial institutions could be held liable for processing credit-card payments to allegedly infringing websites. The court held that the defendants did not "materially contribute" to the alleged infringement, because the credit-card payments did not *directly* assist in the reproduction, distribution or display of the infringing copies.[1216] The court distinguished the search engines in *Amazon.com* and the indexing software in *Napster* and *Grokster*, saying that "[h]elping users to locate an image might substantially assist users to download infringing images, but processing payments does not."[1217] The court acknowledged that "Defendants make it easier for infringement to be *profitable*, which tends to increase financial incentives to infringe,"[1218] but it held that "because infringement of Perfect 10's copyrights can occur without using Defendants' payment system, we hold that payment processing . . . does not constitute a 'material contribution' under the test for contributory infringement of copyrights."[1219] Finally, as in *Amazon.com*, the

---

1115 (D. Nev. 2006), Parker v. Google, Inc., 422 F. Supp. 2d 492, 497 (E.D. Pa. 2006), *aff'd*, 2007 U.S. App. LEXIS 16370 (3d Cir. July 20, 2007).

[1211] *See CoStar*, 373 F.3d at 552–55; 17 U.S.C. § 512(l) (failure to qualify for limitation of liability under § 512 does not adversely affect any other defenses).

[1212] 488 F.3d 1102 (9th Cir. 2007). *See* § 4I[3][b].

[1213] 508 F.3d 1146, 1159–62 (9th Cir. 2007). *See* § 4G[5].

[1214] *Id.* at 1172.

[1215] *Id.* at 1173–75.

[1216] 494 F.3d 788, 796 (9th Cir. 2007).

[1217] *Id.* at 797.

[1218] *Id.* (emphasis in original).

[1219] *Id.* at 798. The ruling drew a strong dissent from Judge Kozinski, who wrote that payment "is not just an economic incentive for infringement; it's an essential step in the infringement process," because the infringing images were not distributed until payment was made. *Id.* at 812 (Kozinski, J., dissenting). He also criticized the majority's suggestion that there were "other viable mechanisms" for

court held that the financial institutions were not vicariously liable, because they did not have the right or ability to control the infringing activity of third-party websites.[1220]

[b] Limitation of Liability for Online Service Providers

Despite the holding in *Netcom*, Internet service providers were concerned that they might be held liable for the infringing activities of those to whom they provided Internet connections and hosting services — either direct liability, because their computers reproduced, distributed and displayed infringing images uploaded by subscribers,[1221] or contributory or vicarious liability.[1222] Accordingly, service providers sought a legislative solution in Congress. The result was the "Online Copyright Infringement Liability Limitation Act," which was enacted as Title II of the Digital Millennium Copyright Act of 1998, and was codified at 17 U.S.C. § 512.

[i] Safe Harbors

Section 512 limits the liability of service providers in four common situations if certain specific conditions are met. In each case, if the service provider meets the conditions, the service provider is only liable for the limited injunctive relief specified in subsection (j).[1223] The four "safe harbors" are as follows:

(a) Transitory Digital Network Communications

A qualifying service provider is not liable for "transmitting, routing, or providing connections for" infringing material by an "automatic technical process," as long as someone other than the service provider initiates the transmission, selects the materials, and chooses the recipient, and the service provider does not modify the contents of the transmission. Further, the service provider is not liable

---

payment, noting that there were other ways of locating infringing copies in *Amazon.com*, *Napster* and *Grokster* as well. *Id.* at 812–14.

[1220] *Id.* at 803. Dissenting, Judge Kozinski pointed out that credit card companies reserve the right to refuse to process payment for gambling websites, or "for any illegal purpose." *Id.* at 817 n.13. However, he agreed that "a utility has no right to stop providing electricity or phone service because it learns that its electrons are being put to illegal use," that "[c]omputer manufacturers don't usually retain the right to reclaim computers they have sold because they are being used unlawfully," and that "software producers and repairmen" would likewise fail the first prong of vicarious liability. *Id.* at 821–22.

[1221] *See, e.g.*, Playboy Enterprises, Inc. v. Frena, 839 F. Supp. 1552, 1556–57 (M.D. Fla. 1993) (operator of a bulletin board service was liable for public distribution and public display of infringing photographs that were posted by subscribers).

[1222] *See, e.g.*, Marobie-FL, Inc. v. National Association of Fire Equipment Distributors, 983 F. Supp. 1167, 1178–79 (N.D. Ill. 1997) (applying *Netcom* analysis and finding triable issue of fact on contributory infringement).

[1223] 17 U.S.C. § 512(j). This section limits an injunction to "[a]n order restraining the service provider from providing access to infringing material or activity residing at a particular online site on the provider's system or network," or access "to a subscriber or account holder of the service provider's system or network who is engaging in infringing activity and is identified in the order," or to other relief "necessary to prevent or restrain infringement, . . . if such relief is the least burdensome to the service provider among the forms of relief" that are available.

for "the intermediate and transient storage of that material" in the course of such activities, as long as "no copy of the material is maintained . . . for a longer period than is reasonably necessary for the transmission, routing, or provision of connections."[1224]

The "intermediate or transient storage" exempted under section 512(a) can be relatively long-lived. A district court has held that AOL was not liable where it maintained USENET messages on its servers for as long as 14 days, because the legislative history indicated that the statute was designed to codify the holding in *Netcom*, in which USENET messages had been maintained for 11 days.[1225] Although the Ninth Circuit reversed the district court on other grounds, it specifically approved this portion of the district court's holding.[1226]

(b)   System Caching

"Caching" refers to the temporary storage of data, such as the contents of frequently visited websites, in order to speed or facilitate user access to that data. A qualifying service provider is not liable for such "intermediate and temporary storage of material" posted online by another person, as long as the storage is carried out through an automatic technical process,[1227] and the service provider (A) does not modify the content; (B) complies with industry standards for refreshing, reloading and updating the material; (C) complies with industry standards for collection of data by the originating website; (D) does not interfere with password protection or other conditions that restrict access to the originating website, such as payment of a fee; and (E) complies with the "notice-and-take-down" provisions of subsection (c), if the material has been removed or disabled on the originating website.[1228]

In the only significant discussion of section 512(b) to date, a district court held that Google was not liable for creating and maintaining a "cache" of websites to facilitate its search engine, and for storing the websites in the cache for approximately 14 to 20 days, "to enable subsequent users to access those pages if they are unsuccessful in requesting the materials from the originating site for whatever reason."[1229]

(c)   Web Hosting

Section 512(c) limits the liability of service providers who provide "hosting" services by allocating server space to customers or clients who wish to make information available to others. A qualifying service provider is not liable "by reason of the storage at the direction of a user of material that resides on a system

---

[1224] 17 U.S.C. § 512(a).

[1225] *See* Ellison v. Robertson, 189 F. Supp. 2d 1051, 1068–70 (C.D. Cal. 2002), *rev'd on other grounds*, 357 F.3d 1072 (9th Cir. 2004).

[1226] 357 F.3d at 1081.

[1227] 17 U.S.C. § 512(b)(1).

[1228] 17 U.S.C. § 512(b)(2).

[1229] Field v. Google, Inc., 412 F. Supp. 2d 1106, 1124 (D. Nev. 2006). *Accord*, Parker v. Google, Inc., 422 F. Supp. 2d 492, 498 (E.D. Pa. 2006), *aff'd on other grounds*, 242 Fed. Appx. 833 (3d Cir. 2007).

or network controlled or operated by or for the service provider," as long as the service provider (A) (i) does not have actual knowledge that the material or an activity using the material is infringing, (ii) is not aware of facts or circumstances from which infringing activity is apparent, and (iii) upon obtaining such knowledge or awareness, acts expeditiously to remove or disable access to the material; (B) does not receive a financial benefit directly attributable to the infringing activity, if the service provider has the right and ability to control that activity; and (C) complies with the notice-and-take-down provisions discussed below.[1230]

The keen-eyed observer will note that the first two conditions bear a strong similarity to contributory infringement and vicarious liability, respectively. With regard to contributory infringement, the statute implicitly assumes that hosting infringing material is a "material contribution," and it removes the safe harbor if the host has (i) actual knowledge or (ii) constructive knowledge that the material is infringing (the knowledge element), and the host fails to "act expeditiously" to remove or disable access to the material upon acquiring such knowledge.[1231] With regard to vicarious liability, two Courts of Appeals have held that, because the statute assumes that the service provider has the ability to remove or disable access to the material (i.e., the right and ability to control the infringement), the statute must require "something more" (such as "exerting substantial influence on the activities of users") in order to disqualify the service provider from the safe harbor.[1232]

Note that under subsection (c)(1)(A), the "actual" knowledge must be knowledge that specific material or activity is infringing, not merely knowledge of an allegation of infringement, or general knowledge that infringing activity is occurring.[1233] Note further that constructive knowledge is defined as awareness of facts "from which infringing activity is apparent." The House Report states that this subsection "can best be described as a 'red flag' test."[1234] It explains that:

> The "red flag" test has both a subjective and an objective element. In determining whether the service provider was aware of a "red flag," the subjective awareness of the service provider of the facts or circumstances in question must be determined. However, in deciding whether those facts or circumstances constitute a "red flag" — in other words, whether infringing activity would have been apparent to a reasonable person . . . — an objective standard should be used.[1235]

[1230] 17 U.S.C. § 512(c)(1).

[1231] This is consistent with Perfect 10, Inc. v. Amazon.com, Inc., 508 F.3d 1146, 1172 (9th Cir. 2007), which held that "a computer system operator can be held contributorily liable if it 'has *actual* knowledge that *specific* infringing material is available using its system,' and can 'take simple measures to prevent further damage' to copyrighted works, yet [it] continues to provide access to infringing works.").

[1232] Viacom Int'l, Inc. v. YouTube, Inc., 676 F.3d 19, 38 (2d Cir. 2012); UMG Recordings, Inc. v. Shelter Capital Partners, LLC, 718 F.3d 1006, 1029–30 (9th Cir. 2013). *See also* Columbia Pictures Indus., Inc. v. Fung, 710 F.3d 1020, 1046 (9th Cir. 2013) (defendant who assisted infringers was disqualified from taking advantage of this safe harbor).

[1233] *Viacom,* 676 F.3d at 30–32; *Shelter Capital,* 718 F.3d at 1021–22.

[1234] H.R. Rep. No. 105-551, Part II, at 54 (1998).

[1235] *Id.*

Because the statute requires that the service provider "remove or disable access to *the* material" when it becomes aware of such "red flags," this subsection "turns on whether the provider was subjectively aware of facts that would have made the *specific* infringement 'objectively' obvious to a reasonable person."[1236]

This subsection has been construed narrowly. Although the House Report states that a website using such words as "pirate," "bootleg" or other slang terms may "make [its] illegal purpose obvious," the Ninth Circuit has held that two softcore porn websites titled "illegal.net" and "stolencelebritypics.com" did *not* raise a "red flag." It explained that "[w]hen a website traffics in pictures that are titillating by nature, describing photographs as 'illegal' or 'stolen' may be an attempt to increase their salacious appeal, rather than an admission that the photographs are actually illegal or stolen."[1237] Similarly, "[p]assword-hacking websites are . . . not *per se* 'red flags' of infringement," because "[t]here is simply no way for a service provider to conclude that the passwords enabled infringement without trying the passwords," but the statute "impose[s] no such investigative duties on service providers."[1238] To the contrary, the statute expressly states that the safe harbors shall *not* be conditioned on "a service provider monitoring its service or affirmatively seeking facts indicating infringing activity."[1239]

In *Viacom Int'l, Inc. v. YouTube, Inc.*, Viacom alleged that "tens of thousands of videos on YouTube . . . were taken unlawfully from Viacom's copyrighted works" and that YouTube was aware of the infringement but failed to do anything about it.[1240] YouTube, in turn, alleged that it had fully complied with the "notice-and-take-down" provisions of the statute after Viacom notified it of infringing material. The Second Circuit held that section 512(c) requires actual or constructive knowledge of specific infringing material, and remanded to determine whether YouTube had such knowledge with regard to any of the copyrighted works at issue.[1241] The court also held that "willful blindness" could substitute for actual knowledge;[1242] that (c)(1)(B) ("right and ability to control") did not require specific knowledge, but that it required "something more" than the ability to remove or disable access to the material;[1243] and that the phrase "by reason of storage" was not limited to storage alone, but also implicitly included reasonable means of "facilitating access to user-stored material," including transmitting the material to users.[1244]

[1236] *Viacom*, 676 F.3d at 31 (emphasis added); *accord, Shelter Capital*, 718 F.3d at 1025. *See also Fung*, 710 F.3d at 1043 (copyrighted movies were sufficiently current and well-known that infringement would have been objectively obvious to a reasonable person).

[1237] Perfect 10, Inc. v. CCBill, LLC, 488 F.3d 1102, 1114 (9th Cir. 2007).

[1238] *Id.*

[1239] 17 U.S.C. § 512(m)(1).

[1240] 718 F. Supp. 2d 514, 518 (S.D.N.Y. 2010), *aff'd in part, vacated and remanded in part*, 676 F.3d 19 (2d Cir. 2012).

[1241] 676 F.3d at 30–34. *See also Shelter Capital*, 718 F.3d at 1021–22 (affirming summary judgment for lack of actual or constructive knowledge).

[1242] *Viacom*, 676 F.3d at 34–35.

[1243] *Id.* at 36–38. *Accord, Shelter Capital*, 718 F.3d at 1029–30.

[1244] *Viacom*, 676 F.3d at 38–40. *Accord, Shelter Capital*, 718 F.3d at 1015–20.

(d) Information Location Tools

A qualifying service provider is not liable for "referring or linking users to an online location containing infringing material or infringing activity, by using information location tools, including a directory, index, reference, pointer, or hypertext link," as long as the service provider satisfies the same three conditions as are set forth in the "hosting" provision. This subsection is potentially available to a search engine that links to infringing material, such as Google.[1245] The House Report gives an example of what would constitute a "red flag" for such a provider:

> The intended objective of this standard is to exclude from the safe harbor sophisticated "pirate" directories — which refer Internet users to other selected Internet sites where pirate software, books, movies, and music can be downloaded or transmitted. Such pirate directories refer Internet users to sites that are obviously infringing because they typically use words such as "pirate," [or] "bootleg," . . . to make their illegal purpose obvious.[1246]

[ii] Eligibility for Safe Harbors

To qualify for one of the safe harbors, a defendant must be a "service provider." For subsection (a), a "service provider" is "an entity offering the transmission, routing, or providing of connections for digital online communications."[1247] For the other three subsections, a "service provider" is defined broadly as "a provider of online services or network access, or the operator of facilities therefore."[1248] This definition applies to a wide variety of Internet businesses, including an online auction site,[1249] an online seller of new and used books,[1250] a peer-to-peer file sharing service,[1251] video-sharing websites,[1252] and a credit-card payment processing service.[1253]

To qualify for the safe harbors, a service provider must have "adopted and reasonably implemented . . . a policy that provides for the termination in appropriate circumstances of subscribers and account holders . . . who are repeat

---

[1245] *See* Perfect 10, Inc. v. Amazon.com, Inc., 508 F.3d 1146, 1175 (9th Cir. 2007).

[1246] H.R. Rep. No. 105-551, Part II, at 57–58 (1998). *See also id.* at 57 ("a directory provider would not be similarly aware merely because it saw one or more well known photographs of a celebrity at a site devoted to that person.").

[1247] 17 U.S.C. § 512(k)(1)(A).

[1248] 17 U.S.C. § 512(k)(1)(B).

[1249] Hendrickson v. eBay, Inc., 165 F. Supp. 2d 1082, 1088 (C.D. Cal. 2001).

[1250] Hendrickson v. Amazon.com, 298 F. Supp. 2d 914, 915 (C.D. Cal. 2003); Corbis Corp. v. Amazon.com, Inc., 351 F. Supp. 2d 1090, 1100 (W.D. Wash. 2004).

[1251] In re Aimster Copyright Litigation, 334 F.3d 643, 655 (7th Cir. 2003).

[1252] Viacom Int'l, Inc. v. YouTube, Inc., 718 F. Supp. 2d 514, 518 (S.D.N.Y. 2010), *aff'd in part, vacated and remanded in part on other grounds*, 676 F.3d 19 (2d Cir. 2012); UMG Recordings, Inc. v. Veoh Networks, Inc., 665 F. Supp. 2d 1099, 1105 (C.D. Cal. 2009), *aff'd sub nom.* UMG Recordings, Inc. v. Shelter Capital Partners, LLC, 718 F.3d 1006, 1015 n.4 (9th Cir. 2013).

[1253] Perfect 10, Inc. v. CCBill, LLC, 340 F. Supp. 2d 1077, 1088 n.8 (C.D. Cal. 2004), *aff'd in part, rev'd in part on other grounds*, 488 F.3d 1102 (9th Cir. 2007). *But see* Perfect 10, Inc. v. Cybernet Ventures, Inc., 213 F. Supp. 2d 1146, 1175 (C.D. Cal. 2002) (questioning, but assuming without deciding, that website providing age-verification service for adult websites was a "service provider").

infringers."[1254] "[A] service provider 'implements' a policy if it has a working notification system, a procedure for dealing with DMCA-compliant notifications, and if it does not actively prevent copyright owners from collecting information needed to issue such notifications."[1255] "[A]n implementation is reasonable if, under 'appropriate circumstances,' the service provider terminates users who repeatedly or blatantly infringe copyright."[1256]

In *Ellison v. Robertson*, the court held that there was a triable issue of fact as to whether AOL "reasonably implemented" its policy, where AOL had changed its e-mail address for notifications, but failed to forward or respond to notices sent to the old address.[1257] In *In re Aimster Copyright Litigation*, the court held that Aimster did not "reasonably implement" its policy, because it instructed users how to encrypt their files, and thereby "disabled itself from doing anything to prevent infringement."[1258] In *Perfect 10, Inc. v. CCBill, LLC*, however, the court held that "a service provider need not affirmatively police its users for evidence of repeat infringement." Instead, it need only respond to notices of infringement that comply with the "notice-and-take-down" provisions described below.[1259] Because Perfect 10's notices did not "substantially comply" with the notice requirements, the court held that "knowledge of infringement may not be imputed to [defendants] based on Perfect 10's communications."[1260] Nonetheless, it remanded to allow the district court to determine whether the defendant had responded to compliant notices that were sent by third parties.[1261]

Several district courts have addressed whether a provider has "reasonably implemented" a policy for terminating repeat infringers. In *Corbis Corp. v. Amazon.com, Inc.*, the court held that "failure to properly implement an infringement policy requires a showing of instances where a service provider fails to terminate a user even though it has sufficient evidence to create actual knowledge of that user's blatant, repeat infringement of a willful and commercial nature."[1262] The court further held that "[a]ctual knowledge of blatant, repeat infringement cannot be imputed merely from the receipt of notices of infringement. Instead, there must be additional evidence available to the service provider to buttress the claim of infringement supplied by the notices."[1263] In *UMG Recordings, Inc. v. Veoh Networks, Inc.*, the court upheld a policy that terminated users only after a second warning triggered by a DMCA-compliant

---

[1254] 17 U.S.C. § 512(i)(1)(A).

[1255] Perfect 10, Inc. v. CCBill, LLC, 488 F.3d 1102, 1108 (9th Cir. 2007).

[1256] *Id.*

[1257] 357 F.3d 1072, 1080 (9th Cir. 2004).

[1258] 334 F.3d 643, 655 (7th Cir. 2003).

[1259] 488 F.3d at 1111–12.

[1260] *Id.* at 1113. *See* 17 U.S.C. § 512(c)(3)(B)(i) ("a notification from a copyright owner . . . that fails to comply substantially with the [notice requirements] . . . shall not be considered . . . in determining whether a service provider has actual knowledge or is aware of facts or circumstances from which infringing activity is apparent.").

[1261] 488 F.3d at 1113.

[1262] 351 F. Supp. 2d 1090, 1104 (W.D. Wash. 2004).

[1263] *Id.* at 1105–06.

notice, even if the first notice listed multiple alleged infringements.[1264] And in *Viacom Int'l, Inc. v. YouTube, Inc.*, the court upheld a "three-strikes" policy that similarly "count[ed] as only one strike . . . both (1) a single DMCA take-down notice identifying multiple videos uploaded by the user, and (2) multiple take-down notices identifying videos uploaded by the user received by YouTube within a two-hour period."[1265] Both the *UMG* and *Viacom* courts also held that automated filtering is not sufficiently reliable to serve as a predicate for a finding of repeat infringement.[1266]

In addition to reasonably implementing a repeat-infringer policy, a service provider must "accommodate and . . . not interfere with standard technical measures" that "are used by copyright owners to identify or protect copyrighted works."[1267] In the only appellate discussion to date, the Ninth Circuit found triable issues of fact whether blocking access to allegedly infringing websites interfered with a "standard technical measure" within the meaning of the statute, and whether the defendant was justified in blocking access because the plaintiff's reversal of credit-card charges had imposed "substantial costs" on the defendant.[1268]

Courts disagree over whether the section 512 safe harbors apply to state-law copyrights in sound recordings fixed before February 15, 1972. Some courts have held that the express language of section 301(c), which provides that state-law causes of action in such works "shall not be annulled or limited by this title until February 15, 2067,"[1269] prevents the application of section 512.[1270] Other courts have reasoned that the purpose of the safe harbors, to protect Internet service providers from liability for the actions of their users, would be thwarted unless section 512 applies to such works.[1271]

[iii]   Notice-and-Take-Down Provisions

Three of the four safe harbors require that the service provider comply with the "notice-and-take-down provisions" in subsection 512(c). That section requires that service provider "has designated an agent to receive notifications of claimed infringement," and has provided the agent's contact information to the Copyright Office and on its website.[1272] It also provides that the copyright owner must

---

[1264] 665 F. Supp. 2d 1099, 1116–18 (C.D. Cal. 2009), *aff'd sub nom.* UMG Recordings, Inc. v. Shelter Capital Partners, LLC, 718 F.3d 1006, 1015 n.5 (9th Cir. 2013).

[1265] 718 F. Supp. 2d 514, 527–28 (S.D.N.Y. 2010), *aff'd in part, vacated and remanded in part on other grounds*, 676 F.3d 19 (2d Cir. 2012).

[1266] 718 F. Supp. 2d at 528; 665 F. Supp. 2d at 1117–18.

[1267] 17 U.S.C. §§ 512(i)(1)(B), (i)(2). Such measures must "have been developed pursuant to a broad consensus of copyright owners and service providers in an open, fair, voluntary, multi-industry standards process" and must "not impose substantial costs on service providers or substantial burdens on their systems or networks." 17 U.S.C. § 512(i)(2)(A), (C).

[1268] Perfect 10, Inc. v. CCBill, LLC, 488 F.3d 1102, 1115 (9th Cir. 2007).

[1269] 17 U.S.C. § 301(c).

[1270] UMG Recordings, Inc. v. Escape Media Group, Inc., 964 N.Y.S.2d 106 (App. Div. 2013).

[1271] Capitol Records, Inc. v. MP3Tunes, LLC, 821 F. Supp. 2d 627, 640–42 (S.D.N.Y. 2011).

[1272] 17 U.S.C. § 512(c)(2).

provide a written notice containing six elements: (i) a physical or electronic signature of the copyright owner or its agent; (ii) identification of the copyrighted work alleged to be infringed, or a representative list of such works; (iii) identification of the material claimed to be infringing, including information reasonably sufficient to permit the service provider to locate the material; (iv) contact information for the complaining party; (v) a "statement that the complaining party has a good faith belief that the use of the material . . . is not authorized by the copyright owner, its agent, or the law"; and (vi) a statement under penalty of perjury that the information is accurate, and that the complaining party is authorized to act on behalf of the copyright owner.[1273] A service provider may not "cobble together [an] adequate notice from separately defective notices."[1274]

Once the copyright owner has served a compliant notice on the service provider, the service provider must "respond[] expeditiously to remove, or disable access to, the material that is claimed to be infringing" in order to benefit from the safe harbor.[1275] If the service provider wishes to avoid liability for taking the material down, it must then "take reasonable steps promptly to notify the subscriber that it has removed or disabled access to the material."[1276] The subscriber may then provide a counter-notification, a written notice containing four elements: (A) a physical or electronic signature of the subscriber; (B) identification of the material which has been removed, and the location of that material before it was removed; (C) a statement under penalty of perjury that the subscriber has a good faith belief that the material was removed or disabled "as a result of mistake or misidentification of the material"; and (D) the subscriber's contact information, and consent to personal jurisdiction.[1277]

Upon receipt of a compliant counter-notification, the service provider must then promptly provide a copy of the counter-notification to the complaining party.[1278] To avoid liability for removing the material, the service provider must then restore the removed material and cease disabling access to it between 10 and 14 business days after notifying the copyright owner, unless the copyright owner notifies the service

---

[1273] 17 U.S.C. § 512(c)(3)(A). Element (vi) reads: "A statement that the information is accurate, and under penalty of perjury, that the complaining party is authorized to act on behalf of the owner." This subsection could easily be read to mean that only the latter statement (concerning authorization) must be made under penalty of perjury. However, in *CCBill*, the Ninth Circuit held that both statements must be made under penalty of perjury, in order to protect the First Amendment rights of the person who posted the material. 488 F.3d at 1112.

[1274] *CCBill*, 488 F.3d at 1113. However, if the notice substantially complies with elements (ii), (iii) and (iv), then the service provider must give the complaining party another opportunity to comply. 17 U.S.C. § 512(c)(3)(B).

[1275] This identical phrase is used in 17 U.S.C. §§ 512(b)(2)(E), (c)(1)(C), and (d)(3). The service provider is not legally obligated to take the material down; but if it fails to do so, it will not be eligible for the safe harbor.

[1276] 17 U.S.C. § 512(g)(2)(A). Again, the service provider is not legally obligated to notify the subscriber, but if it fails to do so, it may be liable in tort for removing or disabling access to non-infringing material.

[1277] 17 U.S.C. § 512(g)(3).

[1278] 17 U.S.C. § 512(g)(2)(B).

provider that it has filed an infringement action seeking an injunction against the subscriber.[1279] If the copyright owner does file an infringement action, the takedown notice, in effect, gives the copyright owner the equivalent of a preliminary injunction without having to prove likelihood of success or likelihood of irreparable harm.

If the service provider complies with all of these conditions, then it is exempt from any liability for removing or disabling access to the material, "regardless of whether the material or activity is ultimately determined to be infringing."[1280] If the material that was removed is not infringing, the subscriber's only recourse is to sue the copyright owner or its agent for "knowingly materially misrepresent[ing] . . . that the material or activity is infringing."[1281] This section requires *subjective* bad faith, not merely objective unreasonableness.[1282] However, "[a]n allegation that a copyright owner acted in bad faith by issuing a takedown notice without proper consideration of the fair use doctrine . . . is sufficient to state a misrepresentation claim."[1283] Thus, in *Online Policy Group v. Diebold, Inc.*, where Diebold used the DMCA notice-and-take-down procedure to get a service provider to remove internal e-mails that disclosed "possible technical problems with Diebold's voting machines," the court held that Diebold "knowingly materially misrepresented" that the e-mails were infringing, "at least with respect to the portions of the email archive clearly subject to the fair use exception."[1284] The court concluded that "Diebold sought to use the DMCA's safe harbor provisions . . . as a sword to suppress publication of embarrassing content rather than as a shield to protect its intellectual property."[1285]

[4]   Digital Millennium Copyright Act

In 1996, the United States persuaded the World Intellectual Property Organization (WIPO) to adopt two new treaties, including the WIPO Copyright Treaty (WCT).[1286] The Digital Millennium Copyright Act of 1998 was enacted to "implement" articles 11 and 12 of the WCT. It contained new provisions against "circumvention of technological protection measures" and protection of "copyright management information," which are codified in Chapter 12 of Title 17.

[1279] 17 U.S.C. § 512(g)(2)(C).

[1280] 17 U.S.C. § 512(g)(1).

[1281] 17 U.S.C. § 512(f)(1). The copyright owner may also sue the subscriber for "knowingly materially misrepresent[ing] . . . that material or activity was removed or disabled by mistake or misidentification." 17 U.S.C. § 512(f)(2).

[1282] Rossi v. Motion Picture Ass'n of America, Inc., 391 F.3d 1000, 1003–05 (9th Cir. 2001) (expressly equating § 512(f) ("knowingly materially misrepresents") with the "good faith belief" required in § 512(c)(3)(A)(v)).

[1283] Lenz v. Universal Music Corp., 572 F. Supp. 2d 1150, 1154–55 (N.D. Cal. 2008).

[1284] 337 F. Supp. 2d 1195, 1204 (N.D. Cal. 2004). The court, however, erroneously appears to have applied an objective standard. *Id.* ("No *reasonable* copyright holder could have believed that the portions of the email archive discussing possible technical problems with Diebold's voting machines were protected by copyright.").

[1285] *Id.* at 1204–05.

[1286] *See* Pam Samuelson, *The U.S. Digital Agenda at WIPO*, 37 Va. J. Int'l L. 369, 409–18 (1997).

[a]   Anti-Circumvention

[i]   In General

Section 1201 contains three causes of action: a prohibition on the circumvention of technological measures that control access to a copyrighted work; a prohibition on trafficking in technology that helps circumvent such access-control measures; and a prohibition on trafficking in technology that helps circumvent copy-protection measures. In practice, however, the distinction between access-protection measures and copy-protection measures tends to blur, because most access-protection measures can also be used to protect against copying.[1287]

Section 1201(a)(1)(A) states that "No person shall circumvent a technological measure that effectively controls access to a work protected under this title."[1288]

Section 1201(a)(2) states that "[n]o person shall manufacture, import, offer to the public, provide, or otherwise traffic in any technology, product, service, device, component, or part" that "(A) is primarily designed or produced for the purpose of circumventing a technological measure that effectively controls access to a work protected under this title; (B) has only limited commercially significant purpose or use other than to circumvent" such a measure; or "(C) is marketed . . . for use in circumventing" such a measure.[1289]

Section 1201(b) imposes an identical prohibition with respect to "a technological measure that effectively protects a right of a copyright owner under this title."[1290] A measure effectively protects a right of a copyright owner "if the measure, in the ordinary course of its operation, prevents, restricts, or otherwise limits the exercise of a right of a copyright owner under this title,"[1291] or in other words, if the measure "prevents, restricts or otherwise limits" the reproduction, adaptation, public distribution, public performance, or public display of a copyrighted work.[1292]

In *Chamberlain Group, Inc. v. Skylink Technologies, Inc.*, the court set forth the elements of the second cause of action under the statute, and the distribution of the burdens of proof:

> A plaintiff alleging a violation of § 1201(a)(2) must prove: (1) ownership of a valid copyright on a work, (2) effectively controlled by a technological measure, which has been circumvented, (3) that third parties can now access (4) without authorization, in a manner that (5) infringes or facilitates infringing a right protected by the Copyright Act, because of a product that

---

[1287] *See, e.g.*, 321 Studios v. Metro-Goldwyn-Mayer Studios, Inc., 307 F. Supp. 2d 1085, 1097 (N.D. Cal. 2004) ("While 321 is technically correct that CSS controls access to encrypted DVDs, the purpose of this access control is to control copying of those DVDs, since encrypted DVDs cannot be copied unless they are accessed."); Apple, Inc. v. Psystar Corp., 673 F. Supp. 2d 931, 941 (N.D. Cal. 2009) ("Although Apple's technological measure may have been primarily aimed at controlling access, it also effectively protected its right to copy"), *aff'd on other grounds*, 658 F.3d 1150 (9th Cir. 2011).

[1288] 17 U.S.C. § 1201(a)(1).

[1289] 17 U.S.C. § 1201(a)(2).

[1290] 17 U.S.C. § 1201(b)(1).

[1291] 17 U.S.C. § 1201(b)(2).

[1292] U.S. v. Elcom Ltd., 203 F. Supp. 2d 1111, 1124 (N.D. Cal. 2002).

(6) the defendant either (i) designed or produced primarily for circumvention; (ii) made available despite only limited commercial significance other than circumvention; or (iii) marketed for use in circumvention of the controlling technological measure. . . . A plaintiff capable of proving elements (1) through (5) need prove only one of (6)(i), (ii), or (iii) to shift the burden . . . to the defendant. At that point, the various affirmative defenses enumerated throughout § 1201 become relevant.[1293]

Each of these elements will be examined in turn.

(a) Ownership of a Valid Copyright

Although *Chamberlain* states that the plaintiff must own a valid copyright in a work,[1294] other courts have allowed manufacturers and suppliers of access-control and copy-control technology to themselves sue defendants for providing or trafficking in technology designed to circumvent the plaintiff's technology.[1295]

(b) Access-Control Measures

"A technological measure 'effectively controls access to a work' if the measure, in the ordinary course of its operation, requires the application of information, or a process or a treatment, with the authority of the copyright owner, to gain access to the work."[1296] The House Report states that "effective" measures include those "based on encryption, scrambling, authentication, or some other measure that requires the use of a 'key' provided by a copyright owner."[1297] An example of such a measure is CSS, the "Content Scramble System" for DVDs.[1298] Another example is "region coding" that only allows games sold in a particular geographic region to be played on consoles sold in that region.[1299] Even simple password-based protection is included.[1300] However, embedded "bits" that encode "permissions" do

---

[1293] 381 F.3d 1178, 1203 (Fed. Cir. 2004). *Compare* CoxCom, Inc. v. Chaffee, 536 F.3d 101, 110 (1st Cir. 2008) (cause of action has only two elements: "(1) defendant trafficked in a technology; and (2) the technology was primarily designed or produced to circumvent conditional access controls to protected works, or has limited commercially significant use other than such circumvention.").

[1294] *Accord*, Lexmark Int'l, Inc. v. Static Control Components, Inc., 387 F.3d 522, 537–42 (6th Cir. 2004) (analyzing whether protection for computer program was eliminated by idea/expression and merger doctrines); *id.* at 550 (if program was not "protected under this title," then "the DMCA necessarily would not protect it.").

[1295] *See, e.g.*, CoxCom, Inc. v. Chaffee, 536 F.3d 101, 106–08, 110 (1st Cir. 2008) (cable TV provider has standing to sue defendants for selling digital cable filters, which enable users to avoid being billed for viewing pay-per-view movies); RealNetworks, Inc. v. Streambox, Inc., 2000 U.S. Dist. LEXIS 1889 (W.D. Wash. Jan. 18, 2000).

[1296] 17 U.S.C. § 1201(a)(3)(B).

[1297] H.R. Rep. No. 105–551 (Part II), at 39–40 (1998).

[1298] Universal City Studios, Inc. v. Reimerdes, 111 F. Supp. 2d 294, 308 (S.D.N.Y. 2000), *aff'd sub nom.* Universal City Studios, Inc. v. Corley, 273 F.3d 429 (2d Cir. 2001). CSS functions as both an access-control measure and a copy-control measure. *Id.*

[1299] *See* Sony Computer Entertainment America, Inc. v. Gamemasters, Inc., 87 F. Supp. 2d 976, 981–82, 987 (N.D. Cal. 1999).

[1300] *See* I.M.S. Inquiry Mgmt. Sys., Ltd. v. Berkshire Info. Sys., Inc., 307 F. Supp. 2d 521, 531–32 (S.D.N.Y. 2004).

not by themselves constitute an "effective" technological measure, because without additional software, there is nothing to prevent anyone from accessing or copying the work in which the bits are embedded.[1301] Likewise, an "authentication sequence" that controls the *use* of a computer program embedded in a laser printer does not "effectively control access" to that program, when anyone who bought the printer could read the literal code of the program directly from the printer's memory, with or without the benefit of the authentication sequence.[1302]

Note that there is a distinction between "encoding" and "encryption." All digital data is "encoded," because it must be translated into 1s and 0s to be reproduced and stored, and it must be translated back into text or images in order to be read, viewed, or listened to. Technically, therefore, all digital data "requires the application of information . . . to gain access to the work," and the statutory definition is hopelessly overbroad. The difference is that with "encoding," the specifications for the encoding algorithm are openly available, so that any manufacturer can make a device to decode the digital data,[1303] whereas with "encryption," the specifications for the encrypting algorithm are kept secret, so that only authorized manufacturers can make a device to decrypt the digital data.[1304] Thus, the fact that a given encryption scheme has already been cracked or "hacked" by others does not mean it is no longer "effective," since it need only be effective "in the ordinary course of its operation."[1305]

(c) Circumvention

"[T]o 'circumvent a technological measure' means to descramble a scrambled work, to decrypt an encrypted work, or otherwise to avoid, bypass, remove, deactivate, or impair a technological measure, without the authority of the copyright owner."[1306] In other words, the prohibition against circumvention

---

[1301] Agfa Monotype Corp. v. Adobe Systems, Inc., 404 F. Supp. 2d 1030, 1035–36 (N.D. Ill. 2005).

[1302] Lexmark Int'l, Inc. v. Static Control Components, Inc., 387 F.3d 522, 546–47 (6th Cir. 2004). *See also* MDY Industries, LLC v. Blizzard Entertainment, Inc., 629 F.3d 928, 952–54 (9th Cir. 2010) (security program for online game *World of Warcraft* did *not* "effectively control access" to the "individual non-literal elements" of the game, but did effectively control access to the real-time "dynamic non-literal elements" of the game).

[1303] *Cf. Agfa*, 404 F. Supp. 2d at 1036 ("Since the specifications for the TrueType Font have been available for free download from the Internet since 1995, it is clearly not secret or undisclosed. Embedding bits are not encrypted, scrambled or authenticated, and software applications, such as Acrobat 5.0, need not enter a password or authorization sequence to obtain access to the embedding bits or the specification for the TrueType font.").

[1304] *Cf.* Universal City Studios, Inc. v. Corley, 273 F.3d 429, 436–37 (2d Cir. 2001) ("CSS is an encryption scheme that employs an algorithm configured by a set of 'keys' to encrypt a DVD's contents. . . . Decryption in the case of CSS requires a set of 'player keys' contained in compliant DVD players, as well as an understanding of the CSS encryption algorithm"; authorized manufacturers are required to keep the algorithm and keys confidential).

[1305] *See* RealNetworks, Inc. v. DVD Copy Control Ass'n, 641 F. Supp. 2d 913, 932 (N.D. Cal. 2009). *Accord*, Universal City Studios, Inc. v. Reimerdes, 111 F. Supp. 2d 294, 317–18 (S.D.N.Y. 2000), *aff'd sub nom.* Universal City Studios, Inc. v. Corley, 273 F.3d 429 (2d Cir. 2001); 321 Studios, Inc. v. Universal City Studios, Inc., 307 F. Supp. 2d 1085, 1094–95 (N.D. Cal. 2004); Apple, Inc. v. Psystar Corp., 673 F. Supp. 2d 931, 941–42 (N.D. Cal. 2009).

[1306] 17 U.S.C. § 1201(a)(3)(A).

prohibits "hacking" in order to gain unauthorized access to a copyrighted work.[1307] Most courts have held that this provision does not apply when the defendant merely uses an authorized password issued to another without "hacking" or otherwise defeating the technological measure by technological means.[1308] Another court, however, disagrees, stating that the statute "provides broad statutory protection against . . . any form of unauthorized use — not just "breaking" — of a technology such as CSS."[1309]

(d)   Authorization

In *Chamberlain*, the manufacturer of a garage door opener used a technology designed to keep the door from being opened by unauthorized persons. The defendant Skylink developed and sold a "universal" remote that allegedly "circumvented" Chamberlain's technology in order to operate the Chamberlain garage door opener. Chamberlain sued, alleging that Skylink's remote control enabled "access" to its copyrighted software without authorization.[1310] The court rejected Chamberlain's argument, noting that "[c]onsumers who purchase a product containing a copy of embedded software have the inherent legal right to use that copy of the software," and that Chamberlain could not revoke that authorization.[1311]

Other courts, however, have rejected the argument that a purchaser of a copyrighted work has an "inherent legal right" to use it in ways not specifically authorized by the copyright owner. In *Universal City Studios, Inc. v. Corley*, the defendant argued "that an individual who buys a DVD has the 'authority of the copyright owner' to view the DVD," and is therefore permitted to "circumvent[] an encryption technology in order to view the DVD on a competing platform (such as Linux)."[1312] The court rejected the argument, saying that "the Defendants offered no evidence that the Plaintiffs have either explicitly or implicitly authorized DVD buyers to circumvent encryption technology to support use on multiple platforms."[1313]

[1307] *See* Healthcare Advocates, Inc. v. Harding, Earley, Follmer & Frailey, 497 F. Supp. 2d 627, 643–46 (E.D. Pa. 2007) (firm that accessed archived images solely because of a server malfunction did not "circumvent" technical measures).

[1308] *See* I.M.S. Inquiry Mgmt. Sys., Ltd. v. Berkshire Info. Sys., Inc., 307 F. Supp. 2d 521, 532–33 (S.D.N.Y. 2004). *Accord*, R.C. Olmstead, Inc. v. CU Interface, LLC, 657 F. Supp. 2d 878, 888–89 (N.D. Ohio 2009), *aff'd on other grounds*, 606 F.3d 262 (6th Cir. 2010); Egilman v. Keller & Heckman, LLP, 401 F. Supp. 2d 105, 112–14 (D.D.C. 2005) (use of a valid user name and password combination, even without authorization, does not constitute circumvention).

[1309] *RealNetworks*, 641 F. Supp. at 934. *But see* MGE UPS Systems, Inc. v. GE Consumer & Industrial, Inc., 622 F.3d 361, 365–66 (5th Cir. 2010) (evidence that plaintiff's technological measure was circumvented at some point was insufficient where the defendant's representatives did not engage in the circumvention, but merely used the altered software after the measure had been circumvented).

[1310] Chamberlain Group, Inc. v. Skylink Technologies, Inc., 381 F.3d 1178, 1183–85 (Fed. Cir. 2004).

[1311] *Id.* at 1202.

[1312] 273 F.3d 429, 444 (2d Cir. 2001).

[1313] *Id.*

(e)   Facilitation of Infringement

In *Chamberlain*, the court held that section 1201 "prohibits only forms of access that bear a reasonable relationship to the protections that the Copyright Act otherwise affords copyright owners."[1314] The court stated that it would be illogical "to hold circumventors liable under § 1201(a) *merely for accessing that work*, even if that access enabled *only* rights that the Copyright Act grants to the public."[1315] Because "[t]he Copyright Act authorized Chamberlain's customers to use the copy of Chamberlain's copyrighted software embedded in the [garage door openers] that they purchased," the court held that it was not unlawful for Skylink to provide a remote that enabled such access.[1316]

Other courts, however, have rejected the argument that there must be a "nexus" between the unauthorized access and facilitation of infringement in order to hold a defendant liable.[1317] For example, in *Universal City Studios, Inc. v. Reimerdes*, the court held that "[w]hether defendants [posted DeCSS decryption code] in order to infringe, or to permit or encourage others to infringe, . . . simply does not matter for purposes of Section 1201(a)(2). The offering or provision of the program . . . is prohibited irrespective of why the program was written."[1318]

(f)   Design, Use, and Marketing of Technology

Finally, as noted above, sections 1201(a)(2) and 1201(b) prohibit trafficking in technology that "(A) is primarily designed or produced for the purpose of circumventing" a technological measure; "(B) has only limited commercially significant purpose or use other than to circumvent" such a measure; or "(C) is marketed . . . for use in circumventing" such a measure.[1319] While the second clause might be interpreted as consistent with the "capable of substantial non-infringing use" standard of *Sony*,[1320] the alternative sections that focus on the primary purpose or marketing of the technology expressly reject the *Sony* standard.[1321]

[1314] Chamberlain Group, Inc. v. Skylink Technologies, Inc., 381 F.3d 1178, 1202 (Fed. Cir. 2004).

[1315] *Id.* at 1200.

[1316] *Id.* at 1204. *Accord*, Lexmark Int'l, Inc. v. Static Control Components, Inc., 387 F.3d 522, 552 (6th Cir. 2004) (Merritt, J., concurring) ("a better reading of the statute is that it requires plaintiffs as part of their burden of pleading and persuasion to show a purpose to pirate on the part of defendants.").

[1317] *See* MDY Industries, LLC v. Blizzard Entertainment, Inc., 629 F.3d 928, 950 (9th Cir. 2010); United States v. Elcom, Ltd., 203 F. Supp. 2d 1111, 1122, 1124 (N.D. Cal. 2002).

[1318] Universal City Studios, Inc. v. Reimerdes, 111 F. Supp. 2d 294, 319 (S.D.N.Y. 2000), *aff'd sub nom.* Universal City Studios, Inc. v. Corley, 273 F.3d 429 (2d Cir. 2001).

[1319] 17 U.S.C. § 1201(a)(2), § 1201(b).

[1320] *See* Sony Corp. of America v. Universal City Studios, Inc., 464 U.S. 417, 442 (1984), discussed at § 4I[2][a].

[1321] Universal City Studios, Inc. v. Reimerdes, 111 F. Supp. 2d 294, 323–24 (S.D.N.Y. 2000), *aff'd sub nom.* Universal City Studios, Inc. v. Corley, 273 F.3d 429 (2d Cir. 2001); *accord*, RealNetworks, Inc. v. DVD Copy Control Ass'n, 641 F. Supp. 2d 913, 941 (N.D. Cal. 2009). Those subsections, however, arguably are consistent with the later-decided case of Metro-Goldwyn-Mayer Studios, Inc. v. Grokster, Ltd., 545 U.S. 913, 919 (2005), which focused on the intent of the defendant rather than the capability of the device. *See* § 4I[2][c].

[ii]   Statutory Exceptions

Statutory exceptions permit circumvention for "any lawfully authorized investigative, protective, information security, or intelligence activity";[1322] for good-faith encryption research[1323] or security testing;[1324] and in order to disable hidden "cookies" that collect personal information about the user of a protected website or other copyrighted work.[1325] In addition, a nonprofit library, archives, or educational institution may circumvent "solely in order to make a good faith determination of whether to acquire a copy of [a] work."[1326] However, there are no exceptions to the "trafficking" provisions for the latter two exceptions, meaning that it is still unlawful to provide libraries, archives, educational institutions, or cookie-disablers with the equipment or software they need to circumvent.

Section 1201(f) permits circumvention "for the sole purpose of identifying and analyzing those elements of [a computer] program that are necessary to achieve interoperability of an independently created computer program with other programs."[1327] This section was held to apply to a defendant who made and sold microchips containing software that enabled refilled printer cartridges to work with the software embedded in the printer.[1328] However, this section "permits reverse engineering of copyrighted computer programs only" and does *not* apply to circumvention to gain "access to other copyrighted works, such as movies."[1329] Thus, a defendant cannot circumvent CSS in order to view movies on a computer running the Linux operating system, even if no authorized player for Linux was available.[1330] In addition, the "acts of identification and analysis" cannot themselves constitute infringement.[1331] Although reverse engineering is generally held to be a fair use,[1332] the court in *Davidson & Associates v. Jung* held that reverse engineering that was prohibited by an end-user license agreement was infringing;[1333] therefore, the defendants could not qualify for this exception.[1334]

[1322] 17 U.S.C. § 1201(e).

[1323] 17 U.S.C. § 1201(g)(2). *See also* Universal City Studios, Inc. v. Reimerdes, 111 F. Supp. 2d 294, 321 (S.D.N.Y. 2000) (exception did not apply where defendants made no effort to obtain authorization, or to share results with copyright owners), *aff'd sub nom.* Universal City Studios, Inc. v. Corley, 273 F.3d 429 (2d Cir. 2001).

[1324] 17 U.S.C. § 1201(j)(2). *See also Reimerdes*, 111 F. Supp. 2d at 321 (rejecting this exception).

[1325] 17 U.S.C. § 1201(i)(1).

[1326] 17 U.S.C. § 1201(d)(1).

[1327] 17 U.S.C. § 1201(f)(1).

[1328] *See* Lexmark Int'l, Inc. v. Static Control Components, Inc., 387 F.3d 522, 550–51 (6th Cir. 2004).

[1329] Universal City Studios, Inc. v. Reimerdes, 82 F. Supp. 2d 211, 218 (S.D.N.Y. 2000).

[1330] *Id. See also* Universal City Studios, Inc. v. Reimerdes, 111 F. Supp. 2d 294, 319–20 (S.D.N.Y. 2000) (rejecting factual premise that DeCSS was developed for the "sole" purpose of playing DVD movies on Linux, and noting that section 1201(f) permits dissemination "solely for the purpose" of achieving interoperability, and does not permit public dissemination), *aff'd sub nom.* Universal City Studios, Inc. v. Corley, 273 F.3d 429 (2d Cir. 2001).

[1331] 17 U.S.C. § 1201(f)(1).

[1332] *See* § 4J[1][c].

[1333] 422 F.3d 630, 639 (8th Cir. 2005).

[1334] Unfortunately, the court in *Davidson* appeared to misunderstand the statute to mean that

Finally, section 1201(c)(1) states that "[n]othing in this section shall affect rights, remedies, limitations, or defenses to copyright infringement, including fair use."[1335] Some courts have viewed this language as simply clarifying that the three causes of action provided by section 1201 are separate from and independent of a cause of action for copyright infringement, and may be violated whether or not copyright infringement has occurred.[1336] In *Chamberlain*, however, the court relied in part on this section in holding that section 1201 "prohibits only forms of access that bear a reasonable relationship to the protections that the Copyright Act otherwise affords copyright owners."[1337] It held that "[a] provision that prohibited access without regard to the rest of the Copyright Act would clearly affect rights and limitations," and that such a construction would "flatly contradict § 1201(c)(1)"[1338]

[iii]   Regulatory Exceptions

In addition to the above exceptions, the DMCA contains a provision requiring the Librarian of Congress and the Copyright Office to conduct a formal rulemaking proceeding every three years, to inquire whether users have been, or in the next three years are likely to be, "adversely affected . . . in their ability to make noninfringing uses . . . of a particular class of copyrighted works."[1339] If the inquiry determines there to be a likely adverse effect, then circumvention to enable those noninfringing uses is permitted during the ensuing three-year period.[1340] However, these regulatory exceptions only permit acts of circumvention; by statute, the exceptions expressly do not provide a defense to anyone who provides devices or services which users might need in order to actually accomplish the permitted circumvention.[1341]

In the 2012 rulemaking, the Librarian recognized exemptions to the prohibition on circumvention for five classes of copyrighted works: (1) electronically distributed literary works, for which the technological measures either prevent read-aloud functionality or otherwise interfere with screen readers used by blind or disabled readers;[1342] (2) software programs for smartphones, when needed to assure interoperability of lawfully purchased "apps";[1343] (3) computer programs

---

reverse engineering for the purpose of interoperability could not *enable* infringement, rather than itself constitute infringement, because its analysis focused on the fact that the reverse engineering enabled unauthorized copies of plaintiff's video games to be played on defendant's servers. *Id.* at 842.

[1335] 17 U.S.C. § 1201(c)(1).

[1336] *See* Universal City Studios, Inc. v. Reimerdes, 111 F. Supp. 2d 294, 322–23 (S.D.N.Y. 2000), *aff'd sub nom.* Universal City Studios, Inc. v. Corley, 273 F.3d 429 (2d Cir. 2001).

[1337] Chamberlain Group, Inc. v. Skylink Technologies, Inc., 381 F.3d 1178, 1202 (Fed. Cir. 2004).

[1338] *Id.* at 1200.

[1339] 17 U.S.C. § 1201(a)(1)(C).

[1340] 17 U.S.C. § 1201(a)(1)(B),(D).

[1341] 17 U.S.C. § 1201(a)(1)(E). *Cf. Reimerdes,* 111 F. Supp. 2d at 324 ("The fact that Congress elected to leave technologically unsophisticated persons who wish to make fair use of encrypted copyrighted works without the technical means of doing so is a matter for Congress unless Congress' decision contravenes the Constitution.").

[1342] 77 Fed. Reg. 65260, 65262–63 (2012).

[1343] *Id.* at 65263–64.

that enable phones to connect to another network;[1344] (4) motion pictures on DVDs, when short portions are needed for criticism or comment in noncommercial videos, documentary films, non-fiction multimedia e-books on film analysis, and for educational purposes in film studies or similar courses;[1345] and (5) motion pictures on DVDs and online, to conduct research and development on players to make audio representations of visual elements for the visually impaired, and visual representations of audio elements for the hearing impaired.[1346]

[iv]   Other Defenses

Several defendants have challenged the anti-circumvention provisions of the DMCA on various Constitutional grounds. All of these challenges have been rejected.

In *United States v. Elcom Ltd.*, the court held that the DMCA was not unconstitutionally vague;[1347] that it did not burden "substantially more speech than is necessary to further the government's interest" in "preventing the unauthorized copying of copyrighted works and promoting electronic commerce"[1348] ; and that it was validly enacted under the Commerce Clause, because it was not "fundamentally inconsistent" with the Patent and Copyright Clause or with any of the limitations contained within it, such as the "limited Times" restriction.[1349]

Similarly, in *Universal City Studios, Inc. v. Corley*, the court held that the government could regulate the "functional" aspects of computer programs, so long as the regulation had only an incidental effect on the "speech" aspects of those programs.[1350] Accordingly, the court upheld an injunction against posting DeCSS decryption code on a website,[1351] and against intentionally linking to a site that provided such decryption code.[1352] The court also held that even if a "fair use" exception was required by the First Amendment, nothing in the Constitution "guarantees copying by the optimum method or in the identical format of the original."[1353]

[1344] *Id.* at 65264–66. This exemption was initially limited to phones purchased before January 26, 2013, and only if the original network provider refused to unlock the phone. *Id.* Congress removed these limitations by enacting the Unlocking Consumer Choice and Wireless Competition Act, Pub. L. No. 113-144, 128 Stat. 1751 (eff. Aug. 1, 2014), which reinstated the 2010 exemption for circumventing such programs, and also expressly allows third parties to provide unlocking services.

[1345] 77 Fed. Reg. at 65266–70.

[1346] *Id.* at 65270–71.

[1347] 203 F. Supp. 2d 1111, 1125 (N.D. Cal. 2002).

[1348] *Id.* at 1129–30.

[1349] *Id.* at 1137–41.

[1350] 273 F.3d 429, 450–54 (2d Cir. 2001).

[1351] *Id.* at 453–55.

[1352] *Id.* at 455–58.

[1353] *Id.* at 459.

[b]   Copyright Management Information

Section 1202(a) prohibits providing, distributing or importing "copyright management information" (or "CMI") that is false, if done "knowingly and with the
intent to induce, enable, facilitate, or conceal infringement."[1354] Section 1202(b)
prohibits (1) intentionally removing or altering CMI, (2) distributing or importing
CMI knowing that CMI has been unlawfully removed or altered, or (3) distributing,
importing or publicly performing works, or copies or phonorecords of works,
knowing that CMI has been unlawfully removed or altered.[1355] Any of these acts
must be done "knowing or . . . having reasonable grounds to know that it will
induce, enable, facilitate, or conceal an infringement."[1356]

CMI is defined to include the title, copyright notice, author, copyright owner,
performers, "terms and conditions for the use of the work," identifying numbers or
symbols, and "such other information as the Register of Copyrights may provide by
regulation."[1357] However, the Register is forbidden from requiring the inclusion of
"any personally identifying information" concerning "the user of a copyrighted
work."[1358] The express language of the definition ("including in digital form")
indicates that it covers analog CMI as well as digital CMI.[1359] Nonetheless, some
courts have held that section 1202 does not apply to "circumstances that have no
relation to the Internet, electronic commerce, automated copyright protection or
management systems, or other technological measures or processes,"[1360] reasoning
that because the *principal* purpose of section 1202 was to facilitate automated
rights management, section 1202 should be *limited* to such uses. This interpretation
is inconsistent with the express language of the statute and should be rejected.

There are exceptions for "lawfully authorized investigative, protective, information security, or intelligence activity";[1361] for analog cable or broadcast transmis-

---

[1354] 17 U.S.C. § 1202(a).

[1355] 17 U.S.C. § 1202(b). According to one court, subsection (b)(1) "applies only to the removal of
copyright management information on a plaintiff's product or original work," whereas subsection (b)(3)
covers the distribution of copies or phonorecords of works without CMI. Kelly v. Arriba Soft Corp., 77
F. Supp. 2d 1116, 1122 (C.D. Cal. 1999), *aff'd in part and rev'd in part on other grounds*, 336 F.3d 811
(9th Cir. 2003).

[1356] 17 U.S.C. § 1202(b). *See* Gordon v. Nextel Communications, 345 F.3d 922, 926–27 (6th Cir. 2003)
(even though defendants intentionally removed copyright notice, unlawful intent was lacking where they
believed a license had been obtained); Kelly v. Arriba Soft Corp., 77 F. Supp. 2d 1116 (C.D. Cal. 1999)
(unlawful intent was lacking where defendant linked to originating web site, which contained the
information), *aff'd in part and rev'd in part on other grounds*, 336 F.3d 811 (9th Cir. 2003).

[1357] 17 U.S.C. § 1202(c).

[1358] *Id.*

[1359] *See* Murphy v. Millennium Radio Group, LLC, 650 F.3d 295 (3d Cir. 2011); Associated Press v.
All Headline News Corp., 608 F. Supp. 2d 454 (S.D.N.Y. 2009); McClatchey v. Associated Press, 82
U.S.P.Q.2d (BNA) 1190 (W.D. Pa. 2007).

[1360] Textile Secrets Int'l v. Ya-Ya Brand, Inc., 524 F. Supp. 2d 1184, 1201 (C.D. Cal. 2007). *See also* IQ
Group, Ltd. v. Wiesner Publishing, LLC, 409 F. Supp. 2d 587, 598 (D.N.J. 2006) (removal from a
copyrighted e-mail of IQ's logo and a hyperlink to IQ's website was not actionable, because neither the
logo nor the hyperlink "functioned as a component of an automated copyright protection or management
system.").

[1361] 17 U.S.C. § 1202(d).

sions, if compliance is "not technically feasible or would create an undue financial hardship" and there is no intent to facilitate infringement;[1362] and for digital cable or broadcast transmissions, if compliance "would result in a perceptible visual or aural degradation of the digital signal," would conflict with government regulations or pre-existing industry standards, or the CMI itself does not comply with an industry standard negotiated with copyright owners.[1363]

§ 4J   FAIR USE AND OTHER DEFENSES

After the plaintiff introduces evidence sufficient to demonstrate a *prima facie* case of infringement, the defendant may respond in a variety of ways. First, the defendant may rebut the plaintiff's *prima facie* case by introducing evidence disputing ownership, validity, copying, or substantial similarity of protected expression.[1364] Second, the defendant may try to show that the plaintiff consented to the use by granting the defendant a license to use the plaintiff's work.[1365] Third, the defendant may attempt to establish any of the exceptions and limitations in sections 107 through 122, which are treated as affirmative defenses.[1366] Fourth, the defendant may attempt to establish one of a number of other affirmative defenses to copyright infringement.

The exceptions and limitations in sections 108 through 122 are covered in section 4G. This section begins with the "fair use" doctrine, which is codified in section 107.

[1]   Fair Use

Section 107 of the 1976 Act provides that "the fair use of a copyrighted work . . . is not an infringement of copyright."[1367] The statute does not attempt to define fair use; as the House Report explains, "the endless variety of situations and combinations of circumstances that can arise in particular cases precludes the formulations of exact rules in the statute."[1368] However, the statute does provide two sources of guidance for the courts: first, the "preamble" to section 107 lists six purposes that are illustrative of the types of purposes that may qualify as fair use; and second, section 107 lists four factors that courts should take into account "[i]n determining whether the use of made of a work in any particular case is a fair use."[1369]

In codifying the fair use doctrine in the 1976 Act, Congress "intended to restate the present judicial doctrine of fair use, not to change, narrow, or enlarge it any

---

[1362] 17 U.S.C. § 1202(e)(1).

[1363] 17 U.S.C. § 1202(e)(2).

[1364] *See* § 4H.

[1365] *See* § 4F[2].

[1366] *See* § 4G.

[1367] 17 U.S.C. § 107.

[1368] H.R. Rep. No. 94-1476, at 66 (1976).

[1369] 17 U.S.C. § 107.

way."[1370] The House Report emphasizes that "each case raising the question must be decided on its own facts."[1371] As the Supreme Court has stated, "[t]he task is not to be simplified with bright-line rules, for the statute, like the doctrine it recognizes, calls for case-by-case analysis."[1372] Because "fair use is an affirmative defense," the defendant has "the burden the burden of demonstrating fair use."[1373]

Since the 1976 Act, the Supreme Court has decided three major cases involving fair use.[1374] In *Sony Corp. of America v. Universal City Studios, Inc.*, the Court held 5-4 that home videotaping of copyrighted broadcasts for time-shifting purposes was a fair use.[1375] In *Harper & Row Publishers, Inc. v. Nation Enterprises*, the Court held 6-3 that publication of some 300 words from a stolen copy of a soon-to-be published memoir by former President Gerald Ford was not a fair use.[1376] Most recently, in *Campbell v. Acuff-Rose Music, Inc.*, the Court unanimously held that an alleged parody by the rap group 2 Live Crew of the popular song "Oh, Pretty Woman" could qualify as a fair use.[1377] These cases are discussed in more detail below.

[a]   Preamble

The "preamble" to section 107 states that "the fair use of a copyrighted work, . . . for purposes such as criticism, comment, news reporting, teaching (including multiple copies for classroom use), scholarship, or research, is not an infringement of copyright."[1378] The words "such as" indicate that this sentence is "illustrative and not limitative," and that it "provides only general guidance about the sorts of copying that courts and Congress mostly commonly had found to be fair uses."[1379] The House Report contains additional examples that, "while by no means exhaustive, give some idea of the sort of activities the courts might regard as fair use under the circumstances."[1380] It is clear that these examples do not *automatically* qualify as fair use.[1381] Instead, they might be described as "favored uses" that are

---

[1370] H.R. Rep. No. 94-1476, at 66 (1976).

[1371] *Id.* at 65.

[1372] Campbell v. Acuff-Rose Music, Inc., 510 U.S. 569, 577 (1994).

[1373] *Campbell*, 510 U.S. at 590; *accord*, Harper & Row Publishers, Inc. v. Nation Enterprises, 471 U.S. 539, 561 (1985). *See also* Latimer v. Roaring Toyz, Inc., 601 F.3d 1224, 1238–40 (11th Cir. 2010) (because fair use is an affirmative defense, it must be pleaded under Fed. R. Civ. P. 8(c), and the district court erred by raising the issue *sua sponte*, although on remand it could entertain a motion to amend the pleadings).

[1374] In a fourth case, the Supreme Court easily brushed aside the argument that a major motion picture adaptation of a short story was fair use. *See* Stewart v. Abend, 495 U.S. 207, 237–38 (1990).

[1375] 464 U.S. 417 (1984).

[1376] 471 U.S. 539 (1985).

[1377] 510 U.S. 569 (1994).

[1378] 17 U.S.C. § 107.

[1379] Campbell v. Acuff-Rose Music, Inc., 510 U.S. 569, 577–78 (1994).

[1380] H.R. Rep. No. 94-1476, at 65 (1976).

[1381] *See* Harper & Row Publishers, Inc. v. Nation Enterprises, 471 U.S. 539, 561 (1985) ("This listing was not intended . . . to single out any particular use as presumptively a 'fair' use. . . . The fact that an article arguably is 'news' and therefore a productive use is simply one factor in a fair use analysis.").

somewhat *more likely* to qualify as fair use after an analysis of all of the factors.[1382]

[b]   Factors

Section 107 lists four factors that "shall" be considered in determining whether a use is fair. The factors are neither exclusive nor exhaustive. As a practical matter, however, courts tend to examine each of the factors, and to fit any additional considerations into one of the existing factors.[1383] However, the four factors may not be "treated in isolation. . . . All are to be explored, and the results weighed together, in light of the purposes of copyright."[1384]

[i]   Purpose and Character of the Use

(a)   Transformative Use

The first factor is "the purpose and character of the use."[1385] According to the Supreme Court:

> The central purpose of this investigation is to see . . . whether the new work merely "supersedes the objects" of the original creation, or instead adds something new, with a further purpose or different character, altering the first with new expression, meaning, or message; it asks, in other words, whether and to what extent the new work is "transformative." Although such transformative use is not absolutely necessary for a finding of fair use, the goal of copyright, to promote science and the arts, is generally furthered by the creation of transformative works. . . . [Thus,] the more transformative the new work, the less will be the significance of other factors, like commercialism, that may weigh against a finding of fair use.[1386]

Since the Supreme Court announced the "transformative use" standard in *Campbell*, it has become the central focus in fair use litigation. Unfortunately, lower courts have not always been consistent or predictable in their application of the standard. Works that have selected fragments of protected expression and re-arranged those fragments in new and creative ways have been held *not* to be transformative,[1387] while works that have reproduced the original in its entirety (albeit sometimes in reduced size) have been held to be "transformative."[1388] Thus,

---

[1382] *Cf. Campbell*, 510 U.S. at 578–79 ("The [fair use] enquiry . . . may be guided by the examples given in the preamble to § 107, looking to whether the use is for criticism, or comment, or news reporting, and the like.").

[1383] For example, the defendant's "good faith" or lack thereof tends to be considered as part of the first factor, "the purpose and character of the use." *See* § 4J[b][1](d).

[1384] Campbell v. Acuff-Rose Music, Inc., 510 U.S. 569, 578 (1994).

[1385] 17 U.S.C. § 107(1).

[1386] *Campbell*, 510 U.S. at 579, *citing* Pierre N. Leval, *Toward a Fair Use Standard*, 103 HARV. L. REV. 1105, 1111 (1990).

[1387] *See, e.g.*, Castle Rock Entertainment, Inc. v. Carol Publishing Group, 150 F.3d 132 (2d Cir. 1998) (book of trivia questions about the TV series *Seinfeld* was not "transformative"); Video Pipeline, Inc. v. Buena Vista Home Entertainment, Inc., 342 F.3d 191, 198–200 (3d Cir. 2003) (two-minute unauthorized "clip previews" of movies were not "transformative").

[1388] *See, e.g.*, Kelly v. Arriba Soft Corp., 336 F.3d 811, 818–20 (9th Cir. 2003) (automated reproduction

most courts seem to be ignoring the phrase in *Campbell* asking whether the defendant's work "alter[s] the first with new expression, meaning, or message."[1389] Instead, most courts are asking whether the *purpose* of the defendant's use is the same as or different from the *purpose* of the underlying work.[1390] This approach best explains the most recent holdings of the Courts of Appeals.

For example, in *Bill Graham Archives v. Dorling Kindersley Ltd.*, the Second Circuit held that reproduction of six concert posters "in significantly reduced form" in a biography was "transformative" and was a fair use.[1391] Similarly, in *Kelly v. Arriba Soft Corp.*, the Ninth Circuit held that the automated reproduction by a visual search engine of unauthorized images placed on the Internet was "transformative" and was a fair use, because the thumbnails "served an entirely different function than Kelly's original images."[1392] By contrast, in *Castle Rock Entertainment, Inc. v. Carol Publishing Group*, the court held that *The Seinfeld Aptitude Test*, a book of 634 trivia questions about the TV series *Seinfeld* was *not* a fair use, because "[a]ny transformative purpose possessed by *The SAT* is slight to nonexistent."[1393]

Castle Rock also comments on a semantic dilemma. Derivative works, by definition, are works in which an underlying work has been "recast, *transformed*, or adapted."[1394] Because such works necessarily add "something new, . . . altering the first with new expression, meaning, or message," one could easily conclude that "the goal of copyright, to promote science and the arts, is generally furthered by the creation of" derivative works.[1395] Thus, if applied literally, *Campbell's* "transformative use" standard might overwhelm the copyright owner's exclusive right "to prepare derivative works based upon the copyrighted work."[1396] To avoid this problem, *Castle Rock* concluded, somewhat counter-intuitively, that "[a]lthough derivative works . . . transform an original work into a new mode of presentation, such works — unlike works of fair use — take expression for purposes that are not 'transformative.' "[1397]

---

of full-size images as "thumbnail" images in a visual search engine was "transformative"); Perfect 10, Inc. v. Amazon.com, Inc., 508 F.3d 1146, 1164–66 (9th Cir. 2007) (same); Bill Graham Archives v. Dorling Kindersley Ltd., 448 F.3d 605, 608–11 (2d Cir. 2006) (reproduction of six concert posters in a biography was "transformative"); Nunez v. Caribbean Int'l News Corp., 235 F.3d 18, 23 (1st Cir. 2000) (reproduction of studio photograph in a newspaper was "transformative").

[1389] 510 U.S. at 579.

[1390] This approach is supported not only by the statutory phrase "the purpose and character of the use," but also by *Campbell's* remark that the new work should have "a further purpose or different character." 510 U.S. at 579.

[1391] 448 F.3d 605, 609–10 (2d Cir. 2006).

[1392] 336 F.3d 811, 818 (9th Cir. 2003). *Accord*, Perfect 10, Inc. v. Amazon.com, Inc., 508 F.3d 1146, 1165 (9th Cir. 2007).

[1393] 150 F.3d 132, 142 (2d Cir. 1998).

[1394] 17 U.S.C. § 101 (emphasis added).

[1395] Campbell v. Acuff-Rose Music, Inc., 510 U.S. 569, 579 (1994).

[1396] 17 U.S.C. § 106(2). That this is not the case is amply demonstrated by Stewart v. Abend, 495 U.S. 207, 237–38 (1990), in which the Court easily rejected the argument that a major motion picture adaptation of a short story was a fair use.

[1397] *Castle Rock*, 150 F.3d at 143.

(b)   Commercial Use

The statutory codification of the first factor also directs courts to consider "whether [the] use is of a commercial nature or is for nonprofit educational purposes."[1398] The House Report states that this clause "is an express recognition that . . . the commercial or non-profit character of an activity, while not conclusive with respect to fair use, can and should be weighed along with other factors in fair use decisions."[1399] Thus, although the statute suggests only a single inquiry, it appears that this language really encompasses two separate inquiries: first, whether the use is commercial or nonprofit, and second, whether the use is for education or for entertainment.

With regard to commercial use, the Supreme Court's opinion in *Sony* stated that "every commercial use of copyrighted material is presumptively . . . unfair."[1400] In subsequent opinions, however, the Supreme Court has backtracked considerably from that statement. In *Campbell*, it explained:

> [T]he commercial or nonprofit educational purpose of a work is only one element of the first factor enquiry into its purpose and character. . . . [T]he mere fact that a use is educational and not for profit does not insulate it from a finding of infringement, any more than the commercial character of a use bars a finding of fairness. If, indeed, commerciality carried presumptive force against a finding of fairness, the presumption would swallow nearly all of the illustrative uses listed in the preamble paragraph of § 107, including news reporting, comment, criticism, teaching, scholarship, and research, since these activities are generally conducted for profit in this country.[1401]

Thus, in *Campbell*, the Court held that the lower court erred "[i]n giving virtually dispositive weight to the commercial nature of the parody."[1402]

In *Sony*, the majority held "that time-shifting for private home use must be characterized as a noncommercial, nonprofit activity."[1403] It rejected the argument that "consumptive uses of copyright[ed works] by home VTR users are commercial even if the consumer does not sell the homemade tape because the consumer will not buy tapes separately sold by the copyrightholder," and it also rejected an analogy to theft of personal property, stating that "the timeshifter no more steals the program by watching it once than does the live viewer."[1404] In *Harper & Row*, however, the Court stated that "[t]he crux of the profit/nonprofit distinction is not

---

[1398] 17 U.S.C. § 107.

[1399] H.R. Rep. No. 94-1476, at 66 (1976).

[1400] Sony Corp. of Am. v. Universal City Studios, Inc., 464 U.S. 417, 451 (1984); *see also id.* at 449 ("If the Betamax were used to make copies for a commercial or profit-making purpose, such use would presumptively be unfair.").

[1401] Campbell v. Acuff-Rose Music, Inc., 510 U.S. 569, 584–85 (1994) (internal quotations and citations omitted).

[1402] *Id.* at 584.

[1403] Sony Corp. of Am. v. Universal City Studios, Inc., 464 U.S. 417, 449 (1984).

[1404] *Id.* at 450 n.33.

whether the sole motive of the use is monetary gain but whether the user stands to profit from exploitation of the copyrighted material without paying the customary price."[1405] Nonetheless, it is clear that courts "are free to consider the public benefit resulting from a particular use notwithstanding the fact that the alleged infringer may gain commercially."[1406] Indeed, after *Campbell*, most courts have placed very little weight on the fact that a particular use was "commercial" in nature.[1407]

(c) Educational Use

The reference to "educational use" is somewhat redundant, as the preamble to section 107 already specifies that favored uses include "teaching (including multiple copies for classroom use), scholarship, or research." The principal battleground concerning this sub-factor has been photocopying for educational use. In a case involving reproduction of "coursepacks" for college courses by a commercial copy shop, the Sixth Circuit rejected the argument "that the copying at issue here would be considered 'nonprofit educational' if done by the students or professors themselves," stating that "[t]he courts have . . . properly rejected attempts by for-profit users to stand in the shoes of their customers making nonprofit or noncommercial uses."[1408] By contrast, the Eleventh Circuit held that a state university's reproduction of published works for electronic course reserves was a nonprofit educational use, even though the use was not "transformative" and there was a significant risk of market substitution.[1409]

(d) Good Faith

In *Harper & Row*, the Supreme Court stated that "[f]air use presupposes 'good faith' and 'fair dealing,'"[1410] and it held that "knowingly exploit[ing] a purloined manuscript," by publishing excerpts two weeks prior to the authorized publication, was not a fair use.[1411] Many courts have followed *Harper & Row* in holding that

---

[1405] Harper & Row Publishers, Inc. v. Nation Enterprises, 471 U.S. 539, 562 (1985).

[1406] Sega Enterprises Ltd. v. Accolade, Inc., 977 F.2d 1510, 1523 (9th Cir. 1992).

[1407] *See, e.g.*, Cariou v. Prince, 714 F.3d 694, 708 (2d Cir. 2013) ("Although there is no question that Prince's artworks are commercial, we do not place much significance on that fact due to the transformative nature of the work."); Bill Graham Archives v. Dorling Kindersley Ltd., 448 F.3d 605, 612 (2d Cir. 2006) (reproduction of six concert posters was "incidental to the commercial biographical value of the book"); Kelly v. Arriba Soft, Inc., 336 F.3d 811, 818 (9th Cir. 2003) ("Because the use of Kelly's images was not highly exploitative, the commercial nature of the use only slightly weighs against a finding of fair use.").

[1408] *See* Princeton University Press v. Michigan Document Services, Inc., 99 F.3d 1381, 1389 (6th Cir. 1996). *Accord*, Basic Books, Inc. v. Kinko's Graphics Corp., 758 F. Supp. 1522 (S.D.N.Y. 1991).

[1409] Cambridge Univ. Press v. Patton, 769 F.3d 1232, 1262–67 (11th Cir. 2014). The court reversed and remanded a district court's ruling that 43 of 48 instances of *prima facie* infringement were fair use, holding that the district court erred in 1) giving all four factors equal weight, 2) not assessing the second factor on a case-by-case basis, 3) applying a 10-percent-or-one-chapter "safe harbor" under the third factor, and 4) not affording enough weight to the fourth factor. *Id.* at 1283.

[1410] Harper & Row Publishers, Inc. v. Nation Enterprises, 471 U.S. 539, 562 (1985).

[1411] *Id.* at 563. *But see* Swatch Group Mgmt. Servs. Ltd. v. Bloomberg, L.P., 756 F.3d 73 (2d Cir. 2014) (distinguishing *Harper & Row*; even assuming defendant knew that recording was unauthorized, it did not intend to supplant right of first publication, but only to engage in news reporting).

bad faith is a factor that tends to weigh against fair use. Examples of bad faith include obtaining access to the work by false pretenses or in violation of a non-disclosure agreement,[1412] tearing off the copyright notice before directing others to copy the work,[1413] and failing to credit the original author and "attempt[ing] to pass off the work as his own, substituting his name as author in place of hers."[1414]

In *Campbell*, the Supreme Court rejected the argument that being using material after seeking and being denied permission should be considered bad faith:

> [W]e reject Acuff-Rose's argument that 2 Live Crew's request for permission to use the original should be weighed against a finding of fair use. Even if good faith were central to fair use, 2 Live Crew's actions do not necessarily suggest that they believed their version was not fair use; the offer may simply have been made in a good-faith effort to avoid this litigation. If the use is otherwise fair, then no permission need be sought or granted. Thus, being denied permission to use a work does not weigh against a finding of fair use.[1415]

Similarly, failing to seek permission does not, by itself, constitute bad faith.[1416] Finally, as with other factors, it is clear that a finding of bad faith is not dispositive.[1417]

[ii]   Nature of the Copyrighted Work

"The second statutory factor, 'the nature of the copyrighted work,' . . . recogni[zes] that some works are closer to the core of intended copyright protection than others, with the consequence that fair use is more difficult to establish when the former works are copied."[1418] Courts typically look at two attributes of the plaintiff's work in assessing this factor.

First, "[t]he law generally recognizes a greater need to disseminate factual works than works of fiction or fantasy."[1419] Thus, subsequent authors have relatively greater latitude in copying factual works, such as biographies, histories,

---

[1412] *See* NXIVM Corp. v. Ross Institute, 364 F.3d 471, 478 (2d Cir. 2004) (bad faith if defendant "knew that his access to the manuscript was unauthorized or was derived from a violation of law or breach of duty"); Atari Games Corp. v. Nintendo of America, Inc., 975 F.2d 832, 843 (Fed. Cir. 1992) ("To invoke the fair use exception, an individual must possess an authorized copy of a literary work.").

[1413] Rogers v. Koons, 960 F.2d 301, 309 (2d Cir. 1992).

[1414] Weissmann v. Freeman, 868 F.2d 1313, 1324 (2d Cir. 1989). *Compare* Nuñez v. Caribbean Int'l News Corp., 235 F.3d 18, 23 (1st Cir. 2000) (finding good faith when defendant newspaper obtained photographs lawfully and reproduced them with attribution).

[1415] Campbell v. Acuff-Rose Music, Inc., 510 U.S. 569, 585 n.18 (1994), *citing* Fisher v. Dees, 794 F.2d 432, 437 (9th Cir. 1986). *See also* Maxtone-Graham v. Burtchaell, 803 F.2d 1253, 1264 (2d Cir. 1986).

[1416] Blanch v. Koons, 467 F.3d 244, 256 (2d Cir. 2006).

[1417] *See* NXIVM Corp. v. Ross Institute, 364 F.3d 471, 479 (2d Cir. 2004).

[1418] Campbell v. Acuff-Rose Music, Inc., 510 U.S. 569, 586 (1994), *citing* 17 U.S.C. § 107(2).

[1419] Harper & Row Publishers, Inc. v. Nation Enterprises, 471 U.S. 539, 563 (1985). *See also* Stewart v. Abend, 495 U.S. 207, 237 (1990) ("In general, fair use is more likely to be found in factual works than in fictional works."); Sony Corp. of America v. Universal City Studios, Inc., 464 U.S. 417, 455 n.40 (1984) ("Copying a news broadcast may have a stronger claim to fair use than copying a motion picture.").

and collections of interviews.[1420] However, "[t]he extent to which one must permit expressive language to be copied, in order to assure dissemination of the underlying facts, will . . . vary from case to case."[1421]

Second, "[t]he fact that a work is unpublished is a critical element of its 'nature.' "[1422] Thus, "[w]hile even substantial quotations might qualify as fair use in a review of a published work or a news account of a speech that had been delivered to the public or disseminated to the press, the author's right to control the first public appearance of his expression weighs against such use of the work before its release."[1423] In *Harper & Row*, for example, the Court held that publication of approximately 300 words from former President Gerald Ford's soon-to-be published memoir, two weeks before its official release, did not constitute a fair use.

After *Harper & Row*, a series of cases involving biographies indicated that lower courts were interpreting the decision narrowly to hold that "unpublished works normally enjoy *complete* protection against copying *any* protected expression."[1424] These cases prompted Congress to amend section 107 to add the final sentence, which reads: "The fact that a work is unpublished shall not itself bar a finding of fair use if such finding is made upon consideration of all the above factors."[1425]

Factor two is the least important of the four factors. An empirical study published in 2005 concluded that "factor two typically has no significant effect on the overall outcome of the fair use test."[1426]

[1420] *See, e.g.*, Rosemont Enterprises, Inc. v. Random House, Inc., 366 F.2d 303, 307 (2d Cir. 1966); Maxtone-Graham v. Burtchaell, 803 F.2d 1253, 1263 (2d Cir. 1986); Time, Inc. v. Bernard Geis Associates, 293 F. Supp. 130, 146 (S.D.N.Y. 1968).

[1421] *Harper & Row*, 471 U.S. at 563, *quoting* Robert A. Gorman, *Fact or Fancy? The Implications for Copyright*, 29 J. Copyr. Soc'y USA 560, 563 (1982).

[1422] *Harper & Row*, 471 U.S. at 564.

[1423] *Id.*

[1424] Salinger v. Random House, Inc., 811 F.2d 90, 97 (2d Cir. 1987) (emphasis added). *See also* New Era Publications Int'l, ApS v. Henry Holt & Co., 873 F.2d 576, 583–84 (2d Cir. 1989) (affirming denial of permanent injunction on ground of laches, but declining to recognize any legitimate reasons for quoting unpublished expression), *reh'g en banc denied*, 884 F.2d 659 (2d Cir. 1989) (with concurring and dissenting opinions debating the proper scope of fair use in unpublished material); Wright v. Warner Books, Inc., 953 F.2d 731, 737–38 (2d Cir. 1991) (affirming finding of fair use, but holding defendant's purpose in quoting letters is irrelevant to factor two).

[1425] 17 U.S.C. § 107. *See, e.g.*, Sundeman v. Seajay Society, 142 F.3d 194 (4th Cir. 1998) (scholarly article quoting four to six percent of unpublished first novel of author Marjorie Kinnan Rawlings was fair use).

[1426] Barton Beebe, *An Empirical Study of U.S. Copyright Fair Use Opinions, 1978–2005*, 156 U. Pa. L. Rev. 549, 610 (2008). *See also* Campbell v. Acuff-Rose Music, Inc., 510 U.S. 569, 586 (1994) (second factor "is not much help in this case, or ever likely to help much in separating the fair use sheep from the infringing goats in a parody case, since parodies almost invariably copy publicly known, expressive works.").

[iii]   Amount and Substantiality of the Use

The third factor is "the amount and substantiality of the portion used in relation to the copyrighted work as a whole."[1427] This factor has both a quantitative component (what percentage of the plaintiff's work was used) and a qualitative component (how important to the plaintiff's work was the portion used).[1428] In appropriate circumstances, a component of a larger work may be treated as a separate "work" for fair use purposes.[1429]

"There are no absolute rules as to how much of a copyrighted work may be copied and still be considered a fair use. In some instances, copying a work wholesale has been held to be fair use, while in other cases taking only a tiny portion of the original work has been held unfair."[1430] For example, in *Sony*, the Supreme Court held that videotaping a television broadcast of an entire work for time-shifting purposes was a fair use.[1431] By contrast, in *Harper & Row*, the Court held that copying approximately 300 words from a 200,000 word soon-to-be published memoir by former President Gerald Ford was *not* a fair use. Although "[i]n absolute terms, the words actually quoted were an insubstantial portion of" the memoir, the portion copied (concerning the pardon of former President Nixon) "was essentially the heart of the book."[1432]

The third factor directs courts to assess "the portion used in relation to the *copyrighted* work as a whole."[1433] Nonetheless, many courts use the third factor to compare the portion used with the *allegedly infringing* work, no doubt encouraged by the Supreme Court's lead in doing so.[1434] Although comparison of the portion used with the allegedly infringing work is relevant and is not erroneous, it is misplaced under the third factor, because it is more relevant to the first and fourth factors.[1435] As the Supreme Court explained in *Campbell*,

---

[1427] 17 U.S.C. § 107(3).

[1428] *See* Campbell v. Acuff-Rose Music, Inc., 510 U.S. 569, 587 (1994) ("this factor calls for thought not only about the quantity of the materials used, but about their quality and importance, too.").

[1429] *Compare* American Geophysical Union v. Texaco, Inc., 60 F.3d 913, 925–26 (2d Cir. 1994) (treating individually authored articles as discrete "works," even though journal in which they were published was "marketed only as a periodical by issue or volume") *and* Hustler Magazine, Inc. v. Moral Majority, Inc., 796 F.2d 1148, 1155 (9th Cir. 1986) (parody advertisement in plaintiff's magazine was a single work) *with* NXVIM Corp. v. Ross Institute, 364 F.3d 471, 480–81 (2d Cir. 2004) (refusing to treat individual "modules" or chapters as separate "works") *and* Triangle Publications, Inc. v. Knight-Ridder Newspapers, Inc., 626 F.2d 1171, 1177 n.15 (5th Cir. 1980) (cover of TV Guide magazine was not a separate work).

[1430] Maxtone-Graham v. Burtchaell, 803 F.2d 1253, 1263 (2d Cir. 1986).

[1431] Sony Corp. of Am. v. Universal City Studios, Inc., 464 U.S. 417, 449–50 (1984) ("when one considers . . . that timeshifting merely enables a viewer to see such a work which he had been invited to witness in its entirety free of charge, the fact that the entire work is reproduced . . . does not have its ordinary effect of militating against a finding of fair use."). *See also* Nuñez v. Caribbean Int'l News Corp., 235 F.3d 18, 24 (1st Cir. 2000) (although defendant newspaper "admittedly copied the entire picture . . . to copy any less than that would have made the picture useless to the story.").

[1432] Harper & Row Publishers, Inc. v. Nation Enterprises, 471 U.S. 539, 564–65 (1985).

[1433] 17 U.S.C. § 107(3).

[1434] *See Harper & Row*, 471 U.S. at 565 (13 percent of infringing article consisted of direct quotes).

[1435] *See* Bill Graham Archives v. Dorling Kindersley Ltd., 448 F.3d 605, 611 (2d Cir. 2006).

[W]hether 'a substantial portion of the infringing work was copied verbatim' from the copyrighted work is a relevant question, for it may reveal a dearth of transformative character or purpose under the first factor, or a greater likelihood of market harm under the fourth; a work composed primarily of an original, particularly its heart, with little added or changed, is more likely to be a merely superseding use, fulfilling demand for the original.[1436]

In *Campbell*, the Supreme Court subtly de-emphasized the importance of the third factor by directing courts to consider "whether 'the amount and substantiality of the portion used . . .' are reasonable *in relation to the purpose of the copying.*"[1437] Thus, in parody cases,

[T]he parody must be able to 'conjure up' at least enough of [the] original to make the object of its critical wit recognizable. What makes for this recognition is quotation of the original's most distinctive or memorable features, which the parodist can be sure the audience will know. Once enough has been taken to assure identification, how much more is reasonable will depend . . . on the extent to which the song's overriding purpose and character is to parody the original or, in contrast, the likelihood that the parody may serve as a market substitute for the original.[1438]

Although this language indicates that the "conjure up" test establishes the *minimum* amount of expression that may be copied,[1439] some courts have erroneously interpreted it to establish the *maximum* amount of expression that may be copied.[1440] More generally, some courts have erroneously stated that "the fair use copier must copy *no more than* is reasonably necessary . . . to enable him to pursue an aim that the law recognizes as proper."[1441]

[iv]   Effect on Potential Market

The fourth factor is "the effect of the use upon the potential market for or value of the copyrighted work."[1442] This factor "requires courts to consider not only the extent of market harm caused by the particular actions of the alleged infringer, but also 'whether unrestricted and widespread conduct of the sort engaged in by the defendant . . . would result in a substantially adverse impact on the potential market' for the original."[1443] The inquiry "must take account not only of harm to

---

[1436] *Campbell*, 510 U.S. at 587–88.

[1437] *Id.* at 586 (emphasis added).

[1438] *Id.* at 588.

[1439] *See* Suntrust Bank v. Houghton Mifflin Co., 268 F.3d 1257, 1273–74 (11th Cir. 2001); Leibovitz v. Paramount Pictures Corp., 137 F.3d 109, 114, 116 (2d Cir. 1998).

[1440] *See* Ty, Inc. v. Publications Int'l, Ltd., 292 F.3d 512, 518 (7th Cir. 2002); Dr. Seuss Enterprises, L.P. v. Penguin Books USA, Inc. v. 109 F.3d 1394, 1400 (9th Cir. 1997).

[1441] Chicago Board of Education v. Substance, Inc., 354 F.3d 624, 629 (7th Cir. 2003) (emphasis added). The court cautioned, however, that "reasonably necessary" does not mean "strictly necessary": "room must be allowed for judgment, and judges must not police criticism with a heavy hand." *Id.*

[1442] 17 U.S.C. § 107(4).

[1443] Campbell v. Acuff-Rose Music, Inc., 510 U.S. 569, 590 (1994).

the original but also of harm to the market for derivative works."[1444]

In *Sony*, the Supreme Court placed the burden of showing harm to the potential market on the copyright owner, saying "[i]f the intended use is for commercial gain, [a] likelihood [of harm] may be presumed. But if it is for a noncommercial purpose, the likelihood must be demonstrated."[1445] In *Campbell*, however, the Supreme Court placed the burden of proving *lack* of market harm on the defendant,[1446] and it also limited the *Sony* presumption, saying:

> No "presumption" or inference of market harm that might find support in *Sony* is applicable to a case involving something beyond mere duplication for commercial purposes. . . . [W]hen a commercial use amounts to mere duplication of the entirety of an original, it clearly "supersedes the objects" of the original and serves as a market replacement for it, making it likely that cognizable market harm to the original will occur. But when, on the contrary, the second use is transformative, market substitution is at least less certain, and market harm may not be so readily inferred.[1447]

Campbell also held that "the only harm . . . that need concern us [under the fourth factor] is the harm of market substitution."[1448] As one court stated: "the economic effect . . . with which we are concerned is not [the new work's] potential to destroy or diminish the market for the original — any bad review can have that effect — but rather whether it *fulfills the demand* for the original. Biting criticism suppresses demand; copyright infringement usurps it."[1449] Or, as another court put it (in "economic terminology"), "copying that is complementary to the copyrighted work (in the sense that nails are complements of hammers) is fair use, but copying that is a substitute for the copyrighted work (in the sense that nails are substitutes for pegs or screws), or for derivative works from the copyrighted work, is not fair use."[1450]

The concept of harm to the potential market for derivative works creates a risk of circular reasoning. A copyright owner can always argue that the defendant has

---

[1444] Harper & Row Publishers, Inc. v. Nation Enterprises, 471 U.S. 539, 568 (1985).

[1445] Sony Corp. of Am. v. Universal City Studios, Inc., 464 U.S. 417, 451 (1984). The majority also held that the plaintiff movie studios "failed to carry their burden with regard to home [videotaping for] time-shifting [purposes]." *Id.* It noted that under TV's advertiser-supported business model, "timeshifting merely enables a viewer to see such a work which he had been invited to witness in its entirety free of charge," *id.* at 449, and that that the district court had rejected as speculative the plaintiffs' arguments that home videotaping would decrease the audience for theatrical movies, live broadcasts, and televised reruns. *Id.* at 451–54.

[1446] Campbell v. Acuff-Rose Music, Inc., 510 U.S. 569, 590 (1994). ("Since fair use is an affirmative defense, its proponent would have difficulty carrying the burden of demonstrating fair use without favorable evidence about relevant markets.").

[1447] *Id.* at 591.

[1448] *Id.* at 593; *see also id.* at 591 ("it is more likely that the new work will not affect the market for the original in a way cognizable under this factor, that is, by acting as a substitute for it").

[1449] Fisher v. Dees, 794 F.2d 432, 438 (9th Cir. 1986) (emphasis in original). The second sentence was quoted with approval in *Campbell*, 510 U.S. at 592.

[1450] Ty, Inc. v. Publications Int'l, Ltd., 292 F.3d 512, 517 (2d Cir. 2002).

deprived it of a potential license fee for the use in question;[1451] but if that use is a fair use, then the copyright owner is not entitled to a license fee in the first place.[1452] Thus, there must always be *some* normative judgment as to which potential derivative uses the copyright owner is entitled to monopolize. The Supreme Court recognized this problem in *Campbell* when it held that "[t]he market for potential derivative uses includes only those that creators of original works would *in general* develop or license others to develop."[1453] Thus, the Court in *Campbell* concluded that "the unlikelihood that creators of imaginative works will license critical reviews or lampoons of their own productions removes such uses from the very notion of a potential licensing market."[1454]

While *Campbell* provides some helpful guidance, it does not remove the problem of circularity altogether. A copyright owner can expand its rights and diminish the rights of users simply by routinely demanding a license fee for uses that otherwise might be considered fair. In response to a cease-and-desist letter, most risk-averse users will either cease the use or else will pay a license fee to the copyright owner, in order to avoid litigation. The copyright owner can then point to the behavior of such users as evidence that a licensing market exists.[1455] To allow this to happen uncritically would come perilously close to adopting the view of some law-and-economics scholars that fair use should be recognized only when the transactions costs of private ordering are so great that they will prevent a potential licensing market from forming.[1456] Other scholars, however, have pointed out that since "fair

---

[1451] *See* Cambridge Univ. Press v. Patton, 769 F.3d 1232 (11th Cir. 2014); American Geophysical Union v. Texaco, Inc., 60 F.3d 913, 929 n.17 (2d Cir. 1994).

[1452] Princeton Univ. Press v. Michigan Document Services, 99 F.3d 1381, 1407 (6th Cir. 1996) (Ryan, J., dissenting); *see also id.* at 1387 (majority opinion) ("The defendants contend that it is circular to assume that a copyright holder is entitled to permission fees and then to measure market loss by reference to the lost fees.").

[1453] Campbell v. Acuff-Rose Music, Inc., 510 U.S. 569, 592 (1994) (emphasis added). *See also* Ringgold v. Black Entertainment Television, Inc., 126 F.3d 70, 81 (2d Cir. 1997) ("We have endeavored to avoid the vice of circularity by considering 'only traditional, reasonable, or likely to be developed markets' when considering" the fourth factor), *citing* American Geophysical Union, 60 F.3d at 930 ("Only an impact on potential licensing revenues for traditional, reasonable, or likely to be developed markets should be legally cognizable" under the fourth factor); *accord, Princeton Univ. Press*, 99 F.3d at 1387.

[1454] *Campbell*, 510 U.S. at 592.

[1455] *See* James Gibson, *Risk Aversion and Rights Accretion in Intellectual Property Law*, 116 YALE L.J. 882 (2007). For a real-life example of this phenomenon, *compare* Williams & Wilkins Co. v. United States, 487 F.2d 1345, 1357–59 (Ct. Cl. 1973) (rejecting argument that library photocopying will harm publishers of medical journals), *aff'd by an equally divided Court*, 420 U.S. 376 (1975), *with American Geophysical Union*, 60 F.3d at 931 ("Whatever the situation may have been previously, before the development of a market for institutional users to obtain licenses to photocopy articles, it is now appropriate to consider the loss of licensing revenues in evaluating" the fourth factor) *and Princeton Univ. Press*, 99 F.3d at 1387 ("A licensing market already exists here, as it did not in" *Williams & Wilkins*). *See also Princeton Univ. Press*, 99 F.3d at 1397 (Merritt, J., dissenting) ("Simply because the publishers have managed to make licensing fees a significant source of income from copyshops and other users of their works does not make the income from the licensing a factor on which we must rely in our analysis. If the publishers have no right to the fee in many of the instances in which they are collecting it, we should not validate that practice by now using the income derived from it to justify further imposition of fees.").

[1456] *See* William L. Landes & Richard A. Posner, *An Economic Analysis of Copyright Law*, 18 J. LEGAL STUD. 325 (1989); Ty, Inc. v. Publications Int'l, Ltd., 292 F.3d 512, 518 (7th Cir. 2002).

use" is one of the ways in which we balance copyright against free speech interests, courts should expressly take such interests into account in deciding which potential derivative uses the copyright owner is entitled to monopolize.[1457]

In *Harper & Row*, the Supreme Court stated that the fourth factor "is undoubtedly the single most important element of fair use."[1458] In *Campbell*, however, the Court pointedly avoided repeating this statement,[1459] and other language in *Campbell* has led courts to conclude that the Court has "retreated" from its position in *Harper & Row*.[1460] And while one study has confirmed the importance of the fourth factor as an empirical matter,[1461] in a number of recent cases the first factor (and in particular, a "transformative" purpose) has seemed to assume greater importance.[1462]

[c]   Examples

[i]   Comment and Criticism

The classic example of "fair use" is the quotation of some of the plaintiff's work in a review of that work, such as a book review or a movie review.[1463] Fair use is upheld even for negative reviews that harm the market for a copyrighted work, so long as the harm is due to the effectiveness of the criticism, and not because the

---

[1457] *See, e.g.*, Wendy J. Gordon, *The "Why" of Markets: Fair Use and Circularity*, 116 YALE L.J. POCKET PART 371, 373 (2007) ("there are some things (like the freedom to criticize) that simply shouldn't be sold on any commercial market, whether or not such a market could feasibly arise."); Wendy J. Gordon, *Excuse and Justification in the Law of Fair Use: Transaction Costs Have Always Been Only Part of the Story*, 50 J. COPYR. SOC'Y USA 149 (2003); Wendy J. Gordon, *Fair Use and Market Failure: A Structural and Economic Analysis of the Betamax Case*, 82 COLUM. L. REV. 1600, 1630–35 (1982) (including "nonmonetizable interests" and "anti-dissemination motives" as cases in which "market failure" occurs). For an example, *see* Ty, Inc. v. Publications Int'l, Ltd., 292 F.3d 512, 520 (7th Cir. 2002) (fair use does not apply "to a publisher's attempting to use licensing to prevent critical reviews of its books").

[1458] Harper & Row Publishers, Inc. v. Nation Enterprises, 471 U.S. 539, 566 (1985).

[1459] The Court did observe that the Sixth Circuit had quoted this sentence from *Harper & Row*, but it did not endorse the quotation. Campbell v. Acuff-Rose Music, Inc., 510 U.S. 569, 574 (1994).

[1460] *See* Blanch v. Koons, 467 F.3d 244, 258 n.8 (2d Cir. 2006); Castle Rock Entertainment, Inc. v. Carol Publishing Group, 150 F.3d 132, 145 (2d Cir. 1998); American Geophysical Union v. Texaco, Inc., 60 F.3d 913, 926 (2d Cir. 1996).

[1461] Barton Beebe, *An Empirical Study of U.S. Copyright Fair Use Opinions, 1978–2005*, 156 U. PA. L. REV. 549, 586 (2008) (concluding upon regression analysis that "the outcome of the fourth factor appears to drive the outcome of the test, and that the outcome of the first factor also appears to be highly influential.").

[1462] *See, e.g.*, Bill Graham Archives v. Dorling Kindersley Ltd., 448 F.3d 605, 614–15 (2d Cir. 2006) (finding lack of market harm because purpose was transformative, despite evidence of licensing market for plaintiff's images); Gaylord v. United States, 595 F.3d 1364, 1372–76 (Fed. Cir. 2010) (holding no fair use where purpose was not transformative, despite admitted lack of any market harm).

[1463] While the fact situation has not actually been litigated, it has been mentioned in dicta so many times that it must be considered settled law. *See, e.g.*, Harper & Row Publishers, Inc. v. Nation Enterprises, 471 U.S. 539, 564 (1985); Video Pipeline, Inc. v. Buena Vista Home Entertainment, Inc., 342 F.3d 191, 200 (3d Cir. 2003); Ty, Inc. v. Publications Int'l, Ltd., 292 F.3d 512, 517–18 (7th Cir. 2002); Supermarket of Homes, Inc. v. San Fernando Valley Bd. of Realtors, 786 F.2d 1400, 1408 (9th Cir. 1986); Folsom v. Marsh, 9 F. Cas. 342, 344 (C.C.D.Mass. 1841).

review quotes so much of the work as to effectively serve as a substitute for it.[1464] Courts have also permitted use of copyrighted works in "truthful and nondeceptive" comparative advertising.[1465]

Less likely to be fair use are uses that quote from the plaintiff's work without adding much in the way of comment or criticism. Thus, a series of two-minute "clip previews" of movies that served the same function as authorized movie "trailers" was held not to be a fair use, even though it was being used to promote sales and rentals of those works.[1466] However, "[t]he law imposes no requirement that a work comment on the original or its author in order to be considered transformative."[1467] Thus, in *Cariou v. Prince*, the Second Circuit held that an artist's use of images from a photographer's work was fair use when the images were "collaged" with images from other sources,[1468] but that five works that consisted primarily of the photographer's images with little change should be remanded for trial.[1469]

Viewed in this light, it is quite probable that the news article in *Harper & Row*, which quoted a mere 300 words from a 200,000-word soon-to-be-published memoir (and paraphrased others), would likely have been deemed to be a fair use had it appeared *after* publication of the memoir, instead of two weeks before. Three important factors — good faith, the unpublished nature of the work, and the harm to the market for pre-publication excerpts — would have come out differently if the Nation had not copied a stolen manuscript, but had reviewed a lawfully purchased copy;[1470] and it is also likely that the Nation would have had time to add commentary of its own, instead of merely summarizing what President Ford had to say in his memoir.[1471]

[1464] Campbell v. Acuff-Rose Music, Inc., 510 U.S. 569, 591–92 (1994) ("when a lethal parody, like a scathing theater review, kills demand for the original, it does not produce a harm cognizable under the Copyright Act."); *Ty*, 292 F.2d at 517–18; On Davis v. The Gap, Inc., 246 F.3d 152, 175–76 (2d Cir. 2001); *Folsom*, 9 F. Cas. at 344–45.

[1465] Sony Computer Entertainment America, Inc. v. Bleem, LLC, 214 F.3d 1022 (9th Cir. 2000).

[1466] *Video Pipeline*, 342 F.3d at 200.

[1467] Cariou v. Prince, 714 F.3d 694, 706 (2d Cir. 2013).

[1468] *Id.* at 710–11. *See also* Seltzer v. Green Day, Inc., 725 F.3d 1170 (9th Cir. 2013) (use of photo of poster from a graffiti-strewn wall as a prominent component of a "video backdrop" in rock band's public performances was a fair use); Blanch v. Koons, 467 F.3d 244 (2d Cir. 2006) (use of advertising photo in artistic collage was a fair use).

[1469] *Cariou*, 714 F.3d at 710–11. *See also* Rogers v. Koons, 960 F.2d 301 (2d Cir. 1992) (three-dimensional reproduction of photo of couple holding eight puppies was not a fair use).

[1470] *See* Harper & Row Publishers, Inc. v. Nation Enterprises, 471 U.S. 539, 562 (1985) ("The Nation's use had not merely the incidental effect but the *intended purpose* of supplanting the copyright holder's commercially valuable right of first publication.") (emphasis in original); *id.* at 564 ("While even substantial quotations might qualify as fair use in a review of a published work . . . , the author's right to control the first public appearance of his expression weighs against such use of the work before its release."); *id.* at 569 ("The Court of Appeals erred . . . in overlooking the unpublished nature of the work and the resulting impact on the potential market for first serial rights").

[1471] *Id.* at 543 ("Mr. Navasky attempted no independent commentary, research or criticism, in part because of the need for speed if he was to 'make news' by 'publish[ing] in advance of publication of the Ford book.' ").

[ii] Parody and Satire

In *Campbell*, the Supreme Court held that a rap parody by 2 Live Crew of the popular song "Oh, Pretty Woman" could qualify as a fair use. Because a parody "can provide social benefit, by shedding light on an earlier work, and, in the process, creating a new one," it is "transformative";[1472] and a parody is unlikely to act as a market substitute for the original or licensed derivatives, because it is unlikely "that creators of imaginative works will license critical reviews or lampoons of their own [works]."[1473] Thus, a parody "must be able to 'conjure up' at least enough of that original to make the object of its critical wit recognizable."[1474]

The Court distinguished parody, which criticizes a particular work, from satire, which uses a work to criticize something else.[1475] Some courts have relied on this distinction to deny fair use protection to "satire." For example, in *Dr. Seuss Enterprises, L.P. v. Penguin Books USA, Inc.*, the court denied protection to a satire of the O.J. Simpson murder trial, written in the style of Dr. Seuss.[1476] The Court in *Campbell*, however, expressly refrained from holding that satire was not a fair use,[1477] and elsewhere in the opinion it expressly indicated that satire *could* qualify as a fair use.[1478] Thus, some courts have held that "satire" can be a fair use,[1479] while others have stretched the definition of "parody" to the breaking point to include works that probably should be considered "satire."[1480] For example, courts have approved modified lyrics to popular songs that had nothing to do with the subject of the original compositions, but merely used the initial words, meter and rhymes of the original lyrics for satirical purposes.[1481]

[1472] Campbell v. Acuff-Rose Music, Inc., 510 U.S. 569, 579 (1994).

[1473] *Id.* at 592.

[1474] *Id.* at 588.

[1475] *Id.* at 580–81. Justice Kennedy made this point more forcefully in his concurring opinion. *Id.* at 597 (Kennedy, J., concurring).

[1476] 109 F.3d 1394, 1400–01 (9th Cir. 1997).

[1477] Campbell v. Acuff-Rose Music, Inc., 510 U.S. 569, 592 n.22 (1994). ("We express no opinion as to . . . works using elements of an original as vehicles for satire or amusement, making no comment on the original or criticism of it.").

[1478] *Id.* at 580 n.14 ("when there is little or no risk of market substitution, . . . looser forms of parody may be found to be fair use, as may satire with lesser justification for the borrowing than would otherwise be required."). For an extensive analysis of parody and satire, see Tyler T. Ochoa, *Dr. Seuss, The Juice, and Fair Use: How the Grinch Silenced a Parody*, 45 J. COPYR. SOC'Y USA 546 (1998).

[1479] *See, e.g.*, Blanch v. Koons, 467 F.3d 244, 254 (2d Cir. 2006) (defendant's work "may be better characterized for these purposes as satire"). Rather than ask whether the work was parody or satire, one should ask "whether Koons had a genuine creative rationale for borrowing Blanch's image" for use in his collage. *Id.* at 255.

[1480] *See, e.g.*, Mattel v. Walking Mountain Prods., 353 F.3d 792, 802 n.7 (9th Cir. 2003) (defendant's photos of Barbie dolls "in various absurd and often sexualized positions," including being menaced by kitchen appliances, were parody and fair use, even though the photos used Barbie primarily as a vehicle for "social commentary"); MasterCard Int'l, Inc. v. Nader2000 Primary Committee, 70 U.S.P.Q. 2d (BNA) 1046 (S.D.N.Y. 2004) (TV ad for Ralph Nader's presidential campaign that mimicked Master-Card's "Priceless" ad campaign was a fair use).

[1481] *See* Berlin v. E.C. Publications, Inc., 329 F.2d 541 (2d Cir. 1964) (publication of parody lyrics to 25 copyrighted songs,); Fisher v. Dees, 794 F.2d 432 (9th Cir. 1986). *But see* MCA, Inc. v. Wilson, 677 F.2d 180 (2d Cir. 1980).

The case law reveals a few trends. Media outlets that are well-known for irreverent parody and satire, such as *South Park, Saturday Night Live, Mad* magazine, and *The Family Guy*, are more likely to be found to have engaged in fair use,[1482] even when the ridicule "has [little or] no critical bearing on the substance or style of the original composition."[1483] Courts are less likely to find fair use when well-known children's works are ridiculed by juxtaposing them with adult content that is sexual or criminal in nature.[1484] Indeed, sexual parodies are less likely to be fair use even when the original is not aimed at children.[1485]

"The threshold question when fair use is raised in defense of parody is whether a parodic character may reasonably be perceived."[1486] Thus, while courts have allowed even extensive borrowing in a work that clearly targeted and criticized the original,[1487] courts have been wary of approving works that appeared merely to be remakes or sequels, "contain[ing] no reasonably discernable rejoinder or specific criticism of any character or theme" in the original.[1488]

[1482] *See* Brownmark Films, LLC v. Comedy Partners, Inc., 682 F.3d 687 (7th Cir. 2012); Elsmere Music, Inc. v. National Broadcasting Co., 482 F. Supp. 741 (S.D.N.Y.), *aff'd*, 623 F.2d 252 (2d Cir. 1980); *Berlin*, 329 F.2d 541; Bourne Co. v. Twentieth Century Fox Film Corp., 602 F. Supp. 2d 499 (S.D.N.Y. 2009); Burnett v. Twentieth Century Fox Film Corp., 491 F. Supp. 2d 962 (C.D. Cal. 2007).

[1483] Campbell v. Acuff-Rose Music, Inc., 510 U.S. 569, 580 (1994). Thus, works featuring actor Leslie Nielsen, who was well-known for appearing in parodies of dramatic works, have invariably been found to be fair use. *See* Leibovitz v. Paramount Pictures Corp., 137 F.3d 109 (2d Cir. 1998); Eveready Battery Co. v. Adolph Coors Co., 765 F. Supp. 440 (N.D. Ill. 1991).

[1484] *See, e.g.*, Dr. Seuss Enterprises, L.P. v. Penguin Books USA, Inc., 109 F.3d 1394 (9th Cir. 1997) (satire of O.J. Simpson murder trial in the style of Dr. Seuss); Walt Disney Prods. v. Air Pirates, 581 F.2d 751, 753 (9th Cir. 1978) (a comic book with "a rather bawdy depiction of the Disney characters as active members of a free thinking, promiscuous, drug ingesting counterculture."). *But see* Lyons Partnership v. Giannoulos, 179 F.3d 384 (5th Cir. 1999) (finding no violation of the Lanham Act for performance in which defendant, dressed as a Chicken, "would flip, slap, tackle, trample, and generally assault the Barney look-alike.").

[1485] *See* MCA, Inc. v. Wilson, 677 F.2d 180 (2d Cir. 1980) (song "Cunnilingus Champion of Company C," a take-off of "Boogie Woogie Bugle Boy of Company B," was not a fair use); Dallas Cowboys Cheerleaders, Inc. v. Scoreboard Posters, Inc., 600 F.2d 1184 (5th Cir. 1979) (poster of former Dallas Cowboys cheerleaders, posed in same manner as original poster, but with exposed breasts, was not a fair use). Less explicit sexual content, however, has been held to be a fair use. *See* Mattel, Inc. v. Walking Mountain Prods., 353 F.3d 792 (9th Cir. 2003) (photos of Barbie dolls, often naked and posed in sexualized positions).

[1486] *Campbell*, 510 U.S. at 582.

[1487] *See, e.g.*, Suntrust Bank v. Houghton Mifflin Co., 268 F.3d 1257 (11th Cir. 2001) (*The Wind Done Gone*, a novel which re-tells the story of Margaret Mitchell's *Gone with The Wind* from the point of view of a mulatto half-sister to Scarlett O'Hara, using all of the novel's major characters and plot elements, in order to criticize the novel's depiction of slavery in the Civil War-era American South, was a fair use).

[1488] Salinger v. Colting, 641 F. Supp. 2d 250, 258 (S.D.N.Y. 2009) (enjoining U.S. publication of defendant's novel *60 Years Later: Coming Through the Rye*, which depicts character of Holden Caulfield from plaintiff's novel *Catcher in the Rye* as a senior citizen), *rev'd on other grounds*, 607 F.3d 68, 83 (2d Cir. 2010) ("we conclude, with the District Court, that Defendants are not likely to prevail in their fair use defense.").

[iii]   News Reporting and Documentaries

Although "news reporting" is listed in the preamble to section 107, news reporting is not automatically a fair use. In *Harper & Row*, the Supreme Court rejected the arguments that "copying of [former President] Ford's expression [is] essential to reporting the news story" and that "the public's interest in learning this news as fast as possible outweighs the right of the author to control its first publication."[1489] Instead, it held that "[t]he fact that an article arguably is 'news' and therefore a productive use is simply one factor in a fair use analysis."[1490]

Notwithstanding *Harper & Row*, many cases involving claims of news reporting sustain the fair use defense. For example, in *Nuñez v. Caribbean Int'l News Corp.*, the court held that it was "fair use" to reprint studio photographs of Miss Puerto Rico Universe in a newspaper, when a controversy had arisen whether some of the "nearly naked" photos were inappropriate.[1491] Courts have also permitted film clips of actors to be used in news reports about those actors.[1492] However, when footage was created specifically to be sold to news agencies, it is not fair use to broadcast the footage without compensation.[1493] Claims of news reporting also fail when the work has only minimal newsworthy value.[1494]

Similarly, many courts have allowed short excerpts of copyrighted works to be used in biographies and historical documentaries.[1495] For example, the Second Circuit has held that reproduction of six concert posters "in significantly reduced form" in a biographical book about the Grateful Dead was "transformative" and was a fair use;[1496] and the Ninth Circuit held that use of a seven-second clip from the *Ed Sullivan Show* in a biographical Broadway musical was a fair use.[1497]

[1489] Harper & Row Publishers, Inc. v. Nation Enterprises, 471 U.S. 539, 556 (1985).

[1490] *Id.* at 561. *Cf.* Zacchini v. Scripps-Howard Broadcasting Co., 433 U.S. 562 (1977) (First Amendment does not require that television news be permitted to broadcast plaintiff's "entire act" without his permission; although analyzed as a right of publicity case, rationale is equally applicable to common-law copyright). *See* § 6G[4][b].

[1491] 235 F.3d 18 (1st Cir. 2000). *See also* Swatch Group Mgmt. Servs. Ltd. v. Bloomberg, L.P., 756 F.3d 73 (2d Cir. 2014) (dissemination of unauthorized recording of conference call between management and financial analysts was a fair use).

[1492] *See, e.g.*, Video-Cinema Films, Inc. v. Cable News Network, Inc., 60 U.S.P.Q. 2d 1415 (S.D.N.Y. 2001) (news report on death of actor Robert Mitchum).

[1493] *See* Los Angeles News Service v. Reuters Television Int'l, Ltd., 149 F.3d 987 (9th Cir. 1998) (aerial footage of Reginald Denny beating during 1992 L.A. riots). *But see* Los Angeles News Service v. CBS Broadcasting, Inc., 305 F.3d 924 (9th Cir. 2002) (Court TV's use of a short clip of the same footage in a "video montage" introducing its news program was a fair use).

[1494] *See, e.g.*, Balsley v. LFP, Inc., 691 F.3d 747 (6th Cir. 2012) (photo of newscaster in a wet t-shirt contest); Monge v. Maya Magazines, Inc., 688 F.3d 1164 (9th Cir. 2012) (photo of clandestine wedding of singer). In both cases, the subject of the photo bought the copyright from the photographer and used it to suppress further dissemination of the photo.

[1495] *See, e.g.*, Hofheinz v. A&E Television Networks, 146 F. Supp. 2d 442 (S.D.N.Y. 2001) (biography of actor Peter Graves); Hofheinz v. AMC Prods., Inc., 147 F. Supp. 2d 127 (E.D.N.Y. 2001) (documentary about movie studio); Monster Communications, Inc. v. Turner Broadcasting System, Inc., 935 F. Supp. 490 (S.D.N.Y. 1996) (biography of boxer Muhammed Ali).

[1496] Bill Graham Archives v. Dorling Kindersley Ltd., 448 F.3d 605, 609–10 (2d Cir. 2006).

[1497] SOFA Ent'mt, Inc. v. Dodger Prods., 709 F.3d 1273 (9th Cir. 2013). *See also* Bouchat v. Baltimore

However, when the use is so extensive that it supersedes an important licensing market for the work, fair use may be denied. Thus, a 16-hour video documentary about Elvis Presley that featured clips of "every film and television appearance" was not a fair use, because "significant portions" of many of the clips were shown, often unaccompanied by any scholarly critique or historical analysis.[1498] Courts have also denied "fair use" to a number of "unauthorized" companion books to various movies and television series that contained detailed summaries of the plots of those works.[1499]

[iv]   Litigation Uses

Courts have allowed copyrighted works to be reproduced by law enforcement officers and attorneys and introduced into evidence in court proceedings, where the contents of the work are relevant to the legal issues involved.[1500] Courts have also held that patent attorneys may make copies of scientific articles ("prior art") in the course of their patent prosecution activities,[1501] and that reproduction of legal briefs in online databases is a fair use.[1502] However, when a work has been commissioned specifically for use in litigation, the commissioning party may be barred from using the work in violation of the conditions agreed to by the parties.[1503]

[v]   Reverse Engineering

In *Sega Enterprises, Ltd. v. Accolade, Inc.*, the defendant "decompiled" the machine-readable binary object code (1s and 0s) of three videogame programs, translating them into human-readable source code. The defendant then studied the decompiled programs and used the information to make its own video games compatible with the Sega Genesis videogame console. The court held that this process was a fair use, because "disassembly is the only means of gaining access" to "unprotected ideas and functional concepts embodied in the code," and because "Accolade has a legitimate interest in gaining such access (in order to determine

---

Ravens L.P., 619 F.3d 301 (4th Cir. 2010) (use of infringing logo in historical display was fair use, but use of logo in highlight films was not a fair use); Bouchat v. Baltimore Ravens L.P., 737 F.3d 932 (4th Cir. 2013) (use of infringing logo in historical display and briefly in historical documentary films was a fair use).

[1498] Elvis Presley Enterprises, Inc. v. Passport Video, 349 F.3d 622 (9th Cir. 2003).

[1499] *See, e.g.*, Twin Peaks Prods., Inc. v. Publications Int'l, Ltd., 996 F.2d 1366 (2d Cir. 1993) (TV series "Twin Peaks"); Toho Co. v. William Morrow & Co., 33 F. Supp. 2d 1206 (C.D. Cal. 1998) ("Godzilla"); Paramount Pictures Corp. v. Carol Publishing Co., 11 F. Supp. 2d 329 (S.D.N.Y. 1998) ("Star Trek" TV series and movies), *aff'd mem.*, 181 F.3d 83 (2d Cir. 1999). *See also* Castle Rock Entertainment, Inc. v. Carol Publishing Group, Inc., 150 F.3d 132 (2d Cir. 1998) (denying fair use to trivia book based on TV series "Seinfeld").

[1500] *See, e.g.*, Bond v. Blum, 317 F.3d 385 (4th Cir. 2003); Religious Technology Center v. Wollersheim, 971 F.2d 364, 367 (9th Cir. 1992); Shell v. City of Radford, 351 F. Supp. 2d 510 (W.D. Va. 2005).

[1501] *See* Am. Inst. of Physics v. Schwegman, Lundberg & Woessner, 2013 U.S. Dist. LEXIS 124578 (D. Minn. July 30, 2013); Am. Inst. of Physics v. Winstead, PC, 109 U.S.P.Q.2d 1661 (N.D. Tex. 2013).

[1502] White v. West Publ'g Corp., 111 U.S.P.Q.2d 1405 (S.D.N.Y. 2014). Another court reached a similar result on different grounds, holding that filing a document in court is an irrevocable license allowing the court, all parties to the action and their attorneys, present and future, to use and modify the document for purposes of the litigation. Unclaimed Property Recovery Serv. v. Kaplan, 734 F.3d 132 (2d Cir. 2013).

[1503] Images Audio Visual Prods., Inc. v. Perini Bldg. Co., 91 F. Supp. 2d 1075 (E.D. Mich. 2000).

how to make its cartridges compatible with the Genesis console)."[1504] This holding has been widely followed in other cases involving reverse engineering of software.[1505]

[vi]　　　Personal Uses

In *Sony Corp. of America v. Universal City Studios, Inc.*, the Supreme Court held that home videotaping of copyrighted broadcasts for time-shifting purposes was a fair use.[1506] Although some thought that *Sony* would support a broad application of fair use to permit many personal uses, the ruling now seems to be limited to advertiser-supported television broadcasting, where the district court expressly found that time-shifting would increase viewership.[1507] Efforts to extend *Sony* to other types of personal uses have been largely unavailing.[1508] For example, courts have uniformly rejected arguments that peer-to-peer file sharing of copyrighted musical works and sound recordings is a fair use.[1509]

[vii]　　　Internet and Database Uses

The basic function of the Internet is to reproduce and transmit digital data from one location to another. Many core applications of the Internet, including browsing, linking, and search engines, rely on the ability to copy and store large amounts of data. Problems arise when that data represents a copyrighted work.

In *Kelly v. Arriba Soft Corp.*, the Ninth Circuit held that a search engine makes a fair use of copyrighted images when it copies the images into RAM, processes the images to make "thumbnails," or reduced size images, stores the thumbnails on a server, and transmits the thumbnails to users in response to a search query, along with a link to the full-size images.[1510] This holding was re-affirmed in a case where

---

[1504] 977 F.2d 1510, 1520 (9th Cir. 1992).

[1505] *See, e.g.*, Sony Computer Entertainment, Inc. v. Connectix Corp., 203 F.3d 596 (9th Cir. 2000); Atari Games, Inc. v. Nintendo of America, Inc., 975 F.2d 832 (Fed. Cir. 1992) (agreeing with fair use analysis, but nonetheless holding for plaintiff where code, not just ideas, was copied). *Cf.* Oracle Am., Inc. v. Google, Inc., 750 F.3d 1339 (Fed. Cir. 2014) (desire to make Android partially interoperable with Java was relevant, if at all, only to fair use); *but cf.* DSC Communications Corp. v. Pulse Communications, Inc., 170 F.3d 1354 (Fed. Cir. 1999) (copying for demonstration purposes, rather than reverse engineering, is not fair use).

[1506] 464 U.S. 417 (1984).

[1507] *Id.* at 452–54. In particular, in an era before remote controls were common, the district court expressly found that few viewers would fast-forward past the commercials during playback. *Id.* at 452 n.36.

[1508] *But cf.* Recording Industry Ass'n of Am. v. Diamond Multimedia Systems, Inc., 180 F.3d 1072 (9th Cir. 1999) (copying MP3 files from computer to a portable player "is paradigmatic noncommercial personal use entirely consistent with the purposes of the [Audio Home Recording] Act."). The AHRA does not apply to peer-to-peer file sharing, because computer manufacturers do not pay the royalty that is paid by manufacturers of other digital audio recording devices. *See* § 4I[2][b].

[1509] *See* Arista Records, LLC v. Doe 3, 604 F.3d 110 (2d Cir. 2010); BMG Music v. Gonzalez, 430 F.3d 888 (7th Cir. 2005); A&M Records, Inc. v. Napster, Inc., 239 F.3d 1004 (9th Cir. 2001); Sony Music Entertainment, Inc. v. Tenenbaum, 672 F. Supp. 2d 217 (D. Mass. 2009), *aff'd on other grounds*, 660 F.3d 487 (1st Cir. 2011). *Cf.* Metro-Goldwyn-Mayer, Inc. v. Grokster, Ltd., 545 U.S. 913 (2005) (implicitly assuming that file-sharing is not a fair use).

[1510] 336 F.3d 811 (9th Cir. 2003).

the plaintiff alleged that there was a market for "thumbnail" images for use on cell phones, where the plaintiff failed to show that any actual downloading of thumbnail images from the search engine had taken place.[1511]

Other courts have held that it is a fair use for search engines to make and store copies of the text of websites, where the website owner has the ability to prevent such automated copying by including a "no archive" flag in the HTML code of his website;[1512] and that it is a fair use for a plagiarism detection website to store copies of student papers to compare to others for possible plagiarism.[1513] Some plaintiffs have challenged the practice of search engines and news aggregators copying headlines and topic sentences from news stories, even when a link to the original story is included; but to date, most such cases have settled or been dismissed.[1514] Some courts, however, have found that such a use is a fair use, at least for an individual blogger.[1515]

The most controversial assertion of fair use in this context is the Google Books project, in which Google scanned all of the contents of several major libraries and enabled full-text searches on the Internet. Google displays the full text only for works published before 1923; otherwise, it displays only "snippets," or a few lines of text. The Authors Guild filed a class-action lawsuit against Google for copyright infringement. After a proposed settlement agreement was rejected by the district judge,[1516] he granted a motion for class certification, which was vacated by the Second Circuit.[1517] On remand, the district judge held that Google's use was a fair use, finding that "Google Books provides significant public benefits" by helping readers identify books and providing links where books may be purchased or borrowed, "without adversely impacting the rights of copyright owners" by substituting for purchases of books.[1518] In a companion case, the Second Circuit affirmed a ruling that a similar full-text search feature offered by the HathiTrust Digital Library was a fair use, as was providing full-text copies to visually impaired people.[1519]

[1511] Perfect 10 v. Amazon.com, Inc., 508 F.3d 1146 (9th Cir. 2007).

[1512] Field v. Google, Inc., 412 F. Supp. 2d 1106 (D. Nev. 2006).

[1513] A.V. v. iParadigms, LLC, 562 F.3d 630 (4th Cir. 2009).

[1514] *See, e.g.*, Associated Press v. All Headline News Corp., 608 F. Supp. 2d 454 (S.D.N.Y. 2009) (denying motion to dismiss; case later settled). *See also* Righthaven, LLC v. Majorwager.com, Inc., 96 U.S.P.Q. 2d 1768 (D. Nev. 2010) (denying motion to dismiss); www.righthavenlawsuits.com (last visited March 1, 2015) (listing 276 lawsuits filed by Righthaven, as assignee of copyrights in news stories, including settlement dates).

[1515] *See* Righthaven, LLC v. Realty One Group, Inc., 96 U.S.P.Q. 2d 1516 (D. Nev. 2010). *See also* Righthaven, Inc. v. Hoehn, 792 F. Supp. 2d 1138 (D. Nev. 2011) (posting entire article for discussion is a fair use), *vacated on other grounds*, 716 F.3d 1166 (9th Cir. 2013).

[1516] Authors Guild v. Google, Inc., 770 F. Supp. 2d 666 (S.D.N.Y. 2011).

[1517] Authors Guild v. Google, Inc., 282 F.R.D. 384 (S.D.N.Y. 2012), *vacated and remanded*, 721 F.3d 132 (2d Cir. 2013).

[1518] Authors Guild v. Google, Inc., 954 F. Supp. 2d 282 (S.D.N.Y. 2013).

[1519] *See* Authors Guild, Inc. v. HathiTrust, 755 F.3d 87 (2d Cir. 2014). The Second Circuit also affirmed a ruling that a proposed "orphan works" project was not yet ripe for review, and vacated a holding that copying for preservation purposes was a fair use, for lack of an actual controversy. *Id.*

[2]   Other Defenses

[a]   Inequitable Conduct

Fraud or inequitable conduct in the registration of a copyright is a defense to an infringement charge.[1520] This defense was codified in a 2008 amendment, which provides that a registration certificate is valid, even if it contains inaccurate information, unless "(A) the inaccurate information was included on the application for copyright registration with knowledge that it was inaccurate; and (B) the inaccuracy of the information, if known, would have caused the Register of Copyrights to refuse registration."[1521] In such cases, "the court shall request the Register of Copyrights to advise the court whether the inaccurate information, if known, would have caused the Register of Copyrights to refuse registration."[1522] This defense is less significant in copyright cases than in patent cases, primarily because Copyright Office examination is more limited than Patent and Trademark Office examination.

Fraud or inequitable conduct only invalidates the registration and any rights based on the registration, including the right to commence an infringement action (for United States works) and to recover statutory damages and attorneys fees (for all works).[1523] Any rights that may be enforced without registration, such as moral rights or rights in foreign works, are unaffected.[1524] Presumably, once the fraud is cured and a registration is obtained, the infringement claim may be re-filed,[1525] unless the statute of limitations has run in the meantime.[1526]

[b]   Misuse

Adopted by analogy to the patent misuse defense,[1527] the doctrine of copyright misuse "forbids the use of the [copyright] to secure an exclusive right or limited monopoly not granted by the [Copyright] Office and which it is contrary to public policy to grant."[1528] Misuse has its roots in the equitable doctrine of "unclean hands," which holds that a party who seeks an equitable remedy must not itself have

---

[1520] *See, e.g.*, Masquerade Novelty, Inc. v. Unique Industries, Inc., 912 F.2d 663, 667 (3d Cir. 1990). For a discussion of fraud and inequitable conduct in patent and trademark registration procurement, see §§ 2D[2] and 5J[7][d].

[1521] 17 U.S.C. § 411(b)(1).

[1522] 17 U.S.C. § 411(b)(2).

[1523] 17 U.S.C. § 411(b)(3) ("Nothing in this subsection shall affect any rights, obligations, or requirements . . . except for the institution of and remedies in an infringement actions under this section [411] and section 412.").

[1524] *See* 17 U.S.C. § 411(a) ("Except for an action brought for a violation of the rights of the author under section 106A(a) [moral rights], and subject to the provisions of subsection (b), no civil action for infringement of the copyright in any United States work shall be instituted until . . . registration of the copyright claim has been made").

[1525] Section 411(a) also permits suit to be filed where registration has been refused, if a copy of the complaint is served on the Register of Copyrights, who is permitted to intervene to defend her refusal to register.

[1526] *See* § 4J[2][c].

[1527] *See* § 2F[4][c].

[1528] Lasercomb America, Inc. v. Reynolds, 911 F.2d 970, 972 (4th Cir. 1990).

acted in bad faith or engaged in inequitable conduct. Thus, a finding of copyright misuse does not invalidate the plaintiff's copyright; instead, the copyright owner "is free to bring a suit for infringement once it has purged itself of the misuse."[1529]

For example, in *Lasercomb America, Inc. v. Reynolds*, the defendant successfully asserted a misuse defense, where the plaintiff's end-user license agreement prohibited the licensee from developing or selling any competing software, whether or not the software was copied from or based on Lasercomb's.[1530] Similarly, in *Alcatel USA, Inc. v. DGI Technologies, Inc.*, misuse was found when the plaintiff's end-user license agreement stipulated that its software was licensed for use only with hardware manufactured by the plaintiff.[1531]

Anticompetitive practices in connection with the licensing of copyrighted works may violate the federal antitrust laws,[1532] and misuse often is asserted by parties who also claim that their adversaries have violated the antitrust laws. It is possible, however, to lose on an antitrust claim while succeeding with a factually-related misuse defense.[1533]

[c]   Statute of Limitations

Section 507(a) imposes a five-year statute of limitations on criminal copyright actions, and section 507(b) imposes a three-year statute of limitations on civil copyright actions.[1534]

In common with all statutes of limitation, section 507 presents difficult interpretation and application problems, such as determining when a claim accrues. For example, if an infringer makes multiple copies of a work and sells them over an extended period, there are at least three plausible positions on when the owner's claim "accrued": (1) treat the first infringing act as accrual; (2) treat the last infringing act as accrual; and (3) treat each infringing act (reproduction and distribution) as a separate claim. In *Petrella v. Metro-Goldwyn-Mayer, Inc.*, the Supreme Court endorsed the third position, stating that "when a defendant has engaged . . . in a series of discrete infringing acts, the copyright holder's suit ordinarily will be timely . . . with respect to more recent acts of infringement (i.e., acts within the three-year window), but untimely with respect to prior acts of the same or similar kind."[1535]

[1529] *Id.* at 979 n.22.

[1530] *Id.* at 973.

[1531] 166 F.3d 772, 793 (5th Cir. 1999); *see also* DSC Communications Corp. v. DGI Technologies, Inc., 81 F.3d 597 (5th Cir. 1996).

[1532] *See, e.g.*, Broadcast Music, Inc. v. Columbia Broadcasting System, Inc., 441 U.S. 1, 19 (1979); United States v. Paramount Pictures, Inc., 334 U.S. 131, 143, 158 (1948).

[1533] *See, e.g.*, Practice Management Information Corp. v. American Medical Association, 121 F.3d 516 (9th Cir. 1997) (holding that the AMA misused its copyright by licensing its medical procedure coding system to the federal Health Care Financing Administration in exchange for the agency's agreement not to use any competing system and to require the use of AMA's system by applicants for Medicaid reimbursement).

[1534] 17 U.S.C. § 507. *See* Prather v. Neva Paperbacks, Inc., 446 F.2d 338, 339–40 (5th Cir. 1971).

[1535] 134 S. Ct. 1962, 1970 (2014).

Recovery outside the three-year window may still be possible, however, using the "discovery" rule of accrual, which holds that "[a] cause of action for copyright infringement accrues when one has knowledge of a violation or is chargeable with such knowledge."[1536] Thus, damages may be recovered for acts occurring more than three years before filing, "so long as the copyright owner did not discover — and reasonably could not have discovered — the infringement" at an earlier date.[1537]

The copyright statute of limitations is not limited to infringement claims, but extends as well to claims seeking declarations of copyright ownership.[1538] In such a case, the analogy to "adverse possession" in real property law may counsel use of the discovery rule of accrual.[1539]

[d]   Laches and Estoppel

Laches is an equitable defense which arises when a plaintiff's unreasonable delay in filing suit prejudices the defendant.[1540] In *Petrella*, the Supreme Court held that laches cannot be applied to bar an action for damages brought within the three-year statute of limitations.[1541] In extraordinary circumstances, however, laches may bar a claim for equitable relief at the outset of the case;[1542] and courts may always take the copyright owner's delay into account in awarding equitable relief, such as an injunction and infringer's profits.[1543]

The Court distinguished laches from the doctrine of equitable estoppel, saying:

> [W]hen a copyright owner engages in intentionally misleading representations concerning his abstention from suit, and the alleged infringer detrimentally relies on the copyright owner's deception, the doctrine of estoppel may bar the copyright owner's claims completely, eliminating all potential remedies.[1544]

For example, in *Field v. Google, Inc.*, the plaintiff was estopped from claiming infringement when he posted an article on his website without using the standard

---

[1536] Roley v. New World Pictures, Ltd., 19 F.3d 479, 481 (9th Cir. 1994); *accord*, Psihoyos v. John Wiley Sons, Inc., 748 F.3d 120, 12425 n.3 (2d Cir. 2014) (listing cases); Bridgeport Music, Inc. v. Diamond Time, Ltd., 371 F.3d 883, 889 (6th Cir. 2004). *Cf. Petrella*, 134 S. Ct. at 1969 n.4 (acknowledging the discovery rule, but noting "we have not passed on the question.").

[1537] Polar Bear Prods. v. Timex Corp., 384 F.3d 700, 706 (9th Cir. 2004).

[1538] *See, e.g.*, Merchant v. Levy, 92 F.3d 51, 55–56 (2d Cir. 1996); Santa-Rosa v. Combo Records, 471 F.3d 224 (1st Cir. 2006). *But see* Pritchett v. Pound, 473 F.3d 217 (5th Cir. 2006) (action for declaratory judgment not barred where party seeks no affirmative relief and only asserts ownership as a defense).

[1539] *See* Gaiman v. McFarlane, 360 F.3d 644 (7th Cir. 2004); *accord*, Brownstein v. Lindsay, 747 F.3d 55, 70 (3d Cir. 2014); Ritchie v. Williams, 395 F.3d 283 (6th Cir. 2005). *But see* Advance Magazine Publishers, Inc. v. Leach, 466 F. Supp. 2d 628 (D. Md. 2006) (doctrine of adverse possession does not apply to copyright).

[1540] *See, e.g.*, Chirco v. Crosswinds Communities, Inc., 474 F.3d 227, 234–36 (6th Cir. 2007).

[1541] Petrella v. Metro-Goldwyn-Mayer, Inc., 134 S. Ct. 1962, 1967, 1974 (2014).

[1542] *Id.* at 1967, 1977–78. The Court cited *Chico* as an example of "extraordinary circumstances." In *Chirco*, plaintiff knew of defendant's plans to build allegedly infringing apartments, but he waited until the units were constructed and occupied before bringing suit, and sought destruction as a remedy.

[1543] *Petrella*, 134 S. Ct. at 1967, 1978–79.

[1544] *Id.* at 1977.

"no-archive" Internet protocol of which he was aware, which would have prevented Google from copying his article into its electronic "cache."[1545] Unlike laches, estoppel bars both equitable and monetary relief.[1546]

[e] Abandonment and Forfeiture

The plaintiff's assertion of copyright ownership can be countered, and the claim of infringement defeated, where the plaintiff (or the plaintiff's predecessor) has abandoned or forfeited the copyright. The nomenclature employed in the cases sometimes is less than precise, but abandonment should not be confused with forfeiture. Before March 1, 1989, forfeiture occurred as a consequence of publication without proper copyright notice. The copyright owner's intent was irrelevant: the forfeiture occurred by operation of law.[1547]

Abandonment, on the other hand, requires *intent* by the copyright owner to surrender rights in the work and normally is proved by an *overt act* evidencing such intent (for example, a statement relinquishing any copyright interest in a work or an act destroying the only existing copy of the work).[1548] For example, in *Oravec v. Sunny Isles Luxury Ventures, L.C.*, the plaintiff was held to have abandoned his copyright in an architectural design when he signed a letter stating that he "reserve[d] no patent, trademark, copyright, trade secret, or other intellectual property rights in any of the material that forms or is contained in [his] proposal."[1549]

§ 4K REMEDIES

[1] In General

A court may grant the following remedies for copyright infringement: preliminary and permanent injunctions; impoundment and destruction of infringing articles; monetary damages, consisting of the copyright owner's actual damages plus the infringer's profits, or statutory damages; and costs and attorney's fees. Willful copyright infringement may constitute a criminal offense.

[1545] 412 F. Supp. 2d 1106, 1116–17 (D. Nev. 2006). *See also* HGI Assocs., Inc. v. Wetmore Printing Co., 427 F.3d 867, 875 (11th Cir. 2005) (defendant was estopped from claiming infringement as a defense to breach of contract where it duped the plaintiff into buying counterfeit software); Carson v. Dynegy, Inc., 344 F.3d 446, 453–55 (5th Cir. 2003) (former employee was estopped from claiming infringement by his former employer when he encouraged the creation of a derivative program for other employees to use and never informed his employer that he was claiming sole ownership of the underlying program or any modifications).

[1546] *See* Peter Letterese & Assocs. v. World Inst. of Scientology Enter., Int'l, 533 F.3d 1287, 1321 (11th Cir. 2008).

[1547] *See, e.g.*, Donald Frederick Evans & Assocs., Inc. v. Continental Homes, Inc., 785 F.2d 897 (11th Cir. 1986).

[1548] *See, e.g.*, Seshadri v. Kasraian, 130 F.3d 798 (7th Cir. 1997); Pacific & Southern Co., Inc. v. Duncan, 572 F. Supp. 1186 (N.D. Ga. 1983), *aff'd in part and rev'd in part*, 744 F.2d 1490 (11th Cir. 1984).

[1549] 469 F. Supp. 2d 1148, 1177–78, *aff'd*, 527 F.3d 1218, 1221 n.1 (11th Cir. 2008).

[2]   Injunctions

Section 502 provides that a court may "grant temporary and final injunctions on such terms as it may deem reasonable to prevent or restrain infringement of a copyright."[1550]

[a]   Preliminary Injunctions

Courts apply general preliminary injunction standards to copyright cases. Most courts consider four factors in deciding whether to grant a preliminary injunction: (1) the likelihood that the moving party will succeed on the merits; (2) the threat of irreparable harm to the moving party should a preliminary injunction be denied; (3) the balance between this harm and the harm that granting the injunction will cause to the other party; and (4) the public interest.[1551]

Two courts have modified the four-factor test to indicate more clearly how they would balance the various factors against one another. The Second Circuit requires the moving party to show irreparable harm and either (1) a likelihood of success on the merits or (2) "sufficiently serious questions going to the merits to make them a fair ground for litigation and a balance of hardship tipping decidedly toward" the moving party.[1552] The Ninth Circuit requires either (1) a likelihood of success on the merits and the possibility of irreparable injury, or (2) the existence of serious questions on the merits and the balance of hardships tips in the moving party's favor.[1553] "These two formulations represent two points on a sliding scale in which the required degree of irreparable harm increases as the probability of success decreases."[1554]

Until recently, copyright owners who were able to show a likelihood of success on their copyright infringement claim rarely failed to obtain injunctive relief, because courts were willing to presume the existence of irreparable injury.[1555] In 2006, however, the Supreme Court ruled in a patent case that because a permanent injunction was an equitable remedy, irreparable harm could not be presumed, but had to be demonstrated in each case.[1556] Because "the Court expressly relied upon copyright cases in reaching its conclusion,"[1557] and because it did not distinguish between preliminary and permanent injunctions, the Second Circuit has held that

---

[1550] 17 U.S.C. § 502(a).

[1551] See, e.g., Coquico, Inc. v. Rodriguez-Miranda, 562 F.3d 62, 66 (1st Cir. 2009); Lexmark Int'l, Inc. v. Static Control Components, Inc., 387 F.3d 522, 532 (6th Cir. 2004); Video Pipeline, Inc. v. Buena Vista Home Entertainment, Inc., 342 F.3d 191, 196 (3d Cir. 2003); Taylor Corp. v. Four Seasons Greetings, LLC, 315 F.3d 1039, 1041 (8th Cir. 2003). Some courts, however, treat the four factors as required elements. See, e.g., Suntrust Bank v. Houghton Mifflin Co., 268 F.3d 1257, 1265 (11th Cir. 2001); Mitel, Inc. v. Iqtel, Inc., 124 F.3d 1366, 1370 (10th Cir. 1997); DSC Communications Corp. v. DGI Technologies, Inc., 81 F.3d 597, 600 (5th Cir. 1996); Erickson v. Trinity Theatre, Inc., 13 F.3d 1061, 1067 (7th Cir. 1994).

[1552] See, e.g., NXVIM Corp. v. Ross Institute, 364 F.3d 471, 476 (2d Cir. 2004).

[1553] See, e.g., Perfect 10, Inc. v. Amazon.com, Inc., 508 F.3d 1146, 1158 (9th Cir. 2007).

[1554] Id.

[1555] See Salinger v. Colting, 607 F.3d 68, 75–76 (2d Cir. 2010); Taylor Corp. v. Four Seasons Greetings, LLC, 315 F.3d 1039, 1041–42 (8th Cir. 2003).

[1556] See eBay, Inc. v. MercExchange, LLC, 547 U.S. 388, 391 (2006), discussed at § 2H[1][b].

[1557] Salinger, 607 F.3d at 78.

its "pre-*eBay* standard for when preliminary injunctions may issue in copyright cases is inconsistent with" *eBay* and had to be modified.[1558] The modified standard is consistent with the more general four-factor test applied by other courts, with the major difference being that the Second Circuit is still willing to accept "serious questions going to the merits," rather than a likelihood of success, if the balance of hardships tips "decidedly" in favor of the plaintiff.

[b]   Permanent Injunctions

In *eBay, Inc. v. MercExchange, LLC*, a patent case, the Supreme Court held that a court cannot presume irreparable harm upon a finding of infringement, and that

> [A] plaintiff seeking a permanent injunction must satisfy a four-factor test before a court may grant such relief. A plaintiff must demonstrate: (1) that it has suffered an irreparable injury; (2) that remedies available at law, such as monetary damages, are inadequate to compensate for that injury; (3) that, considering the balance of hardships between the plaintiff and defendant, a remedy in equity is warranted; and (4) that the public interest would not be disserved by a permanent injunction.[1559]

Several Courts of Appeals have already held that this standard applies with equal force to permanent injunctions in copyright cases.[1560]

[3]   Impoundment and Disposition

While the action is pending, section 503(a) permits courts to order the impoundment of "all copies or phonorecords claimed to have been made or used in violation of the exclusive rights of the copyright owner."[1561] This remedy extends as well to "all plates, molds, matrices, masters, tapes, film negatives, or other articles by means of which such copies or phonorecords may be reproduced."[1562] The phrase "made or used" permits a court to seize "articles which, though reproduced and acquired lawfully, have been used for infringing purposes such as rentals, performances and displays."[1563]

Whether impoundment orders can be issued in summary or *ex parte* proceedings, or whether the defendant has a right to an adversarial hearing, was

---

[1558] *Id.* at 79–80. *Accord*, Perfect 10, Inc. v. Google, Inc., 653 F.3d 976 (9th Cir. 2011).

[1559] 547 U.S. 388, 391 (2006).

[1560] *See* CoxCom, Inc. v. Chaffee, 536 F.3d 101, 112 (1st Cir. 2008); Peter Letterese & Assocs. v. World Institute of Scientology Enterprises Int'l, 533 F.3d 1287, 1323 (11th Cir. 2008); Christopher Phelps & Assocs. v. Galloway, 492 F.3d 532, 543 (4th Cir. 2007). The second factor listed in *eBay* would not appear to add much, if anything, to the calculus, because the definition of irreparable injury is that legal remedies are inadequate to compensate for the injury. *See* BLACK'S LAW DICTIONARY 801 (8th ed. 2004) ("an injury that cannot be adequately measured or compensated by money").

[1561] 17 U.S.C. § 503(a)(1)(A).

[1562] 17 U.S.C. § 503(a)(1)(B).

[1563] H.R. Rep. No. 94-1476, at 160 (1976). Note, however, that impoundment *cannot* be ordered against an innocent third party who purchased an infringing copy in good faith, because mere possession of an infringing copy does not violate any of the plaintiff's exclusive rights. *See* Société Civile Succession Richard Guino v. Int'l Foundation for Anticancer Drug Discovery, 460 F. Supp. 2d 1105 (D. Ariz. 2006).

for many years a controversial issue. Several courts suggested that *ex parte* seizures might violate the Due Process Clauses of the Fifth and Fourteenth Amendments.[1564] Today, however, as a result of a 2001 amendment to Federal Rule of Civil Procedure 65,[1565] it is clear that impoundment is subject to the same standards as a motion for preliminary injunction or a temporary restraining order; and that under Rule 65(b), impoundment may be ordered on an *ex parte* basis only when "giving the defendant notice of the application . . . could result in an inability to provide any relief at all,"[1566] and may last "only for so long as is necessary to hold a hearing."[1567]

Upon a finding of infringement, section 503(b) provides that a court, as part of its final judgment or decree, may order "the destruction or other reasonable disposition" of both the infringing articles and the equipment used to produce them.[1568] The House Report states that the court may "order the infringing articles sold, delivered to the plaintiff, or disposed of in some other way that would avoid needless waste and best serve the ends of justice."[1569]

[4]   Monetary Remedies

[a]   In General

Under section 504(a), "an infringer of copyright is liable for either (1) the copyright owner's actual damages and any additional profits of the infringer, as provided by subsection (b); or (2) statutory damages, as provided by subsection (c)."[1570] In other words, while the plaintiff is entitled to recover *both* actual damages plus the infringer's profits, to the extent they do not overlap,[1571] the plaintiff may recover statutory damages only as an *alternative* to a combined award of actual damages plus the infringer's profits.

The plaintiff may make the election "at any time before final judgment is rendered."[1572] Indeed, some courts have held that the plaintiff may elect "whichever type of damages results in the greatest award,"[1573] meaning that the court must determine *both* the amount of actual damages plus defendant's profits *and* the amount of statutory damages that it finds appropriate, so that the plaintiff may choose the larger of the two.[1574] Note, however, that a plaintiff may elect to recover

---

[1564] *See, e.g.*, Paramount Pictures Corp. v. Doe, 821 F. Supp. 82 (E.D.N.Y. 1993); WPOW, Inc. v. MRLJ Enterprises, 584 F. Supp. 132 (D.D.C. 1984).

[1565] *See* Fed. R. Civ. P. 65(f) ("This rule applies to copyright-impoundment proceedings.").

[1566] Adobe Systems, Inc. v. South Sun Prods., Inc., 187 F.R.D. 636, 640 (S.D. Cal. 1999).

[1567] First Tech. Safety Sys., Inc. v. Depinet, 11 F.3d 641, 650 (6th Cir. 1993).

[1568] 17 U.S.C. § 503(b).

[1569] H.R. Rep. No. 94-1476, at 160 (1976).

[1570] 17 U.S.C. § 504(a).

[1571] *See* § 4K[4][b].

[1572] 17 U.S.C. § 504(c).

[1573] RSO Records, Inc. v. Peri, 596 F. Supp. 849, 860 (S.D.N.Y. 1984).

[1574] *Id.* at 864. *See also* Feltner v. Columbia Pictures Television, Inc., 523 U.S. 340, 347 n.5 (1998) ("election may occur even after a jury has returned a verdict on liability and an award of actual

statutory damages only if it registered its copyrights before the infringement began, or for infringement of a published work, within three months after first publication of the work.[1575]

Despite some ill-considered dicta to the contrary,[1576] punitive damages are *not* available under the Copyright Act.[1577] However, punitive damages may be available in state-law actions for infringement of common-law copyright in sound recordings fixed before February 15, 1972.[1578]

Unlike the Patent Act, which expressly provides for prejudgment interest,[1579] "[t]he Copyright Act neither expressly allows nor prohibits awarding prejudgment interest in copyright infringement cases."[1580] Courts disagree whether prejudgment interest may be awarded.[1581]

[b]   Damages and Profits

Plaintiff may recover "the actual damages suffered by him or her as a result of the infringement, and any profits of the infringer that are attributable to the infringement and are not taken into account in computing the actual damages."[1582] "These remedies are two sides of the damages coin — the copyright holder's losses and the infringer's gains."[1583]

---

damages."); Storm Impact, Inc. v. Software of the Month Club, 13 F. Supp. 2d 782, 791–92 (N.D. Ill. 1998) (allowing greater of the two); Branch v. Ogilvy & Mather, Inc., 772 F. Supp. 1359, 1364 (S.D.N.Y. 1991) (allowing election to be made after court ruled on plaintiff's motion for judgment notwithstanding the verdict).

[1575] 17 U.S.C. § 412. This section applies to both foreign and domestic works. *See* Football Ass'n Premier League Ltd. v. YouTube, Inc., 633 F. Supp. 2d 159, 161–63 (S.D.N.Y. 2009).

[1576] *See* Blanch v. Koons, 396 F. Supp. 2d 598 (S.D.N.Y. 2004), *aff'd on other grounds*, 467 F.3d 244 (2d Cir. 2006); TVT Island Records v. Island Def Jam Music Group, 262 F. Supp. 2d 185 (S.D.N.Y. 2003), *rev'd on other grounds*, 412 F.3d 82 (2d Cir. 2005).

[1577] Bucklew v. Hawkins, Ash, Baptie & Co., 329 F.3d 923, 933–34 (7th Cir. 2003); On Davis v. The Gap, Inc., 246 F.3d 152, 172 (2d Cir. 2001); Viacom Intl, Inc. v. YouTube, Inc., 540 F. Supp. 2d 461, 462 (S.D.N.Y. 2008) (disapproving *Blanch* and *TVT*); Calio v. Sofa Express, Inc., 368 F. Supp. 2d 1290, 1291 (M.D. Fla. 2005) (same).

[1578] *See* Bridgeport Music, Inc. v. Justin Combs Publishing, 507 F.3d 470, 477, 486–90 (6th Cir. 2007) (holding punitive damages award of $3.5 million unconstitutionally excessive under Due Process Clause); Capitol Records, Inc. v. MP3Tunes, LLC, 2014 U.S. Dist. LEXIS 140139 (S.D.N.Y. Sept. 29, 2014) (holding punitive damages award of $7.5 million unconstitutionally excessive under Due Process Clause). *See* § 4K[4][c][iv], below.

[1579] 35 U.S.C. § 284.

[1580] Robert R Jones Assocs. v. Nino Homes, 858 F.2d 274, 282 (6th Cir. 1988).

[1581] *Compare Robert R. Jones Assocs.*, 858 F.2d at 282 *and* John G. Danielson, Inc. v. Winchester-Conant Properties, Inc., 322 F.3d 26, 51 (1st Cir. 2003) (disallowing prejudgment interest) *with* Polar Bear Prods., Inc. v. Timex Corp., 384 F.3d 700, 716–18 (9th Cir. 2004); Kleier Advertising, Inc. v. Premier Pontiac, Inc., 921 F.2d 1036, 1040–42 (10th Cir. 1990) (allowing prejudgment interest) *and* McRoberts Software, Inc. v. Media 100, Inc., 329 F.3d 557, 572–73 (7th Cir. 2003) (allowing prejudgment interest for willful infringement). *See also* Frank Music Corp. v. Metro-Goldwyn-Mayer, Inc., 886 F.2d 1545, 1550–52 (9th Cir. 1989) (allowing prejudgment interest under the 1909 Act).

[1582] 17 U.S.C. § 504(b).

[1583] Polar Bear Prods., Inc. v. Timex Corp., 384 F.3d 700, 708 (9th Cir. 2004).

Under the 1909 Copyright Act, the courts did not agree on whether a copyright owner could recover "(1) the greater of either damages or profits or (2) both damages and profits."[1584] If the court awarded the plaintiff actual damages measured wholly or in part by the defendant's sales and also the defendant's profits on those sales, a "double recovery" would occur. The 1976 Act resolves the issue by expressly permitting actual damages and infringer profits as long as double recovery does not occur.[1585]

Under the statute, "actual damages must be suffered 'as a result of the infringement,' and recoverable profits must be 'attributable to the infringement.' From the statutory language, it is apparent that a causal link between the infringement and the monetary remedy sought is a predicate to recovery of both actual damages and profits."[1586] Accordingly, the plaintiff "must establish this causal connection, and . . . this requirement is akin to tort principles of causation and damages."[1587]

Because the Copyright Act does not apply extraterritorially, it is improper to award actual damages resulting from infringement that occurs outside the United States.[1588] However, if there has been a "predicate act" of infringement within the United States, and the defendant earns profits from further exploitation of the infringing copies outside the United States, those profits may be awarded to the plaintiff on a "constructive trust" theory.[1589]

Multiple infringers are jointly and severally liable for the portion of the copyright owner's recovery representing actual damages.[1590] As a result, the amount of pre-trial settlements with other defendants should be deducted from the amount of actual damages found by the jury at trial.[1591] However, each infringer is liable only for its own profits and is *not* jointly or severally liable for other infringers' profits.[1592] "Exceptions to this general rule may be appropriate only where the infringement was not innocent or where the defendants engaged 'in a

---

[1584] Sid & Marty Krofft Television Prods., Inc. v. McDonald's Corp., 562 F.2d 1157, 1176 (9th Cir. 1977) (plaintiff entitled to recover the greater of actual damages or defendant's profits); *see also* Frank Music Corp. v. Metro-Goldwyn-Mayer, Inc., 772 F.2d 505, 512 (9th Cir. 1985) (same); Miller v. Universal Studios, Inc., 650 F.2d 1365, 1376 (5th Cir. 1981) (plaintiff allowed to recover both).

[1585] H.R. Rep. No. 94-1476, at 161 (1976). *See, e.g.*, Abeshouse v. Ultragraphics, Inc., 754 F.2d 467, 470–71 (2d Cir. 1985) (permitting recovery of plaintiff's damages, measured by lost profits it would have made on sales to the defendant, and the profits defendant actually made on retail sales of the infringing posters).

[1586] Polar Bear Prods., Inc. v. Timex Corp., 384 F.3d 700, 708 (9th Cir. 2004).

[1587] *Id.*

[1588] Los Angeles News Service v. Reuters Television Int'l, Ltd., 340 F.3d 926, 929–32 (9th Cir. 2003).

[1589] *Id.* at 930, 931–32; Tire Eng'g & Dist., LLC v. Shandong Linglong Rubber Co., 682 F.3d 292, 306–08 (4th Cir. 2012); Update Art, Inc. v. Modiin Publishing, Ltd., 843 F.2d 67, 73 (2d Cir. 1988); Sheldon v. Metro-Goldwyn Pictures Corp., 81 F.2d 49, 54–56 (2d Cir. 1936).

[1590] Abeshouse v. Ultragraphics, Inc., 754 F.2d 467, 472 (2d Cir. 1985); Nelson-Salabes, Inc. v. Morningside Development, LLC, 284 F.3d 505, 517 (4th Cir. 2002).

[1591] BUC Int'l Corp. v. Int'l Yacht Council Ltd., 517 F.3d 1271, 1276–78 (11th Cir. 2008). *Accord*, Screen Gems-Columbia Music, Inc. v. Metlis & Lebow Corp., 453 F.2d 552, 553–54 (2d Cir. 1972) (1909 Act).

[1592] *Abeshouse*, 754 F.2d at 472; *Nelson-Salabes*, 284 F.3d at 517.

partnership, joint venture, or similar enterprise.' "[1593]

[i] Actual Damages

Actual damages should reimburse the copyright owner for the "extent to which the market value of the copyrighted work at the time of the infringement has been injured or destroyed by the infringement."[1594] The loss in fair market value is usually measured either "by the profits lost due to the infringement or by the value of the use of the copyrighted work to the infringer."[1595] The value of the use may be measured, in turn, by the license fee that the copyright owner customarily charges others for a similar use, or by what "a willing buyer and a willing seller would have agreed for the use taken by the infringer."[1596]

Because "[t]he plaintiff bears the burden of proving that the infringement was the cause of its loss of revenue, . . . the plaintiff should first establish that the infringement was the cause-in-fact of its loss by showing with reasonable probability that, but for the defendant's infringement, the plaintiff would not have suffered the loss. . . . The plaintiff must also prove that the infringement was a proximate cause of its loss by demonstrating that the existence and amount of the loss was a natural and probable consequence of the infringement."[1597]

(a) Lost Profits

A copyright owner may recover profits on sales he would have made but for the infringement.[1598] If the infringing goods compete directly with the owner's goods and are similar in quality and price, plaintiff can usually show that he would have made every sale the infringer made.[1599] However, if the owner's and infringer's goods differ in quality, price, or intended use, the fact-finder must "necessarily engage in some degree of speculation."[1600]

In order to claim lost profits from lost sales, the plaintiff must show that it had the ability to produce the requisite number of copies it claims it would have sold.[1601] For example, in *Polar Bear Prods. v. Timex Corp.*, the plaintiff claimed "that it could have sold at least 10,000 to 15,000 copies of [the infringed work] at a

---

[1593] *Absehouse*, 754 F.2d at 472. *See also Nelson-Salabes*, 284 F.3d at 517 (exception exists where defendants are "practical partners").

[1594] Fitzgerald Publishing Co., Inc. v. Baylor Publishing Co., Inc., 807 F.2d 1110, 1118 (2d Cir. 1986).

[1595] Polar Bear Prods., Inc. v. Timex Corp., 384 F.3d 700, 708 (9th Cir. 2004), *quoting* McRoberts Software, Inc. v. Media 100, Inc., 329 F.3d 557, 566 (7th Cir. 2003).

[1596] On Davis v. The Gap, Inc., 246 F.3d 152, 167 (2d Cir. 2001). *Accord*, Dash v. Mayweather, 731 F.3d 303, 319 (4th Cir. 2013); Jarvis v. K2, Inc., 486 F.3d 526, 533 (9th Cir. 2007).

[1597] Data General Corp. v. Grumman Systems Support Corp., 36 F.3d 1147, 1170–71 (1st Cir. 1994).

[1598] Fitzgerald Publishing Co. v. Baylor Publishing Co., 807 F.2d 1110, 1118 (2d Cir. 1986).

[1599] *See, e.g.*, RSO Records, Inc. v. Peri, 596 F. Supp. 849, 863 (S.D.N.Y. 1984); Gund, Inc. v. Swank, Inc., 673 F. Supp. 1233, 1237 (S.D.N.Y. 1987).

[1600] Stevens Linen Associates, Inc. v. Mastercraft Corp., 656 F.2d 11, 14 (2d Cir. 1981).

[1601] *See, e.g.*, Banff Ltd. v. Express, Inc., 921. F. Supp. 1065, 1069 (S.D.N.Y. 1995) ("Banff offered little evidence that it could have supplied the quantity of sweaters Express needed. Express purchased between 39,262 and 40,137of the knockoff sweaters. By contrast, Banff sold only about 400 of its cotton sweaters.").

profit of between $20 to $30 per copy, but was unable to do so because it . . . lacked the financial wherewithal to sell the additional videos."[1602] The plaintiff claimed that if the defendant had paid a license fee for its infringing use, the plaintiff "would have had the necessary funds to pay to produce these tapes, thus reaping the profits from its would-be sales."[1603] The court held that "[i]t is too speculative to say that [defendant's] failure to pay license fees for the use of the footage was the cause of [plaintiff's] inability to put 10,000 copies of [the infringed work] on the market."[1604]

(b)   Value of Use

When the copyright owner has regularly licensed third parties to use the copyrighted work in a way comparable to the infringing use, the license royalty rate sets fair market value.[1605] Even if the copyright owner has not yet concluded a license at that rate, evidence that it would have accepted a license fee at a rate quoted before the dispute arose is sufficient to support an award, "unless it exceeds the range of the reasonable market value."[1606] Absent evidence of an actual or quoted license fee, "actual damages may include in appropriate cases the reasonable license fee on which a willing buyer and a willing seller would have agreed for the use taken by the infringer."[1607] It is not necessary for the plaintiff to show that the defendant actually would have been willing to license the work at that price.[1608]

Calculating a reasonable license fee will often depend on the specific circumstances of the use. Where the defendant's unauthorized use in a television commercial destroyed the value of the copyrighted work to others for a similar use, it was proper for the court to award the full market value of a hypothetical license to use the entire work, even though only a portion of the work was used, since "[t]here was no evidence that [defendant] sought, or [plaintiff] was willing to grant,

---

[1602] 384 F.3d 700, 709 (9th Cir. 2004).

[1603] *Id.*

[1604] *Id.* at 710.

[1605] *See, e.g.*, Kleier Advertising, Inc. v. Premier Pontiac, Inc., 921 F.2d 1036, 1039–40 (10th Cir. 1990) (affirming jury's award of "actual damages that resulted from the license fees the . . . defendants should have paid"). *Cf.* Harper & Row Publishers, Inc. v. Nation Enterprises, 471 U.S. 539, 562 (1985) (inquiring in fair use analysis "whether the user stands to profit from exploitation of the copyrighted material without paying the customary price."); *id.* at 567 (affirming district court's finding of actual damages of $12,500, based on license fee that plaintiff would have been paid by Time magazine for the same use if the infringement had not occurred).

[1606] Polar Bear Prods. v. Timex Corp., 384 F.3d 700, 709 (9th Cir. 2004) (affirming jury's award of $37,500 license fee quoted to defendant, because "[t]he proposed license fee was proffered before Timex's infringement. Nothing suggests that the fee was contrived or artificially inflated."). *See also* Fournier v. McCann Erickson, 242 F. Supp. 2d 318, 336–37 (S.D.N.Y. 2003).

[1607] On Davis v. The Gap, Inc., 246 F.3d 152, 167 (2d Cir. 2001). *Accord*, Jarvis v. K2, Inc., 486 F.3d 526, 534 (9th Cir. 2007). *But see* Dash v. Mayweather, 731 F.3d 303 (4th Cir. 2013) (plaintiff could not recover lost licensing fee where there was no evidence plaintiff had ever sold, offered for sale, or licensed any of his works to anyone, and expert report relied only on works which were not comparable).

[1608] Oracle Corp. v. SAP, AG, 765 F.3d 1081, 1087–88 (9th Cir. 2014); Gaylord v. U.S., 678 F.3d 1339, 1343–45 (Fed. Cir. 2012).

a license for use of less than the entire copyrighted work."[1609] By contrast, where there was evidence that the defendant would *not* have paid a fee for the entire work for the right to use only a portion of the work, it was proper for the court to apportion the lost license fee.[1610]

(c) Consequential Damages

Finally, plaintiff is allowed to recover any additional loss that is attributable to the infringement, even if the loss is indirect, so long as it is not unduly speculative. For example, in *Sunset Lamp Corp. v. Alsy Corp.*, the court held that defendant infringed plaintiff's copyright on a floor lamp with banana leaf ornamentation. Plaintiff argued that it should be permitted at trial to prove it lost sales on its entire line of lamps, not just those with the infringing ornamentation. Its damage theory required proof of three facts: the banana leaf floor lamp was a "door opener" into the major department store market; in that market, buyers typically purchased a company's entire product line; and defendant's sale of cheaper, infringing floor lamps disrupted plaintiff's ability to enter that market and sell its entire lamp product line.[1611] The court ruled that this damages theory was permissible, if the plaintiff could "present substantial credible evidence showing a basis for its claim that damages from the infringement include lost sales on non-infringed items."[1612] Similarly, a plaintiff may recover damages for the omission of credit for the use of plaintiff's work, if such damages are not speculative and are supported by evidence.[1613]

[ii] Infringer's Profits

(a) In General

To establish the infringer's profits, "the copyright owner is required to present proof of the infringer's gross revenue, and the infringer is required to prove his or her deductible expenses and the elements of profit attributable to factors other than the copyrighted work."[1614]

Gross revenue means "the gross revenue associated with the infringement, as opposed to the infringer's overall gross sales resulting from all streams of revenue."[1615] Thus, "[i]f General Motors were to steal your copyright and put it in

---

[1609] Cream Records, Inc. v. Joseph Schlitz Brewing Co., 754 F.2d 826, 827–28 (9th Cir. 1985).

[1610] *See* Softel, Inc. v. Dragon Medical & Scientific Communications Ltd., 891 F. Supp. 935, 938–39, 941 (S.D.N.Y. 1995), *rev'd in part on other grounds*, 118 F.3d 955 (2d Cir. 1997). *See also* Frank Music, Inc. v. Metro-Goldwyn-Mayer, Inc., 772 F.2d 505, 513–14 (9th Cir. 1985) (defendant's presentation of six minutes of music from the musical *Kismet* did not cause the plaintiff MGM to lose a licensing fee for the entire musical).

[1611] 749 F. Supp. 520, 521–22 (S.D.N.Y. 1990).

[1612] *Id.* at 525.

[1613] Graham v. James, 144 F.3d 229, 238–39 (2d Cir. 1998).

[1614] 17 U.S.C. § 504(b).

[1615] Polar Bear Prods. v. Timex Corp., 384 F.3d 700, 711 n.8 (9th Cir. 2004). *See also* Nelson-Salabes, Inc. v. Morningside Development, LLC, 284 F.3d 505, 511 n.9 (4th Cir. 2002); On Davis v. The Gap, Inc., 246 F.3d 152, 160 (2d Cir. 2001).

a sales brochure, you could not just put a copy of General Motors' corporate income tax return in the record and rest your case for an award of infringer's profits."[1616] Gross revenue is calculated by multiplying the quantity of sales of the infringing items times the infringer's price.[1617] The plaintiff must make a reasonable showing of gross revenue, even if the defendant's business records make it difficult to do so.[1618]

Once the copyright owner proves gross revenues, the infringer must prove deductible expenses associated with the infringing articles' production.[1619] Deductible expenses include direct costs such as materials, printing costs, and shipping.[1620] "Overhead expense is also a proper deduction from the profits of an infringer," provided that the infringer adequately demonstrates that the overhead "contributed to the production of the infringing items, and . . . offer[s] a fair and acceptable formula for allocating a given portion of overhead to the particular infringing items in issue."[1621] Where the infringer cannot demonstrate that the expenses contributed to production, a deduction for overhead expenses may be denied.[1622] Some courts have suggested that a willful infringer should be barred from deducting overhead expenses.[1623] However, nothing in the text of either the

---

[1616] Taylor v. Meirick, 712 F.2d 1112, 1122 (7th Cir. 1983); Bouchat v. Baltimore Ravens Football Club, Inc., 346 F.3d 514, 521 (4th Cir. 2003) (quoting *Taylor*).

[1617] Abeshouse v. Ultragraphics, Inc., 754 F.2d 467, 470 (2d Cir. 1985) (evidence of sales of 21,500 infringing posters, multiplied by $2.00 price per poster, supported calculation of $43,000 in gross revenue).

[1618] Estate of Vane v. The Fair, Inc., 849 F.2d 186, 188 (5th Cir. 1988).

[1619] "If the infringing defendant does not meet its burden of proving costs, the gross figure stands as the defendant's profits." Frank Music Corp. v. Metro-Goldwyn-Mayer, Inc., 772 F.2d 505, 514 (9th Cir. 1985). *See also* Johnson v. Jones, 149 F.3d 494, 506–07 (6th Cir. 1998); Universal Furniture Int'l, Inc. v. Collezione Europa USA, Inc., 599 F. Supp. 2d 648, 660–61 (M.D.N.C. 2009), *aff'd*, 618 F.3d 417, 440–41 (4th Cir. 2010).

[1620] *See* Sygma Photo News, Inc. v. High Society Magazine, 778 F.2d 89 (2d Cir. 1985).

[1621] In Design v. K-Mart Apparel Corp., 13 F.3d 559, 565–66 (2d Cir. 1994). *Accord*, Hamil America, Inc. v. GFI, 193 F.3d 92, 105 (2d Cir. 1999); Frank Music Corp. v. Metro-Goldwyn-Mayer, Inc., 772 F.2d 505, 516 (9th Cir. 1985). Acceptable means of allocating overhead costs include "the production cost of the infringing product as a percentage of the total production costs," and "the number of infringing products as a percentage of total products." *Hamil America*, 193 F.3d at 105 n.5. *See also Frank Music*, 772 F.2d at 516 (approving allocation "based on a ratio of the revenues from [the infringing] production as compared to MGM Grand's total revenues.").

[1622] *See, e.g., Sygma Photo*, 778 F.2d at 93 (denying deduction for depreciation, rent, and legal fees, but allowing other items of overhead); *Frank Music*, 772 F.2d at 516. *See also* Taylor v. Meirick, 712 F.2d 1112, 1121 (7th Cir. 1983) ("Costs that would be incurred anyway should not be subtracted, because by definition they cannot be avoided by curtailing the profit-making activity."). Taken literally, *Taylor* would suggest that the defendant cannot deduct overhead expenses at all, unless the defendant incurred *additional* overhead as a result of the infringement. To the extent *Taylor* is read that broadly, it conflicts with the law in the other circuits.

[1623] Saxon v. Blann, 968 F.2d 676, 681 (8th Cir. 1992), *citing Frank Music*, 772 F.2d at 515 (stating that overhead may be deducted "at least where the infringement was not willful, conscious, or deliberate"). The *dicta* in *Frank Music* can be traced back to a misreading of Sheldon v. Metro-Goldwyn Pictures Corp., 106 F.2d 45 (2d Cir. 1939), *aff'd* 309 U.S. 390 (1940), which held that because of "deliberate plagiarism," the defendants "can be credited only with such factors as they bought and paid for; the actors, the scenery, the producers, the directors *and the general overhead*." 106 F.2d at 51 (emphasis added). The only thing that *Sheldon* disallowed based on "deliberate plagiarism" was taking

1909 Act or the 1976 Act supports such a rule.[1624]

Courts have held that a "conscious and deliberate" infringer is *not* entitled to deduct federal income taxes paid on sales of infringing products, on the ground that the plaintiff will have to pay taxes on the award when it is received.[1625] However, courts disagree whether a non-willful infringer may deduct taxes. Both the Second and the Ninth Circuit have held that a non-willful infringer may deduct taxes from its infringing profits, on the ground that the defendant should not be required to pay more than he has actually earned from the infringement.[1626] The Sixth Circuit, however, has held that a non-willful infringer should *not* be allowed to deduct taxes, on the ground that when it pays the judgment, it will be allowed to deduct that amount from its income taxes, "allow[ing] the infringer to reap a net gain from his infringing activity."[1627]

(b)   Indirect Profits

"On its face, § 504(b) does not differentiate between 'direct profits' — those that are generated by selling an infringing product — and 'indirect profits' — revenue that has a more attenuated nexus to the infringement."[1628] Consequently, courts have held that section 504(b) is "expansive enough to afford parties an indirect profits remedy under certain conditions."[1629] However, "because the amount of profits attributable to the infringement in an indirect profits case is not always clear, '. . . a copyright holder must establish the existence of a causal link before indirect profits damages can be recovered.' "[1630] Thus, to recover indirect profits, "1) the copyright claimant must first show a causal nexus between the infringement and the gross revenue; and 2) once the causal nexus is shown, the infringer bears the burden of apportioning the profits that were not the result of infringement."[1631]

Copyright owners often argue that the infringer's activity contributed to profits in other business areas. In *Frank Music Corp. v. Metro-Goldwyn-Mayer, Inc.*, for example, the plaintiff sought a portion of the defendant's hotel and gambling

---

into consideration "the effect of [the defendants'] standing and reputation in the industry" as a factor in apportioning profits. *Id.* at 50–51.

[1624] ZZ Top v. Chrysler Corp., 70 F. Supp. 2d 1167, 1168–69 (W.D. Wash. 1999). *Cf. Hamil America*, 193 F.3d at 106–07 (refusing to adopt "a hard and fast rule denying all overhead deductions to willful infringers," but directing the district court to "give extra scrutiny to the categories of overhead expenses claimed by the infringer to insure that each category is directly and validly connected to the sale and production of the infringing product").

[1625] In Design v. K-Mart Apparel Corp., 13 F.3d 559, 566 (2d Cir. 1994), *citing* L.P. Larson, Jr. Co. v. William Wrigley Jr., Co., 277 U.S. 97, 99–100 (1928) (no deduction for taxes for infringing trade dress).

[1626] Three Boys Music Corp. v. Bolton, 212 F.3d 477, 487–88 (9th Cir. 2000); *In Design*, 13 F.3d at 567. However, the Ninth Circuit has disallowed any credit for imputed taxes that were allegedly offset against the defendant's Net Operating Loss (NOL) carry-forward, on the ground that no taxes were actually paid. *Three Boys Music*, 212 F.3d at 488.

[1627] Schnadig Corp. v. Gaines Mfg. Co., 620 F.2d 1166, 1170 (6th Cir. 1980) (design patent infringement).

[1628] Mackie v. Rieser, 296 F.3d 909, 914 (9th Cir. 2002).

[1629] Polar Bear Prods. v. Timex Corp., 384 F.3d 700, 710 (9th Cir. 2004).

[1630] *Polar Bear*, 384 F.3d at 710, *quoting Mackie*, 296 F.3d at 914.

[1631] *Polar Bear*, 384 F.3d at 711.

revenue on the grounds that defendant's infringing floor show drew customers to its hotel and casino. The court held that an owner may recover such "indirect profits" under the 1909 Act if he shows the profits are attributable in part to the infringing activity.[1632] The court found evidence of the requisite "causal nexus" in the defendant's annual report, which stated its hotel and gaming operations were "materially enhanced by the popularity of the hotel's entertainment," including the infringing show.[1633]

Cases involving indirect profits often involve the use of the copyrighted work in advertising some other product. For example, in *Polar Bear Productions v. Timex Corp.*, the court held that the plaintiff adequately demonstrated a "causal nexus" for sales of the defendant's watches that occurred at trade shows at which the infringing video was shown; and for sales of watches that resulted from a promotion with the soft drink Mountain Dew in which an infringing still picture was used.[1634] However, the court held that there was insufficient evidence to support an award based on a "brand premium analysis" that purported to show that the infringing promotions "created excitement about the product . . . and that [increased] consumer enthusiasm permitted Timex to increase prices and generate more revenue."[1635]

Similarly, in *Mackie v. Rieser*, the court held that an artist whose work was infringed in the season brochure of the Seattle Symphony could not recover a percentage of the Symphony's gross revenues, because there were too many factors "to account for an individual's decision to subscribe to the [Symphony] . . . that have nothing to do with the artwork in question."[1636] And in *Bouchat v. Baltimore Ravens Football Club, Inc.*, the court held that the plaintiff failed to offer non-speculative evidence that revenues from ticket sales, broadcast licenses, game programs, parking, and food concessions were attributable to the infringing logo design.[1637] By contrast, in *Andreas v. Volkswagen of America, Inc.*, the jury found that one of the defendant's television commercials for a new model of car infringed the caption in a drawing made by the plaintiff. The court upheld the jury's award of 10% of the gross profits realized from sales of the car, finding there was sufficient evidence of a "causal nexus" between the commercial and sales of the car.[1638] However, the court found that there was no causal connection between the

---

[1632] 772 F.2d 505, 517 (9th Cir. 1985).

[1633] *Id.*

[1634] Polar Bear Prods. v. Timex Corp., 384 F.3d 700, 712–13 (9th Cir. 2004).

[1635] *Id.* at 714. *See also* Business Trends Analysts, Inc. v. Freedonia Group, Inc., 887 F.2d 399, 407 (2d Cir. 1989) (although indirect profits "might include [profits resulting from] enhanced good will or market recognition," evidence introduced was insufficient to support such an award).

[1636] 296 F.3d 909, 916 (9th Cir. 2002).

[1637] 346 F.3d 514, 517–18, 525–26 (4th Cir. 2003). *See also* Dash v. Mayweather, 731 F.3d 303 (4th Cir. 2013) (no evidence that performance of allegedly infringing song affected any of defendants' revenue streams).

[1638] 336 F.3d 789, 795–99 (8th Cir. 2003). This decision can be criticized on the ground that it attributes sales of the car to the commercial rather than to the infringement, which involved only the words spoken in the commercial. It is highly likely that *any* commercial for a new model of car would lead to increased sales of the car, so the proper approach should have been to compare actual sales of the car to what sales would have been with a similar but non-infringing commercial.

infringing commercial and sales of other models of cars.[1639]

(c) Apportionment

An infringer who adds value to the infringing work has the burden of apportioning profits to "factors other than the copyrighted work."[1640] The defendant is entitled to "an apportionment of profits to account for his independent contributions only when 'the evidence is sufficient to provide a fair basis of division so as to give the copyright proprietor all the profits that can be deemed to have resulted from the use of what belonged to him.' "[1641] Because a precise estimate is usually impossible, "a court should err on the side of guaranteeing the plaintiff a full recovery, but want of precision is not a ground for denying apportionment altogether."[1642]

Two examples will suffice to demonstrate the difficulty of making a fair and reasonable apportionment. In *Sheldon v. Metro-Goldwyn Pictures Corp.*, the defendants were held to have infringed the stage play "Dishonored Lady" in producing their motion picture "Letty Lynton." The defendants presented expert testimony that the play was responsible for between 5 and 12 percent of the success of the movie, that the greatest portion of the success should be attributed to the acting stars, and that "the other chief factors were the skill and reputation of the producer and the director, the scenery and costumes, the extent of the advertising and the reputation and standing of the producing company itself."[1643] Because the infringement was deliberate, the Second Circuit refused to take into account the reputation and standing of the defendant,[1644] and it awarded 20 percent of the profits of the motion picture.[1645] The Supreme Court affirmed, saying "what is required is not mathematical exactness but only a reasonable approximation."[1646]

In *Frank Music Corp. v. Metro-Goldwyn-Mayer, Inc.*, the defendants presented a ten-act revue at the MGM Grand Hotel entitled *Hallelujah Hollywood*. Act IV of

---

[1639] *Id.* at 799–800.

[1640] 17 U.S.C. § 504(b).

[1641] Gaste v. Kaiserman, 863 F.2d 1061, 1069 (2d Cir. 1988), *quoting* Sheldon v. Metro-Goldwyn Pictures Corp., 309 U.S. 390 (1940).

[1642] *Id.* at 1070; Sygma Photo News, Inc. v. High Society Magazine, 778 F.2d 89, 95 (2d Cir. 1985). *See also* John G. Danielson, Inc. v. Winchester-Conant Properties, Inc., 322 F.3d 26, 47–50 (1st Cir. 2003) (trial court erroneously instructed jury that contributions had to be "completely separate" from infringing material).

[1643] 106 F.2d 45, 50 (2d Cir. 1939), *aff'd*, 309 U.S. 390 (1940). *See also* Abend v. MCA, Inc., 863 F.2d 1465, 1478 (9th Cir. 1988) ("tremendous success" of motion picture "Rear Window" "is attributable in significant measure to . . . the outstanding performances of its stars — Grace Kelly and James Stewart — and the brilliant directing of Alfred Hitchcock."), *aff'd on other grounds sub nom.* Stewart v. Abend, 495 U.S. 207 (1990).

[1644] *Sheldon*, 106 F.2d at 50–51. *But see* Rogers v. Koons, 960 F.2d 301, 313 (2d Cir. 1992) (factors relevant to apportionment of profits earned for infringing sculpture "may include Koons' own notoriety and his related ability to command high prices for his work.").

[1645] *Sheldon*, 106 F.2d at 51.

[1646] 340 U.S. at 408.

the revue, which consisted of eleven-and-a-half minutes from the musical *Kismet*, was held to be infringing. The entire revue was 100 minutes long, except on Saturdays, when two acts were deleted to make the running time 75 minutes. The revue was performed twice daily and three times on Saturdays. Accepting the district court's implicit conclusion "that all the acts in the show were of substantially equal value," the Ninth Circuit calculated that 12% of the profits from the revue should be apportioned to Act IV.[1647] Moreover, while the district court concluded that 75% of the success of Act IV should be attributed to the defendants, the Ninth Circuit reversed this conclusion, finding that 75% of the success of Act IV should be attributed to the infringing material.[1648] Finally, the court affirmed the district court's conclusion that 2% of the indirect profits from hotel and gaming operations should be attributed to the revue, of which 9% (12% multiplied by 75%) was attributable to the infringing portion of the revue.[1649]

[c]   Statutory Damages

Section 504(c)(1) permits a copyright owner to elect, in lieu of actual damages and profits, "an award of statutory damages for all infringements involved in the action, with respect to any one work, . . . in a sum of not less than $750 or more than $30,000 as the court considers just."[1650] Statutory damages are "intended both to compensate plaintiffs and [to] deter defendants from future infringing conduct."[1651] With respect to compensation, statutory damages serve "to give the owner of a copyright some recompense for injury done him, in a case where the rules of law render difficult or impossible proof of damages or . . . profits."[1652] Accordingly, "[s]tatutory damages may be elected whether or not there is adequate evidence of the actual damages suffered by plaintiff or of the profits reaped by defendant."[1653]

Although Section 504 states that "the court" shall determine the amount of statutory damages, the Supreme Court has held that "the Seventh Amendment provides a right to a jury trial on all issues pertinent to an award of statutory damages under § 504(c) of the Copyright Act, including the amount itself."[1654] Because a plaintiff may elect to recover statutory damages "at any time before final judgment is rendered,"[1655] the plaintiff may ask the court to have the jury

---

[1647] 886 F.2d 1545, 1548–49 & n.2 (9th Cir. 1989).

[1648] *Id.* at 1549–50.

[1649] *Id.* at 1550 & n.4.

[1650] 17 U.S.C. § 504(c)(1). As enacted in 1976, the range was $250 to $10,000. The amounts were increased to $500 to $20,000 in 1988, and to the present amounts in 1999.

[1651] Unicity Music, Inc. v. Omni Communications, Inc., 844 F. Supp. 504, 510 (E.D. Ark. 1994). *See also* Feltner v. Columbia Pictures Television, Inc., 523 U.S. 340, 352 (1998) ("an award of statutory damages may serve purposes traditionally associated with legal relief, such as compensation and punishment.").

[1652] F.W. Woolworth Co. v. Contemporary Arts, 344 U.S. 228, 231 (1952), *quoting* Douglas v. Cunningham, 294 U.S. 207, 209 (1935).

[1653] Harris v. Emus Records Corp., 734 F.2d 1329, 1335 (9th Cir. 1984). *Accord,* Los Angeles New Service v. Reuters Television Int'l, Ltd., 149 F.3d 987, 996 (9th Cir. 1998).

[1654] Feltner v. Columbia Pictures Television, Inc., 523 U.S. 340, 355 (1998).

[1655] 17 U.S.C. § 504(c)(1).

determine *both* actual damages and profits *and* statutory damages before making an election.[1656] However, if a plaintiff seeks only the minimum amount of statutory damages per work infringed, a jury trial is not required if the number of works can be determined on summary judgment.[1657]

To recover statutory damages or attorney fees, section 412 requires an owner to register his work before the defendant's infringing activities began or, for infringement of a published work, within three months of first publication.[1658] The purpose of this statute is to encourage copyright owners to register promptly.[1659] An "infringement 'commences' for the purposes of § 412 when the first act in a series of acts constituting continuing infringement occurs."[1660]

[i]   Number of Works Infringed

The 1909 Act permitted the court to award statutory damages for each infringement of each infringed work. The 1976 Act only permits "an award of statutory damages for all infringements involved in the action, with respect to any one work, for which any one infringer is liable individually, or for which any two or more infringers are liable jointly and severally"[1661] "Both the text of the Copyright Act and its legislative history make clear that statutory damages are calculated according to the number of works infringed, not the number of infringements."[1662]

When questions arise regarding what constitutes one "work," most courts have adopted a test that inquires whether separate works have "separate economic value."[1663] For example, in *Walt Disney Co. v. Powell*, the court found that the defendant had infringed only two copyrights, one each in Mickey and Minnie Mouse, even though the plaintiff had registered six copyrights depicting those characters in various poses.[1664] And in a series of cases, courts have held that each episode of a television show constitutes a separate work, even if there is a continuing storyline and even if an entire season is sold as a unit to broadcasters, because each episode is written, produced, and directed separately and may be rented or viewed separately.[1665]

[1656] *See* § 4K[4][a].

[1657] BMG Music v. Gonzalez, 430 F.3d 888, 892–93 (7th Cir. 2005).

[1658] 17 U.S.C. § 412.

[1659] Derek Andrew, Inc. v. Poof Apparel Corp., 528 F.3d 696, 700 (9th Cir. 2008); Johnson v. Jones, 149 F.3d 494, 505 (6th Cir. 1998); H.R. Rep. No. 94-1476, at 158 (1976).

[1660] Johnson v. Jones, 149 F.3d 494, 506 (6th Cir. 1998). *Accord,* Derek Andrew, Inc. v. Poof Apparel Corp., 528 F.3d 696, 700–01 (9th Cir. 2008); Bouchat v Bon-Ton Dept. Stores, Inc., 506 F.3d 315, 330 (4th Cir. 2007).

[1661] 17 U.S.C. § 504(c)(1).

[1662] Walt Disney Co. v. Powell, 897 F.2d 565, 569 (D.C. Cir. 1990). *See also* H.R. Rep. No. 94-1476, at 162 (1976).

[1663] *Powell*, 897 F.2d at 569.

[1664] *Id.* at 569–70. Arguably this was still erroneous, because Mickey and Minnie were both introduced in the same motion picture, *Steamboat Willie* (1928). While the copyright in a motion picture may protect the distinctive characters depicted in that motion picture, each "character" by itself would not be accepted as a separate "work" for purposes of registration.

[1665] *See, e.g.*, Columbia Pictures Television v. Krypton Broadcasting, 106 F.3d 284, 295 (9th Cir. 1997),

The statute provides little guidance, but it does provide that "all the parts of a compilation or derivative work constitute one work."[1666] Under this clause, if the plaintiff issues a number of songs on one "album" or CD, that album or CD constitutes a single "work," even if the songs are also registered separately.[1667] This clause, however, refers to a compilation or derivative work issued *by the copyright owner*; where the defendant created a new compilation of 13 songs without authorization, an award of statutory damages per song infringed was appropriate.[1668] Courts disagree whether a musical work and a sound recording fixed in a single phonorecord are one work or two works for purposes of statutory damages.[1669]

[ii]   Defendant's Intent

Section 504(c)(2) addresses the effect on statutory damages of the defendant's intent:

> In a case where the copyright owner sustains the burden of proving, and the court finds, that infringement was committed willfully, the court in its discretion may increase the award of statutory damages to a sum of not more than $150,000. In a case where the infringer sustains the burden of proving, and the court finds, that such infringer was not aware and had no reason to believe that his or her acts constituted an infringement of copyright, the court in its discretion may reduce the award of statutory damages to a sum of not less than $200.[1670]

" 'Willful' within the meaning of § 504(c)(2) means 'with knowledge that the defendant's conduct constitutes copyright infringement."[1671] In some cases, how-

---

rev'd on other grounds sub nom. Feltner v. Columbia Pictures Television, Inc., 523 U.S. 340 (1998); MCA Television Ltd. v. Feltner, 89 F.3d 766, 768–70 (11th Cir. 1996); Gamma Audio & Video, Inc. v. Ean-Chea, 11 F.3d 1106, 1117–18 (1st Cir. 1993); Twin Peaks Prods., Inc. v. Publications Int'l, Ltd., 996 F.2d 1366, 1380–81 (2d Cir. 1993). The *Twin Peaks* court, however, left open the possibility that a multi-episode mini-series based on a single novel might be considered to be a single work. 996 F.2d at 1381.

[1666] 17 U.S.C. § 504(c)(1).

[1667] Bryant v. Media Rights Prods., Inc., 603 F.3d 135, 140–42 (2d Cir. 2010). *See also* Xoom, Inc. v. Imageline, Inc., 323 F.3d 279, 285 (4th Cir. 2003) (software package containing multiple "clip art" images constitutes a compilation for which a single award was appropriate).

[1668] WB Music Corp. v. RTV Communications Group, Inc., 445 F.3d 538, 540–41 (2d Cir. 2006). *See also* Venegas-Hernandez v. Sonolux Records, 370 F.3d 183, 191–94 (1st Cir. 2004) (one award of statutory damages per song infringed; where defendants made 16 albums that infringed two songs, 16 awards of $100,000 was improper).

[1669] *Compare* Teevee Tunes, Inc. v. MP3.com, Inc., 134 F. Supp. 2d 546 (S.D.N.Y. 2011) (two works if copyrights are separately owned; one work if copyrights are owned by same person) *with* Capitol Records, Inc. v. MP3Tunes, LLC, 2014 U.S. Dist. LEXIS 143435 (S.D.N.Y. Apr. 7, 2014) (owners of copyright in musical work and sound recording must share a single award of statutory damages).

[1670] 17 U.S.C. § 504(c)(2). As enacted in 1976, the amounts were $50,000 and $100, respectively. The amounts were increased to $100,000 and $200 in 1988, and the maximum amount was increased to $150,000 in 1999.

[1671] Lyons Partnership, L.P. v. Morris Costumes, Inc., 243 F.3d 789, 799 (4th Cir. 2001); Columbia Pictures Television v. Krypton Broadcasting, 106 F.3d 284, 293 (9th Cir. 1997), *rev'd on other grounds sub nom.* Feltner v. Columbia Pictures Television, Inc., 523 U.S. 340 (1998); Peer Int'l Corp. v. Pausa Records, Inc., 909 F.2d 1332, 1335 n.3 (9th Cir. 1990).

ever, the defendant's reckless disregard for whether he is violating copyright may be sufficient to show willfulness.[1672] There is also a rebuttable presumption of willfulness if the defendant "knowingly provided . . . materially false contact information . . . in registering, maintaining, or renewing a domain name used in connection with the infringement."[1673] Absent a good-faith defense such as fair use, knowledge that the plaintiff has terminated an express license agreement or has filed an infringement action is sufficient to demonstrate willfulness.[1674] However, where the defendant was acting under color of rights granted by a license, it cannot be held to have acted willfully, even if it is later determined that the license was invalid.[1675]

To meet Section 504(c)(2)'s "innocence" standard, the infringer "must not only establish its good faith belief in the innocence of its conduct, it must also show that it was reasonable in holding such a belief."[1676] The infringer's sophistication is an important factor.[1677] In *D.C. Comics, Inc. v. Mini Gift Shop*, the court found that retail store owners who sold unauthorized "Batman" goods infringed innocently, where the goods did not bear copyright notices, the store owners were recent immigrants who spoke little English, and the plaintiff's licensing director testified that a layman would "probably not" be able to distinguish licensed from infringing goods based on their style or quality.[1678]

A defendant cannot claim "innocent infringement in mitigation of actual or statutory damages" if "the published copy or copies [or phonorecords] to which [the] defendant . . . had access" bore a proper copyright notice.[1679] Courts have held that the notice requirement was satisfied where all authorized, publicly available copies of the work bore a proper notice, even though the defendant downloaded an infringing electronic file lacking such notice.[1680]

[1672] *Lyons*, 243 F.3d at 799. *See also* Yurrman Design, Inc. v. PAJ, Inc., 262 F.3d 101, 112 (2d Cir. 2001); Dolman v. Agee, 157 F.3d 708, 715 (9th Cir. 1998) (affirming finding of willfulness where counsel advised defendant "that the copyright situation was 'a mess'," and defendant continued to infringe after receiving and acknowledging documentation of plaintiff's ownership).

[1673] 17 U.S.C. 504(c)(3).

[1674] *Krypton*, 106 F.3d at 293. *But see Lyons*, 243 F.3d at 800 (evidence that defendant made a serious attempt to create a similar but non-infringing work supported finding that defendant did not act "willfully," despite receipt of cease-and-desist letter).

[1675] Danjaq, LLC v. Sony Corp., 263 F.3d 942, 958–59 (9th Cir. 2001); Frank Music Corp. v. Metro-Goldwyn-Mayer, Inc., 772 F.2d 505, 515 (9th Cir. 1985).

[1676] Columbia Pictures Television v. Krypton Broadcasting, 106 F.3d 284, 293 (9th Cir. 1997), *rev'd on other grounds sub nom.* Feltner v. Columbia Pictures Television, Inc., 523 U.S. 340 (1998); Peer Int'l Corp. v. Pausa Records, Inc., 909 F.2d 1332, 1336 (9th Cir. 1990).

[1677] D.C. Comics, Inc. v. Mini Gift Shop, 912 F.2d 29, 35–36 (2d Cir. 1990).

[1678] *Id.* at 32.

[1679] 17 U.S.C. § 401(d) (copies); *see also* 17 U.S.C. § 402(d) (same rule for phonorecords).

[1680] *See* Maverick Recording Co. v. Harper, 598 F.3d 193 (5th Cir. 2010); BMG Music v. Gonzalez, 430 F.3d 888, 891–92 (7th Cir. 2005).

[iii]   Amount of Award

The trial court has wide discretion in fixing the amount of statutory damages, and an appeals court will overturn the trial court's award only for abuse of discretion.[1681] Factors to be considered include: "(1) the infringer's state of mind; (2) the expenses saved, and profits earned, by the infringer; (3) the revenue lost by the copyright holder; (4) the deterrent effect on the infringer and third parties; (5) the infringer's cooperation in providing evidence concerning the value of the infringing material; and (6) the conduct and attitude of the parties."[1682]

[iv]   Constitutionality

Although punitive damages are not available under the Copyright Act,[1683] courts have acknowledged that statutory damages may serve the same purposes as punitive damages, namely, to punish and to deter willful infringement.[1684] Accordingly, the question has arisen whether statutory damages are subject to the same constitutional limitations that the U.S. Supreme Court has imposed on punitive damages under the Due Process Clause.[1685]

The Supreme Court has held that punitive damages that are "grossly excessive" violate the Due Process Clause.[1686] In deciding whether an award is "grossly excessive," a court should consider the degree of reprehensibility of the misconduct; the disparity between the harm or potential harm suffered by the plaintiff and the punitive damages award; and the difference between the award and civil penalties authorized or imposed for similar misconduct.[1687] While declining to impose a bright-line limit on the ratio of punitive damages to actual damages, the Court has observed that "in practice, few awards exceeding a single-digit ratio between punitive and compensatory damages . . . will satisfy due process."[1688] Courts have applied this line of cases to limit the amount of punitive damages that may be awarded for infringement of state common-law copyright in sound recordings fixed before February 15, 1972.[1689]

[1681] Bryant v. Media Rights Prods., Inc., 603 F.3d 135, 143 (2d Cir. 2010).

[1682] *Bryant*, 603 F.3d at 144. *Cf.* Dream Games of Ariz., Inc. v. PC Onsite, 561 F.3d 983, 993–94 (9th Cir. 2009) (evidence that plaintiff's video poker game was being operated illegally in two states was irrelevant to the availability or amount of statutory damages).

[1683] *See* § 4K[4][a].

[1684] *See* Feltner v. Columbia Pictures Television, Inc., 523 U.S. 340, 352 (1998); Dream Games of Ariz., Inc. v. PC Onsite, 561 F.3d 983, 992 (9th Cir. 2009).

[1685] *Cf.* Parker v. Time Warner Entertainment Co., 331 F.3d 13, 22 (2d Cir. 2003) (suggesting in *dicta* that statutory damages under the Cable Communications Policy Act may be subject to review under the Due Process clause). Note that the Supreme Court's punitive damages jurisprudence relies on the Due Process Clause of the Fourteenth Amendment, which applies to the States. *See* U.S. Const., Amend. XIV, § 1. Any limitations on statutory damages under the federal Copyright Act would have to be found in the similarly-worded Due Process Clause of the Fifth Amendment, which applies to the federal Government. *See* U.S. Const., Amend. V.

[1686] BMW of North America, Inc. v. Gore, 517 U.S. 559, 568 (1996).

[1687] *Id.* at 575; State Farm Mutual Automobile Ins. Co. v. Campbell, 538 U.S. 408, 418 (2003).

[1688] *Campbell*, 538 U.S. at 425.

[1689] Bridgeport Music, Inc. v. Justin Combs Publishing, 507 F.3d 470, 486–90 (6th Cir. 2007) (finding

Several courts of appeals, however, have held that this line of cases does *not* apply to an award of statutory damages under the Copyright Act.[1690] Instead, these courts have held that an award of statutory damages must not be "so severe and oppressive as to be wholly disproportioned to the offense and obviously unreasonable."[1691] Applying this standard, courts have upheld awards of statutory damages for peer-to-peer file sharing of $222,000 ($9,250 per song)[1692] and $675,000 ($22,500 per song).[1693]

[5]   Costs and Attorney's Fees

Section 505 grants courts discretion to award full costs against "any party" except the United States and also to "award a reasonable attorney's fee to the prevailing party as part of the costs."[1694] Typically, courts grant costs to the prevailing party with little or no discussion, even when attorney fees are not awarded. However, a prevailing copyright owner cannot recover its fees unless it registered its copyright before the infringement commenced, or for infringement of a published work, within three months of the work's first publication.[1695]

Before 1994, many courts applied a dual standard for awarding attorneys' fees, under which prevailing plaintiffs were routinely awarded attorney's fees, while prevailing defendants had to show that the plaintiff's claim was frivolous or was brought in bad faith in order to recover their fees.[1696] In 1994, however, in *Fogerty v. Fantasy, Inc.*, the Supreme Court ruled that "[p]revailing plaintiffs and prevailing defendants are to be treated alike" under section 505,[1697] because "a successful defense of a copyright infringement action may further the policies of the Copyright Act every bit as much as a successful prosecution of an infringement claim by the holder of a copyright."[1698] The Court also stated that in determining when fees should be awarded, courts should consider factors such as "frivolousness, motivation, objective unreasonableness (both in the factual and in the legal components of the case) and the need in particular circumstances to advance considerations of compensation and deterrence . . . so long as such factors are

---

award of $3.5 million in punitive damages unconstitutional, and remanding for district court to offer remittitur); Capitol Records, Inc. v. MP3Tunes, LLC, 2014 U.S. Dist. LEXIS 140139 (S.D.N.Y. Sept. 29, 2014) (finding punitive damages award of $7.5 million violates due process and ordering remittitur to $750,000).

[1690] *See, e.g.*, Sony BMG Music Ent'mt v. Tenenbaum, 719 F.3d 67 (1st Cir. 2013); Capitol Records, Inc. v. Thomas-Rasset, 692 F.3d 899 (8th Cir. 2012); Zomba Enterprises, Inc. v. Panorama Records, Inc., 491 F.3d 574 (6th Cir. 2007).

[1691] *Zomba*, 491 F.3d at 587–88, *quoting* St. Louis, I.M. & S. Ry. Co. v. Williams, 251 U.S. 63 (1919). *Accord, Tenenbaum*, 719 F.3d at 71; *Thomas-Rasset*, 692 F.3d at 907–08.

[1692] *Thomas-Rasset*, 692 F.3d at 908–10.

[1693] *Tenenbaum*, 719 F.3d at 71–72. *See also Zomba*, 491 F.3d at 587–88 (affirming award of $806,000, or $31,000 per work, for making infringing karaoke disks).

[1694] 17 U.S.C. § 505.

[1695] 17 U.S.C. § 412.

[1696] Fogerty v. Fantasy, Inc., 510 U.S. 517, 520–21 nn. 6, 8 (1994) (citing cases).

[1697] *Id.* at 534.

[1698] *Id.* at 527.

faithful to the purposes of the Copyright Act and are applied to prevailing plaintiffs and defendants in an evenhanded manner."[1699] Note, however, that the statute mandates uneven treatment in one respect, because a prevailing copyright owner must register its copyright in order to recover its fees, whereas a prevailing defendant may recover its fees regardless of whether the work is registered. [1700]

Although an award of fees is left to the discretion of the district court, some courts have announced bright-line rules to guide that discretion. The Seventh Circuit has held that, in the case of willful infringements involving small amounts of money, attorneys' fees should be presumed in order to deter willful infringement.[1701] The Seventh Circuit also follows a similar presumption in favor of prevailing defendants, because "without the prospect of such an award, the party might be forced into a nuisance settlement or deterred altogether from enforcing his rights."[1702] If an infringer acts willfully or deliberately, or if the plaintiff's claim is "objectively unreasonable," most courts will award fees.[1703] Courts disagree whether fees should be awarded to a prevailing defendant when the plaintiff's claim was not "objectively unreasonable."[1704]

In determining the *amount* of fees to be awarded, courts consider multiple factors, such as the time and labor required, the novelty and difficulty of the issues, the skill required to perform the legal service properly, the customary fee for similar work, the amount involved and the results obtained, and the experience, reputation, and ability of the attorneys.[1705]

[1699] *Id.* at 534 n.19.

[1700] Latin Am. Music Co. v. ASCAP, 642 F.3d 87 (1st Cir. 2011).

[1701] Gonzales v. Transfer Technologies, Inc., 301 F.3d 608, 609–10 (7th Cir. 2002).

[1702] Assessment Technologies of Wisconsin, LLC v. WIREdata, Inc., 361 F.3d 434, 437 (7th Cir. 2004). *See also* Klinger v. Conan Doyle Estate, Ltd., 761 F.3d 789 (7th Cir. 2014) ("In effect [defendant] was a private attorney general, combating a disreputable business practice — a form of extortion" in which the Estate demanded license fees for the use of characters that were in the public domain).

[1703] *See, e.g.*, Love v. Associated Newspapers, Ltd., 611 F.3d 601, 615 (9th Cir. 2010) ("The mere fact that a plaintiff has statutory standing does not make his legal and factual arguments objectively reasonable."); McRoberts Software, Inc. v. Media 100, Inc., 329 F.3d 557, 572 (7th Cir. 2003) (affirming fee award for willful infringement).

[1704] *Compare* Seltzer v. Green Day, Inc., 725 F.3d 1170 (9th Cir. 2013) (vacating award; fact that plaintiff lost did not mean action was objectively unreasonable); Virgin Records America, Inc. v. Thompson, 512 F.3d 724 (5th Cir. 2008) (affirming denial of fees where action was neither frivolous nor objectively unreasonable); Fogerty v. MGM Group Holdings, Inc., 379 F.3d 348 (6th Cir. 2004) (reversing award); *and* Matthew Bender & Co., Inc. v. West Publishing Co., 240 F.3d 116 (2d Cir. 2001) ("imposition of a fee award against a copyright holder with an objectively reasonable litigation position *generally* will not promote the purposes of the Copyright Act") (emphasis added) *with* Mattel, Inc. v. MGA Ent'mt, Inc., 705 F.3d 1108 (9th Cir. 2013) (affirming award of fees "[e]ven assuming Mattel's claim was objectively reasonable"); Bridgeport Music, Inc. v. WB Music Corp., 520 F.3d 588 (6th Cir. 2008) (affirming award of attorneys' fees to prevailing defendant, even though plaintiff's legal theory was objectively reasonable); Riviera Distributors, Inc. v. Jones, 517 F.3d 926, 928 (7th Cir. 2008) ("objectively unreasonable" standard would resurrect "asymmetric" approach rejected in *Fogerty*).

[1705] *See, e.g.*, Micromanipulator Co. v. Bough, 779 F.2d 255, 259 (5th Cir. 1983) (listing 12 factors); Cable/Home Communication Corp. v. Network Prods., Inc., 902 F.2d 829, 853 n.27 (11th Cir. 1990) (same).

[6] Criminal Penalties

Section 506 provides that criminal penalties are available against "[a]ny person who willfully infringes a copyright . . . for purposes of commercial advantage or private financial gain."[1706] In *United States v. LaMacchia*, the court quashed the prosecution of a computer bulletin-board operator who provided free unauthorized copies of software, on the grounds that his activity was not undertaken for financial gain.[1707] In 1997, Congress closed this perceived loophole by enacting the No Electronic Theft Act, which added criminal penalties for willful infringement "by the reproduction or distribution, including by electronic means, during any 180-day period, of 1 or more copies or phonorecords of 1 or more copyrighted works, which have a total retail value of more than $1,000."[1708] Felony penalties attach to the reproduction or distribution, during any 180-day period, of at least 10 copies or phonorecords which have a total retail value of more than $2,500, whereas reproduction or distribution below that amount is a misdemeanor.[1709] "[T]he term 'willfully' requires the government to prove that a defendant knew he was acting illegally rather than simply that he knew he was making copies."[1710]

In 2005, Congress added a provision criminalizing the unauthorized "distribution of a work being prepared for commercial distribution, by making it available on a computer network accessible to members of the public, if the person knew or should have known that the work was intended for commercial distribution."[1711] This section currently applies only to a computer program, a musical work, a motion picture or other audiovisual work, or a sound recording.[1712]

Additional criminal violations are found in Title 18. Section 2319A makes unlawful the unauthorized fixation or transmission of a live musical performance, or the reproduction or distribution of such a fixation, when done "knowingly and for purposes of commercial advantage or private financial gain."[1713] Section 2319B makes it a felony to knowingly use or attempt to use an audiovisual recording device to record a motion picture in a theater without the authorization of the copyright owner.[1714] In addition, anyone who violates the anti-circumvention or copyright management information provisions of the Digital Millennium Copyright Act "willfully and for purposes of commercial advantage or private financial gain" faces potential criminal liability.[1715]

[1706] 17 U.S.C. § 506(a)(1)(A).

[1707] 871 F. Supp. 535 (D. Mass. 1994).

[1708] 17 U.S.C. § 506(a)(1)(B).

[1709] 18 U.S.C. § 2319(b)(1), (c)(1) (felony); 18 U.S.C. § 2319(b)(3), (c)(3) (misdemeanor).

[1710] United States v. Liu, 731 F.3d 982, 985 (9th Cir. 2013).

[1711] 17 U.S.C. § 506(a)(1)(C).

[1712] 17 U.S.C. § 506(a)(3)(A),(B).

[1713] 18 U.S.C. § 2319A(a). This section has been upheld against Constitutional challenge. *See* § 4C[2][d].

[1714] 18 U.S.C. § 2319B.

[1715] 17 U.S.C. § 1204(a).

Chapter 5

TRADEMARKS

SYNOPSIS

§ 5A INTRODUCTION

§ 5B HISTORICAL DEVELOPMENT

    [1] Early Common Law: Passing Off

    [2] Modern Common Law and State Statutes

    [3] Early Federal Law: *The Trademark Cases*

    [4] The Lanham Act

        [a] Overview

        [b] Recent Amendments

§ 5C PROTECTABILITY

    [1] Requirements for Protection

        [a] In General

        [b] Distinctiveness

        [c] Non-Functionality

         [i] Public Policy

         [ii] The Evolving Definition of Functionality

         [iii] Aesthetic Functionality

    [2] Trademark Subject Matter

        [a] Distinctiveness

         [i] Arbitrary or Fanciful

         [ii] Suggestive

         [iii] Descriptive

          (a) Common Law

          (b) Secondary Meaning

         [iv] Generic Terms

        [b] Words and Slogans

         [i] In General

         [ii] Personal Names

         [iii] Foreign Words

         [iv] Abbreviations of Generic or Descriptive Terms

         [v] Titles

    [c] Non-Verbal Marks
    [i] Numerals and Alphanumeric Combinations
    [ii] Color, Sound, Scent
    [iii] Expressive Works
    [iv] Celebrity Likenesses and Fictional Characters
    [d] Trade Dress
§ 5D ACQUISITION AND MAINTENANCE OF TRADEMARK RIGHTS
  [1] Use in Trade
    [a] Establishing Priority of Use
    [i] Actual Use
    [ii] Reputation and Business Presence
    [iii] Zone of Expansion
    [b] Lanham Act
    [i] Use in Commerce
    [ii] Foreign Use
    [iii] The Famous Marks Doctrine
    [iv] Intent to Use Applications
    [v] Constructive Use
  [2] Distinctiveness
  [3] Maintaining Trademark Rights
  [4] Assignments and Licenses
    [a] Assignments
    [b] Licensing
§ 5E REGISTRATION OF TRADEMARK RIGHTS
  [1] Marks Eligible for Federal Registration
    [a] In General
    [b] Service Marks
    [c] Certification Marks
    [d] Collective Marks
  [2] Marks Ineligible for Federal Registration
    [a] Immoral, Deceptive, Scandalous, or Disparaging Matter
    [b] National, State, or Municipal Insignia
    [c] Name, Portrait, or Signature
    [d] Marks Confusingly Similar to Existing Marks
    [i] Priority of Use
    [ii] Priority Through Analogous Use
    [iii] Factors
    [iv] Concurrent Use
    [e] Descriptive, Misdescriptive, or Functional Marks

     [i]   Descriptive and Misdescriptive Marks

     [ii]   Primarily Geographically Descriptive Marks

     [iii]   Primarily Geographically Deceptively Misdescriptive Marks

     [iv]   Primarily Merely a Surname

     [v]   Functional Marks

    [f]   Secondary Meaning

    [g]   Dilutive Marks

 [3]   Registration Process

    [a]   Use Applications

    [b]   Intent to Use Applications

    [c]   Who May Register a Mark

    [d]   Dividing Applications

    [e]   *Inter Partes* Proceedings

     [i]   Opposition

     [ii]   Interferences

     [iii]   Concurrent Use Proceedings

     [iv]   Cancellation

      (a)   Grounds for Cancellation

      (b)   Procedure

    [f]   Judicial Review

    [g]   Maintaining and Renewing Registration

     [i]   Affidavit of Use

     [ii]   Renewal

 [4]   Incontestability

    [a]   Effect of Incontestable Status

    [b]   Establishing Incontestability

 [5]   The Supplemental Register

    [a]   Eligible Marks

    [b]   Registration Procedure

    [c]   Effect of Supplemental Registration

    [d]   Cancellation

 [6]   Domestic Priority Based on Foreign Registration

    [a]   International Agreements

    [b]   National Treatment

    [c]   Domestic Priority

    [d]   The Madrid Protocol

 [7]   State Trademark Registration

    [a]   State Registration Statutes

     [b] Federal Preemption

  [8] Unregistered Marks

§ 5F INFRINGEMENT

  [1] Effect of Federal Registration

  [2] Ownership of a Valid Mark

  [3] Likelihood of Confusion

     [a] Overview

     [b] Factors

      [i] Similarity of Marks

      [ii] Competitive Proximity

      [iii] Strength of Plaintiff's Mark

      [iv] Consumer Sophistication

      [v] Actual Confusion

      [vi] Bridging the Gap

      [vii] Defendant's Intent

      [viii] Relative Quality of Defendant's Goods or Services

     [c] Jurisdictional Variations on the *Polaroid* Test

     [d] Reverse Confusion

     [e] Confusion Before or After the Purchasing Decision

      [i] Initial Interest Confusion

      [ii] Post-Sale Confusion

  [4] Trademark Use

     [a] Keyword-Triggered Advertising

     [b] Metatags

     [c] Domain Names

     [d] Expressive Works

  [5] Use in Commerce as Jurisdictional Prerequisite

  [6] Territorial Limitations

  [7] Reverse Passing Off

  [8] Adjudication and Procedure

     [a] Subject Matter Jurisdiction

     [b] Standing

      [i] Standing to Cancel or Oppose Federal Registration

      [ii] Standing Under Section 32

      [iii] Standing Under Section 43(a) and Common Law

      [iv] Standing Under Section 43(c)

     [c] Declaratory Judgments

§ 5G DILUTION

  [1] The Concept of Dilution

[2]   Dilution Under State Law
[3]   Federal Trademark Dilution Act
   [a]   History
   [b]   Elements of a Federal Dilution Claim
   [c]   Trademark Use
   [d]   Distinctive and Famous Mark
    [i]   Distinctiveness
    [ii]   Fame
    [iii]   Trade Dress and Other Nontraditional Marks
   [e]   Similarity
   [f]   Actual Dilution Versus Likelihood of Dilution
    [i]   The FTDA and the *Moseley* Decision
    [ii]   Likelihood of Dilution Under the TDRA
    [iii]   Judicial Interpretations
     (a)   Likelihood of Dilution by Blurring
     (b)   Likelihood of Dilution by Tarnishment
   [g]   Effective Date of TDRA
[4]   Exceptions to FTDA
   [a]   Fair Use
   [b]   Noncommercial Use
   [c]   News Reporting and Commentary
   [d]   Federal Registration as a Defense
[5]   Remedies

§ 5H   CYBERSQUATTING
[1]   Anticybersquatting Consumer Protection Act
   [a]   Elements of an ACPA Claim
   [b]   *In Rem* Jurisdiction
   [c]   Personal Names
   [d]   ACPA Remedies
[2]   Alternative Forums for Domain Name Disputes

§ 5I   SECONDARY LIABILITY
[1]   Contributory Infringement
[2]   Vicarious Liability

§ 5J   DEFENSES
[1]   Abandonment
   [a]   Cessation of Use
   [b]   Other Causes of Abandonment
    [i]   Naked Licensing
    [ii]   Assignment in Gross

[2] First Sale Doctrine
   [a] Misrepresentation by Authorized Resellers
   [b] Materially Different Goods
     [i] Used, Altered, or Refurbished Goods
     [ii] Other Non-Genuine Goods
   [c] Undisclosed Repackaging
   [d] Parallel Imports
[3] "Classic" Fair Use
[4] Nominative Fair Use
[5] Comparative Advertising
[6] First Amendment
   [a] Commercial Parodies
     [i] Infringement and Unfair Competition
     [ii] Dilution
   [b] Noncommercial Expression
     [i] Infringement and Unfair Competition
     [ii] Dilution
   [c] Political Speech
   [d] Expressive Merchandise
[7] Other Defenses
   [a] Laches
   [b] Acquiescence
   [c] Statute of Limitations
   [d] Unclean Hands
[8] Federal Preemption
[9] Sovereign Immunity

§ 5K REMEDIES
[1] Non-Monetary Remedies
   [a] Injunctions
   [b] Seizure of Counterfeit Goods and Related Materials
   [c] Destruction of Infringing Articles
   [d] Cancellation of Federal Registration
   [e] Disclaimers
[2] Monetary Remedies
   [a] Actual Damages, Defendant's Profits, and Costs
   [b] Enhanced Damages
   [c] Attorney's Fees
   [d] Statutory Damages
   [e] Enhanced Awards in Counterfeiting Cases

[f] Marking or Actual Notice

[g] Damages Under Federal Dilution Law

[h] False or Fraudulent Registration

[3] Limitations on Remedies Against Certain Defendants

[a] Makers of Labels, Signs, Packaging, or Advertisements

[b] Printers and Publishers

[c] Domain Name Registration Authorities

[d] Family Movie Act of 2005

[e] Remedies Against Federal and State Governments

[4] Criminal Penalties

[a] Counterfeit Marks

[b] Counterfeit Labels

§ 5A INTRODUCTION

Trademark law recognizes exclusive rights to use marks that distinguish the goods and services of one manufacturer, merchant or service provider from those of others. A trademark is typically a brand name, logo, or slogan, but it can consist of any device that serves to distinguish goods or services. Colors, sounds, product packaging, even nonfunctional design features, are potential marks.[1]

Trademark law serves two purposes — to protect consumers from being confused or deceived about the source of goods or services in the marketplace, and to protect the goodwill that merchants have developed in their trademarks.[2] Historically, it is part of the broader law of unfair competition, which is rooted in English common law. By the end of the twentieth century, however, United States trademark and unfair competition law had expanded the scope of their protection to encompass a wider array of source indicators, had begun to protect the goodwill of especially famous trademarks even in the absence of confusion or competition, and had become extensively codified at both the state and federal level. In spite of these changes, many aspects of trademark and unfair competition law still reflect their common law roots.

A merchant, manufacturer, or service provider acquires common-law mark ownership by adopting and using the mark on goods and services.[3] The mark must be distinctive of the goods or services. If a mark is the product's generic name, it cannot serve as a trademark. If it is descriptive of a good's nature or geographic origin, it cannot serve as a trademark for the good unless it has acquired a "secondary meaning," that is, unless it has become distinctive in the public's mind through use as a mark. A mark must not be confusingly similar to marks or trade names others have previously adopted and not abandoned.

---

[1] See § 5C.

[2] Qualitex Co. v. Jacobson Prods. Co. Inc., 514 U.S. 159, 163–64 (1995).

[3] See § 5D.

If a mark ceases to be used as a source indicator, or if the public ceases to recognize it as a source indicator, then it will cease to be protected as a trademark. Thus, trademark owners need to be vigilant in monitoring the use and public perception of their marks. However, regardless of a trademark owner's efforts to police and protect its mark, the consumer remains the ultimate arbiter of whether that mark deserves continued protection or has lost its trademark significance — for example, where the mark has become generic.[4]

A common-law mark owner may acquire important federal statutory benefits by registering the mark with the Patent and Trademark Office.[5] Among the benefits are the ability to file for registration based on a bona fide "intent to use" a mark in interstate commerce (which may be perfected only upon a showing of actual use); constructive use and priority nationwide, subject only to any rights preexisting on the date of the application; and incontestability, which limits certain defenses that may be raised to challenge a mark's validity.

A trademark owner may prevent others from using the same or similar marks that create a likelihood of confusion, mistake or deception.[6] Although originally limited to likelihood of confusion concerning source or origin, the concept of confusion has been broadened to include likelihood of confusion as to sponsorship or endorsement; initial interest confusion that provides a competitor an advantage in the market, even if such confusion has been dispelled at the point of sale; post-sale confusion, when third parties encounter counterfeit goods after the point of sale; and reverse confusion, when a larger and more well-known junior user creates confusion that overwhelms a smaller and less well-known senior user.

The owner of a famous mark may also be able prevent others from using the same or similar marks on other goods and services, even if there is no competition or likelihood of confusion between the mark owner and the defendant, if the use is likely to harm either the distinctiveness or the reputation of the famous mark.[7]

Defenses to trademark infringement and dilution include abandonment of a mark, the first-sale doctrine for resale of genuine goods, and various doctrines designed to reflect First Amendment values, including descriptive fair use and nominative fair use.[8]

§ 5B   HISTORICAL DEVELOPMENT

[1]   Early Common Law: Passing Off

The law of trademarks and unfair competition has its roots in nineteenth-century tort law, specifically the common law tort of passing off (also known as "palming off"), which was concerned with protecting merchants against

---

[4] *See, e.g.*, DuPont Cellophane Co. v. Waxed Prods. Co., 85 F.2d 75, 81 (2d Cir. 1936).

[5] *See* § 5E.

[6] *See* § 5F.

[7] *See* § 5G.

[8] *See* § 5J.

competitors who copied their source-indicating marks in order to capitalize on the merchants' reputations and deceive their customers into purchasing the competitors' deceptively marked goods. Imitation of another's "technical trademark" (a category limited to inherently distinctive words and symbols) constituted trademark infringement, while use of other means to falsely suggest the origin of goods (such as imitating packaging or trade dress) constituted unfair competition. Today, trademark infringement encompasses both the imitation of technical trademarks and the imitation of descriptive terms or features that have acquired secondary meaning.

Throughout the nineteenth century, fraudulent intent was an essential element of passing off (although some English courts were willing to grant injunctions even in the absence of intent to deceive). During the twentieth century, the element of intent gradually decreased in importance, and the concern for avoiding consumer confusion, even where unintentional, became paramount.[9]

[2]   Modern Common Law and State Statutes

Because the law of trademarks is a subset of the larger field of unfair competition, both are governed by essentially the same principles. However, unlike trademark infringement, unfair competition is based on principles of equity and does not always involve the violation of one party's exclusive right to use a specific word, mark, symbol, or device as an indication of origin.

In its narrowest formulation, unfair competition involves a defendant's fraudulent "passing off" (or "palming off") of his or her goods or services as originating from the plaintiff.[10] An unfair competition claim may be based on a defendant's unauthorized use of a distinctive mark that the plaintiff uses to identify its goods or services, or it may be based on the existence of other conduct or contextual factors that are likely to confuse consumers about the source of the defendant's goods or services.[11] Some courts have used the term "unfair competition" more broadly, however, to describe any conduct that they perceive as exceeding the bounds of ethical competition.[12]

The modern common law of trademarks and unfair competition is reflected in the *Restatement (Third) of Unfair Competition*, which defines "passing off" in terms of the effect of the defendant's conduct on consumers' purchasing decisions rather than in terms of the subjective intent of the defendant,[13] and which recognizes other forms of unfair competition such as false advertising (defined by

---

[9] J. Thomas McCarthy, McCarthy on Trademarks and Unfair Competition § 5:2 (4th ed. 2009).

[10] Crowell Pub. Co. v. Italian Monthly Co., 28 F.2d 613 (2d Cir. 1928).

[11] *See, e.g.*, William R. Warner & Co. v. Eli Lilly & Co., 265 U.S. 526 (1924); Murphy Door Bed Co. v. Interior Sleep Sys., Inc., 874 F.2d 95 (2d Cir. 1989); DuPont Cellophane Co. v. Waxed Prods. Co., 85 F.2d 75, 82 (2d Cir. 1936).

[12] *See, e.g.*, Addison-Wesley Pub. Co. v. Brown, 207 F. Supp. 678 (E.D.N.Y. 1962) (publishing answers to the problems presented in another publisher's physics textbook); Merchants' Syndicate Catalog Co. v. Retailers' Factory Catalog Co., 206 F. 545 (N.D. Ill. 1913) (misuse of confidential information).

[13] Restatement (Third) of Unfair Competition § 4 (1995).

the *Restatement* as false statements about a merchant's own goods),[14] reverse passing off (that is, misrepresenting the source of another merchant's goods),[15] and the right of publicity (that is, the unauthorized appropriation of a person's name or likeness for commercial gain).[16] The *Restatement* also recognizes "a residual category encompassing other business practices determined to be unfair," such as (1) threatening to bring a patent infringement claim against resellers of a competitor's product, knowing that the claim of patent infringement is baseless, (2) fraudulently altering a competitor's bid for a supply contract, or (3) submitting a fraudulent change of address in the name of a competitor, thus causing the competitor to lose potential customers.[17]

While trademark law is a subset of the broader category of unfair competition law, it is by far the most significant component of this category, especially under its modern formulation, which recognizes that descriptive terms, product packaging, and even product configuration can serve as trademarks when they acquire secondary meaning. Distinctive product packaging and configuration have become known as "trade dress."

Unregistered trademarks, including trade dress, are protected under state common law, and a related provision in federal law, provided that they are not a functional feature of a product, and provided that they distinguish, in the minds of consumers, the goods or services of one merchant from those of another. In addition to common law doctrines, many states have enacted trademark and unfair competition statutes that apply to unregistered trademarks and trade dress, and many have also enacted state registration systems that provide enhanced protection to registered marks. Many states also recognize the right of publicity as a matter of common law and/or statutory law.[18]

[3]　　Early Federal Law: *The Trademark Cases*

Congress enacted the first federal trademark statute in 1870,[19] providing a system of federal registration for all trademarks used within the United States, regardless of whether they were used in interstate commerce. However, in 1879, the Supreme Court struck down this statute in *The Trademark Cases*[20] on the ground that it exceeded the scope of Congress's authority under either the Patent and Copyright Clause or the Commerce Clause of the Constitution. The statute exceeded Congress's power under the Patent and Copyright Clause because it extended trademark protection without regard to the originality or creativity of the mark. It exceeded Congress's power under the Commerce Clause because it

---

[14] *Id.* § 2. In contrast, the federal law of false advertising now applies to false statements about the defendant's own goods or services or those of another. 15 U.S.C. § 1125(a)(1)(B). *See* § 6E.

[15] RESTATEMENT § 5.

[16] *Id.* § 46. *See, e.g.,* Waits v. Frito-Lay, Inc., 978 F.2d 1093 (9th Cir. 1992); White v. Samsung Electronics America, Inc., 971 F.2d 1395 (9th Cir. 1992). *See* § 6G.

[17] RESTATEMENT § 1, cmt. g.

[18] *See* § 6G.

[19] Act of July 8, 1870, 16 Stat. 198.

[20] 100 U.S. 82 (1879).

appeared to extend federal protection to trademarks without regard to whether they were used in "commerce with foreign nations, and among the several states, and with the Indian tribes."[21] Congress corrected this constitutional defect in 1881 by expressly limiting the scope of federal law to commerce with foreign nations and Indian tribes.

Congress did not permit federal registration of marks used in interstate commerce until the Trademark Act of 1905.[22] The 1905 Act permitted registration only of "technical" trademarks — that is, marks that were inherently distinctive — thus excluding descriptive marks and most types of trade dress regardless of their degree of acquired distinctiveness. Over the next 40 years, the federal trademark statutes were continuously revised, with coverage extended to descriptive marks with secondary meaning in the 1920 Act.[23] Finally, Congress undertook a major overhaul of federal trademark law in the Lanham Trademark Act of 1946.[24]

[4]   The Lanham Act

[a]   Overview

The Lanham Act provides a federal registration scheme for trademarks and service marks that are used in any commerce that Congress has the authority to regulate, and provides an array of remedies against parties that infringe such registered marks. It also provides a federal scheme of protection against certain acts of unfair competition that take place in federally regulated commerce, but that do not involve infringement of federally registered marks. In enacting the Lanham Act, Congress recognized that commercial activities were increasingly taking place on a national scale, so that state-by-state remedial schemes were not necessarily adequate to protect consumers and merchants from injury due to unfair competition.[25]

The three most important sections of the Act are sections 2, 32, and 43(a), although the significance of section 43(a) was less apparent in 1946 than it is today. Section 2 sets forth the standards for registering a trademark or service mark on the Principal Register of the Patent and Trademark Office (PTO). Section 32 protects federally registered trademarks and service marks against unauthorized uses that are likely to confuse or mislead consumers as to the origin of goods or services. Section 43(a) provides a federal unfair competition cause of action for a party that suffers a competitive injury as a result of false statements made by others in connection with the offering of goods or services, including infringement of an unregistered trademark.

---

[21] U.S. Const., Art. I, § 8, cl. 3.

[22] Act of Feb. 20, 1905, 33 Stat. 724.

[23] Act of Mar. 19, 1920, 41 Stat. 533.

[24] Pub. L. No. 79-489, 60 Stat. 427 (1946). Section 45 of the Lanham Act provides that "[t]he intent of this chapter is to regulate commerce within the control of Congress," where " 'commerce' means all commerce which may lawfully be regulated by Congress." 15 U.S.C. § 1127.

[25] H.R. Rep. No. 79-219, at 4 (1945); S. Rep. No. 779-1333, at 5–6 (1946).

Sections 2 and 32 of the Lanham Act have undergone relatively minor modifications since 1946. Section 43(a), in contrast, has continuously expanded in importance, primarily as a result of expansive judicial interpretation. Most of those judicial interpretations were endorsed by Congress in the Trademark Law Revision Act (TLRA) of 1988, which amended the language of section 43(a).

[b] Recent Amendments

Over time, the Lanham Act has been amended to incorporate new types of trademark protection. Two of these changes — the addition of dilution provisions in 1995 (followed by their amendments in 2006), and the addition of cybersquatting provisions in 1999 — represent especially significant expansions of the scope of federal trademark law.

In 1995, Congress followed the lead of states that had enacted dilution laws to protect trademark owners against certain unauthorized uses of their marks that could undermine the selling power, or tarnish the reputation, of their marks even in the absence of competition or likelihood of confusion. In the Federal Trademark Dilution Act (FTDA),[26] Congress added section 43(c) to the Lanham Act,[27] creating a cause of action for dilution of the selling power of "famous" marks.[28] In 2006, Congress enacted the Trademark Dilution Revision Act (TDRA),[29] amending section 43(c) in response to ten years of judicial interpretations.

With the proliferation of commercial transactions on the Internet, existing federal trademark protections under sections 32, 43(a), and 43(c) of the Lanham Act were not always adequate to protect trademark owners against parties that made unauthorized use of their trademarks in domain names in a way that could confuse or mislead consumers, or undermine the selling power of their marks. Congress sought to remedy these problems in 1999 with the Anticybersquatting Consumer Protection Act (ACPA),[30] which added section 43(d) to the Lanham Act.[31] In this provision, Congress sought to define with greater certainty the circumstances in which registration, use, or trafficking in a domain name that resembles a valid trademark violates the rights of a trademark owner, and to establish procedures for enforcing such rights even when the infringer is beyond the personal jurisdiction of the federal courts.[32]

§ 5C PROTECTABILITY

A trademark is a device that, when used on or in connection with goods or services, serves the function of identifying to consumers the source from which those particular goods or services have emanated. Although traditionally a trade-

---

[26] Pub. L. No. 104-98, 109 Stat. 985.

[27] 15 U.S.C. § 1125(c).

[28] Federal dilution law is discussed in § 5G.

[29] Pub. L. No. 109-312, 120 Stat. 1730.

[30] Pub. L. No. 106-113, 113 Stat. 1536.

[31] 15 U.S.C. § 1125(d).

[32] The anti-cybersquatting provisions are discussed in § 5H.

mark consisted of a word or symbol, trademarks today may take many forms, including a sound, a fragrance, or the overall appearance of a product or its packaging (known as trade dress). Although registration of trademarks is possible under both state and federal law, and federal registration can significantly enhance the legal protections available to the trademark owner, registration is not essential to trademark protection in the United States.

[1]   Requirements for Protection

[a]   In General

The function of a trademark or service mark is to inform consumers about the source of the goods or services with which that mark is associated. The trademark is a shorthand form of communication from a merchant to its customers or potential customers, in which the merchant identifies which products or services it stands behind and distinguishes them from competing products or services offered by other merchants. Trademarks also enable consumers to hold merchants accountable for products or services that prove to be disappointing. A consumer can avoid brands that have been unsatisfactory in the past, and can also complain to a merchant whose brand is displeasing.

Goodwill is the reputation that attaches to a trademark. It represents the cumulative experience of consumers who have used the product or service with which the mark is associated, as well as consumer expectations that have been cultivated through marketing efforts.

While trademarks are origin identifiers, their primary importance to the public lies in the indirect assurances of quality and accountability that they provide. Their importance to merchants lies in their ability to capture the goodwill generated by the merchant's efforts and their ability to channel that goodwill toward the merchant that is responsible for creating it rather than toward the merchant's competitors, thus increasing the likelihood that the merchant will enjoy future patronage by satisfied customers. Thus, when a trademark is infringed, "[w]hat truly is infringed is the public's right to be secure from confusion and the corresponding right of each trademark's owner to control its own product's reputation."[33]

[b]   Distinctiveness

A trademark or service mark must be capable of distinguishing the goods or services in connection with which it is used from goods or services offered by another source. If a word, symbol, or other device is incapable of distinguishing the source of goods or services, then it cannot qualify for trademark protection, either at common law or under the Lanham Act.

A mark can be distinctive in either of two ways. It can be inherently distinctive, or it can acquire distinctiveness through use. A mark is inherently distinctive if, starting from the moment its use commences, "[its] intrinsic nature serves to

---

[33] David Berg & Co. v. Gatto Int'l Trading Co., 884 F.2d 306, 310 (7th Cir. 1989).

identify a particular source."[34] Inherently distinctive marks may be fanciful ("Kodak" film), arbitrary ("Camel" cigarettes), or suggestive ("Tide" detergent).[35] Many marks, however, are not inherently distinctive, because when they are first used on a product or service they do not immediately convey to the consumer the message that they are source indicators. A descriptive mark is not inherently distinctive, because it conveys information about the characteristics of the product or service in connection with which it is used. However, a descriptive mark may nonetheless possess acquired distinctiveness — also known as secondary meaning.[36] Secondary meaning arises when, "in the minds of the public, the primary significance of a [mark] is to identify the source of the product rather than the product itself."[37] Acquired distinctiveness, or secondary meaning, arises over time, after consumers have had repeated encounters with the mark.

There are important legal consequences to the determination of: (1) whether a mark is inherently distinctive, (2) whether a descriptive mark has acquired secondary meaning, and (3) whether a word, symbol, or other device is so lacking in distinctiveness that it cannot distinguish one merchant's goods or services from those of another (in which case it is characterized as either "generic" or "merely descriptive"). These consequences are discussed where relevant throughout the remainder of this chapter.

[c]   Non-Functionality

[i]   Public Policy

Under both state and federal law, the functionality bar denies trademark protection to any aspects of an article that contribute to the utility of the article. According to the Supreme Court's most comprehensive effort to define functionality, "a product feature is functional, and cannot serve as a trademark, if it is essential to the use or purpose of the article or if it affects the cost or quality of the article, that is, if exclusive use of the feature would put competitors at a significant non-reputation-related disadvantage."[38]

The proscription against trademark protection for the functional features of an article is a judicially created doctrine that predates the Lanham Act.[39] The functionality prohibition serves two related purposes: (1) it fosters competition by ensuring that all competitors are free to copy the useful features of a product, and

---

[34] Abercrombie & Fitch Co. v. Hunting World, Inc., 537 F.2d 4, 10–11 (2d Cir. 1976).

[35] The "spectrum of distinctiveness" — which indicates the relative strength of arbitrary, fanciful, suggestive, and descriptive marks — is discussed in § 5C[2][a][i].

[36] "The phrase 'secondary meaning' originally arose in the context of word marks, where it served to distinguish the source-identifying meaning from the ordinary, or 'primary,' meaning of the word. 'Secondary meaning' has since come to refer to the acquired, source-identifying meaning of a non-word mark as well." Wal-Mart Stores, Inc. v. Samara Bros., Inc., 529 U.S. 205, 211 (2000).

[37] Inwood Laboratories, Inc. v. Ives Laboratories, Inc., 456 U.S. 844, 851, n. 11 (1982); see also Perini Corp. v. Perini Construction, Inc., 915 F.2d 121, 125 (4th Cir. 1990) ("Secondary meaning is the consuming public's understanding that the mark, when used in context, refers, not to what the descriptive mark ordinarily describes, but to the particular business that the mark is meant to identify.").

[38] Qualitex Co. v. Jacobson Products Co., 514 U.S. 159, 165 (1995) (internal quotation marks omitted).

[39] Wilhelm Pudenz, GmbH v. Littlefuse, Inc. 177 F.3d 1204, 1207 (11th Cir. 1999).

(2) it prevents trademark law from conflicting with the scheme of federal patent protection by ensuring that trademark law does not provide patent-like protection of unlimited duration for the useful features of a product.[40] If a feature is functional, it may be the subject of a monopoly only if and to the extent that it qualifies for federal patent protection, and if it so qualifies, the monopoly should expire at the end of the federal patent term so that all other competitors will be free to incorporate the useful feature. The functionality bar applies to both state and federal law, even though the latter is not subject to Supremacy Clause preemption.[41]

For example, in *William R. Warner & Co. v. Eli Lilly & Co.*,[42] pharmacists had been covertly substituting a cheaper medication for the more expensive brand requested by customers. The deception was facilitated by the fact that the two medications were similar in appearance and flavor because both contained chocolate; indeed, there was some evidence that the defendant had deliberately set out to duplicate the plaintiff's formula as precisely as possible. Although the Supreme Court agreed that the pharmacists had engaged in unfair competition in the nature of passing off, and that the manufacturer of the cheaper medication was liable for the activities of its sales representatives in encouraging the deception, the Court held that it would be improper to enjoin the defendant from continuing to use chocolate in its medication, because chocolate was a functional ingredient that contributed to the taste and appearance of the medication, and also served as a suspension agent for the medicinal ingredients.[43]

[ii]   The Evolving Definition of Functionality

Although the concept of functionality was at the core of the Supreme Court's decision in *William R. Warner*, the Court did not use this term or attempt to define the concept at that time. In its 1982 decision in *Inwood Laboratories, Inc. v. Ives Laboratories, Inc.*, however, the Court held that "a product feature is functional if it is essential to the use or purpose of the article or if it affects the cost or quality of the article."[44] As discussed below, this remains the primary definition of functionality in trademark law, although the Supreme Court has articulated a secondary test as well.

Inwood Laboratories involved an unfair competition claim that arose from the fraudulent activities of pharmacists who were able to pass off the defendant's cheaper medication for the plaintiff's more expensive medication because the capsules were identical in color. The Supreme Court held that the plaintiff's claim was properly rejected by the district court for two reasons, either of which was sufficient by itself: (1) the color of the capsules lacked secondary meaning, and (2) the color of the capsules was functional. The color was functional because patients associated the color with the type of medication, some patients commingled their pills, color helped to identify drugs in emergencies, and uniform colors for brand

---

[40] *Id.* at 1207–08; Qualitex Co. v. Jacobson Products Co., Inc., 514 U.S. 159, 164–65 (1995).

[41] *Wilhelm Pudenz*, 177 F.3d at 1208.

[42] 265 U.S. 526 (1924).

[43] *Id.* at 531.

[44] 456 U.S. 844, 850 n.10 (1982).

name and generic versions of a drug helped to prevent pharmacist errors.[45]

In 1995, the Supreme Court addressed the concept of aesthetic functionality in *Qualitex Co. v. Jacobson Products Co.*,[46] which raised the question whether color alone could be federally registered as a trademark. Although it recognized that "sometimes color plays an important role in making a product more desirable," the Court found that color played no such role in this case. In concluding that color was not a functional feature of the registrant's product (a laundry press pad), the Court quoted the *Inwood Laboratories* standard, but added the language indicated in italics below:

> "[I]n general terms, a product feature is functional," and cannot serve as a trademark, "if it is essential to the use or purpose of the article or if it affects the cost or quality of the article," *that is, if exclusive use of the feature would put competitors at a significant non-reputation-related disadvantage.*[47]

Although the added language was not necessary to hold that the color of the press pad in this case was nonfunctional, it broadened the definition of functionality in important ways. Implicit in this new definition is the concept of "aesthetic functionality" — that is, the concept that certain aesthetic aspects of a product's design or packaging may contribute to its consumer appeal in ways that are unrelated to any origin-identifying function and which, therefore, should be denied trademark protection even if they have acquired secondary meaning.[48]

The Court's 2001 opinion in *TrafFix Devices, Inc. v. Marketing Displays, Inc.*,[49] clarified the functionality analysis, making the original *Inwood Laboratories* test primary, and the *Qualitex* expansion relevant only in cases of aesthetic functionality and in cases where the primary test is not satisfied.[50] In *TrafFix*, the trade dress at issue was an aspect of the product's design that had been the subject of a since-expired utility patent, a dual-spring device that "provide[d] a unique and useful mechanism to resist the force of the wind."[51] The fact that the feature in question had been the subject of a utility patent was, in the Court's view, "strong evidence" that the feature was functional, and warranted imposing a "heavy burden" on the party seeking to refute this evidence of functionality.[52] In this case, the utility of the device established that it was functional, and this made it unnecessary to inquire whether alternative design possibilities were available to competitors.[53] The utilitarian function of the design was therefore distinguishable from the arbitrary selection of a color for the laundry press pad in *Qualitex*, where

---

[45] *Id.* at 853.

[46] 514 U.S. 159 (1995).

[47] *Id.* at 165 (emphasis added).

[48] For more on aesthetic functionality, see § 5C[1][c][iii].

[49] 532 U.S. 23 (2001).

[50] *Id.* at 32–33 (citations omitted).

[51] *Id.* at 33.

[52] *Id.* at 29–30.

[53] *Id.* at 33–35.

the exclusive use of one color by one party still left numerous alternative color choices for competitors.

TrafFix thus appears to make *Inwood Laboratories* the primary test of functionality, so that the availability of alternative designs need not be considered where the *Inwood Laboratories* test is satisfied. Only if a product feature is deemed to be nonfunctional under the strictly utilitarian standard of *Inwood Laboratories* should a court inquire whether copying that feature was a competitive necessity, or whether competitors could instead have used alternative designs. The Fifth and Sixth Circuits have adopted this interpretation of *TrafFix*,[54] and the Second Circuit appears to have embraced it as well.[55]

In contrast, post-*TrafFix* opinions from the Federal Circuit as well as the Fourth and Ninth Circuits have continued to treat the availability of alternative designs as a threshold test of functionality. The Federal Circuit held in *Valu Engineering v. Rexnord Corp.* that the availability of alternative designs can still be considered as "a legitimate source of evidence to determine whether a feature is functional in the first place,"[56] without limiting the relevance of this inquiry to cases involving aesthetic functionality. Accordingly, the Federal Circuit continues to apply the four-factor test articulated by the Court of Customs and Patent Appeals in *In re Morton-Norwich Products, Inc.*,[57] which considers: (1) the existence of a utility patent disclosing the utilitarian advantages of the design; (2) advertising materials in which the originator of the design touts the design's utilitarian advantages; (3) the availability to competitors of functionally equivalent designs; and (4) facts indicating that the design results in a comparatively simple or cheap method of manufacturing the product.[58] In the Federal Circuit's view, *TrafFix* did not alter the *Morton-Norwich* analysis.[59] The Fourth Circuit has adopted the Federal Circuit's approach.[60] The Ninth Circuit, too, continues to treat the availability of alternative designs as evidence of non-functionality, even after *TrafFix*.[61]

Whether or not a feature is functional depends on how it relates to the trademark owner's product or packaging, not how it is used by the accused infringer. Accordingly, the Fourth Circuit reversed a district court's holding that Google's unauthorized use of a trademark as an advertising keyword was non-infringing because Google's use was functional.[62]

---

[54] Eppendorf-Netheler-Hinz GmbH v. Ritter GmbH, 289 F.3d 351 (5th Cir. 2002); Groeneveld Transp. Efficiency, Inc. v. Lubecore Int'l, Inc., 730 F.3d 494 (6th Cir. 2013)

[55] Nora Beverages, Inc. v. Perrier Group of Am., Inc., 269 F.3d 114, 120 n.4 (2d Cir. 2001) (mentioning the relevance of alternative design possibilities only in the context of aesthetic functionality).

[56] 278 F.3d 1268, 1276 (Fed. Cir. 2002).

[57] 671 F.2d 1332, 1340–41 (C.C.P.A. 1982).

[58] *Valu Eng'g*, 278 F.3d at 1274.

[59] *Id.* at 1276.

[60] McAirlaids, Inc. v. Kimberly-Clark Corp., 756 F.3d 307, 312–13 (4th Cir. 2014).

[61] Talking Rain Bev. Co. v. South Beach Bev. Co., 349 F.3d 601, 603 (9th Cir. 2003). Treatise author J. Thomas McCarthy agrees with this approach. J. THOMAS McCARTHY, McCARTHY ON TRADEMARKS AND UNFAIR COMPETITION § 7.75 (2009).

[62] Rosetta Stone v. Google, 676 F.3d 144 (4th Cir. 2012).

[iii] Aesthetic Functionality

The concept of "aesthetic functionality," as opposed to the "utilitarian" type of functionality described in *Inwood Laboratories*, is somewhat controversial. As early as 1938, this concept was recognized in the *Restatement of Torts*, which noted that "[w]hen goods are bought largely for their aesthetic value, their features may be functional because they definitely contribute to that value and thus aid the performance of an object for which the goods are intended."[63] The *Restatement (Third) of Unfair Competition* also recognizes aesthetic functionality, noting that "[a] design is functional because of its aesthetic value only if it confers a significant benefit that cannot practically be duplicated by the use of alternative designs."[64]

Many of the lower federal courts had recognized the concept of aesthetic functionality long before the Supreme Court addressed it in *Qualitex*.[65] Some of these courts found an aesthetic feature to be nonfunctional, and thus eligible for trademark protection, if it was "of such an arbitrary nature that depriving the public of the right to copy it is insignificant";[66] in contrast, if the aesthetic feature was dictated by functional considerations, it was ineligible for trademark protection.[67] Applying this standard in *Keene Corp. v. Paraflex Industries, Inc.*, the Third Circuit denied trademark protection to the aesthetic features of an exterior wall-mounted lighting fixture, because "part of its function includes its architectural compatibility with the structure or building on which it is mounted. Thus its design configuration, rather than serving merely as an arbitrary expression of aesthetics, is intricately related to its function."[68] The court noted that it was entirely possible for an aesthetic feature to be both functional and imbued with secondary meaning, and that in such cases trademark law should not prevent competitors from copying the functional feature. It also rejected a "competitive necessity" standard as "an unnecessarily narrow view of functionality."[69] Similarly, in *Deere & Co. v. Farmhand, Inc.*, the Eighth Circuit denied trademark protection to the particular shade of green used by John Deere for its tractors and other farm equipment, in spite of strong evidence that the color had secondary meaning, because the court found that farmers preferred to buy their equipment in matching colors.[70]

Other courts adopted a slightly different test, treating an aesthetic element as functional if its presence was a "competitive necessity." In *Brunswick Corp. v. British Seagull*,[71] the Federal Circuit upheld the PTO's refusal to register the

---

[63] RESTATEMENT OF TORTS § 742, cmt. a (1938).

[64] RESTATEMENT (THIRD) OF UNFAIR COMPETITION § 17, cmt. c (1993).

[65] *See* Keene Corp. v. Paraflex Indus., Inc., 653 F.2d 822, 825–26 (3d Cir. 1981) (collecting cases).

[66] *Id.* at 825 (quoting *In re* Mogen David Wine Corp., 328 F.2d 925, 933 (C.C.P.A. 1964) (Rich, J., concurring)).

[67] 653 F.2d at 825.

[68] *Id.* at 826.

[69] *Id.* at 827.

[70] 560 F. Supp. 85, 98 (S.D. Iowa 1982) (following *Keene*), *aff'd*, 721 F.2d 253 (8th Cir. 1983) (per curiam).

[71] 35 F.3d 1527 (Fed. Cir. 1994).

color black for outboard motors, on the ground that black was more desirable than other colors because it made the motor appear smaller and because it was compatible with a wider variety of boat colors.[72] The Federal Circuit noted that "[f]unctionality reflects a tension" between "a fundamental right to compete through imitation of a competitor's product" and "the individual's right to protect symbols which identify the source of particular goods."[73] Under the functionality doctrine, the right to protect source indicators as trademarks should, therefore, be limited by "the *need* to copy [articles that are not protected by patent or copyright], which is more properly termed the right to compete *effectively.*"[74]

The Supreme Court has addressed aesthetic functionality in a series of cases — including *William R. Warner, Inwood Laboratories,* and *Qualitex,* as well as dictum in *TrafFix* — that have consistently indicated that aesthetic features such as color (as well as flavor, in *William R. Warner*) may be barred from trademark protection under the functionality doctrine.

The Court's discussion of aesthetic functionality in *Qualitex* provides the most comprehensive guidance to date. Although *Qualitex* was not itself an aesthetic functionality case, addressing instead the threshold question of whether color, by itself, is *per se* unregistrable, the question of functionality arose because the party opposing registration argued that granting trademark protection to colors would have an anticompetitive effect, in that it would deplete the color choices available to competitors of the registrant. In rejecting that argument, the Court observed that "the trademark doctrine of 'functionality' normally would seem available to prevent the anticompetitive consequences" of color depletion,[75] and that a diminishing array of color choices would not hinder competition in cases in which color contributed nothing to the functionality of the product. The Court appeared to endorse the prevailing judicial interpretations of aesthetic functionality by citing *Deere, Brunswick Corp.,* and *Nor-Am Chemical,*[76] and added:

> The Restatement (Third) of Unfair Competition adds that, if a design's "aesthetic value" lies in its ability to "confer a significant benefit that cannot practically be duplicated by the use of alternative designs," then the design is "functional." The "ultimate test of aesthetic functionality," it explains, "is whether the recognition of trademark rights would significantly hinder competition."

> The upshot is that, where a color serves a significant nontrademark function — whether to distinguish a heart pill from a digestive medicine or to satisfy the "noble instinct for giving the right touch of beauty to common

---

[72] *Id.* at 1530–32 (quoting TTAB).

[73] *Id.* at 1530.

[74] *Id.* at 1531, *quoting In re* Morton-Norwich Prods., Inc., 671 F.2d 1332, 1339 (C.C.P.A. 1982) (emphasis in original). *See also* Nor-Am Chem. v. O.M. Scott & Sons Co., 4 U.S.P.Q.2d 1316, 1320 (E.D. Pa. 1987) (applying competitive necessity test to conclude that color blue was functional for fertilizer); *cf.* Warner Lambert Co. v. McCrory's Corp., 718 F. Supp. 389, 396 (D.N.J. 1989) (holding that color is functional for mouthwash, because customers associate certain colors with certain flavors).

[75] Qualitex Co. v. Jacobson Prods. Co., 514 U.S. 159, 169 (1995).

[76] *Id.* at 169–70.

and necessary things," courts will examine whether its use as a mark would permit one competitor (or a group) to interfere with legitimate (nontrademark-related) competition through actual or potential exclusive use of an important product ingredient.[77]

Six years after *Qualitex*, dictum in *TrafFix* confirmed that "[i]t is proper to inquire into a 'significant non-reputation-related disadvantage' in cases of aesthetic functionality."[78] The *TrafFix* opinion specifically refers to this as the "competitive necessity" test.[79]

Even after *Qualitex*, aesthetic functionality remains controversial. Leading commentator and treatise author J. Thomas McCarthy continues to reject the doctrine, arguing that purely ornamental features of trade dress should receive trademark protection when they acquire secondary meaning, and that consumer preferences as to ornamentation should not alter this analysis.[80] Aesthetic functionality was squarely rejected by the Fifth Circuit in 2008.[81]

In those courts that have expressly recognized aesthetic functionality, post-*Qualitex* decisions have revealed some confusion over what test to apply to determine the functionality of aesthetic features.[82] In *Publications Int'l, Ltd. v. Landoll, Inc.*,[83] the Seventh Circuit held that the use of gold-colored gilding on the edges of cookbook pages was aesthetically functional because "[g]old connotes opulence," and is a color commonly used both in food decoration and bookbinding.[84] Calling this "a prime example of aesthetic functionality,"[85] the court observed: "[I]f consumers derive a value from the fact that a product looks a certain way that is distinct from the value of knowing at a glance who made it, then it is a nonappropriable feature of the product."[86] Several years later, in *Eco Mfg., LLC v. Honeywell Int'l, Inc.*,[87] the Seventh Circuit affirmed a district court's finding that the round shape of a thermostat was likely to be functional. Although the district court expressly held that the shape was aesthetically functional because "a substantial minority of customers" preferred the round shape,[88] the court of appeal court found it insufficient that *some* consumers preferred the round appearance,

---

[77] *Id.* at 169–70 (citing RESTATEMENT (THIRD) OF UNFAIR COMPETITION § 17, cmt. c., at 175–76 (1993) (additional citations omitted)).

[78] TrafFix Devices, Inc. v. Marketing Displays, Inc., 532 U.S. 23, 33 (2001).

[79] *Id.*

[80] J. THOMAS MCCARTHY, MCCARTHY ON TRADEMARKS AND UNFAIR COMPETITION § 7:81 (4th ed. 2014).

[81] Board of Supervisors for Louisiana State Univ. v. Smack Apparel Co., 550 F.3d 465, 487–88 (5th Cir. 2008).

[82] *See* Abercrombie & Fitch Stores, Inc. v. American Eagle Outfitters, Inc., 280 F.3d 619, 641–45 (6th Cir. 2002).

[83] 164 F.3d 337 (7th Cir. 1998).

[84] *Id.* at 342.

[85] *Id.* at 339.

[86] *Id.*

[87] 357 F.3d 649 (7th Cir. 2003).

[88] Eco Mfg. LLC v. Honeywell Int'l, Inc., 295 F. Supp. 2d 854, 872 (S.D. Ind. 2003), *aff'd*, 357 F.3d 649 (7th Cir. 2003).

and noted that such a broad understanding of aesthetic functionality "would destroy the protection of trade dress." Resting its analysis only partly on aesthetic functionality, the appellate court suggested that the round shape might be functional because it (1) was easier for some people to use, (2) caused fewer injuries, or (3) better matched other decorative items. While these advantages did not establish that the round shape was *essential* to the thermostat, the court concluded that they could affect its price or quality.[89]

Post-*Qualitex*, the Eleventh Circuit held that functionality barred trademark protection for the color, shape, and size of flash-frozen ice-cream pellets. With regard to colors, the court found that a significant non-reputation-related disadvantage would arise if trademark law gave one competitor the exclusive right to use certain colors to indicate the flavors of its ice cream.[90] The court also applied the "competitive necessity" test to the color, shape, and size of the ice-cream pellets, treating all three as aesthetically functional aspects of the product's design, and essential to the defendant's ability to compete in the flash-frozen ice cream market.[91]

Post-*Qualitex* decisions from courts in the Second Circuit, which had embraced aesthetic functionality even before *Qualitex*,[92] have reflected some confusion as well. In a muddled opinion issued immediately after *Qualitex*, the Court of Appeals held in *Knitwaves, Inc. v. Lollytogs, Ltd.*[93] that granting trade dress protection to a decorative design on a sweater would not hinder competition because alternative designs were available, but it declined to grant such protection because "the designs were not primarily intended as source identification."[94] A later Second Circuit opinion endorsed aesthetic functionality without mentioning intent, citing *Qualitex*'s "non-reputation-related disadvantage" formulation."[95]

In 2012, the Second Circuit skirted the question of aesthetic functionality in fashion design. In *Christian Louboutin S.A. v. Yves Saint Laurent Am., Inc.*,[96] the district court refused to recognize a red sole as a trademark for the plaintiff's shoes because, in the context of fashion design, color by itself can never serve as a trademark due to its aesthetic function. On appeal, the Second Circuit rejected this *per se* rule, but declined to decide whether the red color was aesthetically functional. Instead, because the defendant's shoes were *entirely* red, the court ruled that, in the absence of a contrasting upper, the plaintiff's red soles lacked secondary meaning.[97]

---

[89] 357 F.3d at 654–55.

[90] Dippin' Dots, Inc. v. Frosty Bites Dist., LLC, 369 F.3d 1197, 1203 (11th Cir. 2004).

[91] *Id.* at 1206–07.

[92] *See, e.g.*, Wallace Int'l Silversmiths, Inc. v. Godinger Silver Art Co., 916 F.2d 76, 79–81 (2d Cir. 1990).

[93] 71 F.3d 996, 1006 (2d Cir. 1995).

[94] *Id.* at 1009. The court's requirement that trade dress be *intended* as source designation, rather than that it actually function as source identification, is without foundation in Supreme Court case law.

[95] Yurman Design, Inc. v. PAJ, Inc., 262 F.3d 101, 116 (2d Cir. 2001).

[96] 778 F. Supp. 2d 445 (S.D.N.Y. 2011), *aff'd in part and rev'd in part*, 696 F.3d 206 (2d Cir. 2012).

[97] 696 F.3d at 224.

Confusion also reigns in the Ninth Circuit, where pre-*Qualitex* decisions had recognized aesthetic functionality but had vacillated in determining its scope.[98] A 2001 opinion (issued shortly after *TrafFix*) flatly held that functional features are limited to those that have a utilitarian aspect, and thus do not include features that contribute only to a product's aesthetic appeal.[99] In contrast, a 2006 opinion endorsed a broader view, applying the doctrine to "product features that serve an aesthetic purpose wholly independent of any source-identifying function."[100] Citing *TrafFix*, the court adopted the test of "whether protection of the feature as a trademark would impose a significant non-reputation-related competitive disadvantage."[101]

Although the Sixth Circuit has yet to formally recognize aesthetic functionality, in *Maker's Mark Distillery, Inc. v. Diageo N.A., Inc.*,[102] the court held that the red dripping wax seal on the plaintiff's bourbon bottles was not functional. The court applied two different tests for functionality — the "comparable alternatives" test, which asks whether protecting the feature would leave "a variety of comparable alternative features" for competitors, and the "effective competition" test, which inquires whether protecting the feature would "hinder the ability of another manufacturer to compete effectively." Under either test, the court concluded, the red wax seal was not functional.

One aspect of aesthetic functionality is uncontroversial. Even where individual elements of a design are aesthetically functional, it is well-settled that the functionality test must be applied to the design as a whole. Thus, while individual design elements may be functional, the total combination of those elements may still be subject to trademark protection.[103]

[2]   Trademark Subject Matter

Section 45 of the Lanham Act defines a trademark as "any word, name, symbol, or device, or any combination thereof" which is used by a person "to identify and distinguish his or her goods, including a unique product, from those manufactured or sold by others and to indicate the source of the goods, even if that source is unknown."[104] The federal definition of a service mark is similar, substituting "services" where appropriate, and adding one additional sentence:

---

[98] J. THOMAS MCCARTHY, MCCARTHY ON TRADEMARKS AND UNFAIR COMPETITION § 7:80 (4th ed. 2009).

[99] *See* Clicks Billiards, Inc. v. Sixshooters, Inc., 251 F.3d 1252, 1260 (9th Cir. 2001) (collecting cases). *But see* Vuitton et Fils S.A. v. J. Young Enters., Inc., 644 F.2d 769, 774 (9th Cir. 1981) (suggesting that Ninth Circuit precedent would still prevent "the use of a trademark to monopolize a design feature which, in itself and apart from its identification of source, improves the usefulness or appeal of the object it adorns").

[100] Au-Tomotive Gold, Inc. v. Volkswagen of America, Inc., 457 F.3d 1062, 1073 (9th Cir. 2006).

[101] *Id.* at 1072 (citing both *Qualitex* and *TrafFix*). The opinion relies heavily on *TrafFix*, even though that case was not cited by either of the parties. *Id.* at 1070–72.

[102] 679 F.3d 410, 418 (6th Cir. 2012).

[103] *Dippin' Dots*, 369 F.3d at 1206–07; *Clicks Billiards*, 251 F.3d at 1259; *Landoll*, 164 F.3d at 342; Jeffrey Milstein, Inc. v. Greger, Lawlor, Roth, Inc., 58 F.3d 27, 32 (2d Cir. 1995); Fuddruckers, Inc. v. Doc's B.R. Others, Inc., 826 F.2d 837, 841 (9th Cir. 1987).

[104] 15 U.S.C. § 1127.

Titles, character names, and other distinctive features of radio or television programs may be registered as service marks notwithstanding that they, or the programs, may advertise the goods of the sponsor.[105]

The concept of a trademark or service mark under common law dispenses with the requirement of use in interstate commerce, but otherwise parallels the Lanham Act definition. Thus, common-law marks must be capable of distinguishing the origin of goods or services.

[a]   Distinctiveness

Courts have developed a "spectrum of distinctiveness" to describe the ability of a particular mark to perform an origin-identifying function, as well the relative strength of one mark compared to other marks. Originating at common law, the spectrum of distinctiveness applies under the Lanham Act as well. In descending order of strength, the categories of protectible marks are categorized as (1) arbitrary or fanciful, (2) suggestive, and (3) descriptive. Marks falling into the first two categories are considered inherently distinctive, meaning they may be protected without a showing of secondary meaning, whereas descriptive marks are protectible only if they acquire distinctiveness through secondary meaning.[106] A fourth category consists of generic terms, which are so highly descriptive that they are incapable of acquiring distinctiveness even after prolonged use. Therefore, although such terms are often referred to as "generic marks," as a matter of both state and federal law they are incapable of serving as either trademarks or service marks. The classification of a mark is a question of fact.[107]

Classification of a mark into one of these four categories is an important step in determining whether and under what circumstances it is eligible for protection under state or federal law, and can also be important in determining the relative strength of the mark, an important factor in determining the likelihood of confusion. Classification is easier in some cases than in others. For example, "ivory" would be generic as applied to a product made from elephant tusks, but it is either arbitrary or suggestive as applied to soap; the word "escalator" was originally fanciful or suggestive, but has since become generic; and "aspirin" was fanciful before it became generic.[108]

In some cases, a trademark proponent will adopt an alternate spelling for a descriptive or generic term. Where the two spellings are pronounced the same way, courts have treated these terms as their descriptive or generic equivalents.[109]

---

[105] *Id.*

[106] Secondary meaning is discussed in § 5C[2][a][iii](b).

[107] Bristol-Myers Squibb Co. v. McNeill-P.P.C., Inc., 973 F.2d 1033, 1039–40 (2d Cir. 1992).

[108] Abercrombie & Fitch Co. v. Hunting World, Inc., 537 F.2d 4, 9 nn. 6–8 (2d Cir. 1976).

[109] *See, e.g.*, Nupla Corp. v. IXL Mfg. Co., 114 F.3d 191, 196 (Fed. Cir. 1997) ("Cush-N-Grip"); Soweco, Inc. v. Shell Oil Co., 617 F.2d 1178, 1186 n. 24 (5th Cir. 1980); Miller Brewing Co. v. G. Heileman Brewing Co., 561 F.2d 75, 81 (7th Cir. 1977) ("Lite"); Hesmer Foods, Inc. v. Campbell Soup Co., 346 F.2d 356, 358 (7th Cir. 1965) ("Beanee"); Keller Prods., Inc. v. Rubber Linings Corp., 213 F.2d 382, 385–86 (7th Cir. 1954) (collecting cases).

In the case of a "composite mark" — that is, a mark which consists of several separable components, which may be words, designs, or any combination thereof — the distinctiveness of the mark must be determined by considering the mark as a whole, rather than by considering the distinctiveness of each individual component. Thus, for example, it is possible for a composite mark to be inherently distinctive (*e.g.*, arbitrary or suggestive) even if each of its individual components is merely descriptive.[110] A few courts, however, have held to the contrary.[111]

[i]   Arbitrary or Fanciful

The strongest marks are those that are either arbitrary or fanciful. Both are considered inherently distinctive, and thus are protectible without a showing of secondary meaning.[112]

Fanciful marks are coined terms that have no commonplace or dictionary meaning at all.[113] Examples include "Kodak" for photographic equipment and supplies,[114] "Xerox" for copying equipment and supplies,[115] "Polaroid" for camera equipment,[116] and "Exxon" for oil and gas products and services.[117]

Arbitrary marks are words in common usage, with dictionary meanings that do not in any respect describe the goods or services to which the words are attached.[118] Like fanciful marks, arbitrary marks are inherently distinctive. Unlike a fanciful mark, however, "an arbitrary mark is distinctive only within its product market and entitled to little or no protection outside of that area,"[119] because the determination of arbitrariness depends on the nature of the goods or services to which the mark is applied. Because an arbitrary mark is not a coined word, it has a commonplace meaning that is unrelated to its origin-indicating function;[120] the distinctiveness of an arbitrary mark arises from the fact that its commonplace meaning has no relationship to that product or service.[121] Thus, "Apple" is arbitrary for computers, but would be generic for apples, and descriptive for apple-flavored candy, liquor, or pies.

---

[110] Union Carbide Corp. v. Ever-Ready, Inc., 531 F.2d 366, 379 (7th Cir. 1976); *see, e.g.*, California Cooler, Inc. v. Loretto Winery, Ltd., 774 F.2d 1451, 1455–56 (9th Cir. 1985); Macia v. Microsoft Corp., 335 F. Supp. 2d 507, 513 (D. Vt. 2004), *aff'd*, 164 Fed. Appx. 17 (2d. Cir. 2006); W.W.W. Pharm. Co. v. Gillette Co., 808 F. Supp. 1013, 1022 (S.D.N.Y. 1992), *aff'd*, 984 F.2d 567 (2d Cir. 1993). *See generally* McCarthy on Trademarks and Unfair Competition § 11:26 (2009).

[111] *See, e.g.*, National Conf. of Bar Examiners v. Multistate Legal Studies, Inc., 692 F.2d 478, 488 (7th Cir. 1982).

[112] Secondary meaning is discussed in § 5C[2][a][iii](b).

[113] Kellogg Co. v. Toucan Golf, Inc., 337 F.3d 616, 624 (6th Cir. 2003).

[114] *Id.*

[115] *Id.*

[116] Polaroid Corp. v. Polaraid, Inc., 319 F.2d 830 (7th Cir. 1963).

[117] Sara Lee Corp. v. Kayser-Roth Corp., 81 F.3d 455, 464 (4th Cir. 1996).

[118] *See* Moose Creek, Inc. v. Abercrombie & Fitch Co., 331 F. Supp. 2d 1214, 1222 (C.D. Cal.), *aff'd*, 114 Fed. Appx. 921 (9th Cir. 2004).

[119] Kellogg Co. v. Toucan Golf, Inc., 337 F.3d 616, 626 (6th Cir. 2003).

[120] Abercrombie & Fitch Co. v. Hunting World, Inc., 537 F.2d 4, 11 (2d Cir. 1976).

[121] *Kellogg*, 337 F.3d at 626.

Other examples of arbitrary word marks include "Camel" for cigarettes,[122] "Toucan" for cereal,[123] "Black & White" for scotch whiskey,[124] and "Domino" for sugar.[125]

Non-word marks may be arbitrary or fanciful as well. In determining whether a design is inherently distinctive, some courts have inquired "whether it was a 'common' basic shape or design, whether it was unique or unusual in a particular field, whether it was a mere refinement of a commonly adopted and well-known form of ornamentation for a particular class of goods viewed by the public as a dress or ornamentation for the goods, or whether it was capable of creating a commercial impression distinct from the accompanying words."[126]

[ii]   Suggestive

Like arbitrary and fanciful marks, suggestive marks are considered inherently distinctive, and thus are eligible for trademark protection without a showing of a secondary meaning.[127]

Suggestive marks are considered strong marks, but less so than arbitrary and fanciful marks. This category of marks was not recognized at early common law, but was developed by courts in response to the common-law rule that descriptive marks could not serve as trademarks,[128] a rule that (under section 5 of the 1905 Trademark Act[129]) also prevented descriptive marks from being federally registered until their owner could demonstrate ten years of exclusive use.[130] In order to avoid denying trademark protection to marks that were only somewhat descriptive, courts categorized these marks as suggestive rather than descriptive.[131]

Having created the "suggestive" category, however, courts found it difficult to define.[132] Suggestive marks have a descriptive aspect, but differ from descriptive marks in that they merely suggest, rather than describe, certain qualities of the goods or services to which they are attached. A suggestive mark only indirectly

---

[122] Daddy's Junky Music Stores, Inc. v. Big Daddy's Family Music Center, 109 F.3d 275, 280–81 (6th Cir. 1997).

[123] *Kellogg*, 337 F.3d at 626.

[124] Fleischmann Distilling Corp. v. Maier Brewing Co., 314 F.2d 149 (9th Cir. 1963).

[125] Amstar Corp. v. Domino's Pizza, Inc., 615 F.2d 252, 260 (11th Cir. 1980) (noting, however, that the mark may originally have been descriptive with regard to sugar, because the plaintiff at one time sold sugar in domino-shaped pieces).

[126] Seabrook Foods, Inc. v. Bar-Well Foods, Ltd., 568 F.2d 1342, 1344 (C.C.P.A. 1977).

[127] Blinded Veterans Ass'n v. Blinded American Veterans Found., 872 F.2d 1035, 1040 (D.C. Cir. 1989). Secondary meaning is discussed in § 5C[2][a][iii](b).

[128] *See, e.g.*, William R. Warner & Co. v. Eli Lilly & Co., 265 U.S. 526, 529 (1924); *In re* Anti-Cori-Zine Chem. Co., 34 App. D.C. 191 (1909).

[129] 33 Stat. 726.

[130] *See* Abercrombie & Fitch Co. v. Hunting World, Inc., 537 F.2d 4, 11 (2d Cir. 1976); Pinaud, Inc. v. Huebschman, 27 F.2d 531, 535 (E.D.N.Y.), *aff'd*, 27 F.2d 538 (2d Cir. 1928).

[131] *Abercrombie & Fitch*, 537 F.2d at 10.

[132] *Id.*

conveys an impression of the goods or services to which it is attached,[133] and thus "requires the observer or listener to use imagination and perception to determine the nature of the goods."[134] Most courts have adopted some variation of this "imagination" test to identify suggestive marks and distinguish them from descriptive marks.[135]

Examples of marks that courts have determined to be suggestive include "Goliath" for wood pencils (connoting "a large size"),[136] "Safari" for ice chests, axes, tents, and smoking tobacco (connoting wilderness expeditions),[137] "Roach Motel" for insect traps (connoting housing for roaches),[138] "Q-Tips" for cotton swabs (connoting cuteness and, therefore, babies),[139] "L'eggs" for women's hosiery (connoting attractiveness and legginess),[140] and "Penguin" (for refrigerators).[141]

[iii]   Descriptive

A descriptive mark specifically describes a quality, function, characteristic, or ingredient of a product or service.[142] In contrast to suggestive marks, it takes no imagination to understand what characteristics of a product or service are being conveyed by a descriptive mark. Examples of descriptive marks include "Rich 'N Chips" for chocolate chip cookies,[143] "Rocktober" for an October rock music broadcast,[144] "After Tan" for post-tanning lotion,[145] "Yellow Pages" for a phone directory with yellow-colored pages,[146] and such general laudatory terms as "Best," "Superior," and "Preferred."[147] One court has described "Coca-Cola" as "the paradigm of a descriptive mark that has acquired a secondary meaning."[148]

---

[133] Blinded Veterans Ass'n v. Blinded American Veterans Found., 872 F.2d 1035, 1040 (D.C. Cir. 1989).

[134] Induct-O-Matic Corp. v. Inductotherm Corp., 747 F.2d 358 (6th Cir. 1984).

[135] *See, e.g.*, *Blinded Veterans Ass'n*, 872 F.2d at 1040; Union Carbide Corp. v. Ever-Ready, Inc., 531 F.2d 366, 378–80 (7th Cir. 1976); General Shoe Corp. v. Rosen, 111 F.2d 95, 98 (4th Cir. 1940) (per curiam); Stix Prods., Inc. v. United Merchants & Mfrs., Inc., 295 F. Supp. 479, 488 (S.D.N.Y. 1968). Several courts have adopted a six-factor test suggested by Professor McCarthy. McCarthy on Trademarks and Unfair Competition § 11:71; *see e.g.*, DeGidio v. West Group Corp., 355 F.3d 506, 510–11 (6th Cir. 2004).

[136] *DeGidio*, 355 F.3d at 510–11.

[137] Abercrombie & Fitch Co. v. Hunting World, Inc., 537 F.2d 4, 14 (2d Cir. 1976).

[138] American Home Prods. Corp. v. Johnson Chem. Co., 589 F.2d 103, 106 (2d Cir. 1978) (noting that the mark might even be arbitrary).

[139] Q-Tips, Inc. v. Johnson & Johnson, 206 F.2d 144 (3d Cir. 1953).

[140] Sara Lee Corp. v. Kayser-Roth Corp., 81 F.3d 455, 465 (4th Cir. 1996).

[141] Union Nat'l Bank of Texas v. Union Nat'l Bank of Texas, 909 F.2d 839, 845 (5th Cir. 1990).

[142] Induct-O-Matic Corp. v. Inductotherm Corp., 747 F.2d 358, 362 (6th Cir. 1984); Blinded Veterans Ass'n v. Blinded Am. Veterans Found., 872 F.2d 1035, 1039–40 (D.C. Cir. 1989).

[143] Application of Keebler Co., 479 F.2d 1405 (C.C.P.A. 1973).

[144] Metromedia, Inc. v. American Broadcasting Cos., 210 U.S.P.Q. 21 (S.D.N.Y. 1980).

[145] Sara Lee Corp. v. Kayser-Roth Corp., 81 F.3d 455, 464 (4th Cir. 1996).

[146] *Id.*

[147] Champions Golf Club, Inc. v. The Champions Golf Club, Inc., 78 F.3d 1111, 1117 (6th Cir. 1996).

[148] *Sara Lee*, 81 F.3d at 464. Secondary meaning is discussed in § 5C[2][a][iii](b).

(a)   Common Law

Traditionally, under the common law of trademarks, descriptive marks were considered incapable of serving as trademarks.[149] It was thought that withdrawing a descriptive term from general circulation for the exclusive use of one competitor would impair the ability of other competitors to describe their own goods or services. However, it is now well settled that descriptive marks can be protected as trademarks under state and federal trademark and unfair competition laws once they have achieved distinctiveness in the minds of consumers — that is, once they acquire secondary meaning.[150]

(b)   Secondary Meaning

A descriptive mark, while not inherently distinctive, may nonetheless acquire distinctiveness through use, if the public comes to recognize the mark as an indication of source, thus giving it "secondary meaning." The question of whether a mark has acquired secondary meaning is a question of fact.[151]

For a descriptive mark to have sufficient secondary meaning to serve as a source indicator, it is not necessary that the public be able to identify the source by name; "[i]t is sufficient if the public is aware that the product comes from a single, though anonymous, source."[152] However, it is essential that "the primary significance of the term in the minds of the consuming public is not the product but the producer."[153]

Under both state and federal law, the existence of secondary meaning is determined by considering a number of factors. Although the precise formulation varies by jurisdiction, the factors tend to be similar. For example, the Ninth Circuit considers: survey evidence; direct consumer testimony; exclusivity, manner and length of use of the mark; amount and manner of advertising; amount of sales and number of customers; established place in the market; and proof of intentional copying by the defendant.[154] Although the importance of each secondary meaning factor may vary from case to case, survey evidence often provides the strongest indication of consumer recognition and association.[155]

Where several parties have used the same descriptive mark in the same geographic area, priority will depend not on which party was the first to use the

---

[149] *See, e.g.*, Armstrong Paint & Varnish Works v. Nu-Enamel Corp., 305 U.S. 315, 334 (1938); William R. Warner & Co. v. Eli Lilly & Co., 265 U.S. 526, 529 (1924); Delaware & Hudson Canal Co. v. Clark, 80 U.S. (13 Wall.) 311, 323 (1872); *In re* Anti-Cori-Zine Chem. Co., 34 App. D.C. 191 (1909); *see generally* Blinded Veterans Ass'n v. Blinded Am. Veterans Found., 872 F.2d 1035, 1041 n.11 (D.C. Cir. 1989).

[150] *See, e.g.*, Colston Inv. Co. v. Home Supply Co., 74 S.W.3d 759, 764–65 (Ky. Ct. App. 2001); Yocono's Restaurant v. Yocono, 651 N.E.2d 1347, 100 Ohio App. 3d 11, 17–18 (Ohio Ct. App. 1994); Zapata Corp. v. Zapata Trading Int'l, Inc., 841 S.W.2d 45, 47–48 (Tex. App. 1992).

[151] Japan Telecom, Inc. v. Japan Telecom Am., Inc., 287 F.3d 866, 873 (9th Cir. 2002).

[152] Union Carbide Corp. v. Ever-Ready, Inc., 531 F.2d 366, 380 (7th Cir. 1976) (citing Spangler Candy Co. v. Crystal Pure Candy Co., 353 F.2d 641, 647 (7th Cir. 1965)).

[153] Kellogg Co. v. Nat'l Biscuit Co., 305 U.S. 111 (1938).

[154] Filipino Yellow Pages, Inc. v. Asian Journal Publ'n, Inc., 198 F.3d 1143, 1151 (9th Cir. 1999).

[155] Levi Strauss & Co. v. Blue Bell, Inc., 778 F.2d 1352, 1358 (9th Cir. 1985).

mark in that market, but which party's mark was the first to acquire distinctiveness (secondary meaning) in that market.[156]

Just as a descriptive term may acquire distinctiveness over time, it may also lose that distinctiveness over time. If the secondary meaning of a descriptive mark weakens, so that the public no longer perceives it as an origin indicator, the mark may lose its trademark status, unless it is a federally registered mark that has become incontestable.[157]

Descriptive marks may describe any aspect of a good or service. As discussed below, personal names are typically treated as descriptive marks.[158] So, too, are geographic indicators.[159]

[iv]   Generic Terms

A generic term is one that is commonly used as the name or description of a kind of goods.[160] A generic term may be synonymous with the good or service itself (*e.g.*, "apple" is generic for apples), or may describe a broader category to which the particular good or service belongs (e.g., "fruit" is also generic for apples). It is sometimes said that a generic term describes the *genus* of which a particular merchant's product is a *species*. A term may sometimes be generic if it names a distinctive *characteristic* of the genus of which the product in question is a species; for example, "Matchbox" was held to be generic for toy vehicles because they were sold in matchbox-sized boxes.[161]

Generic terms are *per se* ineligible for trademark protection under either state or federal law. Unlike descriptive terms, which can serve as trademarks if and when they acquire secondary meaning, generic terms are, as a matter of law, incapable of serving as indicators of source.[162]

Examples of generic terms include "cereal" for breakfast cereal,[163] "Bermuda" for shorts,[164] "Light Beer" for low-calorie beer,[165] "Crab House" for a restaurant

---

[156] Investacorp, Inc. v. Arabian Inv. Banking Corp., 931 F.2d 1519, 1524 (11th Cir. 1991); Grupo Gigante S.A. de C.V. v. Dallo & Co., 119 F. Supp. 2d 1083, 1092, *aff'd*, 391 F.3d 1088 (9th Cir. 2004).

[157] Incontestability is discussed in § 5E[4].

[158] *See* § 5C[2][b][ii].

[159] *See, e.g.*, Madison Reprographics v. Cook's Reprographics, 552 N.W.2d 440 (Wis. Ct. App. 1996).

[160] Induct-O-Matic Corp. v. Inductotherm Corp., 747 F.2d 358, 362 (6th Cir. 1984); *accord*, G. Heileman Brewing Co. v. Anheuser-Busch, Inc., 873 F.2d 985, 997 (7th Cir. 1989); Dayton Progress Corp. v. Lane Punch Corp., 917 F.2d 836, 839 (4th Cir. 1990).

Although generic terms are sometimes referred to as "common descriptive" terms, they must be distinguished from the category of descriptive terms, discussed above, which are also called "merely descriptive" terms. Blinded Veterans Ass'n v. Blinded Am. Veterans Found., 872 F.2d 1035, 1039 n.4 (D.C. Cir. 1989).

[161] Sara Lee Corp. v. Kayser-Roth Corp., 81 F.3d 455, 464 n.10 (4th Cir. 1996).

[162] Abercrombie & Fitch Co. v. Hunting World, Inc., 537 F.2d 4, 9 (2d Cir. 1976).

[163] Kellogg Co. v. Toucan Golf, Inc., 337 F.3d 616, 624 (6th Cir. 2003).

[164] *Abercrombie & Fitch*, 537 F.2d at 13.

[165] *Sara Lee*, 81 F.3d at 464.

that serves crab,[166] and "Multistate Bar Examination" for an attorney competency exam used by many states.[167]

A term may be generic for one class of goods, but not for another. For example, "apple" is generic for apples, but it is arbitrary for computers.[168] Conversely, a term may be generic with respect to more than one category of product or service. For example, "safari" is generic not only for an expedition into the African wilderness, but also for a type of clothing that was originally associated with such activities but later became popular with a broader group of consumers.[169] A term may be generic even if there are other synonyms for the product or service.[170]

Although many generic terms are nouns, other types of words, such as verbs[171] or adjectives,[172] can be generic as well. And while case law addressing genericism most frequently involves word marks, designs can also be generic.[173]

Under both state and federal law, a protected trademark will lose its protected status if it becomes generic, that is, if the public begins to use the mark as a synonym for the product itself. A generic mark cannot be federally registered, and if a mark becomes generic after it has been registered, its registration can be cancelled.[174] Genericism is a question of fact.[175] Even diligent efforts to "police" a mark — that is, to maintain the trademark status of the mark by discouraging the public from using the term generically and by taking prompt action against infringers — can be insufficient to prevent the public from adopting the mark as a generic term for the product or service.[176]

Marks associated with unique or patented products or services, and marks that have been featured in particularly strong advertising campaigns, run a particular risk of becoming generic. The term "aspirin," for example, was originally a trademark until, through popular usage, it become the generic term for the pain

---

[166] Hunt Masters, Inc. v. Landry's Seafood Rest., Inc., 240 F.3d 251 (4th Cir. 2001).

[167] National Conference of Bar Examiners v. Multistate Legal Studies, Inc., 692 F.2d 478, 488 (7th Cir. 1982).

[168] For other examples, see Self-Realization Fellowship Church v. Ananda Church of Self-Realization, 59 F.3d 902, 909–10 (2d Cir. 1995); H-D Michigan, Inc. v. Top Quality Serv., Inc., 496 F.3d 755, 761–62 (7th Cir. 2007).

[169] Abercrombie & Fitch Co. v. Hunting World, Inc., 537 F.2d 4, 11–12 (2d Cir. 1976).

[170] Blinded Veterans Ass'n v. Blinded Am. Veterans Found., 872 F.2d 1035, 1041 (D.C. Cir. 1989).

[171] Although no court has held "Xerox" to be generic, at one time the widespread use of this term as a verb meaning "to photocopy" posed a risk of genericide. See Union Nat'l Bank v. Union Nat'l Bank, 909 F.2d 839, 845 n.15 (5th Cir. 1990). "Park 'n Fly" presents a close question as well. See Park 'N Fly, Inc. v. Dollar Park and Fly, Inc., 718 F.2d 327, 330–31 (9th Cir. 1984), rev'd on other grounds, 465 U.S. 1078 (1984).

[172] See, e.g., Rudolph Int'l, Inc. v. Realys, Inc., 482 F.3d 1195, 1198–99 (9th Cir. 2007).

[173] Kendall-Jackson Winery, Ltd. v. E. & J. Gallo Winery, 150 F.3d 1042, 1048–49 (9th Cir. 1998) (grape leaf design for wine).

[174] See § 5E[2][e][i] (registration), § 5E[3][d][iv](a) (cancellation).

[175] Bath & Body Works, Inc. v. Luzier Personalized Cosmetics, Inc., 76 F.3d 743, 748 (6th Cir. 1996).

[176] See Ty, Inc. v. Softbelly's, Inc., 353 F.3d 528, 532 (7th Cir. 2003); King-Seeley Thermos Co. v. Aladdin Indus., Inc., 321 F.2d 577 (2d Cir. 1963).

medication to which it was attached.[177] Other former trademarks that became generic include "yo-yo," "trampoline," "brassiere," "cellophane," "escalator," "shredded wheat," "dry ice," and "thermos."[178]

[b]   Words and Slogans

[i]   In General

Any word or combination of words may qualify as a trademark if it is not generic for the goods or services and it is either inherently distinctive (fanciful, arbitrary, or suggestive), or it has acquired distinctiveness ("secondary meaning"). In addition to brand names and company names, slogans may qualify for trademark protection. Although many slogans are descriptive and therefore require secondary meaning to qualify,[179] other slogans may be considered suggestive or arbitrary. Examples of slogans that qualify for trademark protection are "Just Do It" for athletic shoes and apparel,[180] "Where There's Life, There's Bud" for beer,[181] "The Greatest Show on Earth" for a circus,[182] and "Don't Leave Home Without It" for a credit card.[183]

[ii]   Personal Names

Because a personal name is not considered to be inherently distinctive, a mark consisting of a personal name is generally treated as a descriptive mark that can be protected only upon a showing of secondary meaning.[184] Nonetheless, personal names can be strong marks. "McDonald's" for fast food restaurants exemplifies a personal name mark with extremely strong secondary meaning. Other examples are "Gallo" for wine, "Avery Dennison" for office products, "Howard Johnson" for restaurants and hotels, "Bacardi" for rum, "Liz Claiborne" and "Levi Strauss" for clothing, and "Sardi's" and "Wolfgang Puck" for restaurants.

For a personal name to serve as a mark, it must be associated with the offering of goods or services to the public (and not perceived simply as the identity of an individual), and it must have secondary meaning. For a personal name to have secondary meaning, it is not enough that the public perceives the product or service as emanating from a person that has that particular name; the public must have the impression that this product or service comes from the same source

---

[177] Bayer Co. v. United Drug Co., 272 F. 505 (S.D.N.Y. 1921).

[178] King-Seeley Thermos Co. v. Aladdin Indus., Inc., 321 F.2d 577 (2d Cir. 1963). The court held, however, that "Thermos" (with a capital "T") remains protected.

[179] See Vincent v. City Colleges of Chicago, 485 F.3d 919, 925 (7th Cir. 2007) (phrase "Smart Foreclosure Buying" was descriptive of real estate education and required secondary meaning).

[180] Nike, Inc. v. Just Did It Enterprises, 6 F.3d 1225, 1226–27 (7th Cir. 1993).

[181] Chemical Corp. v. Anheuser-Busch, Inc., 306 F.2d 433, 434–36 (5th Cir. 1962).

[182] Ringling Bros.-Barnum & Bailey Combined Shows, Inc. v. Utah Div. of Travel Development, 170 F.3d 449, 451 (4th Cir. 1999).

[183] American Express Co. v. CFK, Inc., 947 F. Supp. 310, 312 (E.D. Mich. 1996).

[184] See, e.g., E. & J. Gallo Winery v. Gallo Cattle Co., 967 F.2d 1280, 1288 (9th Cir. 1992); Marker Int'l v. DeBruler, 844 F.2d 763 (10th Cir. 1988); Buscemi's, Inc. v. Anthony Buscemi Delicatessen, 96 Mich. App. 2d 714, 717–18 (Mich. Ct. App. 1980). But see Peaceable Planet, Inc. v. Ty, Inc., 362 F.3d 986, 988–90 (7th Cir. 2004) (holding personal names are not always descriptive marks).

whenever it is offered under that name.[185] Thus, for example, even though the name "McDonald's" is a common surname, the public perceives the name "McDonald's" on a fast-food restaurant as an indicator that this restaurant is affiliated with all of the other McDonald's fast-food restaurants, and not as an indicator that one of the many people having the surname McDonald happens to own this particular restaurant.

Individual entertainers and musical groups who establish secondary meaning for their names (including real names, nicknames, and stage names) are entitled to register them on the Principal Register as service marks for their entertainment services (and also as trademarks, if they engage in merchandising).[186] For a musician or musical group to register a name as a mark for sound recordings, the name must have been used on more than one recording, so that it signifies to the public that the entertainer is the source of any recordings that bear his or her name.[187] A similar rule requires authors to use their names on multiple works of authorship in order to qualify for registration.[188] Professional athletes must also show secondary meaning to obtain registration.[189]

In some cases, a mark may have two meanings, only one of which is a personal name.[190] For federal registration purposes, the "primary" significance of the mark is determinative,[191] and there is authority, albeit limited, for applying the same test under the common law.[192]

At one time courts recognized a virtually absolute right to use one's own name as a trademark.[193] Today, however, most courts hold that the ordinary rules of trademark priority apply to personal names; thus, there is no absolute right to use one's own name as a trademark, if such use would conflict with another's prior use of that name as a mark in such a way as to cause consumer confusion.[194] Some courts, however, remain reluctant to enjoin the use of a proprietor's own name to identify the source of his or her goods or services, unless the name was adopted as

---

[185] *See, e.g.*, Lewis v. Marriott Int'l, Inc., 527 F. Supp. 2d 422, 426–27 (E.D. Pa. 2007) (noting that "a personal name acquires secondary meaning as a mark when the name and the business become synonymous in the public mind") (quoting Tillery v. Leonard & Sciolla, LLP, 437 F. Supp. 2d 312, 321 (E.D. Pa. 2006)).

[186] *See, e.g., In re* Carson, 197 U.S.P.Q. 554 (T.T.A.B. 1977).

[187] Trademark Manual of Examining Procedure (TMEP) § 1202.09(a). For the rules governing federal registration of surnames, see § 5E[2][e][iv]. For rules governing the unauthorized use of celebrity names or likenesses, see § 5C[2][c][iv].

[188] *Id.* § 1301.02(b).

[189] *See, e.g., In re* Mancino, 219 U.S.P.Q. (BNA) 1047 (T.T.A.B. 1983); *In re* Lee Trevino Enters., 182 U.S.P.Q. 253 (T.T.A.B. 1974); *see also* Reg. No. 2,442,618 (TIGER WOODS registered for entertainment services).

[190] Peaceable Planet, Inc. v. Ty, Inc., 362 F.3d 986, 992 (7th Cir. 2004); Lane Capital Mgt., Inc. v. Lane Capital Mgt., Inc., 192 F.3d 337, 346 (2d Cir. 1999).

[191] *In re* Hutchinson Tech., Inc., 852 F.2d 552, 554 (Fed. Cir. 1988).

[192] *See, e.g.*, Brody's, Inc. v. Brody Bros., Inc., 454 A.2d 605, 608 (Pa. Super. Ct. 1984).

[193] *See* Basile, S.p.A. v. Basile, 899 F.2d 35, 39 (D.C. Cir. 1990).

[194] *See, e.g.*, John R. Thompson Co. v. Holloway, 366 F.2d 108 (5th Cir. 1966); Little Tavern Shops v. Davis, 116 F.2d 903 (4th Cir. 1941); David B. Findlay, Inc. v. Findlay, 218 N.E.2d 531, 535 (N.Y. 1966).

a mark for the purpose of confusing the public.[195] Thus, where intent to confuse or mislead is absent, an injunction will be "carefully tailored to balance the interest in using one's own name against the interest in avoiding public confusion."[196] Such an injunction may require, for example, that the junior user's name be used in combination with a modifier or disclaimer so that the two marks are distinguishable.[197] In cases involving predatory intent or other equitable considerations, however, more sweeping injunctions are warranted.[198]

[iii]   Foreign Words

When the mark for which protection is sought consists of a word or phrase in a language other than English, in some cases the English translation will determine whether the word or phrase qualifies for trademark protection. Under the "doctrine of foreign equivalents," if the foreign word is from a relatively common language, its English translation will be used to determine genericness and descriptiveness, as well as similarity of connotation in order to assess whether it is confusingly similar to English-language word marks already in use.[199] However, if it is unlikely that "the average American purchaser" will translate the foreign mark, then the doctrine will be withheld.[200] The translation need not be literal; idiomatic uses are sufficient.[201]

In practice, the doctrine of foreign equivalents has been applied somewhat differently in the context of federal registration than it has in the context of protecting unregistered marks. Registration has been refused solely because a foreign word mark and an English-language word mark have the same meaning, even if the two marks are not similar in sight or sound.[202] In contrast, in determining whether an unregistered mark warrants protection under state law or section 43(a), most courts have treated similarity of meaning as just one part of a three-part test, which considers sight, sound, and meaning. Thus, although the

---

[195] *See, e.g.*, E. & J. Gallo Winery v. Gallo Cattle Co., 967 F.2d 1280, 1288 (9th Cir. 1992); Brodys, Inc. v. Brody Bros., Inc., 454 A.2d 605, 607–08 (Pa. Super. Ct. 1982); Poloskey v. Pantano, 25 Pa. D. & C.2d 307, 311–12 (1961); Haltom v. Haltom's Jewelers, Inc., 691 S.W.2d 823, 826–27 (Tex. App. 1985).

[196] *E. & J. Gallo Winery*, 967 F.2d at 1288.

[197] *See, e.g.*, Sardi's Rest. Corp. v. Sardie, 755 F.2d 719, 725 (9th Cir. 1985) (collecting cases). *But see* A.W. Cox Dept Store Co. v. Coxs, Inc., 221 S.E.2d 539, 544–45 (W. Va. 1976) (questioning effectiveness of such "halfway limitations").

[198] *See, e.g.*, Taylor Wine Co. v. Bully Hill Vineyards, Inc., 569 F.2d 731, 735 (2d Cir. 1978) (collecting cases).

[199] Palm Bay Imports, Inc. v. Veuve Clicquot Ponsardin Maison Fondee En 1772, 396 F.3d 1369, 1377 (Fed. Cir. 2005); Otokoyama Co. v. Wine of Japan Import, Inc., 175 F.3d 266 (2d Cir. 1999); *In re* Sarkli, Ltd., 721 F.2d 353 (Fed. Cir. 1983); Blue & White Food Prods. Corp. v. Shamir Food Indus., Ltd., 350 F. Supp. 2d 514 (S.D.N.Y. 2004); Popular Bank of Fla. v. Banco Popular de Puerto Rico, 9 F. Supp. 2d 1347, 1359 (S.D. Fla. 1998).

[200] *Palm Bay Imports*, 396 F.3d at 1377; *see also In re* Tia Maria, Inc., 188 U.S.P.Q. 524 (T.T.A.B. 1975).

[201] Enrique Bernat F., S.A. v. Guadalajara, 210 F.3d 439, 443–45 (5th Cir. 2000) (collecting cases).

[202] *See, e.g., In re* Sarkli, Ltd., 721 F.2d 353, 355 (Fed. Cir. 1983); Weiss Noodle Co. v. Golden Cracknel & Specialty Co., 290 F.2d 845 (C.C.P.A. 1961) (cancelling HA-LUSH-KA mark for noodles because it was phonetic equivalent in English of Hungarian name for noodles); *In re* La Peregrina Ltd., 86 U.S.P.Q.2d 1645 (T.T.A.B. 2008); *In re* Am. Safety Razor Co., 2 U.S.P.Q.2d 1459, 1460 (T.T.A.B. 1987).

English translation of the mark is considered relevant to determining similarity of meaning, most courts will consider the foreign word itself (untranslated) in determining similarity of sight and sound.[203] However, courts will consider the meaning alone when assessing whether the foreign mark is generic or descriptive.[204]

[iv]   Abbreviations of Generic or Descriptive Terms

Courts have not reached a consensus on whether and under what circumstances trademark protection can extend to abbreviations of words or phrases that are themselves either generic or merely descriptive. In the context of federal registration, the CCPA and the TTAB have taken a liberal view, permitting such abbreviations to be registered "unless they have become so generally understood as representing descriptive words as to be accepted as substantially synonymous therewith."[205] In contrast, the Seventh Circuit imposes a "heavy burden" on the trademark proponent to establish that the abbreviation has a meaning distinct from the underlying unprotectable expression.[206] Several courts have suggested that *all* abbreviations of descriptive phrases are inherently descriptive.[207] Others have held that such abbreviations can acquire secondary meaning,[208] and still others have held that they can be suggestive,[209] arbitrary, or fanciful.[210]

[v]   Titles

The titles of literary or artistic works present a special problem in descriptive trademarks. It is clear that the title of a *series* of such works (such as the name of a newspaper, periodical, or a series of books or films) can enjoy trademark protection, including federal registration, if it acquires secondary meaning — that is, if the public perceives the name of the series as an indication that each work in the series "comes from the same source as the others."[211]

However, with respect to the titles of individual works, the standards for federal registration diverge from the standards for providing protection under the common law and section 43(a) of the Lanham Act. Federal registration is not permitted for the title of a single work.[212] Such a title is considered merely

---

[203] *See, e.g.,* Horn's, Inc. v. Sanofi Beaute, Inc., 963 F. Supp. 318, 323 (S.D.N.Y. 1997); *Popular Bank,* 9 F. Supp. 2d at 1359.

[204] *See, e.g., Enrique Bernat,* 210 F.3d at 445.

[205] Modern Optics v. Univis Lens Co., 234 F.2d 504, 506 (C.C.P.A. 1956); *accord,* Racine Indus., Inc. v. Bane-Clene Corp., 35 U.S.P.Q.2d 1832 (T.T.A.B. 1995).

[206] G. Heileman Brewing Co. v. Anheuser-Busch, Inc., 873 F.2d 985, 994 (7th Cir. 1989).

[207] CPP Ins. Agency, Inc. v. General Motors Corp., 212 U.S.P.Q. 257 (C.D. Cal. 1980), *aff'd mem.,* 676 F.2d 709 (9th Cir. 1982); U.S. Conference of Catholic Bishops v. Media Research Center, 432 F. Supp. 2d 616, 624 (E.D. Va. 2006).

[208] Welding Services, Inc. v. Forman, 509 F.3d 1351, 1359 (11th Cir. 2007).

[209] Anheuser-Busch, Inc. v. Stroh Brewery Co., 750 F.2d 631, 635–36 (8th Cir. 1984).

[210] Grove Labs. v. Brewer & Co., 103 F.2d 175 (1st Cir. 1939) (arbitrary or fanciful).

[211] *In re* Cooper, 254 F.2d 611, 615 (C.C.P.A. 1958); *accord, In re* Scholastic, 23 U.S.P.Q.2d 1774, 1779 (T.T.A.B. 1992).

[212] Herbko Int'l, Inc. v. Kappa Books, Inc., 308 F.3d 1156, 1162–63 (Fed. Cir. 2002); TMEP § 1202.08.

descriptive: "Each literary title is regarded as a designation used to describe the literary work itself, rather than a trademark used to identify and distinguish the literary work of one source from that of another."[213] In contrast, courts have held that the titles of individual works can be protected as common-law marks under section 43(a) of the Lanham Act if they acquire secondary meaning.[214]

[c]   Non-Verbal Marks

[i]   Numerals and Alphanumeric Combinations

Numbers and alphanumeric combinations can serve as trademarks under common law as well as federal law, if they have inherent or acquired distinctiveness. The "501" mark for Levi's jeans, for example, is a federally registered mark.[215] In some cases, numeric or alphanumeric marks are arbitrary, in which case no secondary meaning is required.[216] In other cases, however, the mark may have originated as a model number or part number, in which case trademark protection is available only if and when the mark acquires secondary meaning.[217]

[ii]   Color, Sound, Scent

Under federal law, the types of devices capable of serving as trademarks may include color alone (for example, the color of the product's packaging, or even the color of the product itself), sound (a melody or even a single sound), scent, and virtually anything else that is nonfunctional and capable of indicating the source of goods or services

Prior to 1995, the federal courts had split on the question of whether color alone could serve as a trademark. The Supreme Court resolved the split in *Qualitex Co. v. Jacobson Prods. Co.*,[218] in which it held that no *per se* rule precluded the federal registration of a trademark consisting of color. *Qualitex* rejected arguments that allowing registration of color alone would deplete the number of colors available to competitors, that it would lead to confusion where competitors used slightly different shades, and that color marks already had sufficient federal protection under section 43(a).[219] The Court held that, while color alone cannot be inherently distinctive, it can serve as a trademark if it is nonfunctional and acquires secondary

---

[213] *Scholastic*, 23 U.S.P.Q.2d at 1779.

[214] *Herbko Int'l, Inc.*, 308 F.3d at 1162 n.2; *see, e.g.*, Estate of Jenkins v. Paramount Pictures Corp., 90 F. Supp. 2d 706, 709–11 (E.D. Va. 2000), *aff'd sub nom.*, Evans v. Paramount Pictures Corp., 7 Fed. Appx. 270 (4th Cir. 2001); Simon & Schuster v. Dove Audio, 936 F. Supp. 156, 163 (S.D.N.Y. 1996); Tri-Star Pictures, Inc. v. Leisure Time Prods., B.V., 749 F. Supp. 1243 (S.D.N.Y. 1990); Orion Pictures Co. v. Dell Pub. Co., 471 F. Supp. 392, 395 (S.D.N.Y. 1979).

[215] Reg. No. 1,552,985.

[216] Eastman Kodak Co. v. Bell & Howell Document Mgt. Prods. Co., 994 F.2d 1569, 1576 (Fed. Cir. 1993).

[217] Arrow Fastener Co. v. Stanley Works, 59 F.3d 384, 392–93 (2d Cir. 1995); Ideal Indus., Inc. v. Gardner Bender, Inc., 612 F.2d 1018 (7th Cir. 1980).

[218] 514 U.S. 159 (1995).

[219] *Id.* at 166–72.

meaning.[220]

Sound and scent, like color, are not likely to be inherently distinctive, because typically they are not immediately recognizable as source identifiers, but they are capable of serving as trademarks if they are non-functional and acquire secondary meaning.[221] Thus, for example, fragrance cannot serve as a trademark for food, soap or perfume, because in those contexts it would be functional, but it can serve as a trademark for thread.[222]

[iii]   Expressive Works

Works of artistic or musical expression may qualify for common law and federal trademark protection if they acquire distinctiveness.[223] Both artistic designs and musical "jingles" are common types of trademarks.[224] Even the design of a building can qualify as a trademark, if the specific images (drawings, photographs, or other renderings) that are used to indicate the source of goods or services are sufficiently consistent to create a "consistent and distinct commercial impression."[225]

However, the application of trademark concepts to expressive works becomes problematic when the expressive work functions as both the product and the source indicator.

To begin with, classifying such an expressive work along the spectrum of distinctiveness can be difficult. For example, in *Foxworthy v. Custom Tees, Inc.*,[226] a federal district court held that section 43(a) protected the phrase "You might be a redneck . . . ," where comedian Jeff Foxworthy had become well-known for using this phrase in his jokes about rural southerners. Although a strong argument can be made that this phrase is descriptive, and therefore protectible only upon a showing of secondary meaning, the court characterized it as a suggestive mark.

Second, the expressive work can function as a trademark only with respect to goods or services other than the expressive work itself. For example, where an advertising agency invented a slogan for a client, the agency had no trademark rights in the slogan; only the client that actually used the slogan in connection with goods or services could assert trademark rights.[227]

An even greater problem, however, is the potential for conflict between

---

[220] *Id.* at 163–65.

[221] *See. e.g., In re* Vertex Group LLC, 89 U.S.P.Q.2d 1694 (T.T.A.B. 2009).

[222] *In re* Clarke, 17 U.S.P.Q.2d 1238 (T.T.A.B. 1990).

[223] *See, e.g., In re* Swift & Co., 223 F.2d 950 (C.C.P.A. 1955) (red-and-white polka dot design); Oliveira v. Frito-Lay, Inc., 251 F.3d 56, 61–62 (2d Cir. 2001) (musical compositions).

[224] Slogans and catch-phrases, which are widely recognized as trademarks under common law and the Lanham Act, may also be considered types of expressive works, although unlike artistic pictorial and musical works, slogans are expressly excluded from copyright protection. *See* 37 C.F.R. 202.1(a) (excluding "words and short phrases such as names, titles, slogans" from copyright registration).

[225] Rock & Roll Hall of Fame & Museum, Inc. v. Gentile Prods., 134 F.3d 749, 755 (6th Cir. 1988).

[226] 879 F. Supp. 1200 (N.D. Ga. 1995).

[227] American Express Co. v. Goetz, 515 F.3d 156, 159–60 (2d Cir. 2008).

trademark protection and other forms of intellectual property protection for expressive works. Although copyright and trademark protection (as well as design patent protection) are not mutually exclusive, special problems may arise when a claim for trademark protection appears to conflict with the overall scheme of federal copyright law. For example, in *Hartford House, Ltd. v. Hallmark Cards, Inc.*[228] and *Romm Art Creations, Ltd. v. Simcha Int'l, Inc.*,[229] defendants were enjoined under section 43(a) from producing creative works (greeting cards and art posters, respectively) that closely imitated the distinctive style of the plaintiffs' similar products. In contrast, *Leigh v. Warner Bros., Inc.*[230] rejected a section 43(a) claim against a defendant that closely imitated the subject matter and style of the plaintiff's well-known photograph. The court held that the style and subject matter of the photograph did not function as a trademark, but constituted the product itself, and it expressly rejected the *Romm Art* analysis.[231] In addition, the doctrine of aesthetic functionality might be applied to the facts of *Hartford House, Romm Art*, and *Leigh*, to bar trade dress protection for the artistic features of an artistic product, regardless of the distinctiveness of those features.[232]

Another potential conflict with copyright law arises when a party seeks trademark protection for an expressive work after the copyright in that work has expired. In *Fredrick Warne & Co. v. Book Sales, Inc.*,[233] a publisher asserted trademark rights in several of the illustrations in Beatrix Potter's "Peter Rabbit" series, which had originally been published by the plaintiff but were no longer protected by copyright. The defendant reproduced those illustrations in a new volume containing the public domain stories. The court rejected the defendant's argument that the expiration of the copyright prevented the publisher from claiming a trademark right in the illustrations: "[T]he proper factual inquiry in this case is not whether the cover illustrations were once copyrightable and have fallen into the public domain, but whether they have acquired secondary meaning, identifying Warne as the publisher or sponsor of goods bearing those illustrations, and if so, whether defendant's use of these illustrations in 'packaging' or 'dressing' its editions is likely to cause confusion."[234] Other courts, however, have stated broadly that "the Lanham Act cannot be used to circumvent copyright law. If material covered by copyright law has passed into the public domain, it cannot then be protected by the Lanham Act without rendering the Copyright Act a nullity."[235]

The key to resolving this dilemma lies in recognizing what federal copyright policy requires. The purpose of placing expressive works in the public domain is to allow them to be freely reproduced and used by others. All non-fanciful trademarks, however, involve creation of exclusive rights in public domain material

---

[228] 846 F.2d 1268, 1274 (10th Cir. 1988).

[229] 786 F. Supp. 1126 (E.D.N.Y. 1992).

[230] 10 F. Supp. 2d 1371 (S.D. Ga. 1998), *aff'd in relevant part*, 212 F.3d 1210, 1218 (11th Cir. 2000).

[231] 10 F. Supp. at 1381. *See also*, Hughes v. Design Look Inc., 693 F. Supp. 1500, 1505 (S.D.N.Y. 1988); Galerie Furstenberg v. Coffaro, 697 F. Supp. 1282, 1290 (S.D.N.Y. 1988).

[232] *See* § 5C[1][c][iii].

[233] 481 F. Supp. 1191 (S.D.N.Y. 1979).

[234] *Id.* at 1198.

[235] Comedy III Prods., Inc. v. New Line Cinema, 200 F.3d 593, 595 (9th Cir. 2000).

through use. Federal copyright policy does not necessarily bar the adoption and use of a formerly copyrighted work as a trademark for unrelated goods or services. However, federal copyright policy does forbid the use of an expressive work as a mark for the expressive work itself.[236] Enforcement of this policy would prevent the misuse of trademark law to prevent reproduction of the expressive work for a non-trademark purpose.

[iv]   Celebrity Likenesses and Fictional Characters

Most courts hold that the name or likeness of a celebrity can function as a trademark only if it is used to identify the source of particular goods or services (and, in the case of a likeness, only if the same image is consistently used as the source indicator, so as to create a continuing and distinct commercial impression).[237] However, courts have also used a "false endorsement" theory under section 43(a) to extend federal protection to a celebrity's name, nickname, physical likeness, voice, and other identifying characteristics.[238] Such cases often combine section 43(a) claims or state law unfair competition claims with claims arising under a state law "right of publicity" doctrine, which provides an individual with a cause of action against unauthorized commercial uses of his or her name or likeness.[239] Although the right of publicity doctrine varies considerably among the different states where it is recognized, right of publicity claims typically differ from state or federal trademark and unfair competition claims in that they do not require the plaintiff to establish that the defendant's use creates a likelihood of confusion. In addition, some states limit or prohibit the post-mortem assertion of a right of publicity, whereas a section 43(a) false endorsement claim or common law unfair competition claim may be asserted by any party that owns the goodwill associated with the deceased celebrity's identity.

Courts have also extended section 43(a) and state unfair competition laws to the names, images, or characteristics of fictional characters,[240] although not to the copyrighted materials embodying them (because this would conflict with federal copyright law).[241]

[d]   Trade Dress

The term *trade dress* refers to the distinctive features of a product's packaging or the distinctive features of the product configuration itself; it is "the total image of a product and may include features such as size, shape, color or color

---

[236] *See* EMI Catalogue Partnership v. Hill, Holliday, Connors, Cosmopulos, Inc., 228 F.3d 56, 63–64 (2d Cir. 2000).

[237] *See, e.g.,* ETW Corp. v. Jireh Pub., Inc., 332 F.3d 915, 922–23 (6th Cir. 2003); Pirone v. MacMillan, Inc., 894 F.2d 579, 583 (2d Cir. 1990); Estate of Presley v. Russen, 513 F. Supp. 1339, 1363–64 (D.N.J. 1981).

[238] *See, e.g.,* Wendt v. Host Int'l, Inc., 125 F.3d 806 (9th Cir. 1997); White v. Samsung Elecs. America, Inc., 971 F.2d 1395 (9th Cir. 1992); Waits v. Frito-Lay, Inc., 978 F.2d 1093 (9th Cir. 1992); Allen v. National Video, Inc., 610 F. Supp. 612 (S.D.N.Y. 1985).

[239] *See* § 6G.

[240] *See, e.g.,* Edgar Rice Burroughs, Inc. v. Manns Theatres, 195 U.S.P.Q. 159 (C.D. Cal. 1976).

[241] Comedy III Prods., Inc. v. New Line Cinema, 200 F.3d 593, 595–96 (9th Cir. 2000).

combinations, texture, graphics, or even particular sales techniques."[242] Services as well as goods may be associated with a distinctive trade dress; for example, the color brown is widely recognized as trade dress used by United Parcel Service (UPS). The overall appearance of a website may be eligible for trade dress protection as well.[243]

Like other types of trademarks, trade dress is protectible only if it is capable of distinguishing, in the minds of the public, the goods or services of one person from those of another.[244] The appearance of a line of products or its packaging need not be identical; it is enough that the design conveys a recognizable and consistent overall look.[245] If the design is not sufficiently consistent, consumers will fail to recognize that the products come from the same source.

Under federal law, in order for trade dress to qualify for trademark protection, it must be both nonfunctional and distinctive. Thus, a plaintiff seeking trade dress protection under section 43(a) must prove that: (1) the trade dress of the two products is confusingly similar; (2) the features of the trade dress are primarily nonfunctional; and (3) the trade dress is inherently distinctive or has acquired secondary meaning.[246]

Trade dress that is both nonfunctional and distinctive may be registered on the Principal Register if it otherwise satisfies the requirements of section 2 of the Lanham Act.[247] Examples of registered trade dress include bottle shapes,[248] the pink color of fiberglass insulation,[249] the design of a candy bar wrapper,[250] and the design of a faucet and faucet handles.[251]

Unregistered trade dress may also be protected under section 43(a). However, in this case the party asserting trade dress protection must establish, as part of its

---

[242] Two Pesos, Inc. v. Taco Cabana, Inc. 505 U.S. 763, 765 n.1 (1992) (quoting John H. Harland Co. v. Clarke Checks, Inc., 711 F.2d 966, 980 (11th Cir. 1983)).

[243] *See, e.g.*, Express Lien v. Nat'l Ass'n of Credit Mgt., 2013 U.S. Dist. LEXIS 120209 (E.D. La. Aug. 23, 2013); Parker Waichman LLP v. Gilman Law LLP, 2013 U.S. Dist. LEXIS 103684 (E.D.N.Y. July 24, 2013); Blue Nile, Inc. v. Ice.com, Inc., 478 F. Supp. 2d 1240, 1246 (W.D. Wash. 2007).

[244] Publications Int'l, Ltd. v. Landoll, Inc., 164 F.3d 337, 338 (7th Cir. 1998).

[245] *See, e.g.*, Rose Art Indus., Inc. v. Swanson, 235 F.3d 165, 173 (3d Cir. 2000). Maharishi Hardy Blechman Ltd. v. Abercrombie & Fitch Co., 292 F. Supp. 2d 535, 549–550 & n.12 (S.D.N.Y. 2003); Walt Disney Co. v. Goodtimes Home Video Corp., 830 F. Supp. 762, 766–68 (S.D.N.Y. 1993).

[246] Dippin' Dots, Inc. v. Frosty Bites Dist., LLC, 369 F.3d 1197 (11th Cir. 2004).

[247] Wal-Mart Stores, Inc. v. Samara Bros., 529 U.S. 205, 209 (2000); *see, e.g., In re* Owens-Corning Fiberglas Corp., 774 F.2d 1116, 1120 (Fed. Cir. 1985). In the case of trade dress, the functionality bar to registration, as well as the corresponding grounds for cancellation and defense to incontestability, will frequently be implicated. 15 U.S.C. §§ 1052(e)(5), 1064(3), 1115(b)(8); *see* § 5C[1][c]. The eligibility rules for federal trademark registration are discussed in § 5E.

[248] *Ex parte* Haig & Haig, Ltd., 118 U.S.P.Q. 229 (Comm'r Pat. 1958); *In re* Mogen David Wine Corp., 328 F.2d 925 (C.C.P.A. 1964); *In re* Days-Ease Home Products Corp., 197 U.S.P.Q. 566 (T.T.A.B. 1977).

[249] *In re* Owens-Corning Fiberglas Corp., 774 F.2d 1116 (Fed. Cir. 1985).

[250] *In re* World's Finest Chocolate, Inc., 474 F.2d 1012 (C.C.P.A. 1973).

[251] Kohler Co. v. Moen, Inc., 12 F.3d 632 (7th Cir. 1993).

prima facie case, that the trade dress is primarily nonfunctional.[252] In this respect, federal protection of trade dress differs from federal protection of other types of marks.

Federal law treats trade dress differently from other types of trademarks in one other respect. Under the Supreme Court precedents discussed below, trade dress that consists of product configuration (as opposed to product packaging), is protectable only upon a showing of secondary meaning.

In *Two Pesos, Inc. v. Taco Cabana, Inc.*,[253] the Supreme Court held that, like other trademarks, inherently distinctive trade dress may be protected under section 43(a) without regard to whether it has acquired secondary meaning; the Court found nothing in section 43(a) to warrant treating trade dress differently from traditional trademarks in this regard.[254] Just eight years later, however, in *Wal-Mart Stores, Inc. v. Samara Brothers., Inc.*,[255] the Court refined its position, drawing a distinction between product *packaging* and product *configuration*, and holding that, as a matter of law, trade dress protection for product configuration may not be obtained on the basis of inherent distinctiveness, because (1) consumers are not predisposed to regard features of product design as origin indicators, in contrast to features of product packaging, and (2) the threat of suits against new competitors could deter them from copying product designs that serve utilitarian and esthetic purposes.[256]

Accordingly, the party asserting trade dress protection under federal law for an element of its product *design* must establish that the design element has secondary meaning. In contrast, a party may obtain trade dress protection for an element of its product *packaging* on the basis of either inherent or acquired distinctiveness. Thus, the rule of *Two Pesos* now applies only to product packaging, and not to product design.

§ 5D   ACQUISITION AND MAINTENANCE OF TRADEMARK RIGHTS

[1]   Use in Trade

Under common law and state statutes, trademark rights may be established only through actual use of the mark in connection with the offering of goods or services to the public. Subject to limited exceptions, this is true under the Lanham Act as well.[257] The Supreme Court has held that "there is no such thing as

---

[252] 15 U.S.C. § 43(a)(3). *See* Dippin' Dots, Inc. v. Frosty Bites Dist., LLC, 369 F.3d 1197, 1202 (11th Cir. 2004).

[253] 505 U.S. 763 (1992).

[254] *Id.* at 773–74.

[255] 529 U.S. 205 (2000).

[256] *Id.* at 212–14.

[257] The intent-to-use provisions of the Lanham Act provide a limited, and short-term, exception to this rule. *See* § 5E[3][b]. A second exception permits federal registration based on a foreign registration, provided that use commences within six years. *See* § 5E[6].

property in a trade-mark except as a right appurtenant to an established business or trade in connection with which the mark is employed . . . . The right to a particular mark grows out of its use, not its mere adoption."[258]

At common law, trademark rights are limited to the market or markets where the mark is actually being used. A major difference between common law and federal law, however, is that federal registration of a trademark or service mark gives rise to "constructive use" of that mark even in markets where the registrant has not actually used the mark. As between competing users in a particular market, the exclusive right to use the mark (referred to as "priority") belongs to the first user (referred to as the "senior user") of the mark in that market, whether that use is actual or (in the case of federal registration) constructive.

As discussed below, under both common law and the Lanham Act, in order for the use of a mark to be sufficient to establish and maintain trademark rights, the use must be a bona fide use in connection with an actual offering of goods or services, rather than a "token" use designed merely to reserve rights in the mark.

[a] Establishing Priority of Use

At common law, trademark rights are established by the person who is the first to make bona fide use of the mark in connection with offering goods or services to the public.[259] Even before actual sales have occurred, bona fide use may be established through pre-sales publicity or sales solicitation using the mark, combined with intent to continue the use.[260]

The right to the exclusive use of a trademark or service mark is ordinarily founded on priority of use. Thus, "the first to use a mark on a product or service in a particular geographic market acquires rights in the mark in that market."[261] The problem of determining priority rights as between competing users of similar marks was succinctly stated by the Ninth Circuit:

A fundamental principle of trademark law is first in time equals first in right. But things get more complicated when to time we add considerations of place, as when one user is first in time in one place while another is first in time in a different place.[262]

Resolution of priority issues with regard to common-law marks (that is, marks that are not federally registered) is governed by common-law principles based on actual use, business presence and reputation, and, in some cases, a "zone of expansion."[263] Where marks are confusingly similar, the principles that determine

---

[258] United Drug Co. v. Theodore Rectanus Co., 248 U.S. 90, 97 (1918).

[259] Societe de Developments et D'Innovations des Marches Agricoles et Alimentaires — SODIMA — Union des Cooperatives Agricoles v. International Yogurt Co., 662 F. Supp. 839, 853 (D. Or. 1987); Hydro-Dynamics, Inc. v. George Putnam & Co., Inc., 811 F.2d 1470, 1472 (Fed. Cir. 1987); Blue Bell, Inc. v. Farah Mfg. Co., 508 F.2d 1260 (5th Cir. 1975) (applying Texas law).

[260] *Societe de Developments et D'Innovations*, 662 F. Supp. at 853.

[261] Popular Bank of Fla. v. Banco Popular de Puerto Rico, 9 F. Supp. 2d 1347, 1353 (S.D. Fla. 1998).

[262] Grupo Gigante S.A. de C.V. v. Dallo & Co., 391 F.3d 1088, 1093 (9th Cir. 2004).

[263] *Popular Bank*, 9 F. Supp. 2d at 1354.

priority rights in the same or different geographical areas are derived from the Supreme Court's decisions in *Hanover Star Milling Co. v. Metcalf*[264] and *United Drug Co. v. Theodore Rectanus Co.*[265] Where similar marks are used in geographic areas that are remote from one another, each user will enjoy exclusive rights within its geographic area; however, where the geographic areas of use are the same or overlapping, exclusive rights belong to the "senior user" in that market.[266] The senior user in one market may find itself the junior user when it seeks entry in a different market, and may therefore be unable to extend its trademark to the new market.[267]

The geographic area in which the senior user of a mark has established priority of use is determined by considering the area in which the mark is actually used in offering goods or services, the area in which the user has established a reputation and business presence, and the user's natural "zone of expansion" or area of "market penetration," encompassing areas into which the use is likely to expand.[268] The geographic scope of the senior user's priority is a question of fact, and depends on the reputation, advertising, and sales in the area.[269]

[i]   Actual Use

To establish priority through actual use, a party must prove a level of use in the ordinary course of business in that territory that is sufficient to acquire rights in the mark; insignificant or sporadic use is insufficient.[270] The extent of the party's sales in the territory is an important indicator of actual use. Thus, "[t]he number and dollar amounts of the sales in the area, the number of customers, the pattern of sales over time, and the potential growth of sales are all relevant factors that should be considered by the court in determining actual use."[271] Mere "token" sales or intracompany shipments generally will not satisfy the actual use requirement.[272]

[ii]   Reputation and Business Presence

A business may acquire trademark priority in a territory where it has established a reputation for its mark, even though it does not offer its product or service in that area; accordingly, "the extent to which advertising has carried the reputation of the mark into a new territory is a factor to be considered in deciding whether the territory has been successfully appropriated by the mark's owner."[273]

---

[264] 240 U.S. 403 (1916).

[265] 248 U.S. 90 (1918).

[266] *Hanover Star Milling*, 240 U.S. at 416.

[267] *United Drug Co.*, 248 U.S. at 100.

[268] *See, e.g.*, Tally-Ho, Inc. v. Coast Community College Dist., 889 F.2d 1018, 1025–27 (11th Cir. 1989); Spartan Food Sys., Inc. v. HFS Corp., 813 F.2d 1279, 1283 (4th Cir. 1987).

[269] Thrifty Rent-A-Car Sys., Inc. v. Thrift Cars, Inc., 639 F. Supp. 750, 753 (D. Mass. 1986), *aff'd*, 831 F.2d 1177 (1st Cir. 1987).

[270] Restatement (Third) of Unfair Competition § 19 cmt. b (1995).

[271] Popular Bank of Fla. v. Banco Popular de Puerto Rico, 9 F. Supp. 2d 1347, 1354 (S.D. Fla. 1998), *citing* Sweetarts v. Sunline, Inc., 380 F.2d 923, 929 (8th Cir. 1967).

[272] *See, e.g.*, Blue Bell Inc. v. Farah Mfg. Co., 508 F.2d 1260 (5th Cir. 1975) (applying Texas law).

[273] *Popular Bank*, 9 F. Supp. 2d at 1355 (citing *Thrifty Rent-A-Car Sys.*, 639 F. Supp. at 753).

Similarly, if the trademark owner's customers transport their purchases to areas where the trademark owner does not conduct business, or if the business attracts customers from different locations, the trademark may become known in areas beyond the trademark owner's business territory. Thus, in determining the geographic scope of a mark, relevant factors include "the nature and extent of advertising and other promotional activities, the geographic distribution of catalogs and flyers, [and] the geographical origins of orders and customer inquiries."[274]

[iii]   Zone of Expansion

In some cases, courts have recognized common-law priority rights in the trademark owner's natural or probable zone of expansion.[275] Courts adopting this approach have tended to define the zone of expansion narrowly; geographical proximity to areas where the trademark owner actually conducts business or advertises is a significant factor in defining the zone.[276] Courts typically consider the party's: (1) previous business activity; (2) previous expansion or lack thereof; (3) dominance of contiguous areas; (4) presently planned expansion; and, where applicable, (5) possible market penetration by means of products brought in from other areas.[277] In assessing "market penetration," courts typically look to: (1) the volume of sales of the trademarked product; (2) the growth trends in the area; (3) the number of people actually purchasing the product in relation to the potential number of customers; and (4) the amount of product advertising in the area.[278]

[b]   Lanham Act

[i]   Use in Commerce

As under common law, the ownership of trademark rights under the Lanham Act is conditioned on use.[279] Under the Lanham Act, however, the use must be not only a use in trade, but also a use in "commerce."

In general, the use in commerce that is required for federal trademark protection is similar to the use required to obtain common-law rights in the mark.[280] The federal definition of a trademark requires that it be used "to identify and distinguish [one person's] goods, including a unique product, from those manufactured or sold by others and to indicate the source of the goods," and the definition of a service mark requires that it be used "to identify and distinguish the

---

[274] *Popular Bank*, 9 F. Supp. 2d at 1355, *citing* RESTATEMENT (THIRD) OF UNFAIR COMPETITION § 19 cmt. b (1995); *see, e.g.,* Stork Restaurant v. Sahati, 166 F.2d 348 (9th Cir. 1948) (mark was entitled to nationwide protection based on its extensive advertising and national press coverage).

[275] Popular Bank of Fla. v. Banco Popular de Puerto Rico, 9 F. Supp. 2d 1347, 1355 (S.D. Fla. 1998), *citing* Tally-Ho, Inc. v. Coast Community College Dist., 889 F.2d 1018, 1027–28 (11th Cir. 1989).

[276] *Popular Bank*, 9 F. Supp. 2d at 1355–56 (collecting authorities).

[277] Spartan Food Sys., Inc. v. HFS Corp., 813 F.2d 1279, 1283 (4th Cir. 1987).

[278] *Id.*

[279] General Healthcare, Ltd. v. Qashat, 364 F.3d 332, 335 (1st Cir. 2004); United Drug Co. v. Theodore Rectanus Co., 248 U.S. 90, 97 (1918).

[280] Societe de Developments et D'Innovations des Marches Agricoles et Alimentaires — SODIMA — Union des Cooperatives Agricoles v. International Yogurt Co., 662 F. Supp. 839, 853 (D. Or. 1987).

services of one person, including a unique service, from the services of others and to indicate the source of the services."[281]

To qualify for federal registration, however, a trademark or service mark must not only be used to identify the source of goods or services; it must also be "used in commerce,"[282] where "commerce" means "all commerce which may lawfully be regulated by Congress,"[283] thus encompassing "[c]ommerce with foreign Nations, and among the several States, and with the Indian Tribes."[284] Because Congress's authority extends to any activity that "substantially affects" interstate commerce,[285] a service mark used purely for intrastate restaurant services can be federally registered if the restaurant has an interstate clientele.[286]

The Lanham Act defines a "use in commerce" as "the bona fide use of a mark in the ordinary course of trade, and not made merely to reserve a right in a mark."[287] Thus, a mere token or *de minimis* use will not qualify.[288] Furthermore, the use of a mark in advertising, without more, will not qualify as a use in commerce for purposes of federal registration.[289] In the case of services, for example, the advertised services must in fact be provided; announcement of future services is insufficient.[290]

Section 45 of the Lanham Act distinguishes between the activities that constitute a use in commerce in the case of a trademark and those that constitute a use in commerce in the case of a service mark. In the case of goods, the mark must be placed on the goods, their containers, or associated displays, or on tags or labels affixed thereto, or, "if the nature of the goods makes such placement

---

[281] 15 U.S.C. § 1127.

[282] 15 U.S.C. § 1051(a)(1).

[283] 15 U.S.C. § 1127.

[284] U.S. Const., Art. I, § 8, cl. 3.

[285] United States v. Lopez, 514 U.S. 549, 559 (1995). It has been said, however, that the concept of a "use in commerce" for registration purposes is slightly narrower than the "use in commerce" concept for purposes of establishing federal jurisdiction under sections 43(a) and 43(c) of the Lanham Act. *See, e.g.*, Planned Parenthood Fed'n of America v. Bucci, 42 U.S.P.Q.2d 1430 (S.D.N.Y. 1997), *aff'd*, 152 F.3d 920 (2d Cir. 1998); McCarthy on Trademarks and Unfair Competition § 25:57 (2009) ("It is difficult to conceive of an act of infringement which is not 'in commerce' in the sense of the modern decisions. . . . However, the Patent and Trademark Office still appears to adopt a higher standard of use in commerce for purposes of qualifying for federal registration in the first instance."). *See generally* § 5F[5] (discussing federal jurisdiction under section 43 of the Lanham Act).

[286] Larry Harmon Pictures Corp. v. Williams Rest. Corp., 929 F.2d 662, 666 (Fed. Cir. 1991).

[287] 15 U.S.C. § 1127.

[288] *See, e.g.*, Hydro-Dynamics, Inc. v. George Putnam & Co., Inc., 811 F.2d 1470 (Fed. Cir. 1987); Avakoff v. Southern Pacific Co., 765 F.2d 1097 (Fed. Cir. 1985); Gay Toys, Inc. v. McDonalds Corp., 585 F.2d 1067 (C.C.P.A. 1978); Paramount Pictures Corp. v. White, 31 U.S.P.Q.2d 1768, 1772–73 (T.T.A.B. 1994).

[289] *See, e.g.*, *In re* Universal Oil Products Co., 476 F.2d 653 (C.C.P.A. 1973); Lands' End, Inc. v. Manbeck, 797 F. Supp. 511 (E.D. Va. 1992); Koffler Stores, Ltd. v. Shoppers Drug Mart, Inc., 434 F. Supp. 697 (E.D. Mich. 1976), *aff'd mem.*, 559 F.2d 1219 (6th Cir. 1977); Greyhound Corp. v. Armour Life Ins. Co., 214 U.S.P.Q. 473, 474 (T.T.A.B. 1982).

[290] *Greyhound Corp.*, 214 U.S.P.Q. at 474; Aycock Eng'g, Inc. v. Airflite, Inc., 560 F.3d 1350, 1359–61 (Fed. Cir. 2009).

impracticable," on associated documents, and the goods must be "sold or transported in commerce."[291] A sale must be a bona fide business transaction; sham sales are disregarded.[292] Alternatively, transportation alone will qualify, provided that it takes place in commerce,[293] which means that the shipments cannot be purely intrastate. In addition, for the transportation of goods to qualify as a sufficient use in commerce, an element of public awareness is required.[294] The transportation must therefore be "sufficiently public to identify or distinguish the marked goods in an appropriate segment of the public mind as those of the adopter of the mark."[295] Accordingly, although the applicant's use of a mark need not have gained wide public recognition, secret, undisclosed shipments do not qualify.[296] In general, for a shipment to qualify as a "use in commerce," it must not be a purely intra-company shipment.[297]

In the case of services, a mark is "used in commerce" when "it is used or displayed in the sale or advertising of services and the services are rendered in commerce, or the services are rendered in more than one State or in the United States and a foreign country and the person rendering the services is engaged in commerce in connection with the services."[298]

A use in "commerce" need not be a profit-seeking use; accordingly, courts recognize the rights of nonprofit and civic organizations to protect the trademarks they use to identify themselves as the source of their noncommercial activities.[299] However, the use of a term as part of a domain name does not, by itself, constitute use as an indicator of the source of goods or services.[300]

Two other concepts relevant to priority of use are the *related companies* doctrine and the concept of *tacking*.

The related companies doctrine, embodied in section 5 of the Lanham Act, provides that, for purposes of validity and registration, the use of a mark by a company related to the registrant/applicant inures to the benefit of the

---

[291] 15 U.S.C. § 1127; *see, e.g., In re* Marriott Corp., 459 F.2d 525 (C.C.P.A. 1972).

[292] Acme Valve & Fittings Co. v. Wayne, 386 F. Supp. 1162, 1169 (S.D. Tex. 1974).

[293] *See, e.g.,* General Healthcare, Ltd. v. Qashat, 364 F.3d 332, 335 (1st Cir. 2004); New England Duplicating Co. v. Mendes, 190 F.2d 415, 417 (1st Cir. 1951); Ideal Toy Corp. v. Cameo Exclusive Prods., Inc., 170 U.S.P.Q. 596 (T.T.A.B. 1971).

[294] *General Healthcare*, 364 F.3d at 335 (collecting cases).

[295] *Mendes*, 190 F.2d at 418; *accord, General Healthcare*, 364 F.3d at 336.

[296] *General Healthcare*, 364 F.3d at 335 (citing Blue Bell, Inc. v. Farah Mfg. Co., 508 F.2d 1260 (5th Cir. 1975)).

[297] Sterling Drug, Inc. v. Knoll A.G. Chemische Fabriken, 159 U.S.P.Q. 628, 631 (T.T.A.B. 1968).

[298] 15 U.S.C. § 1127.

[299] *See, e.g.,* United We Stand Am., Inc. v. United We Stand, Am., N.Y., Inc., 128 F.3d 86, 92–93 (2d Cir. 1997); Kappa Sigma Fraternity v. Kappa Sigma Gamma Fraternity, 654 F. Supp. 1095, 1101 (D.N.H. 1987); American Diabetes Ass'n, Inc. v. Nat'l Diabetes Ass'n, 533 F. Supp. 16, 20 (E.D. Pa. 1981), *aff'd*, 681 F.2d 804 (3d Cir. 1982); United States Jaycees v. Philadelphia Jaycees, 490 F. Supp. 688, 691 (E.D. Pa. 1980), *rev'd on other grounds*, 639 F.2d 134 (3d Cir. 1981).

[300] *In re* Roberts, 87 U.S.P.Q.2d 1474 (T.T.A.B. 2008); Brookfield Comms., Inc. v. West Coast Entert. Corp., 174 F.3d 1036, 1051 (9th Cir. 1999).

registrant/applicant, unless the mark has been used in a deceptive manner.[301] A "substantial relationship" between the parties is required.[302] The Lanham Act defines a "related company" as "any person whose use of a mark is controlled by the owner of the mark with respect to the nature and quality of the goods or services on or in connection with which the mark is used."[303] Where the mark is used by a licensee that is subject to quality controls, the licensee's use inures to the benefit of the registrant or applicant.[304]

A trademark user that was not the first to use the exact mark at issue may still be able to establish priority based on its earlier use of a similar though technically distinct mark. However, the user may "tack" its rights in the later mark to its use of the earlier mark only if the marks are so similar that the relevant consumers consider them to be the same mark.[305]

[ii]   Foreign Use

Section 45 defines "commerce" broadly, as "all commerce which may lawfully be regulated by Congress."[306] However, under the well-established "territoriality principle," the use of a mark exclusively outside the United States is not a "use in commerce," and thus will not establish ownership rights in the United States, either at common law or for purposes of the Lanham Act.[307]

In applying the territoriality principle, the question has arisen whether a use in commerce can be established where the goods and services associated with the mark are advertised or promoted in the United States, but are offered exclusively overseas.

The Trademark Trial and Appeal Board (TTAB) has consistently held that where a mark is used exclusively for services offered outside the United States, a use in commerce cannot be established solely through advertising to United States consumers. In *Mother's Restaurants, Inc. v. Mother's Other Kitchen, Inc.*, for example, the mark in question was used for a restaurant located in Canada. Although ads for the restaurant were broadcast only by Canadian radio stations, some of these broadcasts reached the United States. Promotional materials and coupons for the restaurant were distributed in southern Ontario along major tourist routes from the United States. The TTAB ruled that these activities did not

---

[301] 15 U.S.C. § 1055.

[302] Secular Orgs. for Sobriety, Inc. v. Ullrich, 213 F.3d 1125 (9th Cir. 2000).

[303] 15 U.S.C. § 1127. The D.C. Circuit applied the related companies doctrine to nonprofit entities in Estate of Coll-Monge v. Inner Peace Movement, 524 F.3d 1341, 1347 (D.C. Cir. 2008).

[304] Turner v. H M H Pub. Co., 380 F.2d 224 (5th Cir. 1967).

[305] Brookfield Comms., Inc. v. West Coast Entert. Corp., 174 F.3d 1036, 1047–48 (9th Cir. 1999). For a detailed discussion of tacking, see § 5F[2].

[306] 15 U.S.C. § 1127.

[307] *See, e.g.*, Grupo Gigante S.A. de C.V. v. Dallo & Co., 391 F.3d 1088, 1097–98 (9th Cir. 2004); Person's Co. v. Christman, 900 F.2d 1565, 1568–69 (Fed. Cir. 1990); Fuji Photo Film Co., Inc. v. Shinohara Shoji Kabushiki Kaisha, 754 F.2d 591, 599 (5th Cir. 1985); Empresa Cubana Del Tabaco v. Culbro Corp., 70 U.S.P.Q.2d 1650, 1675 (S.D.N.Y. 2004), *aff'd in part and rev'd in part*, 399 F.3d 462 (2d Cir. 2005); Tactica Int'l, Inc. v. Atlantic Horizon, Int'l, Inc., 154 F. Supp. 2d 586, 599 (S.D.N.Y. 2001).

establish a use in commerce.[308]

The Second Circuit adopted the rule of *Mother's Restaurant* in *Buti v. Impressa Perosa, S.R.L.*,[309] holding that no Lanham Act priority was established where the "Fashion Café" service mark was used for restaurant services offered exclusively in Italy, and where the restaurant was not the subject of a formal advertising campaign in the United States, even though during visits to the United States the operator of the restaurant had distributed "literally thousands of T-shirts, cards, and key chains with the Fashion Café name and logo to persons associated with the modeling and fashion industry which entitled them to free meals" at the restaurant.[310]

The Fourth Circuit, however, takes a broader view. In *International Bancorp, LLC v. Society des Bains de Mer et du Cercle des Etrangers a Monaco*,[311] the court held that a mark was used "in commerce" where it identified the source of services that a foreign casino operator offered to United States citizens. Although the casino operator provided its services exclusively overseas, it advertised in the United States through its New York office. The court concluded that the casino's services were provided "in commerce" because: (1) "United States citizens went to and gambled at the casino," and (2) the casino used its mark in its United States advertising for the casino.[312] The casino's gambling services therefore constituted "foreign trade," falling within the scope of the Commerce Clause.[313] The Fourth Circuit emphasized, however, that both the services and the advertising must take place in qualifying commerce in order to qualify.[314]

The Fourth's Circuit's interpretation of "use in commerce" has been criticized as overbroad on the ground that it could require a party seeking to use a trademark in the United States to cede priority to a party that has used the mark exclusively overseas.[315]

[iii] The Famous Marks Doctrine

Several state and federal courts have recognized a controversial exception to the territoriality principle known as the "famous marks" doctrine (or alternatively, the "well-known marks" doctrine). Under this doctrine, use of a mark exclusively overseas may give the owner of that mark priority in the United States if the mark

---

[308] 218 U.S.P.Q. 1046, 1048 (T.T.A.B. 1983). *Accord*, Linville v. Rivard, 41 U.S.P.Q.2D 1731, 1735–37 (T.T.A.B. 1997), *aff'd*, 133 F.3d 1446 (Fed. Cir. 1998); Techex, Ltd. v. Dvorkovitz, 220 U.S.P.Q. 81, 83 (T.T.A.B. 1983); Intermed Communications, Inc. v. Chaney, 197 U.S.P.Q. 501, 507–08 (T.T.A.B. 1977); Oland's Breweries [1971] Ltd. v. Miller Brewing Co., 189 U.S.P.Q. 481, 489 (T.T.A.B. 1976).

[309] 139 F.3d 98 (2d Cir. 1998).

[310] *Id.* at 100. *See also* Morningside Group, Ltd. v. Morningside Capital Group, LLC, 182 F.3d 133, 138 (2d Cir. 1999).

[311] 329 F.3d 359 (4th Cir. 2003).

[312] *Id.* at 365.

[313] *Id.*

[314] *Id.* at 381.

[315] *See, e.g., Int'l Bancorp*, 329 F.3d at 388 (Motz, J., dissenting); Empresa Cubana Del Tabaco v. Culbro Corp., 70 U.S.P.Q.2d 1650, 1675 n.8 (S.D.N.Y. 2004), *aff'd in part and rev'd in part*, 399 F.3d 462 (2d Cir. 2005); McCarthy on Trademarks and Unfair Competition § 29:4 (2009).

is sufficiently well-known to U.S. consumers, even if the goods and services are not offered in the United States.

The famous marks doctrine was first recognized by New York trial courts under the common law of unfair competition. In *Maison Prunier v. Prunier's Restaurant & Cafe*,[316] the trial court granted preliminary relief to a Paris restauranteur against a New York restaurant that was using a confusingly similar name and slogan and promoting itself as "The Famous French Sea Food Restaurant." In the court's view, the defendant's bad faith justified creating an exception to the territoriality principle. In *Vaudable v. Montmartre, Inc.*,[317] another New York court enjoined the use of the name "Maxim's" for a restaurant in New York, because the Paris restaurant of that name had long held a "unique and eminent position as a restaurant of international fame and prestige,"[318] even though its services were offered exclusively in Paris.[319]

Federal courts have reached conflicting conclusions on whether the famous marks exception should apply to the Lanham Act. The TTAB has applied the doctrine in several opposition proceedings,[320] and it has also been invoked by several federal district courts.[321] Among the courts of appeal, however, only the Ninth Circuit has embraced the doctrine. In its 2004 decision in *Grupo Gigante S.A. de C.V. v. Dallo & Co.*, it observed: "An absolute territoriality rule without a famous-mark exception would promote consumer confusion and fraud."[322] Accordingly, where a large Mexican grocery chain had used the "Gigante" mark exclusively in Mexico, but its reputation had spread to San Diego, the Ninth Circuit held that the Mexican trademark owner could have priority in San Diego if its mark had become sufficiently well-known to consumers in that market before the arrival of the junior user.

In contrast, in 2007 the Second Circuit expressly held that the famous marks exception does *not* apply to the Lanham Act in *ITC Ltd. v. Punchgini, Inc.*[323] While acknowledging that "a persuasive policy argument can be advanced" in support of the doctrine, the court held that Congress had not yet incorporated the doctrine into the Lanham Act. However, the court left open the possibility that the famous marks exception might apply to an unfair competition claim brought under *common* law. When the Second Circuit certified this question to the New York Court of Appeals, the latter court held that, while the famous marks doctrine was not recognized as an independent theory of liability under New York's common law

---

[316] 159 Misc. 551, 557–58, 288 N.Y.S. 529, 535–36 (N.Y. Sup. Ct. 1936).

[317] 193 N.Y.S.2d 332, 334–36 (N.Y. Sup. Ct. 1959).

[318] *Id.* at 334.

[319] *See also Maison Prunier*, 288 N.Y.S. at 537.

[320] London Regional Transport v. The William A. Berden & Edward C. Goetz, III Partnership, 2006 TTAB LEXIS 272 (June 20, 2006); The All England Lawn Tennis Club (Wimbledon) Ltd. v. Creations Aromatiques, Inc., 220 U.S.P.Q. 1069, 1072 (T.T.A.B. 1983).

[321] *See, e.g.*, Koffler Stores, Ltd. v. Shoppers Drug Mart, Inc., 434 F. Supp. 697, 704 (E.D. Mich. 1976), *aff'd mem.*, 559 F.2d 1219 (6th Cir. 1977).

[322] 391 F.3d 1088, 1094–95 (9th Cir. 2004).

[323] 482 F.3d 135 (2d Cir. 2007).

of unfair competition, nonetheless a plaintiff could make out a common law claim of unfair competition by showing that the defendant deliberately copied the plaintiff's mark or trade dress, and that the mark or trade dress had secondary meaning among the relevant New York consumers.[324]

Even where the famous marks exception has been recognized, there is little authority addressing the degree of fame necessary for a mark to qualify. Some courts have suggested that secondary meaning in the relevant United States market is sufficient.[325] In *Grupo Gigante*, however, the Ninth Circuit rejected this view, because setting the standard this low "would effectively cause the exception to eclipse the territoriality rule entirely."[326] Instead, the court held that the trademark owner must show, by a preponderance of the evidence, that "a *substantial* percentage of consumers in the relevant American market is familiar with the foreign mark."[327] Relevant factors include (1) intentional copying by the defendant, and (2) whether the defendant's customers of the American company are likely to think that they are patronizing the same firm that uses the mark overseas.[328]

In *ITC v Punchgini*, the Second Circuit certified to the New York Court of Appeals the question of what degree of fame is necessary to invoke the famous marks exception under New York common law. The state court responded that, at a minimum, United States consumers of the goods or services in question "must primarily associate the mark with the foreign plaintiff."[329] Factors relevant to this determination would include:

> (1) evidence that "the defendant intentionally associated goods with those of the foreign plaintiff in the minds of the public, such as public statements or advertising stating or implying a connection with the foreign plaintiff"; (2) "direct evidence, such as consumer surveys, indicating that consumers of defendant's goods or services believe them to be associated with the plaintiff"; and (3) "evidence of actual overlap between customers of the New York defendant and the foreign plaintiff."[330]

[iv]   Intent to Use Applications

Until 1989, applicants with similar marks sometimes found themselves in a "race" to be the first to use their mark in commerce in order to be the first to register the mark on the Principal Register. They sometimes resorted to "token" interstate uses of their trademarks, leading to costly litigation over whether these

---

[324] ITC Ltd. v. Punchgini, Inc., 518 F.3d 159 (2d Cir. 2008) (citing ITC Ltd. v. Punchgini, Inc., 880 N.E.2d 852 (N.Y. 2007)).

[325] *See* ITC Ltd. v. Punchgini, 373 F. Supp.2d 275, 287–88 (S.D.N.Y. 2005) (collecting cases), *aff'd in part*, 482 F.3d 135 (2d Cir. 2007).

[326] 391 F.3d at 1096.

[327] *Id.* at 1098. Professor McCarthy agrees with the requirement that a "substantial percentage" of the relevant American consumers should be familiar with the foreign mark, and suggests a threshold of 50%. McCarthy on Trademarks § 29:4.

[328] 391 F.3d at 1098.

[329] 518 F.3d at 161 (quoting ITC Ltd. v. Punchgini, Inc., 880 N.E.2d 852, 859–60 (N.Y. 2007)).

[330] 518 F.3d at 161 (quoting *Punchgini*, 880 N.E.2d 852, 859–61)).

uses were sham transactions or bona fide uses in commerce as required by the Lanham Act's definition of a "use in commerce."[331] Even in the absence of such contrivances, aspiring trademark applicants risked losing their investment in developing new trademarks if another applicant for the same or a confusingly similar mark edged them out in being the first to make a bona fide use of the mark.

In addition, domestic trademark applicants filing applications based on actual use in commerce sometimes found themselves edged out by applicants for foreign trademark registrations for the same or similar marks because, as discussed below,[332] in many cases the latter are entitled to federal registration priority based on their foreign application dates even if they have not yet used their marks anywhere in the world.

In response to these concerns, in the Trademark Law Revision Act of 1988, Congress amended section 1 of the Lanham Act to permit the filing of "intent to use" (ITU) applications for registration on the Principal Register. The ITU provisions, codified in section 1(b),[333] took effect in 1989. The ITU application allows a trademark applicant to file an application for registration on the Principal Register before the date on which the mark is first used in trade. If the ITU application eventually ripens into a valid trademark registration, the effective date of that registration will be the date on which the ITU application was filed. Accordingly, by using the ITU process, the successful applicant obtains a priority date for nationwide constructive use that corresponds to the applicant's ITU filing date, which is earlier than the date of the first actual use of the mark in trade. The ITU application process is discussed in detail below.[334]

[v]   Constructive Use

Although actual use in commerce is a prerequisite to registration of a mark on the Principal Register, registration of the mark constitutes constructive use of the mark throughout the United States, thus giving the registrant priority against later adopters of confusingly similar marks even in areas where the registrant has not actually used the mark.[335] Constructive use is discussed in more detail below.[336]

[2]   Distinctiveness

As discussed above,[337] a trademark or service mark must distinguish the goods or services in connection with which it is used from goods or services offered by another source. A mark can be distinctive in either of two ways: it can be inherently distinctive, in which case trademark rights arise when it is first used in

---

[331] 15 U.S.C. § 1127 (defining "use in commerce"); *see, e.g.*, Blue Bell, Inc. v. Jaymar-Ruby, Inc., 497 F.2d 433, 437 (2d Cir. 1974).

[332] *See* § 5E[6].

[333] 15 U.S.C. § 1051(b).

[334] *See* § 5E[3][b].

[335] 15 U.S.C. § 1057(c).

[336] *See* § 5E[1].

[337] *See* § 5C[1][b], § 5C[2][a].

commerce;[338] or it can acquire distinctiveness ("secondary meaning") through use, in which case trademark rights arise when secondary meaning arises.[339]

[3]   Maintaining Trademark Rights

Unlike patents and copyrights, which have statutorily limited terms of protection, trademark rights have indefinite duration, both at common law and under the Lanham Act. However, once trademark rights have been established, they must also be maintained, or they will be lost. Because trademark rights are established through: (1) use and (2) distinctiveness, they can be lost through: (1) non-use or (2) loss of distinctiveness.

A loss of trademark rights through cessation of use is referred to as "abandonment." This topic is addressed in § 5J[1].

Trademark rights can also be lost if a mark loses its ability to distinguish the trademark owner's goods or services from those of another. This can occur if consumers begin to perceive the mark not as an origin indicator, but merely as a description of, or a synonym for, the goods or services in question. These topics are discussed in §§ 5C[2][a][iii] and [iv].

Although trademarks and service marks can be assigned or licensed, the ability to assign or license a mark is not unfettered. If the assignment or license causes the mark to become separated from its underlying goodwill, so that consumer expectations are frustrated, the mark may lose its protection. These topics are addressed in the next section.

In the case of a federally registered mark, the registrant must also file periodic renewals and statements of use in order to maintain the federal registration and to continue to enjoy the legal benefits of that registration. This topic is addressed in § 5E[3][f].

[4]   Assignments and Licenses

[a]   Assignments

Under both common law and the Lanham Act, any assignment of a mark (that is, any transfer of ownership) must include a transfer of the accompanying goodwill of the line of business in which the mark is used. An attempt to transfer rights in the mark without the accompanying goodwill constitutes an "assignment in gross," and results in abandonment of the mark.[340] However, where some of the goodwill of a business is not associated with the mark that is being assigned — for example, where the mark is used in one line of business but not another, or where some of the goodwill of the business is associated with other marks — only the goodwill

---

[338] Grupo Gigante S.A. de C.V. v. Dallo & Co., 119 F. Supp. 2d 1083, 1088–89, *aff'd*, 391 F.3d 1088 (9th Cir. 2004).

[339] Investacorp, Inc. v. Arabian Inv. Banking Corp., 931 F.2d 1519, 1524 (11th Cir. 1991); *Grupo Gigante*, 119 F. Supp. 2d at 1092.

[340] Assignments in gross are discussed in more detail in § 5J[1][b][ii].

associated with the particular mark being assigned must be included in the transfer.[341]

Because of the prohibition against assignments in gross, an intent-to-use application under section 1(b)[342] cannot be assigned until the verified statement of use has been filed under section 1(d)[343] or the application has been amended to allege use pursuant to section 1(c).[344] The only exception is when the application is assigned to a successor to the business of the applicant to which the mark pertains, if the business is ongoing.[345]

Assignments of registered marks, or of marks that are the subject of pending applications, must be in writing and duly executed.[346] Recording of the assignment in the PTO's Assignments Services Branch is *prima facie* evidence of execution.[347] An assignment is void against any subsequent purchaser for valuable consideration without notice, unless the assignment is properly recorded in the PTO within three months after the assignment or prior to the subsequent purchase.[348] In contrast, no writing requirement applies to assignments of common-law marks.

If a mark is assigned while federal registration is still pending, the assignee should record the assignment in the PTO so that the registration will ultimately issue in the assignee's name.[349] The assignee becomes entitled to prosecute the application.[350]

If the ownership of a registration changes with respect to some, but not all, of the goods and services listed in the registration, then the owners may, upon recording these assignment(s), request that the registration be divided into two or more separate registrations.[351]

[b]   Licensing

A trademark can be validly licensed provided that the licensor maintains adequate control over the licensee's use of the mark.[352] Neither common law nor the Lanham Act imposes specific formalities on the licensing of trademarks or service marks. However, it is essential that the licensor exercise adequate quality control over the licensee's use of the mark. Failure to exercise quality control constitutes

---

[341] 15 U.S.C. §§ 1060(a)(1)–(2).

[342] 15 U.S.C. § 1051(b).

[343] 15 U.S.C. § 1051(d).

[344] 15 U.S.C. § 1051(c); Clorox Co. v. Chemical Bank, 40 U.S.P.Q.2d 1098 (T.T.A.B. 1996).

[345] 15 U.S.C. § 1060(a)(1).

[346] 15 U.S.C. § 1060(a)(3).

[347] *Id.*

[348] 15 U.S.C. § 1060(a)(4).

[349] 15 U.S.C. § 1057(d); TMEP § 501.01(a).

[350] 37 C.F.R. § 3.71.

[351] TMEP §§ 501.06, 1615–1615.02; *see* Visa, USA, Inc. v. Birmingham Trust Nat'l Bank, 696 F.2d 1371 (Fed. Cir. 1982).

[352] Dawn Donut Co. v. Hart's Food Stores, Inc., 267 F.2d 358, 366 (2d Cir. 1946).

"naked licensing," which will lead to a finding of abandonment.[353]

§ 5E   REGISTRATION OF TRADEMARK RIGHTS

Although federal registration is not a prerequisite to protecting a trademark under section 43 of the Lanham Act or under state law, registration does confer significant benefits.

First, under sections 7(b) and 33(a), registration on the Principal Register is *prima facie* evidence that the mark in question is valid and owned by the registrant, and that the latter has the exclusive right to use the mark in commerce on or in connection with the goods or services for which it is registered, subject to any conditions or limitations stated in the registration.[354] Thus, in an action for infringement, the registered mark will be presumed valid for the goods or services for which it is registered, and the registrant need not affirmatively prove validity in order to make out a *prima facie* case of infringement. Instead, the defendant bears the burden of showing that the mark should not have been registered in the first place, or that it was valid when registered but subsequently lost its validity.

Second, section 7(c) provides that, subject to several exceptions, if the application to register a mark on the Principal Register is ultimately successful, then the filing of the application will constitute constructive use of the mark, conferring nationwide priority with respect to the goods or services for which the mark is registered, as of the date on which the application was filed.[355] The exceptions to this rule apply when another party has taken any one of the following actions *prior to* the applicant's filing date: (1) used the mark; (2) filed an application to register the mark, which either is pending or has resulted in registration of the mark; or (3) filed a foreign application to register the mark on the basis of which that party has acquired a right of priority, and has timely filed a registration application under 15 U.S.C. § 1126(d), which either is pending or has resulted in registration of the mark. For any of the exceptions to apply, however, the party taking one of these three actions must not have subsequently abandoned the mark.[356]

Third, under section 22, registration on the Principal Register constitutes constructive notice of the registrant's ownership of the mark, thus giving the registrant priority over junior users even in markets where the registrant has not yet used the mark.[357] It also precludes a subsequent user from arguing that it adopted the mark in good faith and without knowledge of the registration.[358] Prior to enactment of the Lanham Act in 1946, there was no constructive notice provision;

---

[353] Naked licensing is discussed in more detail in § 5J[1][b][i].

[354] 15 U.S.C. §§ 1057(b), 1115(a); Coca-Cola Co. v. Overland, Inc., 692 F.2d 1250, 1254 (9th Cir. 1982).

[355] 15 U.S.C. § 1057(c).

[356] *Id.* Priority based on foreign applications is discussed at § 5[E][7].

[357] 15 U.S.C. § 1072; Value House v. Phillips Mercantile Co., 523 F.2d 424, 429 (10th Cir. 1975); Old Dutch Foods, Inc. v. Dan Dee Pretzel & Potato Chip Co., 477 F.2d 150, 156–57 (6th Cir. 1973); John R. Thompson Co. v. Holloway, 366 F.2d 108, 115 (5th Cir. 1966); Dawn Donut Co. v. Hart's Food Stores, Inc., 267 F.2d 358, 362 (2d Cir. 1959).

[358] *Value House,* 523 F.2d at 429.

thus, a party that was the first to use a mark in a particular region could obtain rights in the mark within that region if it adopted the mark without actual notice of an existing registration.[359] However, for post-1989 applications, the constructive notice provision has reduced importance in light of the more powerful constructive use provision in section 7(c).

Fourth, once a mark has been registered on the Principal Register for five years, it can become incontestable,[360] as discussed in § 5E[4].

Fifth, under section 42, federal registration significantly improves the trademark owner's ability to block the importation of infringing goods.[361]

Finally, in an infringement action, the owner of a mark that is registered on the Principal Register has access to a broader array of remedies under sections 34(d), 35(b), and 35(c) than does the owner of an unregistered mark.[362]

Where a trademark owner brings an infringement action for use of its registered mark on goods or services other than those for which the mark is registered, the advantages of federal registration do not apply, and the mark will be treated as an unregistered mark. The trademark owner's rights and remedies, therefore, will be limited to those available under the applicable state law and section 43(a) of the Lanham Act.[363]

The benefits of federal registration provide trademark owners with an incentive to seek registration rather than rely on protection under state law or section 43(a). Federal registration also benefits the public, by providing notice of which marks are in use and by whom, by discouraging infringing conduct, and by helping entrepreneurs to select marks that will not conflict with marks already in use.[364]

[1]   Marks Eligible for Federal Registration

[a]   In General

Section 45 of the Lanham Act defines a "trademark" as "any word, name, symbol, or device, or any combination thereof" that is used by a person "to identify and distinguish his or her goods, including a unique product, from those manufactured or sold by others and to indicate the source of the goods, even if that source is unknown."[365] A "service mark" is defined in identical terms, except for the

---

[359] *Dawn Donut*, 267 F.2d at 362.

[360] 15 U.S.C. § 1065.

[361] 15 U.S.C. § 1124. In addition, only registered marks can be recorded with the U.S. Customs Service, and once the mark is recorded, Customs agents can seize infringing goods under 19 U.S.C. § 1526.

[362] 15 U.S.C. §§ 1116(d), 1117(b), (c). For more on remedies, see § 5K.

[363] Natural Footwear Ltd. v. Hart, Schaffner & Marx, 760 F.2d 1383, 1396–97 (3d Cir. 1985); Universal Nutrition Corp. v. Carbolite Foods, Inc., 325 F. Supp. 2d 526, 532 (D.N.J. 2004).

[364] Bongrain Int'l Corp. v. Delice de France, Inc., 811 F.2d 1479, 1485 (Fed. Cir. 1987); *Natural Footwear*, 760 F.2d at 1395.

[365] 15 U.S.C. § 1127.

substitution of "services" for "goods."[366] Thus, a trademark or service mark must be used to identify and distinguish the applicant's goods or services, and to indicate their source. If the applicant's mark does not serve this function, it cannot be registered.

Although this standard is similar to the general standard used to determine whether a mark qualifies for protection under the common law or section 43(a),[367] the PTO in some circumstances interprets this standard more narrowly in the registration context. For example, titles of individual books or movies generally cannot be registered, but have been protected under section 43(a).[368]

If an applicant's mark satisfies the federal definition of a trademark or service mark, it must still run the gauntlet of the bars to registration under sections 2(a) through (e). The bars to registration reflect a variety of concerns related to public policy or international law.[369]

[b] Service Marks

The definition of a "service mark" in section 45 of the Lanham Act is identical to that of a "trademark," except for the substitution of "services" for "goods."[370] Service marks may be registered, subject to all of the same rules and protections that apply to trademarks for goods.[371] If the same mark is used for both goods and services, two separate registrations may be obtained.[372]

For a mark to be registered as a service mark, the owner must use the mark in connection with offering bona fide services, as opposed to activities that constitute merely the advertising, promotion, or aftermarket support of the merchant's goods.[373] In some cases, this distinction can be difficult to draw — for example, where the mark is used in connection with a contest or a sporting event that provides entertainment services to the public while simultaneously promoting the merchant's goods.[374]

Advertising agencies may not register marks for their advertising services if the marks are simply licensed to their clients for use in promoting the clients' own goods or services.[375] In contrast, an advertising agency may register a mark that it uses to promote its advertising services, even if it *also* uses (or allows clients to use)

---

[366] *Id.*

[367] *See* § 5C.

[368] *See* § 5C[2][b][v].

[369] *See* § 5E[2].

[370] 15 U.S.C. § 1127.

[371] 15 U.S.C. § 1053.

[372] *In re* Burger King of Florida, Inc., 136 U.S.P.Q. 396 (T.T.A.B. 1963).

[373] *See, e.g., In re* Orion Research, Inc., 669 F.2d 689 (C.C.P.A. 1980).

[374] *See, e.g., In re* Dr. Pepper Co., 836 F.2d 508 (Fed. Cir. 1987); *In re* Heavenly Creations, Inc., 168 U.S.P.Q. 317 (T.T.A.B. 1971).

[375] *In re* Local Trademarks, Inc., 220 U.S.P.Q. 728 (T.T.A.B. 1983); *In re* Application of Admark, Inc., 214 U.S.P.Q. 302 (T.T.A.B. 1982).

the same mark to promote the goods or services of the clients.[376]

[c] Certification Marks

A mark may be registered as a certification mark, rather than as a trademark or service mark, pursuant to section 4 of the Lanham Act.[377] Section 45 defines a certification mark as "any word name, symbol, or device, or any combination thereof" that is "used by a person other than its owner . . . to certify regional or other origin, material, mode of manufacture, quality, accuracy, or other characteristics of such person's goods or services or that the work or labor on the goods or services was performed by members of a union or other organization."[378]

Examples of certification marks include the "Underwriters Laboratory" or "UL" mark, which signifies that a product complies with certain safety standards,[379] and the "Roquefort" mark, which signifies that a cheese has been manufactured according to a particular process and within a particular region of France.[380]

The otherwise-applicable prohibition against registering primarily geographically descriptive marks contains an exception for certification marks, which can be registered even if they describe the geographic origin of goods or services and lack secondary meaning.[381] However, a non-geographic mark that is generic or primarily descriptive cannot be registered as a certification mark, because consumers would not recognize such a mark as a certification of quality.[382]

A certification mark is neither a trademark nor a service mark, and will become invalid if it is used as such. Thus, the owner of a certification mark is prohibited from producing or marketing the goods or services to which that mark is applied; such activities are grounds for refusal or cancellation of a certification mark's registration.[383] However, a certification mark registrant is not prohibited from using its certification mark in advertising or promoting its certification program or the goods or services meeting its certification standards, provided that the registrant does not itself produce, manufacture, or sell any of the certified goods or services to which its certification mark is applied.[384]

Under section 14(5),[385] registration of a certification mark may also be cancelled if the registrant: (1) does not control, or is not able legitimately to exercise control

---

[376] *In re* Advertising & Marketing Dev., Inc. 821 F.2d 614, 620–21 (Fed. Cir. 1987).

[377] 15 U.S.C. § 1054.

[378] 15 U.S.C. § 1127.

[379] Midwest Plastic Fabricators, Inc. v. Underwriters Laboratories, Inc., 906 F.2d 1568 (Fed. Cir. 1990).

[380] Community of Roquefort v. William Faehndrich, Inc., 303 F.2d 494 (2d Cir. 1962).

[381] *Id.*

[382] *In re* Prof'l Photographers of Ohio, Inc., 149 U.S.P.Q. 857 (T.T.A.B. 1966).

[383] *In re* Florida Citrus Comm'n, 160 U.S.P.Q. 495 (T.T.A.B. 1968).

[384] 15 U.S.C. § 1064(5).

[385] *Id.*

over, the use of such mark;[386] (2) permits the use of the certification mark for purposes other than to certify; or (3) discriminately refuses to certify or to continue to certify the goods or services of any person who maintains the standards or conditions that such mark certifies. A certification mark must be made available, without discrimination, to any product or service that meets the certification standards.[387]

[d]   Collective Marks

Section 4 of the Lanham Act also permits registration of collective marks, which are trademarks or service marks indicating that the user is a member of the particular association or collective group that owns the mark. Thus, the origin-signifying function of a collective mark is not to signify that the goods or services come from a particular source, but to indicate that their source is affiliated with a particular group. Unlike certification marks, collective marks do not signify that the product or service bearing the mark has particular qualities or characteristics.

Section 45 defines a collective mark as "a trademark or service mark" that is "used by the members of a cooperative, an association, or other collective group or organization," including "marks indicating membership in a union, an association, or other organization."[388]

A collective mark's registration may be canceled if the association (as distinguished from individual members) begins to use the mark on goods or services, or transfers ownership of the mark to a particular member of the group.[389] However, the association is free to license its mark to nonmembers subject to the generally applicable rule requiring trademark licensors to exercise proper control over licensees' use of the mark.[390] Like trademarks and service marks, a collective mark must be distinctive in order to be registered on the Principal Register.[391]

Examples of collective marks include "Realtor" and "Realtors," registered by the National Association of Realtors,[392] and "Lions International," registered by the International Association of Lions Clubs.[393]

---

[386] *See* Midwest Plastic Fabricators, Inc. v. Underwriters Laboratories, Inc., 906 F.2d 1568, 1573 (Fed. Cir. 1990).

[387] 15 U.S.C. § 1064(5); Community of Roquefort v. William Faehndrich, Inc., 303 F.2d 494, 497 (2d Cir. 1962).

[388] 15 U.S.C. § 1127.

[389] F.R. Lepage Bakery, Inc. v. Roush Bakery Prods. Co., 851 F.2d 351 (Fed. Cir.), *modified and remanded*, 863 F.2d 43 (Fed. Cir. 1988).

[390] Professional Golfers Ass'n of America v. Bankers Life & Cas. Co., 514 F.2d 665, 668 (5th Cir. 1975).

[391] Racine Industries Inc. v. Bane-Clene Corp., 35 U.S.P.Q.2d 1832, 1837 (T.T.A.B. 1994).

[392] Zimmerman v. National Ass'n of Realtors, 70 U.S.P.Q.2d 1425 (T.T.A.B. 2004).

[393] Int'l Ass'n of Lions Clubs v. Mars, Inc., 221 U.S.P.Q. 187 (T.T.A.B. 1984).

[2]   Marks Ineligible for Federal Registration

Section 2 of the Lanham Act sets forth the general substantive standards for registering a mark on the Principal Register of the PTO. It is structured, however, as a series of rules specifying which marks will be refused registration. The general standard that precedes the specific bars to registration simply states that "[n]o trademark by which the goods of the applicant may be distinguished from the goods of others shall be refused registration on the principal register on account of its nature" unless it falls within one of the ineligible categories listed in sections 2(a) through (e).[394] Section 3 makes clear that the registration rules of section 2 apply equally to service marks.[395]

Thus, if a mark is capable of distinguishing the applicant's goods or services from those of another, the mark may be registered on the Principal Register unless it falls within one of the five categories described in sections 2(a) through (e). With respect to the first four of these categories, sections 2(a) through (d), registration of a mark falling into that category is completely prohibited. With respect to marks that are barred from registration under section 2(e), however, section 2(f) distinguishes between marks that are completely unregistrable and those that may overcome the presumption of unregistrability if they have acquired secondary meaning.

"Composite marks" are marks which consist of several separable components, which may be words, designs, or combinations thereof. When an applicant seeks to register a composite mark that includes some components that are unregistrable, the applicant may disclaim, or may be required by the Director of the PTO to disclaim, the portions of the mark that are unregistrable.[396] With respect to the disclaimed portions of the mark, the applicant surrenders any entitlement to exclusivity that would otherwise arise from the fact of registration.[397] The disclaimer does not prejudice the applicant's ability to seek registration of the disclaimed matter at another time — for example, where the disclaimed matter is descriptive but later acquires secondary meaning.[398] However, a disclaimer may not be used to avoid a rejection based on deceptiveness under section 2(a),[399] or based on a determination that a mark is primarily geographically deceptively misdescriptive under section 2(e)(3).[400] The rationale for these exceptions is that

---

[394] 15 U.S.C. § 1052.

[395] 15 U.S.C. § 1053.

[396] 15 U.S.C. § 1056 (a); see, e.g., In re Best Software, Inc., 63 U.S.P.Q.2d 1109 (T.T.A.B. 2002). Sometimes, the registrable and unregistrable components of a composite mark are so interdependent (either graphically or semantically) that the mark is considered "unitary," in which case a disclaimer will not be required. For example, the term BLACK MAGIC would be considered unitary, because the meaning of the two words combined has nothing to do with the color black; thus, although BLACK is a descriptive term it would not have to be disclaimed even if the BLACK MAGIC mark were applied to goods that were black in color. Trademark Manual of Examining Procedure (TMEP) § 1213.05 (5th ed.).

[397] United States Steel Corp. v. Vasco Metals Corp., 394 F.2d 1009, 1012 (C.C.P.A. 1968).

[398] 15 U.S.C. § 1056(b).

[399] American Speech-Language-Hearing Ass'n v. National Hearing Aid Soc'y, 224 U.S.P.Q. 798 (T.T.A.B. 1984).

[400] In re Wada, 48 U.S.P.Q.2d 1689 (T.T.A.B. 1998).

the public that encounters the trademark will be unaware that any portion of it has been disclaimed; thus, permitting registration of a mark that contains a deceptive component would lead to consumer confusion notwithstanding the disclaimer.[401]

There are conflicting authorities on the question of whether an applicant may disclaim each individual component of a composite mark, but still obtain registration for the mark as a whole. For example, registration of the mark MINITMIX was permitted, subject to disclaimers of both MINIT and MIX,[402] but a registration for PILATES STUDIO was cancelled, notwithstanding disclaimers of both PILATES and STUDIO, on the ground that "a composite mark cannot be amended to disclaim all portions of the mark individually and remain valid."[403]

Only one mark can be registered in a single application.[404] In *In re International Flavors & Fragrances, Inc.*, the Federal Circuit invoked this rule to bar "phantom" registrations, in which an applicant seeks to register an incomplete mark so that the registered mark can be used in combination with various other terms in order to obtain protection for an open-ended "family" of related marks in a single registration. In that case, the applicant applied for three registrations — for LIVING XXXX FLAVOR, LIVING XXXX FLAVORS, and LIVING XXXX. In each case, XXXX was merely a placeholder for the name of "a specific herb, fruit, plant or vegetable" or "a botanical or extract thereof" that the applicant would later insert for each product marketed under the mark — for example, LIVING GREEN BELL PEPPER FLAVORS. The Federal Circuit held that these applications were unregistrable, because allowing registrations in this incomplete and indefinite form would make trademark searches too difficult, and would thus fail to provide the public with constructive notice of what was registered.[405]

Failure of a mark to qualify for registration on the Principal Register does not preclude protection for such marks under section 43(a) of the Lanham Act, or under state common law or statutory law. In addition, some marks that fail to qualify for the Principal Register may obtain a lesser degree of protection by being registered on the Supplemental Register.[406]

[a]   Immoral, Deceptive, Scandalous, or Disparaging Matter

Section 2(a) bars registration of a mark that comprises any of the following: (1) immoral, deceptive, or scandalous matter; (2) matter that may disparage, or falsely suggest a connection, with persons (either living or dead), institutions, beliefs, or national symbols, or bring them into "contempt, or disrepute"; or (3) with respect to marks used on or in connection with wines or spirits, a geographical indication that is not the place where the goods originated, but only if such use of the mark by

---

[401] *Wada*, 48 U.S.P.Q. 2d at 1692.

[402] *Ex parte* Pillsbury Flour Mills Co., 23 U.S.P.Q. 168 (Comm'r 1934).

[403] Pilates, Inc. v. Georgetown Bodyworks Deep Muscle Massage Ctrs., Inc., 157 F. Supp. 2d 75, 82 (D.D.C. 2001). *See also In re* Midy Labs, 104 F.2d 617, 618 (C.C.P.A. 1939).

[404] *In re* International Flavors & Fragrances, Inc., 183 F.3d 1361, 1366 (Fed. Cir. 1999).

[405] *Id.* at 1368 & n.6 (Fed. Cir. 1999).

[406] *See* § 5E[5].

the applicant commenced on or after January 1, 1995 (the effective date of the WTO Agreement in the U.S.).[407]

A mark is immoral or scandalous if "the mark would be offensive to the conscience or moral feelings of a substantial composite of the general public."[408] Whether a particular mark is so immoral or scandalous as to be unregistrable is a somewhat subjective judgment, and changing social and cultural norms may lead to different decisions over time. According to the Federal Circuit, "whether the mark consists of or comprises scandalous matter must be determined from the standpoint of a substantial composite of the general public . . . and in the context of contemporary attitudes, keeping in mind changes in social mores and sensitivities."[409]

The Federal Circuit has held that a finding that a mark is vulgar is sufficient to establish that it is immoral or scandalous.[410] Although the personal opinion of the examining attorney cannot be the basis for a determination that a mark is scandalous, where the evidence shows that a mark has only one pertinent meaning, the dictionary meaning alone can satisfy the PTO's burden of proof for a section 2(a) refusal, because "dictionary definitions represent an effort to distill the collective understanding of the community with respect to language."[411]

Registration has been denied for the term "BUBBY TRAP" for brassieres,[412] for an image of a man and woman kissing that displayed full frontal nudity,[413] for an image of a defecating dog,[414] and for the terms "BULLSHIT"[415] and "JACK-OFF."[416] Registrations of "MADONNA"[417] and "MESSIAS"[418] for wine were refused, on the ground that the juxtaposition would be offensive or scandalous. However, the term "BLACK TAIL"[419] and the image of a condom with stars and stripes resembling an American flag[420] were both held to be registrable.

To determine whether a mark is disparaging, the Federal Circuit and the Trademark Trial and Appeal Board (TTAB) make the following inquiry:

 (1) what is the likely meaning of the matter in question, taking into account not

---

[407] 15 U.S.C. § 1052(a).

[408] *In re* Wilcher Corp., 40 U.S.P.Q.2d 1929 (T.T.A.B. 1996).

[409] *In re* Boulevard Entertainment, Inc., 334 F.3d 1336, 1340 (Fed. Cir. 2003).

[410] *Id.*

[411] *Id.*

[412] *In re* Runsdorf, 171 U.S.P.Q. 443 (T.T.A.B. 1971).

[413] *In re* McGinley, 660 F.2d 481 (C.C.P.A. 1981).

[414] Greyhound Corp. v. Both Worlds, Inc., 6 U.S.P.Q.2d 1635 (T.T.A.B. 1988).

[415] *In re* Tinseltown, Inc., 212 U.S.P.Q. 863 (T.T.A.B. 1981).

[416] *In re* Boulevard Entertainment, Inc., 334 F.3d 1336 (Fed. Cir. 2003).

[417] *In re* Riverbank Canning Co., 95 F.2d 327 (C.C.P.A. 1938); *In re* P.J. Valckenbeg, GmbH, 122 U.S.P.Q. 334 (T.T.A.B. 1959).

[418] *In re* Sociedade Agricola v. Commercial Dos Vinhos Messias, S.A.R.L., 159 U.S.P.Q. 275 (T.T.A.B. 1968).

[419] Boswell v. Mavety Media Group, Ltd., 52 U.S.P.Q.2d 1600 (T.T.A.B. 1999).

[420] *In re* Old Glory Condom Corp., 26 U.S.P.Q.2d 1216 (T.T.A.B. 1993).

only dictionary definitions, but also the relationship of the matter to the other elements in the mark, the nature of the goods or services, and the manner in which the mark is used in the marketplace in connection with the goods or services; and

(2)   if that meaning is found to refer to identifiable persons, institutions, beliefs or national symbols, whether that meaning may be disparaging to a substantial composite of the referenced group.[421]

Thus, in contrast to scandalous marks, a disparaging mark must be perceived as such by a substantial composite of the allegedly disparaged group rather than the general public.

In litigation that has been ongoing since 1992, the TTAB has twice ruled that the term "REDSKINS" for a football team was disparaging to Native Americans at the time of registration, and should therefore be cancelled. Applying the "substantial composite" standard, the TTAB held that 30% was "without doubt" a substantial composite of Native Americans.[422]

Recent litigation has raised, but not resolved, the question whether 2(a) rejections based on disparagement violate the First Amendment.[423]

The test of whether a mark is "deceptive" is somewhat more objective. To be deceptive, (1) the mark must falsely describe the goods or services, (2) the misdescription must be one that the prospective purchaser is likely to believe is true, and (3) that mistaken belief must be likely to materially affect the consumer's purchasing decision.[424] For example, the mark "LOVEE LAMB" for car seat covers made of fuzzy synthetic material was held to be unregistrable as deceptive, because purchasers were likely to believe the material was lambskin, and this belief was likely to have a material effect on their purchasing decision.[425]

The test used by the TTAB to determine whether a mark falsely suggests a connection with persons, institutions, beliefs, or national symbols is also objective. In order to establish a false connection, the TTAB must find that: (1) the applicant's mark is the same as, or closely approximates, another's previously used name or identity; (2) the mark would be recognized as such; (3) the other party (person, institution, etc.) is not connected with the activities performed by the applicant under the mark; and (4) the name or identity of the other party is of sufficient fame or reputation that when the applicant's mark is used on goods or services, a connection with the other party would be presumed.[426]

---

[421] *In re* Geller, 751 F.3d 1355 (Fed. Cir. 2014).

[422] Blackhorse v. Pro-Football, Inc., 111 U.S.P.Q.2d 1080 (T.T.A.B. 2014). The earlier proceeding was Pro-Football, Inc. v. Harjo, 284 F. Supp. 2d 96 (D.D.C. 2003).

[423] *See In re* Geller, 751 F.3d 1355 (Fed. Cir. 2014), *petition for cert. filed* (Aug. 11, 2014); Blackhorse v. Pro-Football, Inc., 111 U.S.P.Q.2d 1080 (T.T.A.B. 2014), *appeal filed*, 2014 U.S. Dist. Ct. Pleadings (E.D. Va. Aug. 14, 2014) Civil Action No. 1:14-cv-01043-GBL-IDD.

[424] *In re* Budge Mfg. Co., 857 F.2d 773 (Fed. Cir. 1988).

[425] *Id.* at 775–77.

[426] Buffett v. Chi-Chi's, Inc., 228 U.S.P.Q. 428, 429 (T.T.A.B. 1985).

[b]   National, State, or Municipal Insignia

Section 2(b) bars registration of a mark that comprises or simulates the flag, coat of arms, or insignia of the United States, any state or municipality, or any foreign nation.[427] Thus, for example, the predecessor to section 2(b) barred registration of the official seals of England[428] and the United States Department of Justice,[429] and the seal and coat of arms of the state of Maryland,[430] but section 2(b) did not bar registration of an image of the Statue of Liberty, which was found to be, at most, a "national symbol" subject to evaluation under section 2(a).[431]

[c]   Name, Portrait, or Signature

Section 2(c) bars registration of any mark that comprises (1) a name, portrait, or signature identifying a particular living individual, except with that person's written consent, or (2) the name, signature, or portrait of a deceased U.S. President during the life of his or her surviving spouse, except with the spouse's written consent.[432] The purpose of this bar is to protect individuals' rights of privacy and publicity.[433]

[d]   Marks Confusingly Similar to Existing Marks

Section 2(d) incorporates the common law "likelihood of confusion" test, barring registration of any mark which so resembles a mark already registered at the PTO, or already used in the United States by another and not abandoned, as to be likely, when used on or in connection with the applicant's goods or services, to cause confusion or mistake, or to deceive.[434] To enjoy a right of priority under section 2(d), a party must show that it was the first to establish proprietary rights in the mark. Proprietary rights "may arise from a prior registration, prior trademark or service mark use, prior use as a trade name, prior use analogous to trademark or service mark use, or any other use sufficient to establish proprietary rights."[435]

[i]   Priority of Use

When two or more parties seek to register confusingly similar marks for similar goods or services, based on either intended or actual use in commerce, the question of which party has the right of priority will depend on which party used the mark first. Although use *in commerce* is essential to obtaining trademark registration, an applicant who is the first to use a mark in commerce may be denied registration under section 2(d) if another party has used a confusingly similar mark on similar goods or services *anywhere* in the United States, even if that use was not "in

---

[427] 15 U.S.C. § 1052(b).

[428] *In re* Gorham Mfg. Co., 41 App. D.C. 263 (1913) (noting that the lion is "[t]he official emblem of the British Assay Office").

[429] *In re* William Connors Paint Mfg. Co., 27 App. D.C. 389 (1906).

[430] *In re* Cahn, Belt, & Co., 27 App. D.C. 173 (1906).

[431] Liberty Mutual Ins. Co. v. Liberty Ins. Co., 185 F. Supp. 895 (E.D. Ark. 1960).

[432] 15 U.S.C. § 1052(c).

[433] University of Notre Dame du Lac v. J.C. Gourmet Food Imports Co., Inc., 703 F.2d 1372, 1376 (Fed. Cir. 1983); Canovas v. Venezia, 220 U.S.P.Q. 660, 661 (T.T.A.B. 1983).

[434] 15 U.S.C. § 1052(d).

[435] Herbko Int'l, Inc. v. Kappa Books, Inc., 308 F.3d 1156, 1162 (Fed. Cir. 2002).

commerce" because it was purely intrastate.[436] In the case of an intent-to-use application, the applicant's priority date will be either the filing date of the intent-to-use application, or the date on which that applicant commenced use of the mark in connection with goods and services (whether or not that use was interstate), whichever is earlier.[437]

[ii] Priority Through Analogous Use

Although technical trademark use is a prerequisite to registration, prior use of a mark in interstate or intrastate commerce can defeat another user's registration (or attempted registration) of a similar mark if the prior use is analogous to trademark use.[438] Under the doctrine of "analogous use," a use that would not by itself be a technical trademark use may nonetheless be sufficient, under section 2(d), to establish which party is the senior user of the mark — that is, which party has priority in the mark.[439] For example, using a mark merely to advertise goods, without actually affixing the mark to the goods and shipping them to consumers or retailers, is not a technical trademark use, and thus is not a sufficient use in commerce to permit registration of the mark. However, if the use "was of such nature and extent as to create an association by the purchasing public of the goods with the user,"[440] then it is an analogous use.[441] The analogous use need not be in the context of advertising, and it need not even be a use by the party claiming priority; for example, a third-party use of the mark by the news media or by the public can inure to the benefit of the party claiming priority by virtue of analogous use, even if that party has not itself used the term.[442] It does not matter whether the analogous use is purely intrastate.[443]

In an opposition or interference proceeding, an analogous use by the party seeking to register a mark may establish the applicant's priority date, regardless of whether the application is based on actual use or intent to use.[444] Likewise, an analogous use by an opposer may establish the opposer's right of priority for

---

[436] First Niagara Ins. Brokers, Inc. v. First Niagara Financial Group, Inc., 476 F.3d 867, 870–71 (Fed. Cir. 2007).

[437] Aktieselskabet AF 21.November 2001 v. Fame Jeans, Inc., 525 F.3d 8, 18–20 (D.C. Cir. 2008); Fair Indigo LLC v. Style Conscience, 85 U.S.P.Q.2d 1536, 1539 (T.T.A.B. 2007); Corporate Document Services, Inc. v. I.C.E.D. Management, Inc., 48 U.S.P.Q.2d 1477, 1479 (T.T.A.B. 1998).

[438] Jimlar Corp. v. Army & Air Force Exchange Serv., 24 U.S.P.Q.2d 1216, 1221 (T.T.A.B. 1992).

[439] Aktieselskabet, 525 F.3d at 20.

[440] IT&T Corp. v. General Instr. Corp., 152 U.S.P.Q. 821 (T.T.A.B. 1967).

[441] See Goetz v. American Express, 515 F.3d 156, 161–62 (2d Cir. 2008); T.A.B. Sys. v. Pactel Teletrac, 77 F.3d 1372, 1376 (Fed. Cir. 1996); Jim Dandy Co. v. Martha White Foods, 458 F.2d 1397, 1398 (C.C.P.A. 1972); Dyneer Corp. v. Automotive Prods. PLC, 37 U.S.P.Q.2d 1251 (T.T.A.B. 1995); Era Corp. v. Electronic Realty Associates, Inc., 211 U.S.P.Q. 734, 745 (T.T.A.B. 1981); Liqwacon Corp. v. Browning-Ferris Industries, Inc., 203 U.S.P.Q. 305, 308 (T.T.A.B. 1979).

[442] National Cable Television Ass'n, Inc. v. American Cinema Editors, Inc., 937 F.2d 1572, 1577–78 (Fed. Cir. 1991); American Stock Exch., Inc. v. American Express Co., 207 U.S.P.Q. 356, 364 (T.T.A.B. 1980).

[443] L. & J.G. Stickley, Inc. v. Cosser, 81 U.S.P.Q.2d 1956, 1965 (T.T.A.B. 2007); Corporate Document Services Inc. v. I.C.E.D. Management Inc., 48 U.S.P.Q.2d 1477, 1479 (T.T.A.B. 1998).

[444] Fair Indigo LLC v. Style Conscience, 85 U.S.P.Q.2d 1536 (T.T.A.B. 2007).

purposes of preventing another's registration of a confusingly similar mark for similar goods or services.[445] Citing analogous use to antedate actual use (or constructive use, in the case of an intent-to-use application) is a species of "tacking."[446]

Analogous use may be tacked to actual use (or constructive use based on the filing date of an intent-to-use application) even if there is a delay between the analogous use and the actual or constructive use, provided that the delay is commercially reasonable.[447] The user "need not necessarily have a capacity to produce goods for sale under the involved mark at the time of the analogous use."[448] However, in the event of delay, the TTAB will inquire whether the user "had a continuing intent to cultivate an association of the mark with itself and its goods and whether members of the relevant purchasing public in fact made such an association."[449] This inquiry is analogous to the analysis of abandonment.[450]

[iii]   Factors

In determining whether a likelihood of confusion exists under section 2(d), the PTO focuses on how the marks will be perceived by consumers in the marketplace, and specifically considers the following list of factors (known as the *DuPont* factors), to the extent that relevant evidence is present in the record:

(1)   The similarity or dissimilarity of the marks in their entireties as to appearance, sound, connotation, and commercial impression.

(2)   The similarity or dissimilarity and nature of the goods or services as described in an application or registration or in connection with which a prior mark is in use.

(3)   The similarity or dissimilarity of established, likely-to-continue trade channels.

(4)   The conditions under which and buyers to whom sales are made, i.e., "impulse" versus careful, sophisticated purchasing.

(5)   The fame of the prior mark (sales, advertising, length of use).

(6)   The number and nature of similar marks in use on similar goods.

(7)   The nature and extent of any actual confusion.

(8)   The length of time and conditions under which there has been concurrent use without evidence of actual confusion.

---

[445] IT&T Corp. v. General Instr. Corp., 152 U.S.P.Q. 821 (T.T.A.B. 1967).

[446] Tacking is discussed further in § 5F[2].

[447] Dyneer Corp. v. Automotive Prods. PLC, 37 U.S.P.Q.2d 1251 (T.T.A.B. 1995); *see also* Evans Chemetics, Inc. v. Chemetics International Ltd., 207 U.S.P.Q. 695, 700 (T.T.A.B. 1980); Computer Food Stores Inc. v. Corner Store Franchises, Inc., 176 U.S.P.Q. 535, 538 (T.T.A.B. 1973).

[448] *Dyneer Corp*, 37 U.S.P.Q.2d at 1255, *citing* PacTel Teletrac v. T.A.B. Systems, 32 U.S.P.Q.2d 1668 (T.T.A.B. 1994).

[449] *Dyneer Corp*, 37 U.S.P.Q.2d at 1255.

[450] *Id.* For a discussion of abandonment, see § 5J[1].

(9) The variety of goods on which a mark is or is not used (house mark, "family" mark, product mark).

(10) The market interface between applicant and the owner of a prior mark, including:

(a) a mere "consent" to register or use.

(b) agreement provisions designed to preclude confusion, i.e., limitations on continued use of the marks by each party.

(c) assignment of mark, application, registration and goodwill of the related business.

(d) laches and estoppel attributable to owner of prior mark and indicative of lack of confusion.

(11) The extent to which applicant has a right to exclude others from use of its mark on its goods.

(12) The extent of potential confusion, i.e., whether *de minimis* or substantial.

(13) Any other established fact probative of the effect of use.[451]

The weight accorded to each factor will vary, depending on the particular circumstances of the case.[452] Typically, however, the similarity of the marks and the similarity of the goods or services are especially important.[453]

[iv] Concurrent Use

If the Director of the PTO determines that the confusion, mistake, or deception can be avoided by imposing certain conditions on the parties' use of the same or similar marks, concurrent registrations can be issued. The Director may also issue concurrent registrations when a court of competent jurisdiction determines that more than one person is entitled to use the same or similar marks in commerce. In either case, for concurrent registrations to issue, the Director must impose conditions and limitations (1) as to either the mode or the place of use of each mark,[454] or (2) as to the goods in connection with which each mark is registered.[455] These provisions are intended to provide an equitable resolution of the problems which arise when two or more persons independently adopt similar marks for use in similar markets.[456]

Concurrent registrations will issue only to applicants that became entitled to use the marks as a result of their concurrent lawful use in commerce prior to the earliest of (1) the filing dates of the pending applications, or (2) any registration

---

[451] *In re* E.I. DuPont de Nemours & Co., 476 F.2d 1357, 1361 (C.C.P.A. 1973).

[452] *Id.* at 1361–62.

[453] *In re* Azteca Rest. Enters., Inc., 50 U.S.P.Q.2d 1209 (T.T.A.B. 1999); *see, e.g., In re* Dixie Rests., 105 F.3d 1405 (Fed. Cir. 1997).

[454] Old Dutch Foods, Inc. v. Dan Dee Pretzel & Potato Chip Co., 477 F.2d 150 (6th Cir. 1973).

[455] *See, e.g.,* Alfred Dunhill of London, Inc. v. Dunhill Tailored Clothes, Inc., 293 F.2d 685 (C.C.P.A. 1961); Avon Shoe Co. v. David Crystal, Inc., 279 F.2d 607 (2d Cir. 1960).

[456] Application of Beatrice Foods, 429 F.2d 466, 472 (C.C.P.A. 1970).

actually issued for the mark. This timing requirement is waived if the owner of such registration or pending application consents to the granting of a concurrent registration to the applicant.

The leading case on this topic, *Application of Beatrice Foods*, involved co-pending applications by two parties who had been using the same mark concurrently for dairy products since 1953 and 1956, respectively. Although the parties reached an agreement to divide the United States into two geographic territories, the TTAB refused to grant their requested registrations, because the designated regions included several states where neither party was using the mark.[457] The Court of Customs and Patent Appeals (CCPA) reversed the TTAB, on the ground that leaving territories unallocated would simply increase the potential for consumer confusion.[458] The CCPA outlined the principles that should determine whether to grant concurrent use applications:

1. The parties must already be entitled to use their respective marks concurrently, meaning that each party must already have made more than a token use of its mark in commerce.

2. Continued concurrent use must not create a likelihood of confusion, mistake, or deception as to the source of the parties' goods.

3. The respective territories must then be restricted as necessary to avoid a likelihood of confusion.[459]

Where neither party owns a registration for the mark, the court held, the following rules should govern the allocation of the parties' territories:

1. The prior user is *prima facie* entitled to nationwide registration.

2. If the prior user applies for registration before registration is granted to another party, then the prior user should be granted nationwide registration, *except* to the extent that another user

    (a) has established common law priority in a particular territory through actual use before the registrant's application date, *and*

    (b) establishes that granting the registrant exclusive rights in the other user's territory would create a likelihood of confusion, mistake, or deception.[460]

However, if the prior user does *not* apply for registration before registration is granted to another, the court noted that "there may be valid grounds, based on a policy of rewarding those who first seek federal registration, and a consideration of the rights created by the existing registration, for limiting [the prior user's] registration to the area of actual use and permitting the prior registrant to retain

---

[457] *Id.* at 470–71.

[458] *Id.* at 473.

[459] *Id.* at 473–74.

[460] *Id.* at 474.

the nationwide protection of the act restricted only by the territory of the prior user."[461]

In determining how to restrict the parties' respective territories so as to avoid confusion, mistake, or deception, *Beatrice Foods* notes that the PTO may consider, although it is not required to adopt, any restrictions that have been agreed upon by the parties themselves.[462] The concurrent registrations should, together, encompass all parts of the United States except those areas where another user has established common law rights through actual use.[463]

Beatrice Foods also considered "what circumstances, if any, short of actual use of the trademark, may create rights in a territory sufficient to warrant inclusion of that territory in a geographically restricted registration, and up to what time prior to registration may proof regarding the territorial extent of trademark rights be submitted."[464] Evidence of a user's likelihood of expansion, the court concluded, is an important consideration in light of the goal of preventing confusion, mistake, or deception.[465]

Beatrice Foods also held that, in determining the conditions and limitations of each party's registration, the PTO should also consider any expansion of a party's exclusive use that took place *after* the filing of the registration application.[466] Although use in commerce prior to registration is essential to establishing the *right* to register the mark, in allocating territories between parties that have already satisfied this requirement the PTO should take account of any changes in their areas of use that take place during the examination process.[467]

[e]   Descriptive, Misdescriptive, or Functional Marks

The section 2(e) bar applies to a variety of marks that are descriptive, misdescriptive, or functional, and to any mark that is primarily merely a surname.[468] In some cases, such marks are completely unregistrable. Under section 2(f), however, some marks that are presumptively barred under section 2(e) can be registered on the Principal Register once they have acquired secondary meaning.[469]

---

[461] *Id.* at 474 & n.13.

[462] Application of Beatrice Foods, 429 F.2d 466, 474 (C.C.P.A. 1970).

[463] *Id.*

[464] *Id.* at 475.

[465] *Id. Accord*, Old Dutch Foods, Inc. v. Dan Dee Pretzel & Potato Chip Co., 477 F.2d 150 (6th Cir. 1973).

[466] *Beatrice Foods*, 429 F.2d at 475.

[467] *Id.*

[468] 15 U.S.C. § 1052(e).

[469] *See* § 5E[2][f].

[i]   Descriptive and Misdescriptive Marks

Subsection (e)(1) bars registration of a mark that is "merely descriptive" of the goods or services for which the mark is to be registered.[470] Any mark denied registration under section (e)(1) is still eligible for registration if and when it acquires distinctiveness (that is, secondary meaning) pursuant to section 2(f).[471] In fact, many descriptive marks have been successfully registered upon a showing of secondary meaning.[472] However, if the mark is so descriptive as to be generic, no amount of secondary meaning will make it registrable.[473] Thus, "COCOA PUFFS" is a registered trademark for breakfast cereal,[474] while "CORN FLAKES" (except as part of the composite mark "KELLOGG'S CORN FLAKES"[475]) is not.

Subsection (e)(1) also bars registration of a mark that is "deceptively misdescriptive" of the applicant's goods or services. A mark is deceptively misdescriptive if (1) it misdescribes the goods or services to which it is affixed, and (2) the public is likely to believe the misdescription to be true. The difference between a mark that is deceptively misdescriptive under section 2(e)(1) and one that is deceptive under section 2(a) is that, in the latter case, the consumer's mistaken belief also has a material effect on the decision to purchase. Thus, for example, the "GLASS WAX" mark for a glass cleaner that contained no wax was held to be deceptively misdescriptive under (e)(1), but not deceptive under (a), because there was no evidence that consumers would be influenced to purchase the product based on the belief that it contained wax.[476]

A mark may be misdescriptive without being deceptively so. For example, the trademark "SOLID GOLD" for a chocolate bar would be misdescriptive, but consumers would be unlikely to believe that the chocolate bar is really made of gold. Similarly, the mark "APPLE" for computers is misdescriptive but not deceptively so, because no one would believe that the computers were made of apples. A mark that is misdescriptive but not deceptively so is, in fact, a type of arbitrary mark.

A mark that is merely deceptively misdescriptive, such as "GLASS WAX," can be registered on the Principal Register if it acquires secondary meaning pursuant to section 2(f). In contrast, a mark that is deceptive under section 2(a) cannot be registered at all.[477]

---

[470] 15 U.S.C. § 1052(e)(1). For the standards used in determining whether a mark is descriptive, see §§ 5C[2][a][ii] and [iii].

[471] 15 U.S.C. § 1052(f); Roux Labs., Inc. v. Clairol, Inc., 427 F.2d 823, 829 (C.C.P.A. 1970).

[472] *See, e.g.,* Union Carbide Corp. v. Ever-Ready, Inc., 531 F.2d 366 (7th Cir. 1976) (EVEREADY for batteries and light bulbs).

[473] *Roux Labs.,* 427 F.2d at 829.

[474] Reg. No. 902,727.

[475] Reg. No. 1,411,563.

[476] Gold Seal Co. v. Weeks, 129 F. Supp. 928 (D.D.C. 1955), *aff'd sub nom.* S.C. Johnson & Son, Inc. v. Gold Seal Co., 230 F.2d 832 (D.C. Cir. 1956).

[477] 15 U.S.C. § 1052(f).

[ii] Primarily Geographically Descriptive Marks

Subsection (e)(2) bars registration of a mark that is "primarily geographically descriptive" of the applicant's goods or services. As in the case of other descriptive marks, allowing one competitor to monopolize a mark that describes the geographic origin of goods or services would make it difficult for competitors to accurately describe their goods or services that have a similar geographic origin. The prohibition applies only when the term is "primarily" geographically descriptive with respect to the goods or services in question; it does not apply when the geographic meaning of the mark is obscure or remote, or when the mark has a popular significance apart from its geographic meaning.[478] The bar is also inapplicable to certification marks.[479]

[iii] Primarily Geographically Deceptively Misdescriptive Marks

Subsection (e)(3) bars registration of a mark that is "primarily geographically deceptively misdescriptive" of the applicant's goods or services. Although at one time such marks could be registered after they acquired secondary meaning, in 1993 the North American Free Trade Agreement (NAFTA) amendments to section 2 changed subsection (e)(3) to an absolute registration bar, comparable to that of section 2(a). Accordingly, marks in this category may not be registered even if they have become distinctive, subject to a narrow exception in the nature of a grandfather clause, spelled out in subsection (f), for marks that became distinctive of the applicant's goods before NAFTA's enactment date (December 8, 1993).

Prior to 2003, the courts and the PTO used a two-part test for determining whether a mark was "primarily geographically deceptively misdescriptive," requiring that the mark "(1) have as its primary significance a generally known geographic place, and (2) identify products that purchasers are likely to believe mistakenly are connected with that location."[480] A TTAB decision distinguished such marks from marks that are deceptive under section 2(a):

> If the evidence shows that the geographical area named in the mark is an area sufficiently renowned to lead purchasers to make a goods-place association but the record does not show that goods like applicant's or goods related to applicant's are a principal product of that geographical area, then the deception will most likely be found not to be material and the mark, therefore, not deceptive. On the other hand, if there is evidence that goods like applicant's or goods related to applicant's are a principal product of the geographical area named by the mark, then the deception will most likely be found material and the mark, therefore, deceptive.[481]

In 2003, however, the Federal Circuit held in *In re California Innovations* that

---

[478] *In re* Int'l Taste, Inc., 53 U.S.P.Q.2d 1604 (T.T.A.B. 2000) (popular significance of the term "Hollywood" prevents it from being primarily geographically descriptive).

[479] 15 U.S.C. § 1052(e)(2) (referencing 15 U.S.C. § 1054).

[480] *In re* Wada, 194 F.3d 1297, 1300 (Fed. Cir. 1999).

[481] *In re* House of Windsor, Inc., 221 U.S.P.Q. 53, 57 (T.T.A.B. 1983).

the two-part test ceased to be appropriate once the NAFTA amendments converted the defeasible registration bar for primarily geographically deceptively misdescriptive marks into a complete bar analogous to that of section 2(a). Instead, under the new test imposed by *California Innovations*, in order for a misdescriptive geographic mark to fall within section 2(e)(3), not only must the mark satisfy the two-part test set forth above, but the misrepresentation of geographic origin must also be "a material factor in the consumer's decision" to purchase the applicant's goods or services.[482] Thus, the new test for "primarily geographically deceptively misdescriptive" marks is now identical to the test for deceptive marks under section 2(a). If the Federal Circuit stands by its ruling, it will have rendered section 2(e)(3) largely superfluous. Furthermore, if the section 2(e)(3) bar now applies only to deceptive marks, then the grandfather clause of section 2(f) (for marks that became distinctive before NAFTA's enactment) may be completely inoperative. Indeed, in applying the *California Innovations* standard, the TTAB has held that a primarily geographically deceptively misdescriptive mark cannot be registered, even if it became distinctive prior to December 8, 1993.[483]

In the case of services, the second prong of the test for primarily geographically deceptively misdescriptive marks, both before and after *California Innovations*, differs slightly from the test that applies to goods. With respect to goods, this part of the test — which asks whether purchasers are likely to believe the goods came from the location implied by the mark — often requires little more than a showing that the place is a known source for the product.[484] In the case of services, however, there must be some additional reason for the consumer to associate the services with the geographic location.[485] In the case of a restaurant, for example, the patrons must be likely to believe that the restaurant's services somehow originated in that location:

> For example, the PTO might find a services-place association if the record shows that patrons, though sitting in New York, would believe the food served by the restaurant was imported from Paris, or that the chefs in New York received specialized training in the region in Paris, or that the New York menu is identical to a known Parisian menu, or some other heightened association between the services and the relevant place.[486]

The new third prong of the (e)(3) test — the materiality requirement — applies equally to both goods and services, but again its application to services appears to differ slightly from its application to goods. In the case of goods, the materiality test is likely to be satisfied where the geographic area in question "is famous as a source of the goods at issue."[487] In the case of services, the Federal Circuit requires either "a particularly strong services-place association" or "direct evidence of material-

---

[482] 329 F.3d 1334, 1338 (Fed. Cir. 2003). *Accord, In re* Les Halles de Paris, J.V., 334 F.3d 1371 (Fed. Cir. 2003) (applying same test to service marks).

[483] *In re* Beaverton Foods, Inc., 84 U.S.P.Q.2d 1253 (T.T.A.B. 2007).

[484] *In re* Les Halles de Paris J.V., 334 F.3d 1371, 1374 (Fed. Cir. 2003).

[485] *Id.*

[486] *Id.*

[487] *Id.*

ity."[488] In the case of restaurant services, the court stated that materiality "might" be established by a "particularly convincing showing" that (1) the relevant place is famous for its specialized culinary training, and (2) this fact is advertised as a reason to choose the restaurant.[489]

In 2009, the Federal Circuit clarified that the materiality test of (e)(3) requires that "a substantial portion of the relevant consumers" are likely to be deceived.[490]

[iv] Primarily Merely a Surname

Subsection (e)(4) bars registration of a mark that is "primarily merely a surname." Such marks may still be registered, however, if they acquire sufficient secondary meaning to satisfy section 2(f). The rationale for the (e)(4) bar is that the primary significance of a surname is to identify an individual's family name. Only when the public begins to recognize the surname as an indication of the origin of specific goods or services is the surname capable of serving a trademark function. The "McDonald's" mark for fast-food restaurants is an example of a surname that has acquired strong secondary meaning.

Some marks may have several meanings, only one of which is a surname. In such cases, the test under subsection (e)(4) is whether the purchasing public perceives the mark as "primarily" a surname when it is used in association with goods or services, or whether the other meanings of the word are more significant.[491] In fact, the surname significance of some words may not be recognized by consumers at all; in such cases, the mark would not fall under subsection (e)(4).[492]

The TTAB considers five factors in determining whether a mark is primarily merely a surname: (1) the degree of the surname's rareness; (2) whether anyone connected with the applicant uses the term as a surname; (3) whether the mark has any recognized meaning other than as a surname; (4) whether the mark has the "look and sound" (or the "structure and pronunciation") of a surname; and (5) whether the manner in which the mark is displayed may negate any surname significance.[493] The Examining Attorney has the initial burden to make a *prima facie* showing of surname significance.[494]

---

[488] *Id.* at 1374–75.

[489] *Id.*

[490] *In re* Spirits Int'l, N.V., 563 F.3d 1347, 1353 (Fed. Cir. 2009).

[491] *See, e.g.*, Savin Corp. v. Savin Group, 391 F.3d 439, 451 (2d Cir. 2004); Williamson-Dickie Mfg. Co. v. Davis Mfg. Co., 149 F. Supp. 852 (E.D. Pa.), *aff'd*, 251 F.2d 924 (3d Cir. 1957).

[492] *See, e.g.*, IMAF, S.P.A. v. J.C. Penney Co., 806 F. Supp. 449, 455 (S.D.N.Y. 1992).

[493] *In re* Benthin Mgmt. GmbH, 37 U.S.P.Q.2d 1332 (T.T.A.B. 1995).

[494] *In re* Yeley, 85 U.S.P.Q.2d 1150 (T.T.A.B. 2007).

[v]   Functional Marks

Subsection (e)(5) bars registration of a mark if it "comprises any matter that, as a whole, is functional."[495]

Functionality issues arise most often in the case of trade dress, either product packaging or product configuration. However, in the case of product configurations, the Federal Circuit and the TTAB distinguish between designs that are *"de jure"* functional and those that are *"de facto"* functional; only *de jure* functionality will trigger the subsection (e)(5) bar.[496]

A product configuration is *de jure* functional if it is "a superior design essential for competition"; in contrast, if the configuration "merely performs some function or utility," but is not significantly better than other possible configurations, it is only *de facto* functional, and will not be subject to the registration bar.[497] For example, the shape of a bottle may be *de facto* functional, because it enables the bottle to hold a liquid,[498] but it may not be *de jure* functional, because the particular bottle design chosen by the manufacturer may serve a purpose other than enhancing the bottle's ability to hold liquid.[499] In contrast, the design of a drinking bottle was held to be *de jure* functional where it made the bottle easier for a bicycle rider to use while cycling.[500] Where a design is *de jure* functional, the Supreme Court's decision in *TrafFix Devices, Inc. v. Marketing Displays, Inc.* indicates that the existence of alternative designs that would perform the same function is irrelevant.[501]

If a design combines significant functional elements with insignificant nonfunctional elements, the Federal Circuit has held that the design as a whole is *de jure* functional.[502]

Because section 2(f) does not apply to marks determined to be *de jure* functional, the subsection (e)(5) bar is insurmountable even if the mark has acquired distinctiveness.

[f]   Secondary Meaning

With respect to most of the section 2 registration bars, the prohibition against registration applies regardless of whether the mark has acquired secondary meaning. The bars that are absolute in this respect are subsections (a), (b), (c), (d),

---

[495] 15 U.S.C. § 1052(e)(5). *See, e.g.*, Talking Rain Bev. Co. v. South Beach Bev. Co., 349 F.3d 601, 604 (9th Cir. 2003); Tie Tech, Inc. v. Kinedyne Corp., 296 F.3d 778, 786 (9th Cir. 2002); Valu Eng'g, Inc. v. Rexnord Corp., 278 F.3d 1268, 1274 (Fed. Cir. 2002). For a detailed discussion of functionality, see § 5C[1][c].

[496] *In re* Morton-Norwich Prods., Inc., 671 F.2d 1332, 1337–41 (C.C.P.A. 1982).

[497] *In re* Ennco Display Sys., Inc., 56 U.S.P.Q.2d 1279 (T.T.A.B. 2000); *Valu Eng'g, Inc.*, 278 F.3d at 1274.

[498] *In re* R.M. Smith, Inc., 734 F.2d 1482, 1484 (Fed. Cir. 1984).

[499] *Valu Eng'g*, 278 F.3d at 1274.

[500] *Talking Rain*, 349 F.3d at 603–05.

[501] 532 U.S. 23, 33–34 (2001), *cited in Talking Rain*, 349 F.3d at 604.

[502] *In re* Becton, Dickinson & Co., 102 U.S.P.Q.2d 1372 (Fed. Cir. 2012).

(e)(3) and (e)(5).[503] In contrast, the bars under (e)(1), (e)(2), and (e)(4) are all subject to section 2(f), which allows an otherwise unregistrable mark to be registered if it has in fact become distinctive of the applicant's goods.[504] This acquired distinctiveness corresponds to secondary meaning under the common law.

In order to demonstrate acquired distinctiveness under subsection (f), an applicant must establish, by a preponderance of the evidence, that the mark has acquired secondary meaning.[505] Relevant evidence includes the amount and manner of advertising, the volume of sales, the length and manner of the applicant's use of the mark, direct consumer testimony, and consumer surveys.[506]

As an alternative, however, subsection (f) provides that the Director of the PTO may accept, as *prima facie* evidence that a mark has become distinctive of the applicant's goods, proof of *substantially exclusive and continuous use* thereof as a mark by the applicant in commerce for the five years immediately preceding the date on which the claim of distinctiveness is asserted. However, the Director is not *required* to accept this as proof of distinctiveness.[507]

In light of section 2(f), it is crucial to distinguish between, on the one hand, the subsection (a) prohibition against registering "deceptive" marks and, on the other hand, the subsection (e)(1) prohibition against registering "deceptively misdescriptive" marks. Whereas the latter can be overcome by a showing of secondary meaning under subsection (f), the former cannot. Thus, if a mark is deceptively misdescriptive, but not deceptive, it can be registered once it acquires secondary meaning. In contrast, a mark that is *both* deceptively misdescriptive *and* deceptive poses a greater risk of misleading consumers, and cannot be registered even if it acquires secondary meaning.

In the case of the subsection (e)(3) bar against registering a mark that is "primarily geographically deceptively misdescriptive," the prohibition is absolute *only* if the mark in question became distinctive of the applicant's goods in commerce on or after December 8, 1993 (the effective date of the North American Free Trade Agreement (NAFTA)). Marks that became distinctive before that date, therefore, can overcome the (e)(3) bar if they satisfy the secondary meaning requirement of section 2(f). After *California Innovations*, however, these marks may also be subject to the absolute bar of section 2(a).[508]

Marks that have been denied registration under subsection (e)(1), (e)(2), or (e)(4), as well as pre-NAFTA marks denied registration under subsection (e)(3), can be registered on the Supplemental Register until they meet the section 2(f) requirements.[509] In contrast, marks that have been denied registration under any other

---

[503] 15 U.S.C. § 1052(f).

[504] *Id.*

[505] *In re* Rogers, 53 U.S.P.Q.2d 1741 (T.T.A.B. 1999).

[506] Union Carbide Corp. v. Ever-Ready, Inc., 531 F.2d 366 (7th Cir. 1976).

[507] *In re* Deister Concentrator Co., 289 F.2d 496 (C.C.P.A. 1961); *In re* Garcia, 175 U.S.P.Q. (BNA) 732 (T.T.A.B. 1972).

[508] *See* § 5E[2][e][iii].

[509] *See* § 5E[5].

provision of section 2 are eligible for neither the Principal nor the Supplemental Register.

[g]   Dilutive Marks

Section 2 also permits the PTO to refuse registration of a mark which would be likely to cause dilution by blurring or dilution by tarnishment under section 43(c).[510] However, such refusal may occur only pursuant to an opposition proceeding under section 13.[511]

For a dilution-based opposition to succeed against an intent-to-use application, the opposer's mark must have become famous before the filing date of the application.[512] Where the application is based on actual use, however, the opposer's mark must have become famous prior to the applicant's first use of its mark.[513]

[3]   Registration Process

Under section 1 of the Lanham Act, there are two types of applications for registration on the Principal Register of the PTO — one based on use, and the other based on intent to use.[514] An application may also be based on the existence of a foreign or international trademark registration, or an application therefor; these applications are filed under section 44 or section 66 of the Act, rather than section 1.[515]

[a]   Use Applications

An application based on use must contain all the information required by section 1(a) of the Lanham Act, including, *inter alia*, the date of the applicant's first use of the mark,[516] the goods or services with which the mark is used, a drawing of the mark,[517] and a specimen.[518] In the case of sound, scent, or other nonvisual marks, a detailed description is required in place of a drawing.[519] If the applicant intends to rely on section 2(f) to establish acquired distinctiveness, the application may also

---

[510] Dilution under section 43(c) is discussed in § 5G.

[511] 15 U.S.C. § 1063. Similarly, a registration may be *cancelled* on these same grounds only pursuant to cancellation proceedings brought under 15 U.S.C. § 1064 (generally limited to the first five years after registration), or 15 U.S.C. § 1092 (applicable to marks registered on the Supplemental Register).

[512] Toro Co. v. ToroHead Inc., 61 U.S.P.Q.2d 1164, 1174–75 (T.T.A.B. 2001).

[513] Enterprise Rent-A-Car Co. v. Advantage Rent-A-Car, Inc., 330 F.3d 1333 (Fed. Cir. 2003); *Toro*, 61 U.S.P.Q.2d at 1174 n.9.

[514] *See* § 5E[3][a],[b].

[515] *See* § 5E[6][c] (section 44), § 5E[6][d] (section 66).

[516] The application must indicate the date of the applicant's first use of the mark *anywhere* (even intrastate) in connection with the specified goods or services, as well as the date of its first use in commerce. 37 C.F.R. § 2.34.

[517] The requirements for the drawing vary depending on whether the mark is a simple word mark or requires such elements as color, motion, three dimensions, or a specific font. 37 C.F.R. § 2.52. Where a drawing cannot adequately capture the significant features of the mark, a verbal description may also be required. 37 C.F.R. § 2.52(b)(5).

[518] 37 C.F.R. § 2.56(a).

[519] 37 C.F.R. § 2.52(e).

include evidence of such distinctiveness.[520] An application for concurrent use must also provide the information necessary for the PTO to determine the appropriate restrictions on that registration.[521] Similarly, applications to register collective marks or certification marks must provide the information necessary to determine whether the marks qualify for the type of registration requested.[522]

If the PTO examiner determines that the mark is entitled to registration, the mark is published in the Official Gazette of the PTO.[523] If no opposition is filed within the statutory period (30 days, subject to extensions for good cause), the certificate of registration will issue.[524] If the examiner determines that the mark is not entitled to registration, the applicant may appeal that decision to the Trademark Trial and Appeals Board (TTAB).[525]

[b]   Intent to Use Applications

An application based on intent to use a mark in commerce is governed by section 1(b) of the Lanham Act. In general, the requirements are similar to those for an application based on actual use. However, rather than assert the date of first use in commerce, the intent-to-use (ITU) applicant must state a bona fide intent to use the mark in commerce. In addition, no specimen is required at the time of filing.[526] A complete ITU application must specify the goods or services for which the mark will be used, and must include a drawing of the mark, the filing fee, a statement of the applicant's bona fide intention to use the mark, and a statement that the applicant knows of no other party that is entitled to use the same or a confusingly similar mark in commerce.[527]

Once the ITU application is filed, the PTO conducts an initial examination of the mark and, if the trademark examiner determines that the applicant will be entitled to register the mark on the Principal Register upon commencing use of the mark in commerce, the mark will be published in the PTO's Official Gazette.[528] (An intent-to-use application may also be amended to allege actual use at any time before the examiner approves the mark for publication; this converts the ITU application in a regular use-based application.[529]) If no opposition is filed within the post-publication statutory period (30 days, subject to extensions for good cause), or if any opposition filed is unsuccessful, then a Notice of Allowance (rather than a certificate of registration) will issue.[530]

---

[520] 37 C.F.R. §§ 2.41, 2.43.

[521] 37 C.F.R. § 2.42.

[522] 37 C.F.R. §§ 2.44–2.45.

[523] 15 U.S.C. § 1062.

[524] 15 U.S.C. § 1063.

[525] 15 U.S.C. § 1070; 37 C.F.R. § 2.141.

[526] 37 C.F.R. §§ 2.33(b)(2), 2.56(a).

[527] 15 U.S.C. § 1051(b)(1)–(3).

[528] 15 U.S.C. § 1062(a).

[529] 15 U.S.C. § 1051(c); 37 C.F.R. § 2.76.

[530] 15 U.S.C. § 1063(b). In contrast, at this point in the application process for an application based on use, the mark would be registered on the Principal Register. *Id.*

Within six months of the date on which the Notice of Allowance is issued, the applicant must file a verified statement that the mark is being used in commerce, indicating the first date on which such use occurred, and describing the goods or services on which the mark is being used (which must correspond to goods or services specified in the Notice of Allowance).[531] The applicant must also submit specimens or facsimiles of the mark used in commerce.[532] An applicant who is unable to meet the six-month deadline may obtain a six-month extension upon filing a timely written request.[533] Further six-month extensions totaling no more than 24 months are available for good cause and upon timely request.[534] Every extension request must comply with additional conditions spelled out in the statutes and regulations.[535]

If the actual use and specimen requirements are satisfied within the statutory period (including any extensions), the PTO will then determine whether the marks, as used, qualify for registration pursuant to section 2 of the Lanham Act.[536] If so, then a certificate of registration will issue, but only with respect to the goods or services that were specified in the applicant's statement of use.[537] The notice of registration will be published in the PTO's Official Gazette.[538] The effective date of this registration will be the filing date of the ITU. Thus, a successful ITU application permits the applicant to establish nationwide constructive use, and therefore nationwide priority, prior to the date on which the mark was actually used in commerce.[539]

An adverse decision on an ITU application may be appealed to the TTAB.[540]

[c]   Who May Register a Mark

Only the *owner* of a mark is entitled to register the mark.[541] In the case of an intent-to-use application, the applicant must be "the person who is entitled to use the mark in commerce."[542] A licensee — even an exclusive licensee — is not entitled to register the licensed mark.[543] An application from an applicant who is not the owner of the mark (or the person entitled to use it) at the time of filing is void, and cannot be amended, because the application right is not assignable; however, an

---

[531] 15 U.S.C. § 1051(d)(1); 37 C.F.R. § 2.88.

[532] 15 U.S.C. § 1051(d)(1).

[533] 15 U.S.C. § 1051(d)(2).

[534] 15 U.S.C. § 1051(d)(2); 37 C.F.R. § 2.89(c),(d).

[535] 15 U.S.C. §§ 1051(d)(2), (4); 37 C.F.R. §§ 2.66, 2.89(f).

[536] 15 U.S.C. §§ 1051(d)(1), 1052.

[537] 15 U.S.C. § 1051(d)(1).

[538] *Id.*

[539] 15 U.S.C. § 1057(c).

[540] 15 U.S.C. § 1070; 37 C.F.R. § 2.141.

[541] 15 U.S.C. § 1051(a)(1); Huang v. Tzu Wei Chen Food Co., 849 F.2d 1458 (Fed. Cir. 1988).

[542] TMEP § 803.01.

[543] *In re* Phillips Beverage Co., 2000 TTAB LEXIS 656 (Sept. 13, 2000); Marcon Ltd. v. Avon Prods., Inc., 4 U.S.P.Q.2d 1474 (T.T.A.B. 1987).

error in the manner of setting forth the applicant's name is correctable.[544] Joint owners of a mark may file a joint application.[545]

[d]   Dividing Applications

Pending trademark applications (based on use or intent to use) may be divided into two or more separate applications. In the case of intent-to-use applications, division is mandatory if the applicant files an amendment to allege use under section 1(c) before making use of the mark on all of the goods or services listed in the application, or files a statement of use under section 1(d) before using the mark on all of the goods specified in the notice of allowance.[546]

[e]   *Inter Partes* Proceedings

[i]   Opposition

In the case of both use and intent-to-use applications, the opposition period begins on the date the mark is published in the Official Gazette, and is limited to 30 days unless extensions are granted. After notice to all parties, the TTAB conducts an *inter partes* opposition proceeding to determine whether the opposed mark should be registered, and what, if any, restrictions to impose on the registration.[547]

An opposition may be filed by any person who anticipates being damaged (for example, due to likelihood of confusion with, or dilution of, another mark) by the registration of the applicant's mark on the Principal Register.[548] To have standing to bring an opposition, an opposer must have a "real interest" in the proceeding.[549] The nature of that interest will depend on the grounds for the opposition. For example, where the opposer claims priority in a confusingly similar mark under section 2(d), the opposer must have "a real commercial interest in its own mark or trade name, plus a reasonable basis for its belief that it would be damaged by the registration in question."[550] In an opposition based on section 2(d) or the false suggestion of an affiliation under section 2(a), the opposer must have a proprietary right in the mark at issue.[551] Where the opposer alleges that the applicant's mark is merely descriptive (or generic), the opposer must be a competitor of the applicant with respect to the goods or services in question.[552] Standing to oppose a mark that is merely a surname, or that is geographically merely descriptive, can be

---

[544] TMEP § 803.01; 37 C.F.R. § 2.71(d).

[545] TMEP § 803.03(d).

[546] TMEP §§ 1104.03(a), 1109.03, 1110; 37 C.F.R. §§ 2.76(c), 2.87(a), 2.88(c).

[547] 15 U.S.C. § 1067.

[548] 15 U.S.C. § 1063(a).

[549] Lipton Industries, Inc. v. Ralston Purina Co., 670 F.2d 1024, 1028 (C.C.P.A. 1982); Compuclean Mktg. & Design v. Berkshire Prods., Inc., 1 U.S.P.Q.2d 1323 (T.T.A.B. 1986).

[550] National Ass'n of Certified Home Inspectors, Inc. v. American Soc'y of Home Inspectors, Inc., Opposition No. 91166484 (T.T.A.B. Aug. 28, 2008).

[551] Jewelers Vigilance Comm., Inc. v. Ullenberg Corp., 229 U.S.P.Q. 860 (T.T.A.B. 1987).

[552] No Nonsense Fashions, Inc. v. Consolidated Foods Corp., 226 U.S.P.Q.2d 502, 504 (T.T.A.B. 1985); Fioravanti v. Fioravanti Corrado S.R.L., 230 U.S.P.Q. 36 (T.T.A.B. 1986).

asserted by a competitor with the same surname, or whose goods come from the same geographic area, respectively.[553]

An opposition under section 2(d) may be brought by either the owner or the exclusive licensee of a mark that is confusingly similar to the mark sought to be registered.[554] Whether a non-exclusive licensee has standing to oppose remains unsettled.[555]

[ii]   Interferences

The Director may declare an interference between two applications for registration, or between an application and a not-yet-incontestable registration, if the marks are similar enough to give rise to a likelihood of confusion when applied to the respective applicants' goods or services, but only upon a showing of extraordinary circumstances that would unduly prejudice a party in the absence of an interference. Because the availability of an opposition or cancellation proceeding will normally eliminate such prejudice,[556] typically an interference is declared only where a party would otherwise have to engage in multiple opposition or cancellation proceedings in which the issues are substantially the same.[557] An interference can be declared only upon petition to the Director.[558] Once the examiner determines that each of the marks in question is registrable, the marks will be published in the Official Gazette for opposition, and, upon notice to the parties, the TTAB will conduct an *inter partes* interference proceeding to determine the parties' respective rights.[559]

[iii]   Concurrent Use Proceedings

Under section 2(d), concurrent use proceedings may be instituted where an applicant seeks to register a mark that resembles another mark already registered or in use, but the Director determines that confusion, mistake, or deception will not arise from concurrent registrations if appropriate conditions and limitations are imposed on the use of each mark. Concurrent registrations are permitted only if (a) both users became entitled to use their respective marks through concurrent lawful use prior to the earliest filing date to which either is entitled, or (b) the user with the earlier filing date consents to concurrent registration by the other user. The Director may also issue concurrent registrations when a court of competent jurisdiction determines that more than one party is entitled to use the same or similar marks in commerce. In either case, the Director may limit the mode or place of use of each mark, or the range of goods or services encompassed by each

---

[553] Fioravanti v. Fioravanti Corrado S.R.L., 230 U.S.P.Q. 36 (T.T.A.B. 1986).

[554] J.L. Prescott Co. v. Blue Cross Laboratories (Inc.), 216 U.S.P.Q. 1127, 1128 (T.T.A.B. 1982).

[555] *See, e.g.*, National Ass'n of Certified Home Inspectors, Inc. v. American Soc'y of Home Inspectors, Inc., Opposition No. 91166484 (T.T.A.B. Aug. 28, 2008); Ramex Records, Inc. v. Guerrero, 2002 TTAB LEXIS 407 (June 26, 2002); William & Scott Co. v. Earl's Restaurants Ltd., 30 U.S.P.Q.2d 1870, 1872 n.2 (T.T.A.B. 1994).

[556] 37 C.F.R. § 2.91.

[557] TMEP § 1507; *In re* Family Inns of America, Inc., 180 U.S.P.Q. 332 (Comm'r of Patents 1974).

[558] TMEP § 1507; 37 C.F.R. § 2.91(a).

[559] 15 U.S.C. § 1067; 37 C.F.R. §§ 2.92–.93.

registration.[560] The substantive standards for granting concurrent use registrations are discussed in § 5E[2][d][iv].

Concurrent use applications are published in the Official Gazette for opposition. If there are no successful oppositions, concurrent use proceedings will be initiated upon notice to all concurrent users and registrants, unless a court of competent jurisdiction has already resolved the respective rights of the concurrent users, and the concurrent use application complies with the court's decree.[561]

[iv]   Cancellation

(a)   Grounds for Cancellation

Although a trademark registered on the Principal Register is presumed valid,[562] the registration may be cancelled under the circumstances set forth in section 14.[563] Some grounds for cancellation apply regardless of the length of time the mark has been registered, while others apply only during the first five years of registration.

Under section 14(3), a mark may be cancelled *at any time* on one of the following grounds, even after it has become incontestable: if the mark becomes generic, if it is functional, if it has been abandoned, if its registration was obtained fraudulently, if its registration was obtained contrary to section 4 of the Lanham Act (dealing with collective and certification marks) or the registration prohibitions of sections 2(a), (b), or (c), or if it is being used by, or with the permission of, the registrant to misrepresent the source of the goods or services with respect to which it is used.[564] If a mark becomes generic with respect to some, but not all, of the goods or services for which it is registered, then it is subject to cancellation only with respect to those goods or services as to which it has become generic.[565]

Under section 14(5), a certification mark may also be cancelled at any time if the registrant (1) does not control, or is unable legitimately to exercise control, over the use of the mark, (2) engages in the production or marketing of any goods to which the certification mark is applied, (3) permits the use of the mark for purposes other than to certify, or (4) discriminately refuses to certify or continue to certify goods that meet the standards or conditions that the mark certifies.[566]

In addition to the grounds on which a mark may be cancelled at any time, a mark that has been registered on the Principal Register for less than five years may be cancelled if it becomes subject to any of the bars to registration under section 2 — for example, if it is found to be merely descriptive under section

---

[560] 15 U.S.C. § 1052(d).

[561] 37 C.F.R. § 2.99.

[562] 15 U.S.C. § 1057(b).

[563] 15 U.S.C. § 1064.

[564] 15 U.S.C. §§ 1064(3), 1065.

[565] *See, e.g.*, Abercrombie & Fitch Co. v. Hunting World, Inc., 537 F.2d 4, 13 (2d Cir. 1976).

[566] 15 U.S.C. § 1064(5); *see, e.g.*, Midwest Plastic Fabricators Inc. v. Underwriters Labs., Inc., 906 F.2d 1568 (Fed. Cir. 1990).

2(e)(1), or if it is found, under section 2(d), to bear a confusing resemblance to a mark already in use in the United States.[567]

Sections 2, 14, and 24 of the Lanham Act permit cancellation of a registered mark that would be likely to cause dilution by blurring or dilution by tarnishment under section 43(c).[568] A dilution-based cancellation petition may be filed against any registration that was filed on or after January 16, 1996.[569] In order to prevail, however, the petitioning party must establish that its mark became famous prior to the registrant's first use of the allegedly dilutive mark.[570]

(b)   **Procedure**

A petition for cancellation may be filed by any person who believes he or she has been, or will be, damaged by the registration of a mark on the Principal Register, including as a result of dilution under section 43(c).[571] The TTAB conducts an *inter partes* proceeding to rule on the petition, and its decision is subject to judicial review by the Federal Circuit.[572]

In a court action involving a registered mark, a court may order full or partial cancellation of a registration if it determines that the registration is wholly or partly invalid.[573]

Because a registration is entitled to a presumption of validity, the Federal Circuit requires the petitioner in a cancellation proceeding to establish grounds for cancellation by a preponderance of the evidence.[574] Although several other courts agree,[575] some circuits require "clear and convincing" evidence, at least where the ground for cancellation is fraud or abandonment.[576] Even where the preponderance of the evidence standard applies, the longer a party waits to commence a cancellation proceeding, the more persuasive that party's evidence will need to be, due to the presumption of validity and the likelihood that the trademark

---

[567] These grounds for cancellation cease to be available once the mark has been registered in the Principal Register for five years, regardless of whether the registrant has also filed for incontestable status under section 15. 15 U.S.C. § 1065. *See, e.g.*, Gracie v. Gracie, 67 U.S.P.Q.2d (BNA) 1702 (T.T.A.B. 2003).

[568] 15 U.S.C. § 1092.

[569] Toro Co. v. ToroHead, Inc., 61 U.S.P.Q.2d 1164, 1172 (T.T.A.B. 2001).

[570] *Id.* at 1174 n.9.

[571] 15 U.S.C. § 1064.

[572] 15 U.S.C. §§ 1067(a), 1071.

[573] 15 U.S.C. § 1119; Abercrombie & Fitch Co. v. Hunting World, Inc., 537 F.2d 4, 13(2d Cir. 1976).

[574] West Fla. Seafood v. Jet Restaurants, 31 F.3d 1122, 1128 (Fed. Cir. 1994); Cerveceria Centroamericana, S.A. v. Cerveceria India, Inc., 892 F.2d 1021, 1023 (Fed. Cir. 1989).

[575] Creative Gifts, Inc. v. UFO, 235 F.3d 540, 545 (10th Cir. 2000); Pro-Football, Inc. v. Harjo, 284 F. Supp. 2d 96, 102, 122 (D.D.C. 2003).

[576] *Pro-Football*, 284 F. Supp. 2d at 122; Woodstock's Enters., Inc. v. Woodstock's Enters., Inc., (T.T.A.B. 1997); *compare* Eurostar, Inc. v. "Euro-Star" Reitmoden GMBH & Co., 34 U.S.P.Q.2d 1266 (T.T.A.B. 1995), *with Cerveceria Centroamericana*, 892 F.2d at 1024, *and* Auburn Farms, Inc. v. McKee Foods Corp., 51 U.S.P.Q.2d 1439 (T.T.A.B. 1999).

owner has built up goodwill in the registered mark in the time since registration.[577]

[f] Judicial Review

Two alternative routes of appeal from decisions of the TTAB or the PTO Director are available to an applicant for trademark registration or renewal, a party to an interference or cancellation proceeding, a party to a concurrent use application, or a registrant who has filed a continuing use affidavit under section 8.[578] The dissatisfied party may appeal to the United States Court of Appeals for the Federal Circuit, in which case the court will limit its review to the PTO record, or the party may commence a civil action in federal district court.[579]

In an appeal to the Federal Circuit, decisions on questions of law are reviewed *de novo*. However, PTO findings of fact are subject to the Administrative Procedure Act's "substantial evidence" standard of review,[580] under which the court must uphold the PTO's findings if "a reasonable person might find that the evidentiary record supports the agency's conclusion."[581]

If a party elects to commence a civil action in federal district court, the standard of review for questions of law is *de novo*, but the standard of review for findings of fact is somewhat unsettled. The weight of authority holds that the "substantial evidence" standard applies; however, because the parties may also submit new evidence, the court may make new findings of fact based on the newly submitted evidence.[582] In addition, several circuits have held that a party may introduce new issues not brought before the TTAB.[583]

For purposes of appellate review, the Federal Circuit has treated PTO determinations under sections 2(a) and 2(d) as questions of law based on underlying factual findings.[584] However, at least one district court has treated such determinations as questions of fact.[585]

[g] Maintaining and Renewing Registration

To maintain a federal trademark registration, the owner of the registration must periodically file: (1) an affidavit of use and (2) a renewal application. Because the time frames for these filings coincide, registrants may choose to combine them into

---

[577] *See Cerveceria Centroamericana*, 892 F.2d at 1023–24; *Pro-Football*, 284 F. Supp. 2d at 123.

[578] 15 U.S.C. §§ 1058, 1071.

[579] 15 U.S.C. § 1071(a)(4), (b).

[580] 5 U.S.C. § 706; *see* Dickinson v. Zurko, 527 U.S. 150 (1999) (holding that APA applies); *In re* Gartside, 203 F.3d 1305, 1315 (Fed. Cir. 2000) ("substantial evidence"); Recot, Inc. v. M.C. Becton, 214 F.3d 1322 (Fed. Cir. 2000) (similar).

[581] On-Line Careline, Inc. v. America Online, Inc., 229 F.3d 1080, 1085–86 (Fed. Cir. 2000).

[582] Pro-Football, Inc. v. Harjo, 284 F. Supp. 2d 96, 102, 115–16 (D.D.C. 2003).

[583] Aktieselskabet AF 21 November 2001 v. Fame Jeans, Inc., 525 F.3d 8, 12 (D.C. Cir. 2008); CAE, Inc. v. Clean Air Eng'g, Inc., 267 F.3d 660, 674 (7th Cir. 2001); PHC, Inc. v. Pioneer Healthcare, Inc., 75 F.3d 75, 80 (1st Cir. 1996).

[584] *See, e.g., In re* Mavety Media Group Ltd., 33 F.3d 1367, 1371 (Fed. Cir. 1994); Weiss Assocs., Inc. v. HRL Assocs. Inc., 902 F.2d 1546, 1547–48 (Fed. Cir. 1990).

[585] *Pro-Football, Inc.*, 284 F. Supp. 2d at 116–17 (collecting cases).

a single document, if it meets the statutory requirements for both filings.[586]

[i]   Affidavit of Use

Under section 8 of the Lanham Act, the owner must file an affidavit of use (and pay the applicable fee) at multi-year intervals (subject to grace periods) which are prescribed by statute.[587] The affidavit must indicate those goods or services for which the mark is registered and in actual use (accompanied by proof), or those goods or services for which the mark is registered but not in actual use (in which case the registrant must demonstrate special circumstances excusing the non-use, to avoid abandonment).[588] Noncompliance will lead to cancellation.[589]

Affidavits of use are also required to maintain registrations arising from extensions of protection under the Madrid Protocol.[590]

[ii]   Renewal

A registration must be timely renewed at ten-year intervals, or it will be cancelled.[591] If a renewal application is rejected, the Director must notify the registrant of the reasons for the rejection.[592] The registrant may renew the registration for fewer than all of the classes of goods or services covered by the initial registration or prior renewals thereof.[593] If the mark has been assigned since its initial registration (or any subsequent renewal thereof), the assignee can become the owner of record only by recording the document of title with the PTO and notifying the post-registration examiner at the time of the renewal application.[594]

These renewal provisions apply to all registrations except for extensions of protection under the Madrid Protocol, which must be renewed by application to WIPO's International Bureau.[595]

[4]   Incontestability

[a]   Effect of Incontestable Status

Section 15 permits certain registered marks to become *incontestable*.[596] Subject to several exceptions, incontestable status conclusively establishes that the registered mark is valid, and that the registrant owns the mark and has the exclusive

---

[586] TMEP § 1606.15.

[587] 15 U.S.C. § 1058.

[588] 15 U.S.C. § 1058(b).

[589] 15 U.S.C. § 1058(a).

[590] 15 U.S.C. § 1141k; TMEP § 1613.

[591] 15 U.S.C. § 1059; 37 C.F.R. § 2.182; TMEP § 1606.03 (collecting cases).

[592] 15 U.S.C. § 1059(b).

[593] 37 C.F.R. § 2.183; TMEP § 1606.02.

[594] TMEP § 1606.06.

[595] TMEP § 1606.01(b).

[596] 15 U.S.C. § 1065.

right to use it in commerce with respect to the goods or services for which it has become incontestable.[597] The conclusive presumptions of validity, ownership, and exclusivity do not apply to the extent that grounds exist for cancelling the mark under paragraphs (3) or (5) of section 14.[598] They also do not apply to the extent, if any, that the use of the registered mark infringes any common-law right established by another's continuous use of a mark from a date prior to the registration date.[599]

Under section 14 of the Lanham Act, an incontestable mark can be cancelled only on the following grounds: (1) with respect to any goods or services as to which it becomes generic; (2) if it is functional; (3) if it is abandoned; (4) if its registration was obtained fraudulently or in violation of section 2(a), (b), or (c); (5) in the case of collective or certification marks, if the registration was obtained contrary to the requirements of section 4; or (6) if the mark is used by, or with the permission of, the registrant in a manner that misrepresents the source of goods or services.[600] However, an incontestable mark cannot be cancelled on the ground that it was granted in violation of section 2(d).

Incontestability offers a significant benefit to descriptive marks. Until they achieve incontestable status, such marks are vulnerable to invalidation, and thus cancellation, upon a showing that they are insufficiently distinctive to maintain their registration. Once such a mark becomes incontestable, however, mere descriptiveness (short of genericness) is insufficient grounds for cancellation.

Incontestability also limits the defenses available to an alleged infringer. Under section 33(b), defenses to infringement of incontestable marks are limited to the following:

(1) that the registration, or incontestable status, was obtained fraudulently;[601]

(2) that the registrant has abandoned the mark;[602]

(3) that the registrant (or a party acting with the consent of, or in privity with, the registrant) is using the mark to misrepresent the source of goods or services;

(4) that the defendant's use of the mark is a fair use;[603]

(5) that the mark used by the defendant was adopted without knowledge of the registrant's prior use, and has been used continuously by the adopter, or those in privity with the adopter, since a date prior to the effective date of registration of the mark alleged to be infringed;

---

[597] 15 U.S.C. § 1115(b).

[598] 15 U.S.C. § 1064(3), (5).

[599] 15 U.S.C. § 1065.

[600] 15 U.S.C. § 1064(3).

[601] Fraud on the PTO occurs when an applicant makes material representations of fact with the intent to deceive. *In re* Bose, 580 F.3d 1240, 1244–45 (Fed. Cir. 2009) (rejecting the "knew or should have known" standard).

[602] Abandonment is discussed at § 5J[1].

[603] The fair use defense is discussed at §§ 5J[4] & [5].

(6) that the mark used by the defendant was registered and used before the registration of the mark alleged to be infringed, and was not abandoned;

(7) that the mark has been or is being used to violate federal antitrust laws;

(8) that the mark is functional;[604] or

(9) that equitable principles (including laches, estoppel, and acquiescence) are applicable.

The prior use defenses under subsections (5) and (6) — which differ in that subsection (6) requires both prior use and prior registration — apply only to the areas in which the defendant's prior use is established.[605]

The Supreme Court's decision in *Park N' Fly v. Dollar Park and Fly* established that descriptiveness is not a defense to infringement of an incontestable mark.[606] In contrast, genericness is grounds for cancellation of an incontestable mark as well as a defense to infringement of an incontestable mark. Even though genericness is not specifically mentioned as a defense in section 33(b), courts have inferred its availability as a defense from the language of section 15(4), which provides that "no incontestable right shall be acquired in a mark which is the generic name of the goods or services or a portion thereof, for which it is registered,"[607] and from section 14(3), which permits cancellation of an incontestable mark that becomes generic.[608]

For purposes of the likelihood-of-confusion test for infringement,[609] the fact that a mark is incontestable does not necessarily establish that it is a strong mark.[610]

[b]   Establishing Incontestability

To become incontestable with respect to goods and services for which it is registered, a mark must have been in continuous use in commerce with respect to those goods or services for at least five consecutive years from the date of registration on the Principal Register.[611] In addition, there must not have been any final decision adverse to the registrant's right to claim of ownership in the mark or right to obtain or maintain the mark's registration, and there must be no pending proceeding in the courts or the PTO with respect to those rights.[612] The registrant must file an affidavit with the Director within one year after the end of this five-year

---

[604] *See, e.g.*, Baughman Tile Co. v. Plastic Tubing, Inc., 211 F. Supp. 2d 720 (E.D.N.C. 2002).

[605] 15 U.S.C. §§ 1115(b)(5), (6); *see, e.g.*, Burger King of Fla., Inc. v. Hoots, 403 F.2d 904 (7th Cir. 1968); Lucky Brand Dungarees, Inc. v. Ally Apparel Resources LLC, 2008 U.S. Dist. LEXIS 8210 (S.D.N.Y. Feb. 5, 2008) (unpub.).

[606] 469 U.S. 189, 201 (1985).

[607] 15 U.S.C. § 1065(4).

[608] 15 U.S.C. § 1064(3); *see, e.g.*, Te-Ta-Ma Truth Foundation v. World Church of the Creator, 297 F.3d 662, 665 (7th Cir. 2002).

[609] The likelihood-of-confusion test is discussed in § 5F[2].

[610] *Compare* Oreck Corp. v. U.S. Floor Sys., Inc., 803 F.2d 166 (5th Cir. 1986) *and* American Soc'y of Plumbing Eng'rs v. TMB Publ'g., Inc., 109 Fed. Appx. 781 (7th Cir. 2004) (unpub.) *with* Dieter v. B&H Indus. of Southwest Fla., Inc., 880 F.2d 322 (11th Cir. 1989).

[611] 15 U.S.C. § 1065.

[612] 15 U.S.C. § 1065(1), (2).

period, asserting that the mark has been in continuous use for this period, and is still in use, and specifying the goods or services for which the mark is registered and has been in continuous use.[613]

[5] The Supplemental Register

Registration on the Supplemental Register offers benefits for certain marks that lack the distinctiveness to be registered on the Principal Register, but that nonetheless have the capacity to acquire distinctiveness through use.[614] The Supplemental Register provides a searchable public record of marks that have been adopted for use in commerce, and prevents the registration of confusingly similar marks. Registration on the Supplemental Register can also help some trademark owners qualify for foreign registrations, although this function has diminished in importance due to changes in foreign trademark systems.

[a] Eligible Marks

Marks that are ineligible for registration on the Principal Register may be registered on the Supplemental Register unless they are functional or barred by sections 2(a), (b), (c), (d), or (e)(3).[615] The Supplemental Register primarily benefits marks that lack sufficient secondary meaning to satisfy section 2(f). A mark that is merely descriptive, or primarily merely a surname, may be registered on the Supplemental Register prior to acquiring distinctiveness, provided the PTO considers it to be capable of becoming distinctive. Once such a mark acquires distinctiveness, the owner of the mark may pursue its registration on the Principal Register under section 2(f). In contrast, marks that are deceptive under section 2(a), and marks that are generic, cannot be registered on either the Principal or the Supplemental Register.[616]

To be eligible for supplemental registration, a mark must be in lawful use in commerce in connection with the goods or services for which it is registered.[617] Although applications for the Supplemental Register may be filed under section 44 (foreign registrations),[618] they may not be filed under section 66(a) (the Madrid Protocol).[619]

---

[613] 15 U.S.C. § 1065(3).

[614] *In re* Simmons Co., 278 F.2d 517 (C.C.P.A. 1960).

[615] 15 U.S.C. § 1091. The section 2(e)(3) bar is inapplicable, however, to marks that were in lawful use in commerce in connection with goods or services prior to December 8, 1993 (the effective date of NAFTA). 15 U.S.C. § 1091(a).

[616] *See, e.g., In re* Helena Rubenstein, Inc., 410 F.2d 438 (CCPA 1969); Clairol, Inc. v. Roux Distr. Co., Inc., 280 F.2d 863 (CCPA 1960); *In re* Sealol, Inc., 168 U.S.P.Q. 320 (T.T.A.B. 1970).

[617] 15 U.S.C. §§ 1091(a), 1094; 37 C.F.R. §§ 2.47(a), (d).

[618] 15 U.S.C. § 1126; *see* § 5E[6][c].

[619] 15 U.S.C. § 1141f; 37 C.F.R. §§ 2.47(b)–(c); *see* § 5E[6][d].

[b]   Registration Procedure

A mark may be registered on the Supplemental Register after it is examined for eligibility, and upon compliance with sections 1(a) and 1(e) of the Lanham Act, to the extent applicable.[620] Such marks are not subject to opposition, and are not published in the PTO's Official Gazette until after registration.[621] They are, however, subject to cancellation.[622] If a mark is refused registration on the Supplemental Register, the applicant may appeal.[623]

[c]   Effect of Supplemental Registration

Under section 26,[624] a mark registered on the Supplemental Register is denied many of the benefits conferred by registration on the Principal Register. The certificate of supplemental registration does not constitute *prima facie* evidence of the validity, ownership, or exclusive right to use the mark. The constructive notice and constructive use provisions do not apply, and the mark may not become incontestable. Under section 28,[625] the owner of a supplemental registration may not invoke the provisions of section 42,[626] which bars importation of counterfeit goods.

Except as provided in section 26, if a mark is registered on the Supplemental Register, it constitutes a "registered" mark for purposes of Title 15. Thus, it can be the basis for refusing registration on the Principal Register to a confusingly similar[627] or dilutive mark (although refusing registration on dilution grounds requires an opposition proceeding).[628] A mark registered on the Supplemental Register can also be the basis for a refusal to register a confusingly similar mark on the Supplemental Register itself.

Although supplemental registration does not provide constructive notice of ownership under section 22, it does provide a searchable database that enables potential adopters of a mark to determine whether a similar mark is already in use.

[d]   Cancellation

A mark registered on the Supplemental Register is not published for opposition, and may not be the subject of an opposition proceeding, but it will be published in the Official Gazette upon registration. Any person who believes that he or she is or will be damaged by registration of that mark on the Supplemental Register may

---

[620] 15 U.S.C. § 1091(a), (b).

[621] 15 U.S.C. § 1092.

[622] 15 U.S.C. § 1092; *see, e.g.*, Professional Economics Inc. v. Professional Economic Servs., Inc., 205 U.S.P.Q. 368 (T.T.A.B. 1979).

[623] 15 U.S.C. §§ 1091(b), 1062(b), 1071. For the appeal procedures, see § 5E[[3]][f].

[624] 15 U.S.C. § 1094.

[625] 15 U.S.C. § 1096.

[626] 15 U.S.C. § 1124.

[627] 15 U.S.C. § 1052(d).

[628] 15 U.S.C. § 1052 (language following subsection (f)).

then file a petition to cancel the registration under section 24.[629] However, if cancellation is sought on the ground that the registered mark is likely to dilute a famous mark by blurring or tarnishment under section 43(c), then cancellation is allowed only if the petitioner's mark became famous *before* the effective filing date of the registration on the Supplemental Register.[630]

[6]   Domestic Priority Based on Foreign Registration

[a]   International Agreements

The United States is a signatory to a number of international agreements pertaining to trademarks and unfair competition, including the International Convention for the Protection of Industrial Property (the "Paris Convention"), the General Inter-American Convention for Trade Mark and Commercial Protection, and the Madrid Protocol.

Under the 1883 Paris Convention, which pertains to trademarks as well as other forms of industrial property, the United States and the other 167 member nations must provide "national treatment" to one another's nationals (including corporations), meaning that foreign nationals must be afforded trademark rights at least equal to those provided to the member's own nationals.[631] In addition, a national of any signatory country who applies to register a trademark in one member nation may use that filing to establish an effective filing date in any other member nation where that applicant applies for registration within six months of the first filing.[632] However, the Paris Convention (unlike the Madrid Agreement and the Madrid Protocol, which are discussed below) does not provide a mechanism for filing a multinational application.

The requirements of these international agreements have been incorporated throughout the Lanham Act, most notably in section 44.[633]

[b]   National Treatment

Section 44(b) provides that nationals of a country that (1) is a party to a trademark treaty or convention to which the United States is a party, or that (2) extends reciprocity to United States nationals, are entitled to "the rights to which any owner of a mark is otherwise entitled" under the Lanham Act.[634] They also enjoy certain additional rights specifically provided to such foreign persons by section 44. Section 44(g) provides that trade names or commercial names of such parties are protected even without registration; even if these do not constitute trademarks, section 44(h) entitles them to "effective protection against unfair competition," including the remedies afforded by the Lanham Act.[635]

---

[629] 15 U.S.C. § 1094.

[630] 15 U.S.C. § 1092.

[631] Paris Convention, Art. 2(1).

[632] Paris Convention, Art. 4(A)(1)(C); 15 U.S.C. § 1441g.

[633] 15 U.S.C. § 1126.

[634] 15 U.S.C. § 1126(b).

[635] Havana Club Holding, S.A. v. Galleon, S.A., 203 F.3d 116 (2d Cir. 2000).

[c]   Domestic Priority

Under section 44(d), nationals of trademark treaty partners or countries providing reciprocity (as prescribed by section 44(b)) may take advantage of an exception (in addition to the section 1(b) intent-to-use exception that is available to all applicants) to the general rule that a mark can be federally registered only after its use in commerce has commenced.[636] Section 44(d) gives foreign nationals registration priority for six months after filing a foreign application, even if the applicant has not yet used the mark anywhere in the world. To invoke section 44(d), both the applicant and the country where the foreign application is filed must be eligible under section 44(b),[637] and the United States application must include a statement of bona fide intent to use the mark in commerce.[638] Where these conditions are satisfied, a domestic application that is filed within six months after the foreign application will be treated as having the same filing date as the foreign application, and the foreign application date becomes the effective date of the applicant's constructive use in the United States.[639] However, a federal registration will not issue until either (1) the mark has been registered in the applicant's country of origin, or (2) the applicant alleges use of the mark in commerce.[640] Once the mark is registered in the country of origin, it may be registered on the Principal Register (if eligible) or the Supplemental Register, provided that the foreign applicant states a bona fide intent to use the mark in commerce, even if the mark has not yet been used anywhere in the world.

A foreign applicant that obtains a federal registration under section 44(e) may maintain that registration for up to six years without actually using the mark in commerce; upon proof of use in commerce before the end of that six-year period, the registration will be subject to the same rules as a use-based registration.[641]

[d]   The Madrid Protocol

In 2003, the United States joined the Protocol Relating to the Madrid Agreement Concerning the International Registration of Marks (1989) (the Madrid Protocol), which permits a party to file a single international trademark application and to request an extension of the resulting registration to any other signatory country.[642] As a result, section 66 of the Lanham Act permits any party that obtains an international trademark registration from a Protocol country to request an extension of that protection to the United States.[643] The applicant must declare a bona fide intent to use the mark in commerce, but actual use in commerce is not

---

[636] Crocker Nat'l Bank v. Canadian Imperial Bank of Commerce, 223 U.S.P.Q. 909 (T.T.A.B. 1984).

[637] 15 U.S.C. § 1126(d).

[638] 15 U.S.C. § 1126(d)(2).

[639] 15 U.S.C. § 1126(d); *see, e.g.*, SCM Corp. v. Langis Foods, Ltd., 539 F.2d 196 (D.C. Cir. 1976).

[640] 15 U.S.C. § 1126(c); *see also In re* Societe d'Exploitation de da Marque le Fouquet's, 67 U.S.P.Q.2d 1784 (T.T.A.B. 2003).

[641] 15 U.S.C. § 1058(a),(b).

[642] Madrid Protocol, Art. 2(1); 15 U.S.C. § 1141a(a).

[643] 15 U.S.C. § 1141e.

required.[644] If the trademark examiner determines that the mark does not meet the requirements of section 2 of the Lanham Act, then the extension of protection will be refused.[645] If section 2 is satisfied (apart from use in commerce), then the mark will be published in the Official Gazette, and will be subject to opposition. If the PTO Director does not send a notice of refusal to the World Intellectual Property Organization (WIPO) within the statutory time limits, then the extension of protection must be granted,[646] and the PTO must issue a "certificate of extension of protection" for the mark, which has the same effect as a registration on the Principal Register.[647] Unless the request for extension of protection is refused, the filing of the request for extension of protection constitutes constructive use of the mark under section 7(c) of the Lanham Act.[648]

All international registrations under the Protocol last for ten years,[649] and may be renewed in a single application.[650] During the first five years, however, the international registration will be cancelled if the home country application is rejected, withdrawn, or lapses, or if the home country registration is cancelled or otherwise terminates; the same consequences follow if the home country rejection or cancellation occurs after the end of the five-year period, if this resulted from a legal action that commenced during the five-year period.[651] If a mark loses its international registration as a result of such adverse action, the applicant has a three-month grace period in which to file country-by-country applications in the Protocol nations without losing the application's original priority date.[652]

[7]   State Trademark Registration

[a]   State Registration Statutes

Many states have supplemented common-law protection of trademarks by enacting their own registration systems. Often, these state registration requirements are modeled after, and closely resemble, the federal scheme,[653] including preclusions similar to those in section 2 of the Lanham Act,[654] and in such cases their terms are typically interpreted *in pari materia*. State trademark registration can benefit parties that cannot use the federal registration system because they do

---

[644] 15 U.S.C. §§ 1141f (a), 1141h(a)(3).

[645] 15 U.S.C. § 1141h(a)(4).

[646] 15 U.S.C. § 1141h.

[647] 15 U.S.C. § 1141i.

[648] 15 U.S.C. § 1057(c); *see id.* §§ 1141f(b), (g) (rules for determining effective date of constructive use).

[649] Madrid Protocol, Art. 6(1).

[650] *Id.* Art. 7.

[651] *Id.* Art. 6(3).

[652] *Id.* Art. 9*quinquies.*

[653] *See, e.g.*, Cal. Bus. & Prof. Code § 14220 (2005); § 765 I.L.C.S. 1036/10 (2005); N.Y. Gen. Bus. L. § 360-a (2005).

[654] 15 U.S.C. § 1052.

not use their marks in interstate commerce. State registration schemes typically do not displace common-law rights.[655]

[b]   Federal Preemption

In general, state common law and state statutes addressing trademarks and unfair competition are not preempted by the Lanham Act, regardless of whether they parallel the Lanham Act or depart from it, except to the extent that they interfere with rights conferred under the Lanham Act. Thus, common-law trademarks are typically protected by both state law and section 43(a) of the Lanham Act. Likewise, the same activities by a junior user of a mark may serve as the basis for infringement (or dilution) claims under both state and federal law, although the standards for establishing liability may differ under the two regimes, and a particular plaintiff may prevail on state law claims but not federal claims, or vice versa.

If, however, in a particular situation, the enforcement of state trademark law would interfere with rights conferred under the Lanham Act, federal law will preempt the state law provisions. For example, trademark registration systems in some states may give state registrants a right of priority throughout the state, even in parts of the state where the registrant does not actually use the mark.[656] If another party were to obtain federal registration for the same (or a confusingly similar) mark, the nationwide priority rights of the federal registrant would supersede the statewide priority rights of the state registrant in any territory where the state registrant had not established common law priority through actual use. Thus, in a battle for priority based on constructive use, federal registration "trumps" state registration, even if the federal registration took place *after* the effective date of the state registration.[657]

Although the Lanham Act makes clear that a federal registrant has nationwide priority, some courts will not enjoin (or award damages for) the use of the mark by a junior user unless and until the registrant shows a likelihood of entry into the junior user's trading territory.[658] The leading case articulating this position is *Dawn Donut Co. v. Hart's Food Stores, Inc.*[659] In that case, the owner of the federal registration for a mark had not exploited the mark at the retail level in a particular geographic area for some 30 years. Even though the Second Circuit held that the plaintiff's mark was not abandoned (because abandonment due to cessation of use occurs only when the registrant no longer uses the mark anywhere in the United States),[660] the court found that there was "no present likelihood" that the plaintiff would expand its retail use of the mark into the junior user's market area, and

---

[655] *See, e.g.*, Cal. Bus. & Prof. Code § 14210 (2005); § 765 I.L.C.S. 1036/80 (2005); N.Y. Gen. Bus. L. § 360-o (2005).

[656] *See, e.g.*, First Nat'l Bank v. First Wyo. S&L Ass'n, 592 P.2d 697, 704–05 (Wyo. 1979) (noting that Wyoming statutes do not have this effect, but that statutes in other states may).

[657] Burger King of Fla., Inc. v. Hoots, 403 F.2d 904 (7th Cir. 1968); *accord* Spartan Food Sys., Inc. v. HFS Corp., 813 F.2d 1279 (4th Cir. 1987).

[658] KeyCorp. v. Key Bank & Trust, 99 F. Supp. 2d 814, 822 n. 5 (N.D. Ohio 2000).

[659] 267 F.2d 358 (2d Cir. 1959).

[660] *Id.* at 363.

refused to issue an injunction to prevent the junior user from using the same mark at the retail level in that territory.[661] The court also refused to award damages. The court noted, however, that the junior user's right to exploit the mark in the limited trading area would cease if and when the federal registrant expanded its retail activities to that area.[662]

While *Dawn Donut* has been endorsed by the majority of circuits,[663] the Sixth Circuit has rejected it, holding instead that injunctive relief is warranted whenever infringement is established under the circuit's multi-factor likelihood-of-confusion analysis.[664]

[8]   Unregistered Marks

Even in states with registration systems, unregistered marks that are capable of distinguishing a merchant's goods or services are still protected under the common law, under principles similar to those of section 43(a) of the Lanham Act.[665]

Sections 43(a) and 43(c) of the Lanham Act also protect unregistered marks against unfair competition and dilution, respectively.[666] These provisions are discussed below.[667]

§ 5F   INFRINGEMENT

A cause of action for infringement of trademarks and service marks may arise under common law, state statutes, or the Lanham Act. Under all three sources of law, traditional trademark infringement claims require the senior user of a mark to establish that the junior user's mark creates a likelihood of confusion with regard to the origin of the latter's goods or services, and that this confusion is likely to cause a competitive injury to the senior user.

However, modern trademark and unfair competition laws are even broader in scope. Under the broadly interpreted unfair competition provisions of the Lanham Act, and comparable provisions of state statutes and common law, false or

---

[661] *Id.* at 360.

[662] *Id.*

[663] *See, e.g.,* Comidas Exquisitos, Inc. v. O'Malley & McGee's, Inc., 775 F.2d 260, 262 (8th Cir. 1985); Pizzeria Uno Corp. v. Temple, 747 F.2d 1522, 1536 (4th Cir. 1984); Foxtrap, Inc. v. Foxtrap, Inc., 671 F.2d 636, 640 (D.C. Cir. 1982) (per curiam); Value House, Inc. v. Phillips Mercantile Co., 523 F.2d 424, 429 (10th Cir. 1975); Holiday Inns of America, Inc. v. B & B Corp., 409 F.2d 614, 618–19 (3d Cir. 1969); Mister Donut of America, Inc. v. Mr. Donut, Inc., 418 F.2d 838, 844 (9th Cir. 1969); American Foods, Inc. v. Golden Flake, Inc., 312 F.2d 619, 625–26 (5th Cir. 1963); *cf.* Citibank, N.A. v. Citibanc Group, Inc., 724 F.2d 1540, 1546 (11th Cir. 1984) (implicitly endorsing *Dawn Donut*). *Compare* Members First Fed. Credit Union v. Members 1st Fed. Credit Union, 54 F. Supp. 2d 393, 402 (M.D. Pa. 1999) (questioning *Dawn Donut*'s continuing applicability in the Third Circuit) *with* Commerce Bancorp, Inc. v. BankAtlantic, 285 F. Supp. 2d 475, 501 n.12 (D.N.J. 2003) (applying *Dawn Donut*).

[664] Circuit City Stores, Inc. v. CarMax, Inc., 165 F.3d 1047, 1056 (6th Cir. 1999).

[665] *See, e.g.,* HQM, Ltd. v. Hatfield, 71 F. Supp. 2d 500, 504 n.17 (D. Md. 1999); Great South Bank v. First South Bank, 625 So. 2d 463, 466–67 (Fla. 993).

[666] 15 U.S.C. § 1125(a), § 1125(c).

[667] *See* § 5F (unfair competition), § 5G (dilution).

misleading representations about the source, sponsorship, or affiliation of goods, services, or commercial activities are actionable even where no trademark misuse occurs, provided that the representations are likely to cause confusion. Furthermore, under the dilution provisions of the Lanham Act, as well as statutes that have been adopted by a majority of states, an actionable injury to the rights of a trademark owner may arise in the absence of a likelihood of confusion, if the plaintiff can establish that the defendant's activities diluted the selling power of the plaintiff's mark or tarnished the reputation of that mark; under many dilution statutes, however, this extraordinary protection is limited to marks that are especially strong and/or "famous."[668] In addition, the Lanham Act contains a false advertising provision that provides a cause of action for false or misleading statements made about products or services in the context of commercial advertising or promotion.[669] Finally, under the Lanham Act's cybersquatting provisions, certain unauthorized uses of another person's mark in a domain name are actionable as well.[670]

[1]   Effect of Federal Registration

In the case of federally registered marks (on the Principal or the Supplemental Register), a federal cause of action for infringement arises under section 32 of the Lanham Act.[671]

Where the mark in question is not registered, but nonetheless qualifies as a mark at common law, the owner of the mark can bring an unfair competition claim under section 43(a) of the Lanham Act or under the state law of unfair competition.[672] The elements of an unfair competition claim under state law are similar to those of section 43(a), regardless of whether the state law claim arises under the common law or under an unfair competition statute.[673] In fact, courts typically use the principles of section 43(a) as a "measuring stick" for analyzing state law unfair competition claims, and will frequently dispense with analyzing the plaintiff's state law claims once they have reached a decision on the Lanham Act claims.[674]

Section 32(1)(a) gives the owner of a federal trademark registration a cause of action against:

Any person who shall, without the consent of the registrant—

---

[668] For the elements of a dilution claim, see § 5G.

[669] For the elements of a federal false advertising claim, see § 6E.

[670] For the elements of a cybersquatting claim, see § 5H.

[671] 15 U.S.C. § 1114. In the case of registered marks, certain federal causes of action may also arise under section 43(a) — for example, claims of false advertising. See 15 U.S.C. § 1125(a)(1)(B).

[672] 15 U.S.C. § 1125(a). In the case of both registered and common law marks, claims of dilution or cybersquatting, which differ from traditional trademark infringement, arise under sections 43(c) and 43(d), respectively, 15 U.S.C. § 1125(c), (d). See § 5G (dilution), § 5H (cybersquatting).

[673] See, e.g., Ohio Rev. Code Ann. § 4165.02 (2005) (codifying unfair competition principles).

[674] See, e.g., Planetary Motion, Inc. v. Techsplosion, Inc., 261 F.3d 1188, 1193 n.4 (11th Cir. 2001).

(a) use in commerce any reproduction, counterfeit, copy, or color-able imitation of a registered mark in connection with the sale, offering for sale, distribution, or advertising of any goods or services on or in connection with which such use is likely to cause confusion, or to cause mistake, or to deceive . . . .[675]

Similarly, section 43(a)(1) authorizes the owner of a common-law mark to bring an infringement claim against

Any person who, on or in connection with any goods or services, or any container for goods, uses in commerce any word, term, name, symbol, or device, or any combination thereof, or any false designation of origin, false or misleading description of fact, or false or misleading representation of fact, which—

(A) is likely to cause confusion, or to cause mistake, or to deceive as to the affiliation, connection, or association of such person with another person, or as to the origin, sponsorship, or approval of his or her goods, services, or commercial activities by another person . . . .[676]

Section 43(a) is, however, more than a trademark infringement statute. It also provides a remedy for false or misleading representations that do not involve unauthorized use of a trademark.[677] The misrepresentations may pertain to the origin of goods or services, the affiliation of one business with another,[678] or, under the false advertising provisions of section 43(a)(1)(B), the qualities or characteristics, or even the geographic origin, of any merchant's goods or services.[679]

Under both federal law and state law, claims of trademark infringement (other than dilution claims) generally involve a two-step analysis: First, the plaintiff must establish that its mark is valid and enforceable, and that the plaintiff is the owner of that mark, with a right of priority over the defendant with respect to that mark.[680] Second, the plaintiff must establish that the defendant has used the mark in connection with goods or services in a way that is likely to cause consumer confusion as to the origin of those goods or services.[681] The analysis under the first step — validity and priority — depends on whether the claim is brought under state or federal law, and on whether the mark has been registered on the Principal Register. These differences are noted in the discussion that follows. However, the analysis of the likelihood of confusion remains essentially the same regardless of

---

[675] 15 U.S.C. § 1114(1)(a).

[676] 15 U.S.C. § 1125(a)(1)(A).

[677] Zyla v. Wadsworth, 360 F.3d 243, 251 (1st Cir. 2004); Dastar Corp. v. Twentieth Century Fox Film Corp., 539 U.S. 23, 25–28 (2003).

[678] Schlotzky's Ltd. v. Sterling, 520 F.3d 393, 399 (5th Cir. 2008).

[679] Empresa Cubana Del Tabaco v. Culbro Corp., 399 F.3d 462, 478 (2d Cir. 2005); Gnesys, Inc. v. Greene, 437 F.3d 482, 488–89 (6th Cir. 2005).

[680] Custom Mfg. & Eng'g, Inc. v. Midway Servs., 508 F.3d 641, 648 & n.8 (11th Cir. 2007).

[681] *See, e.g.*, Lamparello v. Falwell, 420 F.3d 309, 313 (4th Cir. 2005); SunAmerica Corp. v. Sun Life Assurance Co. of Canada, 77 F.3d 1325, 1334 (11th Cir. 1996).

whether the mark is registered,[682] and regardless of whether the claim is brought under state statute, common law, or the Lanham Act.[683]

In addition to establishing ownership of a valid mark, and a likelihood of confusion arising from the defendant's activities, a plaintiff bringing a trademark infringement claim under either section 32 or section 43(a) of the Lanham Act must also establish that the defendant's infringing activities took place "in commerce." Likewise, an unfair competition claim under section 43(a) must also involve activities taking place in commerce. In contrast, a claim of trademark infringement or unfair competition that is brought under state law may arise from activities that are purely intrastate, and thus do not meet the "in commerce" jurisdictional requirement of federal law.

[2] Ownership of a Valid Mark

If a mark is registered on the Principal Register, section 7(b) of the Lanham Act provides that the certificate of registration is *prima facie* evidence of the validity of the mark and its registration, of the registrant's ownership of the mark, and of the registrant's exclusive right to use the registered mark in commerce.[684] However, this applies only to the goods or services specified on the registration certificate. Thus, if the trademark owner uses the registered mark on other goods or services, it will not be entitled to the presumption of validity. When the presumption applies to a registered mark, it shifts the burden of production to the infringement defendant, who must present evidence that the mark is invalid — for example, because the mark is descriptive and lacks secondary meaning.[685] The presumption of validity does not apply to marks that are registered only on the Supplemental Register.[686]

If a mark registered on the Principal Register has become incontestable, the registration is *conclusive* evidence of the validity of the mark and its registration, of the registrant's ownership of the mark, and of the registrant's exclusive right to use the mark in commerce, subject only to a narrow list of exceptions.[687]

However, in the case of a common-law mark, or a mark that is registered on the Supplemental Register, the plaintiff bears the burden of establishing ownership of a valid mark. Thus, the plaintiff must establish that it has used the mark in connection with the offering of goods or services to the public, and that its mark either (1) is inherently distinctive (that is, arbitrary, fanciful, or suggestive) or (2)

---

[682] *See, e.g.*, Louis Vuitton Malletier v. Dooney & Bourke, Inc., 454 F.3d 108, 114 (2d Cir. 2006); Matrix Motor Co. v. Toyota Jidosha Kabushiki Kaisha, 290 F. Supp. 2d 1083, 1090 (C.D. Cal. 2003), *aff'd mem.*, 120 Fed. Appx. 30 (9th Cir. 2005) (unpub.); Rolls-Royce Motors, Ltd. v. A & A Fiberglass, Inc., 428 F. Supp. 689 (N.D. Ga. 1977).

[683] As discussed in § 5F[3][c], each federal court of appeals and each state uses a multi-factor analysis to determine whether the activities of the junior user give rise to a likelihood of consumer confusion. *See, e.g., Matrix Motor*, 290 F. Supp. 2d at 1090 n.7.

[684] 15 U.S.C. § 1057(b).

[685] Custom Vehicles, Inc. v. Forest River, Inc., 476 F.3d 481, 486 (7th Cir. 2007).

[686] 15 U.S.C. § 1094; E.T. Browne Drug Co. v. Cococare Prods., 538 F.3d 185, 190 (3d Cir. 2008).

[687] 15 U.S.C. § 1115(b).

has acquired secondary meaning. The date on which the plaintiff began using its mark, and the market in which it uses the mark, will determine whether it is in fact the senior user, with priority over the accused infringer.

Sometimes, a trademark owner will make minor changes to its mark over time. In the context of an infringement action, the trademark owner may argue that its priority rights should be based on the earlier versions of the mark, rather than the most recent version. Under the practice known as "tacking," a trademark owner may claim priority in a mark based on the date on which it commenced use of a similar but not identical mark. However, tacking is permitted only when "the previously used mark is 'the legal equivalent of the mark in question or indistinguishable therefrom' such that consumers 'consider both as the same mark.' "[688] Where consumers regard the new and old marks as essentially the same, tacking furthers the goals of trademark law by protecting consumers from confusion while allowing some flexibility to trademark owners: "Without tacking, a trademark owner's priority in his mark would be reduced each time he made the slightest alteration to the mark, which would discourage him from altering the mark in response to changing consumer preferences, evolving aesthetic developments, or new advertising and marketing styles."[689]

The standard for tacking, however, has been described as "exceedingly strict."[690] The degree of similarity required is greater than the similarity required under the "likelihood of confusion" test.[691] The earlier and later versions of the mark "must create the same, continuing commercial impression, and the later mark should not materially differ from or alter the character of the mark attempted to be tacked."[692] Consistent with the strictness of this standard, tacking is rarely allowed.[693] Courts are especially reluctant to tack an earlier mark with a "narrow commercial impression" to a later mark with a "broader commercial impression."[694] The question whether tacking is warranted is a question of fact.[695]

In a section 43(a) action for infringement of unregistered trade dress, establishing ownership of a valid mark requires one additional element: the

---

[688] Brookfield Comms., Inc. v. West Coast Entertainment Corp., 174 F.3d 1036, 1047–48 (9th Cir. 1999) (quoting Data Concepts, Inc. v. Digital Consulting, Inc., 150 F.3d 620, 623 (6th Cir. 1998)); *accord*, Van Dyne-Crotty, Inc. v. Wear-Guard Corp., 926 F.2d 1156, 1159 (Fed. Cir. 1991)).

[689] *Brookfield*, 174 F.3d at 1048.

[690] *Id.*

[691] *Id.*

[692] *Id. (quoting Van Dyne-Crotty*, 926 F.2d at 1159); *accord Data Concepts*, 150 F.3d at 623.

[693] Sufficient similarity to support tacking was found in Hess's of Allentown, Inc. v. National Bellas Hess, Inc., 169 U.S.P.Q. 673, 674–75 (T.T.A.B. 1971), and Laura Scudder's v. Pacific Gamble Robinson Co., 136 U.S.P.Q. 418, 419–20 (T.T.A.B. 1962). In contrast, sufficient similarity to support tacking was absent in *Brookfield*, 174 F.3d at 1049; *Data Concepts*, 150 F.3d at 623–24; *Van Dyne-Crotty*, 926 F.2d at 1160; Pro-Cuts v. Schilz-Price Enters., 27 U.S.P.Q.2d 1224, 1227 (T.T.A.B. 1993); and American Paging, Inc. v. American Mobilphone, Inc., 13 U.S.P.Q.2d 2036 (T.T.A.B. 1989), *aff'd*, 17 U.S.P.Q.2d 1726 (Fed. Cir. 1990).

[694] *See* Van Dyne-Crotty, Inc. v. Wear-Guard Corp., 926 F.2d 1156, 1160 (Fed. Cir. 1991) (giving examples).

[695] Hana Financial, Inc. v. Hana Bank, 135 S. Ct. 907 (Jan. 21, 2015).

plaintiff must establish, as part of its *prima facie* case, that the trade dress it seeks to protect is not functional.[696] In contrast, under state law, while functionality will bar an infringement claim, it is up to the individual states to determine whether nonfunctionality is part of the plaintiff's *prima facie* case or whether the plaintiff need address it only to rebut a functionality defense.

[3]   Likelihood of Confusion

[a]   Overview

In a cause of action for infringement of a registered or common-law trademark, or for a false designation of origin claim under unfair competition doctrine, the key inquiry is whether the defendant's false or misleading representation as to the origin of goods or services is likely to confuse the consuming public. More specifically, the likelihood-of-confusion test inquires whether "an appreciable number of ordinarily prudent consumers" are likely to be misled or confused into believing that the junior user's product or service either originated with the senior user, or had some connection (such as sponsorship, endorsement, or affiliation) to the senior user.[697]

Under this test, the likelihood of confusion is evaluated from the point of view of the "ordinarily prudent consumer."[698] The ordinarily prudent consumer is not necessarily assumed to be highly intelligent, or to exercise a high degree of care in purchasing decisions, but is instead assumed to possess those characteristics that are typical of buyers for the particular goods or services at issue.[699] The question of what characteristics typify this consumer is incorporated into the likelihood-of-confusion analysis.[700] However, courts express varying views on the extent to which careless consumers should be considered in determining the likelihood of confusion. Some decisions have held that a probability of confusion on the part of careless consumers argues in favor of likelihood of confusion,[701] while others suggest that careless consumers should be disregarded.[702] In some cases, the nature of a product

---

[696] 15 U.S.C. § 1125(a)(3). For a discussion of functionality, *see* § 5C[1][c].

[697] *See, e.g.*, Mushroom Makers, Inc. v. R.G. Barry Corp., 580 F.2d 44, 47 (2d Cir. 1978); HMH Pub. Co. v. Lambert, 482 F.2d 595 (9th Cir. 1973); J.R. Wood & Sons, Inc. v. Reese Jewelry Corp., 278 F.2d 157 (2d Cir. 1960); CBS, Inc. v. Liederman, 866 F. Supp. 763 (S.D.N.Y. 1994), *aff'd*, 44 F.3d 174 (2d Cir. 1995) (per curiam); Toys "R" Us, Inc. v. Canarsie Kiddie Shop, Inc., 559 F. Supp. 1189, 1195 (E.D.N.Y. 1983).

[698] *See, e.g.*, S.S. Kresge Co. v. Winget Kickernick Co., 96 F.2d 978 (8th Cir. 1938); Walgreen Drug Stores v. Obear-Nester Glass Co., 113 F.2d 956 (8th Cir. 1940).

[699] *See, e.g.*, Volkswagenwerk Aktiengesellschaft v. Tatum, 344 F. Supp. 235, 237 (S.D. Fla. 1972); Stork Rest. v. Sahati, 166 F.2d 348 (9th Cir. 1948); Coca-Cola Co. v. Snow Crest Beverages, Inc., 162 F.2d 280 (1st Cir. 1947); Drexel Enters., Inc. v. Hermitage Cabinet Shop, Inc., 266 F. Supp. 532 (N.D. Ga. 1967); Ralston Purina Co. v. Saniwax Paper Co., 26 F.2d 941 (W.D. Mich. 1928).

[700] *See* § 5F[3][b][iv].

[701] *See, e.g.*, Fleischmann Distilling Corp. v. Maier Brewing Co., 314 F.2d 149, 156 (9th Cir. 1963); Harold F. Ritchie, Inc. v. Chesebrough-Pond's, Inc., 281 F.2d 755 (2d Cir. 1960); American Chicle Co. v. Topps Chewing Gum, Inc., 208 F.2d 560 (2d Cir. 1953); Stork Restaurant v. Sahati, 166 F.2d 348, 359 (9th Cir. 1948).

[702] *See, e.g.*, Indianapolis Colts, Inc. v. Metropolitan Baltimore Football Club L.P., 34 F.3d 410,

as an "impulse purchase" has led courts to assume that even the ordinarily prudent consumer would be somewhat careless.[703]

There is no fixed standard as to what constitutes an "appreciable number" of confused consumers.[704] Most courts do not require that a majority of consumers be confused.[705] Surveys showing relatively low percentages of actual confusion (15 to 20%, and sometimes even lower) are typically deemed persuasive evidence of actual confusion, which, in turn, is strongly probative of the likelihood of confusion.[706]

Confusion must be probable, not merely possible.[707] "The test . . . is not whether confusion is possible; nor is it whether confusion is probable among customers who are not knowledgeable. Rather, the test . . . is whether confusion is probable among numerous customers who are ordinarily prudent."[708]

It is not necessary for a plaintiff to prove that consumers would erroneously believe that the plaintiff actually produced the goods or services in question; it is enough that consumers would believe that the plaintiff endorsed or was affiliated with those goods or services.[709] Although the most common type of confusion is that which occurs at the time of purchasing — sometimes called "point of sale" confusion — infringement claims may also be based on initial interest confusion (that is, pre-sale confusion that dissipates before the purchase is made) or post-sale (or "aftermarket") confusion.[710]

[b] Factors

The federal courts of appeals, and the courts of each state, have developed their own versions of a multi-factor balancing test that functions as a flexible guide for evaluating the likelihood of confusion under federal or state law, respectively. Although the tests used in different jurisdictions differ as to the precise factors, the overall analysis is largely the same. Furthermore, jurisdictions generally agree that (1) no single factor is decisive, (2) evidence of actual confusion is helpful but not essential, (3) the list of factors adopted in any particular jurisdiction is non-exhaustive, and (4) on any given set of facts, some of the factors may be more significant than others. Ultimately, the likelihood of confusion depends on the

---

414–415 (7th Cir. 1994); Dawn Donut Co. v. Day, 450 F.2d 332 (10th Cir. 1971); Oriental Foods, Inc. v. Chun King Sales, Inc. 244 F.2d 909 (9th Cir. 1957); Life Savers Corp. v. Curtiss Candy Co., 182 F.2d 4 (7th Cir. 1950).

[703] Beer Nuts, Inc. v. Clover Club Foods Co., 805 F.2d 920 (10th Cir. 1986); Playboy Enters., Inc. v. Chuckleberry Pub., Inc., 687 F.2d 563 (2d Cir. 1982); Beech-Nut, Inc. v. Warner-Lambert Co., 480 F.2d 801 (2d Cir. 1973).

[704] Alderman v. Iditarod Props., 32 P.3d 373, 390 (Alaska 2001).

[705] Id.

[706] Id.; see § 5F[3][v] (discussing survey evidence of actual confusion).

[707] A&H Sportswear Co. v. Victoria's Secret Stores, Inc., 166 F.3d 197, 205–06 (3d Cir. 1999); Elvis Presley Enters. v. Capece, 141 F.3d 188, 193 (5th Cir. 1998); Alderman, 32 P.3d at 390.

[708] Estee Lauder v. Gap, Inc., 108 F.3d 1503, 1511 (2d Cir. 1997).

[709] See, e.g., Conagra, Inc. v. Singleton, 743 F.2d 1508, 1512 n.2 (11th Cir. 1984).

[710] See, e.g., Louis Vuitton Malletier v. Dooney & Bourke, Inc., 340 F. Supp. 2d 415, 431 (S.D.N.Y. 2004), aff'd in part, vacated and remanded in part, 454 F.3d 108 (2d Cir. 2006). Initial interest confusion and post-sale confusion are discussed in § 5F[3][e].

circumstances of the particular case, and must be "proved by inference drawn from the totality of relevant facts."[711]

In the Second Circuit, the following factors (known as the *Polaroid* factors) are considered in assessing the likelihood of confusion: (1) the strength of the senior mark; (2) the degree of similarity between the two marks; (3) the proximity of the products or services; (4) the likelihood that the prior owner will "bridge the gap"; (5) evidence of actual confusion; (6) the defendant's good faith (or bad faith) in adopting the mark in question; (7) the quality of defendant's product or service; and (8) the sophistication of the buyers.[712] Depending on the complexity of the issues, "the court may have to take still other variables into account."[713]

Outside of the Second Circuit, each federal court of appeals, and each state, has adopted some variation on the *Polaroid* test. Several of the *Polaroid* factors are universally recognized — *i.e.*, the strength of the senior mark, the similarity of the marks, the similarity of the parties' goods or services, evidence of actual confusion, and the junior user's intent. One factor — the quality of the junior user's goods or services — has received little attention outside the Second Circuit. Beyond these factors, there are slight variations among the different jurisdictions, but these generally amount to different categorizations rather than differences in substance.[714]

For example, the Ninth Circuit uses the *Sleekcraft* factors: (1) the similarity of the marks; (2) the relatedness or proximity of the two parties' products or services; (3) the strength of the senior user's mark; (4) the marketing channels used; (5) the degree of care likely to be exercised by the purchaser in selecting the goods or services; (6) the accused infringer's intent in selecting its mark; (7) evidence of actual confusion; and (8) the likelihood of expansion in product lines (that is, "bridging the gap").[715]

Although district courts are expected to analyze each factor in the likelihood-of-confusion analysis with care,[716] and must justify the conclusion that a particular factor is inapplicable in a given case,[717] courts have repeatedly cautioned against

---

[711] A&H Sportswear Co. v. Victoria's Secret Stores, Inc., 166 F.3d 197, 206–07 (3d Cir. 1999) (quoting Richard L. Kirkpatrick, *Likelihood of Confusion in Trademark Law* § 1.8 (PLI 1997); Dieter v. B&H Indus., Inc., 880 F.2d 322, 326 (11th Cir. 1989)).

[712] Polaroid Corp. v. Polarad Elecs. Corp., 287 F.2d 492, 495 (2d Cir. 1961).

[713] *Id.*

[714] For tests used in other federal circuits, *see* AMF Inc. v. Sleekcraft Boats, 599 F.2d 341, 346 (9th Cir. 1979) (8-factor test); Scott Fetzer Co. v. House of Vacuums, Inc., 381 F.3d 477 (5th Cir. 2004) (7-factor test); Sullivan v. CBS Corp., 385 F.3d 772, 776–77 (7th Cir. 2004) (7-factor test); Palm Bay Imports, Inc. v. Veuve Clicquot Ponsardin Maison Fondee en 1772, 396 F.3d 1369 (Fed. Cir. 2005) (13-factor test, developed by Federal Circuit's predecessor in *In re* E.I. DuPont de Nemours & Co., 476 F.2d 1357, 1361 (C.C.P.A. 1973)); Frisch's Restaurants v. Elby's Big Boy, 670 F.2d 642, 648 (6th Cir. 1982) (8-factor test); SquirtCo v. Seven-Up Co., 628 F.2d 1086, 1091 (8th Cir. 1980) (6-factor test); and Jellibeans, Inc. v. Skating Clubs of Georgia, Inc., 716 F.2d 833 (11th Cir. 1983) (7-factor test).

[715] *Sleekcraft*, 599 F.2d at 346.

[716] *See, e.g.*, New Kayak Pool v. R & P Pools, Inc., 246 F.3d 183, 185 (2d Cir. 2001); Sunbeam Prods., Inc. v. West Bend Co., 123 F.3d 246, 257 (5th Cir. 1997).

[717] *See, e.g., New Kayak Pool*, 246 F.3d at 185.

rigid application of any particular test.[718]

In reviewing trial court decisions regarding the likelihood of confusion, appellate courts treat determinations under each individual factor as questions of fact, reviewable only for clear error.[719] However, appellate courts disagree on the standard of review that applies to the ultimate conclusion of whether a likelihood of confusion exists.[720] Although a majority of courts treat this as a question of fact,[721] others treat it as a question of law subject to *de novo* review.[722] Even where the ultimate conclusion is treated as a question of fact, *de novo* review is proper if this conclusion was premised on an incorrect legal standard.[723]

[i] Similarity of Marks

Although likelihood of confusion, and infringement, may be found even though the junior and senior users' marks are not identical, the similarity of the junior and senior users' marks receives considerable weight in the likelihood-of-confusion analysis.[724]

A few courts have expressed the view that, in the case of directly competing goods, a strong showing of similarity or dissimilarity of the marks can obviate the need to undertake the rest of the likelihood-of-confusion analysis,[725] but such a foreshortened analysis is uncommon.[726] Extreme dissimilarity of marks will almost always dictate a finding of non-infringement even under the full likelihood-of-confusion analysis, but determining what degree of dissimilarity is sufficient to make further analysis unnecessary would be a somewhat subjective determination. In the case of extremely *similar* marks used on directly competing goods, it would be highly unlikely that federal registrations could be validly obtained for both marks under section 2(d) of the Lanham Act.[727] Where similar marks are *un*registered, the full likelihood-of-confusion analysis is not foreclosed, because even identical unregistered marks on directly competing goods may be non-

---

[718] *See, e.g.*, Indianapolis Colts, Inc. v. Metropolitan Baltimore Football Club L.P., 34 F.3d 410, 414 (7th Cir. 1994); Bristol-Myers Squibb. Co. v. McNeil-P.P.C., Inc., 973 F.2d 1033, 1044 (2d Cir. 1992).

[719] *See, e.g.*, Tumblebus, Inc. v. Cranmer, 399 F.3d 754, 764 (6th Cir. 2005).

[720] *See* ConAgra, Inc. v. George A. Hormel & Co., 990 F.2d 368 (8th Cir. 1993) (collecting cases).

[721] *See* 3 RONALD S. GILSON, TRADEMARK PROTECTION AND PRACTICE § 8.14 (Matthew Bender 2005); *see, e.g.*, Facenda v. N.F.L. Films, Inc., 542 F.3d 1007, 1024 (3d Cir. 2008); General Motors Corp. v. Urban Gorilla, LLC, 500 F.3d 1222, 1227 (10th Cir. 2007); Everest Capital, Ltd. v. Everest Funds Mgt., L.L.C., 393 F.3d 755 (8th Cir. 2005); Thane Int'l v. Trek Bicycle Corp., 305 F.3d 894, 901 (9th Cir. 2002); Elvis Presley Enters. v. Capece, 141 F.3d 188, 196 (5th Cir. 1998); Scandia Down Corp. v. Euroquilt, Inc., 772 F.2d 1423, 1428 (7th Cir. 1985); Jellibeans, Inc. v. Skating Clubs of Georgia, Inc., 716 F.2d 833, 840 n.16 (11th Cir. 1983) (rejecting earlier precedents to the contrary).

[722] Leelanau Wine Cellars v. Black & Red, 502 F.3d 504, 515 (6th Cir. 2007); China Healthways Inst., Inc., v. Wang, 491 F.3d 1337, 1339 (Fed. Cir. 2007).

[723] Elvis Presley Enters. v. Capece, 141 F.3d 188, 196 (5th Cir. 1998).

[724] Daddy's Junky Music Stores, Inc. v. Big Daddy's Family Music Center, 109 F.3d 275, 283 (6th Cir. 1997).

[725] *See, e.g.*, A & H Sportswear, Inc. v. Victoria's Secret Stores, Inc., 237 F.3d 198, 214 (3d Cir. 2000); Brookfield Communs., Inc. v. West Coast Ent. Corp., 174 F.3d 1036, 1054, 1056 (9th Cir. 1999).

[726] *See, e.g.*, Dippin' Dots, Inc. v. Frosty Bites Dist., LLC, 369 F.3d 1197, 1208 n.13 (11th Cir. 2004).

[727] 15 U.S.C. § 1052(d).

infringing under appropriate circumstances, such as where the marks are relatively weak and are used in remote geographic locations.

In assessing the similarity of trademarks, or trade dress, courts have stressed that each mark must be considered as a whole.[728] In the case of a composite mark (that is, a mark consisting of a combination of words and/or images), the "anti-dissection" rule requires courts to "view marks in their entirety and focus on their overall impressions, not individual features."[729] Only by viewing the marks in their entirety can a court understand the overall impression that each would make on a consumer in the marketplace.

Similarly, where one of the marks at issue is a subordinate mark — that is, a mark that is always used in conjunction with another mark — this may undercut the similarity between the senior and junior users' marks. For example, where the defendant always used its "Alpha" mark for cameras in conjunction with its "Polaroid" mark, this reduced the likelihood that its cameras would be confused with the plaintiff's cameras, which were sold under the "Alpha" mark.[730]

The anti-dissection rule applies even in the case of a registered composite mark in which part of the mark has been disclaimed. In comparing the registered mark with the allegedly infringing marks, courts consider the plaintiff's mark as a whole, including the disclaimed portion, because this is how consumers experience the plaintiff's mark.[731]

Notwithstanding the anti-dissection rule, "[i]f one word or feature of a composite trademark is the salient portion of the mark, it may be given greater weight than the surrounding elements."[732] This is particularly true where the surrounding elements are very weak. For example, in *International Kennel Club, Inc. v. Mighty Star, Inc.*, the Seventh Circuit found that the only significant difference between the plaintiff's "International Kennel Club of Chicago" mark and the defendant's "International Kennel Club" mark was "the common geographic term 'of Chicago,' " and concluded, therefore, that the "similarity" factor weighed in the plaintiff's favor because the defendant had appropriated "the dominant

---

[728] Clicks Billiards, Inc. v. Sixshooters, Inc., 251 F.3d 1252, 1259 (9th Cir. 2001); *see also* The Forschner Group, Inc. v. Arrow Trading Co., Inc., 124 F.3d 402, 409 (2d Cir. 1997); Union Carbide Corp. v. Ever-Ready, Inc., 531 F.2d 366, 379 (7th Cir. 1976).

[729] *Daddy's Junky Music Stores, Inc.*, 109 F.3d at 283–84; *see, e.g.*, AutoZone, Inc. v. Tandy Corp., 373 F.3d 786, 795–96 (6th Cir. 2004); AM General Corp. v. DaimlerChrysler Corp., 311 F.3d 796, 825 (7th Cir. 2002); Packman v. Chicago Tribune Co., 267 F.3d 628, 644 (7th Cir. 2001); Little Caesar Enters., Inc. v. Pizza Caesar, Inc. 834 F.2d 568, 571 (6th Cir. 1987); Henri's Food Prods. Co., Inc. v. Kraft, Inc., 717 F.2d 352, 355 (7th Cir. 1983); Sweetwater Brewing Co. LLC v. Great American Restaurants, Inc., 266 F. Supp. 2d 457, 462 (E.D. Va. 2003); MB Financial Bank, N.A. v. MB Real Estate Services, L.L.C., 2003 U.S. Dist. LEXIS 21051 (N.D. Ill. Nov. 20, 2003).

[730] Pignons S.A. de Mecanique de Precision v. Polaroid Corp., 657 F.2d 482, 487 (1st Cir. 1981); *see also* Fisher Stoves, Inc. v. All Nighter Stove Works, Inc., 626 F.2d 193, 194–95 (1st Cir. 1980); Keebler Co. v. Rovira Biscuit Corp., 624 F.2d 366, 378–79 (1st Cir. 1980); Alpha Indus., Inc. v. Alpha Steel Tube & Shapes, Inc., 616 F.2d 440, 444 (9th Cir. 1980); Bose Corp. v. Linear Design Labs, Inc., 467 F.2d 304, 310 (2d Cir. 1972); R.G. Barry Corp. v. A. Sandler Co., 406 F.2d 114, 116 (1st Cir. 1969).

[731] *See, e.g.*, Sleeper Lounge Co. v. Bell Mfg. Co., 253 F.2d 720 (9th Cir. 1958).

[732] *Sullivan*, 385 F.3d at 777.

portion" of the plaintiff's mark.[733] Similarly, courts routinely disregard top-level domain names (that is, ".com," ".org," etc.) in assessing similarity between domain names and trademarks.[734] Where a portion of a mark has been disclaimed, the non-disclaimed portion is generally considered to be dominant.[735]

In *Daddy's Junky Music Stores, Inc. v. Daddy's Junky Music Center*, the Sixth Circuit outlined several important principles that guide the assessment of similarity:

> When analyzing similarity, courts should examine the pronunciation, appearance, and verbal translation of conflicting marks. The appearance of the litigated marks side by side in the courtroom does not accurately portray market conditions. Rather, courts must determine whether a given mark would confuse the public when viewed alone, in order to account for the possibility that sufficiently similar marks may confuse consumers who do not have both marks before them but who may have a general, vague, or even hazy, impression or recollection of the other party's mark. Moreover, courts must view marks in their entirety and focus on their overall impressions, not individual features.[736]

In addition, in order to assess the similarity of the marks as the consumer would actually experience them, the comparison must be made "in light of what happens in the marketplace and not merely by looking at the two marks side-by-side."[737] Thus, where consumers do not normally encounter the marks together, minor stylistic differences between the marks should be disregarded.[738]

In some cases, a trademark owner may establish rights in an entire family of marks sharing a common and distinctive characteristic, which is called the "formative." The owner of rights in a family of marks may obtain trademark protection against a party whose mark uses the same formative in a manner that is likely to lead consumers to believe that its goods or services emanate from the same

---

[733] 846 F.2d 1079, 1088 (7th Cir. 1988); *see also* Meridian Mut. Ins. Co. v. Meridian Ins. Group, Inc., 128 F.3d 1111, 1116 (7th Cir. 1997); Induct-O-Matic Corp. v. Inductotherm Corp., 747 F.2d 358, 361 (6th Cir. 1984); MB Financial Bank, N.A. v. MB Real Estate Services, L.L.C., 2003 U.S. Dist. LEXIS 21051 (N.D. Ill. Nov. 20, 2003); Sweetwater Brewing Co. LLC v. Great American Restaurants, Inc., 266 F. Supp. 2d 457, 462 (E.D. Va. 2003).

[734] *See, e.g.*, Brookfield Communications, Inc. v. West Coast Entertainment Corp., 174 F.3d 1036, 1055 (9th Cir. 1999); Public Serv. Co. v. Nexus Energy Software, Inc., 36 F. Supp. 2d 436 (D. Mass. 1999); Minnesota Mining & Mfg. Co. v. Taylor, 21 F. Supp. 2d 1003, 1005 (D. Minn. 1998); Interstellar Starship Servs. Ltd. v. Epix, Inc., 983 F. Supp. 1331, 1335 (D. Or. 1997); Planned Parenthood Federation of America, Inc. v. Bucci, 1997 U.S. Dist. LEXIS 3338 (S.D.N.Y. Mar. 24, 1997), *aff'd*, 152 F.3d 920 (2d Cir. 1998).

[735] Citigroup Inc. v. City Holding Co., 2003 U.S. Dist. LEXIS 1845, *63 (S.D.N.Y. Feb. 10, 2003); *see, e.g.*, Quantum Fitness Corp. v. Quantum Lifestyle Ctrs., L.L.C., 83 F. Supp. 2d 810, 824 (S.D. Tex. 1999); Am. Throwing Co. v. Famous Bathrobe Co., 250 F.2d 377, 381–82 (C.C.P.A. 1957).

[736] 109 F.3d 275, 283 (6th Cir. 1997) (citations and internal quotes omitted). The three characteristics "pronunciation, appearance, and verbal translation" are more frequently referred to as "sight, sound, and meaning."

[737] Sullivan v. CBS Corp., 385 F.3d 772, 777 (7th Cir. 2004).

[738] *Sullivan*, 385 F.3d at 777; International Kennel Club, Inc. v. Mighty Star, Inc., 846 F.2d 1079, 1088 (7th Cir. 1988).

"family."[739] The existence of a family of marks is a question of fact based on "the distinctiveness of the common formative component and other factors, including the extent of the family's use, advertising, promotion, and its inclusion in a number of registered and unregistered marks owned by a single party."[740] Furthermore, courts have held that the existence of third-party uses or registrations of marks using the same formative does not preclude recognition of a party's rights to a family of marks using that formative.[741]

For example, in *J&J Snack Foods Corp. v. McDonald's Corp.*, the Federal Circuit held that the McDonald's restaurant chain had established a family of marks that consisted of a variety of generic food names preceded by the "Mc" prefix, even if it had not used or registered the "Mc" prefix by itself. The court explained that, for a family of marks to be protected, the public must recognize "the common characteristic of the family" as an indication of origin; relevant factors include "the use, advertisement, and distinctiveness of the marks, including assessment of the contribution of the common feature to the recognition of the marks as of common origin."[742]

[ii]   Competitive Proximity

Competitive proximity refers to the likelihood that consumers will assume that the junior user's product or service is associated with the senior user.[743] In determining the proximity of the goods or services associated with the junior and senior users' marks, courts consider the "content, geographic distribution, market position, and audience appeal," of those goods or services.[744] In *CBS v. Liederman*, the district court found little proximity between a California television production facility and a television-themed restaurant in New York, because the services were very different, and the locations were far apart. Thus, there was little market overlap.[745]

When goods are in direct competition, the degree of similarity between the marks that is necessary to establish a likelihood of confusion is lower than in the case of dissimilar products.[746] In contrast, where the parties' goods or services do

---

[739] *See* McDonald's Corp. v. McBagel's, Inc., 649 F. Supp. 1268, 1271–72 (S.D.N.Y. 1986); Medical Modalities Association, Inc. v. ARA Corporation, 203 U.S.P.Q. 295 (T.T.A.B. 1979). The fact that a party has not registered the formative by itself does not preclude recognition that it owns a family of marks using that formative. Toys "R" Us v. Abir, 1997 U.S. Dist. LEXIS 22431, *7–*8 (S.D.N.Y. Dec. 19, 1997).

[740] *McBagel's*, 649 F. Supp. at 1272.

[741] J&J Snack Foods Corp. v. McDonald's Corp., 932 F.2d 1460, 1463 (Fed. Cir. 1991); *accord* McDonald's Corp. v. McKinley, 13 U.S.P.Q.2d 1895 (T.T.A.B. 1989).

[742] 932 F.2d 1460, 1463 (Fed. Cir. 1991); *accord* International Diagnostics Technology, Inc. v. Miles Labs., Inc., 746 F.2d 798, 800 (Fed. Cir. 1984); McDonald's Corp. v. Dorothy Jill McKinley dba McKinley & Co., 13 U.S.P.Q.2d 1895 (T.T.A.B. 1989); *see also* Phat Fashions, LLC v. Phat Game Athletic Apparel, Inc., 2002 U.S. Dist. LEXIS 15734, *25–*27 (E.D. Cal. Mar. 19, 2002); AMF, Inc. v. American Leisure Prods., Inc., 474 F.2d 1403, 1406 (C.C.P.A. 1973); Motorola, Inc. v. Griffiths Elecs., Inc., 317 F.2d 397, 399 (C.C.P.A. 1963).

[743] CBS v. Liederman, 866 F. Supp. 763, 767 (S.D.N.Y. 1994), *aff'd*, 44 F.3d 174 (2d Cir. 1995).

[744] *Id.*

[745] *Id.*

[746] Sara Lee Corp. v. Kayser-Roth Corp., 81 F.3d 455, 465–66 (4th Cir. 1996).

not directly compete, a higher degree of similarity between the marks will normally be necessary.[747] Although ordinarily the similarity between marks must be weighed against the other likelihood-of-confusion factors, some courts have gone so far as to state that, where the parties' goods or services are directly competing, a court rarely needs to look beyond the similarity of the marks.[748]

Even where goods or services do not directly compete, if they serve the same purpose, are closely related, or are likely to be used together, this can contribute to a likelihood of confusion.[749] In *E. & J. Gallo Winery v. Gallo Cattle Co.*, wine, cheese, and salami were found to be complementary goods because they are often served together, a fact that increased the likelihood of confusion where similar marks were used on these goods.[750]

There is wide variation in what courts consider to be similar or related goods or services; especially in older cases, where the user's mark is particularly strong, courts have found non-competing goods to be related even where the relationship is quite tenuous.[751] Such cases today would more likely be litigated under dilution laws, which protect especially strong marks against non-competing uses even in the absence of a likelihood of confusion.[752]

This aspect of the likelihood-of-confusion analysis also takes account of the marketing channels through which the senior and junior users advertise and sell their goods or services. In some jurisdictions, such as the Second Circuit, this factor is subsumed in the analysis of the proximity of the parties' goods or services,[753] while in others the similarity of the parties' marketing channels is treated as a separate factor.[754] Where there is no overlap between the marketing channels for the parties' goods, confusion is less likely. For example, where one

---

[747] Kellogg Co. v. Toucan Golf, Inc., 337 F.3d 616, 625 (6th Cir. 2003); *see, e.g.*, Recot, Inc. v. Becton, 214 F.3d 1322, 1328 (Fed. Cir. 2000); Hunt Foods & Indus., Inc. v. Gerson Stewart Corp., 367 F.2d 431, 435, 54 C.C.P.A. 751 (C.C.P.A. 1966); American Sugar Refining Co. v. Andreassen, 296 F.2d 783, 784, 49 C.C.P.A. 782 (C.C.P.A. 1961); Yale Elec. Corp. v. Robertson, 26 F.2d 972, 974 (2d Cir. 1928); Quality Inns Int'l, Inc. v. McDonald's Corp., 695 F. Supp. 198, 221–22 (D. Md. 1988); John Walker & Sons, Ltd. v. Bethea, 305 F. Supp. 1302, 1307–08 (D.S.C. 1969); *see also* Daddy's Junky Music Stores, Inc. v. Big Daddy's Family Music Center, 109 F.3d 275, 282 (6th Cir. 1997).

[748] *See, e.g.*, A & H Sportswear Co. v. Victoria's Secret Stores, Inc., 166 F.3d 197, 202 (3d Cir. 1999); Interpace Corp. v. Lapp, Inc., 721 F.2d 460, 462 (3d Cir. 1983); Members First Federal Credit Union v. Members 1st Federal Credit Union, 54 F. Supp. 2d 393, 402 n.15 (M.D. Pa. 1999).

[749] RESTATEMENT (THIRD) OF UNFAIR COMPETITION § 21, cmt. j (1995); *see, e.g.*, Lange v. Retirement Living Pub. Co., 949 F.2d 576, 582 (2d Cir. 1991); *Yale Electric Corp.*, 26 F.2d at 974; Aunt Jemima Mills Co. v. Rigney & Co., 247 F. 407, 409–10 (2d Cir. 1917); Schieffelin & Co. v. Jack Co., 850 F. Supp. 232, 244–45 (S.D.N.Y. 1994). *Compare* Time, Inc. v. Life Television Corp., 123 F. Supp. 470, 475 (D. Minn. 1954) (finding likely confusion between Life magazine and Life television sets), *with* Time, Inc. v. T.I.M.E., Inc., 123 F. Supp. 446, 456–57 (S. Cal. 1954) (finding no likely confusion between Time magazine and T.I.M.E. trucking service).

[750] 967 F.2d 1280, 1291 (9th Cir. 1992).

[751] *See* Fleischmann Distilling Corp. v. Maier Brewing Co., 314 F.2d 149, 153 n.2A (9th Cir. 1963) (collecting cases).

[752] *See* § 5G.

[753] *See, e.g.*, Patsy's Brand, Inc. v. I.O.B. Realty, Inc., 317 F.3d 209, 218 (2d Cir. 2003).

[754] *See, e.g.*, Dippin' Dots, Inc. v. Frosty Bites Dist., LLC, 369 F.3d 1197, 1207 (11th Cir. 2004).

party sold its food products directly to consumers, while another sold exclusively to commercial food brokers, the Second Circuit held that there was no consumer who would encounter both marks, and thus no consumer to be confused.[755] On the other hand, the fact that the parties' goods are sold in the same types of stores does not necessarily receive great weight, because "modern marketing methods tend to unify widely different types of products in the same retail outlets or distribution networks"[756] — for example, selling groceries, DVDs, fishing gear, computers, and home improvement supplies in a single "big box" store or on Amazon.com.

[iii]   Strength of Plaintiff's Mark

The "strength" of a trademark refers to its distinctiveness or, more precisely, its tendency to identify the goods or services sold under the mark as emanating from a particular, although possibly anonymous, source.[757] As a general rule, the stronger the plaintiff's mark, the greater the likelihood of confusion: "The more deeply a plaintiff's mark is embedded in the consumer's mind, the more likely it is that the defendant's mark will conjure up the image of the plaintiff's product instead of that of the junior user."[758]

A mark's strength is measured by two factors: (1) the degree to which it is inherently distinctive (that is, arbitrary, fanciful, or suggestive); and (2) the degree to which it is distinctive in the marketplace.[759] Thus, while the spectrum of distinctiveness provides a useful guide to the strength of a plaintiff's mark for purposes of the likelihood of confusion test, the extent of the mark's recognition in the marketplace is also important.[760] Some courts refer to a mark's position on the spectrum of distinctiveness as its "conceptual strength," and its degree of recognition by consumers as its "commercial strength."[761] (The concept of commercial strength is virtually synonymous with secondary meaning.) A mark may be conceptually strong, yet commercially weak, or vice versa.[762] For example, a mark may be fanciful, and thus inherently distinctive, but may not be known to a large number of consumers, or may be considered relatively weak for other

---

[755] Dawn Donut Co. v. Hart's Food Stores, Inc., 267 F.2d 358 (2d Cir. 1959).

[756] Vitarroz Corp. v. Borden, Inc., 644 F.2d 960, 967 (2d Cir. 1981) (quoting Continental Connector Corp. v. Continental Specialties Corp., 492 F. Supp. 1088, 1096 (D. Conn. 1979)).

[757] McGregor-Doniger, Inc. v. Drizzle, Inc., 599 F.2d 1126, 1131 (2d Cir. 1979).

[758] Hormel Foods Corp. v. Jim Henson Prods., 73 F.3d 497, 503 (2d Cir. 1996); accord, McGregor-Doniger, Inc., 599 F.2d at 1132. However, parody can be an exception to this rule. Hormel, 73 F.3d at 503. See § 5J[3].

[759] Virgin Enters., Ltd. v. Nawab, 335 F.3d 141, 147–48 (2d Cir. 2003); W.W.W. Pharm. Co. v. Gillette, 984 F.2d 567, 572 (2d Cir. 1993); Kraft Gen. Foods, Inc. v. Allied Old English, Inc., 831 F. Supp. 123, 128 (S.D.N.Y. 1993).

[760] "The more likely a mark is to be remembered and associated in the public mind with the mark's owner, the greater protection the mark is accorded by trademark law." GoTo.com v. Walt Disney Co., 202 F.3d 1199, 1207 (9th Cir. 2000); accord, Miss World (UK), Ltd. v. Mrs. America Pageants, Inc., 856 F.2d 1445, 1449 (9th Cir. 1988).

[761] See, e.g., Moose Creek, Inc. v. Abercrombie & Fitch Co., 331 F. Supp. 2d 1214, 1224 (C.D. Cal.), aff'd, 114 Fed. Appx. 921 (9th Cir. 2004).

[762] See, e.g., Oxford Indus., Inc. v. JBJ Fabrics, Inc., 6 U.S.P.Q.2d 1756 (S.D.N.Y. 1988); McGregor-Doniger, Inc. v. Drizzle, Inc., 599 F.2d 1126, 1131–32 (2d Cir. 1979).

reasons. Likewise, a descriptive mark with strong secondary meaning may qualify as a very strong mark for purposes of the likelihood-of-confusion analysis because, while it lacks conceptual strength, it has a high degree of commercial strength.

In the case of federally registered marks, section 7(b) provides that registration on the Principal Register creates a rebuttable presumption of validity.[763] Incontestability makes this presumption conclusive, subject to the defenses of section 33(b).[764] In addition, several circuits have held that the PTO's decision to register a mark on the Principal Register without requiring proof of secondary meaning gives rise to a rebuttable presumption that the mark is inherently distinctive (that is, arbitrary, fanciful, or suggestive) rather than descriptive.[765] The fact that a registered mark has become incontestable may be relevant to an assessment of its strength, but it is far from conclusive.[766]

In the case of a composite mark, validity and distinctiveness must be tested by considering the mark as a whole, rather than by dissecting it into its component parts.[767] When considered as a whole, a composite mark may be stronger than its individual components.[768] For example, a combination of two descriptive terms may result in a suggestive mark.[769]

Evidence of a mark's strength can take many forms. Evidence of long and continuous use, extensive advertising, sales, and recognition in the commercial field of use, and use on a broad variety of products can all help to establish the extent of its secondary meaning.[770] Even if a mark is otherwise strong, however, its strength may be undermined where other parties have used the same or similar marks at the same time as the plaintiff.[771]

[iv]   Consumer Sophistication

In general, more sophisticated consumers are presumed to be less easily confused than consumers who are less sophisticated, because the former are presumed to have greater powers of discrimination, and thus to exercise a higher

---

[763] 15 U.S.C. § 1057(b); Zyla v. Wadsworth, 360 F.3d 243 (1st Cir. 2004).

[764] Retail Servs. v. Freebies Pub'g, 364 F.3d 535, 548 (4th Cir. 2004).

[765] See, e.g., GTE Corp. v. Williams, 904 F.2d 536, 538–39 (10th Cir. 1990); Pizzeria Uno Corp. v. Temple, 747 F.2d 1522, 1528–29 (4th Cir. 1984); Money Store v. Harriscorp Fin., Inc., 689 F.2d 666, 673 (7th Cir. 1982); Abercrombie & Fitch Co. v. Hunting World, Inc., 537 F.2d 4, 11 (2d Cir. 1976).

[766] Therma-Scan, Inc. v. Thermoscan, 295 F.3d 623, 632–33 (6th Cir. 2002).

[767] GoTo.com, Inc. v. Walt Disney Co., 202 F.3d 1199, 1207 (9th Cir. 2000); Courtenay Comms. Corp. v. Hall, 334 F.3d 210, 215 (2d Cir. 2003).

[768] Union Carbide Corp. v. Ever-Ready, Inc., 531 F.2d 366, 379 (7th Cir. 1976).

[769] See, e.g., Banff, Ltd. v. Federated Dept. Stores, Inc., 841 F.2d 486, 489 (2d Cir. 1988); Macia v. Microsoft, 335 F. Supp. 2d 507, 514–15 (D. Vt. 2004); W.W.W. Pharm. Co. v. Gillette Co., 808 F. Supp. 1013, 1022 (S.D.N.Y. 1992), aff'd, 984 F.2d 567 (2d Cir. 1993).

[770] See, e.g., Scarves by Vera, Inc. v. Todo Imports, Ltd., 544 F.2d 1167 (2d Cir. 1976); Levi Strauss & Co. v. Blue Bell, Inc., 632 F.2d 817 (9th Cir. 1980); Minnesota Mining & Mfg. Co. v. 3M Electrical Corp., 184 U.S.P.Q. 470 (S.D. Fla. 1974).

[771] See, e.g., Sun Banks of Florida, Inc. v. Sun Federal Sav. & Loan Ass'n, 651 F.2d 311 (5th Cir. 1981); Amstar Corp. v Domino's Pizza, Inc., 615 F.2d 252 (5th Cir. 1980).

degree of care in making their purchasing decisions.[772] Thus, in evaluating the likelihood of confusion, courts consider the sophistication of the typical consumer who would encounter the junior user's product or service.

The nature of the junior user's goods or services is often relevant to the question of consumer sophistication.[773] Certain products or services (high-end designer clothing or certain financial services, for example) may be of interest largely to sophisticated consumers, while others (such as laundry detergent, standard grocery items, or plumbing repair services) are of interest to a broader demographic, and still others may be marketed to relatively unsophisticated people, such as children. Where a product is relatively expensive, the process of purchasing it typically involves a higher level of purchaser engagement (sometimes referred to as the "degree of care") that will tend to mitigate the likelihood of confusion.[774] In contrast, confusion is more likely in the case of impulse purchases.[775] The average educational level of the relevant consumers can also be an important indicator of sophistication.[776]

[v] Actual Confusion

Where evidence of actual confusion exists, it will often be the best evidence of likelihood of confusion,[777] and as a result it receives substantial weight in the likelihood-of-confusion analysis.[778] However, evidence of actual confusion is not required to establish likelihood of confusion, both because such evidence can be difficult to obtain,[779] and because requiring such evidence would compel plaintiffs to postpone legal action until both they and the consumer have suffered harm from the defendant's infringing activities. Indeed, in many cases, actual confusion will be difficult or impossible to demonstrate, because the senior user brings the infringement claim before the junior user has commenced its use of the mark in question, or shortly after the use has commenced but before there has been an opportunity for significant confusion to arise.[780] Because the policy of trademark law is to encourage trademark owners to take legal action before they suffer actual injury from the infringing use, the absence of evidence of actual confusion in such a case will have little or no impact on the likelihood-of-confusion analysis.[781]

---

[772] *See, e.g.*, Virgin Enters. v. Nawab, 335 F.3d 141, 151 (2d Cir. 2003); TCPIP Holding Co. v. Haar Communications, Inc., 244 F.3d 88, 102 (2d Cir. 2001); Ashe v. Pepsico, Inc., 205 U.S.P.Q. 451 (S.D.N.Y. 1979); Reddy Comms., Inc., v. Environmental Action Foundation, 477 F. Supp. 936 (D.D.C. 1979).

[773] *See, e.g.*, Merriam-Webster, Inc. v. Random House, Inc., 35 F.3d 65, 72 (2d Cir. 1994).

[774] *See, e.g.*, Deere & Co. v. MTD Holdings, Inc., 70 U.S.P.Q.2d 1009, 1023–24 (S.D.N.Y. 2004).

[775] *See, e.g.*, *id.*; Citigroup, Inc. v. City Holding Co., 171 F. Supp. 2d 333, 349 (S.D.N.Y. 2001).

[776] *See, e.g.*, Information Clearing House, Inc. v. Find Magazine, 492 F. Supp. 147, 163 (S.D.N.Y. 1980).

[777] Amstar Corp. v. Domino's Pizza, Inc., 615 F.2d 252, 263 (5th Cir. 1980).

[778] International Kennel Club v. Mighty Star, Inc., 846 F.2d 1079, 1089–90 (7th Cir. 1988).

[779] *See, e.g.*, Brookfield Comms., Inc. v. West Coast Entert. Corp., 174 F.3d 1036, 1050 (9th Cir. 1999); Eclipse Assocs. Ltd. v. Data Gen. Corp., 894 F.2d 1114, 1118–19 (9th Cir. 1990); AMF Inc. v. Sleekcraft Boats, 599 F.2d 341, 353 (9th Cir. 1979).

[780] *See, e.g.*, Lobo Enters., Inc. v. Tunnel, Inc., 822 F.2d 331, 333 (2d Cir. 1987).

[781] CBS v. Liederman, 866 F. Supp. 763, 768 (S.D.N.Y. 1994), *aff'd*, 44 F.3d 174 (2d Cir. 1995) (per curiam).

However, the absence of evidence of actual confusion can weaken a plaintiff's case where the competing marks have been in concurrent use for an extended period; if long-term concurrent use has not yet yielded actual confusion, this suggests that future confusion is unlikely.[782]

The strength of the actual confusion evidence will influence the weight it receives in the overall likelihood-of-confusion analysis. Isolated instances of confusion, or evidence of confusion that is unclear or insubstantial, will be given little weight.[783] In addition, the weight given to evidence of actual confusion will vary according to the identity of those confused, the value of the services involved, and the context in which the confusion occurs.[784] Courts have given little weight to the absence of actual confusion evidence where the goods in question were inexpensive impulse purchases, because consumers are less likely to report confusion in such cases.[785]

Evidence of actual confusion may take the form of anecdotal accounts by actual consumers, or survey evidence.[786] If a survey is well-constructed, survey evidence can be especially persuasive evidence of actual confusion.[787] When survey evidence is used, the question arises as to what percentage of survey respondents must have been confused in order for the evidence to be persuasive; in general, percentages of 15 to 20 percent or higher have been deemed persuasive,[788] although in some instances lower percentages have been deemed persuasive.[789] Questions may also arise regarding the manner in which the survey was constructed or administered, and expert testimony may be important in determining what, if any, weight to assign to the survey evidence.[790] Flawed survey methodologies may undermine or

---

[782] *See, e.g.,* Libman Co. v. Vining Indus., Inc., 69 F.3d 1360, 1361 (7th Cir. 1995).

[783] *See, e.g.,* Alpha Industries, Inc. v. Alpha Steel Tube & Shapes, Inc., 616 F.2d 440, 445 (9th Cir. 1980); *Sleekcraft,* 599 F.2d at 352; De Costa v. Columbia Broadcasting System, Inc., 520 F.2d 499, 514–15 (1st Cir. 1975); McFly, Inc. v. Universal City Studios, 228 U.S.P.Q. 153 (C.D. Cal. 1985); Schwartz v. Slenderella Systems of California, Inc., 271 P.2d 857 (Cal. 1954).

[784] Imperial Service Systems, Inc. v. ISS Int'l Service System, Inc., 701 F. Supp. 655, 659 (N.D. Ill. 1988); *see, e.g.,* A La Carte, Inc. v. Culinary Enters., Inc., 1997 U.S. Dist. LEXIS 12755, *20 n.1 (N.D. Ill. Aug. 21, 1997).

[785] *See, e.g.,* AmBrit, Inc. v. Kraft, Inc., 805 F.2d 974, 987–88 (11th Cir. 1986); Foxworthy v. Custom Tees, 879 F. Supp. 1200, 1216–17 (N.D. Ga. 1995).

[786] *See, e.g.,* Resource Developers Inc. v. Statue of Liberty-Ellis Island Foundation, Inc., 926 F.2d 134, 140 (2d Cir. 1991); Schieffelin & Co. v. Jack Co., 850 F. Supp. 232, 245 (E.D.N.Y. 1994).

[787] *See, e.g.,* Blockbuster Entertainment Group v. Laylco, Inc., 869 F. Supp. 505 (E.D. Mich. 1994).

[788] *See, e.g.,* Novartis Consumer Health, Inc. v. Johnson & Johnson-Merck Consumer Pharms. Co., 290 F.3d 578, 594 (3d Cir. 2002); Sara Lee Corp. v. Kayser-Roth Corp., 81 F.3d 455, 466–67 & n. 15 (4th Cir. 1996); Exxon Corp. v. Texas Motor Exch., Inc., 628 F.2d 500, 507 (5th Cir. 1980); RJR Foods, Inc. v. White Rock Corp., 603 F.2d 1058 (2d Cir. 1979); James Burrough, Ltd. v. Sign of Beefeater, Inc., 540 F.2d 266 (7th Cir. 1976); Schieffelin & Co. v. Jack Company of Boca, 850 F. Supp. 232, 247 (S.D.N.Y. 1994); *Blockbuster,* 869 F. Supp. at 513.

[789] *See, e.g.,* Mutual of Omaha Ins. Co. v. Novak, 836 F.2d 397, 400 (8th Cir. 1987) (10%); Coca-Cola Co. v. Tropicana Prods., Inc., 690 F.2d 312 (2d Cir. 1982) (7.5%); Goya Foods, Inc. v. Condal Distribs., Inc., 732 F. Supp. 453, 457 n. 7 (S.D.N.Y. 1990) (9–10%); Nat'l Football League Props., Inc. v. New Jersey Giants, Inc., 637 F. Supp. 507, 517 (D.N.J. 1986) (8.5–15%); Grotrian, Helfferich, Schulz, Th. Steinweg Nachf. v. Steinway & Sons, 365 F. Supp. 707, 716 (S.D.N.Y. 1973) (8.5%).

[790] *See, e.g., Blockbuster,* 869 F. Supp. at 514.

negate the evidentiary value of the survey.[791]

[vi] Bridging the Gap

This factor considers whether the senior user is likely to expand into the junior user's market.[792] If the two fields are closely related, this factor will tend to favor the senior user. In *Scarves by Vera, Inc. v. Todo Imports, Ltd.*, for example, the Second Circuit held that the fact that other women's fashion designers had crossed over into cosmetics, perfume, and toiletries, together with evidence that the plaintiff (a women's fashion designer) was exploring that market, helped to establish that perfumes were sufficiently related to women's fashion products that the parties' use of VERA in both fields was likely to cause confusion.[793] In contrast, if the parties' fields are unrelated, the senior user is unlikely to prevail on this factor.[794]

Bridging the gap applies to geographic markets as well as product markets. Thus, if the parties are not currently operating in the same territories, courts may consider the likelihood that the senior user will enter the junior user's territory in the future.[795]

[vii] Defendant's Intent

This factor considers whether the junior user adopted its mark "with the intention of capitalizing on plaintiff's reputation and goodwill and any confusion between [the junior user's] and the senior user's" goods or services.[796] Although a finding of bad faith is not necessary to finding a likelihood of confusion,[797] if the junior user adopted its mark with the intent of capitalizing on consumer confusion, this will weigh in favor of the senior user.

Typically there will be no direct evidence of the junior user's intent in adopting the mark. However, courts have held that a rebuttable presumption of bad faith may be warranted when the junior user's mark is identical to another mark that was already well-known and had acquired a secondary meaning at the time the

---

[791] Indianapolis Colts, Inc. v. Metropolitan Baltimore Football Club L.P., 34 F.3d 410, 414–15 (7th Cir. 1994); Anheuser-Busch, Inc. v. Balducci Pubs., 28 F.3d 769, 775 n. 4 (8th Cir. 1994); Lois Sportswear, U.S.A., Inc. v. Levi Strauss & Co., 799 F.2d 867, 875 (2d Cir. 1986); ConAgra, Inc. v. Geo. A. Hormel & Co., 784 F. Supp. 700, 734 (D. Neb. 1992), *aff'd*, 990 F.2d 368 (8th Cir. 1993); Conopco, Inc. v. Cosmair, Inc., 49 F. Supp. 2d 242, 252–55 (S.D.N.Y. 1999).

[792] CBS, Inc. v. Liederman, 866 F. Supp. 763, 767 (S.D.N.Y. 1994), *aff'd*, 44 F.3d 174 (2d Cir. 1995).

[793] 544 F.2d 1167, 1173 (2d Cir. 1976).

[794] *See, e.g.*, McGregor-Doniger, Inc. v. Drizzle, Inc., 599 F.2d 1126, 1135–36 (2d Cir. 1979); Westward Coach Mfg. Co. v. Ford Motor Co., 388 F.2d 627, 635 (7th Cir. 1968); *Liederman*, 866 F. Supp. at 767; Procter & Gamble Co. v. Johnson & Johnson, Inc., 485 F. Supp. 1185 (S.D.N.Y.), *aff'd without op.*, 636 F.2d 1203 (2d Cir. 1979).

[795] *See, e.g.*, Sun Banks of Florida, Inc. v. Sun Federal Sav. & Loan Ass'n, 200 U.S.P.Q. 758 (N.D. Fla. 1978); Cork 'N Cleaver of Colorado, Inc. v. Keg 'N Cleaver of Utica, Inc., 192 U.S.P.Q. 148 (N.D.N.Y. 1975).

[796] W.W.W. Pharmaceutical Co. v. Gillette Co., 984 F.2d 567, 575 (2d Cir. 1993); *accord*, Lang v. Retirement Living Pub. Co., 949 F.2d 576, 583 (2d Cir. 1991); Macia v. Microsoft, 335 F. Supp. 2d 507 (D. Vt. 2004); Edison Bros. Stores, Inc. v. Cosmair, Inc., 651 F. Supp. 1547, 1560 (S.D.N.Y. 1987).

[797] Tisch Hotels, Inc. v. Americana Inn, Inc., 350 F.2d 609, 613 (7th Cir. 1965).

junior user adopted it.[798] Bad faith may also be inferred from a junior user's continued use of a mark after being notified of the senior user's objections.[799]

Mere knowledge that another party is already using a similar mark, however, does not necessarily establish a junior user's bad faith. Courts have held that bad faith was not established where the junior user relied on legal advice that confusion with the senior user's mark was unlikely,[800] and where a junior user failed to conduct a trademark search before adopting a mark.[801] Conversely, where a junior user seeks advice of counsel and undertakes a trademark investigation before determining that adoption of a mark will not lead to confusion, this has been treated as evidence of good faith.[802]

Bad faith in the context of trademark infringement or unfair competition under state law or under sections 32 or 43(a) of the Lanham Act should not be confused with "bad faith intent to profit" under the cybersquatting provisions of section 43(d). The latter is discussed in § 5H.

[viii]　　Relative Quality of Defendant's Goods or Services

Although the quality of the defendant's goods or services is one of the *Polaroid* factors used by the Second Circuit, its role in the analysis is somewhat ambiguous, and it seems to have little relevance in other jurisdictions.

The ambiguity of this factor arises from the fact that a marked difference in quality between the senior and junior users' goods cuts both ways. It can reduce the likelihood of confusion, but where the junior user's goods are significantly lower in quality, any confusion that does occur will not only divert sales from the senior user, but will also tend to injure the senior user's reputation.[803]

Yet, when courts consider quality in the traditional likelihood-of-confusion analysis, they do not always acknowledge the ambiguous role of this factor. In some cases, courts have squarely held that there is less likelihood of confusion when the defendant's goods are at least equal in quality to the plaintiff's, because in such a case any consumer confusion about the origin of the defendant's goods is less likely to injure the plaintiff's reputation.[804] Other courts have squarely held that there is

---

[798] Stern's Miracle-Gro Prods., Inc. v. Shark Prods., Inc., 823 F. Supp. 1077, 1087 (S.D.N.Y 1993); Toys "R" Us, Inc. v. Canarsie Kiddie Shop, Inc., 559 F. Supp. 1189, 1199 (E.D.N.Y. 1983).

[799] *Stern's Miracle-Gro*, 823 F. Supp. at 1088; *see also* Mobil Oil Corp. v. Pegasus Petroleum Corp., 818 F.2d 254, 258–59 (2d Cir. 1987); Eastman Kodak Co. v. Rakow, 739 F. Supp. 116, 119 (W.D.N.Y. 1989).

[800] *See, e.g.*, W.W.W. Pharmaceutical Co. v. Gillette Co., 984 F.2d 567 (2d Cir. 1993); Procter & Gamble Co. v. Johnson & Johnson, Inc., 485 F. Supp. 1185, 1202 (S.D.N.Y. 1979).

[801] Paco Sport, Ltd. v. Paco Rabanne Parfums, 86 F. Supp. 2d 305 (S.D.N.Y.), *aff'd*, 2000 U.S. App. LEXIS 29570 (2d Cir. Nov. 16, 2000).

[802] *See, e.g.*, AMF, Inc. v. Sleekcraft Boats, 599 F.2d 341, 353–54 (9th Cir. 1979); Drexel Enterprises, Inc. v. Hermitage Cabinet Shop, Inc., 266 F. Supp. 532 (N.D. Ga. 1967).

[803] Savin Corp. v. Savin Group, 391 F.3d 439, 460–61 (2d Cir. 2004); Hormel Foods Corp. v. Jim Henson Prods., Inc., 73 F.3d 497, 505 (2d Cir. 1996); New Colt Holding Corp. v. RJG Holdings of Fla., Inc., 312 F. Supp. 2d 195, 227 (D. Conn. 2004).

[804] *See, e.g.*, Gruner + Jahr USA Pub'g v. Meredith Corp., 991 F.2d 1072, 1079 (2d Cir. 1993); W.W.W.

less likelihood of confusion where the defendant's goods are inferior to the plaintiff's, because this makes the goods (and their likely purchasers) dissimilar.[805] On other occasions, courts have acknowledged that this factor is more relevant to assessing the extent of the senior user's injury, and fashioning an appropriate remedy, than to determining the existence of likelihood of confusion, because the plaintiff's reputation might have been tarnished if the defendant's goods were of low quality.[806]

Where inferior quality is reflected in the price of the defendant's goods, however, courts generally hold that a significant price differential reduces the likelihood of confusion.[807] The same applies if the defendant's goods are higher in price.[808]

Similarity in quality may be especially significant in the post-sale context, where it will tend to increase the likelihood of confusion by nonpurchasers, because, unlike the purchasers, they do not benefit from knowing the price differential.[809]

[c] Jurisdictional Variations on the *Polaroid* Test

Outside of the Second Circuit, the list of factors considered by some jurisdictions includes factors that, while not expressly listed in the *Polaroid* test, are nonetheless subsumed under the broad sweep of such factors as the proximity of the goods and the sophistication of the consumers.[810]

For example, several jurisdictions explicitly consider the "degree of care" exercised by consumers in selecting goods or services of the type in question,[811] an important element that, in the *Polaroid* analysis, is usually considered under the "sophistication of the consumers" factor.[812] When a high degree of care is exercised at the time of purchase, this generally reduces the likelihood of confusion.[813] For example, consumers are thought to exercise a higher degree of care in selecting

---

Pharm. Co. v. Gillette Co., 984 F.2d 567, 575 (2d Cir. 1993); Lever Bros. Co. v. American Bakeries Co., 693 F.2d 251, 258 (2d Cir. 1982); Scarves by Vera, Inc. v. Todo Imports, Ltd., 544 F.2d 1167, 1172 (2d Cir. 1976); M&G Elecs. Sales Corp. v. Sony Kabushiki Kaisha, 250 F. Supp. 2d 91, 104 (E.D.N.Y. 2003).

[805] Plus Prods. v. Plus Discount Foods, Inc., 722 F.2d 999, 1007 (2d Cir. 1983).

[806] Virgin Enters., Ltd. v. Nawab, 335 F.3d 141, 152 (2d Cir. 2003).

[807] *See, e.g.*, McGregor-Doniger, Inc. v. Drizzle, Inc., 446 F. Supp. 160 (S.D.N.Y.), *aff'd*, 599 F.2d 1126 (2d Cir. 1978); Field Enters. Educ. Corp. v. Cove Industries, Inc., 297 F. Supp. 989 (E.D.N.Y. 1969); Field Enters. Educ. Corp. v. Grosset & Dunlap, Inc., 256 F. Supp. 382 (S.D.N.Y. 1966).

[808] *See, e.g.*, W.F. & John Barnes Co. v. Vandyck-Churchill Co., 207 F. 855 (S.D.N.Y.), *aff'd*, 213 F. 637 (2d Cir. 1913); Gort Girls Frocks, Inc. v. Princess Pat Lingerie, Inc., 73 F. Supp. 364 (S.D.N.Y. 1947).

[809] Lois Sportswear, U.S.A., Inc. v. Levi Strauss & Co., 799 F.2d 867, 875 (2d Cir. 1986).

[810] For authorities listing some of the multi-factor tests used outside the Second Circuit, see § 5F[3][b].

[811] *See, e.g.*, Sullivan v. CBS Corp., 385 F.3d 772, 776–77 (7th Cir. 2004); Frisch's Restaurants v. Elby's Big Boy, 670 F.2d 642, 648 (6th Cir. 1982); AMF Inc. v. Sleekcraft Boats, 599 F.2d 341, 353–54 (9th Cir. 1979).

[812] *See, e.g.*, Deere & Co. v. MTD Holdings, Inc., 70 U.S.P.Q.2d 1009, 1023–24 (S.D.N.Y. 2004); Tommy Hilfiger Licensing, Inc. v. Nature Labs, LLC, 221 F. Supp. 2d 410, 420 (S.D.N.Y. 2002).

[813] Sally Beauty Co. v. Beautyco, Inc., 304 F.3d 964, 975 (10th Cir. 2002); Heartsprings, Inc. v. Heartspring, Inc., 143 F.3d 550, 557 (10th Cir. 1998).

banking or financial services,[814] educational services,[815] or other expensive items,[816] than they do in making inexpensive impulse purchases.[817]

Several jurisdictions also list an additional likelihood of confusion factor, which they describe as either the "marketing channels used" by the junior and senior user in promoting their goods,[818] or the "area and manner of concurrent use" of the parties' marks.[819] In the Second Circuit's *Polaroid* test, this consideration is subsumed under the broader "proximity of the goods" factor.

[d] Reverse Confusion

Trademark infringement under sections 32 or 43(a) of the Lanham Act may be based on either "forward" or "reverse" confusion.[820] Forward (or "ordinary") confusion is the more common type of confusion, in which the junior user adopts a mark that so closely resembles the senior user's mark that consumers are likely to be misled into believing that the senior user is the source of the junior user's goods or services. In reverse confusion, the similarity between the marks has the opposite effect: consumers are likely to be misled into believing that the senior user's goods originate with the junior user.[821] In other words, "consumers encountering Plaintiff's products will assume that they are made by Defendant."[822] Most commonly, this results from the junior user's marketing success, which causes the junior user to become better known than the senior user.

Where reverse confusion occurs, the junior user's goodwill may so overwhelm that of the senior user that consumers may mistakenly believe that the senior user and the junior user are the same or related entities,[823] or even that the senior user is infringing the junior user's mark.[824] The senior user's ability to move into new markets may also be impaired.[825]

---

[814] *See, e.g.*, Sioux Falls v. First National Bank, South Dakota, 153 F.3d 885, 889–90 (8th Cir. 1998); First Franklin Fin. Corp. v. Franklin First Fin., LTD, 356 F. Supp. 2d 1048 (N.D. Cal. 2005).

[815] *Heartsprings*, 143 F.3d at 557.

[816] *Sally Beauty Co.*, 304 F.3d at 975; *Tommy Hilfiger*, 221 F. Supp. 2d at 420.

[817] *Sally Beauty Co.*, 304 F.3d at 975; Beer Nuts, Inc. v. Clover Club Foods Col, 805 F.2d 920, 926 (10th Cir. 1986).

[818] *See, e.g.*, AMF Inc. v. Sleekcraft Boats, 599 F.2d 341, 353 (9th Cir. 1979).

[819] *See, e.g.*, Sullivan v. CBS Corp., 385 F.3d 772, 776–77 (7th Cir. 2004).

[820] Trouble v. Wet Seal, 179 F. Supp. 2d 291, 295–96 (S.D.N.Y. 1991).

[821] Dreamwerks Prod. Group v. SKG Studio, 142 F.3d 1127, 1130 (9th Cir. 1998); Sterling Drug, Inc. v. Bayer AG, 14 F.3d 733, 741 (2d Cir. 1994); Lange v. Retirement Living Pub. Co., 949 F.2d 576, 583 (2d Cir. 1991); Banff, Ltd. v. Federated Dept. Stores, Inc., 841 F.2d 486, 490 (2d Cir. 1988); Fuji Photo Film Co. v. Shinohara Shoji Kabushiki Kaisha, 754 F.2d 591, 596 (5th Cir. 1985); Trustees of Columbia University v. Columbia/HCA Healthcare Corp., 964 F. Supp. 733, 743 (S.D.N.Y. 1997); Sunenblick v. Harrell, 895 F. Supp. 616, 625–26 (S.D.N.Y. 1995), *aff'd without op.*, 101 F.3d 684 (2d Cir. 1996); RESTATEMENT (THIRD) OF UNFAIR COMPETITION § 20(1)(c) & cmt. f (1995).

[822] Becoming, Inc. v. Avon Products, Inc., 2001 U.S. Dist. LEXIS 11929, *28 (S.D.N.Y. Aug. 15, 2001).

[823] Home Box Office, Inc. v. Showtime/The Movie Channel, Inc., 832 F.2d 1311, 1314 (2d Cir. 1987).

[824] *See, e.g.*, W.W.W. Pharm. Co. v. Gillette Co., 984 F.2d 567, 571 (2d Cir. 1993); Banff, Ltd. v. Federated Dept. Stores, Inc., 841 F.2d 486, 490 (2d Cir. 1988); *Sunenblick*, 895 F. Supp. at 625–26.

[825] Ameritech, Inc. v. American Information Technologies Corp., 811 F.2d 960, 964 (6th Cir. 1987); *Sunenblick*, 895 F. Supp. at 625.

Courts have applied the Lanham Act to encompass claims of reverse confusion because providing such protection to trademark owners "comports with the dual purposes of the Act — namely, to protect the public from confusion as to the source of goods, and at the same time to protect the trademark holder from misappropriation of its mark."[826]

In contrast to forward confusion, the injury to the senior user arising from reverse confusion may not involve an immediate diversion of sales. Instead, it typically involves an erosion of the senior user's goodwill or a loss of control over the senior user's reputation.[827] For example, consumers may come to believe that the senior user is an infringer trying to ride the coattails of the junior user.[828] Alternatively, if the junior user engages in conduct that gives rise to negative public opinion, this could tarnish the reputation of the senior user by eroding the goodwill associated with the mark.[829]

In determining the likelihood of reverse confusion, courts generally consider the same likelihood of confusion factors that they apply to claims of "ordinary" confusion,[830] with occasional modification.[831] However, with respect to one of these factors — the strength of the mark — courts disagree on whether the reverse confusion analysis should focus on the strength of the senior user's mark or that of the junior user's mark.[832] When the focus is on the senior user's mark, often that mark is too weak for the senior user to prevail.[833]

---

[826] *Sterling Drug*, 14 F.3d at 741; *see, e.g.*, Plus Products v. Plus Discount Foods, Inc., 722 F.2d 999, 1003–04 (2d Cir. 1983); Big O Tire Dealers, Inc. v. Goodyear Tire & Rubber Co., 561 F.2d 1365, 1372 (10th Cir. 1977).

[827] *See, e.g.*, Sands, Taylor & Wood Co. v. Quaker Oats Co., 978 F.2d 947, 957 (7th Cir. 1992); Lange v. Retirement Living Pub. Co., 949 F.2d 576, 583 (2d Cir. 1991); Ameritech, Inc. v. American Information Technologies Corp., 811 F.2d 960, 964 (6th Cir. 1987).

[828] Banff, Ltd. v. Federated Dep't Stores, Inc., 841 F.2d 486, 490 (2d Cir. 1988); W.W.W. Pharm. Co. v. Gillette Co., 984 F.2d 567, 571 (2d Cir. 1993); Sunenblick v. Harrell, 895 F. Supp. 616, 625 (S.D.N.Y. 1995), *aff'd without op.*, 101 F.3d 684 (2d Cir. 1996).

[829] Dreamwerks Prod. Group v. SKG Studio, 142 F.3d 1127, 1129 (9th Cir. 1998) (also suggesting that senior user could be harmed if junior user's dominance impedes senior user from expanding into junior user's line of business).

[830] *See, e.g.*, *Dreamwerks Prod. Group*, 142 F.3d at 1129; Sands, Taylor & Wood Co. v. Quaker Oats Co., 978 F.2d 947, 959 (7th Cir. 1992); *Banff*, 841 F.2d at 491; M & G Elecs. Sales Corp. v. Sony Kabushiki Kaisha, 250 F. Supp. 2d 91, 100 (E.D.N.Y. 2003).

[831] *See, e.g.*, Commerce Nat'l Ins. Servs. v. Commerce Ins. Agency, 214 F.3d 432, 444 (3d Cir. 2000). In the Ninth Circuit, three of the likelihood-of-confusion factors are considered especially important in determining the likelihood of reverse confusion: (1) the strength of the marks, (2) the relatedness of the goods, and (3) the similarity of the marks. *Dreamwerks Prod. Group*, 142 F.3d at 1130; Matrix Motor Co., Inc. v. Toyota Jidosha Kabushiki Kaisha, 290 F. Supp. 2d 1083, 1090 (C.D. Cal. 2003), *aff'd*, 120 Fed. Appx. 30 (9th Cir. 2005).

[832] *Compare Commerce Nat'l Ins.*, 214 F.3d at 444 (senior user's mark); Trustees of Columbia University v. Columbia/HCA Healthcare Corp., 964 F. Supp. 733, 744–45 (S.D.N.Y. 1997) (same); *and* Ernst Hardware Co. v. Ernst Home Ctr., 895 P.2d 1363, 1364–65 (Or. Ct. App. 1995) (same), *with Dreamwerks*, 142 F.3d at 1130 n.5 (junior user's mark); Sands, Taylor & Wood Co. v. Quaker Oats Co., 978 F.2d 947, 959 (7th Cir. 1992); *and* Sunenblick v. Harrell, 895 F. Supp. 616, 626 (S.D.N.Y. 1995) (same), *aff'd without op.*, 101 F.3d 684 (2d Cir. 1996).

[833] *See, e.g.*, J.T. Colby & Co. v. Apple, Inc., 2014 U.S. App. LEXIS 18527 (2d Cir. Sept. 29, 2014); Kaufman v. Bausch & Lomb, Inc., 2013 U.S. Dist. LEXIS 131532 (M.D. Fla. July 25, 2013); Scorpiniti v.

Although reverse confusion is now well-recognized under the Lanham Act, only a few decisions have discussed its viability under state law. The majority of these cases have concluded that the state laws in question encompassed reverse confusion.[834]

[e]   Confusion Before or After the Purchasing Decision

Consumer confusion occurring at the time a transaction takes place (sometimes called "point of sale" confusion) is not the only type of consumer confusion recognized under the Lanham Act. As discussed below, a number of courts have recognized "initial interest confusion" and "post-sale confusion." This expansive view of confusion has been traced to the 1962 amendments to section 2 of the Lanham Act, which removed references to "purchasers" being confused.[835]

[i]   Initial Interest Confusion

Initial interest confusion occurs when one party has used another's mark "in a manner calculated 'to capture initial consumer attention, even though no actual sale is finally completed as a result of the confusion.' "[836] Here, the similarity between a junior user's mark and a senior user's mark is what draws the consumer's initial attention to the goods or services of the junior user, but the consumer is no longer confused by the time the purchasing decision is made.[837] To employ the Ninth Circuit's now-famous analogy:

> Suppose [Blockbuster Video] puts up a billboard on a highway reading — "West Coast Video: 2 miles ahead at Exit 7" — where West Coast is really located at Exit 8 but Blockbuster is located at Exit 7. Customers looking for West Coast's store will pull off at Exit 7 and drive around looking for it. Unable to locate West Coast, but seeing the Blockbuster store right by the highway entrance, they may simply rent there. . . . Customers are not confused in the narrow sense: they are fully aware that they are purchasing from Blockbuster and they have no reason to believe that Blockbuster is

---

Fox Television Studios, Inc., 918 F. Supp. 2d 866 (N.D. Iowa 2013); Kate Spade LLC v. Saturdays Surf LLC, 950 F. Supp. 2d 639 (S.D.N.Y. 2013); *but see* Boldface Licensing & Branding v. By Lee Tillet, Inc., 940 F. Supp. 2d 1178 (C.D. Cal. 2013) (granting preliminary injunction because of strong showing on other factors).

[834] *See, e.g.*, Ameritech, Inc. v. American Info. Tech. Corp., 811 F.2d 960 (6th Cir. 1987) (Ohio); Capital Films Corp. v. Charles Fries Productions, 628 F.2d 387 (5th Cir. 1980) (Texas); Big O Tire Dealers, Inc. v. Goodyear Tire & Rubber Co., 561 F.2d 1365, 1371 (10th Cir. 1977) (Colorado); *cf.* Ernst Hardware Co. v. Ernst Home Ctr., 895 P.2d 1363, 1364–65 (Or. Ct. App. 1995).. *But see* Westward Coach Mfg. Co. v. Ford Motor Co., 388 F.2d 627, 633–34 (7th Cir. 1968) (concept not recognized under Indiana law).

[835] *See* Checkpoint Sys. v. Check Point Software Techs., Inc., 269 F.3d 270, 295 (3d Cir. 2001). The Federal Circuit disagrees, however, noting that the term "purchasers" was deleted from section 2 in order to make clear that the Lanham Act's protection also extends to *potential* purchasers. Electronic Design & Sales, Inc. v. Electronic Data Sys. Corp., 954 F.2d 713, 716 (Fed. Cir. 1992) (citing S. Rep. No. 87-2107, at 4 (1962), *reprinted in* 1962 U.S.C.C.A.N. 2844, 2847).

[836] Brookfield Comms., Inc. v. West Coast Ent. Corp., 174 F.3d 1036, 1062 (6th Cir. 1999), *quoting* Dr. Seuss Enters. v. Penguin Books, 109 F.3d 1394, 1405 (9th Cir. 1997).

[837] *See* Playboy Enters. v. Netscape Communs. Corp., 354 F.3d 1020, 1025 (9th Cir. 2004); *accord*, Mobil Oil Corp. v. Pegasus Petroleum Corp., 818 F.2d 254, 259 (2d Cir. 1987).

related to, or in any way sponsored by, West Coast. Nevertheless, the fact that there is only initial consumer confusion does not alter the fact that Blockbuster would be misappropriating West Coast's acquired goodwill.[838]

For example, in *Elvis Presley Enterprises, Inc. v. Capece*, the Fifth Circuit found that initial interest confusion was likely to arise from the defendant's use of the name "The Velvet Elvis" for its restaurant. Even though, once having entered the bar, consumers would realize that it was not affiliated with the plaintiff, their initial confusion was enough to bring them in the door.[839] Similarly, in *Grotrian, Helfferich, Schulz, Th. Steinweg Nachf. v. Steinway & Sons*, the Second Circuit found that, despite the high degree of care exercised by consumers in purchasing pianos, the resemblance between the Steinway mark and the Grotrian-Steinweg mark could initially confuse consumers into considering the latter brand. While closer examination of the latter product would eliminate their initial confusion, some of them might decide to purchase it based on cost and quality; this impermissibly allowed the maker of the Grotrian-Steinweg piano to benefit from confusion with the Steinway mark.[840]

At least seven circuits now recognize initial interest confusion as a valid basis for an infringement claim.[841]

Because the likelihood of initial interest confusion depends on the familiar likelihood-of-confusion factors, the analysis in any given case will be highly fact-specific. For example, the likelihood of initial interest confusion presented a close question where a grocery store's house brand adopted trade dress that was similar to that of a name brand competitor.[842] Although consumers may be highly sophisticated about house brands, and the store may present the competing goods in a way that draws attention to the fact that they are different brands and invites customers to make comparisons, this does not always outweigh the similarities between the marks.[843]

Initial interest confusion has played a significant role in infringement claims arising from the unauthorized use of trademarks in Internet domain names and metatags. A consumer looking for a senior user's website may search for a domain name incorporating the familiar trademark. A junior user may divert that consumer

---

[838] *Brookfield*, 174 F.3d at 1064.

[839] 141 F.3d 188, 204 (5th Cir. 1998).

[840] 523 F.2d 1331, 1341–42 (2d Cir. 1975).

[841] *See* Australian Gold v. Hatfield, 436 F.3d 1228, 1238–39 (10th Cir. 2006); Brookfield Comm'ns., Inc. v. West Coast Ent. Corp., 174 F.3d 1036 (9th Cir. 1999); Elvis Presley Enters., Inc. v. Capece, 141 F.3d 188, 204 (5th Cir. 1998); Forum Corp. of N. Am. v. Forum, Ltd., 903 F.2d 434, 442 n.2 (7th Cir. 1990); Mobil Oil Corp. v. Pegasus Petroleum Corp., 818 F.2d 254 (2d Cir. 1987); SecuraComm. Consulting, Inc. v. SecuraCom Inc., 984 F. Supp. 286 (D.N.J. 1997), *rev'd on other grounds*, 166 F.3d 182 (3d Cir. 1999), *appeal after remand*, 224 F.3d 273 (3d Cir. 2000); HRL Assocs., Inc. v. Weiss Assocs., Inc., 12 U.S.P.Q.2d 1819 (T.T.A.B. 1989), *aff'd on other grounds*, 902 F.2d 1546 (Fed. Cir. 1990). The Sixth Circuit has implicitly recognized it as well. *See* Gibson Guitar Corp. v. Paul Reed Smith Guitars, LP, 423 F.3d 539, 549–50 (6th Cir. 2005); PACCAR, Inc. v. TeleScan Techs., LLC, 319 F.3d 243, 253 (6th Cir. 2003).

[842] McNeil Nutritionals, LLC v. Heartland Sweeteners, LLC, 512 F. Supp. 2d 217 (E.D. Pa. 2007), *aff'd in part and rev'd in part*, 511 F.3d 350 (3d Cir. 2007).

[843] 511 F.3d at 367–69.

to its own website by incorporating the senior user's trademark, or a common misspelling, into the domain name, or by incorporating the trademark in the text of the web page or as a metatag. Depending on the search engine's methodology, a trademark that appears prominently in the text or metatags may cause the search engine to assign the web page a high ranking in the list of search results it provides to the user[844] (although as search engines have become more sophisticated they are less easily misled than in the past). Even where a consumer (or a search engine utilized by the consumer) is confused only briefly by a junior user's use of a misleading domain name, metatag or similar device, the consumer may remain on the junior user's website long enough to learn about its products or services, or those that it is advertising, and may even decide to make a purchase; thus, the temporary nature of the confusion does not preclude a finding that the junior user has misappropriated the senior user's goodwill, and thereby infringed.[845]

A leading case involving initial interest confusion on the Internet is *Brookfield Communications, Inc. v. West Coast Entertainment Corp.*,[846] in which a video rental company planned to use "moviebuff.com" as the domain name for its website, and to use a similar term as a metatag. The Ninth Circuit held that the defendant's actions infringed the plaintiff's rights in its registered "MovieBuff" trademark, which it used in connection with software and databases related to the entertainment industry. The court noted that several types of confusion were possible: consumers reaching the defendant's website might believe it was the plaintiff's website, or that it was licensed by or affiliated with the plaintiff, or they might believe that the defendant had purchased the plaintiff's business, or that the plaintiff had gone out of business. These consumers might decide to use the defendant's services rather than continue to search for the plaintiff's website. In the court's view, because it takes so little effort to reach a website, "Web surfers are more likely to be confused as to the ownership of a web site than traditional patrons of a brick-and-mortar store would be of a store's ownership."[847]

The Ninth Circuit extended its *Brookfield* analysis to banner ads in *Playboy Enters. v. Netscape Communs. Corp.*,[848] which held that the provider of an Internet search engine could be liable for allowing banner ads to be triggered when consumers entered certain search terms. The practice at issue involved "keying" banner ads to related search terms — for example, causing banner ads for seed companies to be displayed whenever a user enters gardening-related search terms into the search engine.[849] The court agreed with the plaintiff that the keying of banner ads to Playboy's marks could lead to initial interest confusion, because consumers might initially believe that the banner ads were links to websites affiliated with Playboy, and even if their confusion was dissipated after reaching the

---

[844] Brookfield Comm'ns., Inc. v. West Coast Ent. Corp., 174 F.3d 1036, 1045 (9th Cir. 1999).

[845] Promatek Indus., Ltd. v. Equitrac Corp., 300 F.3d 808, 812–13 (7th Cir. 2002).

[846] 174 F.3d 1036 (9th Cir. 1999).

[847] *Id.* at 1057–58.

[848] 354 F.3d 1020 (9th Cir. 2004).

[849] *Id.* at 1022–23.

competitors' websites, they might be content to patronize those sites.[850] The court noted, however, that initial interest confusion would not arise if a keyword-triggered banner ad conveyed sufficient information to alleviate confusion *before* the user clicked on the link contained in the banner ad and was taken to the advertiser's website — for example, where the banner ad clearly identified its source or overtly compared its own goods or services with those offered by the owner of the trademarked keyword.[851] In general, recent case law reveals that plaintiffs are having difficulty establishing a likelihood of confusion in keyword advertising cases.[852]

In *Brookfield* and several later cases, the Ninth Circuit emphasized three of its eight likelihood-of-confusion factors (the *Sleekcraft* factors[853]) as especially relevant to initial interest confusion on the Internet: (1) the similarity of the marks, (2) the relatedness of the goods or services, and (3) the parties' simultaneous use of the Internet as a marketing channel. The Sixth Circuit also endorsed this "Internet trinity."[854] Although the Ninth Circuit initially applied this approach in a variety of Internet contexts,[855] it reconsidered its position in *Network Automation, Inc. v. Advanced Systems Concepts, Inc.*, holding that the trinity factors were no longer the most important factors in the keyword advertising context, and that they should not automatically be considered the most important factors in other Internet contexts; instead, all eight of the *Sleekcraft* factors should be considered.[856] The court also introduced an additional factor that should be considered in evaluating the likelihood of confusion in the context of keyword advertising: "the labeling and appearance of the advertisements and the surrounding context on the screen displaying the results page."[857]

Another aspect of *Brookfield* — its conclusion that initial interest confusion can arise from the use of a mark solely in a metatag — has met with mixed reviews.[858]

---

[850] *Id.* at 1025–26.

[851] *Id.* at 1025 n.16, 1030 n.44.

[852] *See, e.g.*, 1-800 Contacts v. Lens.com, Inc., 722 F.3d 1229 (10th Cir. 2013); Allied Interstate LLC v. Kimmel & Silverman, 2013 U.S. Dist. LEXIS 113465 (S.D.N.Y. Aug. 12, 2013); Gen'l Steel Domestic Sales LLC v. Chumley, 2013 U.S. Dist. LEXIS 172290 (D. Colo. May 7, 2013). *But see* Rosetta Stone Ltd. v. Google, Inc. (4th Cir. 2012) (material issues of fact precluded summary judgment for defendant).

[853] AMF Inc. v. Sleekcraft Boats, 599 F.2d 341 (9th Cir. 1979). The *Sleekcraft* factors are listed in § 5F[3][b].

[854] *See* PACCAR, Inc. v. Telescan Techs., LLC, 319 F.3d 243, 254–55 (6th Cir. 2003).

[855] *See, e.g.*, Interstellar Starship Servs. v. Epix, Inc., 304 F.3d 936, 942 (9th Cir. 2002); GoTo.com, Inc. v. Walt Disney Co., 202 F.3d 1199, 1205–07 (9th Cir. 2000); SMC Promotions, Inc. v. SMC Promotions, 355 F. Supp. 2d 1127 (C.D. Cal. 2005); *see also* Nissan Motor Co. v. Nissan Computer Corp., 378 F.3d 1002, 1019 (9th Cir. 2004) (finding initial interest confusion when website offered goods related to trademark owner's, but not when it offered different goods).

[856] 638 F.3d 1137, 1148–49 (9th Cir. 2011).

[857] *Id.* at 1154.

[858] Agreeing with *Brookfield*: North Am. Med. Corp. v. Axiom Worldwide, Inc., 522 F.3d 1211, 1222 (11th Cir. 2008) (dicta); Australian Gold, Inc. v. Hatfield, 436 F.3d 1228, 1240 (10th Cir. 2007); Promatek Indus., Ltd. v. Equitrac Corp., 300 F.3d 808 (7th Cir. 2002); Eli Lilly & Co. v. Natural Answers, Inc., 86 F. Supp. 2d 834, 844 (S.D. Ind.), *aff'd on other grounds*, 233 F.3d 456 (7th Cir. 2000); Tdata Inc. v. Aircraft Technical Publishers, 411 F. Supp. 2d 901, 907 (S.D. Ohio 2006). Disagreeing: Playboy Enters., Inc. v.

The likelihood that confusion will result from unauthorized use of a mark in a metatag has probably decreased in recent years, because most search engines such as Google have changed their methodologies so that metatags no longer significantly influence their search results.[859]

The Sixth Circuit has held that the use of another's trademark in the *post*-domain URL path of a website does not constitute infringement, because it is not likely to be perceived by consumers as an indication of source.[860]

Because initial interest confusion is actionable even if the confusion ends before the purchasing decision takes place, disclaimers on a website are considered ineffective to negate the possibility of initial interest confusion.[861]

The doctrine of initial interest confusion is not universally recognized, nor is the scope of its application entirely clear. In *Lamparello v. Fallwell*, for example, the Fourth Circuit questioned the validity of the doctrine, but also suggested, in the alternative, that the doctrine should be applied only to defendants with a profit motive.[862] In *Gibson Guitar Corp. v. Paul Reed Smith Guitars*, the Sixth Circuit questioned whether initial interest confusion should apply at all outside of the Internet context and, more specifically, whether it should apply to trade dress.[863]

[ii]   Post-Sale Confusion

Consumer confusion about the origin of goods or services may occur even after the purchasing decision has been made.[864] Typically, the consumer experiencing such post-sale (or "aftermarket") confusion is not the same consumer who made the purchasing decision. One court has described the injury as arising from the likelihood that "the senior user's potential purchasers or ongoing customers might

---

Netscape Comm'ns Corp., 354 F.3d 1020, 1035–36 (9th Cir. 2004) (Berzon, J., concurring); J.G. Wentworth, S.S.C. Ltd. P'ship v. Settlement Funding LLC, 85 U.S.P.Q.2d 1780, 1786 (E.D. Pa. 2007); *see also* North Am. Med. Corp. v. Axiom Worldwide, Inc., 522 F.3d 1211, 1224 n.10 (11th Cir. 2008); J. Thomas McCarthy, McCarthy on Trademarks § 25:69 n.17.

[859] Eric Goldman, *Deregulating Relevancy in Internet Trademark Law*, 54 Emory L.J. 507, 567 (2005); McCarthy on Trademarks, at § 25:69.

[860] Interactive Prods. Corp. v. A2Z Mobile Office Solutions, Inc., 326 F.3d 687, 696–98 (6th Cir. 2003).

[861] *See, e.g.*, Australian Gold, Inc. v. Hatfield, 436 F.3d 1228 (10th Cir. 2006); SMC Promotions, Inc. v. SMC Promotions, 355 F. Supp. 2d 1127 (C.D. Cal. 2005); 1-800 Contacts, Inc. v. WhenU.com, 309 F. Supp. 2d 467 (S.D.N.Y. 2003); OBH, Inc. v. Spotlight Magazine, Inc., 86 F. Supp. 2d 176, 190 (W.D.N.Y. 2000); Toys "R" Us v. Abir, 1997 U.S. Dist. LEXIS 22431, *12 (S.D.N.Y. Dec. 19, 1997); Planned Parenthood v. Bucci, 1997 U.S. Dist. LEXIS 3338, *12 (S.D.N.Y. Mar. 19, 1997), *aff'd*, 152 F.3d 920 (2d Cir. 1998).

[862] 420 F.3d 309, 316 (4th Cir. 2005).

[863] 423 F.3d 539, 551 n.15 (6th Cir. 2005).

[864] Section 43(a) refers to false designations of origin or other false or misleading representations that are likely to cause confusion as to, *inter alia*, "affiliation, connection, or association," or "origin, sponsorship, or approval." 15 U.S.C. § 1125(a)(1)(A). Section 32 of the Lanham Act refers to any use of a registered mark that "is likely to cause confusion, or to cause mistake, or to deceive." 15 U.S.C. § 1114(1)(a). Prior to its amendment in 1962, section 32 specifically required confusion "of purchasers as to the source of origin of such goods or services." Pub. L. No. 87-772, 76 Stat. 769, 773 (1962). The 1962 amendment made clear that section 32 extends to confusion by nonpurchasers. Payless Shoesource, Inc. v. Reebok Int'l, Ltd., 998 F.2d 985, 989 (Fed. Cir. 1993); Lois Sportswear, U.S.A., Inc. v. Levi Strauss & Co., 799 F.2d 867, 872–73 (2d Cir. 1986).

mistakenly associate the inferior quality work of the junior user with the senior user and, therefore, refuse to deal with senior user in the future."[865] Many courts have recognized the likelihood of post-sale confusion as a valid basis for an infringement claim under the Lanham Act.[866]

The likelihood-of-confusion analysis will often lead to different results with respect to purchasers and nonpurchasers; for example, the fact that the senior user and junior user sell their products in completely different packaging, with different labels, at different prices, or in different stores will often make point-of-sale confusion unlikely, while consumers who encounter the products after they have been purchased will not have the benefit of these signals as to origin. Thus, the consumer who purchases a knock-off Gucci bag from a street vendor is less likely to be confused than the person who receives that bag as a gift and finds that the stitching has unraveled after a few weeks of use. It is said that the failure to protect trademark owners from post-sale confusion can undermine their incentive to produce high-quality goods.[867]

In *Payless Shoesource v. Reebok Int'l*, shoe manufacturer Reebok alleged that retailer Payless sold shoes that infringed Reebok's trademarks and trade dress in violation of sections 32 and 43(a) of the Lanham Act. Applying the traditional likelihood-of-confusion factors, the district court concluded that confusion at the point of sale was "inconceivable."[868] The appellate court agreed that point-of-sale confusion was unlikely, but it found that the district court had given inadequate consideration to the possibility of post-sale confusion; if someone observed the purchaser wearing the Payless shoes and believed them to be Reeboks, the observer might "attribute any perceived inferior quality of Payless shoes to Reebok, thus damaging Reebok's reputation and image."[869] Similarly, in *Karl Storz-Endoscopy America, Inc. v. Surgical Technologies, Inc.*, post-sale confusion was likely where hospitals used refurbished endoscopes that still displayed the original manufacturer's trademark, and were not marked as having been refurbished.[870] Although the hospitals knew of the refurbishment, the doctors did not, and they attributed defects in the equipment to the trademark owner.

Not all instances of post-sale confusion will support an infringement action; the confusion must be "commercially relevant." Confusion is commercially relevant if the defendant's use of the mark "could inflict commercial injury in the form of . . . a diversion of sales, damage to goodwill, or loss of control over reputation."[871] The trademark owner alleging aftermarket confusion need not prove an actual loss of

---

[865] Acxiom Corp. v. Axiom, Inc., 27 F. Supp. 2d 478, 497 (D. Del. 1998).

[866] *See, e.g.*, General Motors Corp. v. Urban Gorilla, LLC, 500 F.3d 1222, 1227 (10th Cir. 2007); Chrysler Corp. v. Silva, 118 F.3d 56, 59 (1st Cir. 1997); Esercizio v. Roberts, 944 F.2d 1235, 1244–45 (6th Cir. 1991); Polo Fashions v. Craftex, Inc., 816 F.2d 145, 148 (4th Cir. 1987); *Lois Sportswear*, 799 F.2d at 871.

[867] United States v. Torkington, 812 F.2d 1347, 1353 n.6 (11th Cir. 1987).

[868] 804 F. Supp. 206, 212 (D. Kan. 1992), *vacated and remanded on other grounds*, 998 F.2d 985 (Fed. Cir. 1993).

[869] 998 F.2d at 989.

[870] 285 F.3d 848, 854–55 (9th Cir. 2002).

[871] Beacon Mut. Ins. Co. v. OneBeacon Ins. Group, 376 F.3d 8, 15 (1st Cir. 2004) (quoting The Sports

sales in order to establish the requisite injury; damage to goodwill or reputation will suffice.[872] This view is in accord with the *Restatement (Third) of Unfair Competition*, which treats confusion as relevant when it creates "a significant risk to the sales or good will of the trademark owner," and notes that actionable confusion "must threaten the commercial interests of the owner of the mark, but it is not limited to the confusion of persons doing business directly with the actor."[873]

Because the potentially confused parties in a post-sale scenario are not actual purchasers, it is not always clear whose confusion should "count." Certainly, any party that has the potential to be a future customer of the senior user should count. Also, as illustrated by *Karl Storz-Endoscopy America*, when an infringing product is purchased for use by a third party whose satisfaction or dissatisfaction with the product may influence the purchaser's future decisions, any confusion experienced by the third-party user has the potential to harm the trademark owner. Thus, courts have held that the post-sale confusion inquiry extends to foreseeable users.[874] However, some parties who encounter the mark in a post-sale context may be so unlikely to purchase, or to influence purchasers of, the product or service in question that their potential confusion should be disregarded.[875]

Some courts have implied that commercially relevant post-sale confusion, and thus actionable injury, may arise even if the junior use's merchandise is not inferior to that of the senior user, because the value of the senior user's merchandise may be due in part to its scarcity, which is undermined by the availability of knock-offs; also, consumers may become reluctant to buy the senior user's merchandise if they fear that they cannot distinguish genuine goods from knock-offs.[876]

[4]   Trademark Use

In order for an infringement (or dilution) claim to arise, a defendant must use another's registered or unregistered trademark to identify the source or affiliation of goods or services that are offered to the public. In most cases, the question of whether the defendant is using the mark to identify the source of goods or services

---

Authority, Inc. v. Prime Hospitality Corp., 89 F.3d 955, 963 (2d Cir. 1996) (internal quotation marks omitted)).

[872] *See, e.g.*, Balance Dynamics Corp. v. Schmitt Indus., Inc., 204 F.3d 683, 693 (6th Cir. 2000); Landscape Forms, Inc. v. Columbia Cascade Co., 113 F.3d 373, 382–83 (2d Cir. 1997); Meridian Mutual Ins. Co. v. Meridian Ins. Group, Inc., 128 F.3d 1111, 1118 (7th Cir. 1997); Insty*Bit, Inc. v. Poly-Tech Indus., 95 F.3d 663, 672 (8th Cir. 1996); Champions Golf Club, Inc. v. The Champions Golf Club, Inc., 78 F.3d 1111, 1119–20 (6th Cir. 1996); Perini Corp. v. Perini Constr., Inc., 915 F.2d 121, 128 (4th Cir. 1990); International Kennel Club of Chicago, Inc. v. Mighty Star, Inc., 846 F.2d 1079, 1091 (7th Cir. 1988).

[873] *See, e.g.*, CMM Cable Rep., Inc. v. Ocean Coast Props., 888 F. Supp. 192, 200 (D. Me. 1995), *aff'd*, 97 F.3d 1504 (1st Cir. 1996); *see also* RESTATEMENT (THIRD) OF UNFAIR COMPETITION § 20 cmt. b (1995). Commercially relevant nonpurchaser confusion "may well extend beyond the confusion of those persons positioned to influence directly the decisions of purchasers." *Beacon Mut. Ins. Co.*, 376 F.3d at 16–17.

[874] Custom Mfg. & Eng'g, Inc. v. Midway Servs., 508 F.3d 641, 651 & n.9 (11th Cir. 2007).

[875] *Id.*

[876] Hermes, Int'l v. Lederer de Paris Fifth Ave., Inc., 219 F.3d 104, 108 (2d Cir. 2000); Lois Sportswear, U.S.A., Inc. v. Levi Strauss & Co., 799 F.2d 867, 875 (2d Cir. 1986); Mastercrafters Clock & Radio Co. v. Vacheron & Constantin-Le Coutre Watches, Inc., 221 F.2d 464, 466 (2d Cir. 1955); Foxworthy v. Custom Tees, 879 F. Supp. 1200, 1216 (N.D. Ga. 1995).

is fairly clear-cut. For example, this requirement is generally not satisfied where a defendant uses another's trademark on a website that is devoted purely to commentary about that party's goods or services.[877] In contrast, if the website also offers goods or services to the public, or if it contains commercial advertising, courts typically treat this as satisfying the threshold requirement.

Other cases, however, present a closer question — for example, where one party uses another's trademark in an expressive work that is offered for sale to the public,[878] where a trademark is used in the domain name of a noncommercial website that contains links to commercial websites[879] or solicits contributions for a cause antithetical to that of the trademark owner,[880] or where an Internet search engine triggers pop-up advertising for a merchant's goods or services whenever a user enters a competitor's trademark as a search term.[881] Some courts have held that the unauthorized use of a merchant's trademark in a domain name may be a use in connection with goods or services if it tends to impede or frustrate consumers trying to find the merchant's official website.[882]

In analyzing these claims, an important threshold question is whether the unauthorized use of the trademark is a "use in connection with . . . goods or services" so as to be actionable under section 32, 43(a), or 43(c). Some courts phrase the question differently, asking whether the defendant's activity involves a "use in commerce" as that term is defined in section 45 of the Lanham Act.[883] In this context, however, the focus of the analysis is not whether the defendant's use of the mark involves commerce that Congress has the authority to regulate, but whether it involves "commerce" in the dictionary sense — offering goods or services to the public.[884] As a result, the issue of trademark "use" arises even

---

[877] *See, e.g.,* Utah Lighthouse Ministry v. Found. for Apologetic Info & Research, 527 F.3d 1045 (10th Cir. 2008); Bosley Medical Inst., Inc. v. Kremer, 403 F.3d 672 (9th Cir. 2005); Savannah College of Art & Design, Inc. v. Houeix, 369 F. Supp. 2d 929 (S.D. Ohio 2004).

[878] *See, e.g.,* Felix the Cat Prods., Inc. v. New Line Cinema Corp., 54 U.S.P.Q. 2d 1856, 1857 (C.D. Cal. 2000).

[879] *Compare Bosley Medical Inst.,* 403 F.3d at 677–80; *and Savannah College,* 369 F. Supp. 2d at 944–48 *with* Nissan Motor Co. v. Nissan Computer Corp., 378 F.3d 1002 (9th Cir. 2004); Taubman Co. v. Webfeats, 319 F.3d 770, 775 (6th Cir. 2003); PETA v. Doughney, 263 F.3d 359 (4th Cir. 2001); OBH, Inc. v. Spotlight Magazine, Inc. 86 F. Supp. 2d 176 (N.D.N.Y. 2000); *and* Jews for Jesus v. Brodsky, 993 F. Supp. 282 (D.N.J.), *aff'd,* 159 F.3d 1351 (3d Cir. 1998).

[880] *See, e.g.,* Planned Parenthood Federation of America, Inc. v. Bucci, 42 U.S.P.Q.2d 1430, 1435 (S.D.N.Y. 1997), *aff'd,* 152 F.3d 920 (2d Cir. 1998).

[881] *See, e.g.,* 1-800 Contacts, Inc. v. WhenU.com, Inc., 414 F.3d 400, 408 (2d Cir. 2005); Google, Inc. v. American Blind & Wallpaper Factory, Inc., 74 U.S.P.Q. 1385 (N.D. Cal. 2005); U-Haul Int'l, Inc. v. WhenU.com, Inc., 279 F. Supp. 2d 723, 731 (E.D. Va. 2003); Wells Fargo & Co. v. WhenU.com, Inc., 293 F. Supp. 2d 734, 760 (E.D. Mich. 2003); GEICO v. Google, Inc., 330 F. Supp. 2d 700, 703 (E.D. Va. 2004). *But see* Rescuecom Corp. v. Google, Inc., 562 F.3d 123, 128–29 (2d Cir. 2009).

[882] *See, e.g.,* PETA v. Doughney, 263 F.3d 359, 365 (4th Cir. 2001); *but see* Bosley Medical Inst., Inc. v. Kremer, 403 F.3d 672, 679–80 (9th Cir. 2005) (rejecting this argument); Ford Motor Co. v. 2600 Enterprises, 177 F. Supp. 2d 661, 664 (E.D. Mich. 2001) (similar).

[883] *See, e.g.,* Boston Duck Tours, LP v. Super Duck Tours, LLC, 527 F. Supp. 2d 205 (D. Mass. 2007); Merck & Co. v. Mediplan Health Consulting, 425 F. Supp. 2d 402, 415 (S.D.N.Y. 2006).

[884] Bosley Medical Inst., Inc. v. Kremer, 403 F.3d 672, 677 (9th Cir. 2005).

where the trademark, unfair competition, or dilution claims arise under state rather than federal law.[885]

The requirement that a mark be used "in commerce" does not limit the protections of the Lanham Act to profit-seeking activities; thus, the Lanham Act also applies to nonprofit activities that involve the offering of goods or services.[886] However, using a registered or unregistered mark in a context that does not involve the sale, distribution, or advertising of goods or services does not constitute infringement under section 32 or 43(a) of the Lanham Act because it does not involve the use of a mark in commerce. For example, the use of a well-known cartoon character to "set the mood" of a film, rather than to indicate its source, was held not to be a use in commerce;[887] however, if such a mark is used to suggest a false or misleading source or affiliation for a work of entertainment, such a use is considered to be "in commerce" and can constitute an infringement.[888]

The discussion that follows focuses on four areas of ostensible trademark use: keyword advertising, metatags, domain names, and expressive works.

[a] Keyword-Triggered Advertising

Internet search engines such as Google and Yahoo often sell advertisers "keyword" rights in the trademarks or service marks of others. Under these arrangements, when a user enters that keyword as a search term, this triggers the appearance of links to the advertiser's website (referred to as "sponsored links"). In other situations, software (sometimes called "adware") is used to detect trademarks or service marks that are being used in Internet searches and to trigger banner or pop-up advertisements for competing or related goods and services. When, as is typically the case, the advertisements or sponsored links are not authorized by the owner of the trademark or service mark, this can give rise to an infringement claim based on likelihood of consumer confusion, most often in the nature of "initial interest confusion."[889] Dilution claims may arise as well.[890]

Thus far, the most thorough consideration of keyword advertising as trademark use has come from two cases in the Second Circuit. In the first of these, *1-800 Contacts v. WhenU.com, Inc.*,[891] the Second Circuit addressed the question whether trademark use occurred when the defendant's adware triggered pop-up ads of the plaintiff's competitors whenever a user visited the plaintiff's website. The adware functioned by maintaining a directory of website addresses, including the plaintiff's.

---

[885] *See, e.g.*, FragranceNet.com, Inc. v. FragranceX.com, Inc., 493 F. Supp. 2d 545, 547 n.4 (E.D.N.Y. 2007).

[886] United We Stand America, Inc. v. United We Stand, America New York, Inc., 128 F.3d 86, 92–93 (2d Cir. 1997).

[887] Felix the Cat Prods., Inc. v. New Line Cinema Corp., 54 U.S.P.Q.2d 1856, 1858 (C.D. Cal. 2000); *accord*, Lucasfilm, Ltd. v. High Frontier, 622 F. Supp. 931, 934 (D.D.C. 1985).

[888] *Felix the Cat Prods.*, 54 U.S.P.Q.2d at 1858.

[889] *See* § 5F[3][e][i].

[890] *See, e.g.*, Playboy Enters. v. Netscape Comm. Corp., 354 F.3d 1020, 1023 (9th Cir. 2004); Rescuecom Corp. v. Google, Inc., 456 F. Supp. 2d 393, 404 (N.D.N.Y. 2006), *vacated and remanded*, 562 F.3d 123, 128–29 (2d Cir. 2009).

[891] 414 F.3d 400 (2d Cir. 2005).

Because the plaintiff's website address incorporated its trademark, the plaintiff argued that the adware's use of its website address to trigger pop-up ads constituted trademark use. The Second Circuit held that no trademark use occurred, because the adware did not "place" the plaintiff's mark on any goods or services to indicate their origin, and indeed did not display the mark to the user.[892] In addition, however, the court noted that what triggered the pop-up ads was not the plaintiff's mark but the plaintiff's web address, which was slightly different from its mark. Accordingly, the court expressly declined to decide whether the inclusion of the actual trademark in the adware directory would constitute trademark use.[893] The court also noted that the ads for the plaintiff's competitors would also be triggered when a user entered a search for purely generic terms relevant to those products or services — *e.g.*, "contacts" or "eye care."[894] Because the adware did not alter or interfere with the plaintiff's website, did not divert or misdirect consumers away from that website, did not alter the results of a search using the plaintiff's mark or web address, and did not involve the sale of trademarks as keywords triggering pop-up ads, the court held that there was no basis for finding trademark use.[895]

In 2009, however, in *Rescuecom Corp. v. Google, Inc.*,[896] the Second Circuit distinguished *1-800 Contacts* and held that Google's keyword advertising system involved trademark use. Google's system had two components — AdWords and Keyword Suggestion Tool. AdWords allowed an advertiser to purchase keywords — including a competitor's trademark — which, when entered as search terms in Google's search engine, would cause the advertiser's ad and link to be displayed in the user's search results, generally accompanied by the label "sponsored link." The Keyword Suggestion Tool actively suggested to each advertiser certain keywords which that advertiser might be interested in purchasing; these suggestions sometimes included the trademarks of the advertiser's competitors. The district court had dismissed the plaintiff's infringement claim on the ground that, under *1-800 Contacts*, Google's activities did not involve a "trademark use." On appeal, however, the Second Circuit reversed. The court distinguished *1-800 Contacts* on two grounds: (1) the advertisers' pop-up ads in that case were triggered when users entered a competitor's website address, not its trademark (although the court acknowledged that the two were often very similar); and (2) instead of being triggered by specific keywords, the pop-up ads in *1-800 Contacts* were triggered by the general category of goods or services that corresponded to the search term or website address entered by a user. In contrast, Google's keyword system recommended, displayed, and "sold" the plaintiff's mark to advertisers; thus, in the court's view, Google's use of the plaintiff's mark fit literally within the language of § 1127's definition of a "use in commerce," because Google used the plaintiff's mark "in the sale of [Google's advertising] services . . . rendered in commerce."[897] The court

---

[892] *Id.* at 408–09.

[893] *Id.* at 409 & n.11.

[894] *Id.* at 410.

[895] *Id.* at 411–12.

[896] 562 F.3d 123 (2d Cir. 2009).

[897] *Id.* at 128–29.

declined to rule on the narrower question whether the inclusion of a trademark in Google's internal search algorithm, without more, could constitute trademark use. It also rejected the argument that Google's scheme was analogous to a retail store's side-by-side display of brand name and generic products.

In *Network Automation, Inc. v. Advanced System Concepts*, the Ninth Circuit agreed with the Second Circuit that the purchase of keywords by advertisers constitutes trademark use.[898] The other circuit courts of appeal, however, have offered little analysis of the issue. The Tenth Circuit has twice assumed, without deciding, that keyword-triggered sponsored links involve trademark use,[899] and the Fourth Circuit expressly made no determination as to trademark use when Google failed to raise the issue on appeal in *Rosetta Stone Ltd. v. Google, Inc.*[900]

Despite extensive litigation on the question, district courts remain divided. District courts in the First,[901] Third,[902] and Eighth[903] Circuits have held, and a district court in the Seventh[904] Circuit has expressly assumed, that keyword-triggered advertising constitutes trademark use. A district court in the Sixth Circuit reached the opposite conclusion, on the ground that when the mark is used merely as a keyword it is not being displayed to consumers, and thus is not being used to indicate source.[905] In the Fourth Circuit, two district courts have held that sponsored linking involves trademark use,[906] while another has held that no trademark use occurs when user-installed software employs a directory of trade-marks to generate pop-up ads related to the user's searches or website visits.[907]

While district courts in the Second Circuit typically found that keyword advertising was not a trademark use prior to the *Rescue.com* decision,[908] subse-quent decisions have held that the purchase of keywords by advertisers constitutes

---

[898] 638 F.3d 1137, 1145 (9th Cir. 2011).

[899] 1-800 Contacts, Inc. v. Lens.com, Inc., 722 F.3d 1229, 1242 (10th Cir. 2013); *Australian Gold v. Hatfield*, 436 F.3d 1228, 1239 (10th Cir. 2006).

[900] 676 F.3d 144, 152 n.4 (4th Cir. 2012).

[901] Hearts on Fire Co., LLC v. Blue Nile, Inc., 603 F. Supp. 2d 274 (D. Mass. 2009); Boston Duck Tours, LP v. Super Duck Tours, LLC, 527 F. Supp. 2d 205 (D. Mass. 2007).

[902] J.G. Wentworth, S.S.C. Ltd. P'ship v. Settlement Funding LLC, 2007 U.S. Dist. LEXIS 288, at *16–17 (E.D. Pa. Jan. 4, 2007); Buying for the Home, LLC v. Humble Abode, LLC, 459 F. Supp. 2d 310, 323 (D.N.J. 2006); 800-JR Cigar, Inc., v. GoTo.com, Inc., 437 F. Supp. 2d 273 (D.N.J. 2006).

[903] Edina Realty, Inc. v. TheMLSonline.com, 2006 U.S. Dist. LEXIS 13775, *9–*10 (D. Minn. Mar. 20, 2006).

[904] International Profit Assocs., Inc. v. Paisola, 461 F. Supp. 2d 672, 677 n.3 (N.D. Ill. 2006).

[905] Wells Fargo & Co. v. WhenU.Com, Inc., 293 F. Supp. 2d 734, 762 (E.D. Mich. 2003).

[906] Market America v. Optihealth Prods., 2008 U.S. Dist. LEXIS 95337, *17–*19 (M.D.N.C. Nov. 21, 2008); Gov't Employees Ins. Co. v. Google, Inc., 330 F. Supp. 2d 700, 704 (E.D. Va. 2004).

[907] U-Haul Intern. Inc. v. WhenU.com, Inc., 279 F. Supp. 2d 723, 728 (E.D. Va. 2003).

[908] Rescue.com Corp. v. Google, Inc., 456 F. Supp. 2d 393, 404 (N.D.N.Y. 2006), *vacated and remanded*, 562 F.3d 123 (2d Cir. 2009); S&L Vitamins, Inc. v. Australian Gold, Inc., 521 F. Supp. 2d 188, 199–202 (E.D.N.Y. 2007); Site Pro-1, Inc. v. Better Metal, LLC, 506 F. Supp. 2d 123 (E.D.N.Y. 2007); FragranceNet.com, Inc. v. FragranceX.com, Inc., 493 F. Supp. 2d 545, 550 (E.D.N.Y. 2007); Merck & Co., Inc. v. Mediplan Health Consulting, Inc., 425 F. Supp. 2d 402, 415 (S.D.N.Y. 2006), *on reconsideration*, 431 F. Supp. 2d 425, 427 (S.D.N.Y. 2006).

trademark use.[909] Accordingly, the courts of the Second Circuit treat both the sale of keywords and their use by advertisers as trademark use.

Even when a court decides that trademark use has occurred within the meaning of the Lanham Act, this does not necessarily mean that the use is infringing or dilutive; these are separate determinations.[910] Also, at least one court has held that even if sponsored linking does not, by itself, involve trademark use, if the plaintiff's mark is also displayed in the advertiser's sponsored link when it appears in the list of search results, this display can constitute trademark use.[911]

[b]   Metatags

Courts are less divided on the question whether incorporating trademarks into a website's metatags constitutes trademark use, generally answering in the affirmative. Metatags are computer codes, invisible to the average user, that give search engines information about the content of a website. A search engine may use this information in determining how high to rank the website when displaying search results. Thus, if a website contains a metatag that incorporates a trademark, that website could appear high on the list of search results displayed to a user who is searching for products bearing that trademark; as discussed above, this has led to claims of initial interest confusion.[912]

The Ninth[913] and Eleventh[914] Circuits have held that metatags involve trademark use, as have district courts in the First[915] and Third[916] Circuits. The First,[917] Seventh,[918] and Tenth[919] Circuits, and a district court in the Fourth Circuit,[920] have tacitly assumed trademark use. In the Second Circuit, while early district court

---

[909] LBF Travel v. Fareportal, Inc., 2014 U.S. Dist. LEXIS 156583 (S.D.N.Y. Nov. 5, 2014); Allied Interstate LLC v. Kimmel & Silverman P.C., 2013 U.S. Dist. LEXIS 113465 (S.D.N.Y. Aug. 12, 2013); CJ Prods. LLC v. Snuggly Plushez LLC, 809 F. Supp. 2d 127, 158 (E.D.N.Y. 2011).

[910] For the likelihood of confusion analysis as applied to keyword advertising, see § 5F[3][e][i].

[911] Hamzik v. Zale Corp./Delaware, 2007 U.S. Dist. LEXIS 28981, at *3 (N.D.N.Y. Apr. 19, 2007); see also Tiffany, Inc. v. eBay, Inc., 576 F. Supp. 2d 463 (S.D.N.Y. 2008) (implying agreement with Hamzik).

[912] See § 5F[3][e][i].

[913] Brookfield Communs., Inc. v. West Coast Entertainment Corp., 174 F.3d 1036, 1064–66 (9th Cir. 1999).

[914] North American Medical Corp. v. Axiom Worldwide Inc., 522 F.3d 1211 (11th Cir. 2008).

[915] Niton Corp. v. Radiation Monitoring Devices, Inc., 27 F. Supp. 2d 102 (D. Mass. 1998).

[916] J.G. Wentworth S.S.C. LP v. Settlement Funding LLC, 2007 U.S. Dist. LEXIS 288, *16–*17 (E.D. Pa. Jan. 4, 2007).

[917] Venture Tape Corp. v. McGills Glass Warehouse, 540 F.3d 56, 60 & n.5 (1st Cir. 2008).

[918] Promatek Indus., LTD v. Equitrac Corp., 300 F.3d 808, 812–13 (7th Cir. 2002); Eli Lilly & Co. v. Natural Answers, Inc., 233 F.3d 456 (7th Cir. 2000).

[919] Australian Gold v. Hatfield, 436 F.3d 1228, 1239 (10th Cir. 2006).

[920] Playboy Enters., Inc. v. Asiafocus Int'l, Inc., 1998 U.S. Dist. LEXIS 10359, *8 (E.D. Va. Apr. 10, 1998); see also Deltek, Inv. v. Iuvo Sys., 2009 U.S. Dist. LEXIS 33555, *18 (E.D. Va. Apr. 20, 2009) (defendant conceded trademark use); Market America v. Optihealth Prods., 2008 U.S. Dist. LEXIS 95337, *17–*19 (M.D.N.C. Nov. 21, 2008) (finding trademark use for purposes of determining personal jurisdiction).

decisions either held[921] or tacitly assumed[922] that metatags involve trademark use, later decisions reached the opposite conclusion, relying on the Second Circuit's analysis of keyword advertising in *1-800-Contacts*.[923]

Courts that treat metatags as trademark use do not necessarily find such uses to be infringing. Courts have held that the unauthorized use of another's mark in a metatag can be a fair use, if the mark fairly and in good faith describes the contents of the website.[924]

The use of trademarks in metatags is unlikely to be extensively litigated in the future; due to changes in searching methodology, search engines today place little or no reliance on metatags.[925]

[c]   Domain Names

Courts have also failed to reach consensus on whether the use of a trademark in a domain name, without more, constitutes trademark use. The question is whether the mere presence of a trademark in a domain name involves using the mark to indicate the origin of goods or services. If the website itself is considered a good or service, then trademark use would be established. However, if the website itself is not considered a good or service, then trademark use would turn on whether consumers encountering the website would perceive the trademark in question as indicating the origin of the goods or services offered or promoted on the website. Unless trademark use is established, claims of likelihood of confusion or dilution cannot be based solely on the presence of the mark in the domain name.

Some courts have held that incorporating a trademark into a domain name involves trademark use because consumers searching for the trademark owner's official website will mistakenly encounter the unauthorized website, frustrating their efforts to reach the official website, thus interfering with the trademark owner's offering of goods or services (although in most of these cases the defendant's website also included links to commercial websites).[926] Other courts have rejected this analysis.[927] Courts are especially reluctant to adopt this theory

---

[921] Bihari v. Gross, 119 F. Supp. 2d 309, 318 (S.D.N.Y. 2000).

[922] New York State Soc'y of CPA's, 79 F. Supp. 2d 331, 341–42 (S.D.N.Y. 1999).

[923] FragranceNet.com, Inc. v. FragranceX.com, Inc., 493 F. Supp. 2d 545, 550 (E.D.N.Y. 2007); S&L Vitamins, Inc. v. Australian Gold, Inc., 521 F. Supp. 2d 188 (E.D.N.Y. 2007); Site Pro-1, Inc. v. Better Metal, LLC, 506 F. Supp. 2d 123 (E.D.N.Y. 2007). These cases adopted the reasoning of the Second Circuit in 1-800 Contacts, Inc. v. WhenU.com, 414 F.3d 400 (2d Cir. 2005), even though that case involved adware rather than metatags.

[924] *See, e.g.*, Playboy Enters., Inc. v. Welles, 279 F.3d 796 (9th Cir. 2002); Bijur Lubricating Corp. v. Devco Corp., 332 F. Supp. 2d 722 (D.N.J. 2004); Trans Union L.L.C. v. Credit Research, Inc., 142 F. Supp. 2d 1029 (N.D. Ill. 2001); Bihari v. Gross, 119 F. Supp. 2d 309, 321–23 (S.D.N.Y. 2000); *accord, Promatek*, 300 F.3d at 814 & n.3; *Brookfield Communs.*, 174 F.3d at 1065–66. Fair use is discussed in § 5J[4] and [5].

[925] Standard Process, Inc. v. Banks, 554 F. Supp. 2d 866, 871 (E.D. Wis. 2008).

[926] *See, e.g.*, PETA v. Doughney, 263 F.3d 359, 366 (4th Cir. 2001); OBH, Inc. v. Spotlight Magazine, Inc., 86 F. Supp. 2d 176, 185–86 (W.D.N.Y. 2000); Jews for Jesus v. Brodsky, 993 F. Supp. 282, 309 (D.N.J. 1998); Planned Parenthood Fed'n v. Bucci, 1997 U.S. Dist. LEXIS 3338, *14 (S.D.N.Y. Mar. 19, 1997), *aff'd*, 152 F.3d 90 (2d Cir. 1998).

[927] *See, e.g.*, Utah Lighthouse Ministry v. Found. for Apologetic Info & Research, 527 F.3d 1045,

of trademark use where the website whose domain name incorporates the trademark is devoted to criticizing or parodying the trademark owner or its goods or services.[928] In contrast, courts have held that registering a domain name incorporating another's trademark in order to compel the trademark owner to purchase the domain name is trademark use, regardless of whether any goods or services are offered or advertised on the website.[929]

The problem of determining whether a domain name constitutes unauthorized trademark use has been somewhat alleviated by the Anticybersquatting Consumer Protection Act ("ACPA"),[930] which creates a specific cause of action for use of a trademark in a domain name with a "bad faith intent to profit" from the mark, without requiring the plaintiff to establish that the defendant was using the mark to indicate the origin of goods or services. The ACPA is discussed in § 5H.

[d] Expressive Works

Although the unauthorized use of trademarks in expressive works also implicates important First Amendment issues,[931] a few courts have held, as a threshold matter, that no trademark use is involved, because the mark is being used in connection with ideas rather than goods or services.[932] In other cases, however, courts have proceeded directly to the infringement or dilution analysis and the First Amendment considerations.[933]

[5] Use in Commerce as Jurisdictional Prerequisite

In an infringement action under section 32 or section 43(a) of the Lanham Act, or in a dilution action under section 43(c), the defendant's infringing conduct must take place "in commerce." This phrase refers to the offering of goods or services in those markets that Congress has the authority to regulate. The reason for this requirement is that Congress's authority to regulate trademarks derives from its powers under the Commerce Clause of the Constitution.[934] Under the Commerce Clause, Congress may regulate commerce among the states, with foreign nations,

---

1053–54 (10th Cir. 2008); Bosley Medical Inst., Inc. v. Kremer, 403 F.3d 672, 679 (9th Cir. 2005).

[928] *See, e.g., Utah Lightbouse Ministry*, 527 F.3d at 1053; *Bosley Medical Inst.*, 403 F.3d at 679; Taubman Co. v. Webfeats, 319 F.3d 770, 777–778 (6th Cir. 2003); Savannah College of Art & Design, Inc. v. Houeix, 369 F. Supp. 2d 929, 947–48 (W.D. Ohio 2004); Ford Motor Co. v. 2600 Enters., 177 F. Supp. 2d 661, 664–65 (E.D. Mich. 2001); Northland Ins. Cos. v. Blaylock, 115 F. Supp. 2d 1108, 1122–23 (D. Minn. 2000).

[929] *See, e.g.*, Panavision International, L.P. v. Toeppen, 141 F.3d 1316, 1325 (9th Cir. 1998); Intermatic Inc. v. Toeppen, 947 F. Supp. 1227, 1239 (N.D. Ill. 1996).

[930] 15 U.S.C. § 1125(d).

[931] *See* § 5J[3].

[932] *See, e.g.*, L.L. Bean Inc. v. Drake Publishers, Inc., 811 F.2d 26 (1st Cir. 1987); Felix the Cat Prods. v. New Line Cinema, 54 U.S.P.Q.2d 1856 (C.D. Cal. 2000); Lucasfilm, Ltd. v. High Frontier, 622 F. Supp. 931, 934 (D.D.C. 1985).

[933] *See, e.g.*, Mattel, Inc. v. MCA Records, 296 F.3d 894, 900–01 (9th Cir. 2002); Dr. Seuss Enters. L.P. v. Penguin Books USA, Inc., 109 F.3d 1394, 1403–04 (9th Cir. 1997); Hormel Foods Corp. v. Jim Henson Prods., Inc., 73 F.3d 497 (2d Cir. 1996); Dallas Cowboys Cheerleaders, Inc. v. Pussycat Cinema, Ltd., 604 F.2d 200 (2d Cir. 1979).

[934] *See* § 5B[3].

or with Indian tribes. Congress may not regulate purely *intrastate* commerce. However, it is increasingly rare to find transactions that are purely intrastate. Intrastate activities are considered to be "in commerce" if they have a substantial effect on interstate or foreign commerce.

The "in commerce" requirement for establishing subject matter jurisdiction for an infringement or dilution action under the Lanham Act is different from the "use in commerce" requirement for establishing ownership of a trademark for purposes of federal registration.[935] The latter, embodied in the section 45 definition of a "use in commerce," inquires whether the applicant for registration has made a qualifying use of the mark in commerce that Congress has the authority to regulate. In contrast, the "in commerce" requirement for infringing or dilutive activities focuses on whether a defendant's allegedly infringing activities have taken place in commerce that Congress has the authority to regulate. The jurisdictional scope of this "in commerce" requirement is broader than the definition of a "use in commerce" for registration purposes.[936]

Because purely intrastate disputes do not fall within the Commerce Clause, they cannot serve as the basis for infringement or dilution claims under the Lanham Act.[937] However, the jurisdictional scope of the Lanham Act has been construed to be "at least as broad as the definition of commerce employed in any other federal statute."[938] Courts have held that the "use in commerce" jurisdictional requirement is satisfied when either (1) the defendant's activity takes place in commerce, or (2) the defendant's conduct involves purely intrastate activities that nonetheless have a substantial effect on interstate commerce. In light of the broad sweep of the Commerce Clause, it is difficult to find an infringing activity that does not have a significant effect on commerce.

Courts have found sufficient interstate activity to satisfy the jurisdictional requirement where goods bearing the infringing mark were sold in interstate commerce,[939] where the infringing mark was used in advertisements in more than one state,[940] where infringing goods moved in interstate commerce from manufacturer to reseller,[941] and where infringing goods were shipped from one state to another in an effort to qualify for federal trademark registration.[942]

---

[935] *See* § 5D[1][b][i].

[936] Planned Parenthood Fed. of America v. Bucci, 42 U.S.P.Q.2d 1430, 1437 n.7 (S.D.N.Y. 1997), *aff'd*, 152 F.3d 920 (2d Cir. 1998).

[937] Jellibeans, Inc. v. Skating Clubs of Georgia, Inc., 716 F.2d 833, 838 (11th Cir. 1983); Iding v. Anaston, 266 F. Supp. 1015, 1019 (N.D. Ill. 1967).

[938] *Jellibeans*, 716 F.2d at 838; *accord*, Shatel Corp. v. Mao Ta Lumber & Yacht Corp., 697 F.2d 1352, 1356 n.3 (11th Cir. 1983); Bulova Watch Co. v. Steele, 194 F.2d 567, 570 n.11 (5th Cir.), *aff'd*, 344 U.S. 280 (1952).

[939] *See, e.g.*, Department of Justice v. Calspan Corp., 578 F.2d 295 (C.C.P.A. 1978).

[940] *See, e.g.*, American Hosp. Ass'n v. Bankers Commercial Life Ins. Co., 275 F. Supp. 563 (D. Tex. 1967), *aff'd*, 403 F.2d 718 (5th Cir. 1968).

[941] *See, e.g.*, Admiral Corp. v. Penco, Inc., 203 F.2d 517 (2d Cir. 1953), *overruled on other grounds*, Monsanto Chem. Co. v. Perfect Fit Prods. Mfg. Co., 349 F.2d 389 (2d Cir. 1965), *disapproved on other grounds*, Fleischmann Distilling Corp. v. Maier Brewing Co., 386 U.S. 714 (1967).

[942] *See, e.g.*, Drop Dead Co. v. S.C. Johnson & Son, Inc., 326 F.2d 87 (9th Cir. 1963).

Where the defendant's infringing activity is intrastate, courts generally agree that a substantial effect on interstate commerce is demonstrated where the infringing conduct damages goodwill that the plaintiff built up through the use of its mark in interstate commerce.[943]

Other effects on interstate commerce have also been held to be sufficient. For example, in *University of Florida v. KPB, Inc.*, the defendant's sale of study guides specific to the courses at a single university was found to have a sufficient effect on interstate commerce because (1) 15 percent of the student body was from out of state, and (2) one of the university's employees had a contract to produce a competing product for an out-of-state publisher.[944]

Activities utilizing the Internet are generally considered to be "in commerce" because they reach a national audience. For example, an Internet domain name was held to be used "in commerce" where the website provided news and information to Chinese-speaking people within the United States, even though it did not offer to sell them any goods or services.[945] In *Planned Parenthood Federation of America v. Bucci*, a federal district court held that the defendant's maintenance of a website that used the plaintiff's mark in its domain name satisfied the jurisdictional predicate for an infringement action under the Lanham Act because the website (1) affected the plaintiff's interstate activities, and (2) reached an interstate (as well as international) audience.[946]

[6] Territorial Limitations

The issue of whether, and when, a federal court may adjudicate a Lanham Act claim arising from activities taking place outside of the United States is a question of subject-matter jurisdiction. Today, it is well settled that federal courts may enjoin extraterritorial conduct under the Lanham Act when necessary to prevent harm to commerce in the United States. Although infringement of registered or unregistered marks is actionable under sections 32 or 43(a) of the Lanham Act (and dilution is actionable under section 43(c)) only when the defendant's activities involve a "use in commerce" of the plaintiff's mark, section 45 of the Act defines "commerce" broadly to include "all commerce which may lawfully be regulated by Congress."[947]

---

[943] United We Stand America, Inc. v. United We Stand, America New York, Inc., 128 F.3d 86, 93 (2d Cir. 1997) (quoting Dawn Donut Co. v. Hart's Food Stores, Inc., 267 F.2d 358, 365 (2d Cir. 1959)); Franchised Stores of New York, Inc. v. Winter, 394 F.2d 664 (2d Cir. 1968); Pure Foods, Inc. v. Minute Maid Corp., 214 F.2d 792 (5th Cir. 1954); Tiffany & Co. v. Boston Club, Inc., 231 F. Supp. 836 (D. Mass. 1964).

[944] 89 F.3d 773, 775 n.3 (11th Cir. 1996).

[945] Cable News Network L.P. v. CNNews.com, 177 F. Supp. 2d 506, 516–18 (E.D. Va. 2001), *aff'd in relevant part*, 56 Fed. Appx. 599, 66 U.S.P.Q.2d 1057 (4th Cir. 2003).

[946] 42 U.S.P.Q.2d 1430 (S.D.N.Y. 1997), *aff'd*, 152 F.3d 920 (2d Cir. 1998); *accord*, Intermatic, Inc. v. Toeppen, 947 F. Supp. 1227, 1239 (N.D. Ill. 1996).

[947] 15 U.S.C. § 1127.

The leading case on the extraterritorial reach of the Lanham Act is the Supreme Court's decision in *Steele v. Bulova Watch Co.*[948] In that case, the United States corporation that owned the "Bulova" trademark for watches alleged that the unauthorized use of its registered trademark by the defendant, a citizen and resident of the United States, was actionable under the Lanham Act even though the defendant's use of the mark took place exclusively in Mexico, where he obtained a Mexican registration for the mark, and began assembling and selling watches bearing the mark using components obtained from the United States and elsewhere. The plaintiff learned of these activities when it began to receive reports from retail jewelers in the Mexican border areas that customers were bringing in the defective watches for repair, believing them to be genuine Bulovas. Noting the general principle that "[t]he legislation of Congress will not extend beyond the boundaries of the United States unless a contrary legislative intent appears,"[949] the Court found that such intent was clearly expressed in section 45, and therefore concluded that "Congress has the power to prevent unfair trade practices in foreign commerce by citizens of the United States, although some of the acts are done outside the territorial limits of the United States."[950] Accordingly, the Court held that the defendant's activities in Mexico were actionable under the Lanham Act because (1) the defendant bought component parts in the United States, (2) some of the falsely marked merchandise was re-entering the United States, and (3) the defendant's goods could affect Bulova's reputation in the United States and abroad.[951] It also noted that the issuance of an injunction against the defendant's infringing activities in Mexico would not create a conflict with Mexican law because the Mexican government had already canceled his trademark registration.[952]

Several of the Circuit Courts of Appeal have distilled the *Bulova* analysis into a three-factor test that considers: (1) whether the defendant is a United States citizen; (2) whether the foreign activity has a substantial effect on United States commerce; and (3) whether exercising jurisdiction would interfere with the sovereignty of another nation.[953] Under this standard of extraterritoriality, the infringing conduct must have a "substantial" effect on United States commerce.[954] For example, the Eleventh Circuit found a substantial effect on commerce where foreign-made counterfeit jeans were found at the defendants' premises in the United States and were shipped through the United States, documents connected to the transactions falsely stated that the jeans were made in the United States, and many of the defendants' illegal activities, including locating and negotiating with prospective buyers and arranging shipments, took place in the United

---

[948] 344 U.S. 280 (1952).

[949] *Id.* at 285.

[950] *Id.* at 286 (quoting Branch v. Federal Trade Commission, 141 F.2d 31, 35 (1944)).

[951] 344 U.S. at 286.

[952] *Id.* at 289.

[953] *See* Int'l Café v. Hard Rock Café Int'l, 252 F.3d 1274, 1278 (11th Cir. 2001); Scanvec Amiable, Ltd. v. Chang, 80 Fed. Appx. 171, 181 (3d Cir. 2003) (unpub.); Atl. Richfield Co. v. ARCO Globus Int'l Co., 150 F.3d 189, 192 (2d Cir. 1998); Nintendo of Am., Inc. v. Aeropower Co., 34 F.3d 246, 250–51 (4th Cir. 1994).

[954] *Atl. Richfield Co.*, 150 F.3d at 192.

States.[955] In the Second Circuit, a substantial effect was established where a defendant advertised its product in the United States and sold it by mail to United States customers,[956] and where a defendant's foreign activities created confusion among United States customers as to the source of products sold in the United States.[957]

Applying the same standard, the Second Circuit has held that a substantial effect is *not* established by non-infringing domestic activities that are designed to support infringing foreign activities; the court noted that the Supreme Court's finding of a substantial effect in *Bulova* was not solely based on the fact that the defendant bought some of its watch components in the United States, but also on the fact that the counterfeit watches were coming into the United States and damaging Bulova's domestic goodwill.[958] In the Second Circuit's view:

> Where (i) an alleged infringer's foreign use of a mark does not mislead American consumers in their purchases or cause them to look less favorably upon the mark; (ii) the alleged infringer does not physically use the stream of American commerce to compete with the trademark owner by, for example, manufacturing, processing, or transporting the competing product in United States commerce; and (iii) none of the alleged infringer's American activities materially support the foreign use of the mark, the mere presence of the alleged infringer in the United States will not support extraterritorial application of the Lanham Act.[959]

In determining whether application of the Lanham Act would create a conflict with foreign law, courts applying the *Bulova* analysis have found such a conflict where the defendant is operating under a presumptively valid trademark in its home country.[960] In some cases, a pending application for the foreign registration may suffice to create a conflict,[961] although the opposite result was reached where it appeared that the defendant's foreign application would be rejected based on the plaintiff's priority rights.[962]

The Ninth Circuit has adopted a different test, known as the *Timberlane* factors: (1) there must be some effect on American foreign commerce; (2) the effect must be sufficiently great to present a cognizable injury to plaintiffs under the federal statute; and (3) the interests of and links to American foreign commerce must be sufficiently strong in relation to those of other nations to justify an assertion of extraterritorial authority.[963] In rejecting the approach adopted by other circuits,

---

[955] Levi Strauss & Co. v. Sunrise Int'l Trading Inc., 51 F.3d 982, 985 (11th Cir. 1995). *See also* Babbit Elecs., Inc. v. Dynascan Corp., 38 F.3d 1161, 1179 (11th Cir. 1994).

[956] Vanity Fair Mills, Inc. v. T. Eaton Co., 234 F.2d 633, 643 (2d Cir. 1956).

[957] Sterling Drug v. Bayer AG, 14 F.3d 733, 747 (2d Cir. 1994).

[958] Atl. Richfield Co. v. ARCO Globus Int'l Co., 150 F.3d 189, 192–93 (2d Cir. 1998).

[959] *Id.* at 193.

[960] Vanity Fair Mills, Inc. v. T. Eaton Co., 234 F.2d 633, 643 (2d Cir. 1956); Aerogroup Int'l v. Marlboro Footworks, 955 F. Supp. 220, 229 (S.D.N.Y. 1997).

[961] American White Cross Labs., Inc. v. H.M. Cote, Inc., 556 F. Supp. 753 (S.D.N.Y. 1983).

[962] Les Ballets Trockadero de Monte Carlo, Inc. v. Trevino, 945 F. Supp. 563, 567–68 (S.D.N.Y. 1996).

[963] Wells Fargo & Co. v. Wells Fargo Express Co., 556 F.2d 406 (9th Cir. 1977) (citing Timberlane

the Ninth Circuit noted that, while the effect on United States commerce, the citizenship of defendants, and the existence of a conflict with foreign law were all "relevant to the resolution of the jurisdictional issue," nonetheless "the absence of one of the factors is not necessarily determinative of the issue." Instead, the court treated each of these factors as "just one consideration to be balanced in the 'jurisdictional rule of reason' of comity and fairness."

Under *Timberlane's* "rule of reason," seven factors determine whether "the contacts and interests of the United States are sufficient to support the exercise of extraterritorial jurisdiction:"[964]

> The degree of conflict with foreign law or policy, the nationality or allegiance of the parties and the locations or principal places of business of corporations, the extent to which enforcement by either state can be expected to achieve compliance, the relative significance of effects on the United States as compared with those elsewhere, the extent to which there is explicit purpose to harm or affect American commerce, the foreseeability of such effect, and the relative importance to the violations charged of conduct within the United States as compared with conduct abroad.[965]

Under the Ninth Circuit's approach, it is not necessary that the defendant be a United States citizen; the "nationality or allegiance of the parties and the locations or principal places of business of corporations" is but one factor in the overall comity analysis. Moreover, even where a conflict might exist between plaintiff's and the defendant's registration in a country, jurisdiction to enjoin the defendant's activities is not necessarily foreclosed.[966]

The Fifth Circuit considers three factors as the "primary elements" of its balancing analysis: (1) the defendant's citizenship, (2) the effect on United States commerce, and (3) any conflict with foreign law. The factors are non-exhaustive, and no single factor is dispositive.[967] Notably, both the Ninth and Fifth Circuits have rejected the requirement that the defendant's foreign activities must have a substantial effect on United States commerce; in these circuits, it is sufficient if those activities have "some" effect.[968]

The First Circuit has articulated its own test for extraterritorial application of the Lanham Act where the defendants are not United States citizens, holding in *McBee v. Delica Co.* that the Lanham Act can be applied to extraterritorial conduct by foreign defendants only where their conduct "has a substantial effect on United States commerce."[969] Where such an effect is established, the court may take considerations of comity into account as a prudential matter, but such consider-

---

Lumber Co. v. Bank of America, 549 F.2d 597 (9th Cir. 1976)).

[964] *Wells Fargo*, 556 F.2d at 428–29 (quoting *Timberlane*, 549 F.2d at 614–15 (footnotes omitted)).

[965] Reebok Int'l, Ltd. v. Marnatech Enters., Inc., 970 F.2d 552, 555 (9th Cir. 1992).

[966] *Wells Fargo*, 556 F.2d at 429.

[967] American Rice, Inc. v. Arkansas Rice Growers Co-op. Ass'n, 701 F.2d 408, 414 (5th Cir. 1983) (citing Vanity Fair Mills, Inc. v. T. Eaton Co., 234 F.2d 633, 643 (2d Cir. 1956)).

[968] *Wells Fargo*, 556 F.2d at 428 (citing *Timberlane*, 549 F.2d at 612); *American Rice*, 701 F.2d at 414 & n.8.

[969] 417 F.3d 107, 120 (1st Cir. 2005).

ations do not preclude the court's exercise of Lanham Act jurisdiction.[970]

[7]   Reverse Passing Off

Section 43(a) has been held to apply also to actions for "reverse passing off" (or "reverse palming off"), which are also recognized at common law.[971] Reverse passing off occurs when a defendant offers goods or services produced by another person, but represents them as the defendant's own.[972] In reverse passing off, "the originator of the misidentified product is involuntarily deprived of the advertising value of [his] name and the goodwill," and the consumer "is deprived of knowing the true source of the product," and may even be deceived about the source.[973]

Reverse passing off may be "express" — where the defendant places its own origin indicator on goods produced by someone else — or "implied" — where the defendant omits the plaintiff's origin indicator but does not substitute its own.[974] However, courts disagree on whether and under what circumstances the mere *removal* of origin-identifying information from a product would violate section 43(a).[975]

Although reverse passing off may occur when a defendant passes off the plaintiff's unaltered goods as its own, it may also occur when a defendant modifies the plaintiff's goods before relabeling them as its own.[976] In the latter cases, courts have distinguished between minor modifications, which are insufficient to avoid liability,[977] and more substantial modifications, which create a "new product" and do not amount to reverse passing off.[978]

Courts often use the term "reverse passing off" to describe situations in which a seller merely uses the goods of another as samples or illustrations of its own goods

---

[970] *Id.* at 121.

[971] *See* RESTATEMENT (THIRD) OF UNFAIR COMPETITION § 5 (1995).

[972] *See, e.g.*, Lipscher v. LRP Pubs., Inc., 266 F.3d 1305, 1312 (11th Cir. 2001); Lamothe v. Atlantic Recording Co., 847 F.2d 1403, 1405 (9th Cir. 1998); Cleary v. News Corp., 30 F.3d 1255 (9th Cir. 1994); Smith v. Montoro, 648 F.2d 602, 607 (9th Cir. 1981); Truck Equipment Service Co. v. Fruehauf Co., 536 F.2d 1210, 1216 (8th Cir. 1976); Kasco Corp. v. General Services, Inc., 905 F. Supp. 29, 33–35 (D. Mass. 1995).

[973] *Montoro*, 648 F.2d at 607; *see also* RESTATEMENT (THIRD) OF UNFAIR COMPETITION § 5, cmt. a (1995).

[974] *See, e.g.*, Summit Mach. Tool Mfg. Corp. v. Victor CNC Sys., Inc., 7 F.3d 1434, 1437 (9th Cir. 1993); Roho, Inc. v. Marquis, 902 F.2d 356, 359 (5th Cir. 1990); *Montoro*, 684 F.2d 602.

[975] *Compare* CCS Communications Control, Inc. v. Law Enforcement Assoc., Inc., 628 F. Supp. 1457, 1460 (S.D.N.Y. 1986) (finding no false designation) *and* PIC Design Corp. v. Sterling Precision Corp., 231 F. Supp. 106 (S.D.N.Y. 1964) (similar) *with* Lamothe, 847 F.2d at 1407 n.2 (suggesting disagreement with *CCS Communs.*), *and* Montoro, 648 F.2d at 605 (removing source designation is "implied" reverse passing off). In Commodore Import Co. v. Hiraoka, 422 F. Supp. 628 (S.D.N.Y. 1976), the district court found no section 43(a) violation where the defendant obtained goods that had been abandoned by plaintiff and replaced plaintiff's labels with its own.

[976] *See* General Univ. Sys. v. Lee, 379 F.3d 131, 148 n. 41 (5th Cir. 2004).

[977] *See* Arrow United Indus., Inc. v. Hugh Richards, Inc., 678 F.2d 410, 412, 415 (2d Cir. 1982); Matsushita Elec. Corp. of Am. v. Solar Sound Sys., Inc., 381 F. Supp. 64, 66–67, 70 (S.D.N.Y. 1974).

[978] *Roho, Inc.*, 902 F.2d at 360–61.

in order to solicit customers.[979] In *Bangor Punta Operations, Inc., v. Universal Marine Co.*,[980] for example, the defendant used a picture of plaintiff's trawler in its advertising materials, representing it to be a picture of its own trawler. Although several authorities describe this as "implied reverse passing off,"[981] this is not true reverse passing off, because the defendant did not in fact sell the plaintiff's goods; rather, it is a form of false advertising.[982] True reverse passing off occurs only when a defendant actually sells a plaintiff's goods to consumers under the pretense that they are the defendant's own goods. Cases holding defendants liable for true reverse passing off are rare.[983] However, few courts have recognized this distinction,[984] and for that reason both usages must be recognized in practice.

In order to state a claim for true reverse passing off under section 43(a), a plaintiff must establish that: (1) the defendant misbranded plaintiff's goods; (2) such misbranding was "material"; (3) the defendant caused the plaintiff's goods to enter interstate commerce; and (4) the defendant's misbranding caused a likelihood of confusion.[985]

Until 2003, most true reverse passing-off cases under section 43(a) involved failure to properly attribute authorship of ideas or creative expression. Courts ruled in favor of an actor whose name was replaced in a film's credits and advertising materials,[986] a publisher whose name was replaced in a hymnal,[987] composers whose names were omitted from a record album and sheet music,[988] authors whose names were omitted from a biography,[989] a publisher whose name was replaced on books,[990] a cookbook author whose books were copied without attribution,[991] and a software creator whose software was copied without

---

[979] *See, e.g.,* Alpo Petfoods, Inc. v. Ralston Purina Co., 913 F.2d 958, 963–964, n.6 (D.C. Cir. 1990); Arrow United Indus., Inc. v. Hugh Richards, Inc., 678 F.2d 410, 415 (2d Cir. 1982); Alum-A-Fold Shutter Corporation v. Folding Shutter Corporation, 441 F.2d 556 (5th Cir. 1971); American Precast Corp. v. Maurice Concrete Products, 360 F. Supp. 859 (D. Mass. 1973), *aff'd,* 502 F.2d 1159 (1st Cir. 1974); Crossbow, Inc. v. Dan-Dee Imports Inc., 266 F. Supp. 335, 339–40 & n.1 (S.D.N.Y. 1967) (collecting cases).

[980] 543 F.2d 1107, 1109 (5th Cir. 1976).

[981] Lamothe v. Atlantic Recording Co., 847 F.2d 1403, 1406 (9th Cir. 1998); Smith v. Montoro, 648 F.2d 602, 604 (9th Cir. 1981) (citing 1 Richard Callman, Unfair Competition, Trademarks and Monopolies § 18.2(b)(1), at 294 (1980 Supp. to 3d ed.)).

[982] Restatement (Third) of Unfair Competition § 5 (1995), cmt. a.

[983] Pioneer Hi-Bred Int'l v. Holden Found. Seeds, 35 F.3d 1226, 1242 (8th Cir. 1994); Web Printing Controls Co. v. Oxy-Dry Corp., 906 F.2d 1202, 1203–04 (7th Cir. 1990); Williams v. Curtiss-Wright Corp., 691 F.2d 168, 172–73 (3d Cir. 1982); Federal Elec. Co. v. Flexlume Corp., 33 F.2d 412, 414–15 (7th Cir. 1929).

[984] This distinction was recognized in Bretford Mfg. v. Smith Sys. Mfg. Co., 286 F. Supp. 2d 969, 971–72 (N.D. Ill. 2003).

[985] Web Printing Controls Co. v. Oxy-Dry Corp., 906 F.2d 1202, 1204 (7th Cir. 1990).

[986] Smith v. Montoro, 648 F.2d 602, 607 (9th Cir. 1981).

[987] F.E.L. Publications, Ltd. v. Catholic Bishop of Chicago, 214 U.S.P.Q. 409, 416–17 (7th Cir. 1982).

[988] Lamothe v. Atlantic Recording Co., 847 F.2d 1403, 1405 (9th Cir. 1998).

[989] Dodd v. Fort Smith Special School Dist., 666 F. Supp. 1278, 1284–85 (W.D. Ark. 1987).

[990] Waldman Pub. Corp. v. Landoll, Inc., 43 F.3d 775, 780 (2d Cir. 1994).

[991] Marling v. Ellison, 218 U.S.P.Q. 702 (S.D. Fla. 1982).

attribution.[992]

However, in its 2003 decision in *Dastar Corp. v. Twentieth Century Fox Film Corp.*,[993] the Supreme Court rejected the application of section 43(a) to misattribution of creative or expressive works, thus implicitly overruling all of these precedents. In *Dastar*, the defendant re-edited a television series that had originally been produced by the plaintiff, but that had lost its copyright and entered the public domain. The defendant then released the re-edited series on videocassette, identifying itself as the producer and omitting any reference to the plaintiff. The plaintiff brought a claim of reverse passing off under section 43(a). The Supreme Court rejected the plaintiff's claim, holding that the term "origin" in section 43(a) refers to "the producer of the tangible goods that are offered for sale, and not to the author of any idea, concept, or communication embodied in those goods."[994] The Court noted, in dicta, that reverse passing off would "undoubtedly" have been established if the defendant had repackaged videocassettes that had been physically produced by the plaintiff,[995] but it held that the same conclusion did not follow when the defendant copied only the plaintiff's intangible intellectual property.[996]

In the Court's view, consumers do not normally care about the creative origins of the goods they purchase; thus, full disclosure of creative — as opposed to physical — origins is not required by the Lanham Act.[997] The Court acknowledged that this generalization might not apply to communicative works, whose creative origins might in fact be a matter of concern to consumers.[998] Nonetheless, the Court concluded that giving different treatment to communicative works would create a conflict between the Lanham Act and federal copyright law: "The right to copy, and to copy without attribution, once a copyright has expired, like the right to make [an article whose patent has expired] — including the right to make it in precisely the shape it carried when patented — passes to the public."[999]

Dastar leaves many questions unanswered. For example, although the case involved an expired copyright, much of the Court's reasoning appears equally applicable to subsisting copyrights, and courts have consistently so held.[1000]

Dastar also casts doubt on the application of section 43(a) to traditional passing off claims involving expressive works. For example, *Gilliam v. American Broadcasting Cos.* found false attribution under section 43(a) where a television

---

[992] Montgomery v. Noga, 168 F.3d 1282, 1299 n.27 (11th Cir. 1999).

[993] 539 U.S. 23 (2003).

[994] *Id.* at 37.

[995] *Id.* at 28.

[996] *Id.* at 28–29.

[997] Dastar Corp. v. Twentieth Century Fox Film Corp., 539 U.S. 23, 32 (2005).

[998] *Id.* at 33.

[999] *Id.* (internal quotation marks omitted).

[1000] *See, e.g.*, Zyla v. Wadsworth, 360 F.3d 243, 251–52 (1st Cir. 2004); Antidote Int'l Films, Inc. v. Bloomsbury Pub'g, PLC, 467 F. Supp. 2d 394 (S.D.N.Y. 2007); Beckwith Builders, Inc. v. Depietri, 81 U.S.P.Q.2d 1302 (D.N.H. 2006); Auscape Int'l v. National Geographic Soc'y, 409 F. Supp. 2d 235, 250 (S.D.N.Y. 2004); Williams v. UMG Recordings, 281 F. Supp. 2d 1177 (C.D. Cal. 2003).

network edited a television program without the authors' consent,[1001] and *King v. Innovation Books* held that section 43(a) was violated when the film credits for "Lawnmower Man" implicitly exaggerated Stephen King's creative contribution.[1002] Since these cases involved false designations of origin with respect to the creative source of the works, it is unclear whether these precedents are still good law.[1003]

Although *Dastar* noted that some false attribution claims pertaining to expressive works might still be brought as false advertising claims under section 43(a)(1)(B),[1004] such claims have not succeeded (as discussed in § 6E).

[8]   Adjudication and Procedure

[a]   Subject Matter Jurisdiction

Federal and state courts have concurrent subject matter jurisdiction to adjudicate claims arising under sections 32, 43(a), 43(c), and 43(d) of the Lanham Act.[1005] However, an *in rem* action under section 43(d) should be brought only in a federal district court, because only the latter is empowered to award the statutory remedy under section 43(d)(2)(D). Decisions of the federal district courts in trademark and unfair competition matters are appealable to the regional circuit courts of appeal.

Although the defendant in a section 32(1) infringement action can counterclaim for cancellation of the plaintiff's mark, the plaintiff can defeat the court's subject matter jurisdiction over the cancellation claim, and thus terminate the litigation, by issuing a sufficiently broad covenant not to sue; in *Already, LLC v. Nike, Inc.*, however, the Supreme Court held that the trademark owner has a "formidable burden" to prove that the covenant not to sue eliminates any "case or controversy" between the parties.[1006]

Trademark, unfair competition, and dilution claims arising under state statutes or common law can be adjudicated in federal courts only under two circumstances: (1) where there is diversity of citizenship between the parties and the amount in controversy exceeds $75,000;[1007] or (2) where the complaint also includes federal

---

[1001] 538 F.2d 14 (2d Cir. 1976).

[1002] 976 F.2d 824 (2d Cir. 1992).

[1003] One court has suggested, in brief dicta, that *Gilliam* remains good law. Auscape Int'l v. National Geographic Soc'y, 409 F. Supp. 2d 235, 251 n.85 (S.D.N.Y. 2004).

[1004] Dastar Corp. v. Twentieth Century Fox Film Corp., 539 U.S. 23, 37 (2005). For a discussion of federal false advertising, *see* § 6E.

[1005] 15 U.S.C. § 1121(a) (granting original and appellate jurisdiction to federal courts, but not exclusively); 28 U.S.C. § 1338(a) (same). *See, e.g.*, Aquatherm Indus. v. Florida Power & Light Co., 84 F.3d 1388, 1394 (11th Cir. 1996); La Chemise Lacoste v. Alligator Co., 506 F.2d 339 (3d Cir. 1974); Pennsylvania State University v. University Orthopedics, Ltd., 706 A.2d 863, n.2 (Pa. Super. 1998); Mastro Plastics Corp. v. Emenee Indus., Inc., 19 A.D.2d 600 (N.Y. App. Div. 1963), *aff'd*, 197 N.E.2d 620 (N.Y. 1964); Dell Pub. Co. v. Stanley Pubs., Inc., 172 N.E.2d 656 (N.Y. 1961); Brown & Bigelow v Remembrance Advertising Products, Inc., 279 A.D. 410 (N.Y. App. Div. 1952), *aff'd*, 110 N.E.2d 736 (N.Y. 1953); Thomas J. Valentino, Inc. v. Majar Discs, Inc., 138 N.Y.S.2d 494 (Sup. 1955).

[1006] 133 S. Ct. 721 (2013).

[1007] 28 U.S.C. § 1332(a); *see, e.g.*, Cohn v. Petsmart, Inc., 281 F.3d 837 (9th Cir. 2002).

claims (*e.g.*, Lanham Act claims), in which case the federal court may hear the state claims pursuant to its supplemental jurisdiction.[1008]

In contrast, federal courts have exclusive jurisdiction over claims arising from PTO decisions involving trademark registrations. Decisions of the Trademark Trial and Appeals Board (TTAB), which conducts opposition and cancellation proceedings and hears appeals from registration denials, can be appealed by either of two routes: (1) by direct appeal, on a closed record, to the United States Court of Appeal for the Federal Circuit,[1009] or (2) by filing a civil action in a federal district court,[1010] in which case the review is *de novo*.[1011]

[b] Standing

[i] Standing to Cancel or Oppose Federal Registration

The standing rules for cancelling a registered mark are the same as those for opposing a registration.[1012] In general, a party has standing only if it has "a real commercial interest in its own marks and a reasonable basis for its belief that it would be damaged" by the registration.[1013] Courts have held that this standard is satisfied where: (1) the trademark for which cancellation is sought has been cited against the registration applications of the plaintiff's own trademarks,[1014] or (2) the party seeking cancellation is using the same or a similar mark for the same or similar goods.[1015]

Where the defendant in an opposition seeks to cancel the opposer's mark on the basis of genericness or descriptiveness, the TTAB has held that the defendant need not have any interest in using the mark for which cancellation is sought.[1016]

In the case of a section 2(a) opposition or petition to cancel alleging that a mark

---

[1008] 28 U.S.C. § 1367(a) (supplemental jurisdiction); *cf.* 28 U.S.C. § 1338(b) (expressly granting jurisdiction over claims of "unfair competition" joined with federal claims). Before being codified in section 1367, supplemental jurisdiction was known as pendent jurisdiction. *See, e.g.,* Lone Star Steakhouse & Saloon, Inc. v. Longhorn Steaks, Inc., 106 F.3d 355 (11th Cir. 1997). The decision to exercise supplemental or pendent jurisdiction is discretionary. 28 U.S.C. § 1367(c) (listing factors); *see, e.g.,* United Mine Workers of Am. v. Gibbs, 383 U.S. 715, 726 (1966); Travelers Ins. Co. v. Keeling, 996 F.2d 1485, 1490 (2d Cir. 1993).

[1009] 15 U.S.C. § 1071(a).

[1010] 15 U.S.C. § 1071(b).

[1011] *See, e.g.,* Gillette Co. v. "42" Prods., Ltd., 435 F.2d 1114 (9th Cir. 1970).

[1012] Ritchie v. Simpson, 170 F.3d 1092, 1095 n.2 (Fed. Cir. 1999).

[1013] Citigroup, Inc. v. City Holding Co., 2003 U.S. Dist. LEXIS 1845, *37 (S.D.N.Y. Feb. 7, 2003) (quoting Aerogroup Int'l Inc. v. Marlboro Footworks, Ltd., 977 F. Supp. 264, 266–67 (S.D.N.Y. 1997)); *accord* Lipton Industries, Inc. v. Ralston Purina Co., 670 F.2d 1024, 1026–27 (C.C.P.A. 1982).

[1014] *See, e.g.,* Jewelers Vigilance Comm., Inc. v. Ullenberg Corp. 823 F.2d 490, 493 (Fed. Cir. 1987); Cerveceria Modelo, S.A. de C.V. v. R.B. Marco & Sons, Inc., 55 U.S.P.Q.2d 1298, 1299–1300 (T.T.A.B. 2000); *see also* Syntex (U.S.A.), Inc. v. E.R. Squibb & Sons, Inc., 14 U.S.P.Q.2d 1879 (T.T.A.B. 1990); BankAmerica Corp. v. Invest America, 5 U.S.P.Q.2d 1076 (T.T.A.B. 1987).

[1015] *See, e.g.,* Selva & Sons, Inc. v. Nina Footwear, Inc., 705 F.2d 1316, 1326 (Fed. Cir. 1983).

[1016] BankAmerica Corp. v. Invest America, 5 U.S.P.Q.2d 1076 (T.T.A.B. 1987); *see also* Aruba v. Excelsior Inc., 5 U.S.P.Q.2d 1685, 1686 (T.T.A.B. 1987).

is disparaging or scandalous, or falsely suggests an affiliation with a person or institution, courts have held that a party need not have a "commercial" interest in order to have standing; it is sufficient for the party to have a "real interest" and a "reasonable basis" for believing it will be damaged by the registration.[1017] A party has a "real interest" if it has a "direct and personal stake in the outcome" of the proceeding.[1018] In the case of marks alleged to be disparaging, for example, an opposer (or party seeking cancellation) has standing simply by being a member of the disparaged group.[1019] Where a mark is alleged to falsely suggest an affiliation with the opposer or party seeking cancellation, standing exists if the mark refers "uniquely and unmistakably to the identity or persona" of that party.[1020]

[ii]   Standing Under Section 32

Section 32(1) permits "the registrant" of a trademark to bring an infringement action against unauthorized users.[1021] Accordingly, as a general rule, only the owner of the federal registration has standing to sue under section 32. The owner may be the actual registrant, or one of the registrant's "legal representatives, successors, and assigns."[1022] Thus, assignees have standing to sue.[1023]

As a general rule, mere licensees lack standing to sue under section 32(1).[1024] However, some courts have recognized a limited exception under which an exclusive licensee will have standing if "the licensing agreement grants the licensee either a property interest in the trademark or rights tantamount to an assignment."[1025] Under this approach, an exclusive licensee will have standing if the licensee receives all of the licensor's rights in the use of the trademark,[1026] or receives the exclusive use of the mark without any restrictions on its ability to enforce the mark against infringers.[1027] The following non-exhaustive factors tend to indicate that a license is not sufficiently exclusive to confer standing:[1028] (1) the licensee lacks the power to exclude the licensor from using the mark in the

---

[1017] Ritchie v. Simpson, 170 F.3d 1092, 1095 (Fed Cir. 1999).

[1018] *Id.*

[1019] *See, e.g.*, Bromberg v. Carmel Self-Service, Inc., 198 U.S.P.Q. 176, 177–79 (T.T.A.B. 1978); *see also* Harjo v. Pro Football Inc., 30 U.S.P.Q.2d 1828, 1830 (T.T.A.B. 1994). In *Ritchie v. Simpson*, 170 F.3d 1092, 1095–1097 (Fed. Cir. 1999), standing to oppose registration of marks that allegedly glorified violence against women was granted to a party who alleged that he (and others who shared his beliefs) would be injured through disparagement of his values.

[1020] *See* Internet, Inc. v. Corporation for Nat'l Research Initiatives, 38 U.S.P.Q.2d 1435 (T.T.A.B. 1996); Estate of Biro v. Bic Corp., 18 U.S.P.Q.2d 1382 (T.T.A.B. 1991).

[1021] 15 U.S.C. § 1114(1).

[1022] 15 U.S.C. § 1127; Berni v. International Gourmet Restaurants, Inc., 838 F.2d 642 (2d Cir. 1988).

[1023] Quabaug Rubber Co. v. Fabiano Shoe Co., Inc., 567 F.2d 154, 159–60 (1st Cir. 1977).

[1024] *Id.*; Finance Investment Co. (Bermuda) Ltd. v. Geberit AG, 165 F.3d 526 (7th Cir. 1998); Gruen Marketing Corp. v. Benrus Watch Co., 955 F. Supp. 979, 982 (N.D. Ill. 1997).

[1025] Bliss Clearing Niagara, Inc. v. Midwest Brake Bond Co., 339 F. Supp. 2d 944, 958–60 (W.D. Mich. 2004).

[1026] *Bliss Clearing*, 339 F. Supp. 2d at 958–60.

[1027] *Id.* at 960 (citing Ultrapure Sys., Inc. v. Ham-Let Group, 921 F. Supp. 659, 665–66 (N.D. Cal. 1996)).

[1028] *See generally Bliss Clearing*, 339 F. Supp. 2d at 959–60 (collecting cases).

licensee's territory,[1029] (2) the licensor retains exclusive ownership of the mark,[1030] (3) the license imposes geographical restrictions on the licensee's use of the mark,[1031] (4) the licensee is required to maintain the quality of the mark, or the licensor reserves the right to monitor the quality of the licensee's products,[1032] (5) the license contains duties and rights between the parties that are inconsistent with an assignment,[1033] and (6) the license limits the licensee's ability to enforce the mark.[1034]

A party that lacks standing under section 32(1) because it is not the owner of the federal registration may nonetheless have standing to sue under section 43(a) if it is likely to be injured as a result of the defendant's actions.

[iii]   Standing Under Section 43(a) and Common Law

Under both section 43(a)(1)(A) and the common law of unfair competition, standing is not limited to trademark owners. Under section 43(a)(1)(A), the plaintiff may be "any person who believes that he or she is or is likely to be damaged" by the defendant's actions.[1035] Notwithstanding the breadth of the statutory language, courts have consistently held that consumers do not have standing to sue under section 43(a)(1)(A).[1036] Instead, standing under section 43(a)(1)(A) is limited to parties alleging a competitive or commercial injury (or likelihood thereof).[1037] This can include licensees of a mark, whether exclusive[1038] or non-exclusive.[1039]

For standing to bring a false advertising claim under section 43(a)(1)(B), see § 6E[2][d].

[1029] Quabaug Rubber Co. v. Fabiano Shoe Co., Inc., 567 F.2d 154, 159 (1st Cir. 1977); Icee Distribs., Inc. v. J & J Snack Foods Corp., 325 F.3d 586, 598–99 (5th Cir. 2003).

[1030] Ultrapure Sys., Inc. v. Ham-Let Group, 921 F. Supp. 659, 665 (N.D. Cal. 1996) (*citing* DEP Corp. v. Interstate Cigar Co., 622 F.2d 621, 623 (2d Cir. 1980)).

[1031] Calvin Klein Jeanswear Co. v. Tunnel Trading, 2001 U.S. Dist. LEXIS 18738 (S.D.N.Y. Nov. 16, 2001).

[1032] *Id.* at *5; Gruen Mktg. Corp. v. Benrus Watch Co., 955 F. Supp. 979, 983 (N.D. Ill. 1997).

[1033] Fin. Inv. Co. (Bermuda) Ltd. v. Geberit AG, 165 F.3d 526, 531–32 (7th Cir. 1998).

[1034] STX, Inc. v. Bauer USA, Inc., 1997 U.S. Dist. LEXIS 16250 (N.D. Cal. June 5, 1997).

[1035] 15 U.S.C. § 1125(a).

[1036] *See, e.g.*, Colligan v. Activities Club of New York, Ltd., 442 F.2d 686 (2d Cir. 1971).

[1037] *See, e.g.*, Waits v. Frito-Lay, Inc., 978 F.2d 1093, 1109 (9th Cir. 1992); Dovenmuehle v. Gilldorn Mortg. Midwest Corp., 871 F.2d 697 (7th Cir. 1989); Smith v. Montoro, 648 F.2d 602 (9th Cir. 1981). A non-profit entity may have standing even though it is not a commercial enterprise, provided that it can assert a competitive injury. *See, e.g.*, United We Stand America, Inc. v. United We Stand, America New York, Inc., 128 F.3d 86 (2d Cir. 1997); Gideons Int'l, Inc. v. Gideon 300 Ministries, Inc., 94 F. Supp. 2d 566 (E.D. Pa. 1999); Healing the Children, Inc. v. Heal the Children, Inc., 786 F. Supp. 1209 (W.D. Pa. 1992).

[1038] *See, e.g.*, Frisch's Restaurants v. Elby's Big Boy, 670 F.2d 642 (6th Cir. 1982); Business Trends Analysts v. Freedonia Group, Inc., 650 F. Supp. 1452 (S.D.N.Y. 1987).

[1039] Quabaug Rubber Co. v. Fabiano Shoe Co., 567 F.2d 154 (1st Cir. 1977); Murphy v. Provident Mut. Life Ins. Co., 756 F. Supp. 83, 86 (D. Conn. 1990), *aff'd*, 923 F.2d 923 (2d Cir. 1990).

[iv]   Standing Under Section 43(c)

Standing to bring a federal dilution claim under section 43(c) is limited to "the owner of a famous mark." Thus, in general, an exclusive licensee does not have standing under section 43(c).[1040] However, courts that recognize the standing of certain exclusive licensees under section 32 (as discussed above) have applied a similar approach to dilution claims under section 43(c), requiring that the exclusive license be tantamount to an assignment before standing will be recognized.[1041]

[c]   Declaratory Judgments

The authority of federal courts to issue declaratory judgments is governed by the Declaratory Judgment Act, which provides that "[i]n a case of actual controversy within its jurisdiction," a federal court "may declare the rights and other legal relations of any interested party seeking such declaration, whether or not further relief is or could be sought."[1042] Until 2007, courts held that no justiciable "controversy" existed unless the party seeking the declaratory judgment had a "reasonable apprehension" that litigation was "imminent." This requirement was typically not satisfied unless the party reasonably believed that it was about to be sued (e.g., for infringement or dilution) by the declaratory judgment defendant. However, in its 2007 decision in *MedImmune, Inc. v. Genentech, Inc.*,[1043] the Supreme Court rejected the "reasonable apprehension" test in the context of patent infringement. Instead, the Court held, the dispute must be "definite and concrete, touching the legal relations of parties having adverse legal interests," must be "real and substantial," and must "admit of specific relief through a decree of a conclusive character, as distinguished from an opinion advising what the law would be upon a hypothetical state of facts."[1044]

In *Surefoot LC v. Sure Foot Corp.*,[1045] the Tenth Circuit became the first federal appellate court to apply *MedImmune* to a trademark case. Although it had been seven years since Sure Foot (the declaratory judgment defendant) had threatened the plaintiff Surefoot with infringement litigation, it had recently initiated several oppositions and a cancellation proceeding against Surefoot's registrations. The Tenth Circuit held that the mere passage of time since Sure Foot's litigation threat had not dissipated the controversy, and that Sure Foot's recent opposition and cancellation proceedings, as well as its repeated infringement accusations, were sufficient to satisfy *MedImmune*'s jurisdictional requirement. This did not, however, resolve the question whether, as a prudential matter, the court *should* hear the suit, because the Declaratory Judgment Act does not *require* a district court to hear a request for a declaratory judgment. The Tenth Circuit therefore instructed the district court on remand to consider the following factors:

[1040] *See, e.g.*, STX, Inc. v. Bauer USA, Inc., 1997 U.S. Dist. LEXIS 16250 (N.D. Cal. June 5, 1997).

[1041] *See* Icee Distribs., Inc. v. J & J Snack Foods Corp., 325 F.3d 586, 597–98 (5th Cir. 2003); Bliss Clearing Niagara, Inc. v. Midwest Brake Bond Co., 339 F. Supp. 2d 944, 958–60 & n.4 (W.D. Mich. 2004); World Championship Wrestling v. Titan Sports, Inc., 46 F. Supp. 2d 118, 122 (D. Conn. 1999).

[1042] 28 U.S.C. § 2201(a).

[1043] 549 U.S. 118 (2007).

[1044] *Id.* at 127.

[1045] 531 F.3d 1236 (10th Cir. 2008).

[1] whether a declaratory action would settle the controversy; [2] whether it would serve a useful purpose in clarifying the legal relations at issue; [3] whether the declaratory remedy is being used merely for the purpose of "procedural fencing" or "to provide an arena for a race to *res judicata*"; [4] whether use of a declaratory action would increase friction between our federal and state courts and improperly encroach upon state jurisdiction; and [5] whether there is an alternative remedy which is better or more effective.[1046]

While numerous district courts have applied the *Medimmune* analysis to trademark disputes, the decisions are highly fact-specific.[1047]

§ 5G   DILUTION

[1]   The Concept of Dilution

The concept of trademark dilution gained acceptance in the mid- to late twentieth century, as trademark protection began to expand beyond its traditional goal of preventing consumer confusion and deception, and began to protect particularly strong trademarks as a form of property in themselves, whose value should be protected against unauthorized appropriation by others.

Dilution doctrine recognizes that trademark law should protect "strong, well-recognized marks even in the absence of a likelihood of confusion, if defendant's use is such as to tarnish, degrade or dilute the distinctive quality of the mark."[1048] Whereas traditional trademark infringement law has focused primarily on protecting consumers against confusion or deception about the origin of goods or services, dilution laws protect the trademark owner's investment in the goodwill that is embodied in a mark.[1049] For example, if a cocoa maker adopted the "Rolls Royce" mark for its hot chocolate, consumers would be unlikely to believe that the car maker had expanded into the cocoa business. Nonetheless, according to dilution theory, harm would occur because the cocoa maker would be capitalizing on the mark's association with high quality merchandise, and because the mark would no longer be uniquely associated with expensive automobiles.[1050]

Because it disassociates trademark protection from consumer protection, dilution doctrine has been criticized as anticompetitive and as an unwarranted extension of trademark law. Courts have applied the doctrine warily, "lest it

---

[1046] *Id.* at 1248.

[1047] *Finding jurisdiction*: Water Pik, Inc. v. Med-Systems, Inc., 2011 U.S. Dist. LEXIS 27631 (D. Colo. Mar. 8, 2011); Blue Athletic, Inc. v. Nordstrom, Inc., 2010 U.S. Dist. LEXIS 72615 (D.N.H. July 19, 2010); Venugopal v. Sharadha Terry Prods., Ltd., 2009 U.S. Dist. LEXIS 43534 (W.D.N.Y. May 22, 2009); Floyd's 99 Holdings, LLC v. Woodrum, 2009 U.S. Dist. LEXIS 24271 (D. Colo. Mar. 24, 2009). *Finding no jurisdiction*: Vina Casa Tamaya S.A. v. Oakville Hills Cellar, Inc., 784 F. Supp. 2d 391 (S.D.N.Y.); Bruce Winston Gem Corp. v. Harry Winston, Inc., 2010 U.S. Dist. LEXIS 96974 (S.D.N.Y. Sept. 16, 2010).

[1048] 2 J. Thomas McCarthy, Trademarks & Unfair Competition § 24.13, at 155 (1973).

[1049] *See* I.P. Lund Trading ApS v. Kohler Co. 163 F.3d 27, 50 (1st Cir. 1998); *accord*, Playboy Enters., Inc. v. Welles, 279 F.3d 796, 805 (9th Cir. 2002).

[1050] *Playboy*, 279 F.3d at 805–06.

swallow up all competition in the claim of protection against trade name infringement."[1051] Although no likelihood of confusion is necessary, the senior and junior users' use of the marks must trigger some sort of mental association in the mind of the consumer;[1052] thus, dilution will ordinarily be found only if "there is at least some subliminal connection in a buyer's mind between the two parties' uses of their marks."[1053]

Unlike traditional trademark and unfair competition law, dilution doctrine is not based on common law. Rather, it is a creature of statute that owes its origin largely to an influential 1927 law review article by Frank Schechter, recommending the expansion of unfair competition beyond the common-law tradition of protecting against consumer deception or confusion. Schechter argued that unfair competition law should serve the broader goal of preserving the "uniqueness of a trademark" by protecting the trademark owner against "the gradual whittling away or dispersion of the identity and hold upon the public mind of the mark or name by its use upon non-competing goods."[1054]

Dilution statutes typically encompass two distinct types of injury to the trademark owner, known as "blurring" and "tarnishment."[1055] Blurring has been defined as "the whittling away of an established trademark's selling power through its unauthorized use by others upon dissimilar products."[1056] Hypothetical examples include "Dupont" shoes, "Buick" aspirin tablets, "Schlitz" varnish, "Kodak" pianos, and "Bulova" gowns.[1057] Affording trademark owners a remedy against blurring provides them with protection in situations in which the public knows that the defendant is not affiliated with the plaintiff, so there is no likelihood of confusion as to source, but where "the ability of the plaintiff's mark to serve as a unique identifier of the plaintiff's goods or services is weakened because the relevant public now also associates that designation with a new and different source."[1058]

Tarnishment, in contrast, typically occurs when a plaintiff's mark is "linked to products of shoddy quality, or is portrayed in an unwholesome or unsavory context, with the end result that the public will associate the lack of quality or lack of prestige in the defendant's goods with the plaintiff's unrelated goods."[1059] These negative associations result in injury to the goodwill associated with the plaintiff's

---

[1051] Coffee Dan's, Inc. v. Coffee Don's Charcoal Broiler, 305 F. Supp. 1210, 1217 n.13 (N.D. Cal. 1969).

[1052] Mead Data Central, Inc. v. Toyota Motor Sales, U.S.A., Inc., 875 F.2d 1026, 1031 (2d Cir. 1989).

[1053] Fruit of the Loom, Inc. v. Girouard, 994 F.2d 1359, 1363 (9th Cir. 1993).

[1054] Frank M. Schechter, *The Rational Basis of Trademark Protection*, 40 HARV. L. REV. 813, 825 (1927).

[1055] *See* New York Stock Exch., Inc., v. New York, New York Hotel, LLC, 293 F.3d 550, 557 (2d Cir. 2002).

[1056] Mead Data Central, Inc. v. Toyota Motor Sales, U.S.A., Inc., 875 F.2d 1026, 1031 (2d Cir. 1989).

[1057] *Id.* (quoting the legislative history of New York's dilution statute).

[1058] Mastercard Int'l, Inc. v. Nader 2000 Primary Comm., Inc., 70 U.S.P.Q.2d 1046, 1052 (S.D.N.Y. 2004) (citing Federal Express Corp. v. Federal Espresso, Inc., 201 F.3d 168, 174 (2d Cir. 2000); Sports Auth. v. Prime Hospitality Corp., 89 F.3d 955, 965–66 (2d Cir. 1996)).

[1059] *New York Stock Exch.*, 293 F.3d at 558 (internal quotation marks omitted); *see, e.g.*, Dallas Cowboys Cheerleaders, Inc. v. Pussycat Cinema, Ltd., 604 F.2d 200, 205 & n.8 (2d Cir. 1979); Eastman

mark.[1060] Although tarnishment is routinely found where the defendant uses the plaintiff's mark in connection with pornographic material,[1061] courts have also held that "tarnishment is not limited to seamy conduct."[1062] For example, the Second Circuit allowed the New York Stock Exchange (NYSE) to proceed with its dilution claim against a New York-themed casino for using modified versions of the NYSE's marks in various aspects of its gaming activities. While the court found no blurring of the NYSE's marks, and acknowledged the humorous context in which the casino used the marks, it found that tarnishment was possible because the association with gambling could injure the NYSE's reputation for "integrity and transparency."[1063]

Using the "Tiffany" mark as an example, Circuit Judge Posner has identified three possible rationales for granting trademark owners protection against unauthorized uses that are both non-competing and non-confusing: (1) if "Tiffany" becomes associated with more than one product or service, "consumers will have to think harder" each time they encounter the mark (the "consumer search costs" explanation for blurring); (2) if the "Tiffany" mark were adopted by a striptease joint, this mental association would tarnish the consumer's image of the jewelry store; and (3) even if there is neither blurring nor tarnishment, "someone is still taking a free ride" on the trademark owner's investment in the "Tiffany" mark, thus potentially discouraging other trademark owners from investing in the creation of a prestigious name.[1064]

The question whether trademarks, even famous ones, should be protected against dilution remains controversial. Many respected commentators view the alleged harm from dilution as highly speculative.[1065]

[2]   Dilution Under State Law

The first dilution statute in the United States was enacted by Massachusetts in 1947.[1066] Today, nearly three-quarters of the states have enacted dilution legislation. Most of these statutes encompass both blurring and tarnishment; some statutes refer to the latter as "injury to business reputation."

Like traditional trademark laws, state dilution laws protect only those trademarks that are distinctive — that is, marks that are arbitrary, fanciful, or

---

Kodak Co. v. Rakow, 739 F. Supp. 116 (W.D.N.Y. 1989); Coca-Cola Co. v. Gemini Rising, Inc., 346 F. Supp. 1183, 1191–92 (E.D.N.Y. 1972).

[1060] *New York Stock Exch.*, 293 F.3d at 558; Hormel Foods Corp. v. Jim Henson Productions, Inc., 73 F.3d 497, 507 (2d Cir. 1996).

[1061] *See, e.g.*, Lucent Techs., Inc. v. Johnson, 56 U.S.P.Q.2d 1637 (C.D. Cal 2000); Mattel, Inc. v. Internet Dimensions, Inc., 2000 U.S. Dist. LEXIS 9747 (S.D.N.Y. July 13, 2000); Hasbro Inc. v. Internet Entertainment Group, Ltd., 40 U.S.P.Q.2d 1479, 1480 (W.D. Wash. 1996).

[1062] New York Stock Exch., Inc., v. New York, New York Hotel, LLC, 293 F.3d 550, 558 (2d Cir. 2002) (quoting *Hormel Foods*, 73 F.3d at 507).

[1063] *Id.*

[1064] Ty, Inc. v. Perryman, 306 F.3d 509, 511–12 (7th Cir. 2002).

[1065] *See, e.g.*, J. Thomas McCarthy, Trademarks & Unfair Competition § 24.67 & n.16.

[1066] Mass. Gen. Laws Ann. Ch. 110B, § 12 (2005).

suggestive, or those that, while descriptive, have achieved distinctiveness through the acquisition of secondary meaning in the marketplace.[1067] In some states, any distinctive mark is eligible for dilution protection,[1068] while in others the mark must be "highly distinctive," "strong," or "famous." In some states, this requirement is expressly imposed by the dilution statute,[1069] while in others it results from judicial interpretation.[1070] The trend is increasingly toward incorporating a "fame" requirement into the statute itself, reflecting the tendency of the states after 1995 to conform their dilution laws to the federal statute. Where there have already been some third-party uses of a mark, it can be especially difficult for the senior user to establish that the mark is strong enough to warrant protection against dilution.[1071]

The requirement that a mark be more than merely distinctive in order to be protected from dilution is endorsed by the *Restatement (Third) of Unfair Competition*.[1072] The *Restatement* considers the following factors relevant: the inherent distinctiveness and uniqueness of the mark, the duration and extent of its use, the duration and extent of advertising that emphasizes the mark, the degree of recognition by prospective purchasers, and the extent of third-party uses of the mark "either as a trade symbol or for other purposes."[1073] While noting that "it is possible" that a descriptive word mark may achieve the requisite level of distinctiveness, the Restatement suggests that this is "less likely" due to the many permissible uses of such words.[1074]

Courts generally do not require marks to be identical in order to find dilution under state statutes. Examples of marks found to be sufficiently similar to be dilutive include "Polaroid" and "Polaraid,"[1075] "The Greatest Show on Earth" and "The Greatest Used Car Show on Earth,"[1076] "Saks Fifth Avenue" and "Sacks Thrift Avenue,"[1077] and "Godiva" and "Dogiva" (as well as "Cativa").[1078] In contrast,

---

[1067] *See, e.g.*, O.C.G.A. § 10-1-451(b) (2004); Dolphin Homes Corp. v. Tocome Dev. Corp., 156 S.E.2d 45 (Ga. 1967).

[1068] *See, e.g.*, Or. Rev. Stat. § 647.107 (2003).

[1069] *See, e.g.*, Rev. Code Wash. §§ 19.77.010(6), 19.77.160 (2008).

[1070] *See, e.g.*, Advantage Rent-A-Car, Inc. v. Enter. Rent-A-Car Co., 238 F.3d 378, 381 (5th Cir. 2001); Scholastic, Inc. v. Time Warner Ent. Co., L.P., 221 F. Supp. 2d 425, 437–38 (S.D.N.Y. 2002), *aff'd sub nom.*, Scholastic, Inc. v. Stouffer, 81 Fed. Appx. 396 (2d Cir. 2003); *but see* Wedgwood Homes, Inc. v. Lund, 648 P.2d 393, 396–400 (Or. Ct. App. 1982) (refusing to impose such a gloss on Oregon statute), *aff'd*, 659 P.2d 377 (Or. 1983).

[1071] *See, e.g.*, Astra Pharmaceutical Prods., Inc. v. Beckman Instruments, Inc., 718 F.2d 1201, 1210 (1st Cir. 1983) (applying Massachusetts law).

[1072] RESTATEMENT (THIRD) OF UNFAIR COMPETITION § 25, cmt. e (1995).

[1073] *Id.*

[1074] *Id.*; *see, e.g.*, Great Southern Bank v. First Southern Bank, 625 So. 2d 463, 470–71 (Fla. 1993) (applying analysis of tentative draft of Restatement to Florida statute).

[1075] Polaroid Corp. v. Polaraid, Inc., 319 F.2d 830 (7th Cir. 1963).

[1076] Ringling Bros.-Barnum & Bailey Combined Shows, Inc. v. Celozzi-Ettelson Chevrolet, Inc., 855 F.2d 480 (7th Cir. 1988).

[1077] Saks & Co. v. Hill, 843 F. Supp. 620, 625 (S.D. Cal. 1993), *appeal dismissed*, 65 F.3d 175 (9th Cir. 1995).

[1078] Grey v. Campbell Soup Co., 650 F. Supp. 1166 (C.D. Cal. 1986), *aff'd*, 830 F.2d 197 (9th Cir. 1997).

the Second Circuit held that "LEXIS" and "LEXUS" were not sufficiently similar to support a dilution claim.[1079]

Many state dilution laws provide relief to plaintiffs that establish a *likelihood* of dilution. In those states, a plaintiff need not offer evidence that dilution has already occurred; it is enough to establish that the defendant's activities create a likelihood of dilution either through blurring or tarnishment.[1080] Typically, the courts use multi-factor tests to assess likelihood of dilution. For example, federal courts interpreting New York's dilution statute[1081] often (though not always) consider six "blurring" factors: "(i) the similarity of the marks; (ii) the similarity of the products covered; (iii) the sophistication of the consumers; (iv) the existence of predatory intent; (v) the renown of the senior mark; and (vi) the renown of the junior mark."[1082]

In contrast, the language of some state dilution statutes provides relief against activities that "cause dilution" of a plaintiff's mark. As illustrated by the Supreme Court's interpretation of similar language in the original (1995) version of the federal dilution statute in *Moseley v. V Secret Catalog*,[1083] this language can be interpreted to require proof of *actual* dilution, rather than a mere likelihood of dilution. This is particularly problematic for state dilution statutes that track the language of the original federal statute, and that have not been revised since the 2003 *Moseley* decision or the legislative overruling of that decision in 2006.[1084] As discussed below, actual dilution is significantly harder to prove than mere likelihood of dilution.[1085]

In jurisdictions that require a mark to be highly distinctive, strong, or famous in order to be protected against dilution, the question arises as to what segment of the consuming public must be examined to make this determination. For example, in *Mead Data Central, Inc. v. Toyota Motor Sales, U.S.A., Inc.*, the Second Circuit held that, for purposes of New York's dilution statute, the plaintiff's mark could be protected against dilution only if it had "a distinctive quality for a significant percentage of the defendant's market."[1086] Because the plaintiff's mark was well-known only to a narrow segment of the general public (attorneys and accountants), it did not have sufficient fame to be protected.

Under certain circumstances, federal law provides a complete defense to a state law dilution claim. Despite the variations in state dilution laws, section 43(c) of the

---

[1079] Mead Data Central, Inc. v. Toyota Motor Sales, U.S.A., Inc., 875 F.2d 1026, 1030 (2d Cir. 1989).

[1080] Glen Raven Mills, Inc. v. Ramada Int'l, Inc., 852 F. Supp. 1544, 1556–57 (M.D. Fla. 1994) (applying Florida statute); E. & J. Gallo Winery v. Consorzio Del Gallo Nero, 782 F. Supp. 457, 469 (N.D. Cal. 1991) (applying California statute).

[1081] N.Y. Gen. Bus. L. § 360-l (McKinney Supp. 2004).

[1082] *See, e.g.*, N.Y. Stock Exch., Inc. v. New York, New York Hotel, L.L.C., 293 F.3d 550, 558 (2d Cir. 2002). This list was first set forth in Judge Sweet's concurring opinion in Mead Data Central, Inc. v. Toyota Motor Sales, U.S.A., Inc., 875 F.2d 1026 (2d Cir. 1989).

[1083] 537 U.S. 418 (2003). *See* § 5G[3][f][i].

[1084] *See, e.g.*, Nev. Rev. Stat. § 600.435(1) (2005).

[1085] *See* § 5G[3][f].

[1086] 875 F.2d 1026, 1031 (2d Cir. 1989).

Lanham Act provides that if the allegedly dilutive mark is the subject of a valid registration on the Principal Register,[1087] the owner of the federal registration has a complete defense to any state law claim asserting blurring, tarnishment, or other harm to the distinctiveness or reputation of a mark.[1088]

Unlike the federal dilution statute, many state dilution laws do not contain express exceptions for news reporting or other noncommercial speech.[1089] Nonetheless, state dilution laws should not be enforced where they would interfere with speech protected by the First Amendment.[1090]

[3]   Federal Trademark Dilution Act

[a]   History

In 1995, the Federal Trademark Dilution Act (FTDA)[1091] added section 43(c) to the Lanham Act, affording the owners of both registered and unregistered marks a federal remedy "against another person's commercial use in commerce of a mark or trade name, if such use begins after the mark has become famous and causes dilution of the distinctive quality of the mark,"[1092] regardless of the absence of competition or confusion.[1093] The purpose of the FTDA was "to protect famous trademarks from subsequent uses that blur the distinctiveness of the mark or tarnish or disparage it, even in the absence of a likelihood of confusion."[1094] In 2006, Congress enacted the Trademark Dilution Revision Act (TDRA)[1095] in order to clarify several aspects of section 43(c). In the discussion below, major differences between the 1995 and 2006 versions of the federal dilution statute are noted where relevant.

[b]   Elements of a Federal Dilution Claim

To qualify for relief under the 2006 amendments to section 43(c), the plaintiff must establish that: (1) the plaintiff owns a mark that is both famous and distinctive; and (2) after the plaintiff's mark became famous, the defendant commenced use of a mark or trade name in commerce that is likely to cause dilution of the famous

---

[1087] The defense also applies if the allegedly dilutive mark was registered under the Act of March 3, 1881, or February 20, 1905. 15 U.S.C. § 1125(c)(3).

[1088] 15 U.S.C. § 1125(c)(6).

[1089] *See, e.g.,* N.Y. Gen. Bus. § 360-l (2008); Ann. Laws Mass. ch. 110H, § 13 (2008); 10 Me. Rev. Stat. § 1530 (2008). However, there are exceptions. *See, e.g.,* Pa. C.S. § 1124 (containing exceptions paralleling those in the 1995 version of 15 U.S.C. § 43(c)).

[1090] *See, e.g.,* L.L. Bean, Inc. v. Drake Pub., Inc., 811 F.2d 26 (1st Cir. 1987); American Family Life Ins. Co. v. Hagan, 266 F. Supp. 2d 682, 693 (N.D. Ohio 2002); Mattel, Inc. v. MCA Records, Inc., 28 F. Supp. 2d 1120, 1154 n.53 (C.D. Cal. 1998), *aff'd,* 296 F.3d 894 (9th Cir. 2002); New Kids on the Block v. News America Publishing, Inc., 745 F. Supp. 1540, 1542 n.1 (C.D. Cal. 1990), *aff'd,* 971 F.2d 302 (9th Cir. 1992). For further discussion of conflicts between trademark and unfair competition laws and the First Amendment, see § 5J[3].

[1091] Pub. L. 104-98, § 3(a), 109 Stat. 985 (1995).

[1092] 15 U.S.C. § 1125(c)(1) (as enacted).

[1093] TCPIP Holding Co. v. Haar Communications, Inc., 244 F.3d 88, 95 (2d Cir. 2001).

[1094] H.R. Rep. No. 104-374, at 3 (1995); 1995 U.S.C.C.A.N. 1029, 1030.

[1095] Pub. L. 109-312, 120 Stat. 1730 (2006).

mark by blurring or by tarnishment.[1096] Liability for dilution by blurring or tarnishment may arise even where there is no actual or likely confusion, no competition, and no actual economic injury.

The 1995 version of section 43(c) did not mention blurring or tarnishment, defining dilution simply as "the lessening of the capacity of a famous mark to identify and distinguish goods or services." Although the lower federal courts had interpreted this definition to encompass both blurring and tarnishment,[1097] in 2003 the Supreme Court cast doubt on this conclusion in *Moseley v. V Secret Catalog*.[1098] In the 2006 amendments, Congress made clear that section 43(c) encompasses both blurring and tarnishment claims, and replaced the general definition of dilution with specific definitions of dilution by blurring and dilution by tarnishment. "Dilution by blurring" is an "association arising from the similarity between a mark or trade name and a famous mark that impairs the distinctiveness of the famous mark,"[1099] and "dilution by tarnishment" is an "association arising from the similarity between a mark or trade name and a famous mark that harms the reputation of the famous mark."[1100]

Under the 1995 version of section 43(c)(1), a dilution claim could be brought only where the defendant's use of the famous mark constituted a "commercial use in commerce." As discussed below,[1101] this limitation to "commercial" uses created some confusion, because section 43(c)(4) expressly exempted "any noncommercial use" of a mark. The TDRA reduced this confusion by broadening the language of section 43(c)(1) to refer simply to the "use of a mark or trade name in commerce."[1102]

[c] Trademark Use

Occasionally, courts have considered the question whether a defendant's use of another's famous mark must be a "trademark use" in order to be dilutive.[1103] While the statutory language makes clear that the defendant must be using the famous mark "in commerce," it is not clear whether that use must be as an *origin indicator*. Courts interpreting the original FTDA reached conflicting conclusions on this question.[1104] However, the TDRA is somewhat less ambiguous, and appears to

---

[1096] 15 U.S.C. § 1125(c)(1); PepsiCo, Inc. v. #1 Wholesale, LLC, 84 U.S.P.Q.2d 1040 (N.D. Ga. July 20, 2007).

[1097] *See, e.g.*, Kraft Foods Holdings, Inc. v. Helm, 205 F. Supp. 2d 942 (N.D. Ill. 2002); Deborah Heart & Lung Ctr. v. Children of the World Found., Ltd., 99 F. Supp. 2d 481 (D.N.J. 2000); Hasbro, Inc. v. Internet Ent. Group, Ltd., 1996 U.S. Dist. LEXIS 11626, *2 (W.D. Wash. Feb. 9, 1996).

[1098] 537 U.S. 418, 432 (2003).

[1099] 15 U.S.C. § 1125(c)(2)(B).

[1100] 15 U.S.C. § 1125(c)(2)(C); *see also* Louis Vuitton Malletier S.A. v. Haute Diggity Dog, LLC, 507 F.3d 252, 264–65 (4th Cir. 2007).

[1101] *See* § 5G[4][b].

[1102] A "use in commerce" is defined in 15 U.S.C. § 1127; *see also* § 5F[5].

[1103] *See* Nabisco, Inc. v. PF Brands, Inc., 191 F.3d 208, 223 (2d Cir. 1999) (finding it unnecessary to resolve this "complicated" question). Most state dilution statutes are ambiguous on this point as well. For a broader discussion of "trademark use," see § 5F[4].

[1104] *See, e.g.*, Horphag Research, Ltd. v. Garcia, 475 F.3d 1029, 1033–37 (9th Cir. 2007); Bird v.

encompass the use of a mark other than as an origin indicator, except where one of the statutory exemptions in section 43(c)(3) applies. Several courts have held that liability under the TDRA is not restricted to use of the famous mark as an origin indicator for the defendant's own goods, so long as consumers perceive the mark as *someone's* trademark.[1105]

[d] Distinctive and Famous Mark

Section 43(c) protects only those marks that are both *distinctive* and *famous*. Under the FTDA, the requirement of distinctiveness was implicit; however, the TDRA made this requirement explicit and also clarified its meaning. The TDRA also clarified and narrowed the meaning of fame.

[i] Distinctiveness

Under the FTDA, there were conflicting interpretations of the requirement that the mark be distinctive. Most circuits interpreted this as a requirement that the mark be *either* (1) inherently distinctive, or (2) descriptive with secondary meaning.[1106] Some courts seemed to assume that a famous mark was *per se* distinctive.[1107] In contrast, the Second Circuit required the plaintiff's mark to have *both* inherent and acquired distinctiveness.[1108] Under this approach, federal dilution law protected only arbitrary, fanciful, or suggestive marks.

The TDRA clearly rejects the latter approach. Now, section 43(c)(1) explicitly protects famous marks that are "distinctive, inherently or through acquired distinctiveness." Thus, a famous mark that is descriptive with secondary meaning is entitled to the same federal dilution protection as a famous mark that is arbitrary, fanciful, or suggestive.

[ii] Fame

Although the 1995 statute included a non-exhaustive list of factors that a court could (but was not required to) consider in assessing whether a mark was "both distinctive and famous,"[1109] determining whether a particular mark was famous often proved difficult. Courts generally applied a rigorous standard, reserving dilution protection for "a select class of marks — those marks with such powerful

---

Parsons, 289 F.3d 865, 880 (6th Cir. 2002); Avery Dennison Corp. v. Sumpton, 189 F.3d 868, 880 (9th Cir. 1999); Panavision Int'l, L.P. v. Toeppen, 141 F.3d 1316, 1325 (9th Cir. 1998).

[1105] Rosetta Stone, Ltd. v. Google, Inc., 676 F.3d 144, 169–70 (4th Cir. 2012); Adidas America, Inc. v. Payless Shoesource, Inc., 2008 U.S. Dist. LEXIS 69260, *20–*22 (D. Or. Sept. 12, 2008).

[1106] *See, e.g.*, Thane, Int'l v. Trek Bicycle Corp., 305 F.3d 894, 912 (9th Cir. 2002); Times Mirror Magazines, Inc. v. Las Vegas Sports News, LLC, 212 F.3d 157, 166 (3d Cir. 2000); NBBJ East L.P. v. NBBJ Training Acad., Inc., 201 F. Supp. 2d 800, 806 (S.D. Ohio 2001); Avery Dennison Corp. v. Sumpton, 189 F.3d 868, 876–77 (9th Cir. 1999).

[1107] *See, e.g.*, Ty, Inc. v. Perryman, 306 F.3d 509, 511, 513–14 (7th Cir. 2002); Ringling Bros.-Barnum & Bailey Combined Shows v. Utah Div. of Travel Dev't, 955 F. Supp. 605, 613 & n.4 (E.D. Va. 1997), *aff'd*, 170 F.3d 449 (4th Cir. 1999); *accord*, McCARTHY ON TRADEMARKS § 24:91.

[1108] *See, e.g.*, Savin Corp. v. Savin Group, 391 F.3d 439, 449 (2d Cir. 2004); TCPIP Holding Co. v. Haar Communications, Inc., 244 F.3d 88, 97–98 (2d Cir. 2001).

[1109] 15 U.S.C. § 1125(c)(1) (prior to 2006 amendments).

consumer associations that even non-competing uses can impinge their value."[1110] The 1995 House Report gave the examples of "Buick," "DuPont," and "Kodak."[1111] As indicators of fame, courts typically considered the length of use, the volume of sales, revenues, advertising expenditures, and whether the mark was nationally advertised.[1112] Marks deemed to be famous under the 1995 statute included "Victoria's Secret,"[1113] "Beanie Babies" (and "Beanies"),[1114] "Wawa,"[1115] "Coca-Cola,"[1116] "The Greatest Show on Earth,"[1117] as well as "7-Eleven," "Nike," and "Pinehurst."[1118]

Under the 1995 statute, some courts concluded that section 43(c) protected only those marks that were famous in the *general* marketplace,[1119] while other courts held that it was sufficient for a mark to be famous in a "niche" market.[1120] The TDRA repudiated the concept of niche market fame by adding section 43(c)(2)(A), which provides that "a mark is famous if it is widely recognized by the general consuming public of the United States as a designation of source of the goods or services of the mark's owner." The amendments also revised the statute's non-exhaustive list of "fame" factors to its current form:

(i)   The duration, extent, and geographic reach of advertising and publicity of the mark, whether advertised or publicized by the owner or third parties.

(ii)   The amount, volume, and geographic extent of sales of goods or services offered under the mark.

(iii)   The extent of actual recognition of the mark.

[1110] Everest Capital Ltd. v. Everest Funds Mgt., L.L.C., 393 F.3d 755, 762 (8th Cir. 2005); *see also* Grupo Gigante S.A. de C.V. v. Dallo & Co., Inc., 391 F.3d 1088, 1108 (9th Cir. 2004) (Graber, J., concurring); TCPIP Holding Co., Inc. v. Haar Communs., Inc., 244 F.3d 88, 99 (2d Cir. 2001); Avery Dennison Corp. v. Sumpton, 189 F.3d 868, 876–79 (9th Cir. 1999); I.P. Lund Trading ApS v. Kohler Co., 163 F.3d 27, 46 (1st Cir. 1998); *cf.* Palm Bay Imports, Inc. v. Veuve Clicquot Ponsardin Maison Fondee En 1772, 396 F.3d 1369, 1374–75 (Fed. Cir. 2005).

[1111] H.R. Rep. No. 104-374, at 3 (1995).

[1112] *See, e.g.*, Savin Corp. v. Savin Group, 391 F.3d 439, 450 (2d Cir. 2004); Nabisco, Inc. v. PF Brands, Inc., 50 F. Supp. 2d 188, 202 (S.D.N.Y. 1999), *aff'd*, 191 F.3d 208 (2d Cir. 1999); Best Cellars, Inc. v. Wine Made Simple, Inc., 2003 U.S. Dist. LEXIS 3958, (S.D.N.Y. Mar. 11, 2003); *but see* I.P. Lund Trading ApS v. Kohler Co., 163 F.3d 27, 47 (1st Cir. 1998) (design was not famous even though it had been featured and advertised in national magazines and displayed in museums, and had been used for 20 years).

[1113] Moseley v. V Secret Catalog, Inc., 537 U.S. 418, 432 (2003).

[1114] Ty, Inc. v. Perryman, 306 F.3d 509, 511 (7th Cir. 2002).

[1115] Wawa, Inc. v. Haaf, 40 U.S.P.Q. 2d 1629 (E.D. Pa. 1996), *aff'd mem.*, 116 F.3d 471 (3d Cir. 1997).

[1116] I.P. Lund Trading ApS v. Kohler Co., 163 F.3d 27, 47 (1st Cir. 1998) (dictum).

[1117] Ringling Bros.-Barnum & Bailey Combined Shows, Inc. v. Utah Div. of Travel Dev't, 170 F.3d 449, 453 (4th Cir. 1999).

[1118] Savin Corp. v. Savin Group, 391 F.3d 439, 452 (2d Cir. 2004).

[1119] *See, e.g.*, *Savin Corp.*, 391 F.3d at 450 & n.6; Thane Int'l, Inc. v. Trek Bicycle Corp., 305 F.3d 894 (9th Cir. 2002); TCPIP Holding Co. v. Haar Comms., Inc., 244 F.3d 88, 98–99 (2d Cir. 2001); Sporty's Farm LLC v. Sportsman's Market, Inc., 202 F.3d 489, 497 n.10 (2d Cir. 2000); Ott v. Target Corp., 153 F. Supp. 2d 1055 (D. Minn. 2001).

[1120] *See, e.g.*, Times Mirror Magazines, Inc. v. Las Vegas Sports News, L.L.C., 212 F.3d 157, 174 (3d Cir. 2000); Syndicate Sales, Inc. v. Hampshire Paper Corp., 192 F3d 633, 640–41 (7th Cir. 1999).

(iv) Whether the mark was registered under the Act of March 3, 1881, or the Act of February 20, 1905, or on the principal register.[1121]

Marks held to be famous and distinctive under the 2006 amendments include "eBay,"[1122] "Visa,"[1123] "Nike,"[1124] "Tiffany,"[1125] "Victoria's Secret,"[1126] "Louis Vuitton,"[1127] and the three-stripe mark used by Adidas.[1128] Marks held not to meet this standard include "Milbank,"[1129] "Top,"[1130] "Mensa,"[1131] and "Jarritos."[1132]

[iii]   Trade Dress and Other Nontraditional Marks

Trade dress and other nontraditional marks can qualify for protection under the federal dilution statute. The Second Circuit applied section 43(c) to protect Pepperidge Farm's Goldfish cracker,[1133] and the Tenth Circuit considered a federal dilution claim alleging that after-market car kits diluted General Motors' trade dress in the appearance of its "Hummer" vehicles.[1134] Protection has been granted to the titles of expressive works, as well as the names and images of fictional characters.[1135]

In the case of dilution claims involving unregistered trade dress, the TDRA added section 43(c)(4), expressly requiring the dilution plaintiff to prove not only that its trade dress is famous, but also that it is not functional. If the unregistered trade dress includes any registered marks, then the owner must prove that the unregistered component of the trade dress is famous "separate and apart from" the registered marks.[1136]

[1121] 15 U.S.C. § 1125(c)(2)(A).

[1122] Perfumebay.com, Inc. v. eBay, Inc., 506 F.3d 1165, 1180 & nn.7–8 (9th Cir. 2007) (applying federal standards to state law dilution claim).

[1123] Visa Int'l Serv. Ass'n v. JSL Corp., 610 F.3d 1088, 1090–91 (9th Cir. 2010).

[1124] Nike, Inc. v. Nikepal Int'l, Inc., 84 U.S.P.Q.2d 1521 (E.D. Cal. Sept. 10, 2007).

[1125] Tiffany, Inc. v. eBay, Inc., 576 F. Supp. 2d 463, 523 (S.D.N.Y. 2008).

[1126] V Secret Catalogue, Inc. v. Moseley, 558 F. Supp. 2d 734, 743–44 (W.D. Ky. 2008).

[1127] Louis Vuitton Malletier S.A. v. Haute Diggity Dog, 507 F.3d 252, 265 (4th Cir. 2007).

[1128] Adidas America, Inc. v. Payless Shoesource, Inc., 546 F. Supp. 2d 1029, 1063 (D. Or. 2008).

[1129] Milbank Tweed Hadley & McCloy LLP v. Milbank Holding Corp., 82 U.S.P.Q.2d 1583 (C.D. Cal. 2007).

[1130] Top Tobacco, LP v. North Atlantic Operating Co., 509 F.3d 380, 383–84 (7th Cir. 2007).

[1131] American Mensa, Ltd. v. Inpharmatica, Ltd., 2008 U.S. Dist. LEXIS 99394, *42 (D. Md. Nov. 6, 2008).

[1132] Jarritos, Inc. v. Los Jarritos, 2007 U.S. Dist. LEXIS 32245, *54–*55 (N.D. Cal. May 2, 2007).

[1133] Nabisco, Inc. v. PF Brands, Inc., 191 F.3d 208, 217 (2d Cir. 1999).

[1134] General Motors Corp. v. Urban Gorilla, 500 F.3d 1222 (10th Cir. 2007).

[1135] *See, e.g.*, Dr. Seuss Enters., L.P. v. Penguin Book USA, Inc., 924 F. Supp. 1559, 1570, 1573 (S.D. Cal. 1996), *aff'd*, 109 F.3d 1394 (9th Cir. 1997).

[1136] 15 U.S.C. § 43(c)(4).

[e] Similarity

Although section 43(c) does not specify the degree of similarity necessary to find one mark dilutive of another, under the FTDA courts required a degree of similarity greater than that required to establish a likelihood of confusion,[1137] reasoning that the similarity must be "great enough that even a noncompeting, nonconfusing use is harmful."[1138] Most courts required the marks to be identical, or nearly so,[1139] while others adopted a variety of phrasings, all connoting a high degree of similarity.[1140]

While the TDRA did not expressly alter the standard of similarity, the new multi-factor test for the likelihood of dilution by blurring treats the similarity of the marks as just one of the six factors to be considered. Courts that have considered the effect of this change have concluded that the marks need *not* be identical, nearly identical, or even substantially similar.[1141] The TTAB requires a diluting mark to be "sufficiently similar to trigger consumers to conjure up a famous mark when confronted with the second mark."[1142]

[f] Actual Dilution Versus Likelihood of Dilution

[i] The FTDA and the *Moseley* Decision

Under the FTDA, courts disagreed on whether a dilution plaintiff was required to prove that the defendant's unauthorized use had in fact caused dilution of the plaintiff's famous mark, or merely that such dilution was likely to occur. In 2003, the Supreme Court resolved the circuit split, holding in *Moseley v. V Secret Catalogue, Inc.* that proof of actual dilution was required.[1143] Moreover, proof that consumers made a mental association between the plaintiff's mark and the defendant's mark was not sufficient; objective proof of actual injury to the economic value of the mark was required.[1144]

[1137] *See, e.g.*, Thane Int'l v. Trek Bicycle Corp., 305 F.3d 894, 906 (9th Cir. 2002).

[1138] Jet, Inc. v. Sewage Aeration Sys., 165 F.3d 419, 424–425 (6th Cir. 1999).

[1139] *See, e.g.*, Nissan Motor Co. v. Nissan Computer Corp., 378 F.3d 1002, 1011 (9th Cir. 2004); *Thane Int'l*, 305 F.3d at 905 (9th Cir. 2002); Playboy Enters., Inc. v. Welles, 279 F.3d 796, 806 (9th Cir. 2002); HI Limited Partnership v. Winghouse of Florida, Inc., 347 F. Supp. 2d 1256 (M.D. Fla. 2004); *see also* AutoZone, Inc. v. Tandy Corp., 373 F.3d 786, 806 (6th Cir. 2004) ("Every federal court to decide the issue has ruled that a high degree of similarity, ranging from 'nearly identical' to 'very similar,' is required for a dilution claim to succeed.").

[1140] *See, e.g.*, Eli Lilly & Co. v. Natural Answers, Inc., 233 F.3d 456, 469 (7th Cir. 2000); Ringling Bros.-Barnum & Bailey Combined Shows, Inc. v. Utah Div. of Travel Dev't, 170 F.3d 449, 458 (4th Cir. 1999); Nabisco, Inc. v. PF Brands, Inc., 191 F.3d 208, 218 (2d Cir. 1999); Luigino's, Inc. v. Stouffer Corp., 170 F.3d 827, 832 (8th Cir. 1999); I.P. Lund Trading ApS v. Kohler Co., 163 F.3d 27, 50 (1st Cir. 1998).

[1141] Levi Strauss v. Abercrombie & Fitch Trading Co., 633 F.3d 1158, 1172 (9th Cir. 2011); Starbucks Co. v. Wolfe's Borough Coffee, Inc., 588 F.3d 97, 109 (2d Cir. 2009).

[1142] UMG Recordings, Inc. v. Mattel, Inc., 100 U.S.P.Q.2d 1868, 1888 (T.T.A.B. 2011).

[1143] 537 U.S. 418, 433 (2003).

[1144] *Id.* at 422, 433.

[ii]   Likelihood of Dilution Under the TDRA

In the 2006 TDRA, Congress legislatively overruled *Moseley*'s holding that section 43(c) requires a showing of actual dilution, calling it "an undue burden for trademark holders."[1145] Section 43(c)(1) now expressly permits the owner of a famous mark to obtain injunctive relief against an unauthorized use "that is likely to cause dilution by blurring or dilution by tarnishment."

Whereas the FTDA offered no guidance to courts in assessing the likelihood of dilution, the amended statute provides that courts "may consider all relevant factors" in assessing the likelihood of dilution by blurring, and specifically suggests the following six factors:

(i)   The degree of similarity between the mark or trade name and the famous mark.

(ii)   The degree of inherent or acquired distinctiveness of the famous mark.

(iii) The extent to which the owner of the famous mark is engaging in substantially exclusive use of the mark.

(iv)   The degree of recognition of the famous mark.

(v)   Whether the user of the mark or trade name intended to create an association with the famous mark.

(vi)   Any actual association between the mark or trade name and the famous mark.[1146]

The TDRA also made conforming amendments to sections 2(f), 13(a), 14, and 24 of the Lanham Act, reflecting the adoption of the likelihood of dilution standard.

[iii]   Judicial Interpretations

(a)   Likelihood of Dilution by Blurring

The first case to apply the TDRA's new multifactor test for the likelihood of dilution by blurring, *Louis Vuitton Malletier S.A. v. Haute Diggity Dog LLC*,[1147] did so in the context of a parody. The plaintiff alleged that its famous "Louis Vuitton" mark was likely to be diluted by the defendant's use of the "Chewy Vuiton" mark on dog toys. Because the defendant was using the mark as a source indicator for its own goods, it was not eligible for the "fair use" exception under the 2006 version of section 43(c)(4)(A). Nonetheless, the Fourth Circuit held that the parodic context was relevant to its analysis of the six statutory blurring factors.[1148] Drawing from existing case law on parodies and dilution,[1149] the court noted that "[w]hile a parody intentionally creates an association with the famous mark in

---

[1145] H.R. Rep. No. 109-23, at 5 (2005).

[1146] 15 U.S.C. § 1125(c)(2)(B). No comparable factors are suggested for determining the likelihood of dilution by tarnishment.

[1147] 507 F.3d 252 (4th Cir. 2007).

[1148] *Id.* at 267.

[1149] For a discussion of these cases, see § 5J[3].

order to be a parody, it also intentionally communicates, if it is successful, that it is *not* the famous mark, but rather a satire of the famous mark."[1150] In addition, "by making the famous mark an object of the parody, a successful parody might actually enhance the famous mark's distinctiveness by making it an icon. The brunt of the joke becomes yet more famous."[1151] Applying these principles, the court concluded that the "Chewy Vuiton" mark was unlikely to blur the distinctiveness of the plaintiff's mark because (1) the latter was "particularly strong and distinctive," and (2) the defendant's imitation successfully conveyed the conflicting messages essential to a successful parody.[1152]

The parodic aspect of the "Chewy Vuiton" mark was also relevant to the analysis of factors (v) and (vi) — whether the defendant intended to create an association with the famous mark, and whether there was any actual association between the marks — because the defendant intentionally associated its mark with the plaintiff's mark, but did so "imperfectly," in order to convey the simultaneous messages essential to a successful parody: "[A]s a parody, it separated itself from the LVM marks in order to make fun of them."[1153]

In contrast, a dilution defendant failed to persuade the Second Circuit that its "Mr. Charbucks" mark for coffee should be treated as a parody of the "Starbucks" mark; as a result, the court applied the blurring factors without any of the special considerations that influenced the *Louis Vuitton* decision.[1154]

Other than *Louis Vuitton*, there is not yet significant case law interpreting the new blurring factors. However, a handful of cases have provided some useful perspectives on three of those factors:

Degree of similarity: Because the first blurring factor calls for an analysis of the *degree* of similarity, the Second Circuit has held a likelihood of dilution can be found even where the marks are not "substantially similar"; thus, the lack of substantial similarity between "Starbucks" and "Mr. Charbucks" was not, by itself, sufficient to defeat a dilution claim.[1155] In contrast, district courts in the Ninth Circuit have held that the TDRA did not relax the stringent similarity requirement established by prior law, and that, accordingly, marks must be "nearly identical" for this factor to favor a dilution plaintiff.[1156]

[1150] 507 F.3d at 267 (*citing* People for Ethical Treatment of Animals (PETA) v. Doughney, 263 F.3d 359, 366 (4th Cir. 2001)).

[1151] *Id.* (*citing* Hormel Foods Corp. v. Jim Henson Prods., Inc., 73 F.3d 497, 506 (2d Cir. 1996) (observing that a successful parody "tends to increase public identification" of the famous mark with its source); Yankee Publishing, Inc. v. News America Publishing, Inc., 809 F. Supp. 267, 272–82 (S.D.N.Y. 1992) (suggesting that a sufficiently obvious parody is unlikely to blur the targeted famous mark)).

[1152] *Id.* (citing *PETA*, 263 F.3d at 366).

[1153] *Id.*

[1154] Starbucks Corp. v. Wolfe's Borough Coffee, Inc., 588 F.3d 97, 112–13 (2d Cir. 2009).

[1155] *Id.* at 107 & n.3.

[1156] Nike, Inc. v. Nikepal Int'l, Inc., 84 U.S.P.Q.2d 1521 (E.D. Cal. 2007) (citing Thane Int'l, Inc. v. Trek Bicycle Corp., 305 F.3d 894, 906 (9th Cir. 2002)); Century 21 Real Estate LLC, 2007 U.S. Dist. LEXIS 8434, *5–*6 (D. Ariz. Feb. 5, 2007) (citing Playboy Enters., Inc. v. Welles, 279 F.3d 796, 806 n.41 (9th Cir. 2002)).

Where there are small differences between the marks, courts have considered the context in which those marks appear. When a defendant used the "evisa" mark in the domain name "evisa.com," the district court observed that, while the difference between "Visa" and "evisa" might be significant in some other settings, in the domain name context the two marks were very similar, because consumers would tend to disregard the "e" prefix.[1157] And the similarity between "Victoria's Secret" and "Victor's Little Secret" supported dilution liability where the word "Little" was "substantially smaller" than the rest of the mark.[1158]

Intent to create association: One district court has held that, even if the junior user did not *intend* to create an association with the famous mark, the more important question is the degree to which consumers *actually* associate the two marks.[1159] Also, the Second Circuit has held that a court may find an intent to associate even in the absence of bad faith; thus, this factor favored the owner of the "Starbucks" mark where the defendant adopted the "Mr. Charbucks" mark in order to convey that its coffee resembled the Starbucks product.[1160]

Actual association: In determining the extent of any actual association between the marks, courts have given significant weight to direct consumer testimony and consumer survey evidence.[1161] However, actual association and blurring are not synonymous — for example, tarnishment rather than blurring was indicated where a consumer associated two marks but perceived the defendant's mark as an offensive imitation of the plaintiff's.[1162]

(b) Likelihood of Dilution by Tarnishment

Faced with little statutory guidance on how to assess the likelihood of dilution by tarnishment, the few courts that have considered post-TDRA tarnishment claims have not departed significantly from the pre-TDRA approach, focusing largely on the nature of the junior user's goods, and inclining toward tarnishment whenever they perceive those goods to be unwholesome, offensive, or poor in quality.

In the first decision to address tarnishment under the TDRA, the Fourth Circuit in *Louis Vuitton* found no likelihood of tarnishment, rejecting as "flimsy" the plaintiff's assertion that the defendant's "Chewy Vuiton" dog toys posed a choking hazard.[1163] Although the court acknowledged that a $10 dog toy was inferior in quality to an expensive Louis Vuitton handbag, the court gave no weight to this

---

[1157] Visa Int'l Serv. Ass'n v. JSL Corp., 590 F. Supp. 2d 1306, 1317–18 (D. Nev. 2008), *aff'd*, 610 F.3d 1088 (9th Cir. 2010).

[1158] V Secret Catalogue, Inc. v. Moseley, 558 F. Supp. 2d 734, 745 (W.D. Ky. 2008).

[1159] *Visa Int'l*, 590 F. Supp. 2d at 1320.

[1160] Starbucks Corp. v. Wolfe's Borough Coffee, Inc., 588 F.3d 97, 109 (2d Cir. 2009).

[1161] *See, e.g., Starbucks*, 588 F.3d at 109; *Visa Int'l*, 590 F. Supp. 2d at 1319; *Nike*, 84 U.S.P.Q.2d at 1528.

[1162] V Secret Catalogue, Inc. v. Moseley, 558 F. Supp. 2d 734, 748–49 (W.D. Ky. 2008).

[1163] Louis Vuitton Malletier S.A. v. Haute Diggity Dog LLC, 507 F.3d 252, 268–69 (4th Cir. 2007).

difference, and offered no explanation for disregarding it, although it was probably influenced by the parodic context.[1164]

In the *Starbucks* case, while survey evidence showed that some respondents associated a hypothetical "Charbucks" brand with burnt, bitter coffee, the tarnishment claim failed because there was no indication that this affected their perceptions of the plaintiff's famous mark, and because the actual Charbucks product was of high quality.[1165]

In *Moseley*, on remand, the district court offered only a brief explanation for its conclusion that that a store called "Victor's Little Secret" which sold "adult" novelties was likely to tarnish the reputation of the "Victoria's Secret" mark for lingerie. The only evidence of consumer perception was the testimony of a single customer who was offended by defendant's imitation of the famous mark, but the court found this persuasive.[1166]

[g]   Effective Date of TDRA

In several cases, courts have considered which version of section 43(c) should apply to dilution claims in which the allegedly dilutive activity commenced before the effective date of the TDRA (October 6, 2006). Courts have consistently held that the TDRA applies to such activities with respect to claims for injunctive relief.[1167] With respect to damages claims, however, courts have held that the original FTDA (and, thus, the more stringent actual dilution standard) applies to conduct predating the TDRA.[1168] This conclusion reflects the language of section 43(c)(5)(A), which provides that monetary relief is available only where the defendant's first use in commerce of the mark that is likely to cause dilution takes place after October 6, 2006.

Accordingly, where a trademark owner seeks injunctive relief, the trademark owner is required to show only a likelihood of dilution, rather than actual dilution. However, in order to obtain damages for willful dilution arising from conduct commencing on or before October 6, 2006, the trademark owner would have to establish actual dilution. To recover damages for willful dilution commencing *after* October 6, 2006, however, the applicable standard is likelihood of dilution.

[4]   Exceptions to FTDA

Unlike many state dilution statutes, the federal dilution statute sets forth specific circumstances in which the unauthorized use of a famous mark will not give rise to liability for dilution. The original three exceptions in the FTDA were retained, modified, and renumbered in the TDRA.

[1164] *Id.* at 269. The court's analysis of blurring is discussed in § 5G[3][f][iii](a).

[1165] *Starbucks*, 588 F.3d at 110–11.

[1166] 558 F. Supp. 2d at 750.

[1167] Jada Toys, Inc. v. Mattel, Inc., 518 F.3d 628, 634 n.2 (9th Cir. 2007); Starbucks Corp. v. Wolfe's Borough Coffee, Inc., 477 F.3d 765, 766 (2d Cir. 2007).

[1168] *Starbucks*, 477 F.3d at 766; University of Kansas v. Sinks, 565 F. Supp. 2d 1216, 1258 (D. Kan. 2008); *cf. Jada Toys*, 518 F.3d at 634 n.2 (holding that TDRA applies to pre-TDRA activities where plaintiff seeks injunctive relief, but not explicitly addressing which statute applies to damages claims).

Section 43(c)(4) of the FTDA exempted:

(A) Fair use of a famous mark by another person in comparative commercial advertising or promotion to identify the competing goods or services of the owner of the famous mark;

(B) Noncommercial use of a mark; and

(C) All forms of news reporting and news commentary.

Post-TDRA, section 43(c)(3) now exempts:

(A) Any fair use, including a nominative or descriptive fair use, or facilitation of such fair use, of a famous mark by another person other than as a designation of source for the person's own goods or services, including use in connection with—

(i) advertising or promotion that permits consumers to compare goods or services; or

(ii) identifying and parodying, criticizing, or commenting upon the famous mark owner or the goods or services of the famous mark owner.

(B) All forms of news reporting and news commentary.

(C) Any noncommercial use of a mark.

Each of these exceptions is discussed below.

[a]   Fair Use

The Ninth Circuit described the reasoning behind the 1995 version of the fair use exception as follows: "Uses that do not create an improper association between a mark and a new product but merely identify the trademark holder's products should be excepted from the reach of the anti-dilution statute. Such uses cause no harm."[1169] For example, the exception allows a merchant to use a competitor's trademark to describe the merchant's own products as identical or comparable to, or as replacements for, the competitor's trademarked goods.[1170]

In 2002, the Ninth Circuit held that nominative fair uses are non-dilutive as a matter of law.[1171] Thus, where a former "Playboy Playmate" maintained a website in which she described herself by that title and made other uses of Playboy's trademarked terms, including uses in metatags and banner advertising for her site, the court held that most of these uses were nominative, and therefore non-dilutive.[1172] However, her repeated use of the abbreviation "PMOY" (for "Playmate of the Year") in the wallpaper of her website was held not to be a nominative use,

---

[1169] Playboy Enters., Inc. v. Welles, 279 F.3d 796, 806 (9th Cir. 2002).

[1170] *See, e.g.,* Bijur Lubricating Corp. v. Devco Corp., 332 F. Supp. 2d 722, 733–34 (D.N.J. 2004); Avery Dennison Corp. v. Acco Brands, Inc., 1999 U.S. Dist. LEXIS 21464, *28–*29 (C.D. Cal. Oct. 12, 1999); Cumberland Packing Corp. v. Monsanto Co., 32 F. Supp. 2d 561, 581 (E.D.N.Y. 1999).

[1171] *Playboy Enters.,* 279 F.3d at 806. Nominative fair use is discussed in § 5J[5].

[1172] *Playboy Enters.,* 279 F.3d at 806.

and thus was not exempt from dilution liability.[1173]

The 2006 amendments expressly extend the fair use exception beyond traditional comparative advertising to encompass nominative fair use as well as parodies or criticisms of famous marks.[1174] However, the exception expressly does not apply if the person accused of dilution uses the mark as a source designation for that person's own goods or services — for example, where the defendant in *Louis Vuitton* used "Chewy Vuiton" as a mark for dog toys.[1175]

[b]   Noncommercial Use

The scope of the "noncommercial use" exception is somewhat unsettled. In the original FTDA, it was unclear why Congress thought it necessary to include a noncommercial use exception at all, because section 43(c)(1) allowed dilution claims only where the defendant engaged in a "commercial use in commerce."[1176] (In contrast, the TDRA deleted the phrase "commercial use," requiring only that the defendant make a dilutive use of the mark "in commerce.") Based in part on the FTDA's legislative history, the Ninth Circuit concluded that "noncommercial use" referred to "a use that consists entirely of noncommercial, or fully constitutionally protected, speech."[1177] Thus, the noncommercial use exception functioned as a catch-all for speech that was protected by the First Amendment but that fell outside of the FTDA's exceptions for comparative advertising and news reporting.[1178] Courts interpreted this exception to include comedy, parody, satire, consumer criticism, editorial commentaries, and other forms of expression, even when they were sold for profit.[1179] This interpretation appears to be correct under the TDRA as well.

Courts have applied this exception to uses that are partly commercial but that nonetheless enjoy a high degree of First Amendment protection, such as the use of Mattel's "Barbie" trademark in a pop song,[1180] and a literary parody of O.J. Simpson's murder trial incorporating characters and other elements from books by "Dr. Seuss."[1181] The exception has also been applied to political speech, including a candidate's television commercial that imitated a credit card company's television

---

[1173] *Id.*

[1174] For a detailed discussion of comparative advertising and nominative uses, see §§ 5J[5] and [6].

[1175] Louis Vuitton Malletier S.A. v. Haute Diggity Dog LLC, 507 F.3d 252, 266 (4th Cir. 2007); *accord*, Starbucks Corp. v. Wolfe's Borough Coffee, Inc., 588 F.3d 97, 112 (2d Cir. 2009).

[1176] Mattel, Inc. v. MCA Records, Inc., 296 F.3d 894, 904 (9th Cir. 2002).

[1177] *Id.* at 905; *accord*, American Family Life Ins. Co. v. Hagan, 266 F. Supp. 2d 682, 695–98 (N.D. Ohio 2002).

[1178] *Mattel*, 296 F.3d at 905–06 (collecting sources); *see also* 141 Cong. Rec. S19310 (daily ed. Dec. 29, 1995) (statement of Sen. Hatch).

[1179] Ford Motor Co. v. 2600 Enters., 177 F. Supp. 2d 661, 664–65 (E.D. Mich. 2001); Charles Atlas, Ltd. v. D.C. Comics, Inc., 112 F. Supp. 2d 330, 336 (S.D.N.Y. 2000); Northland Ins. Cos. v. Blaylock, 115 F. Supp. 2d 1108, 1122–23 (D. Minn. 2000); World Championship Wrestling v. Titan Sports, Inc., 46 F. Supp. 2d 118, 122–23 (D. Conn. 1999); Bally Total Fitness Holding Corp. v. Faber, 29 F. Supp. 2d 1161, 1166–67 (C.D. Cal. 1998); Dr. Seuss Enterprises v. Penguin Books USA, Inc., 924 F. Supp. 1559, 1574 (S.D. Cal. 1996); Panavision Int'l, L.P. v. Toeppen, 945 F. Supp. 1296, 1303 (C.D. Cal. 1996).

[1180] *Mattel*, 296 F.3d at 906–07.

[1181] *Dr. Seuss Enterprises*, 924 F. Supp. at 1573–74.

ads,[1182] and a candidate's Internet commercials that included a quacking cartoon duck "highly reminiscent" of the duck character featured in an insurance company's television ads.[1183]

The noncommercial use exception is frequently applied to websites that incorporate famous marks in their domain names and contain criticism or commentary aimed at the owners of those marks. As one court noted, "[i]f the FTDA's 'commercial use' requirement is to have any meaning, it cannot be interpreted so broadly as to include any use that might disparage or otherwise commercially harm the mark owner."[1184] In contrast, commercial use has been found where a defendant used a plaintiff's trademark in a domain name in order to redirect consumers to another website in order to solicit contributions or sell merchandise.[1185]

[c] News Reporting and Commentary

The FTDA's exception for news reporting and news commentary, which was unaltered by the TDRA, makes explicit what is already required by the First Amendment. Issues have arisen regarding its scope, particularly where a defendant's "news" reporting has commercial aspects. Where a website devoted to reporting real estate transactions identified by name the law firm that employed several attorneys who were involved in these transactions, and included links to the law firm's website, the parties disputed whether these references constituted news reporting or a dilutive use, and the dilution claims survived a motion to dismiss.[1186] Another court applied the news reporting exception to a blog; while noting that not every blog will qualify, the court based its decision on the blog's content and the intent of its author.[1187]

[d] Federal Registration as a Defense

Under the original FTDA, ownership of a valid registration on the Principal Register (or under the 1881 or 1905 Trademark Acts) was a complete bar to any *state law* claim, with respect to that mark, brought against the owner of the registration and seeking "to prevent dilution of the distinctiveness of a mark, label, or form of advertisement."[1188] The registration defense did not preclude *federal* dilution claims.

[1182] Mastercard Int'l Inc. v. Nader 2000 Primary Comm., Inc., 70 U.S.P.Q.2d 1046, 2004 U.S. Dist. LEXIS 3644 (S.D.N.Y. 2004).

[1183] American Family Life Ins. Co. v. Hagan, 266 F. Supp. 2d 682, 686, 698–701 (N.D. Ohio 2002); *accord*, Griffith v. Fenrick, 486 F. Supp. 2d 848, 853 (W.D. Wis. 2007) (use of famous actor's name by political candidate was noncommercial use).

[1184] *Ford Motor Co.*, 177 F. Supp. 2d at 665; *see also* Bally Total Fitness Holding Corp. v. Faber, 29 F. Supp. 2d 1161, 1166–67 (C.D. Cal. 1998); Savannah College of Art & Design, Inc. v. Houeix, 369 F. Supp. 2d 929, 957–58 (S.D. Ohio 2004).

[1185] *See, e.g.*, Jews for Jesus v. Brodsky, 993 F. Supp. 282 (D.N.J.), *aff'd*, 159 F.3d 1351 (3d Cir. 1998); Planned Parenthood Federation of America, Inc. v. Bucci, 1997 U.S. Dist. LEXIS 3338 (S.D.N.Y. Oct. 12, 1997), *aff'd*, 152 F.3d 920 (2d Cir. 1998).

[1186] Jones Day v. Blockshopper, LLC, 2008 U.S. Dist. LEXIS 94442, *8–11 (N.D. Ill. Nov. 13, 2008).

[1187] BidZirk, LLC v. Smith, 2007 U.S. Dist. LEXIS 78481, *16–19 (D.S.C. Oct. 22, 2007).

[1188] 15 U.S.C. § 1125(c)(3) (prior to 2006 amendments).

However, a drafting error in the TDRA revised the wording of the registration defense so that, under a literal reading, federal registration precluded federal as well as state dilution claims. Congress corrected this error in 2012, but the correction applied only to actions filed on or after October 5, 2012.[1189]

[5]   Remedies

The remedies available to plaintiffs under section 43(c) of the Lanham Act are more limited than those available for claims under sections 32 or 43(a).[1190] Unless the defendant's dilutive activity is willful, the plaintiff is entitled only to injunctive relief under section 34.[1191] The plaintiff may also bar importation of diluting goods.[1192]

The TDRA amended the dilution statute's provisions on monetary awards in order to clarify the meaning of willfulness. Under section 43(c)(5), the owner of a famous mark may recover damages and/or profits, costs and attorney fees under section 35(a),[1193] and may obtain an order for destruction of infringing articles under section 36,[1194] only if, in the case of a blurring claim, the defendant "willfully intended to trade on the recognition of the famous mark,"[1195] or, in the case of a tarnishment claim, the defendant "willfully intended to harm the reputation of the famous mark."[1196] As discussed above, the availability of these additional remedies depends on whether the defendant first used the dilutive mark in commerce before or after October 6, 2006.[1197]

§ 5H   CYBERSQUATTING

[1]   Anticybersquatting Consumer Protection Act

Cybersquatting occurs, in the words of one court, "when a person other than the trademark holder registers the domain name of a well-known trademark and then attempts to profit from this by either ransoming the domain name back to the trademark holder or by using the domain name to divert business from the trademark holder to the domain name holder."[1198]

In 1999, Congress enacted section 43(d) of the Lanham Act, the Anticybersquatting Consumer Protection Act (ACPA), to clarify and strengthen

---

[1189] Pub. L. No. 112-190, 112th Cong., 2d Sess. (Oct. 5, 2012).

[1190] For a detailed discussion of Lanham Act remedies, see § 5K.

[1191] 15 U.S.C. §§ 1116, 1125(c)(1), (c)(5).

[1192] 15 U.S.C. § 1125(b).

[1193] 15 U.S.C. § 1117(a).

[1194] 15 U.S.C. § 1118.

[1195] 15 U.S.C. § 1125(c)(5)(B)(i).

[1196] 15 U.S.C. § 1125(c)(5)(B)(ii).

[1197] 15 U.S.C. § 1125(c)(5)(A). *See* § 5G[3][g].

[1198] DaimlerChrysler v. The Net, Inc., 388 F.3d 201, 204 (6th Cir. 2004); *see also* Virtual Works, Inc. v. Volkswagen of America, Inc. 238 F.3d 264 (4th Cir. 2001).

the remedies available against users of domain names that incorporate registered marks or marks that are protected under section 43(a) or (c). Congress was concerned with three types of conduct in particular: (1) registering domain names that are similar to famous marks in order to profit by selling those domain names to the owners of the marks; (2) attaching offensive (*e.g.*, pornographic) matter to an infringing domain name in order to tarnish the mark; and (3) attempting to divert a trademark owner's customers to a competitor's website.[1199]

The legislative history of the ACPA defines cybersquatters as those who: (1) "register well-known brand names as Internet domain names in order to extract payment from the rightful owners of the marks;" (2) "register well-known marks as domain names and warehouse those marks with the hope of selling them to the highest bidder;" (3) "register well-known marks to prey on consumer confusion by misusing the domain name to divert customers from the mark owner's site to the cybersquatter's own site;" or (4) "target distinctive marks to defraud consumers, including to engage in counterfeiting activities."[1200]

[a]   Elements of an ACPA Claim

Section 43(d) gives the trademark owner a cause of action against anyone who, with a bad faith intent to profit from the mark, registers, traffics in, or uses a domain name that (1) is identical or confusingly similar to a mark that was distinctive at the time the defendant's domain name was registered; or (2) is identical or confusingly similar to, or dilutive of, a mark that was famous at the time the defendant's domain name was registered.[1201] A trademark owner asserting a claim under the ACPA must therefore establish the following: (1) it has a valid trademark entitled to protection; (2) its mark is distinctive or famous; (3) the defendant's domain name is identical or confusingly similar to, or in the case of famous marks, dilutive of, the owner's mark; and (4) the defendant used, registered, or trafficked in the domain name; (5) with a bad faith intent to profit.[1202] Liability under section 43(d) may be imposed only on the domain name registrant or an authorized licensee of the registrant.[1203]

The question whether a domain name is "confusingly similar" to a famous mark is not analyzed under the traditional likelihood-of-confusion analysis for trademark infringement, which considers a wide variety of factors that may affect a consumer's perception of the junior user's mark, including the similarity of the goods or services.[1204] Instead, the question of confusing similarity under the ACPA looks only at the similarity between the senior user's mark and the junior user's domain

---

[1199] Coca-Cola Co. v. Purdy, 382 F.3d 774, 778 (8th Cir. 2004); *see also* Lucent Techs., Inc. v. Lucentsucks.com, 95 F. Supp. 2d 528, 530 n.1 (E.D. Va. 2000); H.R. Rep. No. 106-412, at 6 (1999).

[1200] S. Rep. No. 106-140, at 5–6 (1999), quoted in Lucas Nursery and Landscaping, Inc. v. Grosse, 359 F.3d 806, 809 (6th Cir. 2004).

[1201] 15 U.S.C. § 1125(d)(1)(A). This provision also applies to registration, trafficking, or use of a mark, word, or name protected under 18 U.S.C. § 706 (the Red Cross) or 36 U.S.C. § 220506 (the Olympics).

[1202] DaimlerChrysler v. The Net, Inc., 388 F.3d 201, 204 (6th Cir. 2004).

[1203] 15 U.S.C. § 1125(d)(1)(D).

[1204] *See* § 5F[3].

name.[1205] The fact that a consumer's confusion could be alleviated by actually visiting the junior user's website is therefore irrelevant.[1206] Courts generally hold that a domain name is confusingly similar to a senior user's trademark if "consumers might think that [the domain name] is used, approved, or permitted" by the senior user.[1207] In making this assessment, courts consider only the second-level domain name (for example, "pepsi" in pepsi.com), and disregard the top-level domain name (for example, .com, .org, .net).[1208] They also disregard "slight differences" between the domain name and the senior user's mark, "such as the addition of minor or generic words,"[1209] or common misspellings or similar errors.[1210]

Domain names may also violate the ACPA if they are "dilutive" of a senior user's mark. Pornographic websites, for example, are routinely held to be dilutive when they incorporate well-known trademarks in their domain names.[1211]

The statutory phrase "traffics in" includes, without limitation, sales, purchases, loans, pledges, licenses, exchanges of currency, and "any other transfer for consideration or receipt in exchange for consideration."[1212]

Congress imposed the threshold requirement of "bad faith intent to profit" in order to target cybersquatters who act with an "intent to trade on the goodwill of another's mark."[1213] In determining whether a defendant acted with such bad faith intent, courts may consider the following non-exhaustive[1214] list of factors: (1) the defendant's intellectual property rights, if any, in the domain name; (2) the extent to which the domain name constitutes the defendant's legal name or a name commonly used to identify the defendant; (3) the defendant's prior use of the domain name in connection with the bona fide offering of goods or services; (4) the defendant's bona fide noncommercial use or fair use of the mark in a site accessible under the domain name; (5) the defendant's intent to divert customers from the

---

[1205] Coca-Cola Co. v. Purdy, 382 F.3d 774, 783 (8th Cir. 2004); Northern Light Tech., Inc. v. Northern Lights Club, 236 F.3d 57, 66 (1st Cir. 2001).

[1206] Coca-Cola, 382 F.3d at 783; People for Ethical Treatment of Animals v. Doughney, 263 F.3d 359 (4th Cir. 2001); Virtual Works, Inc. v. Volkswagen of Am., Inc., 238 F.3d 264, 266 (4th Cir. 2001); Sporty's Farm LLC v. Sportsman's Market, Inc., 202 F.3d 489, 497–98 (2d Cir. 2000).

[1207] DaimlerChrysler, 388 F.3d at 205–06 (citing Ford Motor Co. v. Greatdomains.com, Inc., 177 F. Supp. 2d 635, 641 (E.D. Mich. 2001); Harrods Ltd. v. Sixty Internet Domain Names, 157 F. Supp. 2d 658, 677 (E.D. Va. 2001)).

[1208] Coca-Cola, 382 F.3d at 783–84.

[1209] See, e.g., DaimlerChrysler, 388 F.3d at 205–06; Ford Motor Co., 177 F. Supp. 2d at 641; Spear, Leeds, & Kellogg v. Rosado, 122 F. Supp. 2d 403, 406 (S.D.N.Y. 2000).

[1210] See, e.g., Shields v. Zuccarini, 254 F.3d 476, 483–84 (3d Cir. 2001).

[1211] See, e.g., Lucent Techs., Inc. v. Johnson, 56 U.S.P.Q.2d 1637 (C.D. Cal 2000); Mattel, Inc. v. Internet Dimensions, Inc., 2000 U.S. Dist. LEXIS 9747 (S.D.N.Y. July 13, 2000); Hasbro Inc. v. Internet Entertainment Group, Ltd., 40 U.S.P.Q.2d 1479, 1480 (W.D. Wash. 1996).

[1212] 15 U.S.C. § 1125(d)(1)(E).

[1213] S. Rep. No. 106-140, at (1999); see Ford Motor Co. v. Catalanotte, 342 F.3d 543, 549 (6th Cir. 2003).

[1214] As permitted by the ACPA, courts have considered factors other than the nine listed. See, e.g., Virtual Works, Inc. v. Volkswagen of America, Inc., 238 F.3d 264 (4th Cir. 2001).

mark owner's online location to a site accessible under the domain name that could harm the goodwill represented by the mark, either for commercial gain or with the intent to tarnish or disparage the mark, by creating a likelihood of confusion as to the source, sponsorship, affiliation, or endorsement of the defendant's site; (6) the defendant's offer to assign the domain name for financial gain without having used, or having an intent to use, the domain name in the bona fide offering of goods or services, or a pattern of such conduct; (7) the defendant's provision of material and misleading false contact information when applying for the domain name's registration, intentional failure to maintain accurate contact information, or prior conduct indicating a pattern of such conduct; (8) the defendant's registration or acquisition of multiple domain names with the knowledge that those names were identical or confusingly similar to distinctive marks of others, or dilutive of famous marks of others, without regard to the goods or services of the parties; and (9) the extent to which the mark incorporated in the defendant's domain name is or is not distinctive and famous within the meaning of section 43(c) (the federal dilution statute).[1215] The first four factors represent reasons why a defendant, acting in good faith, might register a domain name that incorporates another's mark, while the last five factors are considered indicia of bad faith.[1216] In applying these factors, courts consider the totality of the circumstances, including "the purely circumstantial indicia of bad faith, as well as the direct evidence of the statements made at the time of registration and the direct evidence regarding terms of the sale" of the domain name.[1217]

Courts have found bad faith where defendants registered domain names similar to the plaintiffs' marks (1) to divert customers to non-commercial websites carrying an anti-abortion message;[1218] (2) for the purpose of selling the domain name back to the trademark owner;[1219] (3) to deprive the trademark owner of the ability to use the domain name;[1220] (4) to confuse consumers into believing the website was affiliated with the plaintiff;[1221] and (5) on a pornographic website.[1222]

In contrast, courts have *not* found bad faith intent to profit where the defendant has incorporated a trademark into its domain name for the purpose of criticizing the owner of that mark.[1223] The question of whether a domain name is being used for a legitimate "gripe site" is not always clear-cut; an ACPA violation may be found

---

[1215] 15 U.S.C. § 1125(d)(1)(B)(i); *See, e.g.*, Shields v. Zuccarini, 254 F.3d 476, 485 (3d Cir. 2001); People for the Ethical Treatment of Animals v. Doughney, 263 F.3d 359, 369 (4th Cir. 2001).

[1216] Coca-Cola Co. v. Purdy, 382 F.3d 774, 785 (8th Cir. 2004) (citing Lucas Nursery & Landscaping, Inc. v. Grosse, 359 F.3d 806, 809–10 (6th Cir. 2004)).

[1217] *Virtual Works*, 238 F.3d at 270.

[1218] *Coca-Cola*, 382 F.3d at 785.

[1219] People for the Ethical Treatment of Animals v. Doughney, 263 F.3d 359 (4th Cir. 2001); *see also* BroadBridge Media, L.L.C. v. Hypercd.com. 106 F. Supp. 2d 505 (S.D.N.Y. 2000).

[1220] Sporty's Farm LLC v. Sportsman's Market, 202 F.3d 489, 499 (2d Cir. 2000).

[1221] Harrods, Ltd. v. Sixty Internet Domain Names, 302 F.3d 214, 233–34 (4th Cir. 2002).

[1222] *See, e.g.*, Lucent Techs., Inc. v. Johnson, 56 U.S.P.Q.2d 1637 (C.D. Cal 2000).

[1223] *See, e.g.*, Coca-Cola Co. v. Purdy, 382 F.3d 774, 786–87 (8th Cir. 2004); Lucas Nursery & Landscaping, Inc. v. Grosse, 359 F.3d 806, 811 (6th Cir. 2004); TMI, Inc. v. Maxwell, 368 F.3d 433 (5th Cir. 2004); Mayflower Transit, LLC v. Prince, 314 F. Supp. 2d 362, 369–71 (D.N.J. 2004).

where the criticisms on a website are merely "a pretext disguising an underlying profit motive."[1224]

Under the ACPA's "safe harbor" provision, bad faith intent to profit may not be found where a defendant "believed and had reasonable grounds to believe that the use of the domain name was fair use or otherwise lawful."[1225] For example, a mere offer to sell a domain name, without more, does not necessarily establish bad faith intent.[1226] However, courts have held that a defendant "who acts even partially in bad faith in registering a domain name is not, as a matter of law, entitled to benefit from [the ACPA's] safe harbor provision."[1227]

[b] *In Rem* Jurisdiction

When a defendant is beyond the reach of a court's *in personam* jurisdiction, the ACPA permits the exercise of *in rem* jurisdiction over the domain name itself.[1228] Where the conditions for *in rem* jurisdiction are satisfied, the plaintiff may file the *in rem* action in the judicial district in which the domain name registrar, domain name registry, or other domain name authority that registered or assigned the domain name is located (which, for ".com" top-level domains, is the Northern District of California or the Eastern District of Virginia).[1229] *In rem* jurisdiction is authorized only if the court finds that the plaintiff (1) cannot obtain *in personam* jurisdiction over the party that is acting in violation of section 43(d); or (2) through due diligence was unable to find that person by (a) sending notice to the domain name registrant at the postal and e-mail addresses that the latter provided to the registrar and (b) by publishing notice of the action, as directed by the court, promptly after filing.[1230] Although several district courts have held that the publication requirement is mandatory even when the registrant receives actual notice,[1231] others have held that, upon a motion by the plaintiff, the court can waive the publication requirement if actual notice is established.[1232]

[1224] *Mayflower Transit*, 314 F. Supp. 2d at 372 (quoting S. Rep. No. 106-140, at 9); *see, e.g.*, Toronto-Dominion Bank v. Karpachev, 188 F. Supp. 2d 110, 111–14 (D. Mass. 2002); *Lucas Nursery*, 359 F.3d at 810–11; Shields v. Zuccarini, 254 F.3d 476, 485 (3d Cir. 2001); *cf.* People for the Ethical Treatment of Animals v. Doughney, 263 F.3d 359, 369 (4th Cir. 2001) ("PETA").

[1225] 15 U.S.C. § 1125(d)(1)(B)(ii).

[1226] Virtual Works, Inc. v. Volkswagen of America, Inc., 238 F.3d 264, 270 (4th Cir. 2001) (citing H.R. Conf. Rep. No. 106-464, at 111 (1999)).

[1227] *Id.*; *accord*, *PETA*, 263 F.3d at 369.

[1228] *See, e.g.*, Porsche Cars N.A., Inc. v. Porsche.net, 302 F.3d 248 (4th Cir. 2002).

[1229] 15 U.S.C. § 1125(d)(2)(A). A domain name registrar "is one of several entities, for a given TLD, that is authorized by ICANN [Internet Corporation for Assigned Names and Numbers] to grant registration of domain names to registrants." FleetBoston Financial Corp. v. FleetBostonFinancial.com, 138 F. Supp. 2d 121, 123 n.2 (D. Mass. 2001). In contrast, a domain name registry "is the single official entity that maintains all official records regarding registrations in the TLD (top level domain)." *Id.* (internal citations and quotation marks omitted). There is one registry for each TLD, such as ".com," ".org," and ".edu." *See generally* Cable News Network, LP, LLLP v. CNNews.com, 162 F. Supp. 2d 484, 486 n.4 (E.D. Va. 2001), *aff'd in relevant part*, 56 Fed. Appx. 599 (4th Cir. 2003).

[1230] 15 U.S.C. § 1125(d)(2)(A).

[1231] *See, e.g.*, Investools, Inc. v. Investtools.com, 81 U.S.P.Q.2d 2019 (E.D. Va. 2006).

[1232] *See, e.g.*, Yahoo!, Inc. v. Yahooahtos.com, 82 U.S.P.Q.2d 1361 (E.D. Va. 2006).

Subsection (d)(2)(C) further provides that the "situs" of a domain name is the judicial district where either (i) the domain name authority that registered or assigned the domain name is located, or (ii) documents sufficient to establish control and authority regarding disposition of the registration and use of the domain name are deposited with the court.[1233] The relationship between subsections (d)(2)(A) (the jurisdictional provision) and (d)(2)(C) (the situs provision) is ambiguous, but courts have generally concluded that subsection (d)(2)(C) does not provide an alternative basis for *in rem* jurisdiction.[1234] To conclude otherwise, courts have noted, would render subsection (d)(2)(C)(i) superfluous,[1235] and treating (d)(2)(C)(ii) as an independent basis for *in rem* jurisdiction would violate the "minimum contacts" requirement of due process.[1236] It appears that a proper reading of the statute treats the question of the domain name's legal "situs" as separate from the question of jurisdiction. The registrar's act of depositing the appropriate documents with a court that *already* has jurisdiction establishes that the domain name's situs is in the judicial district that has jurisdiction, and this gives the court authority to exercise control over the domain name throughout the litigation, even if the location of the registrar or registry changes after the litigation commences.[1237]

The ACPA is ambiguous with respect to the substantive scope of the *in rem* cause of action. Initially, district courts disagreed on whether the *in rem* cause of action was available *only* in cases involving "bad faith intent to profit" under section 43(d)(1), or whether it could also be invoked against domain names that violated section 32, 43(a), or 43(c) even without a showing of bad faith.[1238] In 2002, the Fourth Circuit adopted the latter interpretation in *Harrods, Ltd. v. Sixty Internet Domain Names*,[1239] and treatise author Thomas McCarthy agrees with that analysis.[1240] Because most *in rem* actions are brought in the Fourth Circuit (where the ".com" registry is located), this probably settles the matter. Thus, where personal jurisdiction cannot be obtained over a defendant, plaintiffs may invoke the *in rem* cause of action against domain names in order to remedy trademark infringement, dilution, and unfair competition claims under the Lanham Act, as well as "bad faith intent to profit" claims.

[1233] 15 U.S.C. § 1125(d)(2)(C).

[1234] *See, e.g.*, Mattel, Inc. v. Barbie-Club.com, 310 F.3d 293, 299–301 (2d Cir. 2002); Ford Motor Co. v. Greatdomains.com, 177 F. Supp. 2d 656, 658–60 (E.D. Mich. 2001); FleetBoston Financial Corp. v. FleetBostonFinancial.com, 138 F. Supp. 2d 121, 124–29 (D. Mass. 2001); Cable News Network, LP, LLLP v. CNNews.com, 162 F. Supp. 2d 484, 489 n.15 (E.D. Va. 2001), *aff'd in relevant part*, 56 Fed. Appx. 599 (4th Cir. 2003).

[1235] *See, e.g., Cable News Network*, 162 F. Supp. 2d at 489 n. 15; *Ford Motor Co.*, 177 F. Supp. 2d at 659 n.4; *Mattel*, 310 F.3d at 301.

[1236] *Ford Motor Co.*, 177 F. Supp. 2d at 658–60; *FleetBoston Financial Corp.*, 138 F. Supp. 2d at 125.

[1237] *Mattel*, 310 F.3d at 303–06.

[1238] *Compare* V'soske, Inc. v. Vsoske.com, 2001 U.S. Dist. LEXIS 6675, *20 (S.D.N.Y. 2001) (bad faith required); Hartog & Co. v. swix.com, 136 F. Supp. 2d 531, 539 (E.D. Va. 2001) (similar); *and* Broadbridge Media, LLC v. Hypercd.com, 106 F. Supp. 2d 505, 511 (S.D.N.Y. 2000) (similar) *with* Jack in the Box, Inc. v. Jackinthebox.org, 143 F. Supp. 2d 590, 591 (E.D. Va. 2001) (*in rem* provision not limited to section 43(d) claims).

[1239] 302 F.3d 214, 228, 232 (4th Cir. 2002); *accord* Cable News Network, L.P. v. CNNews.com, 56 Fed. Appx. 599, 603 (4th Cir. 2003) (unpub.).

[1240] *See* McCarthy on Trademarks § 25:79 (4th ed. 2009).

Conversely, there is some uncertainty as to whether an *in rem* action can be predicated *solely* on the act of registering a domain name, regardless of whether the registrant has a bad intent to profit. Based on a difference in wording between the *in rem* and *in personam* provisions of the ACPA, one district court held that an *in rem* cause of action could be based on the act of registration alone.[1241] In that court's view, the mere act of registering another person's mark as a domain name was a "use in commerce" that was likely to cause confusion, mistake, or deception within the meaning of section 32(1) or section 43(a).[1242] Another district court disagreed, holding that *in rem* proceedings are limited to actions under section 43(d).[1243] The Fourth Circuit's ruling in *Harrods*, discussed above, did not resolve the question whether domain name registration, without more, is a sufficient basis for trademark owner to bring an *in rem* proceeding.

[c] Personal Names

With respect to unauthorized domain name registrations of personal names, both the civil action under section 43(d)(1)(A) and the *in rem* action under section 43(d)(2) apply to "a personal name which is protected as a mark" under section 43.[1244] With respect to personal names that lack sufficient secondary meaning to qualify as trademarks, however, the ACPA affords a narrower range of protection. In contrast to section 43(d)(1), which provides a cause of action whenever a trademark-protected personal name is used in a domain name with a "bad faith intent to profit," section 47 of the Lanham Act provides a cause of action for unauthorized use of a personal name (or a confusingly similar name) in a domain name *only* where the defendant has registered the domain name "with the specific intent to profit from such name by selling the domain name for financial gain."[1245]

In addition to these restrictions, one court has held that no liability arises under section 43(d) where a political figure's name is used as the domain name for a noncommercial website devoted to criticism of that person, because, *inter alia*, such use is protected by the First Amendment.[1246]

[d] ACPA Remedies

Where a violation of section 43(d) is established, the court may order the forfeiture or cancellation of the domain name, or may order that it be transferred to the owner of the mark.[1247] In an action under section 43(d)(2), these remedies are exclusive.[1248] In an action under section 43(d)(1), however, the full array of Lanham

---

[1241] Jack in the Box, Inc. v. Jackinthebox.org, 143 F. Supp. 2d 590, 591–92 (E.D. Va. 2001).

[1242] 143 F. Supp. 2d at 592; *see* § 5F[5] (discussing the "use in commerce" requirement for violations of sections 32, 43(a), and 43(c)).

[1243] Broadbridge Media, LLC v. Hypercd.com, 106 F. Supp. 2d 505, 511 (S.D.N.Y. 2000).

[1244] 15 U.S.C. § 1125(d)(1)(A).

[1245] 15 U.S.C. § 1129(1)(A); *see, e.g.*, Schmidheiny v. Weber, 285 F. Supp. 2d 613 (E.D. Pa. 2003).

[1246] Ficker v. Tuohy, 305 F. Supp. 2d 569, 572 (D. Md. 2004).

[1247] 15 U.S.C. § 1125(d)(1)(C).

[1248] 15 U.S.C. § 1125(d)(2)(D); *see* Harrods Ltd. v. Sixty Internet Domain Names, 302 F.3d 214, 232 (4th Cir. 2002).

Act remedies are available.[1249] In addition, section 35(d) permits a plaintiff bringing a claim under section 43(d)(1) to elect statutory damages in place of actual damages and profits; a court may award an amount of statutory damages between $1,000 and $100,000 per domain name, as the court considers just.[1250]

[2]   Alternative Forums for Domain Name Disputes

The ACPA does not preclude states from providing their own remedies for cybersquatting. However, the main mechanism for resolving domain name disputes outside of the Lanham Act is the Uniform Domain Name Dispute Resolution Policy (UDRP) of the Internet Corporation for the Assigned Names and Numbers (ICANN), a non-profit, non-governmental organization that administers the domain name registration system. The UDRP provisions, which have been incorporated into all domain name registration agreements since 1999, give trademark owners a non-judicial option for resolving domain name disputes quickly and inexpensively through non-binding arbitration. Remedies are limited to cancellation or transfer of the domain name registration. Trademark owners are not required to utilize the UDRP, and may pursue their legal claims in court instead of, or in addition to, initiating a UDRP proceeding.[1251]

To prevail under the UDRP, the complainant generally must establish (1) that the domain name is identical or confusingly similar to a trademark or service mark in which the complainant has rights (either through trademark registration or under common law), (2) that the domain name holder does not have legitimate interests in the domain name, and (3) that the domain name was registered and is being used in bad faith.[1252] The policy sets forth a non-exhaustive list of bad faith indicia.[1253] The domain name holder must respond by demonstrating a legitimate interest in the domain name. Proof of such a legitimate interest should include (1) whether the name used in the domain name is connected to the bona fide offering of goods or services; (2) whether the domain name holder is commonly known by the name used as a domain name; or (3) whether the domain name holder is making a legitimate noncommercial or a fair use of the domain name without intent to divert consumers or tarnish the trademark in question.[1254]

A party that is dissatisfied with the outcome of a UDRP proceeding may pursue a separate legal action in a court of competent jurisdiction. If the UDRP panel orders cancellation or transfer of the domain name registration, the domain name registrar will implement that decision within ten business days unless it receives official documentation (such as a copy of the complaint) indicating that the registrant has commenced legal action.

[1249] For a detailed discussion of Lanham Act remedies, see § 5K.

[1250] 15 U.S.C. § 1117(d).

[1251] BroadBridge Media, L.L.C. v. Hypercd.com, 106 F. Supp. 2d 505, 509 (S.D.N.Y. 2000).

[1252] UDRP, ¶ 4(a), available at http://www.icann.org/en/dndr/udrp/policy.htm.

[1253] *Id.* ¶ 4(b).

[1254] *Id.* ¶ 4(c).

§ 51 SECONDARY LIABILITY

Although the Lanham Act contains no statutory provisions for imposing liability on parties other than direct infringers, the courts have turned to the common law of torts in order to develop doctrines of contributory and vicarious liability that apply to claims involving registered trademarks as well as violations of section 43(a).

[1] Contributory Infringement

Even prior to the Lanham Act, the common law recognized contributory liability in the context of unfair competition when a party supplied goods to another knowing or intending that the latter would pass off the goods as those of a competitor.[1255] As discussed below, it is now well settled that contributory liability under section 32 or 43(a) of the Lanham Act arises when a defendant either: (1) actively induces another to infringe, or (2) continues to supply a product to a party that it knows or has reason to know is using the product in an infringing activity. More recently, the latter test has been extended to the provision of services.

In the leading case, *Inwood Laboratories v. Ives Laboratories*,[1256] a drug manufacturer continued to supply generic drugs to pharmacists who were allegedly mislabeling them with another maker's trademark. In determining whether the manufacturer/supplier could be held liable under section 32 for the infringing actions of the pharmacists, the Supreme Court held that:

> [I]f a manufacturer or distributor intentionally induces another to infringe a trademark, or if it continues to supply its product to one whom it knows or has reason to know is engaging in trademark infringement, the manufacturer or distributor is contributorily responsible for any harm done as a result of the deceit.[1257]

Both prongs of the *Inwood Labs* formulation have been extended beyond the manufacturer/supplier context.[1258] In the franchising context, for example, the Eleventh Circuit held that "under appropriate facts, contributory trademark infringement might be grounded upon a franchisor's bad faith refusal to exercise a clear contractual power to halt the infringing activities of its franchisees," but it refused to impose on franchisors an affirmative "duty to supervise with reasonable diligence."[1259] Similarly, the Seventh Circuit held that the operator of a flea market

---

[1255] *See* William R. Warner & Co. v. Eli Lilly & Co., 265 U.S. 526, 530–31 (1924); Smith, Kline & French Labs. v. Clark & Clark, 157 F.2d 725, 731 (3d Cir. 1946); F.W. Fitch Co. v. Camille, Inc., 106 F.2d 635, 640 (8th Cir. 1939); Coca-Cola Co. v. Gay-Ola Co., 200 F. 720, 722–23 (6th Cir. 1912); N.K. Fairbank Co. v. R.W. Bell Manuf'g. Co., 77 F. 869, 875, 877–78 (2d Cir. 1896); Hiram Walker & Sons v. Grubman, 224 F. 725, 733–34 (S.D.N.Y. 1915); Enoch Morgan's Sons Co. v. Whittier-Coburn Co., 118 F. 657, 661–62 (N.D. Cal. 1902); Hostetter Co. v. Brueggeman-Reinert Distilling Co., 46 F. 188, 189 (E.D. Mo. 1891); Robert Reis & Co. v. Herman B. Reiss, Inc., 63 N.Y.S.2d 786, 798–803 (N.Y. Sup. Ct. 1946) (collecting cases).

[1256] 456 U.S. 844 (1982).

[1257] *Id.* at 854–55.

[1258] *See* Procter & Gamble Co. v. Haugen, 317 F.3d 1121, 1129–30 (10th Cir. 2003); AT&T v. Winback & Conserve Program, 42 F.3d 1421, 1432 (3d Cir. 1994).

[1259] Mini Maid Servs. Co. v. Maid Brigade Sys., Inc., 967 F.2d 1516, 1519–22 (11th Cir. 1992).

could be contributorily liable for violations of sections 32 and 43(a) by one of its vendors,[1260] under the common law rule that a company "is responsible for the torts of those it permits on its premises 'knowing or having reason to know that the other is acting or will act tortiously.' "[1261] Absent proof that the flea-market operator had actual knowledge of the infringements, the court held that contributory liability could be imposed if the operator was "willfully blind" to the infringing activities, because "willful blindness is equivalent to actual knowledge for purposes of the Lanham Act."[1262] To be willfully blind, "a person must suspect wrongdoing and deliberately fail to investigate."[1263] Thus, the flea-market operator had "no affirmative duty to take precautions against the sale of counterfeits."[1264] The Seventh Circuit's expansion of *Inwood Labs* to flea-market operators was later adopted by the Ninth Circuit.[1265]

Several courts have examined the application of *Inwood Labs* to Internet-related services. In *Lockheed Martin Corp. v. Network Solutions, Inc.*,[1266] the Ninth Circuit held that a domain name registrar could not be liable for contributory infringement simply because it registered, and refused to cancel, certain infringing domain names. The "supplying a product" aspect of the *Inwood Labs* test, in the court's view, would be satisfied only if the registrar directly controlled and monitored the infringing activities,[1267] as might be the case with an Internet service provider (ISP) whose storage or communication services involved infringing content.[1268] The court noted, however, that even an ISP "cannot be held liable merely for failing to monitor the information posted on their computers for tortious content."[1269] A few years later, the Ninth Circuit applied *Lockheed Martin* to hold that a web hosting service cannot be contributorily liable for the activities of its customers unless it has "reasonable means to withdraw services to the direct infringers."[1270]

In *Playboy Enterprises v. Netscape Communications Corp.*,[1271] the Ninth Circuit allowed Playboy Enterprises to proceed against service provider Netscape for trademark infringement and dilution, when the Netscape browser caused banner ads from Playboy's competitors to "pop up" when users conducted keyword searches on a Netscape search engine using Playboy's trademarks. While the Ninth Circuit held that triable issues of fact existed with respect to Netscape's liability,

---

[1260] Hard Rock Café Licensing Corp. v. Concession Servs., Inc., 955 F.2d 1143, 1149 (7th Cir. 1992).

[1261] *Id.* at 1149 (quoting RESTATEMENT (SECOND) OF TORTS § 877(c) & cmt. d (1979)).

[1262] *Hard Rock Café*, 955 F.2d at 1149.

[1263] *Id.*

[1264] *Id.* (citing RESTATEMENT (SECOND) OF TORTS § 12(1) & cmt. a (1965)).

[1265] Fonovisa, Inc. v. Cherry Auction, Inc., 76 F.3d 259, 265 (9th Cir. 1996).

[1266] 194 F.3d 980 (9th Cir. 1999).

[1267] *Id.* at 984–85 (citations omitted).

[1268] Lockheed Martin Corp. v. Network Solutions, Inc., 985 F. Supp. 949, 962 (C.D. Cal. 1997), *aff'd*, 194 F.3d 980 (9th Cir. 1989).

[1269] *Id.* at 962 n.7.

[1270] Louis Vuitton Malletier, S.A. v. Akanoc Solutions, Inc., 658 F.3d 936, 942 (9th Cir. 2011).

[1271] 354 F.3d 1020 (9th Cir. 2004).

either as a direct infringer or as a contributory infringer, the court declined to decide which theory of liability applied.

Two district courts have held that that the operator of a search engine can be liable for infringements by its advertisers. In *Government Employees Insurance Co. v. Google, Inc.* ("*GEICO*"), the court held that Google could be liable under a theory of contributory or vicarious liability — the court did not specify which — for the actions of advertisers that used the plaintiff's trademarks in their banner ads in a way that was likely to confuse consumers.[1272] The court based its conclusion on the fact that Google "exercise[d] significant control over the content of advertisements that appear on their search results pages," because it monitored and controlled the third-party advertisements.[1273] In *Google, Inc. v. American Blind & Wallpaper Factory, Inc.*,[1274] the court applied *Netscape* and *GEICO* to hold that Google could be contributorily liable for infringement arising from its keyword-triggered advertising program. Google encouraged its advertisers to "purchase" trademarked keywords that, when entered into a search engine, would generate "sponsored links" to the advertisers' websites, and Google received a payment each time a user clicked on a sponsored link.

In *Perfect 10, Inc. v. Visa Int'l Serv. Ass'n*,[1275] the Ninth Circuit considered a contributory infringement claim against credit-card companies that processed payments for customers who made purchases from websites that infringed the plaintiff's mark. Because there was no indication that the defendants intentionally induced the websites' infringing activities, the court applied the *Lockheed Martin* version of *Inwood Labs*: "When the alleged direct infringer supplies a service rather than a product, under the second prong of this test, the court must 'consider the extent of control exercised by the defendant over the third party's means of infringement.' For liability to attach, there must be '[d]irect control and monitoring of the instrumentality used by a third party to infringe the plaintiff's mark.'"[1276] Since the payment network was not the instrument that was used to infringe the plaintiff's mark, the infringement "occur[red] without any involvement of Defendants and their payment systems."[1277] Although the defendants might have the power to stop processing payments to the websites, which could then have the practical effect of stopping or reducing the infringing activity, the court held that "[t]his, without more, does not constitute 'direct control.'"[1278]

In *Tiffany, Inc. v. eBay, Inc.*,[1279] the Second Circuit considered whether Internet auction site eBay was contributorily liable for sales of counterfeit Tiffany goods by merchants using its website. Tiffany did not allege inducement; thus, the contribu-

---

[1272] 330 F. Supp. 2d 700, 704 (E.D. Va. 2004).

[1273] *Id.* at 705 (citing Size v. Network Solutions. Inc., 255 F. Supp. 2d 568, 573 (E.D. Va. 2003); Lockheed Martin Corp. v. Network Solutions, Inc., 194 F.3d 980 (9th Cir. 1999)).

[1274] 74 U.S.P.Q.2d 1385 (N.D. Cal. 2005) (unpub.).

[1275] 494 F.3d 788 (9th Cir. 2007).

[1276] *Id.* at 807 (quoting *Lockheed Martin*, 194 F.3d at 984).

[1277] *Id.*

[1278] *Id.*

[1279] 600 F.3d 93 (2d Cir. 2010).

tory liability question turned on whether eBay continued to supply its services to vendors that it knew or had reason to know were infringing. Although eBay promptly removed, without question, any listings that Tiffany identified as infringing, Tiffany argued that eBay was required to monitor its website and to preemptively remove any listings that *might* be infringing based on its generalized knowledge that infringing activities were taking place. Tiffany had notified eBay that there were no authorized third-party vendors for Tiffany merchandise and, therefore, that any vendor offering five or more Tiffany items was almost certainly selling counterfeit goods; in Tiffany's view, this imposed on eBay an affirmative duty to monitor its website and remove listings from merchants offering multiple Tiffany items, even without having specific knowledge that the items were counterfeit. The Second Circuit disagreed, applying *Inwood Labs*:

> For contributory trademark infringement liability to lie, a service provider must have more than a general knowledge or reason to know that its service is being used to sell counterfeit goods. Some contemporary knowledge of which particular listings are infringing or will infringe in the future is necessary.[1280]

The court noted, however, that eBay might be contributorily liable if it chose to be "willfully blind" to infringing activities by its vendors.[1281]

Courts and commentators have only recently begun to explore the concept of contributory liability for dilution.[1282] Although several cases have discussed the possibility of contributory dilution,[1283] only two district courts have actually recognized this cause of action.[1284]

While several district courts have recognized the possibility of contributory liability for cybersquatting under the ACPA,[1285] the Ninth Circuit has expressly rejected the concept.[1286]

[1280] *Id.* at 107.

[1281] *Id.* at 109.

[1282] *See, e.g.*, John T. Cross, *Contributory and Vicarious Liability for Trademark Dilution*, 80 OR. L. REV. 625 (2001).

[1283] *Lockheed Martin*, 194 F.3d at 986; Tiffany, Inc. v. eBay, Inc., 576 F. Supp. 2d 463, 526 (S.D.N.Y. 2008), *aff'd on other grounds*, 600 F.3d 93, 112 (2d Cir. 2010) (declining to reach the issue); Medline Indus., Inc. v. Strategic Commercial Solutions, Inc., 553 F. Supp. 2d 979, 992 (N.D. Ill. 2008); Google, Inc. v. American Blind & Wallpaper Factory, Inc., 74 U.S.P.Q.2d 1385, 1394 (N.D. Cal. 2005); Academy of Motion Picture Arts & Sciences v. Network Solutions, Inc., 989 F. Supp. 1276, 1278–81 (C.D. Cal. 1997).

[1284] Coach, Inc. v. Gata Corp., 2011 U.S. Dist. LEXIS 45093 (D.N.H. Apr. 26, 2011); Kegan v. Apple Computer Inc., 42 U.S.P.Q.2d 1053, 1062 (N.D. Ill. 1996).

[1285] Verizon Cal., Inc. v. Above.com Pty Ltd, 881 F. Supp. 2d 1173 (C.D. Cal. 2011); Microsoft Corp. v. Shah, 2011 U.S. Dist. LEXIS 2995 (W.D. Wash. Jan. 12, 2011); Solid Host, NL v. Namecheap, Inc., 652 F. Supp. 2d 1092 (C.D. Cal. 2009); Ford Motor Co. v. Greatdomains.com, Inc., 177 F. Supp. 2d 635 (E.D. Mich. 2011) (limiting the doctrine to "exceptional circumstances").

[1286] Petroliam Nasional Berhad v. GoDaddy.com, 737 F.3d 546 (9th Cir. 2013).

[2]   Vicarious Liability

Because courts generally apply common-law principles of agency in determining whether, and under what circumstances, to impose vicarious liability under state trademark law and the Lanham Act,[1287] the concept of vicarious liability in trademark law is narrower than the corresponding concept in federal copyright law.[1288]

Where an infringement action concerns common-law trademarks under section 43(a), some courts have expressed uncertainty on the question of whether the pertinent agency principles are governed by federal common law or by the common law of the state where the infringing conduct took place.[1289] Where the action involves federally registered marks under section 32, however, state-law principles would not appear to be relevant.

The seminal case on vicarious liability under the Lanham Act is *Hard Rock Café Licensing Corp. v. Concession Services, Inc.*, in which the Seventh Circuit considered whether to hold a flea-market operator vicariously liable for violations of section 32 and 43(a) by a vendor who operated a booth at the market. Applying common law, the court held that vicarious liability would apply only if the vendor and the flea-market operator was a joint tortfeasor — that is, only if "the defendant and the infringer have an apparent or actual partnership, have authority to bind one another in transactions with third parties or exercise joint ownership or control over the infringing product."[1290] Applying the same standard, a district court held that apparel maker Reebok was not vicariously liable for violations of sections 32 and 43(a) by third-party websites, absent evidence that Reebok either supplied the products offered on the websites or "authorized, licensed, permitted or encouraged the use of" its marks on the websites, nor was it liable for infringements by a basketball player's promotional company, even though Reebok had occasional business dealings with that company and an endorsement deal with the player.[1291]

In *Perfect 10, Inc. v. Visa Int'l Serv. Ass'n*, the Ninth Circuit rejected a vicarious liability claim against the credit-card companies that processed customers' payments for purchases made on websites that infringed the plaintiff's mark, because the payment processing services did not amount to a "symbiotic" relationship or a "joint ownership and control" relationship with the infringing websites; rather, the services merely provided a means to settle the customer's debt.[1292] Dissenting, Judge Kozinski argued that the relationship was symbiotic

---

[1287] AT&T v. Winback & Conserve Program, 42 F.3d 1421, 1433–34 (3d Cir. 1994).

[1288] Hard Rock Café Licensing Corp. v. Concession Servs., Inc., 955 F.2d 1143, 1150 (7th Cir. 1992).

[1289] *See AT&T*, 42 F.3d at 1435 n.16; W.T. Rogers Co., Inc. v. Keene, 778 F.2d 334 (7th Cir. 1985); Fare Deals, Ltd. v. World Choice Travel.com, Inc., 180 F. Supp. 2d 678, 684 n.2 (D. Md. 2001). In many cases, of course, the law will be the same. *See, e.g., AT&T*, 42 F.3d at 1435 n.16; *Fare Deals*, 180 F. Supp. 2d at 684 n.2; Procter & Gamble Co. v. Haugen, 317 F.3d 1121, 1127–28 (10th Cir. 2003).

[1290] 955 F.2d at 1150 (citation omitted); *accord, AT&T*, 42 F.3d at 1441 n.22; David Berg & Co. v. Gatto Int'l Trading Co., 884 F.2d 306, 311 (7th Cir. 1989).

[1291] SB Designs v. Reebok Int'l, Ltd., 338 F. Supp. 2d 904, 910–11 (N.D. Ill. 2004).

[1292] 494 F.3d 788, 808 (9th Cir. 2007).

because the actions of the credit-card companies bound the websites to deliver the content to purchasers.[1293]

Although vicarious liability has been difficult to establish, it is not impossible. One district court refused to dismiss a vicarious liability claim against Internet search engines that sold trademarks as keywords that triggered advertising ("sponsored links") by competitors of the trademark owner, finding that "joint ownership and control over the infringing product" could be established where the search engine and the advertisers controlled the appearance of the advertisements on the search results page and the use of the plaintiff's trademarks in those advertisements.[1294]

When a claim of vicarious liability is premised on a principal-agent relationship, courts look to the common law of agency to determine whether the direct infringer was acting as an agent for the defendant when it engaged in the infringing activities.[1295] Common-law agency principles are complex and multi-faceted, extending to situations involving both actual and apparent authority.[1296] As a result, agency determinations are highly fact-specific.

Although no court has yet imposed vicarious liability for trademark dilution, and only one court has considered such a claim,[1297] there would appear to be no legal barrier to imposing such liability where the common-law standard is satisfied.

§ 5J DEFENSES

The infringement defenses listed in section 33(b) with respect to incontestable marks[1298] are available for contestable marks as well.[1299] Unless otherwise indicated, the defenses discussed below apply to an action for infringement of any trademark or service mark, without regard to whether the mark is registered or, if registered, has become incontestable.

[1] Abandonment

Abandonment is both a defense to infringement of a mark and a ground for cancelling a federal registration.[1300] Common law has long recognized abandonment as a defense to trademark infringement. This rule derives from the basic principle that trademark rights arise from use.[1301] However, non-use does not, by itself, constitute abandonment; instead, common-law abandonment requires

---

[1293] *Id.* at 822–23 (Kozinski, J., dissenting).

[1294] Government Employees Insurance Co. v. Google, 330 F. Supp. 2d 700, 705 (E.D. Va. 2004).

[1295] *See, e.g.*, AT&T v. Winback & Conserve Program, 42 F.3d 1421, 1434–40 (3d Cir. 1994) (collecting authorities).

[1296] *See, e.g., id.*; 1-800 Contacts, Inc. v. Lens.com, Inc., 722 F.3d 1229, 1250–52 (10th Cir. 2013).

[1297] *See* Fare Deals, Ltd. v. World Choice Travel.com, Inc., 180 F. Supp. 2d 678, 685–86 (D. Md. 2001).

[1298] 15 U.S.C. § 1115(b); *see* § 5E[5] (discussing the effect of incontestability).

[1299] Matador Motor Inns, Inc. v. Matador Motel, Inc., 376 F. Supp. 385, 388 (D.N.J. 1974).

[1300] 15 U.S.C. §§ 1115(b)(2), 1064(3).

[1301] United Drug Co. v. Theodore Rectanus Co., 248 U.S. 90, 97 (1918).

that the cessation of use be coupled with an intent not to resume use.[1302]

Abandonment may be raised as an affirmative defense to infringement, or as a ground for cancelling a mark's registration, even after the party that abandoned the mark has resumed use of the mark in commerce.[1303] This is because the mark, once abandoned, loses its trademark status and enters the public domain, at which point it becomes available for adoption by any party, including, but not limited to, its previous owner.[1304] A right of priority in a previously abandoned mark will therefore belong to whichever party, if any, first establishes trademark rights through use of the mark on goods or services after the abandonment takes place.[1305] Thus, where a trademark owner abandons a mark and then wishes to resume use of the mark at a later date, an intervening use by another party may give the latter a right of priority in the mark, enabling it to enjoin the original owner's resumption of use or cancel the original owner's registration.[1306] If the abandonment leads to cancellation of the existing registration, then even if the original owner resumes use before another party establishes priority in the mark, the original owner's rights will be limited to those arising from use of an unregistered mark; once registration has been cancelled due to abandonment, the mark must be registered anew to enjoy the benefits of registration.[1307]

Courts disagree on the standard of proof that applies to the abandonment defense. Some courts require "clear and convincing evidence" of abandonment,[1308] while others require only a "preponderance of the evidence."[1309] Still others have been less precise, asserting that the proponent of the defense bears a "stringent," "heavy," or "strict" burden of proof.[1310]

The concept of abandonment under federal trademark law is derived from the common-law rule. Under section 45 of the Lanham Act, a mark is deemed abandoned under either of two circumstances: (1) when its bona fide use in the ordinary course of trade has been discontinued with intent not to resume such use, or (2) when the conduct of the mark's owner, including acts of commission or omission, causes the mark to become generic.[1311] These rules, discussed below,

---

[1302] Beech-Nut Co. v. Lorillard Co., 273 U.S. 629, 633 (1926); Baglin v. Cusenier Co., 221 U.S. 580, 598 (1910).

[1303] *See, e.g.,* Ambrit, Inc. v. Kraft, Inc., 812 F.2d 1531, 1551 (11th Cir. 1986) (collecting cases).

[1304] Major League Baseball Properties, Inc. v. Sed Non Olet Denarius, Ltd., 817 F. Supp. 1103, 1132–33 (S.D.N.Y. 1993), *vacated pursuant to settlement,* 859 F. Supp. 80 (S.D.N.Y. 1994).

[1305] *Id.*

[1306] *Id.*; Conwood Corp. v. Loew's Theatres, Inc., 173 U.S.P.Q. 829, 830 (T.T.A.B. 1972).

[1307] *Ambrit,* 812 F.2d at 1551 n.114.

[1308] *See, e.g.,* Saratoga Vichy Spring Co., Inc. v. Lehman, 625 F.2d 1037, 1044 (2d Cir. 1980).

[1309] *See, e.g.,* West Florida Seafood, Inc. v. Jet Restaurants, Inc., 31 F.3d 1122, 1124 (Fed. Cir. 1994).

[1310] *See, e.g.,* Grocery Outlet, Inc. v. Albertson's, Inc., 497 F.3d 949 (9th Cir. 2007); Cumulus Media, Inc. v. Clear Channel Communs., Inc., 304 F.3d 1167, 1175 & n.12 (11th Cir. 2002); Moore Business Forms, Inc. v. Ryu, 960 F.2d 486 (5th Cir. 1992); Conagra, Inc. v. Singleton, 743 F.2d 1508, 1516 (11th Cir. 1984); Citibank, N.A. v. Citibanc Group, Inc., 724 F.2d 1540, 1545 (11th Cir. 1984); Lipton Indus., Inc. v. Ralston Purina Co., 670 F.2d 1024, 1031 (C.C.P.A. 1982).

[1311] 15 U.S.C. § 1127 (defining "abandonment").

apply to both registered and unregistered marks.[1312]

[a]   Cessation of Use

Abandonment under subsection (1) of the Lanham Act definition may occur either through express abandonment, such as the owner's cancellation of the mark, or through cessation of use with intent not to resume use.[1313]

Intent not to resume use of a mark may be inferred from circumstances; and nonuse for three (formerly two) consecutive years constitutes *prima facie* evidence that the mark has been abandoned.[1314] Where the *prima facie* case of abandonment based on three years of nonuse cannot be established, the party challenging a trademark must show that the trademark owner is not using the mark and has no intention to resume its use in the reasonably foreseeable future.[1315] Where a mark is used legitimately and in a nondeceptive manner by a related company, such use will inure to the benefit of the trademark owner under section 5 of the Lanham Act,[1316] and will defeat a claim of abandonment due to nonuse.[1317]

The federal courts appear to have reached a general consensus that a *prima facie* showing of abandonment under the three-year rule does not shift the ultimate burden of persuasion to the trademark owner, but merely the burden of production.[1318] Thus, the trademark owner need only produce some evidence to rebut the *prima facie* case of abandonment — such as evidence of intent to resume use — and the challenger still bears the burden of proving that abandonment occurred.[1319]

To rebut a *prima facie* case of abandonment based on cessation of use, the trademark owner must demonstrate that there were reasonable grounds for suspending use of the mark,[1320] and must produce evidence of an intent to resume use of the mark "within the reasonably foreseeable future."[1321] A bare assertion of

---

[1312] Sweetheart Plastics, Inc. v. Detroit Forming, Inc., 743 F.2d 1039, 1047 n.4 (4th Cir. 1984).

[1313] Sands, Taylor & Wood Co. v. Quaker Oats Co., 978 F.2d 947 (7th Cir. 1992); Defiance Button Mach. Co. v. C&C Metal Prods. Corp., 759 F.2d 1053, 1059 (2d Cir. 1985); Major League Baseball Properties, Inc. v. Sed Non Olet Denarius, Ltd., 817 F. Supp. 1103 (S.D.N.Y. 1993), *vacated pursuant to settlement*, 859 F. Supp. 80 (S.D.N.Y. 1994).

[1314] 15 U.S.C. § 1127.

[1315] Stetson v. Howard D. Wolf & Assocs., 955 F.2d 847, 850 (2d Cir. 1992).

[1316] 15 U.S.C. § 1055.

[1317] Turner v. HMH Pub. Co., 380 F.2d 224 (5th Cir. 1967); Alligator Co. v. Robert Bruce, Inc., 176 F. Supp. 377 (E.D. Pa. 1953).

[1318] *See* Cumulus Media, Inc. v. Clear Channel Communs., Inc., 304 F.3d 1167, 1177 (11th Cir. 2002); Emergency One, Inc. v. American FireEagle, Ltd., 228 F.3d 531, 536 (4th Cir. 2000); Cerveceria Centroamericana, S.A. v. Cerveceria India, Inc., 892 F.2d 1021, 1025 (Fed Cir. 1989); Silverman v. CBS Inc., 870 F.2d 40, 47 (2d Cir. 1989); Roulo v. Russ Berrie & Co., 886 F.2d 931, 938 (7th Cir. 1989); Star-Kist Foods, Inc. v. P.J. Rhodes & Co., 769 F.2d 1393, 1396 (9th Cir. 1985); Exxon Corp. v. Humble Exploration Co., 695 F.2d 96, 99 (5th Cir. 1983); Saratoga Vichy Spring Co. v. Lehman, 625 F.2d 1037, 1043–44 (2d Cir. 1980); Sterling Brewers, Inc. v. Schenley Industries, Inc., 441 F.2d 675, 679 (C.C.P.A. 1971); Societe de Developments et D'Innovations des Marches Agricoles et Alimentaires-SODIMA-Union de Cooperatives Agricoles v. International Yogurt Co., 662 F. Supp. 839, 844–45 (D. Or. 1987) (collecting cases).

[1319] *Societe de Developments et D'Innovations*, 662 F. Supp. at 845.

[1320] Silverman v. CBS, 870 F.2d 40, 47 (2d Cir. 1989).

[1321] *Emergency One*, 228 F.3d at 537; *Silverman*, 870 F.2d at 46–47; *see also* ITC Ltd. v. Punchgini,

possible future use is insufficient, and the trademark owner must produce more than conclusory testimony or affidavits of intent.[1322] There is no hard-and-fast rule as to what constitutes "the reasonably foreseeable future," and courts have held that this determination "will vary depending on the industry and the particular circumstances of the case."[1323]

Mere token or sporadic use is insufficient to overcome a showing of abandonment due to nonuse.[1324] Moreover, once a mark has been abandoned, subsequent commercial use cannot retroactively cure the abandonment.[1325]

In appropriate cases, the concept of trademark tacking[1326] may be invoked to overcome a defense of abandonment.[1327] Thus, if the trademark owner makes only minor changes to a mark that do not change its overall commercial impression, the altered version of the mark will be treated as a continuing use of the earlier mark.[1328]

[b] Other Causes of Abandonment

Abandonment under subsection (2) of the federal definition arises from acts of commission or omission by the trademark owner that cause the mark to become generic or otherwise to lose its significance as a mark.[1329] Mere failure to pursue infringers does not, by itself, constitute abandonment of a mark. Such unauthorized uses can lead to a weakening of the strength of the mark, however, and this weakening can, in turn, cause the mark to become generic; genericism, whatever its cause, will lead to a finding of abandonment under subsection (2), because the mark will have lost its significance as an origin indicator.[1330]

Abandonment will also be found under section (2) when a mark loses its significance as an indicator of goods or services through (a) unrestricted ("naked") licensing, (b) assignment of the mark without an accompanying assignment of the

---

Inc., 482 F.3d 135, 149 n.9 (2d Cir. 2007) (intent to resume use must exist during the 3-year period of non-use); Imperial Tobacco, Ltd. v. Philip Morris, Inc., 899 F.2d 1575, 1580–81 (Fed. Cir. 1990) (similar).

[1322] *Silverman*, 870 F.2d at 47; *Imperial Tobacco*, 899 F.2d at 1581; Rivard v. Linville, 133 F.3d 1446, 1449 (Fed. Cir. 1998); Hughes v. Design Look, Inc., 693 F. Supp. 1500, 1506 (S.D.N.Y. 1988) (citation omitted).

[1323] *Emergency One*, 228 F.3d at 537; *accord*, Defiance Button Mach. Co. v. C & C Metal Prods. Corp., 759 F.2d 1053, 1060–62 (2d Cir. 1985).

[1324] *See, e.g.*, Pilates, Inc. v. Current Concepts, Inc., 120 F. Supp. 2d 286, 307–10 (S.D.N.Y. 2000); *accord*, Kusek v. Family Circle, Inc., 894 F. Supp. 522 (D. Mass. 1995); Hughes v. Design Look Inc., 693 F. Supp. 1500, 1506 (S.D.N.Y. 1988).

[1325] Societe de Developments et D'Innovations des Marches Agricoles et Alimentaires-SODIMA-Union de Cooperatives Agricoles v. International Yogurt Co., 662 F. Supp. 839, 851 (D. Or. 1987).

[1326] For a general discussion of tacking, see § 5F[2].

[1327] Sands, Taylor & Wood Co. v. Quaker Oats Co., 978 F.2d 947, 955 (7th Cir. 1992); Children's Legal Services PLLC v. Kresch, 87 U.S.P.Q.2d 1765 (E.D. Mich. 2008); Paris Glove of Canada Ltd. v. SBC/Sporto Corp., 84 U.S.P.Q.2d 1856 (T.T.A.B. 2007).

[1328] Miyano Mach. USA, Inc. v. Miyanohitec Mach., Inc., 576 F. Supp. 2d 868, 882 (N.D. Ill. 2008).

[1329] 15 U.S.C. § 1127.

[1330] *See* Exxon Corp. v. Oxxford Clothes, Inc., 109 F.3d 1070, 1080 (5th Cir. 1997); Sweetheart Plastics, Inc. v. Detroit Forming, Inc., 743 F.2d 1039, 1047–48 (4th Cir. 1984); *see generally* § 5C[2][a][iv] (discussing genericism).

goodwill that is associated with it ("assignment in gross"), or (c) any circumstance that causes the mark to become generic.[1331]

[i]   Naked Licensing

Naked licensing occurs "when a trademark owner fails to exercise reasonable control over the use of a mark by a licensee," so that "the presence of the mark on the licensee's goods or services misrepresents their connection with the trademark owner since the mark no longer identifies goods or services that are under the control of the owner of the mark," and the mark can no longer provide "a meaningful assurance of quality."[1332] The underlying policy concern is that "if a trademark owner allows licensees to depart from his quality standards, the public will be misled, and the trademark will cease to have utility as an informational device."[1333]

A minority of courts have held that, to defeat a naked licensing defense, the licensor must have contractually reserved the right to control the licensee's use of the mark.[1334] Under the majority view, however, the crucial question is whether the licensor in fact exercised such control; the contractual reservation of a right to control is neither necessary nor sufficient.[1335] While there are no clear-cut rules for determining whether the licensor has exercised sufficient quality control, courts have considered the actual quality of the goods produced, the existence or absence of consumer complaints about quality, and the extent to which the licensor actually inspected the goods or the facilities where they were produced.[1336] In appropriate circumstances, such as where there is a close working relationship between the parties, or where the licensor is familiar with the quality control practices of the licensee, it may be reasonable for the licensor to rely on the quality control measures of the licensee.[1337]

[1331] Defiance Button Mach. Co. v. C & C Metal Prods. Corp., 759 F.2d 1053, 1059 (2d Cir. 1985).

[1332] Tumblebus, Inc. v. Cranmer, 399 F.3d 754, 764 (6th Cir. 2005) (quoting RESTATEMENT (THIRD) OF UNFAIR COMPETITION § 33 cmt. b (1995)). Some courts cite section 5 of the Lanham Act, 15 U.S.C. § 1055, often together with the statutory definition of abandonment, as the statutory basis for the naked licensing defense under the Lanham Act. See Exxon Corp. v. Oxxford Clothes, Inc., 109 F.3d 1070, 1079 n.12 (5th Cir. 1997). In the case of certification marks, the general principle that naked licensing is grounds for canceling a federal registration is expressly incorporated in section 14(5)(A) of the Lanham Act, 15 U.S.C. § 1064(5)(A).

[1333] Exxon, 109 F.3d at 1079 (quoting Kentucky Fried Chicken Corp. v. Diversified Packaging Corp., 549 F.2d 368, 387 (5th Cir. 1977)); accord, Dawn Donut Co. v. Hart's Food Stores, Inc., 267 F.2d 358, 367 (2d Cir. 1959) (citing S. Rep. No. 79-1333 (1946)).

[1334] See, e.g., E. I. Du Pont de Nemours & Co. v. Celanese Corp. of America, 167 F.2d 484 (C.C.P.A. 1948); Robinson Co. v. Plastics Res. & Dev. Corp., 264 F. Supp. 852 (W.D. Ark. 1967).

[1335] See, e.g., Barcamerica Int'l USA Trust v. Tyfield Imps., Inc., 289 F.3d 589, 596–97 (9th Cir. 2002); Dawn Donut Co. v. Hart's Food Stores, Inc., 267 F.2d 358 (2d Cir. 1959); Carl Zeiss Stiftung v. V.E.B. Carl Zeiss, Jena, 293 F. Supp. 892 (S.D.N.Y. 1968), supp. op. at 298 F. Supp. 1309 (S.D.N.Y. 1969), mod., 433 F.2d 686 (2d Cir. 1970).

[1336] See, e.g., Exxon, 109 F.3d at 1077; Carl Zeiss Stiftung, 293 F. Supp. at 918.

[1337] See, e.g., Barcamerica Int'l USA Trust v. Tyfield Imps., Inc., 289 F.3d 589, 596–97 (9th Cir. 2002); Transgo, Inc. v. Ajac Transmission Parts Corp., 768 F.2d 1001, 1017–18 (9th Cir. 1985); Taco Cabana Int'l, Inc. v. Two Pesos, Inc., 932 F.2d 1113, 1121 (5th Cir. 1991), aff'd, 505 U.S. 763 (1992); Taffy Original Designs, Inc. v. Taffy's Inc., 161 U.S.P.Q. 707, 713 (N.D. Ill. 1966).

A naked license must be distinguished from a consent-to-use agreement, which "is not an attempt to transfer or license the use of a trademark . . . but fixes and defines the existing trademark of each [party] . . . [so] that confusion and infringement may be prevented."[1338] To avoid being recharacterized as a naked license, a consent-to-use agreement must be "structured in such a way as to avoid misleading or confusing consumers as to the origin and/or nature of the respective parties' goods."[1339] In contrast, the permitted use under a licensing agreement is one that would be an infringing use but for the existence of the license; that is, it could mislead customers as to the origin or quality of the goods if the licensor did not exercise sufficient control over the licensee's use of the mark.[1340]

Courts have construed a wide variety of agreements and relationships entered into for a range of reasons, including the cessation or forbearance of litigation, as trademark licenses that are subject to the naked licensing defense.[1341] Whether a particular agreement constitutes a license is a question of fact that depends on the particular facts and circumstances of the case.[1342]

Just as rights in a mark may be established in one geographic market but not in others, a number of courts have recognized that a mark may be abandoned in fewer than all of the markets where it has been used.[1343] Thus, naked licensing in one territory may lead to a finding of abandonment in that territory but not in others.[1344]

[ii] Assignment in Gross

Under both common law and the Lanham Act, a mark is deemed to be abandoned when it is transferred separately from the goodwill that it represents — in other words, when it is the subject of an "assignment in gross."[1345] Because a trademark has no independent significance apart from its function as a symbol of

---

[1338] Exxon Corp. v. Oxxford Clothes, Inc., 109 F.3d 1070, 1076 (5th Cir. 1997) (quoting Waukesha Hygeia Mineral Springs Co. v. Hygeia Sparkling Distilled Water Co., 63 F. 438, 441 (7th Cir. 1894)).

[1339] Exxon, 109 F.3d at 1076.

[1340] Id.

[1341] Id. at 1078 n.9; see, e.g., E. & J. Gallo Winery v. Gallo Cattle Co., 967 F.2d 1280, 1289–1290 (9th Cir. 1992); Stock Pot Restaurant, Inc. v. Stockpot, Inc., 737 F.2d 1576, 1579–1580 (Fed. Cir. 1984); United States Jaycees v. Philadelphia Jaycees, 639 F.2d 134, 139 n.7 (3d Cir. 1980); Professional Golfers Ass'n v. Bankers L. & C. Co., 514 F.2d 665, 668–669 (5th Cir. 1975); Sheila's Shine Products, Inc. v. Sheila Shine, Inc., 486 F.2d 114, 123 (5th Cir. 1973); Express, Inc. v. Sears, Roebuck & Co., 840 F. Supp. 502, 509–510 (S.D. Ohio 1993); Engineered Mechanical Servs., Inc. v. Applied Mechanical Tech., Inc., 584 F. Supp. 1149, 1158–1159 (M.D. La. 1984); Universal City Studios, Inc. v. Nintendo Co., 578 F. Supp. 911, 929 (S.D.N.Y. 1983), aff'd, 746 F.2d 112 (2d Cir. 1984); Hodge Chile Co. v. KNA Food Distributors, Inc., 575 F. Supp. 210, 213 (E.D. Mo. 1983), aff'd, 741 F.2d 1086 (8th Cir. 1984); Acme Valve & Fittings Co. v. Wayne, 386 F. Supp. 1162, 1165–1166 (S.D. Tex. 1974); Naclox, Inc. v. Lee, 231 U.S.P.Q. 395, 399 (T.T.A.B. 1986).

[1342] Exxon, 109 F.3d at 1076–78.

[1343] See, e.g., Tumblebus, Inc. v. Cranmer, 399 F.3d 754, 765–66 (6th Cir. 2005); Sheila's Shine Prods., 486 F.2d at 124–25; E. F. Prichard Co. v. Consumers Brewing Co., 136 F.2d 512, 522 (6th Cir. 1943); RESTATEMENT (THIRD) OF UNFAIR COMPETITION § 30 cmt. a, § 33 cmt. b.

[1344] See, e.g., Sheila's Shine Prods., 486 F.2d at 123–24.

[1345] Sands, Taylor & Wood Co. v. Quaker Oats Co., 978 F.2d 947, 956 (7th Cir. 1992); Money Store v. Harriscorp Finance, Inc., 689 F.2d 666, 676 (7th Cir. 1982).

the goodwill associated with the goods or services to which it is attached, the mark cannot be sold or otherwise assigned apart from the business with which it is associated.[1346] Thus, a mark is assigned "in gross" when it is assigned "separately from the essential assets used to make the product or service that the trademark identifies," because in such a case "[t]he consumer would have no assurance that he was getting the same thing (more or less) in buying the product or service from its new maker."[1347]

An assignment of physical assets is not essential to a valid trademark assignment, as long as the assignment includes the goodwill of the business in connection with which the mark is used.[1348] However, where no physical assets are transferred, it can be difficult to determine whether the goodwill has been assigned.[1349] Although a trademark assignment agreement typically recites that the associated goodwill is being assigned, such a recitation is not sufficient; instead, courts will look at the reality of the transaction as a whole.[1350]

Goodwill has been defined as "the advantage obtained from use of a trademark," where the advantage arises from "public confidence in the quality of the product and in the warranties made on behalf of the product, and the 'name recognition' of the product that differentiates that product from others."[1351] Professor McCarthy describes goodwill as "a business value that reflects the basic human propensity to continue doing business with a seller who has offered goods and services that the customer likes and has found adequate to fulfill his needs."[1352]

An assignment of a mark unaccompanied by the associated physical assets will typically *not* be an assignment in gross if the assignee "is producing a product or providing a service which is substantially similar to that of the assignor and where consumers will not be deceived or harmed."[1353] In contrast, where the assignee uses the mark on a substantially different product or service, then the assignment is treated as an assignment in gross.[1354]

[1346] Dial-A-Mattress Operating Corp. v. Mattress Madness, Inc., 841 F. Supp. 1339, 1350 (E.D.N.Y. 1994); *see also* 15 U.S.C. § 1060(a); United Drug Co. v. Theodore Rectanus Co., 248 U.S. 90, 97 (1918).

[1347] Green River Bottling Co. v. Green River Corp., 997 F.2d 359, 362 (7th Cir. 1993).

[1348] *See, e.g.*, Sands, Taylor & Wood Co. v. Quaker Oats Co., 978 F.2d 947, 956 (7th Cir. 1992).

[1349] Money Store v. Harriscorp Finance, Inc., 689 F.2d 666, 676 (7th Cir. 1982).

[1350] *Money Store*, 689 F.2d at 676; Haymaker Sports, Inc. v. Turian, 581 F.2d 257 (C.C.P.A. 1978); Colonial Elec. & Plumbing Supply v. Colonial Elec., 2007 U.S. Dist. LEXIS 94417, *17 (D.N.J. Dec. 27, 2007).

[1351] Premier Dental Prods. Co. v. Darby Dental Supply Co., 794 F.2d 850, 853 n.3 (3d Cir. 1986).

[1352] McCarthy on Trademarks § 2.17.

[1353] *Colonial Elec.*, 2007 U.S. Dist. LEXIS 94417 at *16–*17; Pilates, Inc. v. Current Concepts, Inc., 120 F. Supp. 2d 286, 311 (S.D.N.Y. 2000); *accord* Defiance Button Machine Co. v. C & C Metal Prods. Corp., 759 F.2d 1053, 1059 (2d Cir. 1985); *see also* InterState Net Bank v. NetB@nk, Inc., 348 F. Supp. 2d 340 (D.N.J. 2004).

[1354] *See, e.g.*, Pepsico, Inc. v. Grapette Co., 416 F.2d 285, 289–90 (8th Cir. 1969).

[2] First Sale Doctrine

Under common law as well as the Lanham Act, the first sale doctrine permits a purchaser of lawfully trademarked goods to display, offer, and sell those goods under their original trademark.[1355] The rationale is that "when a retailer merely resells a genuine, unaltered good under the trademark of the producer, the use of the producer's trademark by the reseller will not deceive or confuse the public as to the nature, qualities, and origin of the good."[1356]

The first sale doctrine does not apply (1) when a reseller uses the mark in a manner that is likely to cause the public to believe that the reseller was part of the producer's authorized sales force or one of its franchisees,[1357] or (2) when the goods sold are materially different from those that the trademark owner has authorized for sale.[1358] Also, several courts have held that the doctrine does not apply to goods that have been repackaged if there is inadequate notice of the repackaging.[1359] Each of these exceptions is discussed below.

[a] Misrepresentation by Authorized Resellers

Under the first sale doctrine, the mere sale of a lawfully trademarked product by an unauthorized reseller does not, by itself, constitute trademark infringement or unfair competition.[1360] Even if purchasers mistakenly believe that the reseller is authorized by or affiliated with the trademark owner, this does not give rise to actionable misrepresentation if the reseller has done no more than stock, display, and resell the goods.[1361] However, if the reseller falsely represents to purchasers that the reseller is an authorized agent of the trademark holder, the first sale defense does not apply. For example, courts have imposed liability where a reseller's print advertising implied that the reseller was a franchisee of the trademark owner,[1362] and where a reseller used the maker's trademark at a trade show and in a trade journal ad, and stamped the reseller's name on the maker's promotional literature.[1363]

[1355] Tumblebus, Inc. v. Cranmer, 399 F.3d 754, 766–67 (6th Cir. 2005); Sebastian Int'l, Inc. v. Longs Drug Stores Corp., 53 F.3d 1073, 1076 (9th Cir. 1995); NEC Electronics v. CAL Circuit Abco, 810 F.2d 1506, 1509 (9th Cir. 1987); see also PACCAR Inc. v. TeleScan Techs., L.L.C., 319 F.3d 243, 257 (6th Cir. 2003); Restatement (Third) of Unfair Competition § 24 cmt. b (1995).

[1356] Tumblebus, 399 F.3d at 766; see also NEC Electronics, 810 F.2d at 1509; Restatement (Third) of Unfair Competition § 24 cmt. b.

[1357] PACCAR, 319 F.3d at 257. Cf. H.L. Hayden Co. of New York, Inc. v. Siemens Med. Sys., Inc., 879 F.2d 1005, 1023–24 (2d Cir. 1989).

[1358] Brilliance Audio Inc. v. Haights Cross Commun., Inc., 474 F.3d 365, 369 (6th Cir. 2007).

[1359] Prestonettes, Inc. v. Coty, 264 U.S. 359, 368–69 (1924); Brilliance Audio, 474 F.3d at 369; Enesco Corp. v. Price/Costco Inc., 146 F.3d 1083, 1085–86 (9th Cir. 1998).

[1360] Matrix Essentials v. Emporium Drug Mart, 988 F.2d 587, 593 (5th Cir. 1993); H.L. Hayden Co. v. Siemens Medical Sys., 879 F.2d 1005, 1023 (2d Cir. 1989); NEC Electronics v. CAL Circuit Abco, 810 F.2d 1506, 1508–09 (9th Cir. 1987).

[1361] Sebastian Int'l v. Longs Drug Stores Corp., 53 F.3d 1073, 1076 (9th Cir. 1995).

[1362] Bandag, Inc. v. Al Bolser's Tire Stores, 750 F.2d 903, 911, 916 (Fed. Cir. 1984).

[1363] Stormor, a Div. of Fuqua Indus. v. Johnson, 587 F. Supp. 275, 279 (W.D. Mich. 1984).

[b]   Materially Different Goods

The first sale defense applies only when the reseller's goods are lawfully trademarked, or "genuine." As discussed below, the question whether goods are genuine may arise when the goods have been altered after their initial manufacture, or when, at some point in the chain of manufacturing and distribution, they have not been subjected to the quality control standards imposed by the trademark owner on its licensees.

[i]   Used, Altered, or Refurbished Goods

In the case of used, altered, or refurbished goods, courts generally examine the extent to which the goods differ from their new, unaltered, counterparts in order to determine whether the use of the original manufacturer's mark is infringing.[1364] Two unsettled issues are: (1) the type and degree of differences or alterations that can give rise to infringement, and (2) the question whether the same legal standards should apply to both used and new goods.

Champion Spark Plug Co. v. Sanders,[1365] the leading case on refurbished goods, involved the repair, reconditioning, and resale of used spark plugs under the original manufacturer's trademark. The district court issued an injunction requiring, *inter alia*, that the defendant remove the manufacturer's trademark and other identifying marks from the spark plugs, repaint them, stamp them prominently as "repaired," and print a legend on the package identifying the repair company by name and address.[1366] On appeal, the Second Circuit eliminated the requirement that the original manufacturer's trademark and other identifying marks be removed, and replaced the district court's precise legend with a more general one indicating that the plugs: (1) were used, and (2) had been reconditioned by the defendants.[1367] The Supreme Court upheld these modifications, holding that the sale of used or refurbished goods under their original trademark is not an infringement, even if the secondhand goods are inferior to their newly manufactured counterparts, provided that the seller does not misrepresent the goods as new, and has not made material alterations to the goods. While noting that "[c]ases may be imagined where the reconditioning or repair would be so extensive or so basic that it would be a misnomer to call the article by its original name, even though the words 'used' or 'repaired' were added," the Court held that, in the absence of such material change, "[f]ull disclosure gives the manufacturer all the protection to which he is entitled."[1368]

Several appellate courts have considered *Champion*'s observation that some

---

[1364] Davidoff & Cie, S.A. v. PLD Int'l Corp., 263 F.3d 1297 (11th Cir. 2001); Nitro Leisure Prods., LLC v. Acushnet Co., 341 F.3d 1356 (Fed. Cir. 2003); Champion Spark Plug Co. v. Sanders, 331 U.S. 125 (1947).

[1365] 331 U.S. 125 (1947).

[1366] *Id.* at 126–27.

[1367] *Id.* at 127–28.

[1368] 331 U.S. at 129–30. The Court in *Champion* relied in part on Prestonettes, Inc. v. Coty, 264 U.S. 359 (1924), which held that a reseller of trademarked perfume and face powder could rebottle the perfumes and combine the face powder with other ingredients, without removing the original trademarks, if the products were accurately labeled to indicate the changes made by the reseller.

alterations might be "so extensive or so basic that it would be a misnomer to call the article by its original name," even with full disclosure. In cases involving reconditioned Rolex and Bulova watches, the Fifth, Seventh, and Ninth Circuits held that the sale of such watches under their original trademarks creates a likelihood of confusion that cannot be negated by a disclosure that the original watches have been altered or that they contain some non-original components.[1369] In these cases, the defendant's alterations resulted in a "new product" that could not be sold under the original manufacturer's trademark.[1370]

In contrast to cases addressing the sale of used or refurbished goods, the Eleventh Circuit applied a "material differences" test to the resale of *new* goods in *Davidoff & Cie, S.A. v. PLD Int'l Corp.*,[1371] which held that etching the glass on a fragrance bottle in order to remove the original batch code degraded the appearance of the product, creating a "material difference," and therefore gave rise to a likelihood of confusion: "[T]he resale of a trademarked product that is materially different can constitute a trademark infringement . . . because materially different products that have the same trademark may confuse consumers and erode consumer goodwill toward the mark."[1372] A finding of material differences, it noted, can be based on differences in quality control or in the goods themselves. The court defined a material difference as "one that consumers consider relevant to a decision about whether to purchase a product," but noted that "the threshold of materiality must be kept low," and that any alteration "resulting in physical differences" should be considered material.[1373]

The Federal Circuit has suggested that *Davidoff*'s material differences standard should not apply to used or refurbished goods. In *Nitro Leisure Products, LLC v. Acushnet Co.*,[1374] the defendant reconditioned golf balls by removing and replacing the outer layers of paint, and reapplying the manufacturer's trademark. Prior to sale, the defendant marked the balls and their packaging with legends clearly indicating that the balls had been refurbished. The Federal Circuit held that, under *Champion*, the alterations to the balls were not so substantial as to create a likelihood of consumer confusion.[1375] Furthermore, because the case involved used

---

[1369] Rolex Watch, U.S.A., Inc. v. Michel Co., 179 F.3d 704 (9th Cir. 1999); Rolex Watch USA, Inc., v. Meece, 158 F.3d 816 (5th Cir. 1998); Bulova Watch Co. v. Allerton Co., 328 F.2d 20 (7th Cir. 1964).

[1370] *Michel*, 179 F.3d at 710.

[1371] 263 F.3d 1297 (11th Cir. 2001).

[1372] *Id.* at 1301–02.

[1373] *Id.* at 1302. The court's definition of a material difference is consistent with the standard adopted in five other circuits; many, though not all, of those cases involved "gray goods" imported without the consent of the trademark owner. *See, e.g.*, Enesco Corp. v. Price/Costco Inc., 146 F.3d 1083, 1087 (9th Cir. 1998); Iberia Foods Corp. v. Romeo, 150 F.3d 298, 302 (3d Cir. 1998); Martin's Herend Imports Inc. v. Diamond & Gem Trading USA, Co., 112 F.3d 1296, 1302 (5th Cir. 1997); Societe des Produits Nestle, S.A. v. Casa Helvetia, Inc., 982 F.2d 633, 644 (1st Cir. 1992); Original Appalachian Artworks, Inc. v. Granada Elecs., Inc., 816 F.2d 68, 73 (2d Cir. 1987); Graham Webb International Ltd. Partnership v. Emporium Drug Mart, Inc., 916 F. Supp. 909 (E.D. Ark. 1995); John Paul Mitchell Systems v. Pete-N-Larry's Inc., 862 F. Supp. 1020, 1027 (W.D.N.Y. 1994); John Paul Mitchell Systems v. Randall's Food Markets, Inc., 17 S.W.3d 721 (Tex. App. 2000).

[1374] 341 F.3d 1356 (Fed. Cir. 2003).

[1375] *Id.* at 1362.

goods rather than new, it was not strictly necessary to apply the "material differences" standard: "According to *Champion*, what is more telling on the question of likelihood of confusion in the context of used goods is whether the used or refurbished goods are so different from the original that it would be a misnomer for them to be designated by the original trademark."[1376] In this case, "the differences in the goods were nothing more than what would be expected for used golf balls."[1377]

In *Karl Storz Endoscopy-America, Inc. v. Surgical Technologies, Inc.*,[1378] which involved a contractor that provided repair services for endoscopes, the Ninth Circuit distinguished between normal repairs — in which a product is repaired and returned to its owner — and the defendant's repairs, which involved replacing every essential component of the device. The reconstructed product, which still bore the manufacturer's trademark, was "so altered as to be a different product," and the defendant's repair therefore constituted the functional equivalent of a sale, making it a "use in commerce."[1379] Even though the customer requesting the repair (a hospital, for example) might not be confused about the origin of the reconstructed endoscope, an actual user of the endoscope (such as a surgeon working at the hospital) who was unaware of the full extent of the repair might experience post-sale confusion, and might therefore blame the original manufacturer for any defects in the product.[1380] The court distinguished the right of property owners to repair or alter trademarked goods without incurring liability for trademark infringement, noting that when the repairs or alterations are done by an outside contractor, "the question is whether the trademarked product is so altered that the substance of the transaction is a sale, and it would be misleading to sell the product without noting the alterations."[1381] Merely cleaning, sterilizing, and resharpening medical instruments, for example, would not constitute trademark infringement.[1382]

Eschewing any bright-line test, the *Karl Storz* court suggested that a number of factors should be considered in determining whether the contractor "has made a different product":

> Those factors include the nature and extent of the alterations, the nature of the device and how it is designed (whether some components have a shorter useful life than the whole), whether a market has developed for service and spare parts, and, most importantly, whether end users of the product are likely to be misled as to the party responsible for the composition of the product.[1383]

[1376] *Id.* at 1362–63.

[1377] *Id.* at 1364.

[1378] 285 F.3d 848 (9th Cir. 2002).

[1379] *Id.* at 856.

[1380] *Id.* at 855–56.

[1381] *Id.* at 856.

[1382] *Id.* (citing U.S. Surgical Corp. v. Orris, Inc., 5 F. Supp. 2d 1201, 1209 (D. Kan. 1998)).

[1383] *Id.* at 856–57 (citations omitted).

The court relied in part on the factors that are used by the Federal Circuit to distinguish a permissible repair from an infringing reconstruction for purposes of federal patent law.[1384]

[ii]   Other Non-Genuine Goods

In some cases, an unauthorized reseller may be ineligible for the first sale defense because its merchandise has not been subjected to the quality control standards that the trademark owner imposes on its licensees, even if there is no evidence that the goods have in fact been altered since their initial manufacture. The failure of quality control may occur at any point in the manufacturing and distribution process. In these cases, courts have held that the first sale defense does not apply, because the goods are not "genuine." The rationale underlying these decisions is that the sale of such goods under the original trademark falsely implies to consumers that the goods have been subjected to the trademark owner's quality control standards from the point of manufacture to the point of sale. For example, a retailer was held to be selling nongenuine goods when it obtained and resold a batch of trademarked shoes that had never been subjected to the final quality control inspection at the factory.[1385]

In another case, Shell motor oil that was genuine when it left the refinery ceased to be genuine when a reseller purchased it and then transported it in containers that failed to meet Shell's cleanliness standards.[1386] Another court held that the Coors beer sold by a distributor was not genuine because the distributor failed to abide by Coors' standards for transporting and storing the product.[1387]

In contrast, it appears that some restrictions imposed by trademark owners on their licensed distributors may be ignored without affecting the "genuineness" of the merchandise. For example, where a retailer sold but did not install the plaintiff's trademarked dental equipment, the Second Circuit held that the equipment was still genuine, even though the plaintiff required its authorized distributors to install the equipment they sold. In the court's view, customers were not deceived if they understood that the product they purchased under the plaintiff's trademark included only the equipment and not the installation.[1388]

[c]   Undisclosed Repackaging

Several courts have recognized a "repackaging" exception to the first sale rule. Under this exception, a reseller can repackage lawfully trademarked goods only if the reseller adequately discloses to consumers that the goods have been repackaged by someone other than the trademark owner. This rule appears to be grounded in the concern that a reseller's repackaging may be inadequate or inappropriate. For example, the new packaging may provide inadequate damage protection, or may permit the product to deteriorate more quickly after purchase, leading consumers

---

[1384] *Id.* at 857 (citing Bottom Line Mgmt., Inc. v. Pan Man, Inc., 228 F.3d 1352, 1355–56 (Fed. Cir. 2000)).

[1385] El Greco Leather Prods. Co. v. Shoe World, Inc., 806 F.2d 392, 395–96 (2d Cir. 1986).

[1386] Shell Oil Co. v. Commercial Petroleum, Inc., 928 F.2d 104, 106–108 (4th Cir. 1991).

[1387] Adolph Coors Co. v. A. Genderson & Sons, Inc., 486 F. Supp. 131 (D. Colo. 1980).

[1388] H.L. Hayden Co. v. Siemens Med. Sys., Inc., 879 F.2d 1005, 1023 (2d Cir. 1989).

to blame their dissatisfaction on the trademark owner.[1389]

The repackaging exception is derived from the Supreme Court's decision in *Prestonettes, Inc. v. Coty*,[1390] in which the defendant repackaged Coty's powders and perfumes for resale. The plaintiff did not allege that the defendant had materially altered the products, although it implied that the new packaging might hasten their deterioration. The Court held that the defendant was permitted to identify the repackaged goods as Coty products provided that consumers were aware that the defendant was responsible for the repackaging.[1391]

In *Brilliance Audio, Inc. v. Haight Cross Communications, Inc.*,[1392] the Sixth Circuit considered an allegation of improper repackaging that did not necessarily affect the quality of the product. The plaintiff had packaged its audiobooks in two versions — library and retail editions. The defendant purchased the plaintiff's retail editions and repackaged them as library editions, which it then resold under the plaintiff's trademark. The plaintiff argued that this repackaging vitiated the first sale defense, because "the notice of repackaging is inadequate because it creates the misrepresentation that '[d]efendants have a long-standing relationship with Plaintiff and that the activities of Defendants are authorized and sponsored by Plaintiff' [and] . . . the inadequate packaging is likely to result in consumer confusion that will dilute the value of the trademark."[1393] Applying *Coty*, the Sixth Circuit held that, even though it was unclear whether the products themselves were materially different, the allegation of differences in "packaging and marketing" was sufficient to withstand a motion to dismiss.[1394]

[d] Parallel Imports

The problem of "gray market goods" represents a special application of the first sale rule. Gray market goods, also known as "parallel imports," are goods that bear a legitimate trademark, but that are manufactured outside the United States under a restricted trademark license that prohibits their importation into the United States. Because the use of the trademark on the licensed goods is authorized, the mark is not counterfeit. However, the question arises whether the subsequent importation of those goods infringes the rights of the domestic trademark owner. If it does, then the trademark owner may bring an action for trademark infringement, or may be able to invoke Customs laws to prevent the goods from entering the United States. Possible avenues of relief include sections 32, 42, 43(a), and 43(b) of the Lanham Act,[1395] as well as section 526 of the 1930 Tariff Act.[1396]

[1389] *See, e.g.*, Enesco Corp. v. Price/Costco, Inc., 146 F.3d 1083, 1085–86 (9th Cir. 1998).

[1390] 264 U.S. 359 (1924).

[1391] *Id.* at 369.

[1392] 474 F.3d 365 (6th Cir. 2007).

[1393] *Id.* at 371.

[1394] *Id.* at 370–71.

[1395] *See, e.g.*, R.J. Reynolds Tobacco Co. v. Premium Tobacco Stores, Inc., 52 U.S.P.Q.2d 1052 (N.D. Ill. 1999), *dismissed in part on other grounds*, 1999 U.S. Dist. LEXIS 19641 (N.D. Ill. Dec. 16, 1999); Societe Des Produits Nestle, S.A. v. Casa Helvetia, Inc., 982 F.2d 633 (1st Cir. 1992).

[1396] 19 U.S.C. § 1526. Under section 526(a) of the Tariff Act, it is "unlawful to import into the United States any merchandise of foreign manufacture if such merchandise . . . bears a trademark owned by

Under sections 32, 43(a), and 43(b),[1397] the plaintiff must establish that the importation of the gray market goods creates a likelihood of confusion, which generally requires a showing that the imported goods are "materially different" from the authorized goods.[1398] In the context of gray market goods, even "subtle differences" can be material.[1399]

Where courts have required a showing of "material differences" between the domestic goods and the imported goods, they have not required the plaintiff to establish that the gray market goods are inferior in quality; it is sufficient that the goods are different.[1400] Furthermore, courts have not limited their analysis to physical differences; "differences in . . . warranty protection or service commitments . . . may well render products non-identical in the relevant Lanham Act sense."[1401] For example, in *Original Appalachian Artworks, Inc. v. Granada Electronics, Inc.*, the court upheld a finding of infringement where a defendant imported "Cabbage Patch" dolls that bore a lawful trademark (licensed from the plaintiff) but which were manufactured abroad under a license prohibiting their sale in the United States. The defendant's dolls were materially different from the plaintiff's because their "birth certificates," "adoption papers," and instructions were in Spanish, and domestic fulfillment houses were not always willing to process these "adoptions." This created consumer confusion over the source of the products, potentially injuring the plaintiff's domestic goodwill.[1402]

Even where the packaging of gray market goods clearly identifies their geographic origin, courts have held that actionable confusion regarding the source of materially different goods can still arise from the use of similar trademarks or trade dress.[1403]

---

a citizen of, or by a corporation or association created or organized within, the United States," if the trademark is properly registered, unless the owner of the registration provides written consent. Section 526(b) subjects such merchandise to seizure and forfeiture. Section 526(c) provides that any person dealing in such merchandise may be enjoined from doing so or may be required to export or destroy the merchandise or remove the trademark; and subjects the vendor to liability for the same damages and profits as in an action for trademark infringement.

[1397] Section 43(b) prohibits importation of goods that are marked in contravention of section 43, and provides that such goods shall not be admitted into the country by U.S. Customs. 15 U.S.C. § 1125(b); *see* United States v. Nippon Miniature Bearing Corp., 155 F. Supp. 2d 707 (C.I.T. 2001) (allowing Customs to exercise this authority without a court order, but subject to appeal).

[1398] *See, e.g., Societe des Produits Nestle*, 982 F.2d at 638; Shell Oil Co. v. Commercial Petroleum, Inc., 928 F.2d 104, 107 (4th Cir. 1991); Weil Ceramics & Glass, Inc. v. Dash, 878 F.2d 659, 668 (3d Cir. 1989); Lever Bros. Co. v. United States, 877 F.2d 101, 105–07 (D.C. Cir. 1989); NEC Elecs., Inc. v. Cal Circuit Abco, 810 F.2d 1506 (9th Cir. 1987); Olympus Corp. v. United States, 792 F.2d 315, 321 (2d Cir. 1986).

[1399] *Societe des Produits Nestle*, 982 F.2d at 641.

[1400] *Id.* at 640. For examples of material differences, see Martin's Herend Imports, Inc. v. Diamond and Gem Trading USA, Co., 112 F.3d 1296 (5th Cir. 1997); Lever Brothers Co. v. United States, 981 F.2d 1330 (D.C. Cir. 1993); *Societe Des Produits Nestle*, 982 F.2d at 641–44; Lever Brothers Co. v. United States, 877 F.2d 101 (D.C. Cir. 1989); and Philip Morris Inc. v. Allen Distributors, Inc., 48 F. Supp. 2d 844 (S.D. Ind. 1999).

[1401] *Societe des Produits Nestle*, 982 F.2d at 639 n.7.

[1402] 816 F.2d 68, 73 (2d Cir. 1987).

[1403] *See, e.g.*, Societe Des Produits Nestle, S.A. v. Casa Helvetia, Inc., 982 F.2d 633, 639 (1st Cir.

In applying the material differences test to gray market goods, the standard of materiality is low: "[A]ny difference between the registrant's product and the allegedly infringing gray good that consumers would likely consider to be relevant when purchasing a product creates a presumption of consumer confusion sufficient to support a Lanham Act claim."[1404] In addition, mere failure of the goods to meet the trademark owner's quality standards can constitute a material difference, even if this difference is not blatant enough to frustrate the expectations of the average consumer.[1405]

In the case of registered marks, the trademark owner also has the option of blocking their importation under section 42, which bars importation of goods that "copy or simulate" a registered trademark.[1406] Courts have held that even when imported goods bear non-counterfeit marks, they may be found to "copy or simulate" registered marks. Although section 42 does not expressly articulate a "likelihood of confusion" standard, courts appear to have reached a consensus that section 42 is violated only when there are material differences between the imported goods and the goods authorized for domestic distribution.[1407]

In contrast, under section 526 of the Tariff Act,[1408] if a United States person owns a trademark that is registered with the PTO, the parallel importation of foreign-made goods bearing that trademark is prohibited absent the written consent of the U.S. trademark owner, even if the goods are *identical* to the domestically authorized goods, and without regard to the presence or absence of a likelihood of confusion.[1409]

A crucial difference between section 526 and the Lanham Act provisions pertaining to gray market goods (which apply only when there are material differences between the domestic and imported goods) is that section 526 applies only to goods that are *manufactured outside the United States*.[1410] Section 526 does

---

1992); Ferrero U.S.A., Inc. v. Ozak Trading, Inc., 753 F. Supp. 1240, 1243, 1247 (D.N.J.), *aff'd*, 935 F.2d 1281 (3d Cir. 1991).

[1404] *Societe des Produits Nestle*, 982 F.2d at 641; *see also* Gamut Trading Co. v. ITC, 200 F.3d 775, 779 (Fed. Cir. 1999); El Greco Leather Products Co. v. Shoe World Inc., 806 F.2d 392 (2d Cir. 1986); *Lever Bros.*, 877 F.2d at 103, 108; *Ferrero U.S.A.*, 753 F. Supp. at 1247; PepsiCo, Inc. v. Nostalgia Prods. Corp., 18 U.S.P.Q.2d 1404, 1405 (N.D. Ill. 1991); PepsiCo v. Giraud, 7 U.S.P.Q.2d 1371, 1373 (D.P.R. 1988); Dial Corp. v. Encina Corp., 643 F. Supp. 951, 952 (S.D. Fla. 1986).

[1405] Abercrombie & Fitch Trading Co. v. Fashion Shops, Inc., 363 F. Supp. 2d 952, 966 (S.D. Ohio 2005).

[1406] 15 U.S.C. § 1124. The prohibition also applies to imported goods that "copy or simulate the name of any domestic manufacture, or manufacturer, or trader," even if it is not registered as a trademark. *Id.*

[1407] Lever Bros. Co. v. United States, 877 F.2d 101, 111 (D.C. Cir. 1989); *accord, Societe des Produits Nestle*, 982 F.2d at 639; Weil Ceramics & Glass, Inc. v. Dash, 878 F.2d 659, 668 (3d Cir. 1989); Olympus Corp. v. United States, 792 F.2d 315, 321 (2d Cir. 1986); Lever Bros. Co. v. United States, 981 F.2d 1330 (D.C. Cir. 1993).

[1408] 19 U.S.C. § 1526.

[1409] Premier Dental Prods. Co. v. Darby Dental Supply Co., 794 F.2d 850, 857–59 (3d Cir. 1986); United States v. Eighty-Nine (89) Bottles of "Eau de Joy," 797 F.2d 767, 771 (9th Cir. 1986). *Cf.* K-Mart Corp. v. Cartier, Inc., 486 U.S. 281 (1988) (addressing validity of Customs regulations under § 526).

[1410] 19 U.S.C. § 1526 (referring to "merchandise of foreign manufacture"); *see* Bourdeau Bros. v. ITC, 444 F.3d 1317, 1322 (Fed. Cir. 2006).

not apply where goods are manufactured in the United States for sale in foreign territories, and then are re-imported without the trademark owner's consent. In addition, in construing the Customs regulations issued under section 526,[1411] the Supreme Court has held that the "extraordinary protection" provided by these regulations applies only when the domestic trademark owner has no corporate affiliation with the foreign manufacturer.[1412] Some of the lower federal courts have treated this restriction as implicit in the statute itself.[1413]

[3] "Classic" Fair Use

Section 33(b)(4) of the Lanham Act provides an affirmative "fair use" defense to trademark infringement, which applies when "the use of the name, term, or device charged to be an infringement is a use, otherwise than as a mark, . . . of a term or device which is descriptive of and used fairly and in good faith only to describe the goods or services of such party, or their geographic origin."[1414] Like the other section 33(b) defenses, fair use is available even if the plaintiff's mark has become incontestable.[1415] The fair use defense of section 33(b)(4) is sometimes called "classic" fair use or "descriptive" fair use, to distinguish it from "nominative" fair use, discussed in the next section.

Classic fair use applies when the defendant has used the plaintiff's trademark only to describe the defendant's own goods or services, and not to describe or identify the plaintiff's goods or services.[1416] This defense exists both at common law and under the Lanham Act; thus, it applies to both registered and unregistered marks.[1417] It protects a junior user's right "to use a descriptive term in good faith in its primary, descriptive sense other than as a trademark."[1418] As one court has noted, "[t]he 'fair-use' defense, in essence, forbids a trademark registrant to appropriate a descriptive term for his exclusive use and so prevent others from accurately describing a characteristic of their goods."[1419]

To establish classic fair use, a defendant must prove that: (1) its use of the plaintiff's mark was not as a trademark or service mark, (2) it is using the mark "fairly and in good faith," and (3) it is using the mark only to describe its goods or services.[1420]

[1411] 19 C.F.R. § 133.23 (2009).

[1412] K Mart Corp. v. Cartier, Inc., 486 U.S. 281, 291 (1988).

[1413] *See, e.g.*, Weil Ceramics & Glass, Inc. v. Dash, 878 F.2d 659, 665 n.6 (3d Cir. 1986).

[1414] 15 U.S.C. § 1115(b)(4).

[1415] Abercrombie & Fitch Co. v. Hunting World, Inc., 537 F.2d 4, 12 (2d Cir. 1976).

[1416] Cairns v. Franklin Mint Co., 292 F.3d 1139, 1150 (9th Cir. 2002).

[1417] *Id.*; Car-Freshner Corp. v. S.C. Johnson & Son., Inc., 70 F.3d 267, 269 (2d Cir. 1995); Soweco, Inc. v. Shell Oil Co., 617 F.2d 1178, 1190 (5th Cir. 1980); Ideal Indus., Inc. v. Gardner Bender, Inc., 612 F.2d 1018, 1027 (7th Cir. 1979); Robert B. Vance & Assocs., Inc. v. Baronet Corp., 487 F. Supp. 790, 797 (N.D. Ga. 1979); RESTATEMENT (THIRD) UNFAIR COMPETITION § 28 comment (a) (1995).

[1418] *Cairns*, 292 F.3d at 1150.

[1419] Soweco, Inc. v. Shell Oil Co., 617 F.2d 1178, 1185 (5th Cir. 1980).

[1420] *Cairns*, 292 F.3d at 1151; *see, e.g.*, Victoria's Secret Stores v. Artco Equip. Co., 194 F. Supp. 2d 704 (S.D. Ohio 2002).

For example, in *In re Dual-Deck Video Cassette Recorder Antitrust Litigation*, the plaintiff argued that its "VCR-2" trademark for dual-deck videocassette recorders was infringed by another merchant whose audiovisual devices — to which two videocassette recorders could be connected simultaneously — included connection terminals that were labeled "VCR-1" and "VCR-2." The Ninth Circuit held that the defendant's use of the term "VCR-2" was descriptive, and that there was no evidence from which bad faith could be inferred.[1421] Similarly, fair use protected defendants that used the term "fish fry" (which was similar to the plaintiff's trademark "Fish-Fri") to describe their batter mixes for coating fish,[1422] as well as a defendant that used the plaintiff's incontestable "Safari" mark, in combination with other words, on hunting boots imported from Africa.[1423] In the latter case, the court noted that the defendant's use was "a purely descriptive use to apprise the public of the type of product by referring to its origin and use."[1424]

In other cases, a fair use defense has failed because the defendant did not use the plaintiff's mark primarily to describe the defendant's goods or services, but as a trademark. Such a conclusion typically follows where the defendant has used the mark in a way that "attracts public attention, is the most prominent element on the package, and dominates the package as a whole."[1425] For example, a fair use defense failed where the term "Brew Nuts" (which was similar to the plaintiff's mark "Beer Nuts") was especially prominent on the defendant's packaging, and was separate from the descriptive phrase "sweetened salted peanuts."[1426]

Although there is limited authority on the question, it appears that the classic fair use defense is not limited to word marks, but may be applied to trade dress as well.[1427]

Courts disagree on whether the fair use defense applies only to descriptive, or perhaps suggestive, trademarks, or whether it extends also to arbitrary and fanciful marks, which have no descriptive aspect.[1428] The text of section 33(b)(4) implies no such limitation, and the better answer appears to be that the defense applies without regard to the nature of the plaintiff's mark, so long as the defendant is using it descriptively. However, the defense will succeed most often in cases involving descriptive marks, because marks that are already descriptive will

---

[1421] 11 F.3d 1460, 1467 (9th Cir. 1993).

[1422] Zatarain's, Inc. v. Oak Grove Smokehouse, Inc., 698 F.2d 786 (5th Cir. 1983).

[1423] Abercrombie & Fitch Co. v. Hunting World, Inc., 537 F.2d 4 (2d Cir. 1976).

[1424] *Id.* at 12.

[1425] Beer Nuts, Inc. v. Clover Club Foods Co., 711 F.2d 934, 938 (10th Cir. 1983); *see also* Sands, Taylor & Wood Co. v. Quaker Oats Co., 978 F.2d 947, 953–54 (7th Cir. 1992); Venetianaire Corp. v. A & P Import Co., 429 F.2d 1079, 1082 (2d Cir. 1970); Feathercombs, Inc. v. Solo Prods. Corp., 306 F.2d 251, 256 (2d Cir. 1962).

[1426] *Beer Nuts*, 711 F.2d at 938 (10th Cir. 1983).

[1427] *See* Mattel Inc. v. Walking Mountain Prods., 353 F.3d 792, 810 (9th Cir. 2003); Car-Freshner Corp. v. S.C. Johnson & Son, Inc., 70 F.3d 267 (2d Cir. 1995).

[1428] *See, e.g.*, *Car-Freshner Corp.*, 70 F.3d at 269; DowBrands, L.P. v. Helene Curtis, Inc., 863 F. Supp. 963, 967–69 (D. Minn. 1994); National Football League Properties v. Playoff Corp., 808 F. Supp. 1288, 1293 (N.D. Tex. 1992).

be the ones most often needed by competitors to describe their own goods and services.

In 2004, the Supreme Court resolved a longstanding circuit split regarding the classic fair use defense, holding in *KP Permanent Make-Up, Inc. v. Lasting Impression I* that a defendant may prevail on a fair use defense without being required to prove the absence of a likelihood of confusion.[1429] Thus, a defendant's unauthorized use of another's trademark can be a permissible fair use even if it creates a likelihood of confusion. The Court acknowledged this possibility, but it concluded that some confusion must be tolerated in order to preserve the rights of competitors to describe their goods and services accurately: "If any confusion results, that is a risk the plaintiff accepted when it decided to identify its product with a mark that uses a well known descriptive phrase."[1430] The Court noted, however, that the *degree* of likely confusion may be relevant to the determination of whether a particular use is fair.[1431]

The concept of fair use is also incorporated into one of the statutory exceptions to the federal dilution statute.[1432]

[4]   Nominative Fair Use

Some courts have recognized a second type of fair use defense, known as "nominative fair use." Nominative fair use, which is not grounded specifically in section 33(b)(4), applies when the defendant has used the plaintiff's trademark to describe or identify the *plaintiff's* goods or services, even if the defendant's ultimate goal is to describe the defendant's own goods or services.[1433] Typically, this use occurs because the plaintiff's mark is the only practical way to refer to a particular subject matter.[1434] In contrast to classic fair use under common law and section 33(b)(4), where the defendant uses the plaintiff's mark in its primary, descriptive sense, in nominative fair use the defendant uses the plaintiff's mark in its trademark sense.[1435]

The leading case on nominative fair use is the Ninth Circuit's decision in *New Kids on the Block v. News America Publishing, Inc.*,[1436] in which defendant newspapers used the trademarked name of a popular musical group to promote their telephone polls regarding the relative popularity of the individual band members. The Ninth Circuit held that the newspapers were using the trademarked name to describe the plaintiff's goods or services (that is, the musical group itself)

[1429] 543 U.S. 111, 114 (2004).

[1430] *Id.* at 122 (quoting Cosmetically Sealed Industries, Inc. v. Chesebrough-Pond's USA Co., 125 F.3d 28, 30 (2d Cir. 1997)).

[1431] 543 U.S. at 123.

[1432] *See* § 5G[4][a].

[1433] *See, e.g.*, Cairns v. Franklin Mint Co., 292 F.3d 1139, 1151 (9th Cir. 2002).

[1434] *See, e.g.*, New Kids on the Block v. News Am. Publ'g, Inc., 971 F.2d 302, 308 (9th Cir. 1992).

[1435] Brother Records, Inc. v. Jardine, 318 F.3d 900, 908 (9th Cir. 2003).

[1436] 971 F.2d 302 (9th Cir. 1992).

for the ultimate purpose of describing the defendants' own goods or services — the telephone polls. The court explained:

> [I]t is often virtually impossible to refer to a particular product for purposes of comparison, criticism, point of reference or any other such purpose without using the mark. . . . Much useful social and commercial discourse would be all but impossible if speakers were under threat of an infringement lawsuit every time they made reference to a person, company or product by using its trademark.[1437]

To establish nominative fair use, the Ninth Circuit held that a defendant must establish: (1) that the plaintiff's goods or services at issue are not readily identifiable without use of the plaintiff's trademark; (2) that the defendant used only as much of the mark as was reasonably necessary to identify the plaintiff's goods or services; and (3) that the defendant did nothing that would, in conjunction with the mark, suggest sponsorship or endorsement by the mark owner.[1438]

The Ninth Circuit applied the nominative fair use defense to reject a claim of trade dress infringement where a photographer used images of Mattel's "Barbie" doll in a series of satirical photos.[1439] Nominative fair use was also found where a maker of memorabilia used the name and likeness of Diana, Princess of Wales, on merchandise commemorating the late princess;[1440] and where a former Playboy "Playmate" used the terms "Playboy" and "Playmate" to describe herself on her website.[1441] The defense failed, however, where a defendant's ads for car wax prominently featured the trade dress and trademarks of the Porsche 911;[1442] and where a defendant's commercial website repeatedly used the name of a competitor's product in metatags that "spawn[ed] confusion as to sponsorship and attempt[ed] to appropriate the cachet of the trademark."[1443] A triable issue of fact as to the third element was found where an automobile maker referred to basketball star Kareem Abdul-Jabbar, who won an award three years in a row, in a commercial for a car that won an award three years in a row.[1444]

In the Ninth Circuit, when a defendant raises a nominative fair use defense, the three-part *New Kids* test for nominative fair use *replaces* the likelihood-of-confusion analysis. Thus, instead of assessing the likelihood of confusion under the usual multifactor tests, under *New Kids* the burden is on the defendant to establish the elements of nominative fair use.[1445]

[1437] *Id.* at 306–07.

[1438] *Cairns*, 292 F.3d at 1151; *New Kids*, 971 F.2d at 308.

[1439] Mattel, Inc. v. Walking Mountain Prods., 353 F.3d 792, 812 (9th Cir. 2003).

[1440] Cairns v. Franklin Mint Co., 292 F.3d 1139, 1153 (9th Cir. 2002).

[1441] Playboy Enters., Inc. v. Welles, 279 F.3d 796, 803–04 (9th Cir. 2002).

[1442] Liquid Glass Enters., Inc. v. Dr. Ing. h.c. F. Porsche AG, 8 F. Supp. 2d 398, 402–03 (D.N.J. 1998).

[1443] Horphag Research, Ltd. v. Pellegrini, 337 F.3d 1036, 1041 (9th Cir. 2003).

[1444] Abdul-Jabbar v. Gen. Motors Corp., 85 F.3d 407, 412–13 (9th Cir. 1996).

[1445] *Cairns*, 292 F.3d at 1151; *Welles*, 279 F.3d at 801; New Kids on the Block v. News Am. Publ'g, Inc., 971 F.2d 302, 308 (9th Cir. 1992).

In *Century 21 Real Estate Corp. v. Lending Tree, Inc.*, the Third Circuit disagreed with the Ninth Circuit's approach, for several reasons. First, "even an accurate nominative use could potentially confuse consumers about the plaintiff's endorsement or sponsorship of the defendant's products or services."[1446] Second, the court suggested that the Supreme Court's decision in *KP Permanent Make-Up*, holding that a classic fair use defense under section 33(b)(4) does not require a defendant to prove the absence of a likelihood of confusion, should also apply to nominative fair use.[1447] Finally, the court believed that the Ninth Circuit's three-part test was unclear. Accordingly, the Third Circuit adopted a two-step approach to claims of nominative fair use: First, the court considers only those likelihood-of-confusion factors which it deems most relevant to the nominative use in question; the specific factors will vary according to the case.[1448] Second, if a likelihood of confusion exists under the modified test, then the burden shifts to the defendant to show that: (1) the use of the plaintiff's mark is necessary to describe both the plaintiff's product or service and the defendant's product or service; (2) the defendant uses only so much of the plaintiff's mark as is necessary to describe the plaintiff's product; and (3) the defendant's conduct or language reflects the true and accurate relationship between the plaintiff and the defendant's products or services.[1449]

The nominative fair use defense has won increasing acceptance outside the Third and Ninth Circuits. The Third Circuit's approach has been applied by a district court in the Eighth Circuit.[1450] The Ninth Circuit's approach has been adopted by district courts in the Sixth[1451] and Seventh[1452] Circuits, although it was rejected by a district court in the Fourth Circuit.[1453] In the context of comparative advertising, the Fifth Circuit applied only the second and third prongs of the *New Kids* test in *Pebble Beach Co. v. Tour 18 I, Ltd.*,[1454] but it also declined to dispense with the traditional likelihood-of-confusion factors.[1455]

The Second Circuit has expressly declined to endorse nominative fair use in any formulation, but it has acknowledged the underlying principle that "a defendant may lawfully use a plaintiff's trademark where doing so is necessary to describe the plaintiff's product and does not imply a false affiliation or endorsement by the plaintiff of the defendant" — for example, where the defendant sells the plaintiff's

---

[1446] 425 F.3d 211, 221 & n.1 (3d Cir. 2005).

[1447] *Id.* at 222 & n.3. In *KP Permanent Make-Up*, the Supreme Court specifically declined to address nominative fair use. 543 U.S. 111, 115 n.3 (2004).

[1448] 425 F.3d at 225–26.

[1449] *Id.* at 222.

[1450] Edina Realty v. TheMLSOnline.com, 80 U.S.P.Q.2d 1039 (D. Minn. 2006).

[1451] Romantics v. Activision Publishing, 532 F. Supp. 2d 884, 890 (E.D. Mich. 2008). The Sixth Circuit had declined to recognize nominative fair use in PACCAR, Inc. v. TeleScan Techs., 319 F.3d 243, 256 (6th Cir. 2003), *overruled on other grounds*, KP Permanent Make-Up, Inc. v. Lasting Impression I, Inc., 543 U.S. 111 (2004), but it also found that the Ninth Circuit's test was not satisfied on the facts of that case.

[1452] World Impressions Corp. v. McDonald's Corp., 235 F. Supp. 2d 831, 844 (N.D. Ill. 2002).

[1453] Nat'l Fed. of the Blind, Inc. v. Loompanics Enters., Inc., 936 F. Supp. 1232, 1241 (D. Md. 1996).

[1454] 155 F.3d 526, 545 (5th Cir. 1998).

[1455] *Id.* at 546–47.

products.[1456] This principle was widely recognized both before and after the *New Kids* decision, although not formally denominated in those cases as "fair use."[1457]

In the 2006 amendments to the federal dilution statute, Congress modified the statutory exemptions in section 43(c) to expressly include nominative fair use.[1458]

[5] Comparative Advertising

Although the Ninth Circuit's approach to nominative fair use has not received universal acceptance, the underlying principle from which it is derived has been widely employed to permit the use of trademarks in order to draw truthful comparisons between one merchant's goods and those of a competitor, provided that the use is not likely to create consumer confusion as to source. This is the principle of comparative advertising:

> An imitator may use in a truthful way an originator's trademark when advertising that the imitator's product is a copy so long as that use is not likely to create confusion in the consumer's mind as to the source of the product being sold. . . . The underlying rationale is that an imitator is entitled to truthfully inform the public that it believes that it has produced a product equivalent to the original and that the public may benefit through lower prices by buying the imitation.[1459]

For example, courts have held that it is permissible for a maker of a "knock-off" perfume to identify the brand-name perfume that it imitates,[1460] for a party that sells imitations of designer clothing to identify the famous couturier whose designs are being copied,[1461] for a seller of "artificial" water to identify the brand of natural spring water that its product resembles,[1462] and for a seller of a pharmaceutical product to identify the brand-name medicine for which it can be substituted.[1463] In contrast, the bounds of truthful comparative advertising were exceeded where a maker of knock-off perfumes used the name-brand perfume's exact mark on its

---

[1456] Tiffany (NJ) Inc. v. eBay, Inc., 600 F.3d 93, 102–03 (2d Cir. 2010).

[1457] *See, e.g.,* Universal Commun. Sys. v. Lycos, Inc., 478 F.3d 413, 424 (1st Cir. 2007); Scott Fetzer Co. v. House of Vacuums, Inc., 381 F.3d 477, 484–85 (5th Cir. 2004); WCVB-TV v. Boston Athletic Association, 926 F.2d 42 (1st Cir. 1991); Volkswagenwerk Aktiengesellschaft v. Church, 411 F.2d 350, *as amended,* 413 F.2d 1126 (9th Cir. 1969); Smith v. Chanel, Inc. 402 F.2d 562 (9th Cir. 1968).

[1458] *See* § 5G[4][a].

[1459] Calvin Klein Cosmetics Corp. v. Lenox Labs., Inc., 815 F.2d 500, 503 (8th Cir. 1987) (citations omitted); *see, e.g.,* Pebble Beach Co. v. Tour 18 I, Ltd. 155 F.3d 526, 545–46 (5th Cir. 1998) (collecting cases); Lindy Pen Co. v. Bic Pen Corp., 725 F.2d 1240 (9th Cir. 1984); Mattel, Inc. v. Azrak-Hamway Int'l, Inc., 724 F.2d 357, 361 (2d Cir. 1983); SSP Agricultural Equipment, Inc. v. Orchard-Rite Ltd., 592 F.2d 1096, 1103 (9th Cir. 1979); Anti-Monopoly, Inc. v. General Mills Fun Group, 611 F.2d 296, 301 n.2 (9th Cir. 1979); Saxony Products, Inc. v. Guerlain, Inc., 513 F.2d 716, 722 (9th Cir. 1975); Smith v. Chanel, Inc., 402 F.2d 562, 563 (9th Cir. 1968).

[1460] Smith v. Chanel, Inc., 402 F.2d 562 (9th Cir. 1968).

[1461] Societe Comptoir de l'Industrie Cotonniere Etablissements Boussac v. Alexander's Dept. Stores, Inc., 299 F.2d 33, 36 (2d Cir. 1962).

[1462] Saxlehner v. Wagner, 216 U.S. 375, 380–81 (1910).

[1463] Viavi Co. v. Vimedia Co., 245 F. 289, 292 (8th Cir. 1917).

packaging with an inconspicuous disclaimer,[1464] and where a golf course that replicated the designs of golf holes at famous courses displayed the marks of those courses so prominently in its materials that consumers perceived them as indications of endorsement or approval.[1465]

As discussed above, the express exemptions in the federal dilution statute include any "fair use" in the context of comparative advertising.[1466]

[6]   First Amendment

Because trademark and unfair competition laws regulate speech, these laws are sometimes in tension with the First Amendment. As discussed in this section, courts have adopted a number of different approaches to resolving these conflicts. Their approaches, however, are not always consistent.

Although it is convenient to discuss First Amendment concerns in connection with defenses to trademark and unfair competition claims, in many cases courts have treated First Amendment considerations as distinct from true affirmative defenses. For example, as discussed below,[1467] where a defendant has used another's trademark in the context of literary and artistic expression, some courts have held that trademark and unfair competition laws either do not apply, or must be narrowly construed, because the defendant is not using the mark to indicate the origin of goods or services. Other courts have engaged in a balancing analysis, weighing the rights of the trademark owner (and the public interest in avoiding consumer confusion) against the public interest in free expression. In contrast, where the defendant uses another's trademark in a parodic fashion either in commercial advertising or on ordinary merchandise, courts will generally treat this as a commercial use that falls within the scope of trademark and unfair competition laws; however, courts disagree on the extent to which the parodic context of this commercial use warrants special consideration.[1468] Another context in which courts have not reached a consensus is that of expressive merchandise (such as posters and T-shirts), which are commercial goods but often have a strong expressive component.[1469] And while political speech normally receives a high degree of First Amendment protection, courts generally have not treated it as outside the scope of trademark laws.[1470]

In the context of infringement and unfair competition claims, courts also disagree on whether the analysis of First Amendment issues should be integrated with the analysis of the likelihood of confusion,[1471] or whether consideration of

---

[1464]   Charles of the Ritz Group, Ltd. v. Quality King Distrs., Inc., 832 F.2d 1317, 1324 (2d Cir. 1987).

[1465]   Pebble Beach Co. v. Tour 18 I, Ltd., 942 F. Supp. 1513, 1553 (S.D. Tex. 1996), aff'd, 155 F.3d 526 (5th Cir. 1998).

[1466]   See § 5G[4].

[1467]   See § 5J[6][b].

[1468]   See § 5J[6][a].

[1469]   See § 5J[6][d].

[1470]   See § 5J[6][c].

[1471]   See, e.g., Elvis Presley Enters. v. Capece, 141 F.3d 188, 200 n.5 (5th Cir. 1998); Dr. Seuss Enters.,

these issues should be undertaken only if a likelihood of confusion is found to exist.[1472] The Eighth Circuit, for example, has held that failure to separate the parody analysis from the standard likelihood-of-confusion analysis is reversible error.[1473]

[a]   Commercial Parodies

Allegations of trademark infringement or unfair competition sometimes arise in a commercial context that involves a parody of a protected mark. Such cases require courts to determine whether and to what extent the parodic aspect of the defendant's actions should affect the traditional likelihood-of-confusion analysis. A similar problem arises when the trademark parody gives rise to a dilution claim, although the analysis in those cases does not involve a likelihood of confusion.

[i]   Infringement and Unfair Competition

In the context of trademark infringement or unfair competition claims, parody is generally not treated as an affirmative defense. Rather, it serves as an additional consideration in the likelihood-of-confusion analysis,[1474] one that tends to weigh against a finding that consumers are likely to be confused as to the source, sponsorship, or approval of the defendant's goods or services.[1475]

For example, in *Hormel Foods Corp. v. Jim Henson Productions*,[1476] the defendant parodied the plaintiff's SPAM trademark for canned meat products by introducing a wild boar "Muppet" character named "Spa'am" in a children's movie and related merchandise. Although the district court rejected the plaintiff's claims of trademark infringement and dilution arising from the movie itself (which it analyzed as a work of artistic expression), additional issues involved the movie company's use of this character in merchandise related to the film. The Second Circuit applied the traditional likelihood-of-confusion factors to the movie merchandise; however, in evaluating each factor it gave significant weight to the parodic context. The court emphasized that, well before the release of the Muppets movie and merchandise, the SPAM mark was already a frequent target of ridicule. Because the defendant's parody was not subtle, the court found that consumers would clearly understand that the character was a parody, and they would not be

---

L.P. v. Penguin Books USA, Inc., 109 F.3d 1394, 1407 (9th Cir. 1997); Nike, Inc. v. "Just Did It" Enters., 6 F.3d 1225, 1231 (7th Cir. 1993); Jordache Enters. v. Hogg Wyld, Ltd., 828 F.2d 1482, 1486 (10th Cir. 1987).

[1472] *See, e.g.*, Anheuser-Busch, Inc. v. Balducci Pubs., 28 F.3d 769, 775 (8th Cir. 1994).

[1473] *Balducci*, 28 F.3d at 775.

[1474] *See, e.g.*, Utah Lighthouse Ministry v. Found. for Apologetic Info. & Resch., 527 F.3d 1045, 1057 (10th Cir. 2008); Louis Vuitton Malletier S.A. v. Haute Diggity Dog, LLC, 507 F.3d 252, 263 (4th Cir. 2007); Elvis Presley Enters. v. Capece, 141 F.3d 188, 194 (5th Cir. 1998); Dr. Seuss Enters. v. Penguin Books USA, Inc., 109 F.3d 1394, 1407 (9th Cir. 1997); Nike, Inc. v. "Just Did It" Enters., 6 F.3d 1225, 1231 (7th Cir. 1993); Anheuser-Busch, Inc. v. L & L Wings, Inc., 962 F.2d 316, 321 (4th Cir. 1992); Jordache Enters. v. Hogg Wyld, Ltd., 828 F.2d 1482, 1486 (10th Cir. 1987); Mutual of Omaha Ins. Co. v. Novak, 648 F. Supp. 905, 910 (D. Neb. 1986), *aff'd*, 836 F.2d 397 (8th Cir. 1987).

[1475] *See, e.g.*, Utah Lighthouse Ministry, 527 F.3d at 1057; Elvis Presley Enters., 141 F.3d at 198–99; Dr. Seuss Enters., 109 F.3d at 1405; Mutual of Omaha, 648 F. Supp. at 910.

[1476] 73 F.3d 497, 503 (2d Cir. 1996).

confused as to the origin or sponsorship of the movie-related merchandise.[1477]

Some decisions analyzing commercial parodies have drawn guidance from the Supreme Court's decision in *Campbell v. Acuff-Rose Music*,[1478] which analyzed a copyright infringement claim involving a parody. There, the Supreme Court distinguished parody from satire, noting that "[p]arody needs to mimic an original to make its point," whereas, in the case of a satire that "has no critical bearing on the substance or style of the original composition, . . . the claim to fairness in borrowing from another's work diminishes accordingly."[1479] Applying this approach to infringement claims against an Elvis Presley-themed bar, the Fifth Circuit held that this use of the plaintiff's Elvis-related marks was not a parody, because the true object of the defendant's humorous message was not the marks, but "the faddish bars of the sixties."[1480]

The more obvious the parody, the less likely it is that consumers will be confused about its source.[1481] A true parody is "so obvious and heavy-handed that a clear distinction [is] preserved in the viewer's mind between the source of the actual product and the source of the parody."[1482] Conversely, a parody that is too subtle is more likely to give rise to liability, and a defendant's parody argument will be disregarded completely if the court does not perceive the mark as a true parody in the first place.[1483] As the Second Circuit has noted: "A parody must convey two simultaneous — and contradictory — messages: that it is the original, but also that it is *not* the original and is instead a parody."[1484] Under this approach, in jurisdictions that consider the defendant's good or bad faith as one of the likelihood-of-confusion factors, an intent to parody is not equated with an intent to confuse or mislead.[1485]

In a minority of cases, courts or the PTO have completely disregarded the parodic nature of the defendant's mark,[1486] or have expressly held it irrelevant.[1487]

[1477] *Id.* For a discussion of the plaintiff's dilution claim, *see* § 5J[6][a][ii].

[1478] 510 U.S. 569 (1994).

[1479] *Id.* at 580–81.

[1480] Elvis Presley Enterprises v. Capece, 141 F.3d 188, 199–200 (5th Cir. 1998); *accord*, Harley-Davidson, Inc. v. Grottanelli, 164 F.3d 806, 813 (2d Cir. 1999); Anheuser-Busch, Inc. v. L & L Wings, Inc., 962 F.2d 316, 321 (4th Cir. 1992).

[1481] New York Stock Exch., Inc. v. New York, New York Hotel, LLC, 69 F. Supp. 2d 479, 487 (S.D.N.Y. 1999), *aff'd in relevant part*, 293 F.3d 550 (2d Cir. 2002); *see, e.g.*, Cardtoons, L.C. v. Major League Baseball Players Ass'n, 95 F.3d 959, 967 (10th Cir. 1996); Tommy Hilfiger Licensing, Inc. v. Nature Labs, LLC, 221 F. Supp. 2d 410, 416 (S.D.N.Y. 2002).

[1482] Mutual of Omaha Ins. Co. v. Novak, 648 F. Supp. 905, 910 (D. Neb. 1986), *aff'd*, 836 F.2d 397 (8th Cir. 1987); *accord*, Hard Rock Licensing Corp. v. Pacific Graphics, Inc., 776 F. Supp. 1454, 1462 (W.D. Wash. 1991).

[1483] *See, e.g.*, *Hard Rock Licensing*, 776 F. Supp. at 1462.

[1484] Hormel Foods Corp. v. Jim Henson Prods., 73 F.3d 497, 503 (2d Cir. 1996) (quoting Cliff Notes, Inc. v. Bantam Doubleday Dell Publishing Group, Inc., 886 F.2d 490, 494 (2d Cir. 1989)).

[1485] *See, e.g.*, *Tommy Hilfiger*, 221 F. Supp. 2d at 418–20; *Jordache*, 828 F.2d at 1486.

[1486] *See, e.g.*, Grey v. Campbell Soup Co., 650 F. Supp. 1166, 1173 (C.D. Cal. 1986), *aff'd without op.*, 830 F.2d 197 (9th Cir. 1987); Recot, Inc. v. Becton, 56 U.S.P.Q.2d 1859 (T.T.A.B. 2000).

[1487] Gucci Shops, Inc. v. R.H. Macy & Co., 446 F. Supp. 838, 840 (S.D.N.Y. 1977).

In these situations, a finding of likelihood of confusion is almost inevitable, due to the similarity between the defendant's mark and the parodied mark, and the defendant's intentional copying.

[ii] Dilution

Because dilution claims do not require a likelihood of consumer confusion, the scope of First Amendment protection for commercial activities involving allegedly dilutive uses of trademarks has been difficult for courts to define. Unlike the federal statute, most state dilution statutes do not contain explicit exemptions for expressive or noncommercial works; thus, the vulnerability of such works to state dilution depends on courts' sensitivity to First Amendment considerations.

Several cases from the Second Circuit provide useful, and contrasting, illustrations. In *Deere & Co. v. MTD Products*,[1488] a television commercial poked fun at the plaintiff's well-known deer trademark by depicting the deer as cowardly. Although no blurring was involved, and the court rejected a tarnishment claim (based on its narrow view of tarnishment as requiring "a context of sexual activity, obscenity, or illegal activity"[1489]), the court held that the defendant had diluted the plaintiff's mark because "alterations of that sort, accomplished for the sole purpose of promoting a competing product . . . risk the possibility that consumers will come to attribute unfavorable characteristics to a mark and ultimately associate the mark with inferior goods and services."[1490] The fact that the parties were competitors was critical.[1491]

However, in *Hormel Foods Corp. v. Jim Henson Productions*,[1492] the same court held that the plaintiff's "SPAM" trademark for canned meat products was not diluted when a film company sold merchandise (related to a children's movie) that featured a comical movie character named "Spa'am." The court concluded that blurring would not occur, because (1) the defendant's parody was so obvious that it would strengthen rather than weaken the association of the mark with the plaintiff's products; (2) the marks were dissimilar, because the name "Spa'am" would always appear together with the character's image and other source identifiers; and (3) the defendant was not using "Spa'am" as a product brand name, but as a character in products bearing the defendant's own trademark.[1493]

On the tarnishment claim, *Hormel* distinguished the defendant's use of the "Spa'am" character from the depiction of the cowardly deer in *Deere* because (1) the "Spa'am" character was depicted in a positive, likeable way, which would not cause consumers to develop negative associations with SPAM-branded meat products; and (2) the defendant's film-related products did not directly compete with the plaintiff's products. Thus, the defendant was not ridiculing the plaintiff's

---

[1488] 41 F.3d 39 (2d Cir. 1994).

[1489] *Id.* at 44.

[1490] *Id.* at 45.

[1491] *Id.*

[1492] 73 F.3d 497, 503 (2d Cir. 1996).

[1493] *Id.* at 506–08.

mark in order to sell more of its own competing goods.[1494]

A third parody case from the Second Circuit reached opposite conclusions on the blurring and tarnishment aspects of a dilution claim. In *New York Stock Exchange v. New York, New York Hotel, LLC*,[1495] the plaintiff brought a state-law dilution claim against a New York-themed casino for using the terms "NY$E" and "New York $lot Exchange" in connection with its gambling services and related merchandise. In the court's view, the "humor or parody" in the casino's modification of the plaintiff's marks prevented any diminution in the capacity of those marks to serve as unique identifiers of the plaintiff's stock trading services; thus, no blurring occurred. However, the court held that this same "humorous analogy" could injure the plaintiff's reputation; accordingly, the plaintiff could proceed to trial on the question of tarnishment.[1496]

The relationship between dilution theory and parodic purpose created analytical problems for the Tenth Circuit in *Jordache Enters. v. Hogg Wyld, Ltd.*, in which a blue jeans maker brought a state law dilution claim against a competitor that marketed blue jeans for larger women with the word "Lardashe" on the seat of the pants, accompanied by an image of a smiling pig. The appellate court held that no blurring occurred, because "parody tends to increase public identification of a plaintiff's mark with the plaintiff."[1497] The court also rejected the tarnishment claim, but in doing so the court applied a narrow concept of tarnishment that resembles a likelihood of confusion as to source, saying that "[i]f the public associates the two marks for parody purposes only and does not associate the two sources of the products, appellant suffers no actionable injury."[1498]

In contrast to the state dilution laws at issue in these cases, when claims against commercial uses are brought under the federal dilution statute, First Amendment considerations tend to be subsumed under the statutory exceptions. As discussed above,[1499] the 2006 amendments to section 43(c) exempt not only "any noncommercial use" of a famous mark,[1500] but also "any fair use . . . other than as a designation of source for the person's own goods or services . . . including use in connection with . . . identifying and parodying, criticizing, or commenting upon the famous mark owner or the goods or services of the famous mark owner."[1501] While this new parody exception may ultimately be applied to some commercial parodies, it does not apply to a commercial parody that uses another party's famous mark as an origin indicator for the defendant's products. Thus, in *Louis Vuitton Malletier S.A. v. Haute Diggity Dog LLC*, the Fourth Circuit held that that the federal parody exception did not apply to a defendant's use of "Chewy

---

[1494] *Id.*

[1495] 293 F.3d 550 (2d Cir. 2002).

[1496] *Id.* at 558. *See also* Gucci Shops, Inc. v. R.H. Macy & Co., 446 F. Supp. 838, 840 n.6 (S.D.N.Y. 1977) (sale of "Gucchi Goo" diaper bags "would debilitate the potency of plaintiff's mark").

[1497] 828 F.2d 1482, 1490 (10th Cir. 1987).

[1498] *Id.* at 1490–91.

[1499] *See* § 5G[4].

[1500] 15 U.S.C. § 1125(c)(3)(C).

[1501] 15 U.S.C. § 1125(c)(3)(A)(ii).

Vuiton" as a trademark for dog toys.[1502] In contrast, as applied to the *Deere* case, the federal parody exception would probably allow the defendant to prevail against a federal dilution claim, even without resort to First Amendment arguments.

[b] Noncommercial Expression

Where a defendant uses a plaintiff's trademark in a work of literary or artistic expression in order to convey an idea, rather than for a purely commercial purpose, First Amendment considerations tend to weigh heavily in the defendant's favor. Therefore, in contrast to cases involving parodic uses of trademarks in connection with the advertising or sale of merchandise, courts have generally applied a different analysis where a trademark is used in a traditional expressive work — typically, a work of artistic, musical, or literary expression.

[i] Infringement and Unfair Competition

When a plaintiff alleges that the use of its mark in a work of artistic expression gives rise to a likelihood of confusion as to origin or sponsorship, most courts employ a balancing test that weighs the public interest in free expression against the public interest in avoiding consumer confusion.[1503] Courts are generally willing to tolerate some degree of consumer confusion in order to avoid chilling protected speech.[1504]

In a leading case, *Rogers v. Grimaldi*,[1505] the Second Circuit considered a film depicting fictional ballroom dancers who became known in Italy as "Ginger and Fred," which was also the title of the movie. Ginger Rogers brought suit, arguing that the film's title violated her rights under section 43(a) and the common-law right of publicity. The Second Circuit affirmed a grant of summary judgment to the defendant on the ground that the film and its title were works of artistic expression rather than commercial speech. While the First Amendment did not completely insulate artistic speech from Lanham Act claims, the expressive element of the film's title warranted "more protection than the labeling of ordinary commercial products."[1506] The court concluded that the Lanham Act should not apply to titles "unless the title has no artistic relevance to the underlying work whatsoever, or, if it has some artistic relevance, unless the title explicitly misleads as to the source or the content of the work."[1507] The court rejected the narrower test proffered by the plaintiff, under which First Amendment considerations would be "implicated only where a title is so intimately related to the subject matter of a work that the author has no alternative means of expressing what the work is about," holding that this

---

[1502] 507 F.3d 252, 266 (4th Cir. 2007). The court nonetheless held that the use did not constitute dilution, and that the parody could affect the court's evaluation of the six factors relevant to dilution. *Id.* at 266–67.

[1503] Cliffs Notes, Inc. v. Bantam Doubleday Dell Publishing Group, Inc., 886 F.2d 490, 494 (2d Cir. 1989).

[1504] *Id.* at 495.

[1505] 875 F.2d 994 (2d Cir. 1989).

[1506] 875 F.2d at 998.

[1507] *Id.*; *accord*, Twin Peaks Productions v. Publications Intern., 996 F.2d 1366, 1379 (2d Cir. 1993).

approach would not "sufficiently accommodate the public's interest in free expression."[1508]

The Second Circuit expanded the *Rogers* balancing approach in *Cliffs Notes, Inc. v. Bantam Doubleday Dell Publishing Group, Inc.*,[1509] where the defendant had published a parody that spoofed the plaintiff's notorious study aids. Although the defendant's cover design was very similar to the plaintiff's, the Second Circuit noted that the defendant must be permitted to "conjure up" the original in order to parody it successfully, and the fact that the defendant's work was prominently marked "A Satire" reduced the likelihood of confusion. Even if some consumers might be confused, the court found it sufficient that "most consumers will realize it is a parody,"[1510] and the "slight risk of consumer confusion" was "outweighed by the public interest in free expression, especially in a form of expression that must to some extent resemble the original."[1511] In so holding, the court expanded the *Rogers* balancing test beyond the context of titles to include all works of artistic expression, including but not limited to parodies.[1512]

The Ninth Circuit applied the *Rogers* approach to the lyrics of a musical work in *Mattel, Inc. v. MCA Records, Inc.*,[1513] in which toy manufacturer Mattel brought trademark infringement and dilution claims against the record companies that produced and distributed a song that poked fun at Mattel's famous "Barbie" doll. Because the song was a work of artistic expression, and because the "Barbie" mark had achieved independent cultural significance apart from its origin-identifying function, the court held, "the trademark owner does not have the right to control public discourse whenever the public imbues his mark with a meaning beyond its source-identifying function."[1514] The Ninth Circuit has also extended the *Rogers* approach to video games, treating them as works of artistic expression.[1515]

The Sixth Circuit applied the *Rogers* approach to works of artistic expression in *ETW Corp. v. Jireh Publishing, Inc.*,[1516] which held that, with respect to a limited edition print of a painting that depicted champion golfer Tiger Woods, the slight risk that some members of the public would believe that Woods endorsed the painting was outweighed by the public interest in artistic expression. The Eleventh Circuit followed suit in *University of Alabama Board of Trustees v. New Life Art, Inc.*, holding that the depiction of college football uniforms in paintings, prints, and calendars reproducing famous football scenes from the college's history was

---

[1508] 875 F.2d at 998–99.

[1509] 886 F.2d 490 (2d Cir. 1989).

[1510] *Id.* at 496.

[1511] *Id.* at 497.

[1512] *Id.* at 494–95.

[1513] 296 F.3d 894 (9th Cir. 2002).

[1514] *Id.* at 900 (citations omitted). The Sixth Circuit applied *Rogers* but distinguished *Mattel* in Parks v. LaFace Records, 329 F.3d 437 (6th Cir. 2003), where it found less justification for the use of a celebrity's name in a song title.

[1515] Brown v. Electronic Arts, Inc., 724 F.3d 1235 (9th Cir. 2013); E.S.S. Entertainment 2000, Inc. v. Rock Star Videos, Inc., 547 F.3d 1095, 1099–1101 (9th Cir. 2008); *see also* Romantics v. Activision Pub., Inc., 574 F. Supp. 2d 758, 768–69 (E.D. Mich. 2008).

[1516] 332 F.3d 915 (6th Cir. 2003).

protected by the First Amendment because the interest in artistic expression outweighed the risk of consumer confusion as to endorsement.[1517]

A few courts have been less solicitous of First Amendment considerations, even where purely expressive works are involved. In *Anheuser-Busch, Inc. v. Balducci Publications*,[1518] the Eighth Circuit held that a humor magazine infringed the plaintiff's marks when it published a fictitious print ad for a beer called "Michelob Oily." Based on the authentic-looking design and the location of the ad within the magazine, as well as consumer survey evidence, the court concluded that the likelihood of confusion was strong,[1519] and that the risk of consumer confusion outweighed the public interest in free expression.[1520] While acknowledging that the fictitious ad was a type of editorial parody, providing social commentary on environmental concerns and "brand proliferation," the court held, in effect, that the parody was too subtle to satisfy the *Rogers* balancing test.[1521]

In some cases, an expressive work is considered so obvious a parody that it eliminates any likelihood of confusion as to source or sponsorship, in which case some courts will rule in the defendant's favor without even applying a First Amendment analysis.[1522] For example, in *Pillsbury Co. v. Milky Way Productions, Inc.*,[1523] a district court found no likelihood of confusion when a pornographic magazine published a fictional advertisement featuring an unsavory depiction of Pillsbury's distinctive characters "Poppin' Fresh" and "Poppie Fresh," together with additional Pillsbury trade-marks. Even though the plaintiff's marks were strong, and the defendant's depiction of them was intentional and nearly identical, the court noted that (1) the defendant's "product" was the expressive work itself, (2) the fictional "ad" was not offering any real goods or services, (3) the defendant did not intend to deceive consumers, (4) the defendant's magazine was offered in different retail outlets, (5) there was little evidence of actual confusion, and (6) most of Pillsbury's customers would never even see the defendant's magazine. Accordingly, the court found it unnecessary even to consider a First Amendment defense.[1524]

In contrast, a parody defense was rejected in *Dallas Cowboys Cheerleaders, Inc. v. Pussycat Cinema, Ltd.*,[1525] in which the defendant's adult film featured a

---

[1517] 683 F.3d 1266 (11th Cir. 2012). However, this holding did not extend to mugs and other "mundane products" depicting the football uniforms; because the defendant did not assert the First Amendment defense with respect to these items on appeal, the Fourth Circuit did not disturb the district court's conclusion that these items infringed.

[1518] 28 F.3d 769 (8th Cir. 1994).

[1519] *Id.* at 774–75.

[1520] *Id.* at 775–76.

[1521] *Id.* at 776.

[1522] *See, e.g.*, Anheuser-Busch, Inc. v. L&L Wings, Inc., 962 F.2d 316, 321 n.2 (4th Cir. 1992); Walt Disney Productions v. Air Pirates, 581 F.2d 751 (9th Cir. 1978) (no likelihood of confusion where defendant's adult-oriented comic book imitated Disney's trademarked characters); Burnett v. Twentieth Century Fox Film, 491 F. Supp. 2d 962 (C.D. Cal. 2007).

[1523] 215 U.S.P.Q. 124 (N.D. Ga. 1981).

[1524] However, the court upheld a claim for dilution by tarnishment. *See* 5J[6][b][ii].

[1525] 604 F.2d 200 (2d Cir. 1979).

promiscuous cheerleader character wearing a costume that resembled the distinctive uniform of the Dallas Cowboys Cheerleaders. The Second Circuit found that confusion was likely because the public would believe that the plaintiff sponsored or was somehow connected with the film. The court discerned no element of parody in the film, and found no other basis for a First Amendment defense, holding that the rights of a trademark owner "need not 'yield to the exercise of First Amendment rights under circumstances where adequate alternative avenues of communication exist.' "[1526]

Few courts have applied this "alternative avenues" test to expressive works. One district court applied it to a movie title,[1527] and the Eighth Circuit applied it to satirical T-shirts.[1528] Most courts that have considered the "alternative avenues" test have rejected it as insufficiently sensitive to First Amendment values in the context of expressive works.[1529] Indeed, the Second Circuit itself arguably retreated from this standard some years later, when it articulated the *Rogers* balancing test and stated: "We do not read *Dallas Cowboys Cheerleaders* as generally precluding all consideration of First Amendment concerns whenever an allegedly infringing author has 'alternative avenues of communication.' "[1530]

[ii]   Dilution

The application of dilution laws to traditional expression has an even greater potential to chill protected speech than the application of trademark infringement or unfair competition doctrines, because dilution (or the likelihood thereof) can be established without any likelihood of consumer confusion or deception. As the Ninth Circuit has observed, "dilution law protects only the distinctiveness of the mark, which is inherently less weighty than the dual interest of protecting trademark owners and avoiding harm to consumers that is at the heart of every trademark claim."[1531]

Furthermore, when traditional expression or expressive merchandise parodies or otherwise criticizes a plaintiff's trademark, this can damage the prestige of the mark, thus establishing one important element of a tarnishment claim. Thus, there is an inherent tension between dilution law's goal of protecting the reputation of a mark and the First Amendment's goal of fostering criticism and commentary. The *Restatement (Third) of Unfair Competition* advises that this tension should be resolved against the trademark owner, on the ground that expressive uses simply do not use the mark *as a trademark*.[1532]

As discussed above, the federal dilution statute contains specific exemptions for

---

[1526] *Id.* at 206 (quoting Lloyd Corp. v. Tanner, 407 U.S. 551, 567 (1972)).

[1527] American Dairy Queen Corp. v. New Line Prods., Inc., 35 F. Supp. 2d 727, 734 (D. Minn. 1998).

[1528] Mutual of Omaha Ins. Co. v. Novak, 836 F.2d 397, 402 (8th Cir. 1987).

[1529] *See, e.g.*, Parks v. LaFace Records, 329 F.3d 437, 448–50 (6th Cir. 2003); Westchester Media v. PRL USA Holdings, Inc., 214 F.3d 658, 672 (5th Cir. 2000); L.L. Bean, Inc. v. Drake Publishers, Inc., 811 F.2d 26, 29 (1st Cir. 1987).

[1530] Rogers v. Grimaldi, 875 F.2d 994, 999 n.4 (2d Cir. 1989).

[1531] Mattel, Inc. v. MCA Records, 296 F.3d 894, 905 (9th Cir. 2002).

[1532] RESTATEMENT (THIRD) UNFAIR COMPETITION § 25 cmt. i (1995).

news reporting and other noncommercial speech, as well as comparative advertising and criticism, including parody.[1533] Even in a case where none of these exceptions applied, because the defendant was using its parody as an origin indicator for its own goods, the Fourth Circuit in *Louis Vuitton Malletier S.A. v. Haute Diggity Dog, LLC* gave significant weight to the parodic context in evaluating the likelihood of dilution by blurring.[1534]

Most state dilution laws, however, contain no specific exemptions distinguishing expressive uses from purely commercial uses, and courts applying these laws have shown varying degrees of solicitude for First Amendment considerations.

An early and influential case involving an allegedly dilutive parody is *L.L. Bean, Inc. v. Drake Publishers, Inc.*, in which the plaintiff brought a tarnishment claim under Maine's dilution statute against a magazine that used its trademarks in "a prurient parody of Bean's famous catalog."[1535] Because the products listed in the fictitious catalog were not actually offered for sale, it was clear that the purpose of the defendant's parody was to spoof the plaintiff's catalog rather than to sell merchandise. This was an expressive use that warranted a substantial degree of First Amendment protection. In ruling for the defendant, the court rejected the argument that the First Amendment could not shield the defendant's parody because "alternative avenues of communication" were available for the defendant to convey its message.[1536] Because the plaintiff and its trademark were the specific targets of the parody, the defendant's message necessitated the use of the identifying trademark.[1537] The Court noted, however, that its analysis did not extend to traditional infringement claims premised on a likelihood of confusion, because "[a] parody which causes confusion in the marketplace implicates the legitimate commercial and consumer protection objectives of trademark law."[1538]

The *L.L. Bean* case arguably represents the high water mark in First Amendment defenses against dilution claims. As discussed below, several other courts have held trademark parodies to be actionable because they potentially have a negative effect on consumer perceptions of a mark, even when the parody takes the form of traditionally protected expression.

In *Anheuser-Busch, Inc. v. Balducci Publications*,[1539] the defendant's fictitious ad (appearing in a humor magazine) parodied various trademarks associated with Michelob beer, and implied that the beer was made from water polluted by an oil spill. There was no evidence that the parody led consumers to believe that the plaintiff's beer was actually tainted. Nonetheless, the Eighth Circuit held that the plaintiff's claim under Missouri's dilution law should not have been dismissed, because the mere suggestion that a product is tainted, regardless of its

---

[1533] *See* § 5G[4].

[1534] 507 F.3d 252 (4th Cir. 2007). For a full discussion, see § 4G[3][f][iii](a).

[1535] 811 F.2d 26, 27 (1st Cir. 1987).

[1536] *Id.* at 32.

[1537] *Id.* at 34.

[1538] *Id.* at 32 n.3.

[1539] 28 F.3d 769 (8th Cir. 2001).

believability, "obviously tarnishes the marks' well-developed images."[1540] The court rejected the defendant's First Amendment arguments, and distinguished *L.L. Bean*, noting that the *L.L. Bean* parody (1) "made no derogatory comment about Bean's products' quality," and (2) was a more obvious parody.[1541]

The First Amendment also provided no defense against dilution claims in *Pillsbury Co. v. Milky Way Productions, Inc.*, in which a sexually explicit cartoon in a humor magazine targeted Pillsbury's "Poppin' Fresh" Dough Boy character. The district court granted a preliminary injunction under the Georgia dilution statute, limiting its analysis to a conclusory statement that the cartoon "could injure the business reputation of the plaintiff or dilute the distinctive quality of its trademarks."[1542] The court made no mention of First Amendment considerations.

In evaluating state-law dilution claims against motion pictures, courts have been unreceptive to First Amendment arguments when the film is sexually exploitative. In *Dallas Cowboys Cheerleaders, Inc. v. Pussycat Cinema, Ltd.*,[1543] in which the defendants' adult film purported to portray a promiscuous Dallas Cowboys Cheerleader (wearing the plaintiff's distinctive costume), in addition to finding a likelihood of confusion as to sponsorship, the Second Circuit upheld a preliminary injunction under the New York dilution statute, offering no analysis separate from its likelihood-of-confusion analysis other than noting that no likelihood of confusion was required. The court had already rejected the defendants' First Amendment arguments in analyzing the traditional infringement claim, holding that the film was not a parody, and that it could not satisfy the "adequate alternative avenues of communication" standard.[1544] The court implicitly applied the same standard to the dilution claim.

Where a motion picture targets a famous trademark in a humorous but disparaging way, but does not involve sexual exploitation, one might expect courts evaluating state dilution claims to be more receptive to First Amendment considerations. However, such a trend has not yet emerged.[1545]

[c]   Political Speech

Political speech is the one area in which courts have consistently subordinated the rights of trademark owners to the public interest in free expression, regardless of whether the claim is based on infringement/unfair competition or dilution. The outcomes in these cases are more consistent than in cases involving artistic and literary expression, because courts generally view political speech as entirely noncommercial, while artistic and literary expression often have a commercial

---

[1540] *Id.* at 777.

[1541] *Id.* at 778.

[1542] 215 U.S.P.Q. 124, 135 (N.D. Ga. 1981).

[1543] 604 F.2d 200 (2d Cir. 1979).

[1544] *See* 5J[6][b][i].

[1545] *See* American Dairy Queen Corp. v. New Line Prods., 35 F. Supp. 2d 727, 735 (D. Minn. 1998) (granting preliminary injunction against film titled "Dairy Queens," based on "adequate alternative avenues" test); Hormel Foods Corp. v. Jim Henson Prods., Inc., 36 U.S.P.Q.2d 1812 (S.D.N.Y. 1995) (rejecting dilution claims without discussing First Amendment considerations), *aff'd*, 73 F.3d 497 (2d Cir. 1996).

aspect. Some of these decisions, however, rest solely on the plaintiff's failure to make out the elements of its claim, without any express mention of the First Amendment.

For example, one district court held that the use of the term "Star Wars" by public interest groups in "political propaganda, newspapers or noncommercial, non-trade references" to the Reagan administration's Strategic Defense Initiative neither infringed nor diluted the plaintiff's trademark in the title of its motion picture.[1546] The court did not expressly rely on the First Amendment, relying instead on the conclusory statement that political speech of this nature would "not affect the distinct, and still strong secondary meaning of STAR WARS in trade and entertainment."[1547] The court also noted that "[i]t would be wholly unrealistic and unfair to allow the owner of a mark to interfere in the give-and-take of normal political discourse."[1548]

In two cases rejecting infringement and dilution claims arising from campaign ads, the district courts did not explicitly mention the First Amendment, holding instead that the plaintiffs failed to make the necessary showing as to likelihood of confusion or dilution; both courts also applied the "noncommercial use" exception to the plaintiffs' federal dilution claims.[1549]

In contrast, political and public service organizations have been held liable for infringement and dilution when they adopt names that are likely to cause confusion as to source or affiliation. The courts in these cases have reasoned that the use of another party's mark as the organization's name constitutes its use as a source identifier, rather than as a means of expressing an idea, and thus is not protected by the First Amendment.[1550]

[d]   Expressive Merchandise

Between the two extremes of purely commercial speech and traditional forms of artistic, political, or literary expression lies the realm of what might be "expressive merchandise" — a wide variety of items such as posters, T-shirts, and coffee mugs, which may carry parodic or satirical messages incorporating well-known trademarks.

The analyses of infringement and dilution claims in cases involving expressive merchandise have been inconsistent. For example, in *Girl Scouts of United States of America v. Personality Posters Mfg. Co.*,[1551] where a poster depicted a pregnant Girl Scout along with the message "Be Prepared," the court found no likelihood of confusion because the outraged members of the public fully understood that the

---

[1546] Lucasfilm, Ltd. v. High Frontier, 622 F. Supp. 931 (D.D.C. 1985).

[1547] *Id.* at 935.

[1548] *Id.*

[1549] Mastercard Int'l, Inc. v. Nader 2000 Primary Comm., Inc., 70 U.S.P.Q.2d 1046 (S.D.N.Y. 2004); American Family Life Insurance Company v. Hagan, 266 F. Supp. 2d 682 (N.D. Ohio 2002).

[1550] *See, e.g.*, United We Stand America, Inc. v. United We Stand, America New York, Inc., 128 F.3d 86, 93 (2d Cir. 1997); MGM-Pathe Communications v. Pink Panther Patrol, 774 F. Supp. 869 (S.D.N.Y. 1991); Tomei v. Finley, 512 F. Supp. 695, 698 (N.D. Ill. 1981).

[1551] 304 F. Supp. 1228 (S.D.N.Y. 1969).

Girl Scouts were not the source of the poster. A dilution claim was rejected because, at that time, courts interpreted New York's dilution law as requiring a likelihood of confusion. Two remaining causes of action, however, more closely resembled modern dilution claims — a defamation claim, and a state statutory claim alleging unauthorized commercial exploitation of a nonprofit organization's identity. With respect to both of these claims, the court held that injunctive relief would constitute an unlawful prior restraint under the First Amendment; the poster was "satirical expression 'deserving of substantial freedom — both as entertainment and as a form of social . . . criticism.'"[1552] The court relied specifically on New York case law holding that posters were "a form of expression which may be constitutionally protected."[1553] In addition, the court found no evidence that the poster would injure the Girl Scouts' reputation. The court's conclusion hints that the iconic status of the Girls Scouts made their trademarks a legitimate target for parody.[1554]

Three years later, in *Coca-Cola Co. v. Gemini Rising, Inc.*, another district court in the same circuit granted a preliminary injunction against distribution of a poster that closely mimicked Coca-Cola's marks as well as its distinctive typeface and trade dress, except that in place of the plaintiff's "Enjoy Coca-Cola" slogan it displayed the message "Enjoy Cocaine."[1555] The plaintiff asserted both a likelihood of confusion and dilution. When the defendant asserted that it intended the poster to be "satirical," the court described this as "predatory intent."[1556] Although the court concluded that there was "a high probability of confusion,"[1557] its analysis also suggests concern over tarnishment: "To associate such a noxious substance as cocaine with plaintiff's wholesome beverage as symbolized by its 'Coca-Cola' trademark and format would clearly have a tendency to impugn that product and injure plaintiff's business reputation, as plaintiff contends."[1558] The court rejected the argument that injunctive relief would be an unconstitutional prior restraint, and held that Coca-Cola was entitled to injunctive relief because of "special circumstances" that were absent in the *Girl Scouts* case — an "imitative use of [a] trademark in a manner injurious to the mark and to plaintiff's business reputation and good will."[1559]

A more recent pair of decisions again illustrates sharply different approaches to expressive merchandise. In *Mutual of Omaha Ins. Co. v Novak*,[1560] (which did not involve a dilution claim) the Eighth Circuit permanently enjoined a defendant from distributing T-shirts, caps, buttons, and coffee mugs displaying the words "Mutant of Omaha" and "Nuclear Holocaust Insurance," and depicting an emaciated, feather-bonneted human head that imitated Mutual of Omaha's distinctive "Indian

---

[1552] *Id.* at 1235.

[1553] *Id.*

[1554] *Id.* at 1235–36.

[1555] 346 F. Supp. 1183, 1192 (E.D.N.Y. 1972).

[1556] *Id.* at 1187.

[1557] *Id.* at 1190.

[1558] *Id.* at 1189.

[1559] *Id.* at 1193.

[1560] 836 F.2d 397 (8th Cir. 1987).

head" logo. Holding that the rights of the trademark owner "need not yield to the exercise of First Amendment rights under circumstances where adequate alternative avenues of communication exist," the court noted that the injunction applied only to the defendant's sale of "services and products," and that the defendant was free to express his views through "an editorial parody in a book, magazine, or film."[1561] The court distinguished cases such as *L.L. Bean* as involving "editorial or artistic" use of a mark "solely for noncommercial purposes."[1562]

The Fourth Circuit's 1992 decision in *Anheuser-Busch, Inc. v. L&L Wings, Inc.*[1563] addressed expressive T-shirts. The plaintiff in *L&L Wings* brought a trademark infringement claim (but no dilution claim) against a defendant that sold souvenir T-shirts with a design that imitated Budweiser's beer label in promoting Myrtle Beach, South Carolina, as the "King of Beaches." Ruling for the defendant, the majority concluded that a reasonable jury could find that the differences between the designs were sufficient to dispel confusion. It also noted, however, that the traditional confusion factors are "at best awkward in the context of parody," and that while successful parodies necessarily imitate the original trademarks, they also "dispel consumer confusion by conveying just enough of the original design to allow the consumer to appreciate the point of the parody."[1564]

[7]   Other Defenses

[a]   Laches

Laches is an equitable defense that can be invoked when a plaintiff has failed to act diligently in asserting its rights. It is a valid defense to trademark, false advertising, and unfair competition claims under both state law and the Lanham Act.[1565] The laches defense is available even when the mark alleged to have been infringed is incontestable.[1566]

To establish laches, a defendant must show that: (a) the claimant unreasonably delayed in filing suit, and (b) as a result of the delay, the defendant suffered prejudice.[1567] Whether the plaintiff's delay was unreasonable depends on when the plaintiff first had knowledge of the defendant's infringing activity.[1568] That knowledge may be actual or constructive.[1569] For example, where the infringing activity was evident from a prominent national advertising campaign, the plaintiff was

---

[1561] 836 F.2d at 402.

[1562] *Id.* at 403 n.9.

[1563] 962 F.2d 316 (4th Cir. 1992).

[1564] *Id.* at 321.

[1565] *See, e.g.,* Danjaq LLC v. Sony Corp., 263 F.3d 942, 955 (9th Cir. 2001); Conopco, Inc. v. Campbell Soup Co., 95 F.3d 187 (2d Cir. 1996); Tillamook Country Smoker, Inc. v. Tillamook County Creamery Ass'n, 311 F. Supp. 2d 1023, 1030 (D. Or. 2004), *aff'd,* 465 F.3d 1102, 1111 (9th Cir. 2006).

[1566] 15 U.S.C. § 1115(b)(9).

[1567] *Tillamook,* 311 F. Supp. 2d at 1030; *see also* Carl Zeiss Stiftung v. VEB Carl Zeiss Jena, 433 F.2d 686, 704 (2d Cir. 1970).

[1568] Chattanooga Mfg., Inc. v. Nike, Inc., 301 F.3d 789, 793 (7th Cir. 2002).

[1569] *Id.*

deemed to have constructive notice of the infringement beginning with the first year of the campaign.[1570] The Fourth Circuit has emphasized that laches is measured not from the date on which the trademark owner knows of the defendant's use, but from the date on which the trademark owner knows (or should know) that the defendant's use is *infringing* — in other words, that it creates a likelihood of confusion.[1571]

In evaluating a laches defense, courts may consider all relevant circumstances. However, some courts, such as the Ninth Circuit, have enumerated a specific list of factors that should be considered.[1572] Ultimately, the doctrine of laches requires "a consideration of the circumstances of each particular case and a balancing of the interests and equities of the parties."[1573]

Even though laches is an equitable defense, most courts permit laches as a defense *only* to a damages claim, and not as a defense to a claim for injunctive relief, because injunctive relief protects the public from the harm that may arise from future infringement.[1574] This view is endorsed by the *Restatement (Third) of Unfair Competition.*[1575] Courts that treat laches as a bar only to damages typically require the stronger showing of acquiescence in order to bar injunctive relief.[1576] Other courts, however, will deny injunctive relief on the basis of laches alone, at least where the defendant would be prejudiced by an injunction.[1577] In the Ninth Circuit, laches will bar injunctive relief unless the suit alleges "that the product is harmful or otherwise a threat to public safety and well being."[1578]

In determining whether a defendant has been prejudiced by a plaintiff's delay, courts consider whether "a defendant has changed his position in a way that would not have occurred if the plaintiff had not delayed."[1579] Typically, prejudice is established where the plaintiff's unexcused delay "caused the defendant to rely to

---

[1570] *Id.*

[1571] Ray Comm'ns, Inc. v. Clear Channel Comm'ns, Inc., 673 F.3d 294, 301–02 (4th Cir. 2012).

[1572] *See, e.g.,* Grupo Gigante SA de CV v. Dallo & Co., 391 F.3d 1088, 1102 (9th Cir. 2004) (applying a six-factor test).

[1573] Tillamook Country Smoker, Inc. v. Tillamook County Creamery Ass'n, 311 F. Supp. 2d 1023, 1030–31 (D. Or. 2004) (internal quotation marks omitted), *aff'd,* 465 F.3d 1102 (9th Cir. 2006).

[1574] *See, e.g.,* Kellogg Co. v. Exxon Corp., 209 F.3d 562, 568 (6th Cir. 2000); Sara Lee Corp., v. Kayser-Roth Corp., 81 F.3d 455 (4th Cir. 1996); TWM Mfg. Co., Inc. v. Dura Corp., 592 F.2d 346, 349–50 (6th Cir. 1979); *see also* Kason Indus. v. Component Hardware Grp., 120 F.3d 1199, 1207 (11th Cir. 1997); SunAmerica Corp. v. Sun Life Assurance Co. of Can., 77 F.3d 1325, 1334 (11th Cir. 1996). *But see* University of Pittsburgh v. Champion Products, Inc., 686 F.2d 1040, 1044–45 (3d Cir. 1982) (noting a "narrow class of cases where the plaintiff's delay has been so outrageous, unreasonable and inexcusable as to constitute a virtual abandonment of its right"); Anheuser-Busch, Inc. v. DuBois Brewing Co., 175 F.2d 370, 374 (3d Cir. 1949) (similar).

[1575] RESTATEMENT (THIRD) OF UNFAIR COMPETITION § 31, cmt. e (1995); *accord,* Profitness Physical Therapy Ctr. v. Pro-Fit Orthopedic & Sports Physical Therapy P.C., 314 F.3d 62, 68 (2d Cir. 2002).

[1576] *See* § 5J[7][b].

[1577] *See, e.g.,* Abraham v. Alpha Chi Omega, 708 F.3d 614, 626 (5th Cir. 2013) (adopting this position but granting injunctive relief); Jarrow Formulas, Inc. v. Nutrition Now, Inc., 304 F.3d 829, 840 (9th Cir. 2002).

[1578] Tillamook Country Smoker, Inc. v. Tillamook County Creamery Ass'n, 465 F.3d 1102, 1111 (9th Cir. 2006); *Jarrow Formulas,* 304 F.3d at 841.

[1579] Chattanooga Mfg. Co. v. Nike, Inc., 301 F.3d 789, 795 (7th Cir. 2002).

its detriment and build up a valuable business around its trademark."[1580] Because laches is "a question of degree," courts often apply a sliding scale to determine whether the defense should apply — *e.g.*, requiring a stronger showing of prejudice if the plaintiff's delay was brief.[1581]

Because the Lanham Act does not contain a statute of limitations, federal courts have looked to analogous state limitations statutes to determine whether a presumption of laches should apply.[1582] However, a laches defense is not *per se* unavailable for claims brought within the limitations period; rather, courts use the state limitations period as a "baseline" for determining whether a presumption of laches is appropriate.[1583] Accordingly, while federal courts will typically "presume that an action is barred if not brought within the period of the statute of limitations and is alive if brought within the period,"[1584] that presumption is rebuttable.[1585]

Courts will also consider whether laches "is equitable in light of the public's interest in being free from confusion and deception."[1586] While the importance of this factor has been described as "paramount,"[1587] concerns about the public interest must be well-founded.[1588]

The laches defense may be negated if the plaintiff establishes "progressive encroachment" by the defendant. Progressive encroachment occurs when the defendant's initial use is not extensive enough to warrant an infringement action, but the defendant later expands its use in some way. For example, progressive encroachment may occur when the defendant alters its mark so that it more closely resembles the plaintiff's mark, or where the defendant expands its market to compete more directly with the plaintiff.[1589] Market expansion that constitutes progressive encroachment occurs when the junior user expands into a different region or a different market; mere growth in the junior user's existing business does not qualify.[1590]

[1580] *Id.*

[1581] Hot Wax, Inc. v. Turtle Wax, Inc., 191 F.3d 813, 824 (7th Cir. 1999).

[1582] *Id.* at 820–21.

[1583] *Id.* at 821–22.

[1584] *Id.* at 821 (quoting Tandy Corp. v. Malone & Hyde, Inc., 769 F.2d 362, 365 (6th Cir. 1985)).

[1585] Chattanooga Mfg. Co. v. Nike, Inc., 301 F.3d 789, 793–94 (7th Cir. 2002).

[1586] Conopco, Inc. v. Campbell Soup Co., 95 F.3d 187, 193 (2d Cir. 1996); *accord*, Hot Wax, Inc. v. Turtle Wax, Inc., 191 F.3d 813, 826 (7th Cir. 1999).

[1587] *Conopco*, 95 F.3d at 193.

[1588] *See, e.g., Hot Wax*, 191 F.3d at 826–27.

[1589] Kellogg Co. v. Exxon Corp., 209 F.3d 562, 570–73 (6th Cir. 2003) (collecting cases).

[1590] Tillamook Country Smoker, Inc. v. Tillamook County Creamery Ass'n, 465 F.3d 1102, 1109–10 (9th Cir. 2006); Grupo Gigante S.A. de C.V. v. Dallo & Co., 391 F.3d 1088, 1103 (9th Cir. 2004); ProFitness Phys. Therapy Ctr. v. Pro-Fit Orthopedic & Sports Phys. Therapy P.C., 314 F.3d 62, 65 (2d Cir. 2002); Westchester Media v. PRL USA Holdings, Inc., 214 F.3d 658 (5th Cir. 2000).

[b]   Acquiescence

In contrast to laches, the defense of acquiescence arises only if the plaintiff gave the defendant an express or implied assurance that the plaintiff would not assert its trademark rights against the defendant.[1591] Thus, acquiescence involves active consent, while laches is passive.[1592] However, acquiescence need not be explicit, and can be inferred from the trademark owner's affirmative conduct toward the defendant.[1593] Several federal courts of appeals have set forth strict criteria for acquiescence, requiring three elements: (1) the senior user actively represented that it would not assert a right or a claim; (2) the delay between the active representation and assertion of the right or claim was not excusable; and (3) the delay caused the defendant undue prejudice.[1594] However, some courts are less precise, and occasionally use the term acquiescence as a synonym for laches.[1595]

Acquiescence may bar injunctive relief as well as monetary damages.[1596] However, even where a finding of acquiescence is otherwise warranted, a strong showing of likelihood of confusion may persuade a court to grant injunctive relief in order to protect the public.[1597] As with laches, a showing of progressive encroachment may negate acquiescence.[1598]

[c]   Statute of Limitations

The Lanham Act does not have its own statute of limitations, and federal courts have developed two approaches to filling this void. Some circuits follow the Supreme Court's instruction in *Wilson v. Garcia*, applicable generally to federal statutes that fail to specify limitations periods, to "adopt a local time limitation as federal law if it is not inconsistent with federal law or policy to do so."[1599] Accordingly, courts in these circuits follow the statute of limitations that applies to the most closely analogous action under state law.[1600] Other courts apply the equitable doctrine of

---

[1591] Creative Gifts, Inc. v. UFO, 235 F.3d 540 (10th Cir. 2000); Sweetheart Plastics, Inc. v. Detroit Forming, Inc., 743 F.2d 1039, 1046 (4th Cir. 1984) (citing Carl Zeiss Stiftung v. VEB Carl Zeiss Jena, 433 F.2d 686, 704 (2d Cir. 1970); Exxon Corp. v. Humble Exploration Co., Inc., 524 F. Supp. 450, 467 (N.D. Tex. 1981), *aff'd in part, rev'd and remanded in part*, 695 F.2d 96 (5th Cir. 1983)).

[1592] Profitness Physical Therapy Ctr. v. Pro-Fit Orthopedic & Sports Physical Therapy P.C., 314 F.3d 62, 67–68 (2d Cir. 2002); Kellogg Co. v. Exxon Corp., 209 F.3d 562, 569 n.2 (6th Cir. 2000); Sara Lee Corp. v. Kayser-Roth Corp., 81 F.3d 455, 460, 462 (4th Cir. 1996).

[1593] *Sweetheart Plastics*, 433 F.2d at 1046; *see, e.g.*, Ambrosia Chocolate Co. v. Ambrosia Cake Bakery, 165 F.2d 693 (4th Cir. 1947); Tillamook Country Smoker, Inc. v. Tillamook County Creamery Ass'n, 311 F. Supp. 2d 1023, 1031 & n.2 (D. Or. 2004), *aff'd*, 465 F.3d 1102 (9th Cir. 2006).

[1594] *See, e.g.*, Times Mirror Magazines, Inc. v. Field & Stream Licenses Co., 294 F.3d 383, 395 (2d Cir. 2002); SunAmerica Corp. v. Sun Life Assurance Co. of Can., 77 F.3d 1325 (11th Cir. 1996).

[1595] *See, e.g.*, University of Pittsburgh v. Champion Prods., Inc., 686 F.2d 1040, 1045 (3d Cir. 1982).

[1596] *Kellogg*, 209 F.3d at 574.

[1597] *See, e.g.*, *Profitness*, 314 F.3d at 68; *Sara Lee*, 81 F.3d at 463; Coach House Rest., Inc. v. Coach & Six Rests., Inc., 934 F.2d 1551 (11th Cir. 1991).

[1598] *Profitness*, 314 F.3d at 68; *Kellogg*, 209 F.3d at 570.

[1599] 471 U.S. 261, 266–67 (1985); *accord* Reed v. United Transp. Union, 488 U.S. 319, 334 (1989).

[1600] *See, e.g.*, Santana Prods. v. Bobrick Washroom Equip., Inc., 401 F.3d 123, 135 (3d Cir. 2005); Jarrow Formulas, Inc. v. Nutrition Now, Inc., 304 F.3d 829, 836 (9th Cir. 2002); Island Insteel Sys., Inc. v. Waters, 296 F.3d 200, 203 (3d Cir. 2002); Beauty Time v. VU Skin Sys., 118 F.3d 140, 143 (3d Cir. 1997);

laches in place of a formal limitations period.[1601] These courts typically treat the analogous state limitations statute as relevant to determining whether a "presumption of laches" should apply.[1602]

[d] Unclean Hands

Unclean hands is an equitable defense against trademark or unfair competition claims under state or federal law. Although the scope of conduct by a plaintiff that warrants invocation of this doctrine is not well defined, it is not limited to illegal conduct. Rather, the Supreme Court has described it as "any willful act concerning the cause of action which rightfully can be said to transgress equitable standards of conduct."[1603] Intentional misrepresentations regarding a product have been held to constitute unclean hands, provided they pertain to the subject matter of the plaintiff's cause of action.[1604] Thus, for example, plaintiffs may be denied relief on the grounds that their marks are deceptive.[1605] The defense may also apply where marks have been used in violation of antitrust laws.[1606] Fraud in obtaining federal trademark registration can also provide an unclean hands defense to infringement of the registered mark; however, this will not bar an action based on common-law rights in that mark.[1607]

[8] Federal Preemption

In certain circumstances, state trademark or unfair competition laws may be preempted by federal patent or copyright law. For example, the functionality bar to trademark protection, discussed above,[1608] illustrates the preemptive effect of federal patent law.

The principal cases on federal preemption of state unfair competitions laws are the Supreme Court's decisions in *Sears, Roebuck & Co. v. Stiffel Co.*,[1609] *Compco*

Lamparello v. Falwell, 360 F. Supp. 2d 768, 775 (E.D. Va. 2004), *rev'd on other grounds*, 420 F.2d 309 (4th Cir. 2005); Unlimited Screw Products, Inc. v. Malm, 781 F. Supp. 1121, 1125 (E.D. Va. 1991); Fox Chemical Co. v. Amsoil, Inc., 445 F. Supp. 1355, 1357 (D. Minn. 1978).

[1601] Ford Motor Co. v. Catalanotte, 342 F.3d 543, 550 (6th Cir. 2003); Hot Wax, Inc. v. Turtle Wax, Inc., 191 F.3d 813, 820–21 (7th Cir. 1999); Conopco, Inc. v. Campbell Soup Co., 95 F.3d 187, 191 (2d Cir. 1996); AmBrit, Inc. v. Kraft, Inc., 812 F.2d 1531, 1546 (11th Cir. 1986); Tandy Corp. v. Malone & Hyde, Inc., 769 F.2d 362, 365 (6th Cir. 1985). For a discussion of laches, see § 5J[7][a].

[1602] *Hot Wax*, 191 F.3d at 820–21; *AmBrit*, 812 F.2d at 1545; *Tandy*, 769 F.2d at 365.

[1603] Precision Instr. Mfg. Co. v. Automotive Maint. Mach. Co., 324 U.S. 806, 815 (1945).

[1604] Havana Club Holding S.A. v. Galleon S.A., 49 U.S.P.Q.2d 1296, 1300–01 (S.D.N.Y. 1998) (plaintiff's alleged use of "HAVANA CLUB" mark for Panamanian rum adequately pleaded an unclean hands defense).

[1605] *See, e.g., id.*; Worden v. California Fig Syrup Co., 187 U.S. 516 (1903); Holeproof Hosiery Co. v. Wallach Bros., 172 F. 859 (2d Cir. 1909).

[1606] Phi Delta Theta Fraternity v. J. A. Bochroeder & Co., 251 F. Supp. 968 (W.D. Mo. 1966); Sanitized, Inc. v. S.C. Johnson & Sons, Inc., 23 F.R.D. 230, 231 (S.D.N.Y. 1959).

[1607] Orient Express Trading Co. v. Federated Dept. Stores, Inc., 842 F.2d 650 (2d Cir. 1988). Fraud as grounds for cancelling a federal registration and as a defense to infringement of an incontestable mark is discussed at §§ 5E[3][d][iv][a] and 5E[4][a].

[1608] *See* 5C[1][c].

[1609] 376 U.S. 225 (1964).

Corp. v. Day-Brite Lighting, Inc.,[1610] and *Bonito Boats, Inc. v. Thunder Craft Boats, Inc.*[1611] These cases are discussed in § 1D[3][a].

Some courts have suggested that the scope of federal preemption and the functionality bar are coextensive.[1612] It is true that the Court's analysis in *Bonito Boats* emphasizes that states should not interfere with the free circulation of designs that are "useful" or "functional." Moreover, the Court specifically noted that states may impose "limited regulations" on the use of designs in order to prevent consumer confusion, even though the designs might be the subject of design patent protection.[1613] However, federal preemption is not necessarily limited to state laws protecting the functional aspects of an article. In both *Sears* and *Compco*, the lamp designs that were held to be unworthy of utility patents had received design patents that were later held to be invalid. In a case decided before *Bonito Boats*, the Federal Circuit held in *Litton Systems, Inc. v. Whirlpool Corp.* that federal law preempted a state law that prohibited the copying of product configuration trade dress.[1614] In decisions issued after *Bonito Boats*, several courts have suggested that state trade dress protection of product configuration (as opposed to product packaging) is preempted.[1615] And one federal district court has held that federal patent law preempts the application of New York's dilution statute to protect the decorative shape of a fragrance bottle.[1616]

Because nonfunctional aspects of product configuration can be protected under section 43(a) of the Lanham Act,[1617] a plaintiff that seeks to protect a distinctive product configuration can bring its claims under section 43(a) and/or section 43(c) to avoid potential preemption of corresponding claims brought under state law.[1618]

Federal copyright law can also preempt the enforcement of some state trademark and unfair competition laws, because some trademarks are also copyrightable works of authorship, and some unfair competition claims may involve false representations about copyrightable works of authorship. Preemption arguments based on copyright law may involve either express preemption or conflict preemption.

[1610] 376 U.S. 234 (1964).

[1611] 489 U.S. 141 (1989).

[1612] *See, e.g.*, I.P. Lund Trading ApS v. Kohler Co., 163 F.3d 27, 36 (1st Cir. 1998).

[1613] 489 U.S. at 154.

[1614] 728 F.2d 1423, 1448 (Fed. Cir. 1984).

[1615] Landscape Forms, Inc. v. Columbia Cascade Corp., 113 F.3d 373, 383 (2d Cir. 1997); PAF S.r.l. v. Lisa Lighting Co., 712 F. Supp. 394, 412 n.19 (S.D.N.Y. 1989).

[1616] Escada AG v. Limited, Inc., 810 F. Supp. 571 (S.D.N.Y. 1993).

[1617] *See* TrafFix Devices, Inc. v. Marketing Displays, Inc., 532 U.S. 23 (2001); Wal-Mart Stores, Inc. v. Samara Bros., Inc., 529 U.S. 205 (2000). For a more detailed discussion of the Lanham Act's application to trade dress, see § 5C[2][c].

[1618] I.P. Lund Trading ApS v. Kohler Co., 163 F.3d 27, 45, 50 (1st Cir. 1998); Sunbeam Prods., Inc. v. West Bend Co., 39 U.S.P.Q.2d 1545, 1555 (S.D. Miss. 1996), *aff'd on other grounds*, 123 F.3d 246 (5th Cir. 1997), *overruled in part on other grounds*, *TrafFix*, 523 U.S. at 28; *see also* GMC v. Urban Gorilla, LLC, 500 F.3d 1222, 1228–9 (10th Cir. 2007); Hammerton, Inc. v. Heisterman, 2008 U.S. Dist. LEXIS 38036 (D. Utah May 8, 2008).

The express preemption provision of the copyright act prohibits enforcement of any state-law claim that: (1) is the equivalent of any of the exclusive rights of a copyright owner and (2) involves a work that falls within the general scope of copyrightable subject matter[1619] (which encompasses original works of authorship fixed in any tangible medium of expression[1620]). The purpose of the express preemption provisions is to prevent states from duplicating or expanding the scope of federal copyright protection. Thus, a state-law claim is not preempted if it involves an "extra element" that makes it qualitatively different from a copyright claim.[1621] Most trademark infringement and false designation of origin claims avoid express preemption because they require proof of a likelihood of confusion.[1622] In contrast, courts have held that copyright law preempts state law "reverse passing off" claims arising from the unauthorized and uncredited copying of copyrightable expression.[1623] The scope of copyright preemption of state dilution laws is unclear; while dilution claims do not require a likelihood of confusion, a dilution plaintiff must still establish that its mark is distinctive (and famous, under some statutes), and that the mark will be diluted or tarnished by the unauthorized use. These "extra elements" have led several courts to hold that a dilution claim is not subject to express preemption.[1624]

Even where a claim is not expressly preempted, conflict preemption will prevent enforcement of state trademark and unfair competition claims that would unduly interfere with the purposes underlying the federal scheme of copyright protection — for example, by preventing the public from freely reproducing works that have entered the public domain, or by allowing someone other than the copyright owner to control the exploitation of a copyrighted work.

Although, in general, Lanham Act claims are not subject to preemption by other federal laws,[1625] the federal courts have applied a principle analogous to conflict preemption in order to reject Lanham Act claims that interfere with the general scheme of copyright protection. In *Dastar Corp. v. Twentieth Century Fox Film Corp.*,[1626] discussed in § 5F[7], the Supreme Court rejected a claim of reverse passing off under section 43(a) of the Lanham Act, where the defendant had reproduced the plaintiff's videos (which had entered the public domain due to failure to renew the copyright registration) and represented itself as the author of those videos, saying that a false designation of origin claim under the Lanham Act could not be used to create a "mutant" form of copyright protection for public domain works. *Dastar* specifically held that the "origin" of goods for purposes of

---

[1619] 17 U.S.C. § 301 (2009). For a detailed discussion of copyright preemption, see § 1D[3][c].

[1620] 17 U.S.C. § 102(a) (2009).

[1621] Computer Assocs. Int'l v. Altai, Inc., 982 F.2d 693, 716 (2d Cir. 1992).

[1622] *See, e.g.*, Warner Bros. v. American Broadcasting Co., 720 F.2d 231, 247 (2d Cir. 1983).

[1623] *See, e.g.*, Waldman Pub. Corp. v. Landoll, Inc., 848 F. Supp. 498, 505 (S.D.N.Y. 1994), *vacated and remanded on other grounds*, 43 F.3d 775 (2d Cir. 1994).

[1624] *See, e.g.*, Eliya, Inc. v. Kohl's Dep't Stores, 82 U.S.P.Q.2d 1088 (S.D.N.Y. 2006); Gateway 2000 v. Cyrix Corp., 942 F. Supp. 985, 995 (D.N.J. 1996).

[1625] *Cf.* 17 U.S.C. § 301(d) ("Nothing in this title [Copyright Act and related rights] annuls or limits any rights or remedies under any other Federal statute.").

[1626] 539 U.S. 23 (2003).

section 43(a) refers to the origin of *tangible* goods, and not to the ideas or intangible intellectual property content of those goods; thus, it does not permit authors to bring reverse passing off claims based on misattribution of authorship.[1627] Lower federal courts have broadened the *Dastar* analysis to encompass Lanham Act claims involving copyrighted works regardless of whether those works have entered the public domain.[1628]

[9]   Sovereign Immunity

Although the Lanham Act expressly provides that States and state officers may be liable for trademark infringement, the Supreme Court has held that the Lanham Act's abrogation of state sovereign immunity for false advertising claims violates the Eleventh Amendment,[1629] and lower courts have extended the holding to trademark claims. For details, see § 1D[5][a].

The United States has expressly waived its sovereign immunity to all claims made under the Lanham Act, including trademark infringement, dilution, and false advertising.[1630]

§ 5K   REMEDIES

[1]   Non-Monetary Remedies

[a]   Injunctions

Under both state and federal law, injunctions are the predominant and most traditional remedy for violations of trademark and unfair competition law. Injunctive relief, unlike monetary damages, protects the consuming public from the danger of continuing confusion and deception. It also protects the trademark owner from the irreparable injury that could be caused by another party's appropriation or tarnishment of the goodwill embodied in the mark.[1631]

Under section 34(a) of the Lanham Act, both permanent and temporary injunctions are available for infringements of registered trademarks under section 32, as well as for violations of sections 43(a), (c), or (d) with respect to both registered and unregistered marks. Section 34 grants state and federal courts broad powers to fashion injunctions "according to the principles of equity and upon such terms as the court may deem reasonable." A federal injunction is nationwide

---

[1627] *Id.* at 37.

[1628] *See, e.g.*, Sybersound Records, Inc. v. UAV Corp., 517 F.3d 1137, 1143–44 (9th Cir. 2008); Richard Feiner & Co. v. New York Times Co., 88 U.S.P.Q.2d 1951 (S.D.N.Y. 2008) (collecting cases).

[1629] College Savings Bank v. Florida Prepaid Postsecondary Education Expense Board, 527 U.S. 666 (1999).

[1630] 15 U.S.C. § 122(a), (c).

[1631] *See, e.g.*, Times Mirror Magazines, Inc. v. Las Vegas Sports News, 212 F.3d 157, 169 (3d Cir. 2000); Lone Star Steakhouse & Saloon v. Alpha of Virginia, 43 F.3d 922 (4th Cir. 1995); Opticians Ass'n v. Independent Opticians, 920 F.2d 187, 195 (3d Cir. 1990); Century 21 Real Estate Corp. v. Sandlin, 846 F.2d 1175 (9th Cir. 1988).

in effect, and may be enforced by proceedings for contempt.[1632]

In exercising their broad discretion under section 34(a), courts will consider all of the equities of a case, including but not limited to the extent of the injury that the plaintiff and the public would suffer from continuing concurrent use of the mark under limitations or conditions (such as concurrent uses in distinct geographic territories), and the good or bad faith of the defendant in adopting the mark.[1633] Some courts will decline to enjoin the junior user of a federally registered mark unless and until the registrant shows a likelihood of actually using the mark in the junior user's territory.[1634]

While a permanent injunction will be issued only after a plaintiff has prevailed on the merits, the court may grant a preliminary injunction prior to the resolution of the case, based on the following criteria: (1) the likelihood that the plaintiff will ultimately succeed on the merits; (2) whether the plaintiff is likely to suffer irreparable harm if the defendant is permitted to continue the allegedly infringing activities during the litigation; (3) whether the hardship to the plaintiff in the absence of a preliminary injunction is likely to be greater than the hardship to the defendant that will result from preliminary injunction; and (4) whether a preliminary injunction would serve the public interest (e.g., by preventing consumer confusion during pendency of the litigation).[1635]

In the past, most federal and state courts routinely granted permanent injunctions to prevailing plaintiffs in trademark cases, on the ground that irreparable harm to the plaintiff could be presumed once a likelihood of confusion was established.[1636] Some courts applied this presumption to dilution and cybersquatting claims as well, once the plaintiff had prevailed on the merits.[1637] Preliminary

---

[1632] 15 U.S.C. § 1116(a).

[1633] See, e.g., King-Seeley Thermos Co. v. Aladdin Industries, Inc., 321 F.2d 577 (2d Cir. 1963). The flexibility afforded to courts fashioning injunctions under the Lanham Act reflects the traditionally broad discretion afforded by the common law of unfair competition. See, e.g., David B. Findlay, Inc. v. Findlay, 258 A.D. 1089 (N.Y. App. Div. 1940).

[1634] See, e.g., Dawn Donut Co. v. Hart's Food Stores, Inc., 267 F.2d 358 (2d Cir. 1959). For a fuller discussion, see § 5E[7][b].

[1635] While these criteria represent the most common formulation, see, e.g., Abbott Laboratories v. Mead Johnson & Co., 971 F.2d 6 (7th Cir. 1992), the federal circuits (and some state courts) have each developed their own version of these factors. See, e.g., Beltran v. Myers, 677 F.2d 1317, 1320 (9th Cir. 1982).

[1636] See, e.g., Brennan's, Inc. v. Brennan's Rest., LLC, 360 F.3d 125, 129 (2d Cir. 2004); Ty, Inc. v. Jones Group, Inc., 237 F.3d 891, 902 (7th Cir. 2001); GoTo.com, Inc. v. Walt Disney Co., 202 F.3d 1199, 1209 (9th Cir. 2000); Circuit City Stores, Inc. v. CarMax, Inc., 165 F.3d 1047, 1056 (6th Cir. 1999); McDonald's Corp. v. Robertson, 147 F.3d 1301, 1310 (11th Cir. 1998); Pappan Enters., Inc. v. Hardee's Food Sys., Inc., 143 F.3d 800, 805 (3d Cir. 1998); Societe Des Produits Nestle, S.A. v. Casa Helvetia, Inc., 982 F.2d 633, 640 (1st Cir. 1992); Black Hills Jewelry Mfg. Co. v. Gold Rush, Inc., 633 F.2d 746, 753 n.7 (8th Cir. 1980). The Fifth Circuit, in contrast, has never adopted this presumption. Paulsson Geophysical Servs., Inc. v. Sigmar, 529 F.3d 303 (5th Cir. 2008). In false advertising cases, some courts have limited the presumption to claims of false comparative advertising. See Scotts Co. v. United Indus. Corp., 315 F.3d 264, 273–74 (4th Cir. 2002) (collecting cases).

[1637] See, e.g., Verizon Calif., Inc. v. Navigation Catalyst Sys., Inc., 568 F. Supp. 2d 1088 (C.D. Cal. 2008); AM Gen. Corp. v. DaimlerChrysler Corp., 311 F.3d 796, 832 (7th Cir. 2002); Asia Apparel, LLC v. RIPSwear, Inc., 2004 U.S. Dist. LEXIS 29208 (W.D.N.C. 2004), aff'd sub nom. Asia Apparel, LLC v.

injunctions, too, were routinely granted once the plaintiff established a likelihood of success on the merits; here, as well, irreparable harm was generally presumed.[1638] However, as a result of the Supreme Court's decisions in *eBay, Inc. v. MercExchange, LLC*,[1639] and *Winter v. National Resources Defense Council, Inc.*,[1640] most courts have concluded that such presumptions are no longer permissible. In *eBay*, a patent infringement case, the Court disapproved the Federal Circuit's policy of routinely granting permanent injunctions against infringers absent "exceptional circumstances," and instead ordered the Federal Circuit to apply the traditional principles of equity in determining whether injunctive relief is warranted; one such principle is the requirement that the plaintiff establish that it has suffered irreparable harm.[1641] In *Winter*, a case involving environmental protection laws, the Court held that a preliminary injunction should be granted only if irreparable harm is "likely"; a mere "possibility" of such harm is not sufficient.[1642]

It is now well settled that the principles of *eBay* apply to the granting of permanent injunctions in trademark infringement actions,[1643] and at least one court has applied *eBay* to a federal dilution claim.[1644]

Likewise, the decision in *Winter* has altered the standard for granting preliminary injunctions. In the past, courts considering motions for preliminary injunctions in trademark, unfair competition, false advertising, cybersquatting, and dilution cases typically presumed irreparable injury once a plaintiff demonstrated a likelihood of success on the merits. While some courts continued this practice post-*eBay*,[1645] a larger number have concluded that *eBay* and *Winter* make this presumption impermissible.[1646]

Cunneen, 118 Fed. Appx. 782 (4th Cir. 2005); Nabisco, Inc. v. PF Brands, Inc., 50 F. Supp. 2d 188, 210 (S.D.N.Y.), *aff'd*, 191 F.3d 208 (2d Cir. 1999); Deere & Co. v. MTD Prods., Inc., 860 F. Supp. 113, 122 (S.D.N.Y.), *aff'd*, 41 F.3d 39 (2d Cir. 1994).

[1638] *See, e.g.*, Tally-Ho, Inc. v. Coast Cmty. Coll. Dist., 889 F.2d 1018, 1029 (11th Cir. 1989).

[1639] 547 U.S. 388 (2006).

[1640] 555 U.S. 7 (2008).

[1641] 547 U.S. at 391.

[1642] 555 U.S. at 22.

[1643] *See, e.g.*, Abraham v. Alpha Chi Omega, 708 F.3d 614 (5th Cir. 2013); Reno Air Racing Ass'n, Inc. v. McCord, 452 F.3d 1126 (9th Cir. 2006); Audi AG v. D'Amato, 469 F.3d 534, 550 (6th Cir. 2006); Coach, Inc. v. O'Brien, 2012 U.S. Dist. LEXIS 52565 (S.D.N.Y. Apr. 13, 2012); Funai Elec. Co., LTD v. Daewoo Elecs. Corp., 593 F. Supp.2d 1088 (N.D. Cal. 2009); Microsoft Corp. v. AGA Solutions, Inc., 589 F.Supp.2d 195 (E.D.N.Y. 2008); American Taxi Dispatch, Inc. v. American Metro Taxi & Limo Co., 582 F. Supp. 2d 999 (N.D. Ill. 2008).

[1644] *See* Nike, Inc. v. Nikepal Intern., Inc., 84 U.S.P.Q.2d 1521 (E.D. Cal. 2007).

[1645] *See, e.g.*, Lorillard Tobacco Co. v. Amouri's Grand Foods, Inc., 453 F.3d 377 (6th Cir. 2006); Canfield v. Health Communs., Inc., 2008 U.S. Dist. LEXIS 28662, *6 (C.D. Cal. Apr. 1, 2008); Verizon Calif., Inc. v. Navigation Catalyst Sys., Inc., 568 F. Supp. 2d 1088 (C.D. Cal. 2008).

[1646] *See, e.g.*, Herb Reed Enters., LLC v. Florida Ent't Mgt, 736 F.3d 1239 (9th Cir. 2013); North American Medical Corp. v. Axiom Worldwide, Inc., 522 F.3d 1211, 1228 (11th Cir. 2008); Lorillard Tobacco Co. v. Engida, 213 Fed. Appx. 654 (10th Cir. 2007) (unpub.); C.J. Prods. LLC v. Snuggly Plushez LLC, 809 F. Supp. 2d 127 (E.D.N.Y. 2011); Auburn Univ. v. Moody, 2008 U.S. Dist. LEXIS 89578, *28–29 (M.D. Ala. Nov. 4, 2008); MyGym, LLC v. Engle, 2006 U.S. Dist. LEXIS 88375 (D. Utah Dec. 6, 2006); Harris Research, Inc. v. Lydon, 505 F. Supp. 2d 1161 (D. Utah 2007).

[b]   Seizure of Counterfeit Goods and Related Materials

Upon *ex parte* application, section 34(d) authorizes seizure of any goods bearing counterfeit marks, as well as the counterfeit marks themselves, the means for making the counterfeit marks, and any related records, provided that certain specified conditions are satisfied.[1647] For this purpose, a "counterfeit" mark is a spurious mark that is identical to, or substantially indistinguishable from, a mark that is: (1) in use, and (2) registered in the Principal Register for the same goods or services, regardless of whether the counterfeiter knew that the mark was registered, except that a mark is *not* counterfeit if, at the time the goods or services in question were manufactured or produced, the holder of the right to use the genuine mark had authorized the maker or producer of the goods or services in question to use that mark.[1648]

The party requesting an order for seizure must provide security adequate to pay any damages arising from wrongful seizure,[1649] and the court must issue any protective orders necessary to prevent disclosure of confidential information.[1650] The defendant is entitled to a post-seizure hearing.[1651] A person harmed by a wrongful seizure may recover such relief as the court finds appropriate, including lost profits, cost of materials, loss of good will, punitive damages if the seizure was sought in bad faith, prejudgment interest, and, absent extenuating circumstances, a reasonable attorney's fee.[1652]

[c]   Destruction of Infringing Articles

In a cause of action under section 32 or 43(a), or a willful violation of section 43(c), a court may order the surrender and destruction of all infringing materials in the defendant's possession, together with all means of making the infringing marks.[1653]

[d]   Cancellation of Federal Registration

Under section 37 of the Lanham Act, a court's authority to order cancellation of a federal registration is concurrent with that of the PTO, and may be exercised on the same grounds.[1654]

[1647] 15 U.S.C. § 1116(d)(4)(B).

[1648] 15 U.S.C. §§ 1116(d)(1)(B), 1127.

[1649] 15 U.S.C. § 1116(d)(4)(A).

[1650] 15 U.S.C. §§ 1116(d)(7),(9).

[1651] 15 U.S.C. § 1116(d)(10).

[1652] 15 U.S.C. § 1116(d)(11).

[1653] 15 U.S.C. § 1118.

[1654] 15 U.S.C. § 1119. *See, e.g.*, Brittingham v. Jenkins, 914 F.2d 447, 453 (4th Cir. 1990); Loctite Corp. v. National Starch & Chemical Corp., 516 F. Supp. 190 (S.D.N.Y. 1981); Polaroid Corp. v. Berkey Photo, Inc., 425 F. Supp. 605 (D. Del. 1976). Grounds for cancellation are discussed in § 5E[3][d][iv](a).

[e]   Disclaimers

In appropriate cases, a court may determine that a disclaimer will be sufficient to alleviate any likelihood of confusion.[1655] A court is particularly likely to reach this conclusion where the likelihood of confusion is modest,[1656] or where other equitable considerations weigh in favor of allowing concurrent use — for example, where the mark in question is the legitimate surname of the junior user.[1657] Often, however, courts hold that a disclaimer is an inadequate remedy, because it may not be used consistently,[1658] it may not be noticed by consumers,[1659] it may not be incorporated in every channel of communication with consumers,[1660] or it may simply be insufficient to completely eliminate confusion.[1661]

[2]   Monetary Remedies

[a]   Actual Damages, Defendant's Profits, and Costs

In the case of infringement of a registered mark under section 32(1)(a), a violation of section 43(a) or 43(d), or a willful violation of section 43(c), section 35 of the Lanham Act permits a plaintiff to recover the defendant's profits, the plaintiff's damages, and costs.[1662] However, duplicative recoveries (for example, defendant's profits plus damages representing plaintiff's lost profits for the same sales) are not permitted.[1663] In an action under section 32(1), damages or profits are awarded only for infringing activities that took place after the plaintiff became the owner of the federal registration.[1664]

[1655] *See, e.g.*, Champion Spark Plug Co. v. Sanders, 331 U.S. 125 (1947); Nitro Leisure Prods., LLC v. Acushnet Co., 341 F.3d 1356 (Fed. Cir. 2003); Soltex Polymer Corp. v. Fortex Indus., Inc., 832 F.2d 1325, 1329 (2d Cir. 1987); Springs Mills, Inc. v. Ultracashmere House, Ltd., 724 F.2d 352, 355 (2d Cir. 1983); Berlitz Schools of Languages v. Everest House, 619 F.2d 211, 215 (2d Cir. 1980); Mushroom Makers, Inc. v. R. G. Barry Corp., 441 F. Supp. 1220 (S.D.N.Y. 1977), *aff'd*, 580 F.2d 44 (2d Cir. 1978).

[1656] *See, e.g.*, Soltex Polymer Corporation v. Fortex Industries, Inc., 832 F.2d 1325 (2d Cir. 1987).

[1657] *See, e.g.*, Joseph Scott Co. v Scott Swimming Pools, Inc., 764 F.2d 62 (2d Cir. 1985); Taylor Wine Co. v. Bully Hill Vineyards, Inc., 590 F.2d 701 (2d Cir. 1978); Coty, Inc. v. Parfums De Grande Luxe, Inc., 298 F. 865 (2d Cir. 1924); G. & C. Merriam Co. v. Saalfield, 198 F. 369 (6th Cir. 1912); G. & C. Merriam Co. v. Ogilvie, 170 F. 167 (1st Cir. 1909).

[1658] *See, e.g.*, International Kennel Club, Inc. v. Mighty Star, Inc., 846 F.2d 1079, 1093 (7th Cir. 1988).

[1659] *See, e.g., International Kennel Club*, 846 F.2d at 1093; Home Box Office, Inc. v. Showtime/Movie Channel, Inc., 832 F.2d 1311, 1315 (2d Cir. 1987); Gilliam v. American Broadcasting Cos., 538 F.2d 14, 25 n.13 (2d Cir. 1976).

[1660] *See, e.g.*, Volkswagenwerk Aktiengesellschaft v. Karadizian, 170 U.S.P.Q. 565, 567 (C.D. Cal. 1971).

[1661] *See, e.g.*, Profitness Phys. Therapy Ctr. v. Pro-Fit Orthopedic & Sports Phys. Therapy P.C., 314 F.3d 62, 70–71 (2d Cir. 2002); Charles of the Ritz Group, Ltd. v. Quality King Distribs., Inc., 832 F.2d 1317, 1324 (2d Cir. 1987); *Home Box Office*, 832 F.2d at 1315–16; United States Jaycees v. Philadelphia Jaycees, 639 F.2d 134, 142 (3d Cir. 1981); Miss Universe, Inc. v. Flesher, 605 F.2d 1130, 1134–35 (9th Cir. 1979); *Gilliam*, 538 F.2d at 25 n.13; Boston Pro Hockey Association v. Dallas Cap & E. Manufacturing, Inc., 510 F.2d 1004, 1013 (5th Cir. 1975).

[1662] 15 U.S.C. § 1117(a).

[1663] *See, e.g.*, United Phosphorus, Ltd. v. Midland Fumigant, Inc., 205 F.3d 1219 (10th Cir. 2000).

[1664] *See, e.g.*, Reliable Tire Distributors, Inc. v. Kelly Springfield Tire Co., 592 F. Supp. 127 (E.D. Pa. 1984).

In assessing damages, courts will consider a plaintiff's lost sales, as well as other damage to the plaintiff's goodwill, provided that these were a proximate result of the infringing activity.[1665] The damages award may include the costs of corrective advertising to restore the value that the plaintiff's trademark has lost due to the defendant's infringement.[1666]

Prior to 1999, courts interpreted section 35(a) as authorizing an accounting of profits in actions under section 32 or section 43(a) only if the defendant acted willfully or in bad faith,[1667] even though section 35(a) did not expressly impose such a requirement. However, after Congress amended section 35(a) in 1999 to authorize an award of profits for infringement of a registered mark or for "a violation under section 43(a), or a willful violation under section 43(c),"[1668] the Third and Fifth Circuits concluded, by reverse implication, that willfulness was no longer a prerequisite to an award of profits in actions under section 32(1)(a) or section 43(a).[1669] The First and Tenth Circuits, in contrast, continue to require willfulness.[1670] In other circuits, district courts have reached conflicting conclusions.[1671]

Subsection (e), which was added to section 35 in 2004, creates a rebuttable presumption of willfulness where a defendant knowingly provides materially false contact information to a domain name registration authority in connection with a domain name used in connection with "a violation referred to in this section."[1672] Because section 35 refers to "willful" violations in two contexts — dilution claims and counterfeiting claims — it appears that the rebuttable presumption of

---

[1665] Ramada Inns, Inc. v. Gadsden Motel Co., 804 F.2d 1562 (11th Cir. 1986); Heaton Distrib. Co. v. Union Tank Car Co., 387 F.2d 477 (8th Cir. 1967); Aladdin Mfg. Co. v. Mantle Lamp Co., 116 F.2d 708 (7th Cir. 1941); Tillman & Bendel, Inc. v. California Packing Co., 63 F.2d 498 (9th Cir. 1933); Lawrence-Williams Co. v. Societe Enfants Gombault et Cie, 52 F.2d 774 (6th Cir. 1931).

[1666] Adray v. Adry-Mart, Inc., 68 F.3d 362 (9th Cir. 1995), *as amended*, 76 F.3d 984, 988–89 (9th Cir. 1996); Zazu Designs v. L'Oreal, S.A., 979 F.2d 499, 506 (7th Cir. 1992); U-Haul Int'l, Inc. v. Jartran, Inc., 793 F.2d 1034, 1041 (9th Cir. 1986); Cher v. Forum Int'l., Ltd., 213 U.S.P.Q. 96, 103 (C.D. Cal.), *aff'd in pertinent part*, 692 F.2d 634, 640 (9th Cir. 1982); Big O Tire Dealers, Inc. v. Goodyear Tire & Rubber Co., 561 F.2d 1365, 1374–76 (10th Cir. 1977).

[1667] International Star Class Yacht Racing Ass'n v. Tommy Hilfiger U.S.A., 146 F.3d 66 (2d Cir. 1998); Banff, Ltd. v. Colberts, Inc., 996 F.2d 33 (2d Cir. 1993); George Basch Co. v. Blue Coral, Inc., 968 F.2d 1532 (2d Cir. 1992); ALPO Petfoods, Inc. v. Ralston Purina Co., 913 F.2d 958, 968 (D.C. Cir. 1990).

[1668] Pub. L. No. 106-43, § 3(b), 113 Stat. 219 (1999). In later amendments, Congress replaced "section 43(a)" with "section 43(a) or (d)" in order to authorize an award of profits in cybersquatting cases.

[1669] *See, e.g.*, Banjo Buddies, Inc. v. Renosky, 399 F.3d 168, 174–75 (3d Cir. 2005); Quick Technologies, Inc. v. Sage Group PLC, 313 F.3d 338, 347–48 (5th Cir. 2002).

[1670] Fishman Transducers, Inc. v. Paul, 684 F.3d 187, 191 (1st Cir. 2012) (holding that "preponderance of the evidence" standard of proof applies to willfulness determination); Western Diversified Servs., Inc. v. Hyundai Motor America, Inc., 427 F.3d 1269, 1272–73 (10th Cir. 2004).

[1671] *See, e.g.*, Life Services Supps., Inc. v. Natural Organics, Inc., 86 U.S.P.Q.2d 1639 (S.D.N.Y. 2007); Louis Vuitton Malletier v. Dooney & Bourke, Inc., 500 F. Supp. 2d 276 (S.D.N.Y. 2007); Hipsaver Co., Inc. v. J.T. Posey Co., 497 F. Supp. 2d 96, 107 (D. Mass. 2007); Gucci America, Inc. v. Exclusive Imports Int'l, 2007 U.S. Dist. LEXIS 19532, *26 (S.D.N.Y. Mar. 14, 2007); Nike, Inc. v. Top Brand Co., 2005 U.S. Dist. LEXIS 42374 (S.D.N.Y. July 13, 2005); MasterCard Int'l, Inc. v. First Nat'l Bank of Omaha, Inc., 2004 U.S. Dist. LEXIS 2485 (S.D.N.Y. Feb. 23, 2004).

[1672] 15 U.S.C. § 1117(e).

willfulness applies to both dilution and counterfeiting claims.[1673]

Even if willfulness is no longer required for an award of profits in actions under sections 32(1)(a), 43(a), and 43(d), section 35(a) nonetheless provides that any award of profits, damages, or costs is "subject to the principles of equity." In making this equitable determination, the factors that courts may consider "include, but are not limited to (1) whether the defendant had the intent to confuse or deceive, (2) whether sales have been diverted, (3) the adequacy of other remedies, (4) any unreasonable delay by the plaintiff in asserting his rights, (5) the public interest in making the misconduct unprofitable, and (6) whether it is a case of palming off."[1674] Courts considering such a monetary award may therefore consider a defendant's willfulness or bad faith as one factor in weighing the equities.[1675] Courts typically justify awarding a defendant's profits based on theories of unjust enrichment or deterrence of willful infringement.[1676]

In establishing the amount of an infringer's profits, the plaintiff need only establish the amount of the defendant's sales; the defendant must prove any elements of cost or deduction claimed.[1677] Courts generally apply a rebuttable presumption that all of the infringer's profits resulted from the infringing activity;[1678] the burden falls on the infringer to establish the portion that was not attributable to the infringement.[1679]

[b]   Enhanced Damages

With respect to damages awards, section 35(a) of the Lanham Act permits a court, "according to the circumstances of the case," to award more than the amount found as actual damages, but not more than three times that amount.[1680] Trebling of damages is normally reserved for cases of willful infringement.[1681] A different rule applies to an award of defendant's profits: if the court finds that the amount of profits is inadequate or excessive to compensate the plaintiff, the court may award any amount that is just, based on the circumstances of the case.[1682] With respect to both damages and profits, however, these enhancements must be compensatory

---

[1673] 15 U.S.C. §§ 1117(a), (c)(2).

[1674] Banjo Buddies, Inc. v. Renosky, 399 F.3d 168, 175 (3d Cir. 2005) (quoting Quick Technologies, Inc. v. Sage Group PLC, 313 F.3d 338, 349 (5th Cir. 2002)) (internal quotation marks and citations omitted).

[1675] See, e.g., Banjo Buddies, 399 F.3d at 175–76; Quick Technologies, 313 F.3d at 349.

[1676] See, e.g., Estate of Bishop v Equinox Int'l Corp., 256 F.3d 1050 (10th Cir. 2001).

[1677] 15 U.S.C. § 1117(a); see, e.g., Wynn Oil Co. v. American Way Service Corp., 943 F.2d 595 (6th Cir. 1991).

[1678] Mishawaka Rubber & Woolen Mfg. Co. v. S. S. Kresge Co., 316 U.S. 203, 206–07 (1942); Century Distilling Co. v. Continental Distilling Corp., 205 F.2d 140, 146 (3d Cir. 1953); Obear-Nester Glass Co. v. United Drug Co., 149 F.2d 671 (8th Cir. 1945).

[1679] Mishawaka Rubber, 316 U.S. at 206–07; see, e.g., WMS Gaming, Inc. v. WPC Productions Ltd., 542 F.3d 601 (7th Cir. 2008); Maier Brewing Co. v. Fleischmann Distilling Corp., 390 F.2d 117 (9th Cir. 1968).

[1680] 15 U.S.C. § 1117(a).

[1681] See, e.g., Scovill Mfg. Co. v. United States Electric Mfg. Corp., 47 F. Supp. 619 (C.D.N.Y. 1942).

[1682] 15 U.S.C. § 1117(a); see Thompson v. Haynes, 305 F.3d 1369 (Fed. Cir. 2002).

rather than punitive.[1683]

Under section 35(b), the court must, in the absence of extenuating circumstances, award the plaintiff treble damages or profits (whichever is greater), as well as a reasonable attorney's fee, against a defendant that either (1) violates section 32(1)(a) by intentionally using a mark, knowing it to be a counterfeit mark within the meaning of section 34(d), or (2) provides goods or services necessary to the commission of such a violation, with the intent that those goods or services would be used in that violation.[1684] A counterfeit mark is a spurious mark that is "identical with, or substantially indistinguishable from," a mark registered on the Principal Register.[1685]

Although section 35(b) requires a showing that the defendant used a counterfeit mark "knowing such mark . . . is counterfeit," the knowledge requirement will be satisfied if the defendant was willfully blind — that is, if the defendant "failed to inquire further because he was afraid of what the inquiry would yield."[1686] At the court's discretion in such cases, the court may also award prejudgment interest.[1687]

In contrast to the Lanham Act, which does not provide for punitive damages, some states authorize punitive damages for trademark infringement or unfair competition.[1688]

[c]　　　Attorney's Fees

Section 35(a) provides that, in "exceptional" cases, a court may award reasonable attorney's fees to the prevailing party, who may be either the plaintiff or the defendant.[1689] Typically, a plaintiff will recover attorney's fees when the infringing conduct was malicious, fraudulent, deliberate, or willful;[1690] attorney's fees may also be awarded to the prevailing party (plaintiff or defendant) when the opponent engaged in bad faith or vexatious litigation,[1691] or litigation misconduct.[1692] Courts

---

[1683] 15 U.S.C. § 1117(a); see ALPO Petfoods, Inc. v. Ralston Purina Co., 997 F.2d 949, 955 (D.C. Cir. 1993); ALPO Petfoods, Inc. v. Ralston Purina Co., 913 F.2d 958, 970 & n.13 (D.C. Cir. 1990).

[1684] 15 U.S.C. § 1117(b).

[1685] 15 U.S.C. §§ 1116(d), 1127. These provisions also apply to counterfeiting of various names and symbols pertaining to the Olympics. 15 U.S.C. § 1116(d).

[1686] Louis Vuitton S.A. v. Lee, 875 F.2d 584, 590 (7th Cir. 1989).

[1687] 15 U.S.C. § 1117(b).

[1688] See JCW Invs., Inc. v. Novelty, Inc., 482 F.3d 910 (7th Cir. 2007); Gai Audio of New York, Inc. v. Columbia Broadcasting Sys., Inc., 340 A.2d 736, 753–54 (Md. Ct. Spec. App. 1975) (collecting cases).

[1689] 15 U.S.C. § 1117(a).

[1690] Hard Rock Café, Int'l, Inc. v. Texas Pig Stands, Inc., 951 F.2d 684, 697 (5th Cir. 1992); Reader's Digest Assoc. v. Conservative Digest, 821 F.2d 800, 808 (D.C. Cir. 1987); Nike, Inc. v. Variety Wholesalers, Inc., 274 F. Supp. 2d 1352 (S.D. Ga. 2003), aff'd, 107 Fed. Appx. 183 (11th Cir. 2004); S. Rep. No. 93-1400, reprinted in 1974 U.S.C.C.A.N. 7132, 7136.

[1691] See, e.g., Mattel, Inc. v. Walking Mountain Prods., 353 F.3d 792, 816 (9th Cir. 2003); SecuraComm Consulting, Inc. v. Securacom, Inc., 224 F.3d 273 (3d Cir. 2000); Universal City Studios, Inc. v. Nintendo, Inc., 797 F.2d 70, 77 (2d Cir. 1986).

[1692] TE-TA-MA Truth Foundation-Family of URI, Inc. v. World Church of the Creator, 392 F.3d 248, 261–63 (7th Cir. 2004); Patsy's Brand, Inc. v. I.O.B. Realty, Inc., 317 F.3d 209 (2d Cir. 2003); SecuraComm Consulting, 224 F.3d at 281–82.

disagree on whether "exceptional" circumstances must be proven by clear and convincing evidence, or whether a lesser standard of proof should apply.[1693] In contrast, section 35(b) provides that, in the absence of extenuating circumstances, an award of attorney's fees is *mandatory* when the defendant intentionally uses a mark registered on the Principal Register, knowing it to be a counterfeit mark.[1694]

The Ninth Circuit has held that attorney's fees cannot be awarded to a plaintiff that elects statutory damages under section 35(c) in place of actual damages or profits under section 35(a).[1695] Elsewhere, the issue is unsettled.[1696] However, the Third Circuit has allowed attorney's fees in conjunction with statutory damages in a cybersquatting case.[1697]

[d]   Statutory Damages

In two situations, a prevailing plaintiff may elect, any time before the trial court renders final judgment, to recover statutory damages in place of actual damages and profits. In a case involving the use of a counterfeit mark as defined in section 34(d),[1698] the court has broad discretion to award statutory damages of $1,000 to $200,000[1699] (or up to $2,000,000 if the infringement was willful[1700]) per counterfeit mark per type of goods or services sold, offered for sale, or distributed. In a cybersquatting case under section 43(d)(1), the court may award statutory damages of $1,000 to $100,000 per domain name.[1701]

It is well settled that the Seventh Amendment right to a jury trial applies to awards of actual damages in trademark cases. Based on the Supreme Court's ruling in a 1998 copyright infringement case, *Feltner v. Columbia Pictures Television, Inc.*,[1702] the same rule should also apply to statutory damages.[1703]

[1693] *See, e.g.*, Eagles, Ltd. v. Am. Eagle Found., 356 F.3d 724, 729 (6th Cir. 2004); Procter & Gamble Co. v. Amway Corp., 280 F.3d 519, 526 (5th Cir. 2002); Finance Investment Co. v. Geberit AG, 165 F.3d 526, 533 (7th Cir. 1998).

[1694] 15 U.S.C. § 1117(b); *see also* 15 U.S.C. §§ 1116(d), 1127 (defining counterfeit marks). These provisions also apply to counterfeiting of various names and symbols pertaining to the Olympics. 15 U.S.C. § 1116(d).

[1695] K & N Eng'g, Inc. v. Bulat, 510 F.3d 1079, 1082 (9th Cir. 2007).

[1696] The Fifth and Seventh Circuits have affirmed awards of statutory damages and attorney's fees to prevailing Lanham Act plaintiffs, but these appellants did not argue that such awards could not be combined. Kiva Kitchen & Bath, Inc. v. Capital Distrib., Inc., 319 Fed. Appx. 316 (5th Cir. 2009); Lorillard Tobacco Co., Inc. v. A & E Oil, Inc., 503 F.3d 588 (7th Cir. 2007).

[1697] Shields v. Zuccarini, 254 F.3d 476, 481–82 (3d Cir. 2001).

[1698] 15 U.S.C. § 1116(d).

[1699] Before October 13, 2008, the effective date of the Pro IP Act, these amounts were $500 and $100,000, respectively.

[1700] 15 U.S.C. § 1117(c); *see, e.g.*, Taylor Made Golf Co. v. MJT Consulting Group, 265 F. Supp. 2d 732 (N.D. Tex. 2003).

[1701] 15 U.S.C. § 1117(d); *see, e.g.*, Bellagio v. Denhammer, 2001 U.S. Dist. LEXIS 24764, *12 (D. Nev. July 10, 2001).

[1702] 523 U.S. 340, 353–54 (1998).

[1703] *See* Bar-Meir v. North Am. Die Casting Ass'n, 55 Fed. Appx. 389, 390–91 (8th Cir. 2003) (per curiam); Microsoft Corp. v. Ion Technologies Corp., 2003 U.S. Dist. LEXIS 9946, *20 (D. Minn. May 30, 2003).

[e]   Enhanced Awards in Counterfeiting Cases

Under sections 35(a)–(d),[1704] monetary awards arising from the use of counterfeit marks are more generous than those arising from other infringements of registered marks, in several respects: first, attorney's fees are mandatory (absent extenuating circumstances) in counterfeiting cases, but are available for other infringements only in exceptional cases; second, treble damages or profits are mandatory (absent extenuating circumstances) in counterfeiting cases, but enhancements of damages are left to the court's discretion in other infringement cases; third, prejudgment interest is available only in counterfeiting cases; and fourth, statutory damages are available for counterfeiting claims (as well as cybersquatting claims under section 43(d)), but not for other infringements.

These enhancements give owners of registered marks an incentive to characterize their section 32(1) infringement claims as counterfeiting claims. However, a mark is a "counterfeit" mark only if it is "identical with, or substantially indistinguishable from," the plaintiff's registered mark.[1705] Accordingly, courts have rejected plaintiffs' efforts to characterize infringing marks as counterfeits when the marks, while similar, are nonetheless distinguishable.[1706]

[f]   Marking or Actual Notice

In an action for infringement of a registered mark under section 32, a plaintiff can recover profits or damages only if the defendant had either actual or statutory notice of the trademark registration.[1707] The requirement of statutory notice is satisfied when the mark is accompanied by the words "Registered in U.S. Patent and Trademark Office," or "Reg. U.S. Pat. & Tm. Off.," or the ® symbol.[1708] In the absence of statutory notice, damages or profits may be recovered only for infringing acts that occurred after the defendant received actual notice of the registration.[1709] Failure to provide notice of registration does not preclude recovery of attorney's fees.[1710]

The notice requirement does not apply to a section 43(a) claim involving an unregistered mark. Several courts have held that the notice requirement also does not apply to recovery of statutory damages for counterfeiting under section 35(c).[1711]

[1704] 15 U.S.C. § 1117(a)–(d).

[1705] 15 U.S.C. §§ 1116(d), 1127.

[1706] *See, e.g.*, Louis Vuitton Malletier v. Haute Diggity Dog, LLC, 507 F.3d 252 (4th Cir. 2007); Colgate-Palmolive Co. v. J.M.D. All-Star Import & Export, Inc., 486 F. Supp. 2d 286 (S.D.N.Y. 2007).

[1707] 15 U.S.C. § 1111.

[1708] *Id.*

[1709] *Id.*; Stark Bros. Nurseries & Orchards Co. v. Stark, 255 U.S. 50 (1921); Treasure Imports, Inc. v. Henry Amdur & Sons, Inc., 127 F.2d 3 (2d Cir. 1942); G. Heileman Brewing Co. v. Independent Brewing Co., 191 F. 489 (9th Cir. 1911); Bambu Sales, Inc. v. Sultana Crackers, Inc., 683 F. Supp. 899 (E.D.N.Y. 1988); Scovill Mfg. Co. v. United States Elec. Mfg. Corp., 47 F. Supp. 619 (S.D.N.Y. 1942).

[1710] Schroeder v. Lotito, 747 F.2d 801 (1st Cir. 1984).

[1711] Diane Von Furstenberg Studio v. Snyder, 2007 U.S. Dist. LEXIS 45941 (E.D. Va. June 25, 2007);

[g]   Damages Under Federal Dilution Law

Ordinarily, injunctive relief is the sole remedy available for dilution under section 43(c)(1).[1712] However, if the dilution was willful, then, subject to the principles of equity and the discretion of the court, the full array of remedies under section 35(a)[1713] (damages, profits, costs, and, in exceptional cases, attorneys fees) and section 36[1714] (destruction of infringing articles) are available.[1715] As discussed above,[1716] because the meaning of willfulness was revised in the 2006 TDRA, the rules governing remedies for willful dilution depend on whether the willful conduct commenced before and after the effect date of this amendment.

[h]   False or Fraudulent Registration

Section 38 permits any person injured by another party's false or fraudulent federal trademark registration to bring a civil action for damages.[1717] According to the Tenth Circuit, a plaintiff must prove that: (1) the registrant made a representation to the PTO during the registration process that was false and material, (2) the registrant knew or believed that its representation was false, (3) the registrant intended to induce action or forbearance in reliance on the false representation, (4) the PTO reasonably relied on the false representation, and (5) the plaintiff's damages resulted from this reliance.[1718]

[3]   Limitations on Remedies Against Certain Defendants

[a]   Makers of Labels, Signs, Packaging, or Advertisements

Section 32(1)(b) imposes liability on parties that do no more than "reproduce, counterfeit, copy, or colorably imitate a registered mark" and apply that mark to labels, signs, packaging, or advertisements intended for use in connection with goods or services offered to the public, if such use is likely to cause confusion, mistake, or deception.[1719] Only injunctive relief is available, unless the defendant acted "with knowledge that such imitation is intended to be used to cause confusion, or to cause mistake, or to deceive," in which cases profits or damages may be

---

Playboy Enterprises, Inc. v. Universal Tel-A-Talk, Inc., 1999 U.S. Dist. LEXIS 6124 (E.D. Pa. Apr. 26, 1999).

[1712] 15 U.S.C. § 1125(c)(1).

[1713] 15 U.S.C. § 1117(a).

[1714] 15 U.S.C. § 1118.

[1715] 15 U.S.C. § 1125(c)(2); *see, e.g.*, Sporty's Farm, L.L.C. v. Sportsman's Market, Inc., 202 F.3d 489, 500 (2d Cir. 2000).

[1716] *See* § 5G[3][g], § 5G[5].

[1717] 15 U.S.C. § 1120.

[1718] San Juan Prods., Inc. v. San Juan Pools, Inc., 849 F.2d 468, 473 (10th Cir. 1988) (citing McCarthy on Trademarks § 31:21).

[1719] 15 U.S.C. § 1114(1)(b).

awarded.[1720]

[b]   Printers and Publishers

Section 32(2) limits the remedies available under section 32(1), 43(a), and 43(d) against a defendant that is engaged solely in the printing or publishing of infringing materials.[1721] Subsections (A) and (B) of section 32(2) apply only to defendants that qualify as "innocent infringers" or "innocent violators" (where "violators" refers to parties liable under section 43(a)).

Under subsection (A), if a defendant is engaged solely in the business of printing the mark or violating matter for others, and qualifies as an innocent infringer (or an innocent violator), remedies are limited to an injunction against future printing.[1722] If the infringement is contained in paid advertising material in a newspaper, magazine, or similar periodical, or in an electronic communication (as defined in 18 U.S.C. § 2510(12)), and the defendant is an innocent infringer or innocent violator, limitations on remedies are imposed by subsections (B) and (C). Subsection (B) limits the remedies to an injunction against the presentation of this advertising matter in future issues of the periodical(s) or future transmissions of such electronic communications.[1723] Subsection (C) provides that injunctive relief will not be available where it would delay the delivery of the periodical or electronic transmission.[1724]

The Lanham Act does not define an "innocent" infringer or violator. Some courts have held that innocence consists of the absence of "actual malice" in the defamation sense, so that a defendant is innocent unless he or she acted with knowledge of the infringement or with reckless disregard as to whether the material was infringing.[1725] Other courts take an objective approach that disregards the defendant's state of mind, treating the defendant as innocent if his or her conduct is "reasonable."[1726]

[c]   Domain Name Registration Authorities

Section 32(2)(D) limits the liability of domain name registration authorities arising from actions they may take in response to infringement or dilution claims brought against domain names. In general, registration authorities are immune from both monetary and injunctive relief if they refuse to register a domain name, remove it from registration, or transfer, temporarily disable, or cancel a domain name either: (1) in compliance with a court order under section 43(d), or (2) pursuant to a "reasonable policy" under which they prohibit registration of domain

---

[1720] *Id.; see, e.g.,* Union Tank Car Co. v. Lindsay Soft Water Corp. of Omaha, Inc., 257 F. Supp. 510, 517 (D.C. Neb. 1966), *aff'd,* 387 F.2d 477 (8th Cir. 1967).

[1721] 15 U.S.C. § 1114(2).

[1722] 15 U.S.C. § 1114(2)(A).

[1723] 15 U.S.C. § 1114(2)(B).

[1724] 15 U.S.C. § 1114(2)(C).

[1725] *See, e.g.,* Gucci Am., Inc. v. Hall & Assocs., 135 F. Supp. 2d 409, 420 (S.D.N.Y. 2001); World Wrestling Fed. Inc. v. Posters Inc., 58 U.S.P.Q.2d 1783, 1785 (N.D. Ill. 2000).

[1726] *See, e.g.,* Dial One of the Mid-South, Inc. v. Bellsouth Telecomm'ns, Inc., 269 F.3d 523, 525 (5th Cir. 2001).

names that are identical or confusingly similar to, or dilutive of, another's mark.[1727] If a domain name is suspended, disabled, or transferred under such a policy, the domain name registrant may, upon notice to the trademark owner, bring a civil action to establish that its use or registration of the domain name is lawful, and if the action succeeds, the court may order that the domain name be reactivated or transferred back to the domain name registrant.[1728] Furthermore, if the domain name registration authority undertakes any of these actions based on a "knowing and material misrepresentation" by another person regarding the infringing or dilutive nature of the domain name, the party making the misrepresentation will be liable for any damages, including costs and attorneys' fees, incurred by the domain name registrant, and the court may order the domain name reactivated or transferred back to the domain name registrant.[1729]

Notwithstanding the general bar on injunctive relief against domain name registration authorities under subsection (D)(ii), injunctive relief may be imposed on a registration authority that has: (1) failed to comply with the requirement of section 43(d)(2)(D) that it expeditiously deposit with the court those documents that enable the court to establish its control or authority over the domain name; (2) transferred, suspended, or modified the domain name during the pendency of the legal action, except upon court order; or (3) willfully failed to comply with any such court order.[1730]

Registration authorities are not liable for damages for registering or maintaining a domain name unless they act with a bad faith intent to profit from these actions.[1731]

[d]   Family Movie Act of 2005

The Family Movie Act of 2005 (FMA) added another limited-liability provision to the Lanham Act, section 32(3),[1732] which immunizes certain types of unauthorized film editing from liability under the Lanham Act. Section 32(3) is a companion provision to section 110(11) of the Copyright Act, which permits home viewers to block portions of a motion picture performance in their home, and allows third parties to create and market the technology that makes this possible,[1733] so that home viewers of a DVD may "skip" or "mute" specific portions of a motion picture that might be considered offensive. Section 32(3) grants Lanham Act immunity to any manufacturer, licensee, or licensor of technology permitted by the FMA, but only if that party "ensures that the technology provides a clear and conspicuous notice at the beginning of each performance that the performance of the motion

---

[1727] 15 U.S.C. § 1114(2)(D)(ii).

[1728] 15 U.S.C. § 1114(2)(D)(v); *see, e.g.*, Sallen v. Corinthians Licenciamentos LTDA, 273 F.3d 14 (1st Cir. 2001).

[1729] 15 U.S.C. § 1114(2)(D)(iv).

[1730] 15 U.S.C. § 1114(2)(D)(i)(II).

[1731] 15 U.S.C. § 1114(2)(D)(iii).

[1732] 15 U.S.C. § 1114(3).

[1733] 17 U.S.C. § 110(11).

picture is altered from the performance intended by the director or copyright holder of the motion picture."[1734]

[e]   Remedies Against Federal and State Governments

Under section 40 of the Lanham Act, the federal government and persons acting on its behalf are subject to the full array of remedies for Lanham Act violations.[1735]

Although section 40 contains a similar provision for state governments,[1736] the Eleventh Amendment makes this provision largely ineffective. Eleventh Amendment immunity does not, however, extend to state and county governments, except where they act as an arm of the state.[1737] For a more detailed discussion of Eleventh Amendment immunity, see § 1D[5][a].

[4]   Criminal Penalties

[a]   Counterfeit Marks

In 1984, Congress enacted the Trademark Counterfeiting Act, codified in 18 U.S.C. § 2320, which imposes criminal penalties on "[w]hoever intentionally traffics or attempts to traffic in goods or services and knowingly uses a counterfeit mark on or in connection with such goods or services."[1738] Penalties for individuals include a fine of up to $2 million and/or up to 10 years in prison; for corporate violators, the penalty is a fine of up to $5 million. For a subsequent violation following a conviction, an individual may be fined up to $5 million and/or imprisoned for up to 20 years, and a corporation may be fined up to $15 million.[1739] The penalties of forfeiture, destruction and restitution also apply to proceedings under section 2320.[1740]

For purposes of section 2320, a "counterfeit mark" is defined as a mark: (1) that is used in connection with trafficking in goods or services; (2) that is identical with, or substantially indistinguishable from, a mark registered for those goods or services on the Principal Register, and in use, whether or not the defendant knew the mark was so registered; and (3) the use of which is likely to cause confusion, to cause mistake, or to deceive.[1741] The government must establish that the defendant had knowledge or intent with respect to every element of this definition.[1742] Courts generally apply the same likelihood-of-confusion analysis in analyzing section 2320 violations that they apply to infringement actions under the Lanham Act.[1743]

[1734] 15 U.S.C. §§ 1114(3)(A)–(C).

[1735] 15 U.S.C. § 1122(a).

[1736] 15 U.S.C. § 1122(b).

[1737] Monell v. Dep't of Soc. Servs., 436 U.S. 658, 690 n.54 (1978); Mt. Healthy City Sch. Dist. Bd. of Educ. v. Doyle, 429 U.S. 274, 280 (1977).

[1738] 18 U.S.C. § 2320(a); *see* United States v. Sultan, 115 F.3d 321, 325 (5th Cir. 1997).

[1739] 18 U.S.C. § 2320(a).

[1740] 18 U.S.C. §§ 2320(b), 2323.

[1741] 18 U.S.C. § 2320(e)(1)(A). Section 2320(e)(1)(B) extends coverage also to counterfeiting of Olympics trademarks, under 36 U.S.C. § 220506.

[1742] United States v. Infurnari, 647 F. Supp. 57 (W.D.N.Y. 1986).

[1743] *See, e.g.*, United States v. Foote, 413 F.3d 1240, 1246 (10th Cir. 2005); United States v Hon, 904

Counterfeit marks do not include "any mark or designation used in connection with goods or services of which the manufacturer or producer was, at the time of the manufacture or production in question, authorized to use the mark or designation for the type of goods or services so manufactured or produced, by the holder of the right to use such mark or designation."[1744] However, counterfeit marks do include genuine trademarks that are attached to the packaging of products that were not made by or under license from the trademark owner.[1745]

Because section 2320(a) requires that the defendant both traffic in goods or services and use a counterfeit mark in connection with those goods or services, it has been held that a defendant who merely traffics in counterfeit labels or tags, unattached to any goods, does not violate section 2320, both because labels or tags are not "goods," and because a spurious mark is not counterfeit unless the defendant uses it in connection with the goods or services for which the genuine mark is registered.[1746]

All defenses, affirmative defenses, and limitations on remedies under the Lanham Act apply to prosecutions under section 2320, and the defendant must prove them by a preponderance of the evidence.[1747]

[b]   Counterfeit Labels

In the Anti-Counterfeiting Amendments Act of 2004,[1748] Congress amended 18 U.S.C. § 2318 to provide both criminal and civil penalties for trafficking in counterfeit labels, documentation, or packaging designed to accompany copyrighted works; such counterfeit labels and packaging facilitate copyright infringement. Section 2318 applies to knowingly trafficking in counterfeit physical documentation or packaging, or counterfeit or illicit labels, designed to accompany a phonorecord, a copy of a computer program, a copy of a motion picture or other audiovisual work, a copy of a literary work, a copy of a pictorial, graphic, or sculptural work, a work of visual art, or documentation or packaging.[1749] "Illicit" labels, for this purpose, are certificates, licensing documents, registration cards, or similar labeling components that are genuine rather than counterfeit, and that are ordinarily used by copyright owners to identify authorized copies of their works, but that are being distributed separately from the authorized copies of these works, without the authority of the copyright owner, or that have been knowingly falsified to designate a larger number

---

F.2d 803 (2d Cir. 1990); United States v. Torkington, 812 F.2d 1347 (11th Cir. 1987); United States v. Infurnari, 647 F. Supp. 57 (W.D.N.Y. 1986).

[1744] 18 U.S.C. § 2320(e)(1).

[1745] United States v. Petrosian, 126 F.3d 1232 (9th Cir. 1997).

[1746] United States v. Giles, 213 F.3d 1247, 1251–53 (10th Cir. 2000) (noting, however, that such a defendant might be charged with "aiding and abetting"); *but see* United States v. Nunez, 127 F. Supp. 2d 53 (D.P.R. 2000) (treating counterfeit tax stamps as "goods"); *cf.* Boston Professional Hockey Ass'n v. Dallas Cap & Emblem Mfg., Inc., 510 F.2d 1004 (5th Cir. 1975) (treating "patches" bearing sports team logos, which purchasers could sew onto jackets or caps, as "goods" for purposes of civil liability under section 32).

[1747] 18 U.S.C. § 2320(c).

[1748] Intellectual Property Protection and Courts Amendments Act of 2004, Title I, Pub. L. 108-482, 118 Stat. 3915 (2004).

[1749] 18 U.S.C. § 2318(a).

of licensed users or copies than the copyright owner has authorized.[1750]

While section 2318 is not limited to counterfeit labels that display registered marks, it applies only to labels, documentation, and packaging that are associated with the specified categories of copyrightable works; its purpose is to enhance the remedies available for unauthorized duplication and distribution of such works. It provides both criminal penalties and civil remedies.[1751]

[1750] 18 U.S.C. § 2318(b)(4).

[1751] 18 U.S.C. § 2318(a), (f). Criminal penalties include fines and/or imprisonment for up to 5 years. 18 U.S.C. § 2318(a).

Chapter 6

OTHER INTELLECTUAL PROPERTY RIGHTS

SYNOPSIS

§ 6A   INTRODUCTION

§ 6B   DESIGN PROTECTION

    [1]   Historical Background

    [2]   Design Patentability Requirements

        [a]   Article of Manufacture

        [b]   Ornamentality

        [c]   Nonfunctionality

        [d]   Novelty and Statutory Bars

        [e]   Nonobviousness

    [3]   Application and Examination

    [4]   Exclusive Rights and Remedies — Infringement

    [5]   Conclusion

§ 6C   PLANT PROTECTION

    [1]   Plant Patent Act

        [a]   Requirements

        [b]   Application and Examination

        [c]   Exclusive Rights — Infringement

    [2]   Plant Variety Protection Act

        [a]   Requirements

        [b]   Application and Examination

        [c]   Exclusive Rights — Infringement

        [d]   Essentially Derived Varieties

    [3]   Utility Patents for Plants

    [4]   Protection Source Choice Factors

    [5]   Plant Breeders Rights Under TRIPS

§ 6D   SEMICONDUCTOR CHIP PROTECTION

    [1]   Introduction

    [2]   Protection Requirements

        [a]   Definitions

        [b]   Originality

        [c] Owner Nationality
    [3] Registration
    [4] Exclusive Rights — Infringement
        [a] Rights Granted
        [b] Limitations
            [i] Reverse Engineering
            [ii] First Sale
            [iii] Innocent Infringement
            [iv] Ideas, Procedures, and Principles
        [c] Infringement Actions
        [d] Remedies
            [i] Injunctive Relief
            [ii] Damages — Attorney's Fees
            [iii] International Trade Commission Remedies
    [5] International Protection for Semiconductor Chips
§ 6E FALSE ADVERTISING
    [1] Historical Development
    [2] Current Federal Law
        [a] Falsity
        [b] Commercial Advertising or Promotion
        [c] Other Commercial Activities
        [d] Standing
§ 6F MISAPPROPRIATION
    [1] The *INS* Decision
    [2] From *INS* to *Sears-Compco*
    [3] *Sears-Compco* and Federal Preemption
    [4] Contemporary Applications
§ 6G RIGHTS OF PUBLICITY
    [1] Introduction
    [2] Historical Development
    [3] Rights
        [a] Names
        [b] Likenesses
        [c] Roles
        [d] Voice and Vocal Imitations
    [4] Infringement and Defenses
        [a] *Prima Facie* Case
        [b] Newsworthiness
        [c] First Amendment

      [i]   Works of Art

      [ii] Parody and Satire

      [iii] Other Uses

    [d] Other Defenses

      [i]   Copyright Preemption

      [ii] First Sale Doctrine

      [iii] Antitrust

      [iv] Statute of Limitations and Laches

      [v] Other Defenses

  [5] Remedies

  [6] Ownership and Transfer

§ 6H IDEA SUBMISSION

  [1] Novelty and Concreteness

    [a] Novelty

    [b] Concreteness

  [2] Express Contracts

    [a] Novelty and Concreteness

    [b] Standard Release Forms

  [3] Implied Contracts

    [a] Unsolicited Submissions

      [i] Involuntarily Received

      [ii] Failure to Reject After Notice

    [b] Solicited Submissions

    [c] Confidential Relationship

  [4] Unjust Enrichment

  [5] Property Theory

  [6] Remedies

  [7] Federal Preemption

§ 6A INTRODUCTION

The four major areas of intellectual property protection — utility patents, trade secrets, copyrights and trademarks — dominate United States intellectual property law, but there are other important rights involving particular situations or subject matter. Three are federal statutory creations: design patents,[1] plant patents and plant variety protection,[2] and semiconductor chip protection.[3] Three are state

---

[1] *See* § 6B.

[2] *See* § 6C.

[3] *See* § 6D.

common law or statutory creations: misappropriation,[4] rights of publicity,[5] and idea submission.[6] One, false advertising, is a blend of state unfair competition law and a federal statute, Lanham Act Section 43(a).[7] With the exception of the design patent statute, these special protection systems are twentieth century innovations, relatively young compared to the patent, trade secret, copyright and trademark systems.[8]

These systems are worth study not only for their direct applications, but also for the lessons they provide on how intellectual property law can effectively accomplish its major task: providing adequate incentives to create, disclose, and market valuable new works, inventions, products, and information without unduly dampening economic competition or discouraging creation of improvements on prior creations.

When technology and society make available new means of creating and efficiently reproducing technology and information, the question arises: should the incentive-competition balance be achieved by applying or expanding the established general systems or should a special (*"sui generis"*) scheme be adopted? The successes and failures of these existing special systems provide guidance.

§ 6B DESIGN PROTECTION

A design may be generally defined as the visual appearance or "look" of a utilitarian object, as distinguished from the underlying object itself or its functionality. United States law provides three forms of intellectual property protection for designs: (1) design patents, (2) copyright, and (3) trade dress protection. Each form of protection has its own distinct scope, requirements, and limitations.

A design patent protects the ornamental appearance of an article of manufacture, and does not extend to any functional features.[9] To obtain a design patent, the creator of the design must apply to the United States Patent and Trademark Office, submitting a set of detailed drawings showing the design. The design must satisfy the novelty, nonobviousness, and disclosure requirements for patentability, much like inventions in utility patents.[10] A design patent filed before December 18, 2013 has a term of 14 years from the date of issuance, and a design patent filed on or after December 18, 2013 has a term of 15 years from the date of issuance.[11] During the term of the design patent, the patent owner can exclude others from making, using,

---

[4] *See* § 6F.

[5] *See* § 6G.

[6] *See* § 6H.

[7] *See* § 6E.

[8] The United States' first patent and copyright statutes were enacted in 1790. *See* §§ 2B and 4B. Common-law trademark and trade secret protection developed in the 19th century, but statutory coverage did not become significant until this century. *See* §§ 3B and 5B.

[9] 35 U.S.C. § 171.

[10] *Id.*

[11] 35 U.S.C. § 173; Patent Law Treaties Implementation Act, Pub. L. No. 112-211, § 102(7), 126 Stat. 1532 (2012).

offering for sale, selling, or importing the patented design.[12]

Copyright protection is available for a "design of a useful article,"[13] but "only if, and only to the extent that, such design incorporates pictorial, graphic, or sculptural features that can be identified separately from, and are capable of existing independently of, the utilitarian aspects of the article."[14] This separate identification-independent existence requirement can exclude from copyright protection some designs that are a merger of form and function, as opposed to "applied art."[15] Like all copyrights, the exclusive rights vest upon creation, without any formal registration with the United States Copyright Office.[16]

Trade dress protection is available for distinctive product designs, provided that the design features are distinctive and are nonfunctional.[17] The rights generally accrue from use in commerce, and last as long as the features are being used.[18] Trade dress rights may be asserted to prevent others from using the trade dress in a way that causes a likelihood of confusion in the pertinent marketplace.[19] The right to exclude does not arise, however, until the design has acquired distinctiveness, or secondary meaning.[20] In other words, unless the public has come to perceive the design as a brand or an indication of source, it cannot be protected as trade dress.

Many other countries have specially tailored design registration laws that are separate from patent, trademark, or copyright laws, but include some similar features. For example, the European Union recently implemented a Community Design Right system.[21] This system provides patent-like protection to nonfunc-

---

[12] 35 U.S.C. § 271(a).

[13] 17 U.S.C. § 101 (defining a "useful article" as "an article having an intrinsic utilitarian function that is not merely to portray the appearance of the article or to convey information.").

[14] 17 U.S.C. § 101 (definition of "pictorial, graphic, or sculptural work"). This standard is typically referred to as a test of either "physical or conceptual separability" from the underlying utilitarian article. *See, e.g.,* Carol Barnhart, Inc. v. Economy Cover Corp., 773 F.2d 411, 414 (2d Cir. 1985). *See* § 4C[4][a][v](b), above.

[15] *See, e.g.,* Mazer v. Stein, 347 U.S. 201, 217–18 (1954) (holding that a base of a table lamp styled to look like a dancing woman was entitled to copyright protection); Universal Furniture Int'l Inc. v. Collezione Europa USA Inc., 618 F.3d 417, 434 (4th Cir. 2010) (holding that furniture ornamentation such as "a carved scroll of leaves on a nightstand post" is protectable because it "does nothing to improve the utilitarian aspect thereof," and "reflects an "artistic judgment exercised independently of functional influences."); *but see* Brandir International v. Cascade Pacific Lumber Co., 834F.2d 1142, 1147–48 (2d Cir. 1987) (holding that an undulating metal bike rack was not protectable because the design features were influenced by functional concerns in accommodating bicycles, and did not reflect unconstrained artistic choices). For a more extensive discussion, see § 4C[4][a][v](b)(3), above.

[16] For a discussion of the role of formalities in copyright, including registration, *see* § 4D, above.

[17] 15 U.S.C. § 1125(a); Two Pesos, Inc. v. Taco Cabana, Inc., 505 U.S. 763, 769 (1992). *See* §§ 5C[1][c] and 5C[2][c], above.

[18] *See* § 5D, above.

[19] Wal-Mart Stores, Inc. v. Samara Bros., Inc., 529 U.S. 205, 214 (2000). For more on likelihood of confusion, see § 5F[3], above.

[20] *Wal-Mart,* 529 U.S. at 214.

[21] Council Regulation 6/2006, Community Designs, 2001 O.J. (L 3) 1 (EC), *available at* http://oami.europa.eu/en/design/pdf/reg2002_6.pdf.

tional designs that are new and have "individual character."[22] EU Community Design Rights initially last for five years, and may be renewed for five year terms up to a total of 25 years.[23] As a registration system, applications are reviewed only for formal requirements, and no substantive evaluation is performed until after registration, in the context of a post-registration opposition or infringement proceeding.[24]

For nearly a century, design protection proponents have urged the United States Congress to enact its own *sui generis* design registration laws. In a worldwide economy where design is becoming an increasingly important competitive factor, these proponents remain hopeful that the United States will, at long last, join its major trading partners in enacting design registration laws separate from the existing patent, trademark, or copyright system.

United States copyright and trade dress protection for useful articles is discussed in greater detail in other sections.[25] The remainder of this section covers only United States design patent law.

[1]   Historical Background

In 1842, at the request of the Commissioner of Patents, Congress enacted the first design patent law to fill a gap between copyright protection for authors and patent protection for inventors in the mechanical arts.[26] The original statute provided protection for "any new and original design for a manufacture."[27]

In *Gorham Mfg. Co. v. White*,[28] which involved a patent on a spoon and fork handle design, the Supreme Court reviewed the statute's purpose:

> The [act was] plainly intended to give encouragement to the decorative arts. . . . The law manifestly contemplated that giving certain new and original appearances to a manufactured article may enhance its salable value, may enlarge the demand for it, and may be meritorious service to the public. . . . The appearance may be the result of peculiarity of configuration, or of ornament alone, or of both conjointly . . . .[29]

The Court adopted an ordinary observer test for design patent infringement:

> [I]f, in the eye of an ordinary observer, giving such attention as a purchaser usually gives, two designs are substantially the same, if the resemblance is

---

[22] *Id.* arts. 3, 4, 5, 6, 8. A design is deemed to have individual character when "the overall impression it produces on the informed user differs from the overall impression produced on such a user by any design which has been made available to the public." *Id.* art. 4.

[23] *Id.* art. 12.

[24] *Id.* arts. 52.1 and 24.1.

[25] *See* §§ 4C[4][a][v](b) and 5C[2][c].

[26] Act of August 29, 1842, ch. 263, § 2, 5 Stat. 543 (codified as amended at 35 U.S.C. § 171).

[27] *Id.*

[28] 81 U.S. (14 Wall.) 511 (1871).

[29] *Id.*

such as to deceive such an observer, inducing him to purchase one supposing it to be the other, the first one patented is infringed by the other.[30]

Although this test includes language reminiscent of copyright law's substantial similarity test[31] and trademark law's likelihood of confusion test,[32] neither proof of copying nor proof of consumer confusion is necessary to establish design patent infringement.[33] Design patent infringement is a strict liability claim, and design patent owners are not required to actually sell their patented designs in the marketplace.[34] The degree of similarity between the patented design and the accused design, in the eyes of an ordinary observer, is the determinative issue for design patent infringement.[35]

[2] Design Patentability Requirements

To be patentable, a design must be for an "article of manufacture" and satisfy four substantive requirements: ornamentality, nonfunctionality, novelty, and nonobviousness. Aside from certain specific exceptions, all provisions in the Patent Act directed to utility inventions apply to designs.[36]

[a] Article of Manufacture

A patentable design must be "for an article of manufacture,"[37] which is essentially "anything made by the hands of man from raw materials, whether literally by hand or by machinery or by art."[38] The design "may relate to the

---

[30] *Id.*

[31] *See* § 4H[3].

[32] *See* § 5F[3].

[33] 35 U.S.C. § 271(a) (requiring only that the infringing act occur "without [the] authority" of the patent owner); Braun Inc. v. Dynamics Corp. of Am., 975 F.2d 815, 828 (Fed. Cir. 1992) (noting that design patent infringement "does not concern itself with the broad issue of consumer behavior in the marketplace"); Unette Corp. v. Unit Pack Co., Inc., 785 F.2d 1026, 1029 (Fed. Cir. 1986) ("Likelihood of confusion as to the source of the goods is not a necessary or appropriate factor for determining infringement of a design patent.").

[34] *Unette*, 785 F.2d at 1029 ("Likelihood of confusion as to the source of the goods is not a necessary or appropriate factor for determining infringement of a design patent. The holder of a valid design patent need not have progressed to the manufacture and distribution of a 'purchasable' product for its design patent to be infringed by another's product.").

[35] *See* § 6B[4].

[36] 35 U.S.C. § 171.

The design patent statutes expressly vary certain requirements from those of utility patents. The Section 119 priority right (*see* § 2H[2][b]) and Section 102(d) bar provision (*see* § 2C[5][b][vii]) are six months rather than a year. A design patent's term is 14 years from issuance rather than 20 years from filing. 35 U.S.C. § 173. The specification and disclosure requirements for patent applications necessarily also vary in the case of designs. *See* § 6B[3].

Because Congress has not provided an exception for designs, the substantive patentability requirements of novelty and nonobviousness for utility inventions apply to designs. *See* §§ 6B[2][d]–[e].

[37] 35 U.S.C § 171.

[38] *In re* Hruby, 373 F.2d 997, 999 (C.C.P.A. 1967) (holding that a fountain water pattern was an article of manufacture design, reversing the Patent Office's view that the claimed design was a mere "fleeting

configuration or shape of an article, to the surface ornamentation applied to an article, or to the combination of configuration and surface ornamentation."[39] A design need not encompass an entire article — patent protection is available for a design of a portion of an article, such as a handle of a tool.[40]

[b]   Ornamentality

A patentable design must be "ornamental."[41] The ornamentality requirement is satisfied when the appearance of the design is not solely dictated by the utilitarian necessities of the underlying article, but includes at least some decorative or arbitrary element.[42] A design need not be aesthetically pleasing, beautiful, or artistic to be deemed ornamental, as long as it is "not the only form of the article that could perform its function."[43]

Designs that are not intended to be visible during the normal and intended use of the article, such as internal hidden components of a machine, are generally not considered ornamental.[44] In *In re Webb*,[45] however, a grooved femoral hip stem prosthesis satisfied the ornamentality requirement because the design was visible in advertisements and at trade shows.[46] The court held that the normal and intended use of an article includes commercial activity during the "period in the article's life, beginning after completion of manufacture or assembly and ending with the ultimate destruction, loss, or disappearance of the article."[47] If the article's appearance may be observed or is intended to be noticed during such commercial activity, the design will satisfy the ornamentality requirement.[48]

---

product of nozzle arrangements") (quotations omitted).

[39] U.S. PATENT & TRADEMARK OFFICE, MANUAL OF PATENT EXAMINING PROCEDURE § 1502 (8th ed., July 2010 rev.). Computer generated icons and user interfaces may also be considered patent-eligible designs "for articles of manufacture," provided that the computer generated images are shown and claimed in the context of a computer display, and not in the abstract. *Id.* § 1504.01(a).

[40] *In re* Zahn, 617 F.2d 261, 267–69 (C.C.P.A. 1980) (holding that the shank portion of a drill bit may be properly protected by a design patent). See the discussion below in section 6B[3] regarding the disclosure requirements for claiming designs that constitute only portions of articles.

[41] 35 U.S.C. § 171.

[42] Seiko Epson Corp. v. Nu-Kote Int'l, Inc., 190 F.3d 1360, 1368 (Fed. Cir. 1999).

[43] *Id.*

[44] *In re* Cornwall, 230 F.2d 457, 459 (C.C.P.A. 1956) ("It is well settled that patentability of a design cannot be based on elements which are concealed in the normal use of the device to which the design is applied."); *In re* Stevens, 173 F.2d 1015, 1019–20 (C.C.P.A. 1949) ("Almost every article is visible when it is made and while it is being applied to the position in which it is to be used. Those special circumstances, however, do not justify the granting of a design patent on an article such as that here under consideration which is always concealed in its normal and intended use. The ornamental appearance of such an article is a matter of such little concern that it cannot be said to possess patentability as a design.").

[45] *In re* Webb, 916 F.2d 1553 (Fed. Cir. 1990).

[46] *Id.* at 1558.

[47] *Id.*

[48] *Id.*

[c]   Nonfunctionality

A design may not be patented if its form is dictated by the functional requirements of the underlying article.[49] For example, the basic shape of the tip of a Phillips head screwdriver is a functional requirement of the article that cannot be covered by a design patent.

Because a patentable design is by definition a design "for a [utilitarian] article of manufacture,"[50] the article typically includes both functional and ornamental features. The mere presence of functional features in the article does not defeat the patentability of the design as a whole, as long as the design includes some nonfunctional elements. The scope of a design patent for an article having both functional and ornamental features, however, is limited to the ornamental features only.[51] For example, in *Richardson v. Stanley Works, Inc.*, a case involving a patent on a design for a multi-function tool, the court ignored the purely functional features of the hammerhead and crow bar, and the patent was construed to cover essentially only the design of the blunt edges and contours of portions extending between the functional components.[52]

[d]   Novelty and Statutory Bars

Patent law's novelty[53] and statutory bar[54] requirements for utility inventions apply to designs.[55] For a claimed design to be anticipated by a prior art design, the two designs must be substantially the same in the eyes of an ordinary observer of the design.[56] This standard is the same as that for infringement under *Gorham Mfg. Co. v. White*,[57] based on the fundamental principle that "[t]hat which infringes, if later, would anticipate, if earlier."[58]

---

[49] Richardson v. Stanley Works, Inc. 597 F.3d 1288, 1293–94 (Fed. Cir. 2010) ("If the patented design is primarily functional rather than ornamental, the patent is invalid."); Hupp v. Siroflex of America, Inc., 122 F.3d 1456, 1460 (Fed. Cir. 1997) ("[A] design or shape that is entirely functional, without ornamental or decorative aspect, does not meet the statutory criteria of a design patent.").

[50] 35 U.S.C. § 171.

[51] *Richardson*, 597 F.3d at 1294. In practice, this means that the court must ignore the functional elements of the design and focus only on the ornamental features when construing the design claim to evaluate the validity or infringement of the patent.

[52] *Id.* at 1294–96; U.S. Design Patent No. D507,167.

[53] *See* § 2C[3].

[54] *See* § 2C[5][b][ii]. The "experimental use" exception to the public use and on sale bars has limited application to designs, since the primary purpose of a design is to be observed. *In re* Mann, 861 F.2d 1581 (Fed. Cir. 1988).

[55] 35 U.S.C. § 171.

[56] Int'l Seaway Trading Corp. v. Walgreens Corp., 589 F.3d 1233, 1237–41 (Fed. Cir. 2009); Door-Master Corp. v. Yorktowne, Inc., 256 F.3d 1308, 1312–13 (Fed. Cir. 2001).

[57] *See* § 6B[1] and § 6B[4].

[58] *Door-Master Corp.*, 256 F.3d at 1312 (quoting Peters v. Active Mfg. Co., 129 U.S. 530, 537 (1889)).

[e]   Nonobviousness

Patent law's requirement that a claimed invention be nonobvious in view of the prior art[59] applies to designs.[60] In analyzing obviousness in the design patent context, "the ultimate inquiry . . . is whether the claimed design would have been obvious to a designer of ordinary skill who designs articles of the type involved."[61] When combining multiple prior art references or teachings to show the obviousness of a design, the analysis requires a two-step process. First, "one must find a single reference, 'a something in existence, the design characteristics of which are basically the same as the claimed design.' "[62] This reference is known as the primary reference, or the *Rosen* reference. Then other "secondary" references may be used to modify the primary reference to create a design having the same overall appearance as the patented design, thereby rendering the design obvious.[63] Importantly, such secondary references may only be used to modify the primary reference if the primary and secondary references are "so related . . . that the appearance of certain ornamental features in one would suggest the application of those features to the other."[64]

[3]   Application and Examination

To obtain a design patent, one must file an application with the United States Patent and Trademark Office disclosing the design. A patent examiner will then analyze the application to determine whether it meets all of the patentability

---

[59] *See* § 2C[4].

[60] 35 U.S.C. § 171; Int'l Seaway Trading Corp. v. Walgreens Corp., 589 F.3d 1233, 1238–39 (Fed. Cir. 2009); Titan Tire Corp. v. Case New Holland, Inc., 566 F.3d 1372, 1380–81 (Fed. Cir. 2009). The application of the nonobviousness requirement to designs may be traced back to the landmark case of *Smith v. Whitman Saddle Co.*, which held that "[m]ere mechanical skill is insufficient [for a design to be patentable]. There must be something akin to genius — an effort of the brain as well as the hand. The adaptation of old devices of forms to new purpose, however convenient, useful or beautiful they may be in their new role, is not invention." 148 U.S. 674, 679 (1893).

[61] Apple, Inc. v. Samsung Elecs. Co., 678 F.3d 1314, 1329 (Fed. Cir. 2012) (quoting *Titan Tire Corp.*, 566 F.3d at 1375).

[62] *Apple*, 678 F.3d at 1329 (quoting *In re* Rosen, 673 F.2d 388, 391 (C.C.P.A. 1982)). In *Apple*, the Federal Circuit held that a 1994 "Fidler" computer tablet design did not qualify as a primary reference to Apple's patented iPad design because Apple's design was highly symmetrical and included an uninterrupted glass surface extending edge-to-edge, both of which being important visual features lacking in the 1994 tablet. *Id.* at 1330–31. The Federal Circuit explained:

> Fidler does not qualify as a primary reference simply by disclosing a rectangular tablet with four evenly rounded corners and a flat back. Rather than looking to the 'general concept' of a tablet, the district court should have focused on the distinctive 'visual appearances' of the reference and the claimed design.

Id. at 1332 (citation omitted).

[63] *Apple*, 678 F.3d at 1329.

[64] *Apple*, 678 F.3d at 1329–30 (quoting *In re* Borden, 90 F.3d 1570, 1575 (Fed. Cir. 1996)). In *Apple*, the Federal Circuit held that an alleged secondary reference — the TC1000 tablet — was "so different in visual appearance from the Fidler reference that it does not qualify as a comparison reference under that standard." *Id.* at 1331 (emphasizing the "flat glass front," "wide rounded-over metallic rim," and front-facing indicator lights of the TC1000, all of which features were visually prominent in the TC1000 but absent in the Fidler tablet).

requirements. If all of the requirements are satisfied, the application will issue as a design patent.

Patent applications for designs are considerably simpler than those for utility inventions. A utility patent application requires a detailed written description, a set of claims, and generally at least one drawing.[65] For designs, patent law's disclosure and claiming requirements are fulfilled almost entirely by the drawings, which illustrate the ornamental appearance of the design.[66] Accordingly, the application must contain "a sufficient number of views to constitute a complete disclosure of the appearance of the design," including whatever surface shading is necessary to show all the character and contours of the surfaces represented.[67] If a design is insufficiently clear in the drawings, the application will be rejected for lack of enablement and indefiniteness.[68]

Design patent applications may contain only a single claim, which is directed to the ornamental design of the article "as shown" in the drawings.[69] If a design is directed to only a portion of an article, other portions of the article may be included for environmental or illustrative purposes, but these other portions must be shown in broken lines.[70]

[4] Exclusive Rights and Remedies — Infringement

The provisions regarding exclusive rights, remedies, and infringement for utility patents apply to design patents.[71] A design patentee generally has the right to prevent others from making, using, offering for sale, selling, or importing an article having the same appearance as the patented design, with injunctive relief or money damages being available remedies for infringement.[72] Section 289 provides an

---

[65] *See* § 2D[3]; U.S. PATENT & TRADEMARK OFFICE, MANUAL OF PATENT EXAMINING PROCEDURE § 601 (8th ed., July 2010 rev.).

[66] 37 C.F.R. § 1.153(a) ("No description, other than a reference to the drawing, is ordinarily required."); U.S. PATENT & TRADEMARK OFFICE, MANUAL OF PATENT EXAMINING PROCEDURE § 1503.01(II) (8th ed., July 2010 rev.) ("No description of the design in the specification beyond a brief description of the drawing is generally necessary, since as a rule the illustration in the drawing views is its own best description.").

[67] 37 C.F.R. § 1.152; U.S. PATENT & TRADEMARK OFFICE, MANUAL OF PATENT EXAMINING PROCEDURE § 1503.02 (8th ed., July 2010 rev.).

[68] 35 U.S.C. § 112, ¶¶ 1–2; U.S. PATENT & TRADEMARK OFFICE, MANUAL OF PATENT EXAMINING PROCEDURE § 1504.04 (8th ed., July 2010 rev.).

[69] 37 C.F.R. § 1.153(a); *In re* Mann, 861 F.2d 1581, 1582 (Fed. Cir. 1988) ("The claim [of a design patent application] . . . is limited to what is shown in the application drawings.").

[70] U.S. PATENT & TRADEMARK OFFICE, MANUAL OF PATENT EXAMINING PROCEDURE § 1503.02 (8th ed., July 2010 rev.) ("Structure that is not part of the claimed design, but is considered necessary to show the environment in which the design is associated, may be represented in the drawing by broken lines."). *See, e.g.*, U.S. Design Patent No. D603,842.

[71] 35 U.S.C. § 171 directs that Title 35's provision on patents for inventions apply to designs "except as otherwise provided." For a discussion of utility patent exclusive rights, infringement, and remedies, see §§ 2E and 2F[5].

[72] 35 U.S.C. § 271; 35 U.S.C. § 283; 35 U.S.C. § 284. In *Apple*, the Federal Circuit made clear that the mere existence of infringement of a patent, including a design patent, does not warrant an injunction — any alleged irreparable harm offered to demonstrate the need for an injunction must have a "nexus" to

additional remedy that allows a design patentee to recover the infringer's total profits, if the infringer reproduces, sells, or offers for sale any article of manufacture bearing the patented design.[73]

Infringement of a design patent is determined by comparing the patented design, as shown in the drawings, with the accused design.[74] To perform this analysis, first the court must properly construe the claimed design to discount any functional features and identify the protectable ornamentation.[75] Once the design claim is so construed, it must be determined whether an ordinary observer would regard the designs as being substantially the same, applying the standard set forth in *Gorham*.

Under the *Gorham* ordinary observer test for infringement, two designs are substantially the same "if, in the eye of an ordinary observer, giving such attention as a purchaser usually gives . . . the resemblance is such as to deceive such an observer, inducing him to purchase one supposing it to be the other."[76] The patented design and the accused design should be compared "as a whole," considering their overall appearances rather than a feature-by-feature comparison of each design detail.[77]

The hypothetical "ordinary observer" is generally the ordinary purchaser of the product in which the claimed design is embodied.[78] In the landmark decision of

---

the infringement. 678 F.3d at 1324 ("To show irreparable harm, it is necessary to show that the infringement caused harm in the first place. Sales lost to an infringing product cannot irreparably harm a patentee if consumers buy that product for reasons other than the patented feature.").

[73] 35 U.S.C. § 289. *See* Trans-World Mfg. Corp. v. Al Nyman & Sons, Inc., 750 F.2d 1552 (Fed. Cir. 1984).

[74] The patentee's commercial embodiment of the claimed design, if any, is irrelevant to the analysis. *See* Sun Hill Industries, Inc. v. Easter Unlimited, Inc., 48 F.3d 1193, 1196–97 (Fed. Cir. 1995). Features such as color, size, or material that are not apparent from the design patent drawings are not to be considered part of the claimed design.

Because a design patent's scope is limited by the patent drawings, infringement is not likely to be found where the accused design is applied to an article other than the type in the patent, due to the inherent differences in appearance of different types of articles. *But see* Avia Group International, Inc. v. L.A. Gear California, Inc., 853 F.2d 1557, 1565 (Fed. Cir. 1988) (holding that a design patent directed to an adult's tennis shoe was infringed by a children's shoe); Goodyear Tire & Rubber Co. v. Hercules Tire & Rubber Co., 162 F.3d 1113, 1116–17 (Fed. Cir. 1998) (holding that a design patent for a "tire tread" was not limited to truck tires only, but included car tires).

[75] *See* § 6B[2][b]–[c]; Richardson v. Stanley Works, Inc. 597 F.3d 1288, 1293–94 (Fed. Cir. 2010).

[76] Gorham Mfg. Co. v. White, 81 U.S. (14 Wall.) 511, 528 (1871).

[77] Egyptian Goddess, Inc. v. Swisa, Inc., 543 F.3d 665, 677 (Fed. Cir. 2008) (*en banc*) (explaining that design patent infringement is not a determination of "whether the accused design has appropriated a single specified feature of the claimed design," but "whether the accused design has appropriated the claimed design as a whole"); Int'l Seaway Trading Corp. v. Walgreens Corp., 589 F.3d 1233, 1243 (Fed. Cir. 2009) (Under the ordinary observer test, "[t]he mandated overall comparison is a comparison taking into account significant differences between the two designs, not minor or trivial differences that necessarily exist between any two designs that are not exact copies of one another."); Litton Systems, Inc. v. Whirlpool Corp., 728 F.2d 1423 (Fed. Cir. 1984) ("[M]inor differences between a patented design and an accused article's design cannot, and shall not, prevent a finding of infringement.").

[78] Arminak & Assoc., Inc. v. Saint-Gobain Calmar, Inc., 501 F.3d 1314, 1322 (Fed. Cir. 2007) ("[T]he focus of the ordinary observer test is 'on the actual product that is presented for purchase, and the ordinary purchaser of *that* product.'") (emphasis in original).

Egyptian Goddess, Inc. v. Swisa, Inc.,[79] the Federal Circuit clarified that the ordinary observer must also be deemed "familiar with the prior art."[80] Such an ordinary observer, comparing the patented and accused designs in light of the prior art, would tend to attach more visual importance to design features that are novel, making it more likely that an accused design including such novel features will be found to infringe.[81]

[5] Conclusion

Design patents can provide valuable intellectual property protection for a vast array of objects, whenever the appearance of an object is of concern. Because design patents are generally more quickly and inexpensively obtained than utility patents, and can be enforced without proof of copying or consumer confusion, they can typically afford some basic protection to a design before other intellectual property rights vest. Because their scope is limited to the appearance of the object shown in the patent drawings, however, design patents are most helpful to prevent exact copies or colorable imitations of a design, and can sometimes be difficult to

---

Although the ordinary observer of a designed product is often the retail level consumer, sometimes the ordinary observer may be a person who is higher up on the supply chain, and who has substantially greater familiarity or expertise with designs in the field of the patent at issue. Such sophisticated ordinary observers tend to make it substantially more difficult to prove infringement. For example, in *Arminak* the claimed design was directed to a sprayer shroud for use in a cleaning product bottle, but did not claim the bottle in its entirety. 501 F.3d at 1317–18. The court found that retail level consumers do not ordinarily buy such shrouds alone, outside the context of a completely assembled cleaning product. *Id.* at 1323–24. Rather, industrial purchasing agents ordinarily bought the shrouds for assembly into their cleaning product bottles. *Id.* Because such persons are more likely to notice differences between designs, the Federal Circuit affirmed the finding of noninfringement, noting that "[t]here is essentially no question that a corporate buyer purchasing these trigger sprayers with these specific shrouds would be able to tell the difference easily." *Id.* at 1324.

[79] 543 F.3d 665 (Fed. Cir. 2008) (*en banc*).

[80] *Id.* at 677, 681.

[81] *Id.* at 677 ("An ordinary observer, comparing the claimed and accused designs in light of the prior art, will attach importance to differences between the claimed design and the prior art depending on the overall effect of those differences on the design.").

Before *Egyptian Goddess*, courts would apply both the ordinary observer test of *Gorham* and a so-called "points of novelty test" to determine whether an accused design infringed a patent. *Egyptian Goddess*, 543 F.3d at 671 (citing cases). Even if an ordinary observer would have found the designs to be substantially similar, the design would not infringe unless it also included one or more of the "points of novelty" of the claimed design, *i.e.*, the ornamental features of the claimed design that were absent in the prior art. *See* Litton Systems, Inc. v. Whirlpool Corp., 728 F.2d 1423, 1444 (Fed. Cir. 1984).

In *Egyptian Goddess*, the Federal Circuit concluded that the points of novelty test placed undue focus on individual features of the design, and emphasized that design infringement requires appropriation of the overall appearance of the claimed design "as a whole." 543 F.3d at 677. Accordingly, the Federal Circuit abrogated the points of novelty test and held that the ordinary observer test of *Gorham* is the sole test for design patent infringement. *Id.* at 678. However, to ignore the prior art and compare only the claimed design and the accused design could result in an accused design being found to infringe when in fact the accused design was actually in prior art (*i.e.*, in the public domain). Thus, the ordinary observer must be deemed "familiar with the prior art," such that he or she would attach more visual importance to the novel aspects of a claimed design, and would tend not to find infringement if the accused design does not include such novel features. *Id.* at 677.

enforce against non-trivial variations of a design.[82]

§ 6C PLANT PROTECTION

United States law provides three potential sources of statutory protection[83] for plant-related inventions: (1) the Plant Patent Act;[84] the Plant Variety Protection Act (PVPA);[85] and (3) the general utility patent statute.[86]

[1]   Plant Patent Act

In 1930, Congress provided for patents on asexually reproduced distinct and new plant varieties, such as flowering plants and fruit trees.[87] The purpose was to "afford agriculture, so far as practicable, the same opportunity to participate in the benefits of the patent system as has been given industry."[88] Without intellectual property protection, a plant breeder would have "no adequate financial incentive to enter upon his work,"[89] because those who purchased his new varieties could use asexual reproduction techniques, such as budding and grafting, to multiply copies of the variety.

[a]   Requirements

Section 161 provides:

> Whoever invents or discovers and asexually reproduces any distinct and new variety of plant, including cultivated sports, mutants, hybrids, and newly found seedlings, other than a tuber propagated plant or a plant found in an uncultivated state, may obtain a patent therefor, subject to the conditions and requirements of this title.[90]

---

[82] See In re Mann, 861 F.2d 1581, 1582 (Fed. Cir. 1988) (observing that "[d]esign patents have almost no scope. The claim at bar, as in all design cases, is limited to what is shown in the application drawings.")

[83] Common law theories, such as trade secret law, see Chapter 3, contract law, and unfair competition law, see § 6F, may also protect against unauthorized misappropriation of plant technology. Trade secret protection can be important for hybrid plants, the parents of which (needed to produce the hybrid) can be maintained as publicly inaccessible lines. See, e.g., Pioneer Hi-Bred Int'l v. Holden Found. Seeds, 35 F.3d 1226, 1235 (8th Cir. 1994); Doebler's Pa. Hybrids, Inc. v. Doebler, 2003 U.S. Dist. LEXIS 27097 at *35 (M.D. Pa. Sept. 23, 2003), aff'd, 2004 U.S. App. LEXIS 2420 (3d Cir. Feb. 12, 2004).

[84] 35 U.S.C. §§ 161–164.

[85] 7 U.S.C. § 2321 et seq.

[86] 35 U.S.C. § 101. For a discussion of utility patent law, see Chapter 2.

[87] See generally D. Chisum, Patents § 1.05.

[88] S. Rep. No. 71-315, at 1 (1930).

[89] Id. In testimony in support of the Act, Thomas Edison claimed: "Nothing that Congress could do to help farming would be of greater value and permanence than to give the plant breeder the same status as the mechanical and chemical inventors now have through the patent law. There are but few plant breeders. This [bill] will, I feel sure, give us many Burbanks," referring to Luther Burbank, America's preeminent plant breeder. H.R. Rep. No. 71-1129, at 3 (1930).

[90] 35 U.S.C. § 161. Note that tuber-propagated plants, such as potatoes, are covered by the PVPA (even though potato "seeds" are not true "seeds", and potatoes are vegetatively propagated). See 7 U.S.C. § 2402(a).

To be eligible for plant patent protection, subject matter must meet several requirements. First, it must be a variety of "plant."[91] In *In re Arzberger*,[92] the court held that a bacterium species cultured from Louisiana cane field soil was not a "plant" because the statute contemplated only plants in the ordinary common-sense meaning.

Second, the inventor must asexually reproduce the new variety, that is, by "means other than from seeds, such as by the rooting of cuttings, by layering, budding, grafting, inarching, etc."[93] Asexual reproduction is necessary to preserve the unique genetic structure of a plant, including hybrids, mutants or sports: "For example, without asexual reproduction, there would have been but one true McIntosh or Greening apple tree."[94]

Third, the subject matter must be a "distinct and new variety."[95] It must "have characteristics clearly distinguishable from those of existing varieties."[96] A distinguishing characteristic may be disease immunity, flower color, flavor or productivity. Further, the plant must either have been "cultivated" (that is, created by the breeder) or be a seedling found upon cultivated land; in other words, it must not have been found "in an uncultivated state."[97]

Fourth, the plant variety must be new and must not be subject to a Section 102(b) statutory bar.[98] Publicly using or selling a plant variety in the United States more than one year prior to the application date bars a patent unless the experimental use doctrine excuses the use or sale.[99] A prior art publication illustrating the plant variety will not necessarily constitute an anticipation because the publication may not be sufficient to enable a person of ordinary skill in the art to reproduce the plant.[100] However, while prior art publication disclosures alone are not enabling for

---

[91] The patent claim is to "the plant shown and described" in the inventor's specification, 35 U.S.C. § 162.

[92] *In re* Arzberger, 112 F.2d 834 (C.C.P.A. 1940).

[93] U.S. Patent & Trademark Office, Manual of Patent Examining Procedure § 1601 (8th ed. rev. 6 2001). Asexual reproduction is analogous to reduction to practice of an invention. *See* D. Chisum, Patents § 1.05[1][b][ii].

[94] S. Rep. No. 71-315, at 4 (1930); *see also* Nicholas O. Seay, *Protecting the Seeds of Innovation: Patenting Plants*, 16 A.I.P.L.A. Q.J. 418 (1989).

[95] 35 U.S.C. § 162.

[96] S. Rep. No. 71-315, at 4 (1930).

[97] 36 U.S.C. § 161; *In re* Beinecke, 690 F.3d 1344 (Fed. Cir. 2012) (newly-discovered oak trees had existed long before land was cultivated and were not eligible for protection).

[98] For a discussion of prior art and statutory bars, see § 2C[5].

[99] *See* Delano Farms Co. v. Calif. Table Grape Comm'n, 940 F. Supp. 2d 1229 (E.D. Cal. 2013) (finding triable issue of fact on whether certain uses were "public," but granting summary judgment that certain other uses were "experimental").

[100] *See In re* Elsner, 381 F.3d 1125, 1129 (Fed. Cir. 2004) (requiring availability of plant material in order for publication to be enabling); *In re* Le Grice, 301 F.2d 929, 938 (C.C.P.A. 1962) (full color photograph of the new rose variety more than one year before the patent application filing date is not a bar). In *Le Grice*, the court noted that Congress altered the enabling disclosure requirement for plant patent specifications, see § 6C[1][b], but made no similar alteration of the anticipatory effect of publications.

statutory bar purposes, they may be sufficient to satisfy the written description requirement for a plant patent.[101]

Fifth, the plant must meet patent law's nonobviousness requirement. The Plant Patent Act does not mention the nonobviousness requirement but does state that "the provisions of this title relating to patents for inventions shall apply to patents for plants, except as otherwise provided." In *Yoder Bros. Inc. v. California-Florida Plant Corp.*,[102] the Fifth Circuit applied a modified version of the *Graham v. John Deere Co.* nonobviousness analysis[103] to determine the patentability of several chrysanthemum varieties.

[b]   Application and Examination

To obtain a patent, a plant developer must file an application with the PTO, which examines the application and issues a patent if patentability conditions are met.[104]

As with design patents,[105] drawings (which include photographs) in addition to a written description fulfill patent law's disclosure and claiming requirements.[106] The drawings must be "artistically and competently executed," "disclose all the distinctive characteristics of the plant capable of visual representation" and be done in color if color is a distinguishing characteristic of the variety.[107]

Section 162 relaxes the enabling disclosure requirement: "No plant patent shall be declared invalid for noncompliance with § 112 of this title if the description is as complete as is reasonably possible."[108]

Only one claim is permitted in plant patent applications, and must be expressed in botanical terms rather than in terms commonly found in nursery or seed catalogs.[109]

---

[101] 35 U.S.C. § 162; *see* § 6C[1][b], below.

[102] 537 F.2d 1347 (5th Cir. 1976).

[103] 383 U.S. 1 (1966).

[104] For a discussion of the patenting process, see § 2D[1].

[105] *See* § 6B.

[106] 35 U.S.C. § 162 ("The claim in the specification shall be in formal terms to the plant shown and described.").

[107] 37 C.F.R. § 1.165.

[108] 35 U.S.C. § 162.

In Diamond v. Chakrabarty, 447 U.S. 303, 311 (1980), the Supreme Court noted that easing the written description requirement was a major reason Congress passed the Plant Patent Act: "Because new plants may differ from old only in color or perfume, differentiation by written description was often impossible."

The Court's description of the problem of describing new plant varieties is not fully accurate. The difficulty is not so much describing the new variety's characteristics as providing sufficient information to enable practitioners to reproduce the variety without direct access to the patentee's actual plant stock. Court decisions recognize that the plant inventor must "clearly and precisely describ[e] those characteristics which define the new variety." *In re* Greer, 484 F.2d 488, 491 (C.C.P.A. 1973)).

[109] 37 C.F.R. 1.164; Manual of Patent Examining Procedure § 1605 (8th ed. rev. 6 2001).

[c]   Exclusive Rights — Infringement

Comparable to a utility patent's five rights to exclude — making, using, selling, offering to sell, and importing — a plant patent confers the right to exclude others from asexually reproducing the plant, and from using, offering for sale, selling, or importing the plant so reproduced,[110] or any of its parts, in the United States.[111] Under some circumstances, aiding and abetting any of these activities constitutes contributory infringement.[112]

In patent law generally, "independent development" is not a defense, and one who without authority makes, uses or sells a product or process covered by another's patent infringes even if he did not directly or indirectly copy the patent's disclosures.[113] This may not be true of plant patent infringement: "It is quite possible that infringement of a plant patent would occur only if stock obtained from one of the patented plants is used, given the extreme unlikelihood that any other plant could actually infringe."[114] Infringement can still be innocent because "[a] direct infringer need not have knowledge of the patent or the source of the plant which is asexually reproduced, sold, or used."[115] Although trial courts had been divided as to whether a plant patent covers independent derivation,[116] the Federal Circuit has held that "in order for there to be infringement . . . the infringing plant must be an asexual reproduction of the plant claimed . . . [and not an] asexual reproduction of *a* plant having the same essential characteristics as the patented plant."[117] Proof of genetic relatedness between the claimed and potentially infringing plant and will likely be necessary to satisfy this requirement.[118]

[2]   Plant Variety Protection Act

In 1970, Congress enacted the Plant Variety Protection Act (PVPA), recognizing plant breeders' ability to produce seeds expressing stable genetic characteristics. It authorized patent-like protection to *sexually* reproduced plants in the form of plant variety protection certificates, which the Secretary of Agriculture, rather than the Patent and Trademark Office, issues. The PVPA's purpose is "[t]o encourage the development of novel varieties of sexually reproduced plants and to

---

[110] The importation right was added by amendment in 1998.

[111] 35 U.S.C. § 163. *See* Yoder Bros., Inc. v. California-Florida Plant Corp., 537 F.2d 1347 (5th Cir. 1976) (sale of immature cuttings infringes; "the act of asexual reproduction was complete at the time the cutting was taken").

[112] *See* Armstrong Nurseries, Inc. v. Smith, 170 F. Supp. 519 (E.D. Tex. 1958). For there to be contributory infringement, there must be an act of direct infringement, which may not occur if the reproduction, use, or sale occurs outside the United States.

[113] *See* § 2F[3][b].

[114] Yoder Bros., Inc. v. California-Florida Plant Corp., 537 F.2d 1347, 1380 (5th Cir. 1976). *See* D. CHISUM, PATENTS § 1.05[1][d].

[115] D. CHISUM, PATENTS § 1.05[1][d]. *See also* Kim Bros. v. Hagler, 167 F. Supp. 665, 668 (S.D. Cal. 1958), *aff'd*, 276 F.2d 259 (9th Cir. 1960).

[116] Cole Nursery, Co. v. Youdath Perennial Gardens, Inc., 17 F. Supp. 159 (N.D. Ohio 1936); Pan-American Plant Co. v. Matsui, 433 F. Supp. 693 (N.D. Cal. 1977).

[117] Imazio Nursery, Inc. v. Dania Greenhouses, 69 F.3d 1560 (Fed. Cir. 1995).

[118] *See* Pioneer Hi-Bred Int'l v. Holden Found. Seeds, 35 F.3d 1226, 1235 (8th Cir. 1994).

make them available to the public, providing protection available to those who breed, develop, or discover them, and thereby promoting progress in agriculture."[119]

[a]   Requirements

The PVPA covers seed-bearing plant varieties (plus tuber-propagated plant varieties) but excludes fungi and bacteria.[120]

To be eligible for PVPA certification, the subject matter must be a "novel variety." The novelty requirement includes statutorily defined distinctiveness, uniformity, and stability criteria.[121] Patent law's nonobviousness requirement does not apply.[122]

Other countries' nationals are eligible for plant variety certification protection only if a treaty applies[123] or reciprocity conditions are met.[124]

The PVPA contains statutory bar provisions similar to the utility patent statute. For example, certification is barred if, "more than one year prior to the date of filing," the variety was "sold...for purposes of exploitation" in the United States with

---

[119] Preamble to Pub. L. 91-577, 84 Stat. 1542 (1970). *See also* Diamond v. Chakrabarty, 447 U.S. 303, 313 (1980) ("sexually reproduced plants were not included under the 1930 Act because new varieties could not be reproduced true-to-type through seedlings. . . . By 1970, however, it was generally recognized that true-to-type reproduction was possible and that plant patent protection was therefore appropriate."); Public Varieties of Mississippi Inc. v. Sun Valley Seed Co. Inc., 734 F. Supp. 250 (N.D. Miss. 1990).

[120] Because both the Plant Patent Act and the PVPA exclude new bacteria, isolated from nature or genetically-altered, the utility patent statute is the only statutory protection source for bacteria. *See* Diamond v. Chakrabarty, 447 U.S. 303 (1980), discussed at § 2C[1][d]; *see also In re* Bergy, 596 F.2d 952 (C.C.P.A. 1979), *vacated on other grounds*, 44 U.S. 1028 (1980).

[121] 7 U.S.C. § 2402(a). *See In re* John Walker, 40 Agric. Dec. 1017 (1981) (novelty requirement met if variety differs from known varieties by even a single distinct, uniform, and stable characteristic).

[122] In eliminating the nonobviousness requirement, the PVPA considerably simplifies the protectability issue. A novelty-only standard for intellectual property eligibility is balanced by the relatively narrow scope of protection.

Is the PVPA's elimination of a nonobviousness-type standard constitutional? In the copyright and patent arenas, the Supreme Court has indicated that there is a constitutional floor of innovation and creativity. Feist Publications v. Rural Telephone Service Co., 499 U.S. 340 (1991); Graham v. John Deere Co., 383 U.S. 1 (1966).

It may be pertinent that in enacting the PVPA, Congress invoked not only its Article I, Sec. 8, cl. 8 Patent-Copyright Clause powers but also its Article I power to regulate interstate and foreign commerce. *See* 7 U.S.C. § 2581:

> It is the intent of Congress to provide the indicated protection for new varieties by exercise of any constitutional power needed for that end, so as to afford adequate encouragement for research, and for marketing when appropriate, to yield for the public the benefits of new varieties. Constitutional clauses 3 and 8 of article I, section 8 are both relied upon.

[123] The United States is a party to the International Union for the Protection of New Varieties of Plants (UPOV). UPOV provides for Plant Breeders' Rights (PBR) protection for plant varieties, both sexually and asexually propagated. Counterpart foreign filings for PBR rights can be made for varieties which are the subject of U.S. plant patents, PVPs or utility patents, and can establish a priority filing date for U.S. plant patents or utility patents. Manual of Patent Examining Procedure § 1613 (8th ed. rev. 6 2001); 7 C.F.R. § 97.5.

[124] 7 U.S.C. § 2403.

the consent of the breeder.[125] However, publication is generally insufficient to serve as an enabling reference under the PVPA, in contrast with statutory bar requirements for utility patents.[126]

Substantial amendments were made to the PVPA in 1994, with applications filed on or after April 4, 1995 subject to the 1994 amendments. Varieties protected under the 1970 PVPA and varieties for which applications were submitted prior to the effective date of the 1994 amendments, continue to be governed by the 1970 PVPA.

[b]   Application and Examination

The new plant variety "owner"[127] may file an application for certification with the Department of Agriculture's Plant Variety Protection Office (PVPO) setting forth (1) the variety's name or temporary designation, (2) a description setting forth distinctiveness, uniformity, and stability, and the genealogy and breeding procedure if known, (3) a statement of the basis of the claim that the variety is new, (4) a declaration that "a viable sample of basic seed necessary for propagation of the variety" will be deposited with a public repository and replenished periodically,[128] and (5) a statement of the basis of applicant's ownership.[129] The PVPO examines certification applications in a fashion comparable to PTO examination and issues a certificate if it determines that the variety meets the statutory requirements.[130]

[c]   Exclusive Rights — Infringement

The PVPA specifically defines a certificate owner's exclusive rights in the protected new variety and what constitutes infringement. Section 2483 confers rights to exclude others from selling, offering for sale, reproducing (either sexually or asexually), importing, exporting, or using the variety to produce hybrid or different varieties.[131] Section 2541 lists ten infringing acts, some of which are broader than rights under a utility patent.[132] Section 2541 also exempts authorized

---

[125] 7 U.S.C. § 2402(a)(1). The Act contains an analog of the experimental use exception. *See* § 2F[4][d]. It provides that sale for experimentation or testing of a variety is not a sale "for purposes of exploitation." 7 U.S.C. § 2401(b)(1),(2). The requirement that the breeder consent to the disclosure is in contrast with utility patent law.

[126] *See* Star Fruits S.N.C. v. United States, 280 F. Supp. 2d 512, 514–15 (E.D. Va. 2003), *aff'd on other grounds*, 393 F.3d 1277 (Fed. Cir. 2005).

[127] "The owner is the breeder of the variety, but by statute a principal is considered to be the breeder where the relevant actions are by an agent on the principal's behalf." D. CHISUM, PATENTS § 1.05[2][c]. *See* 7 U.S.C. § 2401(a)(2).

[128] The certificate may expire if the owner fails to comply with the replenishment requirement (7 U.S.C. § 2483(c)) and samples that are not retained by the Plant Variety Protection Office or requested by the owner are destroyed. 7 C.F.R. § 97.8(c).

For a discussion of biological material deposits for utility patent purposes, see § 2D[3][a][vi].

[129] 7 U.S.C. §§ 2421, 2422.

[130] 7 U.S.C. § 2441.

[131] 7 U.S.C. § 2483.

[132] 7 U.S.C. § 2541(a). These include (1) selling, offering, or exposing for sale; (2) importing or exporting; (3) sexually multiplying for growing purposes; (4) using in production of hybrids; (5) using seed for propagation; (6) dispensing without notice of protection; (7) conditioning for propagation; (8) stocking; (9) asexual reproduction; and (10) inducing any for these acts.

uses,[133] private non-commercial uses,[134] and, once authorized plants have been placed in the stream of commerce, any acts that do not involve further propagation.[135]

The protection term expires 20 years after the certificate's issue date, but may be shortened if the certificate does not issue within three years from filing and the delay is attributable to the applicant.[136] In the case of trees or vines, the term of the plant variety protection is 25 years from the date of issue.[137] Unlike patent owners (except for provisional rights under 35 U.S.C. § 154(d)), variety owners may recover for infringements occurring before the certificate issues but after distribution of the variety with notice.[138]

Section 2543 grants farmers a limited right to save and sell seeds, but only for non-reproductive purposes.[139] Section 2544 provides a research exemption: "The use and reproduction of a protected variety for plant breeding or other bona fide research shall not constitute an infringement. . . ."[140]

The PVPA's infringement remedies are substantially the same as those for utility patent infringement.[141]

[d]   Essentially Derived Varieties

The PVPA provides infringement protection for "essentially derived varieties" (EDV) which is any variety that is predominantly derived from another variety and retains its essential characteristics, but is nevertheless clearly distinguishable from the initial variety.[142] This protection does not extend to varieties themselves derived

---

[133] 7 U.S.C. § 2541(b); AGSouth Genetics, LLC v. Georgia Farm Services, LLC, 2014 U.S. Dist. LEXIS 68806 (M.D. Ga. May 20, 2014) (sales made to investigator hired by plaintiff were not "authorized" sales).

[134] 7 U.S.C. § 2541(e).

[135] 7 U.S.C. § 2541(d); AGSouth Genetics, 2014 U.S. Dist. LEXIS 68806 (sale of seed "involves" further propagation; no evidence of actual propagation is required).

[136] 7 U.S.C. § 2483(b).

[137] 7 U.S.C. § 2483(b)(1)(B).

[138] 7 U.S.C. §§ 2541(a), 2567. By using the notice, the owner obtains protection for more than 20 years. The owner must apply for a certificate within one year of public distribution. 7 U.S.C. § 2402(a)(1).

[139] 7 U.S.C. § 2543. In 1983, the Fifth Circuit held that Congress had intended that the "farmer's exemption" was meant to be read narrowly and required sales be made directly from farmer to farmer, see Delta and Pine Land Co. v. People Gin Co., 694 F.2d 1012 (5th Cir. 1983). Section 2543 was amended in 1994 to eliminate the infringement exemption that allowed farmers growing patented seed for non-reproductive purposes to sell their seed to other non-reproductive use farmers to use for planting their crops (a reproductive use). The amendment added further statutory support to the holding in Asgrow Seed Co. v. Winterboer, 513 U.S. 179 (1995), in which the Supreme Court held that sale for reproductive use under the unamended statute is limited to that which the farmer can grow himself. This decision interpreted the prohibition against sexually propagating a protected variety "as a step in marketing (for growing purposes) the variety" to mean a prohibition against selling the variety for reproductive purposes, with the sale of seed saved for replanting the farmer's own acreage the only permitted use.

[140] 7 U.S.C. § 2544.

[141] 7 U.S.C. §§ 2561–2570. See § 2F[5].

[142] 7 U.S.C. §§ 2401(a)(3), 2541(c).

from essentially derived varieties. While this provision appears to allow for broad protection in the way that the doctrine of equivalents broadens utility patent protection, it is unclear that this expansion has been utilized to any extent in infringement suits in the United States. The scope of EDV protection, however, continues to be of interest to those who use material taken from seed banks such as the international network of seed germplasm banks of the Consultative Group on International Agricultural Resources (CGIAR), as well as in national seed libraries like the U.S. Seed Bank at Fort Collins, Colorado. Users of this material agree to not seek intellectual property protection on the material received, which allows potential protection for EDVs of this material. The scope of EDV protection in this context has been controversial.

[3]   Utility Patents for Plants

The PTO now recognizes that plant matter falls within the subject-matter definitions of the utility patent statute, and that a new plant may receive a utility patent even though it is also eligible for protection under the plant patent or plant variety protection statutes. Satisfaction of the written description requirement for plants generally requires a deposit of plant material in a publicly accessible depository, or evidence that the claimed plant is known and readily available.[143] This construction of the utility patent statute has been confirmed in a series of court cases.

In *Diamond v. Chakrabarty*,[144] the Supreme Court held that genetically-altered microorganisms, which are living organisms but fall outside the coverage of the two plant statutes, were Section 101 patentable subject matter as either "compositions of matter" or "manufactures." It rejected the PTO's argument that Congress intended the Plant Patent Act and the Plant Variety Protection Act to be the exclusive means for protecting living subject matter.[145] In particular, the Court held that the exclusion of bacteria "may simply reflect congressional agreement with . . . *In re* Arzberger, 112 F.2d 834 (C.C.P.A. 1940), which held that bacteria were not plants for the purposes of the 1930 Act. Or it may reflect the fact that prior to 1970 the Patent Office had issued patents for bacteria under § 101."[146]

In *Ex parte Hibberd*,[147] the PTO's Board of Patent Appeals and Interferences extended *Chakrabarty* to hold that plants, plant seeds, and plant tissue cultures constituted Section 101 patentable subject matter. The applicants developed technology for plants that produced corn with increased tryptophan, which has

---

[143] 37 C.F.R. § 1.801 et seq.; U.S. Patent & Trademark Office, Manual of Patent Examining Procedure § 1601 (8th ed. rev. 6 2001); 54 Fed. Reg. 34,864 (August 22, 1989).

There are established procedures and depositories for seed crops (i.e., seed deposit), but deposits for asexually propagated plants may be less straightforward in terms of what is deposited and who maintains it (e.g., a frozen tissue-culture deposit). 7 C.F.R. § 97.7; U.S. Patent & Trademark Office, Manual of Patent Examining Procedure § 2403.02 (8th ed. rev. 6 2001).

[144] 447 U.S. 303 (1980), discussed at § 2C[1][d].

[145] 447 U.S. at 311–314.

[146] *Id.* at 114.

[147] 227 U.S.P.Q. 443 (PTO Bd. Pat. App. & Int'f 1985).

greater nutritional value than ordinary corn. The applicants presented claims specifying the corresponding tryptophan content, including claims to: (1) maize seed, (2) a maize plant, (3) a maize tissue culture, (4) a hybrid seed, (5) a hybrid plant, (6) a method for producing a maize plant, and (7) a method for producing hybrid seed. The examiner rejected the maize seed, plant, and tissue culture claims on the ground that subject matter potentially protectable under either PVPA or the Plant Patent Act (PPA) was not eligible for patent protection under the general ("utility") patent statute.[148] The Board reversed the examiner's rejections (though it did enter a new ground for rejection based on deficiencies in the evidence as to the adequacy of a deposit of seeds with a public depository in order to comply with the enablement requirement).

In 2001, in *J.E.M. Ag Supply, Inc. v. Pioneer Hi-Bred Int'l, Inc.*,[149] the Supreme Court confirmed the holding of *Hibberd* that plants, plant seeds, and plant tissue cultures constituted § 101 patentable subject matter. The Court expressly held that protection under the PPA or PVPA does not limit protection under 35 U.S.C. § 101.

In *J.E.M.*, Pioneer, a large plant breeder, sued J.E.M. for infringing its utility patents for inbred and hybrid corn lines after J.E.M. resold Pioneer's hybrid seed. Pioneer sold its seed under a limited license with a specific prohibition against using it for propagation. J.E.M. defended by asserting invalidity of Pioneer's patents as unpatentable subject matter under § 101. In particular, J.E.M. argued that sexually reproduced plants are not covered by § 101 because the PPA and PVPA provide the exclusive means for patenting plant life.

The Court rejected J.E.M.'s argument. It first affirmed the expansive reading of § 101 given in *Chakrabarty*, emphasizing that the principal distinction necessary for patentable subject matter is between natural products and human-made inventions, and not between living and non-living matter. As such, as long as the plant invention can satisfy the requirements of novelty, utility, non-obviousness, and the written description, it is patentable subject matter.[150]

The Court then held that neither the PPA nor the PVPA forecloses utility patent coverage for plants. The Court noted that neither statute explicitly excludes utility patent protection, and it held that neither statute precludes utility protection by implication. First, although the history of the PPA revealed that in 1930, Congress believed that sexually-reproduced plants could not be stably reproduced and that plants could not meet the stringent written description requirements for utility patents, both of those limitations were later disproved.[151] Second, the differences in the protection available under the PVPA and the utility patent statute "do not present *irreconcilable* conflicts because the requirements for obtaining a utility patent under § 101 are more stringent than those for obtaining a PVP certificate, and the protections afforded by a utility patent are greater than those afforded by

---

[148] The examiner also argued that Section 101 protection for plants would violate the International Union for the Protection of New Plant Varieties (UPOV) Article 2. The Board held that UPOV was an unratified executive agreement that could not override conflicting statutory law.

[149] 534 U.S. 124 (2001).

[150] *Id.* at 130–31.

[151] *Id.* at 132–38.

a PVP certificate.[152] In particular, the PVPA includes exemptions for saving seed and for research which are not available as defenses to a utility patent.[153] Finally, the Court emphasized that although the PTO had granted utility patents for plant material as process-product claims (the product of hybrid processes) and as products since *Hibberd*, Congress expressed no indication that "such coverage is inconsistent with the PVPA or the PPA," and in fact recognized the availability of utility patents for plants when it enacted 35 U.S.C. § 119(f), which provides that applications for plant breeder's rights in any WTO nation may establish a right of priority for a domestic utility patent application.[154]

Neither *Hibberd* nor *J.E.M.* directly addresses the problem of election — that is, whether one must elect one form of protection or may seek several forms of protection concurrently. If a person seeks both a utility patent and a plant patent for similar subject matter, the problem would presumably be handled by applying the double patenting doctrine, as is done with utility and design patents.[155] Multiple protection will be allowed provided the two patents do not claim identical subject matter and provided a terminal disclaimer is entered if the claimed subject matter of one patent would be obvious in view of the claimed subject matter of the other patent. If a person seeks both a utility patent and PVPA protection, the problem is more difficult. Is the appropriate analogy that between design patent protection and copyright[156] (where nothing equivalent to a terminal disclaimer is required) — or between multiple patents?

[4]   Protection Source Choice Factors

In choosing among utility, plant, and PVPA protection for plant-related inventions, the utility patent option has several advantages. First, in a utility patent, the inventor may claim multiple plant parts, including plant genomes coding for nonplant proteins, cells and cell cultures, and plant tissue. Further, with a utility patent, methods may be claimed, and there may be multiple claims to methods and/or products. Both plant patents (which have a single claim) and PVPs (which have no "claim" in the patent sense) are directed to a single variety, although the rights extend to plant parts as well.[157]

Second, a utility patent may cover multiple varieties, an entire species, or even a genus if the applicant can show disclosure support sufficient to satisfy the enablement requirement.

Third, like a PVPA certification but unlike a plant patent, a utility patent protects against sexual as well as asexual reproduction.

---

[152] *Id.* at 142.

[153] *Id.* at 140.

[154] *Id.* at 144–45.

[155] *See* § 2D [3][a][iv]. The MPEP, however, does not specifically address double patenting in the plant-utility patent context, as it does with design-utility patents.

[156] *See* Mazer v. Stein, 347 U.S. 201 (1954); *In re* Yardley, 493 F.2d 1389 (C.C.P.A. 1974).

[157] *See* 35 U.S.C. § 161; 7 U.S.C. § 2541.

Fourth, like a plant patent, a utility patent is not subject to the PVPA's specific farmers' surplus seed sale exemption.[158]

The plant patent option eases the enabling disclosure requirement. Both the PVPA and utility patents require a seed stock deposit, but plant patents do not.[159] Biological material deposits are expensive and may cause surrender of otherwise valuable proprietary advantages.

The PVPA certification option has the advantage that the nonobviousness patentability requirement need not be met.

[5]   Plant Breeders Rights Under TRIPS

Under the Agreement on Trade-Related Aspects of Intellectual Property (TRIPS), members of the World Trade Organization (WTO) "shall provide for the protection of plant varieties either by patents or by an effective *sui generis system* or by any combination thereof."[160] Because the U.S. provides several methods for plant patent protection, TRIPS does not substantially affect plant patent rights in the United States.

§ 6D   SEMICONDUCTOR CHIP PROTECTION

[1]   Introduction

The 1984 Semiconductor Chip Protection Act (SCPA)[161] established a special form of intellectual property protection for "masks" used to create semiconductor chips' electronic circuitry.[162] Semiconductors are used in computers and many other products, such as televisions, telephones, medical equipment, industrial control systems, machine tools, microwave ovens, and automobiles.

Congress enacted the SCPA because of concern that existing law did not adequately protect United States companies' huge investment in chip development and manufacture.[163] A single chip costing up to $100 million to develop could be copied for a fraction of that cost. Congress feared patent law did not adequately protect this investment because chip layouts, though time-consuming and costly to

---

[158] *See* Monsanto v. McFarling, 363 F.3d 1336 (Fed. Cir. 2004), in which the Federal Circuit held that the seed-saving provisions of the PVPA do not preempt and invalidate all prohibitions on seed saving under utility patent protection. The court also rejected the argument that patents for genetically modified plants cover only the gene technology and not the germplasm (the seeds).

[159] U.S. Patent & Trademark Office, Manual of Patent Examining Procedure § 2403.02 (8th ed. rev. 6 2001).

[160] TRIPS Agreement, art. 27(b)(3).

[161] 17 U.S.C. § 901–914.

[162] The SCPA covers all mask works "first commercially exploited or . . . registered under this chapter, or both, on or after" its enactment date (November 8, 1984). 17 U.S.C. § 913(c). It also has limited retroactive application, covering chips exploited on or after July 1, 1983, provided the owner registered his protection claim before July 1, 1985, and subject to the right of others to import and distribute chips made before the enactment date on payment of a reasonable royalty. 17 U.S.C. § 913(d).

[163] H.R. Rep. No. 98-781, at 2 (1984).

produce, usually lacked patentable novelty and nonobviousness over the prior art.[164] Copyright law was inadequate because it traditionally did not cover utilitarian items such as semiconductor chips, and any protection was limited to copying the chips' drawings, not the final chip product.[165]

Congress considered but rejected amending the Copyright Act to cover semiconductor chips[166] for two reasons: to maintain copyright law's "integrity"[167] and to avoid automatic extension of United States protection to foreign nationals' mask works under international copyright law's national treatment principle.[168] Instead, it created a new form of legal protection that borrows many copyright law concepts but also includes patent concepts and new concepts.[169] The SCPA's purpose is "to protect semiconductor chip products in such a manner as to reward creativity, encourage innovation, research and investment in the semiconductor industry, prevent piracy, while at the same time protecting the public."[170]

The SCPA has an extensive legislative history that offers guidance on its interpretation, but there is only two appellate decisions applying it.[171] Many issues remain unclear.

[2]   Protection Requirements

[a]   Definitions

The SCPA protects "mask works" that are "fixed" in a "semiconductor chip product." It defines a "mask work" as:

"a series of related images, however fixed or encoded—

(A) having or representing the predetermined, three-dimensional pattern of metallic, insulating, or semiconductor material present or removed from the layers of a semiconductor chip product; and

---

[164] See § 2C[4].

[165] H.R. Rep. No. 98-781, at 3–4, 8, (1984). See also Brooktree Corp. v. Advanced Micro Devices, Inc., 977 F2d 1555, 1562 (Fed. Cir. 1992). For discussions of the copyrightability of useful articles, depiction of useful articles, and computer programs, see §§ 4C[4][a][i](b) and 4C[4][a][v].

[166] The Senate favored a copyright approach but acceded to the House of Representative's insistence on a sui generis approach.

[167] "Rather than risk confusion and uncertainty in, and distortion of, existing copyright law as a result of attempting to modify fundamental copyright principles to suit the unusual nature of chip design, . . . a new body of statutory and decisional law should be developed." H.R. Rep. No. 98-781, at 10 (1984).

[168] "If the United States enacts copyright legislation to protect mask works, we would be required to give equivalent protection under the UCC [Universal Copyright Convention]. . . . The United States could be required to protect, for example, the mask works of Japan, West Germany, and the Soviet Union, and receive no protection in return." Id. at 7.

[169] See Brooktree, 977 F.2d at 1563.

[170] H.R. Rep. No. 98-781, at 1 (1984).

[171] Brooktree Corp. v. Advanced Micro Devices, Inc., 977 F.2d 1555 (Fed. Cir. 1992); Altera Corp. v. Clear Logic, Inc., 424 F.3d 1079 (9th Cir. 2005).

(B) in which series the relation of the images to one another is that each image has the pattern of the surface of one form of the semiconductor chip product.[172]

It defines a "semiconductor chip product" as:

(A) having two or more layers of metallic, insulating, or semiconductor material, deposited or otherwise placed on, or etched away or otherwise removed from, a piece of semiconductor material in accordance with a predetermined pattern; and

(B) intended to perform electronic circuitry functions."[173]

A mask work is "fixed" in a semiconductor product when "its embodiment in the product is sufficiently permanent or stable to permit the mask work to be perceived or reproduced from the product for a period of more than transitory duration."[174]

The House Report explains that masks are the stencils used to etch an electronic circuit on a semiconductor chip.[175] A mask work is "the layout determination and the sum total of the individual masks, set upon each other, used to fabricate the entire chip."[176]

The SCPA was "drafted flexibly so as not to freeze into place existing technologies," and is intended to cover new semiconductor manufacturing technologies.[177] Because the mask work definition covers a series of related images "however fixed or encoded," some commentators suggest that the definition is broad enough to cover the layout of the electronic circuit itself, and thus protects against circuit design copying by techniques that do not use masks to create the circuit design.[178]

[b]   Originality

A mask work is not eligible for protection if it is not "original," or "consists of designs that are staple, commonplace, or familiar in the semiconductor industry, or variations of such designs, combined in a way that, considered as a whole, is not original."[179]

The SCPA's legislative history indicates that its originality standard is lower than patent law's nonobviousness requirement,[180] but the mask work must display "some

---

[172] 17 U.S.C. § 901(a)(2).

[173] 17 U.S.C. § 901(a)(1).

[174] 17 U.S.C. § 901(a)(3). This is nearly identical to the copyright definition of "fixed." *See* § 4C[2], above.

[175] H.R. Rep. No. 98-781, at 12–13 (1984).

[176] *Id.* at 13–14.

[177] *Id.* at 14.

[178] Charles M. McManis, *International Protection for Semiconductor Chip Designs and the Standard of Judicial Review of Presidential Proclamations Issued Pursuant to the Semiconductor Chip Protection Act of 1984*, 22 Geo. Wash. J. Int'l L. & Econ. 331, 338 (1988); Note, *Semiconductor Protection: Foreign Response to a U.S. Initiative*, 25 Colum. J. Transnat'l L. 345, 360–61 (1987).

[179] 17 U.S.C. § 902(b).

[180] H.R. Rep. No. 98-781, at 19–20 (1984).

minimum of creativity" to qualify for protection.[181] One commentator states that this creativity requirement is higher than the copyright law's *de minimis* originality standard.[182] The Ninth Circuit, however, has applied the copyright standard,[183] holding that

> A mask work is original as long as it exhibits any minimal degree of creativity in any aspect of the mask work layout. The requisite level of creativity for originality is extremely low; even a slight amount will suffice.[184]

As with copyrighted works, mask work protection does not extend to "any idea, procedure, process, system, method of operation, concept, principle, or discovery, regardless of the form in which it is described, explained, illustrated or embodied in [the] work."[185]

[c]   Owner Nationality

The SCPA encourages other countries to adopt similar legislation. A mask work qualifies for protection only if one of three alternative conditions is met. The first two alternatives are that the work is (1) first commercially exploited in the United States or (2) owned by a national or domiciliary of the United States, a stateless person, or a national or domiciliary of a country that has signed a treaty protecting mask works to which the United States is a party.[186]

These alternatives initially had limited significance for non-United States mask work owners, who ordinarily first commercially exploit a mask work outside the United States.[187] The United States is not a party to the 1989 Washington Treaty on Intellectual Property in Respect of Integrated Circuits (IPIC),[188] which never entered into force because fewer than five nations have ratified it.[189] In 1994, however, the World Trade Organization (WTO) adopted the TRIPS Agreement, which incorporates many of the substantive provisions of the IPIC Treaty, and also requires member states to adopt additional protection sought by the United

---

[181] *Id.* at 19.

[182] RICHARD STERN, SEMICONDUCTOR CHIP PROTECTION § 5.3(A)(1) (1986).

[183] The House Report explained that an "original" mask work is "the independent creation of an author who did not copy it," adopting "the essence of the customary copyright law concept of originality and appl[ying] it to mask works, to the extent it is appropriate and feasible to do so." *See* H.R. Rep. No. 98-781, at 17 (1984).

[184] Altera Corp. v. Clear Logic, Inc., 424 F.3d 1079, 1087 (9th Cir. 2005) (quoting district court's jury instruction), *id.* at 1088 (approving this portion of jury instruction); *see also id.* (holding that "only minimal ingenuity is necessary for a second chip to qualify as original").

[185] 17 U.S.C. § 902(c). *See* § 6D[4][b][iv].

[186] 17 U.S.C. § 902(a)(1)(A), (B). The SCPA defines an "owner" as the work's creator or the creator's legal representative or assignee, except that a work created in the course of a person's employment is owned by the employer or the employer's assignee. 17 U.S.C. § 901(a)(6).

For a discussion of ownership of other intellectual property rights arising from employment, see §§ 2G[1] (patents), 3D[6] (trade secrets), 4F[1][a] (copyright).

[187] For the definition of commercial exploitation, see § 6D[3].

[188] For details on the United States' objections to the Treaty, see § 6D[5], below.

[189] *See* www.wipo.int/treaties/en/ip/washington (last visited Dec. 31, 2010).

States.[190] As a result, in 1995 President Clinton issued a Presidential proclamation recognizing SCPA protection for mask work owners in all present and future members of the WTO.[191]

A third alternative is that a mask work may qualify for protection if the owner is a national of a country covered by a Presidential proclamation finding that the nation protects mask works of United States owners (a) on substantially the same basis as mask works of its own nationals; or (b) on substantially the same basis as the SCPA.[192] One might interpret the test's first part to mean that a country offering little or no protection to mask works could obtain a Presidential proclamation if it made the "protection" equally available to its nationals and United States nationals. This interpretation is not consistent with the SCPA's purpose, and United States government practice to date makes clear that it does not interpret the statute in this manner.[193] In any case, this alternative is of limited significance after the TRIPS Agreement.

Prior to 1995, there was a fourth alternative. The SCPA authorized the Secretary of Commerce to extend protection on an interim basis to countries making good faith progress towards entering a semiconductor protection treaty or adopting legislation complying with the SCPA's reciprocity requirements, provided that that country's nationals were not engaged in infringing activities and that the extension promoted the SCPA's purposes.[194] The Secretary's authority was extended twice, but it expired in 1995 and was not renewed.[195]

[3]   Registration

A mask work owner automatically receives two years of protection after first commercially exploiting the work anywhere in the world.[196] The SCPA defines "commercially exploit" as "to distribute to the public for commercial purposes a semiconductor chip product embodying the mask work; except that such term includes an offer to sell or transfer a semiconductor chip product only when the offer is in writing and occurs after the mask work is fixed in the semiconductor chip product."[197] If the owner fails to register the work during this two-year grace period, protection terminates.[198] To receive the full 10-year period of protection, the owner must register the mask work with the Register of Copyrights (the U.S.

---

[190] TRIPS Agreement, arts. 35–38. For details, see § 6D[5], below.

[191] Presidential Proclamation No. 6780, 60 Fed. Reg. 16,845 (March 23, 1995), at ¶ 6. Technically, the TRIPS Agreement is not a treaty, so this proclamation should instead be seen as an instance of the third alternative, below.

[192] 17 U.S.C. § 902(a)(1)(C), (a)(2).

[193] See, e.g., Erstling, The Semiconductor Chip Protection Act and Its Impact on the International Protection of Chip Designs, 15 RUTGERS COMP. & TECH. L. J. 303, 312–13 (1989).

[194] 17 U.S.C. § 914(a).

[195] 17 U.S.C. § 914(c),(e).

[196] 17 U.S.C. §§ 904(a), 908(a).

[197] 17 U.S.C. § 901(a)(5). For a discussion of patent law's "on sale" and "public use" concepts, see § 2C[5][b].

[198] 17 U.S.C. § 908(a).

Copyright Office) within two years after first commercially exploiting the work anywhere in the world.[199]

If the Register approves the application, the owner receives a registration certificate, effective from the date the Register received the application.[200] The certificate is *prima facie* evidence of the mask owner's rights and the facts stated in the certificate.[201] If the Register refuses registration or fails to act within four months, the owner may seek judicial review.[202]

Mask work registration procedure is similar to copyright, in that the Office only examines the information on the application and conducts no prior art search.[203] As a result, the Register grants almost all registration requests.[204]

[4]   Exclusive Rights — Infringement

[a]   Rights Granted

The SCPA grants a protected mask owner:

"[T]he exclusive rights to do and to authorize any of the following:

(1) reproduce the mask work by optical, electronic, or any other means;

(2) to import or distribute a semiconductor chip product in which the mask work is embodied; and

(3) to induce or knowingly to cause another person to do any of the acts described in paragraphs (1) and (2)."[205]

These rights begin upon registration or commercial exploitation anywhere in the world, whichever occurs first, and end ten years after protection begins.[206] As noted above, protection terminates if the mask work is not registered within two years of commercial exploitation.[207]

To "reproduce" a mask work or to "embody" a mask work in a chip means to copy the work. Two copyright-like concepts are implicit in the SCPA's structure, if not explicit from its language. First, an infringing mask or chip must be substantially similar, though not identical, to the protected mask work.[208] The SCPA's reverse

---

[199] *Id.*

[200] 17 U.S.C. § 908(e).

[201] 17 U.S.C. § 908(f).

[202] 17 U.S.C. § 908(g).

[203] For a discussion of patent examination and copyright registration, see §§ 2D[1] and 4D[3][b], above.

[204] For example, in Fiscal Year 2009, the Copyright Office received 281 applications to register mask works, and registered 270. U.S. Copyright Office, 2009 Annual Report, at 31–32.

[205] 17 U.S.C. § 905.

[206] 17 U.S.C. § 904(a), (b). The protection term is actually slightly longer than 10 years because registrations run "to the end of the calendar year in which they would otherwise expire." 17 U.S.C. 904(c).

[207] 17 U.S.C. § 908(a).

[208] *See* Brooktree Corp. v. Advanced Micro Devices, Inc., 977 F.2d 1555, 1564 (Fed. Cir. 1992)

engineering limitation[209] and its legislative history[210] recognize that a functionally equivalent but different design will not infringe. The House Report indicates that the substantial similarity principles of copyright law as applied to fact-based and functional works should provide guidance:

> Legal concepts used to establish infringement in copyright law — substantial similarity, ideas versus expression, and merger of idea and expression when function dictates form — are all carried forward, insofar as applicable, to the new law for mask works. . . .

> While . . . the courts may usefully consider the copyright law precedents concerning substantial similarity, . . . [they] should have sufficient flexibility to develop a new body of law specifically applicable to semiconductor chip infringement. Moreover, the concept of "substantial similarity" varies depending upon the nature of the work. Cases concerning fictional or imaginative works are not necessarily relevant to semiconductor chip infringement. . . . [T]he line of cases regarding infringement of fact-based works, compilations, and directories provides precedents more applicable to semiconductor chips.[211]

Second, an independently-produced chip design will not infringe a mask work right even though the second design is in fact substantially similar to the first protected work.[212] If the second chip's creator had no access to the protected design, directly or indirectly, there can be no infringement. The point may be academic because of the extreme improbability that a design meeting the SCPA's originality standard, which excludes standard industry designs, would be independently created by more than one person or company.

The House Report notes that special substantial similarity problems may arise with "cells," discrete functional portions of chips.[213] In *Brooktree Corp. v. Advanced Micro Devices, Inc.*, the alleged infringement related to a single cell of only ten

---

("Although the Semiconductor Chip Protection Act does not use the word 'copy' to describe infringement, the parallel language reflects the incorporation of the well-explicated copyright principle of substantial similarity into the Semiconductor Chip Protection Act."). *See also* H.R. Rep. No. 98-781, at 20 (1984):

> Complete reproduction of a mask work is not required in order to constitute an infringement of the owner's exclusive right of reproduction. Unless a valid defense is presented, a judge or jury could find an infringement if the mask work embodied in the "copied" semiconductor chip is substantially similar to the registered mask work. If this was otherwise, an infringer could immunize himself by adding a mistake to a mask work copied in its entirety.

[209] *See* § 6D[4][b][i].

[210] "If the mask work embodied in the alleged infringing chip is not substantially similar to the registered work, there could be no infringement. The second manufacturer is simply engaged in privileged, and socially valuable, free competition from which the public benefits." H.R. Rep. No. 98-781, at 26 (1984).

[211] H.R. Rep. No. 98-781, at 26 (1984).

[212] For a discussion of copyright law's concept of independent creation, see §§ 4C[1][a] and 4H[2]. In this respect, the Copyright Act and the SCPA different from patent law. *See* § 2F[3][b].

[213] "Mask works sometimes contain substantial areas of (so-called 'cells') whose layouts involve creativity and are commercially valuable. [Footnote 51: For example, the layout for a counter of an oscillator may be contained in a mask work along with many other 'cells' or other parts that together comprise the entire semiconductor chip product. Such a cell may be usable in other chips, and may be the subject of a 'cell library license.'] In appropriate fact settings, the misappropriation of such a cell —

transistors that was "repeated over six thousand times in an array covering about eighty percent of the chip area."[214] After trying and rejecting designs based on six and eight transistors, AMD produced competing chips with cells of ten transistors configured in a similar way.[215] At trial, the jury found infringement. The Federal Circuit upheld the verdict, rejecting AMD's argument that the SCPA "requires copying of the entire chip" in order to find infringement, and instead concluding that infringement "does not require that all parts of the accused chip be copied."[216]

[b]   Limitations

The SCPA provides four express limitations on exclusive rights: (1) reverse engineering; (2) the first sale doctrine; (3) innocent infringement; and (4) ideas, procedures, and principles.

[i]   Reverse Engineering

It is not an infringement to reproduce a mask work for "teaching, analyzing, or evaluating the concepts or techniques embodied in the mask work or the circuitry, logic flow, or organization of components used in the mask work."[217] It is also not an infringement to incorporate the results of such analysis in another original mask work.[218]

The "reverse engineering" exception[219] endorses the existing industry practice of photographing and analyzing an existing chip to create chips with the same external specifications — "form, fit, and function" compatibility.[220] Congress found that this practice promotes fair competition and often provides a needed second source for chips.[221] The limitation permits reverse engineering, even when substantial parts of the first chip design are incorporated into the second design, provided the second design is itself original and not merely a copy of the first design.[222]

---

assuming it meets the originality standards of this chapter — could be the basis for an infringement action." H.R. Rep. No. 98-781, at 26–27 (1984).

[214] Brooktree Corp. v. Advanced Micro Devices, Inc., 977 F.2d 1555, 1563 (Fed. Cir. 1992).

[215] *Id.* at 1567–69.

[216] *Id.* at 1564; *see also id.* (quoting jury instruction: "Substantial similarity may exist where an important part of the mask work is copied, even though the percentage of the entire chip which is copied may be relatively small.").

[217] 17 U.S.C. § 906(a)(1).

[218] 17 U.S.C. § 906(a)(2).

[219] The phrase "reverse engineering" does not appear in the statute but is in its title ("Limitation on exclusive rights: reverse engineering; first sale."). 17 U.S.C. § 906.

For a discussion of "reverse engineering" in trade secrets and copyright law, see §§ 3E[3] and 4J[1][c].

[220] H.R. Rep. No. 98-781, at 21–22 (1984).

[221] *Id.* at 22.

[222] "It is the intent of the Committee to permit . . . the 'unauthorized' creation of a second mask work whose layout, in substantial part, is similar to the layout of the protected mask work — if the second mask work was the product of substantial study and analysis, and not the mere result of plagiarism accomplished without such study or analysis." *Id. See also* Brooktree Corp. v. Advanced Micro Devices, Inc., 977 F.2d 1555, 1566 (Fed. Cir. 1992) (quoting Explanatory Memorandum — Mathias-Leahy Amendment to S. 1201, 130 Cong. Rec. S12,916, S12,917 (daily ed. Oct. 3, 1984):

The House Report asserts that the reverse engineering limitation should not be difficult to apply, emphasizing that legitimate reverse engineering can be distinguished from mere piracy by the enormous "paper trail" of computer simulations, time records, and other documents showing the effort involved in analyzing the chip.[223]

Brooktree Corp. v. Advanced Micro Devices, Inc., shows that the reverse engineering limitation may not be as easy to apply as the House Report suggests. After a jury found AMD had infringed Brooktree's cell design, AMD moved for judgment notwithstanding the verdict, arguing that its design was original as a matter of law, and it supported its motion with a "paper trail" showing that it took two-and-a-half years and three million dollars to develop its design.[224] Brooktree responded that AMD's paper trail related mostly to AMD's "lengthy and expensive failures" to develop a competing chip, and it "pointed to the rapidity with which AMD changed to Brooktree's layout when the error in analysis was discovered, [when] AMD immediately [began] producing, without further experimentation, a substantially identical SRAM cell."[225] The Federal Circuit upheld the verdict, finding that a reasonable jury could reject the reverse engineering defense based on its evaluation of the conflicting evidence.[226]

[ii]   First Sale

The SCPA contains a first sale doctrine analogous to that of patent and copyright law.[227] An owner of "a particular semiconductor chip product" that is made "by the owner of the mask work, or by any person authorized by the owner of the mask work," may "import, distribute or otherwise dispose of or use, but not reproduce, that particular semiconductor chip product without the authority of the owner of the mask work."[228]

The end product of the reverse engineering process is not an infringement, and itself qualifies for protection under this Act, if it is an original mask work, as contrasted with a substantial copy. If the resulting semiconductor chip product is not substantially identical to the original, and its design involved significant toil and investment so that it is not a mere plagiarism, it does not infringe the original chip, even if the layout of the two chips is, in substantial part, similar.

Accord, Altera Corp. v. Clear Logic, Inc., 424 F.3d 1079, 1087 (9th Cir. 2005).

[223] "The Committee intends that the courts, in interpreting section 906(a), should place great weight on objective documentary evidence of this type." H.R. Rep. No. 98-781, at 21 (1984).

[224] 977 F.2d 1555, 1567 (Fed. Cir. 1992).

[225] *Id.* at 1567–68.

[226] *Id.* at 1568.

[227] 17 U.S.C. § 906(b). For a discussion of first sale in patent and copyright law, see §§ 2E[3] and 4G[3][c].

[228] 17 U.S.C. § 906(b). *See also* H.R. Rep. No. 98-781, at 23 (1984):

As in the case of copyrighted products, the owner of a mask work has no right to try to exercise 'remote control' over the pricing or other business conduct of its semiconductor chip customers, once the semiconductor chips have passed into their hands. Except where the Congress expressly orders otherwise, the exhaustion of any rights by the first authorized sale is a basic tenet of our intellectual property law. . . . Accordingly, the Act specifies that purchasers of semiconductor chips have the right to use and resell them freely (whether as chips or incorporated into other products which contain chips).

The first sale limitation's language confirms that it does not apply to reproduction; one purchasing a product lawfully embodying a mask work has no right to copy it except as the owner authorizes or the reverse engineering exception permits.

The language of the SCPA's first sale provision's language resolves the parallel importation (grey market) problem that plagues other intellectual property areas.[229] One who purchases abroad a chip made by the mask work owner's licensee may import the chip into the United States even if the mask owner attempts by contract to establish exclusive territories.

[iii]   Innocent Infringement

The SCPA limits the liability of an "innocent purchaser," defined as "a person who purchases a semiconductor chip product in good faith and without having notice of protection with respect to the semiconductor chip product."[230] The innocent purchaser limitation protects not only persons directly purchasing chips but also those who purchase for resale products, such as computers, televisions, and automobiles, that contain infringing chips.

An innocent purchaser has no liability for chips he resells before receiving notice of protection and is liable only for a reasonable royalty for products it resells after that date.[231] The innocent purchaser limitation extends to "any person who directly or indirectly purchases an infringing semiconductor chip product from an innocent purchaser."[232]

The innocent purchaser limitation applies only to products purchased before the purchaser receives notice of protection.[233] Once a company receives notice of protection, it can no longer be an innocent purchaser and will be liable in full for all products purchased after that date. The SCPA defines "notice of protection" as "having actual knowledge that, or reasonable grounds to believe that, a mask work is protected under this chapter."[234] Placing a mask work notice on products embodying the mask work is "*prima facie* evidence of notice of protection."[235] An infringing product, of course, is unlikely to bear a notice, and one who purchases it may never have seen a product legitimately embodying the mask work. A purchaser may be able to overcome the *prima facie* evidence of notice of protection by showing that it never saw the marked products and did not otherwise have reason to believe that the mask work was protected.

The innocent purchaser limitation, like that on first sale, relates only to distribution and not to reproduction. An innocent purchaser who improperly

---

[229] *See, e.g.,* § 4G[3][d].

[230] 17 U.S.C. § 901(a)(7).

[231] 17 U.S.C. § 907(a).

[232] 17 U.S.C. § 907(c).

[233] 17 U.S.C. § 907(d).

[234] 17 U.S.C. § 901(a)(8).

[235] 17 U.S.C. § 909(a). A mask work notice consists of the words "mask work," the symbol M*, or the symbol Ⓜ (the letter M in a circle), and the name of the owner or owners of the mask work. 17 U.S.C. § 909(b). No date is required.

reproduces a protected mask is subject to full liability even if the purchaser had no notice of protection.

[iv]   Ideas, Procedures, and Principles

Mask work protection does not extend to "any idea, procedure, process, system, method of operation, concept, principle, or discovery, regardless of the form in which it is described, explained, illustrated or embodied in [the] work."[236] This limitation overlaps the reverse engineering defense. A mask work's ideas are not protected, and it is lawful to extract them by reverse engineering and incorporate them into an original mask work.

The idea limitation is also related to the SCPA's originality requirement.[237] A mask work is not eligible for protection if it consists merely of unprotected ideas and procedures, for example, reproduction of commonplace industry designs.

In *Altera Corp. v. Clear Logic, Inc.*,[238] Altera made programmable logic devices (PLDs), chips that could be programmed using software to perform multiple functions. Clear Logic took the output of that software, known as a bitstream, and used it to manufacture Altera-compatible, application-specific integrated circuits (ASICs) to perform specific functions. The resulting chips were similar to Altera's chips only in "the placement of groupings of transistors on the chip," and not with respect to "the layout of the transistors within those groupings."[239] On appeal from a jury verdict of infringement, the Ninth Circuit rejected Clear Logic's argument that "the placement of the groupings is a system or an idea and is not entitled to protection under the SCPA."[240] Instead, it held that "[t]he placement of logic groupings in a mask work is not an abstract concept; it is embodied in the chip and affects the chip's performance and efficiency as well as the chip's timing."[241]

[c]   Infringement Actions

The SCPA provides that "[e]xcept as otherwise provided in this chapter, any person who violates any of the exclusive rights of the owner of a mask work under this chapter, by conduct in or affecting commerce, shall be liable as an infringer of such rights."[242]

---

[236] 17 U.S.C. § 902(c).

[237] *See* § 6D[2][b].

[238] 424 F.3d 1079 (9th Cir. 2005).

[239] *Id.* at 1085.

[240] *Id.*

[241] *Id.* at 1086. Arguably, this conclusion is inconsistent with the court's later conclusion that "only minimal ingenuity is necessary for a second chip to qualify as original," *id.* at 1088. If the layout of specific transistors in the second chip is different, that should suffice for the "minimal" creativity needed to make the second chip "original."

[242] 17 U.S.C. § 910(a). The reference to "conduct in or affecting commerce" reflects the Congressional decision to base the SCPA on its constitutional authority to regulate commerce, as well as on its authority to protect the rights of patent and copyright holders. *See generally* Burchfiel, *The Constitutional Intellectual Property Power: Progress of Useful Arts and the Legal Protection of Semiconductor Technology*, 28 Santa Clara L. Rev. 473 (1988). Congress made a similar decision with respect to the 1970 Plant Variety Protection Act. *See* § 6C[2][a].

A mask work owner or his exclusive licensee may bring a federal court civil action or seek International Trade Commission relief against infringement.[243] As with the Copyright Act,[244] an owner may sue only if the Copyright Office has issued a registration certificate,[245] or, if the Office refuses registration, by serving notice of the action on the Register of Copyrights.[246] The SCPA imposes a statute of limitations; an infringement action is barred "unless commenced within three years after the claim accrues."[247]

A person accused of infringement may assert as defenses the four SCPA limitations to the extent they apply. He may also assert other defenses similar to those of copyright and patent law. For example, he may argue that the registration is invalid because the mask work fails to meet the SCPA's protection requirements.[248] One commentator suggests that the courts will likely recognize patent and copyright defenses such as inequitable conduct in procurement and misuse.[249]

[d]   Remedies

[i]   Injunctive Relief

The SCPA authorizes federal courts to grant "temporary restraining orders, preliminary injunctions, and permanent injunctions on such terms as the court may deem reasonable to prevent or restrain infringement."[250] Ancillary to a preliminary injunction or temporary restraining order, the court may impound allegedly infringing semiconductor chip products, masks, and drawings.[251] It may order infringing products destroyed as part of a final judgment.[252]

The SCPA's general language suggests that usual preliminary injunction standards should apply.[253] In *Brooktree Corp. v. Advanced Micro Devices, Inc.*, the district court found before trial that the mask owner failed to demonstrate a strong likelihood of success on the merits in light of the accused infringer's evidence that it engaged in legitimate reverse engineering or to demonstrate that a preliminary injunction was necessary to prevent irreparable harm that could not be

---

[243] 17 U.S.C. § 910(b), (c).

[244] *See* § 4D[3][b].

[245] 17 U.S.C. § 910(b)(1).

[246] 17 U.S.C. § 910(b)(2). The Register may join the action but is not required to do so.

[247] 17 U.S.C. § 911(d).

[248] *See* § 6D[2]. As noted above, the registration is *prima facie* evidence that the registrant has met the SCPA's requirements. For a discussion of copyright law's validity presumption of validity, see § 4H[1].

[249] RICHARD STERN, SEMICONDUCTOR CHIP PROTECTION § 5.4 (1986). *See* §§ 2F[4][b], 2F[4][c], 4F[4][b] and 4F[4][c]. The Ninth Circuit has rejected a claim that copyright misuse bars enforcement of a license agreement to use programmable logic devices (PLDs), chips that can be programmed to perform multiple functions and can be used to design other chips. Altera Corp. v. Clear Logic, Inc., 424 F.3d 1079, 1090 (9th Cir. 2005). Apparently, however, the defendant did not argue copyright misuse with respect to the SPCA itself.

[250] 17 U.S.C. § 911(a).

[251] 17 U.S.C. § 911(e)(1).

[252] 17 U.S.C. § 911(e)(2).

[253] For a discussion of preliminary injunction standards in patent infringement suits, see § 2F[5][a][i].

compensated by monetary damages.[254] Applying an alternate preliminary injunction standard, it found that the owner raised serious question on the merits but failed to show that the balance of hardships tipped sharply in its favor.[255]

[ii] Damages — Attorney's Fees

The court "shall award [the mask work owner's] actual damages suffered . . . as a result of the infringement" and "the infringer's profits that are attributable to the infringement and are not taken into account in computing the award of actual damages."[256] Alternatively, the owner may elect to recover statutory damages of up to $250,000 for "all infringements involved in the action, with respect to any one mask work for which any one infringer is liable individually, or for which any two or more infringers are liable jointly and severally."[257]

In *Brooktree Corp. v. Advanced Micro Devices, Inc.*,[258] the jury awarded $25 million in damages for mask work and patent infringement. The district court held that prejudgment interest could be awarded only on the damage award's patent portion[259] and directed the mask owner to submit "data that clearly shows the allocation of damages between the patent and mask work claims."[260] The owner submitted a declaration segregating the damages.

On appeal in *Brooktree*, the infringer challenged the jury's award on the ground that it included losses incurred after it announced its competing product but before the infringing chips appeared on the market. The Federal Circuit rejected this argument, holding that "a reasonable jury could have concluded that Brooktree's price reductions were made as a result of AMD's actual and announced marketing of the infringing chips."[261]

The SCPA grants a court discretion to "allow the recovery of full costs, including reasonable attorneys' fees, to the prevailing party."[262] The House Report states

---

[254] 705 F. Supp. 491, 496–97 (S.D. Cal. 1988), *later proceeding at* 757 F. Supp. 1088 (S.D. Cal. 1990), *aff'd*, 977 F.2d 1555 (Fed. Cir. 1992). In so holding, the district court rejected a presumption of irreparable harm, which is consistent with the Supreme Court's subsequent decision in eBay, Inc. v. MercExchange, LLC, 547 U.S. 388 (2006). *See* § 2F[5][a][ii].

[255] 705 F. Supp. at 497.

[256] 17 U.S.C. § 911(b). In establishing profits, the owner need only show the infringer's gross revenues, and "the infringer is required to prove his or her deductible expenses and the elements of profit attributable to factors other than the mask work." *Id.* These provisions are nearly identical to those for copyright infringement.

For a discussion of damages for patent, copyright, trademark infringement, see §§ 2F[5][b], 4K[4] and 5K[2].

[257] 17 U.S.C. § 911(c).

[258] 757 F. Supp. 1088 (S.D. Cal. 1990), *aff'd*, 977 F.2d 1555 (Fed. Cir. 1992).

[259] "[G]iven that the Chip Act itself is silent as to the award of prejudgment interest, this court should not imply an additional remedy without some indication in the statute or the legislative history." 757 F. Supp. at 1099.

For a discussion of prejudgment interest in patent and copyright cases, see §§ 2F[5][d], 4K[4][a].

[260] 757 F. Supp. at 1100.

[261] 977 F.2d at 1580–81.

[262] 17 U.S.C. § 911(f).

that this section is similar to Copyright Act Section 505.[263] In *Brooktree*, the Federal Circuit upheld the district court's decision not to award attorney's fees, because the suit involved complex and novel issues of law.[264]

[iii]   International Trade Commission Remedies

As an alternative or in addition to bringing a federal court infringement suit, a protected mask work owner may petition the International Trade Commission (ITC) to preclude importation of infringing products. ITC relief is available only if the petitioner's case meets ITC statutory requirements, including that there be imported products and the mask work relates to a domestic (United States) industry.[265] The ITC cannot award damages, but ITC actions offer mask work owners substantial advantages over district court infringement suits. An important advantage is that statutory deadlines require the ITC to render a decision promptly. ITC's rapid actions pressure accused infringers to settle on terms favorable to an intellectual property owner.

[5]   International Protection for Semiconductor Chips

Although the Washington Treaty on Intellectual Property in Respect of Integrated Circuits (IPIC) never entered into force,[266] many of the substantive provisions of the IPIC Treaty were incorporated into the TRIPS Agreement.[267] In addition, the TRIPS Agreement provides all of the additional protection that the United States unsuccessfully sought to have incorporated into the Washington Treaty.[268] In particular, the TRIPS Agreement provides that Member states "shall consider unlawful" any importing, selling, or commercial distribution of a protected layout design, an integrated circuit incorporating such design, or an article incorporating such an integrated circuit.[269] Innocent infringers are protected from liability, by they must pay a reasonable royalty after receiving notice of the infringement,[270] and compulsory licensing is restricted in the same manner that TRIPS restrict compulsory licensing for patents.[271] The term of protection is ten years after registration or first commercial exploitation, although members may

---

[263] H.R. Rep. No. 98-781, at 28 (1984).

[264] Brooktree Corp. v. Advanced Micro Devices, Inc., 977 F.2d 1555, 1582–83 (Fed. Cir. 1992).

[265] *See* § 2E[2][b][ii].

[266] *See* § 6D[2][c], above.

[267] TRIPS Agreement, art. 35.

[268] The United States objected to the Washington Treaty because (1) it provided for broad compulsory licensing; (2) it did not adequately deal with importation and distribution of products containing infringing chips; (3) innocent infringers were not required to pay a reasonable royalty after receiving notice of protection; (4) protection was limited to eight rather than ten years; and (5) the dispute resolution procedure was too politicized as it involved the WIPO assembly. *See U.S., Japan Refuse to Sign WIPO Treaty on Protection of Semiconductor Chips*, 38 Pat. Trademark & Copyright J. (BNA) No. 933, at 123–24 (June 1, 1989).

[269] TRIPS Agreement, art. 36.

[270] TRIPS Agreement, art. 37(1).

[271] TRIPS Agreement, art. 37(2).

allow protection to lapse 15 years after the creation of the layout-design.[272] Finally, as with other TRIPS provisions, disputes concerning protection for semiconductor chips are subject to the dispute-resolution mechanism of the World Trade Organization.

§ 6E   FALSE ADVERTISING

[1]   Historical Development

Before the Lanham Act's passage in 1943, any false and misleading advertising claim was brought as a common law unfair competition or trade disparagement claim and was generally restricted to situations where defendant had "passed-off" its goods as those of the plaintiff.[273] In the leading case articulating this limited view, *American Washboard Co. v. Saginaw Mfg. Co.*,[274] the sole manufacturer of aluminum washboards sought relief against a manufacturer who falsely advertised that its washboards were made from aluminum. In rejecting the claim, the court stated that "it is only where . . . deception induces the public to buy the goods as those of complainant that a private right of action arises."[275]

Later decisions expanded the common law false advertising unfair competition remedy in certain respects,[276] but *American Washboard* continued to limit false advertising claims for more than 50 years.[277]

Commentators heralded Lanham Act Section 43(a) as a significant revision of the *American Washboard* doctrine,[278] but courts and practitioners were slow to recognize the breadth of Section 43(a)'s condemnation of "any false description or representation, including words or other symbols tending falsely to describe or represent . . . goods or services."[279] Ten years after its enactment, Judge Clark noted "there is indication here and elsewhere that the bar has not yet realized the

---

[272] TRIPS Agreement, art. 38.

[273] *See, e.g.*, Johnson & Johnson v. Carter-Wallace, Inc. 631 F.2d 186, 189 (2d Cir. 1980). For a discussion of "passing off" and the origins of trademark and unfair competition law, see § 5B.

[274] 103 F. 281 (6th Cir. 1900).

[275] *Id.* at 284–85.

[276] In Ely-Norris Safe Co. v. Mosler Safe Co., 7 F.2d 603 (2d Cir. 1925), *rev'd*, 273 U.S. 132 (1927), Judge Learned Hand held that the plaintiff could sue a defendant who falsely described his goods as having the same qualities as plaintiff's when plaintiff had a monopoly on the goods, thereby making it more certain that defendant's falsity caused plaintiff to lose customers. The Supreme Court granted certiorari to reconcile the conflict between *Eli-Norris* and *American Washboard*, 268 U.S. 684 (1925), but instead reversed on a different ground. *See also* American Philatelic Society v. Claibourne, 46 P.2d 135 (Cal. 1935); Motor Improvements, Inc. v. A.C. Spark Plug Co., 80 F.2d 385 (6th Cir. 1936).

[277] *See* California Apparel Creators v. Wieder of California, Inc., 162 F.2d 893 (2d Cir. 1947) (no relief for false advertising can be granted absent a showing of actual diversion of trade).

[278] *See, e.g.*, ROBERT, THE NEW TRADE-MARK MANUAL 186–88 (1947); Callmann, *The New Trade-Mark Act of July 5, 1946*, 46 COL. L. REV. 929, 931 (1946).

[279] 15 U.S.C. § 43(a) (as enacted).

potential impact of this statutory provision."[280]

Modern Section 43(a) false advertising liability law began with *L'Aiglon Apparel, Inc. v. Lana Lobell, Inc.*[281] Plaintiff accused defendant of using a likeness of plaintiff's dress in advertisements for defendant's cheaper dress. The district court dismissed plaintiff's Section 43(a) claim because defendant used its own name and thus had not "passed-off" its goods as those of plaintiff. The appeals court reversed:

> It seems to us that Congress has defined a statutory civil wrong of false representation of goods in commerce and has given a broad class of suitors injured or likely to be injured by such wrong the right to relief in the federal courts. This statutory tort is defined in language which differentiates it in some particulars from similar wrongs which have developed and have become defined in the judge made law of unfair competition.[282]

Over the subsequent decades, and particularly in the 1970s and 1980s, false advertising claims proliferated and encompassed new and different factual situations.[283] The enactment of the Trademark Law Revision Act of 1988 (TLRA)[284] precluded any argument that false advertising claims under Section 43(a) were limited to "passing off" by codifying the primary substantive theories of the non-passing off cases.

The TLRA split former Section 43(a) into two parts. The first part, section 43(a)(1)(A), pertains to false designations of origin and provides a cause of action for infringement of unregistered trademarks and trade dress.[285] The second part, section 43(a)(1)(B), permits a plaintiff to bring a federal claim for false advertising against a defendant that uses, in connection with any goods or services in commerce, "any false designation of origin, false or misleading description of fact, or false or misleading representation of fact . . . which, in commercial advertising or promotion, misrepresents the nature, characteristics, qualities, or geographic origin of his or her or another person's goods, services, or commercial activities."[286] The false or misleading representation may pertain to either the plaintiff's or the defendant's goods, services, or commercial activities.

---

[280] Maternally Yours, Inc. v. Your Maternity Shop, Inc., 234 F.2d 538, 546 (2d Cir. 1956) (Clark, J., concurring).

[281] 214 F.2d 649 (3d Cir. 1954).

[282] 214 F.2d at 651. The Third Circuit thereby aligned itself with the view that § 43(a) signified a new federal tort that was not limited to the common-law elements of pre-Lanham Act unfair competition claims. *See* S.C. Johnson & Son, Inc. v. Johnson, 175 F.2d 176, 178 (2d Cir. 1949) (Clark, J. dissenting); Dad's Root Beer Co. v. Doc's Beverages, Inc., 193 F.2d 77, 80 (2d Cir. 1951).

[283] *See, e.g.*, McNeilab Inc. v. American Home Products, Inc., 848 F.2d 34, 37 (2d Cir. 1988) (advertisements that deceive only a "not insubstantial fraction" of viewers); Allen v. National Video, Inc., 610 F. Supp. 612, 625 (S.D.N.Y. 1985) (misleading use of celebrity likeness); Gucci Shops, Inc. v. R.H. Macy & Co., 446 F. Supp. 838, 840 n.4 (S.D.N.Y. 1977) (parody as actionable false and misleading statement); Zandelin v. Maxwell Bentley Mfg. Co., 197 F. Supp. 608, 612 (S.D.N.Y. 1961) (use of retouched photographs of competitor's product).

[284] Pub. L. No. 100-667, 102 Stat. 3935 (1988).

[285] 15 U.S.C. § 1125(a)(1)(A); *see* §§ 5B[4][a], 5F[1], above.

[286] 15 U.S.C. § 1125(a)(1)(B).

[2] Current Federal Law

To prevail on a false advertising claim, a plaintiff must prove by a preponderance of the evidence (1) that the defendant has made false or misleading statements as to his own product (or another's); (2) that there is actual deception of, or at least a tendency to deceive, a substantial portion of the intended audience; (3) that the deception is material in that it is likely to influence purchasing decisions; (4) that the advertised goods traveled in interstate commerce; and (5) that there is a likelihood of injury to the plaintiff (*e.g.*, declining sales or loss of good will).[287]

Mere "puffery" is not actionable. Puffery consists of "exaggerated advertising, blustering, and boasting upon which no reasonable buyer would rely,"[288] and includes representations of product superiority that are vague or highly subjective.[289] In contrast, false statements regarding specific or absolute characteristics of a product, and specific, measurable claims of product superiority that are based on product testing are not puffery and are actionable.[290]

[a] Falsity

To prove that a defendant's statements were false or misleading, the plaintiff must establish either that (1) the advertisement is literally false, or (2) although the advertisement is literally true or ambiguous, it is likely to deceive or confuse consumers.[291] Where the advertised claim is literally false, the court may enjoin the continued assertion of the false claim "without reference to the advertisement's impact on the buying public,"[292] — that is, without proof of consumer deception.[293] However, in the absence of such literal falsity, the plaintiff must show that the public was actually misled.[294] Such proof may take the form of consumer testimony, marketing surveys, proof of lost sales, or other evidence of consumer deception.[295] Thus, a false advertising plaintiff must prove either literal falsity or consumer confusion.[296]

---

[287] *See, e.g.*, AT&T v. Winback & Conserve Program, 42 F.3d 1421, 1428 n.9 (3d Cir. 1994).

[288] United Indus. Corp. v. Clorox Co.,140 F.3d 1175, 1180 (8th Cir. 1998) (quoting Southland Sod Farms v. Stover Seed Co., 108 F.3d 1134, 1145 (9th Cir. 1997)); *see also* Castrol Inc. v. Pennzoil Co., 987 F.2d 939, 945 (3d Cir. 1993).

[289] *United Indus. Corp.*, 140 F.3d at 1180 (citing *Southland*, 108 F.3d at 1145); *see also* Cook, Perkiss & Liehe, Inc. v. Northern California Collection Serv., Inc., 911 F.2d 242, 246 (9th Cir. 1990).

[290] *United Indus. Corp.*, 140 F.3d at 1180; *see also Southland*, 108 F.3d at 1145; *Castrol*, 987 F.2d at 945.

[291] Lipton v. Nature Co., 71 F.3d 464, 474 (2d Cir. 1995).

[292] McNeil-P.C.C., Inc. v. Bristol-Myers Squibb Co., 938 F.2d 1544, 1549 (2d Cir. 1991) (quoting Coca-Cola v. Tropicana Prods., Inc., 690 F.2d 312, 317 (2d Cir. 1982)).

[293] Vidal Sassoon, Inc. v. Bristol-Myers Co., 661 F.2d 272, 277 (2d Cir. 1981).

[294] Clorox Co. v. Procter & Gamble Commercial Co., 228 F.3d 24, 36 (1st Cir. 2000); United Indus. Corp. v. Clorox Co., 140 F.3d 1175, 1182 (8th Cir. 1998).

[295] *See, e.g.*, Warner-Lambert Co. v. BreathAsure, Inc., 204 F.3d 87, 96 (3d Cir. 2000); McNeilab, Inc. v. American Home Prods. Corp., 501 F. Supp. 517, 525 (S.D.N.Y. 1980).

[296] Castrol Inc. v. Pennzoil Co., 987 F.2d 939, 943 (3d Cir. 1993). In the Eighth Circuit, proof that the defendant acted willfully and in bad faith can substitute for proof of consumer confusion. United Indus. Corp. v. Clorox Co., 140 F.3d 1175, 1183 (8th Cir. 1998).

In determining whether claims are literally false, a court will first identify the unambiguous claims made by the advertisement or by the product's name, and then determine whether those claims are false.[297] A literally false claim need not be explicit; it may be "conveyed by necessary implication when, considering the advertisement in its entirety, the audience would recognize the claim as readily as if it had been explicitly stated."[298] However, the claim must still be unambiguous in order to be literally false: "The greater the degree to which a message relies upon the viewer or consumer to integrate its components and draw the apparent conclusion, . . . the less likely it is that a finding of literal falsity will be supported."[299]

The question whether a false claim is necessarily implied by a product's name or advertisement depends on whether, "based on a facial analysis of the product name or advertising, the consumer will unavoidably receive a false message from the product's name or advertising."[300] In *Novartis Consumer Health, Inc. v. Johnson & Johnson-Merck Pharms. Co.*, the Third Circuit considered whether the name and/or advertising of the defendant's "Mylanta Night Time Strength" heartburn remedy were "literally false by necessary implication," because they implied two claims: (1) that the product was "specially formulated" for nighttime relief, and (2) that the product was superior to competing products at providing nighttime relief.[301] The court concluded that the first claim indeed followed by necessary implication from the use of the term "Night Time" in the product's name, but held that the second claim did not follow by necessary implication from either the name of the product or its advertising.[302] Because the message of superior performance was not literally conveyed (explicitly or implicitly) by the defendant's statements, the plaintiff was required to prove that consumers were likely to be misled by the product's name and advertising.[303]

The plaintiff's burden in establishing literal falsehood depends on the nature of the false claim. A defendant's advertising may falsely claim that its product has a certain superior characteristic, or, instead, it may falsely claim that "tests prove" that the product has the claimed characteristic. Where the defendant's advertising asserts only the characteristic, and not the existence of probative tests, the plaintiff must adduce evidence affirmatively proving that the advertised assertion is false.[304]

---

[297] Clorox Co. v. Procter & Gamble Commercial Co., 228 F.3d 24, 34 (1st Cir. 2000); Novartis Consumer Health, Inc. v. Johnson & Johnson-Merck Consumer Pharms. Co., 290 F.3d 578, 586 (3d Cir. 2002).

[298] *Clorox*, 228 F.3d at 35.

[299] *Novartis*, 290 F.3d at 587.

[300] *Id.; see, e.g.*, Vidal Sassoon, Inc. v. Bristol-Myers Co., 661 F.2d 272, 277 (2d Cir. 1981); Warner-Lambert Co. v. BreathAsure, Inc., 204 F.3d 87, 96–97 (3d Cir. 2000); Cuisinart, Inc. v. Robot-Coupe Int'l Corp., 1982 U.S. Dist. LEXIS 13594 (S.D.N.Y. June 9, 1982).

[301] 290 F.3d 578, 587 (3d Cir. 2002).

[302] *Id.* at 588–89.

[303] *Id.*

[304] Castrol, Inc. v. Quaker State Corp., 977 F.2d 57, 63 (2d Cir. 1992); Procter & Gamble Co. v. Chesebrough-Pond's, Inc., 747 F.2d 114, 119 (2d Cir. 1984); BASF Corp. v. Old World Trading Co., 41 F.3d 1081, 1090–91 (7th Cir. 1994); United Indus. Corp. v. Clorox, 140 F.3d 1175, 1182 (8th Cir. 1998). In the

In contrast, where the advertising asserts that "tests prove" that its product has the superior characteristic, the plaintiff need only establish that the tests on which the defendant rests its claim "were not sufficiently reliable to permit one to conclude with reasonable certainty that they established the proposition for which they were cited."[305] Once the plaintiff challenges the defendant's tests, the defendant must identify the tests on which it relied.[306] The plaintiff may then satisfy its burden of proof by showing either (1) that the tests are insufficiently reliable to prove the defendant's claim, or (2) that, even if reliable, the test results do not support the defendant's claim.[307]

If an advertisement is not literally false, then the plaintiff may still prevail by demonstrating that the statement has a tendency to confuse or deceive consumers. To prevail on this basis, the plaintiff must establish that (1) the defendant has made false or misleading statements of fact concerning his own product or another's; (2) the statement actually or tends to deceive a substantial portion of the intended audience; (3) the statement is material; (4) the advertisements were introduced into interstate commerce; and (5) there is some causal link between the challenged statements and injury to the plaintiff (or likelihood thereof).[308] A false or misleading statement is material if it is likely to influence a consumer's purchasing decision.[309]

With respect to food and beverage labels, the federal Food, Drug and Cosmetics Act (FDCA) and regulations promulgated by the Food and Drug Administration (FDA) establish certain minimum standards of disclosure for the purpose of consumer protection. In the 2014 case of *POM Wonderful LLC v. Coca-Cola Co.*,[310] the Supreme Court held that a misleading food or beverage label may be actionable as false advertising under the Lanham Act even if it complies with this regulatory scheme. Accordingly, the FDCA and FDA regulations do not provide food and beverage makers with a safe harbor against federal false advertising claims.

[b]   Commercial Advertising or Promotion

Misrepresentations are actionable under section 43(a)(1)(B) only if they take place in "commercial advertising or promotion." In determining whether a particular activity constitutes commercial advertising or promotion, some courts have adopted the following approach:

> In order for representations to constitute "commercial advertising or promotion" under Section 43(a)(1)(B), they must be: (1) commercial speech;

Third Circuit, however, a plaintiff may establish literal falsity simply by proving that the defendant's claim is unsubstantiated. Novartis Consumer Health, Inc. v. Johnson & Johnson-Merck Pharms. Co., 290 F.3d 578, 589 (3d Cir. 2002).

[305] *Castrol*, 977 F.2d at 63; *accord, Chesebrough-Pond's*, 747 F.2d at 119; *BASF*, 41 F.3d at 1090–91; *United Indus. Corp.*, 140 F.3d at 1182.

[306] *Castrol*, 977 F.2d at 63.

[307] *Id.*

[308] American Council of Certified Podiatric Physicians & Surgeons v. American Bd. of Podiatric Surgery, Inc., 185 F.3d 606 (6th Cir. 1999); *accord* Pizza Hut, Inc. v. Papa John's Int'l, Inc., 227 F.3d 489 (5th Cir. 2000); *Novartis*, 290 F.3d at 590.

[309] Cashmere & Camel Hair Mfrs. Inst. v. Saks Fifth Ave., 284 F.3d 302 (1st Cir. 2002).

[310] 134 S. Ct. 2228 (2014).

(2) by a defendant who is in commercial competition with plaintiff; (3) for the purpose of influencing consumers to buy defendant's goods or services. While the representations need not be made in a "classic advertising campaign," but may consist instead of more informal types of "promotion," the representations (4) must be disseminated sufficiently to the relevant purchasing public to constitute "advertising" or "promotion" within that industry.[311]

Other courts have adopted only three prongs of this test, dispensing with the requirement that the parties be competitors.[312] For purposes of this test, courts generally follow the Supreme Court's definition of commercial speech as "speech which does no more than propose a commercial transaction."[313]

Nontraditional activities that may qualify as commercial advertising or promotion have been held to include disparaging comments made about competitors in a variety of contexts — e.g., in the course of phone conversations with customers,[314] in a trade publication,[315] and in an anonymous memorandum.[316] However, courts have cautioned against interpreting commercial advertising or promotion so broadly as to encompass protected speech. For example, where an article in a trade publication contained comments by the owners of one art gallery challenging the authenticity of works offered by a competing gallery, the Second Circuit held that these statements were not commercial speech even if they were widely disseminated and were intended to influence purchasers to choose the defendants' gallery over the competing gallery, because the statements were made "in a forum that has traditionally been granted full protection under the First Amendment."[317]

Statements may be actionable under section 43(a)(1)(B) even if the speaker has not yet begun to compete in the same market as the party whose commercial activities it is disparaging.[318] Otherwise, a business entity could "destroy an anticipated competitor through false representations made during the period before the commencement of the new business, and then pick up the pieces of the ruined business."[319]

---

[311] Procter & Gamble Co. v. Haugen, 222 F.3d 1262, 1273–74 (10th Cir. 2000); accord, Coastal Abstract Serv., Inc. v. First Am. Tit. Ins. Co., 173 F.3d 725, 734 (9th Cir. 1999); Seven-Up Co. v. Coca-Cola Co., 86 F.3d 1379, 1384 (5th Cir. 1996); Gordon & Breach Sci. Pubs., S.A. v. American Inst. of Physics, 859 F. Supp. 1521, 1535–36 (S.D.N.Y. 1994).

[312] See, e.g., Galerie Gmurzynska v. Hutton, 355 F.3d 206, 210 (2d Cir. 2004).

[313] Id. (quoting City of Cincinnati v. Discovery Network, Inc., 507 U.S. 410, 422 (1993) (internal quotation marks omitted)).

[314] National Artists Mgt. Co. v. Weaving, 769 F. Supp. 1224 (S.D.N.Y. 1991).

[315] Semco, Inc. v. Amcast, Inc., 52 F.3d 108, 113–14 (6th Cir. 1995); Fuente Cigar, Ltd. v. Opus One, 985 F. Supp. 1448, 1456 (M.D. Fla. 1997); contra, Gordon & Breach Sci. Pubs., 859 F. Supp. at 1541–42.

[316] H&R Indus. v. Kirshner, 899 F. Supp. 995, 1006 (E.D.N.Y. 1995).

[317] Boule v. Hutton, 328 F.3d 84, 91–92 (2d Cir. 2003) (quoting Groden v. Random House, Inc., 61 F.3d 1045, 1052 (2d Cir. 1995)); see also Galerie Gmurzynska v. Hutton, 355 F.3d 206 (2d Cir. 2004) (per curiam).

[318] See, e.g., Fuente Cigar, Ltd. v. Opus One, 985 F. Supp. 1448, 1456 (M.D. Fla. 1997); National Artists Mgt. Co. v. Weaving, 769 F. Supp. 1224, 1233 (S.D.N.Y. 1991).

[319] Fuente Cigar, 985 F. Supp. at 1456 (quoting National Artists, 769 F. Supp. at 1234).

[c]   Other Commercial Activities

Actionable misrepresentations under section 43(a)(1)(B) may pertain to goods, services, or "commercial activities."[320] Courts have interpreted the latter phrase as encompassing a variety of commercial activities other than those that involve the offering of goods or services to the public.[321] Typically, actionable false statements pertaining to "commercial activities" are those that have the effect of tarnishing the plaintiff's general business reputation. Examples include allegations of improper and unethical practices,[322] of failure to pay bills,[323] and of improper solicitation of customers,[324] as well as an allegation that a competitor donated a share of its profits to "the church of Satan."[325]

Another variety of false advertising takes place when a party presents its potential customers with a picture or sample of a competitor's product, implying that this is a picture or sample of its own product, in order to solicit their patronage.[326] This type of false advertising has sometimes been treated instead as a false designation of origin under Section 43(a)(1)(A).[327]

As noted above,[328] the Supreme Court in *Dastar Corp. v. Twentieth Century Fox Film Corp.* held that a false attribution of the authorship of an expressive work is not actionable as a false designation of origin under section 43(a)(1)(A), but that it might (if material) constitute false advertising under section 43(a)(1)(B).[329] Thus far, however, post-*Dastar* attempts to bring false advertising claims for false attribution of authorship have been unsuccessful.[330]

---

[320] 15 U.S.C. § 1125(a)(1)(B).

[321] Procter & Gamble Co. v. Haugen, 222 F.3d 1262 (10th Cir. 2000); *see also* Fuente Cigar, Ltd. v. Opus One, 985 F. Supp. 1448, 1454 (M.D. Fla. 1997).

[322] *National Artists*, 769 F. Supp. at 1229–36.

[323] Coastal Abstract Serv., Inc. v. First Am. Tit. Ins. Co., 173 F.3d 725, 732 (9th Cir. 1999).

[324] H & R. Indus., Inc. v. Kirshner, 899 F. Supp. 995, 1005–06 (E.D.N.Y. 1995).

[325] *Haugen*, 222 F.3d at 1272–73.

[326] *See, e.g.*, Innovative Design Enters. v. Circulair, Inc. 1997 U.S. Dist. LEXIS 12799, *39–*40 (N.D. Ill. Aug. 20, 1997); Accurate Leather & Novelty Co. Inc. v. LTD Commodities Inc., 18 U.S.P.Q. 2d 1327, 1329 (N.D. Ill. 1990).

[327] *See, e.g.*, Truck Equipment Service Co. v. Fruehauf Corp., 536 F.2d 1210, 1216 (8th Cir. 1976); *Innovative Design*, 1997 U.S. Dist. LEXIS 12799 at *39–40. Courts have sometimes characterized these claims as "implied reverse passing off." *See* § 5F[7], above.

[328] *See* § 5F[7].

[329] 539 U.S. 23, 37 (2003).

[330] *See, e.g.*, Sybersound Records, Inc. v. UAV Corp., 517 F.3d 1137, 1143–44 (9th Cir. 2008); Zyla v. Wadsworth, 360 F.3d 243, 251–52 & n.8 (1st Cir. 2004); Wilchcombe v. Teevee Toons, Inc., 515 F. Supp. 2d 1297, 1305–06 (N.D. Ga. 2007); Antidote Int'l Films, Inc. v. Bloomsbury Pub'g, PLC, 467 F. Supp. 2d 394 (S.D.N.Y. 2007); Monsanto Co. v. Syngenta Seeds, Inc., 443 F. Supp. 2d 648, 652–53 (D. Del. 2006), *aff'd*, 503 F.3d 1352 (Fed. Cir. 2007); Radolf v. University of Connecticut, 364 F. Supp. 2d 204, 222 (D. Conn. 2005).

[d]   Standing

In its 2014 decision in *Lexmark International, Inc. v. Static Control Components*, the Supreme Court resolved a three-way circuit split regarding standing to bring a Lanham Act false advertising claim, holding that standing is not limited to direct competitors.[331] Instead, a party has standing if it suffers a business injury that is proximately caused by the defendant's false statements.

Where a false advertising claim is raised by a competitor of the defendant, it can be difficult for the plaintiff to establish a commercial injury in a market where there are sellers other than the plaintiff and the defendant. Under the proximate causation requirement, the plaintiff may be denied standing because it cannot establish that, but for the defendant's false statements, customers would have dealt with the plaintiff rather than the defendant.[332] In contrast, a plaintiff typically will have standing to sue where it is the only source of the goods or services to which a competitor's false advertising pertains, or where the plaintiff and the false advertiser are the only sources of those goods or services.[333]

§ 6F   MISAPPROPRIATION

The law regards competition, even competition calculated to eliminate competitors, as lawful and in the public interest.[334] Early unfair competition law focused narrowly on two "unfair" competitive methods: deception as to the origin or nature of goods and use of breaches of confidence and improper means to obtain competitively useful information. The former, known as the "passing off" or "palming off" tort, is the foundation of modern trademark law.[335] The latter is the foundation of modern trade secret law.[336]

The deception branch of unfair competition law later expanded to encompass a competitor's remedy for a rival's false advertising and labeling, that is, a defendant's misrepresentations as to the nature or qualities of his own goods that tended to divert plaintiff's sales.[337]

The Supreme Court's 1918 decision in *International News Service v. Associated Press*[338] provoked debate on whether unfair competition law could go beyond

---

[331] 134 S. Ct. 1377 (2014).

[332] *See, e.g.*, Burndy Corp. v. Teledyne Industries, Inc., 584 F. Supp. 656 (D. Conn. 1984), *aff'd*, 748 F.2d 767 (2d Cir. 1984); Construction Technology v. Lockformer Co., 704 F. Supp. 1212 (S.D.N.Y. 1989).

[333] *See, e.g.*, Mosler Safe Co. v. Ely-Norris Safe Co., 273 U.S. 132 (1927); Electronics Corp. of America v. Honeywell, Inc., 428 F.2d 191 (1st Cir. 1970).

[334] *See, e.g.*, Tuttle v. Buck, 119 N.W. 946, 948 (Minn. 1909) ("To divert to one's self the customers of a business rival by the offer of goods at lower prices is in general a legitimate mode of serving one's own interest, and justifiable as fair competition"; recognizing as an exception that "when a man starts an opposition place of business, not for the sake of profit to himself, but regardless of loss to himself, and for the sole purpose of driving his competitor out of business.").

[335] *See* Chapter 5.

[336] *See* Chapter 3.

[337] *See* § 6E.

[338] 248 U.S. 215 (1918).

deception to encompass "misappropriation," that is, a second competitor's unauthorized taking of publicly disclosed information that a first competitor invests time and effort to create, when the taking diminishes or eliminates the first competitor's incentive to continue to create the information.

Since *INS*, the misappropriation doctrine has had uncertain status. After *Erie* decreed that there is no general federal common law,[339] the misappropriation doctrine's existence and scope became a question of state law. Decisions in some states, particularly New York, relied on the *INS* misappropriation doctrine to provide relief when no other theory adequately supported relief against improper copying. Other decisions restricted *INS* to its specific facts[340] or held federal patent and copyright policy preempted the doctrine.[341]

More recent decisions do not reject the doctrine entirely but confine it to situations in which the alleged misappropriator's use of information is in direct competition with the producer's primary use of the information and there is a clear threat that unchecked misappropriation will diminish the producer's incentive to produce the information.[342]

[1]   The *INS* Decision

International News Service v. Associated Press[343] involved a clash between competing news-gathering services, the Associated Press (AP) and the International News Service (INS), over news reporting in the European theater during the First World War. AP was a collective of 950 daily newspapers that shared its news gathering costs, with the member newspapers agreeing not to permit pre-publication disclosure of AP stories. AP sought an injunction restraining INS from pirating AP news.

AP complained of three practices. First, INS allegedly bribed employees of AP member newspapers to furnish news to INS's clients. Second, it allegedly induced AP members to violate AP by-laws and permit INS to obtain AP news. The district court's injunction restraining these practices was not a point of controversy.

The point of controversy was INS's third practice: "copying news from bulletin boards and from early editions of [AP member] newspapers and selling this, either bodily or after rewriting it, to defendant's customers." Following this practice, INS's customer newspapers could report the news almost as soon as AP members; and INS's west coast newspapers could report stories simultaneously or earlier than their AP competitors because of the three-hour time difference from the east to the west coast of the United States.

AP did not rely on copyright infringement. Whether or not AP sought copyright in its stories as literary works, it could not obtain copyright protection for the news

---

[339] Erie R.R. v. Tompkins, 304 U.S. 64 (1938).

[340] Cheney Brothers v. Doris Silk Corp., 35 F.2d 279 (2d Cir. 1929).

[341] *See, e.g.*, Columbia Broadcasting Sys., Inc. v. DeCosta, 377 F.2d 315 (1st Cir. 1967). *See* § 1D[3][c].

[342] *See* National Basketball Ass'n v. Motorola, Inc., 105 F.3d 841, 852 (2d Cir. 1997); § 6F[4], below.

[343] 248 U.S. 215 (1918).

described in its stories: news consists of facts and ideas, and copyright law protects only the *expression* of facts and ideas.[344] Instead, AP relied on unfair competition law principles. It sought, and the appeals court awarded, a preliminary injunction "against any bodily taking of the words or substance of complainant's news until its commercial value as news had passed away."[345]

On certiorari, the Supreme Court affirmed. The majority opinion addressed three questions in AP's argument:

> (1) Whether there is any property in news; (2) Whether, if there be property in news collected for the purpose of being published, it survives the instant of its publication in the first newspaper to which it is communicated by the news-gatherer; and (3) whether defendant's admitted course of conduct in appropriating for commercial use matter taken from bulletins or early editions of Associated Press publications constitutes unfair competition in trade.[346]

The need to resolve the status of news as "property" arose from the historic equity requirement that an injunction would only issue in aid of property rights. The Court clearly did not wish to say that AP or anyone else had an absolute property right in disclosed news. Instead, it characterized the news as "quasi property." Between either party and the public, disclosed news could not be property;[347] but between the parties as competitors, the news was "stock in trade, to be gathered at the cost of enterprise, organization, skill, labor, and money, and to be distributed and sold to those who will pay money for it, as for any other merchandise."[348]

The key question was the third one of "unfair competition in business." Upholding the claim, the Court put forth an agricultural metaphor:

> [Defendant] admits that it is taking material that has been acquired by complainant as the result of organization and the expenditure of labor, skill, and money, and which is salable by complainant for money, and that defendant in appropriating it and selling it as its own *is endeavoring to reap where it has not sown, and . . . is appropriating to itself the harvest of those who have sown.* Stripped of all disguises, the process amounts to an unauthorized interference with the normal operation of complainant's legitimate business precisely at the point where the profit is to be reaped, in order to divert a material portion of the profit from those who have earned it to those who have not; with special advantage to defendant in the competition because of the fact that it is not burdened with any part of the

---

[344] *See* §§ 4C[3] and 4H[3][a].

[345] 248 U.S. at 232.

[346] *Id.*

[347] *Id.* at 234 ("But the news element — the information respecting current events contained in the literary production — is not the creation of the writer, but is a report of matters that ordinarily are *publici juris*; it is the history of the day. It is not to be supposed that the framers of the Constitution . . . intended to confer upon one who might happen to be the first to report a historic event the exclusive right for any period to spread the knowledge of it.").

[348] *Id.* at 236.

expense of gathering the news. The transaction speaks for itself and a court of equity ought not to hesitate long in characterizing it as unfair competition in business.[349]

There were two dissents. Justice Holmes wrote that AP's only ground of complaint was against INS's false implied representation that it was the source of news stories it in fact derived from AP[350] — a theory that today would be characterized as "reverse passing off" or false advertising. Justice Brandeis more directly challenged the majority's "misappropriation" theory:

> [T]he fact that a product of the mind has cost its producer money and labor, and has a value for which others are willing to pay, is not sufficient to ensure to it this legal attribute of property. The general rule of law is, that the noblest of human productions — knowledge, truths ascertained, conceptions, and ideas — became, after voluntary communication to others, free as the air to common use. Upon these incorporeal productions the attribute of property is continued after such communication only in certain classes of cases where public policy has seemed to demand it. . . . The creations which are recognized as property . . . have also protection under the copyright statutes. The inventions and discoveries upon which this attribute of property is conferred only by statute, are the few comprised within the patent law.[351]

In other words, intangible property rights after public disclosure should be confined to those created by statute, and should not be extended by judicial fiat.[352] Justice Brandeis also challenged the majority's apparent view that "free riding" ought to be condemned:

> To appropriate and use for profit, knowledge and ideas produced by other men, without making compensation or even acknowledgment, may be inconsistent with a finer sense of propriety; but, with the exceptions indicated above, the law has heretofore sanctioned the practice. Thus . . . one may ordinarily make and sell anything in any form, may copy with exactness that which another has produced, or may otherwise use his ideas without his consent and without the payment of compensation, and yet not inflict a legal injury.[353]

[2]   From *INS* to *Sears-Compco*

"The language of the *I.N.S.* opinion is very broad, and courts have struggled over the years to define the limits of the doctrine."[354]

---

[349] International News Service v. Associated Press, 248 U.S. 215, 239–40 (1918) (emphasis added).

[350] *Id.* at 246–48 (Holmes, J., joined by McKenna, J., dissenting).

[351] *Id.* at 250 (Brandeis, J., dissenting).

[352] *Id.* at 262–63, 264–67.

[353] *Id.* at 257.

[354] United States Golf Ass'n v. St. Andrews Systems, Data-Max, Inc., 749 F.2d 1028, 1035–36 (3d Cir. 1984).

Although some courts applied the misappropriation doctrine to fact patterns resembling *INS*,[355] the Second Circuit gave the misappropriation doctrine narrow scope. In *Cheney Brothers v. Doris Silk Corp.*,[356] the plaintiff, a manufacturer of "silks," put out new patterns each season. Because of the short product life, plaintiff did not seek design patents, and many of its designs would not have met patentability standards.[357] The Copyright Office views clothing designs as uncopyrightable subject matter.[358] The Second Circuit, in an opinion by Judge Learned Hand, found no common-law basis for relief even though plaintiff sought protection for only a short period of time:

> The plaintiff asks for protection only during the season, and needs no more, for the designs are all ephemeral. . . . But the reasoning which would justify any interposition at all demands that it cover the whole extent of the injury. A man whose designs come to harvest in two years, or in five, has *prima facie* as good right to protection as one who deals only in annuals. Nor could we consistently stop at designs; processes, machines, and secrets have an equal claim. The upshot must be that, whenever any one has contrived any of these, others may be forbidden to copy it. That is not the law. In the absence of some recognized right at common law, or under the statutes — and the plaintiff claims neither — a man's property is limited to the chattels which embody his invention. Others may imitate these at their pleasure.[359]

Plaintiff relied upon *INS.*, but the court essentially limited *INS* to its facts:

> Although [*INS*] concerned another subject-matter — printed news dispatches — we agree that, if it meant to lay down a general doctrine, it would cover this case; at least, the language of the majority opinion goes so far. We do not believe that it did. While it is of course true that law ordinarily speaks in general terms, there are cases where the occasion is at once the justification for, and the limit of, what is decided. This appears to us such an instance; we think that no more was covered than situations substantially similar to those then at bar. The difficulties of understanding it otherwise are insuperable. We are to suppose that the court meant to create a sort of common-law patent or copyright for reasons of justice. Either would flagrantly conflict with the scheme which Congress has for more than a century devised to cover the subject-matter.[360]

---

[355] *See, e.g.*, Associated Press v. KVOS, Inc., 80 F.2d 575 (9th Cir. 1935) (radio broadcast of news taken from AP newspaper), *rev'd on other grounds*, 299 U.S. 269 (1936).

[356] 35 F.2d 279 (2d Cir. 1929).

[357] For the standards applicable to design patents, see § 6B.

[358] *See* § 4C[4][a][v](b). It is unclear whether the case involved dress designs, which are still uncopyrightable, or printed patterns on fabric, which are copyrightable today, but may not have been in the 1920s.

[359] 35 F.2d at 279–80.

[360] *Id.* at 280; *see also id.* ("To exclude others from the enjoyment of a chattel is one thing; to prevent any imitation of it, to set up a monopoly in the plan of its structure, gives the author a power over his fellows vastly greater, a power which the Constitution allows only Congress to create.").

Many other courts also rejected misappropriation arguments.[361] Courts in New York, however, tended to apply the misappropriation doctrine expansively. In *Metropolitan Opera Ass'n v. Wagner-Nichols Recorder Corp.*,[362] the New York courts granted the Metropolitan Opera and Columbia Records, its authorized recording company, an injunction restraining the defendant from recording and distributing phonorecords of the Met's opera performances, which American Broadcasting Company broadcast with the Met's permission. Defendant's records were cheaper, and, according to plaintiffs, inferior in quality to plaintiffs' authorized records. The case's facts suggested implied misrepresentation about the source of defendant's recordings and direct competition between plaintiff Columbia Records and defendant, but the court refused to limit its holding to cases of palming off[363] or directive competitive injury.[364] Many subsequent New York cases relied on this case in granting relief against unauthorized copying.[365]

[3]   *Sears-Compco* and Federal Preemption

In *Sears, Roebuck & Co. v. Stiffel Co.*,[366] and *Compco Corp. v. Day-Brite Lighting, Inc.*,[367] the United States Supreme Court held that federal patent and copyright policy preempted state unfair competition law insofar as it would bar copying of publicly distributed products not covered by a valid patent or copyright.[368] The decisions dealt a blow to the misappropriation doctrine,[369] but it

---

[361] *See, e.g.*, RCA Manufacturing Co. v. Whiteman, 114 F.2d 86 (2d Cir. 1940) (rebroadcast of recordings); Addressograph-Multigraph Corp. v. American Expansion Bolt & Mfg. Co., 124 F.2d 706 (7th Cir. 1941) (applying Illinois law); Triangle Publications v. New England Newspaper Publishing Co., 46 F. Supp. 198 (D. Mass. 1942) (applying Massachusetts law); *cf.* Fashion Originators' Guild of Am. v. Federal Trade Commission, 312 U.S. 457 (1941) (commercial boycott by fashion designers against "style piracy" violates antitrust laws); Millinery Creators' Guild, Inc. v. Federal Trade Commission, 109 F.2d 175 (2d Cir. 1940), *aff'd*, 312 U.S. 469 (1941) (same with respect to designs of high-priced hats). *But see* Waring v. WDAS Broadcasting Station, Inc., 194 A. 631 (Pa. 1937) (enjoining radio broadcast of phonograph records).

[362] 199 Misc. 786 (N.Y. Sup. Ct. 1950), *aff'd*, 279 A.D. 632 (1951).

[363] 199 Misc. 786 at 791–93.

[364] *Id.* at 795–96.

[365] *See, e.g.*, Capitol Records, Inc. v. Mercury Records Corp., 221 F.2d 657 (2d Cir. 1955) (holding that *Metropolitan Opera* case undermined *RCA* and was controlling New York law under *Erie*); Roy Export Co. v. Columbia Broadcasting Sys., Inc., 672 F.2d 1095, 1105 (2d Cir. 1982) (unauthorized broadcast of a compilation of Charlie Chaplin's films after his death constitutes misappropriation under New York law); Bond Buyer v. Dealers Digest Publishing Co., 25 A.D.2d 158, 267 N.Y.S.2d 944 (1966); New York World's Fair 1964–1965 Corp. v. Colour Picture Publishers, Inc., 21 A.D.2d 896, 251 N.Y.S.2d 885 (1964); Madison Sq. Garden Corp. v. Universal Pictures Co., 255 A.D. 459, 7 N.Y.S.2d 845 (1938); Columbia Broadcasting System Inc. v. Documentaries Unlimited, Inc., 42 Misc. 2d 723 (N.Y. Sup. Ct. 1964); Capitol Records, Inc. v. Greatest Records, Inc., 43 Misc. 2d 878 (N.Y. Sup. Ct. 1964).

[366] 376 U.S. 225 (1964).

[367] 376 U.S. 234 (1964).

[368] For a discussion of *Sears* and *Compco*, see § 1D[3][a][i], above.

[369] *See, e.g.*, Columbia Broadcasting Sys., Inc. v. DeCosta, 377 F.2d 315, 318–19 (1st Cir. 1967) (no unfair competition for copying plaintiff's publicly disclosed character; *INS* "is no longer authoritative for at least two reasons: it was decided as a matter of general federal law before the decision in *Erie R.R. v. Tompkins*; and, as it prohibited the copying of published written matter that had not been copyrighted (indeed, as news it could not be copyrighted), it has clearly been overruled by the Supreme Court's recent

was not fatal.[370] And although the Supreme Court later reconfirmed that federal policy restricts state-law anti-copying remedies as applied to subject matter potentially eligible for patent protection,[371] the status of misappropriation was left unclear by the Court's holding that federal copyright law did *not* preempt state laws concerning record piracy (at a time when sound recordings were not eligible for copyright).[372]

Misappropriation's status arose during Congressional consideration of the 1976 Copyright Act, which preempts state common law and statutory rights that are "equivalent to any of the exclusive rights within the general scope of copyright . . . in works of authorship that are fixed in a tangible medium of expression and come within the subject matter of copyright."[373] Section 301(b)(3), however, saves state rights and remedies against "activities violating legal or equitable rights that are not equivalent to any of the exclusive rights within the general scope of copyright."[374]

The bill that became the 1976 Act, as it went to the House floor, had a clause at the end of Section 301(b)(3) listing saved state-created rights, "including rights against misappropriation not equivalent to any of such exclusive rights . . . ." The Justice Department objected to the reference to misappropriation. On the House floor, Congressman Seiberling amended Section 301(b) to delete the entire "including" clause. Unfortunately, the House floor remarks of Seiberling and other Congressmen left the purpose of the amendment unclear as it relates to preemption of misappropriation.[375]

[4]   Contemporary Applications

Faced with the ambiguous legislative history, courts have reached differing decisions on whether and when a state law cause of action for misappropriation should be allowed, and whether and when it is preempted by federal copyright law. One of the difficulties is that the label "misappropriation" has been used in a wide range of situations, including traditional actions for "passing off" and common-law trademark infringement, which are not preempted because they require the "extra elements" of trademark rights and likelihood of confusion;[376] and actions for misappropriation of trade secrets, which are not preempted because they require

---

decisions in" *Sears* and *Compco*) (citations omitted).

[370] *See, e.g.*, United States Golf Association v. St. Andrews Systems, Data-Max, Inc., 749 F.2d 1028, 1036 (3d Cir. 1984) ("The Court has not . . . clearly defined where the power of the states to protect interests in intellectual property ends, and where the realm of federal preemption begins.").

[371] *See* Bonito Boats, Inc. v. Thunder Craft Boats, Inc., 489 U.S. 141 (1989), discussed in § 1D[3][a].

[372] *See* Goldstein v. California, 412 U.S. 546 (1973), discussed in § 1D[3][a].

[373] 17 U.S.C. § 301(a). For a discussion of Section 301, see § 1D[3][c].

[374] 17 U.S.C. § 301(b)(3).

[375] *See* 122 Cong. Rec. H10,910 (Sept. 22, 1976).

[376] *See, e.g.*, Donald Frederick Evans & Assocs., Inc. v. Continental Homes, Inc., 785 F.2d 897, 914 (11th Cir. 1986); Warner Bros. Inc. v. American Broadcasting Cos., 720 F.2d 231, 247 (2d Cir. 1983). For a discussion of the "extra element" test, see § 1D[3][c][ii].

the "extra elements" of secrecy (undisclosed information) and improper means.[377] However, the effect of Section 301 on pure misappropriation claims of the *INS* variety is considerably more uncertain.

In *National Basketball Ass'n v. Motorola, Inc.*, the NBA sought to enjoin Motorola from offering a pager service "which displays updated information of professional basketball games in progress."[378] The Second Circuit held that federal copyright law preempts almost all misappropriation claims under state law. Specifically,

> We hold that the surviving "hot-news" *INS*-like claim is limited to cases where: (i) a plaintiff generates or gathers information at a cost; (ii) the information is time-sensitive; (iii) a defendant's use of the information constitutes free riding on the plaintiff's efforts; (iv) the defendant is in direct competition with a product or service offered by the plaintiffs; and (v) the ability of other parties to free-ride on the efforts of the plaintiff or others would so reduce the incentive to produce the product or service that its existence or quality would be substantially threatened.[379]

Because Motorola gathered the facts and statistics itself (by paying individuals to watch games and enter data), rather than "free-riding" by copying data compiled by the NBA, and because the data reporting would not deter the NBA from continuing to present professional basketball games, the court held that the NBA's misappropriation claim was preempted.[380]

Similarly, in *Barclay's Capital, Inc. v. Theflyonthewall.com, Inc.*, plaintiff financial institutions issued daily research reports to their investor clients that often contained recommendations to "buy" or "sell" certain stocks.[381] The Second Circuit held that the plaintiffs' claims for misappropriation, based on defendant's republication (for profit) of those "recommendations" (but not the reports themselves) to its own clients as part of its subscription news service, were preempted by the Copyright Act.[382] The recommendations were considered "facts" that by themselves could move the market,[383] and the court likened the defendant's conduct to traditional news reporting of those "facts," with attribution to the firms that generated them.[384]

---

[377] *See, e.g.*, Stromback v. New Line Cinema, 384 F.3d 283, 302–04 (6th Cir. 2004) (citing cases); Dun & Bradstreet Software Services, Inc. v. Grace Consulting, Inc., 307 F.3d 197, 218 (3d Cir. 2002); Computer Associates Int'l, Inc. v. Altai, Inc., 982 F.2d 693, 717 (2d Cir. 1992). *See* Chapter 3.

[378] 105 F.3d 841, 843 (2d Cir. 1997).

[379] *Id.* at 845; *see also id.* at 852. *But see* Barclay's Capital, Inc. v. Theflyonthewall.com, Inc., 650 F.3d 876, 898–901 (2d Cir. 2011) (criticizing this summary of the holding in *Motorola* as *dicta*); *id.* at 908–12 (concurring opinion) (expressing doubt about this holding in *Motorola*, but following it as binding authority).

[380] *Id.* at 853–54. *See also* National Football League v. Governor of Delaware, 435 F. Supp. 1372 (D. Del. 1977) (state lottery based on outcomes of professional football games does not constitute misappropriation).

[381] 650 F.3d 876, 878–79 (2d Cir. 2011).

[382] *Id.* at 882–84, 902–06.

[383] *Id.* at 879, 902.

[384] *Id.* at 903–04 ("We do not perceive a material difference between [defendant's conduct and] . . .

A number of cases have applied misappropriation to bar unauthorized use of stock market indices to create publicly traded securities, such as futures contracts. In *Standard & Poor's Corp. v. Commodity Exchange, Inc.*, the Second Circuit upheld a preliminary injunction barring the defendant (Comex) from offering a futures contract based on the Standard & Poor's 500 index, in direct competition with S&P's licensee, the Chicago Mercantile Exchange.[385] Under the governing preliminary injunction standard, it did not decide whether S&P's misappropriation claim was valid; it was sufficient that "the record indicates the presence of sufficiently serious questions going to the merits of S&P's misappropriation claim to make them fair grounds for litigation."[386] Similarly, in *Board of Trade of the City of Chicago v. Dow Jones & Co.*, the Illinois Supreme Court held that the Board's proposal to offer a futures contract based on the Dow Jones Industrial Average without the defendant's permission would constitute misappropriation.[387] The court refused to confine misappropriation to cases in which the copier directly competes in the producer's primary market.[388]

Most recently, in *Chicago Board Options Exchange, Inc. v. International Securities Exchange, LLC*, an Illinois appellate court held that "Congress intended for misappropriation to avoid preemption in cases such as this one."[389] In *CBOE*, the owners of the Dow Jones average and the S&P 500 index gave CBOE an exclusive license to offer "index options" based on those indices. When ISE sought to offer unlicensed index options in competition with them, CBOE and its licensors sued. The court characterized ISE's conduct as "unauthorized *use* of the research, expertise, reputation, and goodwill associated with the plaintiff's product for ISE's own gain," rather than mere reproduction, distribution, or display of the index values themselves.[390] Accordingly, it held that that the claim survived preemption, because "ideas, systems, and concepts . . . do not fall under the Copyright Act."[391]

---

what appears to be unexceptional and easily recognized behavior by members of the traditional news media."); *see also id.* at 905 ("Fly's employees are engaged in the financial-industry equivalent of observing and summarizing facts about basketball games and selling those packaged facts to consumers.").

One concurring judge would have decided the case on the alternative ground that the defendant was not in direct competition with the plaintiffs, because the plaintiffs made money from their recommendations only when clients bought or sold stocks, and the defendants did not offer brokerage services. *Id.* at 912–16.

[385] 683 F.2d 704, 710 (2d Cir. 1982).

[386] *Id.* at 712. Comex had not yet received regulatory approval to offer its futures contract, so the preliminary injunction essentially preserved the status quo.

[387] 456 N.E.2d 84, 85 (Ill. 1983). Plaintiff initially developed its own stock average, but regulatory authorities required that stock market index contracts be based on well-known averages. 456 N.E.2d at 86.

[388] 456 N.E.2d at 90.

[389] 973 N.E.2d 390, 400 (Ill. Ct. App. 2012). In so holding, the court relied on the House Report on the 1976 Copyright Act, and ignored the fact that the language which the House Report was explaining was deleted from the final version of the Act passed by Congress. *See* § 6F[3], above.

[390] 973 N.E.2d at 398.

[391] *Id.* In so holding, the court aligned itself with the minority position. Most courts hold that claims based on misappropriation of ideas and concepts are nonetheless preempted, because Congress intended ideas and concepts to be placed in the public domain. *See* § 1D[3][c][i], above.

However, in *Dow Jones & Co. v. International Securities Exchange, Inc.*, the Second Circuit held that ISE could lawfully issue and trade options on the shares of exchange trading funds (ETFs) that were licensed by Dow Jones and S&P.[392] The court did not discuss preemption; instead, it held for ISE by analogy to the doctrine of exhaustion:

> By authorizing the creation of ETFs using their proprietary formulas, and the sale of the ETF shares to the public, the plaintiffs have relinquished any right to control resale and public trading of those shares, notwithstanding the fact that plaintiffs' intellectual property may be embedded in the shares. Owners and would-be owners of ETF shares are free to negotiate with one another for the purchase and sale of the ETF shares plaintiffs have sold to the public. Because plaintiffs have permitted the buying and selling of the ETF shares, plaintiffs may not prevent exchanges from offering marketplaces for buyers and sellers to come together to effectuate their transactions.[393]

Two courts have split over whether the United States Golf Association (USGA) may prevent others from using its mathematical formula for calculating golf "handicaps" for amateur golfers. In *United States Golf Ass'n v. St. Andrews Systems, Data-Max, Inc.*, the Third Circuit rejected the misappropriation claim under New Jersey law, "largely because in using the formula Data-Max will not compete directly with the U.S.G.A., and thus will not interfere with the economic incentives of the U.S.G.A. to maintain and update its handicap formula."[394] The court explained:

> Because the U.S.G.A. formula is the equivalent of an "industry standard" for the golfing public, preventing other handicap providers from using it would effectively give the U.S.G.A. a national monopoly on the golf handicapping business. Where such a monopoly is unnecessary to protect the basic incentive for the production of the idea or information involved, we do not believe that the creator's interest in its idea or information justifies such an extensive restraint on competition.[395]

By contrast, in *United States Golf Ass'n v. Arroyo Software Corp.*, the California Court of Appeal enjoined Arroyo from offering software that used the USGA's formula, holding that California misappropriation law did not impose a requirement of direct competition.[396] The court also rejected an argument that the claim was preempted by federal copyright law.[397]

Courts have also evoked the misappropriation doctrine to suppress unauthorized reproduction and broadcast of pre-1972 sound recordings,[398] which federal copy-

---

[392] 451 F.3d 295 (2d Cir. 2006).

[393] *Id.* at 302–03.

[394] 749 F.2d 1028, 1029–30 (3d Cir. 1984).

[395] *Id.* at 1040–41.

[396] 69 Cal. App. 4th 607, 618–19 (1999).

[397] 69 Cal. App. 4th at 62123.

[398] *See, e.g.*, Capitol Records, Inc. v. Naxos of America, Inc., 830 N.E.2d 250 (N.Y. 2005); Flo & Eddie,

right law does not cover.[399] Given the express exception in Section 301 preserving state common-law copyright in pre-1972 sound recordings until December 31, 2067,[400] this application of the misappropriation doctrine is clearly permissible, although certainly not compelled.

It should be noted that the *Restatement (Third) of Unfair Competition* takes the position that "the principle of unjust enrichment does *not* demand restitution of every gain derived from the benefits of others," and concludes that "[t]he better approach, and the one most likely to achieve an appropriate balance between the competing interests, does *not* recognize a residual common law tort of misappropriation."[401]

§ 6G   RIGHTS OF PUBLICITY

[1]   Introduction

A right of publicity is the right of a person to use his or her identity for commercial purposes. Like trade secret law,[402] rights of publicity are governed by state, not federal law and vary from state to state. Some states have publicity statutes;[403] in others, courts recognize a common-law publicity right.[404] In all, more than 30 of the 50 states have recognized a right of publicity.[405] Rights of publicity protect a person's name, voice, signature, photograph, or likeness,[406] and any other aspects of a person's "identity."[407]

Inc. v. SiriusXm Radio, Inc., 2014 U.S. Dist. LEXIS 166492 (S.D.N.Y. Nov. 14, 2014); Columbia Broadcasting Sys. v. Melody Recordings, Inc., 341 A.2d 348 (N.J. Super Ct. 1975); Capitol Records, Inc. v. Spies, 264 N.E.2d 874 (Ill. Ct. App. 1970); Capitol Records, Inc. v. Mercury Records Corp., 221 F.2d 657 (2d Cir. 1955) (New York law).

[399] *See* § 4C[4][a][vii].

[400] 17 U.S.C. § 301(c).

[401] RESTATEMENT (THIRD) OF UNFAIR COMPETITION § 38 cmt. b (1995) (emphasis added). *See also* Richard A. Posner, *Misappropriation: A Dirge*, 40 HOUS. L. REV. 621, 633 (2003) ("I am hard pressed to find a case in which a claim of misappropriation should have succeeded.").

[402] *See* Chapter 3.

[403] *See, e.g.*, Cal. Civ. Code §§ 3344, 3344.1; Fla. Stat. § 540.08; 765 Ill. Comp. Stat. 1075/10; Ind. Code. § 32-36-1-8; Ky. Rev. Stat. § 391.170; Mass. General Laws ch. 214 § 3A; Neb. Rev. Stat. § 20-202; Nev. Rev. Stat. § 597.790; N.Y. Civ. Rights Law § 51; Ohio Rev. Code § 274.02; Okla. Stat. tit. 21, §§ 839.1–839.3, 1448; 42 Pa. Cons. Stat. § 8316; R.I. Gen. Laws § 9-1-28; Tenn. Code Ann. §§ 47-25-1103; Tex. Prop. Code § 26.002 (protecting rights of deceased persons); Utah Code § 45-3-3; Va. Code Ann. §§ 8.01-40, 18.2-216.1; Wash. Rev. Code § 63.60.010; Wis. Stat. § 895.50.

In California, Florida, Illinois, Kentucky, Ohio, Pennsylvania, Texas, and Wisconsin, rights of publicity have also been recognized in common law.

[404] *See* J. THOMAS MCCARTHY, THE RIGHTS OF PUBLICITY AND PRIVACY § 6.3 (2d ed. 2010) (listing cases from Arizona, Alabama, California, Connecticut, Florida, Georgia, Hawaii, Illinois, Kentucky, Michigan, Minnesota, Missouri, New Hampshire, New Jersey, Ohio, Pennsylvania, Texas, Utah, West Virginia, and Wisconsin).

[405] *Id.*

[406] *See, e.g.*, Cal. Civ. Code §§ 3344(a), 3344,1(a).

[407] *See* § 6G[3], below.

Courts and scholars have articulated several rationales for granting individuals control over the commercial exploitation of their identities. Under one theory, human identity is a self-evident natural property right.[408] This theory is closely linked with theories of misappropriation and unjust enrichment,[409] which posit that celebrities are entitled to the fruits of their labors, and that anyone who benefits from exploiting a celebrity identity should compensate the celebrity for such "free riding."[410] Another theory posits that talented individuals should be given an economic incentive to undertake socially beneficial activities that require entering the public scene.[411] A law-and-economics view is that publicity rights promote the efficient allocation of resources by preventing the dissipation of value through overuse.[412] Some have suggested that publicity rights are necessary to prevent fraudulent or misleading business practices,[413] although this rationale is largely superfluous in light of state and federal actions for false endorsement.[414] Finally, rights of publicity may protect the feelings of celebrities who do not want to endorse products,[415] or do not want to be associated with products that might change their image or diminish their reputation.[416] The latter rationale closely resembles the rationale for trademark dilution.[417]

Unfair competition law and trademark law can overlap publicity rights. For a right of publicity claim to arise, the plaintiff need not show likelihood of confusion, only that his or her identity was used without authorization. However, if an unauthorized use of a celebrity name is also likely to confuse consumers as to the endorsement of goods or services, a claim may arise under both a right of publicity and unfair competition law, including Lanham Act § 43(a).[418] If the celebrity's name is also a registered trademark or service mark, unauthorized use may also be

---

[408] *See, e.g.*, Pavesich v. New England Life Insurance Co., 50 S.E. 68, 79 (Ga. 1905); McCarthy, The Rights of Publicity and Privacy § 2.2.

[409] *See* § 6F.

[410] *See, e.g.*, Zacchini v. Scripps-Howard Broadcasting Co., 433 U.S. 562, 576 741 (1977) ("The rationale for protecting the right of publicity is the straightforward one of preventing unjust enrichment by the theft of good will."); McCarthy, The Rights of Publicity and Privacy § 2.5; *but see* Cardtoons, L.C. v. Major League Baseball Players Ass'n, 95 F.3d 959, 975–76 (10th Cir. 1996).

[411] *See, e.g.*, Zacchini, 433 U.S. at 576 (right of publicity "provides an economic incentive for [plaintiff] to make the investment required to produce a performance of interest to the public."); McCarthy, The Rights of Publicity and Privacy § 2.6; *but see* Cardtoons, 95 F.3d at 973–74.

[412] *See, e.g.*, Matthews v. Wozencraft, 15 F.3d 432, 437–38 (5th Cir. 1994); McCarthy, The Rights of Publicity and Privacy § 2.6; *but see* Cardtoons, 95 F.3d at 974–75.

[413] *See, e.g.*, Felcher & Rubin, *Privacy, Publicity, and the Portrayal of Real People by the Media*, 88 Yale L. J. 1566, 1600 (1979).

[414] *See* § 5C[2][c][iv], above.

[415] *See, e.g.*, Waits v. Frito-Lay, Inc., 978 F.2d 1093, 1103 (9th Cir. 1992).

[416] *Cf.* Newcombe v. Adolf Coors Co., 157 F.3d 686 (9th Cir. 1998) (plaintiff, a recovering alcoholic, was depicted in a beer advertisement); Carson v. Here's Johnny Portable Toilets, Inc., 698 F.2d 831, 834 (6th Cir. 1983); Ali v. Playgirl, Inc., 447 F. Supp. 723 (S.D.N.Y. 1978) (plaintiff depicted nude in a boxing ring).

[417] *See* § 5G.

[418] 15 U.S.C. § 1125(a). *See, e.g.*, Allen v. National Video, Inc., 610 F. Supp. 612 (S.D.N.Y. 1985); McCarthy, The Rights of Publicity and Privacy § 5.31; *see also* § 5C[2][c][iv], above.

trademark infringement.[419]

Similarly, unauthorized copying of a live performance could infringe the performer's common-law copyright as well as a right of publicity right.[420] If the performance is fixed in a tangible medium of expression, such as a film, then some publicity rights may be preempted by federal copyright law.[421]

Publicity rights have stimulated scholarly commentary and, as discussed below, the right developed in response to this commentary.[422]

[2]   Historical Development

The roots of publicity rights lie in the law of privacy. Both ancient Jewish and Roman law recognized an individual's right to be left alone,[423] but the English common law did not. Samuel Warren and Louis Brandeis' seminal 1890 Harvard Law Review article introduced the concept of the right of privacy to the United States. Warren and Brandeis argued that the law should "protect the privacy of private life. . . . [T]he matters of which the publication should be repressed may be described as those which concern the private life, habits, acts and relations of an individual."[424]

In *Roberson v. Rochester Folding Box Co.*,[425] the New York Court of Appeals specifically rejected the Warren-Brandeis article in a case involving unauthorized use of a young woman's photograph in flour advertisements. The court noted the "so-called 'right of privacy' has not as yet found an abiding place in our jurisprudence."[426] In response to *Roberson*, in 1903 New York's legislature enacted a statute making use of a person's name or picture for advertising purposes without consent a tort and a misdemeanor.[427] Following *Roberson*, the New York courts have yet to recognize a common law privacy or publicity right.

---

[419] McCarthy, The Rights of Publicity and Privacy § 5.14; *see also* § 5C[2][c][iv], above. Under Lanham Act Section 2(c), 15 U.S.C. § 1052(c), a person can prevent another from registering a mark comprising his or her name, portrait, or signature. *See* §§ 5C[2][b][ii], 5E[2][c].

[420] *See, e.g.*, Zacchini v. Scripps-Howard Broadcasting Co., 351 N.E.2d 454 (Ohio 1976), *rev'd on other grounds*, 433 U.S. 562 (1977). Some commentators suggest that because the subject matter of copyright and publicity rights are different — "expression" as opposed to "identity" — there is no overlap between the two, and cases suggesting such overlap are mislabeling the legal theories involved. *See* McCarthy, The Rights of Publicity and Privacy § 5.45, 5.46. Under this argument, *Zacchini*, involving the news broadcast of a 15-second human cannonball act, is not really a right of publicity right case at all, but a mislabeled common-law copyright case. *See also* Melville B. Nimmer & David Nimmer, Nimmer on Copyright §§ 1.01[B], 2.12, 2.13.

[421] *See* §§ 1D[3][c][iii] and 6G[4][c][ii]. For a discussion of the fixation requirement, see § 4C[2], above.

[422] The authoritative contemporary work is J. Thomas McCarthy, The Rights of Publicity and Privacy (2d ed. 2010).

[423] Samuel H. Hofstadter & George Horowitz, The Right to Privacy 9 (1964).

[424] Samuel Warren & Louis Brandeis, *The Right to Privacy*, 4 Harv. L. Rev. 193, 195 (1890).

[425] 171 N.Y. 538, 64 N.E. 442 (1902).

[426] 64 N.E. at 447.

[427] This statute, as amended, is now codified at N.Y. Civ. Rights Law §§ 50–51.

In *Pavesich v. New England Life Insurance Co.*,[428] the Georgia Supreme Court became the first court in the United States to recognize a common-law right of privacy, in a case involving unauthorized use of the plaintiff's photograph and a false testimonial in an advertisement.

In the ensuing years, other courts divided. Those courts following *Pavesich* viewed violation of the right of privacy as a personal tort in which the injury was the damage "to an individual's self respect in being made a public spectacle."[429] Accordingly, courts awarded damages only for mental anguish. Some courts refused to find injury when an advertiser used a celebrity's name or photograph without authority, reasoning that because celebrities seek publicity, they cannot be harmed by additional, albeit unauthorized, publicity.[430]

In *Haelan Laboratories, Inc. v. Topps Chewing Gum Inc.*, the Second Circuit rejected the limited mental anguish view and predicted under the *Erie* doctrine that New York would recognize a common-law property right in a person's identity, calling it "the right of publicity."[431] The following year, Melville Nimmer wrote an influential article highlighting the deficiencies of traditional privacy and trademark laws in protecting the commercial interest of individuals in their identities.[432] The right of publicity right received additional legitimacy in 1960 when William Prosser included as the fourth of his four privacy torts: "Appropriation, for the defendant's advantage, of the plaintiff's name or likeness."[433]

During the 1960s and 1970s, many other courts and legislatures recognized rights of publicity, either as a separate cause of action, or as part of a broader privacy right. Publicity rights became firmly entrenched in American jurisprudence with *Zacchini v. Scripps-Howard Broadcasting Co.*,[434] the only Supreme Court case involving the right of publicity. *Zacchini* involved an unauthorized broadcast of Zacchini's 15-second "human cannonball" act on a local television news program, rather than the more typical situation of unauthorized use of a name or likeness in advertising or merchandising.[435] The Court held that the First Amendment did not permit the station to broadcast Zacchini's "entire act" and discussed some of the rationales for recognizing a right of publicity.[436]

Ironically, in 1984 the New York Court of Appeals (the highest court in New York) rejected *Haelan Laboratories*, holding that there is no common-law right of publicity in New York (although it also held that the New York right of privacy

---

[428] Pavesich v. New England Life Insurance Co., 50 S.E. 68 (Ga. 1905).

[429] Edward Bloustein, *Privacy as an Aspect of Human Dignity: An Answer to Dean Prosser*, 39 N.Y.U. L. Rev. 962, 981 (1964).

[430] *See, e.g.*, O'Brien v. Pabst Sales Co., 124 F.2d 167 (5th Cir. 1941).

[431] 202 F.2d 866, 868 (2d Cir. 1953).

[432] Melville B. Nimmer, *The Right of Publicity*, 19 Law & Contemp. Probs. 203 (1954).

[433] Prosser, *Privacy*, 48 Calif. L. Rev. 383, 389 (1960). The Second Restatement of Torts also included the four Prosser privacy torts. Restatement (Second) of Torts §§ 652A–652I (1977).

[434] 433 U.S. 562 (1977).

[435] As noted in § 6G[1], *Zacchini* arguably is not a publicity right case, but a common-law copyright case.

[436] 433 U.S. at 575–78.

statute covered celebrities as well as non-celebrities).[437] By that time, however, the right of publicity was firmly implanted in the law of several states. It received a further boost that same year when California enacted an influential statute recognizing a post-mortem right of publicity.[438] The right of publicity is also recognized in the *Restatement (Third) of Unfair Competition*, which states simply that "One who appropriates the commercial value of a person's identity by using without consent the person's name, likeness, or other indicia of identity for purposes of trade is subject to liability."[439]

[3]   Rights

Rights of publicity grant an individual exclusive control over the commercial use of his or her identity.[440] The subject matter of publicity rights can include any element that identifies a person, such as name, likeness, voice, performing style, or signature. In a given case, an identity element's protectability turns on whether the element in fact identifies the individual.[441]

[a]   Names

Any name by which a person is known to the public is protectable, including a single name,[442] a nickname,[443] or a stage name. For example, one court held that the name "Crazylegs," adopted for women's moisturizing shaving gel, sufficiently identified football player Elroy "Crazylegs" Hirsch.[444] Because many persons have the same name, a plaintiff must show more than that the defendant used his name. Rather, plaintiff must show from the use's context that he was identifiable. For example, one court held that a fictional policeman named "T.J. Hooker," did not refer to plaintiff T.J. Hooker, a woodcarver.[445] However, modifying a name — for example, using "Charlie Aplin" instead of "Charlie Chaplin" — will not shield a

---

[437] Stephano v. News Group Publications, Inc., 474 N.E.2d 580 (N.Y. 1984).

[438] The California post-mortem publicity statute is now codified at Cal. Civ. Code § 3344.1.

[439] *See* Restatement (Third) of Unfair Competition § 46 (1995).

[440] Some decisions hold that only "celebrities" have publicity rights, *see, e.g.*, Curran v. Amazon.com, Inc., 86 U.S.P.Q.2d 1784 (S.D.W.V. 2008); People for the Ethical Treatment of Animals v. Berosini, 895 P.2d 1269, 1283–85 (Nev. 1995); but the majority of courts recognize publicity rights for non-celebrities as well. McCarthy, The Rights of Publicity and Privacy § 4.16. Several decisions extend publicity right protection to music groups. *See, e.g.*, Bi-Rite Enterprises, Inc. v. Button Master, 555 F. Supp. 1188 (S.D.N.Y. 1983). To date, neither courts nor legislatures have recognized a publicity right in animals, corporations or institutions. McCarthy, §§ 4.36, 4.39. Institutions, such as universities and companies, can use trademark, unfair competition, and dilution principles to attempt to suppress unauthorized use of their names and symbols. *See* §§ 5F, 5G, above.

[441] The number of people who identify plaintiff from the use has no bearing on whether the use identifies the plaintiff: "the question is whether the figure is recognizable, not the number of people who recognized it." Negri v. Schering Corp., 333 F. Supp. 101, 104 (S.D.N.Y. 1971). The number of people that could identify plaintiff does influence the amount of damages awarded. *Id.*

[442] *See, e.g.*, Cher v. Forum Int'l Ltd., 692 F.2d 634 (9th Cir. 1982).

[443] *See, e.g.*, McFarland v. Miller, 14 F.3d 912 (3d Cir. 1994) (child actor "Spanky" McFarland). Some courts have found that the New York statute protects only names, not nicknames. *See, e.g.*, Geisel v. Poynter Prods., Inc., 295 F. Supp. 331, 355–56 (S.D.N.Y. 1968) (pen name "Dr. Seuss").

[444] Hirsch v. S.C. Johnson & Sons, Inc., 280 N.W.2d 129 (Wisc. 1979).

[445] Hooker v. Columbia Pictures Indus., Inc., 551 F. Supp. 1060 (N.D. Ill. 1982).

defendant if the plaintiff is still identifiable from the modified use.[446]

In *Carson v. Here's Johnny Portable Toilets, Inc.*, the court held that the defendant's use of the phrase "Here's Johnny!" identified television host Johnny Carson, who was introduced with the phrase every night on the Tonight Show.[447] Defendant admitted "that the public tends to associate the words 'Johnny Carson' [and] the words 'Here's Johnny' with plaintiff," and it used the slogan "The World's Foremost Commodian" to emphasize the connection.[448] In dicta, however, the court suggested that Carson would *not* have been identified by his full legal name, John William Carson, or by the variations J. William Carson or J.W. Carson.[449]

[b]   Likenesses

A person's likeness — his or her facial and other physical features — is protected against unauthorized use, whether by photograph,[450] drawing,[451] or celebrity look-alike.[452]

Identifiability is less of a problem with photographs than with names because facial and physical features are more distinctive than names, but it can be an issue with drawings and photographs that do not include the plaintiff's face.[453] In *Motschenbacher v. R.J. Reynolds Tobacco Co.*, the court held that race-car driver Lothar Motschenbacher was identifiable from the distinctive appearance of his race car, even though his face was not visible;[454] and in *Newcombe v. Adolf Coors Co.*, the court held there was a triable issue of fact whether former baseball pitcher Don Newcombe was "readily identifiable" from his pitching stance, as depicted in a drawing based on an actual photograph of Newcombe.[455]

More controversial was the holding in *White v. Samsung Electronics America, Inc.*, in which a robot wearing a blond wig, evening gown, and jewels was depicted standing next to the "Wheel of Fortune" game board.[456] The majority held that the robot was *not* a "likeness" of Wheel of Fortune hostess Vanna White under the California statute,[457] but it held that "the common law right of publicity is not so

---

[446] Chaplin v. Amador, 269 P. 544 (Cal. 1928).

[447] 698 F.2d 831, 835–36 (6th Cir. 1983).

[448] *Id.* at 836.

[449] *Id.* at 837.

[450] Grant v. Esquire, Inc., 367 F. Supp. 876 (S.D.N.Y. 1973) (photograph of actor Cary Grant).

[451] Ali v. Playgirl, Inc., 447 F. Supp. 723 (S.D.N.Y. 1978) (drawing of boxer Muhammad Ali).

[452] Allen v. National Video, Inc., 610 F. Supp. 612 (S.D.N.Y. 1985) (look-alike of actor Woody Allen); Onassis v. Christian Dior-New York, Inc., 472 N.Y.S.2d 254 (1984), *aff'd without opinion*, 110 A.D.2d 1095 (N.Y. App. Div. 1985) (look-alike of former First Lady Jacqueline Kennedy Onassis).

[453] *See, e.g.*, Cohen v. Herbal Concepts, Inc., 100 A.D.2d 175 (N.Y. App. Div.), *aff'd*, 472 N.E.2d 307 (N.Y. 1984) (photograph of plaintiff's nude back).

[454] 498 F.2d 821, 826–27 (9th Cir. 1974).

[455] 157 F.3d 686, 692–93 (9th Cir. 1998). The court borrowed the "readily identifiable" standard from Cal. Civ. Code § 3344(b), which applies to photographs.

[456] 971 F.2d 1395, 1396 (9th Cir. 1992), *reh'g en banc denied*, 989 F.2d 1512 (9th Cir. 1993) (Kozinski, J., joined by O'Scannlain & Kleinfeld, JJ., dissenting). The robot is shown at 989 F.2d at 1523.

[457] 971 F.2d at 1397 (citing Cal. Civ. Code § 3344(a)).

confined," and that White had alleged sufficient facts to show that the defendant's had appropriated her "identity."[458] Dissenting from denial of rehearing *en banc*, Judge Kozinski accused the majority of "creating a new and much broader property right" by giving White "an exclusive right to *anything that reminds the viewer of her.*"[459]

[c] Roles

A role with which an actor is closely identified can be the subject of a publicity right, especially if it is a "self-created" and consistent persona, such as Charlie Chaplin's "Little Tramp,"[460] Laurel and Hardy,[461] or the Marx Brothers.[462] A more difficult issue is presented by fictional roles in copyrighted works, especially roles that have been played by more than one actor over time. In *Wendt v. Host International, Inc.*, the court held that two robots depicting the characters "Norm" and "Cliff" from the TV series "Cheers" sufficiently resembled actors George Wendt and John Ratzenberger to be actionable;[463] and in *Lugosi v. Universal Pictures*, a majority of the judges to address the issue agreed with the trial court's finding that "Universal did not license the use of an undifferentiated Count Dracula character, but the distinctive and readily recognizable portrayal of Lugosi as the notorious Transylvanian count."[464]

[d] Voice and Vocal Imitations

Some state statutes grant an individual a publicity right in his or her "voice," but these statutes have been interpreted to prevent unauthorized use of the actual voice, not imitations.[465] Nonetheless, in *Midler v. Ford Motor Co.*, the Ninth Circuit held that "when a distinctive voice of a professional singer is widely known and is deliberately imitated in order to sell a product, the sellers have appropriated what is not theirs and have committed a tort in California."[466]

---

[458] *Id.* at 1397–99.

[459] 989 F.2d at 1515 (Kozinski, J, dissenting) (emphasis in original).

[460] Chaplin v. Amador, 269 P. 544 (Cal. 1928).

[461] Price v. Hal Roach Studios, Inc., 400 F. Supp. 836 (S.D.N.Y. 1975).

[462] Groucho Marx Prod., Inc. v. Day & Night Co., 523 F. Supp. 485, 491 (S.D.N.Y. 1981), *rev'd on other grounds*, 689 F.2d 317 (2d Cir. 1982).

[463] 125 F.3d 806, 810–11 (9th Cir. 1997), *reh'g en banc denied*, 197 F.3d 1284 (9th Cir. 1999) (Kozinski, J., joined by Kleinfeld & Tashima, JJ., dissenting). Judge Kozinski's dissenting opinion focused on the conflict between the actors and the copyright holder, who owned the rights to the characters, saying "it is impossible to recreate the character without evoking the image of the actor in the minds of viewers." 197 F.3d at 1286.

[464] 603 P.2d 425, 445 (Cal. 1979) (Bird, C.J., joined by Tobriner & Manuel, JJ., dissenting). *But see* 603 P.2d at 432 (Mosk, J., concurring) ("Merely playing a role . . . creates no inheritable property right in an actor, absent a contract so providing."). A plurality did not reach the issue, holding that California did not recognize a post-mortem right of publicity at common law. 602 P.2d at 430. That holding is still good law; but five years later, the California legislature enacted a statutory post-mortem right of publicity. *See* Cal. Civ. Code § 3344.1.

[465] Midler v. Ford Motor Co., 849 F.2d 460, 463 (9th Cir. 1988).

[466] *Id. See also* Waits v. Frito-Lay, Inc., 978 F.2d 1093, 1099–1100 (9th Cir. 1992) (reaffirming *Midler*); Lahr v. Adell Chemical Co., 300 F.2d 256, 259 (1st Cir. 1962) (deliberate imitation of distinctive speaking voice is unfair competition under Massachusetts law). *But see* Sinatra v. Goodyear Tire & Rubber Co.,

Some courts have also held celebrity impersonators may violate the right of publicity outside the context of advertising. In *Estate of Presley v. Russen*, the court enjoined presentation of "The Big El Show," a 90-minute concert featuring an actor impersonating Elvis Presley;[467] and in *Groucho Marx Prods. v. Day & Night Co.*, the district court held that a non-biographical play in which actors imitated the Marx Brothers violated their rights of publicity.[468] Another district court, however, held that a biographical play about singer Janis Joplin, which included a concert performance as the second act, was exempt under California law.[469] Nevada has a specific statutory exception for celebrity impersonators, "except where the use is directly connected with commercial sponsorship."[470]

[4] Infringement and Defenses

[a] *Prima Facie* Case

Publicity right infringement consists of defendant making a commercial use of some element of plaintiff's identity without authorization in such a way that plaintiff is identifiable from defendant's use.[471] In some states, the right is even broader: any unauthorized use of the plaintiff's identity "to defendant's advantage, commercially or otherwise," may be a violation.[472] The "core" types of infringing conduct are use of the defendant's identity in advertising and in merchandising.[473] However, the scope of potential violations is so broad that often the only real limitation on the right of publicity is the First Amendment's guarantee of freedom of expression.

Courts typically have *not* included intent to identify plaintiff as a necessary element of a *prima facie* case.[474] The California statute does require that defendant "knowingly" make use of plaintiff's identity for an infringement to occur;[475] but this statute supplements, rather than supersedes, the common-law action, which does not require knowledge.[476] In Missouri, the plaintiff does not need to show that the defendant intended to injure or that it actually derived a commercial advantage;

---

435 F.2d 711, 716–18 (9th Cir. 1970) (dismissing claim of unfair competition where singer alleged that copyrighted song had become so identified with her that any use of it evoked her identity).

[467] 513 F. Supp. 1339 (D.N.J. 1981).

[468] 523 F. Supp. 485, 491 (S.D.N.Y. 1981), *rev'd on other grounds*, 689 F.2d 317 (2d Cir. 1982). The Second Circuit reversed the ruling on the ground that California law applied, and that California did not recognize a post-mortem right of publicity at common law. Ironically, today California has a statutory post-mortem right of publicity, while New York's statutory right (which is exclusive) does not apply to deceased people.

[469] Joplin Enterprises v. Allen, 795 F. Supp. 349 (W.D. Wash. 1992).

[470] 52 Rev. Stat. Nev. § 597.790(2)(d).

[471] McCarthy, The Rights of Publicity and Privacy § 3.2.

[472] *See, e.g.*, Eastwood v. Superior Court, 149 Cal. App. 3d 409 (1983).

[473] *See, e.g.*, Cal. Civ. Code § 3344(a) ("on or in products, merchandise, or goods, or for purposes of advertising or selling, or soliciting purchases of, products, merchandise, goods or services").

[474] *See, e.g.*, Welch v. Mr. Christmas, Inc., 440 N.E.2d 1317, 1319 (1982) ("Knowledge is not an element of the cause of action for compensatory damages or injunctive relief under the [New York] statute.").

[475] Cal. Civ. Code § 3344(a). The use need not be "knowing" to violate a publicity right relating to a deceased person. Cal. Civ. Code § 3344.1(a).

[476] *See* Eastwood v. Superior Court, 149 Cal. App. 3d 409 (1983).

instead, the plaintiff must show "the defendant's intent or purpose to obtain a commercial benefit from use of the plaintiff's identity."[477] However, where the use would otherwise be newsworthy and protected speech, it is necessary to show that the defendant knew the information was false or acted with reckless disregard as to its truth or falsity.[478]

Even where intent is not an element of a *prima facie* case, it can be probative of the fact that plaintiff is identifiable from the use.[479] Proof of knowledge or intent is needed to support an award of punitive damages.[480]

In some states, knowledge may be required in order for secondary infringers — those who merely print or publish the infringing material — to be held liable.[481] Likewise, section 230 of the Communications Decency Act expressly provides that, in most cases, Internet service providers are not liable for information provided by others.[482] Section 230 contains an exception for "any law pertaining to intellectual property";[483] however, the Ninth Circuit has held that this exception applies only to federal intellectual property, and not state rights of publicity.[484] Other courts have disagreed, holding that the exception covers state rights of publicity as well.[485]

[b]   Newsworthiness

In order to avoid conflicts with the First Amendment, most states have an express exception for news reporting,[486] or else they construe their statutes narrowly to exclude newsworthy information. For example, in *Messenger v. Gruner + Jahr Printing & Publishing*, the New York Court of Appeals held that use "for advertising purposes or for purposes of trade" under the New York statute does not include "reports of newsworthy events or matters of public interest," even if the plaintiff's photograph creates a false impression, as long as there is "a real relationship between the article and the photograph" and the article is not "an advertisement in disguise."[487] The "newsworthiness" exception in New York is

---

[477] Doe v. TCI Cablevision, 110 S.W.3d 363, 370–71 (Mo. 2003).

[478] *See* § 6G[4][b].

[479] *See, e.g.,* Carson v. Here's Johnny Portable Toilets, Inc., 698 F.2d 831, 836 (6th Cir. 1983).

[480] *See* § 6G[5], below.

[481] *See, e.g.,* Cal. Civ. Code §§ 3344(f), 3344.1(l); Tenn. Code § 47-25-1107(c); Cabaniss v. Hipsley, 151 S.E.2d 496, 506–07 (Ga. Ct. App. 1966).

[482] 47 U.S.C. § 230(c)(1) ("No provider or use of an interactive computer service shall be treated as the publisher or speaker of any information provided by another information content provider.").

[483] 47 U.S.C. § 230(e)(2).

[484] Perfect 10, Inc. v. CCBill, LLC, 488 F.3d 1102, 1118–19 (9th Cir. 2007).

[485] *See* Atlantic Recording Corp. v. Project Playlist, Inc., 603 F. Supp. 690, 704 (S.D.N.Y. 2009); Doe v. Friendfinder Network, Inc., 540 F. Supp. 2d 288, 302 (D.N.H. 2008).

[486] *See, e.g.,* Cal. Civ. Code § 3344(d) (exempting "any news, public affairs, or sports broadcast or account, or any political campaign"); § 3344.1(j) (same). *See also* Neb. Rev. Stat. § 597.790(2)(c); Tenn. Code § 47-25-1107(a).

[487] 727 N.E.2d 549, 552–53 (N.Y. 2000); *see also* Tyne v. Time Warner Entertainment Co., 901 So.2d 802, 810 (Fla. 2005) (statute prohibiting use "for purposes of trade or for any commercial or advertising purpose" "does not apply to publications, including motion pictures, which do not directly promote a product or service.").

construed broadly; for example, it has been held that a photo of plaintiff wearing a "bomber jacket" designed by Giorgio Armani, accompanied by a column listing the price of the jacket and where it could be purchased, was not an "advertisement in disguise" because no consideration was paid for the column or photo.[488]

Nonetheless, it is clear that the First Amendment does not automatically immunize any uses of newsworthy information. In *Zacchini v. Scripps-Howard Broadcasting Co.*,[489] the Supreme Court held that the First Amendment did not require a state to dismiss a suit to recover damages for an unauthorized television news broadcast of the plaintiff's entire 15-second "human cannonball" act. The court reasoned that "[t]he broadcast of a film of petitioner's entire act poses a substantial threat to the economic value of that performance," and that "the Constitution does not prevent Ohio from . . . deciding to protect the entertainer's incentive in order to encourage the production of this type of work."[490] The Court also held that the "actual malice" standard applicable to cases of defamation and false-light privacy did not apply.[491]

In *Eastwood v. Superior Court*,[492] actor Clint Eastwood alleged that the supposedly newsworthy information printed about him in the National Enquirer was not news because it was false, and therefore it was simply commercial exploitation in disguise. Distinguishing *Zacchini*, the court held that where the action requires proof of falsity in order to succeed, then the plaintiff must prove "actual malice," *i.e.*, that the defendant knew that the material was false or acted with reckless disregard as to its truth or falsity.[493] "Actual malice" must be proved by clear and convincing evidence, and on appeal the appellate court must review the evidence *de novo* and "independently decide" whether the evidence is sufficient to meet this standard.[494]

Even uses that might otherwise be seen as "commercial" exploitation may be entitled to a newsworthiness defense. In *C.B.C. Distribution & Marketing, Inc. v. Major League Baseball Advanced Media, L.P.*, the Eighth Circuit held that use of baseball players' names and statistics as part of an online "fantasy baseball" game was protected by the First Amendment;[495] and in *Montana v. San Jose Mercury News*, the court held that a newspaper was entitled to sell a poster-sized reproduction of a newspaper page featuring an artist's rendition of quarterback Joe Montana, "first, because the posters themselves report newsworthy items of public

---

[488] *See* Stephano v. News Group Publications, Inc., 474 N.E.2d 580, 585–86 (N.Y. 1984).

[489] 433 U.S. 562, 578 (1977).

[490] *Id.* at 575–77.

[491] *Id.* at 570–75.

[492] 149 Cal. App. 2d 409 (1983).

[493] 149 Cal. App. 2d at 425–26; *see also* Lerman v. Flynt Distributing Co., 745 F.2d 123, 138–40 (2d Cir. 1984).

[494] *See* Eastwood v. National Enquirer, Inc., 123 F.3d 1249, 1251–52 (9th Cir. 1997); *Lerman*, 745 F.2d at 140–41.

[495] 505 F.3d 818 (8th Cir. 2007). *See also* Gionfriddo v. Major League Baseball, 94 Cal. App. 4th 400, 411 (2001) (names, likenesses, statistics, and performances of former baseball players on MLB website were newsworthy; "the public interest is not limited to current events; the public is also entitled to be entertained and informed about our history.").

interest; and second, because a newspaper has a constitutional right to promote itself by reproducing its originally protected articles or photographs."[496]

[c]   First Amendment

Use of a celebrity likeness in an advertisement often does not raise any First Amendment issues, because "commercial speech" (i.e., speech that "does no more than propose a commercial transaction") is entitled to lesser protection under the First Amendment.[497] Courts have also given short shrift to arguments that celebrity merchandise violates the First Amendment,[498] even though the content of the speech (a photograph or likeness) would be protected in other contexts. More recently, courts have reached differing views on whether and when the First Amendment shields the use of celebrity likenesses against liability under state law.

[i]   Works of Art

In *Comedy III Prods., Inc. v. Gary Saderup, Inc.*, the California Supreme Court held that lithographs, prints, posters, and t-shirts bearing a reproduction of defendant's charcoal drawing of the Three Stooges violated the California right of publicity statute and were not shielded from liability by the First Amendment.[499] Although the court held that the portraits were fully protected speech rather than commercial speech,[500] it nonetheless held that "when artistic expression takes the form of a literal depiction or imitation of a celebrity for commercial gain," then the right of publicity "outweighs the expressive interests of the imitative artist."[501] However, when a work is "transformative" within the meaning of the Supreme Court's opinion in *Campbell v. Acuff Rose Music, Inc.*,[502] such as "works of parody or other distortions of a the celebrity figure," then the First Amendment "outweighs whatever interest the state may have in enforcing the right of publicity."[503] The court also suggested that "courts may find useful a subsidiary inquiry": whether "the marketability and economic value of the challenged work derive primary from the fame of the celebrity depicted" or "from the creativity, skill, and reputation of the artist."[504]

---

[496] 34 Cal. App. 4th 790, 797 (1995). *See also* Namath v. Sports Illustrated, 48 A.D.2d 487 (N.Y. App. Div. 1975).

[497] *See* White v. Samsung Electronics America, Inc., 971 F.2d 1395, 1400 & n.3 (9th Cir. 1992), *reh'g en banc denied*, 989 F.2d 1512 (9th Cir. 1993) (Kozinski, J., joined by O'Scannlain & Kleinfeld, JJ., dissenting) (criticizing the majority for failing to apply the Supreme Court's *Central Hudson* test); *cf.* Central Hudson Gas & Elec. Corp. v. Public Serv. Comm'n, 447 U.S. 557 (1980).

[498] *See, e.g.*, Brinkley v. Casablancas, 80 A.D.2d 428, 43234 (N.Y. App. Div. 1981) (poster of model Christie Brinkley); Factors Etc., Inc. v. Pro Arts, Inc., 579 F.2d 215, 222 (2d Cir. 1978) (poster of Elvis Presley), *overruled on other grounds*, 652 F.2d 278 (2d Cir. 1981); Lugosi v. Universal Pictures, 603 P.2d 425, 449 (Cal. 1979) (Bird, C.J., joined by Tobriner & Manuel, dissenting) (merchandise featuring Lugosi as Dracula is not protected by First Amendment; majority did not reach the issue).

[499] 21 P.3d 797 (Cal. 2001).

[500] 21 P.3d at 802, 804, 810.

[501] 21 P.3d at 808.

[502] 510 U.S. 569, 579 (1994). *See* § 4J[1] (discussing the role of "transformative" in copyright fair use).

[503] *Saderup*, 21 P.3d at 808.

[504] 21 P.3d at 810.

In contrast, in *ETW Corp. v. Jireh Publishing, Inc.*, the Sixth Circuit held that limited-edition prints of a painting of golfer Tiger Woods by sports artist Rick Rush were protected by the First Amendment.[505] The court borrowed a test from *Rogers v. Grimaldi*,[506] which concerned a movie titled "Ginger and Fred" that was not about famed dancing duo Gingers Rogers and Fred Astaire, but was instead about "two fictional Italian cabaret performers who imitated Rogers and Astaire."[507] The *Rogers* court held that allegedly misleading titles using a celebrity's name were protected "unless the title has no artistic relevance to the underlying work . . . [or] unless the title explicitly misleads as to the source or content of the work."[508] The *ETW* court held that Rush's print satisfied this standard, and also contained "significant transformative elements" under the *Saderup* test.[509]

[ii]   Parody and Satire

In *White v. Samsung Electronics America, Inc.*, Samsung was sued by TV game-show hostess Vanna White when it published an advertisement for its VCRs featuring a robot dressed in a blond wig, evening gown, and jewelry standing next to the "Wheel of Fortune" game board. The panel majority summarily rejected a First Amendment defense, primarily because the ad was commercial speech.[510] Dissenting from denial of rehearing *en banc*, Judge Kozinski took the panel to task for failing to apply the Supreme Court's *Central Hudson* test,[511] which asks whether a speech restriction is "narrowly tailored" to and "directly advances" a "substantial state interest."[512]

Four years later, in *Cardtoons L.C. v. Major League Baseball Players Ass'n*, the Tenth Circuit held that parody baseball cards that lampooned familiar baseball players were protected by the First Amendment.[513] The court rejected an analogy to *Lloyd Corp. v. Tanner*, in which the Supreme Court held that protesters were not entitled to use real property belonging to another as long as there were "adequate alternative avenues of expression."[514] Instead, the court balanced "the importance of Cardtoons' right to free expression and the consequences of limiting that right" against "the effect of infringing on MLBPA's right of publicity."[515] The court then systematically evaluated seven different rationales for the right of publicity, finding most of them unpersuasive and all of them weaker in the context

---

[505] 332 F.3d 915, 924–25 (6th Cir. 2003).

[506] 875 F.2d 994 (2d Cir. 1989).

[507] *ETW*, 332 F.3d at 926.

[508] *Rogers*, 875 F.2d at 999. *See also* RESTATEMENT (THIRD) OF UNFAIR COMPETITION § 47, cmt. c (1995).

[509] *ETW*, 332 F.3d at 937–38.

[510] 971 F.2d 1395, 1400 & n.3 (9th Cir. 1992), *reh'g en banc denied*, 989 F.2d 1512 (9th Cir. 1993) (Kozinski, J., joined by O'Scannlain & Kleinfeld, JJ., dissenting).

[511] *See* Central Hudson Gas & Elec. Corp. v. Public Serv. Comm'n, 447 U.S. 557 (1980).

[512] *White*, 989 F.2d at 1519–21 (Kozinski, J., joined by O'Scannlain & Kleinfeld, JJ., dissenting).

[513] 95 F.3d 959 (10th Cir. 1996).

[514] 407 U.S. 551, 567 (1972).

[515] *Cardtoons*, 95 F.3d at 972.

of parody than in other contexts.[516] The court also expressly rejected *White*,[517] and relied instead on the Supreme Court's subsequent decision in *Campbell v. Acuff-Rose Music, Inc.*, which held that parody could qualify for the "fair use" defense to copyright law.[518]

In *Winter v. DC Comics*, the California Supreme Court unanimously held that defendants were entitled to summary judgment under the *Saderup* standard when they published comic books that depicted the plaintiffs, rock musicians Johnny and Edgar Winter, as "villainous half-worm, half-human offspring . . . who engage in wanton acts of violence, murder and bestiality for pleasure."[519] The court held the comic books "are not just convention depictions of plaintiffs but . . . are distorted for purposes of lampoon, parody, or caricature."[520]

In contrast, in *Doe v. TCI Cablevision*, the Missouri Supreme Court held that the comic book *Spawn* violated the Missouri right of publicity by using the name of professional hockey player Tony Twist as the name for a fictional mafia Don and was not protected by the First Amendment.[521] The principal defendant, author Todd McFarlane, denied that the comic book character was "about" the real-life Twist (perhaps to avoid a defamation claim), and the plaintiffs introduced evidence that *Spawn* merchandise was marketed to hockey fans.[522] Rejecting the "relatedness" test of *Rogers* and the "transformative" test of *Saderup*, the court instead applied a "predominant use" test that asks whether the predominant purpose of the product is to "exploit the commercial value of an individual's identity" or "to make an expressive comment on or about a celebrity."[523]

[iii]   Other Uses

As a practical matter, traditional expressive works, such as movies, books, and plays, receive greater First Amendment protection than do "nontraditional" media such as t-shirts and coffee mugs.[524] Courts have almost uniformly held that the First Amendment protects traditional works about celebrities, whether truthful biographies,[525] dramatized "docudramas,"[526] or even pure works of fiction.[527] The

---

[516] *Id.* at 973–76.

[517] *Id.* at 970–72.

[518] 510 U.S. 569 (1994). *See* § 4J[1] (discussing fair use).

[519] 69 P.3d 473, 476 (Cal. 2003).

[520] 69 P.3d at 479.

[521] 110 S.W.3d 363 (Mo. 2003).

[522] *Id.* at 367.

[523] *Id.* at 374.

[524] *See* McCarthy, Rights of Publicity and Privacy §§ 7.22, 7.24.

[525] *See, e.g.*, Frosch v. Grosset & Dunlap, Inc., 75 A.D.2d 768 (N.Y. App. Div. 1980) (biography of Marilyn Monroe); Rosemont Enterprises, Inc. v. Random House, Inc., 58 Misc. 2d 1 (N.Y. Sup. Ct. 1968), *aff'd without opinion*, 32 A.D.2d 892 (N.Y. App. Div. 1969) (biography of Howard Hughes).

[526] *See, e.g.*, Tyne v. Time Warner Entertainment Co., 901 So.2d 802 (Fla. 2005) (fishermen depicted in movie *The Perfect Storm*); Taylor v. National Broadcasting Co., 22 Media L. Rep. 2433 (Cal. Super. Ct. 1980) (miniseries about life of actress Elizabeth Taylor).

[527] *See, e.g.*, Guglielmi v. Spelling-Goldberg Prods., 603 P.2d 454 (Cal. 1979) (Bird, C.J., joined by Tobriner, Manuel, & Newman, concurring) (TV movie entitled *Valentino: A Romantic Fiction*); Hicks v.

sole exception is fiction that is presented as truthful, which is subject to the "actual malice" standard applicable to defamation claims.[528]

This dichotomy leaves cases involving "new media" to be classified in one category or the other. In *Hoffman v. Capital Cities/ABC, Inc.*, the court held that a still photo of actor Dustin Hoffman in drag from the movie "Tootsie," digitally altered to make it appear he was wearing a modern evening gown, was protected by the First Amendment.[529] Bizarrely, the court applied the "actual malice" standard to what was admittedly a digitally modified work; but instead of inquiring whether the defendant knew the portrayal was false, the court asked whether it "knew (or purposefully avoided knowing) that the photograph would mislead its readers" into thinking that Hoffman had actually participated in the manipulation[530] — a strange amalgamation of the "actual malice" standard and the likelihood of confusion standard for false endorsement.

A series of recent cases has raised the issue of whether athlete likenesses may be used in video games depicting real college and professional teams. In two cases, courts have held that the *Saderup* "transformative use" standard should be applied to right of publicity claims; and they concluded that the games were not protected by the First Amendment, because the athletes were depicted playing the same sports and the same positions as they did in real life.[531] In a companion case, however, the Ninth Circuit held that the *Rogers* standard should be applied to claims based on section 43(a) of the Lanham Act; and it dismissed such a claim under the First Amendment because the athlete's depiction had "artistic relevance" to the game.[532] Similar claims have been raised by professional singers depicted in video games, with varying results.[533]

[d]   Other Defenses

[i]   Copyright Preemption

Section 301(a) of the Copyright Act[534] preempts state law rights of publicity if a work is fixed in a tangible medium of expression, the work comes within the subject matter of copyright, and the state law grants rights in the work that are

---

Casablanca Records, 464 F. Supp. 426 (S.D.N.Y. 1978) (fictional novel inspired by real-life 11-day disappearance of mystery writer Agatha Christie).

[528] *See, e.g.*, Spahn v. Julian Messner, Inc., 233 N.E.2d 840 (N.Y. 1967) (fictional biography of pitcher Warren Spahn). *See* § 6G[4][b], above.

[529] 255 F.3d 1180 (9th Cir. 2001). The photo was one a series of photos from famous movies, digitally altered to substitute current fashions.

[530] *Id.* at 1187–89.

[531] *See* Hart v. Electronic Arts, Inc., 717 F.3d 141 (3d Cir. 2013); *In re* Student-Athlete Name & Likeness Licensing Litigation (Keller v. Electronic Arts, Inc.), 724 F.3d 1268 (9th Cir. 2013).

[532] *See* Brown v. Electronic Arts, Inc., 724 F.3d 1235 (9th Cir. 2013).

[533] *See* Kirby v. Sega of America, Inc., 144 Cal. App. 4th 47 (2006) (assuming space-age character was based on plaintiff, significant differences in physique, hairstyle, costume, and dance moves rendered character "transformative"); No Doubt v. Activision Pub'g, Inc., 192 Cal. App. 4th 1018 (2011) (literal recreations of band members were not "transformative," even though they could be made to perform different songs in fanciful locales).

[534] 17 U.S.C. § 301(a).

"equivalent" to rights in the Copyright Act.[535]

Unfortunately, the state of the law with regard to copyright preemption of publicity rights claims is a confused mess. Where the basis of the claim is merely the reproduction of a copyrighted work, and the person's likeness was fixed in the work with authorization, such claims are usually (but not always) held preempted.[536] However, where the basis of the claim is the use of a person's likeness or identity for advertising purposes, the claim is typically *not* preempted,[537] even though right of publicity claims do not require any showing of false endorsement or likelihood of confusion. Some courts have held that right of publicity claims are not preempted because the subject matter of the claim, the "name or likeness" of a person (or, more broadly, his or her "persona") is not "fixed,"[538] even when it is embodied in a copyrighted work, such as a photo.[539] This rationale is overbroad, because it would preclude preemption of any right of publicity claim.[540] Other courts have held, more sensibly, that the rights involved are not "equivalent" when the photo is being used to advertise an unrelated product.[541]

[ii]   First Sale Doctrine

The first-sale doctrine, which limits federal patent, copyright, and trademark rights, likewise applies to state-law rights of publicity. Thus, when a celebrity likeness has lawfully been incorporated into merchandise, that merchandise can be re-sold without violating the celebrity's right of publicity.[542] For example, trading cards may be mounted on plaques (even plaques with clocks) and re-sold; but the cards may not be used to advertise a separate product in a manner that would create a false impression of celebrity endorsement of the product.[543]

---

[535] For a discussion of copyright preemption generally, *see* § 1D[3][c].

[536] *See, e.g.*, Jules Jordan Video, Inc. v. 144942 Canada Inc., 617 F.3d 1146, 1153–55 (9th Cir. 2010) (reproduction of DVD); Laws v. Sony Music Entertainment, Inc., 448 F.3d 1134, 1139–45 (9th Cir. 2006) (reproduction of sound recording); Baltimore Orioles, Inc. v. Major League Baseball Players Ass'n, 805 F.2d 663, 674–79 (7th Cir. 1986) (telecasts of baseball games); Fleet v. CBS, Inc., 50 Cal. App. 4th 1911, 1919–21 (1996) (distribution of motion picture).

[537] *See, e.g.*, Toney v. L'Oreal USA, Inc., 406 F.3d 905, 910 (7th Cir. 2005); Downing v. Abercrombie & Fitch, 265 F.3d 994, 1003–04 (9th Cir. 2001); Brown v. Ames, 201 F.3d 654, 657–59 (5th Cir. 2000); Waits v. Frito-Lay, Inc., 978 F.2d 1093, 1100 (9th Cir. 1992) (claim based on imitation of celebrity's distinctive voice in advertisement was not preempted); Midler v. Ford Motor Co., 849 F.2d 460, 462 (9th Cir. 1988) (same).

[538] *See Midler*, 849 F.2d at 462.

[539] *See Toney*, 406 F.3d at 910; *Downing*, 265 F.3d at 1000–04.

[540] *But see* Facenda v. NFL Films, Inc., 542 F.3d 1007, 1027–32 (3d Cir. 2008) (dismissing statutory preemption for lack of fixation, but engaging in lengthy "conflict preemption" analysis).

[541] *See, e.g., Toney*, 406 F.3d at 910. *See also Waits*, 978 F.2d at 1100 (elements of distinctive voice and deliberate imitation were sufficiently "different in kind" from copyright infringement).

[542] *See* Allison v. Vintage Sports Plaques, 136 F.3d 1443 (11th Cir. 1998).

[543] *Id.* at 1450–51.

[iii]   Antitrust

Publicity right licensing programs have faced antitrust challenges. The courts and the Federal Trade Commission have held that baseball players' exclusive contracts licensing their identities in connection with baseball cards and chewing gum violated neither Sherman Act Section 1 or Section 2[544] nor Federal Trade Commission Act Section 5.[545]

[iv]   Statute of Limitations and Laches

In many states, courts apply the relatively short (often one- or two-year) libel and invasion of privacy statute of limitations periods to publicity right cases;[546] elsewhere, courts apply the longer "property" torts statute of limitations.[547] For statute of limitations purposes, the cause of action accrues upon the infringing "publication." Under the rule most states follow,[548] any "one edition of a book or newspaper, or any radio or television broadcast, exhibition of a motion picture or similar aggregate communication" constitutes a "single publication."[549] Application of this rule can pose difficulties in particular cases. For example, in *Christoff v. Nestle Corp.*, the California Supreme Court remanded for the lower court to determine whether production over a period of years of labels and multiple advertising campaigns for Taster's Choice coffee, featuring a photo of the plaintiff, constituted a "single publication" or not.[550]

Unreasonable delay in bringing suit may lead to a denial of relief based on the equitable doctrine of laches. For example, in *Miller v. Glenn Miller Prods.*, the court held that where the children of bandleader Glenn Miller had been aware of the allegedly unauthorized sub-licensing and sale of merchandise for over 20 years, a laches defense was appropriate.[551]

[v]   Other Defenses

In a case involving the use of basketball star Kareem Abdul-Jabbar's former name (Lew Alcindor) in a television ad, the Ninth Circuit held that abandonment was *not* a valid defense to either right of publicity or Lanham Act claims involving

---

[544] Fleer Corp. v. Topps Chewing Gum, Inc., 658 F.2d 139 (3d Cir. 1981); Topps Chewing Gum, Inc. v. Fleer Corp., 799 F.2d 851 (2d Cir. 1986); Topps Chewing Gum, Inc. v. Major League Baseball Players Ass'n, 641 F. Supp. 1179 (S.D.N.Y. 1986).

[545] *In re* Topps Chewing Gum, Inc., 67 F.T.C. 744 (1965).

[546] *See, e.g.*, Lugosi v. Universal Pictures, Inc., 603 P.2d 425, 451 (Cal. 1979) (Bird, C.J., joined by Tobriner & Manuel, dissenting); Neb. Rev. Stat. § 20-211 (1987).

[547] Canessa v. J.I. Kislak, Inc., 235 A.2d 62, 65–76 (N.J. Super. Ct. 1967) (applying New Jersey's six-year statute).

[548] *See* Keeton v. Hustler Magazine, Inc., 465 U.S. 770, 777 n.8 (1984); McCarthy, The Rights of Publicity and Privacy §§ 11.20, 11.11.

[549] Uniform Single Publication Act § 1, 14 Uniform Laws Annotated 351 (1980) (in effect in Arizona, California, Idaho, Illinois, New Mexico, North Dakota and Pennsylvania). Only one damages action can be maintained per publication. *Id.*; Restatement (Second) of Torts § 577A(3) (1977).

[550] 213 P.3d 132 (Cal. 2009).

[551] 454 F.3d 975, 996–1000 (9th Cir. 2005).

celebrity names.[552] The court also analyzed and rejected a "nominative fair use" defense to the Lanham Act claim;[553] but by omission it implicitly held that this defense did not apply to a state-law right of publicity claim.

[5]   Remedies

The standard remedy for infringement of the right of publicity is an injunction. Money damages for personal identity infringement are typically inadequate and difficult to measure.[554] However, the U.S. Supreme Court has held that a court may not presume irreparable harm in patent cases; instead, the plaintiff must offer proof of irreparable harm for which monetary damages are inadequate, and show that the balance of hardships and the public interest favor issuance of an injunction.[555] These principles may be applied in publicity rights cases as well.[556]

A preliminary injunction can issue if the plaintiff shows a likelihood of success on the merits and the other factors are in his favor;[557] but a request for one may trigger the rule against prior restraints.[558] Courts have the power to issue extraterritorial or nationwide injunctions,[559] but they should decline to do so in cases in which the conduct may not violate other states' laws.[560]

In addition to an injunction, courts may award damages for violations of the right of publicity. Damages can be awarded for emotional distress,[561] or for commercial loss. Courts use a reasonable royalty or market value test to measure

---

[552] Abdul-Jabbar v. General Motors Co., 85 F.3d 407, 411–12, 415 (9th Cir. 1996).

[553] *Id.* at 412–13.

[554] *See* Ali v. Playgirl, Inc., 447 F. Supp. 723, 729 (S.D.N.Y. 1978); Uhlaender v. Henrickson, 316 F. Supp. 1277, 1283 (D. Minn. 1970); McCarthy, The Rights of Publicity and Privacy § 11.22.

[555] eBay, Inc. v. MercExchange, LLC, 547 U.S. 388, 391 (2006).

[556] *See, e.g.*, Comedy III Prods. v. Gary Saderup, Inc., 25 Cal. 4th 387 (2001).

[557] Some courts have held that "sufficiently serious questions going to the merits to make them a fair ground for litigation" is enough to support a preliminary injunction, if the balance of hardships tips strongly in the plaintiff's favor. *See, e.g.*, Ali v. Playgirl, Inc., 447 F. Supp. 723, 729 (S.D.N.Y. 1978). This more lenient standard may be inconsistent with the Supreme Court's subsequent decision in Winter v. Natural Resources Defense Council, Inc., 555 U.S. 7 (2008), in which the Court required that irreparable harm be "likely" and rejected the Ninth Circuit's dictum that a "possibility" of irreparable harm is sufficient. *Id.* at 21–22.

[558] *See, e.g.*, Taylor v. National Broadcasting Co., 22 Media L. Rep. 2433 (Cal. Super. Ct. 1994); Rosemont Enterprises, Inc. v. McGraw-Hill Book Co., 85 Misc. 2d 583, 586–87 (N.Y. Sup. Ct. 1975).

[559] *See, e.g.*, Carson v. Here's Johnny Portable Toilets, Inc., 810 F.2d 104, 105 (6th Cir. 1987); Ali v. Playgirl, Inc., 447 F. Supp. 723, 731, n.10 (S.D.N.Y. 1978).

[560] *See, e.g.*, Herman Miller, Inc. v. Palazzetti Imports & Exports, Inc., 270 F.3d 298, 326 & n.16 (6th Cir. 2001); Rosemont Enterprises v. Urban Systems, Inc., 42 A.D.2d 544, 345 N.Y.S.2d 17, 18 (N.Y. App. Div. 1973); *see also* Restatement (Third) of Unfair Competition § 48 cmt. c (1995) ("an injunction protecting the right of publicity should ordinarily be limited to conduct in jurisdictions that provide protection comparable to the former state.").

[561] McCarthy, The Rights of Publicity and Privacy § 11.27. Although damages for emotional distress are most often awarded to non-celebrities, celebrities may recover such damages, particularly when they have taken a public position against the use of their identity for advertising purposes. *See, e.g.*, Waits v. Frito-Lay, Inc., 978 F.2d 1093, 1103 (9th Cir. 1992); Grant v. Esquire, Inc., 367 F. Supp. 876, 881 (S.D.N.Y. 1973).

commercial loss. Courts look to amounts comparable persons receive for comparable uses,[562] or, if possible, to amounts plaintiff received for similar authorized use of his or her identity.[563] Damages can also be awarded to compensate for injury to professional standing or future income.[564] Some state statutes provide statutory damages as an alternative to actual damages;[565] and some allow plaintiff to recover the infringer's profits in addition to actual damages.[566]

Most states allow the plaintiff to recover punitive or exemplary damages for publicity right violations. Plaintiff must show the defendant acted with culpable intent, but the exact state of mind necessary varies from state to state.[567] Excessive punitive damages may violate the Due Process Clause of the Fourteenth Amendment.[568] Finally, many state statutes permit the prevailing party to recover his or her attorney's fees.[569]

[6]   Ownership and Transfer

In a majority of the states that have considered the issue, publicity rights are descendible property interests that can be exploited for a limited time period after the person's death.

Because publicity rights originated from traditional, personal privacy rights that protected dignity and reputation, some courts held that the right could not be asserted by relatives or after a person's death.[570] Some courts, drawing upon principles of unfair competition, suggested that post-mortem publicity rights were limited to cases in which the person exploited the publicity rights during his or her lifetime,[571] or transferred the publicity rights in connection with a transfer of other

---

[562] *See, e.g.*, National Bank of Commerce v. Shaklee Corp., 503 F. Supp. 533, 546–47 (W.D. Tex. 1980).

[563] *See, e.g.*, Clark v. Celeb Publishing, Inc., 530 F. Supp. 979, 983 (S.D.N.Y. 1981).

[564] *See, e.g.*, Waits v. Frito-Lay, Inc., 978 F.2d 1093, 1104 (9th Cir. 1992); Hirsch v. S.C. Johnson & Son, Inc., 90 Wis. 2d 379, 400, 280 N.W.2d 129, 138 (1979).

[565] *See, e.g.*, Cal. Civ. Code §§ 3344(a) 3344.1(a) ($750).

[566] *See, e.g.*, Tenn. Code Ann. § 47-25-1106(d); Wis. Stat. Ann. § 895.50(1)(b). Under California's statute, plaintiff need only prove defendant's total revenues; the defendant then has the burden of showing its deductible expenses. Cal. Civ. Code §§ 3344(a) 3344.1(a).

[567] *Compare* N.Y. Civ. Rights Law § 51 (McKinney Supp. 1991) ("knowingly used") *with* Cal. Civ. Code § 3294(a) ("oppression, fraud, or malice."); Cal. Civ. Code § 3294(c)(1) (defining malice as "despicable conduct which is carried on by the defendant with a willful and conscious disregard of the rights or safety of others."); Waits v. Frito-Lay, Inc., 978 F.2d 1093, 1104–04 (9th Cir. 1992).

[568] *See* BMW of North America, Inc. v. Gore, 517 U.S. 559 (1996); State Farm Mutual Auto Ins. Co. v. Campbell, 538 U.S. 408 (2003); Philip Morris USA, Inc. v. Williams, 549 U.S. 346 (2007).

[569] *See, e.g.*, Cal. Civ. Code §§ 3344(a), 3344.1(a); 12 Okla. Stat. § 1449(A); Wash. Rev. Code § 63.60.060(5). In Wisconsin, a "successful plaintiff" may recover fees as a matter of course, but the defendant may recover fees only if the action was "frivolous." Wis. Stat. § 995.50(1)(c), (6)(a).

[570] *See, e.g.*, Reeves v. United Artists Corp., 765 F.2d 79 (6th Cir. 1985) (Ohio law); Memphis Development Foundation v. Factors Etc. Inc., 616 F.2d 956 (6th Cir. 1980) (Tennessee law); Guglielmi v. Spelling-Goldberg Prods., 603 P.2d 454 (Cal. 1979); Maritote v. Desilu Productions, Inc., 345 F.2d 418, 420 (7th Cir. 1965) (Illinois law).

[571] *See, e.g.*, Lugosi v. Universal Pictures, Inc., 603 P.2d 425 (Cal. 1979); Factors Etc., Inc. v. Pro Arts,

assets.[572] Other courts, recognizing that the right of publicity more closely resembles a "property" right, held that the common-law right may be exercised by a person's heirs after the person's death.[573]

One of the principal objections to recognizing a post-mortem right by common law is the difficulty of determining how long the right should last.[574] In *Hebrew University of Jerusalem v. General Motors LLC*, a federal court applying New Jersey law held that Albert Einstein's common-law post-mortem right expired 50 years after his death.[575] The court borrowed the term of federal copyright law that existed when the plaintiff acquired Einstein's rights upon his death in 1982.[576]

Although the existence of a post-mortem right at common law is hotly debated, many state legislatures have taken the initiative to provide for a fixed period of post-mortem rights. To date, fourteen states have enacted post-mortem right of publicity statutes,[577] with durations ranging from 20 years[578] to 100 years.[579] Tennessee has a unique provision: the rights lasts for 10 years after death, but "commercial exploitation of the property right" maintains the right indefinitely, until the right is abandoned by non-use for two consecutive years.[580] Five other states recognize post-mortem rights under their common law.[581] Of the six states in which courts have held that there is no post-mortem right under common law, four have now recognized post-mortem rights by statute.[582] Only two states, New York and Wisconsin, continue to hold that there is no post-mortem right, because the statutes in those states limit the right to "any living person."[583]

Inc., 579 F.2d 215, 222 & n.11 (2d Cir. 1978); Hicks v. Casablanca Records, 464 F. Supp. 426, 429–30 (S.D.N.Y. 1978).

[572] Hanna Mfg. Co., v. Hillerich & Bradsby Co., 78 F.2d 763, 766–67 (5th Cir. 1935).

[573] *See, e.g.*, Martin Luther King, Jr. Center for Social Change, Inc. v. American Heritage Products, Inc., 296 S.E.2d 697, 705 (Ga. 1982); State ex rel. Elvis Presley Int'l Memorial Foundation v. Crowell, 733 S.W.2d 89 (Tenn. Ct. App. 1987) (overruling *Memphis Development Foundation*); Estate of Presley v. Russen, 513 F. Supp. 1339, 1355 (D.N.J. 1981).

[574] *See, e.g.*, Lugosi, 603 P.2d at 433–34 (Mosk, J., concurring); *but see* 603 P.2d at 446–47 (Bird, C.J., joined by Tobriner & Manuel, JJ., dissenting) (suggesting adoption of the statutory copyright term).

[575] 903 F. Supp. 2d 932 (C.D. Cal. 2012). The court could not certify the question to the New Jersey Supreme Court, because that court only accepts certified questions from the U.S. Court of Appeals for the Third Circuit. N.J. Ct. R. 2:12A-1 (2012).

[576] 903 F. Supp. 2d at 938–39.

[577] *See* McCarthy, Rights of Publicity and Privacy § 9.18.

[578] *See* Va. Code Ann. §§ 8.01-40.

[579] *See* Ind. Code. § 32-36-1-8; Okla. Stat. tit. 21, § 1448(G).

[580] *See* Tenn. Code Ann. §§ 47-25-1104.

[581] *See* McCarthy, Rights of Publicity and Privacy § 9.18.

[582] *See* Cal. Civ. Code § 3344.1; 765 Ill. Comp. Stat. 1075/30; Ohio Rev. Code § 274.02(A); Tenn. Code Ann. § 47-25-1104.

[583] *See* Stephano v. News Group Publications, Inc., 474 N.E.2d 580, 584 (N.Y. 1984) (rejecting common law right of publicity as separate from statutory privacy rights); Hagen v. Dahmer, 38 U.S.P.Q.2d 1146 (E.D. Wis. 1995).

Publicity rights are property rights that may be assigned[584] or licensed.[585] In those states with post-mortem rights, the rights can be passed by will to testamentary beneficiaries, or else they descend to the person's heirs. In most states, however, property rights may only pass by will if they existed at the time of the person's death. Because of this rule, it was held that Marilyn Monroe's post-mortem rights did not validly pass to her testamentary beneficiaries, because she died in 1962, long before the California post-mortem rights statute was enacted.[586] After a flurry of lobbying activity, the California legislature amended its statute to expressly provide that the right was retroactive.[587] Nonetheless, two courts have held that Monroe does not have a post-mortem right of publicity, because she was domiciled in New York at the time of her death.[588]

To determine whether a celebrity's estate has a post-mortem right of publicity, California applies the law of the state in which the celebrity was domiciled at the time of his or her death.[589] At least two states, however, have statutes that purport to apply without regard to the person's domicile at the time of death.[590] Although "Washington's approach to post-mortem personality rights raises difficult questions regarding whether another state must recognize the broad personality rights that Washington provides," the Ninth Circuit held that the Washington statute could constitutionally be applied to "the narrow, non-speculative circumstances presented by this case," namely, the unauthorized license of Jimi Hendrix merchandise for sale in Washington state.[591]

---

[584] Haelan Laboratories, Inc. v. Topps Chewing Gum, Inc., 202 F.2d 866, 868 (2d Cir. 1953); Acme Circus Operating Co. v. Kuperstock, 711 F.2d 1538 (11th Cir. 1983); Factors Etc., Inc. v. Pro Arts, Inc., 579 F.2d 215, 221 (2d Cir. 1978). Unlike trademarks, a person may assign publicity rights "in gross," that is, without also transferring a business. *See* McCarthy, The Rights of Publicity and Privacy § 10.13.

[585] Douglass v. Hustler Magazine, Inc., 769 F.2d 1128, 1138 (7th Cir. 1985). *See generally* McCarthy, The Rights of Publicity and Privacy § 10.15 *et seq.*

[586] *See* Shaw Family Archives, Ltd. v. CMG Worldwide, Inc., 486 F. Supp. 2d 309 (S.D.N.Y. 2007); Milton H. Green Archives, Inc. v. CMG Worldwide, Inc., Case No. CV 05-2200 MMM (C.D. Cal. May 14, 2007), *aff'd on other grounds sub nom.* Milton H. Green Archives, Inc. v. Marilyn Monroe, LLC, 692 F.3d 983 (9th Cir. 2012).

[587] *See* Cal. Civ. Code § 3344.1(b),(p).

[588] *See Milton H. Green Archives*, 692 F.3d at 987–90, 1000; Shaw Family Archives, Ltd. v. CMG Worldwide, Inc., 2008 U.S. Dist. LEXIS 67529 (S.D.N.Y. Sept. 2, 2008).

[589] Cairns v. Franklin Mint Co., 292 F.3d 1139, 1146–49 (9th Cir. 2002). *See also* Factors Etc., Inc. v. Pro Arts, Inc., 652 F.2d 278, 280–81 (2d Cir. 1981) (predicting New York would apply Tennessee law to determine the existence and scope of Elvis Presley's post-mortem rights).

[590] *See* Ind. Code § 32-36-1-1 ("This chapter applies to an act or event that occurs within Indiana, regardless of a personality's domicile, residence, or citizenship."); Wash. Rev. Code § 63.60.010 ("This chapter is intended to apply to all individuals and personalities, living and deceased, regardless of place of domicile or place of domicile at time of death.").

[591] Experience Hendrix, LLC v. Hendrixlicensing.com, Ltd., 762 F.3d 829, 836 (9th Cir. 2014).

§ 6H   IDEA SUBMISSION

Traditional intellectual property law typically does not protect ideas.[592] In some instances, however, state law affords alternative ways to protect people who develop or offer ideas, usually for some business purpose. Idea submission claims often arise in the context of the entertainment business; for instance, a person submits a proposal for a TV show or a radio program and later claims similarity between his or her idea and an actual show or program and demands compensation. The main challenge that the law faces is striking a balance between creating incentives to create new ideas and allowing free access to ideas to nurture the progress of knowledge and market competitiveness.

Idea submission law relies on common-law theories of express and implied contract, quasi-contract, and property. Courts do not always carefully distinguish the theories and may use elements commonly associated with one theory to grant or deny recovery under a different theory, and many cases decided under one theory contain facts that would support recovery under another theory as well.[593] Many jurisdictions impose requirements of novelty and concreteness as a prerequisite to recovery under some or all of these theories.[594] Depending on whether the plaintiff makes a contract or tort claim, different statutes of limitations and types of relief may apply.

A question of growing interest concerns the relationship between the common law of idea submission and federal intellectual property law. Idea submitters may sometimes seek to protect rights similar to the exclusive rights granted under federal copyright law. In those situations, a question arises whether the idea submitter's claims are preempted by the federal Copyright Act.[595]

[1]   Novelty and Concreteness

Many jurisdictions require that an idea be novel and concrete for the plaintiff to obtain relief under both contract and property theories.

---

[592] Patent law does not protect abstract ideas, as such; but it can protect more specific ideas that meet the requirements of utility, novelty, and non-obviousness. *See* § 2C[1]. Copyright law protects only original expression, and not ideas. *See* § 4C[3]. Trademark law protects business and product identifiers, but does not protect functional matter. *See* § 5C[1][c]. Trade secret law can protect ideas, but only when they are kept secret and are disclosed to others only in the context of a confidential relationship or express contract prohibiting further use or disclosure. *See* § 3C[1][b].

[593] Nimmer adds a fifth theory: confidential relationships. 3 MELVILLE B. NIMMER & DAVID NIMMER, NIMMER ON COPYRIGHT § 16.02. Epstein properly considers confidential relationships to be a subset of implied contracts. MICHAEL A. EPSTEIN, EPSTEIN ON INTELLECTUAL PROPERTY § 7 (5th ed. 2010).

[594] *See, e.g.*, Downey v. General Foods Corp., 286 N.E.2d 257, 259 (N.Y. 1972) ("when one submits an idea to another, no promise to pay for its use may be implied, and no asserted agreement enforced, if the elements of novelty and originality are absent, since the property right in an idea is based upon these two elements.").

[595] *See* § 6H[7].

[a]   Novelty

Ideas that are commonly used, well-known, or variations of old familiar themes may not qualify for protection. As with trade secret law,[596] idea submission law's novelty standard should not be as strict as patent law's novelty and nonobviousness requirements. Some jurisdictions have suggested that an idea must simply be original to the plaintiff without necessarily being innovative.[597] Others have applied novelty standards as demanding as those of patent law.[598] Courts have also differed in whether the idea must be unknown to the public in general or only to the defendant.[599]

Examples of ideas found to be novel include: writing a magazine article about the bat mitzvah of a Down Syndrome afflicted girl;[600] holding auditions in a high school assembly format to select student talent for a radio show;[601] a sales incentive program offering a resort vacation in lieu of small monthly prizes;[602] and a concept for using cassette tapes to train sales personnel.[603] Examples of ideas found to be not novel include: a plan for the takeover of a food service company and the partial sale of its operations;[604] a plan to furnish cosmetics customers with a videotape of a "makeover";[605] and a greeting card character with a halo and wings called "Little Angel Food Cake."[606]

Murray v. National Broadcasting Co.[607] is a good example of a case in which a court denied recovery for lack of novelty. Plaintiff claimed that the producers of the "Cosby Show" improperly took her idea for a television sitcom centered on a wholesome, intact, non-stereotypical Black American family. The court found that the idea lacked novelty because (1) Bill Cosby had publicly espoused the idea twenty years earlier, and (2) the idea represented an "adaptation of existing knowledge" using "known ingredients": When "an idea consists in essence of nothing more than a variation on a basic theme — in this case, the family situation comedy — novelty cannot be found."[608]

---

[596] *See* § 3C[1][c][vi].

[597] *See, e.g.*, Stevens v. Continental Can Co., 308 F.2d 100, 104 (6th Cir. 1962).

[598] *See* Tate v. Scanlan International, Inc., 403 N.W.2d 666, 671 (Minn. Ct. App. 1987) ("A novel idea is an original idea, something that is not already known or in use. . . . The novelty essential to a protected property right cannot arise solely from the fact that something already known and in use is put to a new use.")

[599] Nadel v. Play-By-Play Toys & Novelties, Inc., 208 F.3d 368, 380 (2d Cir. 2000).

[600] Werlin v. Reader's Digest Ass'n, 528 F. Supp. 451 (S.D.N.Y. 1981).

[601] Hamilton National Bank v. Belt, 210 F.2d 706 (D.C. Cir. 1953).

[602] Bergman v. Electrolux, 558 F. Supp. 1351 (D. Nev. 1987) (plaintiff presented enough evidence to raise a question of fact as to novelty).

[603] Educational Sales Programs, Inc. v. Dreyfuss Corp., 65 Misc. 2d 412 (N.Y. Sup. Ct. 1970).

[604] Orderline Wholesale Distributors Inc. v. Gibbons, Green, van Amerongen Ltd., 675 F. Supp. 122 (S.D.N.Y. 1987).

[605] Ring v. Estee Lauder, Inc., 702 F. Supp. 76, 78 (S.D.N.Y. 1988), *aff'd*, 874 F.2d 109 (2d Cir. 1984).

[606] Pittman v. American Greeting Corp., 619 F. Supp. 939 (W.D. Ky. 1985).

[607] 844 F.2d 988 (2d Cir. 1988).

[608] *Id.* at 992–93. The New York courts later clarified that, for claims based on an express or implied

[b]   Concreteness

In addition to novelty, some courts also require that the submitted idea be concrete, not abstract. There are two general approaches to this requirement.

Under one approach, concreteness means only that the idea should be sufficiently developed so as to be ready for implementation.[609] For example, in *Hamilton National Bank v. Belt*, the court found that the plaintiff's plan for a weekly radio program was sufficiently concrete, where the idea called for local high school talent to be "presented and recorded as a student assembly, retaining the atmosphere of a school by referring to the show as a class, to the acts as assignments and to the action as recitations."[610] Similarly, a California court held that a partially developed idea that gave insight into a final product was sufficiently concrete.[611]

Other courts have applied a stricter standard of concreteness. For example, in *Smith v. Recrion Corp.*, the Supreme Court of Nevada held that an idea must be "ready for immediate use without embellishment."[612] In that case, the court rejected a proposal, illustrated with a detailed brochure, to construct and operate a recreational vehicle park in connection with defendant's luxury hotel. Under a similarly demanding standard, another court held that the suggested advertising slogan for Haberle beer, "Neighborly Haberle," was not sufficiently concrete.[613]

In assessing concreteness, the form in which the idea is presented is not crucial. Courts have found that concrete ideas can be submitted in a variety of forms: an oral presentation of a radio program idea;[614] a letter describing an idea for a new detergent combining two other products;[615] or a drawing and a non-workable mock-up.[616] Some courts, however, require that the idea be embodied in some tangible form, such as a writing or a finished product.[617] In assessing concreteness, courts may consider custom and industry practice regarding idea submissions.[618]

---

contract, the idea did not have to be novel generally, but only unknown to the defendant. *See* Nadel v. Play-By-Play Toys & Novelties, Inc., 208 F.3d 368, 379–80 & n.9 (2d Cir. 2000).

[609] *See, e.g.*, Hamilton National Bank v. Belt, 210 F.2d 706, 709 (D.C. Cir. 1953) ("in the field of radio broadcasting concreteness may lie between the boundaries of mere generality on the one hand and, on the other, a full script containing the words to be uttered and delineating the action to be portrayed.").

[610] *Id.* at 709.

[611] Fink v. Goodson-Todman Ent. Ltd., 9 Cal. App. 3d 996 (1970).

[612] 541 P.2d 663, 665 (Nev. 1975).

[613] Baily v. Haberle Congress Brewing Co., 193 Misc. 723 (N.Y. Sup. Ct. 1941).

[614] Hamilton National Bank v. Belt, 210 F.2d 706, 709 (D.C. Cir. 1953).

[615] Galanis v. Procter & Gamble Corp., 153 F. Supp. 34, 38 (S.D.N.Y. 1957).

[616] Dewey v. American Stair Glide Corp., 557 S.W.2d 643, 646–47 (Mo. App. 1977).

[617] *See, e.g.*, Bailey v. Haberle Congress Brewing Co., 193 Misc. 723 (N.Y. Sup. Ct. 1948) (reduction of idea into writing required); O'Brien v. RKO Radio Pictures Inc., 68 F. Supp. 13, 14 (S.D.N.Y. 1946); Tutelman v. Stokowski, 44 U.S.P.Q. 47, 48 (Pa. C.P. 1939) (incorporation into tangible product required).

[618] Tate v. Scanlan Int'l, Inc., 403 N.W.2d 666, 672 (Minn. Ct. App. 1987) ("The undisputed testimony . . . was that 'concrete' in the field of medical marketing meant that the concept was very well defined, with reasonable access to all parts necessary to develop it. He also testified that in this field a working model of an idea was rarely presented."); Hamilton Nat'l Bank v. Belt, 210 F.2d 706, 709 (D.C. Cir. 1953).

[2]   Express Contracts

An offeree may expressly agree to compensate the submitter for the disclosure or use of an idea. Some courts may impose limiting conditions on an express contract, such as novelty and concreteness of the idea.

[a]   Novelty and Concreteness

Courts split on whether an idea must be novel and concrete before an express contract for its submission will be enforced. Some hold that if parties expressly contract for the disclosure of an idea, lack of novelty or concreteness will not vitiate the obligation.[619] Others disagree.[620]

In *Masline v. New York, New Haven & Hartford Railroad*,[621] the Connecticut Supreme Court denied recovery, holding that novelty and concreteness were required to enforce an express contract. Plaintiff, a railroad employee, informed defendant, a railroad, that he had "information of value" and if defendant used it, it would earn at least $100,000. The parties entered into an express oral agreement that if defendant used the idea, plaintiff would receive five percent of the revenue derived from his idea. Plaintiff disclosed his idea: selling advertising space in and on the railroad's stations, depots, cars, fences, and the like. The railroad had not sold advertising space before and immediately began to do so, earning a large amount of money from advertising, but refused to pay the plaintiff. The court found plaintiff's idea was not novel or original. Because the idea was common knowledge, plaintiff had no property right in it, and the defendant's promise to pay was unenforceable for lack of consideration.[622]

Other courts have enforced express contracts for the submission of a non-novel idea where the idea's value to the defendant came from the timing of the disclosure or the manner of presentation. In *Nadel v. Play-By-Play Toys & Novelties, Inc.*,[623] the Second Circuit held that a showing of novelty to the buyer will supply sufficient consideration for an agreement. *Nadel* extended the rule of *Apfel v. Prudential-Bache Securities, Inc.*[624] that novelty was not required where the parties entered into a separate post-disclosure agreement for use of the idea. The *Apfel* court noted that the buyer of the idea may find value not necessarily in the novelty of the idea but "by not having to expend resources to pursue the idea through other channels

---

[619] *See, e.g.*, Vantage Point, Inc. v. Parker Bros., Inc., 529 F. Supp. 1204, 1216 (E.D.N.Y. 1981), *aff'd without op.*, 697 F.2d 301 (2d Cir. 1982); Donahue v. Ziv Television Programs, Inc., 245 Cal. App. 2d 593 (1966).

[620] *See, e.g.*, Tate v. Scanlan International Inc., 403 N.W.2d 666, 671 (Minn. Ct. App. 1987); Bergman v. Electrolux Corp., 558 F. Supp. 1351, 1353 (D. Nev. 1983).

[621] Masline v. New York, New Haven and Hartford R.R., 95 Conn. 702, 112 A. 639 (1921).

[622] Many criticize *Masline. See, e.g.*, 3 NIMMER ON COPYRIGHT § 16.04 ("The . . . decision [is] unsound, since it seems to ignore the fact that defendant promised to pay for the idea without conditioning such promise upon plaintiff producing an idea which would be regarded as property."); Havighurst, *The Right to Compensation for an Idea*, 49 N.W.U. L. REV. 295 (1954); Stanley v. Columbia Broadcasting Sys., 221 P.2d 73, 85 (Cal. 1950) (Traynor, J., dissenting).

[623] 208 F.3d 368 (2d Cir. 2000). *But see* Lapine v. Seinfeld, 918 N.Y.S.2d 313 (Sup. Ct. 2011) (criticizing *Nadel* as a misreading of New York law).

[624] 616 N.E.2d 1095 (N.Y. 1993).

or by having a profit-making idea implemented sooner rather than later."[625]

[b] Standard Release Forms

Companies often require all idea submitters to sign a standard release form with language disclaiming or limiting liability for using the idea. Typically, courts will not enforce such release forms unless they are completely unambiguous. Some courts impose a reasonableness requirement even if the defendant's exculpatory language is unambiguous.

The case law shows a wide range of approaches to release forms.[626] In one case, the court implied a reasonableness standard in interpreting defendant's exculpatory release form, which read: "the use, if any, to be made of this suggestion by . . . [defendant] and the compensation to be paid therefore, if any, if . . . [defendant] uses it, are matters solely in . . . [the defendant's] discretion."[627] The court construed this to mean that defendant had sole discretion whether to use the idea but must pay a reasonable amount if it decided to use it. Other courts, however, have construed similar discretionary language literally to allow the defendant to avoid contractual liability.[628]

Burten v. Milton Bradley Co.[629] is an example of the high standards for unambiguous language that courts sometimes apply. The plaintiffs alleged that they revealed their computerized board game idea to defendant in confidence and that defendant breached the confidence by marketing the idea without compensating plaintiffs. To avoid liability, defendant argued that plaintiffs signed a release form that precluded recovery on the theory of confidential relationship. The form stated that plaintiff's submission "does not . . . establish or create by implication or otherwise any relationship" between the parties.[630] The court held that this language could be construed "to embrace only those ties and obligations established by consensual understanding or course of dealing and not those legal constructs which may be triggered by unanticipated, covert, and devious misuse."[631]

---

[625] 616 N.E.2d at 1098.

[626] *See, e.g.,* Welles v. Columbia Broadcasting Sys., 308 F.2d 810 (9th Cir. 1962); Burten v. Milton Bradley Co., 592 F. Supp. 1021 (D.R.I. 1984), *rev'd,* 763 F.2d 461 (1st Cir. 1985) (applying Massachusetts law).

[627] Downey v. General Foods Corp., 37 A.D.2d 250, 255 (N.Y. App. Div. 1971), *rev'd on other grounds,* 286 N.E.2d 257 (N.Y. 1972).

[628] *See* Davis v. General Foods Corp., 21 F. Supp. 445 (S.D.N.Y. 1937) (where release form read: "We shall be glad to examine your idea for a new food product, but only with the understanding that the use to be made of it by us, and the compensation, if any, are matters resting solely in our discretion."); *see also* Lueddecke v. Chevrolet Motor Co., 70 F.2d 345 (8th Cir. 1934); Thomas v. R.J. Reynolds Tobacco Co., 38 A.2d 61 (Pa. 1944).

[629] 763 F.2d 461 (1st Cir. 1985).

[630] *Id.* at 464 n.3.

[631] *Id.* at 465. *Compare* Crown Industries v. Kawneer, 335 F. Supp. 749, 754 (N.D. Ill. 1971) ("No confidential relationship is to be created by such submission."; agreement enforced); Kearns v. Ford Motor Co., 203 U.S.P.Q. 884, 886 (E.D. Mich. 1978) ("Ford Motor Company cannot receive suggestions in confidence."; same) *with* Gordon v. Vincent Youmans Inc., 358 F.2d 261 (2d Cir. 1965) (suggesting "the broad language of a release form was mere boilerplate"); Houser v. Snap-On Tools Corp., 202 F. Supp. 181 (D. Md. 1962) (signing parties did not waive all rights by signing release; doubtful whether such a

[3]   Implied Contracts

In an implied contract, the parties' agreement is expressed through their conduct rather than through their words.[632] In deciding whether the parties' conduct involving idea submission showed intent to enter into a contract, courts consider a number of factors: whether the idea was solicited;[633] whether the defendant had an opportunity to prevent disclosure;[634] whether the parties have engaged in negotiations;[635] the parties' expectations;[636] and whether the industry's customs would support finding an agreement.[637] As with express contracts, some courts require that an idea be novel and concrete before they will find an implied contract to pay for the script's use.[638]

[a]   Unsolicited Submissions

[i]   Involuntarily Received

Courts generally do not find an implied contract when the defendant receives an idea without solicitation and without warning,[639] and may deny compensation even if the plaintiff submits a truly valuable idea expecting compensation and the defendant, aware of plaintiff's expectation, uses the idea.[640] In *Desny v. Wilder*, the

---

document "would give a manufacturer the right to expropriate a disclosure without remuneration, where the course of dealings between the parties indicates . . . that the disclosing party was seeking remuneration for the use of his creation.").

[632] *See* 3 NIMMER ON COPYRIGHT § 16.05. General contract law principles apply in idea submission cases. *See* Faris v. Enberg, 97 Cal. App. 3d 309, 318 (1979) ("for an implied contract, one must show: that he or she prepared the work; that he or she disclosed the work to the offeree for sale; under all the circumstances attending disclosure it can be concluded that the offeree voluntarily accepted the disclosure knowing the conditions on which it was tendered (*i.e.* the offeree must have the opportunity to reject the attempted disclosure if the conditions are unacceptable); and the reasonable value of the work.").

[633] *See, e.g.*, Gunther-Wahl Prods., Inc. v. Mattel, Inc., 104 Cal. App. 4th 27, 36 & n.14, 42–43 (2002).

[634] *See, e.g.*, Desny v. Wilder, 299 P.2d 257, 270 (Cal. 1956).

[635] *See, e.g.*, Landsberg v. Scrabble Crossword Game Players Inc., 736 F.2d 485, 489 (9th Cir. 1984); Smith v. Weinstein, 578 F. Supp. 1297, 1305 (S.D.N.Y. 1984), *aff'd*, 738 F.2d 414 (2d Cir. 1984); Annisgard v. Bray, 419 N.E.2d 315, 318 (Mass. Ct. App. 1981).

[636] Liggett & Meyer Tobacco Co. v. Meyer, 194 N.E. 206 (Ind. Ct. App. 1939). *Cf.* Aliotti v. R. Dakin & Co., 831 F.2d 898, 902 (9th Cir. 1987) ("no contract may be implied where an idea has been disclosed not to gain compensation for that idea but for the sole purpose of inducing the defendant to enter a future business relationship."), *citing* Faris v. Enberg, 97 Cal. App. 3d 309, 318 (1979).

[637] *See, e.g.*, Forest Park Pictures v. Universal Television Network, Inc., 683 F.3d 424, 435 (2d Cir. 2012); Nadel v. Play-by-Play Toys & Novelties, Inc., 208 F.3d 368, 376 n.5 (2d Cir. 2000); Whitfield v. Lear, 751 F.2d 90, 93 (2d Cir. 1984).

[638] *See, e.g.*, Marcus Advertising Inc. v. M.M. Fisher Assoc. Inc., 444 F.2d 1061, 1064 (7th Cir. 1971); Stevens v. Continental Can Co., 308 F.2d 100, 104 (6th Cir. 1962); Victor G. Reiling Assocs. v. Fisher-Price, Inc., 450 F. Supp. 2d 175, 177–80 (D. Conn. 2006); Tate v. Scanlan International Inc., 403 N.W.2d 666, 674 (Minn. Ct. App. 1987); Fleming v. Ronson Corp., 258 A.2d 153, 157, *aff'd*, 275 A.2d 759 (N.J. Super. Ct. 1969).

[639] *See, e.g.*, Aliotti v. R. Dakin & Co., 831 F.2d 898, 903 (9th Cir. 1987).

[640] 3 NIMMER ON COPYRIGHT § 16.32. *See also* Smith v. Recrion Corp., 541 P.2d 663 (Nev. 1975); Bowen v. Yankee Network, 46 F. Supp. 62 (D. Mass. 1942); O'Brien v. RKO Radio Pictures, 68 F. Supp. 13 (S.D.N.Y. 1946); Davies v. Carnation Co., 352 F.2d 393 (9th Cir. 1965); Thompson v. California Brewing

California Supreme Court noted: "The idea man who blurts out his idea without having first made his bargain has no one but himself to blame for the loss of his bargaining power . . . even though the conveyance has been made with the hope or expectation that some obligation will ensue."[641]

Courts will imply a contract if the circumstances justify the implication. In *Landsberg v. Scrabble Crossword Game Players, Inc.*, the court suggested that even if plaintiff had not submitted his unsolicited idea in confidence, defendant's request for a second copy of plaintiff's manuscript may have created an implied-in-fact contract.[642] In several cases, industry practice or custom may lead to a finding of implied contract.[643] If defendant usually pays for unsolicited ideas of the kind the plaintiff submitted, this may be sufficient to create an implied contract.[644]

[ii]   Failure to Reject After Notice

If a defendant receives advance notice of an unsolicited submission and fails to reject it before disclosure, the defendant's conduct may be sufficient to create an implied contract to compensate the submitter for use of his idea. In some jurisdictions, if the recipient knows the submitter expects compensation and the idea is used, inaction in failing to reject before disclosure can lead to implication of a promise to pay.[645] Where "the idea purveyor has clearly conditioned his offer to convey the idea upon an obligation to pay for it if it is used by the offeree and the offeree, knowing the condition before he knows the idea, voluntarily accepts its disclosure . . . and uses it," the law will imply an agreement.[646]

In a case concerning a television program, the defendant received plaintiff's mailgram announcing that a script would arrive, opened the script, and reviewed it.[647] There was evidence that in the television industry, studios not seeking unsolicited submissions explicitly say so and return unsolicited submissions without opening them. Thus, the court concluded that there was sufficient evidence to show an implicit agreement to pay for its use.[648]

Co., 310 P.2d 436 (Cal. 1957); Official Airlines Schedule Information Service v. Eastern Airlines, 333 F.2d 672 (5th Cir. 1964); Landsberg v. Scrabble Crossword Game Players, Inc., 802 F.2d 1193, 1196 (9th Cir. 1986).

[641] 299 P.2d 257, 270 (Cal. 1956).

[642] 736 F.2d 485, 490 (9th Cir. 1984). On remand, the district court found for plaintiff but on a different theory. Plaintiff's second disclosure was confidential, and this created an implied contract. The appeals court affirmed. Landsberg v. Scrabble Crossword Game Players, Inc., 802 F.2d 1193, 1196 (9th Cir. 1986).

[643] *See, e.g.*, Nadel v. Play-by-Play Toys & Novelties, Inc., 208 F.3d 368, 376 n.5 (2d Cir. 2000) (New York law); Victor G. Reiling Assocs. v. Fisher-Price, Inc., 450 F. Supp. 2d 175, 185 (D. Conn. 2006) (New York law).

[644] Kurlan v. Columbia Broadcasting System, Inc., 256 P.2d 962 (Cal. 1953); Vantage Point Inc. v. Parker Bros., Inc., 529 F. Supp. 1204 (E.D.N.Y. 1981), *aff'd sub nom.* Vantage Point, Inc. v. Milton Bradley Co., 697 F.2d 301 (2d Cir. 1982); McGhan v. Ebersol, 608 F. Supp. 277, 285 (S.D.N.Y. 1985).

[645] Donahue v. Ziv Television Prog. Inc., 245 Cal. App. 2d 593 (1966). *See also* Smith v. Weinstein, 578 F. Supp. 1247 (S.D.N.Y. 1984), *aff'd without op.*, 738 F.2d 419 (2d Cir. 1984).

[646] Desny v. Wilder, 299 P.2d 257, 270 (Cal. 1956).

[647] Whitfield v. Lear, 751 F.2d 90, 93 (2d Cir. 1984).

[648] *Id.* Nimmer argues for limiting the failure-to-reject a contract implication theory: "Suppose a man is wandering through Central Park, looking for a bench to rest. At this point, a woman emerges and

[b]   Solicited Submissions

If a person requests that another reveal an idea, most courts consider the solicitation sufficient to imply a promise to pay for the idea if used. In *Moore v. Ford Motor Co.*,[649] defendant solicited plaintiff's submission, but specified that there was an understanding that there was "no obligation on our part." Plaintiff responded that he understood "that there is no obligation on your part." The court interpreted this language to mean that defendant had no obligation to use plaintiff's idea or to compensate plaintiff for the mere submission; but defendant still had a legal obligation to pay plaintiff if the idea was used.[650] Although "use" of the idea may be inferred from evidence of access to the plaintiff's idea and substantial similarity between the defendant's work and the plaintiff's idea, uncontroverted evidence of independent creation will negate the inference and justify judgment in the defendant's favor.[651]

[c]   Confidential Relationship

A variation on the implied contract theory is the implied promise to keep the submitted idea confidential.[652] "An actionable breach of confidence will arise when an idea, whether or not protectable [by copyright], is offered to another in confidence, and is voluntarily received by the offeree in confidence with the understanding that it is not to be disclosed to others, and is not to be used by the offeree for purposes beyond the limits of the confidence without the offeror's permission."[653] As with other implied contracts, courts consider various factors in determining whether such a confidential relationship exists, including evidence "that the material submitted was protected by reason of sufficient novelty and elaboration," and evidence "of a particular relationship such as partners, joint adventurers, principal and agent or buyer and seller under certain circumstances."[654] If defendant, by using the idea, discloses it to others, defendant has breached the contract.[655]

---

states 'I expect to be paid for what I'm about to disclose unless you tell me not to speak.' The man says nothing. The woman goes on to say 'There is an unoccupied bench beyond the hedge.' Now, if the man uses the bench, is he obligated to pay the woman?" 3 Nimmer on Copyright § 16.03.

[649] 43 F.2d 685 (2d Cir. 1930).

[650] *Id.* at 686–87.

[651] *See* Spinner v. American Broadcasting Cos., 215 Cal. App. 4th 172 (2013).

[652] *See, e.g.,* Faris v. Enberg, 97 Cal. App. 2d 309, 320–23 (1979); Davies v. Krasna, 245 Cal. App. 2d 535, 546–48 (1966). The California Supreme Court has expressly refrained from endorsing this theory. *See* Davies v. Krasna, 535 P.2d 1161, 1164–65 n.3 (Cal. 1975) (assuming without deciding that California law recognizes such a theory, it was barred by the statute of limitations).

[653] *Faris,* 97 Cal. App. 2d at 323. *See also* Aliotti v. R. Dakin & Co., 831 F.2d 898, 902 (9th Cir. 1987).

[654] *Faris,* 97 Cal. App. 2d at 323.

[655] *See also* Gilbert v. General Motors Corp., 32 F. Supp. 502 (W.D.N.Y. 1940); Carneval v. William Morris Agency, Inc., 124 N.Y.S.2d 319 (1953), *aff'd,* 284 A.D. 1041 (N.Y. App. Div. 1954); Sloan v. Mud Products Inc., 114 F. Supp. 916 (N.D. Okla. 1953); Official Airlines Schedule Information Service, Inc. v. Eastern Airlines, 333 F.2d 672 (5th Cir. 1964).

[4]   Unjust Enrichment

Unjust enrichment, or quasi-contract, is an equitable theory. Some courts will impose quasi-contractual obligations even in the absence of an express or implied contract where there is a risk that one party might receive an unfair advantage or benefit over another party. The plaintiff must convince the court that the idea bestowed a benefit on the recipient, that the recipient retained the benefit, and that it would be unjust not to compensate the idea submitter.[656]

In practice, although plaintiffs often make idea submission claims under quasi-contract, courts rarely grant relief under this theory. For example, in *Reeves v. Alyeska Pipeline Service Co.*, the plaintiff alleged that defendants used his idea for a visitor center at the Trans-Alaska pipeline without compensation. The court held that an unjust enrichment claim for the idea could not be sustained without proof that the idea disclosed was novel or original, which was lacking. However, the court held that plaintiff could recover for the reasonable value of his services if defendant benefitted from those services or from his experience in the Alaska tourist industry, rather than from the intrinsic value of the idea.[657]

[5]   Property Theory

The property theory focuses primarily on the idea's nature, unlike the other three theories, which focus on the parties' relationship. Although a number of jurisdictions recognize a "property" right in ideas,[658] many do not.[659] In discussing idea submissions, courts often use the term "property" loosely, recognizing it is more a legal conclusion than a factual description.[660]

Most courts applying a property theory agree the idea must be novel and original, and concrete.[661] Once an idea is recognized as property, the submitter

---

[656] *See, e.g.*, Reeves v. Alyeska Pipeline Service Co., 926 P.2d 1130, 1143 (Alaska 1996); Werlin v. Reader's Digest Association, Inc., 528 F. Supp. 451, 465 (S.D.N.Y. 1981); Vantage Point, Inc. v. Parker Bros., Inc., 529 F. Supp. 1204, 1216–17 (E.D.N.Y. 1981), *aff'd without op.*, 697 F.2d 301 (2d Cir. 1982).

[657] *Reeves*, 926 P.2d at 1143–44.

[658] *See, e.g.*, Educational Sales Program, Inc. v. Dreyfus Corp., 65 Misc. 2d 412, 412–414 (N.Y. Sup. Ct. 1970); Peunte v. President and Fellows of Harvard College, 248 F.2d 799, 802 (1st Cir. 1957); Wilson v. Barton & Ludwiz, Inc., 296 S.E.2d 74 (Ga. Ct. App.1982); Davies v. Carnation Co., 352 F.2d 393 (9th Cir. 1965); Boop v. Ford Motor Co., 278 F.2d 197, 199 (7th Cir. 1960).

[659] *See, e.g.*, Whitfield v. Lear, 751 F.2d 90 (2d Cir. 1984) (refusing property theory recovery because California does not recognize property in ideas, but granting implied contract recovery); Weitzenkorn v. Lesser, 256 P.2d 947 (Cal. 1953); B & M Die Co. v. Ford Motor Co., N.W.2d 620, 623 (Mich. Ct. App. 1988). Some courts refrain from using the property label but apply property theory's three-element analysis — novelty and originality, concreteness, and unauthorized use.

[660] *See* Desny v. Wilder, 299 P.2d 257, 264–265 (Cal. 1965) ("An idea is usually not regarded as property, because all sentient beings may conceive and evolve ideas throughout the gamut of their powers of cerebration and because our concept of property implies something which may be owned and possessed to the exclusion of all other persons.").

[661] Novelty and concreteness are also sometimes requisites for recovery under express, implied, and quasi-contract theories.

must show that it was used without his or her authority.[662] An idea submitter can prove use by showing that the alleged user had access to the submitted idea and that there is substantial similarity between the submitted idea and defendant's product.[663]

[6]   Remedies

Idea submitters typically seek relief in the form of monetary compensation. Damages measures that courts have actually used or discussed include: the reasonable value of an ad slogan;[664] the actual value of the benefit to defendant, rather than the market value of the magazine article;[665] the actual value to defendant of a radio program;[666] fair value for the use of a television program based on defendant's typical royalty and percentage of profits;[667] expectation damages;[668] and the full profits of defendant plus attorney's fees and prejudgment interest.[669]

In *Tate v. Scanlan International, Inc.*,[670] the court, in an implied contract context, applied patent law's reasonable royalty standard to affirm a jury verdict awarding a 30% royalty, in view of defendant's 60% profit on sale of the product.[671] Punitive damages may not be awarded for a breach of express or implied contract, although they may be awarded under a property theory.[672]

In some instances, idea submission plaintiffs may also apply for injunctive relief, or an order of the court prohibiting the defendant to use or disclose an idea. Courts evaluate four factors in determining whether to grant a preliminary injunction: the idea submitter's likelihood of prevailing on the merits; the threat of irreparable harm to the submitter in the absence of an injunction; the balance between this harm and the injury that granting the injunction will inflict on other interested parties; and the public interest in the grant or denial of an injunction.[673] While no

---

[662] *See, e.g.*, McGhan v. Ebersol, 608 F. Supp. 277, 286 (S.D.N.Y. 1985). This is akin to a conversion claim, but courts do not label it as such.

[663] Fleming v. Ronson Corp., 258 A.2d 153, 157 (N.J. Super. Ct. 1969), *aff'd*, 275 A.2d 759 (N.J. Super. Ct. 1971). This proof rule resembles that for copyright infringement. *See* § 4K.

[664] Healy v. R.H. Macy & Co., 14 N.E.2d 388 (N.Y. 1938) (property theory); Matarese v. Moore-McCormack Lines Inc., 158 F.2d 631 (2d Cir. 1946) (quasi-contract).

[665] Werlin v. Reader's Digest Ass'n, 528 F. Supp. 451 (S.D.N.Y. 1981) (quasi-contract).

[666] Stanley v. Columbia Broadcasting System, Inc., 221 P.2d 73 (Cal. 1950).

[667] Donahue v. UA Corp., 2 Cal. App. 3d 794 (1969) (implied contract).

[668] Elfenbein v. Luckenbach Terminals Inc., 166 A. 91 (N.J. 1933) (express contract).

[669] Landsberg v. Scrabble Crossword Game Players, Inc., 802 F.2d 1193, 1196 (9th Cir. 1986) (implied contract).

[670] 403 N.W.2d 666 (Minn. Ct. App. 1987).

[671] For a discussion of damages in patent and copyright cases, see §§ 2F[5] and 4K[4][b].

[672] *See* RESTATEMENT (SECOND) OF CONTRACTS § 355 (1979) ("Punitive damages are not recoverable for a breach of contract unless the conduct constituting the breach is also a tort for which punitive damages are recoverable."); Reeves v. Alyeska Pipeline Service Co., 56 P.3d 660, 671–72 (Alaska 2002).

[673] *See* Novo Nordisk of North Am., Inc. v. Genentech, Inc., 77 F.3d 1364, 1367 (Fed. Cir. 1996); Dataphase Sys., Inc. v. CL Sys., Inc., 640 F.2d 109, 114 (8th Cir. 1981).

single factor is dispositive, a moving party is required to show a threat of irreparable harm.[674] Injunctive relief is regarded as a "drastic and extraordinary remedy"[675] and may be particularly difficult to obtain in the context of idea submission, where a showing of irreparable harm can be problematic.[676] Since idea-submission claims are typically made under an express or implied contract theory, courts are likely to find that damages are quantifiable and adequate.[677]

For example, in *Cargo Protectors, Inc. v. American Lock Co.*, the court denied a preliminary injunction to the submitter of design ideas for a lock guard device to a large lock manufacturer under a Submission of Idea Agreement.[678] The lock manufacturer used the design in its production without authorization from the submitter. The court found that despite the plaintiff's likelihood of success on a claim for a breach of the agreement, it suffered no irreparable harm in reputation but could easily determine lost profits based on sales of the device to other customers and the value of time spent developing the prototypes for the defendant.[679]

[7]   Federal Preemption

In situations where an idea is contained in a copyrighted work, a question arises whether the idea submitter's claims are preempted by the federal law. The subject matter of the federal Copyright Act of 1976 encompasses all original works of authorship fixed in a tangible medium of expression,[680] although the Act expressly excludes ideas from copyright protection.[681] The author of such a work holds exclusive rights of reproduction, adaptation, public distribution, public performance, and public display.[682] Under section 301 of the Copyright Act, state-law rights that are "equivalent" to the exclusive rights, in works that are fixed in a tangible medium and come within the subject matter of copyright, are preempted.[683]

Courts have rarely reached preemption issues in the idea submission context, and those that have ruled on the subject are split in opinion. Some courts read the express exclusion of ideas from the subject matter of the Copyright Act as an indication that the lawmakers did not intend preemption of idea submission claims.[684] Other courts hold that federal law preempts claims regarding ideas contained in copyrighted works even though ideas themselves are outside the

---

[674] Cargo Protectors, Inc. v. American Lock Co., 92 F. Supp. 2d 926, 929 (D. Minn. 2000); *see also* Modern Computer Sys., Inc. v. Modern Banking Sys., Inc., 871 F.2d 734, 737 (8th Cir. 1989).

[675] Intel Corp. v. ULSI System Tech., Inc., 995 F.2d 1566, 1568 (Fed. Cir. 1993).

[676] *See, e.g.*, Cargo Protectors, Inc. v. American Lock Co., 92 F. Supp. 2d 926, 934–35 (D. Minn. 2000).

[677] *See Cargo Protectors, Inc.*, 92 F. Supp. 2d at 935.

[678] 92 F. Supp. 2d 926 (D. Minn. 2000).

[679] *Id.* at 935.

[680] 17 U.S.C. § 102(a). *See* § 4C.

[681] 17 U.S.C. § 102(b). *See* § 4C[3].

[682] 17 U.S.C. § 106. *See* § 4[G].

[683] 17 U.S.C. § 301(a). *See* § 1D[3][c].

[684] *See, e.g.*, Dunlap v. G&L Holding Group, Inc., 381 F.3d 1285 (11th Cir. 2004).

subject matter of the Act.[685] This view is supported by the House Report to the 1976 Act.[686] It is clear, however, that if the idea is not fixed in a tangible medium, then statutory preemption does not apply,[687] although principles of conflict preemption might still come into play.[688]

Even if a work comes within the subject matter of copyright, however, the state-law right must still be "equivalent" to copyright in order to be preempted. A state-law claim based on an unjust enrichment or quasi-contract theory is typically deemed to be "equivalent" and is therefore preempted.[689] Courts that have found no preemption often focus on the existence of an "extra element" exceeding the requirements of copyright law. For instance, contract claims typically are not preempted because they require the additional element of an express or implied agreement to compensate the submitter.[690] Some courts have suggested that where the implied contract is a promise not to use or disclose an idea, rather than a promise to pay, the claim is "equivalent" to a copyright claim and should be preempted;[691] but other courts have rejected such a distinction.[692]

---

[685] *See* Forest Park Pictures v. Universal Television Network, Inc., 683 F.3d 424, 429–30 (2d Cir. 2012); Montz v. Pilgrim Films & Television, Inc., 649 F.3d 975, 979 (9th Cir. 2011); Briarpatch Ltd. v. Phoenix Pictures, Inc., 373 F.3d 296 (2d Cir. 2004) ("The subject matter requirement is satisfied if the claim applies to a work of authorship fixed in a tangible medium of expression and falling within the ambit of one of the categories of copyrightable works. These categories encompass literary works and motion pictures, 17 U.S.C. § 102(a), including those based on preexisting works . . . . A work need not consist entirely of copyrightable material in order to meet the subject matter requirement, but instead need only fit into one of the copyrightable categories in a broad sense.").

[686] *See* H.R. Rep. No. 94-1476, at 131 ("As long as a work fits within one of the general subject matter categories of sections 102 and 103, the bill prevents the States from protecting it even if it fails to achieve Federal statutory copyright because it is too minimal or lacking in originality to qualify, or because it has fallen into the public domain.").

[687] *Id.* ("On the other hand, section 301(b) expressly preserves common-law copyright protection for one important class of works: works that have not been 'fixed in any tangible medium of expression.' "); *Montz*, 649 F.3d at 979.

[688] *See* § 1D[3][c].

[689] *See, e.g.*, Briarpatch Ltd. v. Phoenix Pictures, Inc., 373 F.3d 296, 306–07 (2d Cir. 2004); NIMMER ON COPYRIGHT § 1.01[B][1][g]. *See also* § 1D[3][c], above.

[690] *See* Forest Park Pictures v. Universal Television Network, Inc., 683 F.3d 424, 431–33 (2d Cir. 2012); Montz v. Pilgrim Films & Television, Inc., 649 F.3d 975, 980–81 (9th Cir. 2011); Wrench LLC v. Taco Bell Corp., 256 F.3d 446, 456–58 (6th Cir. 2004).

[691] *See, e.g.*, *Wrench*, 256 F.3d at 457 ("If the promise amounts only to a promise to refrain from reproducing, performing, distributing or displaying the work, then the contract claim is preempted."); *see also Montz*, 649 F.3d at 983–84 (dissenting opinion).

[692] *See Montz*, 649 F.3d at 979–81 (majority *en banc* opinion).

INDEX

[References are to sections.]

A

ACPA (See ANTICYBERSQUATTING CONSUMER PROTECTION ACT (ACPA))

ANTICYBERSQUATTING CONSUMER PROTECTION ACT (ACPA)
Generally . . . 5H[1]
Elements of . . . 5H[1][a]
In rem jurisdiction . . . 5H[1][b]
Personal names . . . 5H[1][c]
Remedies . . . 5H[1][d]

B

BERNE CONVENTION IMPLEMENTATION ACT
Notice after . . . 4D[2][c]

C

COMMERCE CLAUSE
Generally . . . 1D[2]

CONSTITUTIONAL PROVISIONS
Generally . . . 1D
Commerce Clause . . . 1D[2]
Copyright (See COPYRIGHT)
Eleventh Amendment and sovereign immunity
  Generally . . . 1D[5]
  Claims against
    Federal government . . . 1D[5][b]
    State governments . . . 1D[5][a]
  Federal government, claims against
    . . . 1D[5][b]
  State governments, claims against . . . 1D[5][a]
First Amendment
  Generally . . . 1D[4]
  Copyright . . . 1D[4][b][i]
  Granting or withholding intellectual property
    rights . . . 1D[4][a]
  Rights of publicity (See RIGHTS OF PUBLICITY, subhead: First Amendment)
  Trademarks (See TRADEMARKS, subhead: First Amendment)
Moral rights . . . 1D[3][c][iv]
Patent and Copyright Clause . . . 1D[1]
Preemption under Supremacy Clause
  Contracts . . . 1D[3][b]
  Copying publicly disclosed subject matter
    . . . 1D[3][a]
  Copyright Act
    Generally . . . 1D[3][c]
    Equivalent rights . . . 1D[3][c][ii]
    Examples . . . 1D[3][c][iii]
    Moral rights . . . 1D[3][c][iv]
    Subject matter . . . 1D[3][c][i]
  Trademark laws . . . 5E[7][b]

CONSTITUTIONAL PROVISIONS—Cont.
Sovereign immunity (See subhead: Eleventh Amendment and sovereign immunity)
Subject matter . . . 1D[3][c][i]

CONTRACTS
Idea submission (See IDEA SUBMISSION, subhead: Contracts)
Preemption . . . 1D[3][b]
Trade secrets
  Contract law conflicts . . . 3D[2][c][i]
  Contract law theories . . . 3D[2][a]

COPYRIGHT
Generally . . . 1B[3]; 4A
Actual damages
  Generally . . . 4K[4][b][i]
  Consequential damages . . . 4K[4][b][i][c]
  Lost profits . . . 4K[4][b][i][a]
  Value of use . . . 4K[4][b][i][b]
Additional rights . . . 4G[8]
Aesthetic non-discrimination principle . . . 4C[1][d]
Architectural works
  Generally . . . 4C[4][a][viii]
  Architectural Works Copyright Protection Act
    . . . 4C[4][a][viii][b]
  Pre-1991 law . . . 4C[4][a][viii][a]
Broadcasts
  Compulsory licenses . . . 4G[9]
  Digital audio transmissions . . . 4G[6]
  Public performance rights (See subhead: Public performance rights)
Choreography . . . 4C[4][a][iv]
Collaborative works (See subhead: Joint works)
Collective works . . . 4C[4][b][i]; 4F[1][c]
Compilations . . . 4C[4][b][i]
Compulsory licenses . . . 4G[9]
Computer programs . . . 4C[4][a][i][b]
Constitutional standard . . . 4C[1][a]
Deposit . . . 4D[3][a]
Derivation or copying
  Generally . . . 4H[2]
  Access . . . 4H[2][a]
  Probative similarity . . . 4H[2][b]
Derivative works
  Generally . . . 4C[4][b][ii]; 4G[2][a]
  Exceptions and limitations . . . 4G[2][b]
Digital audio transmissions . . . 4G[6]
Digital Millennium Copyright Act (See DIGITAL MILLENNIUM COPYRIGHT ACT)
Display rights . . . 4G[5]
Distribution rights (See subhead: Public distribution)
Dramatic works . . . 4C[4][a][iii]
Duration . . . 4E[1]
Electronic distribution . . . 4G[3][b]
Exclusive rights and limitations
  Generally . . . 4G
  Additional rights . . . 4G[8]
  Compulsory licenses . . . 4G[9]

[References are to sections.]

COPYRIGHT—Cont.

Exclusive rights and limitations—Cont.

Derivative works

Generally . . . 4G[2][a]

Exceptions and limitations . . . 4G[2][b]

Digital audio transmissions . . . 4G[6]

Display rights . . . 4G[5]

Distribution rights (See subhead: Public distribution)

Moral rights

Generally . . . 4G[7][a]

Visual Artists Rights Act (VARA) . . . 4G[7][b]

Public distribution (See subhead: Public distribution)

Public performance rights (See subhead: Public performance rights)

Reproduction rights (See subhead: Reproduction rights)

Fair use

Generally . . . 4J; 4J[1]

Abandonment . . . 4J[2][e]

Amount and substantiality of use . . . 4J[1][b][iii]

Commentaries . . . 4J[1][c][i]

Commercial use . . . 4J[1][b][i][b]

Criticism . . . 4J[1][c][i]

Database uses . . . 4J[1][c][vii]

Documentaries . . . 4J[1][c][iii]

Educational use . . . 4J[1][b][i][c]

Estoppel . . . 4J[2][d]

Factors

Generally . . . 4J[1][b]

Commercial use . . . 4J[1][b][i][b]

Educational use . . . 4J[1][b][i][c]

Good faith . . . 4J[1][b][i][d]

Transformative use . . . 4J[1][b][i][a]

Forfeiture . . . 4J[2][e]

Good faith . . . 4J[1][b][i][d]

Inequitable conduct . . . 4J[2][a]

Internet uses . . . 4J[1][c][vii]

Laches . . . 4J[2][d]

Litigation uses . . . 4J[1][c][iv]

Marketplace as factor . . . 4J[1][b][iv]

Misuse . . . 4J[2][b]

Nature of copyrighted work . . . 4J[1][b][ii]

News reporting . . . 4J[1][c][iii]

Parody . . . 4J[1][c][ii]

Personal use . . . 4J[1][c][vi]

Preamble . . . 4J[1][a]

Reverse engineering . . . 4J[1][c][v]

Satire . . . 4J[1][c][ii]

Statute of limitations . . . 4J[2][c]

Transformative use . . . 4J[1][b][i][a]

First Amendment . . . 1D[4][b][i]

First-sale doctrine . . . 4G[3][c]

Fixation

Generally . . . 4C[2]

Live broadcasts and transmissions . . . 4C[2][c]

Live performances . . . 4C[2][d]

1976 Act

Generally . . . 4C[2][b]

Random-access memory . . . 4C[2][b][ii]

COPYRIGHT—Cont.

Fixation—Cont.

1976 Act—Cont.

Video games . . . 4C[2][b][i]

Random-access memory . . . 4C[2][b][ii]

Transmissions . . . 4C[2][c]

Video games . . . 4C[2][b][i]

White-Smith v. Appollo . . . 4C[2][a]

Formalities

Notice (See subhead: Notice)

Publication

1909 Act . . . 4D[1][a]

1976 Act . . . 4D[1][b]

Graphic works (See subhead: Pictorial, graphic, and sculptural works)

Historical development

English antecedents . . . 4B[1]

1909 Act . . . 4B[2][b]

1976-today . . . 4B[2][c]

1709-1909 . . . 4B[2][a]

Idea and expression

Baker v. Selden . . . 4C[3][b]

General principle . . . 4C[3][a]

Merger doctrine . . . 4C[3][c]

Scènes à Faire . . . 4C[3][d]

Import and export rights . . . 4G[3][d]

Infringement

Generally . . . 4H

De minimis use . . . 4H[3][c]

Derivation or copying (See subhead: Derivation or copying)

Ordinary observer test . . . 4H[3][b]

Ownership of valid copyright . . . 4H[1]

Protected expression

Abstraction-filtration-comparison . . . 4H[3][a][iii]

Dissection . . . 4H[3][a][i]

Ideas *versus* expression . . . 4H[3][a][ii]

Substantial similarity

Generally . . . 4H[3]

De minimis use . . . 4H[3][c]

Ordinary observer test . . . 4H[3][b]

Protected expression . . . 4H[3][a]

Infringer's profits

Generally . . . 4K[4][b][ii][a]

Apportionment . . . 4K[4][b][ii][c]

Indirect profits . . . 4K[4][b][ii][b]

Initial ownership

Generally . . . 4F[1]

Collective works . . . 4F[1][c]

Joint works (See subhead: Joint works)

Works for hire (See subhead: Works for hire)

Internet, secondary liability and

Generally . . . 4I[3][a]

Online service providers, limitation of liability for (See subhead: Online service providers, limitation of liability for)

Joint works

Generally . . . 4F[1][b]

1909 Act . . . 4F[1][b][i]

1976 Act . . . 4F[1][b][ii]

Literary works

Generally . . . 4C[4][a][i]

[References are to sections.]

COPYRIGHT—Cont.
Literary works—Cont.
  Characters . . . 4C[4][a][i][a]
  Computer programs . . . 4C[4][a][i][b]
Live broadcasts and transmissions . . . 4C[2][c]
Live performances . . . 4C[2][d]
Merger doctrine . . . 4C[3][c]
Monetary remedies
  Generally . . . 4K[4][a]
  Damages and profits
    Generally . . . 4K[4][b]
    Actual damages (See subhead: Actual damages)
    Infringer's profits (See subhead: Infringer's profits)
    Statutory damages (See subhead: Statutory damages)
Moral rights
  Generally . . . 4G[7][a]
  Visual Artists Rights Act (VARA) . . . 4G[7][b]
Motion pictures . . . 4C[4][a][vi]
Musical works . . . 4C[4][a][ii]
Notice
  Generally . . . 4D[2]
  Berne Convention Implementation Act, after . . . 4D[2][c]
  Collective works . . . 4D[2][b][iii]
  Errors in notice . . . 4D[2][b][ii]
  1909 Act, under . . . 4D[2][a]
  1976 Act, under
    Generally . . . 4D[2][b]
    Collective works . . . 4D[2][b][iii]
    Errors in notice . . . 4D[2][b][ii]
    Omission of notice . . . 4D[2][b][i]
  Omission of notice . . . 4D[2][b][i]
  Termination of transfers . . . 4F[3][b]
Online service providers, limitation of liability for
  Notice-and-take-down provisions . . . 4I[3][b][iii]
  Safe harbors
    Generally . . . 4I[3][b][i]
    Eligibility for . . . 4I[3][b][ii]
    Information location tools . . . 4I[3][b][i][d]
    System caching . . . 4I[3][b][i][b]
    Transitory digital network communications . . . 4I[3][b][i][a]
    Web hosting . . . 4I[3][b][i][c]
Originality
  Aesthetic non-discrimination principle . . . 4C[1][d]
  Constitutional standard . . . 4C[1][a]
  Photographs . . . 4C[1][c]
  Words and short phrases . . . 4C[1][b]
Ownership
  Infringement, as prerequisite for . . . 4H[1]
  Initial ownership (See subhead: Initial ownership)
Pantomimes . . . 4C[4][a][iv]
Performance rights (See subhead: Public performance rights)
Photographs . . . 4C[1][c]
Pictorial, graphic, and sculptural works
  Generally . . . 4C[4][a][v][a]

COPYRIGHT—Cont.
Pictorial, graphic, and sculptural works—Cont.
  Useful articles
    Historical development . . . 4C[4][a][v][b][1]
    Separability . . . 4C[4][a][v][b][3]
    Statutory definition . . . 4C[4][a][v][b][2]
Preexisting material, works using
  Generally . . . 4C[4][b]
  Collective works . . . 4C[4][b][i]
  Compilations . . . 4C[4][b][i]
  Derivative works . . . 4C[4][b][ii]
Publication
  1909 Act . . . 4D[1][a]
  1976 Act . . . 4D[1][b]
Public distribution
  Generally . . . 4G[3][a]
  Electronic distribution . . . 4G[3][b]
  First-sale doctrine . . . 4G[3][c]
  Import and export rights . . . 4G[3][d]
Public performance rights
  Generally . . . 4G[4][a]
  Exceptions and limitations . . . 4G[4][c]
  Performing rights organizations . . . 4G[4][d]
  Secondary transmissions
    Generally . . . 4G[4][b]
    1909 Act . . . 4G[4][b][i]
    1976 Act . . . 4G[4][b][ii]
Random-access memory . . . 4C[2][b][ii]
Registration . . . 4D[3][b]
Remedies
  Generally . . . 4K[1]
  Attorney's fees . . . 4K[5]
  Costs and attorney's fees . . . 4K[5]
  Criminal penalties . . . 4K[6]
  Disposition . . . 4K[3]
  Impoundment . . . 4K[3]
  Injunctions
    Generally . . . 4K[2]
    Permanent injunctions . . . 4K[2][b]
    Preliminary injunctions . . . 4K[2][a]
  Monetary remedies (See subhead: Monetary remedies)
Renewal
  Automatic renewal . . . 4E[2][c]
  Derivative works, and . . . 4E[2][b]
  Principles, basic . . . 4E[2][a]
Reproduction rights
  Generally . . . 4G[1][a]
  Electronic reproduction . . . 4G[1][b]
  Exceptions and limitations . . . 4G[1][c]
Restoration of copyright in foreign works . . . 4E[3]
Scènes à Faire . . . 4C[3][d]
Sculptural works (See subhead: Pictorial, graphic, and sculptural works)
Secondary liability
  Generally . . . 4I
  Contributory infringement . . . 4I[1][a]
  Copying devices or software
    Audio Home Recording Act . . . 4I[2][b]
    Peer-to-peer file sharing . . . 4I[2][c]
    Sony decision . . . 4I[2][a]

[References are to sections.]

COPYRIGHT—Cont.

Secondary liability—Cont.

    Digital Millennium Copyright Act (See DIGITAL MILLENNIUM COPYRIGHT ACT)

    Internet, secondary liability and

        Generally . . . 4I[3][a]

        Online service providers, limitation of liability for (See subhead: Online service providers, limitation of liability for)

        Vicarious liability . . . 4I[1][b]

    Sound recordings . . . 4C[4][a][vii]

    Statutory damages

        Generally . . . 4K[4][c]

        Amount of award . . . 4K[4][c][iii]

        Constitutionality . . . 4K[4][c][iv]

        Defendant's intent . . . 4K[4][c][ii]

        Number of works infringed . . . 4K[4][c][i]

    Subject matter, copyrightable

        Generally . . . 4C

        Fixation (See subhead: Fixation)

        Government works . . . 4C[5]

        Idea and expression (See subhead: Idea and expression)

        National eligibility . . . 4C[6]

        Originality (See subhead: Originality)

    Termination of transfers

        Generally . . . 4F[3]

        Agreements to contrary . . . 4F[3][d]

        Effect of termination . . . 4F[3][c]

        Notice . . . 4F[3][b]

        Persons entitled to terminate . . . 4F[3][a]

        Time periods for termination . . . 4F[3][b]

    Transfers

        Licenses, and . . . 4F[2]

        Termination of transfers (See subhead: Termination of transfers)

    Transmissions . . . 4C[2][c]

    Video games . . . 4C[2][b][i]

    Words and short phrases . . . 4C[1][b]

    Works for hire

        Generally . . . 4F[1][a]

        1909 Act . . . 4F[1][a][i]

        1976 Act . . . 4F[1][a][ii]

    Works of authorship

        Architectural works (See subhead: Architectural works)

        Choreography . . . 4C[4][a][iv]

        Dramatic works . . . 4C[4][a][iii]

        Literary works (See subhead: Literary works)

        Motion pictures . . . 4C[4][a][vi]

        Musical works . . . 4C[4][a][ii]

        Pantomimes . . . 4C[4][a][iv]

        Preexisting material, works using (See subhead: Preexisting material, works using)

        Sound recordings . . . 4C[4][a][vii]

        Statutory categories

            Generally . . . 4C[4][a]

            Architectural works (See subhead: Architectural works)

            Choreography . . . 4C[4][a][iv]

            Dramatic works . . . 4C[4][a][iii]

            Literary works (See subhead: Literary works)

            Motion pictures . . . 4C[4][a][vi]

COPYRIGHT—Cont.

Works of authorship—Cont.

    Statutory categories—Cont.

        Musical works . . . 4C[4][a][ii]

        Pantomimes . . . 4C[4][a][iv]

        Pictorial, graphic, and sculptural works (See subhead: Pictorial, graphic, and sculptural works)

        Sound recordings . . . 4C[4][a][vii]

CYBERSQUATTING

Alternative forums for domain name disputes . . . 5H[1][e]

Anticybersquatting Consumer Protection Act (ACPA) (See ANTICYBERSQUATTING CONSUMER PROTECTION ACT (ACPA))

D

DAMAGES

Actual damages . . . 5K[2][a]

Copyright

    Actual damages (See COPYRIGHT, subhead: Actual damages)

    Statutory damages (See COPYRIGHT, subhead: Statutory damages)

Enhanced damages . . . 5K[2][b]

Federal dilution law, under . . . 5K[2][g]

Patents (See PATENTS, subhead: Damages)

Statutory damages . . . 5K[2][d]

Trademarks

    Actual damages . . . 5K[2][a]

    Enhanced damages . . . 5K[2][b]

    Federal dilution law, damages under . . . 5K[2][g]

    Statutory damages . . . 5K[2][d]

Trade secrets

    Compensatory damages (See TRADE SECRETS, subhead: Compensatory damages)

    Punitive damages . . . 3F[2][b]

DESIGN PROTECTION

Generally . . . 6B; 6B[1]; 6B[5]

Application and examination . . . 6B[3]

Exclusive rights . . . 6B[4]

Infringement . . . 6B[4]

Patentability requirements

    Generally . . . 6B[2]

    Article of manufacture . . . 6B[2][a]

    Nonfunctionality . . . 6B[2][c]

    Nonobviousness . . . 6B[2][e]

    Novelty . . . 6B[2][d]

    Ornamentality . . . 6B[2][b]

    Statutory bars . . . 6B[2][d]

Remedies . . . 6B[4]

DIGITAL MILLENNIUM COPYRIGHT ACT

Generally . . . 4I[4]

Anti-circumvention

    Generally . . . 4I[4][a][i]

    Access-control measures . . . 4I[4][a][i][b]

    Authorization . . . 4I[4][a][i][d]

    Circumvention . . . 4I[4][a][i][c]

[References are to sections.]

DIGITAL MILLENNIUM COPYRIGHT ACT—Cont.

Anti-circumvention—Cont.

    Defenses, other . . . 4I[4][a][i][f][iv]

    Design, use, and marketing of technology . . . 4I[4][a][i][f]

    Facilitation of infringement . . . 4I[4][a][i][e]

    Ownership of valid copyright . . . 4I[4][a][i][a]

    Regulatory exceptions . . . 4I[4][a][i][f][iii]

    Statutory exceptions . . . 4I[4][a][i][f][ii]

Copyright management information . . . 4I[4][b]

E

ELEVENTH AMENDMENT (See CONSTITUTIONAL PROVISIONS, subhead: Eleventh Amendment and sovereign immunity)

EQUIVALENT RIGHTS

Copyright Act preemption . . . 1D[3][c][ii]

F

FALSE ADVERTISING

Current federal law

    Generally . . . 6E[2]

    Commercial advertising or promotion . . . 6E[2][b]; 6E[2][c]

    Falsity . . . 6E[2][a]

    Standing . . . 6E[2][d]

Historical development . . . 6E[1]

FIRST AMENDMENT (See CONSTITUTIONAL PROVISIONS, subhead: First Amendment)

I

IDEA SUBMISSION

Generally . . . 6H

Concreteness as prerequisite for protection . . . 6H[1][b]

Contracts

    Express contracts

        Generally . . . 6H[2]

        Novelty and concreteness requirements . . . 6H[2][a]

        Standard release forms . . . 6H[2][b]

    Implied contracts (See subhead: Implied contracts)

Federal preemption . . . 6H[7]

Implied contracts

    Generally . . . 6H[3]

    Confidential relationship . . . 6H[3][c]

    Solicited submissions . . . 6H[3][b]

    Unsolicited submissions

        Failure to reject after notice . . . 6H[3][a][ii]

        Involuntarily received . . . 6H[3][a][i]

Novelty as prerequisite for protection . . . 6H[1][a]

Property theory . . . 6H[5]

Remedies . . . 6H[6]

Unjust enrichment . . . 6H[4]

INFRINGEMENT

Copyright (See COPYRIGHT, subhead: Infringement)

Patents (See PATENTS, subhead: Infringement)

Rights of publicity (See RIGHTS OF PUBLICITY, subhead: Infringement and defenses)

Semiconductor chip protection (See SEMICONDUCTOR CHIP PROTECTION, subhead: Exclusive rights: infringement)

Trademarks (See TRADEMARKS, subhead: Infringement)

INTELLECTUAL PROPERTY LAW (GENERALLY)

Generally . . . 6A

Copyright (See COPYRIGHT)

Design protection (See DESIGN PROTECTION)

False advertising (See FALSE ADVERTISING)

Human creativity, and . . . 1A

Idea submission (See IDEA SUBMISSION)

Misappropriation (See MISAPPROPRIATION)

Moral rights (See MORAL RIGHTS)

Other intellectual property rights . . . 1B[5]

Patents (See PATENTS)

Plant protection (See PLANT PROTECTION)

Policy considerations . . . 1C

Rights . . . 1B

Rights of publicity (See RIGHTS OF PUBLICITY)

Semiconductor chip protection (See SEMICONDUCTOR CHIP PROTECTION)

Trademarks (See TRADEMARKS)

Trade secrets (See TRADE SECRETS)

L

LANHAM ACT (See TRADEMARKS, subhead: Lanham Act)

M

MISAPPROPRIATION

Generally . . . 6F

Contemporary applications . . . 6F[4]

INS decision . . . 6F[1]

INS to *Sears-Compco* . . . 6F[2]

Sears-Compco and federal preemption . . . 6F[3]

Trade secrets (See TRADE SECRETS, subhead: Misappropriation litigation)

MORAL RIGHTS

Generally . . . 4G[7][a]

Copyright Act preemption . . . 1D[3][c][iv]

Visual Artists Rights Act (VARA) . . . 4G[7][b]

P

PATENTS

Generally . . . 1B[1]; 2A; 2C

Abandonment . . . 2C[5][b][vi]

Applications for

    Generally . . . 2D

    Claiming requirements (See subhead: Claiming requirements)

PATENTS—Cont.

Applications for—Cont.

Continuation applications (See subhead: Continuation applications)

Derivation proceedings . . . 2D[5][g]

Disclosure requirements (See subhead: Disclosure requirements)

Double patenting doctrine (See subhead: Double patenting doctrine)

Interferences proceedings (See subhead: Interferences proceedings)

Post-issuance procedures (See subhead: Post-issuance procedures)

Prosecution of patent applications (See subhead: Prosecution of patent applications)

Attorney's fees and expenses . . . 2H[4]

Best mode requirement (See subhead: Disclosure requirements)

Claiming requirements

Generally . . . 2D[3]

Alternative limitations-Markush groups . . . 2D[3][d]

Definiteness . . . 2D[3][a]

Format . . . 2D[3][b]

Functionality-Means-plus-function claims . . . 2D[3][e]

Jepson claims . . . 2D[3][c]

Multiple claims-dependent claims . . . 2D[3][g]

Negative limitations . . . 2D[3][f]

Continuation applications

Generally . . . 2D[4][b]

Copendency . . . 2D[4][b][iii]

Cross references . . . 2D[4][b][ii]

Disclosure continuity . . . 2D[4][b][i]

Inventorship . . . 2D[4][b][iv]

Damages

Compensatory damages . . . 2H[2][a]

Increased damages—willful infringement . . . 2H[2][b]

Notice—patent marking . . . 2H[2][c]

Defenses

Generally . . . 2G

Estoppel . . . 2G[5]

Experimental use . . . 2G[4]

First sale doctrine . . . 2G[6]

Fraud . . . 2G[2]

Implied license . . . 2G[6]

Inequitable conduct . . . 2G[2]

Invalidity

Generally . . . 2G[1]

Judgment, effect of . . . 2G[1][c]

Presumption of validity . . . 2G[1][a]

Standing to challenge validity . . . 2G[1][b]

Laches . . . 2G[5]

Misuse . . . 2G[3]

Personal use . . . 2G[4]

Prior commercial use . . . 2G[7]

Derivation proceedings . . . 2D[5][g]

Disclosure requirements

Generally . . . 2D[2]

Best mode requirement

Generally . . . 2D[2][c][i]

Computer programs . . . 2D[2][c][ii]

PATENTS—Cont.

Disclosure requirements—Cont.

Best mode requirement—Cont.

Time frame . . . 2D[2][c][iv]

Trade secrets . . . 2D[2][c][iii]

Enablement requirement

Generally . . . 2D[2][a]

Biological material, deposit of . . . 2D[2][a][iv]

Claim scope . . . 2D[2][a][i]

Experimentation . . . 2D[2][a][ii]

Other enablement issues . . . 2D[2][a][iii]

Inventor identification

Generally . . . 2D[2][d]

Correcting inventorship . . . 2D[2][d][iv]

Joint invention . . . 2D[2][d][ii]

Separate claims . . . 2D[2][d][iii]

Sole invention . . . 2D[2][d][i]

Written description requirement . . . 2D[2][b]

Double patenting doctrine

Generally . . . 2D[4][a]

Claim comparison . . . 2D[4][a][i]

Design and utility patents . . . 2D[4][a][iv]

Different inventors' commonly assigned applications . . . 2D[4][a][vi]

Identical inventions . . . 2D[4][a][ii]

Obvious variation . . . 2D[4][a][iii]

Terminal disclaimers . . . 2D[4][a][v]

Utility patent . . . 2D[4][a][iv]

Exclusive rights

Generally . . . 2E[2]

Direct infringement . . . 2E[2][a]

Exportation . . . 2E[2][b][i]

Importation . . . 2E[2][b][ii]

Process patent protection . . . 2E[2][b][iii]

Secondary liability

Generally . . . 2E[2][c]

Active inducement . . . 2E[2][c][ii]

Contributory infringement . . . 2E[2][c][iii]

Directors of corporations . . . 2E[2][c][iv]

Officers of corporations . . . 2E[2][c][iv]

Relation to direct infringement . . . 2E[2][c][i]

Territorial rights . . . 2E[2][b]

Experimental use exception . . . 2C[5][b][v]

Foreign patenting . . . 2C[5][b][vii]

Historical development

1836 and 1870 Acts . . . 2B[2]

1880–1892 . . . 2B[4][a]

1892–1930 . . . 2B[4][b]

First invention concept . . . 2B[3]

Leahy-Smith America Invents Act of 2011 . . . 2B[7]

1930–1950 . . . 2B[4][c]

1952 Act . . . 2B[5]

1966 *Graham* trilogy and beyond . . . 2B[6]

1790 and 1793 Acts . . . 2B[1]

Infringement

Generally . . . 2F

Claim language interpretation

Generally . . . 2F[1]

Consistency . . . 2F[1][c]

Differentiation, claim . . . 2F[1][a][i]

[References are to sections.]

PATENTS—Cont.
Infringement—Cont.
  Claim language interpretation—Cont.
    Expert testimony . . . 2F[1][a][iv]
    Lexicographer principle . . . 2F[1][a][ii]
    Means-plus-function limitations . . . 2F[1][b]
    Prosecution history . . . 2F[1][a][iii]
  Design patents . . . 6B[4]
  Doctrine of equivalents
    Generally . . . 2F[2][b]
    "All elements" rule . . . 2F[2][b][iii]
    Comparison standard . . . 2F[2][b][iii]
    Graver Tank . . . 2F[2][b][i]
    Later developed equivalents . . . 2F[2][b][v]
    Prior art constraints . . . 2F[2][b][vii]
    Range of equivalents . . . 2F[2][b][iv]
    Reverse doctrine of equivalents
      . . . 2F[2][b][vi]
    Triple-identity test . . . 2F[2][b][ii]
    Warner-Jenkinson . . . 2F[2][b][i]
  Joinder provisions . . . 2F[4]
  Jurisdiction . . . 2F[4]
  Literal infringement
    Generally . . . 2F[2][a]
    Additions and improvements . . . 2F[2][a][ii]
    Omissions . . . 2F[2][a][i]
  Plant patents . . . 6C[1][c]
  Plant Variety Protection Act (PVPA)
    . . . 6C[2][c]
  Proof of infringing activity
    Agency . . . 2F[3][c]
    Burden of proof . . . 2F[3][a]
    Employees . . . 2F[3][c]
    Intent . . . 2F[3][b]
    Officers of corporations . . . 2F[3][c]
  Prosecution history estoppel
    Generally . . . 2F[2][c]
    Acts giving rise to . . . 2F[2][c][i]
    Effect of . . . 2F[2][c][ii]
  Injunctions
    Generally . . . 2H[1]
    Permanent injunctions . . . 2H[1][b]
    Preliminary injunctions . . . 2H[1][a]
  Interest . . . 2H[3]
  Interferences proceedings
    Generally . . . 2D[5]
    Abandonment . . . 2D[5][f]
    Concealment . . . 2D[5][f]
    Conception . . . 2D[5][b]
    Corroboration . . . 2D[5][e]
    Diligence . . . 2D[5][d]
    First-to-invent rule . . . 2D[5][a]
    Priority rules . . . 2D[5][a]
    Reduction to practice . . . 2D[5][c]
    Suppression . . . 2D[5][f]
  Nonobviousness requirement
    Generally . . . 2C[4]
    Comparative utility
      New and unexpected properties
        . . . 2C[4][c][ii]
      Rationale . . . 2C[4][c][i]
      Undisclosed advantages and properties
        . . . 2C[4][c][iii]

PATENTS—Cont.
Nonobviousness requirement—Cont.
  General test -*Graham v. Deere* . . . 2C[4][a]
  Guidelines, other
    Generally . . . 2C[4][e]
    Chemical compounds and intermediates
      . . . 2C[4][e][iii]
    Combination inventions . . . 2C[4][e][ii]
    Methods of making and using
      . . . 2C[4][e][iv]
    Obvious to try approach . . . 2C[4][e][i]
  Nonanalogous art . . . 2C[4][b]
  Objective evidence
    Generally . . . 2C[4][d]
    Commercial success . . . 2C[4][d][ii]
    Copying by infringer . . . 2C[4][d][iv]
    Laudatory statements by infringer
      . . . 2C[4][d][iv]
    Licensing and acquiescence by competitors
      . . . 2C[4][d][iii]
    Long-felt need—failure of others
      . . . 2C[4][d][i]
    Near simultaneous invention . . . 2C[4][d][v]
Novelty requirement . . . 2C[3]
Ownership and transfer
  Generally . . . 2I
  Ability to sue infringers . . . 2I[2]
  Compulsory licenses . . . 2I[3]
  Employee and contractor inventions . . . 2I[1]
Patentable subject matter
  Generally . . . 2C[1]
  Business methods . . . 2C[1][e]
  Computer software
    Abstract ideas . . . 2C[1][f][i]
    Grams and *Iwahashi* . . . 2C[1][f][iii]
    Supreme Court precedent on software patents
      . . . 2C[1][f][ii]
  Definitions . . . 2C[1][a]
  Exclusions and exceptions . . . 2C[1][b]
  Living organisms, products of . . . 2C[1][d]
  Methods of treatment . . . 2C[1][e]
  Nature and living organisms, products of
    . . . 2C[1][d]
  New uses of old products . . . 2C[1][c]
  Products of nature and living organisms
    . . . 2C[1][d]
Post-issuance procedures
  Inter partes review . . . 2D[6][d]
  Post-grant review . . . 2D[6][c]
  Reexamination . . . 2D[6][a]
  Reissue (See subhead: Reissue)
Prior art before Leahy-Smith America Invents Act
(AIA)
  Generally . . . 2C[5]
  Continuation applications . . . 2C[5][c][iii]
  Derivation—section 102(f) . . . 2C[5][d][ii]
  Documentary sources
    Generally . . . 2C[5][a]
    Patents . . . 2C[5][a][ii]
    Publications . . . 2C[5][a][i]
  Invention date . . . 2C[5][e]
  Inventive entities . . . 2C[5][f]
  Milburn doctrine . . . 2C[5][c][i]

[References are to sections.]

PATENTS—Cont.
Prior art before Leahy-Smith America Invents Act
(AIA)—Cont.
    Patents . . . 2C[5][a][ii]
    Prior invention—section 102(g) . . . 2C[5][d][i]
    Publications . . . 2C[5][a][i]
    Public use and sale
        Abandonment . . . 2C[5][b][vi]
        Experimental use exception . . . 2C[5][b][v]
        Foreign patenting . . . 2C[5][b][vii]
        Known or used by others . . . 2C[5][b][i]
        Sale in United States . . . 2C[5][b][iv]
        Statutory bars . . . 2C[5][b][ii]
        Use in United States . . . 2C[5][b][iii]
    Senior-filed patents
        Generally . . . 2C[5][c]
        Continuation applications . . . 2C[5][c][iii]
        Foreign priority applications . . . 2C[5][c][ii]
        Issuance . . . 2C[5][c][iv]
        Milburn doctrine . . . 2C[5][c][i]
Prior art under Leahy-Smith America Invents Act
(AIA) . . . 2C[6]
Prosecution of patent applications
    Generally . . . 2D[1][a]
    Amendments . . . 2D[1][d]
    Confidentiality . . . 2D[1][c]
    Duty of candor . . . 2D[1][e]
    Unity of invention as condition of filing
        . . . 2D[1][b]
Reissue
    Generally . . . 2D[6][b]
    Claim scope alteration . . . 2D[6][b][ii]
    Effect of . . . 2D[6][b][v]
    Error . . . 2D[6][b][iii]
    Inoperativeness and invalidity . . . 2D[6][b][i]
    Oath or declaration . . . 2D[6][b][iv]
Remedies
    Attorney's fees and expenses . . . 2H[4]
    Damages (See subhead: Damages)
    Injunctions (See subhead: Injunctions)
    Interest . . . 2H[3]
Rights
    Generally . . . 2E
    Duration . . . 2E[1]
    Exclusive rights (See subhead: Exclusive rights)
    Exhaustion of rights . . . 2E[3]
    First sale doctrine . . . 2E[3]
    Government use . . . 2E[4]
    Repair and reconstruction . . . 2E[3]
Utility requirement . . . 2C[2]

PLANT PATENT ACT (See PLANT PROTEC-
TION, subhead: Plant Patent Act)

PLANT PROTECTION
Generally . . . 6C
Plant Patent Act
    Generally . . . 6C[1]
    Application and examination . . . 6C[1][b]
    Exclusive rights . . . 6C[1][c]
    Infringement . . . 6C[1][c]
    Requirements . . . 6C[1][a]

PLANT PROTECTION—Cont.
Plant Variety Protection Act (PVPA)
    Generally . . . 6C[2]
    Application and examination . . . 6C[2][b]
    Exclusive rights . . . 6C[2][c]
    Infringement . . . 6C[2][c]
    Requirements . . . 6C[2][a]
Protection source choice factors . . . 6C[4]
Trade-Related Aspects of Intellectual Property
    (TRIPS), plant breeders rights under . . . 6C[5]
Utility patents for plants . . . 6C[3]

PLANT VARIETY PROTECTION ACT (PVPA)
(See PLANT PROTECTION, subhead: Plant Variety Protection Act (PVPA))

PUBLICITY RIGHTS (See RIGHTS OF PUBLIC-
ITY)

R

RIGHTS OF PUBLICITY
Generally . . . 6G[1]
First Amendment
    Generally . . . 6G[4][c]
    Other uses . . . 6G[4][c][iii]
    Parody and satire . . . 6G[4][c][ii]
    Works of art . . . 6G[4][c][i]
Historical development . . . 6G[2]
Infringement and defenses
    Generally . . . 6G[4][d][v]
    Antitrust . . . 6G[4][d][iii]
    Copyright preemption . . . 6G[4][d][i]
    First Amendment (See subhead: First Amend-
        ment)
    First sale doctrine . . . 6G[4][d][ii]
    Laches . . . 6G[4][d][iv]
    Newsworthiness . . . 6G[4][b]
    Prima facie case . . . 6G[4][a]
    Statute of limitations . . . 6G[4][d][iv]
Likenesses . . . 6G[3][b]
Names . . . 6G[3][a]
Ownership . . . 6G[6]
Remedies . . . 6G[5]
Roles . . . 6G[3][c]
Transfer . . . 6G[6]
Voice and vocal imitations . . . 6G[3][d]

S

SEMICONDUCTOR CHIP PROTECTION
Generally . . . 6D[1]
Exclusive rights: infringement
    Generally . . . 6D[4][c]
    Innocent infringement . . . 6D[4][b][iii]
    International protection for semiconductor chips
        . . . 6D[5]
Limitations
    First sale doctrine . . . 6D[4][b][ii]
    Ideas, procedures and principles
        . . . 6D[4][b][iv]
    Innocent infringement . . . 6D[4][b][iii]
    Reverse engineering . . . 6D[4][b][i]

[References are to sections.]

SEMICONDUCTOR CHIP PROTECTION—Cont.

Exclusive rights: infringement—Cont.
Rights granted . . . 6D[4][a]
Protection requirements
Definitions . . . 6D[2][a]
Originality . . . 6D[2][b]
Owner nationality . . . 6D[2][c]
Registration . . . 6D[3]
Remedies
Attorney fees . . . 6D[4][d][ii]
Damages . . . 6D[4][d][ii]
Injunctive relief . . . 6D[4][d][i]
International Trade Commission Remedies
. . . 6D[4][d][iii]

SOVEREIGN IMMUNITY (See CONSTITU-
TIONAL PROVISIONS, subhead: Eleventh
Amendment and sovereign immunity)

T

**TRADEMARK DILUTION REVISION ACT
(TDRA)**
Generally . . . 5G[3][f][ii]; 5G[3][g]

TRADEMARKS
Generally . . . 1B[4]; 5A
Abandonment
Generally . . . 5J[1]
Assignment in gross . . . 5J[1][b][ii]
Cessation of use . . . 5J[1][a]
Naked licensing . . . 5J[1][b][i]
Other causes of abandonment
Generally . . . 5J[1][b]
Assignment in gross . . . 5J[1][b][ii]
Naked licensing . . . 5J[1][b][i]
Assignments . . . 5D[4][a]
Celebrity likenesses . . . 5C[2][c][iv]
Certification marks . . . 5E[1][c]
Classic fair use . . . 5J[3]
Collective marks . . . 5E[1][d]
Colors . . . 5C[2][c][ii]
Comparative advertising . . . 5J[5]
Constructive use . . . 5D[1][b][v]
Criminal penalties
Counterfeit labels . . . 5K[4][b]
Counterfeit marks . . . 5K[4][a]
Cybersquatting
Alternative forums for domain name disputes
. . . 5H[1][e]
Anticybersquatting Consumer Protection Act
(ACPA) (See ANTICYBERSQUATTING
CONSUMER PROTECTION ACT (ACPA))
Declaratory judgments . . . 5F[5][c]
Defenses
Generally . . . 5J
Abandonment (See subhead: Abandonment)
Acquiescence . . . 5J[7][b]
Classic fair use . . . 5J[3]
Comparative advertising . . . 5J[5]
Federal preemption . . . 5J[8]

TRADEMARKS—Cont.

Defenses—Cont.
First Amendment (See subhead: First Amend-
ment)
First sale doctrine (See subhead: First sale doc-
trine)
Laches . . . 5J[7][a]
Sovereign immunity . . . 5J[9]
Statute of limitations . . . 5J[7][c]
Unclean hands . . . 5J[7][d]
Defined . . . 5C[2]
Destruction of infringing articles . . . 5K[1][c]
Dilution
Concept of . . . 5F[1]
Noncommercial expression . . . 5J[6][b][ii]
Parodies . . . 5J[6][a][ii]
Remedies . . . 5G[5]
State law, under . . . 5F[2]
Disclaimers . . . 5K[1][e]
Distinctiveness
Generally . . . 5C[1][b]; 5C[2][a]; 5D[2]
Arbitrary or fanciful . . . 5C[2][a][i]
Descriptive
Generally . . . 5C[2][a][iii]
Common law . . . 5C[2][a][iii][a]
Secondary meaning . . . 5C[2][a][iii][b]
Generic terms . . . 5C[2][a][iv]
Suggestive . . . 5C[2][a][ii]
Early federal law . . . 5B[3]
Expressive works . . . 5C[2][c][iii]
Famous marks doctrine . . . 5D[1][b][iii]
Federal Trademark Dilution Act (FTDA)
Actual *versus* likelihood of dilution
Blurring . . . 5G[3][f][iii][a]
Judicial interpretations . . . 5G[3][f][iii]
Moseley decision . . . 5G[3][f][i]
Tarnishment . . . 5G[3][f][iii][b]
Trademark Dilution Revision Act (TDRA)
. . . 5G[3][f][ii]; 5G[3][g]
Distinctive and famous mark
Generally . . . 5G[3][d]
Distinctiveness . . . 5G[3][d][i]
Fame . . . 5G[3][d][ii]
Trade dress and other nontraditional marks
. . . 5G[3][d][iii]
Elements of claims . . . 5G[3][b]
Exceptions
Fair use . . . 5G[4][a]
Federal registration as defense . . . 5G[4][d]
News reporting and commentary
. . . 5G[4][c]
Noncommercial use . . . 5G[4][b]
History . . . 5G[3][a]
News reporting and commentary . . . 5G[4][c]
Noncommercial use exception . . . 5G[4][b]
Similarity . . . 5G[3][e]
Trademark Dilution Revision Act (TDRA)
Effective date of . . . 5G[3][g]
Likelihood of dilution under . . . 5G[3][f][ii]
Trademark use . . . 5G[3][c]
Fictional characters . . . 5C[2][c][iv]
First Amendment
Generally . . . 1D[4][b][ii]; 5J[6]

[References are to sections.]

TRADEMARKS—Cont.
First Amendment—Cont.
  Commercial parodies
    Generally . . . 5J[6][a]
    Dilution . . . 5J[6][a][ii]
    Infringement . . . 5J[6][a][i]
    Unfair competition . . . 5J[6][a][i]
  Expressive merchandise . . . 5J[6][d]
  Noncommercial expression
    Dilution . . . 5J[6][b][ii]
    Infringement . . . 5J[6][b][i]
    Unfair competition . . . 5J[6][b][i]
  Political speech . . . 5J[6][c]
First sale doctrine
  Generally . . . 5J[2]
  Authorized resellers, misrepresentation by
    . . . 5J[2][a]
  Materially different goods
    Generally . . . 5J[2][b]
    Altered goods . . . 5J[2][b][i]
    Other non-genuine goods . . . 5J[2][b][ii]
    Refurbished goods . . . 5J[2][b][i]
    Used goods . . . 5J[2][b][i]
  Misrepresentation by authorized resellers
    . . . 5J[2][a]
  Parallel imports . . . 5J[2][d]
  Repackaging, nondisclosure of . . . 5J[2][c]
Foreign use . . . 5D[1][b][ii]
Historical development
  Early federal law . . . 5B[3]
  Lanham Act
    Generally . . . 5B[4][a]
    Recent amendments . . . 5B[4][b]
  Modern common law . . . 5B[2]
  "Passing off" concept . . . 5B[1]
  State statutes . . . 5B[2]
Incontestability
  Effect of incontestable status . . . 5E[4][a]
  Establishing incontestability . . . 5E[4][b]
Infringement
  Generally . . . 5F
  Confusion, likelihood of
    Generally . . . 5F[3][a]
    Actual confusion . . . 5F[3][b][v]
    Bridging gap . . . 5F[3][b][vi]
    Competitive proximity . . . 5F[3][b][ii]
    Consumer sophistication . . . 5F[3][b][iv]
    Defendant's intent . . . 5F[3][b][vii]
    Factors for evaluating . . . 5F[3][b]
    Initial interest confusion . . . 5F[3][e][i]
    Parodies . . . 5J[6][a][i]
    Polaroid test . . . 5F[3][c]
    Post-sale confusion . . . 5F[3][e][ii]
    Relative quality of defendant's goods or services . . . 5F[3][b][viii]
    Reverse confusion . . . 5F[3][d]
    Similarity of marks . . . 5F[3][b][i]
    Strength of plaintiff's mark . . . 5F[3][b][iii]
  Declaratory judgments . . . 5F[5][c]
  Federal registration, effect of . . . 5F[1]
  Jurisdiction
    Commerce as jurisdictional prerequisite, use in
      . . . 5F[5]

TRADEMARKS—Cont.
Infringement—Cont.
  Jurisdiction—Cont.
    Subject matter jurisdiction . . . 5F[8][a]
    Noncommercial expression . . . 5J[6][b][ii]
    Ownership of valid mark . . . 5F[2]
    Reverse passing off . . . 5F[7]
    Standing for causes of action . . . 5F[5][b]
    Territorial limitations . . . 5F[6]
    Use of mark as prerequisite
      Generally . . . 5F[4]
      Commerce as jurisdictional prerequisite, use in
        . . . 5F[5]
      Domain names . . . 5F[4][c]
      Expressive works . . . 5F[4][d]
      Keyword-triggered advertising . . . 5F[4][a]
      Metatags . . . 5F[4][b]
  Injunctions . . . 5K[1][a]
  Intent to use (ITU) applications . . . 5D[1][b][iv]
  Lanham Act
    Generally . . . 5B[4][a]
    Constructive use . . . 5D[1][b][v]
    Famous marks doctrine . . . 5D[1][b][iii]
    Foreign use . . . 5D[1][b][ii]
    Intent to use (ITU) applications
      . . . 5D[1][b][iv]
    Recent amendments . . . 5B[4][b]
    Use in commerce . . . 5D[1][b][i]
  Licensing . . . 5D[4][b]
  Maintaining trademark rights . . . 5D[3]
  Modern common law . . . 5B[2]
  Monetary remedies
    Actual damages . . . 5K[2][a]
    Attorney's fees . . . 5K[2][c]
    Awards in counterfeiting cases, enhanced
      . . . 5K[2][e]
    Costs . . . 5K[2][a]
    Damages under federal dilution law
      . . . 5K[2][g]
    Defendant's profits . . . 5K[2][a]
    Enhanced damages . . . 5K[2][b]
    False registration . . . 5K[2][h]
    Fraudulent registration . . . 5K[2][h]
    Marking or actual notice . . . 5K[2][f]
    Statutory damages . . . 5K[2][d]
  Non-monetary remedies
    Cancellation of federal registration . . . 5K[1][d]
    Destruction of infringing articles . . . 5K[1][c]
    Disclaimers . . . 5K[1][e]
    Injunctions . . . 5K[1][a]
    Seizure of counterfeit goods . . . 5K[1][b]
  Non-verbal marks
    Celebrity likenesses . . . 5C[2][c][iv]
    Colors . . . 5C[2][c][ii]
    Expressive works . . . 5C[2][c][iii]
    Fictional characters . . . 5C[2][c][iv]
    Numerals and alphanumeric combinations
      . . . 5C[2][c][i]
    Scents . . . 5C[2][c][ii]
    Sounds . . . 5C[2][c][ii]
  Numerals and alphanumeric combinations
    . . . 5C[2][c][i]
  "Passing off" concept . . . 5B[1]

[References are to sections.]

TRADEMARKS—Cont.

Priority of use, establishing
  Generally . . . 5D[1][a]; 5E[2][d][i]
  Actual use . . . 5D[1][a][i]
  Analogous use, through . . . 5E[2][d][ii]
  Concurrent use . . . 5E[2][d][iv]
  Factors . . . 5E[2][d][iii]
  Reputation and business presence as factor
    . . . 5D[1][a][ii]
  Zone of expansion . . . 5D[1][a][iii]
Protectability
  Generally . . . 5C
  Distinctiveness (See subhead: Distinctiveness)
  Non-verbal marks (See subhead: Non-verbal
    marks)
  Requirements for protection
    Generally . . . 5C[1][a]
    Aesthetic functionality . . . 5C[1][c][iii]
    Distinctiveness . . . 5C[1][b]
    Evolving definition of functionality
      . . . 5C[1][c][ii]
    Non-functionality . . . 5C[1][c]
    Public policy . . . 5C[1][c][i]
  Trade dress . . . 5C[2][d]
  Words and slogans (See subhead: Words and slo-
    gans)
Registration
  Generally . . . 5E; 5E[3]; 5K[1][d]
  Cancellation of registration
    Grounds for . . . 5E[3][e][iv][a]
    Procedure . . . 5E[3][e][iv][b]
  Dividing applications . . . 5E[3][d]
  False registration . . . 5K[2][h]
  Foreign registration and domestic priority
    Domestic priority . . . 5E[6][c]
    International agreements . . . 5E[6][a]
    Madrid protocol . . . 5E[6][d]
    National treatment . . . 5E[6][b]
  Fraudulent registration . . . 5K[2][h]
  Incontestability
    Effect of incontestable status . . . 5E[4][a]
    Establishing incontestability . . . 5E[4][b]
  Ineligible marks
    Generally . . . 5E[2]
    Confusion or similarity to existing marks
      . . . 5E[2][d]
    Deceptive misdescriptive marks
      . . . 5E[2][e][iii]
    Descriptive marks . . . 5E[2][e][i];
      5E[2][e][ii]
    Dilutive marks . . . 5E[2][g]
    Functional marks . . . 5E[2][e][v]
    Immoral, deceptive, scandalous or disparaging
      matter . . . 5E[2][a]
    Misdescriptive marks . . . 5E[2][e][i]
    Name, portrait, or signature . . . 5E[2][c]
    National, state, or municipal insignia
      . . . 5E[2][b]
    Secondary meaning . . . 5E[2][f]
    Surnames . . . 5E[2][e][iv]
  Intent to use (ITU) applications . . . 5E[3][b]
  Inter partes proceedings
    Cancellation . . . 5E[3][e][iv]

TRADEMARKS—Cont.

Registration—Cont.
  Inter partes proceedings—Cont.
    Concurrent use proceedings . . . 5E[3][e][iii]
    Interferences . . . 5E[3][e][ii]
    Opposition . . . 5E[3][e][i]
  Judicial review . . . 5E[3][f]
  Maintaining registration
    Generally . . . 5E[3][g]
    Affidavit of use . . . 5E[3][g][i]
    Renewal . . . 5E[3][g][ii]
  Marks eligible for registration
    Generally . . . 5E[1][a]
    Certification marks . . . 5E[1][c]
    Collective marks . . . 5E[1][d]
    Service marks . . . 5E[1][b]
  Persons who may register . . . 5E[3][c]
  Renewal . . . 5E[3][g][ii]
  State registration
    Federal preemption . . . 5E[7][b]
    State statutes . . . 5E[7][a]
  Supplemental register
    Generally . . . 5E[5]
    Cancellation . . . 5E[5][d]
    Effect of registration . . . 5E[5][c]
    Eligible marks . . . 5E[5][a]
    Procedure . . . 5E[5][b]
  Unregistered marks . . . 5E[8]
  Use applications . . . 5E[3][a]
Remedies
  Criminal penalties
    Counterfeit labels . . . 5K[4][b]
    Counterfeit marks . . . 5K[4][a]
  Domain name registration authorities
    . . . 5K[3][c]
  Family Movie Act of 2005 . . . 5K[3][d]
  Federal and state governments, remedies against
    . . . 5K[3][e]
  Limitations against certain defendants
    Domain name registration authorities
      . . . 5K[3][c]
    Family Movie Act of 2005 . . . 5K[3][d]
    Federal and state governments, remedies
      against . . . 5K[3][e]
    Makers of labels, signs, packaging, or adver-
      tisements . . . 5K[3][a]
    Printers and publishers . . . 5K[3][b]
    Publishers . . . 5K[3][b]
  Makers of labels, signs, packaging, or advertise-
    ments . . . 5K[3][a]
  Monetary remedies (See subhead: Monetary rem-
    edies)
  Non-monetary remedies (See subhead: Non-
    monetary remedies)
  Printers . . . 5K[3][b]
  Publishers . . . 5K[3][b]
Rights of publicity and . . . 1D[4][b][ii]
Scents . . . 5C[2][c][ii]
Secondary liability
  Generally . . . 5I
  Contributory infringement . . . 5I[1]
  Vicarious liability . . . 5I[2]
Seizure of counterfeit goods . . . 5K[1][b]

[References are to sections.]

TRADEMARKS—Cont.
Service marks . . . 5E[1][b]
Slogans (See subhead: Words and slogans)
Sounds . . . 5C[2][c][ii]
State statutes . . . 5B[2]
Trade dress . . . 5C[2][d]
Use in commerce . . . 5D[1][b][i]
Use in trade
    Generally . . . 5D[1]
    Lanham Act (See subhead: Lanham Act)
    Priority of use, establishing (See subhead: Prior-
      ity of use, establishing)
Words and slogans
    Generally . . . 5C[2][b][i]
    Abbreviations of generic or descriptive terms
      . . . 5C[2][b][iv]
    Foreign words . . . 5C[2][b][iii]
    Personal names . . . 5C[2][b][ii]
    Titles . . . 5C[2][b][v]

**TRADE-RELATED ASPECTS OF INTELLEC-
TUAL PROPERTY (TRIPS)**
Plant breeders rights under . . . 6C[5]

TRADE SECRETS
Generally . . . 1B[2]; 3A
Commercial value and use as requirement
    Cost of development . . . 3C[1][d][ii]
    Value requirement . . . 3C[1][d][i]
Compensatory damages
    Generally . . . 3F[2][a]
    Calculation of damages . . . 3F[2][a][i]
    Public disclosure, effect of . . . 3F[2][a][ii]
Defenses
    Generally . . . 3E
    Absences of secrecy-public domain . . . 3E[2]
    Equitable defenses
      Estoppel . . . 3E[5][c]
      Laches . . . 3E[5][b]
      Unclean hands . . . 3E[5][a]
    Independent development . . . 3E[1]
    Privilege . . . 3E[4]
    Reverse engineering . . . 3E[3]
Definitions . . . 3C[1][a]
Duration of rights . . . 3C[3]
Eligible subject matter
    Generally . . . 3C[1][b]
    Combinations . . . 3C[1][b][iii]
    Concreteness . . . 3C[1][b][i]
    Continuous use . . . 3C[1][b][v]
    Customer lists . . . 3C[1][b][iv]
    Negative information . . . 3C[1][b][vi]
    Nontechnical information . . . 3C[1][b][ii]
Exclusive rights . . . 3C[2]
Historical development
    Generally . . . 3B
    Early English cases . . . 3B[1]
    Early United States cases . . . 3B[2]
    Restatement . . . 3B[3]
    Uniform Trade Secrets Act . . . 3B[4]
Misappropriation litigation
    Generally . . . 3D; 3D[5]
    Burdens of proof . . . 3D[3]

TRADE SECRETS—Cont.
Misappropriation litigation—Cont.
    Confidential relationship . . . 3D[5][a]
    Definition of misappropriation . . . 3D[1]
    Detrimental use or disclosure . . . 3D[6]
    Disclosure . . . 3D[6]
    Elements . . . 3D[3]
    Improper and proper means
      Generally . . . 3D[5][b]
      Improper means . . . 3D[5][b][i]
      Lawful conduct . . . 3D[5][b][iii]
      Proper means . . . 3D[5][b][ii]
    Innocent receipt . . . 3D[5][c]
    Ownership (See subhead: Ownership)
    Theories of law (See subhead: Theories of law)
Ownership
    Generally . . . 3D[4]
    Common law
      Generally . . . 3D[4][a][ii]
      Employment as confidential relationship
        . . . 3D[4][a][iii]
      Information protectability . . . 3D[4][a][i]
    Express agreements
      Generally . . . 3D[4][b]
      Assignment agreements . . . 3D[4][b][i]
      Consideration . . . 3D[4][b][iii]
      Timing of creation . . . 3D[4][b][ii]
    Non-competition agreements . . . 3D[4][c]
Patent law, relationship with . . . 3A[2]
Punitive damages . . . 3F[2][b]
Remedies
    Generally . . . 3F
    Attorney fees and court costs . . . 3F[3]
    Criminal penalties . . . 3F[5]
    Damages
      Compensatory damages (See subhead: Com-
        pensatory damages)
      Punitive damages . . . 3F[2][b]
    Injunctions
      Generally . . . 3F[1]
      Duration of . . . 3F[1][c]
      Preliminary injunctions . . . 3F[1][a]
      Scope of . . . 3F[1][b]
    Seizure of embodiments . . . 3F[4]
Secrecy
    Generally . . . 3C[1][c]
    Application of secrecy requirement
      . . . 3C[1][c][ii]
    Ascertainability from products and public sources
      . . . 3C[1][c][iii]
    Copyrighted material . . . 3C[1][c][iv]
    Defined . . . 3C[1][c][i]
    Disclosure to government agencies
      . . . 3C[1][c][vii]
    General knowledge, novelty versus
      . . . 3C[1][c][vi]
    Government agencies, disclosure to
      . . . 3C[1][c][vii]
    Laws mandating disclosure . . . 3C[1][c][viii]
    Novelty versus general knowledge
      . . . 3C[1][c][vi]
    Patented material . . . 3C[1][c][v]
Seizure of embodiments . . . 3F[4]

[References are to sections.]

TRADE SECRETS—Cont.
State *versus* federal law . . . 3A[1]
Termination of protection . . . 3C[3]
Theories of law
    Generally . . . 3D[2]
    Conflicts of laws
        Generally . . . 3D[2][c]
        Contract law conflicts . . . 3D[2][c][i]
        Statutes of limitations . . . 3D[2][c][iii]
        Tort law conflicts . . . 3D[2][c][ii]
    Contract law theories . . . 3D[2][a]
    Tort law theories . . . 3D[2][b]
Uniform Trade Secrets Act . . . 3B[4]

TRIPS (See TRADE-RELATED ASPECTS OF IN-
TELLECTUAL PROPERTY (TRIPS))

U

UNIFORM TRADE SECRETS ACT (UTSA)
Generally . . . 3B[4]

UTSA (See UNIFORM TRADE SECRETS ACT
(UTSA))

V

VARA (See VISUAL ARTISTS RIGHTS ACT
(VARA))

VISUAL ARTISTS RIGHTS ACT (VARA)
Moral rights . . . 4G[7][b]

MSU College of Law Library